Y0-ACG-147

Information please business almanac & sourcebook

### Business Law & Government

### Communications

### Corporate Administration

### Finance

### Human Resources

### International

### Manufacturing

### Marketing

### Office Management

### Personal Computing

### Maps

### Reference

## Finance

Pages 165 to 276

*Includes:*
The Stock Market
Initial Public Offerings
Business Incubators
Top Stock Analysts
Futures
Options
Funds
Choosing an Accountant
Insurance Companies
Alternative Financing
Low-Cost Labor Alternatives

## Human Resources

Pages 277 to 354

*Includes:*
Schools
Training
Illiteracy
Personnel Policy
Parental and Medical Leave
Childcare and Eldercare
Headhunters
Job Hunting & Hiring
Labor Union Directory
First Aid
Workers' Compensation

## International

Pages 355 to 434

*Includes:*
NAFTA
Trade Assistance
Government Assistance
Making International Contacts
International Price Comparisons
World Business Languages
Electric Current Conversions
Small Business and Trade
Exporting
Translation Services
Currencies
World Weather

## Personal Computing

Pages 583 to 618

*Includes:*
Product Awards
Used Computers
Shareware
Bulletin Boards
Upgrading an Existing Computer
Products and Services Directory
Online Services
Internet Access Providers
Program Templates

## Maps

Pages 619 to 654

*Includes:*
Atlanta
Boston
Chicago
Cleveland
Columbus
Africa
Asia
Australia
Mileage Table

## Reference

Pages 655 to 735

Glossary
Weights and Measures
The Largest Public Companies
Newsletters
Index

# Praise for
# The 1994 Information Please
# Business Almanac

"As thorough an information compendium as can be found in one volume." — *The Orange County Register*

"An indispensable resource."
— Jay Conrad Levinson, author of *Guerrilla Marketing*

"Highly recommended." — *The Library Journal*

"An excellent addition to the business bookshelf."
— *The Internet Business Journal*

"These facts could make you filthy rich." — *The Wall Street Journal*

"The Business Bible." — CBS Radio

"The best book I have seen since I have opened my store."
— President of Office Max

"It will get much use." — Faith Popcorn

"Wonderful to leaf through but pointedly relevant time and again...
Will become a valued time-saving resource."
— Mitchell T. Rabkin, M.D., President,
Beth Israel Hospital, Boston

"A wonderful book full of great information."
— Small Business Crain's Detroit

"Filled with interesting information."
— Paul Edwards, author of *Working from Home*

"This is an amazingly varied compendium of business information."
— Michael Perish, Business Librarian, University of Indiana

# THE 1995
# INFORMATION PLEASE®
# BUSINESS ALMANAC &
# SOURCEBOOK

# THE 1995 INFORMATION PLEASE®
# BUSINESS ALMANAC &
# SOURCEBOOK

Seth Godin, Editor

**HOUGHTON MIFFLIN COMPANY**

*Boston • New York*

Copyright ©1994 by Seth Godin Productions, Inc.

For information about permission to reproduce selections from this book, write to Permissions, Houghton Mifflin Company, 215 Park Ave. S., New York, NY 10003.

ISBN: 0-395-70110-4

ISSN: 1070-4639

Printed in the United States of America

DOW 10 9 8 7 6 5 4 3 2 1

# CONTENTS

## FINANCE...................................... 165

## HUMAN RESOURCES ............................. 277

# How to Use This Book

There are three easy ways to access the *Almanac*:

## Chapter by Chapter

The front and back inside covers give a map of the organization of the *Almanac*, together with page numbers for each chapter. At the start of each chapter you'll find a listing of every article contained in the chapter.

## The Table of Contents

The *Almanac* is organized in much the same way a company is. Information about doing business abroad is in the International section, while data on brand names and ad agencies are listed under Marketing. The Table of Contents lists each chapter, together with the name of each article in that chapter.

## The Index

A comprehensive index of companies, reference sources, and basic concepts is located at the back of the book, in the Reference section.

# Feedback

The editors of the *Almanac* would like to hear from you. Tell us your likes and dislikes, and let us know what information you'd like to see included in future volumes. While we can't answer every letter, we promise that each suggestion will be carefully reviewed and included wherever possible.

## To reach the editorial staff:

Internet:  almanac@sgp.com
Fax:  (914) 693-8132
Mail:  Box 321, Dobbs Ferry, NY 10522

# FaxSource

The *Information Please Business Almanac* offers a variety of resources by fax. Simply call our fax machine from your machine, and you can receive the desired material.

## How to Receive a FaxSource Document

1. Using the handset on your fax machine, call (815) 229-4911.

2. You will hear, "Welcome to FaxSource. Please enter the number of the first item you wish to receive."

3. Enter the three-digit number you see in the box where your desired item is listed.

4. You will now hear, "Please enter the number of the next item you wish to receive. If you do not have any more requests, press the pound key."

5. Enter the next three-digit number, or press the pound (#) key.

6. If you have entered another number, go to step 4.

7. After you have pressed the pound key, you will hear, "Thank you for using FaxSource. Press the Start key to receive the material you requested."

8. Press the Start key. The material should start to print from your fax machine as a regular fax.

9. If you have any technical problems, call (815) 398-9009 for assistance. You can also write to the *Business Almanac* at Box 321, Dobbs Ferry, NY 10522.

## FaxSource Items

- *Basic Airline Fare Codes*. List of common airline abbreviations and their definitions. Request #684.

- *Causes of Business Failures*. Seven primary reasons for business failure and incidence of failure in nine sectors of business. Request #576.

- *Consumer Price Indexes*. Table of consumer price indexes by major groups. Request #127.

- *Employer Costs*. Tables of employer costs for employee compensation and employees with pension plans or group health plans. Request #431.

- *Family and Medical Leave*. Tables of percent of full-time employees by leave policy and duration of leave policy. Request #998.

- *Fleet Cars*. Explanation of fleet cars and contact numbers. Request #429.

- *Foreign Buyers of U.S. Companies*. Table of foreign buyers: number of transactions, by country. Request #923.

- *Free Government Resources*. List of subject bibliographies available from the Government Printing Office. Request #203.

- *Government Income and Spending*. Tables of federal budget outlays, gross federal debt, and federal receipts by source. Request #202.

- *Internal Revenue Service Centers*. List of regional offices that accept tax returns. Request #104.

- *Labor Force*. Tables of civilian labor force by educational attainment, self-employed workers and employed workers by selected characteristics. Request #126.

- *Largest Airlines Worldwide*. *Fortune*'s ranking by revenue of the top 25 airlines worldwide. Request #888.

- *Law Firm Fees*. Description of types of fees and suggestions for negotiating a billing method. Request #333.

- *Longest Occupational Tenure*. Bar graph of the average number of years in occupation for the top 10 jobs. Request #878.

- *Manhattan Address Locator*. Chart that makes it easy to find a location in Manhattan if you know the address. Request #100.

- *Non-Performing Loans*. Table of percentage of non-performing loans in each state (in FDIC-insured commercial banks). Request #279.

- *Population Data*. Table of resident population by age and state. Request #125.

- *Producer Price Indexes*. Table of producer price indexes, selected commodities. Request #443.

- *State Travel Information Centers*. Phone numbers of travel information offices nationwide. Request #411.

- *Time Spent at Work and Leisure*. Tables of gross average weekly earnings and hours worked for selected non-manufacturing and manufacturing industries. Request #771.

- *Top Brands*. *SuperBrands*' 1994 list of top brands. Request #852.

- *Top 50 Airport Car Rental Markets*. Table of top airport car rental markets by revenue and percent share. Request #321.

- *U.S. Direct Investment Abroad*. Table of U.S. investment abroad, historical cost basis. Request #227.

- *U.S. Exports and Imports by Area*. Table of U.S. exports and imports for six major countries. Request #542.

- *Worldwide Gross Domestic Product*. Table of gross domestic product for 24 major countries. Request #550.

# Editorial and Production Staff

| | |
|---|---|
| Editor in Chief: | Seth Godin |
| Senior Editors: | Ellen Kenny<br>Carol Markowitz<br>Karen Watts |
| Production Editors: | Julie Maner<br>Megan O'Connor |
| Acquisition Editor: | Steve Lewers |
| Editorial Assistance: | Chris Angelilli<br>Meredith Cristiano<br>Lisa DiMona<br>Jennifer Gniady |
| Consulting Editor: | Michael Cader |
| Copy Editing: | Pat Goff<br>Jennifer Landau Jones |
| Proofreading: | David Bloom<br>Gwen Helene Bronson |
| Technical Layout: | Martin Erb |
| Data Entry: | Bill Brandau<br>Lauren Fox<br>Mark Underwager |
| Research: | José Arroyo<br>Kate Grossman<br>Margery Mandell<br>Margaret Talcott |
| Design: | Charles Kreloff |
| Glossary: | Marcia Layton |
| Template Design: | Lisa Jahred |
| Troubleshooting: | Steve Ketchum |
| Security: | Lucy Wood |
| Houghton Mifflin: | Doug Eisenhart<br>Bob Enos<br>Bruce Frost<br>Pat McTiernan<br>Greg Mrozek<br>Marnie Patterson<br>Kristin Robbins<br>Bill Trippe<br>Steve Vana-Paxhia |
| Output: | R.R. Donnelley & Sons |
| Maps: | MicroMaps |

# ACKNOWLEDGMENTS

More than 500 people and organizations contributed valuable insights, information, and advice to the creation of this *Almanac*. This is a partial list of those who were so gracious in their help.

## Individuals:

Kathleen Antonini, United Parcel Service
Talie Bar-Nadav, Organization Resources Counselors
Dr. Beverly Berger, Federal Laboratory Consortium
Rick Boyle, Center for Advanced Purchasing Studies
Shelly Burton, Building Owners and Managers Association
Lisa Cavallari, Frank Russell
Lori Cioffi, Reed Travel Group
Graef Crystal, The Crystal Report
David Cudaback, Institutional Investor
Kathleen Dempsey, NACORE International
Gina Ellrich, United Parcel Service
Carl Frankel, Green MarketAlert
John Gawalt, National Science Foundation
Cindy Giglio, Standard & Poor's
Stephen Gold, Tax Foundation
Nina Gressens, U. S. Bureau of the Census
Sunny Harris, Crawford Associates
Mark Hulbert, The Hulbert Financial Digest
Susan Jacobs, Dun & Bradstreet
Lisa Kay Dowd, Sprint
David Kostin, Salomon Brothers
Katherine Lieber, The Foundation Center
Robert Liu, Securities Data
Dianna Losey, Interior Design Magazine
Lynda Lucker, Philadelphia Stock Exchange
Tom Mariam, American Stock Exchange
Alice Teppler Marlin, Council on Economic Priorities
Ira Mayer, The Licensing Letter
Martha McDonald, International Quality and Productivity Center
John McIlquham, Davis Information Group
Charlie McKuen, GPO Marketing
Meara McLaughlin, Boston Aviation Services
Terry Murphy, National Business Incubation Association
Helen Norton, Women's Legal Defense Fund
Peter Packer, Runzheimer International
Samantha Sanford, London Stock Exchange
Fran Schwartz, Ravelle Brickman P.R.
Art Spinella, CNW Marketing Research
Judith Sussman, Pezzano & Co.
Pam Tverdy, Midwest Stock Exchange
Jennifer Vazzana, Nikkei America
Ed Welch, University of Michigan
Jack Zavada, National Association for the Exchange of Industrial Resources

A particular thank you to the *Almanac* board of advisors: Abby Roeder-Johnson, Barry Bronfin, Beth Emme, Carl Sangree, Chip Conley, Chris Everly, Dan Lovy, Frank Sisco, Jay Levinson, William and Lenore Godin, Neil and Emily Epstein, Eric and Marjorie Bryen, Linda Litner, Lisa Orden Zarin, Kim Takal, Steven Greenstein, Lynne Gordon, Steve Dennis, Nancy Pellowe-Dennis.

Steve Lewers, Kristin Robbins, and Bob Enos were responsible for much of the vision that helped us refine the *Almanac* and bring it to its present form.

Finally, thanks to all the spouses and family members who were so patient, insightful, and supportive.

## Organizations:

3M Commercial Office Supply Division; 9 to 5, Working Women Education Fund; Abelow Response; Advertising Agency Register; Advertising Agency Search Service; Advisory Council on Intergovernmental Relations; AFL-CIO; Air & Waste Management Association; Airship International; Alcoholics Anonymous World Services; Alternative Press Center; American Arbitration Association; American Association for Exporters and Importers; American Association of Advertising Agencies; American Association of Port Authorities; American Bankers Association; American Bar Association; American Civil Liberties Union; American Express Airfare Management Unit; American Express Travel Management Services; American Financial Services Association; American Institute of Architects; American Institute of Certified Public Accountants; American League of Financial Institutions; American League of Lobbyists; American Management Association; American Marketing Association; American Paper Institute; American Passage; American Productivity and Quality Center; American Red Cross; American Society for Industrial Security; American Society for Interior Designers; American Society for Personnel Administration; American Society for Quality Control; American Society for Training and Development; American Society of Interpreters; American Society of Journalists and Authors; American Society of Magazine Photographers; American Stock Exchange; American Translators Association; Amward Publications; Artistic Greetings; Association for Science, Technology, and Innovation; Association of Alternative Newsweeklies; Association of Executive Search Consultants; Association of Management Consulting Firms; Association of National Advertisers; Association of Shareware Professionals; Association of Small Business Development Centers; Association of Venture Clubs; AT&T; Audit Bureau of Circulation; Audrey Reichblum Associates; Automatic Data

Processing; AZ Marketing Services; Bacon's Information; BEI Entertainment Catalog; Berlitz Translation Services; Blenheim Franchise Shows; Boston Stock Exchange; Buck Consultants; Building Owners and Managers Association; Bureau of Economic Analysis; Bureau of Labor Statistics; Business Committee for the Arts; Business Council for International Understanding; Business Information Service for the Newly Independent States; Business Trend Analysts; Buyers Laboratory; Cahner's Publishing; Cass Communications; CDA Investment Technologies; CDC National AIDS Clearing House; Celebrity Service International; Center for Advanced Purchasing Studies; Charter Pacific Book; Chicago Board of Trade; Chicago Mercantile Exchange; Chicago Stock Exchange; Chrysler Corporation; The Cincinnati Stock Exchange; Citibank; Clio Awards; CNW Marketing Research; Coalition for Literacy; Coffee, Sugar & Cocoa Exchange; Color Marketing Group; Committee for Economic Development; Commodity Exchange; Commodity Futures Trading Association; Communication Channels; Compensation and Benefits Consultants; CompuServe; The Conference Board; Conney Safety Products; Consulting Psychologists Press; Continental Dataforms; Copysearch; Corporate Agents; Corporate Resources Group; The Corporate University; Council of Economic Advisors; Council of State Governments; Council on Economic Priorities; Crain Communications; Crawford Associates; Credit Research Foundation; Crestline; Database America Companies; Davis Information Group; DDB Needham; Demand Research; Dominique Licensing Corporation; Dun & Bradstreet; DuPont Quality Management & Technology Center; E.I. DuPont DeNemours and Company; Earth Share; Earthworks Press; Econocolor; Employee Benefit Research Institute; Environmental Action Coalition; Environmental Federation of New York; Equal Employment Opportunity Commission; Executive Enterprises Publications; Export-Import Bank; Families and Work Institute; Faulkner & Gray; Federal Elections Commission, Publications Information; Federal Express; Federal Laboratory Consortium; Federal Reserve Board; Federal Trade Commission; Find SVP; Foundation Center; Frank Russell; Fredonia Group; Freedom of Information Clearinghouse; Frost & Sullivan; Futures Industry Association; Gift Association of America; Gift In Kind Clearing House; Goldhirsh Group; Goodyear; Government Printing Office; Grant Thornton; Greeting Card Association; HarperCollins; Harvard Business Services; Hay/Huggins Company; Health Insurance Association of America; Hewitt Associates; Human Factors Society; IDD Information Service; Industrial Designers Society of America; Inflight Food Service Association; Information Resources; Ingels; Ingram; Inmac; Instant Promotions on Package; Institute of Clean Air Companies; Institute of International Education; Institute of Management and Administration; Institute of Outdoor Advertising; Institute of Real Estate Management; Institute of Scrap Recycling Industries; The Insurance Forum; Insurance Fund Foundation; Insurance Information

Institute; Intercultural Press; Interior Design Magazine; Internal Revenue Service; International Advertising Association; International Air Passengers Association; International Association of Convention and Visitors Bureaus; International Association of Exposition Managers; International Business Brokers Association; International Chamber of Commerce; International Finance/World Bank; International Franchise Association; International Quality and Productivity Center; The International Society for Intercultural Education, Training and Research; Investment Company Institute; Irwin Professional Publishing; J.D. Power and Associates; Jobs for the Future; Judicial Arbitration and Mediation Services; Kaiser Health Reform Project; Kemper National Insurance; Korn/Ferry International; Landauer Real Estate Counselors; Leon Henry; Licensing Executive Society; Lipper Analytical Services; LNA/Arbitron Multimedia Services; London Stock Exchange; Loose Leaf Binder Company; Luce Press Clippings; Magazine Publishers of America; Manufacturers' Agents National Association; Manufacturers' Alliance for Productivity and Innovation; Manufacturing Technology Centers Programs; McGraw-Hill; MCI Telecommunications; Medialink; Meeting Planners International; Memphis Airships; Merrill Lynch & Co.; MidAmerica Commodity Exchange; Midwest Stock Exchange; Minority Business Information Institute; Miracolor; Moody's Investor's Services; Morningstar; Mt. Vernon Public Library; Multiprint; NACORE International; National Airline Passengers Association; National Alliance for Choice in Giving; National Association for Credit Management; National Association for the Exchange of Industrial Resources; National Association of Broadcasters; National Association of Business Travel Agents; National Association of Manufacturers; National Association of Radio Talk Show Hosts; National Association of Realtors; National Association of Securities Dealers; National Association of Small Business Investment Companies; National Association of Temporary Services; National Automated Clearing House Association; National Business Incubation Association; National Career Network; National Center for Standards and Certification Information; National Coalition for Advanced Manufacturing; National Coalition for Advanced Technology; National Commercial Finance Association; National Commission for Cooperative Education; National Committee for Responsive Philanthropy; National Cristina Foundation; National Foreign Trade Council; National Foreman's Institute; National Foundation for Women Business Owners; National Futures Association; National Governor's Association; National Home Study Council; National Institute for Aviation Research; National Institute of Standards and Technology; National Insurance Association; National Insurance Consumer Help Line; National Labor Relations Board; National Leadership Coalition on AIDS; National Mass Retail Association; National Materials Exchange Network; National Organization for Women; National Recycling Coalition; National Register Publishing Company;

National Safety Council; National Science Foundation; National Small Business United; National Society for Experiential Education; National Solid Waste Management Association; National Speakers Association; New York Cotton Exchange; New York Department of Health; New York Mercantile Exchange; New York State Department of Economic Development; New York State Division of Alcoholism and Alcohol Abuse; New York Stock Exchange; Nichols/Feren; Nielsen Media Research; Nightingale-Conant Publishing; Nikkei America; Northwestern National Life; Nutshell; Occupational Safety and Health Administration; Office of Federal Contract Compliance Programs; Office of Management and Budget; Office of the Secretary of Transportation, Department of Transportation; Office Planners and Users Group; Oglivy & Mather; The One Club; Organization for Economic Cooperation and Development; Organization Resources Counselors; Orion Protective Services; Outdoor Advertising Association of America; Overseas Private Investment Corporation; Pacific Bell; Pacific Stock Exchange; Package Design Council/Institute of Packaging Professionals; Paychex; PC Research; Philadelphia Stock Exchange; Prestige Product Placement; Printbooks; Professional Convention Management Association; Promotional Products Association International; Public Relations Society of America; Publishers Information Bureau; Quill, Chiswick's & Reliable; R.R. Bowker; Radio Advertising Bureau; Radio Association Network; Radio Network Association; Random House; Reed Travel Group; Risk and Insurance Management Society; Roeder-Johnson; Rogers and Cowan; Roper Starch; Royal Wholesale Banner; Sales & Marketing Executives of Greater New York; Salomon Brothers; SBC Investment Management; Scangrafics; The Schecter Group; Securities Data; Securities Industry Association; Select Committee on Children, Youth and Family; Sheshunoff Information Services; Small Business Administration; Small Business Foundation of America; Society of the Plastics Industry; Solid Waste Assistance Program; Southern Waste Information Exchange; Specialty Advertising Association of Greater New York; Stafford Publications; Standard & Poor's; Tax Foundation; Thomson & Thomson; Toastmasters International; Tokyo Stock Exchange; Tompkins Associates; Trade Information Center; Trade Show Professionals; Trademark Research Corporation; Travel Industry Association of America; TRW; U.S. Bureau of the Census; U.S. Chamber of Commerce; U.S. Conference of Mayors; U.S. Congress; U.S. Department of Commerce, Advanced Technology Program; U.S. Department of Commerce, Bureau of Economic Analysis; U.S. Department of Commerce, Bureau of the Census; U.S. Department of Commerce, Economics and Statistics Administration, Office of Business Analysis; U.S. Department of Justice, Internal Security Division; U.S. Department of Labor, Bureau of Labor Statistics, Office of International Prices; U.S. Department of Labor, Bureau of Labor Statistics, Office of Productivity and Technology; U.S. Department of Labor, Ergonomics Division; U.S. Department of Labor, Women's Bureau; U.S. Department of State; U.S. Department of Transportation; U.S. Environmental Protection Agency; U.S. Environmental Protection Agency, Office of Solid Waste; U.S. Federal Aviation Administration; U.S. Federal Information Center; U.S. General Services Administration; U.S. Government Printing Office; U.S. International Trade Administration, "E" Awards Program; International Training in Communication; U.S. International Trade Administration, Office of Public Affairs; U.S. International Trade Commission; U.S. Postal Service; U.S. Securities and Exchange Commission; U.S. Trademark Association; U.S. Travel and Tourism Administration; U.S. Travel Data Center; Union Pen Company; United Parcel Service; University of Wisconsin; Urban Land Institute; Video Storyboard Tests; VR Business Brokers; Walter Karl Companies; Walters International Speakers Bureau; Warwick Baker & Fiore; Washington Speakers Bureasu; White Plains Public Libary; William M. Mercer; Wilshire Associates; Working Mother; World Map Company; World Trade Centers Association; Zagat Survey

## Reference Sources

The *Information Please Business Almanac* would also like to mention the following invaluable reference sources:

*43 Proven Ways to Raise Capital for Your Small Business*, Enterprise Publishing
*50 Simple Things You Can Do to Save the Earth*, Earthworks Press
*The 90-Minute Hour*, Plume
*Access EPA*, U.S. Environmental Protection Agency
*Accountant's Desk Handbook*, Prentice-Hall
*Accountant's Handbook of Formulas and Tables*, Prentice-Hall
*Accounting Desk Book*, Prentice-Hall
*Accounting Today*, Faulkner and Gray
*Advanced Selling Power*, The Thompson Group
*Advertising Age*, Crain Communications
*Adweek Agency Directory*, Adweek Magazine
*Adweek Client/Brand Directory*, Adweek Magazine
*Adweek*
*Air Charter Guide*, Boston Aviation Services

*Air Traveler's Handbook*, St. Martin's Press
*Aircraft, Airports and Airways*, U.S. Government Printing Office
*Almanac of Business and Industrial Financial Ratios*, Prentice-Hall
*AMA Guide for Meeting and Event Planners*, Gale Research
*AMA Handbook of Key Management Forms*, American Management Association
*AMA Management Handbook*, American Management Association
*America's New Foundations*, Gale Publishing
*American Academy of Actuaries Yearbook*, American Academy of Actuaries
*The American Almanac 1992-1993*, The Reference Press
*American Almanac of Jobs and Salaries*, Avon Books
*American Business Climate and Economic Profiles*, Gale Research
*American Demographics*
*American Export Register*, Thomas International Publishing
*The American Franchise Catalogue*, TBS Publishing
*An American Guide to Doing Business in Australia*, PacRim Publishing
*American Lawyer*
*American Lobbyists Directory*, Gale Research
*Americans with Disabilities Handbook*, John Wiley & Sons
*Annual Asset Survey*, Salomon Brothers
*Annual of Advertising, Editorial and Television Art and Design*, Art Directors Club
*Architectural Record*, McGraw-Hill
*ASTD Buyer's Guide & Consultant Directory*, American Society for Training and Development
*Auto Rental News*, Bobit Publishing
*Aviation Daily*
*Aviation Directory*
*Bacon's Newspaper/Magazine Directory*, Bacon's Information
*Basic Facts about Trademarks*, US Department of Commerce
*A Basic Guide to Exporting*, U.S. Department of Commerce
*Before & After*
*Bergano's Register of International Importers*, Bergano Books
*Best's Insurance Reports*, A.M. Best
*Best's Review*, A.M. Best
*The Better World Investment Guide*, Prentice-Hall
*Beyond Race and Gender*, American Management Association
*Billboard's International Talent and Touring Directory*, Billboard Publications
*Black Enterprise Magazine*
*The Blue List*, Standard & Poor's
*Board of Governors Report on the Flow of Funds*, Federal Reserve System
*Boardwatch Magazine*
*Bond Guide*, Standard and Poor's
*Book Publishing*, Practicing Law Institute
*Bookazine Ready-Made Computer Book Best Seller List*, Bookazine
*The Bordwin Letter: Preventive Law for Business*
*Breakthrough Strategies*
*Broadcasting & Cable Market Place*, R.R. Bowker
*Bulletin to Management*, Bureau of National Affairs
*Business America*, U.S. Department of Commerce
*Business and Health*, American Health Consultants
*Business Aviation Magazine*
*Business Failure Record*, Dun & Bradstreet
*Business Forms & Systems*
*Business Forms on File*, Facts on File
*Business Franchise Guide*, Commerce Clearing House
*Business History of the World: A Chronology*, Greenwood Publishing Group
*Business Information ALERT*, ALERT Publications
*Business Insurance Magazine*
*Business Marketing*, Crain Communications
*Business One Irwin Business & Investment Almanac*, Business One Irwin
*Business Protocol*, John Wiley & Sons
*Business Rankings and Salaries Index*, Gale Research
*Business Statistics*, U.S. Government Printing Office

*Business to Business Directory*, NYNEX Information Resources
*Business Tokyo*
*Business Travel News*
*Business Week*
*Buyers Laboratory Test Reports: Reports on Office Products*, Buyers Laboratory
*C.Q. Almanac*, Congressional Quarterly
*Career Information Center*, Glencoe Publishing
*Career Track*
*Cavalcade of Acts & Attractions*, Amusement Business
*Celebrity Directory*, Axiom Information Resources
*Census of Manufacturers*, U.S. Government Printing Office
*Change*
*Chronicle of Philanthropy*
*Co-op Source Directory*, National Register Publishing
*College Blue Book: Occupational Education*, Macmillan
*Commerce Business Daily*, U.S. Government Printing Office
*Commerical Atlas & Marketing Guide*, Rand McNally
*Commodity Futures Trading Commission*, U.S. Government Printing Office
*Commodity Price Charts*
*Common Market Reports*, Commerce Clearing House
*Communication Systems and Computer Networks*, Halsted Press
*Compensation and Benefits Manager's Report*, BBP/Prentice-Hall
*Competitive Edge*, Tompkins Associates
*The Complete Investor: Instruments, Markets, and Guides*, Richard D. Irwin
*Computers and Computing Information Resources*, Gale Research
*ComputerWorld*
*Consultants and Consulting Organizations*, Gale Research
*Consumer Magazine and Agri-Media Rates and Data*
*Consumer Reports Travel Buying Guide*, Consumers Union
*Consumer Reports Travel Letter*, Consumers Union
*Consumer Sourcebook*, Gale Research
*Consumers Index to Product Evaluations & Information Sources*, Pierian Press
*Copyright Basics*, U.S. Government Printing Office
*Copyrights, Patents, and Trademarks*, TAB Books
*Copywriter's Handbook*, Dodd, Mead & Co.
*Corporate 500: The Directory of Corporate Philanthropy*, Gale Research
*Corporate Art Consultants*, Art Network
*Corporate ARTnews*, ARTnews
*The Corporate Finance Sourcebook*, National Register Publishing Company
*Corporate Real Estate Executive*, NACORE International
*Corporate Travel*, Miller Freeman
*The Corporate University Guide to Short Management Seminars*, The Corporate University
*Corporation Forms*, Prentice-Hall Information Services
*Crain's New York Business*
*The Crystal Report*
*Datapro Directory of Microcomputer Software*, Datapro Research Corporation
*Deadlines*
*Design Access*, National Endowment for the Arts/National Building Museum
*Design and Drafting News*, American Design and Drafting Association
*Design for a Livable Planet*, HarperCollins
*Direct Mail List Rates and Data*, Standard Rate and Data Service
*Direct Marketing Association Statistical Factbook*, Direct Marketing Association
*Direct Marketing Magazine*
*Directory of Accredited Home Study Schools*, National Home Study Council
*Directory of Accredited Institutions*, Association of Independent Colleges and Schools
*Directory of Conventions*, Bill Communications
*The Directory of Coporate and Foundation Givers*, Gale Publishing
*Directory of Industrial Designers*, Industrial Designers Society of America
*Directory of Lawyers and Law Firms by Specialty*, West Publishing
*Directory of Leading U.S. Export Management Companies*, Bergano Books
*Directory of Mail Order Catalogs*, Grey House Publishing

*Directory of Mailing List Companies*, Todd Publications
*Directory of Manufacturers' Sales Agencies*, Manufacturers' Agents National Association
*Directory of U.S. Importers/Exporters*, Journal of Commerce
*Directory to Industrial Design in the United States*, Van Nostrand Reinhold
*Discount Store News*, Lebhar-Friedman
*Do's and Taboos Around the World*, John Wiley & Sons
*Does Your Business Produce Hazardous Wastes?*, U.S. Environmental Protection Agency
*Dow Jones Guide to Real Estate Investing*, Dow Jones-Irwin
*Dow Jones Investor's Handbook*, Dow Jones
*Dow Jones-Irwin Guide to Bond & Money Market Investments*, Dow Jones-Irwin
*Dun's Employment Opportunities Directory*, Dun's Marketing Services
*Economic Indicators*, U.S. Government Printing Office
*The Economist*
*EDI News*, Phillips Communications
*Editor and Publisher International Yearbook*
*Effective Business Communication*, Houghton -Mifflin
*Electronic Business*, Cahners Publishing
*Emerging Technologies: Survey of Technical and Economic Opportunites*, U.S. Department of Commerce
*Employee Benefits and the Computer*, Advanced Personnel Systems
*Employers' Human Rights & Equity Report*
*Employment and Earnings*, U. S. Department of Labor
*Employment Coordinator*, Research Institute of America
*Employment, Hours, Earnings: United States 1909-1984*, U.S. Government Printing Office
*Engineering News Record*, McGraw-Hill
*English Language Orientation Programs in the U.S.*, Institute of International Education
*Entertainment Weekly*
*The Entrepreneur and Small Business Problem Solver*, John Wiley & Sons
*Entrepreneur Annual Franchise 500*
*Entrepreneur Magazine*
*Environmental Almanac*, Houghton Mifflin
*The Ernst & Young Tax Guide 1994*, John Wiley & Sons
*The Europa World Year Book*, Gale Research
*Every Manager's Guide to Firing*, Irwin Professional Publishing
*The Executive Desk Register of Publicly Held Companies*, Demand Research
*Executive Compensation Alert*, Research Institute of America
*Executive Excellence*, Institute for Principle-Centered Leadership
*Export Profits: A Guide for Small Business*, Upstart Publishing
*Export Programs: A Business Directory of U.S. Government Resources*, U.S. Department of Commerce
*Exportise*, Small Business Foundation of America
*FAA Statistical Handbook of Aviation*, U.S. Government Printing Office
*The Fact Book 1994*, Insurance Information Institute
*Federal Register*, U.S. Government Printing Office
*Federal Regulatory Directory*, Congressional Quarterly
*Financial World*
*Findex*, Cambridge Information Group
*The Five-Minute Interview*, John Wiley & Sons
*Folio*
*Forbes*
*Foreign Trade Barriers*, Office of the United States Trade Representative
*Fortune*
*The Foundation Directory*, The Foundation Center
*Foundation Giving*, The Foundation Center
*Foundation Grants Index*, The Foundation Center
*Franchise Annual*, Info Franchise News
*Franchise Bible: A Comprehensive Guide*, The Oasis Press/PSI Research
*Franchise Opportunities Guide*, International Franchise Association
*Franchise Packet*, Federal Trade Commission
*Franchising World*, International Franchise Association
*Frequent Flyer*, Reed Travel
*Fundamentals of Business Law*, Prentice-Hall
*Futures Industry*, Futures Industry Association

*Futures Magazine*
*Futures Market Directory*, Prentice-Hall
*Gift and Decorative Accessory Buyers Directory*, Geyer McAllister Publications
*Global Investor*
*Graphic Arts Monthly*, Cahners Publishing
*Green Book–International Directory of Marketing*, American Marketing Association
*Green MarketAlert*
*Guerrilla Financing*, Houghton Mifflin
*Guerrilla Marketing*, Houghton Mifflin
*Guide to Corporate Giving*, American Council for the Arts
*Guide to Free Tax Services*, Internal Revenue Service
*Guide to Worldwide Postal Code & Address Formats*
*Guidebook to Fair Employment Practices*, Commerce Clearing House
*Handbook for Raising Capital*, Dow Jones-Irwin
*Handbook of Business Information*, Libraries Unlimited
*Harvard Business Review*
*Herschell Gordon Lewis on the Art of Writing Copy*, Prentice-Hall
*Hiring the Best*, Bob Adams
*Hospital Supervisor's Bulletin*, Bureau of Business Practice
*How to Buy Foreign Stocks and Bonds: A Guide*, HarperCollins
*How to Cut Your Company's Health Care Costs*, Prentice-Hall
*How to Develop an Effective Company Security Program*, The Dartnell Corporation
*How to Develop an Employee Handbook*, The Dartnell Corporation
*How to Do Business with Russians*, Quorum Books
*How to Fire an Employee*, Facts on File
*How to Form Your Own Corporation Without a Lawyer for Under $75.00*, Dearborn Financial Publishing
*How to Get a Business Loan*, Random House
*How to Read the Financial Pages*, Warner Books
*HR Magazine*
*The Hulbert Financial Digest*
*The Human Resources Yearbook*, Prentice-Hall
*ID Magazine*
*Idea Source Guide: A Monthly Report to Executives in Advertising, Merchandising, and Sales Promotion*, Bramlee
*The IMS Ayer Directory of Publications*, IMS Press
*Inc. Magazine*
*Inc. Yourself*, Warner Books
*Incentive Magazine*
*Incorporating Your Business*, Contemporary Books
*Industry Week*
*Industry, the Environment, and Corporate Social Responsibility*, Council of Planning Librarians
*Infomercial Marketing Report*
*Information for the Private Sector and State and Local Governments*, Equal Employment Opportunity Commission
*The Information Please Almanac*, Houghton Mifflin
*Information Week*
*InfoWorld*
*InsideFlyer*
*The Insider's Guide to Franchising*, AMACOM
*Institutional Investor*
*Interior Design Magazine*
*International Business Practices*, U.S. Department of Commerce
*International Business*, American International Publishing
*The International Businesswoman of the 1990s: A Guide to Success in the Global Marketplace*, Praeger Publishers
*International Directory of Corporate Affiliations*, Reed Publishing
*International Marketing Handbook*, Gale Research
*International Price Indexes: Export and Import*, Bureau of Labor Statistics, U.S. Department of Labor
*International Travel to and from the United States: 1994 Outlook*, U.S. Travel and Tourism Administration
*Investing in Employee Health*, Jossey-Bass
*Investment Dealers' Digest*
*The Investment Survey*, Value Line Publishing
*Investor's Daily*
*The Investor's Dictionary*, John Wiley & Sons

*Journal of Accountancy*

*Journal of Commerce*

*The Journal of the Small Business Forum*, University of Wisconsin

*Kiplinger's Personal Finance Magazine*

*Law and Legal Information Directory*, Gale Research

*Law Dictionary for Non-Lawyers*, West Publishing

*Lawyers Almanac*, Prentice-Hall

*The Legal Guide for Starting and Running a Small Business*, Nolo Press

*Legal Research: How to Find and Understand the Law*, Nolo Press

*Legal Thesaurus*, Macmillan

*Lesko's Info-Power*, Information USA

*Licensing Business Databook*, EPM Communications

*The Licensing Journal*

*The Licensing Letter*, EPM Communications

*Lists for Direct Mail and Telemarketing*, Database America Companies

*The Lobbying Handbook*, Professional Lobbying Consulting Center

*Louis Rukeyser's Business Almanac*, Simon & Schuster

*The Mac Shareware 500*, Ventana Press

*MacUser*

*Macweek*

*Mail Order Business Directory*, B. Klein Publications

*Major Companies in Western Europe*

*Managing Foundations Assets*, The Foundation Center

*Marketer's Guide to Media*, Adweek and Mediaweek

*Marketing Made Easier*, Todd Publications

*Marketing News*

*Meetings and Conventions*, Reed Travel Group

*Mergers & Acquisitions*, MLR Publishing Company

*Mergerstat*, Bureau of Labor Statistics, U.S. Department of Labor

*Mergerstat℠ Review*, Merrill Lynch & Co.

*Merrill Lynch Portfolio Strategies*, Merrill Lynch & Co.

*Modern Language Handbook*, Modern Language Association

*The Money Charity Honor Roll*, Money Magazine

*Money Magazine*

*Money Market Dictionary of Pension Funds, and their Investment Managers*, Money Market Directories

*Moody's Bank and Finance Manual*, Moody's Investors Service

*Moody's Bond Record*, Moody's Investors Service

*Moody's Directory of the World's Largest Service Companies*, Moody's Investors Service

*Moody's Handbook of Common Stocks*, Moody's Investors Service

*Moody's Handbook of OTC Stocks*, Moody's Investors Services

*Moody's International Manual*, Moody's Investors Service

*Morgan Stanley Capital Internationals*, Morgan Stanley

*Morningstar Mutual Funds*, Morningstar

*The Motion Picture Almanac*, Quigley Publishing Company

*The Multinational Executive Travel Companion*, Suburban Publishing of Connecticut

*Mutual Fund Fact Book*, Investment Company Institute

*NASDAQ Fact Book and Company Directory*

*Nation's Business*, U.S. Chamber of Commerce

*National Business Education Yearbook*, National Business Education Association

*National Directory of Addresses and Telephone Numbers*, Omnigraphics

*National Directory of Corporate Giving*, The Foundation Center

*National Directory of Minority-Owned Business Firms*, Business Research Services

*National Directory of Women-Owned Business*, Business Research Services

*The National Law Journal*

*National Patterns of R&D Resources*, National Science Foundation

*National Real Estate Investor*

*National Report for Training and Development*, American Society for Training and Development

*National Roster of Realtors Directory*, Stamats Communications

*National Trade Data Bank*, U.S. Department of Commerce

*New York Public Library Book of Chronologies*, Prentice-Hall

*New York Public Library Desk Reference*

*New York Stock Exchange Fact Book*, New York Stock Exchange
*New York Times*
*The Newsletter on Newsletters*
*Nikkei Data Bank*, Nikkei America
*NonProfit Times*
*North American International Business*
*NYNEX Business to Business Yellow Pages*
*O'Dwyer's Directory of Public Relations Firms*, J.R. O'Dwyer
*Occupational Outlook Handbook*, U.S. Government Printing Office
*OEL Insider*, Office of Export Licensing, Bureau of Export Administration
*Office Adminstration Handbook*, The Dartnell Corporation
*Official U.S. Custom House Guide*, North American Publishing
*On Location National Film and Videotape Production Directory*, On Location Publishing
*ONESCO Statistical Yearbook*, UNIPUB
*Opportunity in Mexico: Small Business Guide*, Small Business Administration
*Packaging Magazine*
*The Partnership Book: How to Write a Partnership Agreement*, Nolo Press
*Patent It Yourself*, Nolo Press
*Payroll Tax Guide*, Automatic Data Processing
*PC Computing*
*PC Week*
*PC World*
*Pensions & Investment Age*
*Pensions & Investments*, Crain Communications
*Pensions and Other Retirement Benefits Plans*, Bureau of National Affairs
*Personnel and Human Relations Management*, West Publishing
*Personnel Management Guide*, Prentice-Hall Information Services
*Perspectives*, American Productivity and Quality Center
*Pocket Station Listing Guide*, National Association of Television Program Executives
*Political Finance and Lobby Reporter*, Amward Publications
*Poor's Register of Corporations, Directors, and Executives*, Standard and Poor's
*Popular Names of U.S. Government Reports: A Catalog*, Government Printing Office
*PR/Media Connection*
*Practical Guide to Credit and Collection*, AMACOM
*Pratt's Guide to Venture Capital Sources*, Venture Economics
*Prentice-Hall Tax Strategy Series*, Prentice-Hall
*Productivity and the Economy: A Chartbook*, Bureau of Labor Statistics, U.S. Department of Labor
*Productivity Measures for Selected Industries*, Bureau of Labor Statistics, U.S. Department of Labor
*Protect Your Company from A to Z*, Business Research Publications
*Public Accounting Report*
*Public Relations Journal*
*The Public Warehouse Selection Process*, Affiliated Warehouse Companies
*Publish Magazine*
*Publishers Weekly*
*Quality Systems Update*, CEEM Information Services
*Racism and Sexism in Corporate Life*, Free Press
*Radio and Records Magazine*
*Rand McNally Bankers Directory: International*, Rand McNally
*Rand McNally Bankers Directory: United States*, Rand McNally
*Rating America's Corporate Conscience*, Addison-Wesley
*Rating Guide to Franchises*, Facts on File
*RCRA Orientation Manual*, U.S. Government Printing Office
*Real Estate Market Forecast*, Landauer Real Estate Counselors
*Report of the National Critical Technologies Panel*, Executive Office of the President
*Robert Half on Hiring*, Plume
*Safety Management: Office and Branch Manager's Bulletin*, National Foreman's Institute
*Safety*, Prentice-Hall
*Science & Engineering Indicators*, National Science Foundation
*A Secretary's Handbook: Addressing Overseas Letters*, W. Foulsham & Co.
*Security Dealer*
*Security Distributing & Marketing*

*Security Magazine*
*Selected Data on Research and Development in Industry*, National Science Foundation
*Selling Techniques*, Marketing Technology Corporation
*Sid Cato's Newsletter on Annual Reports*
*Site Selection Magazine*
*The Small Business Advocate*
*Small Business Forms*, LawPrep Press
*Small Business Handbook*, Prentice-Hall
*The Small Business Legal Guide*, Dearborn Financial Publishing
*Small Business Reports*, American Management Association
*Small Business Resource Guide*, U.S. Chamber of Commerce
*Small Business Sourcebook*, Gale Research
*Society of Actuaries Yearbook*, Society of Actuaries
*Software Reviews on File*, Facts on File
*The Source Book of Franchise Opportunities*, Richard D. Irwin
*Spot Television Rates and Data*, Standard Rate and Data Service
*Standard & Poor's 500 Index*, Standard & Poor's
*Standard and Poor's Creditweek*
*Standard Directory of Advertising Agencies: The Agency Red Book*, National Register Publishing Company
*Standard Legal Forms and Agreements for Small Businesses*, Self Counsel Press
*Starting and Operating a Clipping Service*, Pilot Books
*State and Metropolitan Area Databook*, U.S. Government Printing Office
*State Tax Guide*, Commerce Clearing House
*Statistical Abstract of the United States*, U.S. Government Printing Office
*Stocks, Bonds, and Inflation Yearbook*, Ibbotson Associates
*Strategies for Tenant Representatives*, Society of Industrial and Office Realtors
*Stratospheric Ozone Information Hotline*
*Study of Media and Markets*, Simmons Market Research Bureau
*Success Magazine*
*Superbrands: America's Top 2000 Brands*, Brandweek/BPI Communications
*Survey of Current Business*, U.S. Department of Commerce, Bureau of Economic Analysis
*The Telecommuting Resource Guide*, Pacific Bell
*Telemarkerting Buyer's Guide*
*Ten-Second Business Forms*, Bob Adams
*Tenant's Handbook to Office Leasing*, McGraw-Hill Professional Publishing Group
*Thomas Register of American Manufacturers*, Thomas Publishing
*Thomas Register's Inbound Traffic Guide*, Thomas Publishing
*Tokyo Stock Exchange Fact Book*, Tokyo Stock Exchange
*Trade Show and Convention Guide*, Amusement Business
*Traders' Catalog & Resource Guide*
*Tradeshow Services Directory*, Tradeshow Week
*Trading Company Sourcebook*, National Federation of Export Associations
*Training Directory for Employee Development*, Gale Research
*Training Magazine*
*Translator's Handbook*, Learned Information
*Travel Industry World Yearbook*, Child and Waters
*Travel Smart for Business*
*U.S. Customs Guide for Private Flyers*, U. S. Customs Service
*U.S. Department of State Travel Advisory*
*U.S. Industrial Outlook*, U.S. Department of Commerce
*U.S. Leading Management Export Companies*, Bergano Book Company
*U.S. News & World Report*
*U.S. Office Market Survey*, Salomon Brothers
*U.S. Office Market*, Salomon Brothers
*The Ultimate College Shopper's Guide*, Addison-Wesley
*Understanding Wall Street*, TAB Books
*Uninsured in America*, Kaiser Health Reform Project
*Universal Almanac*, Andrews & McNeel
*Urban Land Magazine*, Urban Land Institute (ULI)
*USA Today*
*Value Line Composite Index*

*Variety's Directory of Major U.S. Show Business Awards*, R.R. Bowker
*Variety's Who's Who in Show Business*, R.R. Bowker
*Venture Capital: Where To Find It*, National Association of Small Business Investment Companies
*Venture Economics*, SDC Publishing
*Vest Pocket Business Fact Book*, Prentice-Hall
*Vest Pocket CEO*, Prentice-Hall
*Vest Pocket Marketer*, Prentice-Hall
*Vest Pocket MBA*, Prentice-Hall
*Vital Business Secrets for New and Growing Companies*, Dow Jones-Irwin
*Wall Street Journal*, Dow Jones
*Wall Street Words*, Houghton Mifflin
*Washington Information Directory*, Congressional Quarterly
*Washington Representatives*, Columbia Books
*What Every Executive Better Know About the Law*, Simon & Schuster
*Who Knows What*, Henry Holt
*Who Owns What Is in Your Head?*, Elsevier-Dutton
*Who's Who and What's What in Packaging*, Institute of Packaging Professionals
*Who's Who in Entertainment*, R.R. Bowker
*Who's Who in Professional Speaking*, National Speakers Association
*Who's Who in Venture Capital*, John Wiley & Sons
*Who's Who of Customs Brokers and Forwarding Agents*, National Customs Brokers and Forwarding Agents Association
*Wilshire 5000 Equity Index*, Wilshire Information Services
*Windows Magazine*
*Women and Family Clearinghouse*, Women's Bureau, U.S. Department of Labor
*Workers' Relocation: A Bibliography*, Vance Bibliographies
*Working Woman*
*Workplace Competencies*, U.S. Department of Education
*Worksite AIDS Education and Attitudes Toward People with the Disease*, Georgia Institute of Technology
*Worksite Wellness*, Prentice-Hall
*World Aviation Directory*, McGraw-Hill
*The World Bank Atlas*, The World Bank
*World Currency Yearbook*, International Currency Analysis
*World Technology/Patent Licensing Gazette*, Techni Research Associates
*World Trade*
*Your Company Magazine*, American Express Publishing Corporation
*Your Rights in the Workplace*, Nolo Press
*The Zen of Media Hype*, Citadel Press

# THE 1995
# INFORMATION PLEASE®
# BUSINESS ALMANAC &
# SOURCEBOOK

# BUSINESS LAW & GOVERNMENT

# Legal Issues in Hiring and Firing

THE 1986–1988 COMBINED ANNUAL Report of the Equal Employment Opportunity Commission states that three of the four most frequently cited charges received by the EEOC were related to hiring and firing practices. In 1988 alone 49.5% of these complaints were directed against an employer's discharge practices, followed by 17.8% regarding terms of employment, and 8.8% pertaining to hiring practices. Hiring and firing procedures should be carefully reviewed to assess the potential liability hidden within established practices.

## Hiring

Hiring, in many cases, begins with a job application. Many of the questions found on traditional applications for employment have become sources of discrimination suits. A non-discriminatory job application should not contain questions about the following:

- Race, age, sex, religion, and national origin. An employer can ask if an applicant is 18 years of age or older and has a legal right to work in this country either through citizenship or status as a resident alien.

- Marital status, maiden name, number, names, and ages of children or other dependents.

- Employment of the spouse and child-care arrangements unless such queries are made of both male and female applicants.

- A woman's pregnancy or related condition.

- Arrest records which did not result in convictions. It is permissible to inquire about convictions or pending felony charges.

- The existence, nature, or severity of a disability. An employer may ask about an applicant's ability to perform specific job functions.

- An applicant's height and weight, except in specific professions such as law enforcement, when valid guidelines have been established for various national organizations.

- Organizational affiliations except those pertaining to professional memberships related to the specific job.

- Military history unless the job requires such a background.

- Status as a high school graduate. It is permissible to request the applicant to supply the details of his or her educational history.

- Lowest salary acceptable for a specific position.

An interview can often be more litigiously threatening than the employment application, because uninformed interviewers often ask seemingly harmless questions which may, in fact, be discriminatory. An interviewer may casually ask a 32-year-old female applicant if she anticipates having a family. If she responds affirmatively and subsequently is not hired, she could file suit for discriminatory hiring practices. Experts say the general rule of thumb is: if a question does not have anything to do with the job, or is not vital to determining the applicant's ability to perform the responsibilities associated with the job, do not ask it.

## Firing

Improperly handled employee terminations generate a significant number of lawsuits against corporations. Complete and accurate records of such actions protect the interests of both the employer and the former employee.

Firing generates stress for the employee being discharged, the individual who does the terminating, and the employees who remain with the company. There are several concepts to consider before, during, and after the discharge is completed which can significantly affect the attitudes and reactions of all involved as well as the vulnerability of the employer.

## Before Firing an Employee

- Be sure the action is approved by top management and conforms to written company policy. Corporate legal advice may be sought regarding severance conditions for higher level employees.

- Except in a for-cause dismissal, an employee is entitled to a documented, concise explanation of the reasons for his or her dismissal. Plan the interview carefully to anticipate responses and diffuse reactions.

- Federal law requires a 60-day advance notification of employees affected by layoffs and plant or office closings. Prematurely early notification may significantly affect production and possibly invite undesirable reactions.

- Consider the possibility of an irrational response by a dismissed employee. Take the necessary precautions to change security codes, access codes to computers, and entry to the corporate premises.

## Handling a Termination

- Be honest and completely clear about the reasons for discharge. Avoid personal statements which might degrade or humiliate the individual, or vague statements which might suggest that the situation is reversible.

- It is sometimes helpful to have another individual, such as a professional from human resources,

*Legal Issues in Hiring and Firing (cont'd)*

present as a witness and a support for the employee, particularly if emotional reactions are anticipated.

- Present a precise explanation of severance pay procedures, benefits continuation forms, pension or profit-sharing payouts, and other available assistance, such as outplacement counseling. In larger corporations, the human resources department handles the filling out of the necessary forms and documents.

- Allow the individual to remove personal belongings at a low-visibility time, after hours or on a weekend. Prepare a checklist of company property that should be accounted for, including keys, credit cards, ID cards, computer disks.

- Respond to all questions and discuss the cover story to be presented when future employers inquire about the individual. Be prepared with a version that is supportive of the employee but does not threaten the company's credibility.

## After Firing an Employee

- Document the termination in writing immediately, detailing conversation, reactions, and emotional tone of both parties. This is essential for a response to any future challenge to the termination.

- Inform the staff or co-workers of the termination by word of mouth or by memo. In the case of for-cause termination, the incident should be men-tioned only briefly, in a non-defamatory manner. If performance is the reason, experts suggest that simply stating that the employee and the organization have agreed to part company should suffice.

- In the case of staff reduction or layoffs, the remaining staff should be assured that downsizing was warranted and that no additional layoffs are anticipated at this time. (If additional reductions are expected, employees should be informed that such an action may be required, and that they will be informed on or before a specific date.)

- Invite employees who have additional questions and concerns to meet with specified representatives of the company privately.

- Inform clients or customers who deal with the discharged individual that the company will continue to serve their needs. When necessary, name a specific individual who will replace the terminated employee.

## Recommended Resources

*The Human Resources Yearbook*
Prentice-Hall, $79.95
(800) 223-1360

*Every Manager's Guide to Firing*
Irwin Professional Publishing, $45
(708) 206-2700

# Non-Compete Agreements

LOSING A VALUED EMPLOYEE is disconcerting. Discovering that the individual has defected to a competitor and has taken proprietary information with him or her is shocking and infuriating. Considerable damage can result when an employee takes invaluable company information such as proposed new product lines or strategic planning, and ultimately gives the competition an unfair advantage. Small and large businesses alike are faced with the problem of reducing the risk of losing more than an employee.

One commonly adopted solution is requiring a new employee to sign a non-compete agreement. Such a document is an agreement between the employer and employee stating that, should the employee choose to leave the company, he or she will not go to work for a competitor for a specified period of time, frequently two years.

A non-compete document is particularly useful for employees who have access to critical information, either through job responsibility or through social interactions with owners or high-level executives. While the signed agreement does not provide foolproof protection against such disruption, it deters this type of action by forcing the employee to reconsider the temptations. A signed document is an excellent reminder of one's responsibility.

A standard non-compete agreement might read this way:

---

**Employee agrees as a condition of employment that, in the event of termination for any reason, he/she will not engage in a similar or competitive business for a period of two years, nor will he/she contact or solicit any customer with whom Employer conducted business during his/her employment. This restrictive covenant shall be for a term of two years from termination, and shall encompass an area within a 50-mile radius of Employer's place of business.**

---

Additional clauses might specify the protections desired by an individual business.

*Non-Compete Agreements (cont'd)*

---

**Employee agrees that Employer's customer lists, processes, manufacturing techniques, sales materials, and pricing information constitute the sole and exclusive property of Employer, and that same are 'trade secrets' under the law. Employee promises that under no circumstances shall he/she disclose same, during or after the term hereof, and upon violation of this provision Employee agrees that Employer shall be entitled to an injunction, compensatory and punitive damages, and reimbursement for its counsel fee.**

---

*Source: What Every Executive Better Know About the Law*

It is important to note that non-compete agreements may be illegal in Montana, Nevada, North Dakota, and Oklahoma. Such agreements may be invalid or limited in Colorado, Florida, Hawaii, Louisiana, Oregon, South Dakota, and Wisconsin. While there is no federal law regarding non-compete agreements, employers should consult state regulations before using such a document.

# Employment Contracts

AN EMPLOYMENT CONTRACT spells out the conditions of employment including wages, hours, and type of work.

Depending upon the level of employment, the responsibility of the new employee, and the nature of the business, the conditions of employment should be detailed regarding the following elements:

- Term of employment.

- Duties of the employee including general and specific responsibilities and performance of duties.

- Compensation including monthly salary, automobile expenses, relocation and moving expenses, and a one-time bonus inducement if used. Details such as bonus or incentive plans, stock options, salary deferment plans, disability benefits, and health and retirement plans may or may not be spelled out.

- Confidentiality required of the employee regarding employer's operating expenses, pricing formulas, procedures, trade secrets, and proprietary information. This confidentiality extends to employee lists, customer lists, or prospective customers who become clients of the organization during the individual's term.

- A non-compete clause as described above.

- Provisions for termination including a violation of responsibility, an inability to perform duties, reorganization, or low company profits. Higher-level employees frequently have a clause included in the contract to state a certain amount of money, often from six to twelve months of salary, which will be paid to the employee in the event of termination by disagreement or dispute.

It is important to remember that any item not covered in the original employment contract falls under common law rights. Therefore, an employee owns the rights to all ideas, inventions, or discoveries unless he or she was specifically hired to develop those ideas or inventions. If the idea or invention is the incidental result of his employment, then the rights belong to the employee unless otherwise specified in the employment contract.

---

## The Top Reference Sources

Copyright Clearance Center
222 Rosewood Dr.
Danvers, MA 01923
(508) 750-8400

The Copyright Clearance Center is a non-profit organization created to ease the process of securing copyright permission and collecting fees. Thousands of publishers and users of business magazines, newsletters, books, technical and trade journals, and other publications register with the CCC and allow it to grant permission and collect fees for the right to reproduce copyrighted materials.

# Contracts

JUST AS A BUSINESSPERSON scans the corporate environment for potential legal pitfalls within the organization, so too, he or she must similarly judge the potential liability of decisions involving outside individuals or businesses. While a written contract is not necessary for every action and decision taken by a businessperson, it can prove invaluable when:

- Disputes arise over delivery dates or option terms;
- Clear, precise written proof is required to resolve litigation;
- Complex details are anticipated and dealt with on paper instead of in the courtroom.

There are several instances when it is in an executive's own best interests to have a simple written agreement on file. First, a boilerplate model of a basic agreement should be kept on file and used when a company hires a consultant or independent contractor. Second, a letter of agreement should be used when an executive wants to create a "written handshake" which states the essentials of the agreement without becoming mired in details. Such an agreement states the simple facts in writing, and is confirmed and accepted when signed and returned to the sender.

This simple document should:

- Identify both parties and the role of each in the agreement;
- Describe the nature of the agreement;
- State payment terms, time expectations, and other contingencies of the agreement;
- In the case of independent contractors, the document should include a clause prohibiting the disclosure to a competitor of any work created for this employer.

An early warning system of liability sensitivity requires prudence rather than panic. It isn't necessary to call an attorney before making every decision. Such hesitation affects the spontaneity of business agreements. Yet it is wise to have boilerplate documents reviewed by counsel prior to being used for the first time. When in doubt regarding a simple agreement, it is worth the peace of mind to consult an attorney. Counsel should be sought when complex situations are involved, such as incorporation, partnership, lease agreements, real estate agreements, debt collection, litigation, and labor/management relations.

The Small Business Administration (SBA) has business development specialists who can provide useful information and direction in response to telephone queries. To find a nearby regional office, call the SBA Answer Desk at (800) 827-5722. (*See also* "*Small Business Administration Regional Offices*" on *page 404.*)

## Recommended Resource

*Small Business Legal Handbook*
by Robert Friedman
Dearborn Financial Publishing, $69.95
(800) 533-2665

# Intellectual Property Protection

IF AN INTRUDER STEALS a word processor or piece of equipment from a factory, the owner becomes acutely aware of the loss. Yet the daily misuse of a company's intellectual property, including its logo or trademark, constitutes theft as well and can be far more damaging. An organization's intellectual property is protected by trademarks (on the company name or logo), patents (on its inventions or product designs), and copyrights (on the literary, musical, or photographic products) generated by or for the company.

## Trademarks

A trademark is potentially the most valuable asset of an organization. It is a word, symbol, design, or combination of these elements which identifies one's products and services and distinguishes them from others in the marketplace. The identity created by a distinct trademark is priceless in the customer loyalty and product awareness it generates. Trade-marks extend the company's public image not only through the product or service, but also through printed material, packaging, and advertising which bear that mark.

An owner can protect a trademark by common law or by federal registration. Common law protection begins with the first use of a mark and is indicated by ™ while federal registration requires a more complicated procedure.

## Why Register a Trademark?

An unregistered trademark (™) is protected by common law only within states where it is used. When a trademark is used in interstate commerce, experts suggest that it is in the owner's best interests to register the trademark (®) with the Federal Patent and Trademark Office (PTO). Such registration guarantees ownership of the mark and entitlement to its use throughout the nation. It can be devastating to a corporation to establish a product name and trade-

*Intellectual Property Protection (cont'd)*

mark recognition only to find that its use is challenged by a previously unknown owner. Imagine the effect on Apple Computer if they suddenly discovered, six months after the first computer rolled off the assembly line, that their trademark rainbow apple with one bite missing was legally in use by an obscure organic fruit grower in California. Registration protects against litigation and liability as well as costly damages. When a trademark is to be used in a complicated manner, it is wise to consult a lawyer regarding the value of federally registering the mark.

Once a trademark is registered, ownership continues for a renewable period of ten years. Midway through the first decade, however, the owner must file an affidavit of intent to continue use of the trademark. In the absence of such documentation, the registration is canceled.

## Life Cycle of a Trademark

Whenever a new business is begun or a new product line is established in an existing company, a unique name, trademark, or logo is created. A corporate trademark, name, or symbol evolves out of the following process:

- Possible names are suggested in brainstorming sessions, by use of software designed to generate names or by name-creation consultants.

- Suggestions are screened via trademark directories or on-line research systems to determine the existence of conflicting U.S. federal, state, or international trademark registrations or applications. (See below.)

- Candidates that survive the initial screening are subjected to professional trademark searches and reports on the availability of use of the desired trademark.

- An application and filing fee is presented to the Patent and Trademark Office (PTO) of the U.S. Department of Commerce and is reviewed by its federal staff.

- If no opposition or conflict is found in the application review process, the trademark is presented in the PTO's official gazette for opposition or challenge.

- Having survived this last hurdle, the owner of the proposed trademark is permitted to register the trademark. All subsequent use of the trademark should include the symbol ® as notification that the trademark is protected under federal trademark law. It is important to note, however, that a

mark may be challenged for up to five years under federal law.

## How to File an Application for Registration

The trademark owner can apply for registration independently or may be represented by an attorney. The risks associated with the financial advantages of self-representation include the possibility of having the application rejected and forfeiting the application fee if the PTO attorney discovers a conflicting mark. However, with some reasonable preparation, an enterprising individual can complete the application form and proceed through at least the initial stages of the procedure.

If a reasonably thorough search is conducted and no conflicting marks are uncovered, the application may be completed and submitted with the fee to the PTO for review.

Application for registration requires:

- A completed application form;

- A drawing of the mark to be used;

- Specimens showing intended use of the mark;

- Filing fee ($210 or more; check with the PTO).

The PTO has documented all the pertinent information about trademark registration applications and filing requirements in a useful booklet called *Basic Facts About Trademarks*.

All correspondence with the PTO, as well as requests for this booklet, can be addressed to:

The Commissioner of Patents and Trademarks
Washington, DC 20231

## Contact Options

*Information Hotlines:*

General Trademark or Patent Information
(703) 308-4357

Automated (Recorded) General Trademark or Patent Information
(800) 557-4636

Automated Line for Status Information on Trademark Applications
(703) 305-8747

Copyright Information (Library of Congress)
(202) 707-3000

*America Online offers the Microsoft Small Business Center, an amalgam of information and articles from the American Management Association, Dun & Bradstreet, Nation's Business, the SBA, and others. KEYWORD MSBC.*

*Intellectual Property Protection (cont'd)*

| TRADEMARK/SERVICE MARK APPLICATION, PRINCIPAL REGISTER, WITH DECLARATION | MARK (Word(s) and/or Design) | CLASS NO. (If known) |
|---|---|---|

**TO THE ASSISTANT SECRETARY AND COMMISSIONER OF PATENTS AND TRADEMARKS:**

**APPLICANT'S NAME:**

**APPLICANT'S BUSINESS ADDRESS:**
(Display address exactly as
it should appear on registration)

**APPLICANT'S ENTITY TYPE:** (**Check one** and supply requested information)

Individual - Citizen of (Country):

Partnership - State where organized (Country, if appropriate):
Names and Citizenship (Country) of General Partners:

Corporation - State (Country, if appropriate) of Incorporation:

Other (Specify Nature of Entity and Domicile):

**GOODS AND/OR SERVICES:**

Applicant requests registration of the trademark/service mark shown in the accompanying drawing in the United States Patent and Trademark Office on the Principal Register established by the Act of July 5, 1946 (15 U.S.C. 1051 et. seq., as amended) for the following goods/services (**SPECIFIC GOODS AND/OR SERVICES MUST BE INSERTED HERE):**

**BASIS FOR APPLICATION:** (Check boxes which apply, **but never both the first AND second boxes,** and supply requested information related to each box checked.)

[ ] Applicant is using the mark in commerce on or in connection with the above identified goods/services. (15 U.S.C. 1051(a), as amended.) Three specimens showing the mark as used in commerce are submitted with this application.
 • Date of first use of the mark in commerce which the U.S. Congress may regulate (for example, interstate or between the U.S. and a foreign country):
 • Specify the type of commerce:
 (for example, interstate or between the U.S. and a specified foreign country)
 • Date of first use anywhere (the same as or before use in commerce date):
 • Specify manner or mode of use of mark on or in connection with the goods/services:
 (for example, trademark is applied to labels, service mark is used in advertisements)

[ ] Applicant has a bona fide intention to use the mark in commerce on or in connection with the above identified goods/services. (15 U.S.C. 1051(b), as amended.)
 • Specify intended manner or mode of use of mark on or in connection with the goods/services:
 (for example, trademark will be applied to labels, service mark will be used in advertisements)

[ ] Applicant has a bona fide intention to use the mark in commerce on or in connection with the above identified goods/services, and asserts a claim of priority based upon a foreign application in accordance with 15 U.S.C. 1126(d), as amended.
 • Country of foreign filing: _____ • Date of foreign filing: _____

[ ] Applicant has a bona fide intention to use the mark in commerce on or in connection with the above identified goods/services and, accompanying this application, submits a certification or certified copy of a foreign registration in accordance with 15 U.S.C. 1126(e), as amended.
 • Country of registration: _____ • Registration number: _____

**NOTE: Declaration, on Reverse Side, MUST be Signed**

PTO Form 1478 (REV. 8/92)
OMB No. 0651-0009 (Exp. 6/30/95)

U.S. DEPARTMENT OF COMMERCE/Patent and Trademark Office

*Intellectual Property Protection (cont'd)*

## DECLARATION

The undersigned being hereby warned that willful false statements and the like so made are punishable by fine or imprisonment, or both, under 18 U.S.C. 1001, and that such willful false statements may jeopardize the validity of the application or any resulting registration, declares that he/she is properly authorized to execute this application on behalf of the applicant; he/she believes the applicant to be the owner of the trademark/service mark sought to be registered, or, if the application is being filed under 15 U.S.C. 1051(b), he/she believes applicant to be entitled to use such mark in commerce; to the best of his/her knowledge and belief no other person, firm, corporation, or association has the right to use the above identified mark in commerce, either in the identical form thereof or in such near resemblance thereto as to be likely, when used on or in connection with the goods/services of such other person, to cause confusion, or to cause mistake, or to deceive; and that all statements made of his/her own knowledge are true and that all statements made on information and belief are believed to be true.

_____       _____
DATE                                 SIGNATURE

_____       _____
TELEPHONE NUMBER              PRINT OR TYPE NAME AND POSITION

## INSTRUCTIONS AND INFORMATION FOR APPLICANT

**TO RECEIVE A FILING DATE, THE APPLICATION MUST BE COMPLETED AND SIGNED BY THE APPLICANT AND SUBMITTED ALONG WITH:**

1. The prescribed **FEE ($210.00)** for each class of goods/services listed in the application;
2. A **DRAWING PAGE** displaying the mark in conformance with 37 CFR 2.52;
3. If the application is based on use of the mark in commerce, **THREE (3) SPECIMENS** (evidence) of the mark as used in commerce for each class of goods/services listed in the application. All three specimens may be in the nature of: (a) labels showing the mark which are placed on the goods; (b) photographs of the mark as it appears on the goods, (c) brochures or advertisements showing the mark as used in connection with the services.
4. An **APPLICATION WITH DECLARATION** (this form) - The application must be signed in order for the application to receive a filing date. Only the following person may sign the declaration, depending on the applicant's legal entity: (a) the individual applicant; (b) an officer of the corporate applicant; (c) one general partner of a partnership applicant; (d) all joint applicants.

**SEND APPLICATION FORM, DRAWING PAGE, FEE, AND SPECIMENS (IF APPROPRIATE) TO:**

**U.S. DEPARTMENT OF COMMERCE**
Patent and Trademark Office, Box TRADEMARK
Washington, D.C. 20231

Additional information concerning the requirements for filing an application is available in a booklet entitled **Basic Facts About Trademarks**, which may be obtained by writing to the above address or by calling: (703) 308-HELP.

This form is estimated to take an average of 1 hour to complete, including time required for reading and understanding instructions, gathering necessary information, recordkeeping, and actually providing the information. Any comments on this form, including the amount of time required to complete this form, should be sent to the Office of Management and Organization, U.S. Patent and Trademark Office, U.S. Department of Commerce, Washington, D.C. 20231, and to Paperwork Reduction Project 0651-0009, Office of Information and Regulatory Affairs, Office of Management and Budget, Washington, D.C. 20503. Do NOT send completed forms to either of these addresses.

# Trademark Protection

"ASPIRIN," "THERMOS," "CELLOPHANE," "shredded wheat," "nylon," and "zipper" are examples of the greatest danger facing a trademark holder. Each was once a registered but, unfortunately, poorly protected trademark. Public misuse caused the trademark name to degenerate to a generic term describing the class or nature of an article. Subsequently, the holder was denied the renewal of trademark rights, and the product name became simply a generic term for competitors' products.

A company or individual holding trademark rights should take the following precautions:

- Make sure the mark being used isn't already in use. Protect interests through a trademark search by a professional search organization.

- Use the trademark symbol ™ to indicate that it is the company's selected mark.

- Once registration is complete, use the ® symbol to indicate that the trademark is officially registered.

- Consider the services of a trademark-search firm to monitor the valid and unscrupulous use of the mark.

- Notify in writing anyone who is misusing a trademark.

- In all advertising, use the trademark as an adjective modifier, rather than as a noun or a verb. Xerox®, for example, is careful to remind the public that Xerox® is a type of photocopier, rather than a process of duplicating a document.

Properly protected, a trademark can last indefinitely.

## Contact Option

Patent and Trademark Office
(703) 308-4357, or (703) 557-4636 for recorded system

# Trademark Searches

THE KEY TO THE SUCCESSFUL adoption of a trademark lies in the trademark search. This process ensures that a desired trademark does not infringe on another existing mark. An informal search can be performed independently and is particularly useful when screening suggestions for trademarks. Searches are generally conducted through computer subscriber databases such as Compu-Mark, Dialog, or IntelliGate, using a computer, modem, and printer.

At a cost of between $5 and $10 per search, an individual may uncover duplicate, conflicting trademarks. A search may also be conducted in a state patent and trademark depository library using Cassis, the free government on-line system. Finally, a search may be made in the library used by the PTO. This facility is located on the second floor of the South Tower Building, 2900 Crystal Dr., Arlington, VA 22202. Note: while these libraries have CD-ROMs containing a database of both registered and pending trademarks in written descriptions, they do not contain the graphics of the actual design marks.

While the informal, independent search described above is a sound preliminary step, it is critical to ensure that the search process has been comprehensive. A successful challenge to the use of a trademark can result in staggering damages, legal costs and loss of profits by the party found guilty of infringement. This financial devastation could be compounded by the expense of removing the offending trademark from all advertising materials, labels and packaging, printed corporate stationery, checks, price lists, catalogues, and any other place in which the mark is displayed.

The wise alternative to an informal search is the use of professional trademark-search services, such as those listed below. These organizations serve a wide range of functions designed to determine the availability of a trademark or trade name for use. Such services also monitor the marketplace for infringement of trademark use, supervise the maintenance of an existing trademark and advise a client regarding the possible acquisition of a specific mark. The value of such a service lies in the thoroughness with which trademark candidates are investigated from among common law sources, pending applications, and actual registrations. Investigations can extend to the state, national, or international marketplace, and can be performed in the preliminary screening stage as well as during the critical pre-filing period. Using such a service in the preliminary design stages of trademark development can save dollars in a costly design budget.

Once a trademark is secured, these agencies can provide additional services such as monitoring the activity of competitors, including the application for new marks from within a specific industry.

*Trademark Searches (cont'd)*

## Contact Options

*Trademark-Search Services:*

Thomson & Thomson
500 Victory Rd.
North Quincy, MA 02171
(800) 692-8833 or (617) 479-1600

Trademark Research Corporation
300 Park Ave. S., 8th floor
New York, NY 10010
(800) 872-6275 or (212) 228-4084

Additional organizations may be listed in the business pages of the local telephone directory.

# Filing for a Copyright

THE COPYRIGHT LAW is important to business individuals from two perspectives: as an owner and as a potential user of registered material. A copyright is used to protect the rights of the author of published or unpublished literature, music and lyrics, drama, choreography, graphics and other art forms, motion pictures, and sound recording.

A revision in the copyright law no longer requires copyright owners to mark their works in a special way to qualify for protection. However, many copyright owners continue to indicate their ownership in the work by using a © to indicate copyright protection.

The copyright registration process originates with an application form obtained from the U.S. Copyright Office. Form TX is the most commonly used application for most business uses and covers non-dramatic literary works such as fiction, nonfiction, textbooks, reference works, directories, catalogues, advertising copy, and computer programs.

## Other Common Forms and Their Uses

- Form PA: Material to be performed, including music (with accompanying lyrics), choreography, motion pictures, audio-visuals.

- Form VA: Visual arts. "Pictorial, graphic, or sculptural works," graphic arts, photographs, prints and art reproductions, maps, globes, charts, technical drawings, diagrams, and models.

- Form SR: Sound recordings.

Once the application is completed, it should be sent with the $20.00 application fee, payable to the Register of Copyrights, Copyright Office, Library of Congress, Washington, DC 20559. After the copyright has been issued, the owner has three months to supply two copies of the registered work, one for registration and one for the Library of Congress, to the Copyright Office.

Confusion arises concerning what can and cannot be copyrighted. Phrases, slogans, ideas, and mottoes cannot be copyrighted. Neither can blank forms, methods, systems, concepts, and names of products. Occasionally, a business owner will attempt to copyright a product or service name, only to be informed that such registration is covered under trademark law rather than copyright law.

### Fair Use

The general rule of thumb is that up to 250 words of text from a book or long article may be used without securing permission for such use. Be very careful of poetry, songs, famous individuals, and endorsements, however. Recent case law has made some works (like directories) more open to fair use, and others (like a star's singing style) less open.

### Contact Options

Copyright Office
Public Information Office
(202) 707-3000
To obtain specific copyright forms, call the Forms Hotline (202) 707-9100

Software Publishers Association Piracy Hotline
(800) 388-7478

---

## The Top Reference Sources

*Your Rights in the Workplace*
Nolo Press, $15.95
(800) 992-6656 or (510) 549-1976

Written by Dan Lacey, a workplace consultant, this book is an employee's guide to firing and layoffs, wages and overtime, maternity and parental leave, unemployment and disability insurance, workers' compensation, job safety, sex, race, and age discrimination. It also explains the latest changes in laws passed to protect workers.

While written from an employee's point of view, this book is also an excellent resource for ensuring that an employer doesn't violate the law.

*Filing for a Copyright (cont'd)*

# FORM TX

**For a Literary Work**
UNITED STATES COPYRIGHT OFFICE

REGISTRATION NUMBER

|  | TX | TXU |
|---|---|---|

EFFECTIVE DATE OF REGISTRATION

| Month | Day | Year |
|---|---|---|

**DO NOT WRITE ABOVE THIS LINE. IF YOU NEED MORE SPACE, USE A SEPARATE CONTINUATION SHEET.**

## 1

**TITLE OF THIS WORK ▼**

**PREVIOUS OR ALTERNATIVE TITLES ▼**

**PUBLICATION AS A CONTRIBUTION** If this work was published as a contribution to a periodical, serial, or collection, give information about the collective work in which the contribution appeared.  **Title of Collective Work ▼**

If published in a periodical or serial give:  **Volume ▼**     **Number ▼**     **Issue Date ▼**     **On Pages ▼**

## 2

**a**

**NAME OF AUTHOR ▼**

**DATES OF BIRTH AND DEATH**
Year Born ▼     Year Died ▼

Was this contribution to the work a "work made for hire"?
☐ Yes
☐ No

**AUTHOR'S NATIONALITY OR DOMICILE**
Name of Country
OR { Citizen of ▶
Domiciled in▶

**WAS THIS AUTHOR'S CONTRIBUTION TO THE WORK**
Anonymous?   ☐ Yes  ☐ No
Pseudonymous?   ☐ Yes  ☐ No
If the answer to either of these questions is "Yes," see detailed instructions.

**NATURE OF AUTHORSHIP** Briefly describe nature of material created by this author in which copyright is claimed. ▼

**NOTE**

Under the law, the "author" of a "work made for hire" is generally the employer, not the employee (see instructions). For any part of this work that was "made for hire" check "Yes" in the space provided, give the employer (or other person for whom the work was prepared) as "Author" of that part, and leave the space for dates of birth and death blank.

**b**

**NAME OF AUTHOR ▼**

**DATES OF BIRTH AND DEATH**
Year Born ▼     Year Died ▼

Was this contribution to the work a "work made for hire"?
☐ Yes
☐ No

**AUTHOR'S NATIONALITY OR DOMICILE**
Name of Country
OR { Citizen of ▶
Domiciled in▶

**WAS THIS AUTHOR'S CONTRIBUTION TO THE WORK**
Anonymous?   ☐ Yes  ☐ No
Pseudonymous?   ☐ Yes  ☐ No
If the answer to either of these questions is "Yes," see detailed instructions.

**NATURE OF AUTHORSHIP** Briefly describe nature of material created by this author in which copyright is claimed. ▼

**c**

**NAME OF AUTHOR ▼**

**DATES OF BIRTH AND DEATH**
Year Born ▼     Year Died ▼

Was this contribution to the work a "work made for hire"?
☐ Yes
☐ No

**AUTHOR'S NATIONALITY OR DOMICILE**
Name of Country
OR { Citizen of ▶
Domiciled in▶

**WAS THIS AUTHOR'S CONTRIBUTION TO THE WORK**
Anonymous?   ☐ Yes  ☐ No
Pseudonymous?   ☐ Yes  ☐ No
If the answer to either of these questions is "Yes," see detailed instructions.

**NATURE OF AUTHORSHIP** Briefly describe nature of material created by this author in which copyright is claimed. ▼

## 3

**a** **YEAR IN WHICH CREATION OF THIS WORK WAS COMPLETED** This information must be given
◀ Year in all cases.

**b** **DATE AND NATION OF FIRST PUBLICATION OF THIS PARTICULAR WORK**
Complete this information Month ▶ _____ Day ▶ _____ Year ▶ _____
ONLY if this work has been published.
◀ Nation

## 4

See instructions before completing this space.

**COPYRIGHT CLAIMANT(S)** Name and address must be given even if the claimant is the same as the author given in space 2. ▼

**TRANSFER** If the claimant(s) named here in space 4 is (are) different from the author(s) named in space 2, give a brief statement of how the claimant(s) obtained ownership of the copyright. ▼

**DO NOT WRITE HERE  OFFICE USE ONLY**

APPLICATION RECEIVED

ONE DEPOSIT RECEIVED

TWO DEPOSITS RECEIVED

FUNDS RECEIVED

**MORE ON BACK ▶**   • Complete all applicable spaces (numbers 5-11) on the reverse side of this page.
• See detailed instructions.    • Sign the form at line 10.

**DO NOT WRITE HERE**

Page 1 of _____ pages

*Filing for a Copyright (cont'd)*

| | FORM TX |
|---|---|
| EXAMINED BY | |
| CHECKED BY | |
| ☐ CORRESPONDENCE Yes | FOR COPYRIGHT OFFICE USE ONLY |

**DO NOT WRITE ABOVE THIS LINE. IF YOU NEED MORE SPACE, USE A SEPARATE CONTINUATION SHEET.**

**PREVIOUS REGISTRATION** Has registration for this work, or for an earlier version of this work, already been made in the Copyright Office?
☐ **Yes** ☐ **No** If your answer is "Yes," why is another registration being sought? (Check appropriate box) ▼
**a.** ☐ This is the first published edition of a work previously registered in unpublished form.
**b.** ☐ This is the first application submitted by this author as copyright claimant.
**c.** ☐ This is a changed version of the work, as shown by space 6 on this application.
If your answer is "Yes," give: **Previous Registration Number** ▼          **Year of Registration** ▼

**5**

**DERIVATIVE WORK OR COMPILATION**  Complete both space 6a and 6b for a derivative work; complete only 6b for a compilation.
**a. Preexisting Material** Identify any preexisting work or works that this work is based on or incorporates. ▼

**b. Material Added to This Work** Give a brief, general statement of the material that has been added to this work and in which copyright is claimed. ▼

**6**

See instructions before completing this space.

—space deleted—

**7**

**REPRODUCTION FOR USE OF BLIND OR PHYSICALLY HANDICAPPED INDIVIDUALS**  A signature on this form at space 10 and a check in one of the boxes here in space 8 constitutes a non-exclusive grant of permission to the Library of Congress to reproduce and distribute solely for the blind and physically handicapped and under the conditions and limitations prescribed by the regulations of the Copyright Office: (1) copies of the work identified in space 1 of this application in Braille (or similar tactile symbols); or (2) phonorecords embodying a fixation of a reading of that work; or (3) both.

a ☐ Copies and Phonorecords          b ☐ Copies Only          c ☐ Phonorecords Only

**8**

See instructions.

**DEPOSIT ACCOUNT**  If the registration fee is to be charged to a Deposit Account established in the Copyright Office, give name and number of Account.
**Name** ▼          **Account Number** ▼

**9**

**CORRESPONDENCE** Give name and address to which correspondence about this application should be sent.    Name/Address/Apt/City/State/ZIP ▼

Area Code and Telephone Number ►

Be sure to give your daytime phone ◄ number

**CERTIFICATION\***  I, the undersigned, hereby certify that I am the
Check only one ► { ☐ author
☐ other copyright claimant
☐ owner of exclusive right(s)
☐ authorized agent of
of the work identified in this application and that the statements made by me in this application are correct to the best of my knowledge.          Name of author or other copyright claimant, or owner of exclusive right(s) ▲

**10**

**Typed or printed name and date** ▼ If this application gives a date of publication in space 3, do not sign and submit it before that date.
_____ date ► _____

✍ **Handwritten signature (X)** ▼

**MAIL CERTIFI-CATE TO**
Name ▼

**Certificate will be mailed in window envelope**
Number/Street/Apartment Number ▼

City/State/ZIP ▼

**YOU MUST:**
• Complete all necessary spaces
• Sign your application in space 10
**SEND ALL 3 ELEMENTS IN THE SAME PACKAGE:**
1. Application form
2. Nonrefundable $20 filing fee in check or money order payable to *Register of Copyrights*
3. Deposit material
**MAIL TO:**
Register of Copyrights
Library of Congress
Washington, D.C. 20559-6000

The Copyright Office has the authority to adjust fees at 5-year intervals, based on changes in the Consumer Price Index. The next adjustment is due in 1996. Please contact the Copyright Office after July 1995 to determine the actual fee schedule.

**11**

\*17 U.S.C. § 506(e): Any person who knowingly makes a false representation of a material fact in the application for copyright registration provided for by section 409, or in any written statement filed in connection with the application, shall be fined not more than $2,500.

July 1993—400,000     ♻ PRINTED ON RECYCLED PAPER          ☆U.S. GOVERNMENT PRINTING OFFICE: 1993-342-582/80,020

# Patents

A PATENT IS A GOVERNMENT-GRANTED right which allows the holder to exclude all others from making, using, or selling the registered inventions. Patents are issued to the original inventor, joint inventors, legal representatives, or guardians for a non-renewable period of 17 years. The patent grant allows the owner to pursue litigation against anyone who makes, uses, or sells the patented invention without the written permission of the patent holder. However, patents also lend prestige to a product and are sometimes secured to impress financial investors or consumers of the product.

## Three Types of Patents

- Utility patents cover new inventions that serve a particular useful function, such as Velcro fasteners, paper clips, and automatic transmissions.

- Design patents protect the unique design or shape of an object which is used for an ornamental or aesthetic purpose, such as a computer icon or the shape of a desk lamp. Design patents are granted for only 14 years.

- Plant patents are issued to an individual who has invented or discovered and produced asexually (from a seed) a new variety of plant, such as a flower. This patent type has been extended to include living cells or cell combinations as produced in biochemical research facilities.

The formula for determining the appropriate patent type, design, or utility is simple. Can the invention function without this feature? If the answer is yes, then a design patent is the appropriate protection.

## Seven Important Points about Patents

- Patents are issued for objects or inventions, not ideas. Mental concepts and abstract ideas are not patentable. Protection for written materials and ideas is covered under copyright law while company logos and corporate marks are protected under trademark laws.

- A patent is not necessary to market an invention commercially. An inventor may make, use, or sell an invention without the benefit of a patent, provided it is not covered by an existing patent currently held by another individual.

- It is a criminal offense to use the words "patent pending" in advertising if the patent application is not active.

- If a patent is desired, an application must be made within one year from the time the invention is first commercialized or the right to patent is lost.

- Patented products are not superior products. A patent only guarantees that the product is significantly different from others similar to it. Superiority is determined by the user rather than by the inventor.

- Until the invention is commercialized and in widespread use, the patent has little value. However, consider where Polaroid would be today if Dr. Edwin Land had not patented the company's products.

- Patent protection is only as good as the vigilance one maintains against infringers. The value of a patent lies in its offensive power which becomes apparent when a patent holder warns a violator to discontinue the unauthorized use of the invention or risk litigation. (Unfortunately, all too often the party with the most money prevails.) In court proceedings, patent holders are certainly looked upon more favorably than violators. However, the burden of vigilance falls upon the patent holder.

## Obtaining a Patent

It is safest to file a patent application before an invention is commercialized. Applications are filed with the Patent and Trademark Office (PTO) and include drawings of the invention, specifications, description, explanation of use, and a sworn declaration of origin.

Determining the patentability of the invention and meeting the requirements for application are complex processes that experts believe warrant the assistance of a patent attorney, a lawyer who has a degree in physical science or engineering. A list of attorneys and patent agents (qualified experts in patent applications and procedures who can practice before the Patent and Trademark Office but do not possess a law degree) is available in the following government publication:

*Patent Attorneys and Agents Registered to Practice Before the U.S. Patent and Trademark Office*
#003-004-00662-5, $26
U.S. Government Printing Office
Washington, DC 20402
(202) 783-3238

The explicit directions for filing application materials and the required fees are available from:

Commissioner of Patents and Trademarks
Washington, DC 20231
(703) 308-4357, or (703) 557-4636 for recorded system

## Recommended Resource

*Patent It Yourself*
by David Pressman
Nolo Press, $36.95
(800) 992-6656

# Work for Hire

IF EXECUTIVE RALPH HIRES engineer Susan to create a super gizmo, who owns the rights to the super gizmo? If Susan tinkers in the company laboratory and develops a super widget, who owns the rights to her invention? Suppose, however, that Susan develops the super widget at home using all her own materials. Does Ralph have any rights and ownership to the super widget?

Law journals are full of cases in which employees and employers waged legal battles about the rights to inventions developed by the employee. According to experts, common law provides that the employer may assume title for those inventions developed within the scope of the individual's employment, particularly if "inventing" was included in the job description. In the absence of a contract, ownership of an invention which is outside the scope of the inventor's employment belongs to the inventor, but the employer is given "shop right," or the license to use the invention without paying royalties. If the invention was developed without the employer's resources and is outside the realm of the employer's business, the employer has no rights whatsoever to the employee's invention.

To avoid such disputes and the resulting litigation, the "work for hire" clause was introduced into employment contracts. Such agreements supersede the common law and clear up the misunderstandings regarding the exact nature of the employee's work responsibilities.

A "work for hire" clause entitles the employer to take ownership of all ideas, inventions, and discoveries made by the employee as a condition of employment. It is not uncommon to include a clause in the contract which states that employees agree to sell for the sum of $1.00 any inventions, ideas, and/or improvements developed during the term of employment which relate to products, methods, designs, and equipment used by the company or any of its subsidiaries. The following is an example of a "work for hire" clause.

_____, hereby certifies that (the "Work") was specially commissioned by and is to be considered a "work made for hire" under the Copyright Act of 1976, as amended, for _____ ("Company"), and that company is entitled to the copyright thereto.

Without limiting the foregoing, for good and valuable consideration, receipt of which is hereby acknowledged, the undersigned hereby assigns and transfers to the Company, its successors and assigns, absolutely and forever, all right, title, and interest, throughout the world in and to the Work and each element thereof, including but not limited to the copyright therein, for the full term of such copyright, and any and all renewals or extensions thereof, in each country of the world, together with any and all present or future claims and causes of action against third parties arising from or related to the Work and the copyrights therein, and the right to use and retain the proceeds relating to such claims and causes of action.

# Rights in the Workplace

TREATING EMPLOYEES WITH respect and fairness is critical for two reasons. First, it establishes a company's reputation for fairness and impartiality. This reputation is carefully scrutinized by individuals both within and outside of the organization and is a vital factor in keeping and attracting desirable employees. The second, equally important reason is that identifying and safeguarding employee rights reduces the possibility of the company becoming embroiled in charges of discrimination, lengthy litigation, and costly settlements. Employee rights fall into three categories: the right to job security, the right to fair treatment by the employer, and the right to fair treatment in the workplace.

### Right to Job Security

This right protects the employee from "termination at will" or the previously popular employer practice of discharging an individual for virtually any reason. Legislation, including Title VII of the Civil Rights Act of 1964 and more recent anti-discrimination laws, is being cited in courts around the country in disputes about employee rights.

Court rulings have determined that an employee cannot be fired for:

- Whistle-blowing regarding employer policies or violations of laws;

- Complaints or testimony regarding violations of employee rights;

- Lawful union activities;

- Filing claims for workers' compensation;

- Filing charges of unfair labor practices;

- Reporting OSHA violations;

- Garnishment for indebtedness.

Justifiable terminations should be spelled out in an employee handbook or personnel manual. Some of these reasons include:

- Incompetence or failure to respond to training;

- Gross insubordination;

*Rights in the Workplace (cont'd)*

- Repeated unexcused absences or lateness;
- Sexual harassment;
- Verbal abuse;
- Physical violence;
- Falsification of records;
- Theft;
- Drunkenness on the job.

## Right to Fair Treatment by Employer

Fair treatment of employees includes honoring their rights to privacy and providing feedback regarding their performance in order to enable them to successfully meet job requirements. Employee privacy issues include:

- The right to refuse a polygraph or drug test as a condition for employment;
- The right to access employment records. Although federal agencies and only six states have laws regarding this right, over 50% of major national companies now have written guidelines for allowing employees access to their personnel files;
- The right to prohibit release of information regarding the employee to other organizations without the employee's consent.

Fair treatment of the employee is guaranteed by:

- The right to specific information regarding company expectations and prohibitions as stated in an Employee Manual;
- The right to due process procedures including consistent rules and protocol for grievances;
- The right to a progressive system of discipline including: an oral warning, a written warning, suspension, transfer or demotion, and, as a last resort, discharge.

## Right to Fair Treatment Within the Workplace

Executives often forget that their employees are entitled to an environment in which they are treated with fairness and respect by their fellow workers. Among these workplace rights are:

- The right to equal and impartial treatment by other employees regardless of race, sex, age, national origin, disability, religion;
- The right to be free from sexual harassment;
- The right to information about a plant or office closing. The Plant Closing Act of 1988 requires employers to provide affected employees with 60 days notification of a plant closing;
- The right to knowledge about workplace hazards ranging from warnings about chemicals used in the company to necessary safety precautions and simple guidelines for avoiding accidents.

Federal legislation protects employee rights, and it is the responsibility of the employer to be informed regarding the interpretation of these laws. Violations of workplace rights make the employer liable to charges of discriminatory practices.

## Recommended Resources

*Beyond Race and Gender*
R. Roosevelt Thomas, Jr., $15.95
AMACOM (American Management Association)
(212) 586-8100

*Guidebook to Fair Employment Practices*
Commerce Clearing House, $21
(800) 248-3248, Dept. 3376

# Sexual Harassment

ALTHOUGH NOT A NEW WORKPLACE problem, the most frequently discussed current employment issue is sexual harassment. Studies over the last ten years indicate that 40% to 70% of women interviewed have been exposed to inappropriate sexual behavior on the job. The 1991 Justice Clarence Thomas confirmation hearings raised American consciousness about the issue while the publicity regarding the litigation between Dr. Francis Cooney, an esteemed brain surgeon, and her employer, Stanford University Medical School, demonstrated the presence of harassment at all levels in the workplace. Consequently, every employer must develop an awareness of situations which constitute sexual harassment, and an understanding of accountability and liability.

Sexual harassment is defined in one of two ways: (1) *quid pro quo* situations; and (2) those circum-

stances which create a "hostile environment." In the first category, an individual's employment, advancement, or benefits are dependent upon the employee's submission to unwelcome sexual advances or behavior, including demands for sexual favors, unwanted touching, leering, and sexually suggestive gestures.

The second category, a hostile environment, is created when the victim is subjected to offensive behavior which consistently affects his/her work performance. Such behavior includes sexually explicit graffiti, offensive sexual epithets, abusive language, or vulgarities. The differences between incidents of bad taste and those of sexual harassment are based upon the frequency of behavior, the severity of the incident, the reaction of the victim, and the harasser's recognition of the victim's response.

*Sexual Harassment (cont'd)*

According to the Civil Rights Act of 1991, the potential for employer liability may be unlimited. Employers are liable for the sexual harassment actions of their supervisors, and their liability may extend to the behavior of other employees. Legal experts point out that employers are held responsible if the employer knows or should have been aware of the harassment and took no steps to correct the situation.

In order to avoid liability, an employer should take the following preventive steps:

• Adopt and implement a company policy against sexual harassment;

• Inform all employees about that policy;

• Train all supervisory staff to recognize a hostile environment and to respond sensitively to a complaint of harassment;

• Establish procedures for handling sexual harassment complaints;

• Take investigative and corrective action on any complaints, including discharge of the offender, when warranted.

## How to Handle a Sexual Harassment Complaint

1. The charge should be reported immediately to the company official designated by corporate policy.

2. The designated official should conduct a thorough, documented, but confidential investigation, informing only those individuals considered essential to the investigatory process. Subsequent interviews should be conducted with witnesses or others with knowledge of the incident(s).

3. All information regarding the investigation should be documented and kept in a separate file.

4. Once the investigation is complete, the victim should be informed that appropriate disciplinary action has been taken. The victim does not need to be informed of the exact nature of the discipline.

5. The victim should be reassured that he or she will not be subject to retaliation and that he or she has legitimately pursued employee rights.

## Contact Options

Equal Employment Opportunity Commission
Office of Communications and Legislative Affairs
1801 L St., NW
Washington, DC 20507
(202) 663-4264, or (800) 669-4000 (to contact local EEOC office)

9 to 5, Working Women Education Fund
614 Superior Ave., NW, Room 852
Cleveland, OH 44113
(216) 566-9308
Offers training programs for management and non-management employees.

# Discrimination

TITLE VII OF THE CIVIL RIGHTS ACT OF 1964 prohibits discrimination based on race, color, religion, sex, or national origin. Under this law, companies employing 15 or more individuals are prevented from discriminating in the areas of:

• Hiring and firing;

• Compensation and promotion;

• Transfer or layoff;

• Job advertisements and recruitment;

• Testing;

• Training and apprenticeship programs;

• Use of company facilities;

• Fringe benefits, retirement plans, and disability leave.

## Amendments to the Civil Rights Act of 1964

Illegal discrimination is further prohibited by the following amendments to Title VII, which are monitored by the Equal Employment Opportunity Commission (EEOC):

• The Equal Pay Act (EPA) requires that an employer pay all employees equally for equal work, regardless of gender. The law covers situations where men and women perform jobs which require equal skill, effort, and responsibility. The exception to this law is a pay system which is based on a factor other than gender, such as seniority, or the quantity or quality of items produced or processed. Thus, Jessica cannot be hired as a reservations agent at a base rate which is lower or higher than that of Randy who was hired 2 months earlier. However, Jessica can be hired at a base rate which is lower than Tom, who has been a reservations agent for five years and has received annual salary increases in return for five years of service to the company.

• The Age Discrimination in Employment Act (ADEA) of 1967 protects persons 40 years of age or older from discriminatory practices in hiring, firing, promotions, pay, and reduction in pension benefits.

• The Older Workers Benefit Protection Act of 1990 was established to discourage employers from targeting older workers for staff cutting programs. It

*Discrimination (cont'd)*

prohibits employers from requiring employees who accept a severance pay package, or an early retirement plan, to sign away their rights to pursue legal action against age-based discrimination.

- The Pregnancy Discrimination Act prohibits employers from refusing to hire a pregnant woman, terminating her employment based on her pregnancy or forcing her to take a maternity leave. The law also requires that a pregnant woman be allowed the same medical leave rights available to other employees for medical conditions. An employer may not refuse to provide health care insurance benefits for pregnancy, if such insurance is provided for other medical conditions.

While Title VII forbids an employer from refusing to grant men the same child care leave rights as women, experts report that only 8% of U.S. companies offer the same option to male employees. Individual states, however, have specific laws regarding parental rights for childbirth, adoption, and parental-responsibility leaves. The prudent employer will investigate such specific state laws either through the local library or in recommended resources.

The Americans with Disabilities Act (ADA) enacted on July 26, 1992, prohibits discrimination against qualified individuals who are defined as persons "with a physical or mental impairment that substantially limits one or more major life activities." While job applicants may not be questioned about the existence, nature, or severity of a disability, they may be asked about their ability to perform specific job functions.

Medical examinations may be a condition of employment, but only if all entering employees in the same category are requested to submit to the same exams. Likewise, medical examinations of current employees must be job related and consistent with the employer's business needs. The ADA does not cover employees or applicants who are currently using illegal drugs. Tests for illegal use of drugs are not subject to the ADA's restrictions on medical examinations.

## Often Overlooked Applications of Title VII

There are several other applications of Title VII that may be unknown to employers:

- An employer is required to reasonably accommodate the religious practices of an employee or prospective employee through flexible scheduling, voluntary substitutions or swaps, job reassignments and lateral transfers, unless to do so would create undue hardship(s) on the employer.

- An employee whose religious practices prohibit payment of union dues to a labor organization cannot be required to pay the dues, but may pay an equal sum to a charitable organization.

- Pregnant employees must be permitted to work as long as they are able to perform their jobs. They may not be prohibited from returning to work for a predetermined length of time after childbirth.

- Leave for childcare must be granted on the same basis as leave granted to employees for other non-medical reasons, such as non-job-related travel or education.

- English-only rules in the workplace may constitute illegal discrimination unless an employer can demonstrate that such a practice is necessary for conducting business. In such a situation, employees have to be told when they must speak English and the consequences for violating the rule.

- An "eligible small business" can receive a 50% tax credit for expenditures exceeding $250, but not in excess of $10,250, if those expenses are incurred in order to modify existing environments to comply with the requirements of the Americans with Disabilities Act.

## Informing Employees of EEOC Regulations

An employer is expected to post notices describing the federal laws prohibiting job discrimination based on race, color, sex, national origin, religion, age, and disability, and describing the provisions of the Equal Pay Act. The EEOC provides a poster summarizing the laws and procedures for filing a complaint.

## Contact Option

Equal Employment Opportunity Commission
Office of Communications and Legislative Affairs
1801 L St., NW
Washington, DC 20507
(800) 669-3362 or (202) 663-4264

Provides posters and fact sheets on discrimination law

## Recommended Resource

*Your Rights in the Workplace*
by Dan Lacey
Nolo Press, $15.95
(800) 992-6656

**TIP:** *According to the Family Support Act, an employer must withhold child support money from a deadbeat dad's paycheck and pass it along to the authorities. Any employer who fails to do so may be held responsible for the payments.*

# AIDS

THE 1990s BROUGHT THE BUSINESS world a startling realization of the presence of AIDS in the workplace. The Centers for Disease Control (CDC) reports that more than one million people are infected with the HIV virus in the United States. While 200,000 people have died from AIDS in this country, many more are living with both diagnosed and undiagnosed HIV virus, which can precede the onset of AIDS. The impact on business is staggering in terms of both direct costs (increased costs in medical benefits, short-term and long-term disability coverage, and increased Medicaid costs), as well as indirect costs (lost productivity, lost talent, and increased recruitment and training expenses).

Individuals living with HIV/AIDS are protected under the Americans With Disabilities Act of 1992 and consequently it is illegal for businesses with 15 or more employees to discriminate against applicants or workers because they are infected with HIV or suffering from AIDS. Companies covered by ADA are expected to make reasonable accommodations in order to permit affected employees to continue working. These accommodations include extended leave policies, reassignment to available positions within the company, and flexible work schedules.

Understanding the responsibilities required by law and responding to the very human needs of those employees living with HIV and those who work alongside these individuals, is a daunting task. There are three organizations dedicated to assisting large and small businesses in formulating policy, providing education and planning, and responding to the immediate concerns of companies who suddenly find themselves face to face with this situation. (*See also "Facts about AIDS" on page 341.*)

## The American Red Cross

The American Red Cross will provide facilitators/instructors or train staff members of an individual company to provide a company training program on HIV/AIDS. This consists of a minimum one-hour presentation on the facts of HIV/AIDS infection and transmission. In addition, the Red Cross offers expanded presentations on the rights and responsibilities of businesses, the facts of disclosure, and a particularly useful training program for managers and supervisors. The Red Cross provides assistance to companies in policy planning.

The National Headquarters of the American Red Cross advises that interested individuals should first contact the local chapter of the American Red Cross to obtain advice and plan a program suited to the needs of the specific organization. If there is no local branch of the ARC, the AIDS Education staff at the National Headquarters of the American Red Cross will provide assistance.

American Red Cross National Headquarters
AIDS Education Division
1750 K St., NW, 7th Floor
Washington, DC 20006
(202) 434-4074

## The CDC's National AIDS Clearing House

The CDC's National AIDS Clearing House is a new referral service established under the National AIDS Information and Education Program. This service has divisions for information, education, and experimental drug programs as well as a new division called Business Response to AIDS Resource Service. This division will provide information and local non-health care referrals to individuals in the business community anywhere in the nation. Their referrals regarding business policy and programs, training programs, legal questions, and insurance issues are made on the local, state, and national level. In addition they will refer inquiries to the appropriate state HIV coordinator.

The CDC National AIDS Clearing House
P.O. Box 6003
Rockville, MD 20849
(800) 458-5231

## The National Leadership Coalition on AIDS

The National Leadership Coalition on AIDS offers technical assistance and guidance to businesses in establishing policies and programs tailored to the individual needs of companies ranging from IBM to small businesses. They will send free literature to companies and individuals seeking to be proactive rather than reactive in the face of increasing HIV throughout the workplace. This particular organization is most useful in determining the specific needs of the company seeking to assist its employees. Its information agents offer clear, supportive direction to any and all inquiries regarding people living with HIV/AIDS. They are equipped to meet the immediate and long-term needs of any organization and are most interested in doing so. The Coalition will also provide a free copy for the first request of any printed materials which they publish on the topic of HIV/AIDS.

The National Leadership Coalition on AIDS
1730 M St., NW, Suite 905
Washington, DC 20036
(202) 429-0930

# Acting as Your Own Lawyer

A MAN WHO ACTS AS HIS OWN ATTORNEY has a fool for a client. Obviously, the originator of this quote never had to pay a sizeable legal fee in return for a simple, routine legal procedure.

Armed with general interest, the time to conduct preliminary research, and a desire to save corporate funds, an ambitious business owner can conduct many of his or her own legal matters. The prudent business owner, however, should be aware of the times when one does and does not require the services of an attorney. The key lies in realizing that the most basic business situation can become complicated and require the guidance of an attorney. The following are some examples of such legal situations:

- Choosing among sole proprietorship, partnership, or corporation;

- Structuring a partnership agreement;

- Establishing a corporation;

- Dealing with stock and security laws;

- Registering trademarks, copyrights, and patents;

- Filing for licenses or permits on federal, state, and local levels;

- Fulfilling the basic tax requirements for small businesses;

- Purchasing real estate or a business;

- Leasing real estate or equipment;

- Negotiating a lease;

- Insuring a business;

- Hiring employees and independent contractors;

- Handling labor disagreements;

- Dealing with customer litigation;

- Extending credit and collecting debts;

- Planning for an estate;

- Dealing with criminal proceedings;

- Handling bankruptcy and reorganization proceedings.

In order to determine the extent to which an individual can handle any one of the above situations, he or she should:

- Understand the basic issues;

- Have a clear understanding of the forms and procedures involved in completing the legal transaction;

- Determine which, if any, aspects of the process can be handled by the individual without legal help;

- Evaluate the complexities and honestly assess the need for legal assistance;

- Decide if it is worthwhile in terms of time and savings to proceed independently.

## Recommended Resources

*Complete Small Business Legal Guide*
by Robert Friedman
Dearborn Financial Publishing, $69.95
(800) 533-2665

*The Partnership Book: How to Write a Partnership Agreement*
by Denise Clifford and Ralph Warner
Nolo Press, $24.95
(800) 992-6656 or (510) 549-1976

*Legal Research: How to Find and Understand the Law*
by Stephen Elias and Susan Levinkind
Nolo Press, $19.95
(800) 992-6656 or (510) 549-1976

*The Bordwin Letter: Preventive Law for Business*
by Milton Bordwin
Ounce of Prevention, $65/year
(617) 244-0019
*A newsletter for the layperson*

Another outstanding resource is the U.S. Small Business Administration (SBA). This federal organization is devoted to offering assistance to existing businesses or to aspiring entrepreneurs. The SBA provides information on financial assistance, management, obtaining government contracts, and counseling services and offers many low-cost publications. By calling a local office of the SBA or its toll-free national number (800) 827-5722, the caller can request a list of available publications. These handy publications can be ordered at a low price and provide useful background information.

# Incorporation

## Total Number of Incorporated Businesses (Thousands)

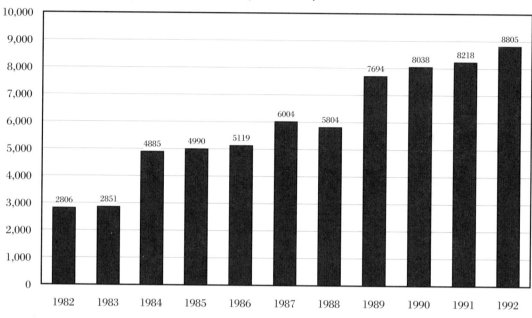

Source: 1993 Statistical Abstract, Table No. 861

SINCE ITS INCEPTION IN THE UNITED STATES over 300 years ago, the corporation has continued to grow and flourish as a legal entity. Experts note that in North America over 50,000 new corporations are formed each month, testifying to sustained commercial growth.

A business owner must choose from among the three types of legal structures (sole proprietorship, partnership, and corporation) when establishing a new firm. The table above demonstrates the growth of business corporations as a popular choice in the U.S. during the last decade.

Forming a corporation can appear to be a formidable task requiring legions of legal assistance, but there are many resources available to those seeking such a legal structure for their businesses. The primary step is to recognize the basic procedure of incorporating. The basic steps include:

- Select and reserve a corporate name;
- Prepare and file articles of incorporation;
- Select the board of directors;
- Establish corporate bylaws;
- Record the minutes of the first meeting of the board of directors;
- Establish a corporate bank account;
- Issue stock certificates to shareholders;
- Create a corporate record book;
- Conform to individual state requirements on incorporation;
- Review bulk sales laws which pertain to the corporation.

The business owner who possesses neither the time nor the inclination to perform these procedures independently, can either enlist the services of a lawyer or can utilize the services of organizations which deal directly with the individual owner in the incorporation process. Such specialists in incorporation can answer a business owner's questions over the telephone and can act as an agent for the company. For nominal fees advertised at $75 to $300, based on required services, these groups will help the organization choose from among the general, the closed, and the non-stock corporation, and will guide the owner through the procedures to incorporation.

## Contact Options

*Incorporation Consultants:*

Corporate Agents
P.O. Box 1281
Wilmington, DE 19899
(800) 877-4224 or (302) 998-0598

*Incorporation (cont'd)*

Harvard Business Services
25 Greystone Manor
Lewes, DE 19958
(800) 345-2677

The more adventurous individual can secure the guidance of several good publications and perform the process on his or her own. These and other self-help books contain step-by-step descriptions of the procedures and, in some cases, provide specimens of the required forms.

### Recommended Resources

*How to Form Your Own Corporation Without a Lawyer for Under $75.00*
by Ted Nicholas
Dearborn Financial Publishing, $19.95
(800) 533-2665

*The Legal Guide for Starting and Running a Small Business*
by Fred S. Steingold
Nolo Press, $22.95
(800) 992-6656 or (510) 549-1976

# Prepared Legal Forms

THE PRESENCE OF THE PHOTOCOPIER as well as the personal computer and its powerful software have threatened the survival of all but the heartiest of suppliers of legal forms and documents. The enterprising business owner can produce the most commonly used documents through a combination of a reasonably powerful PC, a hard disk, and a laser printer. There is software available that allows the user to produce blank electronic forms.

The business owner who infrequently uses legal forms can select either local stationers dealing with legal documents or one of the well-known suppliers of legal forms. Upon request they will send a catalogue and order form.

### Recommended Resources

Blumberg's Law Products (Excelsior Legal)
62 White St.
New York, NY 10013
(800) 221-2972 or (212) 431-5000
*Legal Supply Source*

*Standard Legal Forms and Agreements for Small Businesses*
Self-Counsel Press, $14.95
1704 N. State St.
Bellingham, WA 98225
(800) 663-3007 or (206) 676-4530

# Important Documents for All Firms

CORPORATE RECORDS ARE A VITAL component in an organization's self-defense program. Such documents can ensure that the protective umbrella of the corporation will serve the officers, the employees, the board of directors, and the stockholders.

All businesses should have the following documents in a corporate kit. This is merely a collection of documents held together in a loose-leaf notebook or in a more formal corporate document holder available from a supplier of law products.

The following should be included in the corporate kit:

- Articles of incorporation;

- Amendments to the articles of incorporation;

- Minutes of the stockholders and board of directors meetings;

- Bylaws of the corporation;

- List of the corporation's shareholders;

- Corporate secretary's affidavit of verification of corporate shares of stock;

- All directors' resolutions;

- All stockholders' resolutions;

- Record of dividends;

- Outstanding loans;

- Contracts;

- Ledgers including accounts receivable, accounts payable, and general inventory;

- Insurance policies;

- Resolutions regarding salaries and bonuses of top executives;

- Employment contracts and agreements;

- Stock option plans;

- Medical-dental expense plans;

- Verification of citizenship or right to work according to the Immigration and Reform Control Act (IRCA) of 1986.

# Employee Handbook

WHILE MOST EMPLOYERS ARE AWARE of the importance of adhering to the law when hiring, firing, and paying employees, few recognize the legal value of the employee handbook. This document outlines the company's expectations of all employees and, when signed by the employee, acknowledges agreement to conform to those policies and practices.

A prudent employer will carefully prepare the employee handbook to present specific company policy on the following important topics:

- Administrative policies such as hours, security, and safety procedures;

- Wage and salary information regarding salary increases, shift differential, non-scheduled work reimbursement, pay periods and checks, overtime, deduction types, annual evaluation policy;

- Benefits including parking, paid holidays, vacation policy, sick leave and personal leave policy, workman's compensation, and details of the health care and insurance plans;

- Personnel policies including hiring, performance appraisal, disciplinary procedures, resignation, severance pay, and grievance procedures;

- Causes for immediate dismissal including:
  Falsification of records, particularly application for employment;
  Incompetence in performance despite additional training;
  Repeated or gross insubordination;
  A pattern of unexcused absence or lateness;
  Abusive or threatening language to supervisors or other employees;
  Sexual harassment;
  Unauthorized possession of firearms on the company premises;
  Physical violence or attempted injury to another employee or visitor;
  Drunkenness on the job;
  Theft of company property or property of another employee;
  Receiving three notices of reprimand during any one-year period.

## Recommended Resources

*Complete Small Business Legal Guide*
by Robert Friedman
Dearborn Financial Publishing, $69.95
(800) 533-2665

*How to Develop an Employee Handbook*
by Joseph W. R. Lawson
The Dartnell Corporation, $91.50
(800) 621-5463 or (312) 561-4000

Dartnell also publishes *How to Develop a Personnel Policy Manual* (also $91.50). Under their terminology, an "employee handbook" as described above is actually a "personnel policy manual" whereas an "employee handbook" is a more informal summary of company policy written for employees and their families. For more information, consult these books.

---

## The Top Reference Sources

*The Copyright Handbook*
Nolo Press, $24.95
(800) 992-6656 or (510) 549-1976

This is a very thorough guide to copyright procedures that includes a good summation of copyright laws and requirements. Chapters are included on registration, completing all the necessary forms, what copyright protects, what copyright does not protect, works made for hire, jointly authored works, compilations, automated databases, fair use privilege, uses that are less likely to be deemed fair, fair use and the photocopy machine, obtaining permission to use copyrighted material, and much more.

# Biggest Verdicts of 1993

| Verdict | Plaintiff vs. Defendant | State | Subject | Status |
|---|---|---|---|---|
| $1.2 billion | Litton Systems vs. Honeywell | CA | Patent infringement | Appeal planned |
| $500 million | Rubicon Petroleum vs. Amoco Production | TX | Oil field sale | Appeal planned |
| $425.6 million | Amoco Chemical vs. Lloyd's of London | CA | Indemnity insurance | Appeal planned |
| $404.16 million | Gold Standard vs. Getty Oil | UT | Gold mine dispute | Reversed by trial judge |
| $309.9 million | Avia Dev. Group vs. Amer. General Realty Investment | TX | Airport project financing | Reduced to $176.5 mil. |
| $197.6 million | Cataldo vs. Budget Rent-a-Car | NY | Car crash | Motions pending |
| $116.6 million | Arntz Contracting vs. St. Paul Fire & Marine Insurance | CA | Bond for housing project | Motions pending |
| $114 million | Sullivan vs. National Football League | MA | Antitrust | Reduced to $51 mil.; on appeal |
| $107.28 million | Datskow vs. Teledyne Continental Motors | NY | Fatal airplane crash | Undisclosed settlement |
| $105.24 million | Moseley vs. General Motors | GA | Gas tank product liability | On appeal |

*Source: National Law Journal*

# Alternate Dispute Resolution

WHILE MOST COURT CASES are settled before, during, or after trial, alternate dispute resolution (ADR) can be a faster and less expensive means of reaching a settlement. ADR has been utilized in construction contract disputes, labor-management disagreements, international commerce, insurance claims, and securities cases, to name a few.

Parties involved in dispute or negotiation may be referred to a neutral third party by a court, or one or both parties may use the assistance of an ADR organization. The organization will also assist the parties in choosing an ADR procedure according to the nature of the dispute. The neutral party may be an ex-judge, attorney, or other expert.

The main ADR procedures are as follows:

- Arbitration: The third party hears both sides and gives a specific decision, which is either binding or non-binding (decided in advance).

- Mediation: The third party negotiates a voluntary, non-binding settlement between the two parties.

- Mini-trial: The two parties each have an attorney make a brief presentation of their cases to a panel of representatives from each side of the dispute with a neutral third party. The neutral party then mediates a non-binding settlement.

- Summary jury trial: Similar to a standard jury trial, except the jury delivers a non-binding verdict, and the attorneys can question the jurors after the trial and use their findings in their settlement negotiations.

## Contact Options

Both of these organizations have offices throughout the United States:

American Arbitration Association
140 W. 51st St.
New York, NY 10020
(212) 484-4000

Judicial Arbitration and Mediation Services
345 Park Ave., 8th Floor
New York, NY 10154
(212) 751-2700

## The Top Reference Sources

*The Entrepreneur & Small Business Problem Solver*
John Wiley & Sons, $27.95
(212) 850-6000

Written by marketing professor William A. Cohen, this is a comprehensive guide for entrepreneurs and managers of small businesses. Sections include financial problem solving, legal aspects of going into business, sources of capital, buying insurance, leasing equipment, financial management.

Also included are sections on market research, introducing new products, advertising and publicity, business plans, recruiting, protecting your ideas, and computers.

# Finding a Lawyer

WHILE LARGE CORPORATIONS have equally large legal firms on retainer to answer legal questions and monitor all legal transactions, the small business owner frequently cannot afford this luxury. He or she must analyze the specific needs of the company and carefully enlist the services of a legal professional. Selecting a good lawyer whose skills, experience, and rapport match the needs of the business should begin with a recognition of the legal matters which may require an attorney's assistance.

## Services Provided by a Business Lawyer

- Review partnership agreements or incorporation documents;

- Review proposed leases;

- Interpret zoning ordinances regarding land use;

- Evaluate employment agreements or advise regarding difficult terminations;

- Assist in patent, copyright, trademark, and business name proceedings;

- Represent the company interests in lawsuits or arbitrations;

- Review documents regarding business or real estate sale or purchase;

- Draft or evaluate estate planning documents such as wills and trusts;

- Advise on public offerings of corporate stock.

## How to Select the Right Lawyer

Selecting a lawyer to represent business interests is no casual task, but a business owner should not be intimidated by the process. By following some basic steps, an individual can accumulate a list of prospective attorneys.

- Talk to people in the business community and ask whose legal services they've used and, more important, why they've made those selections.

- Ask a trusted banker, accountant, insurance agent, or real estate broker for a recommendation.

- Inquire among friends, relatives, and business associates for candidate suggestions.

- Solicit the advice of the director of the local chamber of commerce.

- Visit a law librarian to ascertain the names of authors of business law books who may practice in the area. Such recommendations while potentially more difficult to obtain may nonetheless be particularly useful for unusual, specialized businesses.

- If a continuing legal education program (CLE) is available in the area, ask the director to suggest the names of well-qualified individuals.

- In many states, the bar association will provide a Lawyer Referral and Information Service. Where available, the service offers the caller a referral to a local lawyer who provides the type of legal services needed by the caller. Participating lawyers will usually agree to provide an initial consultation for a nominal fee. The rest is up to the individual and the attorney. It is important to note that the state bar associations can provide names of attorneys, but they cannot provide evaluations on these individuals.

## Checking Out the Suggestions

After compiling a list of candidates, it is wise to seek additional information from the Martindale-Hubbell Law Directory, available at most law libraries and some local public libraries. This directory offers a compilation of biographical information, education, professional organizations, and the specialties of all listed lawyers. Each individual is also given a confidential rating solicited from lawyers and judges. While some ratings are not published at the behest of a lawyer or because one is not available, the information and rating system can serve to narrow the list considerably.

## Interview Prospective Candidates

The final step in the selection process is to request interviews from several good prospects, making clear the purpose of the interview and thus avoiding consultation fees. It is important to look for experience, rapport, accessibility, and value by assessing the interview in terms of the following criteria:

- Does the candidate understand your field and the needs of your business?

- How accessible is this attorney to client phone calls, questions, document review?

- Is this attorney willing to assist in your business legal education, or is he or she proprietary and secretive about legal matters?

- Is this candidate willing to allow you to defray some legal costs by performing negotiations and preparing preliminary drafts of documents, and willing to advise, review, and fine tune transactions when necessary?

- Is the candidate a practical problem solver or likely to become mired in legalistic technicalities?

*Finding a Lawyer (cont'd)*

- Is the prospective attorney willing to leave the control of the business to you, as owner, and serve as advisor in legal matters?

- Which services are billed by flat fees, contingency fees, annual fees, and hourly charges? Is the billing method clear and concise?

- Are all your questions answered?

- Is the individual clear and understandable in his or her answers?

- Do you feel comfortable and compatible with this individual?

## Recommended Resource

*The Legal Guide for Starting and Running a Small Business*
by Fred S. Steingold
Nolo Press, $22.95
(800) 992-6656 or (510) 549-1976

# State Bar Association Directory

| State | Bar Association Telephone |
|---|---|
| Alabama | (205) 269-1515 |
| Alaska | (907) 272-7469 |
| Arizona | (602) 252-4804 |
| Arkansas | (501) 375-4605 |
| California | (415) 561-8200 |
| Colorado | (303) 860-1115 |
| Connecticut | (203) 721-0025 |
| Delaware | (302) 658-5279 |
| District of Columbia | (202) 223-6600 |
| | (202) 737-4700 |
| Florida | (904) 561-5600 |
| Georgia | (404) 527-8700 |
| Hawaii | (808) 537-1868 |
| Idaho | (208) 342-8958 |
| Illinois | (217) 525-1760 |
| Indiana | (317) 639-5465 |
| Iowa | (515) 243-3179 |
| Kansas | (913) 234-5696 |
| Kentucky | (502) 564-3795 |
| Louisiana | (504) 566-1600 |
| Maine | (207) 622-7523 |
| Maryland | (410) 685-7878 |
| Massachusetts | (617) 542-3602 |
| Michigan | (517) 372-9030 |
| Minnesota | (612) 333-1183 |
| Mississippi | (601) 948-4471 |
| Missouri | (314) 635-4128 |
| Montana | (406) 442-7660 |
| Nebraska | (402) 475-7091 |
| Nevada | (702) 382-2200 |

| State | Bar Association Telephone |
|---|---|
| New Hampshire | (603) 224-6942 |
| New Jersey | (908) 249-5000 |
| New Mexico | (505) 842-6132 |
| New York | (518) 463-3200 |
| North Carolina | (919) 828-0561 |
| | (919) 828-4620 |
| North Dakota | (701) 255-1404 |
| Ohio | (614) 487-2050 |
| Oklahoma | (405) 524-2365 |
| Oregon | (503) 620-0222 |
| Pennsylvania | (717) 238-6715 |
| Puerto Rico | (809) 721-3358 |
| Rhode Island | (401) 421-5740 |
| South Carolina | (803) 799-6653 |
| South Dakota | (605) 224-7554 |
| Tennessee | (615) 383-7421 |
| Texas | (512) 463-1400 |
| Utah | (801) 531-9077 |
| Vermont | (802) 223-2020 |
| Virginia | (804) 775-0500 |
| | (804) 644-0041 |
| Virgin Islands | (809) 778-7497 |
| Washington | (206) 727-8200 |
| West Virginia | (304) 558-2456 |
| | (304) 342-1474 |
| Wisconsin | (608) 257-3838 |
| Wyoming | (307) 632-9061 |

*Source: 1993/94 ABA Directory*

# Law Firm Billing

## 15 Largest Law Firms (by Partners, Associates)

| Firm | Headquarters | Partners | Associates |
|---|---|---|---|
| Baker & McKenzie | Chicago | 626 | 1,009 |
| Jones, Day, Reavis & Pogue | Cleveland | 386 | 579 |
| Skadden, Arps, Slate, Meagher & Flom | New York | 236 | 777 |
| Sidley & Austin | Chicago | 299 | 339 |
| Weil, Gotshal & Manges | New York | 155 | 504 |
| Gibson, Dunn & Crutcher | Los Angeles | 238 | 349 |
| Fulbright & Jaworski | Houston | 271 | 314 |
| Morgan, Lewis & Bockius | Philadelphia | 256 | 346 |
| Pillsbury Madison & Sutro | San Francisco | 239 | 362 |
| Shearman & Sterling | New York | 132 | 408 |
| Morrison & Foerster | San Francisco | 218 | 342 |
| Mayer, Brown & Platt | Chicago | 253 | 303 |
| Latham & Watkins | Los Angeles | 222 | 335 |
| Vinson & Elkins | Houston | 217 | 294 |
| O'Melveny & Myers | Los Angeles | 184 | 344 |

*Source: National Law Journal, September 27, 1993*

Cities with at least three law firms in the top 250 where the firms had the largest average increase in number of attorneys:

Tampa
Atlanta
Washington, DC
St. Louis
Milwaukee
New York
Boston

Cities with at least three law firms in the top 250 where the firms had the largest average decrease in number of attorneys:

Cleveland
San Francisco
Baltimore
Detroit
Houston
Los Angeles
Philadelphia

*Source: National Law Journal, September 27, 1993*

# Specialty Law Firms

FINDING A LAW FIRM that deals with the specific needs of a company can appear to be a formidable process. A simple way to accomplish this process is to call the county or state bar association. Ask if they have a lawyer referral system. If it is available, ask for a list of attorneys or firms which handle the particular specialty you need.

Frequently these services will provide a printed listing of attorneys by specialty. The referrals include attorneys who have agreed to offer an initial consultation for a nominal fee to the prospective client.

---

**FAX** **Law Firm Fees.** Request #333. See p. xi for instructions.
Description of types of fees and suggestions for negotiating a billing method.

# U.S. Law Firms with Foreign Offices

THE FOLLOWING DATA WERE COMPILED from *National Law Journal*'s top 250 law firms by size.

| | Argentina | Australia | Belgium | Brazil | Canada | China | Czech Republic | Egypt | England | France | Germany | Hong Kong | Hungary | Indonesia | Italy | Japan | Lithuania | Mexico | Netherlands | Poland | Russia | Saudi Arabia | Singapore | Spain | Sweden | Switzerland | Taiwan | Thailand |
|---|---|---|---|---|---|---|---|---|---|---|---|---|---|---|---|---|---|---|---|---|---|---|---|---|---|---|---|---|
| Altheimer & Gray | | | | | | | • | | | | | | | | | | | | | • | | | | | | | | |
| Baker & McKenzie | • | • | • | • | • | • | | | • | • | • | • | • | | | • | | • | • | • | • | • | • | • | • | • | • | • |
| Bryan, Cave | | | | | | | | | • | | • | | | | | | | | | | | | • | | | | | |
| Cleary, Gottlieb | | | • | | | | | | • | • | • | • | | | | • | | | | | | | | | | | | |
| Coudert Brothers | | • | • | | | • | | | • | • | | • | | | | • | | | | | • | | • | | | | | • |
| Cravath, Swaine & Moore | | | | | | | | | • | | | | | | | | | | | | | | | | | | | |
| Davis Polk & Wardwell | | | | | | | | | • | • | • | • | | | | • | | | | | | | | | | | | |
| Debevoise & Plimpton | | | | | | | | | • | • | | | • | | | | | | | | | | | | | | | |
| Dechert Price & Rhoads | | | • | | | | | | • | | | | | | | | | | | | | | | | | | | |
| Dewey Ballantine | | | | | | | • | | • | | | | | • | | | | | | • | | | | | | | | |
| Dorsey & Whitney | | | • | | | | | | • | | | | | | | | | | | | | | | | | | | |
| Fulbright & Jaworski | | | | | | | | | • | | | • | | | | | | | | | | | | | | | | |
| Gibson, Dunn & Crutcher | | | • | | | | | | • | • | | • | | | | • | | | | | | | • | | | | | |
| Graham & James | | | | | | • | | | • | | | • | • | | • | • | | | | | | | • | | | | • | • |
| Hogan & Hartson | | | • | | | | • | | • | • | | | | | | | | | | • | | | | | | | | |
| Hunton & Williams | | | • | | | | | | | | | | | | | | | | | • | | | | | | | | |
| Jones, Day | | | • | | | | | | • | • | • | • | | | | • | | | | | | | • | | | | • | • |
| Kaye, Scholer | | | • | | | | | | | | | • | | | | | | | | | | | | | | | | |
| Kelley Drye & Warren | | | • | | | | | | | | | | | | | • | | | | | | | | | | | | |
| Latham & Watkins | | | | | | | | | • | | | | | | | | | | | | • | | | | | | | |
| LeBoeuf, Lamb | | | • | | | | | | • | | | | | | | | | | | | • | | | | | | | |
| Mayer, Brown & Platt | | | • | | | | | | • | | | | | | | • | | | | | | | | | | | | |
| Milbank, Tweed | | | | | | | | | • | | | • | | | | • | | | | | | | • | • | | | | |
| Morgan, Lewis & Bockius | | | • | | | | | | • | | • | | | | | • | | | | | | | | | | | | |
| Morrison & Foerster | | | • | | | | | | • | | | • | | | | • | | | | | | | | | | | | |
| O'Melveny & Myers | | | • | | | | | | • | | | | | | | • | | | | | | | | | | | | |
| Oppenheimer, Wolff | | | • | | | | | | • | • | | | | | | • | | | | | | | | | | | | |
| Paul, Weiss, Rifkind | | | | | | • | | | • | • | | | | | | • | | | | | | | | | | | | |
| Rogers & Wells | | | | | | | | | • | • | • | | | | | | | | | | | | | | | | | |
| Shearman & Sterling | | | | | • | | | | • | • | • | | • | | | • | | | | | | | | | • | | | |
| Sidley & Austin | | | | | | | | | • | | | | | | | • | | | | | | | | • | | | | |
| Simpson, Thacher | | | | | | | | | • | | • | | | | | • | | | | | | | | | | | | |
| Skadden, Arps | | • | • | | • | • | • | | • | • | • | • | | • | | • | | | | | • | | | | | | | |
| Squire, Sanders | | | | | | | | | • | | | | | • | | | | | | | | | | | | | | |
| Stroock & Stroock | | | | | | | | | | | | | | • | | | | | | | | | | | | | | |
| Sullivan & Cromwell | | • | | | | | | | • | • | • | | | | | • | | | | | | | | | | | | |
| Vinson & Elkins | | | | | | | | | • | | | | | | | | | | | | • | • | | | | | | |
| Weil, Gotshal & Manges | | | • | | | | | | | | | | | • | | | | | | | | | | | | | | |
| White & Case | | | • | | | • | | | • | • | • | • | | • | | • | | • | | • | | • | • | • | • | • | | |
| Wilmer, Cutler | | | • | | | | | | • | | • | | | | | | | | | | | | | | | | | |
| Wilson, Elser, Moskowitz | | | | | | | | | • | | | | | | | • | | | | | | | | | | | | |
| Winthrop, Stimson | | | • | | | | | | • | | • | | | | | • | | | | | | | | | | | | |

*Source: National Law Journal, September 27, 1993*

# Federal Information Center

KNOWING EXACTLY WHOM TO CALL is the first step in obtaining information. When an individual is searching for information from the Federal Government, the task of finding the appropriate office can be overwhelming. The General Services Administration has set up a clearinghouse for such needs. The Federal Information Center is a telephone service that is staffed with individuals who can direct a caller to the appropriate federal agency.

The attractive feature of this service is the availability of regional offices serving the larger metropolitan areas of over 35 states. The following numbers all connect the caller to the same office, but they also offer recorded information about local services. If there is no number for a certain location, the individual can call the main FIC center at (301) 722-9000.

## U.S. Federal Information Center

| State | Telephone | Metropolitan Area Served |
|---|---|---|
| AK | (800) 729-8003 | Anchorage |
| AL | (800) 366-2998 | Birmingham, Mobile |
| AR | (800) 366-2998 | Little Rock |
| AZ | (800) 359-3997 | Phoenix |
| CA | (800) 726-4995 | Los Angeles, San Diego, San Francisco, Santa Ana, Sacramento |
| CO | (800) 359-3997 | Colorado Springs, Denver, Pueblo |
| CT | (800) 347-1997 | Hartford, New Haven |
| DC | (800) 347-1997 | Washington metropolitan area |
| FL | (800) 347-1997 | Fort Lauderdale, Jacksonville, Miami, Orlando, St. Petersburg, Tampa, W. Palm Beach |
| GA | (800) 347-1997 | Atlanta |
| HI | (800) 733-5996 | Honolulu |
| IA | (800) 735-8004 | All points in Iowa |
| IL | (800) 366-2998 | Chicago |
| IN | (800) 366-2998 | Gary |
| IN | (800) 347-1997 | Indianapolis |
| KS | (800) 735-8004 | All points in Kansas |
| KY | (800) 347-1997 | Louisville |
| LA | (800) 366-2998 | New Orleans |
| MA | (800) 347-1997 | Boston |
| MD | (800) 347-1997 | Baltimore |
| MI | (800) 347-1997 | Detroit, Grand Rapids |
| MN | (800) 366-2998 | Minneapolis |
| MO | (800) 366-2998 | St. Louis |
| MO | (800) 735-8004 | Other points in Missouri |
| NC | (800) 347-1997 | Charlotte |
| NE | (800) 366-2998 | Omaha |
| NE | (800) 735-8004 | Other points in Nebraska |
| NJ | (800) 347-1997 | Newark, Trenton |
| NM | (800) 359-3997 | Albuquerque |
| NY | (800) 347-1997 | Albany, Buffalo, New York City, Rochester, Syracuse |
| OH | (800) 347-1997 | Akron, Cincinnati, Cleveland, Columbus, Dayton, Toledo |
| OK | (800) 366-2998 | Oklahoma City, Tulsa |
| OR | (800) 726-4995 | Portland |
| PA | (800) 347-1997 | Philadelphia, Pittsburgh |
| RI | (800) 347-1997 | Providence |
| TN | (800) 347-1997 | Chattanooga |
| TN | (800) 366-2998 | Memphis, Nashville |
| TX | (800) 366-2998 | Austin, Dallas, Fort Worth, Houston, San Antonio |
| UT | (800) 359-3997 | Salt Lake City |
| VA | (800) 347-1997 | Norfolk, Richmond, Roanoke |
| WA | (800) 726-4995 | Seattle, Tacoma |
| WI | (800) 366-2998 | Milwaukee |

# Regulatory Agencies

Consumer Product Safety Commission
Washington, DC 20207
(301) 504-0580

Environmental Protection Agency
401 M St., SW
Washington, DC 20460
(202) 260-4454

Equal Employment Opportunity Commission
Office of Communications and Legislative Affairs
1801 L St., NW
Washington, DC 20507
(202) 663-4264, or (800) 669-4000 (to contact local
EEOC office)

Federal Communications Commission
1919 M St., NW
Washington, DC 20554
(202) 632-7000

Federal Deposit Insurance Corporation
550 17th St., NW
Washington, DC 20429
(202) 393-8400

Federal Energy Regulatory Commission
825 N. Capitol St., NE
Washington, DC 20426
(202) 208-1371

Federal Reserve System
20th and C Sts., NW
Washington, DC 20551
(202) 452-3215

Federal Trade Commission
6th St. and Pennsylvania Ave., NW
Washington, DC 20580
(202) 326-2222

Food and Drug Administration
5600 Fishers Ln.
Rockville, MD 20857
(301) 443-3170

Immigration and Naturalization Service
U.S. Dept. of Justice
425 I St., NW, Room 7116
Washington, DC 20536
(800) 755-0777

Interstate Commerce Commission
12th St. and Constitution Ave., NW
Washington, DC 20423
(202) 927-7600

National Credit Union Administration
1775 Duke St.
Alexandria, VA 22314
(703) 518-6300

National Labor Relations Board
1099 14th St., NW
Washington, DC 20570
(202) 273-1000

National Transportation Safety Board
490 L'Enfant Plaza, SW
Washington, DC 20594
(202) 382-6600

Occupational Safety and Health Administration
200 Constitution Ave., NW
Washington, DC 20210
(202) 219-8148

Pension Benefit Guaranty Corporation
Office of Coverage and Inquiries
1200 K St., NW
Washington, DC 20005
(202) 326-4000

Resolution Trust Corporation
801 17th St., NW
Washington, DC 20434
(202) 416-6900

Securities and Exchange Commission
450 5th St., NW
Washington, DC 20549
(202) 272-7440

Small Business Administration
409 3rd St., SW
Washington, DC 20416
(202) 205-7717, or (800) 827-5722 or
(202) 205-7701 for recorded information

United States International Trade Commission
500 E St., SW
Washington, DC 20436
(202) 205-2000

U.S. Postal Service (Current Rates, Fees, and
Services)
475 L'Enfant Plaza, SW
Washington, DC 20260
(202) 636-9595

*Regulatory Agencies (cont'd)*

*Other Useful Federal Offices:*

Bureau of Export Administration (Commerce Dept.)
P. O. Box 273
Washington, DC 20044
(202) 482-4811

Economic Development Administration
(Commerce Dept.)
14th and Constitution Ave., NW
Washington, DC 20230
(202) 482-2000

Patent and Trademark Office (Commerce Dept.)
Washington, DC 20231
(703) 308-4357, or (703) 557-4636 for
recorded information

Trade Regulation Enforcement (Federal Trade
Commission)
Enforcement Division
6th & Pennsylvania Ave., NW
Washington, DC 20580
(202) 326-2000

Office for Civil Rights (Health and Human
Services Dept.)
330 Independence Ave., SW
Washington, DC 20201
(202) 619-0585

Public Health Service (Health and Human
Services Dept.)
5600 Fishers Ln.
Rockville, MD 20857
(301) 443-2403

Social Security Administration (Health and
Human Services Dept.)
6401 Security Blvd.
Baltimore, MD 21235
(410) 965-7700 or (800) 772-1213

Government National Mortgage Association
(Housing and Urban Development Dept.)
451 7th St., SW
Washington, DC 20410
(202) 708-0980

Employment Standards Administration
(Labor Dept.)
200 Constitution Ave., NW
Washington, DC 20210
(202) 219-8743

Employment and Training Administration
(Labor Dept.)
200 Constitution Ave., NW
Washington, DC 20210
(202) 219-6871

Pension and Welfare Benefits Administration
(Labor Dept.)
200 Constitution Ave., NW
Washington, DC 20210
(202) 219-8776

Veterans' Employment and Training Services
(Labor Dept.)
200 Constitution Ave., NW
Washington, DC 20210
(202) 219-9116

Internal Revenue Service (Treasury Dept.)
1111 Constitution Ave., NW
Washington, DC 20224
(800) 829-1040

United States Customs Service (Treasury Dept.)
1301 Constitution Ave., NW
Washington, DC 20229
(202) 927-2095

*Hotlines:*

Small Business Administration Answer Desk
(202) 205-7717, or (800) 827-5722 or
(202) 205-7701 for recorded information

Small Business Export/Import Advisory Service
(800) 424-5201

---

## The Top Reference Sources

*Congressional Quarterly's Washington
Information Directory*
Congressional Quarterly, $89.95
(202) 887-8500

This directory lists the departments and agencies
of the federal government, congressional committees, and private, nonprofit organizations in the

nation's capital. Each chapter covers a broad
subject area, such as health, energy, or science.
Entries include the name, address, and telephone number of the organization; the name and
title of the best person to contact for information;
and a brief description of the work performed by
the organization.

# State Information Offices

EACH STATE HAS AN INFORMATION office staffed by operators who can direct the caller to the appropriate office based on his or her stated purpose. The Information Office numbers for each of the state offices are as follows:

| State | Telephone |
|---|---|
| Alabama | (205) 242-8000 |
| Alaska | (907) 465-2111 |
| Arizona | (602) 255-4900 |
| Arkansas | (501) 682-3000 |
| California | (916) 322-9900 |
| Colorado | (303) 866-5000 |
| Connecticut | (203) 240-0222 |
| Delaware | (302) 739-4000 |
| District of Columbia | (202) 727-1000 |
| Florida | (904) 488-1234 |
| Georgia | (404) 656-2000 |
| Hawaii | (808) 548-6222 |
| Idaho | (208) 334-2411 |
| Illinois | (217) 782-2000 |
| Indiana | (317) 232-1000 |
| Iowa | (515) 281-5011 |
| Kansas | (913) 296-0111 |
| Kentucky | (502) 564-3130 |
| Louisiana | (504) 342-6600 |
| Maine | (207) 582-9500 |
| Maryland | (410) 974-2000 |
| Massachusetts | (617) 722-2000 |
| Michigan | (517) 373-1837 |
| Minnesota | (612) 296-6013 |
| Mississippi | (601) 359-1000 |

| State | Telephone |
|---|---|
| Missouri | (314) 751-2000 |
| Montana | (406) 444-2511 |
| Nebraska | (402) 471-2311 |
| Nevada | (702) 687-5000 |
| New Hampshire | (603) 271-1110 |
| New Jersey | (609) 292-2121 |
| New Mexico | (505) 827-4011 |
| New York | (518) 474-2121 |
| North Carolina | (919) 733-1110 |
| North Dakota | (701) 224-2000 |
| Ohio | (614) 466-2000 |
| Oklahoma | (405) 521-1601 |
| Oregon | (503) 378-3131 |
| Pennsylvania | (717) 787-2121 |
| Rhode Island | (401) 277-2000 |
| South Carolina | (803) 734-1000 |
| South Dakota | (605) 773-3011 |
| Tennessee | (615) 741-3011 |
| Texas | (512) 463-4630 |
| Utah | (801) 538-3000 |
| Vermont | (802) 828-1110 |
| Virginia | (804) 786-0000 |
| Washington | (206) 753-5000 |
| West Virginia | (304) 558-3456 |
| Wisconsin | (608) 266-2211 |
| Wyoming | (307) 777-7011 |

# OSHA

THE OCCUPATIONAL SAFETY AND Health Administration (OSHA) is the arm of the U.S. Department of Labor which deals with maintaining health and safety in the workplace. Established under the OSHA act of 1970, this agency was set up to:

- Reduce workplace hazards.

- Establish minimum standards for health and safety for industries.

- Regularly inspect workplace sites to ensure compliance with standards. Note: Any business with ten or fewer employees is not subject to these inspections. However, OSHA produces a checklist for self-inspections of premises which can assist the small business owner in maintaining a hazard-free workplace.

- Maintain a systematic method of reporting incidents of on-the-job or work-related illnesses or injuries, including those which entitle an individual to compensation.

In order to provide businesses with information about OSHA requirements, free consultation assistance is available to employers. Representatives of OSHA will assist in identifying specific and potential hazards which may exist in the workplace. They will also assist in implementing health and safety programs, particularly concerning issues such as maintaining a smoke-free environment. To obtain a list of free OSHA publications as well as information regarding on-site consultation, interested individuals should contact:

*OSHA (cont'd)*

OSHA Publications
Occupational Safety and Health Administration
Department of Labor
200 Constitution Ave., NW, Room N4101
Washington, DC 20210
(202) 219-4667

To obtain information regarding OSHA programs, and to be referred to the appropriate department of OSHA, the interested individual should call the Information Office at OSHA at (202) 219-8148.

The upside of the OSHA safety regulations is a program called Voluntary Protection Program (VPP) which rewards companies for maintaining safer workplace environments. Those companies which have effective health and safety programs, and a lower than average injury and illness rate, may be eligible for the program. The benefits for participants in the program are reduced worker compensation costs, a reduction in workday injuries with potential for reduced insurance rates, and possible automatic exemption from OSHA's programmed inspections.

To find out about the program write or call:

Occupational Safety and Health Administration
Department of Labor
200 Constitution Ave., NW, Room N3700
Washington, DC 20210
(202) 219-7266

Statistics collected by the Insurance Information Institute suggest that awareness of safety in the workplace is beginning to produce favorable results in a reduced number of accidental deaths.

## Accidental Deaths in the U.S.

|  | 1992 | 1991 | % Change |
|---|---|---|---|
| All Accidents | 83,000 | 88,000 | -6 |
| Motor Vehicles | 40,300 | 43,500 | -7 |
| Home | 19,500 | 20,500 | -5 |
| Work | 8,500 | 9,900 | -14 |
| Public | 18,000 | 18,000 | 0 |

*Source: National Safety Council*

---

**FAX**    **Government Income and Spending.** Request #202. See p. xi for instructions.

Tables of federal budget outlays, gross federal debt, federal receipts by source.

---

## The Top Reference Sources

*Access EPA*
National Technical Information Service, $24
(703) 487-4650
Stock #055-000-00437-4

First published in 1991, this annual directory of U.S. Environmental Protection Agency (EPA) and other public sector environmental information resources contains information for everyone interested in the environment.

Chapters include major EPA dockets, clearinghouses and hotlines, major EPA environmental databases, library and information services, state environmental libraries, alternate state environmental contacts, and EPA scientific models.

# Governors, Mayors, Congress

## U.S. Governors

| State | Governor | Phone |
| --- | --- | --- |
| Alabama | Jim Folsom, Jr. | (205) 242-7100 |
| Alaska | Walter J. Hickel | (907) 465-3500 |
| Arizona | Fife Symington | (602) 542-4331 |
| Arkansas | Jim Guy Tucker | (501) 682-2345 |
| California | Pete Wilson | (916) 445-2841 |
| Colorado | Roy R. Romer | (303) 866-2471 |
| Connecticut | Lowell P. Weicker, Jr. | (203) 566-4840 |
| Delaware | Thomas Carper | (302) 739-4101 |
| Florida | Lawton Chiles | (904) 488-2272 |
| Georgia | Zell Miller | (404) 656-1776 |
| Hawaii | John D. Waihee, III | (808) 586-0034 |
| Idaho | Cecil D. Andrus | (208) 334-2100 |
| Illinois | Jim Edgar | (217) 782-6830 |
| Indiana | Evan Bayh | (317) 232-1048 |
| Iowa | Terry E. Branstad | (515) 281-5211 |
| Kansas | Joan Finney | (913) 296-3232 |
| Kentucky | Brereton Jones | (502) 564-2611 |
| Louisiana | Edwin W. Edwards | (504) 342-7015 |
| Maine | John R. McKernan, Jr. | (207) 287-3531 |
| Maryland | William Donald Schaefer | (410) 974-3901 |
| Massachusetts | William F. Weld | (617) 727-3600 |
| Michigan | John Engler | (517) 373-3400 |
| Minnesota | Arne Carlson | (612) 296-3391 |
| Mississippi | Kirk Fordice | (601) 359-3150 |
| Missouri | Mel Carnahan | (314) 751-3222 |
| Montana | Marc Racicot | (406) 444-3111 |
| Nebraska | E. Benjamin Nelson | (402) 471-2244 |
| Nevada | Bob Miller | (702) 687-5670 |
| New Hampshire | Stephen Merrill | (603) 271-2121 |
| New Jersey | Christine Todd Whitman | (609) 292-6000 |
| New Mexico | Bruce King | (505) 827-3000 |
| New York | Mario M. Cuomo | (518) 474-8390 |
| North Carolina | James B. Hunt, Jr. | (919) 733-4240 |
| North Dakota | Edward T. Schafer | (701) 224-2200 |
| Ohio | George V. Voinovich | (614) 466-3555 |
| Oklahoma | David Walters | (405) 521-2342 |
| Oregon | Barbara Roberts | (503) 378-3111 |
| Pennsylvania | Robert P. Casey | (717) 787-2500 |
| Puerto Rico | Pedro Rossello | (809) 721-7000 |
| Rhode Island | Bruce G. Sundlun | (401) 277-2080 |
| South Carolina | Caroll A. Campbell, Jr. | (803) 734-9818 |
| South Dakota | Walter D. Miller | (605) 773-3212 |
| Tennessee | Ned McWherter | (615) 741-2001 |
| Texas | Ann W. Richards | (512) 463-2000 |
| Utah | Mike Leavitt | (801) 538-1000 |
| Vermont | Howard Dean | (802) 828-3333 |
| Virginia | George Allen | (804) 786-2211 |
| Washington | Mike Lowry | (206) 753-6780 |
| West Virginia | Gaston Caperton | (304) 558-2000 |
| Wisconsin | Tommy G. Thompson | (608) 266-1212 |
| Wyoming | Michael J. Sullivan | (307) 777-7435 |

*Governors, Mayors, Congress (cont'd)*

# Mayors of Major U.S. Cities

| City | Mayor | Phone |
|------|-------|-------|
| Atlanta | Bill Campbell | (404) 330-6100 |
| Baltimore | Kurt Schmoke | (410) 396-3835 |
| Boston | Thomas M. Menino | (617) 635-4000 |
| Buffalo | Anthony Masiello | (716) 851-4841 |
| Chicago | Richard M. Daley | (312) 744-3300 |
| Cincinnati | Roxanne Qualls | (513) 352-3250 |
| Cleveland | Michael R. White | (216) 664-2220 |
| Columbus | Greg Lashutka | (614) 645-7671 |
| Dallas | Steve Bartlett | (214) 670-4054 |
| Denver | Wellington E. Webb | (303) 640-2721 |
| Detroit | Dennis Archer | (313) 224-6340 |
| Hartford | Mike Peters | (203) 543-8500 |
| Honolulu | Frank F. Fasi | (808) 523-4141 |
| Houston | Bob Lanier | (713) 247-2200 |
| Indianapolis | Stephen Goldsmith | (317) 327-3601 |
| Jacksonville | Edward Austin | (904) 630-1776 |
| Los Angeles | Richard Riordan | (213) 485-3311 |
| Memphis | Willie W. Herenton | (901) 576-6000 |
| Miami | Steve Clark | (305) 250-5300 |
| Milwaukee | John O. Norquist | (414) 278-2200 |
| Minneapolis | Sharon Sayles Belton | (612) 673-2100 |
| Nashville | Philip N. Bredesen | (615) 862-6000 |
| New Orleans | Sidney Barthelemy | (504) 565-6400 |
| New York | Rudolph Giuliani | (212) 788-3000 |
| Norfolk | Mason C. Andrews | (804) 441-2679 |
| Orlando | Glenda Hood | (407) 246-2221 |
| Philadelphia | Edward Rendell | (215) 686-2181 |
| Phoenix | Paul Johnson | (602) 262-7111 |
| Pittsburgh | Tom Murphy | (412) 255-2626 |
| Portland, OR | Vera Katz | (503) 823-4120 |
| Sacramento | Joseph Serna, Jr. | (916) 264-5407 |
| St. Louis | Freeman R. Bosley, Jr. | (314) 622-3201 |
| Salt Lake City | Deedee Corradini | (801) 535-7704 |
| San Antonio | Nelson W. Wolff | (210) 299-7060 |
| San Diego | Susan Golding | (619) 236-6330 |
| San Francisco | Frank Jordan | (415) 554-6141 |
| Seattle | Norman Rice | (206) 684-4000 |
| Tampa | Sandra W. Freedman | (813) 223-8251 |
| Washington, DC | Sharon Pratt Kelly | (202) 727-6319 |

*Source: U.S. Conference of Mayors*

*Compuserve offers access to Findex, McGraw Hill, PTS Mars and other business-related databases. GO MGMTRC.*

*Governors, Mayors, Congress (cont'd)*

## U.S. Senators

| Senator | State | Party | Phone | Senator | State | Party | Phone |
|---------|-------|-------|-------|---------|-------|-------|-------|
| Murkowski, Frank H. | AK | R | (202) 224-6665 | Baucus, Max | MT | D | (202) 224-2651 |
| Stevens, Ted | AK | R | (202) 224-3004 | Burns, Conrad | MT | R | (202) 224-2644 |
| Heflin, Howell | AL | D | (202) 224-4124 | Faircloth, Lauch | NC | R | (202) 224-3154 |
| Shelby, Richard C. | AL | D | (202) 224-5744 | Helms, Jesse | NC | R | (202) 224-6342 |
| Bumpers, Dale | AR | D | (202) 224-4843 | Conrad, Kent | ND | D | (202) 224-2043 |
| Pryor, David H. | AR | D | (202) 224-2353 | Dorgan, Byron L. | ND | D | (202) 224-2551 |
| Deconcini, Dennis | AZ | D | (202) 224-4521 | Exon, J. James | NE | D | (202) 224-4224 |
| McCain, John | AZ | R | (202) 224-2235 | Kerrey, J. Robert | NE | D | (202) 224-6551 |
| Boxer, Barbara | CA | D | (202) 224-3553 | Gregg, Judd | NH | R | (202) 224-3324 |
| Feinstein, Dianne | CA | D | (202) 224-3841 | Smith, Bob | NH | R | (202) 224-2841 |
| Brown, Hank | CO | R | (202) 224-5941 | Bradley, Bill | NJ | D | (202) 224-3224 |
| Campbell, Ben N. | CO | D | (202) 224-5852 | Lautenberg, Frank R. | NJ | D | (202) 224-4744 |
| Dodd, Christopher J. | CT | D | (202) 224-2823 | Bingaman, Jeff | NM | D | (202) 224-5521 |
| Lieberman, Joseph I. | CT | D | (202) 224-4041 | Domenici, Pete V. | NM | R | (202) 224-6621 |
| Biden, Joseph R., Jr. | DE | D | (202) 224-5042 | Bryan, Richard H. | NV | D | (202) 224-6244 |
| Roth, William V., Jr. | DE | R | (202) 224-2441 | Reid, Harry | NV | D | (202) 224-3542 |
| Graham, Bob | FL | D | (202) 224-3041 | D'Amato, Alfonse M. | NY | R | (202) 224-6542 |
| Mack, Connie | FL | R | (202) 224-5274 | Moynihan, Daniel P. | NY | D | (202) 224-4451 |
| Coverdell, Paul | GA | R | (202) 224-3643 | Glenn, John | OH | D | (202) 224-3353 |
| Nunn, Sam | GA | D | (202) 224-3521 | Metzenbaum, Howard | OH | D | (202) 224-2315 |
| Akaka, Daniel K. | HI | D | (202) 224-6361 | Boren, David L. | OK | D | (202) 224-4721 |
| Inouye, Daniel K. | HI | D | (202) 224-3934 | Nickles, Don | OK | R | (202) 224-5754 |
| Grassley, Charles E. | IA | R | (202) 224-3744 | Hatfield, Mark O. | OR | R | (202) 224-3753 |
| Harkin, Tom | IA | D | (202) 224-3254 | Packwood, Bob | OR | R | (202) 224-5244 |
| Craig, Larry E. | ID | R | (202) 224-2752 | Specter, Arlen | PA | R | (202) 224-4254 |
| Kempthorne, Dirk | ID | D | (202) 224-6142 | Wofford, Harris | PA | D | (202) 224-6324 |
| Moseley-Braun, Carol | IL | D | (202) 224-2854 | Chafee, John H. | RI | R | (202) 224-2921 |
| Simon, Paul | IL | D | (202) 224-2152 | Pell, Claiborne | RI | D | (202) 224-4642 |
| Coats, Dan | IN | R | (202) 224-5623 | Hollings, Ernest F. | SC | D | (202) 224-6121 |
| Lugar, Richard G. | IN | R | (202) 224-4814 | Thurmond, Strom | SC | R | (202) 224-5972 |
| Dole, Robert | KS | R | (202) 224-6521 | Daschle, Thomas A. | SD | D | (202) 224-2321 |
| Kassebaum, Nancy L. | KS | R | (202) 224-4774 | Pressler, Larry | SD | R | (202) 224-5842 |
| Ford, Wendell H. | KY | D | (202) 224-4343 | Mathews, Harlan | TN | D | (202) 224-4944 |
| McConnell, Mitch | KY | R | (202) 224-2541 | Sasser, Jim | TN | D | (202) 224-3344 |
| Breaux, John B. | LA | D | (202) 224-4623 | Hutchison, Kay Bailey | TX | R | (202) 224-5922 |
| Johnston, J. Bennett | LA | R | (202) 224-5824 | Gramm, Phil | TX | R | (202) 224-2934 |
| Kennedy, Edward M. | MA | D | (202) 224-4543 | Bennett, Robert F. | UT | R | (202) 224-5444 |
| Kerry, John F. | MA | D | (202) 224-2742 | Hatch, Orrin G. | UT | R | (202) 224-5251 |
| Mikulski, Barbara A. | MD | D | (202) 224-4654 | Robb, Charles S. | VA | D | (202) 224-4024 |
| Sarbanes, Paul S. | MD | D | (202) 224-4524 | Warner, John W. | VA | R | (202) 224-2023 |
| Cohen, William S. | ME | R | (202) 224-2523 | Jeffords, James M. | VT | R | (202) 224-5141 |
| Mitchell, George J. | ME | D | (202) 224-5344 | Leahy, Patrick J. | VT | D | (202) 224-4242 |
| Levin, Carl | MI | D | (202) 224-6221 | Gorton, Slade | WA | R | (202) 224-3441 |
| Riegle, Donald W., Jr. | MI | D | (202) 224-4822 | Murray, Patty | WA | D | (202) 224-2621 |
| Durenberger, Dave | MN | R | (202) 224-3244 | Feingold, Russell D. | WI | D | (202) 224-5323 |
| Wellstone, Paul | MN | D | (202) 224-5641 | Kohl, Herb | WI | D | (202) 224-5653 |
| Bond, Christopher S. | MO | R | (202) 224-5721 | Byrd, Robert C. | WV | D | (202) 224-3954 |
| Danforth, John C. | MO | R | (202) 224-6154 | Rockefeller, John D., IV | WV | D | (202) 224-6472 |
| Cochran, Thad | MS | R | (202) 224-5054 | Simpson, Alan K. | WY | R | (202) 224-3424 |
| Lott, Trent | MS | R | (202) 224-6253 | Wallop, Malcolm | WY | R | (202) 224-6441 |

*Governors, Mayors, Congress (cont'd)*

## U.S. Representatives

| Representative | State | Party | Phone |
|---|---|---|---|
| Young, Don | AK | R | (202) 225-5765 |
| Bachus, Spencer T., III | AL | R | (202) 225-4921 |
| Bevill, Tom | AL | D | (202) 225-4876 |
| Browder, Glen | AL | D | (202) 225-3261 |
| Callahan, Sonny | AL | R | (202) 225-4931 |
| Cramer, Robert E., Jr. | AL | D | (202) 225-4801 |
| Everett, Terry | AL | R | (202) 225-2901 |
| Hilliard, Earl F. | AL | D | (202) 225-2665 |
| Dickey, Jay | AR | R | (202) 225-3772 |
| Hutchinson, Y. Tim | AR | R | (202) 225-4301 |
| Lambert, Blanche M. | AR | D | (202) 225-4076 |
| Thornton, Ray | AR | D | (202) 225-2506 |
| Faleomavaega, Eni F.H. | AS | C | (202) 225-8577 |
| Coppersmith, Sam | AZ | D | (202) 225-2635 |
| English, Karan | AZ | D | (202) 225-2190 |
| Kolbe, Jim | AZ | R | (202) 225-2542 |
| Kyl, Jon | AZ | R | (202) 225-3361 |
| Pastor, Ed | AZ | D | (202) 225-4065 |
| Stump, Bob | AZ | R | (202) 225-4576 |
| Baker, William P. | CA | R | (202) 225-1880 |
| Becerra, Xavier | CA | D | (202) 225-6235 |
| Beilenson, Anthony C. | CA | D | (202) 225-5911 |
| Berman, Howard L. | CA | D | (202) 225-4695 |
| Brown, George E., Jr. | CA | D | (202) 225-6161 |
| Calvert, Ken | CA | R | (202) 225-1986 |
| Condit, Gary A. | CA | D | (202) 225-6131 |
| Cox, Christopher | CA | R | (202) 225-5611 |
| Cunningham, Randy | CA | R | (202) 225-5452 |
| Dellums, Ronald V. | CA | D | (202) 225-2661 |
| Dixon, Julian C. | CA | D | (202) 225-7084 |
| Dooley, Calvin M. | CA | D | (202) 225-3341 |
| Doolittle, John T. | CA | R | (202) 225-2511 |
| Dornan, Robert K. | CA | R | (202) 225-2965 |
| Dreier, David | CA | R | (202) 225-2305 |
| Edwards, Don | CA | D | (202) 225-3072 |
| Eshoo, Anna G. | CA | D | (202) 225-8104 |
| Farr, Sam | CA | D | (202) 225-2861 |
| Fazio, Vic | CA | D | (202) 225-5716 |
| Filner, Bob | CA | D | (202) 225-8045 |
| Gallegly, Elton | CA | R | (202) 225-5811 |
| Hamburg, Dan | CA | D | (202) 225-3311 |
| Harman, Jane | CA | D | (202) 225-8220 |
| Herger, Wally | CA | R | (202) 225-3076 |
| Horn, Stephen | CA | R | (202) 225-6676 |
| Huffington, Michael | CA | R | (202) 225-3601 |
| Hunter, Duncan | CA | R | (202) 225-5672 |
| Kim, Jay | CA | R | (202) 225-3201 |
| Lantos, Tom | CA | D | (202) 225-3531 |
| Lehman, Richard H. | CA | D | (202) 225-4540 |
| Lewis, Jerry | CA | R | (202) 225-5861 |
| Martinez, Matthew G. | CA | D | (202) 225-5464 |
| Matsui, Robert T. | CA | D | (202) 225-7163 |
| McCandless, Alfred A. | CA | R | (202) 225-5330 |
| McKeon, Howard P. | CA | R | (202) 225-1956 |
| Miller, George | CA | D | (202) 225-2095 |
| Mineta, Norman Y. | CA | D | (202) 225-2631 |
| Moorhead, Carlos J. | CA | R | (202) 225-4176 |
| Packard, Ron | CA | R | (202) 225-3906 |
| Pelosi, Nancy | CA | D | (202) 225-4965 |
| Pombo, Richard W. | CA | R | (202) 225-1947 |
| Rohrabacher, Dana | CA | R | (202) 225-2415 |
| Roybal-Allard, Lucille | CA | D | (202) 225-1766 |
| Royce, Edward R. | CA | R | (202) 225-4111 |
| Schenk, Lynn | CA | D | (202) 225-2040 |
| Stark, Fortney Pete | CA | D | (202) 225-5065 |
| Thomas, William M. | CA | R | (202) 225-2915 |
| Torres, Esteban Edward | CA | D | (202) 225-5256 |
| Tucker, Walter R., III | CA | D | (202) 225-7924 |
| Waters, Maxine | CA | D | (202) 225-2201 |
| Waxman, Henry A. | CA | D | (202) 225-3976 |
| Woolsey, Lynn C. | CA | D | (202) 225-5161 |
| Allard, Wayne | CO | R | (202) 225-4676 |
| Hefley, Joel | CO | R | (202) 225-4422 |
| McInnis, Scott | CO | R | (202) 225-4761 |
| Schaefer, Dan | CO | R | (202) 225-7882 |
| Schroeder, Patricia | CO | D | (202) 225-4431 |
| Skaggs, David E. | CO | D | (202) 225-2161 |
| DeLauro, Rosa L. | CT | D | (202) 225-3661 |
| Franks, Gary A. | CT | R | (202) 225-3822 |
| Gejdenson, Sam | CT | D | (202) 225-2076 |
| Johnson, Nancy L. | CT | R | (202) 225-4476 |
| Kennelly, Barbara B. | CT | D | (202) 225-2265 |
| Shays, Christopher | CT | R | (202) 225-5541 |
| Norton, Eleanor Holmes | DC | C | (202) 225-8050 |
| Castle, Michael N. | DE | R | (202) 225-4165 |
| Bacchus, Jim | FL | D | (202) 225-3671 |
| Bilirakis, Michael | FL | R | (202) 225-5755 |
| Brown, Corrine | FL | D | (202) 225-0123 |
| Canady, Charles T. | FL | R | (202) 225-1252 |
| Deutsch, Peter | FL | D | (202) 225-7931 |
| Diaz-Balart, Lincoln | FL | R | (202) 225-4211 |
| Fowler, Tillie K. | FL | R | (202) 225-2501 |
| Gibbons, Sam | FL | D | (202) 225-3376 |
| Goss, Porter J. | FL | R | (202) 225-2536 |
| Hastings, Alcee L. | FL | D | (202) 225-1313 |
| Hutto, Earl | FL | D | (202) 225-4136 |
| Johnston, Harry | FL | D | (202) 225-3001 |
| Lewis, Tom | FL | R | (202) 225-5792 |
| McCollum, Bill | FL | R | (202) 225-2176 |
| Meek, Carrie P. | FL | D | (202) 225-4506 |
| Mica, John L. | FL | R | (202) 225-4035 |
| Miller, Dan | FL | R | (202) 225-5015 |
| Peterson, Douglas | FL | D | (202) 225-5235 |
| Ros-Lehtinen, Ileana | FL | R | (202) 225-3931 |
| Shaw, E. Clay, Jr. | FL | R | (202) 225-3026 |
| Stearns, Cliff | FL | R | (202) 225-5744 |
| Thurman, Karen L. | FL | D | (202) 225-1002 |
| Young, C.W. Bill | FL | R | (202) 225-5961 |
| Bishop, Sanford D., Jr. | GA | D | (202) 225-3631 |
| Collins, Michael A. | GA | R | (202) 225-5901 |

*Governors, Mayors, Congress (cont'd)*

## U.S. Representatives

| Representative | State | Party | Phone |
|---|---|---|---|
| Darden, George | GA | D | (202) 225-2931 |
| Deal, Nathan | GA | D | (202) 225-5211 |
| Gingrich, Newt | GA | R | (202) 225-4501 |
| Johnson, Don | GA | D | (202) 225-4101 |
| Kingston, Jack | GA | R | (202) 225-5831 |
| Lewis, John | GA | D | (202) 225-3801 |
| Linder, John | GA | R | (202) 225-4272 |
| McKinney, Cynthia A. | GA | D | (202) 225-1605 |
| Rowland, J. Roy | GA | D | (202) 225-6531 |
| Underwood, Robert A. | GU | C | (202) 225-1188 |
| Abercrombie, Neil | HI | D | (202) 225-2726 |
| Mink, Patsy T. | HI | D | (202) 225-4906 |
| Grandy, Fred | IA | R | (202) 225-5476 |
| Leach, Jim | IA | R | (202) 225-6576 |
| Lightfoot, Jim | IA | R | (202) 225-3806 |
| Nussle, Jim | IA | R | (202) 225-2911 |
| Smith, Neal | IA | D | (202) 225-4426 |
| Crapo, Michael D. | ID | R | (202) 225-5531 |
| LaRocco, Larry | ID | D | (202) 225-6611 |
| Collins, Cardiss | IL | D | (202) 225-5006 |
| Costello, Jerry F. | IL | D | (202) 225-5661 |
| Crane, Philip M. | IL | R | (202) 225-3711 |
| Durbin, Richard J. | IL | D | (202) 225-5271 |
| Evans, Lane | IL | D | (202) 225-5905 |
| Ewing, Thomas W. | IL | R | (202) 225-2371 |
| Fawell, Harris W. | IL | R | (202) 225-3515 |
| Gutierrez, Luis V. | IL | D | (202) 225-8203 |
| Hastert, J. Dennis | IL | R | (202) 225-2976 |
| Hyde, Henry J. | IL | R | (202) 225-4561 |
| Lipinski, William O. | IL | D | (202) 225-5701 |
| Manzullo, Donald A | IL | R | (202) 225-5676 |
| Michel, Robert H. | IL | R | (202) 225-6201 |
| Porter, John Edward | IL | R | (202) 225-4835 |
| Poshard, Glenn | IL | D | (202) 225-5201 |
| Reynolds, Mel | IL | D | (202) 225-0773 |
| Rostenkowski, Dan | IL | D | (202) 225-4061 |
| Rush, Bobby L. | IL | D | (202) 225-4372 |
| Sangmeister, George E. | IL | D | (202) 225-3635 |
| Yates, Sidney R. | IL | D | (202) 225-2111 |
| Burton, Dan | IN | R | (202) 225-2276 |
| Buyer, Stephen E. | IN | R | (202) 225-5037 |
| Hamilton, Lee H. | IN | D | (202) 225-5315 |
| Jacobs, Andrew, Jr. | IN | D | (202) 225-4011 |
| Long, Jill L. | IN | D | (202) 225-4436 |
| McCloskey, Frank | IN | D | (202) 225-4636 |
| Myers, John T. | IN | R | (202) 225-5805 |
| Roemer, Tim | IN | D | (202) 225-3915 |
| Sharp, Philip R. | IN | D | (202) 225-3021 |
| Visclosky, Peter J. | IN | D | (202) 225-2461 |
| Glickman, Dan | KS | D | (202) 225-6216 |
| Meyers, Jan | KS | R | (202) 225-2865 |
| Roberts, Pat | KS | R | (202) 225-2715 |
| Slattery, Jim | KS | D | (202) 225-6601 |
| Baesler, Scotty | KY | D | (202) 225-4706 |
| Barlow, Thomas J., III | KY | D | (202) 225-3115 |

| Representative | State | Party | Phone |
|---|---|---|---|
| Bunning, Jim | KY | R | (202) 225-3465 |
| Mazzoli, Romano L. | KY | D | (202) 225-5401 |
| Natcher, William H. | KY | D | (202) 225-3501 |
| Rogers, Harold | KY | R | (202) 225-4601 |
| Baker, Richard H. | LA | R | (202) 225-3901 |
| Fields, Cleo | LA | D | (202) 225-8490 |
| Hayes, James A. | LA | D | (202) 225-2031 |
| Jefferson, William J. | LA | D | (202) 225-6636 |
| Livingston, Bob | LA | R | (202) 225-3015 |
| McCrery, Jim | LA | R | (202) 225-2777 |
| Tauzin, W. J. | LA | D | (202) 225-4031 |
| Blute, Peter | MA | R | (202) 225-6101 |
| Frank, Barney | MA | D | (202) 225-5931 |
| Kennedy, Joseph P., II | MA | D | (202) 225-5111 |
| Markey, Edward J. | MA | D | (202) 225-2836 |
| Meehan, Martin T. | MA | D | (202) 225-3411 |
| Moakley, John Joseph | MA | D | (202) 225-8273 |
| Neal, Richard E. | MA | D | (202) 225-5601 |
| Olver, John W. | MA | D | (202) 225-5335 |
| Studds, Gerry E. | MA | D | (202) 225-3111 |
| Torkildsen, Peter G. | MA | R | (202) 225-8020 |
| Andrews, Thomas H. | ME | D | (202) 225-6116 |
| Snowe, Olympia J. | ME | R | (202) 225-6306 |
| Bartlett, Roscoe G. | MD | R | (202) 225-2721 |
| Bentley, Helen Delich | MD | R | (202) 225-3061 |
| Cardin, Benjamin L. | MD | D | (202) 225-4016 |
| Gilchrest, Wayne T. | MD | R | (202) 225-5311 |
| Hoyer, Steny H. | MD | D | (202) 225-4131 |
| Mfume, Kweisi | MD | D | (202) 225-4741 |
| Morella, Constance A. | MD | R | (202) 225-5341 |
| Wynn, Albert Russell | MD | D | (202) 225-8699 |
| Barcia, James A. | MI | D | (202) 225-8171 |
| Bonior, David E. | MI | D | (202) 225-2106 |
| Camp, Dave | MI | R | (202) 225-3561 |
| Carr, Bob | MI | D | (202) 225-4872 |
| Collins, Barbara-Rose | MI | D | (202) 225-2261 |
| Conyers, John, Jr. | MI | D | (202) 225-5126 |
| Dingell, John D. | MI | D | (202) 225-4071 |
| Ford, William D. | MI | D | (202) 225-6261 |
| Henry, Paul B. | MI | R | (202) 225-3831 |
| Hoekstra, Peter | MI | R | (202) 225-4401 |
| Kildee, Dale E. | MI | D | (202) 225-3611 |
| Knollenberg, Joe | MI | R | (202) 225-5802 |
| Levin, Sander M. | MI | D | (202) 225-4961 |
| Smith, Nick | MI | R | (202) 225-6276 |
| Stupak, Bart | MI | D | (202) 225-4735 |
| Upton, Fred | MI | R | (202) 225-3761 |
| Grams, Rod | MN | R | (202) 225-2271 |
| Minge, David | MN | D | (202) 225-2331 |
| Oberstar, James L. | MN | D | (202) 225-6211 |
| Penny, Timothy J. | MN | D | (202) 225-2472 |
| Peterson, Collin C. | MN | D | (202) 225-2165 |
| Ramstad, Jim | MN | R | (202) 225-2871 |
| Sabo, Martin Olav | MN | D | (202) 225-4755 |
| Vento, Bruce F. | MN | D | (202) 225-6631 |

*Governors, Mayors, Congress (cont'd)*

## U.S. Representatives

| Representative | State | Party | Phone |
|---|---|---|---|
| Clay, William | MO | D | (202) 225-2406 |
| Danner, Pat | MO | D | (202) 225-7041 |
| Emerson, Bill | MO | R | (202) 225-4404 |
| Gephardt, Richard A. | MO | D | (202) 225-2671 |
| Hancock, Mel | MO | R | (202) 225-6536 |
| Skeleton, Ike | MO | D | (202) 225-2876 |
| Talent, James M. | MO | R | (202) 225-2561 |
| Volkmer, Harold L. | MO | D | (202) 225-2956 |
| Wheat, Alan | MO | D | (202) 225-4535 |
| Montgomery, G.V. | MS | D | (202) 225-5031 |
| Parker, Mike | MS | D | (202) 225-5865 |
| Taylor, Gene | MS | D | (202) 225-5772 |
| Thompson, Bennie G. | MS | D | (202) 225-5876 |
| Whitten, Jamie L. | MS | D | (202) 225-4306 |
| Williams, Pat | MT | D | (202) 225-3211 |
| Ballenger, Cass | NC | R | (202) 225-2576 |
| Clayton, Eva M. | NC | D | (202) 225-3101 |
| Coble, Howard | NC | R | (202) 225-3065 |
| Hefner, W. G. | NC | D | (202) 225-3715 |
| Lancaster, H. Martin | NC | D | (202) 225-3415 |
| McMillan, J. Alex | NC | R | (202) 225-1976 |
| Neal, Stephen L. | NC | D | (202) 225-2071 |
| Price, David E. | NC | D | (202) 225-1784 |
| Rose, Charlie | NC | D | (202) 225-2731 |
| Taylor, Charles H. | NC | R | (202) 225-6401 |
| Valentine, Tim | NC | D | (202) 225-4531 |
| Watt, Melvin, L. | NC | D | (202) 225-1510 |
| Pomeroy, Earl | ND | D | (202) 225-2611 |
| Barrett, Bill | NE | R | (202) 225-6435 |
| Bereuter, Doug | NE | R | (202) 225-4806 |
| Hoagland, Peter | NE | D | (202) 225-4155 |
| Swett, Dick | NH | D | (202) 225-5206 |
| Zeliff, William H., Jr. | NH | R | (202) 225-5456 |
| Andrews, Robert E. | NJ | D | (202) 225-6501 |
| Franks, Bob | NJ | R | (202) 225-5361 |
| Gallo, Dean A. | NJ | R | (202) 225-5034 |
| Hughes, William J. | NJ | D | (202) 225-6572 |
| Klein, Herb | NJ | D | (202) 225-5751 |
| Menendez, Robert | NJ | D | (202) 225-7919 |
| Pallone, Frank, Jr. | NJ | D | (202) 225-4671 |
| Payne, Donald M. | NJ | D | (202) 225-3436 |
| Roukema, Marge | NJ | R | (202) 225-4465 |
| Saxton, Jim | NJ | R | (202) 225-4765 |
| Smith, Christopher H. | NJ | R | (202) 225-3765 |
| Torricelli, Robert G. | NJ | D | (202) 225-5061 |
| Zimmer, Dick | NJ | R | (202) 225-5801 |
| Richardson, Bill | NM | D | (202) 225-6190 |
| Schiff, Steven | NM | R | (202) 225-6316 |
| Skeen, Joe | NM | R | (202) 225-2365 |
| Bilbray, James H. | NV | D | (202) 225-5965 |
| Vucanovich, Barbara F. | NV | R | (202) 225-6155 |
| Ackerman, Gary L. | NY | D | (202) 225-2601 |
| Boehlert, Sherwood L. | NY | R | (202) 225-3665 |
| Engel, Eliot L. | NY | D | (202) 225-2464 |
| Fish, Hamilton, Jr. | NY | R | (202) 225-5441 |

| Representative | State | Party | Phone |
|---|---|---|---|
| Flake, Floyd H. | NY | D | (202) 225-3461 |
| Gilman, Benjamin A. | NY | R | (202) 225-3776 |
| Hinchey, Maurice D. | NY | D | (202) 225-6335 |
| Hochbrueckner, George J. | NY | D | (202) 225-3826 |
| Houghton, Amo | NY | D | (202) 225-3161 |
| King, Peter T. | NY | R | (202) 225-7896 |
| LaFalce, John J. | NY | D | (202) 225-3231 |
| Lazio, Rick | NY | R | (202) 225-3335 |
| Levy, David A. | NY | R | (202) 225-5516 |
| Lowey, Nita M. | NY | D | (202) 225-6506 |
| Maloney, Carolyn B. | NY | D | (202) 225-7944 |
| Manton, Thomas J. | NY | D | (202) 225-3965 |
| McHugh, John M. | NY | R | (202) 225-4611 |
| McNulty, Michael R. | NY | D | (202) 225-5076 |
| Molinari, Susan | NY | R | (202) 225-3371 |
| Nadler, Jerrold | NY | D | (202) 225-5635 |
| Owens, Major R. | NY | D | (202) 225-6231 |
| Paxon, Bill | NY | R | (202) 225-5265 |
| Quinn, Jack | NY | R | (202) 225-3306 |
| Rangel, Charles B. | NY | D | (202) 225-4365 |
| Schumer, Charles E. | NY | D | (202) 225-6616 |
| Serrano, José E. | NY | D | (202) 225-4361 |
| Slaughter, Louise McIntosh | NY | D | (202) 225-3615 |
| Solomon, Gerald B.H. | NY | R | (202) 225-5614 |
| Towns, Edolphus | NY | D | (202) 225-5936 |
| Velázquez, Nydia M. | NY | D | (202) 225-2361 |
| Walsh, James T. | NY | R | (202) 225-3701 |
| Applegate, Douglas | OH | D | (202) 225-6265 |
| Boehner, John A. | OH | R | (202) 225-6205 |
| Brown, Sherrod | OH | D | (202) 225-3401 |
| Fingerhut, Eric | OH | D | (202) 225-5731 |
| Gillmor, Paul E. | OH | R | (202) 225-6405 |
| Hall, Tony P. | OH | D | (202) 225-6465 |
| Hobson, David L. | OH | R | (202) 225-4324 |
| Hoke, Martin R. | OH | R | (202) 225-5871 |
| Kaptur, Marcy | OH | D | (202) 225-4146 |
| Kasich, John R. | OH | R | (202) 225-5355 |
| Mann, David | OH | D | (202) 225-2216 |
| Oxley, Michael G. | OH | R | (202) 225-2676 |
| Portman, Rob | OH | R | (202) 225-3164 |
| Pryce, Deborah | OH | R | (202) 225-2015 |
| Regula, Ralph | OH | R | (202) 225-3876 |
| Sawyer, Thomas C. | OH | D | (202) 225-5231 |
| Stokes, Louis | OH | D | (202) 225-7032 |
| Strickland, Ted | OH | D | (202) 225-5705 |
| Traficant, James A., Jr. | OH | D | (202) 225-5261 |
| Brewster, Bill K. | OK | D | (202) 225-4565 |
| English, Glenn | OK | D | (202) 225-5565 |
| Inhofe, James M. | OK | R | (202) 225-2211 |
| Istook, Ernest J., Jr. | OK | R | (202) 225-2132 |
| McCurdy, Dave | OK | D | (202) 225-6165 |
| Synar, Mike | OK | D | (202) 225-2701 |
| DeFazio, Peter A. | OR | D | (202) 225-6416 |
| Furse, Elizabeth | OR | D | (202) 225-0855 |
| Kopetski, Michael J. | OR | D | (202) 225-5711 |

*Governors, Mayors, Congress (cont'd)*

## U.S. Representatives

| Representative | State | Party | Phone |
|---|---|---|---|
| Smith, Robert F. | OR | R | (202) 225-6730 |
| Wyden, Ron | OR | D | (202) 225-4811 |
| Blackwell, Lucien E. | PA | D | (202) 225-4001 |
| Borski, Robert A. | PA | D | (202) 225-8251 |
| Clinger, William F., Jr. | PA | R | (202) 225-5121 |
| Coyne, William J. | PA | D | (202) 225-2301 |
| Foglietta, Thomas M. | PA | D | (202) 225-4731 |
| Gekas, George W. | PA | R | (202) 225-4315 |
| Goodling, William F. | PA | R | (202) 225-5836 |
| Greenwood, James C. | PA | R | (202) 225-4276 |
| Holden, Tim | PA | D | (202) 225-5546 |
| Kanjorski, Paul E. | PA | D | (202) 225-6511 |
| Klink, Ron | PA | D | (202) 225-2565 |
| Margolies-Mezvinsky, M. | PA | D | (202) 225-6111 |
| McDade, Joseph M. | PA | R | (202) 225-3731 |
| McHale, Paul | PA | D | (202) 225-6411 |
| Murphy, Austin J. | PA | D | (202) 225-4665 |
| Murtha, John P. | PA | D | (202) 225-2065 |
| Ridge, Thomas J. | PA | R | (202) 225-5406 |
| Santorum, Rick | PA | R | (202) 225-2135 |
| Shuster, Bud | PA | R | (202) 225-2431 |
| Walker, Robert S. | PA | R | (202) 225-2411 |
| Weldon, Curt | PA | R | (202) 225-2011 |
| Romero-Barcelo, Carlos | PR | C | (202) 225-2615 |
| Machtley, Ronald K. | RI | R | (202) 225-4911 |
| Reed, Jack | RI | D | (202) 225-2735 |
| Clyburn, James E. | SC | D | (202) 225-3315 |
| Derrick, Butler | SC | D | (202) 225-5301 |
| Inglis, Bob | SC | R | (202) 225-6030 |
| Ravenel, Arthur, Jr. | SC | R | (202) 225-3176 |
| Spence, Floyd | SC | R | (202) 225-2452 |
| Spratt, John M., Jr. | SC | D | (202) 225-5501 |
| Johnson, Tim | SD | D | (202) 225-2801 |
| Clement, Bob | TN | D | (202) 225-4311 |
| Cooper, Jim | TN | D | (202) 225-6831 |
| Duncan, John J., Jr. | TN | R | (202) 225-5435 |
| Ford, Harold E. | TN | D | (202) 225-3265 |
| Gordon, Bart | TN | D | (202) 225-4231 |
| Lloyd, Marilyn | TN | D | (202) 225-3271 |
| Quillen, James H. | TN | R | (202) 225-6356 |
| Sundquist, Don | TN | R | (202) 225-2811 |
| Tanner, John S. | TN | D | (202) 225-4714 |
| Andrews, Michael A. | TX | D | (202) 225-7508 |
| Archer, Bill | TX | R | (202) 225-2571 |
| Armey, Richard K. | TX | R | (202) 225-7772 |
| Barton, Joe | TX | R | (202) 225-2002 |
| Bonilla, Henry | TX | R | (202) 225-4511 |
| Brooks, Jack | TX | D | (202) 225-6565 |
| Bryant, John | TX | D | (202) 225-2231 |
| Chapman, Jim | TX | D | (202) 225-3035 |
| Coleman, Ronald D. | TX | D | (202) 225-4831 |
| Combest, Larry | TX | R | (202) 225-4005 |
| de la Garza, E. | TX | D | (202) 225-2531 |
| DeLay, Tom | TX | R | (202) 225-5951 |
| Edwards, Chet | TX | D | (202) 225-6105 |

| Representative | State | Party | Phone |
|---|---|---|---|
| Fields, Jack | TX | R | (202) 225-4901 |
| Frost, Martin | TX | D | (202) 225-3605 |
| Geren, Pete | TX | D | (202) 225-5071 |
| Gonzalez, Henry B. | TX | D | (202) 225-3236 |
| Green, Gene | TX | D | (202) 225-1688 |
| Hall, Ralph M. | TX | D | (202) 225-6673 |
| Johnson, E.B. | TX | D | (202) 225-8885 |
| Johnson, Sam | TX | R | (202) 225-4201 |
| Laughlin, Greg | TX | D | (202) 225-2831 |
| Ortiz, Solomon P. | TX | D | (202) 225-7742 |
| Pickle, J. J. | TX | D | (202) 225-4865 |
| Sarpalius, Bill | TX | D | (202) 225-3706 |
| Smith, Lamar S. | TX | R | (202) 225-4236 |
| Stenholm, Charles W. | TX | D | (202) 225-6605 |
| Tejeda, Frank | TX | D | (202) 225-1640 |
| Washington, Craig A. | TX | D | (202) 225-3816 |
| Wilson, Charles | TX | D | (202) 225-2401 |
| Hansen, James V. | UT | R | (202) 225-0453 |
| Orton, Bill | UT | D | (202) 225-7751 |
| Shepherd, Karen | UT | D | (202) 225-3011 |
| Bateman, Herbert H. | VA | R | (202) 225-4261 |
| Bliley, Thomas J., Jr. | VA | R | (202) 225-2815 |
| Boucher, Rick | VA | D | (202) 225-3861 |
| Byrne, Leslie L | VA | D | (202) 225-1492 |
| Goodlatte, Bob | VA | R | (202) 225-5431 |
| Moran, James P. | VA | D | (202) 225-4376 |
| Payne, L. F. | VA | D | (202) 225-4711 |
| Pickett, Owen B. | VA | D | (202) 225-4215 |
| Scott, Robert C. | VA | D | (202) 225-8351 |
| Sisisky, Norman | VA | D | (202) 225-6365 |
| Wolf, Frank R. | VA | R | (202) 225-5136 |
| de Lugo, Ron | VI | C | (202) 225-1790 |
| Sanders, Bernard | VT | I | (202) 225-4115 |
| Cantwell, Maria | WA | D | (202) 225-6311 |
| Dicks, Norman D. | WA | D | (202) 225-5916 |
| Dunn, Jennifer B. | WA | R | (202) 225-7761 |
| Foley, Thomas S. | WA | D | (202) 225-2006 |
| Inslee, Jay | WA | D | (202) 225-5816 |
| Kreidler, Mike | WA | D | (202) 225-8901 |
| McDermott, Jim | WA | D | (202) 225-3106 |
| Swift, Al | WA | D | (202) 225-2605 |
| Unsoeld, Jolene | WA | D | (202) 225-3536 |
| Barrett, Thomas M. | WI | D | (202) 225-3571 |
| Gunderson, Steve | WI | R | (202) 225-5506 |
| Kleczka, Gerald D. | WI | D | (202) 225-4572 |
| Klug, Scott L. | WI | R | (202) 225-2906 |
| Obey, David R. | WI | D | (202) 225-3365 |
| Petri, Thomas E. | WI | R | (202) 225-2476 |
| Roth, Toby | WI | R | (202) 225-5665 |
| Sensenbrenner, F. James, Jr. | WI | R | (202) 225-5101 |
| Mollohan, Alan B. | WV | D | (202) 225-4172 |
| Rahall, Nick Joe, II | WV | D | (202) 225-3452 |
| Wise, Robert E., Jr. | WV | D | (202) 225-2711 |
| Thomas, Craig | WY | R | (202) 225-2311 |

*C: Resident Commissioner; I: Independent*

# Congressional Chairs

## Senate Committees

| Committee | Chair |
| --- | --- |
| Agriculture, Nutrition, and Forestry | Patrick J. Leahy, D-VT |
| Appropriations | Robert C. Byrd, D-WV |
| Armed Services | Sam Nunn, D-GA |
| Banking, Housing, and Urban Affairs | Donald W. Riegle, Jr., D-MI |
| Budget | Jim Sasser, D-TN |
| Commerce, Science, and Transportation | Ernest F. Hollings, D-SC |
| Energy and Natural Resources | J. Bennett Johnston, R-LA |
| Environment and Public Works | Max Baucus, D-MT |
| Finance | Daniel P. Moynihan, D-NY |
| Foreign Relations | Claiborne Pell, D-RI |
| Government Affairs | John Glenn, D-OH |
| Judiciary | Joseph R. Biden, Jr., D-DE |
| Labor and Human Resources | Edward M. Kennedy, D-MA |
| Rules and Administration | Wendell H. Ford, D-KY |
| Select Ethics | Richard H. Bryan, D-NV |
| Select Indian Affairs | Daniel K. Inouye, D-HI |
| Select Intelligence | Dennis DeConcini, D-AZ |
| Small Business | Dale Bumpers, R-AK |
| Special Aging | David H. Pryor, R-AR |
| Veterans' Affairs | John Rockefeller IV, D-WV |

## House Committees

| Committee | Chair |
| --- | --- |
| Agriculture | E. de la Garza, D-TX |
| Appropriations | William H. Natcher, D-KY |
| Armed Services | Ronald V. Dellums, D-CA |
| Banking, Finance, and Urban Affairs | Henry B. Gonzalez, D-TX |
| Budget | Martin Olav Sabo, D-MN |
| District of Columbia | Fortney Pete Stark, D-CA |
| Education and Labor | William D. Ford, D-MI |
| Energy and Commerce | John D. Dingell, D-MI |
| Foreign Affairs | Lee H. Hamilton, D-IN |
| Government Operations | John Conyers, Jr., D-MI |
| House Administration | Charlie Rose, D-NC |
| Judiciary | Jack Brooks, D-TX |
| Merchant Marine and Fisheries | Gerry E. Studds, D-MA |
| Natural Resources | George Miller, D-CA |
| Post Office and Civil Svc. | William L. Clay, D-MO |
| Public Works and Trans. | Norman Y. Mineta, D-CA |
| Rules | John J. Moakley, D-MA |
| Science, Space, and Technology | George E. Brown, Jr., D-CA |
| Select Intelligence | Dan Glickman, D-KS |
| Small Business | John J. LaFalce, D-NY |
| Standards of Official Conduct | Jim McDermott, D-WA |
| Veterans' Affairs | G.V. Montgomery, D-MS |
| Ways and Means | Sam Gibbons, D-FL |

## Joint Committees of Congress

| Committee | Senate Chair | House Chair |
| --- | --- | --- |
| Economic | Paul S. Sarbanes, MD | David R. Obey, WI |
| Library | Claiborne Pell, RI | Charlie Rose, NC |
| Organization of Congress | David L. Boren, OK | Lee H. Hamilton, IN |
| Printing | Wendell H. Ford, KY | Charlie Rose, NC |
| Taxation | Daniel P. Moynihan, NY | Dan Rostenkowski, IL |

## The Top Reference Sources

*1994 Washington Representatives*
Columbia Books, $70
(202) 898-0662

This essential reference book is a compilation of names of representatives of the major national associations, labor unions, and U.S. companies, registered foreign agents, lobbyists, lawyers, law firms, and special interest groups, together with their clients and areas of legislative and regulatory concerns.

# Small Business Administration

THE U.S. SMALL BUSINESS Administration (SBA) is an independent government agency created by Congress to help small businesses grow and prosper. The SBA has over 100 offices that offer small firms financial assistance through guaranteed loans, management assistance, help in obtaining government contracts, counseling services, and many low-cost publications.

The SBA offers assistance to small businesses and pays particular attention to those owned by ethnic minorities, women, veterans, and others with special needs and circumstances. There are fact sheets available covering each of these and many more categories.

The SBA publishes over 100 business booklets that sell for modest fees (usually under $2.00). They address issues which concern prospective and exist-

ing small business owners. A free directory of Small Business Administration publications may be obtained from the SBA Answer Desk or from any regional SBA office. *(See also "Small Business Administration Regional Offices" on page 404.)*

## Contact Option

Small Business Answer Desk
(202) 205-7717, or (800) 827-5722 or (202) 205-7701 for recorded information

This hotline provides the caller with an automated menu of topics on relevant small business issues. Informative brochures will be sent upon request.

# Getting an SBA Loan

SBA LOANS ARE AVAILABLE to small companies that have sought and been refused financing from other lending institutions prior to applying to the SBA for assistance. Most of the SBA loans are made through the guaranteed loan program, in which the private lender agrees to loan funds to the small business and the SBA agrees to guarantee 90% of a loan under $155,000 and up to 85% of a loan greater than that figure, up to a maximum of $750,000.

Although the interest rates on SBA guaranteed loans are negotiated between the borrower and lender, they are subject to SBA maximums and generally cannot exceed 2.75% over the New York prime rate.

The SBA also provides specialized loan guarantee programs which include:

- Export revolving lines of credit
- International trade loans
- Seasonal lines of credit
- Small general contractor financing
- Lender incentives for small loans of less than $50,000
- Pollution control loans
- Community development loans.

Direct loans of up to $150,000 by the SBA are very limited in number and are available only to applicants unable to secure an SBA-guaranteed loan. Before applying, a small business owner must seek financing from his or her bank of account and, in cit-

ies of over 200,000, from at least one other lender. Direct loan funds are available to businesses located in high-unemployment areas, or owned by low-income or handicapped individuals, Vietnam veterans or disabled veterans. Interest on direct loans is calculated quarterly.

## Eligibility Requirements

To be eligible for SBA loan assistance, a company must be operated for profit and fall within size standards. It cannot be a business involved in the creation or distribution of ideas or opinions such as newspapers, magazines, and academic schools. It cannot be engaged in speculation or investment in rental real estate.

The SBA has other eligibility requirements which qualify a business as a small business:

- Manufacturing: the maximum number of employees may range from 500 to 1,500 depending on the type of product manufactured.

- Wholesaling: the maximum number of employees may not exceed 100.

- Services: the average annual receipts may not exceed $3.5 to $14.5 million depending on the industry.

- Retailing: the average annual receipts may not exceed $3.5 to $13.5 million, depending on the industry.

- Construction: general construction average annual receipts may not exceed $9.5 to $17 million depending on the industry.

*Getting an SBA Loan (cont'd)*

- Special trade construction: average annual receipts may not exceed $7 million.

- Agriculture: average annual receipts range from $1 to $3.5 million, depending on the industry.

## Applying for an SBA Loan

To apply for a loan, a small business owner must do the following:

- Prepare a current business balance sheet listing all assets, liabilities, and net worth. Start-up businesses should prepare an estimated balance sheet including the amount invested by the owner and others.

- Prepare a profit and loss statement for the current period and the most recent three fiscal years. Start-up businesses should prepare a detailed projection of earnings and expenses for at least the first year of operation.

- Prepare a personal financial statement of the proprietor and each partner or stockholder owning 20% or more of the business.

- List collateral to be offered as security for the loan.

- List any existing liens.

- State the amount of the requested loan and the purposes for which it is intended.

- Present the above items to a selected lender. If the loan request is refused, the business owner should contact the local SBA office regarding the guaranteed-loan program.

- If the guaranteed loan is not possible, other loans may be available from the SBA.

# Alternatives to an SBA Loan

ALTHOUGH THE SBA is perhaps the best known "friend" to the small business owner, there are several other governmental and private sector organizations which can offer financial assistance and guidance to individuals requiring it.

SBIC (Small Business Investment Companies) are privately organized and managed firms which make equity capital and long-term credit available to small, independent businesses. SBICs are licensed by the SBA but set their own policies and investment decisions. SSBICs (Special Small Business Investment Companies) invest specifically in socially and economically disadvantaged entrepreneurs. The SBIC can borrow up to four times its private capital through a federally guaranteed funding system, at an interest rate slightly above the cost of money to the U.S., making it an attractive and powerful source of capital for new and growing businesses.

The National Association of Small Business Investment Companies (NASBIC) is the national trade association for the 215 SBICs and 127 SSBICs. It publishes a directory of members, broken down by state, size of financing, industry preference, and geographical preference. The NASBIC directory is entitled: *Venture Capital: Where to Find It.* Phone or credit card orders are not accepted.

To obtain the directory, send a check for $10, payable to NASBIC, to:

NASBIC Directory
POB 2039
Merrifield, VA 22116

For other questions or information, call or write:

National Association of Small Business
Investment Companies
1199 N. Fairfax St., Suite 200
Alexandria, VA 22314
(703) 683-1601

BDCs (Business Development Corporations) are groups affiliated with 30 various state governments and they differ from SBAs. BDCs agree to accept riskier loans, for longer terms. They frequently sell parts of these loans to others on the secondary loan market to offset the risk. Interest rates usually average 2 to 4% above the prime lending rate and some BDCs charge a flat fee.

To locate the BDC within a state, or to obtain assistance in locating other funding sources, an individual should write or call a specific state Small Business Development Center. The national organization will direct the caller to one of 750 state or regional centers. These centers provide assistance in the form of training, counseling, and research assistance in start-up, operation, and expansion of business in all 50 states. While the centers do not provide funding, they do refer individuals to the organizations that can offer the greatest assistance. *(See also "Small Business Development Centers" on page 404.)*

Association of Small Business Development Centers
1313 Farnum, Suite 132
Omaha, NE 68182
(402) 595-2387

# Small Business Support

EACH STATE HAS offices that provide assistance for prospective or existing small business owners. These agencies help businesses to prosper and create and retain jobs. They also increase economic opportunities for communities and populations in need.

The following phone numbers connect to the main business support office in each state. These offices in turn can direct the caller to an appropriate regional or local office, if necessary.

## State-by-State Support

| State | Small Business Assistance Office |
|-------|----------------------------------|
| AK | (907) 465-2500 |
| AL | (205) 242-0400 |
| AR | (501) 682-2052 |
| AZ | (602) 542-1353 |
| CA | (916) 322-3982 |
| CO | (303) 892-3840 |
| CT | (203) 258-4202 |
| DC | (202) 727-6600 |
| DE | (302) 739-4271 |
| FL | (904) 488-6300 |
| GA | (404) 656-3556 |
| HI | (808) 586-2360 |
| IA | (515) 242-4814 |
| ID | (208) 334-2470 |
| IL | (217) 782-7500 |
| IN | (317) 232-8894 |
| KS | (913) 296-3480 |
| KY | (502) 564-7670 |
| LA | (504) 342-5388 |
| MA | (617) 727-8380 |
| MD | (410) 333-6901 |
| ME | (207) 267-2656 |
| MI | (517) 373-0347 |
| MN | (612) 296-6424 |
| MO | (314) 751-3946 |
| MS | (601) 359-3449 |
| MT | (406) 444-3923 |
| NC | (919) 733-4151 |

| State | Small Business Assistance Office |
|-------|----------------------------------|
| ND | (701) 224-2810 |
| NE | (402) 471-3747 |
| NH | (603) 271-2411 |
| NJ | (609) 292-2444 |
| NM | (505) 827-0305 |
| NV | (702) 687-4325 |
| NY | (518) 474-4100 |
| OH | (614) 466-2317 |
| OK | (405) 843-9770 |
| OR | (503) 373-1205 |
| PA | (717) 787-3003 |
| RI | (401) 277-2601 |
| SC | (803) 737-0400 |
| SD | (605) 773-5032 |
| TN | (615) 741-1888 |
| TX | (512) 472-5059 |
| UT | (801) 538-8700 |
| VA | (804) 371-8106 |
| VT | (802) 828-3221 |
| WA | (206) 753-7426 |
| WI | (608) 266-7884 |
| WV | (304) 558-3650 |
| WY | (307) 777-7284 |

## The Top Reference Sources

*The Legal Guide for Starting and Running a Small Business*
Nolo Press, $22.95
(800) 992-6656 or (510) 549-1976

This book contains legal information the small business owner needs to know about partnerships, cor-

porations, buying businesses, franchises, licenses, permits, leases, contracts, hiring and firing, customer relations, independent contractors, insurance, and taxes.

Useful sample forms and letters are also included throughout.

# Minority Contracting Provisions

THE SBA OFFERS SPECIAL assistance to help minority-owned small businesses grow and thrive. The agency acts as the prime contractor for a share of all awards made by federal agencies and subcontracts to firms owned by socially and economically disadvantaged Americans. This SBA program admits small and minority-owned businesses into a program which allows them to negotiate on special contracts. Sources of information include the regional and district offices of the SBA, as well as individual State Information Offices.

# Winning Government Contracts

IN ONE RECENT YEAR, the federal government and its purchasing agents and departments contracted for $184.2 billion worth of goods and services from the private sector. This represents 16% of the total federal outlay. Of that total, $31.6 billion or 17.2% was purchased directly from small businesses. The SBA reports that another $27.2 billion reached small businesses through subcontracts to large, prime contractors to the federal government.

The SBA Answer Desk Hotline can provide prerecorded messages regarding business opportunities in the federal government sector. The regional offices of the SBA can also provide such information. *(See also "Small Business Administration Regional Offices" on page 404.)*

Small Business Answer Desk
(800) 827-5722 or (202) 205-7701

The Small Business Innovation Research Program administers a program among government agencies that provides grants to small businesses for innovation research and development. The Pre-Solicitation Announcement, published by the SBIR in March, June, September, and December lists the needs of 11 federal agencies for R&D activities.

For more information, contact:

Small Business Innovation Research Program
U.S. Small Business Administration
Office of Innovation, Research & Technology
409 Third St., SW, Room 8500
Washington, DC 20416
(202) 205-6450

Each business day, the GPO releases the *Commerce Business Daily*, a publication that provides a daily list of U.S. government procurement invitations, contract awards, subcontracting leads, sales of surplus property, and foreign business opportunities. Each edition contains 500 to 1,000 such notices and each notice appears in the CBD only once. Back issues are available in the public library, and a subscription may be obtained for six-month or one-year time periods.

Information about the rates and service may be obtained from:

The Superintendent of Documents
Government Printing Office
Washington, DC 20402
(202) 783-3238

Other useful documents that are available from the GPO are *U.S. Government Purchasing and Sales Directory* ($5.50) and *Small Business Guide to Federal Research and Development Funding Opportunities* ($6).

Another helpful source is the General Services Administration. It handles the government's purchases, sales, and services. GSA Business Service Centers provide small businesses with information about contracting opportunities. Call the GSA for the phone number of the nearest Business Service Center:

General Services Administration
18th and F Sts., NW
Washington, DC 20405
(202) 708-5804

# GPO Electronic Bulletin Board

DURING 1993, THE GOVERNMENT Printing Office (GPO) established an electronic bulletin board as an efficient way to retrieve government information. Armed with a PC and a modem, the interested user can access information from participating Federal agencies. The Federal Bulletin Board (BBS) is available 22 hours each day, 7 days a week. It is not available from 3:00 A.M. to 5:00 A.M., EST. Users are allowed to browse complementary files, review product announcements through README.doc files and receive a free user's manual, all without a time-based charge. E-mail allows users to place electronic orders for all GPO products using VISA, MasterCard, or GPO account numbers.

Some of the information available to users includes:

- Daily press briefings from the State Department;

- Background information on 170 countries;

- Congressional policy statements, fact sheets, and testimony;

- Clearinghouses and hotlines for EPA information resources.

To use the system call: (202) 512-1387; for user assistance, call (202) 512-1524. A 2400 bps or 9600 bps modem should be set to 8-N-1. The system will adjust to the rate of the incoming modem and allows the user to enter the system. A menu-driven program permits the user to log on and enter information for billing purposes (if billable data is accessed), and browse through a bulletin board of serviceable items.

## Recommended Resource

GPO Office of Electronic Information
Dissemination Services
732 North Capitol St., NW
Mail Stop: SDE
Washington, DC 20401
Information: (202) 512-1265
Order assistance: (202) 512-1526

# CD-ROMs Available from the GPO

THE GPO HAS BEGUN TO MAKE information available on CD-ROM at prices from approximately $13–$40. Generally, these CD-ROM disks are in ISO 9660 format and will run on any IBM-compatible PC with 640K RAM, a minimum of 12 megabytes of free hard disk space, and a CD-ROM reader with MS-DOS extensions. Additional requirements are provided with individual title listings.

While there are a limited number of publications available on CD-ROM at this time, many are timely and pertinent to specific industries. Health care professionals, for example, can find the latest information on the Clinton Health Plan proposals, while those in the food industry may choose to access the latest in food labeling regulations.

The Federal Acquisition Regulation (FAR) and Federal Information Resources Management Regulation (FIRMR) from the General Services Adminis-

tration are now available quarterly on one compact disk for easy access to information needed to sell goods and services to the federal government.

The SIGCAT (Special Interest Group) CD-ROM Compendium (1993) is a useful reference which gives an annotated index of approximately 300 CD-ROM products containing information supplied by federal, state, and other non-profit agencies. The index includes source and vendor information and technical requirements. Available from the GPO for $11.

To get more information about the current and upcoming CD-ROMs, call the GPO Office of Electronic Information Dissemination Services between 8:00 A.M. and 4:00 P.M.
Information: (202) 512-1265
Order assistance: (202) 512-1526

# U.S. Government Subscriptions

SMALL AND LARGE CORPORATIONS alike rely on magazines and periodical publications for the most up-to-date information on the changing climate of the business community. The federal government maintains access to such information and offers it to the general public in periodic publications. The U.S. Government Printing Office offers a quarterly catalogue of periodical and subscription services. The catalogue is available from:

Superintendent of Documents
U.S. Government Printing Office
Washington, DC 20402
(202) 783-3238

Several noteworthy publications of interest to the business community include:

*Business America: The Magazine of International Trade*

A biweekly publication providing American exporters with information on trade opportunities and methods of doing business in foreign countries. A typical issue includes an analytical piece on current U.S. trade policy, a "how to" article for the novice exporter, a picture of the nation's economic health, and news of congressional and government actions affecting trade. Subscriptions can be obtained for $61 per year; issues can be ordered on an individual basis for $2.50 each.

*Census and You*

Monthly newsletter for users of the Census Bureau statistics. A free sample copy is available from DUSD, Bureau of the Census, Washington, DC 20233. Subscriptions cost $21 per year.

*Commerce Publications Update: A Biweekly Listing of Latest Titles from the U.S. Department of Commerce*

Listing of all publications and press releases issued by the U.S. Department of Commerce and providing the latest figures in 19 key areas of business and economic activity. A copy of the update can be purchased for $1.50. Yearly subscriptions cost $31.

*Department of Defense Telephone Directory*

An alphabetical directory of Departments of Army, Navy, and Air Force personnel, and a classified section by agency for the Washington, DC metropolitan area. The directory costs $24 per year.

*Foreign Labor Trends*

American Embassy reports describing labor developments, labor-management relations, trade unions, employment, wages and working conditions, labor and government, training, and a list of key labor indicators for some of the most important foreign countries. The reports cost $36 for approximately 73 issues per year.

*Survey of Current Business*

Monthly report on general trends in industry, the business situation, future outlook, and other points pertinent to the business world. Subscriptions to the monthly report cost $43 per year.

*Federal Acquisition Regulation (FAR) and the Federal Information Resources Management Regulation*

Quarterly listing of primary regulations used by federal executive agencies requesting supplies and services. The listings cost $33 per copy or $106 per year.

# GPO Business Publications

INSTEAD OF BROWSING THROUGH a general catalogue of GPO publications, request the *Catalog of Publications and Subscriptions for Business*. This includes titles on general business reference, publications on import/export, patents and trademarks, selling to the government, employment, health and safety, labor law and statistics, accounting and auditing, as well as regulatory information. The catalogue is available from:

Superintendent of Documents
U.S. Government Printing Office
Washington, DC 20402
(202) 783-3238

# Assistance from the Government

## The Service Corps of Retired Executives (SCORE)

SCORE is a volunteer program of the SBA. The organization matches the skills and experience of the volunteers with a business that needs expert advice. Approximately 14,000 men and women business executives participate in the program and share their management and technical expertise with present and prospective owners and managers of small businesses.

Volunteers are members of 390 locally organized, self-administered chapters offering services in more than 700 locations throughout the U.S. There is no charge for the counseling, but there may be a nominal fee for the training programs. Volunteers offer counseling in distribution channels, expansion potential, product changes. They offer workshops to present and prospective small business entrepreneurs within the local community. An individual currently operating a small business or contemplating a business start-up is eligible for help from SCORE. The service is not tied to any SBA loan. Any local office of the SBA can advise a caller of the availability of a SCORE program.

## Small Business Development Centers (SBDCs)

This branch of the SBA sponsors 57 SBDCs in 50 states as well as the District of Columbia, Puerto Rico, and the Virgin Islands. Through a network of subcenters located at educational institutions, chambers of commerce, economic development corporations, and downtown storefronts, the state SBDCs provide up-to-date counseling and training, and deal with financial, marketing, production, organization, engineering, technical problems, and feasibility studies.

More specialized programs include services to inventors with patentable products, international trade centers for how-to export and import advice, business law information and guidance, procurement matching, venture capital formation, and small business incubators.

The location of a local SBDC can be found by calling the Association of Small Business Development Centers at (402) 595-2387. *(See also "Small Business Development Centers" on page 404.)*

## Small Business Institute (SBI)

The SBA sponsors over 500 SBIs in all states and territories in order to offer small business owners an opportunity to receive intensive management counseling from qualified college level business students working under expert faculty guidance. The studies focus on market studies, accounting systems, personnel policies, production design, product line diversification, exporting, expansion feasibility, and strategy. A local office of the SBA can advise the caller of the availability of an SBI in the area.

# Lobbying

THERE ARE APPROXIMATELY 14,000 individuals in the nation's capital whose profession might be listed as "advocacy." They include persons who work to influence government policies and actions by advocating for their own or their client's interests. They work in government affairs or in public relations departments for trade associations, professional societies, labor unions, corporations, and a wide variety of special interest and public interest groups. Some are registered as lobbyists on Capitol Hill. Others, who represent foreign industry or governments, are registered with the Justice Department as foreign agents. Still others are part of the executive branch of the federal government and act as liaisons between that office and Congress.

The Justice Department requires agents representing foreign countries, foreign companies, and organizations to file forms in their Foreign Agents Registration Unit: (202) 514-1216. These files are open for public inspection at the Justice Department.

Lobbyists also register with the Clerk of the House of Representatives and Secretary of the Senate, indicating the party or individuals in whose interest he or she works, the length of employment, amount of reimbursement received by the lobbyist, and what expenses are covered by this reimbursement. Furthermore, the lobbyist must file quarterly financial reports stating the name and address of each individual who has made a contribution of $500 or more, and the total contributions made during the calendar year.

# Hiring a Lobbyist

THE MOST EFFECTIVE WAY TO HIRE a lobbyist is to contact a Washington, DC law firm that represents national associations, labor unions, U.S. companies, registered foreign agents, lobbyists, or special interest groups. The following are the largest Washington legal firms (as noted by *Legal Times*) that represent special interest clients (as indicated by their listing in *Washington Representatives*, a compilation of such groups).

## Recommended Resources

*Washington Representatives (1994)*
Columbia Books, $70
(202) 898-0662

*Directory of Washington Lobbyists, Lawyers, and Interest Groups*
Amward Publications, $97.50
(703) 525-7227

*The American Lobbyists Directory*
Gale Research, $175
800-877-4253

*Political Finance and Lobby Reporter*
Amward Publications, $327/year
2030 Clarendon Blvd., Suite 305
Arlington, VA 22201
(703) 525-7227
*A semimonthly newsletter*

*The Lobbying Handbook*
by John Zorak
Professional Lobbying Consulting Center, $125
1111 14th St., NW, Suite 1001
Washington, DC 20005
(202) 898-0084

## Largest Washington Legal Firms Ranked by Size

| Legal Firm | Telephone Number |
| --- | --- |
| Covington & Burling | (202) 662-6000 |
| Arnold & Porter | (202) 872-6700 |
| Hogan & Hartson | (202) 637-5600 |
| Shaw, Pittman, Potts & Trowbridge | (202) 663-8000 |
| Arent, Fox, Kintner, Plotkin & Kahn | (202) 857-6000 |
| Akin, Gump, Hauer & Feld | (202) 887-4000 |
| Wilmer, Cutler & Pickering | (202) 663-6000 |
| Steptoe & Johnson | (202) 429-3000 |
| Jones, Day, Reavis & Pogue | (202) 879-3939 |
| Crowell & Moring | (202) 624-2500 |
| Skadden, Arps, Slate, Meagher & Flom | (202) 371-7000 |
| Howrey & Simon | (202) 783-0800 |
| Morgan, Lewis & Bockius | (202) 467-7000 |
| Dickstein, Shapiro & Morin | (202) 785-9700 |
| Dow, Lohnes, & Albertson | (202) 857-2500 |
| Patton, Boggs & Blow | (202) 457-6000 |
| Sutherland, Asbill & Brennan | (202) 383-0100 |
| Williams & Connolly | (202) 434-5000 |
| Sidley & Austin | (202) 736-8000 |
| McKenna & Cuneo | (202) 789-7500 |
| Verner, Lipfert, Bernhard, McPherson & Hand | (202) 371-6000 |
| Fried, Frank, Harris, Shriver & Jacobson | (202) 639-7000 |
| Reed, Smith, Shaw & McClay | (202) 456-6100 |
| Gibson, Dunn & Crutcher | (202) 955-8500 |
| Baker & Hostetler | (202) 861-1500 |
| Miller & Chevalier | (202) 626-5800 |
| Winston & Strawn | (202) 371-5700 |
| Kirkpatrick & Lockhart | (202) 778-9000 |
| Swidler & Berlin | (202) 944-4300 |

*Source: Legal Times*

# Political Action Committees

POLITICAL ACTION COMMITTEES are groups devoted to special interests. These groups raise and distribute funds for political candidates who support their specific concerns, as well as for lobbyists who represent their interests to legislators. PACs can be sponsored by a trade association, a union, special interest group, or a company.

## Contact Options

*Business-Associated PACs:*

AFL-CIO Committee on Political Education
(202) 637-5101

Americans for Free International Trade
(202) 659-8545

Business and Industry
(202) 833-1880

*Political Interest Groups:*

American Conservative Union
(202) 546-6555
    Focuses on defense, foreign policy, economics, and legal issues.

U.S. Chamber of Commerce
(202) 463-5604
    Promotes the enaction of pro-business legislation.

Congressional Economic Leadership Institute
(202) 546-5007
    Nonpartisan group, promotes discussion between Congress and private sector.

Family Research Council
(202) 393-2100
    Advocates the interests of the family in public policy formulation.

Foundation for Public Affairs
(202) 872-1750
    Disseminates information on corporate public affairs programs.

Several organizations monitor the voting records of members of Congress on particular issues and publish the results periodically. Some of those organizations which might be of interest to the business community include:

American Federation of Labor
Congress of Industrial Organizations
(202) 637-5000

Common Cause
(202) 833-1200

Competitive Enterprise Institute
(202) 547-1010

National Federation of Independent Business
(202) 554-9000

National Taxpayers Union
(202) 543-1300

National Women's Political Caucus
(202) 898-1100

## Recommended Resource

*Almanac of Federal PACs*
Amward Publications, $97.50
(703) 525-7227

---

## The Top Reference Sources

*Leadership Directories*
Monitor Leadership Directories, $125–$185
(212) 627-4140

These books provide easy access to decision-makers in business, government, and professional organizations. The books are updated quarterly or semiannually.

Titles include *Corporate Yellow Book, Financial Yellow Book, NASDAQ Yellow Book, International Corporate Yellow Book, Congressional Yellow Book, Federal Yellow Book, Federal Regional Yellow Book, State Yellow Book, Municipal Yellow Book, Law Firms Yellow Book, Associations Yellow Book,* and *News Media Yellow Book.*

# Major Trade Associations

## Selected Associations and Telephone Numbers

| Trade Association | Telephone Number |
|---|---|
| American Advertising Federation | (202) 898-0089 |
| American Bankers Association | (202) 663-5000 |
| American Council of Life Insurance | (202) 624-2000 |
| American Electronics Association | (408) 987-4200 |
| American Farm Bureau Federation | (312) 399-5700 |
| American Financial Services Association | (202) 296-5544 |
| American Health Care Association | (202) 842-4444 |
| American Hotel and Motel Association | (202) 289-3100 |
| American Institute of Certified Public Accountants | (212) 596-6200 |
| American Petroleum Institute | (202) 682-8000 |
| American Society of Association Executives | (202) 626-2723 |
| American Society of Travel Agents | (703) 739-2782 |
| American Trucking Association | (202) 544-6245 |
| American Wholesale Marketers Association | (202) 463-2124 |
| Associated Builders and Contractors | (202) 637-8800 |
| Associated General Contractors of America | (202) 393-2040 |
| Association of American Publishers | (212) 689-8920 |
| Automotive Service Association | (202) 543-1440 |
| Computer and Business Equipment Manufacturers Association | (202) 737-8888 |
| Direct Marketing Association | (202) 347-1222 |
| Electronic Industries Association | (202) 457-4900 |
| Food Marketing Institute | (202) 452-8444 |
| Grocery Manufacturers Association | (202) 337-9400 |
| Health Industry Manufacturers Association | (202) 783-8700 |
| Independent Petroleum Association of America | (202) 857-4722 |
| Information Industry Association | (202) 639-8260 |
| Information Technology Association of America | (703) 522-5055 |
| International Association for Financial Planning | (404) 395-1605 |
| International Communications Industries Association | (703) 273-7200 |
| National Association of Broadcasters | (202) 429-5300 |
| National Association of Chain Drug Stores | (703) 549-3001 |
| National Association of Convenience Stores | (703) 684-3600 |
| National Association of Environmental Professionals | (202) 966-1500 |
| National Association of Home Builders | (202) 822-0200 |
| National Association of Realtors | (312) 329-8200 |
| National Association of Wholesalers-Distributors | (202) 872-0885 |
| National Automobile Dealers Association | (703) 821-7000 |
| National Forest Products Association | (202) 463-2700 |
| National Home Furnishing Association | (919) 883-1650 |
| National Industrial Transportation League | (703) 524-5011 |
| National Restaurant Association | (202) 331-5900 |
| National Retail Federation | (202) 783-7971 |
| Printing Industries of America | (703) 519-8100 |
| Travel Industry Association of America | (202) 293-1433 |

# Government Publications

MORE THAN 12,000 BOOKS, pamphlets, posters, periodicals, subscription services, and other government publications are available for purchase from the Superintendent of Documents, Government Printing Office (GPO). They range from "accidents" to "zoning" and deal with almost every facet of human life. Topics are selected to meet the informational needs of congressional staff members who require sound background in order to propose and prepare legislation. The topics are also a response to the needs and interests of the general public.

The all-time best seller list prepared by the GPO includes the following titles and the number of copies sold:

1. *Metric Conversion Card* (3,977,405)
2. *Federal Benefits for Veterans and Dependents* (2,610,464)
3. *United States Government Manual* (1,732,005)
4. *Occupational Outlook Handbook* (1,677,105)
5. *Economic Report of the President* (1,321,817)
6. *Constitution of the United States* (1,088,796)

Other continuing titles which have a recurring demand include:

1. *Statistical Abstract of the United States*, 1993
2. *United States Industrial Outlook*, 1994
3. *Where to Write for Vital Records*
4. *Eating to Lower Your Blood Cholesterol*
5. *General Information Concerning Patients*

Frequently, a legal or general information question arises that can be resolved by a call to a Federal agency. It is usually worthwhile to request that the agency send any available printed information on a specific topic. Most agencies will gladly oblige such a request. If a charge is attached to a document, the caller will be referred to the Government Printing Office (GPO) and will be given the name of the publication to order.

In addition, depository libraries are designated to store certain federal documents and make them available for public access. There are 1,400 such libraries throughout the country. The reference desk of the local public library should be able to provide the caller with the location of the nearest depository library, where he or she will be assisted in locating the desired publication.

 **FAX** **Free Government Resources.** Request #203. See p. xi for instructions.

List of subject bibliographies available from the Government Printing Office.

## The Top Reference Sources

*How to Form Your Own Corporation Without a Lawyer for Under $75.00*
Dearborn Financial Publishing, $19.95
(800) 533-2665

The kind of information provided in this book previously had to be bought from an attorney.

Author Ted Nicholas explains how to avoid the hassle of lawyers and how to save hundreds or even thousands of dollars by following simple instructions. The book includes a complete set of forms, a certificate of incorporation, minutes, by-laws, and more.

# Government Bookstores

## Branch Bookstores of the U.S. Government Printing Office

| Address | City, State, Zip | Telephone |
| --- | --- | --- |
| 2021 3rd Ave., N | Birmingham, AL 35203 | (205) 731-1056 |
| 505 S. Flower St. | Los Angeles, CA 90071 | (213) 239-9844 |
| 450 Golden Gate Ave. | San Francisco, CA 94102 | (415) 252-5334 |
| 1961 Stout St. | Denver, CO 80294 | (303) 844-3964 |
| 201 W. 8th St. | Pueblo, CO 81003 | (719) 544-3142 |
| 710 N. Capitol St., NW | Washington, DC 20401 | (202) 512-0132 |
| 1510 H St., NW | Washington, DC 20005 | (202) 653-5075 |
| 100 W. Bay St. | Jacksonville, FL 32202 | (904) 353-0569 |
| 999 Peachtree St., NE | Atlanta, GA 30309 | (404) 347-1900 |
| 401 S. State St. | Chicago, IL 60604 | (312) 353-5133 |
| 10 Causeway St. | Boston, MA 02222 | (617) 720-4180 |
| 477 Michigan Ave. | Detroit, MI 48226 | (313) 226-7816 |
| 5600 E. Bannister Rd. | Kansas City, MO 64137 | (816) 765-2256 |
| 26 Federal Plaza | New York, NY 10278 | (212) 264-3825 |
| 1240 E. 9th St. | Cleveland, OH 44199 | (216) 522-4922 |
| 200 N. High St. | Columbus, OH 43215 | (614) 469-6956 |
| 1305 SW First Ave. | Portland, OR 97201 | (503) 221-6217 |
| 100 N. 17th St. | Philadelphia, PA 19103 | (215) 636-1900 |
| 1000 Liberty Ave. | Pittsburgh, PA 15222 | (412) 644-2721 |
| 1100 Commerce St. | Dallas, TX 75242 | (214) 767-0076 |
| 801 Travis St. | Houston, TX 77002 | (713) 228-1187 |
| 915 2nd Ave. | Seattle, WA 98174 | (206) 553-4270 |
| 310 W. Wisconsin Ave. | Milwaukee, WI 53203 | (414) 297-1304 |

# Freedom of Information Act

THE FREEDOM OF INFORMATION Act (FOIA) became law in 1966 and guaranteed the public the right of access to information held by the federal government. According to the act, any individual may request and receive a document, file, or other record held by any agency of the federal government. The burden of proof has shifted from the individual to the government, and the law requires that the government justify the need for secrecy regarding a document. However, there are nine specific exemptions to the access rule, including national defense, foreign policy, trade secrets, and criminal investigations.

The Privacy Act of 1974 enhances the FOIA by permitting individuals access to records about themselves, which are held by federal agencies. Such information must be complete, accurate, and relevant; the law requires that each agency publish a description of its record system and forbids the agency from disclosing personal information except to the individual who is the subject of such informa-

tion. Both laws permit the individual to request access to federal records regarding him or herself and allows the individual to appeal a denial of that request.

The FOIA sets a deadline of ten working days for replying to the information request and a twenty-day deadline on responding to the appeal. The initial request letter and the appeals letter, if necessary, should be clearly and simply written. The Freedom of Information Clearinghouse will provide a brochure detailing how to write a request as well as an appeals letter.

## Recommended Resource

*A User's Guide to the Freedom of Information Act*
Freedom of Information Clearinghouse
P.O. Box 19367
Washington, DC 20036
(202) 833-3000

# COMMUNICATIONS

# Area Codes

## U.S. Area Codes by State

| State | City | Code |
|-------|------|------|
| AL | All points | 205 |
| AK | All points | 907 |
| AZ | All points | 602 |
| AR | All points | 501 |
| CA | Alameda | 510 |
| | Alhambra | 818 |
| | Altadena | 818 |
| | Anaheim | 714 |
| | Arcadia | 818 |
| | Azusa | 818 |
| | Bakersfield | 805 |
| | Baldwin Park | 818 |
| | Bell Gardens | 213 |
| | Bellflower | 310 |
| | Belmont | 415 |
| | Berkeley | 510 |
| | Beverly Hills | 310 |
| | Buena Park | 714 |
| | Burbank | 818 |
| | Burlingame | 415 |
| | Campbell | 408 |
| | Carmichael | 916 |
| | Carson | 213 |
| | Castro Valley | 510 |
| | Chula Vista | 619 |
| | Claremont | 714 |
| | Compton | 310 |
| | Concord | 510 |
| | Corona | 909 |
| | Costa Mesa | 714 |
| | Covina | 818 |
| | Culver City | 310 |
| | Cypress | 714 |
| | Daly City | 415 |
| | Davis | 916 |
| | Downey | 310 |
| | East Los Angeles | 213 |
| | El Cerrito | 510 |
| | El Monte | 818 |
| | Escondido | 619 |
| | Eureka | 707 |
| | Fairfield | 707 |
| | Fountain Valley | 714 |
| | Fremont | 510 |
| | Fresno | 209 |
| | Fullerton | 714 |
| | Gardena | 310 |
| | Garden Grove | 714 |
| | Glendale | 818 |
| | Glendora | 818 |
| | Hacienda Heights | 818 |
| | Hawthorne | 310 |
| | Hollywood | 213 |
| | Huntington Beach | 714 |
| | Huntington Park | 213 |

| State | City | Code |
|-------|------|------|
| CA | Inglewood | 310 |
| | La Habra | 213 |
| | Lakewood | 310 |
| | La Mesa | 619 |
| | La Mirada | 714 |
| | Lancaster | 805 |
| | La Puente | 818 |
| | Lawndale | 213 |
| | Livermore | 510 |
| | Lodi | 209 |
| | Lompoc | 805 |
| | Long Beach | 310 |
| | Los Altos | 415 |
| | Los Angeles | 213 |
| | Los Gatos | 408 |
| | Lynwood | 213 |
| | Manhattan Beach | 213 |
| | Menlo Park | 415 |
| | Merced | 209 |
| | Milpitas | 408 |
| | Modesto | 209 |
| | Monrovia | 818 |
| | Montclair | 714 |
| | Montebello | 213 |
| | Monterey | 408 |
| | Monterey Park | 818 |
| | Mountain View | 415 |
| | Napa | 707 |
| | National City | 619 |
| | Newark | 510 |
| | Newport Beach | 714 |
| | North Highlands | 916 |
| | Norwalk | 310 |
| | Novato | 415 |
| | Oakland | 510 |
| | Oceanside | 619 |
| | Ontario | 714 |
| | Orange | 714 |
| | Oxnard | 805 |
| | Pacifica | 415 |
| | Palm Springs | 619 |
| | Palo Alto | 415 |
| | Palos Verdes | 213 |
| | Paramount | 213 |
| | Pasadena | 818 |
| | Pataluma | 707 |
| | Pico Rivera | 310 |
| | Pleasant Hill | 510 |
| | Rancho Cordova | 916 |
| | Redlands | 909 |
| | Redondo Beach | 310 |
| | Redwood City | 415 |
| | Rialto | 714 |
| | Richmond | 510 |
| | Riverside | 909 |

| State | City | Code |
|-------|------|------|
| CA | Rosemead | 818 |
| | Sacramento | 916 |
| | Salinas | 408 |
| | San Bernardino | 909 |
| | San Bruno | 415 |
| | San Carlos | 415 |
| | San Diego | 619 |
| | San Francisco | 415 |
| | San Gabriel | 818 |
| | San Jose | 408 |
| | San Leandro | 510 |
| | San Lorenzo | 510 |
| | San Luis Obispo | 805 |
| | San Rafael | 415 |
| | Santa Ana | 714 |
| | Santa Barbara | 805 |
| | Santa Clara | 408 |
| | Santa Cruz | 408 |
| | Santa Maria | 805 |
| | Santa Monica | 310 |
| | Santa Rosa | 707 |
| | Seal Beach | 213 |
| | Seaside | 408 |
| | Simi Valley | 805 |
| | Southgate | 213 |
| | South Pasadena | 818 |
| | S. San Francisco | 415 |
| | South Whittier | 213 |
| | Spring Valley | 619 |
| | Stockton | 209 |
| | Sunnyvale | 408 |
| | Temple City | 818 |
| | Thousand Oaks | 805 |
| | Torrance | 310 |
| | Upland | 909 |
| | Vallejo | 707 |
| | Ventura | 805 |
| | Visalia | 209 |
| | Vista | 619 |
| | Walnut Creek | 510 |
| | West Covina | 818 |
| | West Hollywood | 213 |
| | Westminister | 714 |
| | Whittier | 310 |
| CO | Aspen | 303 |
| | Colorado Springs | 719 |
| | Denver | 303 |
| | Grand Junction | 303 |
| | Pueblo | 719 |
| | Vail | 303 |
| | Woodland Park | 719 |
| CT | All points | 203 |
| DE | All points | 302 |
| DC | All points | 202 |
| FL | Boca Raton | 407 |

*Area Codes (cont'd)*

| State | City | Code |
|-------|------|------|
| FL | Carol City | 305 |
| | Clearwater | 813 |
| | Coral Gables | 305 |
| | Daytona Beach | 904 |
| | Fort Lauderdale | 305 |
| | Fort Myers | 813 |
| | Fort Pierce | 407 |
| | Gainesville | 904 |
| | Hallandale | 305 |
| | Hialeah | 305 |
| | Jacksonville | 904 |
| | Kendall | 305 |
| | Key West | 305 |
| | Lake Worth | 407 |
| | Lakeland | 813 |
| | Melbourne | 407 |
| | Merritt Island | 407 |
| | Miami | 305 |
| | Miami Beach | 305 |
| | Miramar | 305 |
| | North Miami | 305 |
| | N. Miami Beach | 305 |
| | Ocala | 904 |
| | Orlando | 407 |
| | Panama City | 904 |
| | Pensacola | 904 |
| | Plantation | 305 |
| | Pompano Beach | 305 |
| | St. Petersburg | 813 |
| | Sarasota | 813 |
| | Tallahassee | 904 |
| | Tampa | 813 |
| | Titusville | 407 |
| | W. Palm Beach | 407 |
| GA | Albany | 912 |
| | Athens | 706 |
| | Atlanta | 404 |
| | Augusta | 706 |
| | Columbus | 706 |
| | East Point | 404 |
| | Fort Benning | 706 |
| | Gainesvillle | 706 |
| | Griffin | 706 |
| | La Grange | 706 |
| | Macon | 912 |
| | Marietta | 404 |
| | Rome | 706 |
| | Savannah | 912 |
| | Valdosta | 912 |
| | Warner Robins | 912 |
| HI | All points | 808 |
| ID | All points | 208 |
| IL | Addison | 708 |
| | Alton | 708 |
| | Arlington Hts. | 708 |
| | Aurora | 708 |
| | Belleville | 618 |
| | Berwyn | 708 |
| | Bloomington | 309 |
| | Blue Island | 708 |

| State | City | Code |
|-------|------|------|
| IL | Calumet City | 708 |
| | Carbondale | 618 |
| | Carpentersville | 708 |
| | Champaign | 217 |
| | Chicago | 312 |
| | Chicago Heights | 708 |
| | Cicero | 708 |
| | Danville | 217 |
| | Decatur | 217 |
| | De Kalb | 815 |
| | Des Plaines | 708 |
| | Dolton | 708 |
| | Downers Grove | 708 |
| | East St. Louis | 618 |
| | Elgin | 708 |
| | Elk Grove Village | 708 |
| | Elmhurst | 708 |
| | Elmwood Park | 708 |
| | Evanston | 708 |
| | Evergreen Park | 708 |
| | Freeport | 815 |
| | Galesburg | 309 |
| | Granite City | 618 |
| | Harvey | 708 |
| | Highland Park | 708 |
| | Hinsdale | 708 |
| | Hoffman Estates | 708 |
| | Joliet | 815 |
| | Kankakee | 815 |
| | La Grange | 708 |
| | Lansing | 708 |
| | Lombard | 708 |
| | Maywood | 708 |
| | Melrose Park | 708 |
| | Moline | 309 |
| | Morton Grove | 708 |
| | Mount Prospect | 708 |
| | Naperville | 708 |
| | Niles | 312 |
| | Normal | 309 |
| | Northbrook | 708 |
| | North Chicago | 708 |
| | Oak Lawn | 708 |
| | Oak Park | 708 |
| | Palatine | 708 |
| | Park Forest | 708 |
| | Park Ridge | 708 |
| | Pekin | 309 |
| | Peoria | 309 |
| | Rantoul | 217 |
| | Rockford | 815 |
| | Rock Island | 309 |
| | Schaumburg | 708 |
| | Skokie | 708 |
| | South Holland | 708 |
| | Springfield | 217 |
| | Urbana | 217 |
| | Villa Park | 708 |
| | Waukegan | 708 |
| | Wheaton | 708 |

| State | City | Code |
|-------|------|------|
| IL | Wilmette | 708 |
| IN | Anderson | 317 |
| | Bloomington | 812 |
| | Columbus | 812 |
| | East Chicago | 219 |
| | Elkhart | 219 |
| | Evansville | 812 |
| | Fort Wayne | 219 |
| | Gary | 219 |
| | Hammond | 219 |
| | Highland | 219 |
| | Indianapolis | 317 |
| | Kokomo | 317 |
| | Lafayette | 317 |
| | Marion | 317 |
| | Merrillville | 219 |
| | Michigan City | 219 |
| | Mishawaka | 219 |
| | Muncie | 317 |
| | New Albany | 812 |
| | Richmond | 317 |
| | South Bend | 219 |
| | Terre Haute | 812 |
| IA | Ames | 515 |
| | Burlington | 319 |
| | Cedar Falls | 319 |
| | Cedar Rapids | 319 |
| | Clinton | 319 |
| | Council Bluffs | 712 |
| | Davenport | 319 |
| | Des Moines | 515 |
| | Dubuque | 319 |
| | Fort Dodge | 515 |
| | Iowa City | 319 |
| | Marshalltown | 515 |
| | Ottumwa | 515 |
| | Sioux City | 712 |
| | Waterloo | 319 |
| KS | Emporia | 316 |
| | Hutchinson | 316 |
| | Kansas City | 913 |
| | Lawrence | 913 |
| | Leavenworth | 913 |
| | Manhattan | 913 |
| | Overland Park | 913 |
| | Salina | 913 |
| | Topeka | 913 |
| | Wichita | 316 |
| KY | Ashland | 606 |
| | Bowling Green | 502 |
| | Covington | 606 |
| | Fort Knox | 502 |
| | Frankfort | 502 |
| | Henderson | 502 |
| | Lexington | 606 |
| | Louisville | 502 |
| | Newport | 606 |
| | Owensboro | 502 |
| | Paducah | 502 |
| | Pleasure Ridge Pk | 502 |

*Area Codes (cont'd)*

| State | City | Code |
|---|---|---|
| KY | Valley Station | 502 |
| LA | Alexandria | 318 |
| | Baton Rouge | 504 |
| | Bossier City | 318 |
| | Gretna | 504 |
| | Houma | 504 |
| | Kenner | 504 |
| | Lafayette | 318 |
| | Lake Charles | 318 |
| | Marrero | 504 |
| | Metairie | 504 |
| | Monroe | 318 |
| | New Iberia | 318 |
| | New Orleans | 504 |
| | Scotlandville | 504 |
| | Shreveport | 318 |
| ME | All points | 207 |
| MD | Annapolis | 410 |
| | Baltimore | 410 |
| | Cumberland | 301 |
| | Frederick | 301 |
| | Hagerstown | 301 |
| | La Plata | 301 |
| | Ocean City | 410 |
| | Rockville | 301 |
| | Salisbury | 401 |
| | Towson | 410 |
| MA | Amherst | 413 |
| | Andover | 508 |
| | Arlington | 617 |
| | Attleboro | 508 |
| | Barnstable | 508 |
| | Belmont | 617 |
| | Beverly | 508 |
| | Boston | 617 |
| | Braintree | 617 |
| | Brookline | 617 |
| | Cambridge | 617 |
| | Chelmsford | 508 |
| | Chelsea | 617 |
| | Chicopee | 413 |
| | Danvers | 508 |
| | Dedham | 617 |
| | Everett | 617 |
| | Fall River | 508 |
| | Fitchburg | 508 |
| | Framingham | 508 |
| | Gardner | 508 |
| | Gloucester | 508 |
| | Greenfield | 413 |
| | Haverhill | 508 |
| | Holyoke | 413 |
| | Lawrence | 508 |
| | Leominster | 508 |
| | Lexington | 617 |
| | Longmeadow | 413 |
| | Lowell | 508 |
| | Lynn | 617 |
| | Malden | 617 |
| | Marblehead | 617 |

| State | City | Code |
|---|---|---|
| MA | Marlborough | 508 |
| | Medford | 617 |
| | Melrose | 617 |
| | Methuen | 508 |
| | Milton | 617 |
| | Nantucket | 508 |
| | Needham | 617 |
| | New Bedford | 508 |
| | Newton | 617 |
| | North Adams | 413 |
| | Northampton | 413 |
| | Norwood | 617 |
| | Paxton | 508 |
| | Pittsfield | 413 |
| | Quincy | 617 |
| | Randolph | 617 |
| | Reading | 617 |
| | Revere | 617 |
| | Roxbury | 617 |
| | Sandwich | 508 |
| | Saugus | 617 |
| | Somerville | 617 |
| | Springfield | 413 |
| | Stoughton | 617 |
| | Taunton | 508 |
| | Tewksbury | 508 |
| | Wakefield | 617 |
| | Waltham | 617 |
| | Watertown | 617 |
| | Wellesley | 617 |
| | West Springfield | 413 |
| | Westfield | 413 |
| | Weymouth | 617 |
| | Woburn | 617 |
| | Worcester | 508 |
| MI | Allen Park | 313 |
| | Ann Arbor | 313 |
| | Battle Creek | 616 |
| | Bay City | 517 |
| | Benton Harbor | 616 |
| | Birmingham | 313 |
| | Dearborn | 313 |
| | Detroit | 313 |
| | East Detroit | 313 |
| | East Lansing | 517 |
| | Ferndale | 313 |
| | Flint | 313 |
| | Garden City | 313 |
| | Grand Rapids | 616 |
| | Hamtramck | 313 |
| | Hazel Park | 313 |
| | Highland Park | 313 |
| | Holland | 616 |
| | Inkster | 313 |
| | Jackson | 517 |
| | Kalamazoo | 616 |
| | Lansing | 517 |
| | Livonia | 313 |
| | Madison Heights | 313 |
| | Marquette | 906 |

| State | City | Code |
|---|---|---|
| MI | Midland | 517 |
| | Monroe | 313 |
| | Muskegon | 616 |
| | Niles | 616 |
| | Oak Park | 313 |
| | Pontiac | 313 |
| | Portage | 616 |
| | Port Huron | 313 |
| | Roseville | 313 |
| | Royal Oak | 313 |
| | Saginaw | 517 |
| | St. Clair Shores | 313 |
| | St. Joseph | 616 |
| | Southfield | 313 |
| | Southgate | 313 |
| | Sterling Heights | 313 |
| | Taylor | 313 |
| | Trenton | 313 |
| | Troy | 313 |
| | Warren | 313 |
| | Westland | 313 |
| | Wyandotte | 313 |
| | Wyoming | 616 |
| | Ypsilanti | 313 |
| MN | Austin | 507 |
| | Bloomington | 612 |
| | Brooklyn Center | 612 |
| | Columbia Hts. | 612 |
| | Coon Rapids | 612 |
| | Crystal | 612 |
| | Duluth | 218 |
| | Edina | 612 |
| | Fridley | 612 |
| | Mankato | 507 |
| | Minneapolis | 612 |
| | Minnetonka | 612 |
| | Moorhead | 218 |
| | New Hope | 612 |
| | Rochester | 507 |
| | Roseville | 612 |
| | St. Cloud | 612 |
| | St. Louis Park | 612 |
| | St. Paul | 612 |
| | White Bear Lake | 612 |
| | Winona | 507 |
| MS | All points | 601 |
| MO | Affton | 314 |
| | Cape Girardeau | 314 |
| | Columbia | 314 |
| | Ferguson | 314 |
| | Florissant | 314 |
| | Ft. Leonard Wood | 314 |
| | Gladstone | 816 |
| | Independence | 816 |
| | Jefferson City | 314 |
| | Joplin | 417 |
| | Kansas City | 816 |
| | Kirkwood | 314 |
| | Lemay | 314 |
| | Overland | 314 |

*Area Codes (cont'd)*

| State | City | Code | State | City | Code | State | City | Code |
|-------|------|------|-------|------|------|-------|------|------|
| MO | Raytown | 816 | NJ | Madison | 201 | NY | Armonk Village | 914 |
| | St. Charles | 314 | | Maplewood | 201 | | Auburn | 315 |
| | St. Joseph | 816 | | Mendham | 201 | | Babylon | 516 |
| | St. Louis | 314 | | Metuchen | 908 | | Baldwin | 516 |
| | Sedalia | 816 | | Middlesex | 201 | | Batavia | 716 |
| | Springfield | 417 | | Millburn | 201 | | Bay Shore | 516 |
| | University City | 314 | | Millville | 609 | | Bedford Village | 914 |
| | Webster Groves | 314 | | Montclair | 201 | | Bellmore | 516 |
| MT | All points | 408 | | Morristown | 201 | | Bethpage | 516 |
| NE | Fremont | 402 | | Mount Holly | 609 | | Binghamton | 607 |
| | Grand Island | 308 | | Newark | 201 | | Brentwood | 516 |
| | Hastings | 402 | | Newark Airport | 201 | | Brewster | 914 |
| | Lincoln | 402 | | New Brunswick | 908 | | Bridgehampton | 516 |
| | North Platte | 308 | | New Milford | 201 | | Bronx | 718 |
| | Omaha | 402 | | North Arlington | 201 | | Bronxville | 914 |
| NV | All points | 702 | | North Plainfield | 908 | | Brooklyn | 718 |
| NH | All points | 603 | | Nutley | 201 | | Brookville | 516 |
| NJ | Asbury Park | 908 | | Old Bridge | 908 | | Buffalo | 716 |
| | Atlantic City | 609 | | Orange | 201 | | Callicoon | 914 |
| | Barnegat | 609 | | Paramus | 201 | | Carmel | 914 |
| | Bayonne | 201 | | Passaic | 201 | | Center Moriches | 516 |
| | Belleville | 201 | | Paterson | 201 | | Central Islip | 516 |
| | Bellmawr | 609 | | Perth Amboy | 908 | | Chappaqua | 914 |
| | Bergenfield | 201 | | Phillipsburg | 908 | | Cohoes | 518 |
| | Bloomfield | 201 | | Plainfield | 908 | | Cold Spring | 914 |
| | Bound Brook | 908 | | Pleasantville | 609 | | Commack | 516 |
| | Bridgeton | 609 | | Point Pleasant | 908 | | Congers | 914 |
| | Burlington | 609 | | Pompton Lakes | 201 | | Copiague | 516 |
| | Camden | 609 | | Princeton | 609 | | Corning | 607 |
| | Carteret | 908 | | Rahway | 908 | | Cortland | 607 |
| | Cliffside Park | 201 | | Red Bank | 908 | | Croton | 914 |
| | Clifton | 201 | | Ridgefield | 201 | | Deer Park | 516 |
| | Collingswood | 609 | | Ridgewood | 201 | | Depew | 716 |
| | Dover | 201 | | Roselle | 908 | | Dobbs Ferry | 914 |
| | Dumont | 201 | | Rutherford | 201 | | Dunkirk | 716 |
| | East Orange | 201 | | Sayreville | 908 | | East Hampton | 516 |
| | East Paterson | 201 | | Somerville | 908 | | East Massapequa | 516 |
| | Eatontown | 908 | | South Amboy | 908 | | East Meadow | 516 |
| | Elizabeth | 908 | | South Orange | 201 | | Eastchester | 914 |
| | Englewood | 201 | | South Plainfield | 908 | | Eastport | 516 |
| | Ewing | 609 | | South River | 908 | | Ellenville | 914 |
| | Fair Lawn | 201 | | Summit | 908 | | Elmira | 607 |
| | Flemington | 908 | | Teaneck | 201 | | Elmsford | 914 |
| | Fort Dix | 609 | | Trenton | 609 | | Elwood | 516 |
| | Fort Lee | 201 | | Union City | 201 | | Endicott | 607 |
| | Garfield | 201 | | Verona | 201 | | Endwell | 607 |
| | Glassboro | 609 | | Vineland | 609 | | Fairmount | 315 |
| | Glen Ridge | 201 | | Weehawken | 201 | | Fallsburg | 914 |
| | Gloucester | 609 | | Westfield | 908 | | Farmingdale | 516 |
| | Hackensack | 201 | | West New York | 201 | | Fire Island | 516 |
| | Haddonfield | 609 | | West Orange | 201 | | Fishers Island | 516 |
| | Hasbrouck Hts. | 201 | | Wildwood | 609 | | Floral Park | 516 |
| | Hawthorne | 201 | | Woodbridge | 908 | | Franklin Square | 516 |
| | Hoboken | 201 | | Woodbury | 609 | | Freeport | 516 |
| | Irvington | 201 | | Wyckoff | 201 | | Fulton | 315 |
| | Jersey City | 201 | NM | All points | 505 | | Garden City | 516 |
| | Kearny | 201 | NY | Albany | 518 | | Garrison | 914 |
| | Lakewood | 908 | | Amagansett | 516 | | Geneva | 315 |
| | Linden | 908 | | Amityville | 516 | | Glen Cove | 516 |
| | Long Branch | 908 | | Amsterdam | 518 | | Glens Falls | 518 |

*Area Codes (cont'd)*

| State | City | Code |
|-------|------|------|
| NY | Gloversville | 518 |
| | Grahamsville | 914 |
| | Great Neck | 516 |
| | Grossinger | 914 |
| | Hamilton | 315 |
| | Hampton Bays | 516 |
| | Harrison | 914 |
| | Hastings | 914 |
| | Haverstraw | 914 |
| | Hempstead | 516 |
| | Hicksville | 516 |
| | Hudson | 518 |
| | Huntington | 516 |
| | Huntington Sta. | 516 |
| | Hurleyville | 914 |
| | Irvington | 914 |
| | Islip | 516 |
| | Ithaca | 607 |
| | Jamestown | 716 |
| | Jeffersonville | 914 |
| | Johnson City | 607 |
| | Kenmore | 716 |
| | Kennedy Airport | 718 |
| | Kerhonkson | 914 |
| | Kiamesha | 914 |
| | Kingston | 914 |
| | Lackawanna | 716 |
| | LaGuardia Airport | 718 |
| | Lake Huntington | 914 |
| | Lakeland | 914 |
| | Lake Success | 516 |
| | Larchmont | 914 |
| | Levittown | 516 |
| | Liberty | 914 |
| | Lindenhurst | 516 |
| | Livingston Manor | 914 |
| | Lockport | 716 |
| | Long Beach | 516 |
| | Long Island | 516 |
| | Lynbrook | 516 |
| | Mahopac | 914 |
| | Mamaroneck | 914 |
| | Manhasset | 516 |
| | Manhattan | 212 |
| | Massapequa | 516 |
| | Massapequa Park | 516 |
| | Massena | 315 |
| | Merrick | 516 |
| | Middletown | 914 |
| | Mineola | 516 |
| | Montauk Point | 516 |
| | Monticello | 914 |
| | Mount Kisco | 914 |
| | Mount Vernon | 914 |
| | Nanuet | 914 |
| | Narrowsburg | 914 |
| | Nassau County | 516 |
| | Newark | 315 |
| | Newburgh | 914 |
| | New City | 914 |

| State | City | Code |
|-------|------|------|
| NY | New Rochelle | 914 |
| | Niagara Falls | 716 |
| | North Babylon | 516 |
| | North Bellmore | 516 |
| | N. Massapequa | 516 |
| | N. Tonawanda | 716 |
| | Norwich | 607 |
| | Nyack | 914 |
| | Oceanside | 516 |
| | Olean | 716 |
| | Oneida | 315 |
| | Oneonta | 607 |
| | Ossining | 914 |
| | Oswego | 315 |
| | Oyster Bay | 516 |
| | Patchogue | 516 |
| | Pearl River | 914 |
| | Peekskill | 914 |
| | Pelham | 914 |
| | Penn Station | 212 |
| | Piermont | 914 |
| | Plainview | 516 |
| | Plattsburgh | 518 |
| | Pleasantville | 914 |
| | Port Chester | 914 |
| | Port Jefferson | 516 |
| | Port Washington | 516 |
| | Potsdam | 315 |
| | Poughkeepsie | 914 |
| | Queens | 718 |
| | Riverhead | 516 |
| | Rochester | 716 |
| | Rockville Centre | 516 |
| | Rome | 315 |
| | Ronkonkoma | 516 |
| | Roosevelt | 516 |
| | Roscoe | 607 |
| | Roslyn | 516 |
| | Rye | 914 |
| | Sag Harbor | 516 |
| | Saratoga Springs | 518 |
| | Sayville | 516 |
| | Scarsdale | 914 |
| | Schenectady | 518 |
| | Seaford | 516 |
| | Shelter Island | 516 |
| | Sloatsburg | 914 |
| | Smithtown | 516 |
| | Southampton | 516 |
| | Spring Valley | 914 |
| | Staten Island | 718 |
| | Stony Point | 914 |
| | Suffern | 914 |
| | Suffolk County | 516 |
| | Syracuse | 315 |
| | Tarrytown | 914 |
| | Ticonderoga | 518 |
| | Tonawanda | 716 |
| | Troy | 518 |
| | Tuckahoe | 914 |

| State | City | Code |
|-------|------|------|
| NY | Uniondale | 516 |
| | Utica | 315 |
| | Valley Stream | 516 |
| | Wantagh | 516 |
| | Watertown | 315 |
| | W. Hempstead | 516 |
| | West Islip | 516 |
| | Westbury | 516 |
| | Westchester | 914 |
| | Westhampton | 516 |
| | Wheatley Hills | 516 |
| | White Lake | 914 |
| | White Plains | 914 |
| | Williamsville | 716 |
| | Woodbourne | 914 |
| | Woodmere | 516 |
| | Woodridge | 914 |
| | Woodstock | 914 |
| | Wyandanch | 516 |
| | Yonkers | 914 |
| | Yorktown Hts. | 914 |
| NC | Asheville | 704 |
| | Burlington | 919 |
| | Camp Le Jeune | 919 |
| | Chapel Hill | 919 |
| | Charlotte | 704 |
| | Durham | 919 |
| | Fayetteville | 919 |
| | Fort Bragg | 919 |
| | Gastonia | 704 |
| | Goldsboro | 919 |
| | Greensboro | 919 |
| | Greenville | 919 |
| | High Point | 919 |
| | Kannapolis | 704 |
| | Kinston | 919 |
| | Lexington | 704 |
| | Raleigh | 919 |
| | Rocky Mount | 919 |
| | Salisbury | 704 |
| | Wilmington | 919 |
| | Wilson | 919 |
| | Winston-Salem | 919 |
| ND | All points | 701 |
| OH | Akron | 216 |
| | Alliance | 216 |
| | Ashtabula | 216 |
| | Athens | 614 |
| | Austintown | 216 |
| | Barberton | 216 |
| | Boardman | 216 |
| | Brook Park | 216 |
| | Canton | 216 |
| | Chillicothe | 614 |
| | Cincinnati | 513 |
| | Cleveland | 216 |
| | Columbus | 614 |
| | Cuyahoga Falls | 216 |
| | Dayton | 513 |
| | East Cleveland | 216 |

*Area Codes (cont'd)*

| State | City | Code |
|---|---|---|
| OH | East Liverpool | 216 |
| | Elyria | 216 |
| | Euclid | 216 |
| | Fair Born | 513 |
| | Findlay | 419 |
| | Garfield Heights | 216 |
| | Hamilton | 513 |
| | Kent | 216 |
| | Kettering | 513 |
| | Lakewood | 216 |
| | Lancaster | 614 |
| | Lima | 419 |
| | Lorain | 216 |
| | Mansfield | 419 |
| | Maple Heights | 216 |
| | Marion | 614 |
| | Massillon | 216 |
| | Mentor | 216 |
| | Middletown | 513 |
| | Newark | 614 |
| | North Olmsted | 216 |
| | Norwood | 513 |
| | Parma | 216 |
| | Parma Heights | 216 |
| | Portsmouth | 614 |
| | Rocky River | 216 |
| | Sandusky | 419 |
| | Shaker Heights | 216 |
| | South Euclid | 216 |
| | Springfield | 513 |
| | Steubenville | 614 |
| | Toledo | 419 |
| | Upper Arlington | 614 |
| | Warren | 216 |
| | Whitehall | 614 |
| | Xenia | 513 |
| | Youngstown | 216 |
| | Zanesville | 614 |
| OK | Altus | 405 |
| | Bartlesville | 918 |
| | Bethany | 405 |
| | Dill City | 405 |
| | Enid | 405 |
| | Lawton | 405 |
| | Midwest City | 405 |
| | Muskogee | 918 |
| | Oklahoma City | 405 |
| | Ponca City | 405 |
| | Shawnee | 405 |
| | Stillwater | 405 |
| | Tulsa | 918 |
| OR | All points | 503 |
| PA | Allentown | 215 |
| | Altoona | 814 |
| | Beaver Falls | 412 |
| | Bellefonte | 814 |
| | Bethel Park | 412 |
| | Bethlehem | 215 |
| | Bloomsburg | 717 |
| | Bradford | 814 |

| State | City | Code |
|---|---|---|
| PA | Chambersburg | 717 |
| | Chester | 215 |
| | Columbia | 717 |
| | DuBois | 814 |
| | Easton | 215 |
| | Erie | 814 |
| | Greensburg | 412 |
| | Harrisburg | 717 |
| | Hazelton | 717 |
| | Indiana | 412 |
| | Johnstown | 814 |
| | Lancaster | 717 |
| | Lebanon | 717 |
| | Levittown | 215 |
| | Lock Haven | 717 |
| | McKeesport | 412 |
| | Monroeville | 412 |
| | New Castle | 412 |
| | Norristown | 215 |
| | Philadelphia | 215 |
| | Pittsburgh | 412 |
| | Pottstown | 215 |
| | Reading | 215 |
| | Scranton | 717 |
| | Sharon | 412 |
| | State College | 814 |
| | Stroudsburg | 717 |
| | Sunbury | 717 |
| | Uniontown | 814 |
| | Warren | 814 |
| | Washington | 412 |
| | Wayne | 215 |
| | West Chester | 215 |
| | West Mifflin | 412 |
| | Wilkes-Barre | 717 |
| | Wilkinsburg | 412 |
| | Williamsport | 717 |
| | York | 717 |
| PR | All points | 809 |
| RI | All points | 401 |
| SC | All points | 803 |
| SD | All points | 605 |
| TN | Chattanooga | 615 |
| | Clarksville | 615 |
| | Jackson | 901 |
| | Johnson City | 615 |
| | Kingsport | 615 |
| | Knoxville | 615 |
| | Memphis | 901 |
| | Murfreesboro | 615 |
| | Nashville | 615 |
| | Oak Ridge | 615 |
| TX | Abilene | 915 |
| | Amarillo | 806 |
| | Arlington | 817 |
| | Austin | 512 |
| | Baytown | 713 |
| | Beaumont | 409 |
| | Big Spring | 915 |
| | Brownsville | 210 |

| State | City | Code |
|---|---|---|
| TX | Bryan | 409 |
| | Corpus Christi | 512 |
| | Dallas | 214 |
| | Denison | 903 |
| | Denton | 817 |
| | El Paso | 915 |
| | Farmers Branch | 903 |
| | Fort Hood | 817 |
| | Fort Worth | 817 |
| | Galveston | 409 |
| | Garland | 903 |
| | Grand Prairie | 903 |
| | Harlingen | 210 |
| | Houston | 713 |
| | Hurst | 817 |
| | Irving | 903 |
| | Killeen | 817 |
| | Kingsville | 512 |
| | Laredo | 210 |
| | Longview | 903 |
| | Lubbock | 806 |
| | Lufkin | 409 |
| | Marshall | 903 |
| | McAllen | 210 |
| | Mesquite | 903 |
| | Midland | 915 |
| | Nacogdoches | 409 |
| | Odessa | 915 |
| | Orange | 409 |
| | Paris | 903 |
| | Pasadena | 713 |
| | Port Arthur | 409 |
| | Richardson | 903 |
| | San Angelo | 915 |
| | San Antonio | 210 |
| | Sherman | 903 |
| | Temple | 817 |
| | Texarkana | 903 |
| | Texas City | 409 |
| | Tyler | 903 |
| | Victoria | 512 |
| | Waco | 817 |
| | Wharton | 409 |
| | Wichita Falls | 817 |
| UT | All points | 801 |
| VT | All points | 802 |
| VI | All points | 809 |
| VA | Alexandria | 703 |
| | Annandale | 703 |
| | Arlington | 703 |
| | Charlottesville | 804 |
| | Chesapeake | 804 |
| | Covington | 703 |
| | Danville | 804 |
| | Hampton | 804 |
| | Hopewell | 804 |
| | Jefferson | 804 |
| | Lynchburg | 804 |
| | Newport News | 804 |
| | Norfolk | 804 |

*Area Codes (cont'd)*

| State | City | Code |
|---|---|---|
| VA | Petersburg | 804 |
| | Portsmouth | 804 |
| | Richmond | 804 |
| | Roanoke | 703 |
| | Staunton | 703 |
| | Virginia Beach | 804 |
| | Woodbridge | 703 |
| WA | Bellevue | 206 |
| | Bellingham | 206 |
| | Bremerton | 206 |
| | Edmonds | 206 |
| | Everett | 206 |
| | Fort Lewis | 206 |
| | Longview | 206 |
| | Olympia | 206 |
| | Renton | 206 |
| | Richland | 509 |
| | Seattle | 206 |
| | Spokane | 509 |
| | Tacoma | 206 |
| | Vancouver | 206 |
| | Walla Walla | 509 |
| | Yakima | 509 |
| WV | All points | 304 |
| WI | Appleton | 414 |

| State | City | Code |
|---|---|---|
| WI | Beloit | 608 |
| | Brookfield | 414 |
| | Eau Claire | 715 |
| | Fond Du Lac | 414 |
| | Green Bay | 414 |
| | Greenfield | 414 |
| | Janesville | 608 |
| | Kenosha | 414 |
| | La Crosse | 608 |
| | Madison | 608 |
| | Manitowoc | 414 |
| | Menomonee Falls | 414 |
| | Milwaukee | 414 |
| | Neenah | 414 |
| | New Berlin | 414 |
| | Oshkosh | 414 |
| | Racine | 414 |
| | Sheboygan | 414 |
| | South Milwaukee | 414 |
| | Stevens Point | 715 |
| | Superior | 715 |
| | Waukesha | 414 |
| | Wausau | 715 |
| | Wauwatosa | 414 |
| | West Allis | 414 |
| WY | All points | 307 |

## Canadian Area Codes

| Province | City | Code |
|---|---|---|
| AB | All points | 403 |
| BC | All points | 604 |
| MA | All points | 204 |
| NB | All points | 506 |
| NF | All points | 709 |
| NS | All points | 902 |
| ON | Ft. William | 807 |
| | London | 519 |
| | North Bay | 705 |
| | Ottawa | 613 |
| | Thunder Bay | 807 |
| | Toronto | 416 |
| PEI | All points | 902 |
| PQ | Montreal | 514 |
| | Quebec | 418 |
| | Sherbrooke | 819 |
| SK | All points | 306 |

## The Top Reference Sources

*Small Business Success*
Pacific Bell Directory, free
(800) 848-8000

This magazine, published every year in April, is replete with information and resources for the small business. Articles in the 1993 edition included "Buying Insurance for Your Small Business," "Boosting Employee Morale," "Marketing to Minorities," "The Wide World of International Trade," and more. Each issue also contains a directory of organizations, publications, and computer resources for the businessperson.

*Small Business Success* is also sponsored by the U.S. Small Business Administration.

*Area Codes (cont'd)*

## Area Codes by Code

| Code | Location |
|------|----------|
| 201 | New Jersey (Newark) |
| 202 | Washington, DC |
| 203 | Connecticut |
| 205 | Alabama |
| 206 | Washington (Seattle) |
| 207 | Maine |
| 208 | Idaho |
| 209 | California (Fresno) |
| 210 | Texas (San Antonio) |
| 212 | New York (Manhattan) |
| 213 | California (Los Angeles) |
| 214 | Texas (Dallas) |
| 215 | Pennsylvania (Phila.) |
| 216 | Ohio (Cleveland) |
| 217 | Illinois (Springfield) |
| 218 | Minnesota (Duluth) |
| 219 | Indiana (South Bend) |
| 301 | Maryland (Bethesda) |
| 302 | Delaware |
| 303 | Colorado (Denver) |
| 304 | West Virginia |
| 305 | Florida (Miami) |
| 307 | Wyoming |
| 308 | Nebraska (North Platte) |
| 309 | Illinois (Peoria) |
| 310 | California (Los Angeles) |
| 312 | Illinois (Chicago) |
| 313 | Michigan (Detroit) |
| 314 | Missouri (St. Louis) |
| 315 | New York (Syracuse) |
| 316 | Kansas (Wichita) |
| 317 | Indiana (Indianapolis) |
| 318 | Louisiana (Shreveport) |
| 319 | Iowa (Dubuque) |
| 401 | Rhode Island |
| 402 | Nebraska (Omaha) |
| 404 | Georgia (Atlanta) |
| 405 | Oklahoma (Oklahoma City) |
| 406 | Montana |
| 407 | Florida (Orlando) |

| Code | Location |
|------|----------|
| 408 | California (San Jose) |
| 409 | Texas (Galveston) |
| 410 | Maryland (Baltimore) |
| 412 | Pennsylvania (Pittsburgh) |
| 413 | Massachusetts (Springfield) |
| 414 | Wisconsin (Milwaukee) |
| 415 | California (San Francisco) |
| 417 | Missouri (Springfield) |
| 419 | Ohio (Toledo) |
| 501 | Arkansas |
| 502 | Kentucky (Louisville) |
| 503 | Oregon |
| 504 | Louisiana (New Orleans) |
| 505 | New Mexico |
| 507 | Minnesota (Rochester) |
| 508 | Massachusetts (Worcester) |
| 509 | Washington (Spokane) |
| 510 | California (Oakland) |
| 512 | Texas (Austin) |
| 513 | Ohio (Cincinnati) |
| 515 | Iowa (Des Moines) |
| 516 | New York (Long Island) |
| 517 | Michigan (Lansing) |
| 518 | New York (Albany) |
| 601 | Mississippi |
| 602 | Arizona |
| 603 | New Hampshire |
| 605 | South Dakota |
| 606 | Kentucky (Newport) |
| 607 | New York (Ithaca) |
| 608 | Wisconsin (Madison) |
| 609 | New Jersey (Trenton) |
| 612 | Minnesota (Minneapolis) |
| 614 | Ohio (Columbus) |
| 615 | Tennessee (Nashville) |
| 616 | Michigan (Grand Rapids) |
| 617 | Massachusetts (Boston) |
| 618 | Illinois (Centralia) |
| 619 | California (San Diego) |
| 701 | North Dakota |

| Code | Location |
|------|----------|
| 702 | Nevada |
| 703 | Virginia (Arlington) |
| 704 | North Carolina (Charlotte) |
| 707 | California (Santa Rosa) |
| 708 | Illinois (Des Plaines) |
| 712 | Iowa (Council Bluffs) |
| 713 | Texas (Houston) |
| 714 | California (Orange County) |
| 715 | Wisconsin (Eau Clair) |
| 716 | New York (Buffalo) |
| 717 | Pennsylvania (Harrisburg) |
| 718 | New York (Brooklyn) |
| 719 | Colorado (Colorado Spr.) |
| 801 | Utah |
| 802 | Vermont |
| 803 | South Carolina |
| 804 | Virginia (Richmond) |
| 805 | California (Bakersfield) |
| 806 | Texas (Amarillo) |
| 808 | Hawaii |
| 812 | Indiana (Evansville) |
| 813 | Florida (Fort Myers) |
| 814 | Pennsylvania (Erie) |
| 815 | Illinois (Rockford) |
| 816 | Missouri (Kansas City) |
| 817 | Texas (Fort Worth) |
| 818 | California (Los Angeles) |
| 901 | Tennessee (Memphis) |
| 903 | Texas (Dallas) |
| 904 | Florida (Jacksonville) |
| 906 | Michigan (Marquette) |
| 907 | Alaska |
| 908 | New Jersey (Elizabeth) |
| 909 | California (San Bernadino) |
| 912 | Georgia (Savannah) |
| 913 | Kansas (Topeka) |
| 914 | New York (White Plains) |
| 915 | Texas (El Paso) |
| 916 | California (Sacramento) |
| 918 | Oklahoma (Tulsa) |

# International Dialing

TRAVELERS CAN SAVE MONEY by using a calling card when making calls from foreign countries to the United States. To reach an operator, an access code must be dialed.

## AT&T Access Codes

| Country | Code |
|---|---|
| Anguilla | 1-800 872 2881 |
| Argentina | 001-800-200-1111 |
| Aruba | 800 1011 |
| Australia | 0014-881-011 |
| Austria | 022-903-011 |
| Bahamas | 1-800-872-2881 |
| Bahrain | 800-001 |
| Belgium | 078-11-0010 |
| Bermuda | 1-800-872-2881 |
| Brazil | 000-8010 |
| British Virgin Islands | 1-800-872-2881 |
| Cayman | 1872 |
| Chile | 00, 0312 |
| China, PRC | 10811 |
| Colombia | 980-11-0010 |
| Costa Rica | 114 |
| Czechoslovakia | 00-420-00101 |
| Denmark | 8001-0010 |
| Dominica | 1-800-872-2881 |
| Dominican Rep. | 1-800-872-2881 |
| Egypt | 510-0200 |
| El Salvador | 190 |
| Finland | 9800-100-10 |
| France | 19-0011 |
| Gambia | 001-199-220-0010 |
| Germany | 0130-0010 |
| Ghana | 0191 |
| Greece | 00-800-1311 |
| Grenada | 872 |
| Guam | 108-872 |
| Guatemala | 190 |
| Haiti | 001-800-872-2881 |
| Honduras | 123 |
| Hong Kong | 800-1111 |
| Hungary | 00-800-01111 |
| India | 000-117 |
| Indonesia | 00-801-10 |
| Ireland | 1-800-550-000 |
| Israel | 177-100-2727 |
| Italy | 172-1011 |
| Jamaica | 0800-872-2881 |
| Japan | 0039-111 |
| Kenya | 0800-10 |
| Korea | 009-11 |
| Liberia | 797-797 |

| Country | Code |
|---|---|
| Macao | 0800-111 |
| Malaysia | 800-0011 |
| Mexico | 95-800-462-4240 |
| Netherlands | 06-022-9111 |
| Netherlands Antilles | 001-800-872-2881 |
| New Zealand | 000-911 |
| Norway | 050-12011 |
| Panama | 109 |
| Peru | 191 |
| Philippines | 105-11 |
| Poland | 0-010-480-0111 |
| Portugal | 05017-1-288 |
| St. Kitts | 1-800-872-2881 |
| Singapore | 800-0011 |
| Spain | 900-9900-11 |
| Suriname | 156 |
| Sweden | 020-795-611 |
| Switzerland | 046-05-0011 |
| Taiwan | 0080-102880 |
| Thailand | 001-999-11111 |
| United Kingdom | 0800-89-0011 |
| United States | (800) 321-0288 |
| Uruguay | 000410 |
| Zimbabwe | 110899 |

*Note: For any countries not listed, call (816) 654-6000 collect from any country.*

*Source: David McCormick, AT&T*

## MCI Access Codes

| Country | Code |
|---|---|
| American Samoa | 633-2624 |
| Antigua | #2 |
| Argentina | 001-800-333-1111 |
| Australia | 1-800-881-100 |
| Austria | 022-903-012 |
| Bahamas | 1-800-624-1000 |
| Bahrain | 1-800-624-1000 |
| Belgium | 78-11-00-12 |
| Bermuda | 1-800-623-0484 |
| Bolivia | 0800-2222 |
| Brazil | 000-8012 |
| Cayman Islands | 1-624 |
| Chile | 00 † 0316 |
| China | 108-12 |
| Colombia | 980-16-0001 |
| Costa Rica | 162 |
| Cyprus | 080-9000 |
| Denmark | 8001-0022 |
| Dominican Rep. | 1-800-751-6624 |
| Ecuador | 170 |

*International Dialing (cont'd)*

| Country | Code |
| --- | --- |
| El Salvador | 195 |
| Finland | 9800-102-80 |
| France | 19-00-19 |
| Gambia | 00-1-91 |
| Germany | 0130-0012 |
| Greece | 00-800-1211 |
| Grenada | 1-800-624-8721 |
| Guam | 950-1022 |
| Guatemala | 189 |
| Haiti | 011-800-444-1234 |
| Honduras | 001-800-674-7000 |
| Hong Kong | 800-1121 |
| Hungary | 00-800-01411 |
| Iceland | 999-002 |
| India | 000-127 |
| Indonesia | 00-801-11 |
| Ireland | 1-800-551-001 |
| Israel | 177-150-2727 |
| Italy | 172-1022 |
| Japan (KDD) | 0039-121 |
| Japan (IDC) | 066-55-121 |
| Kenya | 0800-11 |
| Korea | 009-14 |
| Korea (US bases) | 550-2255 |
| Kuwait | 800-10-624 |
| Lebanon (Beirut) | 600-624 |
| Lebanon | 01-600-624 |
| Liechtenstein | 155-0222 |
| Luxembourg | 0800-0112 |
| Macao | 0800-131 |
| Malaysia | 800-0012 |
| Mexico | 95-800-674-7000 |
| Monaco | 19 † 00-19 |
| Netherlands | 06 † 022-91-22 |
| New Zealand | 000-912 |
| Nicaragua | 166 |
| Norway | 800-19912 |
| Panama | 108 |
| Peru | 1190 |
| Philippines | 10514 |
| Poland | 0 † 01-04-800-112 |
| Portugal | 05-017-1234 |
| Qatar | 0800-012-77 |
| Saipan | 950-1022 |
| San Marino | 172-1022 |
| Singapore | 8000-177-177 |
| Slovakia | 00-42-000112 |
| South Africa | 0800-99-0011 |
| Spain | 900-99-0014 |
| Sweden | 020-795-922 |

| Country | Code |
| --- | --- |
| Switzerland | 155-0222 |
| Syria | 0800 |
| Taiwan | 00801-34567 |
| Thailand | 001-999-1-2001 |
| Turkey | 99-8001-1177 |
| United Arab Emirates | 800-11 |
| United Kingdom | 0800-89-0222 |
| Uruguay | 000412 |
| Vatican City | 172-1022 |
| Venezuela | 800-1114-0 |

*† wait for second dial tone*

## Sprint Access Codes

| Country | Code |
| --- | --- |
| Antigua | #0 |
| Argentina | 001-800-777-1111 |
| Australia | 0014-881-877 |
| Austria | 022-903-014 |
| Bahamas | 1-800-389-2111 |
| Barbados | 1-800-877-8000 |
| Belgium | 078-11-0114 |
| Belize (hotels) | 556 |
| Belize | *4 (star key + 4) |
| Bermuda | 1-800-623-0877 |
| Bolivia | 0800-3333 |
| Brazil | 000-8016 |
| British Virgin Islands | 1-800-877-8000 |
| Cambodia | 80-01-01 |
| Canada | 1-800-877-8000 |
| Chile | 00 † 0317 |
| China | 108-13 |
| Colombia | 980-13-0010 |
| Costa Rica | 163 |
| Cyprus | 080-900-01 |
| Denmark | 8001-0877 |
| Dominican Rep. | 1-800-751-7877 |
| Ecuador | 171 |
| El Salvador | 191 |
| Finland | 9800-1-0284 |
| France | 19 † 0087 |
| Germany | 0130-0013 |
| Greece | 008-001-411 |
| Guatemala | 195 |
| Honduras | 001-800-1212000 |
| Hong Kong | 800-1877 |
| Hungary | 00 † 800-01-877 |
| India | 000-137 |
| Indonesia | 00-801-15 |
| Ireland | 1-800-55-2001 |

*International Dialing (cont'd)*

| Country | Code |
|---------|------|
| Israel | 177-102-2727 |
| Italy | 172-1877 |
| Japan (KDD) | 0039-131 |
| Japan (IDC) | 0066 † 55-877 |
| Kenya | 0800-12 |
| Korea | 009-16 |
| Korea (U.S. bases) | 550-3663 |
| Kuwait | 800-777 |
| Liechtenstein | 155-9777 |
| Luxembourg | 0800-0015 |
| Macao | 0800-121 |
| Malaysia | 800-0016 |
| Monaco | 19 † 0087 |
| Netherlands | 06 † 022-9119 |
| New Zealand | 000-999 |
| Nicaragua (Managua) | 161 |
| Nicaragua | 02-161 |
| Norway | 050-12-877 |
| Panama | 115 |
| Peru | 196 |
| Philippines (ETP) | 105-01 |
| Philippines (PhilCom) | 102-611 |
| Poland | 0010-480-0115 |
| Portugal | 05017-1-877 |
| Puerto Rico | 1-800-877-8000 |

| Country | Code |
|---------|------|
| Saint Lucia | 187 |
| San Marino | 172-1877 |
| Singapore | 8000-177-177 |
| South Africa | 0-800-99-0001 |
| Spain | 900-99-0013 |
| Sweden | 020-799-011 |
| Switzerland | 155-9777 |
| Taiwan | 0080-14-0877 |
| Thailand | 001-999-13-877 |
| Trinidad & Tobago | 23 |
| Turkey | 99800-1-4477 |
| United Arab Emirates | 800-1-0011 |
| United Kingdom | 0800-89-0877 |
| United States | 1-800-877-8000 |
| Uruguay | 000417 |
| U.S. Virgin Islands | 1-800-877-8000 |
| Vatican City | 172-1877 |
| Venezuela | 800-1111-0 |

*†  wait for second dial tone*

*Note: For any countries not listed, call (913) 624-5336 collect from any country.*

# Phone Cards on Other Systems

## AT&T

Dial (800) 225-5288 (CALL-ATT) and follow the instructions (for calling card, credit card, or customer service).

## MCI

Dial (800) 674-7000. Enter MCI card number and then the party's area code and phone number.

For international calls, dial (800) 674-7000. Enter MCI card number, then 011, and then the party's country code and number.

## Sprint

Dial 1-0-333-0 and then the party's area code and number. You should hear "Welcome to Sprint." Then enter Sprint card number. If not, dial (800) 877-8000. At the tone, dial 0 and then the party's area code and number. Then enter Sprint card number.

For international calls, dial 1-0-333-0-1 and then the party's country code and number. Then press the # button. If there is a problem, dial (800) 877-8000 and repeat.

To make another call, do not hang up. Hold down the # key for two seconds. At the tone, dial 0 and then the party's area code and number. For both domestic and international calls.

**TIP:** *To access international directory assistance, dial the operator and ask for an international operator. The international operator will then contact the directory assistance of the desired country.*

# Country Codes

| Country | Access Code |
|---|---|
| Algeria | 213 |
| Argentina | 54 |
| Australia | 61 |
| Austria | 43 |
| Belgium | 32 |
| Belize | 501 |
| Bolivia | 591 |
| Brazil | 55 |
| Chile | 56 |
| China | 86 |
| Colombia | 57 |
| Costa Rica | 506 |
| Denmark | 45 |
| Ecuador | 593 |
| Egypt | 20 |
| Ethiopia | 251 |
| Finland | 358 |
| France | 33 |
| Germany | 37 |
| Greece | 30 |
| Guam | 671 |
| Guatamala | 502 |
| Haiti | 509 |
| Hong Kong | 852 |
| Hungary | 36 |
| Iceland | 354 |
| India | 91 |
| Indonesia | 62 |
| Iran | 98 |
| Iraq | 964 |
| Ireland | 353 |
| Israel | 972 |
| Italy | 39 |
| Japan | 81 |
| Kenya | 254 |
| Korea | 82 |
| Kuwait | 965 |
| Lebanon | 961 |
| Liberia | 231 |
| Libya | 218 |

| Country | Access Code |
|---|---|
| Luxembourg | 352 |
| Malaysia | 60 |
| Malta | 356 |
| Monaco | 33 |
| Morocco | 212 |
| Netherlands | 31 |
| Netherlands Antilles | 599 |
| New Zealand | 64 |
| Nicaragua | 505 |
| Nigeria | 234 |
| Norway | 47 |
| Oman | 968 |
| Pakistan | 92 |
| Panama | 507 |
| Paraguay | 595 |
| Peru | 51 |
| Philippines | 63 |
| Poland | 48 |
| Portugal | 351 |
| Qatar | 974 |
| Romania | 40 |
| Saudi Arabia | 966 |
| Senegal | 221 |
| Singapore | 65 |
| South Africa | 27 |
| Spain | 34 |
| Sri Lanka | 94 |
| Sweden | 46 |
| Switzerland | 41 |
| Taiwan | 886 |
| Thailand | 66 |
| Trinidad | 809 |
| Tunisia | 216 |
| Turkey | 90 |
| Russia | 7 |
| United Kingdom | 44 |
| Uruguay | 598 |
| Vatican | 39 |
| Venezuela | 58 |

*NOTE: Dial 011 before dialing a country code. For most telephone numbers that start with a zero, the zero should not be dialed when calling from abroad. Check with an international operator.*

# Zip Codes

## Manhattan Zip Codes

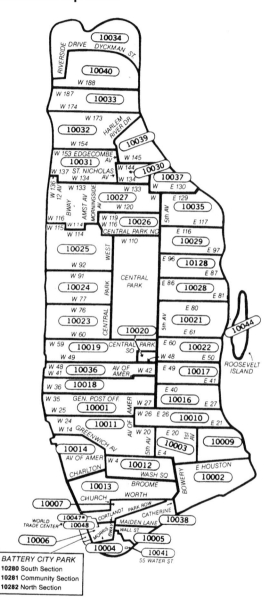

BATTERY CITY PARK
**10280** South Section
**10281** Community Section
**10282** North Section

For fastest service, use the exact zip code for the destination address. The zip codes in this table will bring mail to the main post office in each city, which is faster than no zip code at all.

This table can also be used to send a batch of letters to a central zip code by Express Mail. The local postmaster will then deliver the individual letters locally, saving time and money.

To obtain a zip code for any location, call the U.S. Postal Service at (202) 682-9595 from 8:00 A.M. to 8:00 P.M., Monday through Friday and 8:00 A.M. to 5:00 P.M. on Saturday. After hours, call the Honolulu Post Office at (808) 423-3930.

## Main Post Office Zip Codes

| City | Zip Code |
| --- | --- |
| Atlanta | 30301 |
| Baltimore | 21233 |
| Boston | 02101 |
| Chicago | 60601 |
| Cincinnati | 45202 |
| Cleveland | 44101 |
| Columbus | 43216 |
| Dallas | 75201 |
| Denver | 80201 |
| Detroit | 48231 |
| Houston | 77052 |
| Indianapolis | 46206 |
| Los Angeles | 90086 |
| Miami | 33101 |
| Milwaukee | 53201 |
| Minneapolis | 55401 |
| New York | 10001 |
| Norfolk | 23503 |
| Philadelphia | 19104 |
| Phoenix | 85201 |
| Pittsburgh | 15233 |
| Portland | 97208 |
| Sacramento | 95814 |
| St. Louis | 63166 |
| San Antonio | 78265 |
| San Diego | 92183 |
| San Francisco | 94142 |
| Seattle | 98101 |
| Tampa | 33602 |
| Washington, DC (federal) | 20500 |
| Washington, DC (other) | 20090 |

**FAX** **Manhattan Address Locator.** Request #100. See p. xi for instructions.
Chart that makes it easy to find a location in Manhattan if you know the address.

# Postal Service

FOR MOST USERS, the United States Postal Service offers five classes of mail. From most expensive to least expensive, they are:

• *Express Mail:* overnight, seven days a week

• *Priority Mail:* two-day service to most locations

• *First Class:* quick and relatively inexpensive

• *Third Class:* bulk mail–permit required

• *Fourth Class:* parcel post and books.

In addition to these services, the Postal Service offers insurance, registration, certification, and (though rarely used) Special Delivery.

## First Class Mail (single-piece letter rates)

| Weight in oz | Postage ($) |
|---|---|
| Postcard | 0.19 |
| 1 | 0.29 |
| 2 | 0.52 |
| 3 | 0.75 |
| 4 | 0.98 |
| 5 | 1.21 |
| 6 | 1.44 |
| 7 | 1.67 |
| 8 | 1.90 |
| 9 | 2.13 |
| 10 | 2.36 |
| 11* | 2.59 |

*For pieces weighing more than 11 oz., use priority mail service*

## Priority Mail

| Weight in lbs | Postage ($) |
|---|---|
| 1 | 2.90 |
| 2 | 2.90 |
| 3 | 4.10 |
| 4 | 4.65 |
| 5 | 5.45 |

## Size Requirements

Minimum size pieces must meet the following requirements to be mailable in any class:

• All pieces must be at least .007 inch thick

• Pieces (except keys and identification devices) that are 1/4 inch or less thick must be:

  • rectangular in shape

  • at least 3 1/2 inches high

  • at least 5 inches long.

Pieces greater than 1/4 inch thick can be mailed even if they measure less than 3 1/2 by 5 inches.

## Non-Standard Mail

Mail that doesn't meet the above requirements is subject to a ten cent surcharge in addition to the applicable postage. For Presort First Class and carrier route First Class, the surcharge is five cents in addition to applicable postage.

Mail is characterized as non-standard, First Class mail or single-piece Third Class mail if it weighs one ounce and:

• Any of the following dimensions are exceeded:

  Length: 11 1/2 inches

  Height: 6 1/8 inches

  Thickness: 1/4 inch, or

• The length divided by the height (aspect ratio) is less than 1.3 or more than 2.5.

## Second Class Mail

Second Class mail is only available to newspapers and periodicals that have qualified for second class mail privileges.

## Third Class Mail

Third Class mail is restricted to specific types of matter–circulars, books, catalogues and other printed materials–weighing less than 16 ounces. A permit is required, and the rules governing this class of service are numerous. Contact your postmaster for details.

## Single-Piece Third Class Rates

| Weight not exceeding (oz) | Postage ($) |
|---|---|
| 1 | 0.29 |
| 2 | 0.52 |
| 3 | 0.75 |
| 4 | 0.98 |
| 6 | 1.21 |
| 8 | 1.33 |
| 10 | 1.44 |
| 12 | 1.56 |
| 14 | 1.67 |
| 15 | 1.79 |

## Fourth Class Mail

To the general public, Fourth Class is the cheapest postal rate available for anything weighing over one pound.

For authorized bulk users, there are subrates available for printed matter. This is a single rate charged to the company regardless of the zone.

The Fourth Class rates are based on the distance sent. There are some discounts available.

*Postal Service (cont'd)*

## Special Services (domestic mail only)

- *Certified Mail* allows the sender to receive evidence of delivery for an extra fee. A mailing receipt and delivery record is sent from the destination post office. Available at a rate of $1 in addition to the applicable postage.

- *COD* (collect on delivery): The maximum value for COD service is $600. Consult postmaster for fees and conditions of mailing.

## Insurance

| Liability | Fee in Addition to Postage |
|---|---|
| .01 to 50.00 | 0.75 |
| 50.01 to 100.00 | 1.60 |
| 100.01 to 200.00 | 2.40 |
| 200.01 to 300.00 | 3.50 |
| 300.01 to 400.00 | 4.60 |
| 400.01 to 500.00 | 5.40 |
| 500.01 to 600.00 | 6.20 |

- *Registered Mail* allows the sender maximum protection and security. The letter is signed for at every step of the mailing process to insure that it has been delivered properly. The sender also receives a return receipt upon completion of delivery. There is an additional fee for registered mail.

## Registered Mail Additional Fees

| Value | Insured | Uninsured |
|---|---|---|
| 1 to 100.00 | 4.50 | 4.40 |
| 100.01 to 500.00 | 4.85 | 4.70 |

*\*For higher values, consult postmaster.*

- *Special Delivery* provides expedited delivery to specified zones. First-Class packages up to 2 pounds are $7.65, between 2 and 10 pounds are $7.95, and more than 10 pounds are $8.55.

- *Special Handling* gives preferential handling to Third- and Fourth-Class packages. Packages less than 10 pounds are $1.80 extra. Those over 10 pounds are $2.50 more.

## Additional Services

- *Certificate of Mailing* (for bulk mailing and firm mailing books, see the postmaster). Fifty cents per certificate.

- *Return Receipt* (available for COD, Express Mail, certified, insured for over $50, and registered mail). There are two levels of service:

- Requested at time of mailing, showing to whom (signature) and date delivered, $1.

- Showing to whom (signature), date, and address where delivered, $1.35.

- *Restricted Delivery* (not available for Express Mail). $2.50.

- *Return Receipt for Merchandise* (provides proof of delivery for merchandise shipments only. Cheaper but less secure than certified or registered mail).

- Showing to whom (signature) and date delivered, $1.10.

- Showing to whom (signature), date, and address delivered, $1.50.

## Express Mail

Express mail is available seven days a week, 365 days a year, for mailable items up to 70 pounds in weight and 108 inches in combined length and width. Features include noon delivery between major business markets; merchandise and document reconstruction insurance; Express Mail shipping containers; shipping receipts; special collection boxes; and such options as return receipt service; COD service; waiver of signature; and pickup service. Call (800) 222-1811 for pickup service for a flat fee of $4.50, no matter how many pieces.

*Rates:*
Up to 8 ounces, $9.95
Up to 2 pounds, $13.95
Over 2 pounds, consult your local postmaster.

## Contact Option

U.S. Postal Service
(800) 222-1811
All rates included here are as of May, 1994. Call the postal service to confirm prices.

*Postal Service (cont'd)*

## International Air Mail—Small Packets and Printed Matter

| Weight Not Over | Canada | Mexico | Western Hemisphere (except Canada & Mexico) | Europe | Asia/Africa | Pacific Rim |
|---|---|---|---|---|---|---|
| 1 oz | 0.38 | 0.40 | 0.70 | 0.85 | 0.93 | 0.95 |
| 2 oz | 0.60 | 0.63 | 1.07 | 1.35 | 1.57 | 1.61 |
| 3 oz | 0.82 | 0.85 | 1.44 | 1.85 | 2.21 | 2.27 |
| 4 oz | 1.04 | 1.07 | 1.81 | 2.35 | 2.85 | 2.93 |
| 6 oz | 1.48 | 1.51 | 2.18 | 3.01 | 3.76 | 3.85 |
| 8 oz | 1.92 | 1.95 | 2.55 | 3.67 | 4.67 | 4.77 |
| 10 oz | 2.36 | 2.39 | 2.92 | 4.33 | 5.58 | 5.69 |
| 12 oz | 2.80 | 2.83 | 3.29 | 4.99 | 6.49 | 6.61 |
| 1 lb | 3.12 | 3.55 | 4.03 | 6.31 | 8.31 | 8.45 |
| 1.8 lb | 3.72 | 4.40 | 5.51 | 8.95 | 11.95 | 12.13 |
| 2 lb | 4.32 | 5.25 | 6.99 | 11.59 | 15.59 | 15.81 |
| 2.8 lb | 5.12 | 6.10 | 8.39 | 14.09 | 19.14 | 19.41 |
| 3 lb | 5.92 | 6.95 | 9.79 | 16.59 | 22.69 | 23.01 |
| 3.8 lb | 6.72 | 7.80 | 11.19 | 19.09 | 26.24 | 26.61 |
| 4 lb | 7.52 | 8.65 | 12.59 | 21.59 | 29.79 | 30.21 |
| Each additional 1/2 lb over 4 lbs | .80 | .85 | 1.40 | 2.50 | 3.55 | 3.60 |

## Postal Business Centers

The U.S. Postal Service maintains Business Centers around the country. The sole function of these offices is to provide businesses with help and support in sending bulk mail.

| Location | Phone Number |
|---|---|
| Anchorage, AK | (907) 564-2823 |
| Birmingham, AL | (205) 323-6510 |
| Little Rock, AR | (501) 227-6639 |
| Phoenix, AZ | (602) 225-5454 |
| Tucson, AZ | (602) 620-5108 |
| Long Beach, CA | (310) 494-2301 |
| Los Angeles, CA | (213) 586-1843 |
| Oakland, CA | (510) 874-8600 |
| Sacramento, CA | (916) 923-4357 |
| San Diego, CA | (619) 674-0400 |
| San Francisco, CA | (415) 550-6565 |
| San Jose, CA | (408) 723-6262 |
| Santa Ana, CA | (714) 662-6213 |
| Van Nuys, CA | (818) 787-8948 |
| Denver, CO | (303) 297-6118 |
| Hartford, CT | (203) 524-6491 |
| Fort Lauderdale, FL | (305) 527-6981 |
| Jacksonville, FL | (904) 260-8101 |
| Miami, FL | (305) 470-0803 |
| Orlando, FL | (407) 826-5602 |
| Tampa, FL | (813) 871-6245 |
| West Palm Beach, FL | (407) 697-2118 |
| Macon, GA | (912) 784-3917 |
| North Metro, GA | (404) 717-3440 |
| Savannah, GA | (912) 235-4591 |
| Honolulu, HI | (808) 423-3761 |
| Des Moines, IA | (515) 251-2336 |
| Aurora, IL | (708) 978-4455 |
| Carol Stream, IL | (708) 260-5511 |
| Chicago, IL | (312) 765-4215 |

| Location | Phone Number |
|---|---|
| Indianapolis, IN | (317) 464-6010 |
| Louisville, KY | (502) 473-4200 |
| New Orleans, LA | (504) 589-1366 |
| Boston, MA | (617) 338-9725 |
| Springfield, MA | (413) 731-0306 |
| Woburn, MA | (617) 938-1450 |
| Worcester, MA | (508) 795-3608 |
| Baltimore, MD | (410) 347-4358 |
| South Portland, ME | (207) 767-1282 |
| Birmingham, MI | (810) 901-4525 |
| Detroit, MI | (313) 225-5445 |
| Grand Rapids, MI | (616) 776-6161 |
| Minneapolis, MN | (612) 349-6360 |
| Kansas City, MO | (816) 374-9513 |
| Saint Louis, MO | (314) 534-2678 |
| Jackson, MS | (601) 360-2700 |
| Billings, MT | (406) 255-6432 |
| Missoula, MT | (406) 329-2231 |
| Charlotte, NC | (704) 393-4457 |
| Greensboro, NC | (919) 655-9740 |
| Omaha, NE | (402) 573-2101 |
| Manchester, NH | (603) 644-3838 |
| Bellmawr, NJ | (609) 933-6000 |
| Edison, NJ | (908) 777-0565 |
| West Orange, NJ | (201) 731-4866 |
| Albuquerque, NM | (505) 245-9469 |
| Las Vegas, NV | (702) 361-9318 |
| Albany, NY | (518) 869-6526 |
| Buffalo, NY | (716) 851-2800 |
| Elmsford, NY | (914) 345-1237 |
| Flushing, NY | (718) 321-5700 |
| Hauppauge, NY | (516) 582-7600 |
| New York, NY | (212) 330-2824 |
| Rochester, NY | (716) 272-7220 |
| Akron, OH | (216) 996-9721 |

*Postal Service (cont'd)*

| Location | Phone Number |
|---|---|
| Cincinnati, OH | (513) 684-5791 |
| Cleveland, OH | (216) 443-4401 |
| Columbus, OH | (614) 469-4336 |
| Oklahoma City, OK | (405) 720-2675 |
| Portland, OR | (503) 294-2306 |
| Erie, PA | (814) 878-0018 |
| Harrisburg, PA | (717) 257-2108 |
| Lancaster, PA | (717) 396-6994 |
| Philadelphia, PA | (215) 895-8046 |
| Pittsburgh, PA | (412) 359-7601 |
| Southeastern, PA | (215) 964-6441 |
| Providence, RI | (401) 276-5038 |
| Columbia, SC | (803) 731-5903 |
| Sioux Falls, SD | (605) 339-8854 |
| Memphis, TN | (901) 576-2035 |

| Location | Phone Number |
|---|---|
| Nashville, TN | (615) 885-9399 |
| Coppell, TX | (214) 393-6701 |
| Fort Worth, TX | (817) 625-3600 |
| Houston, TX | (713) 226-3349 |
| North Houston, TX | (713) 985-4108 |
| San Antonio, TX | (210) 657-8578 |
| Salt Lake City, UT | (801) 974-2503 |
| Merrifield, VA | (703) 207-6800 |
| Richmond, VA | (804) 775-6224 |
| Seattle, WA | (206) 625-7016 |
| Spokane, WA | (509) 448-4219 |
| Madison, WI | (608) 246-1245 |
| Milwaukee, WI | (414) 287-2522 |
| Charleston, WV | (304) 340-4233 |

# Postal Abbreviations

| State | Abbr. |
|---|---|
| Alabama | AL |
| Alaska | AK |
| American Samoa | AS |
| Arizona | AZ |
| Arkansas | AR |
| California | CA |
| Colorado | CO |
| Connecticut | CT |
| Delaware | DE |
| District of Columbia | DC |
| Florida | FL |
| Georgia | GA |
| Hawaii | HI |
| Idaho | ID |
| Illinois | IL |
| Indiana | IN |
| Iowa | IA |
| Kansas | KS |
| Kentucky | KY |
| Louisiana | LA |

| State | Abbr. |
|---|---|
| Maine | ME |
| Marshall Islands | TT |
| Maryland | MD |
| Massachusetts | MA |
| Michigan | MI |
| Minnesota | MN |
| Mississippi | MS |
| Missouri | MO |
| Montana | MT |
| Nebraska | NE |
| Nevada | NV |
| New Hampshire | NH |
| New Jersey | NJ |
| New Mexico | NM |
| New York | NY |
| North Carolina | NC |
| North Dakota | ND |
| Ohio | OH |
| Oklahoma | OK |
| Oregon | OR |

| State | Abbr. |
|---|---|
| Pennsylvania | PA |
| Puerto Rico | PR |
| Rhode Island | RI |
| South Carolina | SC |
| South Dakota | SD |
| Tennessee | TN |
| Texas | TX |
| Utah | UT |
| Vermont | VT |
| Virginia | VA |
| Virgin Islands | VI |
| Washington | WA |
| West Virginia | WV |
| Wisconsin | WI |
| Wyoming | WY |

## The Top Reference Sources

*AT&T Toll-Free 800 Directory*
AT&T, business edition $24.99, consumer
edition $14.95, both $34.95
(800) 426-8686

These are essential references for businesses and
consumers. The business edition is a business-to-

business directory, with over 150,000 numbers.
The consumer edition lets the average person
comparison-shop from coast to coast. It contains
over 120,000 numbers.

Listings are alphabetical by company name in
the white pages, and by classified headings in the
yellow pages.

# United Parcel Service

UNITED PARCEL SERVICE (UPS) is one of the most cost-effective ways to move packages across the country. They offer four levels of service:

- Ground

- 3 Day Select

- 2nd Day Air

- Next Day Air

In all instances, the maximum weight of the package is 70 pounds. The maximum size of 130 inches is figured out by a formula: ((longest side) + (next longest side x 2)) + (shortest side x 2).

## Ground Service

Pricing on UPS ground service, the most inexpensive means of shipping most packages, is based on zones. The price of a given shipment changes depending on the origin and destination zip codes. The zone map used by UPS is different in every part of the country.

The charts on the next two pages give the price of sending one-pound and five-pound packages to and from major cities. These numbers are only a guideline—contact UPS for precise figures.

## 3 Day Select

This new service provides guaranteed three-day service throughout the country. Rates are based on the origin and destination zip code. Call (800) 742-5877 for pricing.

## 2nd Day Air (Blue)

All packages sent by this service within the 48 contiguous states are charged a flat rate.

## Next Day Air (Red)

All packages sent by this service within the 48 contiguous states are charged a flat rate.

## UPS Air Pricing

| Weight (lbs) | Next Day Air | Second Day Air |
| --- | --- | --- |
| Letter | 9.00 | 5.75 |
| 1 | 15.25 | 6.00 |
| 2 | 16.00 | 7.00 |
| 3 | 17.50 | 7.75 |
| 4 | 19.00 | 8.25 |
| 5 | 20.75 | 9.00 |
| 6 | 22.75 | 10.25 |
| 7 | 24.75 | 11.50 |
| 8 | 26.50 | 12.75 |
| 9 | 28.50 | 14.00 |
| 10 | 30.25 | 15.25 |

*Note: All rates as of February, 1994*

The costs above do not reflect pick-up charges. With 24 hours' notice, UPS will pick up any number of packages for a flat fee of $5.00. For air packages, UPS will pick up on the same day for a charge of $3.25 per package.

## Contact Option

United Parcel Service
(800) 742-5877

## The Top Reference Sources

*Bacon's Newspaper/Magazine Directory*
Bacon's Information, $250
(312) 922-2400

This annual directory of magazines and newspapers offers descriptive editorial profiles of leading consumer magazines and prominent trade publications.

The reference also contains a listing of Hispanic newspapers, ad rates, and an index of multiple publishers for daily newspaper chains.

*United Parcel Service, (cont'd)*

# UPS Rates, One-Pound Package, Ground Service

| | | Atlanta, 30301 | Baltimore, 21233 | Boston, 02101 | Chicago, 60601 | Cincinnati, 45202 | Cleveland, 44101 | Columbus, 43216 | Dallas, 75201 | Denver, 80201 | Detroit, 48231 | Houston, 77052 | Indianapolis, 46206 | LA, 90806 | Miami, 33101 | Milwaukee, 53201 |
|---|---|---|---|---|---|---|---|---|---|---|---|---|---|---|---|---|
| Atlanta | 30301 | 2.35 | 2.74 | 2.83 | 2.74 | 2.74 | 2.74 | 2.74 | 2.83 | 2.92 | 2.74 | 2.83 | 2.74 | 3.07 | 2.74 | 2.83 |
| Baltimore | 21233 | 2.74 | 2.35 | 2.74 | 2.74 | 2.74 | 2.50 | 2.74 | 2.92 | 3.00 | 2.74 | 2.92 | 2.74 | 3.07 | 2.83 | 2.83 |
| Boston | 02101 | 2.83 | 2.74 | 2.35 | 2.83 | 2.83 | 2.74 | 2.83 | 3.00 | 3.00 | 2.83 | 3.00 | 2.83 | 3.07 | 2.92 | 2.83 |
| Chicago | 60601 | 2.74 | 2.74 | 2.83 | 2.35 | 2.50 | 2.50 | 2.50 | 2.83 | 2.83 | 2.50 | 2.83 | 2.35 | 3.00 | 2.92 | 2.35 |
| Cincinnati | 45202 | 2.74 | 2.74 | 2.83 | 2.50 | 2.35 | 2.50 | 2.35 | 2.83 | 2.92 | 2.50 | 2.83 | 2.35 | 3.07 | 2.83 | 2.50 |
| Cleveland | 44101 | 2.74 | 2.50 | 2.74 | 2.50 | 2.50 | 2.35 | 2.35 | 2.83 | 2.92 | 2.35 | 2.92 | 2.50 | 3.07 | 2.92 | 2.74 |
| Columbus | 43216 | 2.74 | 2.74 | 2.83 | 2.50 | 2.35 | 2.35 | 2.35 | 2.83 | 2.92 | 2.50 | 2.83 | 2.35 | 3.07 | 2.83 | 2.74 |
| Dallas | 75201 | 2.83 | 2.92 | 3.00 | 2.83 | 2.83 | 2.83 | 2.83 | 2.35 | 2.83 | 2.83 | 2.50 | 2.83 | 2.92 | 2.92 | 2.83 |
| Denver | 80201 | 2.92 | 3.00 | 3.00 | 2.83 | 2.92 | 2.92 | 2.92 | 2.83 | 2.35 | 2.92 | 2.83 | 2.83 | 2.83 | 3.00 | 2.83 |
| Detroit | 48231 | 2.74 | 2.74 | 2.83 | 2.50 | 2.50 | 2.35 | 2.50 | 2.83 | 2.92 | 2.35 | 2.92 | 2.50 | 3.07 | 2.92 | 2.50 |
| Houston | 77052 | 2.83 | 2.92 | 3.00 | 2.83 | 2.83 | 2.92 | 2.83 | 2.50 | 2.83 | 2.92 | 2.35 | 2.83 | 2.92 | 2.83 | 2.83 |
| Indianapolis | 46206 | 2.74 | 2.74 | 2.83 | 2.35 | 2.35 | 2.50 | 2.35 | 2.83 | 2.83 | 2.50 | 2.83 | 2.35 | 3.00 | 2.92 | 2.35 |
| Los Angeles | 90086 | 3.07 | 3.07 | 3.07 | 3.00 | 3.07 | 3.07 | 3.07 | 2.92 | 2.83 | 3.07 | 2.92 | 3.00 | 2.35 | 3.07 | 3.00 |
| Miami | 33101 | 2.74 | 2.83 | 2.92 | 2.92 | 2.83 | 2.92 | 2.83 | 2.92 | 3.00 | 2.92 | 2.83 | 2.92 | 3.07 | 2.35 | 2.92 |
| Milwaukee | 53201 | 2.83 | 2.83 | 2.83 | 2.35 | 2.50 | 2.74 | 2.74 | 2.83 | 2.83 | 2.50 | 2.83 | 2.35 | 3.00 | 2.92 | 2.35 |
| Minneapolis | 55401 | 2.83 | 2.83 | 2.92 | 2.74 | 2.74 | 2.83 | 2.74 | 2.83 | 2.83 | 2.74 | 2.92 | 2.74 | 3.00 | 3.00 | 2.50 |
| New York | 10001 | 2.35 | 2.35 | 2.50 | 2.83 | 2.74 | 2.74 | 2.74 | 2.92 | 3.00 | 2.74 | 2.92 | 2.83 | 3.07 | 2.92 | 2.83 |
| Norfolk | 23503 | 2.74 | 2.50 | 2.74 | 2.83 | 2.74 | 2.74 | 2.74 | 2.92 | 3.00 | 2.74 | 2.92 | 2.74 | 3.07 | 2.83 | 2.83 |
| Philadelphia | 19104 | 2.83 | 2.35 | 2.50 | 2.83 | 2.74 | 2.74 | 2.74 | 2.92 | 3.00 | 2.74 | 2.92 | 2.74 | 3.07 | 2.83 | 2.83 |
| Phoenix | 85201 | 3.00 | 3.07 | 3.07 | 3.00 | 3.00 | 3.00 | 3.00 | 2.83 | 2.74 | 3.00 | 2.92 | 3.00 | 2.74 | 3.07 | 3.00 |
| Pittsburgh | 15233 | 2.74 | 2.50 | 2.74 | 2.74 | 2.50 | 2.35 | 2.35 | 2.92 | 2.92 | 2.50 | 2.92 | 2.74 | 3.07 | 2.83 | 2.74 |
| Portland, OR | 97208 | 3.07 | 3.07 | 3.07 | 3.00 | 3.07 | 3.07 | 3.07 | 3.00 | 2.83 | 3.07 | 3.07 | 3.07 | 2.83 | 3.07 | 3.00 |
| Sacramento | 95814 | 3.07 | 3.07 | 3.07 | 3.00 | 3.07 | 3.07 | 3.07 | 3.00 | 2.83 | 3.07 | 3.00 | 3.07 | 2.74 | 3.07 | 3.00 |
| St. Louis | 63166 | 2.74 | 2.83 | 2.92 | 2.50 | 2.50 | 2.74 | 2.74 | 2.74 | 2.83 | 2.74 | 2.74 | 2.83 | 3.00 | 2.92 | 2.74 |
| San Antonio | 78265 | 2.83 | 2.92 | 3.00 | 2.92 | 2.92 | 2.92 | 2.92 | 2.50 | 2.83 | 2.92 | 2.50 | 2.83 | 2.92 | 2.92 | 2.92 |
| San Diego | 92183 | 3.07 | 3.07 | 3.07 | 3.00 | 3.07 | 3.07 | 3.07 | 2.92 | 2.83 | 3.07 | 2.92 | 3.00 | 2.35 | 3.07 | 3.00 |
| San Fran. | 94142 | 3.07 | 3.07 | 3.07 | 3.07 | 3.07 | 3.07 | 3.07 | 3.00 | 2.83 | 3.07 | 3.00 | 3.07 | 2.74 | 3.07 | 3.07 |
| Seattle | 98101 | 3.07 | 3.07 | 3.07 | 3.00 | 3.07 | 3.07 | 3.07 | 3.00 | 2.92 | 3.07 | 3.07 | 3.07 | 2.83 | 3.07 | 3.00 |
| Tampa | 33602 | 2.74 | 2.83 | 2.92 | 2.83 | 2.83 | 2.83 | 2.83 | 2.83 | 3.00 | 2.83 | 2.83 | 2.83 | 3.07 | 2.50 | 2.92 |
| DC | 20090 | 2.74 | 2.35 | 2.74 | 2.74 | 2.74 | 2.50 | 2.74 | 2.92 | 3.00 | 2.74 | 2.92 | 2.74 | 3.07 | 2.83 | 2.83 |

| | | Minneapolis, 55401 | New York, 10001 | Norfolk, 23503 | Philadelphia, 19104 | Phoenix, 85201 | Pittsburgh, 15233 | Portland, OR, 97208 | Sacramento, 95814 | St. Louis, 63166 | San Antonio, 78265 | San Diego, 92183 | San Francisco, 94142 | Seattle, 98101 | Tampa, 33602 | DC, 20900 |
|---|---|---|---|---|---|---|---|---|---|---|---|---|---|---|---|---|
| Minneapolis | 55401 | 2.35 | 2.83 | 2.92 | 2.83 | 2.92 | 2.83 | 3.00 | 3.00 | 2.74 | 2.92 | 3.00 | 3.00 | 2.92 | 2.92 | 2.83 |
| New York | 10001 | 2.83 | 2.35 | 2.50 | 2.83 | 3.07 | 2.74 | 3.07 | 3.07 | 2.83 | 3.00 | 3.07 | 3.07 | 3.07 | 2.83 | 2.50 |
| Norfolk | 23503 | 2.92 | 2.50 | 2.35 | 2.50 | 3.07 | 2.74 | 3.07 | 3.07 | 2.83 | 2.92 | 3.07 | 3.07 | 3.07 | 2.83 | 2.35 |
| Philadelphia | 19104 | 2.83 | 2.83 | 2.50 | 2.35 | 3.07 | 2.50 | 3.07 | 3.07 | 2.83 | 3.00 | 3.07 | 3.07 | 3.07 | 2.83 | 2.35 |
| Phoenix | 85201 | 2.92 | 3.07 | 3.07 | 3.07 | 2.35 | 3.07 | 2.92 | 2.83 | 2.92 | 2.83 | 2.74 | 2.83 | 2.92 | 3.00 | 3.07 |
| Pittsburgh | 15233 | 2.83 | 2.74 | 2.74 | 2.50 | 3.07 | 2.35 | 3.07 | 3.07 | 2.74 | 2.92 | 3.07 | 3.07 | 3.07 | 2.83 | 2.50 |
| Portland, OR | 97208 | 3.00 | 3.07 | 3.07 | 3.07 | 2.92 | 3.07 | 2.35 | 2.35 | 3.00 | 3.00 | 2.83 | 2.35 | 2.35 | 3.07 | 3.07 |
| Sacramento | 95814 | 3.00 | 3.07 | 3.07 | 3.07 | 2.83 | 3.07 | 2.35 | 2.35 | 3.00 | 3.00 | 2.74 | 2.35 | 2.83 | 3.07 | 3.07 |
| St. Louis | 63166 | 2.74 | 2.83 | 2.83 | 2.83 | 2.92 | 2.74 | 3.00 | 3.00 | 2.35 | 2.83 | 3.00 | 3.00 | 3.00 | 2.83 | 2.83 |
| San Antonio | 78265 | 2.92 | 3.00 | 2.92 | 3.00 | 2.83 | 2.92 | 3.00 | 3.00 | 2.83 | 2.35 | 2.92 | 3.00 | 3.00 | 2.83 | 2.92 |
| San Diego | 92183 | 3.00 | 3.07 | 3.07 | 3.07 | 2.74 | 3.07 | 2.83 | 2.74 | 3.00 | 2.92 | 2.35 | 2.74 | 2.92 | 3.07 | 3.07 |
| San Fran. | 94142 | 3.00 | 3.07 | 3.07 | 3.07 | 2.83 | 3.07 | 2.35 | 2.35 | 3.00 | 3.00 | 2.74 | 2.35 | 2.83 | 3.07 | 3.07 |
| Seattle | 98101 | 2.92 | 3.07 | 3.07 | 3.07 | 2.92 | 3.07 | 2.35 | 2.83 | 3.00 | 3.00 | 2.92 | 2.83 | 2.35 | 3.07 | 3.07 |
| Tampa | 33602 | 2.92 | 2.83 | 2.83 | 2.83 | 3.00 | 2.83 | 3.07 | 3.07 | 2.83 | 2.83 | 3.07 | 3.07 | 3.07 | 2.35 | 2.83 |
| DC | 20090 | 2.83 | 2.50 | 2.35 | 2.35 | 3.07 | 2.50 | 3.07 | 3.07 | 2.83 | 2.92 | 3.07 | 3.07 | 3.07 | 2.83 | 2.35 |

*United Parcel Service, (cont'd)*

## UPS Rates, Five-Pound Package, Ground Service

| | | Atlanta, 30301 | Baltimore, 21233 | Boston, 02101 | Chicago, 60601 | Cincinnati, 45202 | Cleveland, 44101 | Columbus, 43216 | Dallas, 75201 | Denver, 80201 | Detroit, 48231 | Houston, 77052 | Indianapolis, 46206 | LA, 90806 | Miami, 33101 | Milwaukee, 53201 |
|---|---|---|---|---|---|---|---|---|---|---|---|---|---|---|---|---|
| Atlanta | 30301 | 2.70 | 3.43 | 3.64 | 3.43 | 3.43 | 3.43 | 3.43 | 3.64 | 3.87 | 3.43 | 3.64 | 3.43 | 4.61 | 3.43 | 3.64 |
| Baltimore | 21233 | 3.43 | 2.70 | 3.43 | 3.43 | 3.43 | 3.00 | 3.43 | 3.87 | 4.18 | 3.43 | 3.87 | 3.43 | 4.61 | 3.64 | 3.64 |
| Boston | 02101 | 3.64 | 3.43 | 2.70 | 3.64 | 3.64 | 3.43 | 3.64 | 4.18 | 4.18 | 3.64 | 4.18 | 3.64 | 4.61 | 3.87 | 3.64 |
| Chicago | 60601 | 3.43 | 3.43 | 3.64 | 2.70 | 3.00 | 3.00 | 3.00 | 3.64 | 3.64 | 3.00 | 3.64 | 2.70 | 4.18 | 3.87 | 2.70 |
| Cincinnati | 45202 | 3.43 | 3.43 | 3.64 | 3.00 | 2.70 | 3.00 | 2.70 | 3.64 | 3.87 | 3.00 | 3.64 | 2.70 | 4.61 | 3.87 | 3.00 |
| Cleveland | 44101 | 3.43 | 3.00 | 3.43 | 3.00 | 3.00 | 2.70 | 2.70 | 3.64 | 3.87 | 2.70 | 3.87 | 3.00 | 4.61 | 3.64 | 3.43 |
| Columbus | 43216 | 3.43 | 3.43 | 3.64 | 3.00 | 2.70 | 2.70 | 2.70 | 3.64 | 3.87 | 3.00 | 3.64 | 2.70 | 4.61 | 3.64 | 3.43 |
| Dallas | 75201 | 3.64 | 3.87 | 4.18 | 3.64 | 3.64 | 3.64 | 3.64 | 2.70 | 3.64 | 3.64 | 3.00 | 3.64 | 3.87 | 3.87 | 3.64 |
| Denver | 80201 | 3.87 | 4.18 | 4.18 | 3.64 | 3.87 | 3.87 | 3.87 | 3.64 | 2.70 | 3.87 | 3.64 | 3.64 | 3.64 | 4.18 | 3.64 |
| Detroit | 48231 | 3.43 | 3.43 | 3.64 | 3.00 | 3.00 | 2.70 | 3.00 | 3.64 | 3.87 | 2.70 | 3.87 | 3.00 | 4.61 | 3.87 | 3.00 |
| Houston | 77052 | 3.64 | 3.87 | 4.18 | 3.64 | 3.64 | 3.87 | 3.64 | 3.00 | 3.64 | 3.87 | 2.70 | 3.64 | 3.87 | 3.64 | 3.64 |
| Indianapolis | 46206 | 3.43 | 3.43 | 3.64 | 2.70 | 2.70 | 3.00 | 2.70 | 3.64 | 3.64 | 3.00 | 3.64 | 2.70 | 4.18 | 3.87 | 2.70 |
| Los Angeles | 90086 | 4.61 | 4.61 | 4.61 | 4.18 | 4.61 | 4.61 | 4.61 | 3.87 | 3.64 | 4.61 | 3.87 | 4.18 | 2.70 | 4.61 | 4.18 |
| Miami | 33101 | 3.43 | 3.64 | 3.87 | 3.87 | 3.87 | 3.64 | 3.64 | 3.87 | 4.18 | 3.87 | 3.64 | 3.87 | 4.61 | 2.70 | 3.87 |
| Milwaukee | 53201 | 3.64 | 3.64 | 3.64 | 2.70 | 3.00 | 3.43 | 3.43 | 3.64 | 3.64 | 3.00 | 3.64 | 2.70 | 4.18 | 3.87 | 2.70 |
| Minneapolis | 55401 | 3.64 | 3.64 | 3.87 | 3.43 | 3.43 | 3.64 | 3.43 | 3.64 | 3.64 | 3.43 | 3.87 | 3.43 | 4.18 | 4.18 | 3.00 |
| New York | 10001 | 2.70 | 2.70 | 3.00 | 3.64 | 3.43 | 3.43 | 3.43 | 3.87 | 4.18 | 3.43 | 3.87 | 3.64 | 4.61 | 3.87 | 3.64 |
| Norfolk | 23503 | 3.43 | 3.00 | 3.43 | 3.64 | 3.43 | 3.43 | 3.43 | 3.87 | 4.18 | 3.43 | 3.87 | 3.43 | 4.61 | 3.64 | 3.64 |
| Philadelphia | 19104 | 3.64 | 2.70 | 3.00 | 3.64 | 3.43 | 3.43 | 3.43 | 3.87 | 4.18 | 3.43 | 3.87 | 3.43 | 4.61 | 3.64 | 3.64 |
| Phoenix | 85201 | 4.18 | 4.61 | 4.61 | 4.18 | 4.18 | 4.18 | 4.18 | 3.64 | 3.43 | 4.18 | 3.87 | 4.18 | 3.43 | 4.61 | 4.18 |
| Pittsburgh | 15233 | 3.43 | 3.00 | 3.43 | 3.43 | 3.00 | 2.70 | 2.70 | 3.87 | 3.87 | 3.00 | 3.87 | 3.43 | 4.61 | 3.64 | 3.43 |
| Portland, OR | 97208 | 4.61 | 4.61 | 4.61 | 4.18 | 4.61 | 4.61 | 4.61 | 4.18 | 3.64 | 4.61 | 4.61 | 4.61 | 3.64 | 4.61 | 4.18 |
| Sacramento | 95814 | 4.61 | 4.61 | 4.61 | 4.18 | 4.61 | 4.61 | 4.61 | 4.18 | 3.64 | 4.61 | 4.18 | 4.61 | 3.43 | 4.61 | 4.18 |
| St. Louis | 63166 | 3.43 | 3.64 | 3.87 | 3.00 | 3.00 | 3.43 | 3.43 | 3.43 | 3.64 | 3.43 | 3.43 | 3.64 | 4.18 | 3.87 | 3.43 |
| San Antonio | 78265 | 3.64 | 3.87 | 4.18 | 3.87 | 3.87 | 3.87 | 3.87 | 3.00 | 3.64 | 3.87 | 3.00 | 3.64 | 3.87 | 3.87 | 3.87 |
| San Diego | 92183 | 4.61 | 4.61 | 4.61 | 4.18 | 4.61 | 4.61 | 4.61 | 3.87 | 3.64 | 4.61 | 3.87 | 4.18 | 2.70 | 4.61 | 4.18 |
| San Fran. | 94142 | 4.61 | 4.61 | 4.61 | 4.61 | 4.61 | 4.61 | 4.61 | 4.18 | 3.64 | 4.61 | 4.18 | 4.61 | 3.43 | 4.61 | 4.61 |
| Seattle | 98101 | 4.61 | 4.61 | 4.61 | 4.18 | 4.61 | 4.61 | 4.61 | 4.18 | 3.87 | 4.61 | 4.61 | 4.61 | 3.64 | 4.61 | 4.18 |
| Tampa | 33602 | 3.43 | 3.64 | 3.87 | 3.64 | 3.64 | 3.64 | 3.64 | 3.64 | 4.18 | 3.64 | 3.64 | 3.64 | 4.61 | 3.00 | 3.87 |
| DC | 20090 | 3.43 | 2.70 | 3.43 | 3.43 | 3.43 | 3.00 | 3.43 | 3.87 | 4.18 | 3.43 | 3.87 | 3.43 | 4.61 | 3.64 | 3.64 |

| | | Minneapolis, 55401 | New York, 10001 | Norfolk, 23503 | Philadelphia, 19104 | Phoenix, 85201 | Pittsburgh, 15233 | Portland, OR, 97208 | Sacramento, 95814 | St. Louis, 63166 | San Antonio, 78265 | San Diego, 92183 | San Francisco, 94142 | Seattle, 98101 | Tampa, 33602 | DC, 20900 |
|---|---|---|---|---|---|---|---|---|---|---|---|---|---|---|---|---|
| Minneapolis | 55401 | 2.70 | 3.64 | 3.87 | 3.64 | 3.87 | 3.64 | 4.18 | 4.18 | 3.43 | 3.87 | 4.18 | 4.18 | 3.87 | 3.87 | 3.64 |
| New York | 10001 | 3.64 | 2.70 | 3.00 | 2.70 | 4.61 | 3.43 | 4.61 | 4.61 | 3.64 | 4.18 | 4.61 | 4.61 | 4.61 | 3.64 | 3.00 |
| Norfolk | 23503 | 3.87 | 3.00 | 2.70 | 3.00 | 4.61 | 3.43 | 4.61 | 4.61 | 3.64 | 3.87 | 4.61 | 4.61 | 4.61 | 3.64 | 2.70 |
| Philadelphia | 19104 | 3.64 | 2.70 | 3.00 | 2.70 | 4.61 | 3.00 | 4.61 | 4.61 | 3.64 | 4.18 | 4.61 | 4.61 | 4.61 | 3.64 | 2.70 |
| Phoenix | 85201 | 3.87 | 4.61 | 4.61 | 4.61 | 2.70 | 4.61 | 3.87 | 3.64 | 3.87 | 3.64 | 3.43 | 3.64 | 3.87 | 4.18 | 4.61 |
| Pittsburgh | 15233 | 3.64 | 3.43 | 3.43 | 3.00 | 4.61 | 2.70 | 4.61 | 4.61 | 3.43 | 3.87 | 4.61 | 4.61 | 4.61 | 3.64 | 3.00 |
| Portland, OR | 97208 | 4.18 | 4.61 | 4.61 | 4.61 | 3.87 | 4.61 | 2.70 | 2.70 | 4.18 | 4.18 | 3.64 | 2.70 | 2.70 | 4.61 | 4.61 |
| Sacramento | 95814 | 4.18 | 4.61 | 4.61 | 4.61 | 3.64 | 4.61 | 2.70 | 2.70 | 4.18 | 4.18 | 3.43 | 2.70 | 3.64 | 4.61 | 4.61 |
| St. Louis | 63166 | 3.43 | 3.64 | 3.64 | 3.64 | 3.87 | 3.43 | 4.18 | 4.18 | 2.70 | 3.64 | 4.18 | 4.18 | 4.18 | 3.64 | 3.64 |
| San Antonio | 78265 | 3.87 | 4.18 | 3.87 | 4.18 | 3.64 | 3.87 | 4.18 | 4.18 | 3.64 | 2.70 | 3.87 | 4.18 | 4.18 | 3.64 | 3.87 |
| San Diego | 92183 | 4.18 | 4.61 | 4.61 | 4.61 | 3.43 | 4.61 | 3.64 | 3.43 | 4.18 | 3.87 | 2.70 | 3.43 | 3.87 | 4.61 | 4.61 |
| San Fran. | 94142 | 4.18 | 4.61 | 4.61 | 4.61 | 3.64 | 4.61 | 2.70 | 2.70 | 4.18 | 4.18 | 3.43 | 2.70 | 3.64 | 4.61 | 4.61 |
| Seattle | 98101 | 3.87 | 4.61 | 4.61 | 4.61 | 3.87 | 4.61 | 2.70 | 3.64 | 4.18 | 4.18 | 3.87 | 3.64 | 2.70 | 4.61 | 4.61 |
| Tampa | 33602 | 3.87 | 3.64 | 3.64 | 3.64 | 4.18 | 3.64 | 4.61 | 4.61 | 3.64 | 3.64 | 4.61 | 4.61 | 4.61 | 2.70 | 3.64 |
| DC | 20090 | 3.64 | 3.00 | 2.70 | 2.70 | 4.61 | 3.00 | 4.61 | 4.61 | 3.64 | 3.87 | 4.61 | 4.61 | 4.61 | 3.64 | 2.70 |

# Federal Express

FEDERAL EXPRESS INVENTED the mass-market overnight delivery business in 1973. They now serve 185 countries and deliver to virtually every location in America. There are three basic classes of service:

- *Priority Overnight Service*: delivered the next business day by 10:30 A.M.

- *Standard Overnight Service*: delivered by 3:00 P.M. the next business day.

- *Economy Two-Day Service*: second business afternoon delivery by 4:30 P.M.

The maximum weight for all three classes of service is 150 pounds per package. The maximum size of 165 inches must be figured out by a formula: (longest side) + (next longest x 2) + (shortest side x 2). Other services offered include:

- *Overnight Freight Service:* Either by noon or 4:30 P.M. the next business day. For packages weighing more than 150 pounds up to 750 pounds or more, with advanced approval. A confirmed flight reservation is required in advance.

- *Two-Day Freight Service:* Second business day delivery by 4:30 P.M. Each piece may weigh more than 150 pounds and up to 1,500 pounds or more, with advanced approval. For delivery commitment to Hawaii call in advance.

## Federal Express Standard Rates

| Weight | Priority Overnight | Standard Overnight | Economy Two-Day |
|---|---|---|---|
| Up to 8 oz | 15.50 | 11.50 | NA |
| 1 lb | 22.50 | 15.50 | 13.00 |
| 2 lb | 24.25 | 16.50 | 14.00 |
| 3 lb | 27.00 | 17.50 | 15.00 |
| 4 lb | 29.75 | 18.50 | 16.00 |
| 5 lb | 32.50 | 19.50 | 17.00 |
| 6 lb | 35.25 | 21.25 | 18.00 |
| 7 lb | 38.00 | 23.00 | 19.00 |
| 8 lb | 40.75 | 24.75 | 20.00 |
| 9 lb | 43.50 | 26.50 | 21.00 |
| 10 lb | 46.25 | 28.25 | 22.00 |

*Note: All prices $2.50 less if dropped off at a service center. Rates as of April, 1994.*

Special services in addition to the regular service charge:

- *Saturday Delivery:* Priority Overnight shipments dropped off on Friday (call for the latest drop-off time) can be delivered on Saturday. Saturday delivery is available for two-day service and must be dropped off by Thursday. (There is an extra charge of $10 per package.)

- *Saturday Pickup:* Priority and Standard packages can be picked up on Saturdays. There is a $10 charge per package. There is no additional charge if the package is dropped off at a Service Center.

- *C.O.D.:* available to destinations in the U.S. including Hawaii and Alaska. A check or money order is collected on delivery. (Charge is $5 per destination)

- *Dangerous Goods Service:* $10 per package

- *Address Correction:* $5

- *Billing Special Handling Fee:* $5

- *SeaTiger Service:* for cargo shipped from Asia to destinations in North America, Latin America, or Europe. Shipments travel by ship to the U.S. and then by air to their final destinations. For more information call (800) 421-7581.

- *Air Charter Services*: (800) 238-0181

- *Telecommunications for the Deaf:* (800) 238-7777

- *Transportation of Animals:* (800) 238-5355

- *International Service:* Federal Express serves more than 185 countries. It offers a variety of services. For more information call (800) 247-4747

## Saving Money on Federal Express

- Drop off packages instead of requesting pickup. If your business ships ten packages a day, you're currently paying as much as $25 per day for pickups.

- Negotiate a discount. Call (800) 238-5355 and ask for the number of your sales rep. Request a face-to-face meeting, and feel free to talk about your other delivery options. There is flexibility built in to the rates.

- Use Standard Overnight instead of Priority.

- Routinely request verbal proof of delivery on all packages, and ask for a refund for all packages delivered late.

## Recommended Resource

Federal Express
General information: (800) 238-5355
Billing and pricing inquiries: (800) 622-1147

# Small Package Rates

## 8-oz Package

|  | Overnight | Next day P.M. | 2-day |
|---|---|---|---|
| UPS* | 15.25 | NA | 6.00 |
| Federal Express | 15.50 | 11.50 | NA |
| Post Office | 9.95 | NA | 2.90 |
| DHL | 11.00 | NA | NA |

## 1-lb Package

|  | Overnight | Next day P.M. | 2-day |
|---|---|---|---|
| UPS* | 16.00 | NA | 7.00 |
| Federal Express | 24.25 | 16.50 | 14.00 |
| Post Office | 13.95 | NA | 2.90 |
| DHL | 19.00 | NA | NA |

## 5-lb Package

|  | Overnight | Next day P.M. | 2-day |
|---|---|---|---|
| UPS* | 20.75 | NA | 9.00 |
| Federal Express | 32.50 | 19.50 | 17.00 |
| Post Office | 19.95 | NA | 5.45 |
| DHL | 29.50 | NA | NA |

*\* UPS rates listed are for drop-off at UPS centers. Consult UPS representative for pick-up surcharge.*

# Postal Answer Line

THE UNITED STATES POSTAL SERVICE has set up an automated telephone system to provide recorded messages regarding the most frequently needed information. The local PAL number is available from your local post office or you may use the number for Manhattan (212) 330-4000 or Los Angeles (213) 587-6142. The recorded instructions will tell the caller when to push the buttons that correspond with the desired message number. The following are some useful messages:

| Message | No. |
|---|---|
| Which class of mail should I use? | 333 |
| First Class Mail and Priority Mail Rates | 323 |
| Second Class (newspapers and magazines) | 336 |
| Third Class and Bulk Business Mail | 322 |
| Fourth Class Parcel Post rates (packages) | 122 |
| Express Mail–P.O. to Addressee–Up to 5 lbs. | 154 |
| Express Mail–P.O. to P.O.–Up to 5 lbs. | 354 |
| Express Mail Same-Day Airport Svc.–Up to 5 lbs. | 302 |

| Message | No. |
|---|---|
| INTERNATIONAL MAIL/SENDING PACKAGES | |
| Rates for First-Class surface mail | 319 |
| Airmail rates and information | 134 |
| Express Mail International Service | 318 |
| Parcel Post rates and information | 317 |
| Customs | 308 |
| Special services available | 142 |
| International Reply Coupons | 302 |
| Which mail option should I select? | 310 |
| Special services available for packages | 143 |
| Removing your name from mailing lists | 140 |
| Mailroom security (business) | 303 |
| Postage meter security (business) | 151 |
| Self-service postal centers | 321 |
| Express Mail Next-Day Service | 332 |
| Express Mail Same-Day Airport Service | 110 |
| Where to deposit Express Mail items | 138 |

## The Top Reference Sources

*The Elements of Style*
Macmillan, $5.95
(212) 702-2000

This classic reference by William Strunk, Jr., and E.B. White is a required text in most high school and college English classes.

In six brief chapters, the book explains the basic rules of grammar and punctuation, plus principles of composition, matters of form, and words and expressions commonly misused. A valuable book for anyone who writes.

# Mailroom Phone Directory

| FREIGHT & PACKAGE SERVICES | |
|---|---|
| A.A. Freight Forwarding | (800) 922-2017 |
| Air Cargo Expeditors | (800) 952-1700 |
| Airborne Express | (800) 222-3049 |
| Airgroup Express | (800) 843-4784 |
| America West Airlines | (800) 228-7862 |
| American Airlines Cargo | (800) 638-7320 |
| American Overseas Movers | (800) 292-3311 |
| American Vanpac Carriers | (800) 877-0444 |
| Amtrak | (800) 523-6590 |
| ATMC | (800) 822-2215 |
| Austrian Airline Cargo Service | (800) 637-2957 |
| Cannonball Air Couriers | (800) 323-6850 |
| Challenger Freight Systems | (800) 225-2836 |
| Coman Courier Service | (800) 824-6420 |
| Consolidated Air Service | (800) 362-1906 |
| Continental Airlines Cargo Center | (800) 421-2456 |
| Courier Express | (800) 243-9773 |
| Delta Airlines | (800) 638-7333 |
| DeSantis Despatch | (800) 962-7260 |
| DHL Worldwide Express | (800) 225-5345 |
| Emery Worldwide ACF | (800) 443-6379 |
| Fast Air Carrier | (800) 327-2578 |
| Federal Express | (800) 238-5355 |
| Global Mail | (800) 426-7478 |
| Griffin Express | (800) 648-2310 |
| Hawaii Air Cargo | (800) 227-3540 |
| International Bonded Couriers | (800) 322-3067 |
| J & B Fast Freight | (800) 841-8029 |
| Jack Rabbit Delivery Service | (800) 782-8149 |
| KLM Royal Dutch Airlines Cargo | (800) 556-9000 |
| Kuwait Airway Cargo Sales | (800) 221-6727 |
| Magic Messenger | (800) 423-7006 |
| Moonlite Courier | (800) 872-4113 |
| Nippon Cargo Airlines | (800) 622-2746 |
| Northwest Airlines Cargo | (800) 692-2746 |
| Philippine Airlines | (800) 227-6144 |
| Primac Courier | (800) 232-6245 |
| Priority Courier Group | (800) 433-4675 |
| Qantas Airways | (800) 227-0290 |

| | |
|---|---|
| Sabena Airlines Cargo | (800) 955-0770 |
| Service by Air | (800) 662-0160 |
| Sky Cab | (800) 631-5488 |
| Sky & Highway Transportation | (800) 328-1972 |
| Southern Air Transport | (800) 327-6456 |
| United Airlines | (800) 631-1500 |
| United Parcel Service | (800) 742-5877 |
| U.S. Express | (800) 468-1012 |
| FACSIMILE COMMUNICATIONS | |
| Mita Copystar America | (800) 222-6482 |
| Omnifax Facsimile | (800) 221-8330 |
| Panafax Fax Machines | (800) 843-0080 |
| Pitney Bowes Facsimile Systems | (800) 672-6937 |
| Sharp | (800) 237-4277 |
| Toshiba Facsimile Systems | (800) 468-6744 |
| FACSIMILE TRANSMISSION SERVICES | |
| Corporate Limited | (800) 322-1017 |
| Facsimile Services | (800) 621-8201 |
| Swift Global Communications | (800) 722-9119 |
| PAGING SYSTEMS | |
| Infopage | (800) 365-2337 |
| Metromedia Paging Services | (800) 437-2337 |
| U.S. Paging Corporation | (800) 473-0846 |
| TELEPHONE CONFERENCE SYSTEMS | |
| AT&T Alliance Teleconference | (800) 544-6363 |
| AT&T Classic Teleconference | (800) 232-1234 |
| American Conferencing | (800) 852-8852 |
| Conference Call Service | (800) 272-5663 |
| Conference Call USA | (800) 654-0455 |
| Darome Teleconferencing | (800) 922-1124 |
| MCI Forum | (800) 475-4700 |
| Sprint Conference Line | (800) 366-2663 |
| CELLULAR PHONE SERVICES | |
| Cellular Communications | (800) 231-9622 |
| Nationwide Cellular Service | (800) 627-2355 |
| Nokia Mobile Phones | (800) 666-5533 |

*Note: For guidelines on choosing a telecommunications service, see Telecommunications Services on page 554.*

# World Time Chart

| Place | If it is 11:00 A.M. EST | Time +/- Hrs. |
|---|---|---|
| Afghanistan | 8:30 P.M. | 9.5 |
| Albania ‡ | 5:00 P.M. | 6 |
| Algeria | 5:00 P.M. | 6 |
| American Samoa | 5:00 A.M. | -6 |
| Andorra ‡ | 5:00 P.M. | 6 |
| Angola | 5:00 P.M. | 6 |
| Anguilla | NOON | 1 |
| Antigua | NOON | 1 |
| Argentina ◊ | 1:00 P.M. | 2 |
| Aruba | NOON | 1 |
| Australia ◊ | | |
|   Northern Territories | 1:30 A.M.* | 14.5 |
|   Western Australia | MIDNIGHT* | 13 |
|   Other | 2:00 A.M.* | 15 |
| Austria ‡ | 5:00 P.M. | 6 |
| Baffin Island | 11:00 A.M. | 0 |
| Bahamas † | 11:00 A.M. | 0 |
| Bahrain | 7:00 P.M. | 8 |
| Baja California | 8:00 A.M. | -3 |
| Bangladesh | 10:00 P.M. | 11 |
| Barbados | NOON | 1 |
| Barbuda | NOON | 1 |
| Belgium ‡ | 5:00 P.M. | 6 |
| Belize | 10:00 A.M. | -1 |
| Benin | 5:00 P.M. | 6 |
| Bermuda † | NOON | 1 |
| Bhutan | 10:00 P.M. | 11 |
| Bikini Island | 4:00 A.M.* | 17 |
| Bolivia | NOON | 1 |
| Bophuthatswana | 6:00 P.M. | 7 |
| Borneo | MIDNIGHT* | 13 |
| Botswana | 6:00 P.M. | 7 |
| Brazil ◊ | | |
|   Fernando de Noronha | 2:00 P.M. | 3 |
|   East | 1:00 P.M. | 2 |
|   West | NOON | 1 |
|   Territory of Acre | 11:00 A.M. | 0 |
| British Guyana | NOON | 1 |
| British Virgin Islands | NOON | 1 |
| Bulgaria ‡ | 6:00 P.M. | 7 |
| Burkina Faso | 4:00 P.M. | 5 |
| Burma | 10:30 P.M. | 11.5 |
| Burundi | 6:00 P.M. | 7 |
| Cameroon | 5:00 P.M. | 6 |
| Canada † | | |

| Place | If it is 11:00 A.M. EST | Time +/- Hrs. |
|---|---|---|
| Atlantic Time | NOON | 1 |
| Eastern Time | 11:00 A.M. | 0 |
| Central Time | 10:00 A.M. | -1 |
| Mountain Time | 9:00 A.M. | -2 |
| Pacific Time | 8:00 A.M. | -3 |
| Canary Islands ‡ | 4:00 P.M. | 5 |
| Cape Verde Islands | 3:00 P.M. | 4 |
| Cayman Island | 11:00 A.M. | 0 |
| Central African Republic | 5:00 P.M. | 6 |
| Chad | 5:00 P.M. | 6 |
| Chile ◊ | NOON | 1 |
| China ◊ | MIDNIGHT* | 13 |
| Colombia | 11:00 A.M. | 0 |
| Congo | 5:00 P.M. | 6 |
| Cook Islands ◊ | 6:00 A.M. | -5 |
| Costa Rica | 10:00 A.M. | -1 |
| Crete | 6:00 P.M. | 7 |
| Cuba ◊ | 11:00 A.M. | 0 |
| Cyprus ‡ | 6:00 P.M. | 7 |
| Czech Republic | 5:00 P.M. | 6 |
| Denmark ‡ | 5:00 P.M. | 6 |
| Djibouti | 7:00 P.M. | 8 |
| Dominica | NOON | 1 |
| Dominican Republic | NOON | 1 |
| Ecuador | 11:00 A.M. | 0 |
| Egypt ◊ | 6:00 P.M. | 7 |
| El Salvador | 10:00 A.M. | -1 |
| Equatorial Guinea | 5:00 P.M. | 6 |
| Ethiopia | 7:00 P.M. | 8 |
| Falkland Islands ◊ | NOON | 1 |
| Fiji | 4:00 A.M.* | 17 |
| Finland ‡ | 6:00 P.M. | 7 |
| France ‡ | 5:00 P.M. | 6 |
| French Antilles | NOON | 1 |
| French Guyana | 1:00 P.M. | 2 |
| French Polynesia | | |
|   Gambier Island | 7:00 A.M.* | -4 |
|   Marquesa Island | 6:30 A.M. | -4.5 |
|   Society Island | 6:00 A.M. | -5 |
| Galapagos Islands | 10:00 A.M. | -1 |
| Germany ‡ | 5:00 P.M. | 6 |
| Ghana | 4:00 P.M. | 5 |
| Gibraltar ‡ | 5:00 P.M. | 6 |
| Great Britain ‡ | 4:00 P.M. | 5 |
| Greece ‡ | 6:00 P.M. | 7 |

*Based on Eastern Standard Time. *Indicates time on the following day.*
*NOTE: Countries around the world shift to daylight savings time on different schedules.*
*† Add one hour to time shown from April 1 to October 27. ‡ Add one hour to time shown from March 25 to September 22.*
*◊ See Non-Standard Daylight Savings on page 79 for details for this country.*

*World Time Chart (cont'd)*

| Place | If it is 11:00 A.M. EST | Time +/- Hrs. |
|---|---|---|
| Greenland | 1:00 P.M. | 2 |
|   Mesters Vig | 4:00 P.M. | 5 |
|   Scoresby Sound | 3:00 P.M. | 4 |
|   Thule | NOON | 1 |
| Grenada | NOON | 1 |
| Guadeloupe | NOON | 1 |
| Guam | 2:00 A.M.* | 15 |
| Guatemala | 10:00 A.M. | -1 |
| Guinea-Bissau | 4:00 P.M. | 5 |
| Guyana | 1:00 P.M. | 2 |
| Haiti † | 11:00 A.M. | 0 |
| Hawaii † | 6:00 A.M. | -5 |
| Hebrides Island, U.K. | 4:00 P.M. | 5 |
| Honduras | 10:00 A.M. | -1 |
| Hong Kong | MIDNIGHT* | 13 |
| Hungary ‡ | 5:00 P.M. | 6 |
| Iceland | 4:00 P.M. | 5 |
| India | 9:30 P.M. | 10.5 |
| Indonesia | | |
|   Jakarta | 11:00 P.M. | 12 |
|   Central | MIDNIGHT* | 13 |
|   East | 1:00 A.M.* | 14 |
| Iran | 7:30 P.M. | 8.5 |
| Iraq ◊ | 7:00 P.M. | 8 |
| Ireland ‡ | 4:00 P.M. | 5 |
| Isle of Man, U.K. | 4:00 P.M. | 5 |
| Isle of Wight, U.K. | 4:00 P.M. | 5 |
| Israel ◊ | 6:00 P.M. | 7 |
| Italy ‡ | 5:00 P.M. | 6 |
| Ivory Coast | 4:00 P.M. | 5 |
| Jamaica † | 11:00 A.M. | 0 |
| Japan | 1:00 A.M.* | 14 |
| Jordan ◊ | 6:00 P.M. | 7 |
| Kamaran Island | 7:00 P.M. | 8 |
| Kenya | 7:00 P.M. | 8 |
| Korea | 1:00 A.M.* | 14 |
| Kuwait | 7:00 P.M. | 8 |
| Laos | 11:00 P.M. | 12 |
| Lebanon ◊ | 6:00 P.M. | 7 |
| Liberia | 4:00 P.M. | 5 |
| Libya ◊ | 5:00 P.M. | 6 |
| Liechtenstein ‡ | 5:00 P.M. | 6 |
| Luxembourg ‡ | 5:00 P.M. | 6 |
| Madagascar | 7:00 P.M. | 8 |
| Malawi | 6:00 P.M. | 7 |

| Place | If it is 11:00 A.M. EST | Time +/- Hrs. |
|---|---|---|
| Malaysia | MIDNIGHT* | 13 |
| Mali | 4:00 P.M. | 5 |
| Malta ‡ | 5:00 P.M. | 6 |
| Marshall Islands | 4:00 A.M.* | 17 |
| Martinique | NOON | 1 |
| Mauritius | 8:00 P.M. | 9 |
| Mexico † | | |
|   Mexico City, Yucatan | 10:00 A.M. | -1 |
|   Baja S., N. Pacific coasts | 9:00 A.M. | -2 |
|   Baja N. above 28th parallel | 8:00 A.M. | -3 |
| Micronesia | | |
|   Kosrae, Ponape Islands | 3:00 A.M. | 16 |
|   Truk, Yap Islands | 1:00 A.M.* | 14 |
| Monaco ‡ | 5:00 P.M. | 6 |
| Mongolia ‡ | MIDNIGHT* | 13 |
| Morocco | 5:00 P.M. | 6 |
| Mozambique | 6:00 P.M. | 7 |
| Mustique, St. Vincent | NOON | 1 |
| Namibia | 6:00 P.M. | 7 |
| Nepal | 9:30 P.M. | 10.5 |
| Netherlands ‡ | 5:00 P.M. | 6 |
| Netherlands, Antilles | NOON | 1 |
| New Britain (Papua N.G.) | 2:00 A.M.* | 15 |
| New Caledonia | 3:00 A.M.* | 16 |
| Newfoundland, Canada | 1:30 P.M. | 2.5 |
| New Zealand ◊ | 4:00 A.M.* | 17 |
| Nicaragua | 10:00 A.M. | -1 |
| Nigeria | 5:00 P.M. | 6 |
| Norfolk Island | 3:30 A.M.* | 16.5 |
| N. Sound Island, British V.I. | NOON | 1 |
| Northern Ireland, U.K. | 4:00 P.M. | 5 |
| Norway ‡ | 5:00 P.M. | 6 |
| Pakistan | 9:00 P.M. | 10 |
| Panama | 11:00 A.M. | 0 |
| Papua New Guinea | 2:00 A.M.* | 15 |
| Paraguay ◊ | NOON | 1 |
| Peru ◊ | 11:00 A.M. | 0 |
| Philippines | MIDNIGHT* | 13 |
| Pitcairn Island | 8:00 A.M. | -3 |
| Poland ‡ | 5:00 P.M. | 6 |
| Portugal ‡ | 4:00 P.M. | 5 |
|   Azores | 3:00 P.M. | 4 |
|   Maderia | 4:00 P.M. | 5 |
| Pr. Edward Is., Canada | NOON | 1 |
| Pr. Edward Is., Indian Ocean | 7:00 P.M. | 8 |

*Based on Eastern Standard Time. *Indicates time on the following day.*
*NOTE: Countries around the world shift to daylight savings time on different schedules.*
*† Add one hour to time shown from April 1 to October 27. ‡ Add one hour to time shown from March 25 to September 22.*
*◊ See Non-Standard Daylight Savings on page 79 for details for this country.*

*World Time Chart (cont'd)*

| Place | If it is 11:00 A.M. EST | Time +/- Hrs. |
|---|---|---|
| Puerto Rico | NOON | 1 |
| Qatar | 7:00 P.M. | 8 |
| Romania ‡ | 6:00 P.M. | 7 |
| Russia | | |
| Moscow, European Part | 7:00 P.M. | 8 |
| Baku, Gorki, Arkhangelsk | 8:00 P.M. | 9 |
| Sverdlovsk | 9:00 P.M. | 10 |
| Tashkent | 10:00 P.M. | 11 |
| Novosibirsk | 11:00 P.M. | 12 |
| Taymyr Pen. | MIDNIGHT* | 13 |
| Vladivostok | 2:00 A.M.* | 15 |
| Magadan, Sakhalin | 3:00 A.M.* | 16 |
| Kamchatka Pen. | 4:00 A.M.* | 17 |
| Saint Barthelemy | NOON | 1 |
| Saint Croix, U.S. V.I. | NOON | 1 |
| Saint Helena Island | 4:00 P.M. | 5 |
| Saint John, U.S. V.I. | NOON | 1 |
| Saint Kitts | NOON | 1 |
| Saint Lucia | NOON | 1 |
| Saint Thomas, U.S. V.I. | NOON | 1 |
| Saint Vincent, Grenadines | NOON | 1 |
| Saudi Arabia | 7:00 P.M. | 8 |
| Scotland, U.K. | 4:00 P.M. | 5 |
| Senegal | 4:00 P.M. | 5 |
| Seychelles | 8:00 P.M. | 9 |
| Shetland Islands, U.K. | 4:00 P.M. | 5 |
| Sicily, Italy | 5:00 P.M. | 6 |
| Sierra Leone | 4:00 P.M. | 5 |
| Singapore | MIDNIGHT* | 13 |
| Somali | 7:00 P.M. | 8 |
| South Africa | 6:00 P.M. | 7 |
| Spain ‡ | 5:00 P.M. | 6 |
| Sri Lanka | 9:30 P.M. | 10.5 |
| Sudan | 6:00 P.M. | 7 |
| Swaziland | 6:00 P.M. | 7 |
| Sweden ‡ | 5:00 P.M. | 6 |
| Switzerland ‡ | 5:00 P.M. | 6 |
| Syria ◊ | 6:00 P.M. | 7 |
| Tahiti | 6:00 A.M. | -5 |
| Taiwan | MIDNIGHT* | 13 |
| Tanzania | 7:00 P.M. | 8 |
| Thailand | 11:00 P.M. | 12 |
| Tibet | 10:00 P.M. | 11 |
| Tierra del Fuego | 1:00 P.M. | 2 |
| Trinidad & Tobago | NOON | 1 |
| Tunisia | 5:00 P.M. | 6 |
| Turkey ‡ | 6:00 P.M. | 7 |
| Turks & Caicos Islands † | 4:00 A.M..* | 17 |
| Uganda | 7:00 P.M. | 8 |
| United Arab Emirates | 8:00 P.M. | 9 |

| Place | If it is 11:00 A.M. EST | Time +/- Hrs. |
|---|---|---|
| United Kingdom | 4:00 P.M. | 5 |
| Uruguay | 1:00 P.M. | 2 |
| USA † | | |
| Eastern Time | 11:00 A.M. | 0 |
| Central Time | 10:00 A.M. | -1 |
| Mountain Time | 9:00 A.M. | -2 |
| Pacific Time | 8:00 A.M. | -3 |
| Alaska Time | 7:00 A.M. | -4 |
| Hawaii Time | 6:00 A.M. | -5 |
| Vancouver Island | 8:00 A.M. | -3 |
| Venezuela | NOON | 1 |
| Vietnam | 11:00 P.M. | 12 |
| Virgin Gorda, Br. V.I. | NOON | 1 |
| Virgin Islands | NOON | 1 |
| Wales | 4:00 P.M. | 5 |
| West Indies | NOON | 1 |
| Zaire | 5:00 P.M. | 6 |
| Zambia | 6:00 P.M. | 7 |
| Zanzibar | 7:00 P.M. | 8 |
| Zimbabwe | 6:00 P.M. | 7 |

*Based on Eastern Standard Time.*

*\*Indicates time on the following day.*

## Non-Standard Daylight Savings

| Country | Daylight Savings Time |
|---|---|
| Argentina | December 1–March 3 |
| Australia | October 8–March 17 |
| Brazil | December 1–March 3 |
| Chile | October 8–March 10 |
| China | April 15–September 15 |
| Cook Islands | October 8–March 17 |
| Cuba | March 18–October 6 |
| Egypt | May 4–September 29 |
| Falkland Islands | September 10–April 14 |
| Iraq | May 4–September 29 |
| Israel | April 29–September 1 |
| Jordan | May 4–September 29 |
| Lebanon | May 1–October 14 |
| Libya | May 1–October 14 |
| New Zealand | October 8–March 17 |
| Paraguay | December 1–March 3 |
| Peru | January 1–March 31 |
| Syria | May 4–September 19 |

*Note: Countries around the world shift to daylight savings time on different schedules. † Add one hour to time shown from April 1 to October 27. ‡ Add one hour to time shown from March 25 to September 22.*

# International Mailing

## European Country Codes

The following codes for mailings into specified European countries have been adopted by the Postal Direct Marketing Service, an association of thirteen European Postal Administrations.

*Code for country where mail is being sent:*

| | |
|---|---|
| Belgium | B |
| Denmark | DK |
| Finland | SF |
| France | F |
| Germany | D |
| Great Britain | GB |
| Ireland | IRL |
| Netherlands | NL |
| Norway | N |
| Portugal | P |
| Spain | (no code) |
| Sweden | S |
| Switzerland | CH |

## International Organizations Providing Postal Information

*Switzerland*
International Bureau
Universal Postal Union
Case Postale
3000 Berne 15
[41] (31) 350-3111

*Venezuela*
IPOSTEL
(Institut Postal Telegrafico de Venezuela)
Edifico Sede
Centro Postal Caracas
Av. Jose Angel Lamas, San Martin
Caracas 1020
[58] (2) 451-8847; 4935

## International Postal Authorities Providing Postal-Code Directories and Information

The following list provides addresses and telephone numbers for postal authorities around the world that generally have printed material about address formats and standards that they will provide upon request. In many countries there is a charge for the material. Some postal administrations also provide the information on tape, diskette, or other magnetic media.

*Algeria*
Ministry of Posts and Telecommunications
4 Boulevard Krim Belkacem
Sept Merveilles
16000 Algiers
[213] 711-220 or 712-900

*Argentina*
ENCOTESA
(National Society of Posts & Telegraphs)
Sarmiento 151
1000 Buenos Aires
[54] (1) 315-1088; 9575

*Australia*
Australian Postal Corporation
GPO Box 1777Q
Melbourne VIC 3001
[61] (3) 204-7171

*Austria*
Ministry of Posts and Telegraphs
1011 Vienna
[43] (1) 515 51 0

*Belgium*
La Poste
General Administration
Centre Monnaie
1000 Brussels
[32] (2) 226-2111

*Bermuda*
Postmaster General
General Post Office
Hamilton HM PM
(809) 295-5151

*Brazil*
Brazil Posts and Telegraphs
SBN - Conjunto 3 - Bloco A
70002-900 Brasilia, DF
[55] (61) 225-0995

*Brunei Darussalam*
Ministry of Communications
Bandar Seri Bagawan 1150
[673] (2) 243-101/2/3/4

*Canada*
Canada Post Corporation
2701 Riverside Dr.
Ottawa, ON K1A 0B1
(613) 734-9000

*Costa Rica*
CORTEL
(Correos y Telégrafos)
San Jose
[506] 239-766

*International Mailing (cont'd)*

*Croatia*
Croatian Posts and Telecommunications
Jurisicéva 13
41001 Zagreb
[38] (41) 435-435

*Czech Republic*
Ministry of Economics
Department of Posts
Vrsovická 65
101 60 Prague 10
[42] (2) 712-1111

*Denmark*
Department of Posts and Telegraphs
Tietgensgade 37
1530 Copenhagen V
[45] 3393-2410

*Egypt*
Ministry of Communications
National Postal Organization
11511 Cairo
[20] (2) 391-4156

*El Salvador*
Department of Posts and Communications
Centro de Gobierno
San Salvador
[503] 711-922

*Finland*
Posts and Telecommunications
P.O. Box 1
00561 Helsinki
[358] (0) 7041

*France*
Ministry of Posts and Telecommunications
75700 Paris
[33] (1) 4564-2222

*Germany*
Deutsche Bundespost
POSTDIENST
C.P. 30 00
53105 Bonn
[49] (228) 1820

*Greece*
Ministry of Transports and Communications
Administration of Posts and Telecommunications
117 80 Athens
[30] (1) 921-5279

*Guatemala*
Department of Posts and Telegraphs
01501 Guatemala City
[502] (2) 28033 or 82975

*Hungary*
Ministry of Transports and Communications
Case Postale 87
1400 Budapest
[36] (1) 122-0220 or 142-0520

*Iceland*
Director of Posts and Telecommunications
150 Reykjavik
[354] (1) 636-000

*India*
Director General of Posts
Dak Tar Bhavan
Parliament Street
New Delhi 110001
[91] (11) 371-0350; 5797

*Indonesia*
Director General of Posts and Telecommunications
37 Jalan Kebon Sirih
Jakarta 10340
[62] (21) 330-008

*Ireland*
An Post
General Post Office
O'Connell St.
Dublin 1
[353] (1) 872-8888

*Israel*
Postal Authority of Israel
237 rue Yafo
91999 Jerusalem
[972] (2) 290-663

*Italy*
Ministry of Posts and Telecommunications
Viale America No. 201
00144 Rome
[39] (6) 59581

*Japan*
Ministry of Posts and Telecommunications
3-2 Kasumigaseki 1 chome
Chiyoda-ku
Tokyo 100-90
[81] (3) 3504-4392; 4793

*Republic of Korea*
Ministry of Communications
Bureau of Posts
Seoul 110-777
[82] (2) 750-2232

*Liechtenstein*
(See Switzerland)

*International Mailing (cont'd)*

*Grand Duchy of Luxembourg*
Posts and Telecommunications
General Administration
2020 Luxembourg
[352] 47651

*Malaysia*
Ministry of Energy, Telecommunications, and Posts
Postal Department
Wisma Damansara
50668 Kuala Lumpur
[60] (3) 256-2222

*Malta*
Postmaster General
Department of Posts
Valleta
[356] 224-421

*Mexico*
SEPOMEX
(Postal Service of Mexico)
Nezahualcoyotl 109 - Piso 8
Centro
06082 Mexico, DF
[52] (5) 761-8439

*Monaco*
Department of Posts and Telecommunications
16 Boulevard de Suisse
98030 Monaco Cedex
[33] (93) 303-371

*Morocco*
Ministry of Posts and Telecommunications
10000 Rabat
[212] (7) 702-091 or 704-311

*Netherlands*
PTT Post BV
P.O. Box 30250
2500 GG The Hague
[31] (70) 334-2805

*New Zealand*
New Zealand Post Limited
Corporate Office
Private Bag 39 990
Wellington 1
[64] (4) 473-8498

*Norway*
Department of Posts
P.O. Box 1181 Sentrum
0107 Oslo 1
[47] (2) 240-9050

*Panama*
Department of Posts and Telegraphs
Postal Service Department
Apartado 3421
Panama 4
[507] 252-825/6

*Peru*
Ministry of Transportation and Communication
Av. 28 de Julio No. 800
Lima 1
[51] (14) 245-088 or 319-206

*Philippines*
Philippine Postal Corporation
Post Office Building
Liwasang Bonifacio
Ermita
1000 Manila
[63] (2) 471-411/2/3

*Poland*
Ministry of Posts and Telecommunications
Department of Posts
Pl. Malachowskiego 2
00-940 Warsaw
[48] (22) 261-411; 071

*Portugal*
CTT
(Correios de Portugal, S.A.)
Rua Conde Redondo 79
1192 Lisbon Codex
[351] (1) 315-4030 or 355-6233

*Russia*
Ministry of Posts and Telecommunications
7 rue Tverskaya
103375 Moscow K-375
[7] (095) 9255-108

*Saudi Arabia*
Director General of Posts
Ryiad 11142
[966] (1) 405-1891; 5671

*Singapore*
Singapore Post Private Ltd.
750 Chai Chee Rd.
Chai Chee Industrial Park
Singapore 1646
[65] 448-7733

*Slovakia*
Ministry of Transport, Posts, and Communications
Department of Posts
Mileticova 19
820 06 Bratislava

*Slovenia*
Composite PTT Enterprises of Slovenia
Cigaletova 15
61000 Ljubljana
[38] (61) 310-166 or 314-455

*South Africa*
Postal Services
South African Post Office Ltd.
Private Bag X377
Pretoria 0001
[27] (12) 31134

*International Mailing (cont'd)*

*Spain*
MOPT (Ministry of Transportation)
Ogranization of Posts and Telegraphs
Calle Aduana 29
28070 Madrid
[34] (1) 522-1812 or 596-3664

*Sweden*
Sweden Post
105 00 Stockholm
[46] (8) 781-1000

*Switzerland*
General Directorate of PTT
Department of the Post
3030 Berne
[41] (31) 62 11 11

*Taiwan*
Directorate General of Posts
Taipei 10603
[886] (2) 392-1310 through 1319

*Thailand*
Ministry of Posts and Telegraphs
Bangkok 10400
[66] (2) 271-3515

*Tunisia*
Ministry of Communications
Department of Posts
1030 Tunis
[216] (1) 660 088

*Turkey*
Ministry of PTT
Department of Posts
06101 Ankara
[90] (4) 311 12 02

*United Kingdom*
Royal Mail
National Postcode Centre
3 & 4 St. Georges Business Centre
St. Georges Square
Portsmouth PO1 3AX

*United States*
For *International Mail Manual*:
Superintendent of Documents
P.O. Box 371954
Pittsburgh, PA 15250
(202) 783-3238

*Uruguay*
Ministry of Communications
Department of Posts
Montevideo
[598] (2) 95 60 24

For *National Five-Digit ZIP Code &
Post Office Directory* (2 volumes, $15.00):
National Address Information Center
U.S. Postal Service
6060 Primacy Parkway, Suite 101
Memphis, TN 38188
(800) 238-3150

Information on mailing internationally is also available from your local Postal Business Center of the United States Postal Service. (See "Postal Business Centers" on page 69.)

The Postal Service provides two guides to international marketing: *Direct Marketing Guide to Canada* and *International Direct Marketing Guide*. These are available at the Business Center, or write:

International Product Management
United States Postal Service
475 L'Enfant Plaza, SW
Washington, DC 20260

## Recommended Resource

*Guide to Worldwide Postal-Code &
Address Formats*, $99.50
Marian Nelson, Editor
35 W. 90th St.
New York, NY 10024
(212) 362-9855

# CORPORATE ADMINISTRATION

# Charity and the Corporation

IN RECENT YEARS, U.S. corporations have continued to make increasingly larger contributions to non-profit charitable organizations. Studies indicate that during the 20 years from 1970 to 1991, contributions rose from $797 million to $6 billion.

Experts point out that the reasons for this largesse range from altruism to practical self-interest and include the following:

• To seek to improve the quality of life in a specific geographic region;

• To ensure a steady supply of future employees from within the community;

• To maintain a favorable corporate perception in the eyes of both employees and customers;

• To qualify for tax advantages by contributing to organizations that are registered with the IRS;

• To enhance a corporate image and influence the opinions of legislators.

Those who assess these trends predict that corporate contributions which have maintained a level of 1.7–1.9 percent of pre-tax income over the last 10 years will continue at this rate.

## Recommended Resource

*The Foundation Directory*
The Foundation Center, $170
79 Fifth Ave.
New York, NY 10003
(212) 620-4230

# Supporters of the Arts & Charities

WHAT TYPES OF CHARITIES have been the recipients of corporate contributions? Research indicates that education has been the main focus of corporate charity. Thirty-five percent of corporate giving has been directed to public education through programs directed at elementary through post-secondary education programs with a major focus given to the pre-college level. Many of these contributions are in the form of human resources such as business/education partnerships. These projects provide personal involvement through programs designed to expand the horizons of the nation's youth in preparation for their participation in the work force.

Health and human services have received 26 percent of the corporate dollar while culture and the arts have accounted for 11 percent. Civic and community activities have received 14 percent of the contributions with a major focus being on the environment.

## Contact Options

Council on Foundations
1828 L St., NW, Suite 300
Washington, DC 20036
(202) 466-6512
Provides information on starting a philanthropic program.

The Foundation Center
79 Fifth Ave.
New York, NY 10003
(212) 620-4230
Provides information on foundations and corporate-giving programs.

## Corporate Philanthropy: Where Are the Dollars Going?*

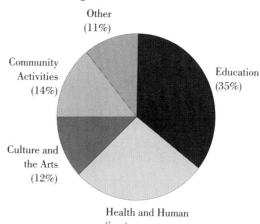

Other (11%)

Community Activities (14%)

Education (35%)

Culture and the Arts (12%)

Health and Human Services (27%)

*\* Figures do not add up to 100% due to rounding.*

*Source: The Conference Board, Corporate Contributions, 1992*

# Charitable Contributions

CORPORATE CITIZENS ARE those businesses that recognize the interconnectedness between industry and the surrounding world. This awareness prompts these companies to make notable philanthropic contributions to charitable organizations that support the major categories of public education, health and human services, culture and the arts, and civic and community activities.

There is sometimes a veil of secrecy regarding a corporation's charitable contributions. The National Committee for Responsive Philanthropy reports that of 200 of the largest profit-making corporations in the country, approximately 25 percent make no contribution information available to grant seekers or to the general public. This reluctance to disclose philanthropic information may be an attempt to discourage those seeking corporate handouts or may be an attempt to obscure the company's parsimony.

The Council on Economic Priorities profiled 100 companies and assessed their records of charitable contributions based on percent of pre-tax income budgeted for charity. According to the Council, an annual outlay of one percent of pre-tax dollars is considered an average charitable program. Fifty-two of the 100 companies surveyed met or exceeded this criteria. The ratings that follow were determined by the amount of giving, based on worldwide taxable earnings, as well as corporate-giving programs which donated millions of dollars worth of drugs, equipment, medical supplies, or food products.

The following companies gave a minimum of 1.6 percent of pre-tax dollars to charity.

These same companies were cited by the CEP for commendable contributions in the area of community outreach.

Aetna Life and Casualty
Anheuser-Busch
Aveda
Avon Products
Baxter International
Ben & Jerry's Homemade
The Body Shop
CPI
Adolph Coors Company

Curtice-Burns
Dayton Hudson
Deluxe
Donaldson
Fred Meyer
General Mills
Grand Metropolitan PLC
Helene Curtis Industries
Herman Miller
Hewlett-Packard
Honeywell
Houghton-Mifflin
J.C. Penney
J.P. Morgan
Johnson Controls
Johnson & Johnson
Johnson & Son
Kellogg
LecTec
Lillian Vernon
McKesson
Merck & Company
Newman's Own
Nordson
Nordstrom
Norwest
Quaker Oats
Rhino Records
St. Paul
Scott Paper
Starbucks
Stride-Rite
Tektronix
Tennant
The Timberland Company
Times Mirror
Tom's of Maine
US West
Upjohn
Whirlpool
Wholesome and Hearty Foods
Xerox
Yamanouchi Pharmaceutical

*Source: Council of Economic Priorities*

## The Top Reference Sources

*National Directory of Corporate Giving*
The Foundation Center, $195
(212) 620-4230

This directory profiles 1,791 companies making contributions to nonprofit organizations. It is intended for use by grantseekers in locating potential support, grantmakers in learning more about other grantseekers, scholars researching the field, journalists reporting on contributions activities of the corporate world, and everyone generally interested in philanthropy.

It lists company, address, contacts, financial data, types of philanthropic support, geographic limitations, and application information.

# The United Way and Alternatives

THE UNITED WAY'S ANNUAL fund-raising totals more than $3 billion. With 2,100 autonomous local agencies and a host of more than 44,000 public service groups supported, the United Way continues to be a significant element in corporate philanthropy.

Less than 16 percent of the money raised by the United Way goes to cover overhead. Because of the large number of volunteers—many of them on loan from corporations—the United Way is able to keep costs low.

In an increasingly aware labor force, employees have expressed concern that the corporate-giving program selected for their company did not represent their charitable interests. As a result, alternative funds have been established. These are umbrella organizations that represent multiple charities with the same focus. Such programs offer an alternative to the donor who prefers to contribute to a specific type of cause not encompassed in another fund.

## Contact Options

The United Way of America
(703) 836-7100
For the local agency in your area, check the white pages of your phone book.

Earth Share
(800) 875-3863
Represents 40 environmental organizations including American Farmland Trust, the National Audubon Society, the Rainforest Alliance, the Sierra Club Foundation, and the Wilderness Society.

Independent Charities of America
(800) 477-0733
Represents 244 organizations including Disabled American Veterans Charitable Service Trust, Toys for Tots, and Ronald McDonald House.

International Service Agencies
(800) 638-8079
Represents 34 groups including CARE, the U.S. Committee of UNICEF, Save the Children, Project Hope, Catholic Relief Services, and Oxfam.

National/United Services Agencies
(800) 458-9505
Represents 65 organizations including the Make-a-Wish Foundation, the Children's Defense Fund, Farm Aid, Covenant House, the NAACP Legal Defense and Education Fund, and Phyllis Schlafly's Eagle Forum.

National Voluntary Health Agencies
(202) 467-5913
Represents Alzheimer's Association, the American Cancer Society, the Muscular Dystrophy Association, and the National Kidney and Myasthenia Gravis foundations.

United Negro College Fund
(212) 326-1100
Represents 41 primarily African-American colleges and universities.

National Coalition of United Arts Funds
(212) 223-2787, ext. 231
Represents 60 funds which support symphonies, the ballet, zoos, museums, the theater, and historical societies.

## Selecting an Alternative Fund

The National Committee for Responsive Philanthropy (NCRP) was organized in 1976 to make more information about philanthropic funds available to the public. As a watchdog group, the NCRP pressed for disclosure of foundation funds available and sought to create alternatives to the corporate charity fund-raising efforts of the United Way. As a result of the organization's efforts, alternative funds were established to organize charities not covered under the United Way. Employees are frequently offered a choice of target funds for their contributions, both through payroll deductions and from direct fund-raisers.

Apple Computer was one of the first Fortune 500 companies to offer employees the opportunity to contribute through their company to alternatives to the United Way. Other companies have followed suit as increasing awareness of employee preferences has occurred.

In order to find alternative funds in a particular area, interested individuals should contact the NCRP which assists in establishing such funds and provides a booklet describing each of the alternative funds.

## Contact Options

National Committee for Responsive Philanthropy
2001 S St., NW, Suite 620
Washington, DC 20009
(202) 387-9177

National Alliance for Choice in Giving
2001 O St., NW
Washington, DC 20036
(202) 296-8470

# The Top Charities

## The Top 25 Charities Ranked by Income

| Rank | Organization | Income ($ millions) | Administrative Costs (%) |
|------|--------------|---------------------|--------------------------|
| 1 | Lutheran Social Ministry Organization | 1,937.8 | NA |
| 2 | Catholic Charities | 1,848.5 | 12 |
| 3 | YMCA of the USA | 1,678.0 | NA |
| 4 | American Red Cross | 1,568.0 | 5 |
| 5 | Salvation Army | 1,399.0 | 7 |
| 6 | UNICEF | 938.0 | 9 |
| 7 | Girl Scouts of the USA | 457.3 | 13 |
| 8 | Boy Scouts of America | 447.0 | NA |
| 9 | Planned Parenthood Federation of America | 446.0 | 12 |
| 10 | Second Harvest of Chicago | 424.3 | <1 |
| 11 | United Cerebral Palsy Association | 417.7 | 10 |
| 12 | United Jewish Appeal | 407.6 | 1 |
| 13 | American Cancer Society | 387.2 | 5 |
| 14 | YWCA of the USA | 377.1 | NA |
| 15 | National Easter Seal Society | 335.0 | 9 |
| 16 | Catholic Relief Services | 290.3 | 4 |
| 17 | American Heart Association | 289.1 | 8 |
| 18 | Nature Conservancy | 274.1 | 6 |
| 19 | Boys and Girls Clubs of America | 272.0 | 15 |
| 20 | World Vision | 250.1 | 10 |
| 21 | Campus Crusade for Christ | 167.1 | 9 |
| 22 | United States Olympic Committee | 145.1 | 4 |
| 23 | American Lung Association | 125.1 | 6 |
| 24 | March of Dimes Birth Defects Foundation | 124.1 | 8 |
| 25 | Habitat for Humanity International | 109.0 | 10 |

*Source: The NonProfit Times, Nov., 1993*

## Top 10 Charities Ranked by Contributions

Total income for these charities may come from public support, government support, investment, or member dues. The *Chronicle of Philanthropy* lists the top ten charities in 1993 based on contributions alone:

| Rank | Organization | Contributions ($ millions) |
|------|--------------|----------------------------|
| 1 | Salvation Army | 726.3 |
| 2 | Catholic Charities USA | 410.9 |
| 3 | United Jewish Appeal | 407.4 |
| 4 | Second Harvest of Chicago | 407.2 |
| 5 | American Red Cross | 394.7 |
| 6 | American Cancer Society | 354.7 |
| 7 | YMCA of the USA | 317.1 |
| 8 | American Heart Association | 235.4 |
| 9 | YWCA of the USA | 217.6 |
| 10 | Boy Scouts of America | 211.0 |

*Source: Chronicle of Philanthropy, Nov. 2, 1993*

## Recommended Resources

*NonProfit Times*, $59/year
190 Tamarack Circle
Skillman, NJ 08558
(609) 921-1251

*Chronicle of Philanthropy*, $67.50/year
1255 23rd St., NW
Washington, DC 20037
(202) 466-1200

# Foundations and Grants

THERE ARE FOUR MAJOR types of foundations in operation throughout the country today.

## Independent or Private Foundations

These foundations are frequently funded through the gift of an individual or a family. The foundations provide grants to individuals or institutions that meet the specific criteria for proposed application of philanthropic funds. The ten largest independent foundations and the total grant amounts are:

| Foundation | Total Grants ($) |
|---|---|
| Ford Foundation | 240,875,343 |
| W.K. Kellogg Foundation | 153,942,541 |
| Lilly Endowment | 131,309,773 |
| J. D. and C. T. MacArthur Foundation | 122,991,197 |
| Pew Charitable Trusts | 109,264,608 |
| Robert Wood Johnson Foundation | 93,531,931 |
| Rockefeller Foundation | 86,906,769 |
| Andrew W. Mellon Foundation | 86,871,015 |
| Kresge Foundation | 58,869,400 |
| Annenberg Foundation | 53,374,300 |

*Source: Foundation Giving, The Foundation Center, 1993*

## Company-Sponsored Foundations

Company-sponsored foundations are funded by endowments and annual contributions of a profit-making corporation. These foundations are generally independent of the corporation. However, the grants awarded by the groups frequently reflect the interests of the corporation and are often made in the community in which the corporation is located.

The largest company-sponsored foundations, based on amount of gifts received, include:

| Foundation | Gifts Received ($) |
|---|---|
| Amoco Foundation | 24,709,623 |
| Morgan Guaranty Trust | 24,100,000 |
| US WEST Foundation | 24,000,000 |
| GTE Foundation | 18,097,648 |
| American Express Foundation | 15,319,879 |
| AT&T Foundation | 15,000,000 |
| General Mills Foundation | 14,700,000 |
| General Electric Foundation | 14,696,000 |
| Johnson & Johnson Family of Companies | 13,401,000 |
| Caring Foundation | 13,000,000 |

*Source: Foundation Giving, The Foundation Center, 1993*

## Community Foundations

Community foundations usually appeal to the general public for contributions that are used annually in support of ongoing local services. Their funds come from many sources rather than a single donor, and they are usually classified as public charities under tax law.

The top ten community foundations or public charities, based on total grants and total assets, are as follows:

| Community Foundation | Total Grants ($ thous.) | Total Assets ($ thous.) |
|---|---|---|
| New York Community Trust | 68,139 | 1,030,579 |
| Chicago Community Trust | 32,490 | 339,971 |
| Marin Community Foundation | 29,800 | 548,900 |
| Cleveland Foundation | 27,458 | 693,600 |
| San Francisco Foundation | 21,855 | 248,550 |
| Communities Foundation of Texas | 212,690 | 17,502 |
| Boston Foundation | 16,980 | 256,248 |
| Hartford Foundation for Public Giving | 13,896 | 209,463 |
| Columbus Foundation | 12,524 | 181,655 |
| Saint Paul Foundation | 9,813 | 183,314 |

*Source: Foundation Giving, The Foundation Center, 1993*

## Operating Foundations

Operating foundations are organizations which use their resources for research or for a specific service. Funding usually comes from an endowment from a single source; however, the foundation is eligible for tax-deductible contributions from the public. These groups provide few grants since the contributions are earmarked for specific purposes.

The largest operating foundations based on assets include:

| Foundations | Assets ($) |
|---|---|
| J. Paul Getty Trust | 3,691,000,000 |
| Norton Simon Foundation | 288,000,000 |
| Robert Welch Foundation | 238,000,000 |
| Amherst H. Wilder Foundation | 206,000,000 |
| Annie E. Casey Foundation | 189,000,000 |
| Norton Simon Art Foundation | 165,000,000 |
| Wunsch Americana Foundation | 142,000,000 |
| Charles F. Kettering Foundation | 104,000,000 |
| Russell Sage Foundation | 97,000,000 |
| Menil Foundation | 93,000,000 |

*Source: Foundation Giving, The Foundation Center, 1993*

# Environmental Awareness

THE AVERAGE WORKER IN AN American office is responsible for discarding 180 pounds of high-grade recyclable paper every year.

While federal laws are designed to protect the environment against unscrupulous industrial pollution, the corporate citizen can take steps to promote environmental awareness both within and outside of the company through the education of its employees.

## Six Simple Projects for Office Conservation

The following are some simple suggestions from conservation specialists regarding ways in which the corporate citizen can protect the environment:

• Ask employees to bring a coffee cup to work instead of using styrofoam or other disposable cups.

• Set up glass and aluminum recycling programs with containers in lunchrooms or next to beverage machines.

• Set up a paper recycling program with containers at each employee's desk or in central locations. The recyclable papers can be collected and placed in outdoor containers by the custodial staff.

• Investigate a two-sided copy machine to reduce the amount of paper used in copying reports.

• Investigate conducting an energy audit to determine what minor changes can result in significant savings in energy and dollars.

• Investigate water-saving measures such as installing faucet aerators and toilet water displacement devices.

## Recommended Resources

*50 Simple Things You Can Do to Save the Earth*
by The Earthworks Group
Earthworks Press, $4.95
(510) 841-5866

*Design for a Livable Planet*
by Jon Naar
HarperCollins Publishing, $12.95
(212) 207-7000

*30 Ways to Use Less Paper*
3M, Commerical Office Supply Division, free
(800) 395-1223

## Directing Corporate Dollars

National organizations will make presentations to companies to promote environmental programs that seek corporate funding. They will readily explain organized programs that can be set up to direct corporate dollars to preserving and enhancing the environment on a national and global level.

## Contact Options

Earth Share
(800) 875-3863
*Umbrella Organization for 40 Environmental Groups*

Independent regional organizations will provide information sessions to corporate employees regarding opportunities to extend their support throughout and beyond the workplace environment.

Environmental Action Coalition
625 Broadway, 2nd Floor
New York, NY 10012
(212) 677-1601

## Environmental Federations

Individuals interested in directing their contributions and efforts to local environmental needs may contact one of several federations that operate in a variety of states. These environmental federations raise funds for regional conservation organizations and will frequently make presentations to corporate gatherings regarding such programs. The following is a list of environmental federations by state.

| Name | Phone |
|------|-------|
| Environmental Fund for Arizona | (602) 254-9330 |
| Earth Share of California | (415) 882-9330 |
| Nature Conservancy of Florida | (407) 628-5887 |
| Environmental Fund for Georgia | (404) 873-3173 |
| Environmental Fund for Illinois | (708) 295-1494 |
| Environmental Fund for Indiana | (317) 349-1062 |
| Environmental Fund for Michigan | (517) 332-3800 |
| Minnesota Environmental Fund | (612) 379-3850 |
| Missouri Coal. for the Environment | (314) 727-0600 |
| Environmental Fed. of New England | (617) 542-3363 |
| Environmental Fed. of New York | (518) 436-0421 |
| Environmental Fed. of North Carolina | (919) 687-4840 |
| Environmental Federation of Oregon | (503) 223-9015 |
| Environmental Fund for Pennsylvania | (717) 975-2998 |
| Environmental Fund for Texas | (512) 472-5518 |
| Environmental Fund for Virginia | (804) 295-6106 |
| Earth Share of Washington | (206) 622-9840 |

# Corporate Responsibility

CORPORATE RESPONSIBILITY CAN BE expressed in a full range of business responses to the needs of society. It can be in the form of direct giving of funds to a targeted nonprofit organization. In addition, a corporation may elect to become directly involved in a project such as the Adopt-a-School Program in which corporations provide services rather than direct dollars to the target school or school district. The participating company supplies mentors, tutors, facilities, equipment, and technology in order to have a positive impact on the educational progress, and consequently exercises considerable control over its own benevolence.

Still other corporations establish company foundations that direct contributions to worthwhile programs or projects. This option offers companies more control over their contribution dollars and permits direction of these funds to specific areas or needs. The largest company-based foundations are listed in "Foundations and Grants" on page 90. Advice on establishing a corporate foundation may be obtained from organizations that monitor and counsel foundations.

## Contact Option

The Foundation Center
79 Fifth Ave., 8th Floor
New York, NY 10013
(212) 620-4230

# Socially Conscious Investments

A HEIGHTENED SENSE OF CIVIC responsibility is being expressed in the types of investments selected by individual and corporate investors. Frequently investors will seek not only a return on their expenditure, but also a vehicle to express their concerns regarding corporate and public policies.

There are several investment funds that deal with socially and environmentally responsible companies.

## Contact Option

Affirmative Investments Group
129 South St.
Boston, MA 02111
(617) 350-0250

Calvert Social Investment Fund
c/o Calvert Group
4550 Montgomery Ave., Suite 1000
Bethesda, MD 20814
(800) 368-2750 or (301) 951-4800

Dreyfus Third Century Fund
200 Park Ave.
New York, NY 10166
(212) 922-6000

Parnassus Fund
244 California St.
San Francisco, CA 94111
(800) 999-3505 or (415) 362-3505

Social Investment Forum
430 First Ave., N
Minneapolis, MN 55401
(612) 333-8338

Socially Responsible Banking Fund
Vermont National Bank
P.O. Box 804-C
Brattleboro, VT 05301
(800) 544-7108

Working Assets Common Holdings
111 Pine St.
San Francisco, CA 94111
(800) 533-3863 or (415) 989-3200

## Recommended Resources

*The Better World Investment Guide*
Council on Economic Priorities, $19.95
(212) 420-1133

*Design for a Livable Planet*
By Jon Naar
Harper Collins Publishing, $12.95
(800) 207-7000

# Corporate Conscience

THE COUNCIL ON ECONOMIC Priorities (CEP) is an independent public interest organization dedicated to researching and reporting on, among other issues, corporate social responsibility. Each year the CEP reviews hundreds of U.S. corporations and selects winners who meet standard criteria for excellence, improvement, and innovation in the areas of charitable contributions, environmental concern, responsiveness to employees, equal opportunity, and community outreach.

## Contact Option

Council on Economic Priorities
30 Irving Pl.
New York, NY 10003
(212) 420-1133

## CEP Corporate Conscience Awards

| 1990 Category | 1990 Winner |
| --- | --- |
| Charitable Contributions | H.B. Fuller |
| Charitable Contributions | Stride-Rite |
| Community Outreach | Foldcraft |
| Responsiveness to Employees | Time Warner |
| Equal Opportunity | Kellogg |
| Environment, Large Co. | Herman Miller |
| Environment, Small Co. | Smith & Hawken |
| Environment, honorable mention | H.J. Heinz |

| 1991 Category | 1991 Winner |
| --- | --- |
| Charitable Contributions | US West |
| Charitable Contributions | Tom's of Maine |
| Community Outreach | Supermarkets General Holdings |
| Community Outreach | Prudential Insurance |
| Responsiveness to Employees | Donnelley |
| Equal Opportunity | General Mills |
| Environment, Large Co. | Church & Dwight |
| Environment, Small Co. | Conservatree Paper |

| 1992 Category | 1992 Winner |
| --- | --- |
| Charitable Contrib., Large Co. | U.S. West |
| Charitable Contrib., Small Co. | Tom's of Maine |
| Community Outreach | Supermarkets General Holdings |
| | Prudential Insurance |
| Responsiveness to Employees | Donnelley |
| Equal Opportunity | General Mills |
| Environment, Large Co. | Church & Dwight |
| Environment, Small Co. | Conservatree Paper |

| 1993 Category | 1993 Winner |
| --- | --- |
| Community Involvement | Clorox |
| Equal Opportunity | Pitney Bowes |
| Responsiveness to Employees | Merck & Co. |
| | Quad/Graphics |
| Environment, Large Co. | Digital Equipment |
| Environment, Small Co. | Aveda |
| Special Recognition for Defense Conversion | Galileo Electro-Optics |
| | Kaman Aircraft |
| | Kavlico |
| | Science Applications International |

| 1994 Category | 1994 Winner |
| --- | --- |
| Community Involvement, Large Co. | Brooklyn Union Gas |
| Community Involvement, Small Co. | America Works |
| Responsiveness to Employees | SAS Institute |
| Environment, Large Co. | S.C. Johnson & Son |
| Environment, Small Co. | Stonyfield Farm |
| International Commitment | Levi Strauss & Co. |

*Source: Council on Economic Priorities*

---

**FAX** **Population Data.** Request #125. See p. xi for instructions.

Table of resident population by age and state.

# Labor Force

## Civilian Labor Force (millions) by Race, Hispanic Origin, Sex, and Age

| Race, Sex, Age | 1970 | 1980 | 1985 | 1990 | 1992 | 2000 (est.) | 2005 (est.) |
|---|---|---|---|---|---|---|---|
| TOTAL | 82.8 | 106.9 | 115.5 | 124.8 | 127.0 | 142.9 | 150.7 |
| White | 73.6 | 93.6 | 99.9 | 107.2 | 108.5 | 120.3 | 125.8 |
| Male | 46.0 | 54.5 | 56.5 | 59.3 | 59.8 | 64.5 | 66.8 |
| Female | 27.5 | 39.1 | 43.5 | 47.9 | 48.7 | 55.8 | 58.9 |
| Black | 9.2 | 10.9 | 12.4 | 13.5 | 13.9 | 16.5 | 17.8 |
| Male | 5.2 | 5.6 | 6.2 | 6.7 | 6.9 | 8.1 | 8.7 |
| Female | 4.0 | 5.3 | 6.1 | 6.8 | 7.0 | 8.4 | 9.1 |
| Hispanic | NA | 6.1 | 7.7 | 9.6 | 10.1 | 14.2 | 16.8 |
| Male | NA | 3.8 | 4.7 | 5.8 | 6.1 | 8.4 | 9.9 |
| Female | NA | 2.3 | 3.0 | 3.8 | 4.0 | 5.8 | 6.9 |
| Male | 51.2 | 61.5 | 64.4 | 68.2 | 69.2 | 75.9 | 79.3 |
| 16 to 19 years | 4.0 | 5.0 | 4.1 | 3.9 | 3.5 | 4.4 | 4.6 |
| 20 to 24 years | 5.7 | 8.6 | 8.3 | 7.3 | 7.2 | 7.2 | 8.0 |
| 25 to 34 years | 11.3 | 17.0 | 18.8 | 19.8 | 19.4 | 17.3 | 17.0 |
| 35 to 44 years | 10.5 | 11.8 | 14.5 | 17.3 | 18.2 | 20.4 | 19.2 |
| 45 to 54 years | 10.4 | 9.9 | 9.9 | 11.2 | 12.2 | 16.5 | 18.6 |
| 55 to 64 years | 7.1 | 7.2 | 7.1 | 6.8 | 6.7 | 7.8 | 9.7 |
| 65 years and over | 2.2 | 1.9 | 1.8 | 2.0 | 2.1 | 2.2 | 2.3 |
| Female | 31.5 | 45.5 | 51.1 | 56.6 | 57.8 | 67.0 | 71.4 |
| 16 to 19 years | 3.2 | 4.4 | 3.8 | 3.5 | 3.2 | 4.1 | 4.2 |
| 20 to 24 years | 4.9 | 7.3 | 7.4 | 6.6 | 6.5 | 6.6 | 7.3 |
| 25 to 34 years | 5.7 | 12.3 | 14.7 | 16.0 | 15.7 | 14.8 | 14.7 |
| 35 to 44 years | 6.0 | 8.6 | 11.6 | 14.6 | 15.4 | 18.4 | 17.8 |
| 45 to 54 years | 6.5 | 7.0 | 7.5 | 9.3 | 10.3 | 15.0 | 17.2 |
| 55 to 64 years | 4.2 | 4.7 | 4.9 | 5.1 | 5.2 | 6.5 | 8.4 |
| 65 years and over | 1.1 | 1.2 | 1.2 | 1.5 | 1.6 | 1.6 | 1.8 |

*Source: 1993 Statistical Abstract, Table No. 622*

**FAX** **Labor Force.** Request #126. See p. xi for instructions.

Tables of civilian labor force by educational attainment, self-employed workers and employed workers by selected characteristics.

## The Top Reference Sources

*Commerce Business Daily*
U.S. Government Printing Office, $324 /year
(202) 783-3238

This extremely useful publication contains a daily list of U.S. Government procurement invitations,

contract awards, subcontracting leads, surplus property, and foreign business opportunities. It is essential reading for anyone who wants to obtain business from the government.

*Labor Force (cont'd)*

## Labor Force Participation Rates (%) by Race, Sex, and Age

| Race, Sex, Age | 1970 | 1980 | 1985 | 1990 | 1992 | 2000 (est.) | 2005 (est.) |
|---|---|---|---|---|---|---|---|
| TOTAL | 60.4 | 63.8 | 64.8 | 66.4 | 66.3 | 68.7 | 69.0 |
| White | 60.2 | 64.1 | 65.0 | 66.8 | 66.7 | 69.3 | 69.7 |
| Male | 80.0 | 78.2 | 77.0 | 76.9 | 76.4 | 76.7 | 76.2 |
| Female | 42.6 | 51.2 | 54.1 | 57.5 | 57.8 | 62.3 | 63.5 |
| Black | 61.8 | 61.0 | 62.9 | 63.3 | 63.3 | 65.7 | 65.6 |
| Male | 76.5 | 70.3 | 70.8 | 70.1 | 69.7 | 71.0 | 70.2 |
| Female | 49.5 | 53.1 | 56.5 | 57.8 | 58.0 | 61.2 | 61.7 |
| Hispanic | NA | 64.0 | 64.6 | 67.0 | 66.5 | 69.3 | 69.9 |
| Male | NA | 81.4 | 80.3 | 81.2 | 80.5 | 81.8 | 81.6 |
| Female | NA | 47.4 | 49.3 | 53.0 | 52.6 | 56.6 | 58.0 |
| Male | 79.7 | 77.4 | 76.3 | 76.1 | 75.6 | 76.0 | 75.4 |
| 16 to 19 years | 56.1 | 60.5 | 56.8 | 55.7 | 53.3 | 57.4 | 57.7 |
| 20 to 24 years | 83.3 | 85.9 | 85.0 | 84.3 | 83.3 | 85.5 | 86.1 |
| 25 to 34 years | 96.4 | 95.2 | 94.7 | 94.2 | 93.8 | 93.9 | 93.6 |
| 35 to 44 years | 96.9 | 95.5 | 95.0 | 94.4 | 93.8 | 93.7 | 93.4 |
| 45 to 54 years | 94.3 | 91.2 | 91.0 | 90.7 | 90.8 | 90.5 | 90.3 |
| 55 to 64 years | 83.0 | 72.1 | 67.9 | 67.7 | 67.0 | 68.2 | 67.9 |
| 65 years and over | 26.8 | 19.0 | 15.8 | 16.4 | 16.1 | 15.8 | 16.0 |
| Female | 43.3 | 51.5 | 54.5 | 57.5 | 57.8 | 62.0 | 63.0 |
| 16 to 19 years | 44.0 | 52.9 | 52.1 | 51.8 | 49.2 | 54.1 | 54.3 |
| 20 to 24 years | 57.7 | 68.9 | 71.8 | 71.6 | 71.2 | 74.3 | 75.3 |
| 25 to 34 years | 45.0 | 65.5 | 70.9 | 73.6 | 74.1 | 78.2 | 79.7 |
| 35 to 44 years | 51.1 | 65.5 | 71.8 | 76.5 | 76.8 | 83.3 | 85.3 |
| 45 to 54 years | 54.4 | 59.9 | 64.4 | 71.2 | 72.7 | 79.0 | 81.5 |
| 55 to 64 years | 43.0 | 41.3 | 42.0 | 45.3 | 46.6 | 51.9 | 54.3 |
| 65 years and over | 9.7 | 8.1 | 7.3 | 8.7 | 8.3 | 8.6 | 8.8 |

*Source: 1993 Statistical Abstract, Table No. 622*

## Labor Force Participation Rates (%) for Wives, Husband Present, by Age of Youngest Child

| Presence, Age of Child | Total 1975 | Total 1985 | Total 1990 | Total 1992 | White 1975 | White 1985 | White 1990 | White 1992 | Black 1975 | Black 1985 | Black 1990 | Black 1992 |
|---|---|---|---|---|---|---|---|---|---|---|---|---|
| Wives, total | 44.4 | 54.2 | 58.2 | 59.3 | 43.6 | 53.3 | 57.6 | 58.7 | 54.1 | 63.8 | 64.7 | 66.8 |
| 0 under 18 | 43.8 | 48.2 | 51.1 | 51.9 | 43.6 | 47.5 | 50.8 | 51.5 | 47.6 | 55.2 | 52.9 | 56.8 |
| All under 18 | 44.9 | 60.8 | 66.3 | 67.8 | 43.6 | 59.9 | 65.6 | 67.3 | 58.4 | 71.7 | 75.6 | 76.0 |
| Under 6 | 36.7 | 53.4 | 58.9 | 59.9 | 34.7 | 52.1 | 57.8 | 59.1 | 54.9 | 69.6 | 73.1 | 73.5 |
| Under 3 | 32.7 | 50.5 | 55.5 | 57.5 | 30.7 | 49.4 | 54.9 | 56.7 | 50.1 | 66.2 | 67.5 | 70.8 |
| 1 yr., under | 30.8 | 49.4 | 53.9 | 56.7 | 29.2 | 48.6 | 53.3 | 55.9 | 50.0 | 63.7 | 64.4 | 68.7 |
| 2 yrs. | 37.1 | 54.0 | 60.9 | 60.9 | 35.1 | 52.7 | 60.3 | 59.8 | 56.4 | 69.9 | 75.4 | 75.0 |
| 3 to 5 yrs. | 42.2 | 58.4 | 64.1 | 63.5 | 40.1 | 56.6 | 62.5 | 62.7 | 61.2 | 73.8 | 80.4 | 77.1 |
| 3 yrs. | 41.2 | 55.1 | 63.1 | 63.5 | 39.0 | 52.7 | 62.3 | 61.8 | 62.7 | 72.3 | 74.5 | 77.6 |
| 4 yrs. | 41.2 | 59.7 | 65.1 | 62.1 | 38.7 | 58.4 | 63.2 | 61.0 | 64.9 | 70.6 | 80.6 | 76.9 |
| 5 yrs. | 44.4 | 62.1 | 64.5 | 65.7 | 43.8 | 59.9 | 62.0 | 65.2 | 56.3 | 79.1 | 86.2 | 80.3 |
| 6 to 13 yrs. | 51.8 | 68.2 | 73.0 | 74.9 | 50.7 | 67.7 | 72.6 | 74.5 | 65.7 | 73.3 | 77.6 | 79.7 |
| 14 to 17 yrs. | 53.5 | 67.0 | 75.1 | 76.6 | 53.4 | 66.6 | 74.9 | 76.9 | 52.3 | 74.4 | 78.8 | 74.0 |

*Source: 1993 Statistical Abstract, Table No. 634*

*Labor Force (cont'd)*

## Unemployed Workers (thousands) by Work Schedules, Sex, and Age

| Characteristic | 1980 | 1985 | 1990 | 1992 |
|---|---|---|---|---|
| TOTAL | 7,637 | 8,312 | 6,874 | 9,384 |
| LOOKING FOR FULL-TIME WORK | 6,269 | 6,793 | 5,541 | 7,746 |
| Male | 3,703 | 3,925 | 3,264 | 4,699 |
| 16 to 19 years old | 537 | 446 | 328 | 360 |
| 20 to 24 years old | 994 | 857 | 582 | 772 |
| 25 to 54 years old | 1,923 | 2,329 | 2,098 | 3,169 |
| 55 years and over | 250 | 292 | 255 | 397 |
| Female | 2,564 | 2,868 | 2,277 | 3,047 |
| 16 to 19 years old | 430 | 331 | 233 | 254 |
| 20 to 24 years old | 636 | 636 | 439 | 509 |
| 25 to 54 years old | 1,363 | 1,727 | 1,491 | 2,087 |
| 55 years and over | 135 | 173 | 115 | 198 |
| PART-TIME | 1,369 | 1,519 | 1,332 | 1,638 |
| Male | 563 | 596 | 535 | 681 |
| 16 to 19 years old | 377 | 360 | 301 | 401 |
| 20 to 24 years old | 81 | 87 | 84 | 112 |
| 25 to 54 years old | 54 | 79 | 89 | 109 |
| 55 years and over | 52 | 70 | 61 | 59 |
| Female | 806 | 923 | 797 | 957 |
| 16 to 19 years old | 326 | 330 | 286 | 338 |
| 20 to 24 years old | 124 | 158 | 116 | 153 |
| 25 to 54 years old | 299 | 359 | 323 | 382 |
| 55 years and over | 57 | 75 | 72 | 84 |

*Source: 1993 Statistical Abstract, Table No. 639*

## Selected Labor Force Characteristics

| Item | Number |
|---|---|
| OCCUPATION | |
| Executive, administrative & managerial | 14,767,000 |
| Professional specialty | 16,386,000 |
| Technicians & related support | 4,253,000 |
| Sales | 13,919,000 |
| Administrative support, including clerical | 18,636,000 |
| Private household | 876,000 |
| Protective service | 2,096,000 |
| Service, except professional & household | 13,124,000 |
| Farming, forestry & fishing | 3,456,000 |
| Precision production, craft & repair | 13,128,000 |
| Machine operators, assemblers & inspect. | 7,524,000 |
| Transportation & material moving | 4,878,000 |
| Handlers, equipment cleaners, laborers | 4,556,000 |
| INDUSTRY | |
| Agriculture, forestry, and fisheries | 3,210,000 |
| Mining | 664,000 |
| Construction | 7,013,000 |
| Manufacturing | 19,972,000 |
| Trans., communs., other public utilities | 8,245,000 |

| Item | Number |
|---|---|
| Wholesale trade | 4,765,000 |
| Retail trade | 19,598,000 |
| Finance, insurance, and real estate | 7,776,000 |
| Business and repair services | 6,553,000 |
| Personal services | 4,400,000 |
| Entertainment and recreation services | 1,957,000 |
| Health services | 9,682,684 |
| Educational services | 9,633,503 |
| Other professional and related services | 27,677,000 |
| Public administration | 5,620,000 |
| CLASS OF WORKER | |
| Private wage and salary workers | 119,164,000 |
| Government workers | 18,554,000 |
| Local government workers | 10,930,000 |
| State government workers | 4,521,000 |
| Federal government workers | 3,103,000 |
| Self-employed workers | 10,017,000 |

*Source: 1993 Statistical Abstract Table Nos. 499, 621, 647*

# Demographics

## Civilian Employment Estimates (thousands)

| Occupation | 1990 Employment | 2005 Low Growth Employment | 2005 Moderate Growth Employment | 2005 High Growth Employment |
|---|---|---|---|---|
| TOTAL | 122,573 | 136,806 | 147,191 | 154,543 |
| LARGEST JOB GROWTH | | | | |
| Salespersons, retail | 3,619 | 4,180 | 4,506 | 4,728 |
| Registered nurses | 1,727 | 2,318 | 2,494 | 2,648 |
| Truck drivers, light and heavy | 2,362 | 2,767 | 2,979 | 3,125 |
| General managers and top executives | 3,086 | 3,409 | 3,684 | 3,871 |
| Janitors and cleaners | 3,007 | 3,332 | 3,562 | 3,728 |
| Nursing aides, orderlies, and attendants | 1,274 | 1,700 | 1,826 | 1,934 |
| Waiters and waitresses | 1,747 | 2,110 | 2,196 | 2,262 |
| Teachers: secondary school | 1,280 | 1,575 | 1,717 | 1,849 |
| Receptionists and information clerks | 900 | 1,228 | 1,322 | 1,394 |
| Systems analysts and computer scientists | 463 | 769 | 829 | 864 |
| Food preparation workers | 1,156 | 1,442 | 1,521 | 1,585 |
| Gardeners and groundskeepers, except farm | 874 | 1,158 | 1,222 | 1,275 |
| Accountants and auditors | 985 | 1,235 | 1,325 | 1,385 |
| Teachers, elementary | 1,362 | 1,538 | 1,675 | 1,803 |
| Teacher aides and educational assistants | 808 | 999 | 1,086 | 1,165 |
| Home health aides | 287 | 512 | 550 | 582 |
| Cooks, restaurant | 615 | 840 | 872 | 898 |
| Secretaries, except legal and medical | 3,064 | 3,065 | 3,312 | 3,488 |
| Lawyers | 587 | 745 | 793 | 830 |
| Marketing, advertising, and P.R. managers | 427 | 582 | 630 | 659 |
| Physicians | 580 | 730 | 776 | 818 |
| Financial managers | 701 | 828 | 894 | 939 |
| Teachers: preschool and kindergarten | 425 | 555 | 598 | 636 |
| Automotive mechanics | 757 | 861 | 923 | 969 |
| Electricians | 548 | 652 | 706 | 748 |
| FASTEST GROWING | | | | |
| Home health aides | 287 | 512 | 550 | 582 |
| Systems analysts and computer scientists | 463 | 769 | 829 | 864 |
| Personal and home care aides | 103 | 170 | 183 | 194 |
| Medical assistants | 165 | 268 | 287 | 306 |
| Human services workers | 145 | 231 | 249 | 264 |
| Radiologic technologists and technicians | 149 | 234 | 252 | 268 |
| Medical secretaries | 232 | 363 | 390 | 415 |
| Psychologists | 125 | 193 | 204 | 214 |
| Travel agents | 132 | 199 | 214 | 224 |
| Correction officers | 230 | 342 | 372 | 400 |
| Flight attendants | 101 | 146 | 159 | 168 |
| Computer programmers | 565 | 811 | 882 | 923 |
| Management analysts | 151 | 218 | 230 | 240 |
| Child care workers | 725 | 1,027 | 1,078 | 1,123 |
| FASTEST DECLINING | | | | |
| Electronic equipment assemblers, precision | 171 | 78 | 90 | 92 |
| Child care workers, private household | 314 | 176 | 190 | 200 |
| Cleaners and servants, private household | 411 | 287 | 310 | 326 |
| Switchboard operators | 246 | 175 | 189 | 198 |
| Typists and word processors | 972 | 805 | 869 | 916 |

*Source: 1993 Statistical Abstract, Table No. 645*

*Demographics (cont'd)*

## Civilian Labor Force Status by Selected Metropolitan Area

| Metropolitan Areas Ranked by Labor Force Size, 1991 | Total Employed | Total Unemployed | Unemployment Rate |
|---|---|---|---|
| U.S. TOTAL | 116,877.0 | 8,426.0 | 6.7 |
| Los Angeles-Long Beach, CA | 4,141.0 | 362.0 | 8.0 |
| New York, NY | 3,643.5 | 319.2 | 8.1 |
| Chicago, IL | 3,025.5 | 224.8 | 6.9 |
| Philadelphia, PA-NJ | 2,274.7 | 156.5 | 6.4 |
| Washington, DC-MD-VA | 2,128.7 | 100.3 | 4.5 |
| Detroit, MI | 1,918.6 | 195.9 | 9.3 |
| Houston, TX | 1,656.9 | 99.1 | 5.6 |
| Boston, MA | 1,422.5 | 119.1 | 7.7 |
| Atlanta, GA | 1,434.1 | 71.0 | 4.7 |
| Dallas, TX | 1,353.6 | 86.3 | 6.0 |
| Minneapolis-St. Paul, MN-WI | 1,354.7 | 65.4 | 4.6 |
| Nassau-Suffolk, NY | 1,283.7 | 82.4 | 6.0 |
| Anaheim-Santa Ana,CA | 1,281.5 | 64.3 | 4.8 |
| St. Louis, MO-IL | 1,193.0 | 87.6 | 6.8 |
| Baltimore, MD | 1,132.6 | 79.6 | 6.6 |
| San Diego, CA | 1,104.2 | 72.1 | 6.1 |
| Seattle, WA | 1,058.9 | 53.7 | 4.8 |
| Oakland, CA | 1,039.3 | 59.2 | 5.4 |
| Riverside-San Bernardino, CA | 988.1 | 100.3 | 9.2 |
| Phoenix, AZ | 1,003.5 | 51.4 | 4.9 |
| Tampa-St. Petersburg-Clearwater, FL | 955.2 | 65.3 | 6.4 |
| Pittsburgh, PA | 944.5 | 60.3 | 6.0 |
| Miami-Hialeah, FL | 878.6 | 83.5 | 8.7 |
| Cleveland, OH | 892.1 | 51.7 | 5.5 |
| Newark, NJ | 873.7 | 64.6 | 6.9 |
| Denver, CO | 851.6 | 41.1 | 4.6 |
| San Francisco, CA | 827.7 | 41.7 | 4.8 |
| Kansas City, MO-Kansas City, KS | 812.1 | 48.5 | 5.6 |
| San Jose, CA | 770.1 | 44.8 | 5.5 |
| Cincinnati, OH-KY-IN | 746.7 | 39.2 | 5.0 |
| Sacramento, CA | 715.9 | 48.9 | 6.4 |
| Milwaukee, WI | 719.4 | 35.2 | 4.7 |
| Columbus, OH | 709.3 | 34.5 | 4.6 |
| Fort Worth-Arlington, TX | 689.7 | 47.8 | 6.5 |
| Portland, OR | 666.0 | 32.9 | 4.7 |
| Bergen-Passaic, NJ | 647.9 | 42.9 | 6.2 |
| Indianapolis, IN | 651.2 | 31.8 | 4.7 |
| Fort Lauderdale-Hollywood-Pompano Beach, FL | 623.7 | 49.8 | 7.4 |
| Norfolk-Virginia Beach-Newport News, VA | 609.2 | 39.2 | 6.1 |
| Charlotte-Gastonia-Rockhill, NC-SC | 610.4 | 33.9 | 5.3 |
| Orlando, FL | 600.0 | 41.5 | 6.5 |
| San Antonio, TX | 566.9 | 39.8 | 6.6 |
| Middlesex-Somerset-Hunterdon, NJ | 559.8 | 30.4 | 5.2 |
| New Orleans, LA | 550.6 | 35.7 | 6.1 |
| Nashville, TN | 502.1 | 27.1 | 5.1 |
| Greensboro-Winston-Salem-High Point, NC | 494.5 | 26.4 | 5.1 |
| Salt Lake City-Ogden, UT | 495.2 | 24.1 | 4.6 |
| Louisville, KY-IN | 481.7 | 31.3 | 6.1 |
| Rochester, NY | 487.4 | 25.5 | 5.0 |
| Mommouth-Ocean, NJ | 460.6 | 31.7 | 6.4 |

*Source: 1993 Statistical Abstract, Table No. 627*

*Demographics (cont'd)*

## Average Hourly and Weekly Earnings in Current Dollars by Private Industry Group

| Private Industry Group | 1970 | 1980 | 1985 | 1989 | 1990 | 1992 |
|---|---|---|---|---|---|---|
| AVERAGE HOURLY EARNINGS | 3.23 | 6.66 | 8.57 | 9.66 | 10.02 | 10.59 |
| Manufacturing | 3.35 | 7.27 | 9.54 | 10.48 | 10.83 | 11.45 |
| Mining | 3.85 | 9.17 | 11.98 | 13.26 | 13.69 | 14.57 |
| Construction | 5.24 | 9.94 | 12.32 | 13.54 | 13.78 | 14.11 |
| Transportation, public utilities | 3.85 | 8.87 | 11.40 | 12.60 | 12.96 | 13.49 |
| Wholesale trade | 3.43 | 6.95 | 9.15 | 10.39 | 10.79 | 11.40 |
| Retail trade | 2.44 | 4.88 | 5.94 | 6.53 | 6.76 | 7.14 |
| Finance, insurance, real estate | 3.07 | 5.79 | 7.94 | 9.53 | 9.97 | 10.82 |
| Services | 2.81 | 5.85 | 7.90 | 9.38 | 9.83 | 10.54 |
| AVERAGE WEEKLY EARNINGS | 120.00 | 235.00 | 299.00 | 334.00 | 346.00 | 364.00 |
| Manufacturing | 133.00 | 289.00 | 386.00 | 430.00 | 442.00 | 469.00 |
| Mining | 164.00 | 397.00 | 520.00 | 570.00 | 604.00 | 638.00 |
| Construction | 195.00 | 368.00 | 464.00 | 513.00 | 526.00 | 536.00 |
| Transportation, public utilities | 156.00 | 351.00 | 450.00 | 490.00 | 504.00 | 523.00 |
| Wholesale trade | 137.00 | 267.00 | 351.00 | 395.00 | 411.00 | 435.00 |
| Retail trade | 82.00 | 147.00 | 175.00 | 189.00 | 195.00 | 206.00 |
| Finance, insurance, real estate | 113.00 | 210.00 | 289.00 | 341.00 | 357.00 | 387.00 |
| Services | 97.00 | 191.00 | 257.00 | 306.00 | 320.00 | 343.00 |

*Source: 1993 Statistical Abstract, Table No. 667*

## The Top Reference Sources

*Martindale-Hubbell Law Directory*
Reed, $645
(800) 521-8110

More than 800,000 lawyers are profiled in this 27-volume set.

In addition to providing valuable information on the background of all lawyers, it provides extensive cross-referencing to make it easier to find specialists in almost any area of the law.

Martindale-Hubbell is updated annually. The hard-cover version is available in most libraries.

 **FAX** **Time Spent at Work and Leisure.** Request #771. See p. xi for instructions.

Tables of gross average weekly earnings and hours worked for selected non-manufacturing and manufacturing industries.

# Unemployment

## Unemployed Persons by Sex and Reason (thousands)

| Sex & Reason Unemployed | 1983 | 1984 | 1985 | 1986 | 1987 | 1988 | 1989 | 1990 | 1992 |
|---|---|---|---|---|---|---|---|---|---|
| MALE | 6,260 | 4,744 | 4,521 | 4,530 | 4,101 | 3,655 | 3,525 | 3,799 | 5,380 |
| Job losers | 4,331 | 2,976 | 2,749 | 2,725 | 2,432 | 2,078 | 1,975 | 2,208 | 3,518 |
| Job leavers | 386 | 375 | 409 | 520 | 494 | 503 | 495 | 511 | 479 |
| Re-entrants | 953 | 867 | 876 | 805 | 761 | 697 | 726 | 782 | 950 |
| New entrants | 589 | 526 | 487 | 480 | 413 | 376 | 328 | 298 | 433 |
| FEMALE | 4,457 | 3,794 | 3,791 | 3,707 | 3,324 | 3,046 | 3,003 | 3,075 | 4,005 |
| Job losers | 1,926 | 1,445 | 1,390 | 1,308 | 1,134 | 1,014 | 1,008 | 1,114 | 1,773 |
| Job leavers | 444 | 449 | 468 | 494 | 471 | 480 | 529 | 503 | 496 |
| Re-entrants | 1,459 | 1,317 | 1,380 | 1,355 | 1,213 | 1,112 | 1,117 | 1,101 | 1,278 |
| New entrants | 627 | 584 | 552 | 549 | 506 | 440 | 349 | 357 | 457 |

## Unemployed Persons by Duration of Unemployment

| Sex & Reason Unemployed | Total Unemployed (thousands) | Less Than 5 Weeks Unemployed (%) | 5 to 14 Weeks Unemployed (%) | 15 Weeks or More Unemployed (%) |
|---|---|---|---|---|
| MALE | 5,380 | 31.7 | 29.2 | 39.0 |
| Job losers | 3,518 | 27.0 | 28.5 | 44.5 |
| Job leavers | 479 | 37.4 | 30.1 | 32.6 |
| Re-entrants | 950 | 39.9 | 30.2 | 29.9 |
| New entrants | 433 | 46.2 | 31.9 | 21.9 |
| FEMALE | 4,005 | 39.0 | 29.7 | 31.3 |
| Job losers | 1,793 | 28.6 | 28.3 | 43.2 |
| Job leavers | 496 | 45.2 | 29.6 | 25.2 |
| Re-entrants | 1,278 | 47.5 | 31.3 | 21.3 |
| New entrants | 457 | 49.2 | 30.9 | 19.9 |

## Unemployment Rates by Industry (%)

| Industry | 1975 | 1980 | 1985 | 1988 | 1989 | 1990 | 1992 |
|---|---|---|---|---|---|---|---|
| ALL UNEMPLOYED | 8.5 | 7.1 | 7.2 | 5.5 | 5.3 | 5.5 | 7.4 |
| Agriculture | 10.4 | 11.0 | 13.2 | 10.6 | 9.6 | 9.7 | 12.3 |
| Mining | 4.1 | 6.4 | 9.5 | 7.9 | 5.8 | 4.8 | 7.9 |
| Construction | 18.0 | 14.1 | 13.1 | 10.6 | 10.0 | 11.1 | 16.7 |
| Manufacturing | 10.9 | 8.5 | 7.7 | 5.3 | 5.1 | 5.8 | 7.8 |
| Transportation and public utilities | 5.6 | 4.9 | 5.1 | 3.9 | 3.9 | 3.8 | 5.5 |
| Wholesale and retail trade | 8.7 | 7.4 | 7.6 | 6.2 | 6.0 | 6.4 | 8.4 |
| Finance, insurance, and real estate | 4.9 | 3.4 | 3.5 | 3.0 | 3.1 | 3.0 | 4.5 |
| Services | 7.1 | 5.9 | 6.2 | 4.9 | 4.8 | 5.0 | 6.5 |
| Government | 4.1 | 4.1 | 3.9 | 2.8 | 2.7 | 2.6 | 3.5 |

*Source: 1993 Statistical Abstract, Table Nos. 653, 655*

*Unemployment (cont'd)*

## Unemployment Rates by Sex

| Industry | Male 1980 | Male 1992 | Female 1980 | Female 1992 |
|---|---|---|---|---|
| ALL UNEMPLOYED | 6.9 | 7.8 | 7.4 | 6.9 |
| Agriculture | 9.7 | 12.1 | 15.1 | 13.8 |
| Mining | 6.7 | 8.3 | 4.5 | 5.7 |
| Construction | 14.6 | 17.2 | 8.9 | 11.0 |
| Manufacturing | 7.4 | 7.2 | 10.8 | 8.8 |
| Transportation and public utilities | 5.1 | 5.5 | 4.4 | 4.7 |
| Wholesale and retail trade | 6.6 | 8.4 | 8.3 | 9.1 |
| Finance, insurance, and real estate | 3.2 | 4.5 | 3.5 | 4.6 |
| Services | 6.3 | 6.5 | 5.8 | 5.9 |
| Government | 3.9 | 3.5 | 4.3 | 3.1 |

*Source: 1993 Statistical Abstract, Table Nos. 653, 655*

# Consumer Trends

## Average Annual Consumer Expenditures by Household ($ thousands)

| Item | 1984 | 1985 | 1988 | 1989 | 1991 | Avg. Annual % Change 1984-91 | Avg. Annual % Change 1990-91 |
|---|---|---|---|---|---|---|---|
| TOTAL EXPENDITURES | 21,975 | 23,490 | 25,892 | 27,810 | 29,614 | 4 | 4 |
| Food, total | 3,290 | 3,477 | 3,748 | 4,152 | 4,271 | 4 | -1 |
| Food at home, total | 1,970 | 2,037 | 2,136 | 2,390 | 2,651 | 4 | 7 |
| Cereal and bakery products | 262 | 283 | 312 | 359 | 404 | 6 | 10 |
| Meats, poultry, fish, and eggs | 586 | 579 | 551 | 611 | 708 | 3 | 6 |
| Dairy products | 253 | 266 | 274 | 304 | 294 | 2 | >.5 |
| Fruits and vegetables | 313 | 322 | 373 | 408 | 429 | 5 | 5 |
| Other food at home | 556 | 585 | 625 | 708 | 815 | 5 | 9 |
| Food away from home | 1,320 | 1,441 | 1,612 | 1,762 | 1,620 | 5 | -11 |
| Alcoholic beverages | 275 | 306 | 269 | 284 | 297 | 1 | 1 |
| Tobacco products and smoking supplies | 228 | 219 | 242 | 261 | 276 | 3 | 1 |
| Housing, total | 6,674 | 7,087 | 8,079 | 8,609 | 9,252 | 5 | 6 |
| Shelter | 3,489 | 3,833 | 4,493 | 4,835 | 5,191 | 6 | 7 |
| Fuels, utilities, and public services | 1,638 | 1,648 | 1,747 | 1,835 | 1,990 | 3 | 5 |
| Household operations and furnishings | 1,241 | 1,282 | 1,477 | 1,546 | 1,648 | 4 | 5 |
| Housekeeping supplies | 307 | 325 | 361 | 394 | 424 | 5 | 4 |
| Apparel and services | 1,319 | 1,420 | 1,489 | 1,582 | 1,735 | 4 | 7 |
| Transportation, total | 4,304 | 4,587 | 5,093 | 5,187 | 5,151 | 3 | 1 |
| Vehicles | 1,813 | 2,043 | 2,361 | 2,291 | 2,111 | 2 | -1 |
| Gasoline and motor oil | 1,058 | 1,035 | 932 | 985 | 995 | -1 | -5 |
| Other transportation | 1,433 | 1,509 | 1,800 | 1,911 | 2,045 | 5 | 5 |
| Health care | 1,049 | 1,108 | 1,298 | 1,407 | 1,554 | 6 | 5 |
| Life insurance | 300 | 278 | 314 | 346 | 356 | 2 | 3 |
| Pensions and Social Security | 1,598 | 1,738 | 1,935 | 2,125 | 2,431 | 6 | 8 |
| Other expenditures | 2,936 | 3,269 | 3,426 | 3,857 | 4,291 | 5 | 7 |

*Source: 1993 Statistical Abstract, Table No. 709*

*Consumer Trends (cont'd)*

## Average Annual Consumer Expenditures for Selected Metropolitan Statistical Areas, 1991

| Metropolitan Statistical Area | Total Expendi- tures | Food | Total Housing | Shelter | Apparel & Services | Total Transpor- tation | Health Care |
|---|---|---|---|---|---|---|---|
| Anchorage, AK | 43,991 | 5,577 | 13,502 | 8,461 | 2,273 | 7,531 | 1,730 |
| Atlanta, GA | 34,163 | 4,187 | 10,788 | 6,051 | 2,306 | 5,807 | 1,778 |
| Baltimore, MD | 33,208 | 4,512 | 11,065 | 6,900 | 1,938 | 5,498 | 1,401 |
| Boston-Lawrence-Salem, MA-NH | 30,835 | 4,183 | 11,341 | 7,582 | 1,855 | 4,696 | 1,498 |
| Buffalo-Niagara Falls, NY | 25,119 | 4,556 | 8,006 | 4,569 | 1,351 | 4,521 | 1,149 |
| Chicago-Gary-Lake County, IL-IN-WI | 32,568 | 5,109 | 10,536 | 6,372 | 2,306 | 4,955 | 1,439 |
| Cincinnati-Hamilton, OH-KY-IN | 27,781 | 4,688 | 8,180 | 4,510 | 1,825 | 4,857 | 1,583 |
| Cleveland-Akron-Lorain, OH | 26,960 | 4,233 | 7,754 | 3,982 | 2,222 | 4,555 | 1,430 |
| Dallas-Fort Worth, TX | 33,500 | 4,741 | 10,097 | 5,358 | 1,999 | 6,413 | 1,543 |
| Detroit-Ann Arbor, MI | 29,732 | 4,123 | 9,698 | 5,687 | 1,573 | 5,748 | 1,304 |
| Honolulu, HI | 36,394 | 5,634 | 11,196 | 7,432 | 1,728 | 6,052 | 1,623 |
| Houston-Galveston-Brazoria, TX | 32,298 | 4,681 | 9,094 | 4,730 | 2,063 | 6,692 | 1,458 |
| Kansas City, MO-Kansas City, KS | 28,189 | 4,427 | 8,679 | 4,776 | 1,485 | 4,661 | 1,964 |
| Los Angeles-Long Beach, Ca | 35,673 | 5,044 | 12,964 | 7,977 | 2,456 | 5,372 | 1,485 |
| Miami-Fort Lauderdale, FL | 32,053 | 5,193 | 10,117 | 5,931 | 1,822 | 5,788 | 1,686 |
| Milwaukee, WI | 27,843 | 4,091 | 9,083 | 5,507 | 1,652 | 4,622 | 1,228 |
| Minneapolis-St. Paul, MN-WI | 34,801 | 4,883 | 10,519 | 6,370 | 1,942 | 5,665 | 1,438 |
| NY-Northern NJ-Long Island, NY-NJ-CT | 34,583 | 5,131 | 12,121 | 7,770 | 2,366 | 4,873 | 1,533 |
| Phil.-Wilmington-Trenton, PA-NJ-DE-MD | 31,795 | 4,526 | 10,350 | 5,710 | 2,103 | 4,832 | 1,648 |
| Pittsburgh-Beaver Valley, PA | 28,626 | 4,458 | 9,104 | 4,254 | 1,886 | 4,699 | 1,290 |
| Portland-Vancouver, OR-WA-CMSA | 29,228 | 4,081 | 8,974 | 5,468 | 1,447 | 5,275 | 1,318 |
| San Diego, CA | 32,983 | 4,457 | 11,365 | 7,691 | 1,808 | 6,076 | 1,178 |
| San Francisco-Oakland-San Jose, CA | 39,707 | 5,284 | 13,883 | 9,417 | 2,413 | 6,116 | 1,536 |
| Seattle-Tacoma, WA | 35,086 | 4,599 | 11,523 | 7,235 | 1,768 | 5,701 | 1,646 |
| St. Louis-East St. Louis-Alton, MO-IL | 27,743 | 3,692 | 8,557 | 4,339 | 1,385 | 4,822 | 1,416 |
| Washington, DC-MD-VA | 38,560 | 4,752 | 12,322 | 7,891 | 2,562 | 6,192 | 1,962 |

*Source: 1993 Statistical Abstract, Table No. 710*

*Compuserve's Business Database Plus allows access to full text from articles in 450+ business and trade publications. GO BUSDB.*

# Per Capita Personal Income

## Average Annual Pay by State

| State | 1990 Avg. Annual Pay | 1991 Avg. Annual Pay | 1992 Avg. Annual Pay | % Change 1990-91 | % Change 1991-92 |
|---|---|---|---|---|---|
| U.S. TOTAL | 23,602 | 24,578 | 25,903 | 4.1 | 5.4 |
| AK | 29,946 | 30,830 | 31,825 | 2.9 | 3.2 |
| AL | 20,468 | 21,287 | 22,340 | 4.0 | 4.9 |
| AR | 18,204 | 19,008 | 20,108 | 4.4 | 5.8 |
| AZ | 21,443 | 22,207 | 23,161 | 3.6 | 4.3 |
| CA | 26,180 | 27,513 | 28,934 | 5.0 | 5.2 |
| CO | 22,908 | 23,981 | 25,040 | 4.7 | 4.4 |
| CT | 28,995 | 30,689 | 32,587 | 5.8 | 6.2 |
| DC | 33,717 | 35,570 | 37,971 | 5.5 | 6.7 |
| DE | 24,423 | 25,647 | 26,596 | 5.0 | 3.7 |
| FL | 21,032 | 21,992 | 23,144 | 4.6 | 5.2 |
| GA | 22,114 | 23,165 | 24,373 | 4.7 | 5.2 |
| HI | 23,167 | 24,104 | 25,613 | 4.0 | 6.3 |
| IA | 19,224 | 19,810 | 20,937 | 3.0 | 5.7 |
| ID | 18,991 | 19,688 | 20,649 | 3.7 | 4.9 |
| IL | 25,312 | 26,317 | 27,910 | 3.9 | 6.1 |
| IN | 21,699 | 22,522 | 23,570 | 3.8 | 4.7 |
| KS | 20,238 | 21,002 | 21,982 | 3.8 | 4.7 |
| KY | 19,947 | 20,730 | 21,858 | 3.9 | 5.4 |
| LA | 20,646 | 21,503 | 22,340 | 4.1 | 3.9 |
| MA | 26,689 | 28,041 | 29,664 | 5.0 | 5.8 |
| MD | 24,730 | 25,962 | 27,145 | 5.0 | 4.6 |
| ME | 20,154 | 20,870 | 21,808 | 3.6 | 4.5 |
| MI | 25,376 | 26,125 | 27,463 | 3.0 | 5.1 |
| MN | 23,126 | 23,962 | 25,315 | 3.6 | 5.6 |
| MO | 21,716 | 22,574 | 23,550 | 3.9 | 4.3 |
| MS | 17,718 | 18,411 | 19,237 | 3.9 | 4.5 |
| MT | 17,895 | 18,648 | 19,378 | 4.2 | 3.9 |
| NC | 20,220 | 21,095 | 22,248 | 4.3 | 5.5 |
| ND | 17,626 | 18,132 | 18,945 | 2.9 | 4.5 |
| NE | 18,577 | 19,372 | 20,355 | 4.3 | 5.1 |
| NH | 22,609 | 23,600 | 24,925 | 4.4 | 5.6 |
| NJ | 28,449 | 29,991 | 32,125 | 5.4 | 7.1 |
| NM | 19,347 | 20,272 | 21,051 | 4.8 | 3.8 |
| NV | 22,358 | 23,083 | 24,743 | 3.2 | 7.2 |
| NY | 28,873 | 30,011 | 32,399 | 3.9 | 8.0 |
| OH | 22,843 | 23,602 | 24,846 | 3.3 | 5.3 |
| OK | 20,288 | 20,968 | 21,699 | 3.3 | 3.5 |
| OR | 21,332 | 22,338 | 23,514 | 4.8 | 5.3 |
| PA | 23,457 | 24,393 | 25,785 | 4.0 | 5.7 |
| RI | 22,388 | 23,082 | 24,315 | 3.1 | 5.3 |
| SC | 19,669 | 20,439 | 21,423 | 3.9 | 4.8 |
| SD | 16,430 | 17,143 | 18,016 | 4.3 | 5.1 |
| TN | 20,611 | 21,541 | 22,807 | 4.5 | 5.9 |
| TX | 22,700 | 23,760 | 25,080 | 4.7 | 5.6 |
| UT | 20,074 | 20,874 | 21,976 | 4.0 | 5.3 |
| VA | 22,750 | 23,805 | 24,937 | 4.6 | 4.8 |
| VT | 20,532 | 21,355 | 22,347 | 4.0 | 4.6 |
| WA | 22,646 | 23,942 | 25,553 | 5.7 | 6.7 |
| WI | 21,101 | 21,838 | 23,022 | 3.5 | 5.4 |
| WV | 20,715 | 21,356 | 22,169 | 3.1 | 3.8 |
| WY | 20,049 | 20,591 | 21,215 | 2.7 | 3.0 |

*Source: 1993 Statistical Abstract, Table No. 669*

# Taxes

**Real Family Income After Taxes, 1980 to 1993 ($)**

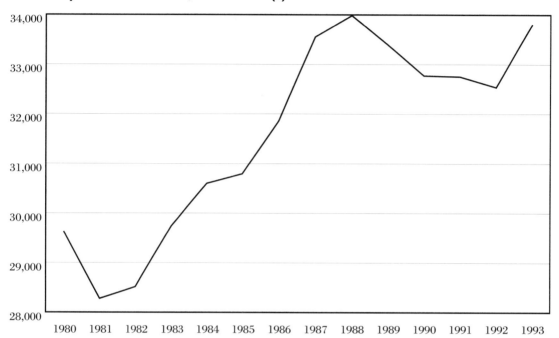

**Typical American Family Budget, 1993**

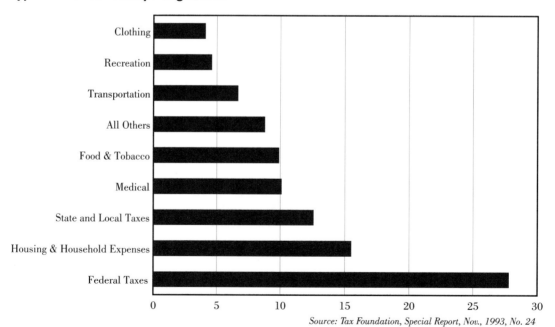

*Source: Tax Foundation, Special Report, Nov., 1993, No. 24*

# State Taxes

## Major State Taxes and Rates as of January, 1994

| State | Corporate (%) | Individual (%) | General Sales and Use Tax (%) | Gasoline Tax (cents per gallon) | Cigarette Tax (cents per pack of 20) |
|---|---|---|---|---|---|
| Alabama | 5.0 | 2 to 5 | 4 | 16 | 16.5 |
| Alaska | 1 to 9.4 | none | none | 8 | 29 |
| Arizona | 9.3 | 3.8 to 7 | 5 | 18 | 18 |
| Arkansas | 1 to 6.5 | 1 to 7 | 4.5 | 18.5 | 31.5 |
| California | 9.3 | 1 to 11 | 6 | 17 | 37 |
| Colorado | 5.0 | 5 | 3 | 22 | 20 |
| Connecticut | 11.5 | 4.5 | 6 | 29 | 47 |
| Delaware | 8.7 | 3.2 to 7.7 | none | 22 | 24 |
| DC | 10.0 | 6 to 9.5 | 6 | 20 | 65 |
| Florida | 5.5 | none | 6 | 12.1 to 16.6 | 33.9 |
| Georgia | 6.0 | 1 to 6 | 5 to 6 | 7.5 | 12 |
| Hawaii | 4.4 to 6.4 | 2 to 10 | 4 | 16 | 60 |
| Idaho | 8.0 | 2 to 8.2 | 5 | 22 | 18 |
| Illinois | 4.8 | 3 | 6.25 | 19 | 44 |
| Indiana | 3.4 | 3.4 | 5 | 15 | 15.5 |
| Iowa | 6 to 12 | .4 to 9.98 | 5 | 20 | 36 |
| Kansas | 4.0 | 4.4 to 7.75 | 4.9 | 18 | 24 |
| Kentucky | 4 to 8.25 | 2 to 6 | 6 | 15 | 3 |
| Louisiana | 4 to 8 | 2 to 6 | 4 | 20 | 20 |
| Maine | 3.5 to 8.93 | 2 to 8.5 | 6 | 19 | 37 |
| Maryland | 7.0 | 2 to 6 | 5 | 23.5 | 36 |
| Massachusetts | 9.5 | 5.95 | 5 | 21 | 51 |
| Michigan | 0.0 to 2.35 | 4.6 | 4 | 15 | 25 |
| Minnesota | 9.8 | 6 to 8.5 | 6.5 | 20 | 48 |
| Mississippi | 3 to 5 | 3 to 5 | 7 | 18 | 18 |
| Missouri | 6.25 | 1.5 to 6 | 4.225 | 13 | 17 |
| Montana | 6.75 | 2 to 11 | none | 24 | 18 |
| Nebraska | 5.58 to 7.81 | 2.62 to 6.99 | 5 | 26 | 37 |
| Nevada | none | none | 6.5 to 7 | 23 | 35 |
| New Hampshire | 0.0 to 7.5 | 5 | none | 18 | 25 |
| New Jersey | 9.0 | 2 to 7 | 6 | 10.5 | 40 |
| New Mexico | 4.8 to 7.6 | 1.8 to 8.5 | 5 | 22 | 21 |
| New York | 9.0 | 4 to 7.875 | 4 | 8 | 56 |
| North Carolina | 7.75 | 6 to 7.75 | 4 | 22 | 5 |
| North Dakota | 3 to 10.5 | 14.70* | 5 | 18 | 44 |
| Ohio | 5.1 to 8.9 | .743 to 7.5 | 5 | 22 | 24 |
| Oklahoma | 6.0 | .5 to 7 | 4.5 | 17 | 23 |
| Oregon | 6.6 | 5 to 9 | none | 24 | 38 |
| Pennsylvania | 12.25 | 2.95 | 6 | 12 | 31 |
| Rhode Island | 9.0 | 27.5* | 7 | 28 | 44 |
| South Carolina | 5.0 | 2.5 to 7 | 5 | 16 | 7 |
| South Dakota | none | none | 4 | 18 | 23 |
| Tennessee | 6.0 | 6 | 6 | 22.4 | 13 |
| Texas | none | none | 6.25 | 20 | 41 |
| Utah | 5.0 | 2.55 to 7.2 | 6 | 19.5 | 26.5 |
| Vermont | 5.5 to 8.25 | 25* | 5 | 15 | 20 |
| Virginia | 6.0 | 2 to 5.75 | 3.5 | 17.5 | 2.5 |
| Washington | none | none | 6.5 | 23 | 54 |
| West Virginia | 9.08 | 3 to 6.5 | 6 | 15.5 | 17 |
| Wisconsin | 7.9 | 4.9 to 6.93 | 5 | 23.2 | 38 |
| Wyoming | none | none | 4 | 9 | 12 |

*of federal income tax liability

Source: Tax Foundation, Special Report, Jan., 1994

*State Taxes (cont'd)*

# Per Capita Federal Tax Burden by State 1993

| State | Per Capita Burden ($) | Per Capita Federal Spending | Per Capita State Rank |
|---|---|---|---|
| U.S. TOTAL | 4,360 | - | - |
| Alabama | 3,348 | 14 | 41 |
| Alaska | 5,502 | 1 | 3 |
| Arizona | 3,488 | 31 | 37 |
| Arkansas | 3,189 | 34 | 46 |
| California | 4,698 | 21 | 11 |
| Colorado | 4,272 | 13 | 19 |
| Connecticut | 6,647 | 15 | 1 |
| Delaware | 5,463 | 42 | 4 |
| DC | 5,826 | NA | 3 |
| Florida | 4,245 | 18 | 20 |
| Georgia | 3,795 | 33 | 32 |
| Hawaii | 4,880 | 5 | 9 |
| Idaho | 3,249 | 27 | 45 |
| Illinois | 5,018 | 44 | 8 |
| Indiana | 3,868 | 50 | 30 |
| Iowa | 3,868 | 36 | 31 |
| Kansas | 4,198 | 26 | 21 |
| Kentucky | 3,316 | 35 | 43 |
| Louisiana | 3,325 | 30 | 42 |
| Maine | 3,593 | 8 | 35 |
| Maryland | 5,120 | 2 | 7 |
| Massachusetts | 5,316 | 6 | 5 |
| Michigan | 4,388 | 46 | 18 |
| Minnesota | 4,458 | 48 | 16 |
| Mississippi | 2,703 | 9 | 50 |
| Missouri | 3,984 | 11 | 27 |
| Montana | 3,413 | 12 | 40 |
| Nebraska | 4,016 | 32 | 26 |
| Nevada | 4,519 | 37 | 13 |
| New Hampshire | 4,757 | 43 | 10 |
| New Jersey | 6,302 | 29 | 2 |
| New Mexico | 3,153 | 3 | 47 |
| New York | 5,290 | 20 | 6 |
| North Carolina | 3,618 | 47 | 34 |
| North Dakota | 3,516 | 7 | 36 |
| Ohio | 4,138 | 39 | 22 |
| Oklahoma | 3,462 | 25 | 38 |
| Oregon | 4,036 | 40 | 25 |
| Pennsylvania | 4,479 | 19 | 14 |
| Rhode Island | 4,464 | 10 | 15 |
| South Carolina | 3,288 | 28 | 44 |
| South Dakota | 3,457 | 16 | 39 |
| Tennessee | 3,655 | 23 | 33 |
| Texas | 3,926 | 38 | 28 |
| Utah | 3,080 | 41 | 48 |
| Vermont | 3,911 | 45 | 29 |
| Virginia | 4,413 | 4 | 17 |
| Washington | 4,666 | 17 | 12 |
| West Virginia | 3,078 | 24 | 49 |
| Wisconsin | 4,103 | 49 | 24 |
| Wyoming | 4,112 | 22 | 23 |

*Source: Tax Foundation, Special Report, May, 1993*

# Gross National Product

THE GROSS NATIONAL PRODUCT (GNP) is the total dollar value of all final goods and services produced for consumption in society during a particular time period. Its rise or fall thus measures economic activity based on the labor and production output within a country. The figures used to assemble data include the manufacture of tangible goods such as cars, furniture, and bread, and the provision of services used in daily living such as education, health care, and auto repair. Intermediate services used in the production of the final product are not separated since they are reflected in the final price of the goods or service. The GNP does include allowances for depreciation and indirect business taxes such as sales and property.

The Gross Domestic Product (GDP) measures output generated through production by labor and property which is physically located within the confines of a country. It excludes such factors as income earned by U.S. citizens working abroad, but does include factors such as the rental value of owner-occupied housing. In December, 1991, the Bureau of Economic Analysis began using the GDP rather than the GNP as the primary measure of United States production. This figure facilitates comparisons between the United States and other countries, since it is the standard used in international guidelines for economic accounting.

# Money Supply, Yield Curve

PAPER MONEY AND COINS WERE originally used as the only mediums of exchange, but the sophistication of financial needs have expanded the types of financial instruments used today. In order to monitor the money supply, the Federal Reserve System, the nation's central bank and controller of the monetary policy of the country, uses four measures:

- M1 is the base measurement of the money supply and includes currency, coins, demand deposits, travelers checks from non-bank issuers, and other checkable deposits.

- M2 is equal to M1 plus overnight repurchase agreements issued by commercial banks, overnight Eurodollars, money market mutual funds, money market deposit accounts, savings accounts, time deposits less than $100,000.

- M3 is M2 plus institutionally held money-market funds, term re-purchase agreements, term Eurodollars, and large time-deposits.

- L, the fourth measure, is equal to M3 plus Treasury bills, commercial paper, bankers acceptances, and very liquid assets such as savings bonds.

## Recommended Resource

*Irwin Business & Investment Almanac*
Irwin Professional Publishing, $75
(800) 634-3966

---

## The Top Reference Sources

*The Vest-Pocket MBA*
Prentice Hall, $11.95
(212) 698-7000

This handy reference contains all the formulas, guidelines, ratios, and rules of thumb needed to evaluate and solve dozens of business problems. The book contains scores of tables, graphs, and charts.

Topics include balance sheet analysis, statistics, break even, working capital, budgeting techniques, margin analysis, and more.

---

**FAX** **Worldwide Gross Domestic Product.** Request #550. See p. xi for instructions.

Table of the gross domestic product for 24 major countries.

# Economic Indicators

ECONOMIC INDICATORS ARE FIGURES used by fore-
casters to predict changes in market economics.
There are eleven leading economic indicators used
to track developments in areas which together predict changes in the overall level of the economy.
These indicators are:

- The length of the average work week of production
  workers in manufacturing settings;

- The average weekly state unemployment insurance claims;

- New orders for consumer goods and materials
  based on 1982 dollars;

- Vendor performance or percentage of companies
  receiving slower deliveries from suppliers;

- Contracts and orders for equipment;

- Index of new private housing units;

- Changes in unfulfilled orders by manufacturers of
  durable goods;

- Changes in sensitive materials prices;

- Index of S&P 500 common stock prices;

- Money supply;

- Index of consumer expectations.

## Producer Price Index

The Producer Price Index (PPI) measures prices
at the wholesale level only. The PPI is viewed as a
leading indicator of inflation.

## Consumer Price Index

The Consumer Price Index (CPI) is also a leading economic indicator. Although changes are
reported from month to month, the more meaningful
analysis is found in charting the percent change
from the same month in the prior year.

Other economic indicators include the index of
industrial materials prices, the Dow Jones Commodity Spot Price Index, Futures Price Index, the
Employment Cost Index, and the Hourly Compensation Index or the Unit Labor Cost Index as a measure
of the change in cost to the labor factor of production. Long-term interest rates are also used to measure changes in the cost of the capital factor of
production.

## The Conference Board

Noted for its carefully managed research program, the Conference Board generates the monthly
"Consumer Confidence Survey" designated by the
Department of Commerce as a leading economic
indicator and predictor of recessions and recovery.

Other services offered consist of timely publications, data collection services for marketing executives, demographic information services, periodic
consumer surveys, and over 100 annual conferences
and seminars.

## Recommended Resources

The Conference Board
845 Third Ave.
New York, NY 10022
(212) 759-0900 or (800) 872-6273

*Economic Indicators*
Council of Economic Advisors, $33/year
Superintendent of Documents
Government Printing Office
Washington, DC 20402
(202) 783-3238
*Monthly publication of national and international
economic statistics*

---

## The Top Reference Sources

*The Conference Board*
845 Third Ave.
New York, NY 10022
(212) 759-0900 or (800) 872-6273

The Conference Board is a nonpartisan, non-
advocacy organization which publishes 20 special
reports and more than 50 surveys a year. The Con-

ference Board is supported by a membership of
more than 2,000 organizations.

The Board offers monthly and quarterly surveys on consumer confidence and other macro-
economic topics, as well as special reports that
discuss these topics in depth.

The Board also sponsors conferences and seminars of interest to executives and economists.

# Consumer Price Index

THE CONSUMER PRICE INDEX (CPI) is a way of tracking the cost of living. It is computed based on prices for the "market basket" of necessities including housing, food and beverages, transportation, apparel, entertainment, medical care, other goods and services. The CPI is updated monthly based on the Department of Labor surveys.

To track the effects of price increases, the years 1982 to 1984 are set as a basis (equal to 100). A price index of 33, therefore, indicates that the price was one-third that of the average in 1982–1984.

## Consumer Price Index for All Urban Consumers

| Average Annual Group | 1991 | 1992 |
|---|---|---|
| ALL ITEMS | 136.2 | 140.3 |
| Food | 136.3 | 137.9 |
| Alcoholic beverages | 142.8 | 147.3 |
| Apparel and upkeep | 128.7 | 131.9 |
| Men's and boys' apparel | 124.2 | 126.5 |
| Women's and girls' apparel | 127.6 | 130.4 |
| Footwear | 120.9 | 125.0 |
| Housing, total | 133.6 | 137.5 |
| Rent | 143.3 | 146.9 |
| Gas and electricity | 112.6 | 114.8 |
| Fuel oil, bottled gas | 94.6 | 90.7 |
| House operation | 116.0 | 118.0 |
| House furnishings | 107.5 | 109.0 |
| Transportation | 123.8 | 126.5 |
| Medical care | 177.0 | 190.1 |
| Personal care | 134.9 | 138.3 |
| Tobacco products | 202.7 | 219.8 |
| Entertainment | 138.4 | 142.3 |
| Personal and educational expenses | 183.7 | 197.4 |

*Source: Monthly Labor Review, Jan., 1994*

FAX **Consumer Price Indexes.** Request #127. See p. xi for instructions.
Table of consumer price indexes by major groups.

# The 1994 Fortune 500

| Rank | Company | Sales ($ millions) | Profits ($ millions) | Assets ($ millions) | Market Value ($ millions) |
|---|---|---|---|---|---|
| 1 | General Motors | 133,621.9 | 2,465.8 | 188,200.9 | 44,556.5 |
| 2 | Ford Motor | 108,521.0 | 2,529.0 | 198,938.0 | 32,543.8 |
| 3 | Exxon | 97,825.0 | 5,280.0 | 84,145.0 | 81,040.5 |
| 4 | Intl. Business Machines | 62,716.0 | -8,101.0 | 81,113.0 | 30,595.4 |
| 5 | General Electric | 60,823.0 | 4,315.0 | 251,506.0 | 89,526.6 |
| 6 | Mobil | 56,576.0 | 2,084.0 | 40,585.0 | 31,554.8 |
| 7 | Philip Morris | 50,621.0 | 3,091.0 | 51,205.0 | 48,130.4 |
| 8 | Chrysler | 43,600.0 | -2,551.0 | 43,830.0 | 21,046.8 |
| 9 | Texaco | 34,359.0 | 1,068.0 | 26,626.0 | 17,095.3 |
| 10 | E. I. Du Pont de Nemours | 32,621.0 | 555.0 | 37,053.0 | 35,657.5 |
| 11 | Chevron | 32,123.0 | 1,265.0 | 34,736.0 | 28,746.5 |
| 12 | Procter & Gamble | 30,433.0 | -656.0 | 24,935.0 | 38,845.5 |
| 13 | Amoco | 25,336.0 | 1,820.0 | 28,486.0 | 26,123.1 |
| 14 | Boeing | 25,285.0 | 1,244.0 | 20,450.0 | 16,029.0 |
| 15 | Pepsico | 25,020.7 | 1,587.9 | 23,705.8 | 30,353.7 |
| 16 | Conagra | 21,519.1 | 270.3 | 9,988.7 | 6,696.0 |
| 17 | Shell Oil | 20,853.0 | 781.0 | 26,851.0 | NA |
| 18 | United Technologies | 20,736.0 | 487.0 | 15,618.0 | 8,523.9 |
| 19 | Hewlett-Packard | 20,317.0 | 1,177.0 | 16,736.0 | 22,525.2 |
| 20 | Eastman Kodak | 20,059.0 | -1,515.0 | 20,325.0 | 14,751.5 |
| 21 | Dow Chemical | 18,060.0 | 644.0 | 25,505.0 | 17,704.3 |
| 22 | Atlantic Richfield | 17,189.0 | 269.0 | 23,894.0 | 15,915.4 |
| 23 | Motorola | 16,963.0 | 1,022.0 | 13,498.0 | 29,183.4 |
| 24 | USX | 16,844.0 | -259.0 | 17,320.0 | NA |
| 25 | RJR Nabisco Holdings | 15,104.0 | -145.0 | 31,295.0 | 7,823.8 |
| 26 | Xerox | 14,981.0 | -126.0 | 38,750.0 | 10,151.9 |
| 27 | Sara Lee | 14,580.0 | 704.0 | 10,862.0 | 10,348.8 |
| 28 | McDonnell Douglas | 14,487.0 | 396.0 | 12,026.0 | 4,655.4 |
| 29 | Digital Equipment | 14,371.4 | -251.3 | 10,950.3 | 4,257.3 |
| 30 | Johnson & Johnson | 14,138.0 | 1,787.0 | 12,242.0 | 25,558.5 |
| 31 | 3M | 14,020.0 | 1,263.0 | 12,197.0 | 22,171.8 |
| 32 | Coca-Cola | 13,957.0 | 2,176.0 | 12,021.0 | 54,006.5 |
| 33 | International Paper | 13,685.0 | 289.0 | 16,631.0 | 8,905.3 |
| 34 | Tenneco | 13,255.0 | 426.0 | 15,373.0 | 9,572.7 |
| 35 | Lockheed | 13,071.0 | 422.0 | 8,961.0 | 4,153.9 |
| 36 | Georgia-Pacific | 12,330.0 | -34.0 | 10,545.0 | 6,420.4 |
| 37 | Phillips Petroleum | 12,309.0 | 243.0 | 10,868.0 | 7,060.0 |
| 38 | AlliedSignal | 11,827.0 | 411.0 | 10,829.0 | 10,962.3 |
| 39 | IBP | 11,671.4 | 90.1 | 1,538.9 | 1,157.6 |
| 40 | Goodyear Tire | 11,643.4 | 387.8 | 8,436.1 | 6,622.7 |
| 41 | Caterpillar | 11,615.0 | 652.0 | 14,807.0 | 11,421.3 |
| 42 | Westinghouse Electric | 11,564.0 | -326.0 | 10,553.0 | 5,106.5 |
| 43 | Anheuser-Busch | 11,505.3 | 594.5 | 10,880.3 | 13,116.4 |
| 44 | Bristol-Myers Squibb | 11,413.0 | 1,959.0 | 12,101.0 | 27,706.9 |
| 45 | Rockwell International | 10,840.0 | 561.9 | 9,885.1 | 9,179.8 |
| 46 | Merck | 10,498.2 | 2,166.2 | 19,927.5 | 38,870.9 |
| 47 | Coastal | 10,136.1 | 115.1 | 10,227.0 | 3,363.5 |
| 48 | Archer Daniels Midland | 9,811.4 | 567.5 | 8,404.1 | 8,333.4 |
| 49 | Ashland Oil | 9,553.9 | 142.2 | 5,551.8 | 2,540.2 |
| 50 | Weyerhaeuser | 9,544.8 | 579.3 | 12,638.5 | 9,767.4 |

*The 1994 Fortune 500 (cont'd)*

| Rank | Company | Sales ($ millions) | Profits ($ millions) | Assets ($ millions) | Market Value ($ millions) |
|------|---------|-------------------|----------------------|---------------------|---------------------------|
| 51 | Martin Marietta | 9,435.7 | 20.9 | 7,744.9 | 4,282.4 |
| 52 | Raytheon | 9,201.2 | 693.0 | 7,257.7 | 8,586.1 |
| 53 | Citgo Petroleum | 9,107.4 | 162.1 | 3,866.3 | NA |
| 54 | Alcoa | 9,055.9 | 4.8 | 11,596.9 | 6,671.4 |
| 55 | Baxter International | 8,879.0 | -198.0 | 10,545.0 | 6,221.6 |
| 56 | Intel | 8,782.0 | 2,295.0 | 11,344.0 | 29,103.3 |
| 57 | Textron | 8,668.5 | 379.1 | 19,658.4 | 5,083.7 |
| 58 | Texas Instruments | 8,523.0 | 472.0 | 5,993.0 | 7,693.2 |
| 59 | Abbott Laboratories | 8,407.8 | 1,399.1 | 7,688.6 | 21,862.6 |
| 60 | American Home Products | 8,304.9 | 1,469.3 | 7,687.4 | 18,425.6 |
| 61 | American Brands | 8,287.5 | 469.8 | 16,339.0 | 6,430.6 |
| 62 | Emerson Electric | 8,173.8 | 708.1 | 7,814.5 | 14,337.0 |
| 63 | General Mills | 8,134.6 | 506.1 | 4,650.8 | 8,764.9 |
| 64 | Occidental Petroleum | 8,116.0 | 283.0 | 17,123.0 | 5,348.1 |
| 65 | Hanson Industries | 8,111.5 | 758.6 | 23,713.7 | NA |
| 66 | Unocal | 8,077.0 | 213.0 | 9,254.0 | 6,696.7 |
| 67 | Apple Computer | 7,977.0 | 86.6 | 5,171.4 | 4,281.2 |
| 68 | TRW | 7,947.9 | 195.4 | 5,336.0 | 4,663.3 |
| 69 | Ralston Purina | 7,902.2 | 122.6 | 5,071.9 | NA |
| 70 | Monsanto | 7,902.0 | 494.0 | 8,640.0 | 8,669.2 |
| 71 | Unisys | 7,742.5 | 565.4 | 7,519.2 | 2,343.0 |
| 72 | Deere | 7,693.8 | -920.9 | 11,351.9 | 7,447.6 |
| 73 | Whirlpool | 7,533.0 | 51.0 | 6,047.0 | 4,986.8 |
| 74 | Pfizer | 7,477.7 | 657.5 | 9,330.9 | 17,411.7 |
| 75 | Sun | 7,297.0 | 288.0 | 5,900.0 | 3,703.0 |
| 76 | Compaq Computer | 7,191.0 | 462.0 | 4,084.0 | 8,339.9 |
| 77 | Colgate-Palmolive | 7,141.3 | 189.9 | 5,761.2 | 9,589.7 |
| 78 | H. J. Heinz | 7,103.4 | 396.3 | 6,821.3 | 8,171.2 |
| 79 | Kimberly-Clark | 6,972.9 | 510.9 | 6,380.7 | 8,812.0 |
| 80 | Hoechst Celanese | 6,899.0 | 101.0 | 7,917.0 | NA |
| 81 | CPC International | 6,738.0 | 454.5 | 5,060.8 | 7,228.7 |
| 82 | Borden | 6,700.0 | -630.7 | NA | 2,098.1 |
| 83 | Campbell Soup | 6,586.2 | 8.2 | 4,897.5 | 10,044.0 |
| 84 | Miles | 6,586.0 | 131.7 | 5,242.3 | NA |
| 85 | Eli Lilly | 6,452.4 | 480.2 | 9,623.6 | 15,808.4 |
| 86 | Kellogg | 6,295.4 | 680.7 | 4,237.1 | 11,343.5 |
| 87 | Cooper Industries | 6,273.8 | 367.1 | 7,147.8 | 4,353.1 |
| 88 | Johnson Controls | 6,181.7 | 15.9 | 3,230.8 | 2,391.2 |
| 89 | Honeywell | 5,963.0 | 322.2 | 4,598.1 | 4,440.1 |
| 90 | Levi Strauss Associates | 5,892.5 | 492.4 | 3,108.7 | NA |
| 91 | Amerada Hess | 5,851.6 | -268.2 | 8,641.5 | 4,363.2 |
| 92 | Warner-Lambert | 5,793.7 | 331.0 | 4,828.0 | 8,467.6 |
| 93 | PPG Industries | 5,753.9 | 22.2 | 5,651.5 | 8,066.5 |
| 94 | W. R. Grace | 5,736.6 | 26.0 | 6,108.6 | 4,035.3 |
| 95 | Quaker Oats | 5,730.6 | 167.1 | 2,815.9 | 4,273.6 |
| 96 | Litton Industries | 5,480.2 | 65.2 | 3,834.4 | 3,085.9 |
| 97 | Coca-Cola Enterprises | 5,465.0 | -15.0 | 8,682.0 | 2,244.5 |
| 98 | Dana | 5,460.1 | 79.6 | 4,631.9 | 2,755.2 |
| 99 | Gillette | 5,410.8 | 288.3 | 5,102.3 | 13,778.0 |
| 100 | American Cyanamid | 5,305.6 | -1,118.5 | 6,057.4 | 4,031.3 |

*The 1994 Fortune 500 (cont'd)*

| Rank | Company | Sales ($ millions) | Profits ($ millions) | Assets ($ millions) | Market Value ($ millions) |
|------|---------|-------------------|---------------------|--------------------|--------------------------|
| 101 | Reynolds Metals | 5,269.2 | -322.1 | 6,708.6 | 3,153.0 |
| 102 | BASF | 5,201.8 | 410.6 | 4,365.7 | NA |
| 103 | Champion International | 5,068.8 | -156.2 | 9,142.8 | 2,790.8 |
| 104 | Northrop | 5,063.0 | 96.0 | 2,939.0 | 1,941.4 |
| 105 | Stone Container | 5,059.6 | -358.0 | 6,836.7 | 1,370.3 |
| 106 | Black & Decker | 4,882.2 | 66.0 | 5,310.6 | 1,665.5 |
| 107 | Mead | 4,790.3 | 124.1 | 4,164.5 | 2,552.4 |
| 108 | Scott Paper | 4,748.9 | -277.0 | 6,625.1 | 3,359.1 |
| 109 | Farmland Industries | 4,722.9 | NA | 1,720.0 | NA |
| 110 | Tyson Foods | 4,707.4 | 180.3 | 3,253.5 | 3,042.2 |
| 111 | Navistar International | 4,694.0 | -501.0 | 5,060.0 | 1,809.8 |
| 112 | General Dynamics | 4,661.0 | 885.0 | 2,635.0 | 2,955.6 |
| 113 | James River (VA) | 4,650.2 | -0.3 | 5,851.3 | 1,561.1 |
| 114 | Union Carbide | 4,640.0 | 58.0 | 4,689.0 | 3,632.0 |
| 115 | Eaton | 4,401.0 | 173.0 | 3,268.0 | 4,242.6 |
| 116 | R. R. Donnelley & Sons | 4,387.8 | 109.4 | 3,654.0 | 4,778.9 |
| 117 | Schering-Plough | 4,341.3 | 730.8 | 4,316.9 | 11,374.0 |
| 118 | Bethlehem Steel | 4,323.4 | -266.3 | 5,876.7 | 1,999.6 |
| 119 | VF | 4,320.4 | 246.4 | 2,877.3 | 3,280.9 |
| 120 | Sun Microsystems | 4,308.6 | 156.7 | 2,767.6 | 2,745.5 |
| 121 | Cummins Engine | 4,247.9 | 177.1 | 2,390.6 | 1,809.5 |
| 122 | Dresser Industries | 4,216.0 | 126.7 | 3,641.9 | 4,131.6 |
| 123 | LTV | 4,163.2 | 4,314.9 | 5,795.1 | 1,361.8 |
| 124 | Crown Cork & Seal | 4,162.6 | 99.1 | 4,216.9 | 3,330.5 |
| 125 | Chiquita Brands International | 4,032.9 | -51.1 | 2,700.0 | 873.2 |
| 126 | Ingersoll-Rand | 4,021.1 | 142.5 | 3,375.3 | 4,092.2 |
| 127 | Rhône-Poulenc Rorer | 4,019.4 | 408.6 | 4,050.0 | 4,730.0 |
| 128 | Avon Products | 4,007.6 | 132.1 | 1,958.0 | 4,091.6 |
| 129 | Corning | 4,004.8 | -15.2 | 5,231.7 | 6,194.6 |
| 130 | Boise Cascade | 3,958.3 | -77.1 | 4,513.0 | 987.7 |
| 131 | Inland Steel Industries | 3,888.2 | -37.6 | 3,435.8 | 1,402.1 |
| 132 | Masco | 3,886.0 | 221.1 | 4,021.1 | 5,330.6 |
| 133 | Lyondell Petrochemical | 3,850.0 | 26.0 | 1,231.0 | 1,850.0 |
| 134 | American Standard | 3,830.5 | -208.6 | 3,046.0 | NA |
| 135 | J. E. Seagram | 3,799.0 | -1,077.0 | 8,027.0 | NA |
| 136 | FMC | 3,753.9 | 36.3 | 2,813.1 | 1,745.7 |
| 137 | Times Mirror | 3,714.2 | 317.2 | 4,606.1 | 4,453.1 |
| 138 | Gannett | 3,641.6 | 397.8 | 3,823.8 | 7,991.3 |
| 139 | Upjohn | 3,611.2 | 392.4 | 4,816.4 | 4,899.5 |
| 140 | Tosco | 3,559.2 | 80.6 | 1,492.9 | 1,060.6 |
| 141 | Pitney Bowes | 3,542.9 | 353.2 | 6,793.8 | 6,920.1 |
| 142 | Owens-Illinois | 3,535.0 | 4.9 | 4,901.4 | 1,427.7 |
| 143 | Hershey Foods | 3,488.2 | 193.3 | 2,855.1 | 4,369.7 |
| 144 | AMP | 3,450.6 | 296.7 | 3,117.9 | 6,779.5 |
| 145 | Fina | 3,416.2 | 70.4 | 2,511.4 | 1,072.1 |
| 146 | Paccar | 3,378.9 | 142.2 | 3,291.2 | 2,234.3 |
| 147 | Varity | 3,374.5 | 27.0 | 2,086.5 | 1,927.4 |
| 148 | Loral | 3,335.4 | -92.1 | 3,228.1 | 3,146.3 |
| 149 | Air Products & Chemicals | 3,327.7 | 200.9 | 4,761.5 | 5,723.7 |
| 150 | Kerr-McGee | 3,281.0 | 77.0 | 3,547.0 | 2,314.6 |

*The 1994 Fortune 500 (cont'd)*

| Rank | Company | Sales ($ millions) | Profits ($ millions) | Assets ($ millions) | Market Value ($ millions) |
|------|---------|--------------------|----------------------|---------------------|---------------------------|
| 151 | Rohm & Haas | 3,269.0 | 107.0 | 3,524.0 | 3,812.0 |
| 152 | Grumman | 3,224.5 | 58.8 | 2,024.4 | 1,357.7 |
| 153 | Illinois Tool Works | 3,159.2 | 206.6 | 2,336.9 | 4,992.7 |
| 154 | Agway | 3,148.7 | NA | 1,204.8 | NA |
| 155 | Union Camp | 3,120.4 | 50.0 | 4,685.0 | 3,404.4 |
| 156 | Tyco International | 3,114.5 | 1.3 | 2,459.3 | 2,497.3 |
| 157 | Harris | 3,099.1 | 111.1 | 2,542.0 | 2,010.5 |
| 158 | Berkshire Hathaway | 3,099.0 | 688.1 | 19,520.5 | 18,019.6 |
| 159 | Premark International | 3,097.3 | 172.5 | 2,117.0 | 2,592.4 |
| 160 | Universal | 3,047.2 | 80.2 | 1,562.0 | 672.6 |
| 161 | Seagate Technology | 3,043.6 | 195.4 | 2,031.2 | 1,963.8 |
| 162 | Maytag | 2,987.1 | 51.3 | 2,479.1 | 1,934.3 |
| 163 | Sherwin-Williams | 2,949.3 | 165.2 | 1,914.7 | 2,920.7 |
| 164 | Jefferson Smurfit | 2,947.6 | -228.9 | 2,584.6 | NA |
| 165 | Owens-Corning | 2,944.0 | 131.0 | 3,013.0 | 1,695.6 |
| 166 | Reader's Digest Association | 2,868.6 | 207.3 | 1,872.4 | 4,957.1 |
| 167 | Hormel Foods | 2,854.0 | -26.8 | 1,093.6 | 1,610.7 |
| 168 | Hercules | 2,773.4 | -33.4 | 3,162.0 | 4,665.6 |
| 169 | Hasbro | 2,747.2 | 200.0 | 2,293.0 | 3,105.8 |
| 170 | Pennzoil | 2,742.2 | 141.9 | 4,886.2 | 2,473.4 |
| 171 | Temple-Inland | 2,735.9 | 117.4 | 3,403.8 | 2,808.7 |
| 172 | Land O'Lakes | 2,733.3 | NA | 866.0 | NA |
| 173 | Mapco | 2,715.3 | 127.0 | 1,940.8 | 1,830.8 |
| 174 | Mattel | 2,704.4 | 117.2 | 2,000.1 | 4,352.9 |
| 175 | Baker Hughes | 2,701.7 | 58.9 | 3,143.3 | 2,633.3 |
| 176 | EG&G | 2,697.9 | 59.1 | 768.8 | 1,024.4 |
| 177 | Ethyl | 2,675.5 | 175.5 | 2,009.2 | 2,116.5 |
| 178 | Willamette Industries | 2,622.2 | 137.0 | 2,804.6 | 3,101.7 |
| 179 | Phelps Dodge | 2,611.1 | 187.9 | 3,720.9 | 3,949.7 |
| 180 | Avery Dennison | 2,608.7 | 84.4 | 1,639.0 | 1,714.1 |
| 181 | Diamond Shamrock | 2,555.3 | 18.4 | 1,349.2 | 841.8 |
| 182 | Whitman | 2,529.7 | 78.2 | 2,103.2 | 1,686.7 |
| 183 | Armstrong World Industries | 2,525.4 | 63.5 | 1,929.3 | 1,991.4 |
| 184 | Louisiana-Pacific | 2,511.3 | 244.0 | 2,466.3 | 4,683.5 |
| 185 | Ball | 2,508.3 | -65.1 | 1,795.6 | 736.2 |
| 186 | Teledyne | 2,491.7 | -116.5 | 1,477.8 | 1,136.5 |
| 187 | Parker Hannifin | 2,489.3 | 65.1 | 1,963.6 | 1,704.4 |
| 188 | Dover | 2,483.9 | 158.3 | 1,773.7 | 3,458.7 |
| 189 | Becton Dickinson | 2,465.4 | 71.8 | 3,087.6 | 2,814.5 |
| 190 | Knight-Ridder | 2,451.3 | 148.1 | 2,431.4 | 3,229.1 |
| 191 | Ultramar | 2,438.3 | 86.5 | 1,724.7 | 1,126.7 |
| 192 | Praxair | 2,438.0 | 118.0 | 3,255.0 | 2,537.7 |
| 193 | Olin | 2,423.0 | -92.0 | 1,930.0 | 931.2 |
| 194 | National Steel | 2,418.8 | -258.9 | 2,304.2 | NA |
| 195 | Brunswick | 2,354.2 | 23.1 | 1,983.7 | 2,131.4 |
| 196 | Alumax | 2,347.3 | -138.3 | 2,958.8 | 1,136.6 |
| 197 | Morton International | 2,330.9 | 32.5 | 2,238.8 | 5,142.6 |
| 198 | Total Petroleum | 2,330.5 | 27.5 | 1,261.4 | 599.3 |
| 199 | Westvaco | 2,329.8 | 104.3 | 3,927.8 | 2,299.9 |
| 200 | Shaw Industries | 2,320.8 | 100.6 | 1,280.4 | 2,744.9 |

*The 1994 Fortune 500 (cont'd)*

| Rank | Company | Sales ($ millions) | Profits ($ millions) | Assets ($ millions) | Market Value ($ millions) |
|------|---------|--------------------|----------------------|---------------------|---------------------------|
| 201 | Manville | 2,275.9 | 47.8 | 3,600.0 | 1,101.0 |
| 202 | Dean Foods | 2,274.3 | 68.4 | 892.8 | 1,261.9 |
| 203 | Stanley Works | 2,273.1 | 84.1 | 1,576.9 | 1,894.0 |
| 204 | Clark Refining & Marketing | 2,258.0 | -8.2 | 811.5 | NA |
| 205 | Nucor | 2,253.7 | 123.5 | 1,829.3 | 5,180.9 |
| 206 | Polaroid | 2,244.9 | -51.3 | 2,212.0 | 1,486.2 |
| 207 | Collins & Aikman Group | 2,225.4 | -271.3 | 1,863.4 | NA |
| 208 | International Multifoods | 2,223.9 | 41.2 | 803.5 | 308.5 |
| 209 | McGraw-Hill | 2,195.5 | 11.4 | 3,084.2 | 3,471.3 |
| 210 | Conner Peripherals | 2,151.7 | -445.3 | 1,464.1 | 954.4 |
| 211 | Engelhard | 2,150.9 | 0.7 | 1,279.1 | 2,662.5 |
| 212 | Witco | 2,142.6 | 19.8 | 1,609.7 | 1,734.8 |
| 213 | E-Systems | 2,097.1 | 121.9 | 1,279.2 | 1,474.0 |
| 214 | Burlington Industries Equity | 2,057.9 | 85.1 | 1,813.3 | 1,073.4 |
| 215 | Cenex | 2,048.0 | NA | 1,099.0 | NA |
| 216 | Dow Corning | 2,043.7 | -287.0 | 3,262.3 | NA |
| 217 | York International | 2,031.9 | 5.2 | 1,335.2 | 1,445.0 |
| 218 | Maxxam | 2,031.1 | -600.2 | 3,500.0 | 355.8 |
| 219 | Tandem Computers | 2,031.0 | -517.7 | 1,685.2 | 1,644.2 |
| 220 | Springs Industries | 2,022.8 | -25.3 | 1,292.1 | 679.1 |
| 221 | New York Times | 2,019.7 | 6.1 | 3,215.2 | 2,906.8 |
| 222 | Dell Computer | 2,013.9 | 101.6 | 927.0 | 1,086.5 |
| 223 | National Semiconductor | 2,013.7 | 130.3 | 1,476.5 | 2,597.6 |
| 224 | Central Soya | 1,981.4 | 15.5 | 865.2 | NA |
| 225 | McDermott | 1,969.6 | -273.8 | 2,345.7 | NA |
| 226 | Rubbermaid | 1,960.2 | 211.4 | 1,513.1 | 4,729.4 |
| 227 | Tribune | 1,952.5 | 188.6 | 2,536.4 | 3,851.4 |
| 228 | Sonoco Products | 1,947.2 | 118.8 | 1,707.1 | 2,099.4 |
| 229 | Echlin | 1,944.5 | 93.6 | 1,263.3 | 1,710.5 |
| 230 | Fleetwood Enterprises | 1,941.9 | 56.6 | 1,061.9 | 1,005.0 |
| 231 | Arvin Industries | 1,939.4 | 40.3 | 1,246.2 | 693.2 |
| 232 | Dow Jones | 1,931.8 | 147.5 | 2,349.5 | 4,053.7 |
| 233 | USG | 1,916.0 | 1,297.0 | 2,163.0 | 1,096.2 |
| 234 | Gencorp | 1,905.0 | 43.0 | 1,164.0 | 464.0 |
| 235 | Fruit of the Loom | 1,884.4 | 207.5 | 2,734.0 | 2,252.8 |
| 236 | Bausch & Lomb | 1,872.2 | 156.5 | 2,511.9 | 2,933.7 |
| 237 | Mid-America Dairymen | 1,825.7 | NA | 385.5 | NA |
| 238 | PET | 1,825.5 | -123.0 | 1,170.5 | 1,907.9 |
| 239 | B. F. Goodrich | 1,818.3 | 128.3 | 2,359.9 | 1,057.8 |
| 240 | Clorox | 1,807.5 | 167.1 | 1,649.2 | 2,822.3 |
| 241 | National Service Industries | 1,804.8 | 75.1 | 1,087.5 | 1,350.8 |
| 242 | Imcera Group | 1,796.3 | -200.4 | 2,177.6 | 2,833.2 |
| 243 | Great Lakes Chemical | 1,792.0 | 272.8 | 1,900.9 | 5,443.6 |
| 244 | Mascotech | 1,774.8 | 47.6 | 1,789.9 | 1,459.5 |
| 245 | Lear Holdings | 1,756.5 | 10.1 | 820.2 | NA |
| 246 | Duracell International | 1,742.2 | 48.5 | 1,997.6 | 4,800.9 |
| 247 | Asarco | 1,736.4 | 15.6 | 3,152.5 | 1,074.2 |
| 248 | Gateway 2000 | 1,731.7 | 66.0 | 564.3 | 1,701.0 |
| 249 | Timken | 1,708.8 | -271.9 | 1,789.7 | 1,087.2 |
| 250 | Quantum | 1,697.2 | 93.8 | 926.6 | 820.6 |

*The 1994 Fortune 500 (cont'd)*

| Rank | Company | Sales ($ millions) | Profits ($ millions) | Assets ($ millions) | Market Value ($ millions) |
|------|---------|-------------------|---------------------|--------------------|--------------------------|
| 251 | SCI Systems | 1,697.1 | 26.6 | 780.3 | 578.2 |
| 252 | Sequa | 1,697.0 | NA | 1,800.0 | 390.2 |
| 253 | Reliance Electric | 1,688.0 | 25.0 | 1,195.0 | 702.2 |
| 254 | Amdahl | 1,680.5 | -580.0 | 1,672.2 | 658.8 |
| 255 | American Greetings | 1,671.7 | 112.3 | 1,548.4 | 2,070.2 |
| 256 | Armco | 1,664.0 | -641.8 | 1,904.7 | 598.7 |
| 257 | Interco | 1,656.8 | 45.4 | 1,205.7 | 743.8 |
| 258 | Advanced Micro Devices | 1,648.3 | 228.8 | 1,929.2 | 2,160.9 |
| 259 | Newell | 1,645.0 | 165.3 | 1,952.9 | 3,250.2 |
| 260 | Trinova | 1,643.8 | -59.7 | 972.2 | 1,097.2 |
| 261 | Cyprus Amax Minerals | 1,639.7 | 100.2 | 5,625.2 | 2,837.6 |
| 262 | Murphy Oil | 1,636.7 | 102.1 | 2,168.9 | 1,848.3 |
| 263 | Cabot | 1,614.3 | 11.3 | 1,489.5 | 995.3 |
| 264 | Freeport-McMoran | 1,610.6 | -103.8 | 3,714.1 | 2,781.7 |
| 265 | Adolph Coors | 1,581.8 | -41.9 | 1,350.9 | 706.7 |
| 266 | Deluxe | 1,581.8 | 141.9 | 1,252.0 | 2,796.3 |
| 267 | Federal-Mogul | 1,575.5 | 40.1 | 1,291.8 | 1,021.4 |
| 268 | M. A. Hanna | 1,560.8 | 2.0 | 1,141.3 | 878.4 |
| 269 | Detroit Diesel | 1,560.1 | 20.7 | 652.7 | 662.9 |
| 270 | McCormick | 1,556.6 | 73.1 | 1,313.2 | 1,762.7 |
| 271 | Del Monte Foods | 1,555.0 | -188.0 | 1,066.0 | NA |
| 272 | Nacco Industries | 1,549.4 | 8.3 | 1,642.5 | 509.6 |
| 273 | Trinity Industries | 1,540.0 | 45.0 | 1,089.1 | 1,704.3 |
| 274 | General Signal | 1,530.0 | 34.7 | 1,224.8 | 1,645.2 |
| 275 | Leggett & Platt | 1,526.7 | 85.9 | 901.9 | 1,804.2 |
| 276 | Lubrizol | 1,517.6 | 45.6 | 1,182.6 | 2,468.5 |
| 277 | Magnetek | 1,512.2 | -21.7 | 1,052.8 | 371.2 |
| 278 | West Point Stevens | 1,501.0 | -402.3 | 1,512.9 | 608.0 |
| 279 | Washington Post | 1,498.2 | 165.4 | 1,622.5 | 2,814.1 |
| 280 | Lafarge | 1,494.5 | 5.9 | 1,673.7 | 1,538.7 |
| 281 | Crown Central | 1,451.2 | -4.3 | 656.2 | 199.1 |
| 282 | Hillenbrand Industries | 1,447.9 | 145.8 | 2,270.7 | 2,946.6 |
| 283 | Maxtor | 1,442.5 | 46.1 | 579.1 | 221.9 |
| 284 | Wm. Wrigley Jr. | 1,428.5 | 174.9 | 815.3 | 5,732.7 |
| 285 | Harsco | 1,422.3 | 87.6 | 1,427.6 | 1,132.9 |
| 286 | Brown-Forman | 1,414.5 | 156.2 | 1,311.0 | 2,321.5 |
| 287 | AST Research | 1,412.2 | -53.7 | 886.2 | 773.5 |
| 288 | Storage Technology | 1,404.8 | -77.8 | 1,793.0 | 1,684.9 |
| 289 | Gold Kist | 1,400.6 | NA | 665.1 | NA |
| 290 | General Instrument | 1,392.5 | 90.6 | 1,776.1 | 2,794.6 |
| 291 | Nalco Chemical | 1,389.4 | 85.6 | 1,212.4 | 2,437.5 |
| 292 | Federal Paper Board | 1,386.4 | 20.8 | 2,570.3 | 1,085.3 |
| 293 | Raychem | 1,385.7 | 9.6 | 1,332.3 | 1,623.8 |
| 294 | Sundstrand | 1,383.1 | 140.7 | 1,511.9 | 1,492.7 |
| 295 | Potlatch | 1,368.9 | 6.6 | 2,066.8 | 1,354.1 |
| 296 | Bowater | 1,353.7 | -64.5 | 2,726.2 | 824.4 |
| 297 | Tecumseh Products | 1,337.3 | 81.4 | 1,132.7 | 1,225.3 |
| 298 | Coltec Industries | 1,334.8 | 47.4 | 806.4 | 1,421.4 |
| 299 | Unifi | 1,332.2 | 128.1 | 970.4 | 1,621.1 |
| 300 | Medtronic | 1,328.2 | 197.2 | 1,286.5 | 4,543.9 |

*The 1994 Fortune 500 (cont'd)*

| Rank | Company | Sales ($ millions) | Profits ($ millions) | Assets ($ millions) | Market Value ($ millions) |
|------|---------|-------------------|----------------------|---------------------|---------------------------|
| 301 | Pentair | 1,328.2 | 46.6 | 958.8 | 671.0 |
| 302 | Varian Associates | 1,311.0 | 45.8 | 893.1 | 1,209.7 |
| 303 | Crane | 1,310.2 | 48.9 | 744.2 | 843.6 |
| 304 | Amgen | 1,306.3 | 383.3 | 1,765.5 | 5,435.7 |
| 305 | Tektronix | 1,302.4 | -55.1 | 984.5 | 810.6 |
| 306 | Walter Industries | 1,291.3 | -58.0 | 3,223.2 | NA |
| 307 | Gerber Products | 1,269.5 | 42.5 | 954.3 | 1,950.2 |
| 308 | E. W. Scripps | 1,259.5 | 128.7 | 1,676.5 | 2,072.9 |
| 309 | Thermo Electron | 1,249.7 | 76.6 | 2,473.7 | 1,988.6 |
| 310 | Burlington Resources | 1,249.0 | 256.3 | 4,447.7 | 5,706.1 |
| 311 | Wang Laboratories | 1,247.0 | -197.2 | 588.8 | 507.7 |
| 312 | Standard Commercial | 1,239.5 | 21.2 | 926.4 | 128.4 |
| 313 | J. M. Huber | 1,238.4 | 29.7 | 876.1 | NA |
| 314 | Great American Mgmt. & Inv. | 1,237.2 | -32.9 | 444.7 | 353.7 |
| 315 | Harnischfeger Ind. | 1,234.7 | -17.7 | 1,334.4 | 663.7 |
| 316 | Triarc | 1,231.9 | -90.9 | 907.0 | 437.1 |
| 317 | Zenith Electronics | 1,228.2 | -97.0 | 559.4 | 464.3 |
| 318 | Western Digital | 1,225.2 | -25.1 | 531.2 | 780.8 |
| 319 | Valero Energy | 1,222.2 | 36.4 | 1,764.4 | 935.2 |
| 320 | Mark IV Industries | 1,222.0 | 42.2 | 1,095.0 | 798.0 |
| 321 | AG Processing | 1,218.6 | NA | 465.8 | NA |
| 322 | Harley-Davidson | 1,217.4 | -11.9 | 583.3 | 1,880.8 |
| 323 | Bemis | 1,203.5 | 44.3 | 789.8 | 1,120.0 |
| 324 | Thiokol | 1,201.7 | 63.8 | 841.0 | 545.5 |
| 325 | Weirton Steel | 1,201.1 | -229.2 | 1,240.7 | 260.1 |
| 326 | A. O. Smith | 1,193.9 | 42.7 | 823.1 | 734.4 |
| 327 | Cooper Tire & Rubber | 1,193.6 | 102.2 | 889.6 | 2,361.2 |
| 328 | Intl. Flavors & Fragrances | 1,188.6 | 202.5 | 1,225.3 | 4,160.2 |
| 329 | Fort Howard | 1,187.4 | -2,052.1 | 1,649.8 | NA |
| 330 | Rohr | 1,175.2 | -254.5 | 1,017.8 | 182.4 |
| 331 | Helene Curtis Industries | 1,167.8 | 22.1 | 600.1 | 253.1 |
| 332 | Ocean Spray | 1,167.6 | NA | 644.3 | NA |
| 333 | Interstate Bakeries | 1,165.6 | 16.7 | 586.8 | 277.0 |
| 334 | Alberto-Culver | 1,148.0 | 41.3 | 593.0 | 629.8 |
| 335 | Smithfield Foods | 1,142.5 | 4.0 | 399.6 | 345.8 |
| 336 | Seaboard | 1,142.1 | 35.9 | 647.3 | 294.5 |
| 337 | Briggs & Stratton | 1,139.5 | 70.3 | 656.1 | 1,229.4 |
| 338 | Vulcan Materials | 1,133.5 | 88.2 | 1,078.6 | 1,762.9 |
| 339 | Snap-On Tools | 1,132.0 | 85.8 | 1,218.9 | 1,862.6 |
| 340 | Anchor Glass Container | 1,126.0 | -34.2 | 1,347.2 | NA |
| 341 | Savannah Foods & Industries | 1,122.9 | 15.2 | 567.9 | 354.2 |
| 342 | Perkin-Elmer | 1,118.0 | -83.1 | 851.1 | 1,592.9 |
| 343 | Worthington Industries | 1,115.7 | 66.2 | 686.1 | 1,764.3 |
| 344 | Allegheny Ludlum | 1,100.2 | 70.8 | 1,174.0 | 1,438.4 |
| 345 | Silicon Graphics | 1,091.2 | 95.2 | 946.1 | 3,414.3 |
| 346 | Applied Materials | 1,080.0 | 99.7 | 1,120.2 | 3,787.5 |
| 347 | Oryx Energy | 1,080.0 | -100.0 | 3,624.0 | 1,732.7 |
| 348 | Data General | 1,077.9 | -60.5 | 866.3 | 296.6 |
| 349 | Kellwood | 1,077.7 | 28.7 | 636.5 | 534.9 |
| 350 | UST | 1,076.1 | 349.0 | 706.2 | 5,349.3 |

*The 1994 Fortune 500 (cont'd)*

| Rank | Company | Sales ($ millions) | Profits ($ millions) | Assets ($ millions) | Market Value ($ millions) |
|------|---------|-------------------|---------------------|---------------------|--------------------------|
| 351 | Thomas & Betts | 1,075.9 | 56.5 | 1,133.2 | 1,205.5 |
| 352 | GAF | 1,069.0 | 14.4 | 2,050.0 | NA |
| 353 | Danaher | 1,067.1 | 17.7 | 872.5 | 955.4 |
| 354 | Sunbeam/Oster | 1,065.9 | 88.8 | 1,006.1 | 1,486.1 |
| 355 | Ferro | 1,065.7 | 37.0 | 767.9 | 1,008.8 |
| 356 | Dibrell Brothers | 1,065.4 | 39.3 | 639.8 | 292.7 |
| 357 | Alliant Techsystems | 1,062.0 | -114.2 | 457.2 | 266.9 |
| 358 | Intergraph | 1,050.3 | -116.0 | 855.3 | 436.5 |
| 359 | Wheeling-Pittsburgh | 1,046.8 | -6.2 | 1,491.6 | 481.1 |
| 360 | First Brands | 1,041.9 | 52.7 | 806.8 | 776.2 |
| 361 | Ecolab | 1,041.5 | 76.6 | 871.5 | 694.2 |
| 362 | United States Surgical | 1,037.2 | -138.7 | 1,170.5 | 961.3 |
| 363 | Outboard Marine | 1,034.6 | -282.5 | 791.8 | 497.7 |
| 364 | Lukens | 1,033.3 | -50.0 | 817.2 | 541.3 |
| 365 | Cincinnati Milacron | 1,029.4 | -101.9 | 729.6 | 813.4 |
| 366 | Fieldcrest Cannon | 1,000.1 | -42.9 | 740.4 | 254.2 |
| 367 | Borg Warner Automotive | 985.4 | -98.0 | 1,159.4 | 681.6 |
| 368 | H. B. Fuller | 975.3 | 10.0 | 564.5 | 521.7 |
| 369 | Geon | 972.5 | 4.9 | 721.2 | 771.5 |
| 370 | C. R. Bard | 970.8 | 56.0 | 798.6 | 1,445.7 |
| 371 | Flowers Industries | 962.1 | 39.2 | 490.9 | 676.3 |
| 372 | Consolidated Papers | 947.3 | 64.2 | 1,467.1 | 1,969.6 |
| 373 | ITT Rayonier | 936.3 | 52.5 | 1,474.8 | NA |
| 374 | Russell | 930.8 | 49.1 | 1,017.0 | 1,207.1 |
| 375 | Hudson Foods | 920.5 | 15.9 | 408.3 | 226.4 |
| 376 | Jostens | 914.8 | -12.1 | 583.3 | 817.2 |
| 377 | International Controls | 909.3 | -43.3 | 517.3 | NA |
| 378 | Uniroyal Chemical | 907.9 | -236.7 | 1,225.4 | NA |
| 379 | CF Industries | 905.5 | NA | 950.6 | NA |
| 380 | Mitchell Energy & Devel. | 902.8 | 18.5 | 2,271.8 | 981.6 |
| 381 | IMC Fertilizer Group | 897.1 | -167.1 | 2,055.6 | 1,074.3 |
| 382 | Cray Research | 894.9 | 60.9 | 1,169.8 | 792.4 |
| 383 | Universal Foods | 891.6 | 33.0 | 730.0 | 871.5 |
| 384 | Allergan | 888.0 | 108.9 | 939.8 | 1,448.0 |
| 385 | Pilgrim's Pride | 887.8 | 21.0 | 442.8 | 234.5 |
| 386 | Dexter | 887.1 | 24.2 | 820.7 | 634.0 |
| 387 | JPS Textile Group | 885.7 | -21.8 | 598.9 | NA |
| 388 | Chesapeake | 885.0 | 10.4 | 919.3 | 572.8 |
| 389 | Beckman Industries | 875.7 | -37.6 | 820.0 | 738.0 |
| 390 | Clark Equipment | 874.9 | 48.0 | 1,001.9 | 1,065.9 |
| 391 | Amsted Industries | 868.1 | 18.7 | 543.5 | NA |
| 392 | General Cable | 859.7 | -57.6 | 620.4 | 58.3 |
| 393 | Molex | 859.3 | 71.1 | 961.8 | 2,241.3 |
| 394 | Vishay Intertechnology | 856.3 | 44.1 | 948.1 | 756.3 |
| 395 | Herman Miller | 855.7 | 22.1 | 484.3 | 787.6 |
| 396 | Lincoln Electric | 846.0 | -37.3 | 572.1 | NA |
| 397 | K-III Comunications | 844.7 | -86.5 | 1,166.7 | NA |
| 398 | Wellman | 842.1 | 31.4 | 1,014.4 | 692.5 |
| 399 | Solectron | 836.3 | 30.6 | 603.3 | 1,237.7 |
| 400 | Hubbell | 832.4 | 66.3 | 874.3 | 1,773.9 |

*The 1994 Fortune 500 (cont'd)*

| Rank | Company | Sales ($ millions) | Profits ($ millions) | Assets ($ millions) | Market Value ($ millions) |
|------|---------|-------------------|---------------------|--------------------|--------------------------|
| 401 | Tesoro Petroleum | 831.0 | 17.0 | 434.5 | 263.8 |
| 402 | Micron Technology | 828.3 | 104.1 | 965.7 | 3,221.2 |
| 403 | Kendall International | 816.3 | 49.2 | 657.7 | 836.8 |
| 404 | Louisiana Land & Exploration | 815.4 | 9.6 | 1,838.7 | 1,244.0 |
| 405 | IMO Industries | 813.7 | -270.6 | 658.4 | 128.9 |
| 406 | Stewart & Stevenson Services | 812.5 | 34.7 | 573.3 | 1,601.8 |
| 407 | Arcadian | 803.2 | 2.5 | 1,104.4 | NA |
| 408 | Safety-Kleen | 794.6 | -101.3 | 995.4 | 858.0 |
| 409 | Kaman | 792.5 | -28.8 | 440.2 | 165.5 |
| 410 | Magma Copper | 792.4 | 21.9 | 1,350.8 | 703.2 |
| 411 | Maxus Energy | 786.7 | -49.4 | 1,987.0 | 636.0 |
| 412 | EMC | 782.6 | 127.1 | 829.6 | 3,512.4 |
| 413 | Valhi | 781.7 | -79.1 | 903.9 | 599.8 |
| 414 | Hon Industries | 780.3 | 45.1 | 352.4 | 966.1 |
| 415 | Cone Mills | 769.2 | 49.6 | 431.6 | 405.8 |
| 416 | Georgia Gulf | 768.9 | 41.9 | 405.3 | 1,141.5 |
| 417 | Meredith | 768.8 | 18.6 | 900.8 | 625.3 |
| 418 | Figgie International | 768.6 | -179.8 | NA | 152.7 |
| 419 | Pittway | 767.6 | 32.8 | 482.0 | 494.9 |
| 420 | Standard Products | 763.8 | 22.6 | 564.9 | 618.6 |
| 421 | Tri Valley Growers | 763.0 | NA | 760.8 | NA |
| 422 | UIS | 761.5 | 43.1 | 511.3 | NA |
| 423 | Quaker State | 759.2 | 13.7 | 783.7 | 374.7 |
| 424 | Huffy | 757.9 | -4.9 | 319.3 | 275.1 |
| 425 | SPX | 756.1 | -40.6 | 1,024.4 | 219.3 |
| 426 | Stanhome | 750.7 | 33.1 | 429.7 | 683.6 |
| 427 | Nortek | 744.1 | -20.8 | 509.2 | 114.4 |
| 428 | Sigma-Aldrich | 739.4 | 96.3 | 675.5 | 2,639.5 |
| 429 | Mary Kay Cosmetics | 737.2 | 4.8 | 542.7 | NA |
| 430 | Gaylord Container | 733.5 | 130.2 | 860.1 | 294.3 |
| 431 | Ametek | 732.2 | -7.3 | 562.7 | 529.1 |
| 432 | Hartmarx | 732.0 | 6.2 | 405.1 | 211.7 |
| 433 | DSC Communications | 730.8 | 81.7 | 900.4 | 2,943.5 |
| 434 | Scientific-Atlanta | 730.6 | 20.0 | 524.2 | 1,165.5 |
| 435 | Tyco Toys | 730.2 | -69.9 | 715.2 | 307.7 |
| 436 | Thorn Apple Valley | 729.9 | 13.9 | 143.9 | 137.8 |
| 437 | Ply Gem | 722.7 | 3.7 | 347.4 | 252.1 |
| 438 | Kimball International | 722.4 | 30.6 | 452.7 | 629.6 |
| 439 | Standard Register | 722.1 | 42.2 | 502.3 | 627.2 |
| 440 | Natl. Coop. Refinery Assn. | 719.6 | NA | 402.2 | NA |
| 441 | LSI Logic | 718.8 | 53.8 | 852.8 | 965.1 |
| 442 | Prairie Farms Dairy | 709.3 | NA | 220.0 | NA |
| 443 | Dr Pepper/Seven-Up | 707.4 | 77.9 | 680.0 | 1,523.8 |
| 444 | Synoptics Communications | 704.5 | 75.9 | 529.4 | 1,569.0 |
| 445 | Warnaco Group | 703.8 | 24.1 | 686.4 | 541.1 |
| 446 | Homestake Mining | 703.5 | 52.5 | 1,121.3 | 2,732.7 |
| 447 | Terex | 700.0 | NA | NA | 88.3 |
| 448 | Banta | 698.0 | 41.0 | 457.4 | 749.9 |
| 449 | Reynolds & Reynolds | 697.0 | 33.4 | 570.6 | 1,000.0 |
| 450 | Foamex | 696.0 | -12.7 | 635.0 | 480.3 |

*The 1994 Fortune 500 (cont'd)*

| Rank | Company | Sales ($ millions) | Profits ($ millions) | Assets ($ millions) | Market Value ($ millions) |
|------|---------|-------------------|---------------------|---------------------|---------------------------|
| 451 | Valspar | 693.7 | 40.2 | 336.8 | 942.1 |
| 452 | A. Schulman | 693.2 | 36.7 | 407.9 | 1,040.4 |
| 453 | Blount | 691.4 | 7.2 | 447.2 | 381.9 |
| 454 | Longview Fibre | 689.6 | 40.3 | 944.4 | 992.2 |
| 455 | Pall | 687.2 | 78.3 | 902.3 | 2,017.6 |
| 456 | Coca-Cola Bottling Co. Consol. | 687.0 | 14.8 | 648.4 | 298.6 |
| 457 | Delta Woodside Industries | 686.2 | 27.3 | 573.9 | 266.5 |
| 458 | Betz Laboratories | 684.9 | 65.5 | 521.1 | 1,462.6 |
| 459 | Toro | 684.3 | 13.0 | 419.2 | 357.2 |
| 460 | La-Z-Boy Chair | 684.1 | 27.3 | 401.1 | 649.8 |
| 461 | Sealy | 683.2 | 25.7 | 823.1 | NA |
| 462 | Riceland Foods | 682.5 | NA | 274.2 | NA |
| 463 | Union Texas | 681.9 | 27.0 | 1,338.7 | 1,698.4 |
| 464 | Interlake | 681.3 | -26.0 | 477.0 | 60.6 |
| 465 | NCH | 679.9 | 37.6 | 467.4 | 470.7 |
| 466 | Oregon Steel Mills | 679.8 | 14.8 | 549.7 | 520.0 |
| 467 | Teleflex | 666.8 | 33.7 | 640.6 | 664.2 |
| 468 | Analog Devices | 666.3 | 44.5 | 678.5 | 1,391.5 |
| 469 | Harman Intl. Industries | 664.9 | 11.2 | 431.7 | 446.5 |
| 470 | Carter-Wallace | 663.5 | 47.2 | 600.6 | 933.0 |
| 471 | Leslie Fay | 661.8 | -95.2 | 421.8 | 70.4 |
| 472 | Eagle-Picher Industries | 661.5 | -1,157.4 | 459.4 | NA |
| 473 | Valassis Communications | 661.4 | 81.9 | 275.2 | 828.1 |
| 474 | Universal Forest Products | 661.0 | 10.4 | 185.7 | 157.1 |
| 475 | Handy & Harman | 658.3 | 9.5 | 412.9 | 210.3 |
| 476 | Guilford Mills | 654.4 | 28.9 | 506.7 | 305.8 |
| 477 | Western Publishing Group | 652.2 | 17.5 | 508.6 | 379.9 |
| 478 | Cisco Systems | 649.0 | 172.0 | 595.2 | 10,082.0 |
| 479 | Sun-Diamond Growers | 648.7 | NA | 352.3 | NA |
| 480 | Doskocil | 648.2 | -32.0 | 316.9 | 85.1 |
| 481 | J & L Specialty Steel | 648.2 | 18.8 | 626.0 | 599.4 |
| 482 | Imperial Holly | 647.8 | -3.4 | 398.2 | 99.9 |
| 483 | Ivax | 645.3 | 84.7 | 658.3 | 2,675.0 |
| 484 | ACX Technologies | 641.9 | 13.0 | 654.0 | 423.3 |
| 485 | Insilco | 641.1 | 402.3 | 517.7 | 159.9 |
| 486 | Oshkosh Truck | 635.0 | 1.1 | 253.0 | 93.4 |
| 487 | Newmont Mining | 634.3 | 133.1 | 1,186.4 | 3,600.3 |
| 488 | Lancaster Colony | 630.6 | 46.2 | 302.1 | 991.8 |
| 489 | Holly | 629.9 | 19.0 | 249.8 | 232.1 |
| 490 | Pope & Talbot | 628.9 | 21.0 | 455.8 | 345.6 |
| 491 | RPM | 625.7 | 39.4 | 584.6 | 1,056.7 |
| 492 | Interface | 625.1 | 13.8 | 642.3 | 261.6 |
| 493 | Block Drug | 624.8 | 61.5 | 726.5 | 630.9 |
| 494 | Diebold | 623.3 | 48.4 | 609.0 | 1,123.4 |
| 495 | Carpenter | 619.0 | 21.0 | 385.0 | NA |
| 496 | 3 Com | 617.2 | 38.6 | 367.6 | 1,804.3 |
| 497 | Harvard Industries | 616.9 | -130.6 | 367.9 | 68.4 |
| 498 | WLR Foods | 616.7 | 14.6 | 265.6 | 334.4 |
| 499 | Quanex | 616.1 | 8.4 | 528.9 | 263.1 |
| 500 | Texas Industries | 614.3 | 1.1 | 757.3 | 399.4 |

# Inc. 500 Fastest Growing Companies

| Rank | Company | 1992 Sales ($ thousands) | 1992 Profit Range | No. of Employees 1992 | % Sales Growth 1988-92 |
|---|---|---|---|---|---|
| 1 | Drypers, Houston, TX | 140,222 | D | 461 | 49,101 |
| 2 | Indeck Energy Systems, Buffalo Grove, IL | 94,743 | D | 154 | 41,637 |
| 3 | Indus Group, San Francisco, CA | 23,911 | A | 177 | 19,499 |
| 4 | Play It Again Sports Franchise, Minneapolis, MN | 27,380 | D | 73 | 12,460 |
| 5 | Galaxy Scientific, Pleasantville, NJ | 11,291 | C | 131 | 10,259 |
| 6 | Gateway 2000, North Sioux City, SD | 1,107,057 | C | 1,847 | 9,307 |
| 7 | Level One Communications, Folsom, CA | 14,075 | B | 70 | 8,752 |
| 8 | Levenger, Delray Beach, FL | 14,004 | B | 37 | 7,637 |
| 9 | Han Corp., Ossining, NY | 11,791 | E | 264 | 7,090 |
| 10 | Trilithic, Indianapolis, IN | 7,537 | E | 87 | 7,078 |
| 11 | Fidelity Technologies, Reading, PA | 9,153 | D | 140 | 6,581 |
| 12 | Travelpro Luggage, Deerfield Beach, FL | 12,624 | A | 30 | 6,341 |
| 13 | Alternative Resources, Lincolnshire, IL | 27,948 | C | 129 | 6,195 |
| 14 | Lokring, Foster City, CA | 6,743 | F | 64 | 6,086 |
| 15 | Micro Design International, Winter Park, FL | 19,209 | A | 64 | 6,037 |
| 16 | Ni-Med, Arnold, MO | 6,556 | F | 70 | 5,702 |
| 17 | Diamond Computer Systems, Sunnyvale, CA | 74,502 | C | 80 | 5,443 |
| 18 | Saint Louis Bread, St. Louis, MO | 13,345 | D | 220 | 5,325 |
| 19 | Labor World of America, Boca Raton, FL | 6,789 | D | 30 | 5,163 |
| 20 | Jelyn & Co., Fort Washington, PA | 13,134 | C | 21 | 5,051 |
| 21 | American Medical Security, Green Bay, WI | 109,558 | C | 890 | 4,912 |
| 22 | FASTech Integration, Lincoln, MA | 7,600 | F | 76 | 4,835 |
| 23 | On Target Media, Cincinnati, OH | 14,569 | B | 60 | 4,789 |
| 24 | Russell Construction, Muskegon, MI | 5,346 | C | 25 | 4,760 |
| 25 | Integrated Services, Lake Oswego, OR | 7,146 | B | 42 | 4,510 |
| 26 | Saber Software, Dallas, TX | 7,153 | C | 52 | 4,427 |
| 27 | CenterLine Software, Cambridge, MA | 18,024 | D | 133 | 4,329 |
| 28 | Ma Laboratories, San Jose, CA | 155,527 | D | 85 | 4,271 |
| 29 | Nationwide Remittance Centers, McLean, VA | 15,106 | F | 475 | 4,266 |
| 30 | CD Plus, New York, NY | 9,674 | D | 70 | 4,070 |
| 31 | First Commonwealth, Chicago, IL | 11,021 | C | 55 | 4,043 |
| 32 | Advanced Systems Technology, Atlanta, GA | 12,372 | D | 197 | 4,038 |
| 33 | Pete's Brewing, Palo Alto, CA | 5,287 | E | 20 | 3,967 |
| 34 | Wastren, Idaho Falls, ID | 9,556 | D | 119 | 3,949 |
| 35 | Elite Computers & Software, Cupertino, CA | 4,745 | D | 13 | 3,921 |
| 36 | Anstec, Fairfax, VA | 22,514 | D | 375 | 3,871 |
| 37 | Digicon, Bethesda, MD | 13,318 | C | 179 | 3,864 |
| 38 | SETA, McLean, VA | 8,629 | C | 106 | 3,822 |
| 39 | Implant Innovations, West Palm Beach, FL | 14,194 | B | 62 | 3,757 |
| 40 | Fiber Spar & Tube, West Wareham, MA | 4,381 | D | 52 | 3,743 |
| 41 | LJL Biosystems, Sunnyvale, CA | 5,172 | D | 30 | 3,703 |
| 42 | Half Off Card Shop, Southfield, MI | 22,545 | D | 200 | 3,633 |
| 43 | Practice Management Information, Los Angeles, CA | 11,098 | B | 54 | 3,612 |
| 44 | McArthur/Glen Group, McLean, VA | 37,000 | F | 120 | 3,600 |
| 45 | Friendship Manor Homes, Madison, WI | 5,002 | D | 400 | 3,578 |
| 46 | Princeton Executive & Management, Fair Lawn, NJ | 5,421 | A | 50 | 3,563 |
| 47 | Roll Systems, Burlington, MA | 19,375 | F | 101 | 3,528 |
| 48 | Space & Asset Management, Dayton, OH | 3,900 | D | 19 | 3,382 |
| 49 | Spectrum Associates, Woburn, MA | 13,904 | B | 102 | 3,333 |
| 50 | Decision Systems Technologies, Greenbelt, MD | 11,165 | D | 184 | 3,243 |

*Profit Range: A-16% or more; B-11% to 15%; C-6% to 10%; D-1%-5%; E-break-even; F-loss*

*Inc. 500 Fastest Growing Companies (cont'd)*

| Rank | Company | 1992 Sales ($ thousands) | 1992 Profit Range | No. of Employees 1992 | % Sales Growth 1988-92 |
|---|---|---|---|---|---|
| 51 | CD Technology Sunnyvale, CA | 3,916 | D | 20 | 3,191 |
| 52 | B&V Technology, Idaho Falls, ID | 37,178 | C | 450 | 3,181 |
| 53 | Cedar Cliff Systems, Springfield, VA | 5,218 | B | 16 | 3,101 |
| 54 | Adnet, La Mirada, CA | 3,679 | A | 16 | 3,044 |
| 55 | Vail Research & Technology, Alexandria, VA | 5,484 | D | 52 | 3,034 |
| 56 | Bergaila & Associates, Houston, TX | 4,788 | F | 90 | 3,029 |
| 57 | Boston Prepatory, New York, NY | 3,835 | A | 4 | 3,018 |
| 58 | Vermont Teddy Bear, Shelburne, VT | 10,603 | D | 170 | 3,009 |
| 59 | Tag Express, Duluth, GA | 4,844 | B | 16 | 2,985 |
| 60 | Skynet Worldwide Courier Group, Miami, FL | 5,335 | C | 70 | 2,966 |
| 61 | General Scientific, Arlington, VA | 6,818 | D | 115 | 2,765 |
| 62 | Ward Petroleum, Enid, OK | 160,231 | D | 80 | 2,739 |
| 63 | Summit Marketing Group, Rochester, NY | 5,281 | D | 168 | 2,694 |
| 64 | National Catastrophe Adjusters, Indianapolis, IN | 7,001 | D | 39 | 2,689 |
| 65 | Trandes, Lanham, MD | 12,661 | D | 172 | 2,677 |
| 66 | SIGS Publications Group, New York, NY | 5,732 | D | 26 | 2,656 |
| 67 | Balboa Capital, Irvine, CA | 2,752 | C | 25 | 2,652 |
| 68 | Forum Financial Group, Richardson, TX | 7,490 | D | 10 | 2,604 |
| 69 | Telecommunication Systems Management, Sterling, VA | 2,928 | C | 49 | 2,562 |
| 70 | Global Computronics, Minneapolis, MN | 3,616 | C | 8 | 2,539 |
| 71 | AJT & Associates, Cape Canaveral, FL | 4,149 | D | 107 | 2,526 |
| 72 | Augustine Medical, Eden Prairie, MN | 14,973 | D | 115 | 2,504 |
| 73 | MVM, Falls Church, VA | 28,438 | D | 1,100 | 2,499 |
| 74 | Maier Group, New York, NY | 13,506 | A | 24 | 2,497 |
| 75 | Oread Laboratories, Lawrence, KS | 6,559 | D | 105 | 2,492 |
| 76 | Value Added Distribution, Gaithersburg, MD | 6,574 | E | 17 | 2,468 |
| 77 | Operator Service, Lubbock, TX | 18,406 | C | 40 | 2,449 |
| 78 | International Pacific, Spokane, WA | 16,353 | C | 102 | 2,447 |
| 79 | Information Systems & Services, Silver Spring, MD | 4,805 | C | 49 | 2,390 |
| 80 | Insight Distribution Network, Tempe, AZ | 117,581 | D | 363 | 2,387 |
| 81 | Penmac Personnel Services, Springfield, MO | 6,267 | D | 19 | 2,387 |
| 82 | Automated Systems Design, Roswell, GA | 5,565 | D | 65 | 2,362 |
| 83 | Waste Reduction Systems, Houston, TX | 10,411 | D | 114 | 2,327 |
| 84 | Environmental Restoration, Fredericksburg, VA | 3,002 | D | 25 | 2,321 |
| 85 | HTS Environmental Group, Columbia, MD | 2,422 | A | 40 | 2,298 |
| 86 | Looney & Co., Houston, TX | 6,485 | D | 170 | 2,293 |
| 87 | SMTEK, Newbury Park, CA | 9,204 | D | 109 | 2,284 |
| 88 | Fusion Systems Group, New York, NY | 10,040 | E | 110 | 2,279 |
| 89 | Contract Manufacturer, Madill, OK | 8,875 | D | 133 | 2,248 |
| 90 | RadiSys, Beaverton, OR | 10,194 | D | 61 | 2,238 |
| 91 | RWD Technologies, Columbia, MD | 12,656 | D | 168 | 2,235 |
| 92 | Staffing Inc., Grand Rapids, MI | 5,821 | D | 31 | 2,228 |
| 93 | Victorian Papers, Kansas City, MO | 2,860 | C | 52 | 2,225 |
| 94 | Health-Tech Systems, Hauppauge, NY | 2,343 | C | 11 | 2,220 |
| 95 | Alternative Pioneering Systems, Chaska, MN | 62,395 | C | 120 | 2,190 |
| 96 | Land Tech Remedial, Monroe, CT | 3,523 | A | 30 | 2,188 |
| 97 | FUNacho, Cincinnati, OH | 2,441 | D | 8 | 2,181 |
| 98 | Bruck Hartman Environmental, Cincinnati, OH | 5,031 | D | 60 | 2,166 |
| 99 | Microbiz, Spring Valley, NY | 6,637 | F | 75 | 2,157 |
| 100 | Softub, Chatsworth, CA | 10,688 | D | 110 | 2,145 |

*Profit Range: A-16% or more; B-11% to 15%; C-6% to 10%; D-1%-5%; E-break-even; F-loss*

*Inc. 500 Fastest Growing Companies (cont'd)*

| Rank | Company | 1992 Sales ($ thousands) | 1992 Profit Range | No. of Employees 1992 | % Sales Growth 1988-92 |
|------|---------|--------------------------|-------------------|-----------------------|------------------------|
| 101 | Team One Plastics, Albion, MI | 2,289 | F | 35 | 2,144 |
| 102 | Triangle Technologies, Downers Grove, IL | 4,218 | F | 21 | 2,120 |
| 103 | Our Secret, Albuquerque, NM | 2,413 | B | 30 | 2,094 |
| 104 | Connecticut Courier, West Hartford, CT | 2,774 | D | 18 | 2,084 |
| 105 | Waltham Technologies, North Chelmsford, MA | 12,154 | D | 217 | 2,078 |
| 106 | Deckers, Carpinteria, CA | 34,900 | B | 248 | 2,074 |
| 107 | Whitlock Group, Glen Allen, VA | 16,182 | D | 63 | 2,040 |
| 108 | Dodson Group, Indianapolis, IN | 4,920 | D | 14 | 2,039 |
| 109 | FWB, San Francisco, CA | 11,708 | C | 28 | 2,025 |
| 110 | Creative Alliance, Louisville, KY | 36,840 | D | 92 | 1,981 |
| 111 | FaxLand, Falls Church, VA | 3,291 | C | 30 | 1,970 |
| 112 | Corporate Child Care Service, Nashville, TN | 10,666 | F | 660 | 1,967 |
| 113 | M.D. Enterprises of Connecticut, North Haven, CT | 105,908 | D | 183 | 1,960 |
| 114 | H.J. Ford Associates, Arlington, VA | 9,077 | B | 90 | 1,949 |
| 115 | RADMAN, Santa Monica, CA | 3,161 | D | 26 | 1,939 |
| 116 | Futron, Bethesda, MD | 5,656 | C | 100 | 1,899 |
| 117 | James P. Walsh & Associates, Boulder, CO | 6,369 | C | 51 | 1,878 |
| 118 | Kingston Technology, Fountain Valley, CA | 253,599 | A | 175 | 1,875 |
| 119 | Advantage KBS, Edison, NJ | 2,560 | C | 25 | 1,869 |
| 120 | GTO, Tallahassee, FL | 3,669 | F | 55 | 1,852 |
| 121 | Metro Services Group, New York, NY | 4,003 | D | 15 | 1,843 |
| 122 | Builders, Designers, Remodelers, Grand Rapids, MI | 3,597 | F | 10 | 1,824 |
| 123 | Diamond Flower (Northeast), East Brunswick, NJ | 27,352 | D | 60 | 1,793 |
| 124 | DRE Environmental Services, Brentwood, TN | 5,254 | D | 47 | 1,776 |
| 125 | StatSci, Seattle, WA | 3,381 | C | 40 | 1,748 |
| 126 | Sweetwater Sound, Fort Wayne, IN | 6,523 | D | 18 | 1,732 |
| 127 | Starpak, Denver, CO | 16,791 | C | 139 | 1,729 |
| 128 | Cutchall Management, Omaha, NE | 3,528 | C | 70 | 1,728 |
| 129 | Collectech Systems, Calabasas, CA | 3,188 | B | 36 | 1,711 |
| 130 | J&M Laboratories, Dawsonville, GA | 7,342 | B | 55 | 1,695 |
| 131 | Parsons Technology, Hiawatha, IA | 35,324 | D | 270 | 1,689 |
| 132 | MacTemps, Cambridge, MA | 20,991 | D | 77 | 1,673 |
| 133 | D&K Enterprises, Carrollton, TX | 3,303 | A | 14 | 1,666 |
| 134 | Peach Industries, Los Angeles, CA | 3,662 | C | 19 | 1,661 |
| 135 | Mega-Sys, Greenwood, IN | 7,795 | D | 18 | 1,652 |
| 136 | Florida Infusion, Palm Harbor, FL | 35,668 | C | 20 | 1,632 |
| 137 | Success Stories, Richmond, VA | 1,860 | A | 28 | 1,622 |
| 138 | Melaleuca, Idaho Falls, ID | 200,359 | A | 903 | 1,622 |
| 139 | DHS & Associates, Des Plaines, IL | 1,999 | F | 25 | 1,594 |
| 140 | National Title Resources, White Bear Lake, MN | 5,024 | C | 90 | 1,592 |
| 141 | Apex Environmental, Rockville, MD | 11,032 | B | 100 | 1,569 |
| 142 | Ralph Marlin & Co., Waukesha, WI | 10,311 | A | 42 | 1,560 |
| 143 | Spray Systems Environmental, Tempe, AZ | 10,801 | D | 150 | 1,559 |
| 144 | STATS, Lincolnwood, IL | 1,766 | C | 18 | 1,550 |
| 145 | Fortitech, Schenectady, NY | 8,596 | C | 27 | 1,544 |
| 146 | Mastech Systems, Pittsburgh, PA | 20,161 | B | 410 | 1,542 |
| 147 | Artisan Freelance, Chicago, IL | 2,569 | D | 8 | 1,536 |
| 148 | Atlantic Network Systems, Cary, NC | 6,786 | D | 17 | 1,535 |
| 149 | Sonic Solutions, San Rafael, CA | 9,449 | A | 33 | 1,535 |
| 150 | MDY Advanced Technologies, Fairlawn, NJ | 3,473 | C | 12 | 1,531 |

*Profit Range: A-16% or more; B-11% to 15%; C-6% to 10%; D-1%-5%; E-break-even; F-loss*

*Inc. 500 Fastest Growing Companies (cont'd)*

| Rank | Company | 1992 Sales ($ thousands) | 1992 Profit Range | No. of Employees 1992 | % Sales Growth 1988-92 |
|------|---------|--------------------------|-------------------|-----------------------|------------------------|
| 151 | GeoTek Engineering & Testing Services, Sioux Falls, SD | 2,983 | A | 35 | 1,521 |
| 152 | Kestrel Associates, Arlington, VA | 2,705 | D | 42 | 1,510 |
| 153 | Cetac Technologies, Omaha, NE | 3,666 | A | 24 | 1,508 |
| 154 | HazWaste Industries, Richmond, VA | 45,567 | D | 266 | 1,504 |
| 155 | Great Valley Products, King of Prussia, PA | 31,163 | C | 70 | 1,490 |
| 156 | Compliance Services International, Tacoma, WA | 2,369 | D | 20 | 1,490 |
| 157 | Q&E Software, Raleigh, NC | 7,265 | B | 100 | 1,490 |
| 158 | Computer Professionals, Lake Wylie, SC | 11,175 | D | 203 | 1,485 |
| 159 | Grand Aire Express, Monroe, MI | 5,360 | C | 45 | 1,481 |
| 160 | Alphatronix, Durham, NC | 11,789 | D | 53 | 1,478 |
| 161 | Geerlings & Wade, Canton, MA | 6,479 | C | 11 | 1,476 |
| 162 | Waldec Group, Tampa, FL | 25,911 | D | 86 | 1,476 |
| 163 | Active Voice, Seattle, WA | 14,369 | B | 102 | 1,472 |
| 164 | Grafton Personnel Service, Kansas City, MO | 1,914 | D | 9 | 1,469 |
| 165 | Ergodyne, St. Paul, MN | 28,960 | B | 81 | 1,465 |
| 166 | Compusist, Dryden, NY | 3,403 | B | 64 | 1,454 |
| 167 | LBS Capital Management, Safety Harbor, FL | 2,787 | A | 18 | 1,448 |
| 168 | Brown's Super Stores, Philadelphia, PA | 23,381 | D | 48 | 1,446 |
| 169 | Teltrust, Salt Lake City, UT | 24,772 | D | 76 | 1,444 |
| 170 | Univenture, Dublin, OH | 1,706 | C | 26 | 1,437 |
| 171 | Williamsburg Winery, Williamburg, VA | 1,811 | D | 30 | 1,422 |
| 172 | Superior Pharmaceutical, Cincinnati, OH | 10,652 | B | 35 | 1,409 |
| 173 | MJD Investments, Irving, TX | 41,632 | D | 650 | 1,405 |
| 174 | Carrio Cabling, Signal Hill, CA | 1,848 | B | 27 | 1,402 |
| 175 | Sunland Computer Services, Phoenix, AZ | 11,213 | D | 92 | 1,401 |
| 176 | Renaissance Design, North Hampton, NH | 1,525 | D | 25 | 1,395 |
| 177 | Link Marketing and Data Services, Cincinnati, OH | 3,116 | C | 35 | 1,391 |
| 178 | RDA Consultants Ltd., Timonium, MD | 2,831 | B | 33 | 1,390 |
| 179 | Morningstar, Chicago, IL | 11,153 | F | 190 | 1,385 |
| 180 | Communique Telecommunications, Ontario, CA | 27,840 | D | 70 | 1,383 |
| 181 | Systems Engineering & Management, Alexandria, VA | 16,395 | D | 260 | 1,376 |
| 182 | Factura Composites, Rochester, NY | 2,008 | B | 36 | 1,366 |
| 183 | Coldwater Creek, Sandpoint, ID | 18,229 | C | 79 | 1,358 |
| 184 | Advanced Engineering & Research, Arlington, VA | 3,771 | C | 50 | 1,345 |
| 185 | Small Systems Management, New Castle, DE | 5,753 | D | 16 | 1,342 |
| 186 | Focus Healthcare Management, Brentwood, TN | 17,639 | C | 297 | 1,341 |
| 187 | Design Construction Services, Akron, OH | 4,136 | C | 7 | 1,336 |
| 188 | Sprint Temporary Services, Tampa, FL | 7,840 | F | 35 | 1,336 |
| 189 | Univest Financial Group, Marietta, GA | 29,865 | A | 102 | 1,327 |
| 190 | Combined Resources Technology, Baton Rouge, LA | 1,492 | B | 12 | 1,321 |
| 191 | CMG Health, Owings Mills, MD | 17,863 | F | 160 | 1,318 |
| 192 | Automation Group, San Francisco, CA | 2,455 | A | 20 | 1,311 |
| 193 | Lam-Tech Industries, Ephrata, PA | 3,342 | D | 59 | 1,304 |
| 194 | Motherwear, Northampton, MA | 1,627 | C | 9 | 1,303 |
| 195 | Yield Techniglobal, Staten Island, NY | 3,379 | B | 6 | 1,296 |
| 196 | Abundant Life Childcare Centers, Kirkland, WA | 2,014 | F | 74 | 1,289 |
| 197 | Maximum Strategy, Milpitas, CA | 10,133 | A | 28 | 1,279 |
| 198 | Medical Equipment Repair Services, Sarasota, FL | 1,480 | D | 16 | 1,270 |
| 199 | ControlAir, Amherst, NH | 1,903 | A | 14 | 1,269 |
| 200 | Sygnetics, Troy, MI | 2,422 | D | 35 | 1,268 |

*Profit Range: A-16% or more; B-11% to 15%; C-6% to 10%; D-1%-5%; E-break-even; F-loss*

*Inc. 500 Fastest Growing Companies (cont'd)*

| Rank | Company | 1992 Sales ($ thousands) | 1992 Profit Range | No. of Employees 1992 | % Sales Growth 1988-92 |
|------|---------|------|------|------|------|
| 201 | Property Sciences Group, Walnut Creek, CA | 5,059 | D | 105 | 1,267 |
| 202 | Executive Mortgage, Melville, NY | 1,365 | A | 18 | 1,265 |
| 203 | Anadigics, Warren, NJ | 20,224 | F | 177 | 1,263 |
| 204 | Canfield & Associates, Cypress, CA | 2,490 | C | 100 | 1,261 |
| 205 | Support Services Alliance, Schoharie, NY | 3,072 | B | 50 | 1,259 |
| 206 | Charles J. Givens Organization, Altamonte Springs, FL | 104,007 | A | 319 | 1,259 |
| 207 | Daydots Label, Fort Worth, TX | 2,330 | A | 21 | 1,255 |
| 208 | Vector Business Systems, York, PA | 1,758 | D | 7 | 1,252 |
| 209 | User Technology Associates, Arlington, VA | 19,503 | C | 330 | 1,250 |
| 210 | Tri-Star Computer, Chandler, AZ | 32,030 | F | 130 | 1,249 |
| 211 | Premiere Merchandising, Inglewood, CA | 7,969 | E | 12 | 1,248 |
| 212 | Technautics, Arlington, VA | 4,690 | D | 53 | 1,248 |
| 213 | U.S. Personnel, Columbia, SC | 7,868 | D | 35 | 1,247 |
| 214 | CompuSense, Nashua, NH | 2,055 | A | 22 | 1,243 |
| 215 | Hub City Indianapolis Terminals, Carmel, IN | 20,538 | D | 15 | 1,242 |
| 216 | Gym Masters, Albany, CA | 7,918 | F | 80 | 1,233 |
| 217 | Digital Network Associates, New York, NY | 8,268 | B | 25 | 1,212 |
| 218 | Eaton Metal Products, Eaton Rapids, MI | 2,033 | C | 27 | 1,212 |
| 219 | Communifax, Warrendale, PA | 2,310 | D | 10 | 1,205 |
| 220 | IMC Networks, Irvine, CA | 5,863 | C | 31 | 1,191 |
| 221 | Family Health Plan, Miami Lakes, FL | 54,843 | D | 193 | 1,191 |
| 222 | High Tide, Seattle, WA | 2,772 | D | 34 | 1,189 |
| 223 | EKS, Naperville, IL | 6,895 | E | 8 | 1,184 |
| 224 | Red Rose Collection, Burlingame, CA | 9,298 | F | 100 | 1,177 |
| 225 | Systems Consulting Group, Miami, FL | 3,665 | C | 50 | 1,177 |
| 226 | United Industrial Temporaries, Springfield, MA | 2,694 | D | 8 | 1,171 |
| 227 | Campbell Services, Southfield, MI | 6,175 | F | 80 | 1,171 |
| 228 | Pet Ventures, Arlington, VA | 10,087 | D | 140 | 1,162 |
| 229 | Di-Mark Group, Houston, TX | 1,598 | B | 3 | 1,148 |
| 230 | Brewer Personnel Services, Fayetteville, AR | 10,860 | D | 33 | 1,145 |
| 231 | Flexible Plan Investments, Bloomfield Hills, MI | 1,724 | F | 13 | 1,140 |
| 232 | Summerlot Engineered Products, Rosedale, IN | 2,787 | C | 28 | 1,139 |
| 233 | Digital DataVoice, Eagan, MN | 1,325 | B | 10 | 1,138 |
| 234 | Maval Manufacturing, Twinsburg, OH | 9,517 | B | 80 | 1,126 |
| 235 | Culver Temporary Workforce, San Diego, CA | 4,655 | D | 17 | 1,125 |
| 236 | Digidesign, Menlo Park, CA | 21,065 | B | 123 | 1,112 |
| 237 | Tomkats, Nashville, TN | 2,681 | F | 31 | 1,108 |
| 238 | Touchstone Research Laboratory, Triadelphia, WV | 2,900 | D | 26 | 1,093 |
| 239 | Hi-Tech Hose, Santa Ana, CA | 2,003 | D | 20 | 1,078 |
| 240 | Replica, Dedham, MA | 5,014 | F | 25 | 1,077 |
| 241 | Pro Mark Technologies, River Forest, IL | 4,149 | C | 24 | 1,075 |
| 242 | FPT Software, North Andover, MA | 33,132 | A | 216 | 1,073 |
| 243 | HCFS, Dallas, TX | 1,240 | A | 29 | 1,070 |
| 244 | Medscribe, Pittsburgh, PA | 1,517 | D | 55 | 1,067 |
| 245 | Mortgage Choice, Durham, NC | 4,036 | A | 28 | 1,066 |
| 246 | Daryan International, Montebello, CA | 8,660 | D | 14 | 1,064 |
| 247 | Meridian Associates, Sarasota, FL | 4,968 | F | 69 | 1,061 |
| 248 | Single Source Systems, Indianapolis, IN | 1,432 | D | 11 | 1,055 |
| 249 | Collins/Reisenbichler Architects, Dallas, TX | 1,297 | A | 17 | 1,048 |
| 250 | Gardner/Fox Associates, Bryn Mawr, PA | 6,739 | D | 40 | 1,046 |

*Profit Range: A-16% or more; B-11% to 15%; C-6% to 10%; D-1%-5%; E-break-even; F-loss*

*Inc. 500 Fastest Growing Companies (cont'd)*

| Rank | Company | 1992 Sales ($ thousands) | 1992 Profit Range | No. of Employees 1992 | % Sales Growth 1988-92 |
|------|---------|--------------------------|-------------------|------------------------|------------------------|
| 251 | MediaMap, Cambridge, MA | 1,896 | D | 25 | 1,042 |
| 252 | Venntronix, Roslyn Heights, NY | 5,390 | C | 85 | 1,040 |
| 253 | Roelynn Business Products, Hazlet, NJ | 1,208 | D | 8 | 1,029 |
| 254 | Home HealthCare Resources, Bensalem, PA | 4,295 | A | 17 | 1,024 |
| 255 | Digital Print, Forth Worth, TX | 2,620 | A | 12 | 1,020 |
| 256 | Barclays Law Publishers, South San Francisco, CA | 8,585 | B | 70 | 1,011 |
| 257 | Key Construction, Wichita, KS | 15,022 | D | 65 | 1,010 |
| 258 | Talan Products, Cleveland, OH | 2,613 | C | 20 | 1,007 |
| 259 | Telamon, Indianapolis, IN | 15,151 | D | 75 | 1,007 |
| 260 | ISYX LAN Systems, Rockville, MD | 6,728 | C | 12 | 999 |
| 261 | Binary Arts, Alexandria, VA | 3,085 | B | 9 | 998 |
| 262 | Rocky Mountain Motorworks, Woodland Park, CO | 2,688 | D | 35 | 997 |
| 263 | Beccorp Transportation Services, Schaumburg, IL | 3,934 | F | 3 | 996 |
| 264 | U.S. Computer, Miama, FL | 153,534 | D | 75 | 994 |
| 265 | Whitacre Trucking, Weston, OH | 6,422 | D | 84 | 992 |
| 266 | Abide International, Kirkland, WA | 4,070 | A | 36 | 980 |
| 267 | Lai, Venuti & Lai, Santa Clara, CA | 2,338 | C | 20 | 977 |
| 268 | Maryland Screen Printers, Baltimore, MD | 6,489 | A | 52 | 976 |
| 269 | AnTel, Plano, TX | 2,080 | F | 20 | 972 |
| 270 | Mustang Engineering, Houston, TX | 24,951 | D | 270 | 972 |
| 271 | MFI Investments, Bryan, OH | 3,288 | D | 16 | 971 |
| 272 | Aroma Vera, Los Angeles, CA | 3,094 | C | 25 | 971 |
| 273 | E. Petrich & Associates, San Luis Obispo, CA | 1,946 | D | 23 | 969 |
| 274 | Environmental Health & Engineering, Newton, MA | 1,623 | D | 22 | 968 |
| 275 | Cavanaugh Enterprises, Half Moon Bay, CA | 1,884 | C | 32 | 964 |
| 276 | Sound Choice Accompaniment Tracks, Pineville, NC | 2,977 | A | 22 | 963 |
| 277 | Lens Express, Deerfield Beach, FL | 19,446 | C | 203 | 960 |
| 278 | JRL Systems, Austin, TX | 4,235 | C | 28 | 956 |
| 279 | Main Tape, Union, NJ | 17,893 | C | 125 | 954 |
| 280 | Hub City Florida Terminals, Orange Park, FL | 25,789 | C | 14 | 950 |
| 281 | Sharon's Finest, Santa Rosa, CA | 2,594 | F | 5 | 950 |
| 282 | ROW Sciences, Rockville, MD | 24,751 | D | 350 | 949 |
| 283 | Northwest Envirocon, Vancouver, WA | 5,822 | E | 122 | 945 |
| 284 | Unipower, Pompano Beach, FL | 16,202 | C | 160 | 933 |
| 285 | Main Street Muffins, Akron, OH | 2,323 | C | 24 | 932 |
| 286 | PAI, Oak Ridge, TN | 10,420 | C | 80 | 932 |
| 287 | Universal Imaging, West Chester, PA | 4,881 | B | 18 | 925 |
| 288 | AVT, Littleton, CO | 2,640 | D | 18 | 923 |
| 289 | MediServe Information Systems, Tempe, AZ | 2,942 | D | 24 | 918 |
| 290 | OCS Group, Pittsford, NY | 8,690 | B | 155 | 918 |
| 291 | Cadapult Graphic Systems, Allendale, NJ | 4,880 | D | 9 | 917 |
| 292 | DCT Systems Group, Marietta, GA | 135,506 | D | 240 | 913 |
| 293 | Direct Air, Gary, IN | 4,820 | F | 100 | 913 |
| 294 | PMT Services, Nashville, TN | 22,200 | D | 84 | 909 |
| 295 | Registry, Newton, MA | 24,021 | D | 78 | 906 |
| 296 | Imedia, Morriston, NJ | 3,066 | A | 18 | 905 |
| 297 | Applied Computer Technologies, Coats, NC | 1,013 | C | 23 | 903 |
| 298 | David Mitchell & Associates, St. Paul, MN | 9,135 | C | 125 | 892 |
| 299 | MAC Management, Oscoda, MI | 3,006 | D | 5 | 889 |
| 300 | Tova Industries, Louisville, KY | 4,055 | C | 35 | 887 |

*Profit Range: A-16% or more; B-11% to 15%; C-6% to 10%; D-1%-5%; E-break-even; F-loss*

*Inc. 500 Fastest Growing Companies (cont'd)*

| Rank | Company | 1992 Sales ($ thousands) | 1992 Profit Range | No. of Employees 1992 | % Sales Growth 1988-92 |
|------|---------|--------------------------|-------------------|------------------------|-------------------------|
| 301 | Technapack, Beaverton, OR | 1,573 | D | 10 | 883 |
| 302 | Staff Leasing, Bradenton, FL | 231,821 | D | 309 | 883 |
| 303 | Data Image, Midland, MI | 1,238 | F | 7 | 883 |
| 304 | K-Whit Tools, Fishers, IN | 48,646 | D | 336 | 882 |
| 305 | Vanguard Automation, Tucson, AZ | 11,360 | D | 120 | 882 |
| 306 | Coverall Cleaning Concepts, San Diego, CA | 22,830 | C | 150 | 880 |
| 307 | Noble Oil Services, Sanford, NC | 4554 | D | 42 | 879 |
| 308 | Sherpa, San Jose, CA | 17,521 | C | 125 | 878 |
| 309 | Jungle Jim's Playlands, San Antonio, TX | 6,555 | F | 49 | 874 |
| 310 | Wright Express, South Portland, ME | 9,197 | D | 77 | 869 |
| 311 | Astea International, Chalfont, PA | 15,981 | B | 150 | 868 |
| 312 | Travel Store, Los Angeles, CA | 34,298 | D | 41 | 863 |
| 313 | American Fastsigns, Dallas, TX | 3,875 | C | 32 | 854 |
| 314 | Marsch Enterprises, Anchorage, AK | 1,452 | A | 15 | 849 |
| 315 | Technical Management Services, Arlington, VA | 6,696 | C | 92 | 848 |
| 316 | Bizware, Englewood Cliffs, NJ | 1,198 | F | 13 | 843 |
| 317 | Beechwood Data Systems, Clark, NJ | 4,102 | A | 52 | 843 |
| 318 | Trapper's Creek, Anchorage, AK | 1,165 | C | 10 | 840 |
| 319 | Union Pointe Construction, Salt Lake City, UT | 12,699 | D | 35 | 839 |
| 320 | CytoDiagnostics, Oklahoma City, OK | 4,813 | F | 75 | 838 |
| 321 | Watsonrise Business Systems, Arlington, TX | 1,387 | C | 6 | 837 |
| 322 | LAN Co., Malvern, PA | 5,538 | D | 28 | 834 |
| 323 | Advanced Cellular Systems, San Juan, PR | 11,755 | D | 53 | 829 |
| 324 | Mytech, Austin, TX | 1,351 | B | 21 | 825 |
| 325 | Govind & Associates, Corpus Christi, TX | 9,550 | F | 210 | 824 |
| 326 | Monterey Homes, Scottsdale, AZ | 35,111 | C | 41 | 823 |
| 327 | Right Byte Computers, Pullman, WA | 1,463 | D | 7 | 820 |
| 328 | Account Pros, Boston, MA | 3,984 | D | 26 | 814 |
| 329 | Antique Gallery, Richmond, VA | 1,833 | D | 6 | 812 |
| 330 | Southern Financial Network, Stone Mountain, GA | 1,593 | B | 24 | 810 |
| 331 | Item Products, Houston, TX | 6,431 | C | 45 | 806 |
| 332 | Information Management Alternatives, Jacksonville, FL | 3,086 | D | 56 | 802 |
| 333 | Patton General Contracting, Summerville, SC | 2,726 | D | 15 | 800 |
| 334 | Tampa Bay Vending, Tampa, FL | 4,008 | B | 30 | 799 |
| 335 | Fastrak Training, Columbia, MD | 1,175 | A | 13 | 797 |
| 336 | Centerline Piping, Center Line, MI | 15,276 | D | 60 | 796 |
| 337 | Cowboy Brothers Trading, Maspeth, NY | 49,096 | D | 90 | 795 |
| 338 | Enter Software, Menlo Park, CA | 1,453 | B | 17 | 791 |
| 339 | R&R Recreation Products, Englewood Cliffs, NJ | 4,447 | C | 5 | 789 |
| 340 | Bruce Co., Washington, DC | 3,518 | D | 73 | 788 |
| 341 | Management Service Systems, Ann Arbor, MI | 1,400 | B | 72 | 786 |
| 342 | Executive Business Services, San Diego, CA | 1,010 | A | 12 | 786 |
| 343 | Retail Resources, Rochester Hills, MI | 6,917 | D | 14 | 783 |
| 344 | Engineering Data Systems, Dubuque, IA | 5,473 | C | 80 | 780 |
| 345 | Florida Island Foods, Fernandina Beach, FL | 3,474 | D | 30 | 779 |
| 346 | AAMP of America, Clearwater, FL | 8,846 | B | 46 | 777 |
| 347 | Englehart, Grand Rapids, MI | 1,149 | C | 15 | 770 |
| 348 | All Green, Marietta, GA | 10,195 | D | 300 | 769 |
| 349 | Phoenix Controls, Newton, MA | 9,814 | D | 83 | 768 |
| 350 | Pest Control Technologies, Dallas, TX | 1,300 | C | 27 | 767 |

*Profit Range: A-16% or more; B-11% to 15%; C-6% to 10%; D-1%-5%; E-break-even; F-loss*

*Inc. 500 Fastest Growing Companies (cont'd)*

| Rank | Company | 1992 Sales ($ thousands) | 1992 Profit Range | No. of Employees 1992 | % Sales Growth 1988-92 |
|------|---------|--------------------------|-------------------|-----------------------|------------------------|
| 351 | Quantum Research International, Huntsville, AL | 3,509 | D | 46 | 766 |
| 352 | Dunsirn Industries, Neenah, WI | 15,634 | C | 111 | 763 |
| 353 | U.S. Computer Maintenance, Farmingdale, NY | 6,916 | C | 55 | 761 |
| 354 | Knowledge Systems, Cary, NC | 3,293 | F | 44 | 760 |
| 355 | DataLOK, Los Angeles, CA | 4,005 | B | 63 | 759 |
| 356 | Keypoint Technology, Walnut, CA | 91,433 | C | 75 | 759 |
| 357 | Saturn Electronics & Engineering, Rochester Hills, MI | 25,842 | C | 325 | 757 |
| 358 | Kirshenbaum & Bond, New York, NY | 7,280 | A | 90 | 752 |
| 359 | Ransom Environmental Consultants, Newburyport, MA | 2,263 | D | 30 | 751 |
| 360 | SalesTalk, Montain View, CA | 9,985 | D | 48 | 750 |
| 361 | Grant Communications, Del Mar, CA | 1,093 | C | 5 | 747 |
| 362 | Comprehensive Technologies International, Chantilly, VA | 39,230 | D | 495 | 746 |
| 363 | Telephone Express, Colorado Springs, CO | 22,872 | D | 117 | 742 |
| 364 | KnowledgePoint, Petaluma, CA | 1,977 | D | 20 | 738 |
| 365 | DCS Software & Consulting, Richardson, TX | 6,212 | D | 103 | 736 |
| 366 | Impact Telemarketing, Woodbury, NJ | 2,223 | D | 20 | 736 |
| 367 | Taggart Ltd., Cody, WY | 15,922 | F | 230 | 731 |
| 368 | Results Marketing Services, Paramus, NJ | 1,129 | A | 16 | 730 |
| 369 | Rock Financial, Bingham Farms, MI | 11,000 | B | 150 | 727 |
| 370 | Peripheral Land, Fremont, CA | 36,512 | D | 167 | 727 |
| 371 | ESE, Marshfield, WI | 3,943 | D | 38 | 723 |
| 372 | Travel 2000, Lansing, MI | 7,404 | D | 44 | 722 |
| 373 | Ethix, Beaverton, OR | 26,196 | C | 400 | 720 |
| 374 | Computer One, Albuquerque, NM | 10,568 | D | 24 | 719 |
| 375 | Maritime Services, Hood River, OR | 5,724 | D | 35 | 719 |
| 376 | Sim Ware, Livonia, MI | 5,529 | D | 73 | 715 |
| 377 | Fisher Industrial Services, Glencoe, AL | 8,452 | C | 145 | 714 |
| 378 | Virtual Services, Rochester Hills, MI | 6,370 | C | 59 | 711 |
| 379 | Dazser & Dazser, M.D., Tampa, FL | 5,723 | E | 16 | 711 |
| 380 | State of the Art Computing, San Diego, CA | 4,822 | E | 46 | 710 |
| 381 | Renaissance, Carmel, IN | 1,731 | F | 30 | 709 |
| 382 | Gail Pittman, Ridgeland, MS | 1,221 | D | 48 | 709 |
| 383 | TERA Systems, Reston, VA | 3,891 | D | 55 | 706 |
| 384 | Proteus, Albuquerque, NM | 5,660 | D | 85 | 704 |
| 385 | Business Psychology Associates, Boise, ID | 1,349 | C | 25 | 703 |
| 386 | Canvasbacks, Milwaukee, WI | 7,371 | B | 63 | 701 |
| 387 | Quintiles Transnational, Morrisville, NC | 47,100 | C | 645 | 698 |
| 388 | Three Springs, Huntsville, AL | 7,013 | A | 120 | 698 |
| 389 | Abacus Technology, Chevy Chase, MD | 15,929 | C | 122 | 688 |
| 390 | Payroll 1, Royal Oak, MI | 4,982 | D | 105 | 687 |
| 391 | Print Mailers, Houston, TX | 1,650 | E | 31 | 686 |
| 392 | Ident-a-Kid Services of America, St. Petersburg, FL | 825 | A | 3 | 686 |
| 393 | Micro Information Services, Mequon, WI | 4,055 | F | 37 | 681 |
| 394 | Mastersoft, Scottsdale, AZ | 3,600 | A | 17 | 681 |
| 395 | Gurney-Kerr Contractors, Willow Grove, PA | 1,045 | E | 9 | 680 |
| 396 | Sherikon, Chantilly, VA | 14,885 | D | 200 | 679 |
| 397 | Securities Service Network, Knoxville, TN | 4,978 | D | 99 | 674 |
| 398 | Teltech Resource Network, Minneapolis, MN | 15,459 | D | 163 | 673 |
| 399 | Global Mail Ltd., Sterling, VA | 12,491 | C | 65 | 672 |
| 400 | American Insurance Management Group, Atlanta, GA | 17,841 | D | 110 | 672 |

*Profit Range: A-16% or more; B-11% to 15%; C-6% to 10%; D-1%-5%; E-break-even; F-loss*

*Inc. 500 Fastest Growing Companies (cont'd)*

| Rank | Company | 1992 Sales ($ thousands) | 1992 Profit Range | No. of Employees 1992 | % Sales Growth 1988-92 |
|---|---|---|---|---|---|
| 401 | Jayline International, Brooklyn, NY | 1,574 | B | 30 | 672 |
| 402 | Cherry Creek Mortgage, Denver, CO | 4,726 | B | 74 | 670 |
| 403 | Quality Composites, Sandy, UT | 2,663 | D | 46 | 670 |
| 404 | Guarantee Insurance Resources, Marietta, GA | 4,077 | A | 41 | 669 |
| 405 | Buckeye Beans & Herbs, Spokane, WA | 2,905 | B | 30 | 669 |
| 406 | Center for Applied Psychology, King of Prussia, PA | 5,879 | D | 30 | 665 |
| 407 | Personnel Management, Shelbyville, IN | 16,242 | D | 70 | 664 |
| 408 | ExecuTrain of Florida, Orlando, FL | 4,011 | C | 55 | 664 |
| 409 | Action Temporary Services, Evansville, IN | 3,911 | D | 8 | 664 |
| 410 | Asay Publishing, Joplin, MO | 1,083 | B | 9 | 657 |
| 411 | Groundwater Protection, Orlando, FL | 9,723 | D | 104 | 657 |
| 412 | Sunrise Terrace, Fairfax, VA | 19,775 | D | 1,050 | 657 |
| 413 | First Benefit, Anderson, IN | 5,588 | D | 119 | 653 |
| 414 | California Investment Trust Fund, San Francisco, CA | 1,580 | B | 12 | 652 |
| 415 | Teubner & Associates, Stillwater, OK | 2,859 | B | 21 | 652 |
| 416 | Adtran, Huntsville, AL | 57,042 | A | 337 | 652 |
| 417 | Munidex, Fort Lee, NJ | 797 | A | 9 | 652 |
| 418 | All Americas, Vancouver, WA | 4,218 | D | 11 | 652 |
| 419 | Flying Colors Painting, Norwalk, CT | 1,383 | C | 2 | 652 |
| 420 | Flash Creative Management, River Edge, NJ | 991 | A | 10 | 651 |
| 421 | Aztech Controls, Mesa, AZ | 6,741 | C | 23 | 650 |
| 422 | Groundwater & Environmental Services, Wall, NJ | 18,003 | D | 175 | 649 |
| 423 | EDECO, Tulsa, OK | 11,250 | D | 177 | 648 |
| 424 | Hernandex Engineering, Houston, TX | 19,670 | D | 350 | 648 |
| 425 | Sherwood Promotions, Aurora, OH | 4,507 | D | 7 | 647 |
| 426 | Source Technologies, Charlotte, NC | 8,782 | D | 24 | 647 |
| 427 | Applied Computer Technology, Fort Collins, CO | 9,842 | D | 45 | 647 |
| 428 | Child Works, Ormond Beach, FL | 2,180 | C | 9 | 647 |
| 429 | Triton Marine Construction, Houston, TX | 25,586 | B | 105 | 643 |
| 430 | RedZone Robotics, Pittsburgh, PA | 1,975 | B | 24 | 642 |
| 431 | System Connection, Provo, UT | 8,736 | C | 70 | 641 |
| 432 | Master Translating Services, Miami, FL | 778 | D | 10 | 641 |
| 433 | American Megatrends, Norcross, GA | 83,876 | A | 151 | 640 |
| 434 | Atkinson-Baker & Associates, Burbank, CA | 5,150 | C | 39 | 636 |
| 435 | Financial Maintenance, Kent, WA | 993 | D | 13 | 636 |
| 436 | Gensym, Cambridge, MA | 13,838 | C | 112 | 633 |
| 437 | Rockwell Construction, Pompano Beach, FL | 27,089 | D | 16 | 630 |
| 438 | ColorAge, Billerica, MA | 6,023 | C | 49 | 628 |
| 439 | Trigen Energy, White Plains, NY | 67,084 | D | 226 | 626 |
| 440 | FitchMeyer Enterprises, Bloomington, IN | 1,001 | F | 22 | 625 |
| 441 | National Register, Lakewood, CO | 1,786 | D | 20 | 623 |
| 442 | Compatible Systems, Boulder, CO | 2,434 | C | 17 | 622 |
| 443 | Recom Technologies, San Jose, CA | 12,644 | C | 250 | 622 |
| 444 | Enrich International, Orem, UT | 24,839 | D | 64 | 622 |
| 445 | Audio Visual Associates, East Hanover, NJ | 1,787 | A | 16 | 621 |
| 446 | BankTemps, Denver, CO | 1,058 | D | 4 | 620 |
| 447 | Intermarket, Miami, FL | 7,230 | D | 16 | 618 |
| 448 | Environmental Operations, St. Louis, MO | 2,861 | D | 35 | 617 |
| 449 | Federal Investment, East Providence, RI | 12,481 | B | 46 | 616 |
| 450 | Kofax Image Products, Irvine, CA | 14,426 | B | 89 | 615 |

*Profit Range: A-16% or more; B-11% to 15%; C-6% to 10%; D-1%-5%; E-break-even; F-loss*

*Inc. 500 Fastest Growing Companies (cont'd)*

| Rank | Company | 1992 Sales ($ thousands) | 1992 Profit Range | No. of Employees 1992 | % Sales Growth 1988-92 |
|------|---------|--------------------------|-------------------|----------------------|------------------------|
| 451 | Payroll 1 Mid-Atlantic, McLean, VA | 3,342 | D | 75 | 613 |
| 452 | Sai Software Consultants, Kingwood, TX | 5,162 | D | 125 | 608 |
| 453 | Landmark Services, Richmond, VA | 1,409 | D | 35 | 608 |
| 454 | Restek, Bellefonte, PA | 9,162 | A | 69 | 605 |
| 455 | Turnkey Environmental Consultants, Mount Prospect, IL | 1,139 | C | 15 | 603 |
| 456 | Docu-Net, Brookfield, WI | 1,426 | D | 17 | 602 |
| 457 | Tycom Limited Partnership, Santa Ana, CA | 16,838 | C | 240 | 602 |
| 458 | Marketplace Promotions, Atlanta, GA | 3,701 | D | 29 | 601 |
| 459 | Label Technology, Merced, CA | 4,380 | D | 32 | 599 |
| 460 | WinterBrook Beverage Group, Bellevue, WA | 15,371 | F | 40 | 596 |
| 461 | Corporate Health Dimensions, Troy, NY | 9,888 | D | 200 | 595 |
| 462 | Joe Koch Construction, Youngstown, OH | 8,746 | C | 21 | 594 |
| 463 | Sterling Information Group, Austin, TX | 1,888 | C | 30 | 594 |
| 464 | Village Homes of Colorado, Littleton, CO | 69,252 | C | 80 | 593 |
| 465 | DeMar Plumbing, Heating & Air-Conditioning, Clovis, CA | 3,324 | C | 44 | 593 |
| 466 | Logmatics, Marietta, GA | 1,925 | D | 20 | 592 |
| 467 | Systems & Programming Solutions, Milwaukee, WI | 2,236 | C | 33 | 592 |
| 468 | Data Sciences, Roseville, MN | 3,008 | C | 36 | 591 |
| 469 | Gap International, Springfield, PA | 3,150 | A | 17 | 591 |
| 470 | Personal Workstations, Kirkland, WA | 7,774 | D | 21 | 590 |
| 471 | Working Assets Funding Service, San Francisco, CA | 15,629 | F | 27 | 589 |
| 472 | State-Line Graphics, Everett, MA | 2,316 | A | 7 | 589 |
| 473 | Eastern Group, Alexandria, VA | 73,148 | D | 60 | 589 |
| 474 | Retail Store Systems, Warwick, RI | 3,889 | C | 15 | 587 |
| 475 | J.D. Edwards & Co., Denver, CO | 170,480 | D | 1,124 | 586 |
| 476 | Promo Magazine, Wilton, CT | 1,551 | D | 7 | 586 |
| 477 | Wild Oats Markets, Boulder, CO | 36,638 | D | 300 | 585 |
| 478 | Greetings Trend Shops, Seattle, WA | 1,090 | D | 12 | 581 |
| 479 | Wasser Industries, Seattle, WA | 4,932 | D | 8 | 581 |
| 480 | Audio Visual Concepts, Tempe, AZ | 1,104 | A | 9 | 577 |
| 481 | HTI Bio-Services, Santa Ysabel, CA | 3,013 | D | 50 | 577 |
| 482 | SWFTE International Ltd., Hockessin, DE | 3,520 | A | 31 | 577 |
| 483 | American Telegram, Beverly Hills, CA | 1,565 | D | 41 | 575 |
| 484 | EnecoTech Group, Denver, CO | 16,565 | D | 195 | 573 |
| 485 | Merritt, Hawkins, & Associates, Irving, TX | 7,643 | D | 75 | 572 |
| 486 | MTI, Anaheim, CA | 115,678 | F | 510 | 566 |
| 487 | MDM Engineering, San Clemente, CA | 10,381 | C | 90 | 564 |
| 488 | Saloom Furniture, Winchendon, MA | 7,554 | D | 75 | 563 |
| 489 | Superior Orthopedic Supplies, Graysville, GA | 1,020 | D | 15 | 562 |
| 490 | Design Basics, Omaha, NE | 3,492 | A | 34 | 561 |
| 491 | POS Systems, Tempe, AZ | 6,730 | D | 231 | 561 |
| 492 | Fencemaster, Jackson, TN | 8,851 | D | 80 | 560 |
| 493 | Fanamation, Compton, CA | 6,600 | F | 27 | 559 |
| 494 | Metters Industries, McLean, VA | 32,979 | D | 475 | 558 |
| 495 | Spray-Tech, Longwood, FL | 17,489 | C | 125 | 553 |
| 496 | International Computer Graphics, Fremont, CA | 44,166 | D | 32 | 553 |
| 497 | Ryan-McGinn, Arlington, VA | 2,252 | A | 13 | 553 |
| 498 | J.B. Dollar Stretcher Magazine, Richfield, OH | 2,688 | D | 8 | 552 |
| 499 | Buschman, Cleveland, OH | 1,883 | A | 17 | 552 |
| 500 | ACS Dataline, Austin, TX | 12,437 | D | 175 | 551 |

*Profit Range: A-16% or more; B-11% to 15%; C-6% to 10%; D-1%-5%; E-break-even; F-loss*        *Source: Inc. Magazine, 1993*

# Black and Female CEOs

Every year, *Black Enterprise* magazine lists the top black-owned businesses ranked by revenue.

| Rank | Company | Location | Staff | 1992 Sales ($) |
|---|---|---|---|---|
| 1 | TLC Beatrice International Holdings | New York, NY | 5,000 | 1,665,000,000 |
| 2 | Johnson Publishing | Chicago, IL | 2,785 | 274,200,000 |
| 3 | Philadelphia Coca-Cola Bottling | Philadelphia, PA | 1,000 | 266,000,000 |
| 4 | H.J. Russell & Company | Atlanta, GA | 825 | 145,610,000 |
| 5 | The Anderson-Dubose Company | Solon, OH | 80 | 110,000,000 |
| 6 | RMS Technologies | Marlton, NJ | 1,176 | 103,300,000 |
| 7 | Gold Line Refining | Houston, TX | 51 | 91,880,000 |
| 8 | Soft Sheen Products | Chicago, IL | 547 | 91,700,000 |
| 9 | Garden State Cable TV | Cherry Hill, NJ | 300 | 91,000,000 |
| 10 | Threads 4 Life Corp. d/b/a Cross Colours | Los Angeles, CA | 250 | 89,000,000 |
| 11 | Barden Communications | Detroit, MI | 328 | 78,600,000 |
| 12 | The Bing Group | Detroit, MI | 210 | 77,630,000 |
| 13 | Burrell Communications | Chicago, IL | 115 | 77,070,000 |
| 14 | Uniworld Group | New York, NY | 85 | 72,420,000 |
| 15 | Pulsar Systems | New Castle, DE | 65 | 67,000,000 |
| 16 | Stop Shop and Save | Baltimore, MD | 600 | 66,000,000 |
| 17 | Black Entertainment Television Holdings | Washington, DC | 328 | 61,660,000 |
| 18 | Mays Chemical | Indianapolis, IN | 75 | 60,800,000 |
| 19 | Essence Communications | New York, NY | 87 | 56,350,000 |
| 20 | Community Foods | Baltimore, MD | 400 | 47,500,000 |
| 21 | Technology Applications | Alexandria, VA | 525 | 46,500,000 |
| 22 | Surface Protection Industries | Los Angeles, CA | 200 | 46,200,000 |
| 23 | Johnson Products | Chicago, IL | 215 | 46,000,000 |
| * | Luster Products | Chicago, IL | 315 | 46,000,000 |
| 25 | The Maxima Corp. | Lanham, MD | 752 | 45,100,000 |
| 26 | Wesley Industries | Flint, MI | 395 | 45,000,000 |
| 27 | Pepsi-Cola of Washington, DC, L.P. | Washington, DC | 138 | 43,870,000 |
| 28 | Integrated Systems Analysts | Arlington, VA | 595 | 43,600,000 |
| 29 | Granite Broadcasting | New York, NY | 364 | 43,110,000 |
| 30 | The Mingo Group | New York, NY | 40 | 42,730,000 |
| 31 | Crest Computer Supply | Skokie, IL | 60 | 42,000,000 |
| 32 | Beauchamp Distributing | Compton, CA | 100 | 40,200,000 |
| 33 | Rush Communications | New York, NY | 65 | 40,000,000 |
| 34 | Grimes Oil | Boston, MA | 18 | 38,700,000 |
| 35 | Westside Distributors | South Gate, CA | 115 | 37,130,000 |
| 36 | Pro-Line | Dallas, TX | 236 | 36,870,000 |
| 37 | Thacker Engineering | Atlanta, GA | 140 | 36,500,000 |
| 38 | Calhoun Enterprises | Montgomery, AL | 578 | 36,480,000 |
| 39 | The Gourmet Companies | Atlanta, GA | 813 | 36,200,000 |
| 40 | Drew Pearson | Addison, TX | 85 | 36,000,000 |
| * | Capsonic Group Division of Gabriel | Elgin, IL | 232 | 36,000,000 |
| 42 | Trumark | Lansing, MI | 300 | 35,300,000 |
| 43 | Network Solutions | Herndon, VA | 380 | 35,000,000 |
| 44 | Am-Pro Protective Agency | Columbia, SC | 1,082 | 32,130,000 |
| 45 | Metters Industries | McLean, VA | 494 | 31,600,000 |
| 46 | Input Output Computer Services | Waltham, MA | 200 | 31,000,000 |
| 47 | Advantage Enterprises | Toledo, OH | 250 | 30,130,000 |
| 48 | Automated Sciences Group | Silver Spring, MD | 300 | 30,000,000 |
| * | Dudley Products | Greensboro, NC | 501 | 30,000,000 |
| 50 | Brooks Sausage | Kenosha, WI | 148 | 29,000,000 |

*Black and Female CEO's (cont'd)*

| Rank | Company | Location | Staff | 1992 Sales ($) |
|------|---------|----------|-------|----------------|
| 51 | Inner City Broadcasting | New York, NY | 200 | 28,000,000 |
| * | Yancy Minerals | Woodbridge, CT | 8 | 28,000,000 |
| 53 | Cimarron Express | Genoa, OH | 85 | 27,770,000 |
| 54 | Queen City Broadcasting | Buffalo, NY | 130 | 26,350,000 |
| 55 | Premium Distributors | Washington, DC | 75 | 26,000,000 |
| * | Integrated Steel | Detroit, MI | 305 | 26,000,000 |
| 57 | African Development Public Investment | Hollywood, CA | 12 | 25,500,000 |
| 58 | Restoration Supermarket | Brooklyn, NY | 178 | 25,460,000 |
| 59 | Navcom Systems | Manassas, VA | 139 | 25,000,000 |
| 60 | Lockhart & Pettus | New York, NY | 32 | 24,890,000 |
| 61 | Parks Sausage | Baltimore, MD | 230 | 24,800,000 |
| 62 | Dick Griffey Productions | Hollywood, CA | 78 | 24,200,000 |
| 63 | R.O.W. Sciences | Rockville, MD | 365 | 24,000,000 |
| 64 | American Development | N. Charleston, SC | 175 | 23,000,000 |
| 65 | Sylvest Management Systems | Lanham, MD | 42 | 22,600,000 |
| 66 | Regal Plastics | Roseville, MI | 222 | 21,710,000 |
| 67 | Simmons Enterprises | Cincinnati, OH | 52 | 21,480,000 |
| 68 | Earl G. Graves | New York, NY | 65 | 21,420,000 |
| 69 | H.F. Henderson Industries | West Caldwell, NJ | 150 | 20,660,000 |
| 70 | Stephens Engineering | Lanham, MD | 140 | 20,500,000 |
| 71 | D-Orum Hair Products | Gary, IN | 150 | 20,000,000 |
| 72 | Bronner Brothers | Atlanta, GA | 250 | 19,500,000 |
| 73 | Dual | Arlington, VA | 241 | 19,310,000 |
| 74 | C.H. James & Company | Charleston, WV | 22 | 18,700,000 |
| 75 | Consolidated Beverage | New York, NY | 24 | 18,500,000 |
| 76 | Watiker & Son | Zanesville, OH | 200 | 18,000,000 |
| 77 | Terry Manufacturing | Roanoke, AL | 300 | 17,500,000 |
| 78 | J.E. Ethridge Construction | Fresno, CA | 25 | 17,300,000 |
| 79 | Burns Enterprises | Louisville, KY | 460 | 17,000,000 |
| * | Ozanne Construction | Cleveland, OH | 130 | 17,000,000 |
| 81 | UBM | Chicago, IL | 53 | 16,670,000 |
| 82 | Amsco Wholesalers | Norcross, GA | 86 | 16,200,000 |
| 83 | Systems Engineering & Management Associates | Alexandria, VA | 260 | 16,000,000 |
| 84 | Mid-Delta Home Health | Belzoni, MS | 345 | 15,000,000 |
| * | Urban Constructors | Miami, FL | 60 | 15,000,000 |
| * | American Urban Radio Networks | New York, NY | 65 | 15,000,000 |
| 87 | Specialized Packaging International | Hamden, CT | 7 | 14,860,000 |
| 88 | A Minority Entity | Norco, LA | 1,200 | 14,750,000 |
| 89 | Tresp Associates | Alexandria, VA | 220 | 14,000,000 |
| 90 | Solo Construction | N. Miami Beach, FL | 46 | 13,960,000 |
| 91 | RPM Supply Company | Philadelphia, PA | 20 | 13,890,000 |
| 92 | Powers & Sons Construction | Gary, IN | 60 | 13,720,000 |
| 93 | Williams Russell and Johnson | Atlanta, GA | 125 | 13,400,000 |
| 94 | Black River Manufacturing | Port Huron, MI | 77 | 13,400,000 |
| 95 | Eltrex Industries | Rochester, NY | 155 | 12,980,000 |
| 96 | Advanced Systems Technology | Atlanta, GA | 200 | 12,700,000 |
| 97 | Advanced Consumer Marketing | Burlingame, CA | 35 | 12,380,000 |
| 98 | Spiral Distribution | Phoenix, AZ | 24 | 12,300,000 |
| 99 | Wise Construction | Dayton, OH | 75 | 12,000,000 |
| * | Systems Management American | Norfolk, VA | 130 | 12,000,000 |

*=tie

Source: *Black Enterprise, May, 1993*

*Black and Women CEO's (cont'd)*

According to statistics generated by the National Foundation for Women Business Owners, women own at least 5.4 million businesses. *Working Woman* in conjunction with NFWBO ranked the top 25 women-owned businesses in the first annual salute to women business owners. To be considered, candidates had to own at least 20 percent of the stock in private companies and 10 percent in public ones and the women had to be top executives running the day-to-day operations.

## Recommended Resource

National Foundation for Women Business Owners
1377 K St., NW, Suite 637
Washington, DC 20005
(301) 495-4975

## The Top 25 Women-Owned Businesses

| Rank | Owner | Business | Employees | % of Ownership |
|------|-------|----------|-----------|----------------|
| 1 | Marian Ilitch | Little Caesar Enterprises | 27,000 | 50 |
| 2 | Joyce Raley Teel | Raley's | 11,000 | 100 |
| 3 | Lynda Resnick | Roll International | 7,500 | 50 |
| 4 | Antonia Axson Johnson | Axel Johnson | 2,000 | 100 |
| 5 | Liz Minyard/Gretchen Minyard Williams | Minyard Food Stores | 6,200 | 67 |
| 6 | Linda Wachner | Warnaco Group | 11,800 | 12 |
| 7 | Jenny Craig | Jenny Craig | 4,910 | >30 |
| 8 | Donna Wolf Steigerwaldt | Jockey International | 5,000 | 100 |
| 9 | Donna Karan | Donna Karan | 1,088 | 50 |
| 10 | Helen Copley | Copley Press | 3,500 | 100 |
| 11 | Barbara Levy Kipper | Chas. Levy | 1,800 | 100 |
| 12 | Bettye Martin Marsham | Gear Holdings | 30 | 20 |
| 13 | Susie Tompkins | Esprit De Corp | 1,250 | 67 |
| 14 | Annabelle Lundy Fetterman | Lundy Packaging | 900 | >20 |
| 15 | Dian Graves Owen | Owen Healthcare | 2,250 | 38 |
| 16 | Carole Little | Carole Little | 850 | 50 |
| 17 | Ellen Gordon | Tootsie Roll Industries | 1,400 | >20 |
| 18 | Josephine Chaus | Bernard Chaus | 750 | 63 |
| 19 | Christel DeHaan | Resort Condominiums International | 2,300 | 100 |
| 20 | Linda Paresky | Thomas Cook Travel | 3,500 | 50 |
| 21 | Patricia Gallup | PC Connection | 450 | 50 |
| 22 | Ebba Hoffman/Sharon Hoffman Avent | Smead Manufacturing | 2,600 | 100 |
| 23 | Sydell Miller | Matrix Essentials | 900 | >50 |
| 24 | Gertrude Boyle | Columbia Sportswear | 700 | >50 |
| 25 | Rachelle Friedman | J&R Music World | 600 | 51 |

*Source: Working Woman Magazine (May, 1994) and*
*National Foundation for Women Business Owners. Reprinted with permission.*

## The Top Reference Sources

*Working Woman*, $11.97/year
(212) 551-9500

This monthly magazine is focused on women and their careers. Features provide guidelines on women's legal rights, management skills, career tactics and developments, plus how to maintain fitness and a positive self-image.

Regular surveys and statistical features, including an annual salary survey, make this an excellent resource.

# The Forbes 400 Wealthiest Ranking

| Name | Worth ($ mil) | Primary Sources |
|------|------|------|
| du Pont family | 9,000 | Du Pont (I) |
| Buffett, Warren | 8,325 | Stock market |
| Gates, William | 6,165 | Microsoft |
| Kluge, John Werner | 5,900 | Metromedia |
| Redstone, Sumner | 5,600 | Viacom, Inc. |
| Rockefeller family | 5,500 | Oil (I) |
| Mellon family | 5,000 | (I) |
| Walton, Jim C. | 4,650 | Wal-Mart (I) |
| Walton, John T. | 4,600 | Wal-Mart (I) |
| Walton, Alice L. | 4,550 | Wal-Mart (I) |
| Walton, Helen | 4,550 | Wal-Mart (I) |
| Walton, S. Robson | 4,550 | Wal-Mart (I) |
| Murdoch, Keith | 4,000 | Publishing |
| Arison, Ted | 3,650 | Cruise ships |
| Perelman, Ronald | 3,600 | Leveraged buyouts |
| Newhouse, Donald | 3,500 | Publishing |
| Newhouse, Samuel, Jr. | 3,500 | Publishing |
| Kerkorian, Kirk | 3100 | Investments |
| Allen, Paul G. | 2,900 | Microsoft |
| Packard, David | 2,750 | Hewlett-Packard |
| Anthony, Barbara Cox | 2,400 | Cox Enterprises (I) |
| Chambers, Anne Cox | 2,400 | Cox Enterprises (I) |
| Hillman, Henry Lea | 2,400 | Industrialist |
| Mars, Forrest Edward, Jr. | 2,400 | Candy (I) |
| Mars, Forrest, Sr. | 2,400 | Candy (I) |
| Mars, John Franklyn | 2,400 | Candy (I) |
| Perot, Henry Ross | 2,400 | Computer services |
| Vogel, Jacqueline Mars | 2,400 | Candy (I) |
| Bronfman, Edgar Miles | 2,300 | Seagram Co. |
| Bass, Robert Muse | 2,200 | Investments |
| Crown, Lester (F) | 2,200 | (I) |
| Pritzker, Jay Arthur | 2,200 | Financier |
| Pritzker, Robert Alan | 2,200 | Financier |
| Turner, Robert (Ted) | 2,200 | Turner Broadcasting |
| Annenberg, Walter | 2,100 | Publishing |
| Hillenbrand family | 1,850 | Caskets |
| Bass, Lee Marshall | 1,750 | Investments |
| Bass, Sid Richardson | 1,750 | Investments |
| DeVos, Richard | 1,750 | Amway |
| Van Andel, Jay | 1,750 | Amway |
| Davis, Marvin Harold | 1,700 | Oil |
| Johnson, Edward | 1,700 | Investments |
| Ellison, Lawrence | 1,600 | Oracle Corp. |
| Scripps (E.W.) family | 1,600 | Newspapers (I) |
| Wexner, Leslie Herbert | 1,600 | The Limited |
| Hunt, Ray Lee (F) | 1,500 | Oil (I) |
| Johnson, Samuel | 1,500 | Johnson Wax |
| Koch, Charles | 1,500 | (I) |
| Koch, David Hamilton | 1,500 | (I) |
| Moore, Gordon Earle | 1,500 | Intel Corp. |

| Name | Worth ($ mil) | Primary Sources |
|------|------|------|
| Smith family | 1,500 | Illinois Tool Works |
| Ziff, William Jr. | 1,500 | Publishing |
| Bacardi family | 1,400 | Liquor |
| Getty, Gordon Peter | 1,400 | Oil (I) |
| Haas, Peter E., Sr. (F) | 1,400 | Levi Strauss |
| Hewlett, William | 1,400 | Hewlett-Packard |
| Knight, Philip | 1,400 | Nike, Inc. |
| Kroc, Joan Beverly | 1,350 | McDonald's (I) |
| Anschutz, Philip | 1,300 | Oil |
| Bren, Donald Leroy | 1,300 | Real estate |
| Gund family | 1,300 | Coffee, banking (I) |
| LeFrak, Samuel Johnson | 1,300 | Real estate |
| Tisch, Laurence Alan | 1,300 | Loews Corp. |
| Tisch, Preston Robert | 1,300 | Loews Corp. |
| Bechtel, Riley P. | 1,250 | Engineering |
| Bechtel, Stephen | 1,250 | Engineering |
| Blaustein family | 1,200 | Oil (I) |
| Chandler family | 1,200 | Times Mirror Co. |
| Collier family | 1,200 | Real estate |
| Donnelley family | 1,200 | R.R. Donnelley |
| Lilly family | 1,200 | Pharmaceuticals |
| Dorrance, Bennett | 1,150 | Campbell Soup (I) |
| Dorrance, John T., III | 1,150 | Campbell Soup (I) |
| Malone, Mary Alice | 1,150 | Campbell Soup (I) |
| Albertson, Kathryn | 1,100 | Albertson's, Inc. |
| Ballmer, Anthony | 1,100 | Microsoft |
| Busch family | 1,100 | Anheuser-Busch |
| Galvin, Robert William | 1,100 | Motorola |
| Murdock, David | 1,100 | Real estate |
| Petrie, Milton | 1,100 | Petrie Stores |
| Rockefeller, David | 1,100 | Oil (I) |
| Soros, George | 1,100 | Money manager |
| Upjohn family | 1,100 | Upjohn Co. (I) |
| Walton, James | 1,100 | Wal-Mart |
| Brown family | 1,000 | Whiskey |
| Carlson, Curtis LeRoy | 1,000 | Entrepreneur |
| Dayton family | 1,000 | Dayton-Hudson |
| Fribourg, Michel | 1,000 | Grain trader |
| Helmsley, Harry | 1,000 | Real estate |
| Hill, Margaret Hunt | 1,000 | Oil (I) |
| Hughes family | 1,000 | Hughes Aircraft |
| Lauder, Estée | 1,000 | Cosmetics |
| Lauder, Leonard | 1,000 | Cosmetics |
| Lauder, Ronald Steven | 1,000 | Cosmetics |
| Marriott family | 1,000 | Hotels |
| McCaw, Craig O. | 1,000 | McCaw Cellular |
| Mellon, Paul | 1,000 | (I) |
| Pitcairn family | 1,000 | PPG Industries (I) |
| Reed family | 1,000 | Lumber, paper |
| Rockefeller, Laurance | 1,000 | Oil (I) |

*(I) = inheritance; (F) = family*

*The Forbes 400 Wealthiest Ranking (cont'd)*

| Name | Worth ($ mil) | Primary Sources | Name | Worth ($ mil) | Primary Sources |
|------|---------------|-----------------|------|---------------|-----------------|
| Schwan family | 1,000 | Schwan's Sales | Scaife, Richard Mellon | 750 | (I) |
| Weyerhaeuser family | 1,000 | Timber (I) | Zell, Samuel | 750 | Real estate |
| Johnson family | 990 | Johnson & Johnson | Hamilton, Dorrance | 740 | Campbell Soup (I) |
| Hall, Donald Joyce | 960 | Hallmark Cards | McCaw, John Elroy | 740 | McCaw Cellular |
| Smith, Richard Alan | 955 | Harcourt General | Dolan, Charles | 735 | Cable television |
| Ingram, Erskine | 950 | Conglomerate | Johnson, Barbara | 735 | Johnson & Johnson |
| Rockefeller, Winthrop | 950 | Oil (I) | Mennen family | 730 | The Mennen Co. |
| Simplot, John | 950 | Potatoes | Mitchell, George | 730 | Oil and gas |
| Nordstrom family | 945 | Retailing | Weber, Charlotte | 730 | Campbell Soup (I) |
| Bass, Edward Perry | 925 | Investments | Harbert, John | 710 | Construction |
| Jordan family | 915 | Media, retailing (I) | Hearst, Randolph (F) | 710 | (I) |
| Ford, William Clay | 900 | Ford Motor Co. (I) | Levine, Stuart Robert | 710 | Cabletron Systems |
| Geffen, David | 900 | Music | McCaw, Bruce | 705 | McCaw Cellular |
| Horvitz family | 900 | Media, real estate | Block family | 700 | Block Drug Co. |
| Lennon, Fred A. | 900 | Valves | Campbell family | 700 | Real Estate |
| Scripps (J.E.) family | 900 | Newspapers (I) | Clapp family | 700 | Weyerhaeuser (I) |
| Searle family | 900 | (I) | Field, Frederick W. | 700 | Department stores |
| Temple family | 900 | Timber (I) | Gore family | 700 | Gore-Tex |
| Wrigley, William | 900 | Wrigley's | Hostetter, Amos, Jr. | 700 | Continental Cable |
| Hixon family | 880 | Connectors | Lauren, Ralph | 700 | Apparel |
| Davidson, William | 870 | Guardian Industries | O'Connor family | 700 | Oil, ranching |
| Greenberg, Hank | 855 | American Int'l | Sammons family | 700 | Sammons |
| Stern, Leonard | 840 | Pet supplies | Whittier family | 700 | Oil (I) |
| Cargill, James R. | 835 | Cargill, Inc | McCaw, Keith W. | 695 | McCaw Cellular |
| Cargill, Margaret | 835 | Cargill, Inc | Sorenson, James | 695 | Medical devices |
| Pigott family | 820 | Paccar (I) | Buffett, Susan | 690 | Berkshire Hathaway |
| Broad, Eli | 810 | Housing | Marcus, Bernard | 690 | Home Depot |
| Magness, Bob John | 810 | Telecommunications | Naify, Robert Allen | 685 | Telecommunications |
| Tyson, Donald John | 810 | Tyson Foods | Gates, Charles, Jr. | 680 | Gates Corp. |
| Cooke, Jack Kent | 800 | Real estate | Heinz, Teresa F. | 675 | H.J. Heinz Co. |
| Feeney, Charles F. | 800 | Duty Free Shoppers | Van Beuren, Hope Hill | 675 | Campbell Soup (I) |
| Green, Pincus | 800 | Commodities trader | Huizenga, Wayne | 670 | Blockbuster Video |
| Kleberg family | 800 | King Ranch (I) | Singleton, Henry | 660 | Teledyne |
| Louis, John Jeffrey | 800 | Johnson Wax (I) | Wilmot family | 660 | Shopping centers |
| Lykes family | 800 | Steel, real estate | Heyman, Samuel J. | 655 | GAF Corp. |
| Meijer family | 800 | Retailing | Tyson, Barbara | 655 | Tyson Foods |
| Rich, Marc | 800 | Commodities | Copley, Helen | 650 | Publishing |
| Richardson family | 800 | Richardson-Vicks | Lindner, Carl, Jr. (F) | 650 | Insurance |
| Stuart family | 800 | Carnation Co. (I) | Noorda, Raymond J. | 650 | Novell Inc. |
| Yates family | 800 | Oil | Norris family | 650 | Lennox Int. |
| Mead family | 785 | Consolidated papers | Rollins family | 650 | (I) |
| Simmons, Harold | 785 | Investments | Pulitzer family | 640 | Publishing (I) |
| Dedman, Robert Sr. | 780 | Country clubs | Cafaro, William (F) | 630 | Shopping malls |
| Gaylord, Edward Lewis | 780 | Broadcasting | Bennett, William | 620 | Circus Circus |
| Hess, Leon | 775 | Amerada Hess | Abramson, Leonard | 610 | U.S. Healthcare |
| Johnson, Charles B. | 775 | Franklin Resources | Batten, Frank | 600 | Publishing |
| Lerner, Alfred | 770 | Banking | Bing family | 600 | Real estate |
| Jenkins family | 755 | Publix Super Mkts. | Durst family | 600 | Real estate |
| Duke, Doris | 750 | (I) | Ilitch, Michael | 600 | Little Caesar |
| Hoyt family | 750 | Carter-Wallace | Jamail, Joseph, Jr. | 600 | Lawyer |

*(I) = inheritance; (F) = family*

*The Forbes 400 Wealthiest Ranking (cont'd)*

| Name | Worth ($ mil) | Primary Sources |
|------|------|------|
| Koch, William | 600 | Oil services (I) |
| Kravis, Henry J. | 600 | Leveraged buyouts |
| May, Cordelia | 600 | (I) |
| McGraw family | 600 | McGraw-Hill |
| Milliken, Roger | 600 | Textiles |
| Moran, James Martin | 600 | Toyota |
| Pohlad, Carl Ray | 600 | Banks |
| Roberts, George R. | 600 | Leveraged buyouts |
| Rowling, Reese (F) | 600 | Oil and gas |
| Sarofim, Fayez Shalaby | 600 | Money management |
| Smith (Charles) family | 600 | Real estate |
| Taylor family | 600 | Publishing (I) |
| Taylor, Jack Crawford | 600 | Enterprise Rentals |
| Terra, Daniel James | 600 | Lawter International |
| Benson, Craig Robert | 590 | Cabletron Systems |
| Johnson, Rupert J. | 585 | Franklin Resources |
| Edson, John Orin | 580 | Manufacturing |
| Freeman, Houghton | 580 | American Int'l |
| Cook, William Alfred | 575 | Catheters |
| Icahn, Carl Celian | 575 | Financier |
| Lindemann, George | 575 | Cable, cellular |
| Barbey Family | 570 | VF Corp. (I) |
| Graham family | 565 | Washington Post Co. |
| Haas, John Charles | 560 | Rohm & Haas |
| Rich, Robert Edward, Sr. | 560 | Food products |
| Skaggs, Leonard Jr. | 560 | American Stores Co. |
| Keinath, Pauline | 555 | Cargill, Inc. (I) |
| MacMillan, Cargill, Jr. | 555 | Cargill, Inc |
| MacMillan, John III | 555 | Cargill, Inc |
| MacMillan, W. Duncan | 555 | Cargill, Inc |
| MacMillan, Whitney | 555 | Cargill, Inc |
| Pictet, Marion | 555 | Cargill, Inc. (I) |
| Bean (Gorman) family | 550 | L.L. Bean |
| Dart, William A. | 550 | Dart Container |
| Dyson, Charles Henry | 550 | Conglomerator |
| Haas, Fritz Otto | 550 | Rohm & Haas |
| Hollingsworth, John D. | 550 | Textile machinery |
| Huntsman, Jon Meade | 550 | Plastics |
| Murphy, Charles, Jr. | 550 | Murphy Oil |
| Park, Roy Hampton | 550 | Park Comm. |
| Wirtz family | 550 | Real estate |
| Houghton family | 545 | Corning Glass |
| Disney, Roy Edward | 540 | Walt Disney (I) |
| Anderson, John Edward | 530 | Beverage dist. |
| Baxter, Arthur | 530 | Home Depot |
| Ford, Josephine | 530 | Ford Motor (I) |
| Fireman, Paul B. | 525 | Reebok |
| Schottenstein family | 525 | Depart. stores |
| Taubman, Adolph | 525 | Real estate |
| Carver, Lucille | 520 | Bandag (I) |

| Name | Worth ($ mil) | Primary Sources |
|------|------|------|
| Fisher, Donald George | 515 | The Gap |
| Fisher, Doris F. | 515 | The Gap |
| Krehbiel, John, Sr. | 515 | Molex |
| Ryan, Patrick George | 515 | Insurance |
| Kelly, William Russell | 510 | Kelly Services |
| Miner, Robert N. | 510 | Oracle Corp. |
| Abraham, S. Daniel | 500 | Slim-Fast Foods |
| Berry, Jack, Sr. | 500 | Yellow Pages |
| Coulter, Wallace | 500 | Blood counters |
| Cowles family | 500 | Newspapers |
| Cullen family | 500 | Oil |
| Davenport, Elizabeth | 500 | Coca-Cola bottler |
| de Menil family | 500 | Schlumberger (I) |
| Dillon family | 500 | Dillon, Read (I) |
| Flagler family | 500 | Oil, real estate (I) |
| Haas, Josephine B. (F) | 500 | Levi Strauss |
| Hobby, Oveta Culp | 500 | Media |
| Hunt, Caroline Rose | 500 | Oil (I) |
| Hunting family | 500 | Steelcase |
| Idema family | 500 | Steelcase |
| Jacobs, Jeremy | 500 | Sports concessions |
| Kauffman, Muriel | 500 | Inheritance |
| Koch, Frederick | 500 | Oil services (I) |
| Kohlberg, Jerome, Jr. | 500 | Leveraged buyouts |
| Kohler family | 500 | Plumbing fixtures |
| Lewis, Peter Benjamin | 500 | Progressive Corp. |
| Litwin, Leonard | 500 | Real estate |
| Lupton, John Thomas | 500 | Coca-Cola bottler |
| Marshall, James, III | 500 | Oil |
| McGovern, Patrick | 500 | Publishing |
| Moore, Jerry J. | 500 | Shopping centers |
| O'Neill family | 500 | Real estate |
| Solheim, Karsten | 500 | Ping golf clubs |
| Washington, Dennis | 500 | Entrepreneur |
| Watson family | 500 | Real estate |
| Wege family | 500 | Steelcase |
| Whitney, Betsey | 500 | Inheritance |
| Mandel, Morton Leon | 490 | Premier Industrial |
| Sulzberger family | 490 | New York Times |
| Coulter, Joseph R. | 480 | Blood counters |
| Ellis, Alpheus Lee | 480 | Banking |
| Marshall, Barbara Hall | 480 | Hallmark (I) |
| Reid, Elizabeth Ann | 480 | Hallmark (I) |
| Brittingham family | 475 | Dal-Tile Group |
| Close family | 475 | Textiles |
| Mandel, Jack N. | 475 | Premier Industrial |
| Spangler, Clemmie, Jr. | 475 | Investments |
| Stephens, Jackson | 475 | Investment banking |
| Manoogian, Richard | 470 | Masco Corp. |
| Naify, Marshall | 470 | Telecomm. |

*(I) = inheritance; (F) = family*

*The Forbes 400 Wealthiest Ranking (cont'd)*

| Name | Worth ($ mil) | Primary Sources | Name | Worth ($ mil) | Primary Sources |
|---|---|---|---|---|---|
| Rainwater, Richard | 470 | Investments | Earheart, Anne Getty | 400 | Oil (I) |
| Kimmel, Sidney | 465 | Jones Apparel | Engelhard, Jane B. | 400 | Inheritance |
| King family | 465 | King World | Flint, Lucille du Pont | 400 | Du Pont (I) |
| Mandel, Joseph C. | 460 | Premier Industrial | Gerry, Alan | 400 | Cable TV |
| Peltz, Nelson | 460 | Leveraged buyouts | Getty, Caroline Marie | 400 | Oil (I) |
| Swig family | 460 | Real estate | Getty, J. Paul, Jr. | 400 | Oil (I) |
| Pennington, William | 455 | Circus Circus | Glazer, Guilford | 400 | Real estate |
| Andersen Family | 450 | Windows | Goldman family | 400 | Real estate (I) |
| Arrillaga, John | 450 | Real estate | Goodson family | 400 | Game shows (I) |
| Aston, Alan C. | 450 | WordPerfect | Hardie, Mary Jane | 400 | Newspapers |
| Bastian, Bruce W. | 450 | WordPerfect | Hoiles, Harry Howard | 400 | Newspapers |
| Clark family | 450 | Singer Manuf. | Mathile, Clayton Lee | 400 | Iams Pet Food |
| Fisher, Lawrence | 450 | Real estate | May, Irene du Pont | 400 | Du Pont (I.) |
| Fisher, Zachary | 450 | Real estate | Milken, Michael Robert | 400 | Financier |
| Hyde, Joseph, III | 450 | Auto Parts | Mills family | 400 | Portrait studios |
| Malone, John C. | 450 | Liberty Media | Moncrief, William Jr. | 400 | Oil and gas |
| McClatchy family | 450 | Newspapers | Pennington, Claude B. | 400 | Oil and gas |
| Monaghan, Thomas | 450 | Pizza | Perry, Claire Getty | 400 | Inheritance (oil) |
| Peery, Richard Taylor | 450 | Real estate | Reinhart, Dewayne B. | 400 | Food wholesaler |
| Perdue, Franklin | 450 | Chickens | Rose family | 400 | Real estate |
| Rosenwald family | 450 | Sears, Roebuck (I) | Rust, Eleanor du Pont | 400 | Du Pont (I) |
| Unanue family | 450 | Goya foods | Schiff family | 400 | Cincinnati Fin. |
| Wolfe family | 450 | Wear-U-Well Shoes | Shorenstein, Walter | 400 | Real estate |
| Simmons, Richard | 445 | Allegheny Ludlum | Silliman, Mariana | 400 | Du Pont (I) |
| Pew family | 440 | Sun Co. (I) | Ueltschi, Albert Lee | 400 | FlightSafety Int. |
| Frist, Thomas F., Jr. | 435 | Hosp. Corp. of Am. | Ward, Louis Larrick | 400 | Russell Stover |
| Roberts, Ralph J. | 435 | Comcast Corp. | Binger, Virginia | 395 | 3M (I) |
| Comer, Gary | 430 | Lands' End | Udvar-Hazy, Steven F. | 395 | Am. Int. Grp. |
| Kelley family | 430 | Hotels | Wasserman, Lewis | 395 | MCA |
| Stempel, Ernest E. | 430 | Am. Int. Grp. | Butt, Charles Clarence | 390 | Grocery stores |
| Farish family | 425 | Oil | Coors family | 390 | Beer |
| Sommer, Viola | 425 | Real estate (I) | Russell family | 390 | Athletic wear |
| Beckerman, David A. | 420 | Starter Corp. | Wexner, Bella | 390 | The Limited |
| Farmer, Richard T. | 420 | Cintas Corp. | Franchetti, Anne (F) | 385 | Milliken & Co. |
| Cook, Jane Bancroft | 415 | Dow Jones (I) | Milliken, Gerrish | 385 | Textiles |
| du Pont, Alexis Jr. | 415 | Du Pont (I) | Weaver, J. Wayne | 385 | Shoes |
| Hunt, Johnnie | 415 | J.B. Hunt | Disney, Walt (heirs) | 380 | Inheritance |
| MacElree, Jane | 415 | Inheritance | Dixon, Fitz Eugene, Jr. | 380 | Inheritance |
| Mills, Alice du Pont | 415 | Du Pont (I) | Stowers, James, Jr. | 380 | Mutual funds |
| Frost, Phillip | 410 | Pharmaceuticals | Catsimatidis, John | 375 | Supermarkets |
| Gottwald family | 410 | Ethyl Corp. | Fisher, Max Martin | 375 | Oil |
| Haas, Peter E., Jr. (F) | 410 | Levi Strauss | Goizueta, Roberto | 375 | Coca-Cola |
| Haas, Robert D. (F) | 410 | Levi Strauss | Herb, Marvin | 375 | Coca-Cola bottler |
| Haas, Walter A., Jr. (F) | 410 | Levi Strauss | Scharbauer, Clarence, Jr. | 375 | Oil, land (I) |
| Weis, Sigfried | 410 | Weis Markets | Connelly, Joohn E. | 370 | Riverboats |
| Bloomberg, Michael | 400 | Financial News | Keck, Howard Brighton | 370 | Superior Oil |
| Bredin, Octavia du Pont | 400 | Du Pont (I) | Munger, Charles T. | 365 | Berkshire Hathaway |
| Connell, Grover | 400 | Equipment leasing | Stein, Jay | 365 | Stein Mart |
| Darden, Constance | 400 | Du Pont (I) | Clayton, James Lee | 360 | Mobile homes |
| du Pont, Irenee, Jr. (F) | 400 | Du Pont (I) | Culverhouse, Hugh | 360 | Real estate |

*(I) = inheritance; (F) = family*

*The Forbes 400 Wealthiest Ranking (cont'd)*

| Name | Worth ($ mil) | Primary Sources |
|---|---|---|
| Steinberg, Saul (F) | 360 | Financier |
| Boudjakdji, Millicent | 355 | Inheritance |
| Cooke, Phoebe Hearst | 355 | Inheritance |
| Goldman, Rhoda (F) | 355 | Levi Strauss |
| Gonda, Leslie L. | 355 | Am. Int. Grp. |
| Gonda, Louis L. | 355 | Am. Int. Grp |
| Hearst, Austin | 355 | Inheritance |
| Hearst, David, Jr. (F) | 355 | Inheritance |
| Hearst, George, Jr. (F) | 355 | Inheritance |
| Hearst, William III | 355 | Inheritance |
| Levine, Leon | 355 | Family Dollar Strs |
| Weis, Robert Freeman | 355 | Weis Markets |
| Cohn, Seymour | 350 | Real estate |
| Day, Robert Addison | 350 | Money management |
| Irvine family | 350 | Lawsuits (I) |
| Kennedy family | 350 | Inheritance |
| Kovner, Bruce | 350 | Trading |
| Lebensfeld, Harry | 350 | UIS, Inc. |
| McGlothlin, James (F) | 350 | Coal |
| Pamplin, Robert, Jr. | 350 | Textiles |
| Pamplin, Robert, Sr. | 350 | Textiles |
| Perenchio, Andrew | 350 | Television |
| Peterson, Robert Einar | 350 | Publishing |
| Sakioka, Roy and family | 350 | Real estate |
| Smith, Frederick | 350 | Federal Express |
| Taper, Sydney Mark | 350 | First Charter |
| Tauber, Laszlo Nandor | 350 | Real estate |
| Diller, Barry | 345 | QVC/HSN stock |
| Schuler, James K. | 345 | Schuler Homes |
| Norris, Diana | 340 | Campbell Soup (I) |
| Allen, Charles, Jr. | 335 | Stock Market |
| Allen, Herbert | 335 | Stock Market |
| Allen, Herbert Anthony | 335 | Stock Market |
| Littlefield, Edmund | 330 | Utah International |
| Marion, Anne Windfohr | 330 | Inheritance |
| Moores, John Jay | 330 | BMC Software |
| Schwab, Charles R. | 330 | Charles Schwab |
| Solomon, Russell | 330 | Tower Records |
| Solow, Sheldon Henry | 330 | Real estate |
| Ackerman, Peter | 325 | Junk bonds |
| Brown, Jack | 325 | Oil |
| Joseph, George | 325 | Mercury General |
| Kamins, Philip Evan | 325 | Plastics |
| Lyon, Frank, Jr. (F) | 325 | Beverage bottling |
| Robinson, Jesse Mack | 325 | Banking |
| Wagner, Cyril, Jr. | 325 | Oil and investments |
| Behring, Kenneth | 320 | Developer |
| Forman, Michael Robert | 320 | Real estate |
| Lurie, Robert Alfred | 320 | Inheritance |
| Milken, Lowell Jay | 320 | Financier |

| Name | Worth ($ mil) | Primary Sources |
|---|---|---|
| Cosby, William, Jr. | 315 | Television |
| du Pont, Willis | 315 | Du Pont (I) |
| Grainger, David William | 315 | W.W. Grainger |
| Guccione, Robert | 315 | Publishing |
| Hammons, John | 315 | Hotels |
| McEvoy, Nan Tucker | 315 | Publishing |
| Pearson, Edith du Pont | 315 | Du Pont (I) |
| Rinker, Marshall, Sr. | 315 | Concrete |
| Huffington, Roy | 310 | Oil |
| Milstein, Monroe Gary | 310 | Retail |
| Hillman, Howard | 305 | Inheritance |
| Hillman, Tatnall Lea | 305 | Inheritance |
| McLane, Robert, Jr. | 305 | Food wholesaling |
| Allbritton, Joe Lewis | 300 | Media |
| Ansin, Edmund Newton | 300 | Sunbeam Television |
| Autry, Orvon Gene | 300 | Broadcasting |
| Bass, Anne Hendricks | 300 | Divorce |
| Block, William | 300 | Media |
| Brennan, Bernard F. | 300 | Montgomery Ward |
| Butler, Sarah Turner | 300 | Coca-Cola stock |
| Cantor, Bernard Gerald | 300 | Cantor Fitzgerald |
| Conover, Catherine | 300 | Inheritance |
| Corn, Elizabeth Turner | 300 | Coca-Cola stock |
| Currier, Andrea | 300 | Inheritance |
| Currier, Lavinia M. | 300 | Inheritance |
| Currier, Michael S. | 300 | Inheritance |
| Daniels, Bill | 300 | Cable TV |
| Davis, Artemus Darius | 300 | Winn-Dixie |
| Ebrahimi, Fred Farhad | 300 | Quark Inc. |
| Eisner, Michael D. | 300 | Disney stock |
| Feld, Kenneth | 300 | Circus |
| Gallo, Ernest | 300 | Wine |
| Gill, Tim | 300 | Quark |
| Hascoe, Norman | 300 | Semiconductor Mat. |
| Howard, Robert Staples | 300 | Publishing |
| Jacobs, Richard E. | 300 | Shopping centers |
| Kaiser, George B. | 300 | Gas |
| Lee, Thomas Haskell | 300 | Leveraged buyouts |
| Maritz, William Edward | 300 | Maritz, Inc. |
| Mellon, Richard | 300 | Inheritance |
| Mellon, Seward | 300 | Inheritance |
| Mellon, Timothy | 300 | Inheritance |
| Milbury, Cassandra | 300 | Inheritance |
| Phipps, Howard Jr. | 300 | Bessemer Trust |
| Saul, Bernard Francis, II | 300 | Inheritance |
| Sidamon-Eristoff, Anne | 300 | Bessemer Trust |
| Simon, Melvin | 300 | Shopping centers |
| Spelling, Aaron | 300 | Television |
| Steinhardt, Michael | 300 | Money management |

*(I) = inheritance; (F) = family*

*Note: Due to multiple entries, rankings have been omitted and more than 400 names appear.*

*Source: Forbes Magazine, Oct. 18, 1993, © Forbes, Inc.*
*Reprinted with permission*

# Business Plan Outline

THE BUSINESS PLAN IS a critical element in planning, growing and financing a business. Here is a sample outline created by Jan W. Zupnick, President of The Entrepreneurship Institute:

I. Overview
  A. Summary of Fundamental Elements Upon Which the Venture Is Built
  B. Background and Critical Success Factors
    1. Introduction
      a. Purpose
      b. History of company
      c. General description of products or services
      d. Benefits
      e. Objectives
      f. Critical success factors
    2. Business Environment
      a. Industry description
      b. Regulatory climate
      c. Market description
      d. Competition
      e. Barriers to achieving objectives
    3. Alternatives (existing businesses)
      a. Business as usual
      b. Growth through expansion
      c. Growth through merger, acquisition, etc.
      d. Contraction
      e. Sell out
    4. Risks and Opportunities
      a. Strengths
      b. Weaknesses
  C. Description of Products and Services
    1. Description of Each Product or Service
    2. Uniqueness and Special Aspects
      a. Features, advantages, benefits
      b. Strengths and weaknesses
      c. Patents, licenses, royalties
    3. Anticipated Changes (existing businesses)
      a. Planned products and services
      b. Discontinued products and services
      c. Life cycles
      d. Environment
    4. Product Strategy
      a. Buy for resale
      b. Make
        – R & D
        – Engineering
      c. Unique or similar
      d. Narrow or broad market
      e. Quality

II. Marketing
  A. Critical Success Factors
  B. Strategy
  C. Market Analysis
    1. Economic Environment
    2. Industry Environment
    3. Customer Base
    4. Market Size, Geography
    5. Market Share
    6. Market Segment and Target Market
    7. Market Needs Analysis
    8. Market Opportunity Trend Analysis
    9. Technological Trends
    10. Growth Trends
    11. Government Regulations
  D. Competition
  E. Sales Tactics
  F. Pricing
  G. Promotion
  H. Packaging
    1. Physical Package for Products
    2. Product and Service Philosophy (Maintenance)
    3. Product or System Philosophy

III. Management and Operational Plan
  A. Management Team
    1. Organization Chart
    2. Key Management Personnel Descriptions
    3. Management Compensation & Ownership
    4. Board of Directors
    5. Supporting Professional Services
  B. Human Resources
    1. Number
    2. Recruitment
    3. Selection
    4. Skills
    5. Training
  C. Facilities and Equipment
    1. Plant, Offices, Warehouse
    2. Capacity, Percent Utilized
    3. Location
    4. Strategy & Plans
    5. Equipment
      a. Production tools and machinery
      b. Inspection equipment
      c. Vendor quality assurance inspection

*Business Plan Outline (cont'd)*

IV. Financial Plan
  A. Financial Situation
    1. Financial History Highlights
    2. Present Financial Condition
    3. Credit Arrangements and Sources
    4. Revenue Projections
    5. Ratios and Comparative Analyses
      a. Internal ratio analysis
      b. External ratio analysis
      c. Budget analysis
    6. Contingent Liabilities
    7. Insurance
    8. Tax Consideration
    9. Review and Control
  B. Financing Requirements
    1. Equity Policy Statement
    2. Capital Requirements
      a. Amount
      b. Purpose
    3. Funding Sources
      a. Internal
      b. External
      c. List of potential sources
    4. Financing Proposal

V. Appendices
  A.  Schedule of Major Events
  B.  Personnel Resources, Key-Person Resumes
  C.  Facilities and Equipment Data
  D.  Financial History
  E.  Revenue Forecast
  F.  Product or Service Cost Analysis
  G.  Expense Budgets
  H.  Income Statement Projection
  I.  Cash Flow Projection
  J.  Balance Sheet Projection
  K.  Financial Ratios
  L.  Collateral
  M.  Organization Chart
  N.  Major Customers
  O.  Principal Suppliers
  P.  Insurance Coverages
  Q.  Formats
  R.  Other Supporting Documents and Data

*Source: © The Entrepreneurship Institute*

## The Top Reference Sources

*Corporate 500: The Directory of Corporate Philanthropy*
Gale Research, $375.00
(800) 877-4253

Compiled by the research staff of the Public Management Institute, this reference is a good source of factual information on the funding programs of the 580 American corporations with the most active philanthropic programs.

Entries include the address and phone number of each corporation, plus contact person, eligibility, number of grants made, application process, sample grants, and more.

# Business Failures

## Number of Business Failures by Industry

| Industry | 1985 | 1986 | 1987 | 1989 | 1990 | 1991 |
|---|---|---|---|---|---|---|
| TOTAL | 57,253 | 61,616 | 61,111 | 50,361 | 60,432 | 81,672 |
| Agriculture, forestry, fishing | 2,699 | 2,649 | 3,766 | 1,540 | 1,727 | 2,256 |
| Mining | 796 | 921 | 627 | 351 | 381 | 411 |
| Construction | 7,005 | 7,109 | 6,735 | 7,120 | 8,072 | 11,963 |
| Manufacturing | 4,869 | 4,772 | 4,273 | 3,933 | 4,709 | 6,595 |
| Food and kindred products | 261 | 239 | 191 | 216 | 226 | 305 |
| Textile mill products | 110 | 72 | 73 | 75 | 101 | 143 |
| Apparel, other textile products | 338 | 287 | 265 | 204 | 318 | 505 |
| Lumber and wood products | 415 | 392 | 374 | 368 | 417 | 576 |
| Furniture and fixtures | 236 | 244 | 200 | 253 | 257 | 383 |
| Paper and allied products | 55 | 46 | 60 | 46 | 66 | 86 |
| Printing and publishing | 659 | 606 | 633 | 679 | 728 | 1,062 |
| Chemicals and allied products | 172 | 129 | 116 | 102 | 134 | 207 |
| Petroleum refining | 26 | 35 | 21 | 21 | 21 | 33 |
| Primary metal products | 122 | 133 | 107 | 71 | 114 | 145 |
| Transportation equipment | 197 | 226 | 175 | 190 | 240 | 318 |
| Instruments and related products | 110 | 140 | 112 | 108 | 119 | 192 |
| Miscellaneous | 271 | 267 | 241 | 206 | 269 | 375 |
| Transportation, public utilities | 2,536 | 2,565 | 2,236 | 2,115 | 2,610 | 3,891 |
| Wholesale trade | 4,836 | 4,869 | 4,336 | 3,687 | 4,376 | 6,170 |
| Retail trade | 13,494 | 13,620 | 12,240 | 11,120 | 12,826 | 17,242 |
| Finance, insurance, real estate | 2,676 | 2,797 | 2,550 | 2,932 | 3,881 | 5,962 |
| Services | 16,649 | 20,967 | 23,802 | 13,679 | 17,673 | 22,852 |

*Source: Business Failure Record, Dun and Bradstreet*

## The Top Reference Sources

*Corporate Meeting Planners*
Reed Publishing, $297
(908) 464-6800

This directory of corporate meeting planners lists approximately 18,090 meeting planners, together with their titles, for over 11,686 top companies in the U.S. Also included are the complete address, telephone number, and type of business for each firm.

Listings also include the number of meetings held during the calendar year, the months and seasons these meetings are held, the number of days, number of attendees, and the location.

**FAX** **Causes of Business Failures.** Request #576. See p. xi for instructions.
Seven primary reasons for business failure and incidence of failure in nine sectors of business.

# 50 Largest Companies Worldwide

## The World's Largest Industrial Companies

| Rank | Company | Country | Sales ($ millions) | Profits ($ millions) | Employees |
|---|---|---|---|---|---|
| 1 | General Motors | U.S. | 132,774.9 | -23,498.3 | 750,000 |
| 2 | Exxon | U.S. | 103,547.0 | 4,770.0 | 95,000 |
| 3 | Ford Motor | U.S. | 100,785.6 | -7,385.0 | 325,333 |
| 4 | Royal Dutch/Shell Group | Britain/Netherlands | 98,935.3 | 5,408.0 | 127,000 |
| 5 | Toyota Motor | Japan | 79,114.2 | 1,812.6 | 108,167 |
| 6 | IRI | Italy | 67,547.4 | -3,811.2 | 400,000 |
| 7 | Intl. Business Machines | U.S. | 65,096.0 | -4,965.0 | 308,010 |
| 8 | Daimler-Benz | Germany | 63,339.5 | 928.6 | 376,467 |
| 9 | General Electric | U.S. | 62,202.0 | 4,725.0 | 268,000 |
| 10 | Hitachi | Japan | 61,465.5 | 619.3 | 331,505 |
| 11 | British Petroleum | Britain | 59,215.7 | -808.4 | 97,650 |
| 12 | Matsushita Electric Industrial | Japan | 57,480.8 | 307.7 | 252,075 |
| 13 | Mobil | U.S. | 57,389.0 | 862.0 | 63,700 |
| 14 | Volkswagen | Germany | 56,734.1 | 49.9 | 274,103 |
| 15 | Siemans | Germany | 51,401.9 | 1,136.1 | 413,000 |
| 16 | Nissan Motor | Japan | 50,247.5 | -448.7 | 143,754 |
| 17 | Philip Morris | U.S. | 50,157.0 | 4,939.0 | 161,000 |
| 18 | Samsung | South Korea | 49,559.6 | 374.2 | 188,558 |
| 19 | Fiat | Italy | 47,928.7 | 446.8 | 285,482 |
| 20 | Unilever | Britain/Netherlands | 43,962.6 | 2,278.6 | 283,000 |
| 21 | Eni | Italy | 40,365.5 | -767.1 | 124,032 |
| 22 | Elf Aquitaine | France | 39,717.8 | 1,166.4 | 87,900 |
| 23 | Nestlé | Switzerland | 39,057.9 | 1,916.9 | 218,005 |
| 24 | Chevron | U.S. | 38,523.0 | 1,569.0 | 49,245 |
| 25 | Toshiba | Japan | 37,471.6 | 164.7 | 173,000 |
| 26 | E.I. Du Pont De Nemours | U.S. | 37,386.0 | -3,927.0 | 125,000 |
| 27 | Texaco | U.S. | 37,130.0 | 712.0 | 37,582 |
| 28 | Chrysler | U.S. | 36,897.0 | 723.0 | 128,000 |
| 29 | Renault | France | 33,884.9 | 1,072.5 | 146,604 |
| 30 | Honda Motor | Japan | 33,369.6 | 306.9 | 90,900 |
| 31 | Philips Electronics | Netherlands | 33,269.7 | -511.6 | 252,200 |
| 32 | Sony | Japan | 31,451.9 | 290.5 | 126,000 |
| 33 | Abb Asea Brown Boveri | Switzerland | 30,536.0 | 505.0 | 213,407 |
| 34 | Alcatel Alsthom | France | 30,529.1 | 1,331.8 | 203,000 |
| 35 | Boeing | U.S. | 30,414.0 | 552.0 | 143,000 |
| 36 | Procter & Gamble | U.S. | 29,890.0 | 1,872.0 | 106,200 |
| 37 | Hoechst | Germany | 29,570.6 | 592.0 | 177,668 |
| 38 | Peugeot | France | 29,387.4 | 636.7 | 150,800 |
| 39 | BASF | Germany | 28,494.3 | 393.3 | 123,254 |
| 40 | Nec | Japan | 28,376.5 | -361.8 | 140,969 |
| 41 | Daewoo | South Korea | 28,333.9 | 383.9 | 78,727 |
| 42 | Fujitsu | Japan | 27,910.7 | -261.2 | 161,974 |
| 43 | Bayer | Germany | 26,625.3 | 970.2 | 156,400 |
| 44 | Mitsubishi Electric | Japan | 26,502.3 | 228.4 | 107,859 |
| 45 | Total | France | 26,141.5 | 537.6 | 51,139 |
| 46 | Amoco | U.S. | 25,543.0 | -74.0 | 46,994 |
| 47 | Mitsubishi Motors | Japan | 25,482.2 | 207.0 | 45,000 |
| 48 | Nippon Steel | Japan | 23,990.8 | 14.6 | 51,900 |
| 49 | Mitsubishi Heavy Industries | Japan | 23,011.3 | 649.7 | 66,000 |
| 50 | Thyssen | Germany | 22,731.5 | 207.9 | 147,279 |

*50 Largest Companies Worldwide (cont'd)*

## Largest Companies in the World by Industry

| Industry | Company | Country | Sales ($ millions) |
|---|---|---|---|
| Aerospace | Boeing | U.S. | 30,414 |
| Apparel | Levi Strauss Associates | U.S. | 5,570 |
| Beverages | PepsiCo | U.S. | 22,084 |
| Building Materials, Glass | Saint-Gobain | France | 14,297 |
| Chemicals | E.I. Du Pont de Nemours | U.S. | 37,386 |
| Computers, Office Equipment | IBM | U.S. | 65,096 |
| Electronics, Electrical Equipment | General Electric | U.S. | 62,202 |
| Food | Philip Morris | U.S. | 50,157 |
| Forest and Paper Products | International Paper | U.S. | 13,600 |
| Industrial and Farm Equipment | Mitsubishi Heavy Industries | Japan | 23,011 |
| Jewelry, Watches | Citizen Watch | Japan | 3,328 |
| Metal Products | Pechiney | France | 12,344 |
| Metals | IRI | Italy | 67,547 |
| Mining, Crude Oil Production | Ruhrkohle | Germany | 15,712 |
| Motor Vehicles and Parts | General Motors | U.S. | 132,775 |
| Petroleum Refining | Exxon | U.S. | 103,574 |
| Pharmaceuticals | Johnson & Johnson | U.S. | 13,846 |
| Publishing, Printing | Matra-Hachette | France | 10,416 |
| Rubber and Plastic Products | Bridgestone | Japan | 13,860 |
| Scientific, Photo, Control Equip. | Eastman Kodak | U.S. | 20,577 |
| Soaps, Cosmetics | Procter & Gamble | U.S. | 29,890 |
| Textiles | Toray Industries | Japan | 7,862 |
| Tobacco | RJR Nabisco Holdings | U.S. | 15,734 |
| Toys, Sporting Goods | Nintendo | Japan | 5,213 |
| Transportation Equipment | Hyundai Heavy Industries | S. Korea | 6,518 |

*Source: Fortune, July 26, 1993, "The Global 500," © 1993 Time, Inc. All rights reserved*

# Worldwide Taxes

## Percent of GDP Collected as National Taxes

| Country | Percentage |
|---|---|
| France | 43.7 |
| Germany | 37.1 |
| Italy | 39.1 |
| Britain | 36.7 |
| Canada | 37.1 |
| Japan | 31.3 |
| U.S. | 29.9 |

## Range of Personal Tax Brackets in the Seven Industrialized Nations (%)

| Country | Lowest | Highest |
|---|---|---|
| Britain | 25 | 40 |
| Canada | 17 | 29 |
| France | 5 | 57 |
| Germany | 22 | 56 |
| Italy | 10 | 50 |
| Japan | 10 | 50 |
| U.S. | 15 | 28 |

*Source: "OECD in Figures" 1993 Edition, supplement to*
*The OECD Observer, No. 182, June/July, 1993*

# Balance of Trade with the World

## National Trade Balances, 1991

| Country | Goods and Services, Imports ($ bil.) | Goods and Services, Exports ($ bil.) |
|---|---|---|
| Australia | 50.9 | 52.6 |
| Austria | 66.2 | 67.6 |
| Belgium | 137.0 | 142.7 |
| Canada | 149.7 | 144.0 |
| Denmark | 39.4 | 47.4 |
| Finland | 27.9 | 27.1 |
| France | 267.0 | 270.5 |
| Germany | 436.4 | 537.3 |
| Greece | 23.3 | 15.9 |
| Iceland | 2.2 | 2.2 |
| Ireland | 23.0 | 26.8 |
| Italy | 223.4 | 224.4 |

| Country | Goods and Services, Imports ($ bil.) | Goods and Services, Exports ($ bil.) |
|---|---|---|
| Japan | 286.0 | 347.5 |
| Luxembourg | 9.3 | 8.8 |
| Netherlands | 142.3 | 157.2 |
| New Zealand | 11.2 | 12.2 |
| Norway | 38.4 | 47.6 |
| Portugal | 28.4 | 21.9 |
| Spain | 107.5 | 91.0 |
| Sweden | 63.1 | 66.9 |
| Switzerland | 78.2 | 81.4 |
| Turkey | 22.6 | 22.6 |
| United Kingdom | 248.7 | 239.6 |
| United States | 620.0 | 589.4 |

*Source: "OECD in Figures" 1993 Edition, supplement to the OECD Observer, No. 182, June/July, 1993*

## U.S. Merchandise Trade ($ billions)

| Commodities | Exports | Imports | Balance |
|---|---|---|---|
| TOTAL TRADE | | | |
| 1990 annual | 393.6 | 495.3 | -101.7 |
| 1991 annual | 421.9 | 488.1 | -66.2 |
| 1992 annual | 448.2 | 532.7 | -84.5 |
| 1993 | | | |
| First Quarter | 453.3 | 557.4 | -104.1 |
| Second Quarter | 460.2 | 582.7 | -122.5 |
| Third Quarter | 456.5 | 573.9 | -117.3 |
| MANUFACTURES TRADE | | | |
| 1990 annual | 315.4 | 388.8 | -73.5 |
| 1991 annual | 345.4 | 393.1 | -47.7 |
| 1992 annual | 368.6 | 434.3 | -65.7 |
| 1993 | | | |
| First Quarter | 376.9 | 739.3 | -62.4 |
| Second Quarter | 395.9 | 473.4 | -77.5 |
| Third Quarter | 370.1 | 491.0 | -120.9 |
| AGRICULTURAL TRADE | | | |
| 1990 annual | 39.6 | 22.3 | 17.3 |
| 1991 annual | 39.3 | 22.2 | 17.1 |
| 1992 annual | 43.1 | 23.4 | 19.7 |
| 1993 | | | |
| First Quarter | 45.7 | 24.5 | 21.2 |
| Second Quarter | 40.7 | 23.9 | 16.8 |
| Third Quarter | 37.0 | 22.1 | 14.9 |

*Source: U.S. Department of Commerce, International Trade Administration*

*Balance of Trade (cont'd)*

## U.S Merchandise Trade with Japan ($ billions)

| Commodities | Exports | Imports | Balance |
|---|---|---|---|
| Total merchandise trade | | | |
| 1991 | 48.1 | 91.6 | -43.5 |
| 1992 | 47.8 | 97.2 | -49.4 |
| Food and beverages | | | |
| 1991 | 8.6 | 0.3 | 8.3 |
| 1992 | 8.2 | 0.3 | 7.9 |
| Capital goods | | | |
| 1991 | 15.1 | 36.1 | -21.0 |
| 1992 | 15.1 | 39.3 | -24.2 |
| Automobile vehicles and parts | | | |
| 1991 | 1.5 | 32.8 | -31.3 |
| 1992 | 1.8 | 33.5 | -31.7 |
| Consumer goods | | | |
| 1991 | 6.1 | 12.5 | -6.4 |
| 1992 | 5.9 | 13.1 | -7.2 |
| Industrial supplies | | | |
| 1991 | 15.3 | 8.5 | 6.8 |
| 1992 | 13.4 | 9.3 | 4.1 |
| Other products | | | |
| 1991 | 1.9 | 1.3 | 0.6 |
| 1992 | 1.9 | 1.7 | 0.2 |

*Source: U.S. Department of Commerce, International Trade Administration*

## The Top Reference Sources

*Co-op Source Directory*
National Register Publishing, $399
(800) 323-6772

The *Co-op Source Directory* provides a comprehensive quick reference guide to manufacturers' cooperative advertising programs. It is divided into 52 product classifications under which co-op summaries appear alphabetically by manufacturer.

The summaries are detailed and include eligible media, regional variations, reimbursement methods, accrual, timing, international availability, media requirements, advertising aids, etc.

*GEnie offers the Dow Jones News Retrieval Service, which provides access to searchable full-text articles from national business newspapers and magazines, as well as market reports, stock and commodities quotes, and more. KEYWORD DOW-JONES.*

*Balance of Trade (cont'd)*

## Composition of U.S. Merchandise Trade ($ billions, annual rates)

| Commoditites | Exports | Imports | Balance |
|---|---|---|---|
| CAPITAL GOODS | | | |
| 1990 annual | 152.7 | 116.4 | 36.3 |
| 1991 annual | 166.8 | 121.4 | 45.4 |
| 1992 annual | 176.7 | 134.2 | 42.5 |
| 1993 | | | |
| First Quarter | 177.2 | 143.1 | 34.1 |
| Second Quarter | 183.0 | 151.3 | 31.7 |
| Third Quarter | 178.6 | 153.2 | 25.4 |
| CONSUMER GOODS | | | |
| 1990 annual | 43.3 | 105.7 | -62.4 |
| 1991 annual | 46.2 | 107.9 | -61.7 |
| 1992 annual | 50.4 | 123.0 | -72.6 |
| 1993 | | | |
| First Quarter | 51.4 | 128.4 | -77.0 |
| Second Quarter | 52.1 | 132.3 | -80.2 |
| Third Quarter | 54.2 | 137.8 | -83.6 |
| AUTOMOTIVE VEHICLES AND PARTS | | | |
| 1990 annual | 37.4 | 87.3 | -49.9 |
| 1991 annual | 40.2 | 85.3 | -45.1 |
| 1992 annual | 47.1 | 91.8 | -44.7 |
| 1993 | | | |
| First Quarter | 51.4 | 100.4 | -49.0 |
| Second Quarter | 51.3 | 102.1 | -50.8 |
| Third Quarter | 48.4 | 100.1 | -51.7 |
| FOOD AND BEVERAGES | | | |
| 1990 annual | 35.1 | 26.7 | 8.4 |
| 1991 annual | 36.3 | 26.5 | 9.8 |
| 1992 annual | 40.2 | 27.9 | 12.3 |
| 1993 | | | |
| First Quarter | 40.8 | 27.4 | 13.4 |
| Second Quarter | 39.5 | 27.5 | 12.0 |
| Third Quarter | 38.8 | 28.4 | 10.4 |
| PETROLEUM AND PRODUCTS | | | |
| 1990 annual | 7.7 | 62.2 | -54.5 |
| 1991 annual | 7.6 | 51.5 | -43.9 |
| 1992 annual | 6.9 | 51.5 | -44.6 |
| 1993 | | | |
| First Quarter | 6.6 | 51.1 | -44.5 |
| Second Quarter | 7.2 | 57.3 | -50.1 |
| Third Quarter | 6.1 | 50.4 | -44.3 |
| OTHER INDUSTRIAL SUPPLIES | | | |
| 1990 annual | 96.8 | 81.0 | 15.8 |
| 1991 annual | 101.6 | 80.1 | 21.5 |
| 1992 annual | 102.4 | 86.8 | 15.6 |
| 1993 | | | |
| First Quarter | 102.8 | 90.0 | 12.8 |
| Second Quarter | 103.3 | 93.3 | 10.0 |
| Third Quarter | 105.5 | 93.9 | 11.6 |

*Source: U.S. Department of Commerce, International Trade Administration*

*Balance of Trade (cont'd)*

## U.S. Merchandise Trade by Area ($ billions, annual rates)

| Area | Exports | Imports | Balance |
|---|---|---|---|
| **WESTERN EUROPE** | | | |
| 1990 annual | 113.1 | 109.0 | 4.1 |
| 1991 annual | 118.7 | 102.6 | 16.1 |
| 1992 annual | 117.1 | 110.7 | 6.4 |
| 1993 | | | |
| First Quarter | 121.0 | 106.7 | 14.3 |
| Second Quarter | 112.2 | 115.9 | -3.7 |
| Third Quarter | 101.7 | 113.6 | -11.9 |
| **JAPAN** | | | |
| 1990 annual | 48.6 | 89.7 | -41.1 |
| 1991 annual | 48.1 | 91.6 | -43.4 |
| 1992 annual | 47.8 | 97.4 | -49.6 |
| 1993 | | | |
| First Quarter | 48.0 | 101.0 | -53.0 |
| Second Quarter | 48.2 | 102.5 | -54.3 |
| Third Quarter | 47.5 | 108.8 | -61.3 |
| **CANADA** | | | |
| 1990 annual | 83.7 | 91.4 | -7.7 |
| 1991 annual | 85.1 | 91.1 | -6.0 |
| 1992 annual | 90.6 | 98.6 | -8.0 |
| 1993 | | | |
| First Quarter | 95.6 | 102.9 | -7.3 |
| Second Quarter | 106.2 | 117.3 | -11.1 |
| Third Quarter | 95.5 | 104.9 | -9.4 |
| **OPEC** | | | |
| 1990 annual | 13.7 | 38.1 | -24.4 |
| 1991 annual | 19.1 | 33.0 | -13.9 |
| 1992 annual | 22.0 | 33.2 | -11.2 |
| 1993 | | | |
| First Quarter | 20.7 | 31.8 | -11.1 |
| Second Quarter | 19.0 | 34.4 | -15.4 |
| Third Quarter | 16.7 | 31.1 | -14.4 |
| **OTHER DEVELOPING COUNTRIES** | | | |
| 1990 annual | 113.6 | 142.4 | -28.8 |
| 1991 annual | 127.7 | 142.1 | -14.4 |
| 1992 annual | 145.1 | 158.3 | -13.2 |
| 1993 | | | |
| First Quarter | 148.5 | 159.1 | -10.6 |
| Second Quarter | 157.4 | 169.2 | -11.8 |
| Third Quarter | 152.7 | 182.3 | -29.6 |
| **EASTERN EUROPE/FORMER U.S.S.R./COMMUNIST ASIA** | | | |
| 1990 annual | 9.0 | 17.4 | -8.4 |
| 1991 annual | 11.1 | 20.8 | -9.7 |
| 1992 annual | 13.0 | 27.7 | -14.7 |
| 1993 | | | |
| First Quarter | 12.3 | 26.9 | -14.6 |
| Second Quarter | 15.3 | 33.0 | -17.7 |
| Third Quarter | 14.5 | 41.6 | -27.1 |

*Source: U.S. Department of Commerce, International Trade Administration*

# World Unemployment

## World Unemployment Rates, (%, 1991 and 1981)

| Country | 1991 Both Sexes | 1981 Both Sexes | 1991 Women | 1981 Women | 1991 Men | 1981 Men | 1991, 12 or More Months Unemployed | 1981, 12 or More Months Unemployed |
|---|---|---|---|---|---|---|---|---|
| Australia | 9.5 | 5.7 | 9.2 | 7.1 | 11.0 | 4.6 | 24.9 | 21.0 |
| Austria | 3.5 | 2.5 | 3.6 | 3.6 | 3.3 | 1.9 | NA | NA |
| Belgium | 9.3 | 10.2 | 13.2 | 15.4 | 6.5 | 7.0 | 69.9 | 61.5 |
| Canada | 10.2 | 7.5 | 9.7 | 8.3 | 10.7 | 6.9 | 7.2 | 4.5 |
| Denmark | 9.1 | 10.3 | 10.0 | 10.7 | 8.3 | 10.0 | 33.7 | 26.2 |
| Finland | 7.5 | 4.8 | 5.7 | 4.6 | 9.1 | 5.0 | 6.9 | 27.0 |
| France | 9.3 | 7.4 | 12.1 | 10.6 | 7.2 | 5.3 | 37.3 | 32.5 |
| Germany | 5.5 | 4.5 | 6.3 | 5.6 | 5.0 | 3.8 | 46.3 | 22.3 |
| Greece | 7.0 | 4.0 | 11.7 | 5.7 | 4.3 | 3.3 | 51.7 | 20.6 |
| Iceland | 2.1 | 0.4 | 1.5 | NA | 1.4 | NA | NA | NA |
| Ireland | 15.7 | 9.9 | 12.1 | 8.9 | 17.3 | 10.3 | 67.2 | 38.2 |
| Italy | 10.8 | 7.8 | 16.7 | 13.4 | 7.4 | 5.0 | 71.1 | 50.2 |
| Japan | 2.1 | 2.2 | 2.2 | 2.1 | 2.0 | 2.3 | 17.9 | 13.5 |
| Luxembourg | 1.2 | 1.3 | 2.0 | 1.3 | 1.1 | 0.8 | NA | NA |
| Netherlands | 7.0 | 8.5 | 9.5 | 9.0 | 5.3 | 8.2 | 48.4 | 29.6 |
| New Zealand | 10.3 | 3.6 | 9.5 | 4.3 | 10.8 | 3.2 | 21.3 | 7.0 |
| Norway | 5.5 | 2.0 | 5.0 | 2.7 | 5.8 | 1.6 | 20.2 | 2.8 |
| Portugal | 4.1 | 7.4 | 5.8 | 12.3 | 2.7 | 4.0 | 48.1 | 56.0 |
| Spain | 16.0 | 13.8 | 23.5 | 15.8 | 12.0 | 12.9 | 51.1 | 40.2 |
| Sweden | 2.7 | 2.5 | 2.3 | 2.6 | 3.0 | 2.3 | 4.8 | 6.0 |
| Switzerland | 1.2 | 0.2 | 1.2 | 0.3 | 1.1 | 0.2 | NA | NA |
| Turkey | 8.0 | 11.3 | 7.3 | NA | 8.3 | NA | NA | NA |
| United Kingdom | 7.9 | 9.0 | 4.4 | 6.0 | 10.5 | 10.9 | 36.0 | 29.3 |
| United States | 6.6 | 7.5 | 6.3 | 7.9 | 6.9 | 7.2 | 6.3 | 6.7 |

Source: "OECD in Figures" 1993 Edition, supplement to The OECD Observer, No. 176, June/July, 1993

**TIP:** *The 1993 Statistical Abstract of the United States is now available on CD-ROM for $50 from the Bureau of the Census, U.S. Department of Commerce. The software requires MS-Dos version 3.0 or 3.1 running on 80286 or higher. To order call Customer Services at (301) 763-4100.*

# Corporate Office Space

## Office Vacancy Rates

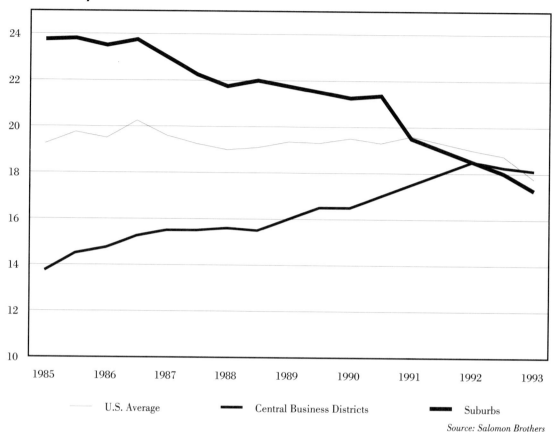

U.S. Average — Central Business Districts — Suburbs

*Source: Salomon Brothers*

## Metropolitan Office Markets Ranked by Vacancy Rates

### Top Ten Markets

| Rank | City | Vacancy June, 1992 |
|---|---|---|
| 1 | Honolulu | 7.2 |
| 2 | Las Vegas | 12.5 |
| 3 | San Francisco | 12.7 |
| 4 | Raleigh-Durham | 13.2 |
| 5 | San Jose | 13.5 |
| 6 | Seattle | 13.8 |
| 7 | Columbus | 14.0 |
| 8 | Portland | 14.1 |
| 9 | Sacramento | 15.6 |
| 10 | Pittsburgh | 15.6 |

*Source: "U.S. Office Market Survey," Jan. 1993, Salomon Brothers*

### Bottom Ten Markets

| Rank | City | Vacancy June, 1992 |
|---|---|---|
| 1 | West Palm Beach | 29.5 |
| 2 | Dallas | 27.6 |
| 3 | New Orleans | 25.8 |
| 4 | San Diego | 25.3 |
| 5 | Fort Lauderdale | 25.1 |
| 6 | Tampa | 24.3 |
| 7 | Houston | 24.1 |
| 8 | Tulsa | 24.0 |
| 9 | Miami | 23.9 |
| 10 | Ventura | 23.7 |

*Source: "U.S. Office Market Survey," Jan. 1993, Salomon Brothers*

*Corporate Office Space (cont'd)*

## Real Office Rents, Vacancy Rates

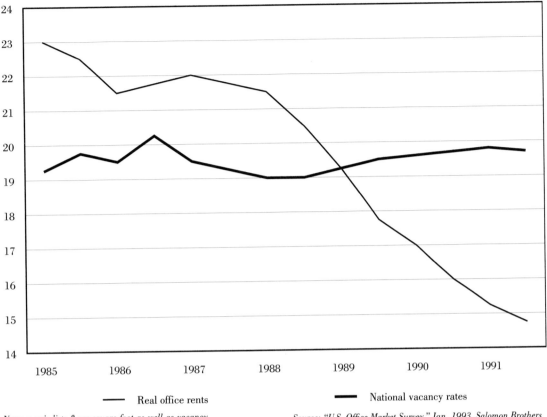

*Note: y axis lists $ per square foot as well as vacancy rate in %.*

*Source: "U.S. Office Market Survey," Jan. 1993, Salomon Brothers*

---

### The Top Reference Sources

*Statistical Forecasts of the United States*
Gale Research, 1993, $89.50
(800) 877-4253

This reference covers population, employment, labor, crime, education, health care, and other key areas. Statistics are compiled from a diverse range of sources, and data is presented in hundreds of charts, graphs, tables, and other statistical illustrations portraying both long- and short-term forecasts of future developments in the United States.

# Vacancy Rates and Rental Costs

| City | Total Office Inventory Surveyed | Office Occupancy Rate (%) | Rental Range ($ per sq. ft.) |
|------|--------------------------------|---------------------------|------------------------------|
| Akron | 1,479,667 | 87.3 | 8.00–21.00 |
| Anchorage, downtown | 2,916,838 | 86.0 | 12.00–25.20 |
| Anchorage, suburban | 4,360,539 | 92.3 | 9.00–25.20 |
| Atlanta, downtown/suburban | 70,392,639 | 82.9 | 12.44–20.14 |
| Baltimore | 36,177,496 | 83.1 | 12.00–20.00 |
| Boston, downtown | 57,657,682 | 83.7 | 21.51 |
| Boston, suburban | 64,653,727 | 81.6 | 13.23 |
| Buffalo | 9,016,309 | 83.8 | 7.00–24.00 |
| Cambridge | 10,380,512 | 85.6 | 17.32 |
| Charlotte, downtown | 10,760,678 | 86.4 | 12.00–24.00 |
| Charlotte, suburban | 12,738,622 | 79.5 | 12.00–21.00 |
| Chicago, downtown | 100,070,500 | 73.9 | 14.50–22.00 |
| Chicago, O'Hare corridor | 3,546,692 | 77.5 | 11.00–28.00 |
| Cincinnati, downtown | 13,979,814 | 83.3 | 14.79 |
| Cincinnati, suburban | 8,081,285 | 83.6 | 13.97 |
| Cleveland, downtown | 22,500,000 | 79.1 | 13.00–21.00 |
| Cleveland, suburban | 13,000,000 | 85.4 | NA |
| Columbus (total) | 22,293,741 | 86.2 | 7.00–19.00 |
| Dallas, downtown | 30,570,125 | 64.0 | 11.00–22.00 |
| Dallas, suburban | 87,664,321 | 75.9 | 10.00–16.50 |
| Denver (total) | 69,663,806 | 82.9 | 9.00–14.00 |
| Detroit, downtown | 14,206,389 | 76.5 | 10.00–20.73 |
| Detroit, suburban | 44,038,042 | 81.4 | 12.00–18.00 |
| Fairfield County, CT | 32,210,000 | 79.4 | 16.44–20.72 |
| Fort Worth, downtown | 7,911,886 | 72.4 | 8.00–17.00 |
| Fort Worth, suburban | 14,592,909 | 81.4 | 4.00–16.00 |
| Hartford, downtown | 11,226,161 | 75.8 | 10.00–28.00 |
| Hartford, suburban | 13,035,528 | 78.2 | 8.00–22.50 |
| Houston (total) | 52,190,992 | 76.4 | 10.00–13.56 |
| Indianapolis, downtown | 9,313,263 | 75.7 | 9.50–22.00 |
| Indianapolis, suburban | 11,653,635 | 80.0 | 10.00–19.00 |
| Kansas City, MO downtown | 12,331,813 | 79.3 | NA |
| Kansas City, MO suburban | 21,968,101 | 89.0 | NA |
| Los Angeles | 243,837,961 | 80.3 | NA |
| Manhattan, midtown | 191,500,000 | 84.8 | 30.95 |
| Milwaukee, downtown | 10,067,160 | 78.9 | NA |
| Milwaukee, suburban | 12,536,491 | 79.1 | NA |
| Minneapolis, downtown | 20,928,119 | 82.5 | 13.50–19.75 |
| Minneapolis, suburban | 20,104,745 | 87.2 | 15.50–21.35 |
| New Orleans, downtown | 16,489,545 | 70.0 | 8.00–15.00 |
| New Orleans, suburban | 6,964,992 | 83.0 | 8.00–18.00 |
| Oakland/ East Bay | 83,400,000 | 85.4 | NA |
| Orlando, downtown | 5,275,000 | 85.8 | 14.55–20.42 |
| Orlando, suburban | 12,387,000 | 85.5 | 12.78–15.85 |
| Phoenix, downtown | 16,100,000 | 74.5 | 11.48–16.73 |
| Phoenix, suburban | 29,900,000 | 77.9 | 12.35–14.82 |
| Pittsburgh, downtown | 24,445,920 | 81.5 | 12.00–27.00 |
| Pittsburgh, suburban | 11,608,631 | 86.7 | 13.50–17.50 |
| Portland, OR downtown | 15,311,205 | 85.2 | 14.00–22.00 |
| Portland, OR suburban | 9,906,274 | 87.4 | 12.00–18.50 |

*Vacancy Rates and Rental Costs (cont'd)*

| City | Total Office Inventory Surveyed | Office Occupancy Rate (%) | Rental Range ($ per sq. ft.) |
|------|-------------------------------|---------------------------|------------------------------|
| Sacramento, downtown | 9,703,220 | 85.4 | 19.00–32.00 |
| Sacramento, suburban | 26,906,803 | 86.3 | 15.00–25.00 |
| Saint Louis, downtown | 12,086,833 | 74.0 | 9.00–25.00 |
| Saint Louis, suburban | 19,400,810 | 87.4 | 13.50–23.50 |
| Saint Paul, downtown | 7,233,151 | 83.3 | 8.25–21.47 |
| Saint Paul, suburban | 5,349,615 | 80.5 | 5.00–18.00 |
| Salt Lake City, downtown | 8,827,702 | 84.5 | NA |
| Salt Lake City, suburban | 6,004,938 | 86.5 | NA |
| San Francisco, downtown | 69,157,256 | 87.3 | 14.00–23.00 |
| Seattle, downtown | 24,108,522 | 86.5 | 9.00–32.50 |
| Seattle, suburban | 6,571,638 | 76.9 | 9.00–18.25 |
| Tucson, downtown | 975,323 | 66.2 | 10.00–15.00 |
| Tucson, suburban | 5,256,203 | 82.6 | 10.00–15.00 |
| Tulsa, downtown | 6,407,694 | 76.2 | 8.50–14.00 |
| Tulsa, suburban | 9,058,750 | 80.8 | 8.25–14.00 |
| Washington, DC, downtown | 79,226,573 | 88.9 | 10.00–60.25 |
| Suburban Virginia | 71,299,474 | 84.4 | 5.00–39.00 |
| Suburban Maryland | 37,615,072 | 84.8 | 9.00–32.50 |
| Westchester County, NY | 25,405,250 | 72.4 | 19.00–22.00 |

*Source: 1993 North American Office Market Review, BOMA*

## Contact Options

Building Owners and Managers Assn. (BOMA)
1201 New York Ave., NW
Washington, DC 20005
(202) 408-2662

Society for Industrial and Office Realtors
777 14th St., NW, Suite 400
Washington, DC 20005
(202) 737-1150

## Recommended Resource

*ULI Market Profiles: 1994*
Urban Land Institute, $329.95/2 volumes
Washington, DC 20005
(800) 321-5011
    Urban Land Institute economic report on 35 major locations plus 13 international markets for real estate development in residential, retail, hotel, office, and industrial sectors.

## The Top Reference Sources

*Comparative Statistics of Industrial and Office Real Estate Markets, 1994*
Society of Industrial and Office Realtors, $70
(202) 737-1150

This publication includes a detailed review and forecast of both industrial and office real estate markets, as well as an analysis of economic trends and their effect on industrial and office markets.
    The book is compiled by a select group of SIOR members in major metropolitan areas in the U.S., Canada, and abroad. The book includes many charts and graphs.

# Construction Starts

**Housing Starts (thousands of units)**

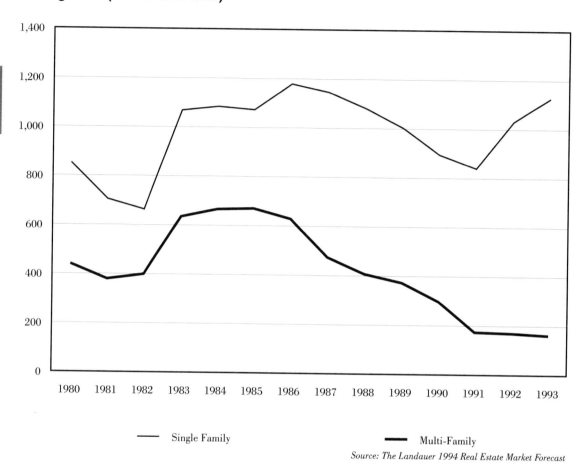

Single Family

Multi-Family

*Source: The Landauer 1994 Real Estate Market Forecast*

## The Top Reference Sources

*Construction Review*
U.S. Government Printing Office, $17/year
(202) 783-3238

This quarterly publication of the International Trade Administration canvasses the major construction series published by the Census Bureau

and Bureau of Labor Statistics. It includes about 50 pages of statistics, from building permits to housing starts, construction materials to price indexes, plus one or two brief articles per issue.

Features include articles on world trade in building materials and non-residential building improvements in the United States.

# Landauer Momentum Index

LANDAUER ASSOCIATES HAS RANKED 24 major metropolitan areas by their real estate momentum. This is computed as the prospective change in supply and demand balance for office space. The median value is set to 100. Therefore, Phoenix has average momentum, while Orlando is expected to see a growth rate that outstrips supply.

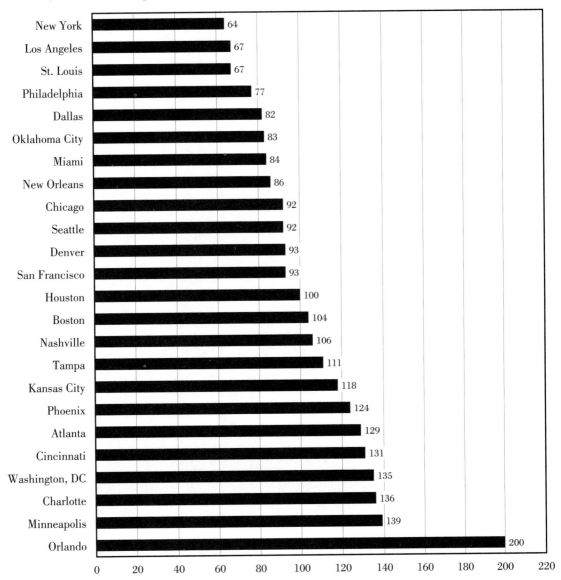

| Metro Area | Index |
|---|---|
| New York | 64 |
| Los Angeles | 67 |
| St. Louis | 67 |
| Philadelphia | 77 |
| Dallas | 82 |
| Oklahoma City | 83 |
| Miami | 84 |
| New Orleans | 86 |
| Chicago | 92 |
| Seattle | 92 |
| Denver | 93 |
| San Francisco | 93 |
| Houston | 100 |
| Boston | 104 |
| Nashville | 106 |
| Tampa | 111 |
| Kansas City | 118 |
| Phoenix | 124 |
| Atlanta | 129 |
| Cincinnati | 131 |
| Washington, DC | 135 |
| Charlotte | 136 |
| Minneapolis | 139 |
| Orlando | 200 |

*Source: 1994 Real Estate Market Forecast, Landauer Associates*

# Major Real Estate Developers

*NATIONAL REAL ESTATE INVESTOR* conducts an annual survey of real estate developers and ranks the respondents based on the total square feet under development in North America. The top ten listings from the 1993 survey are:

Homart Development
55 W. Monroe, Suite 3100
Chicago, IL 60603
(312) 551-5000

Hines Interests Ltd. Partnership
2800 Post Oak Blvd.
Houston, TX 77056
(713) 621-8000

Simon Property Group
115 W. Washington
Indianapolis, IN 46204
(317) 636-1600

The Edward J. DeBartolo
7620 Market St.
Youngstown, OH 44513
(216) 758-7292

Lincoln Property
500 N. Akard, Suite 3300
Dallas, TX 75201
(214) 740-3300

Breslin Realty Development
500 Old Country Rd., Suite 200
Garden City, NY 11530
(516) 741-7400

The Hutensky Group
1 Financial Plaza, 10th Floor
Hartford, CT 06103
(203) 297-4500

The Cafaro Co.
2445 Belmont Ave.
Youngstown, OH 44504
(216) 747-2661

Zeckendorf Realty
55 E. 59th St.
New York, NY 10022
(212) 826-2900

Industrial Developments
3343 Peachtree Rd., Suite 1050
Atlanta, GA 30326
(404) 233-6080

# Major Property Managers

*NATIONAL REAL ESTATE INVESTOR* conducts an annual survey of property managers ranking the respondents based on the amount of space in their management portfolios. The following are the top ten listings from the 1993 survey:

Trammell Crow
2001 Ross Ave., Suite 3500
Dallas, TX 75201
(214) 979-5100

Network Management Group International
9401 LBJ Freeeway, Suite 200
Dallas, TX 75243
(214) 644-5900

Lincoln Property
500 N. Akard, Suite 3300
Dallas, TX 75201
(214) 740-3300

JMB Properties
900 N. Michigan Ave.
Chicago, IL 60601
(312) 915-2500

Cushman & Wakefield
51 W. 52nd St.
New York, NY 10019
(212) 841-7500

The Edward J. DeBartolo Corp.
7620 Market St.
Youngstown, OH 44513
(216) 758-7292

Insignia Management Group
P.O. Box 1089
Greenville, SC 29602
(803) 239-1000

La Salle Partners
11 S. LaSalle St.
Chicago, IL 60603
(312) 782-5800

PM Realty Group
1177 W. Loop South, Suite 1200
Houston, TX 77027
(713) 966-3600

Grubb & Ellis
2800 Two PNC Plaza
Pittsburgh, PA 15222
(412) 281-0100

# Major Real Estate Lenders

## The Top 50 Commerical Banks in Deposits

| Rank | Bank Name | City Location | Telephone | Total Assets* ($) |
|---|---|---|---|---|
| 1 | Citibank, NA | New York | (800) 568-7904 | 168,567,000 |
| 2 | Bank of America NT & SA | San Francisco | (415) 622-6320 | 133,970,000 |
| 3 | Chemical Bank | New York | (212) 310-6161 | 110,375,000 |
| 4 | Morgan Guaranty Trust | New York | (212) 483-2323 | 103,490,418 |
| 5 | Chase Manhattan Bank, NA | New York | (212) 552-2222 | 79,947,495 |
| 6 | Bankers Trust | New York | (212) 250-2500 | 63,853,000 |
| 7 | Wells Fargo Bank, NA | San Francisco | (415) 477-1000 | 49,908,503 |
| 8 | NationsBank of Texas, NA | Dallas | (214) 508-2130 | 36,911,237 |
| 9 | PNC Bank, NA | Pittsburgh | (412) 762-2000 | 36,822,932 |
| 10 | Bank of New York | New York | (212) 495-1041 | 35,775,745 |
| 11 | First National Bank | Chicago | (312) 732-4000 | 34,081,108 |
| 12 | Mellon Bank, NA | Pittsburgh | (412) 234-5000 | 28,553,000 |
| 13 | Republic National Bank of New York | New York | (212) 525-5000 | 28,381,291 |
| 14 | First Union National Bank of Florida | Jacksonville | (904) 361-2265 | 26,197,165 |
| 15 | First National Bank | Boston | (617) 434-8155 | 25,723,006 |
| 16 | NationsBank of North Carolina | Charlotte | (704) 386-8669 | 24,549,294 |
| 17 | NBD Bank, NA | Detroit | (313) 225-1000 | 24,400,120 |
| 18 | Comerica Bank | Detroit | (313) 222-3300 | 22,317,093 |
| 19 | Continental Bank, NA | Chicago | (312) 828-2345 | 22,038,000 |
| 20 | NationsBank of Florida, NA | Tampa | (813) 882-2000 | 22,001,243 |
| 21 | First Union National Bank of North Carolina, NA | Charlotte | (704) 374-6161 | 20,745,048 |
| 22 | First Fidelity Bank, NA | Newark | (201) 565-3223 | 20,179,576 |
| 23 | First Interstate Bank of California | Los Angeles | (213) 614-4111 | 19,526,246 |
| 24 | Wachovia Bank of North Carolina, NA | Winston-Salem | (919) 770-5000 | 18,625,351 |
| 25 | Society National Bank | Cleveland | (216) 689-3000 | 18,528,129 |
| 26 | State Street Bank & Trust | Boston | (617) 654-4000 | 18,267,536 |
| 27 | Bank One, Texas, NA | Dallas | (713) 751-6100 | 17,414,041 |
| 28 | National Westminster Bank USA | New York | (516) 531-7120 | 16,456,767 |
| 29 | Marine Midland Bank, NA | Buffalo | (716) 841-6762 | 16,122,584 |
| 30 | Union Bank | San Francisco | (213) 236-7109 | 16,045,781 |
| 31 | CoreStates Bank, NA | Philadelphia | (215) 973-3512 | 15,492,416 |
| 32 | Seattle-First National Bank | Seattle | (206) 358-3000 | 15,097,315 |
| 33 | Norwest Bank Minnesota, NA | Minneapolis | (612) 667-8123 | 15,097,106 |
| 34 | NationsBank of Georgia, NA | Atlanta | (404) 607-4109 | 14,936,154 |
| 35 | Key Bank of New York | Albany | (518) 486-8159 | 13,924,236 |
| 36 | Shawmut Bank, NA | Boston | (617) 292-2000 | 13,409,650 |
| 37 | First Bank NA | Minneapolis | (612) 370-4141 | 13,380,047 |
| 38 | Northern Trust | Chicago | (312) 630-6000 | 13,115,380 |
| 39 | Shawmut Bank Connecticut, NA | Hartford | (203) 728-2000 | 12,760,674 |
| 40 | Texas Commerce Bank, NA | Houston | (713) 216-4865 | 12,429,701 |
| 41 | Maryland National Bank | Baltimore | (410) 605-6150 | 11,757,845 |
| 42 | Huntington National Bank | Columbus | (614) 463-4424 | 11,717,712 |
| 43 | Bank of Hawaii | Honolulu | (808) 537-8272 | 11,593,218 |
| 44 | NationsBank of Virginia, NA | Richmond | (804) 788-3034 | 11,289,509 |
| 45 | Crestar Bank | Richmond | (804) 782-5000 | 11,118,509 |
| 46 | United States National Bank | Portland | (503) 275-6111 | 10,808,687 |
| 47 | Bank One, Arizona, NA | Phoenix | (602) 221-2900 | 10,694,173 |
| 48 | Wachovia Bank of Georgia, NA | Atlanta | (404) 332-5000 | 10,500,425 |
| 49 | Meridian Bank | Reading | (215) 320-2000 | 10,421,197 |
| 50 | Banco Popular de Puerto Rico | San Juan | (809) 765-9800 | 10,415,633 |

*as of June, 1993*

Source: American Banker

# Lease Negotiation Tips

ACCORDING TO *Corporate Real Estate Executive*, techniques used during negotiations depend on whether you are in the "early," "middle," or "ending" phase of the process.

In the early phase of negotiations, it is important to develop basic trust, spell out realistic objectives, learn relevant facts, and establish procedural guidelines. Careful preparation will set the stage for this process. The one who is best prepared and who has anticipated objections, generally has the advantage right to the end.

There are certain tactics that help. For example, meeting at your place, if possible, or at a neutral location may eliminate distractions or interruptions, may allow you to plan seating or even lighting to your advantage. Because important decisions are best made at mid-day, scheduling the meeting over lunch would enable you to start with some small talk that may reveal more about the other person's needs and personality. Above all, schedule enough time.

The early phase is the time to ask a lot of questions, probe for information, concentrate on what the other party is saying, and how it is being said. Establish reasonable expectations. This is also the time to show how much both sides have in common, as well as learn about related problems. During this phase, listen carefully and attempt to get the other side to talk and make commitments. Save most of your talking for the middle phase when you will concentrate on problem solving.

During the middle phase of negotiations, explore alternatives to show you understand the other party's position. At this point, you can start to narrow down the issues and establish a positive tone and a sense of coming to an agreement. Keep asking the other party to explain the reasoning behind every demand and be ready to explain your own. Observe his eyes and body language carefully when he is making an important point. Try trading small compromises in return for larger ones.

Never concede anything too quickly; be sure each concession is fully appreciated and always made for something in return. Save your energy for what is important—which is usually the price.

Throughout negotiations, it is important to avoid common pitfalls. Don't ask for too little. If you don't ask, you don't get. Don't make excessive demands that destroy your credibility. Know exactly what you will settle for, or you will transfer control of negotiations to the other side. Be prepared to break a stalemate with new information or by changing the subject or by asking questions. Have a deadline to work against. If you are negotiating with more than one principal, leave something for the other principals to negotiate just prior to closing.

When it is time to wrap up the agreement, the parties should review together what is agreed upon and confirm that all the problems are resolved. This is not the time for you to bring up new issues. If you have everything you want, stop negotiating. As you get into the document stage, be prepared to illustrate to the party's lawyer how and why they have a good deal.

In working out the documents, ask the other party's lawyer to note any questions or give you any comments before changing the language. Once the other party is committed to its own language, it is more difficult to reverse direction.

Finally, be available in person when the documents are prepared to answer any last minute questions or to resolve any remaining matters.

When the deal is done, analyze your approach. Remember that hard work, practice, and experience are essential for consistent success. And do not underestimate your ability to earn a reputation as an excellent negotiator.

*Source: NACORE International, reprinted by permission*

## Recommended Resources

*Corporate Real Estate Executive*
NACORE International, $65/year
440 Columbia Dr., Suite 100
West Palm Beach, FL 33409
(407) 683-8111

*Negotiating Commercial Real Estate Leases*
by Martin Zankel
Dearborn Financial Publishing, $34.95
(800) 982-2850
Provides nontechnical guidance to elements in leases and other related topics.

*Tenant's Handbook to Office Leasing*
by Stanley Wolfson
McGraw-Hill, $49.50
(800) 262-4729
Features negotiating tips for leasing contracts enhanced by tables, charts, graphs, and forms.

# Total Personal Income

**Percent Growth, 1991–1992**

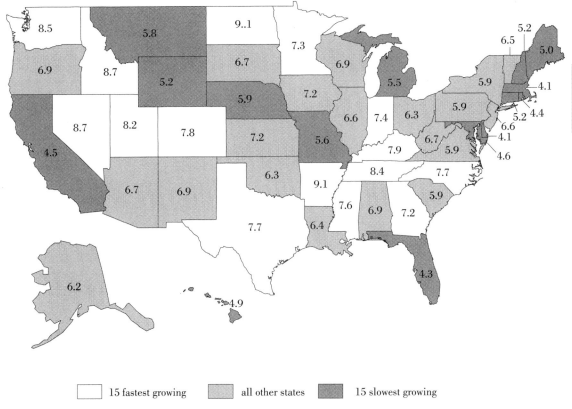

| | | |
|---|---|---|
| □ 15 fastest growing | ▨ all other states | ▨ 15 slowest growing |

*Source: Survey of Current Business*

## The Top Reference Sources

*State and Metropolitan Area Data Book*
U.S. Government Printing Office, $26
(202) 783-3238

A supplement to the *Statistical Abstract*, this publication is compiled by the Economics and Statistics Administration, Bureau of the Census. The data presented comes from over fifty federal and private agencies and represents some of the most up-to-date statistics available.

The statistics included cover a range of topics: commercial office space, manufacturers, personal income, housing, civilian labor force, farms, and retail trade.

The book is updated on a five-year cycle. The next expected update should be available in 1996.

# BOMA Standards

THE BUILDING OWNERS AND MANAGERS Association International (BOMA) is an organization whose purpose is to establish standards through which building owners, managers, tenants, appraisers, architects, lending institutions, and others can communicate and compute on a clear and understandable basis. To achieve that objective, BOMA publishes standards for measuring floor area, calculating and analyzing expenses and income for office buildings, as well as other related tasks. In addition, BOMA provides annual surveys of office space utilization, rental prices/square foot, vacancy rates, and the general rental market in major downtown and suburban locations throughout the nation as well as in Canada.

## Contact Option

Building Owners and Managers Association International (BOMA)
1201 New York Ave., NW, Suite 300
Washington, DC 20005
(202) 408-2662

# Management Consulting Firms

## Major Management Consulting Firms in the U.S.

| Firm | Telephone |
|------|-----------|
| A. Foster Higgins | (212) 574-9000 |
| Alexander Consulting Group | (201) 460-6700 |
| Alexander Proudfoot | (407) 697-9600 |
| Andersen Consulting | (312) 580-0069 |
| Arthur D. Little | (617) 864-5770 |
| Bain & Co. | (617) 572-2000 |
| Booz-Allen & Hamilton | (212) 697-1900 |
| Boston Consulting Group | (617) 973-1200 |
| Coopers & Lybrand | (212) 536-3306 |
| CSC Consulting | (617) 661-0900 |
| Deloitte & Touche | (212) 489-1600 |
| Ernst & Young | (216) 861-5000 |
| Hay Group | (215) 875-2300 |
| Hewitt Associates | (312) 295-5000 |
| KPMG Peat Marwick | (212) 909-5000 |
| McKinsey & Co. | (212) 446-7000 |
| Mercer Consulting Group | (212) 345-4500 |
| Milliman & Robertson | (206) 624-7940 |
| Price Waterhouse | (212) 489-8900 |
| Towers Perrin | (212) 309-3400 |

*Source: Consultants and Consulting Organizations Directory*

# Business Brokers

THE TREND TOWARD INDEPENDENTLY owned and operated small- and medium-sized businesses is increasing dramatically. In fact, small companies created over 13 million jobs in the last decade.

Business brokers bring the buyers and sellers of these businesses together. When the companies that are for sale exceed $1 million in value, the negotiations are usually handled by mergers and acquisitions specialists. Smaller business deals—sales below $1 million—are handled by business brokers.

For sellers, business brokers:

- Advise on how to prepare a business for sale;
- Advise on pricing the business;
- Market the business to potential buyers;
- Keep the sale confidential to protect business standing;
- Pre-qualify prospects to find the right match;
- Negotiate the transaction;
- Manage the close.

For buyers, business brokers:

- Provide access to an inventory of businesses for sale;
- Answer questions about buying a business;
- Match buyer's interests, goals, and desires with the right business;
- Prepare buyers to act quickly when the right opportunity is uncovered;
- Identify financing options;
- Manage the close;
- Support the transition.

## Contact Options

International Business Brokers Association
P.O. Box 704
Concord, MA 01742
(508) 369-2490
The IBBA is a trade association that has a directory of its members arranged alphabetically and by location.

International Association of Merger and Acquisition Consultants
60 Revere Dr., Suite 500
Northbrook, IL 60062
(708) 480-9037

*Business Brokers:*

New England Business Advisors
196 Danbury Rd., P.O. Box 786
Wilton, CT 06897
(203) 834-0070

Corporate Investment International
101 Wymore Rd., Suite 225
Altamonte Springs, FL 32714
(407) 682-9600

Georgia Business Associates
2401 Lake Park Dr., Suite 350
Smyrna, GA 30080
(404) 319-6500

Hoganson Venture Group
15 Salt Creek Ln., Suite 217
Hinsdale, IL 60521
(708) 887-4788

Finn & Associates
545 North Woodlawn
Wichita, KS 67208
(316) 683-3466

UBI of Louisiana
4205 Canal St.
New Orleans, LA 70119
(504) 486-5375

Vernon A. Martin
1 Corporate Pl., 55 Ferncroft Rd.
Danvers, MA 01923
(508) 774-0160

Inexco Business Brokerage & Development
1568 Mt. Mercy Dr., NW
Grand Rapids, MI 49504
(616) 949-4374

Calhoun Companies
4930 W. 77th St., Suite 100
Minneapolis, MN 55435
(612) 831-3300

Opportunities in Business
3433 Broadway St., NE, Suite 555
Minneapolis, MN 55413
(612) 331-8392

Siegel Business Services
One Bala Plaza, Suite 621
Bala-Cynwyd, PA 19004
(215) 668-9780

*Business Brokers (cont'd)*

Landmark Business Brokers
600 W. Park Row
Arlington, TX 76010
(817) 265-9188

Certified Business Brokers
10301 Northwest Freeway, Suite 200
Houston, TX 77092
(713) 680-1200

Country Business
Box 1071
Manchester Center, VT 05255
(802) 362-4710

J.S. Keate & Co.
Croger Bldg., 1014 Vine St., Suite 1600
Cincinnati, OH 45202
(513) 241-3700

Bluestem Resources Group
1427 E. 41st St.
Tulsa, OK 74105
(918) 749-4315

The Hughes Group & Associates
621 N. Robinson
Oklahoma City, OK 73102
(405) 848-1866

Probus/MBI Business Brokers & Consultants
307 Orchard City Dr., Suite 100
Campbell, CA 95008
(408) 370-9500

Geneva Business Services
5 Park Plaza
Irvine, CA 92714
(714) 756-2200

Business Team
3031 Tisch Way, Suite 400
San Jose, CA 95128
(408) 246-1102

DAP Business Services
11314 South St.
Cerritos, CA 90701
(310) 402-2686

Colorado Business Consultants
899 Logan St., Suite 309
Denver, CO 80203
(303) 832-2020

Corporate Finance Associates
1801 Broadway, Suite 1200
Denver, CO 80202
(303) 296-6300

VR Business Brokers
1151 Dove St., Suite 100
Newport Beach, CA 92660
(800) 377-8722
    VR has 82 franchises around the country, each independently owned and operated. It is the only national company of business brokers in the United States.

# Corporate Art

ESTABLISHING A CORPORATE ART collection is no longer the privilege of Fortune 500 companies alone. In recent years, more and more small- and mid-sized firms have begun to collect art, not only to create ambiance in their surrounding office space but because of its potential investment value.

As a result, an entire industry has developed to serve the needs of corporate art collections. The following directories provide information on what other companies are collecting as well as complete listings of the agents, dealers, and consultants who help companies choose their collections.

## Recommended Resources

*ARTnews International Directory of Corporate Art Collections*
ARTnews & International Art Alliance, $109.95
P.O. Box 1608
Largo, FL 34249
(813) 581-7328

This annual directory provides an alphabetical listing by company of major national and international corporate art collections. Each listing includes a brief description of the corporation as well as information pertinent to the collection, including size, year begun, location, source of artwork, loan policy, and selection process.

*Encyclopedia of Living Artists*
ArtNetwork, $17.95
13284 Rices Crossing Rd.
P.O. Box 369
Renaissance, CA 95962
(916) 692-1355

This annual book is a full-color catalogue of the work of American artists, complete with personal profiles, names and addresses of the artists and their agents. It is used as a resource for galleries, publishers, private and corporate collectors, and consultants.

# Choosing an Architect

THERE ARE MANY METHODS of selecting an architect, ranging from formal design competitions to negotiated procurement to competitive bidding. You need to determine which approach fits your requirements and designate an individual or group to manage your selection process. To begin the selection process:

- Make a list of potential architects by asking colleagues for referrals.

- Contact your local chapter of the American Institute of Architects.

- Discover who designed projects similar to yours that appeal to you.

You may want to ask for qualifications and references at this stage. If the scope of the project is still indefinite, narrow the field based on what you learn.

You may want the architect to prepare a preliminary or full proposal explaining how he or she would approach your project. In that case, you may wish to send a written project description to the most promising firms; sending the same information to each architecture firm will make it easier to compare responses.

Decide how much cost information to request and when you want to request it; you may want to know only how the architect will charge for services, or you may need more–like preliminary estimates or even a detailed proposal. The choice is yours to make based on your needs and the nature of your project.

With your in-house team, or whichever staff you delegate to manage the project, review the information you have collected. Useful factors to consider include:

- The size of the firm and the amount of time it has been in practice;

- Experience and past projects;

- Their ability to work within budget/time schedules;

- Cost of services;

- Special expertise including experience in your project type, management ability, and knowledge of building codes/zoning regulations.

Beyond review of the proposal, you may also wish to:

- Visit at least one finished project of each architect under consideration;

- Call client references.

An interview can give you important information on how well you will be able to work with a potential architect. If the written material you have received doesn't tell you all you need to know to select a firm, here is one way to pursue the process further:

- Create a short list of perhaps three to five firms to interview.

- Decide who from your firm will be responsible for the interviewing and final selection.

- Allow at least an hour for the interview.

- Decide on location of interview. At your office the architect can gain a better understanding of you and your project; at the architect's office you can see how the architect and staff work.

- Make sure that the people you interview are the people who will actually be working on your project.

In making your final determination, look at:

- Design quality

- Technical competence

- Experience

- Cost

- Organization.

You will need to evaluate for yourself the weight to give each of the factors.

You will also be looking for an architect who:

- Is responsive to your needs

- Listens carefully

- Seems to understand your company

- Makes you feel comfortable.

You will be working with the architect for a long time and may work with him or her on future projects. It is important that you trust the architect's judgment and ability.

## Recommended Resource

The American Institute of Architects
1735 New York Ave., NW
Washington, DC 20006
(202) 626-7300; 7461
In addition to its role as the national organization of architects, the AIA maintains local and regional offices that will work with a company to help it find an architect. To reach a local office, contact the national headquarters above.

# Interior Design

EVERY JANUARY AND JULY, *Interior Design* ranks the country's top design firms.

## Interior Design's Top 25 Design Firms

| Name of Firm | City | Telephone | Interior Design Fees ($ millions) | No. of Employees |
|---|---|---|---|---|
| Gensler & Associates/Architects | San Francisco, CA | (415) 433-3700 | 42.73 | 267 |
| ISI (Interior Space International) | Chicago, IL | (312) 454-9100 | 24.75 | 25 |
| R.J. Pavlik | Ft. Lauderdale, FL | (305) 523-3300 | 20.22 | 39 |
| Leo A. Daly | Omaha, NE | (402) 391-8111 | 18.33 | 25 |
| HNTB Corporation | Kansas City, MO | (816) 472-1201 | 18.33 | 15 |
| Sverdrup Corporation | St. Louis, MO | (314) 436-7600 | 16.75 | 90 |
| Hellmuth, Obata & Kassabaum | St. Louis, MO | (314) 421-2000 | 15.98 | 51 |
| Retail Planning Associates (RPA) | Columbus, OH | (614) 461-1820 | 14.89 | 26 |
| Space Design International | Cincinnati, OH | (513) 241-3000 | 12.94 | 70 |
| Smith, Hinchman & Grylls Associates | Detroit, MI | (313) 983-3600 | 12.85 | 19 |
| Perkins & Will | Chicago, IL | (312) 977-1100 | 12.05 | 42 |
| NBBJ | Seattle, WA | (206) 223-5555 | 11.40 | 31 |
| Interprise | Chicago, IL | (312) 855-1002 | 11.27 | 38 |
| ODA/Environetics International | New York, NY | (212) 221-7440 | 10.88 | 55 |
| The Phillips Janson Group Architects, P.C. | New York, NY | (212) 768-0800 | 10.42 | 53 |
| Swanke Hayden Connell Architects | New York, NY | (212) 977-9696 | 9.77 | 33 |
| Interior Architects Incorporated (IA) | San Francisco, CA | (415) 434-3305 | 9.07 | 49 |
| Studios Architecture | Washington, DC | (202) 736-5900 | 8.88 | 49 |
| Walker Group/ CNI | New York, NY | (212) 206-0444 | 8.75 | 37 |
| SCR Design Organization | New York, NY | (212) 421-3500 | 8.10 | 38 |
| HLW–Haines Lundberg Waehler | New York, NY | (212) 353-4600 | 7.98 | 39 |
| Griswold Heckel & Kelly | Chicago, IL | (312) 263-6605 | 7.91 | 54 |
| AI/ Boggs | Washington, DC | (202) 737-1020 | 7.77 | 34 |
| Mancini–Duffy | New York, NY | (212) 938-1260 | 7.71 | 31 |
| Henningson, Durham & Richardson | Omaha, NE | (402) 399-1000 | 7.58 | 3 |

## Contact Options

American Society of Interior Designers
608 Massachusetts Ave., NE
Washington, DC 20002
(202) 546-3480
    Provides referrals for interior designers in its local offices around the country.

Office Planners and Users Group
Box 11182
Philadelphia, PA 19136
(215) 335-9400
    Plans and manages office facilities.

## Recommended Resource

*Interior Design*
249 W. 17th St.
New York, NY 10011
(212) 463-6675

**TIP:** *The Business Information Service for the Newly Independent States (BISNIS) is a branch of the U.S. Department of Commerce whose specific purpose is to offers assistance to businesses seeking to establish offices in the newly independent states of the former Soviet Union. It offers directories, sources of news, and information on finance and commercial guidelines to the interested individual. For information, call (202) 484-4655. (See also "The Newly Independent States" on page 427.)*

# Architects/Designers

## 20 Top Design Firms Based on Billings, 1993

| Rank | Name | City |
|------|------|------|
| 1 | ABB Lummus Crest | Bloomfield, NJ |
| 2 | The Parsons Corp. | Pasadena, CA |
| 3 | Bechtel Group | San Francisco, CA |
| 4 | Fluor Daniel | Irvine, CA |
| 5 | Raytheon Eng. & Constructors | Lexington, MA |
| 6 | Jacobs Engineering Group | Pasadena, CA |
| 7 | Foster Wheeler | Clinton, NJ |
| 8 | Stone & Webster Engineering | Boston, MA |
| 9 | Brown & Root | Houston, TX |
| 10 | John Brown E & C | Houston, TX |
| 11 | Litwin Eng. & Constructors | Houston, TX |
| 12 | Rust International | Birmingham, AL |
| 13 | CH2M Hill | Denver, CO |
| 14 | Parsons Brinckerhoff | New York, NY |
| 15 | Law Cos. Group/Sir Alex. Gibb | Atlanta, GA |
| 16 | Sverdrup | Maryland Hts, MO |
| 17 | The Austin Company | Cleveland, OH |
| 18 | ICF Kaiser International | Fairfax, VA |
| 19 | Dames & Moore | Los Angeles, CA |
| 20 | S&B Eng. & Constructors | Houston, TX |

*Source: Engineering News Record, April 5, 1993*

## Award Winners

Almost every year since 1907, the American Institute of Architects has awarded a gold medal to one architect for outstanding design work.

| Year | Architect |
|------|-----------|
| 1981 | Josep Liuis Sert |
| 1982 | Romaldo Giurgola |
| 1983 | Nathaniel A. Owings |
| 1985 | William Wayne Caudill (posthumously) |
| 1986 | Arthur Erickson |
| 1989 | Joseph Esherick |
| 1990 | E. Fay Jones |
| 1991 | Charles W. Moore |
| 1992 | Benjamin Thompson |
| 1993 | Kevin Roche |
| 1994 | Sir Norman Foster |

## Contact Option

The American Institute of Architects
1735 New York Ave., NW
Washington, DC 20006
(202) 626-7300

# Annual Reports

## Sid Cato's Standards for the Best Annual Report

- Does the front cover demand readership? Has the report utilized readership-enhancing devices, including an intriguing cover statement, textual call-outs, boldface lead-ins, action subheads, bulleted paragraphs and the like? Does it contain an open, inviting layout, solicit readership on every page and have an action-filled index—that is, a "talking table of contents"?

- Is the writing sprightly and efficient? How does the text score on readability? Has use of complex words been avoided?

- Does it truly aim to inform fully, presenting items such as a special editorial section, glossary of terms, a mission statement?

- Does it truly shed light on the competition, market position and market share? Also, does it provide a breakdown of operations, results, and prospects?

- Is a photo of the organization's head person used, and does it lead off the shareholder letter?

- Has management wholeheartedly assumed responsibility, alongside the auditors, for the financials?

- Does the report contain biographical data on officers and directors—more than simply age and year of affiliation?

- Has it broken any new ground—in other words, is the report unquestionably other than run-of-the-mill? Does the board include women and/or minorities?

- Does it have a discernible point of view—a theme clearly thought out, delineated, and woven throughout?

- Does it communicate a favorable image—or identity—of the company, through its stature, articulation, point of view, and furtherance of understanding of the entity's business and performance?

- Is financial disclosure extensive—more than the minimum, five-year-data required by the SEC? Are graphs fully explained?

- Does honesty exist throughout, starting with the letter to shareholders? Bad news delivered without subterfuge or delay? Forthrightness to the ultimate—no conflicts between the report's parts, for example?

- Is CEO involvement (whether actual or perceived) displayed in the shareholder letter?

*Annual Reports (cont'd)*

- Is the CEO unequivocally (a) presenting a revelatory view of the company as well as (b) providing substantive insight into where it's headed?

*Copyright © 1984-1993, Cato Communications, Inc. Reprinted by permission.*

Every year, *Institutional Investor* magazine picks what it considers to be the best annual reports. Besides the best annual reports, 22 others were singled out for excellence.

## Best Annual Reports

General Electric
Coca-Cola
Monsanto
Southwest Airlines
Exxon
Northrop

## The Runners-Up

Allegheny Ludlum
Capital Cities/ ABC

CBI
Chevron
Consolidated Rail
General Mills
General Motors
Golden West Financial
Goodyear Tire & Rubber
Knight-Ridder
Magma Copper
Pall
Pfizer
Philip Morris
Phillips Petroleum
Pinnacle West Capital
Promus
Ryder System
Silicon Graphics
Waste Management
Wells Fargo & Co.
Whirlpool

*Source: Institutional Investor, Sept., 1993*

# Annual Report Designers & Writers

## Contact Options

*Graphic design firms specializing in annual reports:*

The Conceptual Communications Group
41 E. 11th St., 2nd Floor
New York, NY 10003
(212) 505-1607

Addison Corporate Annual Reports
791 5th Ave., 6th Floor
New York, NY 10003
(212) 229-5000

WYD
61 Wilton Rd.
Westport, CT 06880
(203) 227-2627

Little & Co.
1010 S. 7th St., Suite 550
Minneapolis, MN 55415
(612) 375-0077

Gunn Associates
275 Newbury St.
Boston, MA 02116
(617) 267-0618

Boller Coates Spadaro
900 N. Franklin St.
Chicago, IL 60610
(312) 787-2783

Curran & Connors
333 Marcus Blvd.
Happauge, NY 11788
(516) 435-0400

## Recommended Resource

*Graphic Arts Monthly Printing Industry Sourcebook*
Cahners Publishing, $50
(800) 637-6089

## The Top Reference Sources

*Directory of Industrial Designers*
Industrial Designers Society of America, $85
(703) 759-0100

This annual directory lists 2,200 industrial designers by their specialty. It includes consumer products, appliances, heavy equipment, computers, toys, furniture, and medical instrument designers, as well as listings by geographical location and by employer.

# FINANCE

# The Stock Market

AT THE EXPLOSIVE PEAK of the '80s bull market, U.S. stock-trading volumes reached a record high of 2 1/4 trillion (1987). For a time after this period, the stock outlook for the nineties appeared bleak, but it seems that the early decade has taken investors by surprise. The markets have done more than rebound from that temporary and terrifying 508-point correction of October 19, 1987, the biggest drop ever. With indexes soaring, the 1991 and 1992 markets have set new records, demonstrating the astonishing strength and sustained power of America's financial system and corporations.

## Market Value of Stocks on U.S. Exchanges

| Year | Value of Stocks ($) |
|------|---------------------|
| 1985 | 1,119,419,614 |
| 1986 | 1,705,123,953 |
| 1987 | 2,284,165,520 |
| 1988 | 1,587,011,727 |
| 1989 | 1,844,768,135 |
| 1990 | 1,611,667,363 |
| 1991 | 1,776,275,383 |

*Source: U.S. Securities and Exchange Commission*
*Annual Report, 1992*

## Volume of Stock Sales on U.S. Exchanges

| Year | Stocks (shares in thousands) |
|------|------------------------------|
| 1985 | 37,046,010 |
| 1986 | 48,337,694 |
| 1987 | 63,770,625 |
| 1988 | 52,533,283 |
| 1989 | 54,238,571 |
| 1990 | 53,337,731 |
| 1991 | 58,031,077 |

## Volume of Stock Sales by Exchange: 1991

| Exchange | Stocks (shares in thousands) |
|----------|------------------------------|
| AMEX | 3,102,872 |
| BSE | 1,030,957 |
| CSE | 501,502 |
| MIDW | 2,715,281 |
| NYSE | 47,673,705 |
| PSE | 2,068,122 |
| PHLX | 929,997 |
| SSE | 2,998 |
| CBOE | 0 |

*Source: U.S. Securities and Exchange Commission*
*Annual Report, 1992*

## Stock Sales on all U.S. Exchanges (total dollar volume in $ billions)

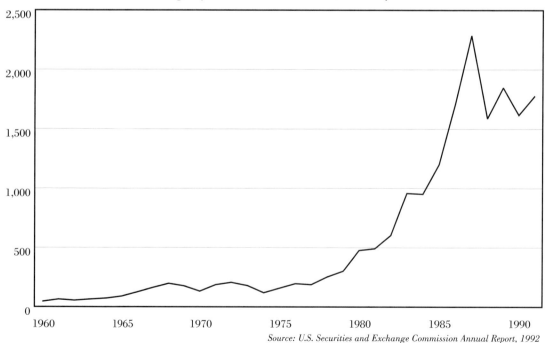

*Source: U.S. Securities and Exchange Commission Annual Report, 1992*

*The Stock Market (cont'd)*

## Share Volume (%) by Exchange, 1945 to 1991

| Year | NYSE | AMEX | MSE | PSE | PHLX | BSE | CSE | Others |
|------|------|------|-----|-----|------|-----|-----|--------|
| 1945 | 65.87 | 21.31 | 1.77 | 2.98 | 1.06 | 0.66 | 0.05 | 6.30 |
| 1950 | 73.32 | 13.54 | 2.16 | 3.11 | 0.97 | 0.65 | 0.09 | 3.16 |
| 1955 | 68.85 | 19.19 | 2.09 | 3.08 | 0.85 | 0.48 | 0.05 | 5.41 |
| 1960 | 68.47 | 22.27 | 2.20 | 3.11 | 0.88 | 0.38 | 0.04 | 2.65 |
| 1965 | 69.90 | 22.53 | 2.63 | 2.33 | 0.81 | 0.26 | 0.05 | 1.49 |
| 1970 | 71.28 | 19.03 | 3.16 | 3.68 | 1.63 | 0.51 | 0.02 | 0.69 |
| 1975 | 80.99 | 8.97 | 3.97 | 3.26 | 1.54 | 0.85 | 0.13 | 0.29 |
| 1980 | 79.94 | 10.78 | 3.84 | 2.80 | 1.54 | 0.57 | 0.32 | 0.21 |
| 1985 | 81.52 | 5.78 | 6.12 | 3.66 | 1.47 | 1.27 | 0.15 | 0.03 |
| 1986 | 81.12 | 6.28 | 5.73 | 3.68 | 1.53 | 1.33 | 0.30 | 0.02 |
| 1987 | 83.09 | 5.57 | 5.19 | 3.23 | 1.30 | 1.28 | 0.30 | 0.04 |
| 1988 | 83.74 | 4.95 | 5.26 | 3.03 | 1.29 | 1.32 | 0.39 | 0.02 |
| 1989 | 81.33 | 6.02 | 5.44 | 3.34 | 1.80 | 1.64 | 0.41 | 0.02 |
| 1990 | 81.86 | 6.23 | 4.68 | 3.16 | 1.82 | 1.71 | 0.53 | 0.01 |
| 1991 | 82.00 | 5.52 | 4.66 | 3.58 | 1.60 | 1.77 | 0.86 | 0.01 |

*Source: U.S. Securities and Exchange Commission Annual Report, 1992*

# New York Stock Exchange (NYSE)

OVER 80% OF AMERICAN SECURITIES are traded on the NYSE, the United States' oldest and largest exchange. In 1991, over 10,000 institutions managing $3.5 trillion in securities had access to and used the NYSE market.

New York Stock Exchange (NYSE)
11 Wall St.
New York, NY 10005
(212) 656-3000
Founded: 1792
Members/Seats: 1,420 members; 1,366 seats
Companies/Issues listed: 1,885 companies; 2,426 issues

## NYSE Record Reported Trades

| Record | Date | No. Trades |
|--------|------|-----------|
| Week Ending | 10/23/87 | 840,246 |
| Month | 1/92 | 3,331,286 |
| Year | 1992 | 30,576,037 |

## NYSE Record Volume

| Record | Date | Volume (shares) |
|--------|------|-----------------|
| First Hour | 6/17/88 | 158,630,000 |
| Day | 10/20/87 | 608,148,710 |
| Year | 1992 | 51,375,671,495 |

## NYSE Record Value of Trading

| Record | Date | Value of Trading ($ millions) |
|--------|------|-------------------------------|
| Day | 10/19/87 | 20,993.0 |
| Year | 1987 | 1,873,597.2 |

*Source: New York Stock Exchange Fact Book, 1992*

*Delphi offers access to continuous 30-minute updates on the Dow Jones Averages. GO BUS DOW.*

*NYSE (cont'd)*

## NYSE Average Share Prices

| End of Year | Average Price ($) |
|---|---|
| 1924 | 62.45 |
| 1950 | 39.86 |
| 1960 | 47.53 |
| 1970 | 39.61 |
| 1975 | 30.48 |
| 1976 | 35.03 |
| 1977 | 30.53 |
| 1978 | 29.84 |
| 1979 | 31.99 |
| 1980 | 36.87 |
| 1981 | 29.87 |
| 1982 | 33.03 |
| 1983 | 35.11 |
| 1984 | 32.31 |
| 1985 | 37.20 |
| 1986 | 36.89 |
| 1987 | 30.87 |
| 1988 | 32.26 |
| 1989 | 36.51 |
| 1990 | 31.08 |
| 1991 | 37.27 |
| 1992 | 34.83 |

*Source: New York Stock Exchange Fact Book, 1992*

## NYSE Seat Sales

| Year | High ($) | Low ($) |
|---|---|---|
| 1955 | 90,000 | 80,000 |
| 1960 | 162,000 | 135,000 |
| 1965 | 250,000 | 190,000 |
| 1970 | 320,000 | 130000 |
| 1971 | 300,000 | 145,000 |
| 1972 | 250,000 | 150,000 |
| 1973 | 190,000 | 72,000 |
| 1974 | 105,000 | 65,000 |
| 1975 | 138,000 | 55,000 |
| 1976 | 104,000 | 40,000 |
| 1977 | 95,000 | 35,000 |
| 1978 | 105,000 | 46,000 |
| 1979 | 210,000 | 82,000 |
| 1980 | 275,000 | 175,000 |
| 1981 | 285,000 | 220,000 |
| 1982 | 340,000 | 190,000 |
| 1983 | 425,000 | 310,000 |
| 1984 | 400,000 | 290,000 |
| 1985 | 480,000 | 310,000 |
| 1986 | 600,000 | 455,000 |
| 1987 | 1,150,000 | 605,000 |
| 1988 | 820,000 | 580,000 |
| 1989 | 675,000 | 420,000 |
| 1990 | 430,000 | 250,000 |
| 1991 | 440,000 | 345,000 |
| 1992 | 600,000 | 410,000 |

*Source: New York Stock Exchange Fact Book, 1992*

## NYSE Reported Share Volume, 1960 to 1991

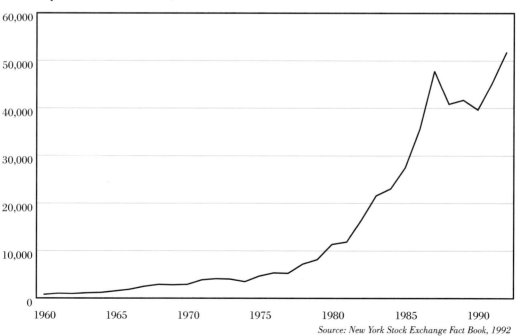

*Source: New York Stock Exchange Fact Book, 1992*

# NYSE Stocks Ranked

## Ten Most Active NYSE Stocks, 1993

| Stock | Share Volume |
|---|---|
| Merck | 728,600,000 |
| RJR Nabisco | 685,300,000 |
| Philip Morris | 642,900,000 |
| Wal-Mart Stores | 600,400,000 |
| Teléfonos de Mexico | 584,100,000 |
| General Motors | 578,600,000 |
| IBM | 566,900,000 |
| Chrysler | 542,400,000 |
| Citicorp | 523,900,000 |
| Glaxo Holdings | 480,500,000 |

*Source: The New York Times, Jan. 3, 1994*

## Ten Most Active NYSE Stocks, 1992

| Stock | Share Volume |
|---|---|
| Glaxo | 569,390,000 |
| RJR Nabisco | 543,230,000 |
| General Motors | 537,620,000 |
| IBM | 512,980,000 |
| Philip Morris | 472,410,000 |
| Teléfonos de Mexico | 464,880,000 |
| Citicorp | 453,480,000 |
| AT&T | 428,890,000 |
| Chrysler | 427,790,000 |
| Merck | 406,010,000 |

*Source: The New York Times, Jan. 4, 1993*

## Ten Best Performers on the NYSE, 1993

| Common Stock | Closing Price ($) | % Change from 1992 |
|---|---|---|
| First USA | 35.75 | 207.4 |
| Callaway Golf | 53.38 | 207.1 |
| Wheeling-Pittsburgh Steel | 17.13 | 197.9 |
| EMC | 16.50 | 177.8 |
| Hospitality Franchise Sys. | 53.13 | 174.1 |
| Timberland | 53.38 | 173.7 |
| Turkish Investment Fund | 14.13 | 169.1 |
| Clark Equipment | 52.38 | 168.6 |
| La Quinta Inns | 35.25 | 164.2 |
| Medusa | 32.38 | 164.1 |

*Source: The New York Times, Jan. 3, 1994*

## Ten Worst Performers on the NYSE, 1993

| Common Stock | Closing Price ($) | % Change from 1992 |
|---|---|---|
| Value Merchants | 0.25 | -97.4 |
| Martech USA | 0.50 | -95.0 |
| Tiphook | 3.00 | -82.2 |
| Merry-Go-Round | 3.25 | -79.2 |
| Leslie Fay | 3.25 | -73.7 |
| Asset Investors | 1.88 | -72.1 |
| He-Ro Group | 1.88 | -68.0 |
| Unionfed Financial | 2.00 | -68.0 |
| U.S. Surgical | 22.50 | -67.3 |
| Robertson-Ceco | 3.63 | -66.4 |

*Source: The New York Times, Jan. 3, 1994*

## Transactions (%) in NYSE-Listed Stock on Participating Markets

| Year | NYSE | AMEX | PSE | MSE | PHLX | BSE | CSE | NASD | INST | Total |
|---|---|---|---|---|---|---|---|---|---|---|
| 1981 | 82.42 | 0.00 | 6.41 | 4.54 | 3.85 | 0.91 | 0.87 | 0.96 | 0.02 | 100.00 |
| 1982 | 78.61 | 0.00 | 8.27 | 5.89 | 3.92 | 1.00 | 0.84 | 1.44 | 0.04 | 100.00 |
| 1983 | 77.68 | 0.00 | 8.58 | 6.81 | 3.88 | 1.25 | 0.49 | 1.28 | 0.04 | 100.00 |
| 1984 | 75.40 | 0.00 | 8.93 | 7.95 | 4.10 | 1.78 | 0.34 | 1.41 | 0.09 | 100.00 |
| 1985 | 74.24 | 0.00 | 9.51 | 8.16 | 3.82 | 2.17 | 0.32 | 1.70 | 0.10 | 100.00 |
| 1986 | 72.68 | 0.00 | 10.57 | 8.52 | 3.65 | 2.25 | 0.29 | 2.00 | 0.03 | 100.00 |
| 1987 | 73.60 | 0.00 | 9.31 | 8.94 | 3.50 | 2.32 | 0.26 | 2.05 | 0.02 | 100.00 |
| 1988 | 72.99 | 0.00 | 8.44 | 9.74 | 3.22 | 2.33 | 0.35 | 2.91 | 0.03 | 100.00 |
| 1989 | 69.23 | 0.00 | 8.35 | 10.43 | 3.39 | 3.16 | 0.44 | 4.98 | 0.03 | 100.00 |
| 1990 | 66.17 | 0.00 | 8.14 | 9.71 | 3.02 | 3.77 | 0.63 | 8.53 | 0.03 | 100.00 |
| 1991 | 67.33 | 0.00 | 8.12 | 8.03 | 2.84 | 3.37 | 0.74 | 9.53 | 0.03 | 100.00 |
| 1992 | 65.17 | 0.00 | 7.55 | 8.34 | 3.31 | 3.17 | 1.85 | 10.57 | 0.03 | 100.00 |

*Source: New York Stock Exchange Fact Book, 1992*

*NYSE Stocks Ranked (cont'd)*

## 50 Leading Stocks by Market Value

| Company | Symbol | Listed Shares (millions) | Market Value 2/93 ($ millions) |
|---|---|---|---|
| Exxon | XON | 1,813 | 110,582 |
| General Electric | GE | 927 | 78,754 |
| Wal-Mart Stores | WMT | 1,150 | 73,155 |
| Philip Morris | MO | 935 | 72,020 |
| Coca-Cola | KO | 1,692 | 70,848 |
| AT&T | T | 1,326 | 67,604 |
| Merck | MRK | 1,367 | 59,459 |
| Procter & Gamble | PG | 730 | 39,247 |
| Johnson & Johnson | JNJ | 767 | 38,560 |
| Bristol-Myers Squibb | BMY | 532 | 35,863 |
| PepsiCo | PEP | 863 | 35,689 |
| GTE | GTE | 945 | 32,836 |
| du Pont de Nemours | DD | 674 | 31,781 |
| International Business Machines | IBM | 572 | 28,804 |
| Mobil | MOB | 440 | 27,755 |
| American International Group | AIG | 225 | 26,090 |
| Abbott Laboratories | ABT | 849 | 25,793 |
| BellSouth | BLS | 489 | 24,862 |
| Chevron | CHV | 356 | 24,759 |
| Amoco | AN | 496 | 24,189 |
| Pfizer | PFE | 332 | 24,100 |
| American Home Products | AHP | 355 | 23,897 |
| 3M | MMM | 236 | 23,748 |
| Walt Disney | DIS | 552 | 23,742 |
| General Motors | GM | 706 | 22,781 |
| Bell Atlantic | BEL | 436 | 22,359 |
| Home Depot | HD | 331 | 22,288 |
| Southwestern Bell | SBC | 301 | 22,266 |
| Federal National Mortgage | FNM | 282 | 21,551 |
| Ameritech | AIT | 294 | 20,934 |
| Kellogg | K | 310 | 20,695 |
| McDonald's | MCD | 415 | 20,239 |
| Anheuser-Busch | BUD | 340 | 19,822 |
| Waste Management | WMX | 496 | 19,724 |
| Pacific Telesis | PAC | 433 | 19,153 |
| Ford Motor | F | 441 | 18,654 |
| Dow Chemical | DOW | 327 | 18,728 |
| Atlantic Richfield | ARC | 161 | 18,445 |
| NYNEX | NYN | 213 | 17,835 |
| Lilly (Eli) | LLY | 293 | 17,788 |
| Hewlett-Packard | HWP | 252 | 17,587 |
| Sears, Roebuck | S | 387 | 17,566 |
| Schlumberger | SLB | 306 | 17,436 |
| Royal Dutch Petroleum | RD | 215 | 17,414 |
| Schering-Plough | SGP | 268 | 17,026 |
| Texaco | TX | 274 | 16,386 |
| US West | USW | 420 | 16,112 |
| BankAmerica | BAC | 346 | 16,070 |
| Gillette | GS | 277 | 15,774 |
| Eastman Kodak | EK | 374 | 15,113 |

*Source: New York Stock Exchange*

# American Stock Exchange (Amex)

The American Stock Exchange (Amex)
86 Trinity Pl.
New York, NY 10006
(212) 306-1000
Members/Seats: 661 regular members; 203 options
principal members
Companies/Issues listed: 860 companies; 1,055
issues

The Amex list includes many younger, smaller
firms and mid-size growth companies, oil, and high
technology issues.

## Typical Amex Company ($ millions)

|                       | Average | Median |
|-----------------------|---------|--------|
| Total Assets          | 347.1   | 62.9   |
| Shareholders' Equity  | 85.1    | 25.9   |
| Sales                 | 245.5   | 49.0   |
| Market Value          | 176.6   | 36.4   |
| Employees             | 2,406.0 | 36.1   |
| Long-Term Debt        | 77.7    | 8.0    |
| Shares Outstanding    | 14.7    | 5.6    |
| Pre-Tax Income        | 4.3     | 0.8    |

## Amex Volume Since 1960

| Year | Volume ($)     |
|------|----------------|
| 1960 | 4,235,685,712  |
| 1965 | 8,874,874,754  |
| 1970 | 14,266,040,599 |
| 1975 | 5,678,028,284  |
| 1980 | 35,788,327,624 |
| 1981 | 24,520,205,419 |
| 1982 | 21,056,649,904 |
| 1983 | 31,237,023,941 |
| 1984 | 21,376,098,408 |
| 1985 | 27,838,566,791 |

| Year | Volume ($)     |
|------|----------------|
| 1986 | 45,356,898,691 |
| 1987 | 50,469,993,686 |
| 1988 | 30,921,806,605 |
| 1989 | 44,401,174,619 |
| 1990 | 37,714,827,819 |
| 1991 | 40,919,297,189 |
| 1992 | 42,238,311,156 |

## Amex Record Volume

| Record     | Date     | Volume        |
|------------|----------|---------------|
| First Hour | 10/20/87 | 143,432,760   |
| Week       | 10/19/87 | 158,680,590   |
| Year       | 1987     | 3,505,954,875 |

## Prices Paid for Amex Seats Since 1960

| Year | High ($) | Low ($) |
|------|----------|---------|
| 1960 | 60,000   | 51,000  |
| 1965 | 80,000   | 55,000  |
| 1970 | 185,000  | 70,000  |
| 1975 | 72,000   | 34,000  |
| 1980 | 252,000  | 95,000  |
| 1981 | 275,000  | 200,000 |
| 1982 | 285,000  | 180,000 |
| 1983 | 325,000  | 261,000 |
| 1984 | 255,000  | 160,000 |
| 1985 | 160,000  | 115,000 |
| 1986 | 285,000  | 145,000 |
| 1987 | 420,000  | 265,000 |
| 1988 | 280,000  | 180,000 |
| 1989 | 215,000  | 155,000 |
| 1990 | 170,000  | 83,500  |
| 1991 | 120,000  | 80,000  |
| 1992 | 110,000  | 76,000  |

*Source: American Stock Exchange Fact Book, 1993*

---

## The Top Reference Sources

*The Business One Irwin Business and Investment
Almanac*
Irwin Professional Publishing, $75
(800) 634-3966

Edited by Sumner N. Levine, this annual publication is a standard reference for the business and
investment community. It includes major and
group stock market averages, reviews of the major
futures markets, charts for futures-traded commodities, the performance of mutual funds, and
performance of leading economies.

The book also contains data on future employment opportunities, U.S. demographics, international stock price indexes, and consumer price
indexes.

# Amex Stocks Ranked

## Ten Most Active Amex Stocks, 1993

| Stock | Share Volume |
|---|---|
| Echo Bay Mines | 265,900,000 |
| Royal Oak Mines | 234,600,000 |
| Energy Services | 181,400,000 |
| Amdahl | 83,700,000 |
| Cheyenne Software | 69,500,000 |
| Atari | 66,800,000 |
| Interdigital Communications | 60,300,000 |
| Hasbro | 59,900,000 |
| Nabors Industries | 58,200,000 |
| NTN Communications | 57,300,000 |

*Source: The New York Times, Jan. 3, 1994*

## Ten Most Active Amex Stocks, 1992

| Stock | Share Volume |
|---|---|
| Chambers Devel. "A" | 105,820,000 |
| Amdahl | 102,890,000 |
| U.S. Bioscience | 81,660,000 |
| Echo Bay Mines | 72,330,000 |
| Sulcus Computer | 71,970,000 |
| Exploration Co. of La. | 68,770,000 |
| Hillhaven | 66,600,000 |
| Ivax | 66,280,000 |
| Fruit of the Loom | 62,490,000 |
| Interdigital Communications | 51,040,000 |

*Source: The New York Times, Jan. 4, 1993*

## Best Performers on the Amex, 1993

| Common Stock | December 31 Closing Price($) | % Change from 1992 |
|---|---|---|
| Fibreboard | 33.75 | 390.6 |
| Bush Industries "A" | 30.88 | 252.9 |
| Rowe Furniture | 21.25 | 235.2 |
| Charter Medical | 25.88 | 223.5 |

*Source: The New York Times, Jan. 3, 1994*

## Worst Performers on the Amex, 1993

| Common Stock | December 31 Closing Price($) | % Change from 1992 |
|---|---|---|
| Health Professionals | 1.13 | -86.5 |
| Advanced Medical | 1.44 | -85.0 |
| Angeles Mortgage Invest. | 2.75 | -82.4 |
| Rx Medical Services | 5.38 | -78.5 |

*Source: The New York Times, Jan. 3, 1994*

## Stocks Outstanding on the Amex, 1980 to 1992 (billions)

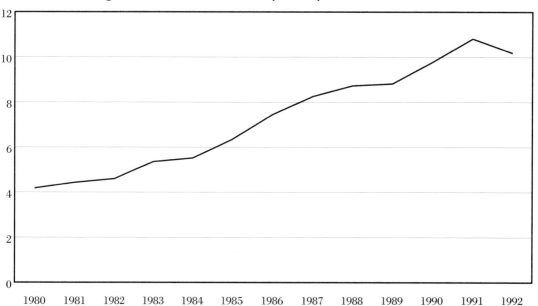

*Source: American Stock Exchange Fact Book, 1993*

*Amex Stocks Ranked (cont'd)*

## Amex Seat Sales, 1970 to 1992

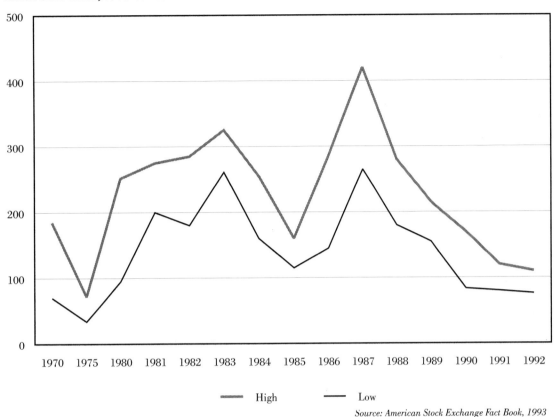

*Source: American Stock Exchange Fact Book, 1993*

## The Top Reference Sources

*Inc. Magazine*
Goldhirsh Group, $19
(800) 234-0999

This popular magazine walks a fine line between feature stories and "how-to" articles. Filled with useful advice and real-life examples, *Inc.* regularly offers the reader excellent insights on topics such as sales and marketing, banking and capital,

management, and financial strategies. *Inc.* is well-known for its annual list of the 500 fastest-growing private companies in the country. Other stories in one typical issue included a comparison of two competitors, their lifestyles and business strategies, the non-traditional organization of fast-growth companies, and financing alternatives available to companies seeking rapid growth.

 **FAX** **Causes of Business Failures.** Request #576. See p. xi for instructions.
Seven primary reasons for business failure and incidence of failure in nine sectors of business.

# The OTC Market: NASDAQ

SHARES OF SMALL AND relatively new companies are traded over-the-counter, in the OTC market. This market has no location: transactions are executed over telephones, private wires, and computers by a vast network of brokers and dealers. Sales and trading information on most (but not all) OTC transactions is received and stored by The National Association of Securities Dealers (NASD). The NASD transmits price and volume data on its computerized quote system: The National Association of Securities Dealers Automated Quotations System (NASDAQ).

The National Assoc. of Securities Dealers (NASD)
1735 K St., NW
Washington, DC 20006
(202) 728-8000
Members: 6,000

NASD is a not-for-profit association of brokers and dealers founded in 1939. A self-regulating organization, the NASD establishes standards of conduct for members trading through NASDAQ and other over-the-counter securities markets. Members of NASD may sell securities to each other at wholesale prices while selling retail to non-members.

NASDAQ is the third-largest market in the world, after the New York and Tokyo exchanges, and handles over 45 percent of all shares traded in the major U.S. markets. There are 5,5401 member firms, 29,137 branch offices, and 406,106 registered representatives on the NASDAQ. More than 4,113 companies have their stocks traded in the NASDAQ; statistics on over 5,300 domestic and foreign securities are transmitted through NASDAQ.

## NASDAQ Single Day Trading Records

| Date | Share Volume |
|------|-------------|
| October 21, 1987 | 288,059,700 |
| October 20, 1987 | 284,117,100 |
| March 6, 1991 | 283,079,300 |
| April 17, 1991 | 267,555,100 |
| January 23, 1987 | 261,850,700 |

## Profile of Typical NASDAQ Company

| | |
|------|------|
| Total Assets ($ mil.) | 582.2 |
| Shareholders' Equity ($ mil.) | 109.0 |
| Total Revenues ($ mil.) | 243.3 |
| P/E ratio | 34.6 |

## Profile of Typical NASDAQ Issue

| | |
|------|------|
| Share Price ($) | 19.57 |
| Number of Market Makers | 12.30 |
| Total Shares Outstanding ($ mil.) | 10.60 |
| Public Float (shares, $ mil.) | 7.80 |
| Market Value of Shares Outstanding ($ mil.) | 208.00 |

*Source: NASDAQ Fact Book & Company Directory, 1993*

## NASDAQ Volume Since 1981 ($ billions)

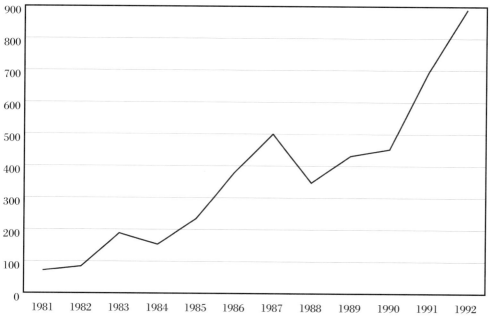

*Source: NASDAQ Fact Book & Company Directory, 1993*

*The OTC Market: NASDAQ (cont'd)*

## Ten Most Active NASDAQ Stocks, 1993

| Stock | Share Volume |
|---|---|
| Intel | 894,100,000 |
| Novell | 735,800,000 |
| Tele-Comm. "A" | 620,300,000 |
| Synoptics Comm. | 571,000,000 |
| Cisco Systems | 554,900,000 |
| MCI Communications | 549,900,000 |
| Microsoft | 503,500,000 |
| Apple Computer | 494,100,000 |
| Amgen | 459,600,000 |
| Oracle Systems | 448,900,000 |

*Source: The New York Times, Jan. 3, 1994*

## Ten Most Active NASDAQ Stocks, 1992

| Stock | Share Volume |
|---|---|
| Intel | 553,720,000 |
| Tele-Comm. "A" | 443,850,000 |
| Novell | 434,320,000 |
| Microsoft | 402,460,000 |
| Seagate Technology | 390,220,000 |
| Sun Microsystems | 384,360,000 |
| Apple Computer | 367,890,000 |
| Oracle Systems | 343,860,000 |
| Teléfonos de Mexico | 339,400,000 |
| Amgen | 329,460,000 |

*Source: The New York Times, Jan. 4, 1993*

## Ten Best Performing NASDAQ Stocks, 1993

| Common Stock | Closing Price ($) | % Change from 1992 |
|---|---|---|
| Whole. & Hearty Foods | 20.50 | 518.8 |
| Glenayre | 43.50 | 467.4 |
| Amer. Mobile Systems | 15.00 | 445.5 |
| Digital Microwave | 29.75 | 440.9 |
| MicroAge | 38.25 | 378.1 |
| Speizman Industries | 13.13 | 377.3 |
| Future Healthcare | 13.00 | 352.2 |
| United Cos. Financial | 39.50 | 338.9 |
| Total-Tel USA | 15.75 | 334.5 |
| Sage Technologies | 19.25 | 320.0 |

*Source: The Wall Street Journal, Jan. 3, 1994*

## Ten Worst Performing NASDAQ Stocks, 1993

| Common Stock | Closing Price ($) | % Change from 1992 |
|---|---|---|
| VideOcart | 0.06 | -98.6 |
| Wolf Financial | 0.09 | -95.3 |
| Sprouse Reitz Stores | 0.13 | -93.8 |
| Hunter Environmental | 0.38 | -93.5 |
| Assix International | 0.19 | -92.1 |
| Amer. Int'l. Petroleum | 2.00 | -89.5 |
| Rose's Stores B | 0.50 | -87.9 |
| Sanborn | 0.81 | -87.5 |
| Modtech | 0.38 | -86.4 |
| All For a Dollar | 1.75 | -86.1 |

*Source: The Wall Street Journal, Jan. 3, 1994*

## The Top Reference Sources

*The NASDAQ Fact Book & Company Directory*
National Association of Securities Dealers, $20
(301) 590-6578

Published annually, this book provides extensive data on the performance of NASDAQ securities and statistics on the NASDAQ market as a whole, as well as information to assist in contacting each company directly.

It is used as a resource by shareholders, corporations, investment analysts, brokerage firms, financial media, government, and educational institutions.

# U.S. Stock Exchanges

## Pacific Stock Exchange (PSE)

618 S. Spring St.
Los Angeles, CA 90014
(213) 977-4500

- Members listed: 551;

- Hours: The PSE is the last full auction U.S. market to close, at 1:50 P.M. Pacific Time, 50 minutes past the New York close;

- Volume: 2.0 billion shares (1989). In 1991, the PSE's average daily volume rose at the highest rate among all use exchanges: 23%;

- Options: 13.9 million contracts (1989).

## Boston Stock Exchange (BSE)

One Boston Pl.
Boston, MA 02109
(617) 723-9500

- Founded: 1834, the third oldest stock exchange in the United States;

- Members/seats: 203 seats held by 144 member firms;

- Companies/issues listed: 127 exclusive listings; over 2,100 issues total;

- Volume: 4,000,00 shares traded daily.

## The Cincinnati Stock Exchange (CSE)

205 Dixie Terminal Building
Cincinnati, OH 45202
(312) 786-8803

- Founded: 1885, the youngest regional exchange in the country;

- Seats: 275;

- Volume: 4,900,000 shares traded in 1993; 8,300 trades daily.

## Chicago Stock Exchange (CHX)

440 LaSalle St.
Chicago, IL 60605
(312) 663-2980

- Founded: 1882 as the Chicago Stock Exchange. In 1949 the St. Louis, Cleveland, and Minneapolis-St. Paul exchanges merged with the Chicago exchange to form the Midwest Stock Exchange. The New Orleans Stock Exchange joined in 1959. In 1993, the name changed back to Chicago Stock Exchange;

- Members/seats: 446 (including specialists, floor brokers, and off-floor members);

- Companies/issues listed: 2,619.

In 1991, block trades represented almost 43% of the total share volume. The average price per share was $28.18.

## Philadelphia Stock Exchange (PHLX)

1900 Market St.
Philadelphia, PA 19103
(215) 496-5000

- Founded: 1790, the oldest security exchange in the United States;

- Volume: 1,303,059,891 shares traded in 1993;

- Companies/issues listed: 2,200.

*Note: The above information was submitted by the public relations departments of the individual exchanges.*

---

## The Top Reference Sources

*The Corporate Finance Sourcebook*
National Register Publishing Company, $425
(708) 256-6067

This annual directory catalogs 19 sources of capital funding and management, including venture capital firms, private lenders, banks, trusts, commercial financing and factoring firms, pension managers, and accounting firms. Listings include the names and numbers of investment officers, industry preference, minimum to maximum investment limits, and lending criteria.

Over 3,600 firms and 20,000 key executives are included in this highly recommended publication.

# U.S. Exchange Markets

## Foreign Stocks Listed on U.S. Exchanges

| Exchange | No. Common Stocks | Value ($ millions) | No. Preferred Stocks | Value ($ millions) |
|----------|-------------------|--------------------|-----------------------|---------------------|
| American | 83 | 25,129 | 3 | 765 |
| Boston | 2 | 57 | 0 | 0 |
| New York | 107 | 162,563 | 16 | 2,816 |
| Pacific | 2 | 33 | 0 | 0 |
| Philadelphia | NA | NA | NA | NA |
| TOTAL | 194 | 187,782 | 19 | 3,581 |

## The Various Markets of the U.S. Exchanges

| | NYSE | AMEX | MSE | PSE | PHLX | BSE | CSE | CBOE | CBOT | CME |
|---|------|------|-----|-----|------|-----|-----|------|------|-----|
| Equities | • | • | • | • | • | • | • | | | |
| Listed Options | | • | | • | • | | | • | | |
| OTC Options | • | • | | • | • | | | • | | |
| Index Options | • | • | | • | • | | | • | • | • |
| Index Futures | • | | | | | | | | | |
| Currency Options | | • | | | • | | | | | • |
| AGRI Options | | | | | | | | | | • |
| AGRI/Currency Futures | | | | | | | | | • | • |
| Options on AGRI/CURR Futures | | | | | | | | | • | |

*Source: U.S. Securities and Exchange Commission Annual Report, 1992*

## Recommended Resources

*New York Stock Exchange Fact Book*
New York Stock Exchange, $10
11 Wall St.
New York, NY 10005
(212) 656-3000

*American Stock Exchange Fact Book*
American Stock Exchange, $15
86 Trinity Pl.
New York, NY 10006
(212) 306-1000

*NASDAQ Fact Book & Company Directory*
The National Association of Securities Dealers, $20
1735 K St., NW, 8th Floor
Washington, DC 20006
(301) 590-6578

## The Top Reference Sources

*The Directory of Corporate Affiliations*
National Register Publishing Company,
$950/six volumes
(800) 521-8110

Published annually, this directory gives a view-at-a-glance of the corporate structure of more than 5,000 major U.S companies and their 50,000 sub-sidiaries, divisions, and affiliates.

Parent company listings contain address, numbers, ticker symbols, stock markets, financial data, number of employees, sales, balance sheet data, SIC codes, a description of the company's line of business, key personnel, and members of the board. Also included are summaries of mergers and acquisitions and name changes.

# Dividends and Splits

A COMPANY'S DIVIDEND PAYMENT to stockholders represents the stockholder's share of the company's net profits. The dividend amount is decided by the company's directors; it is fixed per share and typically paid quarterly in cash (mailed checks). A split is a commensurate increase in the number of shares of outstanding stock without increasing the shareholder's equity. A firm's stock will split to reduce the market price and increase the stock's attractiveness to investors.

## Cash Dividends on NYSE Listed Common Stocks

| Year | Number of Issues Listed at Year End | Number Paying Cash Dividends During Year | Estimated Aggregate Cash Payments ($ millions) |
|------|------|------|------|
| 1929 | 842 | 554 | 2,711 |
| 1935 | 776 | 387 | 1,336 |
| 1940 | 829 | 577 | 2,099 |
| 1945 | 881 | 746 | 2,275 |
| 1950 | 1,039 | 930 | 5,404 |
| 1955 | 1,076 | 982 | 7,488 |
| 1956 | 1,077 | 975 | 8,341 |
| 1957 | 1,098 | 991 | 8,807 |
| 1958 | 1,086 | 961 | 8,711 |
| 1959 | 1,092 | 953 | 9,337 |
| 1960 | 1,126 | 981 | 9,872 |
| 1961 | 1,145 | 981 | 10,430 |
| 1962 | 1,168 | 994 | 11,203 |
| 1963 | 1,194 | 1,032 | 12,096 |
| 1964 | 1,227 | 1,066 | 13,555 |
| 1965 | 1,254 | 1,111 | 15,302 |
| 1966 | 1,267 | 1,127 | 16,151 |
| 1967 | 1,255 | 1,116 | 16,866 |
| 1968 | 1,253 | 1,104 | 18,124 |
| 1969 | 1,290 | 1,121 | 19,404 |
| 1970 | 1,330 | 1,120 | 19,781 |
| 1971 | 1,399 | 1,132 | 20,256 |
| 1972 | 1,478 | 1,195 | 21,490 |
| 1973 | 1,536 | 1,276 | 23,627 |
| 1974 | 1,543 | 1,308 | 25,662 |
| 1975 | 1,531 | 1,273 | 26,901 |
| 1976 | 1,550 | 1,304 | 30,608 |
| 1977 | 1,549 | 1,360 | 36,270 |
| 1978 | 1,552 | 1,373 | 41,151 |
| 1979 | 1,536 | 1,359 | 46,937 |
| 1980 | 1,540 | 1,361 | 53,072 |
| 1981 | 1,534 | 1,337 | 60,628 |
| 1982 | 1,499 | 1,287 | 62,224 |
| 1983 | 1,518 | 1,259 | 67,102 |
| 1984 | 1,511 | 1,243 | 68,215 |
| 1985 | 1,503 | 1,206 | 74,237 |
| 1986 | 1,536 | 1,180 | 76,161 |
| 1987 | 1,606 | 1,219 | 84,377 |
| 1988 | 1,643 | 1,270 | 102,190 |
| 1989 | 1,683 | 1,303 | 101,778 |
| 1990 | 1,741 | NA | 103,150 |
| 1991 | 1,860 | NA | 123,385 |
| 1992 | 2,068 | NA | 109,696 |

*Source: New York Stock Exchange Fact Book, 1992*

*Dividends and Splits (cont'd)*

## Annual Number of Stock Splits on the NYSE

| Year | Total |
|------|-------|
| 1983 | 300 |
| 1984 | 178 |
| 1985 | 166 |
| 1986 | 272 |
| 1987 | 244 |

| Year | Total |
|------|-------|
| 1988 | 104 |
| 1989 | 142 |
| 1990 | 105 |
| 1991 | 107 |
| 1992 | 182 |

*Source: New York Stock Exchange Fact Book, 1992*

# Block Trading

BLOCKS ARE LARGE HOLDINGS OF STOCK, usually 10,000 shares or more. Blocks are most likely owned by institutions; block trades usually occur between institutions.

## Block Trading on the NYSE

| Year | Total Transactions | % of Reported Volume |
|------|--------------------|----------------------|
| 1965 | 2,171 | 3.1 |
| 1970 | 17,217 | 15.4 |
| 1975 | 34,420 | 16.6 |
| 1976 | 47,632 | 18.7 |
| 1977 | 54,27 | 22.4 |
| 1978 | 75,036 | 22.9 |
| 1979 | 97,509 | 26.5 |
| 1980 | 133,597 | 29.2 |
| 1981 | 145,564 | 31.8 |
| 1982 | 254,707 | 41.0 |
| 1983 | 363,415 | 45.6 |
| 1984 | 433,427 | 49.8 |
| 1985 | 539,039 | 51.7 |
| 1986 | 665,587 | 49.9 |
| 1987 | 920,679 | 51.2 |
| 1988 | 768,419 | 54.5 |
| 1989 | 872,811 | 51.1 |
| 1990 | 843,365 | 49.6 |
| 1991 | 981,077 | 49.6 |
| 1992 | 1,134,832 | 50.7 |

*Source: New York Stock Exchange Fact Book, 1992*

## Block Trading on the Amex

| Year | Number of Blocks | % of Total Dollar Volume |
|------|------------------|--------------------------|
| 1970 | 2,260 | 6.9 |
| 1975 | 1,803 | 7.6 |
| 1980 | 9,895 | 11.5 |
| 1981 | 10,463 | 16.2 |
| 1982 | 12,330 | 17.9 |
| 1983 | 20,629 | 21.4 |
| 1984 | 18,820 | 29.2 |
| 1985 | 29,094 | 34.0 |
| 1986 | 44,421 | 35.4 |
| 1987 | 53,814 | 36.0 |
| 1988 | 39,865 | 36.7 |
| 1989 | 51,907 | 33.4 |
| 1990 | 60,830 | 37.7 |
| 1991 | 52,678 | 34.8 |
| 1992 | 54,345 | 31.8 |

*Source: American Stock Exchange Fact Book, 1993*

---

## The Top Reference Sources

*S&P 500 Directory*
Standard & Poor's, $39.95
(212) 208-1649

This annual fact book provides a good overview of the S&P 500 index, including background infor-

mation and methodology. It includes a "year in review" section, plus a directory of S&P index products, and an A–Z listing of the S&P 500 companies.

S&P 500 company reports and statistical tables are also provided.

# Initial Public Offerings

WHEN A COMPANY FIRST OFFERS ITS STOCK for sale to potential investors it conducts what is known as an initial public offering (IPO).

## Total IPO Issuance on NASDAQ

| Year | Proceeds ($ mil.) | Market Share | No. of Issues |
|------|------|------|------|
| 1976 | 79.7 | 0.2 | 3 |
| 1977 | 47.7 | 0.1 | 2 |
| 1979 | 1.6 | 0.0 | 1 |
| 1981 | 25.0 | 0.1 | 1 |
| 1982 | 12.1 | 0.0 | 2 |
| 1983 | 80.3 | 0.2 | 2 |
| 1984 | 167.1 | 0.4 | 4 |
| 1985 | 31.7 | 0.1 | 4 |
| 1986 | 199.2 | 0.5 | 9 |
| 1987 | 294.9 | 0.7 | 12 |
| 1988 | 317.4 | 0.8 | 27 |
| 1989 | 1,910.9 | 4.8 | 112 |
| 1990 | 2,306.0 | 5.8 | 140 |
| 1991 | 7,546.8 | 19.1 | 304 |
| 1992 | 10,977.0 | 27.7 | 424 |
| 1993 | 15,560.1 | 39.3 | 529 |
| TOTAL | 39,557.6 | 100.0 | 1,576 |

## Total IPO Issuance on NYSE

| Year | Proceeds ($ mil.) | Market Share | No. of Issues |
|------|------|------|------|
| 1976 | 73.4 | 0.0 | 2 |
| 1977 | 63.2 | 0.0 | 2 |
| 1980 | 101.6 | 0.1 | 2 |
| 1981 | 60.0 | 0.0 | 1 |
| 1982 | 154.0 | 0.1 | 2 |
| 1983 | 1,141.7 | 0.7 | 14 |
| 1984 | 901.7 | 0.6 | 13 |
| 1985 | 3,994.4 | 2.5 | 25 |
| 1986 | 9,692.8 | 6.1 | 67 |
| 1987 | 17,983.0 | 11.4 | 72 |
| 1988 | 19,501.3 | 12.3 | 72 |
| 1989 | 10,816.1 | 6.8 | 64 |
| 1990 | 7,380.5 | 4.7 | 57 |
| 1991 | 17,406.1 | 11.0 | 87 |
| 1992 | 28,539.0 | 18.1 | 168 |
| 1993 | 40,257.0 | 25.5 | 216 |
| TOTAL | 158,065.8 | 100.0 | 864 |

## Total IPO Issuance on Amex

| Year | Proceeds ($ mil.) | Market Share | No. of Issues |
|------|------|------|------|
| 1976 | 9.9 | 0.1 | 2 |
| 1979 | 20.4 | 0.2 | 2 |
| 1980 | 9.6 | 0.1 | 1 |
| 1981 | 61.9 | 0.6 | 5 |
| 1983 | 129.8 | 1.3 | 7 |
| 1984 | 113.6 | 1.1 | 9 |
| 1985 | 520.4 | 5.2 | 17 |
| 1986 | 2,316.9 | 23.2 | 53 |
| 1987 | 2,008.8 | 20.1 | 52 |
| 1988 | 2,226.3 | 22.2 | 36 |
| 1989 | 346.2 | 3.5 | 10 |
| 1990 | 344.3 | 3.4 | 9 |
| 1991 | 191.3 | 1.9 | 11 |
| 1992 | 428.5 | 4.3 | 12 |
| 1993 | 1,278.3 | 12.8 | 39 |
| TOTAL | 10,006.1 | 100.0 | 265 |

## Total IPO Issuances

| Year | Proceeds ($ mil.) | Market Share | No. of Issues |
|------|------|------|------|
| 1975 | 189.4 | 0.1 | 6 |
| 1976 | 337.2 | 0.1 | 40 |
| 1977 | 221.6 | 0.1 | 32 |
| 1978 | 225.4 | 0.1 | 38 |
| 1979 | 398.4 | 0.2 | 62 |
| 1980 | 1,387.1 | 0.6 | 149 |
| 1981 | 3,114.7 | 1.2 | 348 |
| 1982 | 1,339.1 | 0.5 | 122 |
| 1983 | 12,466.4 | 5.0 | 686 |
| 1984 | 3,868.9 | 1.5 | 357 |
| 1985 | 8,497.6 | 3.4 | 355 |
| 1986 | 22,250.3 | 8.9 | 727 |
| 1987 | 26,847.3 | 10.7 | 556 |
| 1988 | 23,807.5 | 9.5 | 291 |
| 1989 | 13,706.1 | 5.5 | 254 |
| 1990 | 10,117.4 | 4.0 | 213 |
| 1991 | 25,144.2 | 10.0 | 402 |
| 1992 | 39,947.1 | 15.9 | 605 |
| 1993 | 57,437.1 | 22.9 | 818 |
| TOTAL | 251,302.6 | 100.0 | 6,061 |

*Source: Securities Data Company*

*Initial Public Offerings (cont'd)*

## 20 Largest Domestic IPO's, 1985 to 1992 (excluding closed-end funds)

| Date | Issuer | Offering Amount ($ mil.) | No. of Shares Offered (mil.) | Offering Price ($) | Book Manager |
|------|--------|--------------------------|------------------------------|--------------------|--------------|
| 10/30/87 | British Petroleum | 2,864.1 | 42.2 | 68.0 | Goldman, Sachs |
| 06/02/93 | Allstate | 1,849.5 | 68.5 | 27.0 | Goldman, Sachs |
| 03/26/87 | Consolidated Rail | 1,456.0 | 52.0 | 28.0 | Goldman, Sachs |
| 06/28/93 | YPF | 1,235.0 | 65.0 | 19.0 | CS First Bos./Merrill Lynch |
| 05/20/86 | Henley Group | 1,190.0 | 56.0 | 21.3 | Lazard, Freres & Co. |
| 07/27/92 | Wellcome | 1,067.5 | 70.0 | 15.3 | Morgan Stanley |
| 11/21/86 | Coca-Cola Enterprises | 1,001.4 | 60.7 | 16.5 | Allen & Co. |
| 12/02/93 | PacTel | 966.0 | 42.0 | 23.0 | Salomon Bros./Lehman Bros. |
| 01/18/89 | Lyondell Petrochemical | 960.0 | 32.0 | 30.0 | Goldman, Sachs |
| 10/23/85 | Fireman's Fund | 824.0 | 32.0 | 25.8 | Shearson Lehman Brothers |
| 04/20/93 | TIG Holdings | 800.5 | 35.4 | 22.6 | Morgan Stanley |
| 04/09/92 | First Data | 770.0 | 35.0 | 22.0 | Lehman Brothers |
| 09/12/85 | Rockefeller Center Properties | 750.0 | 37.5 | 20.0 | Goldman, Sachs |
| 12/13/93 | Simon Property Group | 713.9 | 32.1 | 22.3 | Merrill Lynch & Co. |
| 02/22/93 | Dean Witter Discover | 695.3 | 25.8 | 27.0 | Dean Witter Reynolds |
| 01/22/91 | MBNA | 689.3 | 30.6 | 22.5 | Goldman, Sachs |
| 10/29/86 | Commercial Credit | 662.2 | 32.3 | 20.5 | CS First Boston |
| 12/13/93 | Grupo Televisa | 640.0 | 10.0 | 64.0 | Goldman, Sachs |
| 02/26/92 | Hospital Corp. of America | 584.8 | 27.2 | 21.5 | Goldman, Sachs |
| 11/06/86 | UNUM | 561.5 | 22.0 | 25.5 | Goldman, Sachs |

*Source: Securities Data Company*

## The Top Reference Sources

Securities Data
1180 Raymond Blvd.
Newark, NJ 07102
(201) 622-3100

Securities Data, a member of the Boston-based Thomson Financial Services family, is the leading provider of merger and financing data worldwide. Its products include on-line databases, publications, and research services covering mergers and acquisitions, corporate and municipal financing, venture capital, restructurings, and corporate governance.

# The World's Stock Exchanges

| Stock Exchange | Tokyo | New York | Toronto | U.K. | Frankfurt | Paris | Zurich |
|---|---|---|---|---|---|---|---|
| No. Stock-Listed Companies (D) | 1,641 | 1,780 | 1,069 | 1,852 | 405 | 551 | 182 |
| No. Stock-Listed Companies (F) | 125 | 105 | 69 | 604 | 359 | 231 | 243 |
| No. Listed Issues, Stocks(D) | 1,650 | 2,303 | 1,464 | 1,927 | 405 | 590 | 326 |
| No. Listed Issues, Stocks (F) | 125 | 123 | 74 | 813 | 359 | 267 | 250 |
| No. Listed Issues, Bonds (D) | 1,257 | 1,773 | 14 | 2,704 | 5,774 | 3,002 | 1,532 |
| No. Listed Issues, Bonds (F) | 159 | 168 | 2 | 1,902 | 1,089 | 267 | 960 |
| Total Mkt. Value, Stocks ($ mil.) | 3,018,565 | 3,547,456 | 266,548 | 991,770 | 361,675 | 348,083 | 179,565 |
| Total Mkt. Value, Bonds ($ mil.) | 1,162,883 | 2,227,010 | NA | 626,846 | 870,383 | 559,758 | 167,097 |
| Trading Value, Stocks ($ mil.) | 827,096 | 1,520,164 | 59,134 | 569,574 | 272,546 | 108,997 | 365,819 |
| Trading Value, Bonds ($ mil.) | 215,270 | 12,698 | NA | 1,042,094 | 459,471 | 566,844 | |
| No. of Member Firms | 124 | 518 | 75 | 405 | 230 | 57 | 24 |

| Stock Exchange | Amsterdam | Milan | Australia | Hong Kong | Singapore | Taiwan | Korea |
|---|---|---|---|---|---|---|---|
| No. Stock-Listed Companies (D) | 263 | 224 | 957 | 333 | 157 | 221 | 686 |
| No. Stock-Listed Companies (F) | 234 | 2 | 37 | 24 | 26 | NA | NA |
| No. Listed Issues, Stocks (D) | 303 | 334 | 1,400 | 344 | 162 | 234 | 1,013 |
| No. Listed Issues, Stocks (F) | 300 | 2 | 46 | 24 | 27 | NA | NA |
| No. Listed Issues, Bonds (D) | 898 | 1,277 | 1,671 | 8 | 44 | 50 | 8,358 |
| No. Listed Issues, Bonds (F) | 176 | 18 | NA | 5 | 113 | 1 | NA |
| Total Mkt. Value, Stocks ($ mil.) | 169,314 | 154,078 | 144,867 | 121,986 | 47,780 | 123,664 | 96,106 |
| Total Mkt. Value, Bonds ($ mil.) | 183,002 | 681,133 | 49,534 | 638 | 100,595 | 13,486 | 80,823 |
| Trading Value, Stocks ($ mil.) | 38,487 | 23,727 | 46,845 | 38,681 | 18,792 | 376,065 | 85,284 |
| Trading Value, Bonds ($ mil.) | 56,803 | 27,681 | 17,266 | 31 | 1,598 | 247 | 2,859 |
| No. of Member Firms | 135 | 105 | 98 | 671 | 26 | 347 | 31 |

*D=Domestic, F=Foreign*                              *Source: Tokyo Stock Exchange Fact Book, 1993*

## Dollar Volume of Equity Trading in Major World Markets (U.S. $ billions)

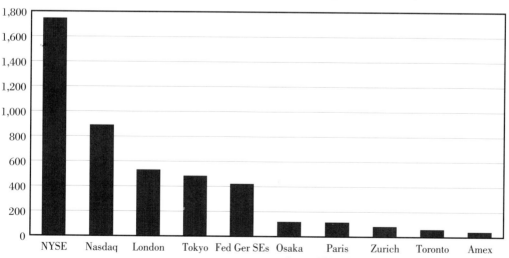

*Source: NASDAQ Fact Book & Company Directory, 1993*

# Major Foreign Exchanges

## London Stock Exchange

The International Stock Exchange of the
United Kingdom and the Republic of Ireland
Old Broad St.
London EC2N 1HP
[44] (71) 797-1000

## Ten Most Active UK Companies

| Company | Value of Turnover (£ mil.) | Shares Traded (mil.) |
|---|---|---|
| British Telecommun. | 18,240.1 | 4,912.2 |
| Glaxo Holdings | 16,674.1 | 2,287.7 |
| HSBC Holdings | 15,220.9 | 2,332.3 |
| British Petroleum | 12,673.5 | 3,335.4 |
| Shell Transport & Trading | 10,533.6 | 1,499.1 |
| Imperial Chemical Ind. | 10,390.9 | 1,022.8 |
| Hanson | 9,896.0 | 4,049.2 |
| BTR | 9,561.7 | 2,979.4 |
| SmithKline Beecham | 9,345.2 | 2,011.7 |
| British Gas | 8,608.1 | 2,569.6 |

*Source: London Stock Exchange Fact Book, 1994*

## Tokyo Stock Exchange

2-1 Nihombashi-Kabuto-Cho
Chuo-ku, Tokyo 103
[81] (3) 3666-0141

New York office:
44 Broadway, 12th Floor
New York, NY 10006
(212) 363-2350

The Tokyo Stock Exchange is divided into two
sections. Approximately 1,220 companies are listed
in the first section, the marketplace for stocks of
larger companies. In the second section, the marketplace for smaller and newly-listed companies,
approximately 420 companies are listed.

Tokyo Stock Price Index (TOPIX) measures the
performance of all stocks listed on the first section of
the Tokyo Stock Exchange. The TOPIX is separated
into 28 sub-indexes by industry groups and size.

The Nikkei Stock Average is the Dow Jones
Average of the Tokyo Stock Market, tracking the
price movements of 225 large, well-known issues in
the first section of the Tokyo Stock Exchange. The
stocks included represent a broad range of industries including foods, textiles, pulp and paper, chemicals, drugs, petroleum, rubber, glass and ceramics,
iron and steel, non-ferrous metals, machinery, elec-
trial equipment, shipbuilding, motor vehicles, transportation equipment, precision instruments, marine
products, mining, construction, trade, retail stores,
banks, securities, insurance, real estate, railroad
and bus, trucking, sea transportation, air transportation, warehousing, communications, electric power,
gas, and services.

## Ten Most Active Tokyo Stock Exchange Issues

| Company | Reported Share Volume |
|---|---|
| Meiji Milk Products | 865,000,000 |
| Nippon Steel | 782,000,000 |
| Toshiba | 655,000,000 |
| Hitachi | 585,000,000 |
| Mitsui Mining and Smelting | 563,000,000 |
| Mitsubishi Heavy Industries | 543,000,000 |
| Okamoto Industries | 518,000,000 |
| Nippon Mining | 509,000,000 |
| The Green Cross | 475,000,000 |
| Nomura Securities | 453,000,000 |

*Source: Tokyo Stock Exchange Fact Book, 1993*

## The Top Reference Sources

*Financial World*
Financial World Partners, $36/year
(212) 594-5030

This monthly magazine concentrates on business,
economic, and financial topics. It includes a focus
on the national economy and effects of Washington policy upon it, statistical analysis of stock,
bond, and mutual fund activity, and the international industrial and financial arena. Highlights
include the list of America's 200 Best Growth
Companies.

*Major Foreign Exchanges (cont'd)*

## Major Foreign Exchanges

*Australia*
Sydney Stock Exchange
Exchange Street
20 Bond St.
Australia Square
P.O. Box H224
Sydney, 2000
Index: Sydney All Ordinaries

*Belgium*
Brussels Stock Exchange
Palais de la Bourse
1000 Brussels
Index: Bel-20 Index

*Canada*
Toronto Stock Exchange
2 First Canadian Pl.
Toronto, Ontario M5X 1J2
Index: 300 Composite

*France*
Bourse De Paris
Paris Stock Exchange
4, Place de la Bourse
F-75080 Paris Cedex 02
Index: CAC 40

*Germany*
Frankfurter Wertpapierbore
Frankfurt Exchange
Börsenplatz 6, P.O. 100811
D-6000 Frankfurt am Main 1
Index: DAX 30

*Hong Kong*
Stock Exchange of Hong Kong
One and Two Exchange Square
Central Hong Kong
Index: Hang Seng

*The Netherlands*
Amsterdamse Effectenbeurs
Amsterdam Stock Exchange
Beursplein 5
1012 JW Amersterdam
Index: ANP-CBS General

*Switzerland*
Zurich Stock Exchange
Bleicherweg 5
P.O. Box CH-8021
Zurich
Index: Swiss Market

## Other Foreign Exchanges

*Asia/Oceania*
Korea Stock Exchange
Kuala Lumpur Stock Exchange (Malaysia)
New Zealand Stock Exchange
Osaka Securities Exchange (Japan)
Stock Exchange of Singapore
Stock Exchange of Thailand
Taiwan Stock Exchange

*Europe*
Barcelona Stock Exchange (Spain)
Bilbao Stock Exchange (Spain)
Copenhagen Stock Exchange (Denmark)
Helsinki Stock Exchange (Finland)
Luxembourg Stock Exchange
Madrid Stock Exchange (Spain)
Oslo Stock Exchange (Norway)
Stockholm Stock Exchange (Sweden)
Vienna Stock Exchange (Austria)
Association of Italian Stock Exchanges
Association of Swiss Stock Exchanges

*Near East/Africa*
Istanbul Stock Exchange (Turkey)
Johannesburg Stock Exchange (South Africa)
Tel Aviv Stock Exchange (Israel)
Tehran Stock Exchange (Iran)

*North and South America*
Buenos Aires Stock Exchange (Argentina)
Mexico Stock Exchange
Montreal Stock Exchange (Canada)
Rio de Janeiro Stock Exchange (Brazil)
Santiago Stock Exchange (Chile)
São Paulo Stock Exchange (Brazil)
Toronto Stock Exchange (Canada)
Vancouver Stock Exchange (Canada)

## The Top Reference Sources

*Tokyo Stock Exchange Fact Book*
Tokyo Stock Exchange, free
(800) 829-5916

This is a useful annual reference for anyone interested in following the Tokyo Stock Exchange.

It is made available in English by the New York Research Office of the Exchange.

Statistical data are provided, along with explanatory comments. The book also includes stock price trends, companies listed, commission rates, investors, and other topics.

*Major Foreign Exchanges (cont'd)*

Just as the Dow Jones Industrial Average is used as a barometer for stock market performance in the U.S., the FT-SE tracks the London Stock Exchange and the Topix and the Nikkei track the Tokyo Stock Exchange.

## FT-SE Financial Times Index, 1984 to 1993

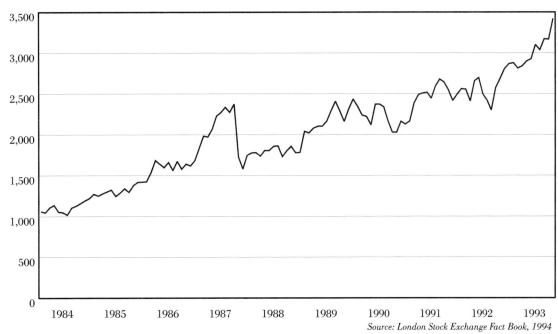

*Source: London Stock Exchange Fact Book, 1994*

## Topix Performance, 1950 to 1992

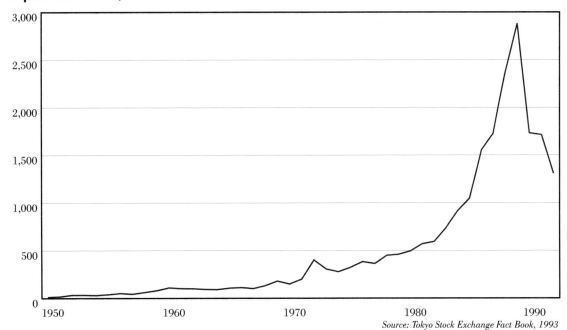

*Source: Tokyo Stock Exchange Fact Book, 1993*

*Major Foreign Exchanges (cont'd)*

## The Nikkei Stock Average: Record One-Day Gains and Losses*

| Date | Average | Percent Gain or Loss |
|------|---------|----------------------|
| December 13, 1991 | 2,298.41 | NA |
| January 31, 1994 | 1,471.24 | NA |
| October 2, 1990 | 2,298.41 | +13.24 |
| December 15, 1949 | 109.62 | +11.29 |
| October 21, 1987 | 2,3947.41 | +9.30 |
| April 16, 1953 | 355.03 | +6.41 |
| March 6, 1953 | 361.88 | +6.31 |
| October 20, 1987 | 2,190.08 | -14.90 |
| March 5, 1953 | 340.41 | -10.00 |
| April 30, 1970 | 2,114.32 | -8.69 |
| August 16, 1971 | 2,530.48 | -7.68 |
| December 14, 1949 | 98.50 | - 6.97 |

*\* as of April, 1994*                                   *Source: Nikkei*

## Nikkei Stock Average Performance

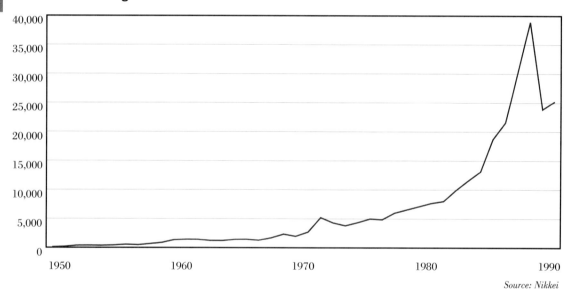

*Source: Nikkei*

## The Top Reference Sources

*The Nikkei Stock Average Data Book*
Nihon Keizai Shimbun America, free
(212) 261-6240

This is a very useful reference for anyone interested in following the Nikkei Stock Average. Periodically updated, it provides a thorough overview of the Stock Average, with performance charts, comparisons with other indexes, stock price rankings, lists of the most advanced and declined stocks, annual quotations, long-term trends, average daily closing prices, largest losses and gains, and other relevant facts.

*Major Foreign Exchanges (cont'd)*

## Foreign Investment (%) in Tokyo Stock Exchange

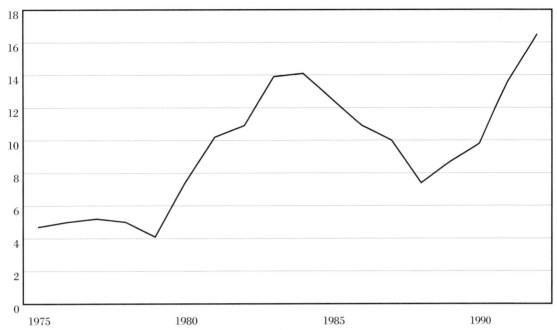

*Source: Tokyo Stock Exchange Fact Book, 1993*

**TIP:** *It may be important for an individual to collect comprehensive data on a company. Mead Data Central's Nexis Express will search through newspapers and periodicals for all references to and mention of a particular company. They will provide a list of all citations and/or the text of the actual article for the client. Fees for this service include $6 per minute search time (the average search ranges from five to 15 minutes) and $2.50 per page of printouts. Additional information is available at (800) 843-6476.*

# The Dow Jones Averages

## The Dow Jones Industrial Average

The Dow Jones Industrial Average ("the Dow") tracks price movements in 30 of the largest blue-chip issues traded on the NYSE, including:

AlliedSignal
Aluminum Company of America
American Express
AT&T
Bethlehem Steel
Boeing
Caterpillar
Chevron
Coca-Cola
Disney (Walt)
DuPont
Eastman Kodak
Exxon
General Electric
General Motors
Goodyear
IBM
International Paper
McDonald's
Merck
3M
Morgan (J.P.)
Philip Morris
Procter & Gamble
Sears
Texaco
Union Carbide
United Technologies
Westinghouse
Woolworth

## The Dow Jones Transportation Average

The Dow Jones Transportation Average was originally of railroads alone. The current index also reflects developments in the airline and trucking business in this mix of twenty transport companies:

AMR
Airborne Freight
Alaska Air
American President
Burlington Northern
Carolina Freight
Consolidated Freightways
Consolidated Rail
CSX
Delta Air Lines
Federal Express
Norfolk Southern
Roadway Services
Ryder Systems
Santa Fe Pacific
Southwest Airlines
UAL
Union Pacific
USAir
XTRA Corporation

## The Dow Jones Utility Average

The Dow Jones Utility Average tracks the following 15 large electricity and natural gas utilities:

American Electric Power
Arkla
Centerior
Commonwealth Edison
Consolidated Edison
Consolidated Natural Gas
Detroit Edison
Houston Industries
Niagara Mohawk Power
Pacific Gas & Electric
Panhandle Eastern
Peoples Energy
Philadelphia Electric
Public Service Enterprises
SCE

## Performance of Dow Jones Industrials, 1993

| Company | 1993 Close ($) | % Change from 1992 |
|---|---|---|
| General Motors | 54.88 | 70.16 |
| Caterpillar | 89.00 | 65.97 |
| Sears Roebuck | 52.88 | 57.46 |
| Kodak | 56.25 | 38.89 |
| Union Carbide | 22.38 | 34.59 |
| Goodyear | 45.75 | 33.82 |
| AlliedSignal | 79.00 | 30.58 |
| United Tech. | 62.00 | 28.83 |
| Bethlehem Steel | 20.38 | 27.34 |
| Chevron | 87.13 | 25.36 |
| American Express | 30.88 | 24.12 |
| General Electric | 104.88 | 22.66 |

| Company | 1993 Close ($) | % Change from 1992 |
|---|---|---|
| McDonald's | 57.00 | 16.92 |
| IBM | 56.50 | 12.16 |
| Texaco | 64.75 | 8.37 |
| 3M | 108.75 | 8.07 |
| Boeing | 43.25 | 7.79 |
| Coca-Cola | 44.63 | 6.57 |
| Procter & Gamble | 57.00 | 6.29 |
| Westinghouse Electric | 14.13 | 5.61 |
| J.P. Morgan | 69.38 | 5.51 |
| Exxon | 63.13 | 3.27 |
| AT&T | 52.50 | 2.94 |
| DuPont | 48.25 | 2.39 |

*The Dow Jones Averages (cont'd)*

| Company | 1993 Close ($) | % Change from 1992 |
|---|---|---|
| Int'l. Paper | 67.75 | 1.69 |
| Disney (Walt) | 42.63 | -0.87 |
| Alcoa | 69.38 | -3.14 |
| Woolworth | 25.38 | -19.76 |

| Company | 1993 Close ($) | % Change from 1992 |
|---|---|---|
| Merck | 34.38 | -20.75 |
| Philip Morris | 55.63 | -27.88 |

*Source: The Wall Street Journal, Jan. 3, 1994*

## Dow Jones Industrial Average Performance Since 1900

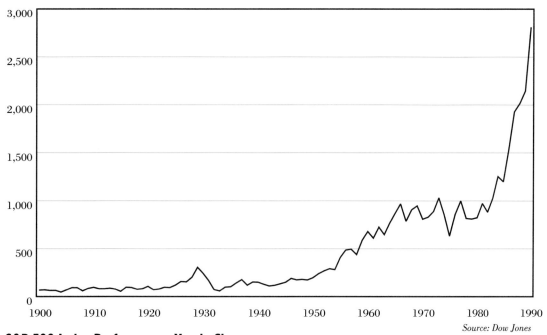

*Source: Dow Jones*

## S&P 500 Index Performance, Yearly Close

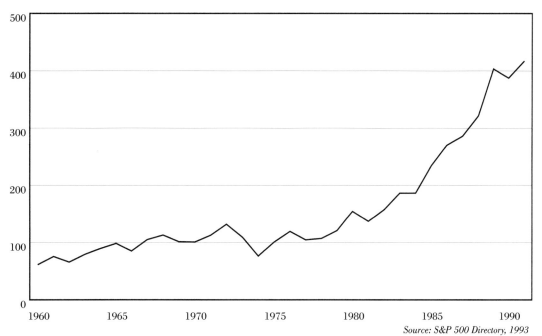

*Source: S&P 500 Directory, 1993*

# Standard & Poor's 500

STANDARD & POOR'S 500 Index (S&P 500) represents approximately 80 percent of the value of all
issues traded on the NYSE, reflecting the performance of 500 stocks including industrials, public
utilities, transportation, and financial companies.

Movement within each of these industry categories
is tracked in sub-indexes.

The S&P 500 index is currently one of the 12
leading economic indicators cited by the U.S. Commerce Department.

## S&P 500 Composite Stock Price Index

| Ticker Symbol | Company Name | Ticker Symbol | Company Name |
|---|---|---|---|
| AMP | AMP | AVP | Avon Products |
| AMR | AMR | BHI | Baker Hughes |
| T | AT&T | BLL | Ball |
| ABT | Abbott Laboratories | BLY | Bally Manufacturing |
| AMD | Advanced Micro Devices | BGE | Baltimore Gas & Electric |
| AET | Aetna Life and Casualty | ONE | Banc One |
| AHM | Ahmanson (H.F.) & Co. | BKB | Bank of Boston |
| APD | Air Products and Chemicals | BAC | BankAmerica |
| ACV | Alberto-Culver | BT | Bankers Trust New York |
| ABS | Albertson's | BCR | Bard (C.R.) |
| AL | Alcan Aluminum Limited | BBI | Barnett Banks |
| ASN | Alco Standard | BSET | Bassett Furniture Industries |
| AAL | Alexander & Alexander Services | BOL | Bausch & Lomb |
| AGN | Allergan | BAX | Baxter International |
| ALD | AlliedSignal | BDX | Becton, Dickinson & Co. |
| AA | Aluminum Co. of America | BEL | Bell Atlantic |
| AZA | Alza | BLS | BellSouth |
| AMX | Amax | BMS | Bemis Company |
| AMH | Amdahl | BNL | Beneficial |
| AHC | Amerada Hess | BS | Bethlehem Steel |
| AMB | American Brands | BEV | Beverly Enterprises |
| ACY | American Cyanamid | BMET | Biomet |
| AEP | American Electric Power | BDK | Black & Decker |
| AXP | American Express | HRB | Block (H&R) |
| AGC | American General | BV | Blockbuster Entertainment |
| AGREA | American Greetings | BOAT | Boatmen's Bancshares |
| AHP | American Home Products | BA | Boeing |
| AIG | American International Group | BCC | Boise Cascade |
| ASC | American Stores | BN | Borden |
| AIT | Ameritech | BGG | Briggs & Stratton |
| AMEN | Amgen | BMY | Bristol-Myers Squibb |
| AN | Amoco | BFD | Brown-Forman |
| ANDW | Andrew | BG | Brown Group |
| BUD | Anheuser-Busch Companies | BFI | Browning-Ferris Industries |
| AAPL | Apple Computer | BRNO | Bruno's |
| ADM | Archer-Daniels-Midland | BC | Brunswick |
| ALG | Arkla | BNI | Burlington Northern |
| AS | Armco | CBS | CBS |
| ACK | Armstrong World Industries | CNA | CNA Financial |
| AR | Asarco | CPC | CPC International |
| ASH | Ashland Oil | CSX | CSX |
| ARC | Atlantic Richfield | CPB | Campbell Soup |
| ACAD | Autodesk | CCB | Capital Cities/ABC |
| AUD | Automatic Data Processing | CPH | Capital Holding |
| AVY | Avery Dennison | CPL | Carolina Power & Light |

*Standard & Poor's 500 (cont'd)*

| Ticker Symbol | Company Name |
|---|---|
| CAT | Caterpillar |
| CTX | Centex |
| CSR | Central & Southwest |
| CEN | Ceridian Corporation |
| CHA | Champion International |
| CHRS | Charming Shoppes |
| CMB | Chase Manhattan |
| CHL | Chemical Banking |
| CHV | Chevron |
| C | Chrysler |
| CB | Chubb |
| CI | Cigna |
| CMZ | Cincinnati Milacron |
| CC | Circuit City Stores |
| CCI | Citicorp |
| CKL | Clark Equipment |
| CLX | Clorox |
| CGP | Coastal |
| KO | Coca-Cola |
| CL | Colgate-Palmolive |
| CG | Columbia Gas System |
| CMCSA | Comcast |
| CWE | Commonwealth Edison |
| CMY | Community Psychiatric Centers |
| CPQ | Compaq Computer |
| CA | Computer Associates International |
| CSC | Computer Sciences |
| CAG | Conagra |
| ED | Consolidated Edison Co. of New York |
| CNF | Consolidated Freightways |
| CNG | Consolidated Natural Gas |
| CRR | Consolidated Rail |
| CIC | Continental |
| CBE | Cooper Industries |
| CTB | Cooper Tire & Rubber |
| ACCOB | Coors (Adolph) |
| CSFN | Corestates Financial |
| GLW | Corning |
| CR | Crane |
| CYR | Cray Research |
| CCK | Crown Cork & Seal |
| CUM | Cummins Engine |
| CYM | Cyprus Minerals |
| DIGI | DSC Communications |
| DCN | Dana |
| DGN | Data General |
| DH | Dayton-Hudson |
| DE | Deere & Company |
| DAL | Delta Air Lines |
| DLX | Deluxe |

| Ticker Symbol | Company Name |
|---|---|
| DTE | Detroit Edison |
| DL | Dial |
| DEC | Digital Equipment |
| DDS | Dillard Department Stores |
| DIS | Disney (Walt) |
| D | Dominion Resources |
| DNY | Donnelley (R.R.) & Sons |
| DOV | Dover |
| DOW | Dow Chemical |
| DJ | Dow Jones & Co. |
| DI | Dresser Industries |
| DUK | Duke Power |
| DNB | Dun & Bradstreet |
| DD | Du Pont (E.I.) De Nemours |
| EGG | EG & G |
| ESY | E-Systems |
| EFU | Eastern Enterprises |
| EK | Eastman Kodak |
| ETN | Eaton |
| ECH | Echlin |
| ECO | Echo Bay Mines |
| ECL | Ecolab |
| EMR | Emerson Electric |
| EC | Engelhard |
| ENE | Enron |
| ENS | Enserch |
| ETR | Entergy |
| EY | Ethyl |
| XON | Exxon |
| FMC | FMC |
| FPL | FPL Group |
| FJQ | Fedders |
| FDX | Federal Express |
| FRE | Federal Home Loan Mortgage |
| FNM | Federal National Mortgage |
| FBO | Federal Paper Board |
| FNB | First Chicago |
| FFB | First Fidelity Bancorp |
| I | First Interstate Bancorp |
| FRM | First Mississippi |
| FTU | First Union |
| FLT | Fleet Financial Group |
| FLE | Fleetwood Enterprises |
| FLM | Fleming Companies |
| FLR | Fluor |
| F | Ford Motor |
| FWC | Foster Wheeler |
| GTE | GTE |
| GCI | Gannett |
| GPS | Gap (The) |

*Standard & Poor's 500 (cont'd)*

| Ticker Symbol | Company Name |
|---|---|
| GCN | General Cinema |
| GD | General Dynamics |
| GE | General Electric |
| GIS | General Mills |
| GM | General Motors |
| GRN | General Re |
| GSX | General Signal |
| GCO | Genesco |
| GPC | Genuine Parts |
| GP | Georgia-Pacific |
| GEB | Gerber Products |
| GFSA | Giant Food |
| GIDL | Giddings & Lewis |
| GS | Gillette |
| GDW | Golden West Financial |
| GR | Goodrich (B.F.) |
| GT | Goodyear Tire & Rubber |
| GRA | Grace (W.R.) & Co. |
| GWW | Grainger (W.W.) |
| GAP | Great Atlantic & Pacific Tea |
| GLK | Great Lakes Chemical |
| GWF | Great Western Financial |
| GQ | Grumman |
| HAL | Halliburton |
| HDL | Handleman |
| JH | Harland (John H.) |
| HPH | Harnischfeger Industries |
| HRS | Harris |
| HMX | Hartmarx |
| HAS | Hasbro |
| HNZ | Heinz (H.J.) |
| HP | Helmerich & Payne |
| HPC | Hercules |
| HSY | Hershey Foods |
| HWP | Hewlett-Packard |
| HLT | Hilton Hotels |
| HD | Home Depot |
| HM | Homestake Mining |
| HON | Honeywell |
| HI | Household International |
| HOU | Houston Industries |
| HUM | Humana |
| ITT | ITT |
| ITW | Illinois Tool Works |
| IMA | Imcera Group |
| N | Inco Limited |
| IR | Ingersoll-Rand |
| IAD | Inland Steel Industries |
| INTC | Intel |
| INGR | Intergraph |
| IK | Interlake |
| IBM | International Business Machines |
| IFF | International Flavors & Fragrances |
| IP | International Paper |
| IPG | Interpublic Group |

| Ticker Symbol | Company Name |
|---|---|
| JWP | JWP |
| JR | James River |
| JP | Jefferson-Pilot |
| JCI | Johnson Controls |
| JNJ | Johnson & Johnson |
| JOS | Jostens |
| KBH | Kaufman & Broad Home |
| K | Kellogg |
| KMG | Kerr-McGee |
| KMB | Kimberly-Clark |
| KWP | King World Productions |
| KM | Kmart |
| KRI | Knight-Ridder |
| KR | Kroger Co. (The) |
| LLY | Lilly (Eli) & Co. |
| LTD | Limited (The) |
| LNC | Lincoln National |
| LIT | Litton Industries |
| LIZC | Liz Claiborne |
| LK | Lockheed |
| LDG | Longs Drug Stores |
| LOR | Loral |
| LOTS | Lotus Development |
| LLX | Louisiana Land & Exploration |
| LPX | Louisiana-Pacific |
| LOW | Lowe's Companies |
| LUB | Luby's Cafeterias |
| MAI | M/A-Com |
| KRB | MBNA |
| MCIC | MCI Communications |
| MNR | Manor Care |
| MHS | Marriott |
| MMC | Marsh & McLennan |
| ML | Martin Marietta |
| MAS | Masco |
| MAT | Mattel |
| MXS | Maxus Energy |
| MA | May Department Stores |
| MYG | Maytag |
| MDR | McDermott International |
| MCD | McDonald's |
| MD | McDonnell Douglas |
| MHP | McGraw-Hill |
| MCK | McKesson |
| MEA | Mead |
| MDT | Medtronic |
| MEL | Mellon Bank |
| MES | Melville |
| MST | Mercantile Stores |
| MRK | Merck & Co. |
| MDP | Meredith |
| MER | Merrill Lynch & Co. |
| MIL | Millipore |
| MMM | 3M |
| MOB | Mobil |

*Standard & Poor's 500 (cont'd)*

| Ticker Symbol | Company Name |
| --- | --- |
| MTC | Monsanto |
| MCL | Moore |
| JPM | Morgan (J.P.) & Co. |
| MRN | Morrison Knudsen |
| MII | Morton International |
| MOT | Motorola |
| NBD | NBD Bancorp |
| NL | NL Industries |
| NC | NACCO Industries |
| NLC | Nalco Chemical |
| NEC | National Education |
| NII | National Intergroup |
| NME | National Medical Enterprises |
| NSM | National Semiconductor |
| NSI | National Service Industries |
| NB | NationsBank |
| NAV | Navistar International |
| NYTA | New York Times (The) |
| NWL | Newell |
| NEM | Newmont Mining |
| NMK | Niagara Mohawk Power |
| GAS | Nicor |
| NIKE | Nike |
| NOBE | Nordstrom |
| NSC | Norfolk Southern |
| NSP | Northern States Power |
| NT | Northern Telecom |
| NOC | Northrop |
| NOB | Norwest |
| NOVL | Novell |
| NUE | Nucor |
| NYN | NYNEX |
| OXY | Occidental Petroleum |
| OG | Ogden |
| OEC | Ohio Edison |
| OKE | Oneok |
| ORCL | Oracle Systems |
| ORX | Oryx Energy |
| GOSHA | Oshkosh B'Gosh |
| OM | Outboard Marine |
| OCF | Owens-Corning Fiberglass |
| PHM | PHM |
| PNC | PNC Financial |
| PPG | PPG Industries |
| PIN | PSI Resources |
| PCAR | Paccar |
| PET | Pacific Enterprises |
| PCG | Pacific Gas & Electric |
| PAC | Pacific Telesis Group |
| PPW | Pacificorp |
| PLL | Pall |
| PEL | Panhandle Eastern |
| PCI | Paramount Communications |
| PH | Parker Hannifin |
| JCP | Penney (J.C.) |

| Ticker Symbol | Company Name |
| --- | --- |
| PZL | Pennzoil |
| PGL | Peoples Energy |
| PBY | Pep Boys (Manny, Moe & Jack) |
| PEP | PepsiCo |
| PKN | Perkin-Elmer |
| PT | PET |
| PFE | Pfizer |
| PD | Phelps Dodge |
| PE | Philadelphia Electric |
| MO | Philip Morris |
| P | Phillips Petroleum |
| PBI | Pitney Bowes |
| PCO | Pittston |
| PDG | Placer Dome |
| PRD | Polaroid |
| PCH | Potlatch |
| PX | Praxair |
| PMI | Premark International |
| PCLB | Price |
| PA | Primerica |
| PG | Procter & Gamble |
| PRI | Promus |
| PEG | Public Service Enterprises |
| OAT | Quaker Oats |
| CUE | Quantum Chemical |
| RAL | Ralston Purina |
| RYC | Raychem |
| RTN | Raytheon |
| RBK | Reebok International |
| RLM | Reynolds Metals |
| RAD | Rite Aid |
| ROAD | Roadway Services |
| ROK | Rockwell International |
| ROH | Rohm & Haas |
| REN | Rollins Environmental Services |
| RDC | Rowan |
| RD | Royal Dutch Petroleum |
| RBD | Rubbermaid |
| RML | Russell |
| RYAN | Ryan's Family Steak Houses |
| R | Ryder Systems |
| SAFC | SAFECO |
| SCE | SCE |
| SPW | SPX |
| SK | Safety-Kleen |
| STJM | St. Jude Medical |
| STPL | St. Paul Companies |
| SB | Salomon |
| SFR | Santa Fe Energy Resources |
| SFX | Santa Fe Pacific |
| SLE | Sara Lee |
| SGP | Schering-Plough |
| SLB | Schlumberger |
| SFA | Scientific-Atlanta |
| SPP | Scott Paper |

*Standard & Poor's 500 (cont'd)*

| Ticker Symbol | Company Name |
|---|---|
| VO | Seagram Company (The) |
| S | Sears, Roebuck & Co. |
| SRV | Service International |
| SMED | Shared Medical Systems |
| SNC | Shawmut National |
| SHW | Sherwin-Williams |
| SHN | Shoney's |
| SKY | Skyline |
| SNA | Snap-On Tools |
| SNT | Sonat |
| SO | Southern |
| SBC | Southwestern Bell |
| SMI | Springs Industries |
| FON | Sprint |
| SWK | Stanley Works |
| STO | Stone Container |
| SRR | Stride-Rite |
| SUN | Sun |
| SUNW | Sun Microsystems |
| STI | Suntrust Banks |
| SVU | Supervalu |
| SYN | Syntex |
| SYY | SYSCO |
| TJX | TJX Companies |
| TRW | TRW |
| TDM | Tandem Computers |
| TAN | Tandy |
| TEK | Tektronix |
| TCOMA | Tele-Communications |
| TDY | Teledyne |
| TIN | Temple-Inland |
| TGT | Tenneco |
| TX | Texaco |
| TXN | Texas Instruments |
| TXU | Texas Utilities |
| TXT | Textron |
| TNB | Thomas & Betts |
| TWX | Time Warner |
| TMC | Times Mirror |
| TKR | Timken |
| TMK | Torchmark |
| TOY | Toys 'R' Us |
| TA | Transamerica |
| E | Transco Energy |
| TIC | Travelers |

| Ticker Symbol | Company Name |
|---|---|
| TRB | Tribune |
| TNV | Trinova |
| TYC | Tyco Laboratories |
| UAL | UAL |
| FG | USF & G |
| UST | UST |
| MRO | USX-Marathon Group |
| X | USX-US Steel Group |
| UN | Unilever |
| UCC | Union Camp |
| UK | Union Carbide |
| UEP | Union Electric |
| UNP | Union Pacific |
| UIS | Unisys |
| USBC | U.S. Bancorp |
| USS | U.S. Surgical |
| USW | US West |
| UTX | United Technologies |
| UCL | Unocal |
| UPJ | Upjohn |
| U | USAir |
| USH | USLife |
| VAT | Varity |
| VFC | V.F. |
| WMT | Wal-Mart Stores |
| WAG | Walgreen |
| WLA | Warner-Lambert |
| WMX | Waste Management |
| WFC | Wells Fargo & Co. |
| WEN | Wendy's International |
| WX | Westinghouse Electric |
| WMOR | Westmoreland Coal |
| W | Westvaco |
| WY | Weyerhaeuser |
| WHR | Whirlpool |
| WH | Whitman |
| WMB | Williams Companies (The) |
| WIN | Winn-Dixie Stores |
| Z | Woolworth |
| WTHG | Worthington Industries |
| WWY | Wm. Wrigley Jr. |
| XRX | Xerox |
| YELL | Yellow Freight Systems |
| ZE | Zenith Electronics |
| ZRN | Zurn Industries |

*Source: S&P 500 Directory, 1993*

*Standard & Poor's 500 (cont'd)*

## S&P 500 by Major Industry Group

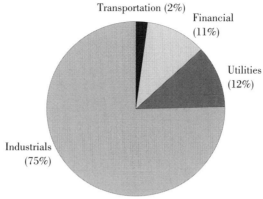

Transportation (2%)

Financial (11%)

Utilities (12%)

Industrials (75%)

*Source: S&P 500 Directory, 1993*

## Most Widely Held S&P Companies, 1992

| Rank | Company | Number of Shareholders |
|------|---------|------------------------|
| 1 | AT&T (T) | 2,486,000 |
| 2 | BellSouth (BLS) | 1,387,800 |
| 3 | Bell Atlantic (BEL) | 1,151,000 |
| 4 | NYNEX (NYN) | 1,093,200 |
| 5 | Ameritech (AIT) | 1,042,200 |
| 6 | Southwestern Bell (SBC) | 1,010,200 |
| 7 | US West (USW) | 1,007,400 |
| 8 | Pacific Telesis (PAC) | 951,900 |
| 9 | General Motors (GM) | 891,600 |
| 10 | International Business Machines (IBM) | 772,000 |
| 11 | Exxon (XON) | 613,700 |
| 12 | Royal Dutch Petroleum (RD) | 500,000 |
| 13 | General Electric (GE) | 490,000 |
| 14 | Occidental Petroleum (OXY) | 487,400 |
| 15 | GTE (GTE) | 442,000 |
| 16 | Sears, Roebuck (S) | 340,300 |
| 17 | Ford Motor (F) | 293,700 |
| 18 | Pacific Gas & Electric (PCG) | 261,000 |
| 19 | Southern (SO) | 254,600 |
| 20 | Philadelphia Electric (PE) | 244,200 |

*Source: S&P 500 Directory, 1993*

*Standard & Poor's 500 (cont'd)*

## S&P 500 Index Performance, Yearly Close, P/E Ratio

| Year | Close | Close P/E Ratio |
|------|-------|-----------------|
| 1960 | 61.49 | 18.14 |
| 1961 | 75.72 | 22.47 |
| 1962 | 66.00 | 17.05 |
| 1963 | 79.25 | 18.69 |
| 1964 | 89.62 | 18.55 |
| 1965 | 98.47 | 17.87 |
| 1966 | 85.24 | 14.47 |
| 1967 | 105.11 | 18.57 |
| 1968 | 113.02 | 18.38 |
| 1969 | 101.49 | 16.45 |
| 1970 | 100.90 | 18.58 |
| 1971 | 112.72 | 18.72 |
| 1972 | 131.87 | 19.31 |
| 1973 | 109.14 | 12.32 |
| 1974 | 76.47 | 7.89 |
| 1975 | 100.88 | 11.80 |
| 1976 | 119.46 | 11.19 |
| 1977 | 104.71 | 9.01 |
| 1978 | 107.21 | 8.17 |
| 1979 | 121.02 | 7.47 |

| Year | Close | Close P/E Ratio |
|------|-------|-----------------|
| 1980 | 154.45 | 9.58 |
| 1981 | 137.12 | 8.29 |
| 1982 | 157.62 | 11.92 |
| 1983 | 186.24 | 12.64 |
| 1984 | 186.36 | 10.36 |
| 1985 | 234.56 | 15.39 |
| 1986 | 269.93 | 18.73 |
| 1987 | 285.86 | 14.09 |
| 1988 | 321.26 | 12.35 |
| 1989 | 403.49 | 15.31 |
| 1990 | 387.42 | 15.90 |
| 1991 | 417.09 | 26.12 |
| 1992 | 435.71 | 22.82 |

*Source: S&P 500 Directory, 1993*

## The Top Reference Sources

*S&P MidCap 400 Directory*
Standard & Poor's, $39.95
(212) 208-1649

Published for the first time in 1992, this annual directory is designed to provide money managers, analysts, institutional and individual investors, corporative executives, journalists, and observers of financial markets and the overall economy with a comprehensive and authoritative analysis of the growing, middle capitalization sector of the U.S. equities market.

The book includes a complete listing of the MidCap 400 companies, company reports, and statistical tables.

**FAX** **Internal Revenue Service Centers.** Request #104. See p. xi for instructions.
List of regional offices that accept tax returns.

# Composite Indexes

## The Amex Market Value Index

The Amex Market Value Index is composed of all common stocks listed on the American Stock Exchange.

## Amex Market Value Index Performance, Yearly Highs

| Year | Index |
|------|-------|
| 1976 | 54.92 |
| 1977 | 63.95 |
| 1978 | 88.44 |
| 1979 | 123.54 |
| 1980 | 185.38 |
| 1981 | 190.18 |
| 1982 | 170.93 |
| 1983 | 249.03 |
| 1984 | 227.73 |
| 1985 | 246.13 |
| 1986 | 285.19 |
| 1987 | 365.01 |
| 1988 | 309.59 |
| 1989 | 397.03 |
| 1990 | 382.45 |
| 1991 | 395.05 |
| 1992 | 418.99 |

*Source: American Stock Exchange Fact Book, 1993*

## The Value Line Composite Index

The Value Line Composite Index tracks the performance of 1,700 stocks listed on the New York Stock Exchange, the American Stock Exchange, the Regional and Canadian Exchanges, and the over-the-counter market.

## The New York Stock Exchange Composite Index

The New York Stock Exchange Composite Index measures price movement of all NYSE-listed common stocks as well as performance in four subgroups: Industrial, Transportation, Utility, and Finance.

## NASDAQ Composite Index

The Nasdaq Composite Index indicates price movements of all domestic OTC common stocks listed on the NASDAQ system. The composite is broken down into six specialized industry indexes.

## NASDAQ Composite Index Classifications

| Index | Number of Issues | Market Value ($ billions) |
|-------|------------------|---------------------------|
| Industrial | 2,860 | 417.6 |
| Other Finance | 614 | 101.4 |
| Bank | 224 | 13.1 |
| Insurance | 106 | 22.7 |
| Utility | 144 | 47.0 |
| Transportation | 65 | 13.3 |
| TOTAL COMPOSITE | 4,013 | 615.1 |
| TOTAL UNASSIGNED | 751 | 7.4 |
| TOTAL ALL NASDAQ | 4,764 | 622.5 |

*Source: NASDAQ Fact Book & Company Directory, 1993*

## NASDAQ Composite Index Market Value, 1981 to 1992

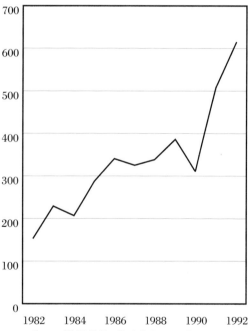

*Source: NASDAQ Fact Book & Company Directory, 1993*

# The Amex Market Value Index

## Index Performance

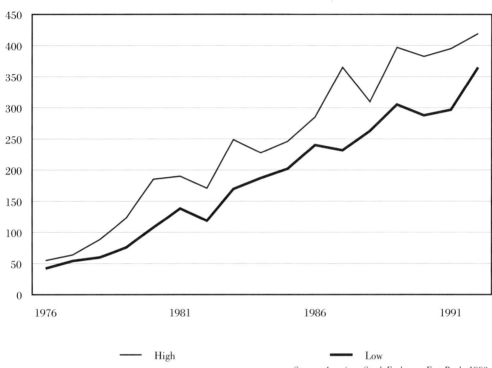

— High　　　　　　　■ Low

*Source: American Stock Exchange Fact Book, 1993*

## The Top Reference Sources

*Pensions & Investments*
Crain Communications, $150/year
(800) 678-9595

This newspaper of corporate and institutional investing includes informative articles on a range of investment topics.
　　Regular features include tracking the changes in the S&P 500, Russell 3000 Stock Index, Morgan Stanley Capital Internationals, and other stock indexes.
　　P&I also sponsors a number of surveys throughout the year, on topics as varied as the largest real estate investors to the popularity of Ross Perot.

# The Wilshire 5000 Equity Index

THE WILSHIRE 5000 EQUITY INDEX measures price movements of all stocks listed on the New York Stock Exchange (85%) and American Stock Exchange (3%) and of most active over-the-counter stocks (12%), or all common equity securities for which pricing is available.

### The Wilshire 5000 Equity Index

*Source: Wilshire Associates*

# The Russell 2000 Index

THE RUSSELL 2000 INDEX TRACKS the stock prices of 2,000 small-capitalization companies (average market capitalization $155 million).

### Russell 2000 Economic Sector Performance: Total Return

| Sector | 4th Qtr. 1993 (%) | Jan.–Dec. (%) | 5 Years Annualized (%) |
| --- | --- | --- | --- |
| Autos and Transportation | 8.27 | 32.13 | 16.62 |
| Health Care | 8.05 | 1.92 | 17.81 |
| Materials and Processing | 6.90 | 23.46 | 7.68 |
| Producer Durables | 5.83 | 17.93 | 6.51 |
| Consumer Discretionary | 5.17 | 17.09 | 12.56 |
| Technology | 3.80 | 20.34 | 15.37 |
| Consumer Staples | 2.18 | -0.49 | 9.88 |
| Financial Services | -2.50 | 22.92 | 18.86 |
| Utilities | -5.49 | 19.90 | 14.34 |
| Integrated Oils | -10.11 | 16.81 | 10.40 |
| Energy* | -12.23 | 26.61 | 9.63 |

*excluding integrated oils

*Source: Frank Russell Company*

*The Russell 2000 Index (cont'd)*

## The Russell 2000 Index Performance

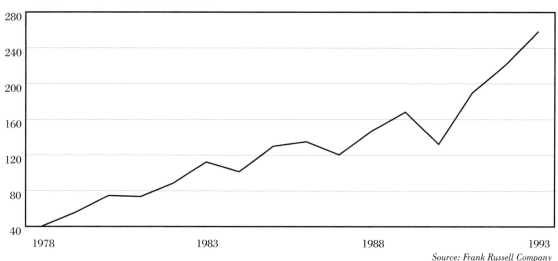

Source: Frank Russell Company

# Stock Indexes Performance

## Performance of Stock Indexes, Year-End

| Year | Dow Jones Industrial Average | S&P 500 | NYSE Composite | Amex Market Value | NASDAQ Composite | Value Line |
|------|------|------|------|------|------|------|
| 1981 | 875.00 | 122.55 | 71.11 | 160.32 | 195.84 | 137.81 |
| 1982 | 1,046.54 | 140.64 | 81.03 | 170.30 | 232.41 | 158.94 |
| 1983 | 1,258.64 | 164.93 | 95.18 | 223.01 | 278.60 | 194.35 |
| 1984 | 1,211.57 | 167.24 | 96.38 | 204.26 | 247.35 | 177.98 |
| 1985 | 1,546.67 | 211.28 | 121.58 | 246.13 | 324.93 | 214.86 |
| 1986 | 1,895.95 | 242.17 | 138.58 | 263.27 | 348.83 | 225.62 |
| 1987 | 1,938.83 | 247.08 | 138.23 | 260.35 | 330.47 | 201.62 |
| 1988 | 2,168.57 | 277.72 | 156.26 | 306.01 | 381.38 | 232.68 |
| 1989 | 2,753.20 | 353.40 | 195.04 | 378.00 | 454.82 | 258.78 |
| 1990 | 2,633.66 | 330.22 | 180.49 | 308.11 | 373.84 | 195.99 |
| 1991 | 3,168.83 | 417.09 | 229.44 | 395.05 | 586.34 | 249.34 |
| 1992 | 3,301.11 | 435.71 | 240.21 | 399.23 | 676.95 | 266.68 |
| 1993 | 3,754.09 | 466.45 | 252.08 | 477.15 | 776.80 | 295.28 |

Source: Securities Industry Association Fact Book, 1994

---

## The Top Reference Sources

*Hulbert Financial Digest*
Hulbert, $135
(703) 683-5905

There are literally hundreds of newsletters written for investors. In most cases, the primary source of income for the editor is not the stock market, but the revenue from the newsletter. In order to separate the pros from the pretenders, the *Hulbert Financial Digest* keeps track of each newsletter's performance. Hulbert's compilations give the regular investor the data needed to choose the best advice available.

*Stock Indexes Performance (cont'd)*

## Performance of Stock Indexes, Annual Percent Change

| Year | Dow Jones Industrial Average | S&P 500 | NYSE Composite | Amex Market Value | NASDAQ Composite | Value Line |
|------|------------------------------|---------|----------------|-------------------|------------------|------------|
| 1981 | -9.2 | -9.7 | -8.7 | -8.1 | -3.2 | -4.4 |
| 1982 | 19.6 | 14.8 | 14.0 | 6.2 | 18.7 | 15.3 |
| 1983 | 20.3 | 17.3 | 17.5 | 31.0 | 19.9 | 22.3 |
| 1984 | -3.7 | 1.4 | 1.3 | 8.4 | -11.2 | -8.4 |
| 1985 | 27.7 | 26.3 | 26.1 | 20.5 | 31.4 | 20.7 |
| 1986 | 22.6 | 14.6 | 14.0 | 7.0 | 7.4 | 5.0 |
| 1987 | 2.3 | 2.0 | -0.3 | -1.1 | -5.3 | -10.6 |
| 1988 | 11.8 | 12.4 | 13.0 | 17.5 | 15.4 | 15.4 |
| 1989 | 27.0 | 27.3 | 24.8 | 23.5 | 19.3 | 11.2 |
| 1990 | -4.3 | -6.6 | -7.5 | -18.5 | -17.8 | -24.3 |
| 1991 | 20.3 | 26.3 | 27.1 | 28.2 | 56.8 | 27.2 |
| 1992 | 4.2 | 4.5 | 4.7 | 1.1 | 15.5 | 7.0 |
| 1993 | 13.7 | 7.1 | 7.9 | 19.5 | 14.7 | 10.7 |

*Source: Securities Industry Association Fact Book, 1994*

## The Top Reference Sources

*The Ernst & Young Tax Guide*
John Wiley & Sons, $13.95
(212) 850-6000

This comprehensive, readable guide is really two books in one. It is the official, annually published IRS tax guide. More important, it is a taxpayer guide which offers explanations, comments, and tax-saving tips. In addition to official tax forms, this very readable book contains pointers and strategies called TaxSavers, TaxPlanners, TaxAlerts and Tax Organizers, all of which offer advice to the individual, the corporate or stock market investor, the real estate investor, the self-employed entrepreneur and the senior citizen.

*Prodigy offers access to current benchmark credit ratings, such as rates for T-bills, U.S. Treasury notes and bonds, and the prime rate. JUMP CREDIT RATES.*

# Financial Ratios by Industry

## Five-Year Average Financial Ratios for Selected Industries

| Financial Ratios | Food, Tobacco | Textile Mill Products | Paper, Allied Products | Printing, Publishing | Chemicals, Allied Products |
|---|---|---|---|---|---|
| Current Ratio | 1.3 | 2.1 | 1.5 | 1.6 | 1.4 |
| Quick Ratio | 0.7 | 1.2 | 0.9 | 1.3 | 0.9 |
| Long-term Debt to Equity (%) | 96.5 | 93.7 | 91.8 | 77.1 | 56.0 |
| Total Liabilities to Total Assets (%) | 66.1 | 63.6 | 62.2 | 59.9 | 59.7 |
| Total Liabilities to Equity (%) | 195.2 | 178.2 | 167.1 | 150.0 | 149.2 |
| Fixed Assets to Equity (%) | 86.5 | 95.3 | 158.0 | 61.4 | 88.2 |
| Current to Total Liabilities (%) | 34.2 | 37.4 | 26.2 | 32.6 | 39.4 |
| Cash Flow to Total Assets (%) | 8.8 | 8.1 | 8.1 | 7.5 | 10.2 |
| Short-term Debt to Total Assets (%) | 7.1 | 8.4 | 4.2 | 4.1 | 7.0 |
| Long-term Debt to Total Assets (%) | 32.6 | 33.3 | 34.1 | 30.8 | 22.4 |
| Equity to Total Assets (%) | 33.9 | 36.3 | 37.7 | 40.1 | 40.2 |
| Average Collection Period (days) | 26.5 | 49.3 | 35.1 | 53.7 | 50.6 |
| Inventory Turnover (times) | 9.9 | 6.6 | 10.0 | 14.8 | 7.9 |
| Fixed Assets Turnover (times) | 4.3 | 4.1 | 1.7 | 3.9 | 2.5 |
| Total Assets Turnover (times) | 1.3 | 1.4 | 1.0 | 1.0 | 0.9 |
| Profit Margin before Taxes (%) | 6.6 | 3.5 | 4.7 | 6.3 | 9.3 |
| Return on Assets before Taxes (%) | 8.5 | 5.0 | 4.9 | 6.1 | 8.5 |
| Return on Assets after Taxes (%) | 5.6 | 3.1 | 3.1 | 3.7 | 6.1 |
| Return on Equity before Taxes (%) | 24.9 | 13.4 | 11.8 | 15.3 | 20.1 |
| Return on Equity after Taxes (%) | 16.4 | 8.1 | 7.3 | 9.2 | 14.6 |

| Financial Ratios | Industrial Chemicals, Synthetics | Drugs | Petroleum, Coal Products | Rubber, Plastic Products | Stone, Clay, Glass Products |
|---|---|---|---|---|---|
| Current Ratio | 1.3 | 1.2 | 1.0 | 1.3 | 1.4 |
| Quick Ratio | 0.9 | 0.8 | 0.7 | 0.8 | 0.9 |
| Long-term Debt to Equity (%) | 67.9 | 27.4 | 52.6 | 72.5 | 111.1 |
| Total Liabilities to Total Assets (%) | 62.7 | 52.5 | 59.0 | 66.6 | 68.9 |
| Total Liabilities to Equity (%) | 171.8 | 110.7 | 144.0 | 199.3 | 223.8 |
| Fixed Assets to Equity (%) | 112.9 | 61.1 | 134.0 | 111.0 | 138.4 |
| Current to Total Liabilities (%) | 33.7 | 55.1 | 31.1 | 49.7 | 32.1 |
| Cash Flow to Total Assets (%) | 8.9 | 15.9 | 9.7 | 7.9 | 5.4 |
| Short-term Debt to Total Assets (%) | 6.1 | 9.8 | 4.6 | 12.2 | 8.1 |
| Long-term Debt to Total Assets (%) | 24.8 | 12.9 | 21.5 | 24.1 | 34.3 |
| Equity to Total Assets (%) | 36.9 | 47.6 | 41.0 | 33.5 | 31.0 |
| Average Collection Period (days) | 56.0 | 46.7 | 34.1 | 49.2 | 51.2 |
| Inventory Turnover (times) | 7.9 | 7.8 | 15.4 | 8.1 | 8.5 |
| Fixed Assets Turnover (times) | 2.0 | 3.0 | 1.6 | 3.8 | 2.2 |
| Total Assets Turnover (times) | 0.8 | 0.9 | 0.9 | 1.4 | 0.9 |
| Profit Margin before Taxes (%) | 6.3 | 19.9 | 5.6 | 2.9 | 1.1 |
| Return on Assets before Taxes (%) | 5.6 | 17.0 | 4.9 | 4.2 | 1.5 |
| Return on Assets after Taxes (%) | 4.0 | 12.8 | 4.1 | 3.0 | 1.0 |
| Return on Equity before Taxes (%) | 12.8 | 35.5 | 11.6 | 11.9 | 3.9 |
| Return on Equity after Taxes (%) | 9.2 | 26.7 | 9.7 | 8.3 | 2.4 |

*Financial Ratios by Industry (cont'd)*

| Financial Ratios | Primary Metal Industries | Iron, Steel | Nonferrous Metals | Fabricated Metal Products | Machinery, Except Electrical |
|---|---|---|---|---|---|
| Current Ratio | 1.7 | 1.7 | 1.6 | 1.9 | 1.7 |
| Quick Ratio | 1.0 | 0.9 | 1.0 | 1.1 | 1.0 |
| Long-term Debt to Equity (%) | 88.3 | 171.4 | 63.3 | 61.5 | 41.1 |
| Total Liabilities to Total Assets (%) | 70.8 | 83.7 | 60.4 | 58.9 | 53.2 |
| Total Liabilities to Equity (%) | 245.5 | 544.6 | 154.7 | 143.6 | 115.0 |
| Fixed Assets to Equity (%) | 148.4 | 285.6 | 107.0 | 69.4 | 51.2 |
| Current to Total Liabilities (%) | 32.8 | 30.3 | 35.7 | 46.2 | 49.6 |
| Cash Flow to Total Assets (%) | 6.0 | 4.4 | 7.2 | 8.5 | 5.2 |
| Short-term Debt to Total Assets (%) | 5.0 | 4.2 | 5.6 | 7.1 | 6.2 |
| Long-term Debt to Total Assets (%) | 25.5 | 26.3 | 24.7 | 25.2 | 19.1 |
| Equity to Total Assets (%) | 29.0 | 15.9 | 39.4 | 41.1 | 46.7 |
| Average Collection Period (days) | 46.6 | 44.9 | 48.0 | 51.6 | 62.8 |
| Inventory Turnover (times) | 7.0 | 6.3 | 7.7 | 6.7 | 6.1 |
| Fixed Assets Turnover (times) | 2.7 | 2.7 | 2.6 | 5.0 | 4.2 |
| Total Assets Turnover (times) | 1.1 | 1.2 | 1.1 | 1.4 | 1.0 |
| Profit Margin before Taxes (%) | 1.6 | 0.2 | 2.7 | 4.5 | 1.1 |
| Return on Assets before Taxes (%) | 2.2 | 0.6 | 3.5 | 6.3 | 1.1 |
| Return on Assets after Taxes (%) | 1.6 | 0.1 | 2.8 | 4.4 | 0.6 |
| Return on Equity before Taxes (%) | 6.0 | -0.1 | 7.3 | 15.4 | 1.5 |
| Return on Equity after Taxes (%) | 4.4 | -2.1 | 6.0 | 10.6 | 0.6 |

| Financial Ratios | Electrical, Electronic Equipment | Transportation Equipment | Motor Vehicles, Equipment | Aircraft, Guided Missiles, Parts | Instruments, Related Products |
|---|---|---|---|---|---|
| Current Ratio | 1.4 | 1.3 | 1.3 | 1.2 | 1.6 |
| Quick Ratio | 0.8 | 0.7 | 1.0 | 0.4 | 1.0 |
| Long-term Debt to Equity (%) | 36.5 | 59.8 | 62.6 | 54.5 | 49.3 |
| Total Liabilities to Total Assets (%) | 56.4 | 73.1 | 72.6 | 72.9 | 55.3 |
| Total Liabilities to Equity (%) | 129.3 | 289.5 | 315.0 | 270.5 | 123.8 |
| Fixed Assets to Equity (%) | 50.8 | 96.5 | 114.6 | 74.7 | 55.3 |
| Current to Total Liabilities (%) | 58.5 | 48.7 | 37.2 | 65.6 | 42.9 |
| Cash Flow to Total Assets (%) | 7.9 | 3.5 | 2.0 | 5.5 | 9.1 |
| Short-term Debt to Total Assets (%) | 9.3 | 3.3 | 3.0 | 3.4 | 5.9 |
| Long-term Debt to Total Assets (%) | 15.9 | 15.2 | 15.0 | 14.6 | 22.0 |
| Equity to Total Assets (%) | 43.6 | 26.1 | 25.3 | 27.0 | 44.7 |
| Average Collection Period (days) | 56.9 | 52.3 | 50.9 | 50.6 | 59.9 |
| Inventory Turnover (times) | 5.7 | 5.4 | 13.2 | 2.7 | 6.0 |
| Fixed Assets Turnover (times) | 4.8 | 4.4 | 4.1 | 5.0 | 3.6 |
| Total Assets Turnover (times) | 1.1 | 1.1 | 1.1 | 1.0 | 0.9 |
| Profit Margin before Taxes (%) | 5.4 | -1.4 | -4.9 | 3.3 | 7.6 |
| Return on Assets before Taxes (%) | 5.8 | -1.1 | -4.5 | 3.3 | 6.8 |
| Return on Assets after Taxes (%) | 3.9 | -0.6 | -2.7 | 2.2 | 5.2 |
| Return on Equity before Taxes (%) | 13.2 | -7.6 | -23.9 | 11.1 | 14.6 |
| Return on Equity after Taxes (%) | 8.9 | -4.5 | -15.1 | 7.3 | 11.3 |

*The financial ratios presented here are based on consistent, seasonally adjusted time series. Source data for the series are published in the Census Bureau's* Quarterly Financial Report. *Corporations are classified in accordance with the* Standard Industrial Classification Manual, *1987. All corporations included in the report receive a greater portion of gross receipts from manufacturing than from other activities; final industry classification is determined by the major source of receipts within the manufacturing sector.*

*Financial Ratios by Industry (cont'd)*

In the calculations on the preceding pages, the federal government uses the following formulas. These formulas are valuable in evaluating the financial reports of any business.

## Formulas for Financial Ratios

*Current Ratio*
Current assets/current liabilities. Measures short-term solvency.

*Quick Ratio*
Current assets less inventories/current liabilities. Measures short-term solvency.

*Long-term Debt to Equity*
Long-term debt/stockholders' equity. Measures the relationship of long-term debt to equity financing.

*Liabilities to Assets*
Total liabilities/total assets. Measures the proportion of assets provided by creditors, or the extent of leverage.

*Liabilities to Equity*
Total liabilities/stockholders' equity. Measures the relationship of debt to equity financing.

*Fixed Assets to Equity*
Net property, plant and equipment/stockholders' equity. Indicates the relative investment in operational assets.

*Current to Total Liabilities*
Current liabilities/total liabilities. Indicates reliance on short-term as opposed to long-term debt.

*Cash Flow to Total Assets*
Net income after tax plus depreciation/total assets. Measures cash flow relative to assets.

*Short-term Debt to Total Assets*
Short-term debt/total assets. Indicates the reliance on short-term debt to support the asset structure.

*Long-term Debt to Total Assets*
Long-term debt/total assets. Indicates the reliance on long-term debt to support the asset structure.

*Equity to Total Assets*
Stockholders' equity/total assets. Measures the stockholders' share of total assets.

*Average Collection Period*
Accounts receivable/sales per day. Indicates the relative level and quality of accounts receivable.

*Inventory Turnover*
Net sales/inventory. Measures the relative efficiency of the use of inventory investment.

*Fixed Assets Turnover*
Net sales/net property, plant and equipment. Measures the relative efficiency of the use of property, plant and equipment.

*Total Assets Turnover*
Net sales/total assets. Measures the relative efficiency of the use of all assets.

*Profit Margin*
Net income/net sales. Measures the percent of profit per sales dollar.

*Return on Assets*
Net income/total assets. Measures the return on total investment.

*Return on Equity*
Net income/stockholders' equity. Measures the return on stockholders' share of total investment.

Source: U.S. Department of Commerce, Office of Business Analysis

---

## The Top Reference Sources

*The American Almanac*
The Reference Press, $14.95
(800) 486-8666

This reference book is based on the *Statistical Abstract of the United States*, which is compiled annually by the Bureau of the Census and published by the U.S. Government Printing Office.

*The American Almanac* contains standard summary statistics on the social, political, and economic organization of the United States, from college enrollment to crop production to population growth rates. This handsome paperback volume is perhaps more reader-friendly than the *Statistical Abstract* and is also available in trade bookstores.

# The Individual Investor

MORE SO THAN IN ANY BULL MARKET in history, individuals were active participants in the 1980s stock surge: between 1980 and mid-1990, the number of individual households investing in the stock market jumped more than 50 percent.

## NYSE Individual Shareholders (thousands)

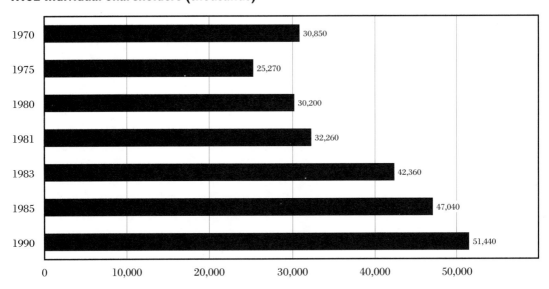

| Year | Value |
|------|-------|
| 1970 | 30,850 |
| 1975 | 25,270 |
| 1980 | 30,200 |
| 1981 | 32,260 |
| 1983 | 42,360 |
| 1985 | 47,040 |
| 1990 | 51,440 |

## NYSE Individual Shareholders by Profession (thousands)

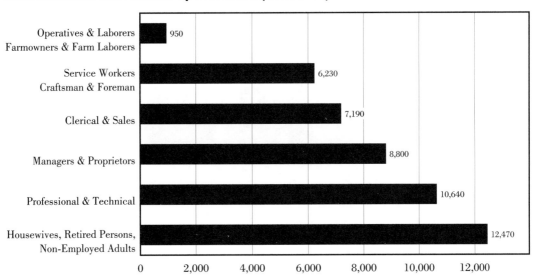

|  |  |
|------------|-------|
| Operatives & Laborers / Farmowners & Farm Laborers | 950 |
| Service Workers / Craftsman & Foreman | 6,230 |
| Clerical & Sales | 7,190 |
| Managers & Proprietors | 8,800 |
| Professional & Technical | 10,640 |
| Housewives, Retired Persons, Non-Employed Adults | 12,470 |

*Source: New York Stock Exchange Fact Book, 1992*

*The Individual Investor (cont'd)*

## NYSE Shareholders by Age

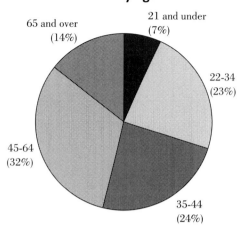

## NYSE Shareholders by Education

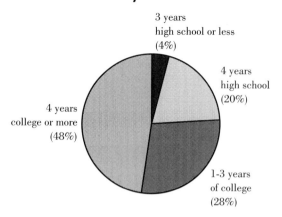

## NYSE Shareholders by Portfolio Size ($)

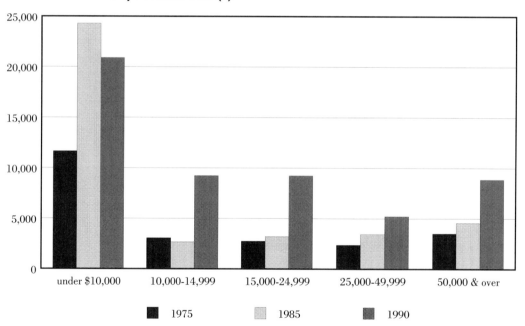

*Source: New York Stock Exchange Fact Book, 1992*

*The Individual Investor (cont'd)*

## NYSE Shareholders by Metropolitan Region (thousands)

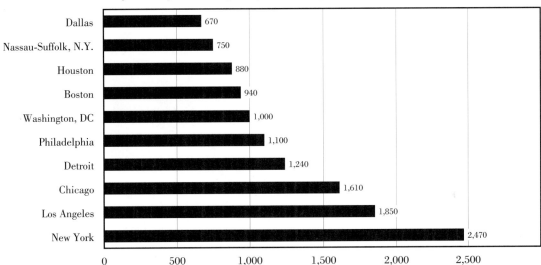

Dallas — 670
Nassau-Suffolk, N.Y. — 750
Houston — 880
Boston — 940
Washington, DC — 1,000
Philadelphia — 1,100
Detroit — 1,240
Chicago — 1,610
Los Angeles — 1,850
New York — 2,470

*Source: New York Stock Exchange Fact Book, 1992*

# The Institutional Investor

## Mutual Fund and Equity Assets of Private Pension Funds, 1977 to 1993

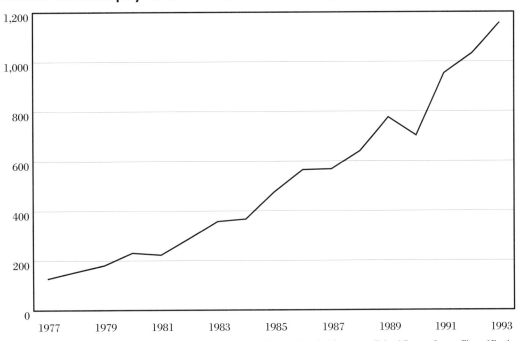

*Source: Board of Governors, Federal Reserve System Flow of Funds*

# The Top Stock Analysts

## Stock Research Departments Ranked

| Rank | Stock Analyst |
|------|---------------|
| 1 | Lehman Brothers |
| 2 | Merrill Lynch |
| 3 | Donaldson, Lufkin & Jenrette |
| 4 | Goldman Sachs |
| 5 | Morgan Stanley |
| 6 | CS First Boston |

| Rank | Stock Analyst |
|------|---------------|
| 7 | Smith Barney Shearson |
| 8 | PaineWebber |
| 9 | Salomon Brothers |
| 10 | Kidder Peabody |
| 10* | Prudential |

*tie*

## The Best Analysts: Stock Pickers

| Name | Industry | Firm |
|------|----------|------|
| Michelle Galanter Applebaum | Steel | Salomon Brothers |
| R. Wayne Atwell | Steel | Morgan Stanley |
| Gary Black | Tobacco | Sanford C. Bernstein |
| Thomas Brown | Banks/regional | DLJ |
| Steven Eisenberg | Gaming & lodging | Oppenheimer & Co. |
| Stephen Girsky | Tire & rubber | PaineWebber |
| Mark Hassenberg | Electrical/consumer | DLJ |
| Dennis Leibowitz | Broadcasting | DLJ |
| Robert Reitzes | Chemicals/major | C.J. Lawrence |
| Scott Smith | Info. tech./software | DLJ |

## The Best Analysts: Written Reports

| Name | Industry | Firm |
|------|----------|------|
| Gary Black | Tobacco | Sanford C. Bernstein |
| Thomas Driscoll | Oil/exploration | Salomon Brothers |
| Joseph Ellis | Retailing/specialty | Goldman Sachs |
| Jonathan Gray | Government sponsored enterprises | Sanford C. Bernstein |
| Thomas Hanley | Banks/money center | CS First Boston |
| Daniel Lemaitre | Medical supplies & technology | Cowen & Co. |
| Ernest Liu | Utilities | Goldman Sachs |
| Peter Marcus | Steel | PaineWebber |
| John Tumazos | Gold mining | DLJ |
| William Young | Chemicals/major | DLJ |

*Source: Institutional Investor, 1993 All-American Research Team*

## The Top Reference Sources

*Standard & Poor's Register of Corporations, Directors and Executives*
Standard & Poor's, $595/year
(212) 208-8702

Published since 1928, this annual, three-volume reference provides information on the nation's major corporations and their key staff.

Volume 1 profiles more than 55,000 corporations in alphabetical order. Volume 2 gives brief biographies of directors and executives. Volume 3 contains indexes by geography and industry, among others. Supplements are published in April, July, and October.

*The Top Stock Analysts (cont'd)*

## The Best Analysts: Overall Service

| Name | Industry | Firm |
| --- | --- | --- |
| Douglas Augenthaler | Pollution control | Oppenheimer & Co. |
| Marc D. Cohen | Coal | Kidder Peabody |
| Laura Conigliaro | Info. tech./mid. sys. | Prudential |
| Thomas Driscoll | Oil/exploration | Salomon Brothers |
| Daniel Mandresh | Info. tech./large sys. | Merrill Lynch |
| J. Clarence Morrison | Nonferrous metals | Prudential |
| Steven Parla | Natural gas | CS First Boston |
| Eric Philo | Publishing | Goldman Sachs |
| Daniel Roling | Coal | Merrill Lynch |
| Linda Runyon | Cellular | Merril Lynch |

*Source: Institutional Investor, 1993 All-American Research Team*

## The All-Star Research Team

| Industry | Name | Firm |
| --- | --- | --- |
| Advertising Agencies | Susan Decker | DLJ |
| Aerospace | Cai von Romohr | Cowen & Co. |
| Airlines | Paul Karas | CS First Boston |
| Autos & Auto Parts | Stephen Girsky | PaineWebber |
| Banks & Money Center | Thomas Hanley | First Boston |
| Banks/Regional | Thomas Brown | DLJ |
| Beverages | Emanuel Goldman | PaineWebber |
| Biotechnology | Teena Lerner | Lehman Bros. |
| Broadcasting | Dennis Leibowitz | DLJ |
| Building | Gregory Nejmeh | Lehman Bros. |
| Cellular | Dennis Leibowitz | DLJ |
| Chemicals/Fertilizers | Charles LoCastro | DLJ |
| Chemicals/Major | William Young | DLJ |
| Chemicals/Specialty | Katharine Plourde | DLJ |
| Coal | Joel Price | DLJ |
| Cosmetics | Joseph Kozloff | Smith Barney Shearson |
| Defense Electronics | Elliott Rogers | Cowen & Co. |
| Electrical/Consumer | Robert Cornell | Lehman Bros. |
| Electrical/Equipment | David Altman | Goldman Sachs |
| Electronics | James Barlage | Smith Barney Shearson |
| Electronics/Connectors | Mark Hassenberg | DLJ |
| Engineering & Construction | Jeanne Gallagher Terrile | Merrill Lynch |
| Financial Services | Lawrence Eckenfelder | Prudential Secutities |
| Food | Nomi Ghez | Goldman Sachs |
| Gaming & Lodging | Steven Eisenberg | Oppenheimer |
| Gold Mining | John Tumazos | DLJ |
| Government Sponsored Enterprises | Eric Hemel | Morgan Stanley |
| Health Care Services | Kenneth Abramowitz | Sanford C. Bernstein |
| Household Products | Jack Salzman | Goldman Sachs |
| Information Technology/Large Systems | Steven Milunovich | Morgan Stanley |
| Information Technology/Midrange Systems | Laura Conigliaro | Prudential Securities |
| Information Technology/Small Systems | David Korus | Kidder Peabody |
| Information Technology/Software & Computer Services | Richard Sherlund | Goldman Sachs |
| Insurance/Life | Margaret Alexandre | Salomon Bros. |
| Insurance/Nonlife | David Seifer | DLJ |

*The Top Stock Analysts (cont'd)*

| Industry | Name | Firm |
|---|---|---|
| Leisure Time | Harold Vogel | Merrill Lynch |
| Machinery | Mitchell Quain | Wertheim Schrader |
| Medical Supplies/Technology | Daniel Lemaitre | Cowen & Co. |
| Natural Gas | Curt Launer | DLJ |
| Nonferrous Metals | John Tumazos | DLJ |
| Oil/Domestic | Frank Kneuttel | Prudential Securities |
| Oil/Exploration | Thomas Driscoll | |
| Oil/International | Bryan Jacobski | Paine Webber |
| Oil/Services & Equipment | James Carroll | Paine Webber |
| Packaging | Timothy Burns | CS First Boston |
| Paper & Forest Products | Richard Schneider | Kidder Peabody |
| Pharmaceuticals | Jerome Brimeyer | Lehman Brothers |
| Photography & Electronic Imaging | B. Alexander Henderson | Prudential Securities |
| Pollution Control | Marc Sulam | Kidder Peabody |
| Publishing | Kevin Gruneich | CS First Boston |
| Railroads | Joel Price | DLJ |
| Restaurants | John Rohs | Wertheim Schroder |
| Retailing/Broadlines | Joseph Ellis | Goldman Sachs |
| Retailing/Food and Drug Chains | Debra Levin | Morgan Stanley |
| Retailing/Specialty | Donald Trott | Dean Witter Reynolds |
| Savings & Loans | Jerry Gitt | Merrill Lynch |
| Steel | Michelle Galanter Applebaum | Salomon Bros. |
| Telecommunications/Equipment & Networking | Joseph Bellace | Merrill Lynch |
| Telecommunications/Services | Robert Morris III | Goldman Sachs |
| Textiles & Apparel | Deborah Bronston | Prudential Securities |
| Tire & Rubber | Steven Girski | PaineWebber |
| Tobacco | Gary Black | Sanford C. Bernstein |
| Trucking | Craig Kloner | Goldman Sachs |
| Utilities | Ernest Liu | Goldman Sachs |

*Source: Institutional Investor, 1993 All-American Research Team*

## The Top Reference Sources

*Institutional Investor*, $375/year
88 Madison Ave.
New York, NY 10022
(212) 303-3300

Published monthly, this magazine is edited for the investor and consumer interested in the current state of the national and international investment world. The magazine focuses on the role of major corporations in high finance through analysis of international banking and business deals. It also features corporate profiles and commentaries on general market trends.

*Institutional Investor* is well known for its annual rankings issues which include the largest employee benefit pension funds, the top money managers, and the well-known "*Institutional Investor*'s All-Star Stock Analyst Team."

# Corporate Activity

## Announced U.S. Mergers and Acquisitions

| Announcement Date | Value ($ mil.) | Market Share | # of Deals | Fees ($ mil.) |
|---|---|---|---|---|
| 1982 | 56,035.1 | 2.4 | 1,932 | NA |
| 1983 | 96,222.7 | 4.2 | 3,387 | NA |
| 1984 | 169,528.9 | 7.3 | 3,621 | 6.9 |
| 1985 | 186,943.5 | 8.1 | ,2257 | 437.4 |
| 1986 | 212,951.6 | 9.2 | 3,142 | 879.3 |
| 1987 | 208,961.9 | 9.1 | ,3324 | 877.9 |
| 1988 | 335,836.9 | 14.5 | ,3922 | 1,580.4 |
| 1989 | 293,199.8 | 12.7 | 5,467 | 946.2 |
| 1990 | 178,938.5 | 7.8 | 5,667 | 402.1 |
| 1991 | 137,299.6 | 5.9 | 5,287 | 289.4 |
| 1992 | 152,455.2 | 6.6 | 5,545 | 265.7 |
| 1993 | 239,059.8 | 10.4 | 6,352 | 287.0 |
| INDUSTRY TOTALS | 2,267,433.5 | 98.2 | 49,903 | 5,972.3 |

## The Ten Largest Completed U.S. Merger & Acquisition Deals, 1984 to 1992

| Date Effective | Acquirer Name | Target Name | Attitude | Value ($ millions) |
|---|---|---|---|---|
| 04/28/89 | Kohlberg Kravis Roberts & Co. | RJR Nabisco | Hostile | 30,598.8 |
| 01/10/90 | Time | Warner Communications | Friendly | 14,110.0 |
| 12/07/88 | Philip Morris | Kraft | Poison Pill | 13,444.0 |
| 06/15/84 | Standard Oil of California | Gulf Oil | Friendly | 13,400.0 |
| 10/04/89 | Bristol Myers | Squibb | Friendly | 12,094.0 |
| 02/17/84 | Texaco | Getty Oil | Friendly | 10,120.0 |
| 07/26/89 | Beecham Group PLC | SmithKline Beckman Group | Friendly | 7,922.0 |
| 09/19/91 | AT&T | NCR | Hostile | 7,893.4 |
| 07/07/87 | BP America | The Standard Oil | Friendly | 7,857.7 |
| 01/03/91 | Matsushita Electric Industrial | MCA | Friendly | 7,406.0 |

## Ten Largest U.S. Merger and Acquisition Deals Completed in 1993

| Date Effective | Acquirer Name | Target Name | Attitude | Value ($ millions) |
|---|---|---|---|---|
| 11/18/93 | Merck & Co | Medco Containment Services | Friendly | 6,225.7 |
| 07/13/93 | Shareholders | Dean Witter Discover & Co | NA | 5,021.0 |
| 09/01/93 | Columbia Hospital | Galen Health Care | Friendly | 4,187.7 |
| 03/09/93 | Sprint | Centel | Friendly | 3,967.0 |
| 12/31/93 | Primerica | Travelers | Friendly | 3,955.9 |
| 10/01/93 | Hanson PLC | Quantum Chemical | Friendly | 3,219.7 |
| 04/02/93 | Martin Marietta | General Electric Aerospace | Friendly | 3,050.0 |
| 10/12/93 | Shareholders | Marriott International | NA | 2,739.6 |
| 11/15/93 | Cyprus Minerals | AMAX | Friendly | 2,657.0 |
| 12/31/93 | Entergy | Gulf States Utilities | Friendly | 2,281.0 |

*Source: Securities Data Company*

*Corporate Activity (cont'd)*

## Announced U.S. LBOs

| Announcement Date | Value ($ mil.) | Market Share | No. of Deals | Fees ($ mil.) |
|---|---|---|---|---|
| 1982 | 2,343.8 | 0.8 | 22 | NA |
| 1983 | 9,191.9 | 3.0 | 62 | NA |
| 1984 | 13,810.4 | 4.5 | 122 | 1.0 |
| 1985 | 28,055.1 | 9.1 | 168 | 140.0 |
| 1986 | 39,211.1 | 12.7 | 254 | 316.8 |
| 1987 | 48,489.2 | 15.7 | 245 | 320.0 |
| 1988 | 93,884.2 | 30.5 | 324 | 691.1 |
| 1989 | 35,551.5 | 11.5 | 342 | 222.3 |
| 1990 | 12,357.7 | 4.0 | 213 | 38.4 |
| 1991 | 5,888.8 | 1.9 | 223 | 1.0 |
| 1992 | 10,438.0 | 3.4 | 252 | 1.9 |
| 1993 | 9,040.4 | 2.9 | 205 | 2.0 |
| INDUSTRY TOTALS | 308,262.1 | 100.0 | 2,432 | 1,734.4 |

## Announced U.S. Divestitures

| Announcement Date | Value ($ mil.) | Market Share | No. of Deals | Fees ($ mil.) |
|---|---|---|---|---|
| 1982 | 11,622.2 | 1.4 | 442 | NA |
| 1983 | 33,511.8 | 4.0 | 1,038 | NA |
| 1984 | 49,463.6 | 6.0 | 1,140 | 4.2 |
| 1985 | 57,537.2 | 6.9 | 929 | 10.2 |
| 1986 | 79,701.0 | 9.6 | 1,216 | 57.0 |
| 1987 | 83,542.7 | 10.1 | 1,142 | 92.1 |
| 1988 | 120,773.4 | 14.5 | 1,452 | 84.3 |
| 1989 | 102,028.4 | 12.3 | 2,087 | 6.6 |
| 1990 | 78,754.4 | 9.5 | 2,259 | 27.7 |
| 1991 | 57,437.8 | 6.9 | 2,204 | 7.1 |
| 1992 | 78,307.1 | 9.4 | 2,111 | 28.3 |
| 1993 | 77,534.3 | 9.3 | 2,403 | 12.5 |
| INDUSTRY TOTALS | 830,214.0 | 100.0 | 18,423 | 330.0 |

*Source: Securities Data Company*

## S&P 500 Company Activity

| Activity | 1989 | 1990 | 1991 | 1992 |
|---|---|---|---|---|
| Mergers and acquisitions among companies in the index | 10 | 8 | 6 | 2 |
| Acquisition by company outside the index | 15 | 2 | 2 | 0 |
| Restructurings | 4 | 2 | 1 | 3 |
| Bankruptcies | 0 | 2 | 3 | 1 |
| TOTAL NUMBER OF COMPANY CHANGES | 29 | 14 | 12 | 6 |

*Source: S&P 500 Directory, 1993*

# Securities and Exchange Commission

THE SECURITIES AND EXCHANGE Commission is the independent, non-partisan, federal agency which administers U.S. laws that provide protection for investors. The SEC was created under the Securities Exchange Act of 1934 to ensure that securities markets are fair and honest. In addition, the SEC acts as an advisor to federal courts in corporate reorganizations proceedings under Chapter 11 of the Bankruptcy Reform Act of 1978. The Commission is composed of five members: a Chairman and four Commissioners. Commission members are appointed by the President, with the advice and consent of the Senate, for five-year terms and the Chairman is designated by the President. Terms are staggered; one expires on June 5th of every year. Not more than three members may be of the same political party.

The Commission meets to deliberate on and resolve issues such as interpretations of federal securities laws, amendments to existing rules under the laws, new rules (often to reflect changed conditions in the marketplace), actions to enforce the laws or to discipline those subject to direct regulation, legislation to be proposed by the Commission, and matters concerning administration of the Commission itself. The Commission staff is organized into divisions including the following:

- The Division of Corporation Finance, which ensures that disclosure requirements are met by publicly held companies registered with the Commission.

- The Division of Market Regulation, which is responsible for overseeing the activity in the secondary markets—registration and regulation of broker-dealers, and supervising self-regulatory organizations (such as the nation's stock exchanges). In addition, the division monitors the activities of other participants in the secondary market, including trading and sales practices, and policies affecting the operating of the securities markets.

- The Division of Investment Management, which ensures compliance with regulations regarding the registration, financial responsibility, sales practices and advertising of mutual funds and of investment advisers. The division's Office of Public Utility Regulation oversees the activities of the 12 active registered holding company systems.

- The Division of Enforcement, which supervises the enforcement of federal securities laws and investigates possible violations of these laws and recommends appropriate remedies for consideration by the Commission.

For public information on the U.S. Securities and Exchange Commission the interested individual can write to:

U.S. Securities and Exchange Commission
450 Fifth St., NW
Washington, DC 20549
(202) 272-3100 (information line)
(202) 272-7460 (publications of SEC educational and informative materials)

Government Printing Office (to order the SEC Annual Report, $5)
(202) 783-3238

## Regional Offices of the SEC

Atlanta Regional Office
3475 Lenox Rd., NE, Suite 1000
Atlanta, GA 30326
(404) 842-7600

Boston Regional Office
John W. McCormack Post Office and Courthouse Building
90 Devonshire St., Suite 700
Boston, MA 02109
(617) 223-9900

Chicago Regional Office
Northwestern Atrium Center
500 W. Madison St., Suite 1400
Chicago, IL 60661
(312) 353-7390

Denver Regional Office
1801 California St., Suite 4800
Denver, CO 80202
(303) 330-6800

Fort Worth Regional Office
411 W. Seventh St., 8th Floor
Fort Worth, TX 76102
(817) 334-3821

Los Angeles Regional Office
5757 Wilshire Blvd., Suite 500 E
Los Angeles, CA 90036
(213) 965-3998

Miami Branch Office
1401 Brickell Ave., Suite 200
Miami, FL 33131
(305) 536-5765

New York Regional Office
75 Park Place, 14th Floor
New York, NY 10007
(212) 264-1636

Philadelphia Regional Office
The Curtis Center, Suite 1005 E
601 Walnut St.
Philadelphia, PA 19106
(215) 597-3100

*Securities and Exchange Commission (cont'd)*

Salt Lake City Branch Office
500 Key Bank Tower
50 S. Main St., Suite 500
Salt Lake City, UT 84144
(801) 524-5796

San Francisco Branch Office
901 Market St., Suite 470
San Francisco, CA 94103
(415) 744-3140

Seattle Regional Office
3040 Jackson Federal Building
915 Second Ave.
Seattle, WA 98174
(206) 442-7990

## Full Disclosure Reviews: Corporate Filings

| Major Filing Review | 1988 | 1989 | 1990 | 1991 | 1992 |
|---|---|---|---|---|---|
| SECURITIES ACT REGISTRATIONS | | | | | |
| New Issuers | 1,444 | 1,177 | 895 | 630 | 831 |
| Repeat Issuers | 640 | 604 | 635 | 776 | 970 |
| Post-Effective Amendments | 1,045 | 929 | 708 | 583 | 347 |
| ANNUAL REPORTS | | | | | |
| Full Reviews | 2,166 | 1,949 | 1,129 | 1,557 | 1,450 |
| Full Financial Reviews | 567 | 388 | 292 | 712 | 1,126 |
| Tender Offers (14D-1) | 254 | 188 | 95 | 37 | 27 |
| Going Private Schedules | 276 | 176 | 108 | 68 | 61 |
| Contested Proxy Solicitations | 93 | 84 | 75 | 65 | 58 |
| MERGER/GOING PRIVATE | | | | | |
| Proxy Statements | 314 | 291 | 240 | 188 | 141 |
| Other | 790 | 428 | 351 | 374 | 395 |

## SEC Total Enforcement Actions Initiated

| Type of Action | 1988 | 1989 | 1990 | 1991 | 1992 |
|---|---|---|---|---|---|
| TOTAL | 252 | 310 | 304 | 320 | 394 |
| Civil Injunctive Actions | 125 | 140 | 186 | 171 | 156 |
| Administrative Proceedings | 109 | 155 | 111 | 138 | 226 |
| Civil and Criminal Contempt Proceedings | 17 | 15 | 7 | 10 | 11 |
| Reports of Investigation | 1 | 0 | 0 | 1 | 1 |

*Source: U.S. Securities and Exchange Commission, Annual Report, 1992*

## The Top Reference Sources

*Moody's Industrial Manual*
Moody's Investors Service, $1,475/year
(800) 342-5647, ext. 0435

Moody's annual bound volume of their twice-weekly publication covers U.S., Canadian, and foreign companies listed on U.S. exchanges.

The listings include corporate history, subsidiaries, principal facilities, products, and financial data.

An excellent resource for broad background data on a wide array of companies.

*Securities and Exchange Commission (cont'd)*

## Enforcement Cases Initiated by the SEC: By Program Area and Percentage

| Program Area in Which a Civil Action or Administrative Proceeding Was Initiated | Total | % of Total Cases |
|---|---|---|
| SECURITIES OFFERING CASES | | 23 |
| Non-Regulated Entity | 41 | |
| Regulated Entity | 49 | |
| TOTAL | 90 | |
| BROKER-DEALER CASES | | 22 |
| Back Office | 10 | |
| Fraud Against Consumer | 41 | |
| Failure to Supervise | 2 | |
| Government Securities | 6 | |
| Other | 15 | |
| TOTAL | 74 | |
| ISSUER FINANCIAL STATEMENT AND REPORTING CASES | | 14 |
| Issuer Financial Disclosure | 58 | |
| Issuer Reporting Other | 9 | |
| Issuer Related Party Transactions | 3 | |
| TOTAL | 70 | |
| Insider Trading Cases | 32 | 8 |
| Market Manipulation Cases | 41 | 10 |
| OTHER REGULATED ENTITY CASES | | |
| Investment Advisors | 39 | |
| Investment Companies | 5 | |
| Total Other Regulated Entity Cases | 52 | 13 |
| Contempt Proceedings | 11 | 2 |
| Corporate Control Cases | 9 | 2 |
| Fraud Against Regulated Entities | 4 | 1 |
| DELINQUENT FILINGS | | |
| Issuer Reporting | 4 | |
| Forms 3 & 4 | 7 | |
| Total Delinquent Filing Cases | 11 | 3 |
| GRAND TOTAL | 449 | 98 |

*Note: The percentages add up to more than 100 due to the rounding of figures.*

## SEC Litigation and Legal Activities: Increase in Matters Handled, 1991 to 1992

| Action Taken | 1991 | 1992 | % Increase |
|---|---|---|---|
| Litigation Matters Opened | 263 | 264 | 0 |
| Litigation Matters Closed | 247 | 267 | 8 |
| Adjudication | | | |
| Cases Received | 30 | 56 | 87 |
| Cases Completed | 39 | 52 | 33 |
| Legislation | | | |
| Testimony | 29 | 16 | -45 |
| Comments to Congress and Others | 29 | 64 | 120 |
| Ethics Matters | 249 | 247 | 1 |

*Source: U.S. Securities and Exchange Commission, Annual Report, 1992*

# Bonds

BONDS ARE LONG-TERM debt obligations issued typically in $1,000 or $5,000 denominations by companies, governments (including the U.S. Treasury), municipalities, or federal agencies. The interest paid on these loans—the coupon or coupon rate—depends upon the amount of risk assumed by the buyer, the loan's backing, and the overall economic climate at the time of issuance. The range of rates offered at any given time is determined in relation to benchmark interest rates set by the U.S. Federal Reserve. But from the date of issuance, a bond's rate of interest remains fixed until maturity. While the prime interest rate may greatly fluctuate over the term of the bond, the rate of interest on the bond remains the same, providing a sure, steady source of income.

The term, repayment schedule, and security of bonds vary widely depending upon the financial needs of the issuer and the bond's intended use, as well as by the type of issuance.

## Interest and Bond Yields, 1981 to 1994

| Period | U.S. Treasury 3-Month Bills | U.S. Treasury 3-yr. Maturity | U.S. Treasury 10-yr. Maturity | High-Grade Muni Bonds | Corp. AAA Bonds | Prime Comm'l Paper | Discount Rate | Prime Rate | New-Home Mortge. Yields |
|---|---|---|---|---|---|---|---|---|---|
| 1981 | 14.03 | 14.44 | 13.91 | 11.23 | 14.17 | 14.76 | 13.42 | 18.87 | 14.70 |
| 1982 | 10.69 | 12.92 | 13.00 | 11.57 | 13.79 | 11.89 | 11.02 | 14.86 | 15.14 |
| 1983 | 8.63 | 10.45 | 11.10 | 9.47 | 12.04 | 8.89 | 8.50 | 10.79 | 12.57 |
| 1984 | 9.58 | 11.89 | 12.44 | 10.15 | 12.71 | 10.16 | 8.80 | 12.04 | 12.38 |
| 1985 | 7.48 | 9.64 | 10.62 | 9.18 | 11.37 | 8.01 | 7.69 | 9.93 | 11.55 |
| 1986 | 5.98 | 7.06 | 7.68 | 7.38 | 9.02 | 6.39 | 6.33 | 8.33 | 10.17 |
| 1987 | 5.82 | 7.68 | 8.39 | 7.73 | 9.38 | 6.85 | 5.66 | 8.21 | 9.31 |
| 1988 | 6.69 | 8.26 | 8.85 | 7.76 | 9.71 | 7.68 | 6.20 | 9.32 | 9.19 |
| 1989 | 8.12 | 8.55 | 8.49 | 7.24 | 9.26 | 8.80 | 6.93 | 10.87 | 10.13 |
| 1990 | 7.51 | 8.26 | 8.55 | 7.25 | 9.32 | 7.95 | 6.98 | 10.01 | 10.05 |
| 1991 | 5.42 | 6.82 | 7.86 | 6.89 | 8.77 | 5.85 | 5.45 | 8.46 | 9.32 |
| 1992 | 3.45 | 5.80 | 7.01 | 6.41 | 8.14 | 3.80 | 3.25 | 6.25 | 8.24 |
| 1993 | 3.02 | 4.44 | 5.87 | 5.63 | 7.22 | 3.30 | 3.00 | 6.00 | 7.20 |
| Mar | 2.97 | 4.40 | 5.98 | 5.65 | 7.58 | 3.24 | 3.00 | 6.00 | 7.46 |
| Apr | 2.89 | 4.30 | 5.97 | 5.78 | 7.46 | 3.19 | 3.00 | 6.00 | 7.46 |
| May | 2.96 | 4.40 | 6.04 | 5.81 | 7.43 | 3.20 | 3.00 | 6.00 | 7.37 |
| June | 3.10 | 4.53 | 5.96 | 5.78 | 7.33 | 3.38 | 3.00 | 6.00 | 7.23 |
| July | 3.05 | 4.43 | 5.81 | 5.60 | 7.17 | 3.35 | 3.00 | 6.00 | 7.20 |
| Aug | 3.05 | 4.36 | 5.68 | 5.50 | 6.85 | 3.33 | 3.00 | 6.00 | 7.05 |
| Sept | 2.96 | 4.17 | 5.36 | 5.31 | 6.66 | 3.25 | 3.00 | 6.00 | 6.95 |
| Oct | 3.04 | 4.18 | 5.33 | 5.29 | 6.67 | 3.27 | 3.00 | 6.00 | 6.80 |
| Nov | 3.12 | 4.50 | 5.72 | 5.47 | 6.93 | 3.43 | 3.00 | 6.00 | 6.80 |
| Dec | 3.08 | 4.54 | 5.77 | 5.35 | 6.93 | 3.40 | 3.00 | 6.00 | 6.92 |
| 1994 | | | | | | | | | |
| Jan | 3.02 | 4.48 | 5.75 | 5.30 | 6.92 | 3.30 | 3.00 | 6.00 | 6.95 |
| Feb | 3.21 | 4.83 | 5.97 | 5.44 | 7.08 | 3.62 | 3.00 | 6.00 | 6.85 |
| Mar | 3.52 | 5.40 | 6.48 | 5.93 | 7.48 | 4.08 | 3.00 | 6.25 | NA |

*Source: Economic Indicators, The Council of Economic Advisers*

# Corporate and Taxable Bonds

CORPORATIONS ISSUE VARIOUS types of debt securities to fund their operations and investments. Their short-term needs are filled by the issuance of commercial paper which can be bought only in $100,000 denominations with a maturity of 90 to 180 days. For the longer term of 20 to 30 years, companies issue bonds in denominations of $1,000 which can be classified by length of time until maturity, and by the type of security put up to secure the bond.

*Debenture Bonds*
A loan not secured by any particular asset but by the company's unpledged assets. The most common type of taxable bond, backed only by the company's word and financial capacity to meet regular principal and interest payments. High-yield and convertible bonds are examples of debentures.

*High-Yield (Junk) Bonds*
An unsecured loan rated higher in risk because of the uncertain financial strength of the issuing company; graded less than BBB.

*Convertible Bond*
A loan that can be converted at the owner's discretion from company debt into a designated amount of equity, e.g. from bonds into stock shareholdings.

*Collateral Trust Bond*
A loan backed by securities, other companies' stocks and bonds, held by the issuing company.

*Mortgage Bond*
A loan secured by a piece of real estate or fixed property, such as a factory, warehouse, or laboratory.

*Equipment Trust Certificate*
A loan secured by movable equipment, such as a fleet of trucks or a locomotive.

*Income Bond*
A loan that is repaid only when the company operates at a profit.

*Senior and Junior or Subordinated Bonds*
Loans that are classified by the issuer according to their seniority. Repayment to senior debt holders takes priority if the company enters into financial trouble.

*Sinking Fund Bond*
A loan that is retired through partial payments over time until final maturity. Repayment usually commences five to ten years after the date of issue.

*Zero-Coupon Bonds*
A corporate, municipal, or treasury bond that is sold at a deeply discounted price, at a fraction of its par value, but pays no interest until final maturity, typically decades from the date of issue.

Secondary markets for corporate bonds are made by investors trading primarily on the New York Stock Exchange and on the American Stock Exchange.

In January, 1993, the corporate bond market set a record for new issuance: $37.1 million total issues for the month, including sales by corporations and government agencies.

## U.S. Domestic Corporate Investment Grade Debt, Sales Volume

| Date | Proceeds ($ mil.) | Market Share | No. of Issues |
|---|---|---|---|
| 1976 | 31,487.0 | 2.2 | 426 |
| 1977 | 25,225.7 | 1.7 | 341 |
| 1978 | 19,934.2 | 1.4 | 230 |
| 1979 | 24,369.3 | 1.7 | 232 |
| 1980 | 35,373.7 | 2.4 | 373 |
| 1981 | 33,864.4 | 2.3 | 346 |
| 1982 | 36,944.7 | 2.5 | 443 |
| 1983 | 30,031.5 | 2.1 | 334 |
| 1984 | 37,718.2 | 2.6 | 321 |
| 1985 | 60,914.7 | 4.2 | 510 |
| 1986 | 113,935.3 | 7.8 | 854 |
| 1987 | 86,891.1 | 6.0 | 669 |
| 1988 | 86,137.3 | 5.9 | 556 |
| 1989 | 95,843.1 | 6.6 | 586 |
| 1990 | 85,184.7 | 5.8 | 591 |
| 1991 | 154,337.7 | 10.6 | 1,361 |
| 1992 | 202,306.8 | 13.9 | 1,390 |
| 1993 | 260,481.1 | 17.9 | 1,807 |
| INDUSTRY TOTALS | 1,420,980.4 | 97.6 | 11,370 |

*Source: Securities Data Company*

*Corporate and Taxable Bonds (cont'd)*

## U.S. Non-Investment Grade Debt, Sales Volume

| Date | Proceeds ($ mil.) | Market Share | No. of Issues |
|------|-------------------|--------------|---------------|
| 1976 | 700.4 | 0.3 | 30 |
| 1977 | 1,030.8 | 0.4 | 61 |
| 1978 | 1,588.2 | 0.6 | 83 |
| 1979 | 1,390.8 | 0.5 | 56 |
| 1980 | 1,374.2 | 0.5 | 45 |
| 1981 | 1,247.2 | 0.5 | 34 |
| 1982 | 2,466.7 | 0.9 | 53 |
| 1983 | 7,406.4 | 2.8 | 95 |
| 1984 | 14,002.7 | 5.3 | 131 |
| 1985 | 14,190.8 | 5.4 | 175 |
| 1986 | 31,905.6 | 12.1 | 226 |
| 1987 | 28,140.1 | 10.7 | 190 |
| 1988 | 27,718.8 | 10.5 | 160 |
| 1989 | 25,426.7 | 9.7 | 131 |
| 1990 | 1,394.9 | 0.5 | 10 |
| 1991 | 9,971.0 | 3.8 | 48 |
| 1992 | 38,185.7 | 14.5 | 236 |
| 1993 | 54,505.9 | 20.7 | 345 |
| INDUSTRY TOTALS | 262,646.9 | 100.0 | 2,109 |

*Source: Securities Data Company*

# Mortgage-Backed Bonds

## Mortgage-Backed Securities, Sales Volume

| Date | Proceeds ($ mil.) | Market Share | No. of Issues |
|------|-------------------|--------------|---------------|
| 1976 | 74.6 | 0.0 | 1 |
| 1977 | 1,338.9 | 0.1 | 13 |
| 1978 | 1,251.7 | 0.1 | 19 |
| 1979 | 1,476.8 | 0.1 | 24 |
| 1980 | 500.2 | 0.0 | 8 |
| 1981 | 512.6 | 0.0 | 12 |
| 1982 | 1,076.8 | 0.1 | 36 |
| 1983 | 8,566.9 | 0.5 | 66 |
| 1984 | 12,069.2 | 0.8 | 117 |
| 1985 | 19,581.3 | 1.2 | 212 |
| 1986 | 57,827.0 | 3.7 | 372 |
| 1987 | 82,321.7 | 5.2 | 469 |
| 1988 | 98,365.1 | 6.2 | 620 |
| 1989 | 110,637.3 | 7.0 | 463 |
| 1990 | 133,996.5 | 8.5 | 474 |
| 1991 | 250,178.0 | 15.9 | 725 |
| 1992 | 376,727.8 | 23.9 | 983 |
| 1993 | 420,665.7 | 26.7 | 1,091 |
| INDUSTRY TOTALS | 1,577,168.2 | 100.0 | 5,705 |

*Source: Securities Data Company*

# Convertible Bonds

## U.S. Convertible Bonds, Sales Volume

| Date | Proceeds ($ mil.) | Market Share | No. of Issues |
|------|-------------------|--------------|---------------|
| 1976 | 932.3 | 1.0 | 25 |
| 1977 | 495.7 | 0.5 | 17 |
| 1978 | 393.4 | 0.4 | 19 |
| 1979 | 724.1 | 0.8 | 31 |
| 1980 | 4,359.6 | 4.8 | 98 |
| 1981 | 4,652.9 | 5.1 | 92 |
| 1982 | 3,201.0 | 3.5 | 67 |
| 1983 | 6,120.3 | 6.7 | 113 |
| 1984 | 4,093.7 | 4.5 | 66 |
| 1985 | 7,484.6 | 8.2 | 139 |
| 1986 | 10,115.9 | 11.1 | 207 |
| 1987 | 9,863.6 | 10.8 | 148 |
| 1988 | 3,136.1 | 3.4 | 36 |
| 1989 | 5,519.9 | 6.1 | 63 |
| 1990 | 4,756.5 | 5.2 | 34 |
| 1991 | 7,478.6 | 8.2 | 49 |
| 1992 | 7,036.2 | 7.7 | 65 |
| 1993 | 9,303.0 | 10.2 | 90 |
| INDUSTRY TOTALS | 89,667.6 | 98.4 | 1,359 |

*Source: Securities Data Company*

# U.S. Government Securities

GUARANTEED BY THE U.S. Government and exempt from state and local income taxes, these securities are some of the safest you can purchase. But because of the near-absence of default risk they offer lower interest rates than do corporate issues. Government issues are actively traded on the over-the-counter market after their initial sale to large investors through an auction conducted by the Treasury.

*Treasury Bills*
Issued at a discount and repaid at face value at final maturity, T-bills pay no interest. They have the shortest maturation of all government securities: 91, 182 or 364 days. $10,000 minimum face value investment.

*Treasury Notes*
Maturing in the range of two to ten years, T-notes yield a steady stream of interest. $1,000 minimum purchase; most notes are sold in $5,000 denominations.

*Treasury Bonds*
Long-term government debt bearing interest, T-bonds generally mature in ten years or longer. Like T-notes they come in denominations of $1,000, $5,000, $10,000, $100,000, and $1,000,000 and are popular with traders and institutional investors. They are highly sensitive to interest-rate movements.

*Zero Coupon Government Bonds*
Long-term government debt bearing interest, with all interest paid in a lump sum at the end of the term. Similar to other zero coupon bonds but tax free.

*Flower Bonds*
This limited series of bonds (the last issue was in 1971) can be redeemed at the time of the holder's death for the payment of estate taxes.

*U.S. Savings Bonds*
Unlike Treasury bills, notes, and bonds, U.S. Savings Bonds cannnot be traded in a secondary market. They are sold mostly to individual investors who buy them directly from the Treasury. The most popular variety of U.S. Savings Bond sells at a 50% discount from its face value and is entirely free of commissions.

*U.S. Government Securities (cont'd)*

Through the sale of securities, the U.S. Government has created more than $200 billion in debt yearly since 1985. Daily volume in U.S. Treasury Securities is up to $100 billion.

## Federal Agency Issues

While the federal government does not back all these issues, they do authorize a variety of their agencies to issue debentures and notes to finance their operations, including:

- U.S. Post Office
- The Tennessee Valley Authority
- The Export-Import Bank

- The Federal Home Loan Mortgage Corporation (FHLMC or Freddie Mac)
- The Federal Intermediate Credit Bank (FICB)
- The Federal National Mortgage Association (FNMA or Fannie Mae)
- The Government National Mortgage Association (GNMA or Ginnie Mae).

As a group, these securities offer a higher rate of interest than direct U.S. Treasury obligations, even though the majority are backed by the full faith and credit of the U.S. Government. Certain issues are also exempt from state and local taxes.

## Federal Agency Issues, Sales Volume

| Date | Proceeds ($ mil.) | Market Share | No. of Issues |
|---|---|---|---|
| 1982 | 707.5 | 0.3 | 4 |
| 1984 | 1,457.0 | 0.5 | 8 |
| 1985 | 1,083.3 | 0.4 | 6 |
| 1986 | 3,985.7 | 1.4 | 24 |
| 1987 | 3,079.0 | 1.1 | 25 |
| 1988 | 6,536.6 | 2.4 | 30 |
| 1989 | 13,560.0 | 4.9 | 64 |
| 1990 | 19,844.3 | 7.2 | 120 |
| 1991 | 36,155.3 | 13.0 | 203 |
| 1992 | 73,405.2 | 26.4 | 518 |
| 1993 | 117,719.7 | 42.4 | 1,086 |
| INDUSTRY TOTALS | 277,533.6 | 100.0 | 2,088 |

*Source: Securities Data Company*

# Municipal Bonds

ISSUED BY STATES, CITIES, towns, counties, and their agencies, municipal bonds (often called munis or tax exempts) are free of federal tax and often from state and local tax in their state of issuance. A new municipal issue subject to federal tax was created out of The Tax Reform Act of 1986. Like corporate issues, municipal bonds are categorized by the form of collateral used to back them and to raise their revenue.

*General Obligation Bonds (GO Bonds)*
GO Bonds represent the largest group of municipal issues. Paid back by general revenues–secured by the government's tax revenue and its ability to impose new taxes–these bonds are only slightly less secure than similar government issues. By law, the government is required to levy taxes in order to pay their bondholders.

*Revenue Bonds*
Used in the development of toll roads, bridges, or tunnels, or any revenue-producing projects, these bonds are paid off by the revenues generated from

the specific development. They typically offer a higher rate of interest than GO Bonds, as payment is more narrowly backed.

*Industrial Development Bonds*
These specific bonds are issued by state and local governnments to fund the construction of new industrial parks, plants, or any development which might attract businesses and increase leasing revenue for the state. The financial strength of the private businesses involved in the project generally determines the quality of the bond. Most are now taxable under The Tax Reform Act of 1986.

*Redevelopment Agency Bonds*
Used for the construction of commercial projects, these bonds are secured by part of the property taxes levied on the development.

*Airport Bonds*
One type of airport bond is used toward, and secured by, general operations and usage. Another,

*Municipal Bonds (cont'd)*

much riskier bond, is tied specifically to facilities leased by individual airlines and is secured by the leasing contract itself.

Bond ratings are listed in *Moody's Bond Record* and *Standard and Poor's Bond Guide*. Weekly newsletters, *Moody's Bond Survey*, and *CreditWeek* (a publication of Standard and Poor's) offer more detailed information of select issues.

As newspapers and financial journals do not carry complete information on municipal bonds, current price, and trading data, investors must turn to specific bond publications to track these issues.

The bible of bond issuance, pricing, and trading is the annual publication *Moody's Municipal & Government Manual*. Organized by state, city, town, and political subdivision, the compendium lists all bond issues (including as well information on Federal Agency issues) and offers information critical to bond buyers, from state tax revenues and census figures to statistics on attendance at local schools. Updates to *Moody's Municipal* are published in a semi-weekly newsletter which lists new and changed issues as well as call notices.

## Recommended Resources

*The Blue List*
Standard & Poor's, $255/year
65 Broadway
New York, NY 10004
(212) 770-4300

*The Daily Bond Buyer*, $1,897
1 State Street Plaza
New York, NY 10004
(212) 943-8200

*Bond Week*, $1,295/year
488 Madison Ave.
New York, NY 10022
(212) 303-3300

*Moody's Municipal & Government Manual*, $2,095
99 Church St.
New York, NY 10007
(800) 342-5647, ext. 0435

## Long-Term Municipal Bond Issues, Sales Volume

| Date | Amount ($ mil.) | % of Total | No. of Issues |
|------|------|------|------|
| 1982 | 70,434.7 | 3.8 | 2,383 |
| 1983 | 76,574.4 | 4.1 | 2,463 |
| 1984 | 94,983.2 | 5.1 | 2,855 |
| 1985 | 201,663.5 | 10.8 | 5,612 |
| 1986 | 148,095.3 | 7.9 | 7,423 |
| 1987 | 101,508.0 | 5.4 | 6,830 |
| 1988 | 115,338.0 | 6.2 | 7,915 |
| 1989 | 121,847.9 | 6.5 | 8,784 |
| 1990 | 126,066.3 | 6.7 | 8,427 |
| 1991 | 171,069.9 | 9.1 | 10,530 |
| 1992 | 232,052.5 | 12.4 | 12,597 |
| 1993 | 289,101.8 | 15.5 | 13,941 |
| 1994* | 40,503.8 | 2.2 | 2,027 |
| TOTAL DOLLAR VOLUME* | 1,789,239.3 | 95.7 | 91,787 |

*\* Year to date as of Mar. 18, 1994*    *Source: Securities Data Company*

## Short-Term Municipal Bond Issues, Sales Volume

| Date | Amount ($ mil.) | % of Total | No. of Issues |
|------|------|------|------|
| 1982 | 16,149.8 | 4.5 | 511 |
| 1983 | 18,870.4 | 5.2 | 541 |
| 1984 | 21,092.8 | 5.8 | 711 |
| 1985 | 21,141.4 | 5.8 | 790 |
| 1986 | 21,115.8 | 5.8 | 1,315 |
| 1987 | 19,652.1 | 5.4 | 1,198 |
| 1988 | 22,302.6 | 6.2 | 1,605 |
| 1989 | 28,872.9 | 8.0 | 2,382 |
| 1990 | 34,134.7 | 9.4 | 2,819 |
| 1991 | 42,277.0 | 11.7 | 3,653 |

*Municipal Bonds (cont'd)*

| Date | Amount ($ mil.) | % of Total | No. of Issues |
|------|-----------------|------------|---------------|
| 1992 | 41,970.5 | 11.6 | 3,398 |
| 1993 | 46,065.8 | 12.7 | 3,526 |
| 1994* | 5,615.5 | 1.6 | 318 |
| TOTAL DOLLAR VOLUME* | 339,261.3 | 93.7 | 22,767 |

*\* Year to date as of 3/18/94*                          *Source: Securities Data Company*

# Bond Performance

## Merrill Lynch Hi-Yield Master Index

| Year | Return (%) |
|------|------------|
| 1985 | 24.61 |
| 1986 | 16.35 |
| 1987 | 4.69 |
| 1988 | 13.47 |
| 1989 | 4.23 |
| 1990 | -4.38 |
| 1991 | 34.58 |
| 1992 | 18.16 |
| 1993 | 17.18 |

## Merrill Lynch Mortgage Master Index

| Year | Return (%) |
|------|------------|
| 1984 | 18.32 |
| 1985 | 25.45 |
| 1986 | 13.14 |
| 1987 | 3.53 |
| 1988 | 9.15 |
| 1989 | 14.60 |
| 1990 | 10.84 |
| 1991 | 15.78 |
| 1992 | 7.33 |
| 1993 | 7.29 |

## Merrill Lynch Agency Master Index

| Year | Return (%) |
|------|------------|
| 1984 | 14.52 |
| 1985 | 17.79 |
| 1986 | 13.87 |
| 1987 | 3.42 |
| 1988 | 4.47 |
| 1989 | 12.93 |
| 1990 | 9.90 |
| 1991 | 15.21 |
| 1992 | 7.27 |
| 1993 | 10.44 |

*Note: Includes Governments, U.S. Agencies (all Maturities)*

## Merrill Lynch Corporate Master Index

| Year | Return (%) |
|------|------------|
| 1984 | 16.21 |
| 1985 | 25.38 |
| 1986 | 16.30 |
| 1987 | 1.84 |
| 1988 | 9.76 |
| 1989 | 14.12 |
| 1990 | 7.37 |
| 1991 | 18.24 |
| 1992 | 9.12 |
| 1993 | 12.43 |

## Merrill Lynch Domestic Master Index

| Year | Return (%) |
|------|------------|
| 1984 | 15.20 |
| 1985 | 22.40 |
| 1986 | 15.22 |
| 1987 | 2.40 |
| 1988 | 8.04 |
| 1989 | 14.18 |
| 1990 | 9.10 |
| 1991 | 15.85 |
| 1992 | 7.58 |
| 1993 | 10.02 |

## Merrill Lynch 1–10 Year Treasury Index

| Year | Return (%) |
|------|------------|
| 1984 | 14.18 |
| 1985 | 18.36 |
| 1986 | 13.20 |
| 1987 | 3.63 |
| 1988 | 6.33 |
| 1989 | 12.60 |
| 1990 | 9.50 |
| 1991 | 13.99 |
| 1992 | 6.94 |
| 1993 | 8.18 |

*Note: Includes Corporate-Government-Mortgage-Bond Index*

*Bond Performance (cont'd)*

## Merrill Lynch 10+ Treasury Index

| Year | Return (%) |
|------|-----------|
| 1984 | 14.95 |
| 1985 | 31.53 |
| 1986 | 23.99 |
| 1987 | -2.66 |
| 1988 | 9.20 |
| 1989 | 18.90 |
| 1990 | 6.46 |
| 1991 | 18.43 |
| 1992 | 7.94 |
| 1993 | 17.23 |

*Government, U.S. Treasury, Intermediate-Term, 1-9.99 years*

## Merrill Lynch 30 Year Treasury Strip

| Year | Return (%) |
|------|-----------|
| 1987 | -31.87 |
| 1988 | -5.76 |
| 1989 | 28.41 |
| 1990 | -4.02 |
| 1991 | 15.36 |
| 1992 | 5.67 |
| 1993 | 36.80 |

*Governments, U.S. Treasury, Intermediate-Term, 10 years and over*

## Merrill Lynch Convertible Securities Index

| Year | Return (%) |
|------|-----------|
| 1989 | 12.46 |
| 1990 | -6.99 |
| 1991 | 31.96 |
| 1992 | 22.41 |
| 1993 | 18.91 |

*Convertible Securities (Bonds and Preferreds) All Qualities*

## Merrill Lynch Eurodollar Index

| Year | Return (%) |
|------|-----------|
| 1984 | 12.68 |
| 1985 | 18.12 |
| 1986 | 13.89 |
| 1987 | 2.63 |
| 1988 | 8.90 |
| 1989 | 12.67 |
| 1990 | 9.37 |
| 1991 | 15.84 |
| 1992 | 8.04 |
| 1993 | 8.87 |

*Eurodollar Straight Bonds*

## Merrill Lynch 1–10 Year Treasury Index (% return)

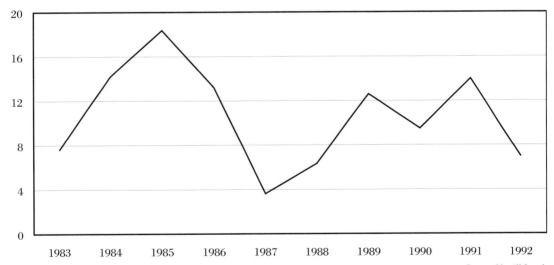

*Source: Merrill Lynch*

*Bond Performance (cont'd)*

## New Security Issues of Corporations: By Type of Offering

| Type of Bond Offering | 1987 | 1988 | 1989 | 1990 | 1991 |
|---|---|---|---|---|---|
| TOTAL | 326.1 | 353.1 | 320.0 | 298.8 | 390.0 |
| Public, domestic | 209.7 | 202.0 | 179.7 | 188.8 | 287.1 |
| Private placement, domestic | 92.1 | 127.7 | 117.4 | 87.0 | 74.9 |
| Sold abroad | 24.3 | 23.1 | 22.9 | 23.1 | 28.0 |

*Source: 1993 Statistical Abstract, Table No. 831*

## New Security Issues of Corporations: By Industry Group

| Industry Group | 1987 | 1988 | 1989 | 1990 | 1991 |
|---|---|---|---|---|---|
| Manufacturing | 60.9 | 70.1 | 74.7 | 51.8 | 86.6 |
| Commercial and miscellaneous | 49.8 | 61.9 | 50.3 | 40.7 | 37.6 |
| Transportation | 12.0 | 10.9 | 10.2 | 12.8 | 13.6 |
| Public utility | 23.0 | 21.1 | 18.6 | 17.6 | 23.9 |
| Communication | 7.3 | 6.0 | 9.3 | 6.7 | 9.4 |
| Real estate and financial | 173.1 | 182.0 | 156.9 | 169.2 | 219.7 |

*Source: 1993 Statistical Abstract, Table No. 831*

## Ownership of Public Debt Securities: By Private Investor

| Investor | 1985 | 1986 | 1987 | 1988 | 1989 | 1990 | 1991 | 1992 |
|---|---|---|---|---|---|---|---|---|
| Total privately held | 1,417 | 1,602 | 1,731 | 1,859 | 2,016 | 2,288 | 2,563 | 2,840 |
| Commercial banks | 189 | 198 | 194 | 185 | 165 | 172 | 222 | 292 |
| Non-bank investors | 1,228 | 1,405 | 1,537 | 1,674 | 1,851 | 2,117 | 2,341 | 2,548 |
| Individuals | 155 | 163 | 172 | 190 | 216 | 234 | 264 | 289 |
| Insurance companies | 81 | 102 | 108 | 119 | 125 | 142 | 168 | 183 |
| Money market funds | 25 | 29 | 15 | 12 | 15 | 46 | 80 | 81 |
| Corporations | 59 | 69 | 85 | 86 | 93 | 109 | 151 | 193 |
| State and local governments | 304 | 347 | 418 | 472 | 488 | 490 | 490 | 532 |
| Foreign and international | 225 | 263 | 300 | 362 | 393 | 422 | 458 | 573 |
| Other investors | 380 | 433 | 439 | 433 | 521 | 674 | 731 | 758 |

*Source: 1993 Statistical Abstract, Table No. 832*

## Household Assets in the Credit Market Instruments

| | 1980 | 1985 | 1988 | 1989 | 1990 | 1991 | 1992 |
|---|---|---|---|---|---|---|---|
| U.S. Government securities | 241 | 427 | 584 | 680 | 771 | 658 | 650 |
| Treasury issues | 194 | 340 | 381 | 393 | 441 | 355 | 344 |
| Savings bonds | 73 | 80 | 110 | 118 | 126 | 138 | 157 |
| Other Treasury | 122 | 260 | 271 | 275 | 315 | 217 | 186 |
| Agency issues | 47 | 87 | 203 | 288 | 330 | 303 | 306 |
| Tax-exempt obligations | 102 | 303 | 465 | 527 | 558 | 579 | 600 |
| Corporate and foreign bonds | 69 | 53 | 81 | 116 | 151 | 150 | 131 |
| Mortgages | 107 | 127 | 182 | 213 | 215 | 245 | 302 |
| Open-market paper | 43 | 122 | 174 | 173 | 188 | 103 | 109 |

*Source: 1993 Statistical Abstract, Table No. 787*

## Bonds Listed on the New York Stock Exchange

| | 1985 | 1986 | 1987 | 1988 | 1989 | 1990 | 1991 | 1992 |
|---|---|---|---|---|---|---|---|---|
| No. of issuers | 1,010.0 | 951.0 | 885.0 | 846.0 | 794.0 | 743.0 | 706.0 | 589.0 |
| No. of issues | 3,856.0 | 3,611.0 | 3,346.0 | 3,106.0 | 2,961.0 | 2,912.0 | 2,727.0 | 1,462.0 |
| Face value ($ bil.) | 1,327.0 | 1,380.0 | 1,651.0 | 1,610.0 | 1,435.0 | 1,689.0 | 2,219.0 | 2,009.0 |
| Market value ($ bil.) | 1,339.0 | 1,458.0 | 1,621.0 | 1,561.0 | 1,412.0 | 1,610.0 | 2,227.0 | 2,044.0 |
| Average price (%) | 100.9 | 105.7 | 98.2 | 97.0 | 98.4 | 95.3 | 100.3 | 101.8 |

*Source: 1993 Statistical Abstract, Table No. 834*

*Bond Performance (cont'd)*

## Foreign Purchases and Sales of U.S. Securities

| Year and Country | Total | Treasury Bonds and Notes | U.S. Government Corporations Bonds | Corporate Bonds | Corporate Stocks |
|---|---|---|---|---|---|
| 1980 | 15.8 | 4.9 | 2.6 | 2.9 | 5.4 |
| 1985 | 78.3 | 29.2 | 4.3 | 39.8 | 4.9 |
| 1987 | 69.4 | 25.6 | 5.0 | 22.5 | 16.3 |
| 1988 | 74.8 | 48.8 | 6.7 | 21.2 | -2.0 |
| 1989 | 96.6 | 54.2 | 15.1 | 17.4 | 9.9 |
| 1990 | 19.4 | 17.9 | 6.3 | 10.4 | -15.1 |
| 1991 TOTAL | 61.1 | 22.5 | 9.8 | 17.7 | 11.1 |
| United Kingdom | 14.6 | 5.7 | 1.3 | 8.0 | -0.3 |
| Japan | 2.9 | -4.1 | 4.7 | 1.1 | 1.2 |
| Canada | 2.4 | -2.7 | 0.3 | 1.0 | 3.8 |
| Bermuda | -1.9 | -2.2 | NA | 0.5 | -0.2 |
| Netherlands Antilles | 7.0 | 6.2 | NA | 0.3 | 0.6 |
| France | -0.2 | -1.0 | 0.4 | 0.4 | NA |
| 1992 TOTAL | 73.2 | 39.0 | 18.3 | 21.1 | -5.2 |
| United Kingdom | 33.9 | 24.2 | 3.8 | 9.1 | -3.3 |
| Japan | 5.6 | 9.5 | 1.5 | -1.7 | -3.6 |
| Canada | 2.2 | 0.6 | 0.1 | 0.1 | 1.4 |
| Bermuda | -2.2 | -5.8 | 1.1 | 1.9 | -1.3 |
| Netherlands Antilles | -1.0 | -1.8 | 0.2 | 0.4 | 0.3 |
| France | -0.3 | -0.2 | 0.4 | 0.8 | 0.8 |

*Source: 1993 Statistical Abstract, Table No. 830*

## U.S. Exchanges Listing Bonds

| Exchange | No. of Listed Bonds | Market Value ($ millions) |
|---|---|---|
| American | 229 | 18,405 |
| Boston | 2 | 18 |
| Cincinnati | 4 | 137 |
| Midwest | 0 | 0 |
| New York | 2,559 | 2,206,173 |
| Pacific | 63 | 4,067 |
| Philadelphia | 47 | NA |
| Spokane | 0 | 0 |
| TOTAL | 2,904 | 2,228,800 |

*Source: U.S. Securities and Exchange Commission, Annual Report, 1992*

**TIP:** *Dun & Bradstreet will prepare a report on any company and include its history and background, payment record, finances, and lawsuits, liens and judgments. The fee for this service is $75.00. Call (800) 362-2255.*

# Bonds on the NYSE

THE NYSE'S BOND MARKET IS the largest of all the U.S. exchanges, offering investors a selection of nearly 2,800 bonds issued by the U.S. government, U.S. corporations, foreign governments, foreign cor-porations, and international banks. In 1991, bond trading on the Exchange reached a record $12.7 billion. About 90% of the NYSE bond volume is in straight or non-convertible debt.

## Groups Listing Bonds on the New York Stock Exchange

| Major Group | Number of Issuers | Number of Issues | Par Value ($ mil.) | Market Value ($ mil.) |
|---|---|---|---|---|
| U.S. companies | 589 | 1,462 | 262,494 | 222,239 |
| Foreign companies | 20 | 27 | 6,388 | 6,173 |
| U.S. government | 1 | 728 | 1,717,191 | 1,796,869 |
| International banks | 5 | 98 | 19,630 | 15,818 |
| Foreign governments | 21 | 39 | 2,932 | 3,023 |
| TOTAL | 636 | 2,354 | 2,008,635 | 2,044,122 |

*Source: New York Stock Exchange Fact Book, 1992*

## 25 Most Active Bonds on the New York Stock Exchange, 1992

| Issue | Par Value of Reported Volume ($ thousands) |
|---|---|
| RJR Nabisco | 588,584 |
| Chrysler | 486,593 |
| General Motors Acceptance | 334,820 |
| General Motors Acceptance | 245,420 |
| Walt Disney | 239,355 |
| USG | 196,992 |
| Chrysler | 195,273 |
| AT&T | 192,663 |
| Chrysler | 162,677 |
| Chrysler | 154,070 |
| Time Warner | 152,535 |
| Stone Container | 141,075 |
| RJR Nabisco | 134,085 |
| Chrysler | 126,917 |
| AT&T | 126,810 |
| USAir | 124,192 |
| Stone Container | 113,208 |
| Federated Department Stores | 100,996 |
| Chrysler Auburn Hills | 95,535 |
| AT&T | 93,256 |
| Owens-Illinois | 89,943 |

*Source: New York Stock Exchange Fact Book, 1992*

## Volume of Bond Trading on the NYSE

| Year | Volume ($ millions) |
|---|---|
| 1983 | 7,572 |
| 1984 | 6,982 |
| 1985 | 9,046 |
| 1986 | 10,464 |
| 1987 | 9,727 |
| 1988 | 7,702 |
| 1989 | 8,836 |
| 1990 | 10,892 |
| 1991 | 12,698 |
| 1992 | 11,629 |

## NYSE Bond Trading Activity Records

| Most Active | Volume ($ millions) |
|---|---|
| DAYS | TOTAL VOLUME |
| February 6, 1991 | 158.4 |
| February 7, 1991 | 128.1 |
| February 5, 1991 | 124.3 |
| July 17, 1990 | 113.9 |
| January 29, 1990 | 111.8 |
| January 30, 1991 | 108.3 |
| July 16, 1990 | 105.2 |
| February 8, 1991 | 102.0 |
| February 11, 1991 | 99.1 |
| February 13, 1990 | 98.7 |
| MONTHS | AVG. DAILY VOLUME |
| February, 1991 | 88.9 |
| February, 1992 | 65.9 |
| March, 1991 | 62.4 |
| YEARS | AVG. DAILY VOLUME |
| 1991 | 50.2 |
| 1992 | 45.8 |
| 1990 | 32.1 |

*Source: New York Stock Exchange Fact Book, 1992*

*Bonds on the NYSE (cont'd)*

## Volume of Bond Trading on the NYSE ($ millions)

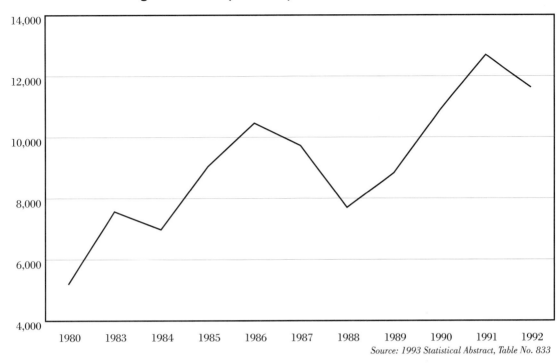

*Source: 1993 Statistical Abstract, Table No. 833*

### The Top Reference Sources

*The Corporate Directory of U.S. Public Companies*
Gale/Walker's Western Research, $360
(800) 877-4253

This mammoth 2-volume set lists the essential facts on every U.S. public company (more than 9,500 in all) with sales greater then $5 million.

Entries include contact data, legal counsel, stock price range, SIC codes, major subsidiaries, and more.

*Bonds on the NYSE (cont'd)*

## Largest Corporate Bond Listings on the New York Stock Exchange, 1992

| Issue | Principal Amount ($ thousands) | Listing Date |
|---|---|---|
| International Bank for Reconstruction & Development | 2,000,000 | 05/19 |
| Time Warner | 1,733,600 | 06/18 |
| International Bank for Reconstruction & Development | 1,500,000 | 07/21 |
| International Bank for Reconstruction & Development | 1,500,000 | 05/19 |
| Federated Department Stores | 1,130,000 | 02/05 |
| International Business Machines | 900,000 | 11/04 |
| RJR Nabisco | 875,000 | 12/09 |
| Automatic Data Processing | 805,000 | 02/14 |
| Home Depot | 805,000 | 02/04 |
| International Business Machines | 750,000 | 11/04 |
| International Business Machines | 750,000 | 08/14 |
| RJR Nabisco | 750,000 | 09/16 |
| News America Holdings | 641,710 | 03/24 |
| RJR Nabisco | 600,000 | 04/03 |
| RJR Nabisco | 600,000 | 04/03 |
| Federated Department Stores | 535,000 | 02/05 |
| American Telephone & Telegraph | 500,000 | 07/27 |
| American Telephone & Telegraph | 500,000 | 01/16 |
| American Telephone & Telegraph | 500,000 | 01/16 |
| Healthtrust | 500,000 | 08/18 |
| Rhone-Poulenc SA | 500,000 | 01/23 |
| Rhone-Poulenc SA | 500,000 | 10/16 |
| Southern Bell Telephone & Telegraph | 500,000 | 12/01 |
| Tenneco | 500,000 | 10/29 |
| Long Island Lighting | 451,000 | 11/27 |

*Source: New York Stock Exchange Fact Book, 1992*

# Bonds on the Amex

THE AMEX OPENED TRADING of U.S. Government securities, Treasury Notes and Bonds in 1975. As of December 31, 1991, 236 corporate and 744 government issues were listed, including U.S. Government Securities in odd-lot denominations, Treasury Notes (2 to 10 years maturity), Treasury Bonds (20 years or more maturity), Federal Agency Securities (Federal Home Loan Banks, Federal National Mortgage Association, Federal Farm Credits, and Federal Land Banks), one-year U.S. Treasury Bills, and three- and six-month Treasury Bills.

## Corporate Bond Trading on the Amex

| Year | Principal Amount ($) |
|---|---|
| 1981 | 301,226,000 |
| 1982 | 325,145,000 |
| 1983 | 395,089,000 |
| 1984 | 371,857,000 |
| 1985 | 644,882,000 |
| 1986 | 810,151,000 |
| 1987 | 686,922,000 |
| 1988 | 603,882,000 |
| 1989 | 708,836,000 |
| 1990 | 767,118,000 |
| 1991 | 952,477,000 |
| 1992 | 894,210,000 |

## Government Bond Trading on the Amex

| Year | Principal Amount ($) |
|---|---|
| 1981 | 964,955,000 |
| 1982 | 1,392,736,000 |
| 1983 | 1,808,921,000 |
| 1984 | 2,086,817,000 |
| 1985 | 2,117,007,000 |
| 1986 | 2,421,255,000 |
| 1987 | 3,016,038,000 |
| 1988 | 3,691,901,000 |
| 1989 | 3,518,454,000 |
| 1990 | 2,719,710,000 |
| 1991 | 2,770,900,000 |
| 1992 | 3,681,143,000 |

*Source: American Stock Exchange Fact Book, 1993*

*Bonds on the Amex (cont'd)*

## Corporate Bond Listings on the Amex

| Year | No. of Issues | Principal Amount Outstanding ($) | Total Market Value ($) | Average Price ($) |
|------|---------------|----------------------------------|------------------------|-------------------|
| 1960 | 63 | 1,064,502,930 | 954,792,454 | 86.69 |
| 1965 | 98 | 1,422,110,590 | 1,319,703,311 | 92.80 |
| 1970 | 169 | 3,178,354,510 | 2,044,735,556 | 64.34 |
| 1975 | 197 | 4,421,821,224 | 2,998,605,993 | 67.82 |
| 1980 | 225 | 6,195,258,443 | 4,853,002,615 | 78.34 |
| 1981 | 237 | 6,863,444,443 | 4,894,243,593 | 71.31 |
| 1982 | 244 | 7,419,099,691 | 6,213,798,988 | 83.75 |
| 1983 | 262 | 8,764,565,391 | 7,443,389,349 | 84.93 |
| 1984 | 290 | 12,670,599,101 | 9,646,216,836 | 76.13 |
| 1985 | 347 | 22,853,452,911 | 17,655,245,818 | 77.25 |
| 1986 | 341 | 24,118,069,806 | 19,845,653,627 | 82.28 |
| 1987 | 324 | 25,461,827,026 | 19,069,341,030 | 74.89 |
| 1988 | 309 | 25,557,448,968 | 20,993,531,457 | 82.14 |
| 1989 | 279 | 27,279,065,889 | 21,443,266,531 | 78.61 |
| 1990 | 260 | 27,195,333,970 | 29,458,671,424 | 108.32 |
| 1991 | 236 | 25,415,012,661 | 18,859,931,447 | 74.21 |
| 1992 | 183 | 23,289,522,693 | 16,862,072,362 | 72.40 |

*Source: American Stock Exchange Fact Book, 1993*

# Bond Ratings

WHILE BOND PRICES AND interest rates are broadly determined by bond categories (zero-coupon, convertible, income, for example); an issue's exact pricing and coupon are determined by a credit rating. Standard & Poor's and Moody's are the best known and most influential credit rating agencies. Their role as raters is to assess the risk of certain bonds through the study of all information provided to the public, and to assign grades to the issue and issuing company which accurately reflect the company's ability to meet the promised principal and interest payments.

While S&P warns investors that a credit rating is not a recommendation to purchase, sell, or hold a particular security, their initial ratings, and revised downgrades and upgrades, greatly affect the success of the issuance in the eyes of both issuers and holders. Bonds with higher ratings offer lower yields and easier money for the issuer. A lower rating usually results in a lower price on the bond–a less expensive purchase for the investor but a riskier investment. In 1991, those who gambled on lower-rated bonds (junk bonds) reaped the highest total returns: an average 34.5 percent. One year later, in a less outstanding year for bonds, junk debt took second place in the race for high returns, 18.2 percent compared to a 22.4 percent return on convertible debt.

Although somewhat different in their letter-usage, Standard & Poor's and Moody's both rate bonds in descending alphabetical order from A to C.

Standard & Poor's rates some 2,000 domestic and foreign companies; 8,000 munipical, state, and supranational entities; and 1,300 commerical-paper-issuing entities. Moody's rates 19,000 long-term debt issues; 28,000 municipals; and 2,000 commercial paper issuers.

## Bond Rating Codes

| Rating | S&P | Moody's |
|--------|-----|---------|
| Highest Quality | AAA | Aaa |
| High Quality | AA | Aa |
| Upper Medium Grade | A | A |
| Medium Grade | BBB | Baa |
| Somewhat Speculative | BB | Ba |
| Low Grade, Speculative | B | B |
| Low Grade, Default Possible | CCC | Caa |
| Low Grade, Partial Recovery Possible | CC | Ca |
| Default, Recovery Unlikely | C | C |

## Recommended Resources

Moody's Investors Service
99 Church St.
New York, NY 10007
(212) 553-0376

*Standard & Poor's Credit Week,* $2,190
25 Broadway
New York, NY 10004
(212) 208-1842

# Commodity and Futures Contracts

A COMMODITY IS a generic good such as grains, metals, and minerals, which is traded in large amounts in financial markets. Futures contracts are agreements between traders which establish a price level at the current time for commodities to be delivered later. These contracts are bought and sold frequently by speculators seeking profit from active, liquid, and competitive markets.

## Major Commodity Futures Traded on the U.S. Exchanges

- Grains and Oilseeds (Barley, Corn , Flaxseed, Oats, Rapeseed, Rye, Sorghum, Soybean Meal, Soybean Oil, Soybeans, Wheat)

- Wood (Lumber, Plywood)

- Metals and Petroleum (Aluminum, Copper, Crude Oil, Gold, Heating Oil, Palladium, Petroleum, Platinum, Propane, Silver, Unleaded Gas)

- Livestock and Meat (Broilers, Feeder Cattle, Pork Bellies, Hogs, Live Cattle)

- Food and Fiber (Cocoa, Coffee, Cotton, Eggs, Orange Juice, Potatoes, Rice, Sugar).

## Major Financial Futures Traded on the U.S. Exchanges

- Interest Rates (Certificates of Deposit, Commercial Paper, GNMA Certificates, T-bills, T-bonds, T-notes)

- Foreign Currencies (British Pound, Canadian Dollar, Deutsche Mark, Dutch Guilder, French Franc, Japanese Yen, Mexican Peso, Swiss Franc)

- Indexes (Consumer Price Index (CPI-W), CRB Futures Index, Municipal Bond Index, NYSE Index, NYSE Beta Index, Standard & Poor's 500 Index, Standard & Poor's 100 Index, Standard & Poor's OTC Index, U.S. Dollar Index).

## Market Volume of Futures Trading (millions)

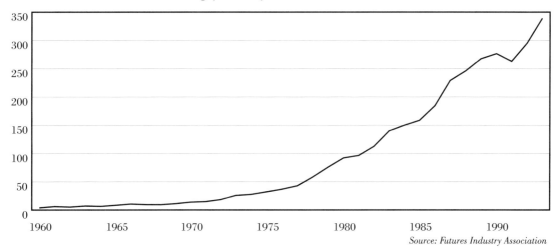

Source: Futures Industry Association

Compuserve's Current Market Snapshot presents hot key data, including highs and lows of Dow Jones 30, the NASDAQ composite indexes, and the S&P 500. GO SNAPSHOT.

*Commodity and Future Contracts (cont'd)*

## U.S. Futures Contracts Traded by Commodity Group

| Rank | Commodity Group | Contracts | Percent |
|---|---|---|---|
| 1989 | | | |
| 1 | Interest Rate | 123,657,483 | 46.25 |
| 2 | Ag Commodities | 54,051,698 | 20.21 |
| 3 | Energy Products | 30,775,659 | 11.51 |
| 4 | Foreign Currency/Index | 26,965,702 | 10.08 |
| 5 | Precious Metals | 16,147,189 | 6.04 |
| 6 | Equity Indexes | 13,290,808 | 4.97 |
| 7 | Non-Precious Metals | 2,097,288 | 0.78 |
| 8 | Other | 398,451 | 0.15 |
| | TOTAL | 267,384,278 | 100.00 |
| 1990 | | | |
| 1 | Interest Rate | 123,419,532 | 44.63 |
| 2 | Ag Commodities | 57,088,348 | 20.64 |
| 3 | Energy Products | 35,441,295 | 12.82 |
| 4 | Foreign Currency/Index | 28,880,894 | 10.44 |
| 5 | Precious Metals | 14,812,847 | 5.36 |
| 6 | Equity Indexes | 14,767,090 | 5.34 |
| 7 | Non-Precious Metals | 1,853,281 | 0.67 |
| 8 | Other | 272,217 | 0.10 |
| | TOTAL | 276,535,504 | 100.00 |
| 1991 | | | |
| 1 | Interest Rate | 119,764,959 | 45.56 |
| 2 | Ag Commodities | 52,229,512 | 19.87 |
| 3 | Energy Products | 33,670,228 | 12.81 |
| 4 | Foreign Currency/Index | 28,715,961 | 10.92 |
| 5 | Equity Indexes | 14,861,067 | 5.65 |
| 6 | Precious Metals | 11,791,525 | 4.49 |
| 7 | Non-Precious Metals | 1,640,065 | 0.62 |
| 8 | Other | 221,706 | 0.08 |
| | TOTAL | 262,895,023 | 100.00 |
| 1992 | | | |
| 1 | Interest Rate | 153,335,831 | 51.93 |
| 2 | Ag Commodities | 51,207,959 | 17.34 |
| 3 | Energy Products | 37,776,601 | 12.79 |
| 4 | Foreign Currency/Index | 26,594,835 | 9.01 |
| 5 | Equity Indexes | 14,685,096 | 4.97 |
| 6 | Precious Metals | 9,754,216 | 3.30 |
| 7 | Non-Precious Metals | 1,674,163 | 0.57 |
| 8 | Other | 263,341 | 0.09 |
| | TOTAL | 295,292,042 | 100.00 |
| 1993 | | | |
| 1 | Interest Rate | 173,768,387 | 51.25 |
| 2 | Ag Commodities | 56,724,601 | 16.73 |
| 3 | Energy Products | 45,618,438 | 13.45 |
| 4 | Foreign Currency/Index | 30,816,446 | 9.09 |
| 5 | Equity Indexes | 14,996,787 | 4.42 |
| 6 | Precious Metals | 14,683,066 | 4.33 |
| 7 | Non-Precious Metals | 2,064,629 | 0.61 |
| 8 | Other | 403,272 | 0.12 |
| | TOTAL | 339,075,626 | 100.00 |

*Source: Futures Industry Association*

*Commodity and Future Contracts (cont'd)*

## U.S. Futures: Contracts with Volume over 100,000

| 1993 Rank | Contracts with Volume over 100,000 | 1993 Contracts | Percent | 1992 Contracts | Percent | 1992 Rank |
|---|---|---|---|---|---|---|
| 1 | T-Bonds, CBOT | 79,428,474 | 23.43 | 70,003,894 | 23.71 | 1 |
| 2 | Eurodollar, CME | 64,411,394 | 19.00 | 60,531,066 | 20.50 | 2 |
| 3 | Crude Oil, NYMEX | 24,868,602 | 7.33 | 21,109,562 | 7.15 | 3 |
| 4 | T-Notes (10-Year), CBOT | 16,601,258 | 4.90 | 11,217,938 | 3.80 | 6 |
| 5 | S&P 500 Index, CME | 13,204,413 | 3.89 | 12,414,157 | 4.20 | 4 |
| 6 | Deutschemark, CME | 12,866,451 | 3.79 | 11,593,174 | 3.93 | 5 |
| 7 | Soybeans, CBOT | 11,649,333 | 3.44 | 9,000,169 | 3.05 | 8 |
| 8 | Corn, CBOT | 11,462,618 | 3.38 | 10,356,632 | 3.51 | 7 |
| 9 | Gold (100 oz), COMEX | 8,916,195 | 2.63 | 6,002,009 | 2.03 | 12 |
| 10 | #2 Heating Oil, NYMEX | 8,625,061 | 2.54 | 8,005,462 | 2.71 | 9 |
| 11 | T-Notes (5-Year), CBOT | 8,123,939 | 2.40 | 6,441,193 | 2.18 | 11 |
| 12 | Unleaded Regular Gas, NYMEX | 7,407,809 | 2.18 | 6,674,757 | 2.26 | 10 |
| 13 | Japanese Yen, CME | 6,023,132 | 1.78 | 4,520,356 | 1.53 | 14 |
| 14 | Swiss Franc, CME | 5,604,841 | 1.65 | 5,134,717 | 1.74 | 13 |
| 15 | Silver (5,000 oz), COMEX | 4,855,924 | 1.43 | 3,016,339 | 1.02 | 21 |
| 16 | Soybean Meal, CBOT | 4,718,095 | 1.39 | 4,145,397 | 1.40 | 16 |
| 17 | Natural Gas, NYMEX | 4,671,533 | 1.38 | 1,920,986 | 0.65 | 23 |
| 18 | Soybean Oil, CBOT | 4,612,229 | 1.36 | 4,282,678 | 1.45 | 15 |
| 19 | Sugar #11, CSC | 4,285,945 | 1.26 | 3,667,481 | 1.24 | 17 |
| 20 | British Pound, CME | 3,701,427 | 1.09 | 3,053,428 | 1.03 | 20 |
| 21 | Live Cattle, CME | 3,306,952 | 0.98 | 3,319,618 | 1.12 | 19 |
| 22 | Wheat, CBOT | 3,019,629 | 0.89 | 3,498,814 | 1.18 | 18 |
| 23 | Coffee C, CSC | 2,489,223 | 0.73 | 2,152,383 | 0.73 | 22 |
| 24 | Cocoa, CSC | 2,128,384 | 0.63 | 1,397,235 | 0.47 | 27 |
| 25 | High Grade Copper, COMEX | 2,064,629 | 0.61 | 1,674,163 | 0.57 | 25 |
| 26 | Cotton, NYCE | 1,603,027 | 0.47 | 1,701,258 | 0.58 | 24 |
| 27 | Canadian Dollar, CME | 1,410,818 | 0.42 | 1,171,640 | 0.40 | 32 |
| 28 | Live Hogs, CME | 1,401,754 | 0.41 | 1,556,092 | 0.53 | 26 |
| 29 | Wheat, KCBT | 1,348,500 | 0.40 | 1,339,842 | 0.45 | 29 |
| 30 | One Month LIBOR, CME | 1,128,321 | 0.33 | 918,593 | 0.31 | 34 |
| 31 | T-Bonds, MIDAM | 1,125,645 | 0.33 | 1,342,251 | 0.45 | 28 |
| 32 | Municipal Bond Index, CBOT | 1,120,510 | 0.33 | 776,205 | 0.26 | 36 |
| 33 | T-Bills (90-Day), CME | 1,017,350 | 0.30 | 1,337,061 | 0.45 | 30 |
| 34 | Soybeans, MIDAM | 966,244 | 0.28 | 1,130,629 | 0.38 | 33 |
| 35 | NYSE Composite Index, NYFE | 848,522 | 0.25 | 1,315,438 | 0.45 | 31 |
| 36 | Wheat, MGE | 822,898 | 0.24 | 742,703 | 0.25 | 37 |
| 37 | Pork Bellies, CME | 698,799 | 0.21 | 784,153 | 0.27 | 35 |
| 38 | Platinum, NYMEX | 651,222 | 0.19 | 577,253 | 0.20 | 39 |
| 39 | Orange Juice (Frozen Conc.), NYCE | 640,131 | 0.19 | 339,230 | 0.11 | 46 |
| 40 | U.S. Dollar Index, NYCE | 599,112 | 0.18 | 678,329 | 0.23 | 38 |
| 41 | T-Notes (2-Year), CBOT | 532,203 | 0.16 | 445,394 | 0.15 | 42 |
| 42 | Oats, CBOT | 455,335 | 0.13 | 459,578 | 0.16 | 40 |
| 43 | Feeder Cattle, CME | 419,888 | 0.12 | 369,042 | 0.12 | 44 |
| 44 | Nikkei 225, CME | 356,523 | 0.11 | 383,755 | 0.13 | 43 |
| 45 | Corn, MIDAM | 276,502 | 0.08 | 458,772 | 0.16 | 41 |
| 46 | S&P MidCap 400 Index, CME | 218,531 | 0.06 | 102,708 | 0.03 | 52 |
| 47 | Australian Dollar, CME | 198,954 | 0.06 | NA | NA | NA |
| 48 | 30-Day Federal Fund, CBOT | 182,319 | 0.05 | 233,727 | 0.08 | 48 |
| 49 | Lumber, CME | 178,184 | 0.05 | 170,534 | 0.06 | 49 |
| 50 | Major Market Index, CBOT | 155,338 | 0.05 | 360,879 | 0.12 | 45 |
| 51 | Sugar #14, CSC | 133,898 | 0.04 | 138,609 | 0.05 | 50 |
| 52 | Deutschemark, MIDAM | 123,573 | 0.04 | 105,543 | 0.04 | 51 |
| 53 | Goldman Sachs Commodity Index, CME | 122,281 | 0.04 | NA | NA | NA |
| 54 | Palladium, NYMEX | 113,681 | 0.03 | NA | NA | NA |
| 55 | Wheat, MIDAM | 101,353 | 0.03 | 239,180 | 0.08 | 47 |

*Source: Futures Industry Association*

# Options

AN OPTION IS A CONTRACT that permits the holder to buy an asset (a *call*) or sell an asset (a *put*) at set price for a specified period of time. Before 1973, options were traded on an unregulated basis through a limited number of firms. Now options are listed and traded on five major U.S. exchanges, including the world's largest, the Chicago Board of Exchange.

## Market Value of Options Sales on U.S. Exchanges: Non-Equity Options

| Calendar Year | Non-Equity Options |
|---|---|
| 1986 | 47,887,805 |
| 1987 | 65,748,621 |
| 1988 | 35,455,956 |
| 1989 | 36,351,306 |
| 1990 | 51,793,712 |
| 1991 | 49,012,406 |

## Market Value of Options Sales on U.S. Exchanges: Equity Options

| Calendar Year | Equity Options Traded |
|---|---|
| 1986 | 40,054,282 |
| 1987 | 53,123,325 |
| 1988 | 27,163,915 |
| 1989 | 40,423,407 |
| 1990 | 27,218,738 |
| 1991 | 27,104,021 |

*Source: U.S. Securities and Exchange Commission*

## Markets Listing Equity Options

| Market | % Share |
|---|---|
| Chicago Board Options Exchange | 42.19 |
| American Stock Exchange | 33.47 |
| Philadelphia Stock Exchange | 10.36 |
| Pacific Stock Exchange | 12.10 |
| New York Stock Exchange | 1.88 |
| TOTAL | 100.00 |

## Markets Listing Index Options

| Market | % Share |
|---|---|
| Chicago Board Options Exchange | 91.88 |
| American Stock Exchange | 7.58 |
| Philadelphia Stock Exchange | 0.35 |
| Pacific Stock Exchange | 0.09 |
| New York Stock Exchange | 0.11 |
| TOTAL | 100.00 |

## Markets Listing All Options

| Market | % Share |
|---|---|
| Chicago Board Options Exchange | 60.20 |
| American Stock Exchange | 21.07 |
| Philadelphia Stock Exchange | 11.14 |
| Pacific Stock Exchange | 6.54 |
| New York Stock Exchange | 1.05 |
| TOTAL | 100.00 |

*Source: Chicago Board Options Exchange*

## U.S. Options Contracts Traded by Commodity Group

| Rank | Commodities Group | Contracts | Percent |
|---|---|---|---|
| 1989 | | | |
| 1 | Interest Rate | 28,073,883 | |
| 2 | Foreign Currency/Index | 9,119,520 | 50.63 |
| 3 | Ag Commodities | 8,113,952 | 14.63 |
| 4 | Energy Products | 6,316,183 | 11.39 |
| 5 | Precious Metals | 2,366,450 | 4.27 |
| 6 | Equity Indexes | 1,201,111 | 2.17 |
| 7 | Non-Precious Metals | 234,035 | 0.42 |
| 8 | Other | 20,996 | 0.04 |
| | TOTAL | 55,446,130 | 100.00 |
| 1990 | | | |
| 1 | Interest Rate | 35,336,832 | 55.13 |
| 2 | Ag Commodities | 9,580,512 | 14.95 |
| 3 | Foreign Currency/Index | 8,588,796 | 13.40 |
| 4 | Energy Products | 6,097,107 | 9.51 |
| 5 | Precious Metals | 2,686,774 | 4.19 |
| 6 | Equity Indexes | 1,672,425 | 2.61 |
| 7 | Non-Precious Metals | 107,387 | 0.17 |
| 8 | Other | 33,261 | 0.05 |
| | TOTAL | 64,103,094 | 100.00 |

*Options (cont'd)*

| Rank | Commodities Group | Contracts | Percent |
|------|------------------|-----------|---------|
| 1991 | | | |
| 1 | Interest Rate | 31,015,006 | 49.86 |
| 2 | Foreign Currency/Index | 11,486,318 | 18.47 |
| 3 | Ag Commodities | 8,860,003 | 14.24 |
| 4 | Energy Products | 6,405,652 | 10.30 |
| 5 | Precious Metals | 2,462,854 | 3.96 |
| 6 | Equity Indexes | 1,863,125 | 3.00 |
| 7 | Non-Precious Metals | 97,163 | 0.16 |
| 8 | Other | 11,784 | 0.02 |
| | TOTAL | 62,201,905 | 100.00 |
| 1992 | | | |
| 1 | Interest Rate | 37,428,654 | 54.05 |
| 2 | Foreign Currency/Index | 10,320,550 | 14.90 |
| 3 | Energy Products | 8,750,896 | 12.64 |
| 4 | Ag Commodities | 8,450,869 | 12.20 |
| 5 | Equity Indexes | 2,273,025 | 3.28 |
| 6 | Precious Metals | 1,916,447 | 2.77 |
| 7 | Non-Precious Metals | 87,324 | 0.13 |
| 8 | Other | 17,010 | 0.02 |
| | TOTAL | 69,244,775 | 100.00 |
| 1993 | | | |
| 1 | Interest Rate | 47,458,153 | 57.98 |
| 2 | Ag Commodities | 9,766,714 | 11.93 |
| 3 | Foreign Currency/Index | 9,588,967 | 11.71 |
| 4 | Energy Products | 8,966,434 | 10.95 |
| 5 | Equity Indexes | 2,965,862 | 3.62 |
| 6 | Precious Metals | 2,888,520 | 3.53 |
| 7 | Non-Precious Metals | 146,594 | 0.18 |
| 8 | Other | 77,391 | 0.09 |
| | TOTAL | 81,858,635 | 100.00 |

*Source: Futures Industry Association*

## U.S. Options: Contracts with Volume over 100,000

| 1993 Rank | Contracts with Volume over 100,000 | 1993 Contracts | Percent | 1992 Contracts | Percent | 1992 Rank |
|-----------|-----------------------------------|----------------|---------|----------------|---------|-----------|
| 1 | S&P 100 Index, CBOE | 64,031,944 | 35.12 | 62,427,272 | 37.78 | 1 |
| 2 | T-Bonds, CBOT | 23,435,164 | 12.85 | 20,258,740 | 12.26 | 2 |
| 3 | Eurodollar, CME | 17,008,764 | 9.33 | 13,762,628 | 8.33 | 3 |
| 4 | S&P 500 Index, CBOE | 16,454,282 | 9.02 | 13,420,174 | 8.12 | 4 |
| 5 | Crude Oil, NYMEX | 7,156,518 | 3.93 | 6,562,163 | 3.97 | 6 |
| 6 | Deutschemark, PHLX | 6,217,792 | 3.41 | 7,966,240 | 4.82 | 5 |
| 7 | Deutschemark, CME | 5,916,463 | 3.24 | 6,354,248 | 3.85 | 7 |
| 8 | T-Notes (10-Year), CBOT | 4,844,272 | 2.66 | 2,564,191 | 1.55 | 8 |
| 9 | French Franc, PSE | 3,978,929 | 2.18 | 1,261,319 | 0.76 | 14 |
| 10 | Soybeans, CME | 2,927,072 | 1.61 | 1,930,334 | 1.17 | 11 |
| 11 | S&P 500 Index, CME | 2,916,047 | 1.60 | 2,209,529 | 1.34 | 10 |
| 12 | Japanese Yen, CME | 2,261,977 | 1.24 | 1,518,409 | 0.92 | 9 |
| 13 | Corn, CBOT | 2,031,284 | 1.11 | 1,833,816 | 1.11 | 12 |
| 14 | T-Notes (5-Year), CBOT | 1,976,924 | 1.08 | 665,587 | 0.40 | 28 |
| 15 | Major Market Index, AMEX | 1,737,250 | 0.95 | 2,713,455 | 1.64 | 9 |
| 16 | Gold (1,000 oz), COMEX | 1,717,015 | 0.94 | 1,152,854 | 0.70 | 17 |
| 17 | Japanese Yen, PHLX | 1,302,396 | 0.71 | 1,305,042 | 0.79 | 13 |
| 18 | Silver (5,000 oz), COMEX | 1,094,702 | 0.60 | 676,543 | 0.41 | 27 |
| 19 | Coffee, CSC | 1,022,017 | 0.56 | 860,943 | 0.52 | 22 |
| 20 | Sugar, CSC | 916,170 | 0.50 | 848,750 | 0.51 | 24 |

*Options (cont'd)*

| 1993 Rank | Contracts with Volume over 100,000 | 1993 Contracts | Percent | 1992 Contracts | Percent | 1992 Rank |
|---|---|---|---|---|---|---|
| 21 | Heating Oil, NYMEX | 803,216 | 0.44 | 1,247,891 | 0.76 | 16 |
| 22 | Japan Index, AMEX | 758,969 | 0.42 | 765,824 | 0.46 | 26 |
| 23 | S&P MidCap Index, AMEX | 720,553 | 0.40 | 1,133,075 | 0.69 | 18 |
| 24 | Wheat, CBOT | 713,670 | 0.39 | 1,108,840 | 0.67 | 19 |
| 25 | Institutional Index, AMEX | 696,894 | 0.38 | 1,255,066 | 0.76 | 15 |
| 26 | Unleaded Regular Gas, NYMEX | 660,886 | 0.36 | 860,086 | 0.52 | 23 |
| 27 | Swiss Franc, CME | 627,923 | 0.34 | 1,026,974 | 0.62 | 20 |
| 28 | British Pound, PHLX | 528,957 | 0.29 | 789,169 | 0.48 | 25 |
| 29 | British Pound, CME | 528,239 | 0.29 | 597,352 | 0.36 | 29 |
| 30 | Live Cattle, CME | 500,664 | 0.27 | 561,058 | 0.34 | 30 |
| 31 | Russell 2000, CBOE | 494,980 | 0.27 | 40,086 | 0.02 | 42 |
| 32 | Swiss Franc, PHLX | 450,105 | 0.25 | 434,432 | 0.26 | 31 |
| 33 | OTC Index, PHLX | 392,330 | 0.22 | 126,745 | 0.08 | 38 |
| 34 | Cotton #2, NYCE | 372,074 | 0.20 | 413,091 | 0.25 | 32 |
| 35 | Natural Gas, NYMEX | 345,814 | 0.19 | NA | NA | NA |
| 36 | Cocoa (10 M Tons), CSC | 326,760 | 0.18 | 209,938 | 0.13 | 34 |
| 37 | Soybean Meal, CBOT | 306,523 | 0.17 | 152,394 | 0.09 | 36 |
| 38 | Gold/Silver Index, PHLX | 298,221 | 0.16 | 65,545 | 0.04 | 40 |
| 39 | OEX Leaps, CBOE | 289,424 | 0.16 | NA | NA | NA |
| 40 | Pharmaceutical Index, PHLX | 271,930 | 0.15 | 889,133 | 0.54 | 21 |
| 41 | Bank Index, PHLX | 236,122 | 0.13 | 7,823 | 0.00 | 44 |
| 42 | Canadian Dollar, PHLX | 220,866 | 0.12 | 188,860 | 0.11 | 35 |
| 43 | Soybean Oil, CBOT | 181,938 | 0.10 | 104,704 | 0.06 | 39 |
| 44 | Canadian Dollar, CME | 176,930 | 0.10 | 306,528 | 0.19 | 33 |
| 45 | Australian Dollar, PHLX | 159,929 | 0.09 | 142,725 | 0.09 | 37 |
| 46 | Wilshire Small Cap Index, PSE | 153,007 | 0.08 | NA | NA | NA |
| 47 | BP/DM, PHLX | 152,641 | 0.08 | 17,714 | 0.01 | 43 |
| 48 | SPX Leaps, CBOE | 146,451 | 0.08 | NA | NA | NA |
| 49 | High Grade Copper, COMEX | 146,060 | 0.08 | NA | NA | NA |
| 50 | Utility Index, PHLX | 124,050 | 0.07 | 40,290 | 0.02 | 41 |
| 51 | Orange Juice (Frozen Conc.), NYCE | 101,214 | 0.06 | NA | NA | NA |

*Source: Futures Industry Association*

# U.S. Futures and Options Exchanges

## The Various Markets of the U.S. Exchanges

| | NYSE | AMEX | MSE | PSE | PHLX | BSE | CBOE | CBOT | CME |
|---|---|---|---|---|---|---|---|---|---|
| Equities | • | • | • | • | • | • | | | |
| Listed Options | | • | | • | • | | • | | |
| OTC Options | • | • | | • | • | | • | | |
| Index Options | • | • | | • | • | | • | • | • |
| Index Futures | • | | | | | | | | |
| Currency Options | | • | | | • | | | | • |
| AGRI Options | | | | | | | | | • |
| AGRI/Currency Futures | | | | | | | | • | • |
| Options on AGRI/CURR Futures | | | | | | | | • | |

*Source: Futures Industry Association*

*U.S. Futures and Options Exchanges (cont'd)*

## Options Traded on U.S. Futures Exchanges: Volume and Market Share, 1993 and 1992

| 1993 Rank | Exchange | 1993 Contracts | Percent | 1992 Contracts | Percent | 1992 Rank |
|---|---|---|---|---|---|---|
| 1 | Chicago Board of Trade | 36,531,698 | 44.63 | 28,701,625 | 41.45 | 1 |
| 2 | Chicago Mercantile Exchange | 30,331,877 | 37.05 | 26,739,210 | 38.62 | 2 |
| 3 | New York Mercantile Exchange | 9,029,095 | 11.03 | 8,790,354 | 12.69 | 3 |
| 4 | Commodity Exchange | 2,960,524 | 3.62 | 1,943,919 | 2.81 | 4 |
| 5 | Coffee Sugar & Cocoa Exchange | 2,265,417 | 2.77 | 1,919,631 | 2.77 | 5 |
| 6 | New York Cotton Exchange | 541,097 | 0.66 | 961,525 | 1.39 | 6 |
| 7 | Kansas City Board of Trade | 89,011 | 0.11 | 86,483 | 0.12 | 7 |
| 8 | Minneapolis Grain Exchange | 37,521 | 0.05 | 16,829 | 0.02 | 10 |
| 9 | New York Futures Exchange | 36,389 | 0.04 | 46,975 | 0.07 | 8 |
| 10 | MidAmerica Commodity Exchange | 36,006 | 0.04 | 38,224 | 0.06 | 9 |
| | TOTAL | 81,858,635 | 100.00 | 69,244,775 | 100.00 | |

## Options Traded on U.S. Securities Exchanges: Volume and Market Share, 1993 and 1992*

| 1993 Rank | Exchange | 1993 Contracts | Percent | 1992 Contracts | Percent | 1992 Rank |
|---|---|---|---|---|---|---|
| 1 | Chicago Board Options Exchange | 81,640,387 | 81.26 | 75,915,781 | 79.09 | 1 |
| 2 | Philadelphia Stock Exchange | 14,246,794 | 14.18 | 12,826,344 | 13.36 | 2 |
| 3 | American Stock Exchange | 4,383,244 | 4.36 | 7,046,479 | 7.34 | 3 |
| 4 | Pacific Stock Exchange | 155,959 | 0.16 | 69,949 | 0.07 | 5 |
| 5 | New York Stock Exchange | 41,745 | 0.04 | 131,324 | 0.14 | 4 |
| | TOTAL | 100,468,129 | 100.00 | 95,989,877 | 100.00 | |

## Options Volume on U.S. Futures and U.S. Securities Exchanges 1989–1993*

| Year | Total Options on Futures Exchanges | Percent Change | Total Options on Securities Exchanges | Percent Change | Grand Total | Percent Change |
|---|---|---|---|---|---|---|
| 1989 | 55,446,130 | 12.84 | 84,910,688 | 2.77 | 140,356,818 | 6.52 |
| 1990 | 64,103,094 | 15.61 | 98,371,455 | 15.85 | 162,474,549 | 15.76 |
| 1991 | 62,201,905 | -2.97 | 93,336,788 | -5.12 | 155,538,693 | -4.27 |
| 1992 | 69,244,775 | 11.32 | 95,989,877 | 2.84 | 165,234,652 | 6.23 |
| 1993 | 81,858,635 | 18.22 | 100,468,129 | 4.67 | 182,326,764 | 10.34 |

*\* Does not include options on individual equities traded on U.S. securities exchanges.*      *Source: Futures Industry Association*

## Futures and Option Contracts by Exchange
## American Stock Exchange

Options
    Computer Technology Index
    Institutional Index
    International Market Index
    Major Market Index (XMI)
    LT-20 Index
    Oil Index
    Chicago Board of Trade
Futures
    Corn
    Oats
    Soybeans
    Soybean Meal, Soybean Oil
    Wheat
    Gold
    Silver
    U.S. Treasury Bonds
    U.S. Treasury Notes
    Two-Year U.S. Treasury Notes
    Five-Year U.S. Treasury Notes
    30-Day Interest Rate

    Major Market Index-Maxi
    Municipal Bond Index
Options on Futures
    Corn
    Oats
    Soybeans
    Soybean Meal, Soybean Oil
    Wheat
    Gold
    Silver
    U.S. Treasury Bonds
    U.S. Treasury Notes
    Five-Year U.S. Treasury Notes
    Municipal Bond Index
    Japanese Government Bonds

## Chicago Board Options Exchange

Options
    Equities
    Long-Term Equities (on selected blue chips)
    Interest Rate (Long-Term, Short-Term)
    S&P 100 Stock Index
    S&P 500 Stock Index

*U.S. Futures and Options Exchanges (cont'd)*

U.S. 30-Year Treasury Bonds
U.S. Five-Year Treasury Notes

## Chicago Mercantile Exchange

Futures and Options on Futures
    Cattle, Feeder
    Cattle, Live
    Hogs, Live
    Lumber
    Pork Bellies
Index and Option Market Division
    Futures and Options on Futures
    Nikkei 225 Stock Average
    Standard & Poor's 500 Stock Index
International Monetary Market Division
    Futures
    Australian Dollar
    British Pound
    Canadian Dollar
    Deutsche Mark
    Dollar/Deutsche Mark DIFF
    Dollar/Sterling DIFF
    Dollar/Yen DIFF
    Eurodollar Time Deposit
    Japanese Yen
    London Interbank Offered Rate
    Swiss Franc
    Treasury Bills
Options on Futures
    Australian Dollar
    British Pound
    Canadian Dollar
    Deutsche Mark
    Eurodollar Time Deposit (3 month)
    Japanese Yen
    Swiss Franc
    Treasury Bills (90 day)

## Coffee, Sugar & Cocoa Exchange

Futures
    Cocoa
    Coffee C
    Sugar No. 11, No. 14, White

## International Market Index

Options on Futures
    Cocoa
    Coffee C
    Sugar No. 11

## Commodity Exchange

Futures
    Aluminum
    Copper
    Gold
    Silver
Options on Futures
    Copper
    Gold
    Silver

## Kansas City Board of Trade

Futures
    Grain Sorghum

Mini Value Line
Stock Index
Value Line
Wheat (Hard red winter)
Options of Futures
    Wheat (Hard red winter)

## MidAmerica Commodity Exchange

Futures
    Cattle, Live
    Hogs, Live
    Corn
    Oats
    CRCE Rough Rice
    Soybeans
    Soybean Meal
    Wheat (Soft winter)
    New York Gold
    New York Silver
    Platinum
    British Pound
    Canadian Dollar
    Deutsche Mark
    Japanese Yen
    Swiss Franc
    U.S. Treasury Bills (90-day)
    U.S. Treasury Bonds
    U.S. Treasury Notes
Options on Futures
    Soybeans
    Wheat (Soft winter)
    New York Gold
    Minneapolis Grain Exchange
Futures
    High Fructose Corn Syrup
    Oats
    Wheat (Hard red spring)
    Wheat (White)
Options of Futures
    Wheat (Hard red spring)
    New York Cotton Exchange
Futures and Options on Futures
    Cotton

## New York Futures Exchange

Futures
    NYSE Composite Stock Index
    CRB Futures Price Index
    U.S. Treasury Bonds
Options on Futures
    NYSE Composite Stock Index
    CRB Futures Price Index
    New York Mercantile Exchange
Futures
    Crude Oil (Light sweet)
    Natural Gas
    No. 2 Heating Oil (New York)
    Palladium
    Platinum
    Propane
    Residual Fuel Oil
    Unleaded Gasoline
Options on Futures
    Crude Oil (Light sweet)
    No. 2 Heating Oil (New York)
    Unleaded Gasoline
    New York Stock Exchange

*U.S. Futures and Options Exchanges (cont'd)*

Options
    NYSE Composite Index

## Pacific Stock Exchange

Options
    Financial News Composite Index
    Philadelphia Board of Trade
Futures
    Australian Dollar
    British Pound
    Canadian Dollar
    Deutsche Mark
    European Currency Unit
    French Franc
    Japanese Yen
National Over-the-Counter Index
    Swiss Franc

## Philadelphia Stock Exchange

Options
    Australian Dollar
    British Pound
    Canadian Dollar
    Deutsche Mark
    European Currency Unit
    French Franc
    Gold/Silver Stock Index
    Japanese Yen
National Over-the-Counter Index
    Swiss Franc
Utility Index (European-style)
Value Line Index (European-style)

## Contact Options

The American Stock Exchange (Amex)
86 Trinity Pl.
New York, NY 10006
(212) 306-1000

Chicago Board of Trade (CBOT)
141 West Jackson Blvd.
Chicago, IL 60604
(312) 435-3500

Chicago Board Options Exchange (CBOE)
LaSalle at Van Buren
Chicago, IL 60605
(312) 786-5600

Chicago Cotton and Rice Exchange (CRCE)
141 West Jackson Blvd.
Chicago, IL 60604
(312) 341-3078

Chicago Mercantile Exchange (CME), International
Monetary Fund, and Index and Option Market
30 South Wacker Dr.
Chicago, IL 60606
(312) 786-5600

Citrus Associates of the New York Cotton Exchange
4 World Trade Center
New York, NY 10048
(212) 938-2702

Coffee, Sugar and Cocoa Exchange (CSCE)
4 World Trade Center
New York, NY 10048
(212) 938-2800

Commodity Exchange (COMEX)
4 World Trade Center
New York, NY 10048
(212)938-2900

Financial Instrument Exchange (FINEX)
4 World Trade Center
New York, NY 10048
(212) 926-2634

Kansas City Board of Trade (KCBT)
4800 Main St.
Kansas City, MO 64112
(816) 753-7500 or (816) 753-1101 (hotline)

MidAmerica Commodity Exchange (MidAm)
141 West Jackson Blvd.
Chicago, IL 60604
(312) 341-3000

Minneapolis Grain Exchange (MGE)
400 S. Fourth St.
Minneapolis, MN 55415
(612) 338-6212

New York Cotton Exchange (NYCE)
4 World Trade Center
New York, NY 10048
(212)938-2650

New York Futures Exchange (NYFE)
20 Broad St.
New York, NY 10005
(212) 623-4949 or (800) 221-7722

New York Mercantile Exchange (NYMEX)
4 World Trade Center
New York, NY 10048
(212) 938-2222

New York Stock Exchange (NYSE)
11 Wall St.
New York, NY 10005
(212) 656-8533 or (800) 692-6973 (out-of-state)

Pacific Stock Exchange (PSE)
301 Pine St.
San Francisco, CA 94101
(415) 393-4000

Philadelphia Board of Trade (PBOT)
1900 Market St.
Philadelphia, PA 19103
(215) 496-5357

Twin Cities Board of Trade (TCBOT)
430 First Ave. North
Minneapolis, MN 55415
(612) 333-6742

# Foreign Options Exchanges

## Futures and Options Exchanges by Year-End Annual Volume

### Australia

Australian Stock Exchange
20 Bridge St.
Sydney, N.S.W. 2000, Australia

Sydney Futures Exchange
Grosvenor St.
Sydney, N.S.W. 2000, Australia

### Canada

Montreal Exchange (ME)
800 Victoria Square
Montreal, Quebec, Canada H4Z 1A9
(514) 871-2424

Toronto Futures Exchange (TE)
2 First Canadian Place, Exchange Tower
Toronto, Ontario, Canada M5X 1J2
(416) 947-4487 or 4585

Toronto Stock Exchange
2 First Canadian Place, Exchange Tower
Toronto, Ontario, Canada M5X 1J2
(416) 947-4700

Vancouver Stock Exchange
609 Granville St.
Vancouver, British Columbia
Canada V7Y 1H1
(614) 689-3334

The Winnipeg Commodity Exchange
500 Commodity Exchange Tower
360 Main St.
Winnipeg, Manitoba
Canada R3C 3Z4
(204) 949-0495

### France

France Matif Automatique
52 Ave des Champs Elysses
75008 Paris, France

### Germany

Deutsche Terminboerse
Grueneburgweg 102, Postfach 17 02 03
D-6000 Frankfurt 1, Germany

### Hong Kong

Hong Kong Futures Exchange
New World Tower
16-18 Queen's Road
Hong Kong

### Japan

Osaka Securities Exchange

8-16 Kitahama, 1-chome, Chuo-ku
Osaka 541, Japan

Tokyo Commodity Exchange
10-8 Nihonbashi Horidomecho
1-chome, Chuo-ku
Tokyo 103, Japan

Tokyo International Financial Futures Exchange
Ntt Data Otemachi Bldg.
2-2-2 Otemachi, Chiyoda-ku
Tokyo 100, Japan

Tokyo Stock Exchange
2-1 Nihombashi-Kabuto-Cho
Chuo-Ku, Tokyo 103

### Netherlands

European Options Exchange (EOE)
Rokin 65, Amsterdam
1012 KK, The Netherlands

Financiele Termijnmarkt Amsterdam N.V.
Nes 49, Amsterdam
1012 KD, The Netherlands

### Singapore

Singapore International Monetary Exchange
1 Raffles Place #07-00
OUB Centre, Singapore 0104

### Switzerland

Swiss Options and Financial Futures Exchange
Neumattstrasse 7
8953 Dietikon, Switzerland

### United Kingdom

Baltic Futures Exchange
24-28 St. Mary Axe
London, England EC3A 8EP

International Petroleum Exchange of London
International House, 1 St. Katharine's Way
London, England E1 9UN

London Futures and Options Exchange
1 Commodity Quay, St. Katharine Docks
London, England E1 9AX

London International Financial Futures Exchange
The Royal Exchange
London, England EC3V 3PJ

London Metal Exchange
Plantation House, Fenchurch St.
London, England EC3M 3AP

London Traded Options Market
Old Broad St.
London, England EC2N 1H

*Source: Futures Industry Association*

# Mutual Fund Rankings and Data

A MUTUAL FUND IS A POOL OF MONEY professionally invested by a money manager. Group performance is measured by 1-year, 3-year, 5-year, and 10-year performance of the following fund categories:

## General Equity Funds

CA–Capital Appreciation Fund
G–Growth Fund
SG–Small Company Growth Fund
GI–Growth and Income Fund
EI–Equity Income Fund

## Specialty Equity-Oriented Funds

H–Health/Biotechnology Fund
NR–Natural Resources Fund
EN–Environmental Fund
TK–Science and Technology Fund
UT–Utility Fund
FS–Financial Services Fund
RE–Real Estate Fund
OI–Option Income Fund
AU–Gold Oriented Fund
GL–Global Fund
IF–International Fund
EU–European Region Fund
PC–Pacific Region Fund
JA–Japanese Fund
LT–Latin America Fund
CN–Canadian Fund

## Other Funds

B–Balanced Fund
CV–Convertible Securities Fund
I–Income Fund

FI–Fixed Income Fund

## Money Market Funds (Taxable)

UST–U.S. Treasury Money Market Funds
USS–U.S. Government Money Market Funds

## Money Market Funds (Municipal)

TEM–Tax-Exempt Money Market Funds

## General Domestic Taxable Fixed-Income Funds

GUT–General U.S. Treasury
GUS–General U.S. Government Funds
GNM–GNMA Funds
USM–U.S. Mortgage Funds
A–Corporate Debt Funds A Rated
BBB–Corporate Debt Funds BBB Rated
GB–General Bond Funds
HY–High Current Yield Funds

## World Taxable Fixed-Income Funds

GWI–General World Income Funds

## General Municipal Debt Funds

GM–General Municipal Debt Funds

## Single State Municipal Debt Funds

AZ, CA, CO, CT, FL, GA, KY, LA, MA, MD, MI, MN, MO, NC, NJ, NY, OH, OR, PA, SC, TX, and VA

## Percent Distribution of Funds by Total Net Assets

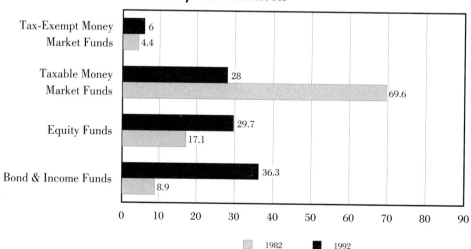

Source: Mutual Fund Fact Book, Investment Company Institute, Washington, DC, 1993. Reprinted with permission.

*Mutual Fund Rankings and Data (cont'd)*

## Number of Mutual Funds by Type of Fund ($ billions)

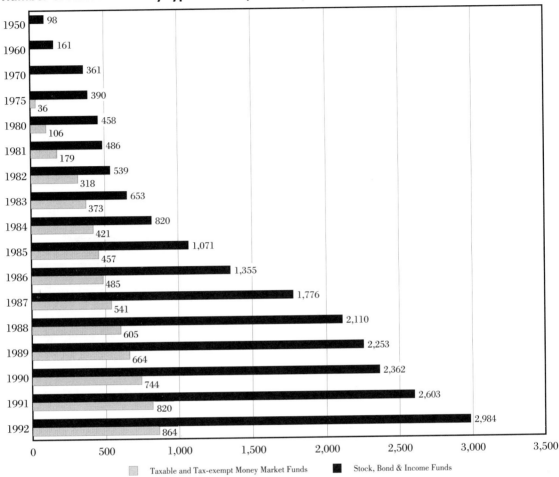

Taxable and Tax-exempt Money Market Funds     Stock, Bond & Income Funds

## Fund Assets: Equity, Income, and Bond Funds ($ billions)

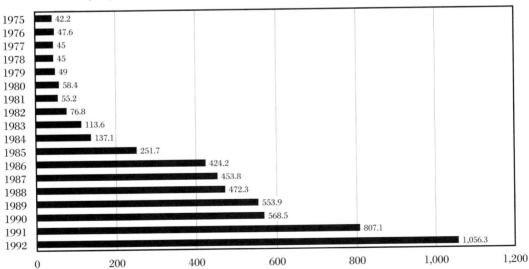

*Source: Mutual Fund Fact Book, Investment Company Institute,
Washington, DC, 1993. Reprinted with permission.*

*Mutual Fund Rankings and Data (cont'd)*

## Fund Assets: Taxable Money Market Funds ($ billions)

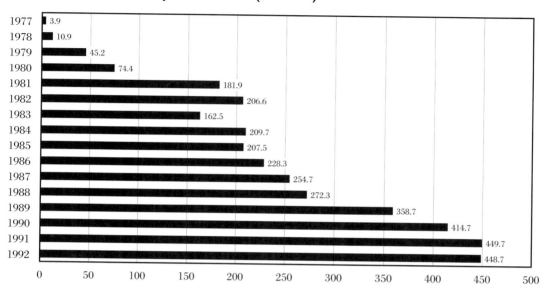

## Fund Assets: Tax-Exempt Money Market Funds ($ billions)

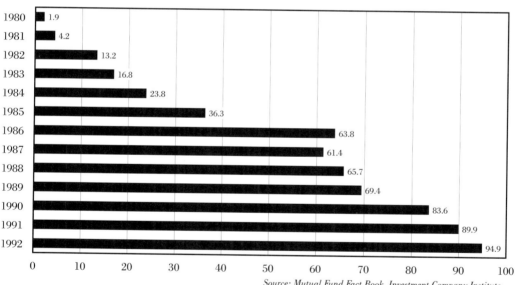

*Source: Mutual Fund Fact Book, Investment Company Institute,*
*Washington, DC, 1993. Reprinted with permission.*

# Eight Types of Mutual Funds

## Aggressive Growth Funds

Aggressive Growth Funds strive to maximize capital gains (they aim to buy low and sell high). These funds may leverage their assets by borrowing funds, and may trade in stock options.

These funds often have low current yields. Because they don't invest for dividend income, and often have little cash in interest-bearing accounts, short-term yield is not optimized.

If you believe that the market is going up, these are the funds that will benefit the most. Conversely, aggressive growth funds are the ones hardest hit in bear markets. The volatility of these funds makes them inappropriate for risk-averse investors.

## Growth Funds

Growth Funds are similar to aggressive growth funds, but do not usually trade stock options or borrow money with which to trade. Most growth funds surpass the S&P 500 during bull markets, but do a little worse than average during bear markets.

Just as in aggressive growth funds, growth funds are not aimed at the short-term market timer. The aggressive investor may find that they are an ideal complement for aggressive growth funds, as the differing investment strategies used by the two types of funds can produce maximum gains.

The volatility of these funds makes them inappropriate as the sole investment vehicle for risk-averse investors.

## Growth-Income Funds

Growth-Income Funds are specialists in blue-chip stocks. These funds invest in utilities, Dow industrials and other seasoned stocks. They work to maximize dividend income while also generating capital gains.

These funds are appropriate as a substitute for conservative investment in the stock market.

## Income Funds

Income funds focus on dividend income, while also enjoying the capital gains that usually accompany investment in common and preferred stocks. These funds are particularly favored by conservative investors.

## International Funds

International Funds hold primarily foreign securities. There are two elements of risk in this invest-ment: the normal economic risk of holding stocks, as well as the currency risk associated with repatriating money after taking the investment profits.

These funds are an important part of many portfolios, but any individual fund may prove too volatile for the average investor as the sole investment.

## Asset Allocation Funds

Asset Allocation Funds don't invest in just stocks. Instead, they focus on stocks, bonds, gold, real estate, and money market funds. This portfolio approach greatly decreases the reliance on any one segment of the marketplace, easing any declines. The upside is limited by this strategy as well.

## Precious Metal Funds

Precious Metal Funds invest in gold, silver, and platinum. Gold and (to a lesser degree) silver often move in the opposite direction from the stock market, and thus these funds can provide a hedge against investments in common stocks.

## Bond Funds

Bond Funds invest in corporate and government bonds. A common misunderstanding among investors is that the return on a bond fund is similar to the returns of the bonds purchased. One might expect that a fund that owns primarily 8 percent yielding bonds would return 8 percent to investors. In fact, the yield from the fund is based primarily on the trading of bonds, which are extraordinarily sensitive to interest rates. Thus, one could find a bond fund that was earning double-digit returns as the prime rate climbed from 4 percent to 6 percent.

In addition to mutual funds, there are money market funds, which are essentially mutual funds that invest solely in government-insured short-term instruments. These funds nearly always reflect the current interest rates, and rarely engage in interest-rate speculation.

## Recommended Resource

*The Mutual Fund Encyclopedia*
by Gerald W. Perritt
Dearborn Financial Publishing, $34.95
(800) 533-2665

# Equity Funds

## 20 Largest Equity Funds

| Fund Name | Objective | 1993 Assets ($ millions) |
|---|---|---|
| Fidelity Magellan Fund | Growth | 31,705.1 |
| Investment Co. of America | Growth & Income | 19,005.0 |
| Washington Mutual Investment | Growth & Income | 12,638.5 |
| Vanguard Windsor | Growth & Income | 10,610.8 |
| Income Fund of America | Equity Income | 10,338.9 |
| Janus Fund | Capital Appreciation | 9,199.6 |
| Fidelity Asset Manager | Flexible Portfolio | 9,094.4 |
| Fidelity Puritan | Equity Income | 8,988.2 |
| Twentieth Century: Ultra Investment | North Carolina | 8,362.4 |
| Vanguard Index: 500 Portfolio | S & P 500 Index | 8,272.7 |
| Vanguard Wellington Fund | Balanced | 8,075.8 |
| Fidelity Growth & Income | Growth & Income | 7,684.0 |
| Vanguard Windsor II | Growth & Income | 7,616.3 |
| Fidelity Equity–Income | Equity Income | 6,641.9 |
| Dean Witter Dividend Group | Growth & Income | 6,549.6 |
| Fidelity Contrafund | Growth | 6,193.3 |
| Vanguard Wellesley Income | Income | 6,011.5 |
| Europacific Growth | Income | 5,803.0 |
| Putnam Growth & Income; A | Growth & Income | 5,327.0 |
| American Mutual | Growth & Income | 5,194.3 |

## 20 Best-Performing Equity Funds, 1993

| Fund Name | Objective | 1993 Return ($) | Five-Year Return ($) |
|---|---|---|---|
| Lexington Strat. Investments | Gold Oriented | 269.78 | 9.39 |
| US: Gold Shares | Gold Oriented | 123.92 | 0.64 |
| Van Eck: International Investment Gold | Gold Oriented | 113.41 | 71.46 |
| Fidelity Select Precious Metals | Gold Oriented | 111.64 | 75.14 |
| Morgan Stanley Institutional: Asian Equity | Pacific Region | 105.71 | NA |
| Keystone Precious Metals | Gold Oriented | 101.89 | 73.35 |
| Blanchard Precious Metals | Gold Oriented | 100.42 | 33.02 |
| Excel Midas Gold Shares | Gold Oriented | 98.76 | 86.34 |
| Dean Witter Pacific Growth | Pacific Region | 94.71 | NA |
| Vanguard Special: Gold | Gold Oriented | 93.36 | 69.95 |
| Thomson: Precious Metals; A | Gold Oriented | 90.91 | NA |
| US: World Gold | Gold Oriented | 89.79 | 46.91 |
| Thomson: Precious Metals; B | Gold Oriented | 89.46 | 36.93 |
| Bull & Bear Gold Investors | Gold Oriented | 87.64 | 42.71 |
| Merrill Dragon Fund; A | Pacific Region | 87.46 | NA |
| Lexington Goldfund | Gold Oriented | 86.96 | 36.83 |
| Merrill Dragon Fund; B | Pacific Region | 86.15 | NA |
| Morgan Stanley Instl.: Emerging Market | Emerging Market | 85.81 | NA |
| Wright Equity: Hong Kong | Pacific Region | 84.32 | NA |
| Fidelity Emerging Markets | Emerging Market | 81.76 | NA |

*Source: Lipper Analytical Services, Inc.*

*Equity Funds (cont'd)*

## 20 Best-Performing Equity Funds: 5-Year

| Name | Objective | Five-Year Return ($) | 1993 Return ($) |
|------|-----------|----------------------|-----------------|
| Fidelity Sel. Biotechnology | Health | 273.38 | 0.70 |
| CGN Capital Development | Growth | 260.03 | 28.66 |
| Twentieth Century: Giftrust | Small Company Growth | 257.65 | 31.41 |
| Thomson: Opportunity; B | Capital Appreciation | 255.92 | 36.16 |
| Berger One Hundred | Growth | 247.78 | 21.20 |
| Oppenheimer Main: 1 & Growth Fund; A | Growth & Income | 246.85 | 35.39 |
| Twentieth Century: Ultra Investment | Mid-cap | 244.43 | 21.81 |
| J. Hancock Special Equity; A | Small Company Growth | 237.29 | 19.74 |
| PBHG Growth Fund | Capital Appreciation | 232.76 | 46.57 |
| Invesco Strat.: Financial | Financial Services | 232.25 | 18.50 |
| Rowe Price Science & Technology | Science/Technology | 228.01 | 24.25 |
| Fidelity Adv. Institutional Equity: Growth | Growth | 225.10 | 15.71 |
| Vista: Growth & Income; A | Growth & Income | 225.04 | 13.00 |
| Kaufmann Fund | Small Company Growth | 224.92 | 18.18 |
| Fidelity Contrafund | Growth | 224.37 | 21.43 |
| MFS Emerging Growth; B | Mid-cap | 221.48 | 24.02 |
| Alger: Small Capital | Small Company Growth | 220.81 | 12.81 |
| Invesco Strat.: Technology | Science/Technology | 218.77 | 15.03 |
| Invesco Strat.: Leisure | Specialty | 214.85 | 35.71 |
| Vista: Capital Growth; A | Mid-cap | 214.69 | 20.18 |

*Source: Lipper Analytical Services, Inc.*

# Taxable Bond Funds

## 20 Largest Taxable Bond Funds

| Fund Name | Objective | 1993 Return ($) |
|-----------|-----------|-----------------|
| CMA Money Fund | Money Market | 25,376.4 |
| Smith Barney/Shearson Daily Dividend | Money Market | 15,313.5 |
| Franklin Custodial: U.S. Government | GNMA | 13,857.1 |
| Vanguard Money Market Fund Reserves: Prime | Money Market | 12,267.3 |
| Dean Witter U.S. Government | General U.S. Government Bond | 12,198.2 |
| Fidelity Cash Reserves | Money Market | 10,096.5 |
| Charles Schwab: Money Market | Money Market | 8,164.6 |
| Dean Witter Liquid Asset | Money Market | 7,768.1 |
| Prudential Moneymart | Money Market | 7,347.9 |
| Merrill Retirement: Reserves | Money Market | 7,123.8 |
| Vanguard Fixed: GNMA Portfolio | GNMA | 7,073.2 |
| AARP GNMA | GNMA | 6,629.9 |
| Merrill Ready Assets | Money Market | 6,523.2 |
| Kemper U.S. Govt. Securities | GNMA | 6,490.0 |
| Temp. Investment Fund: Tempfund; Shearson | Institutional Money Market | 6,423.3 |
| Bond Fund of America | Corporate Debt–A Rated | 5,284.6 |
| Dreyfus Treasury Prime; A | Institutional U.S. Money Market | 5,137.8 |
| Fidelity Institutional: Treasury II; A | Institutional U.S. Money Market | 5,060.9 |
| Fidelity Institutional: U.S. Government; A | Institutional U.S. Money Market | 4,843.4 |
| Dreyfus Liquid Assets | Money Market | 4,840.2 |

*Source: Lipper Analytical Services, Inc.*

*Taxable Bond Funds (cont'd)*

## 20 Best-Performing Taxable Bond Funds, 1993

| Name | Objective | 1993 Return ($) | Five-Year Return ($) |
|---|---|---|---|
| Benham Target: 2020 | Target Maturity | 35.62 | NA |
| Keystone American Str. Income; A | High Yield | 31.69 | 69.58 |
| Dean Witter High Yield | High Yield | 31.59 | 41.32 |
| Alliance Bond: Corporate Bond; A | Corporate Bonds–BBB Rated | 31.07 | 109.17 |
| Benham Target: 2015 | Target Maturity | 30.51 | 122.17 |
| Benham Target: 2010 | Target Maturity | 26.28 | 115.43 |
| Keystone B-4 | High Yield | 26.22 | 56.64 |
| Fidelity Capital & Income | High Yield | 24.91 | 93.23 |
| MAS Funds: High Yield | High Yield | 24.57 | NA |
| Northeast Investment Trust | Flexible Income | 23.60 | 66.78 |
| PaineWebber High Income; A | High Yield | 22.79 | 100.64 |
| AAL Funds: Target 2006 | Science/Technology | 22.71 | NA |
| Paine Webber High Income; D | High Yield | 22.34 | NA |
| Metlife SS: High Income; A | High Yield | 22.32 | 70.31 |
| Loomis Sayles: Bond | Corporate Bonds–BBB Rated | 22.22 | NA |
| M. Stanley Institutional: High Yield | High Yield | 22.12 | NA |
| PaineWebber High Income; B | High Yield | 22.04 | NA |
| Fortis Advantage: High Yield | High Yield | 21.82 | 69.48 |
| T. Rowe Price High Yield | High Yield | 21.82 | 60.51 |
| Fidelity Spartan High Income | High Yield | 21.74 | NA |

## 20 Best-Performing Taxable Bond Funds: 5-Year

| Name | Objective | 1993 Return ($) | Five-Year Return ($) |
|---|---|---|---|
| Fidelity Advantage High Yield | High Yield | 20.41 | 122.33 |
| Benham Target: 2015 | Target Maturity | 30.51 | 122.17 |
| Benham Target: 2010 | Target Maturity | 26.28 | 115.43 |
| Alliance Bond: Corporate Bond; A | Corporate Bonds–BBB Rated | 31.07 | 109.17 |
| Benham Target: 2005 | Target Maturity | 21.56 | 107.59 |
| Kemper Diversified Income | High Yield | 20.88 | 103.82 |
| Oppenheimer Champion High Yield; A | High Yield | 21.37 | 102.19 |
| PaineWebber High Income; A | High Yield | 22.79 | 100.64 |
| Merrill: High Income; A | High Yield | 17.39 | 97.00 |
| Fidelity Capital & Income | High Yield | 24.91 | 93.23 |
| Benham Target: 2000 | Target Maturity | 15.46 | 92.49 |
| Liberty High Income; A | High Yield | 17.42 | 91.84 |
| Piper Jaffrey: Institutional Govt. | Short U.S. Government | 15.60 | 90.84 |
| Kemper Pt.: Diversified; Int'l. | High Yield | 19.86 | 90.53 |
| Merrill: High Income; B | High Yield | 16.66 | 89.91 |
| Scudder Zero Coupon 2000 | Target Maturity | 16.00 | 89.58 |
| American High-Income Trust | High Yield | 17.22 | 87.60 |
| Smith Barney/Shearson Inv. GD; B | Corp. Debt–A Rated | 18.05 | 87.27 |
| Vanguard Preferred Stock | Flexible Income | 13.04 | 87.26 |
| Vanguard Fixed: Long-Term Corporate | Corp. Debt–A Rated | 14.49 | 85.89 |

*Source: Lipper Analytical Services, Inc.*

# Tax-Exempt Funds

## 20 Largest Tax-Exempt Funds

| Fund Name | Objective | Latest TNA |
|---|---|---|
| Franklin CA Tax-Free Income | California Municipal | 14,112.0 |
| Franklin Fed. Tax-Free Income | General Municipal | 7,060.4 |
| CMA Tax-Exempt Fund | Tax-Exempt Money Market | 7,058.6 |
| IDS High Yield Tax-Exempt | High Yield Municipal | 6,845.7 |
| Vanguard Municipal: Intermediate-Term | International Municipal Debt | 5,238.1 |
| Franklin NY Tax-Free Income | New York | 4,779.5 |
| Dreyfus Municipal Bond | General Municipal | 4,559.9 |
| Kemper Municipal Bond | General Municipal | 4,114.9 |
| Vanguard Municipal: Money Market | Tax-Exempt Money Market | 3,878.6 |
| Putnam CA Tax-Exempt Income; A | California Municipal | 3,641.6 |
| Smith Barney/Shearson Municipal MM | Tax-Exempt Money Market | 3,482.9 |
| Colonial Tax-Exempt; A | General Municipal | 3,435.3 |
| Franklin Tax-Free: High Yield | High Yield Municipal | 3,327.3 |
| Fidelity Tax-Exempt Money Market | Tax-Exempt Money Market | 3,024.9 |
| Nuveen Municipal Bond | General Municipal | 2,683.0 |
| Putnam Tax-Exempt Income; A | General Municipal | 2,458.1 |
| Charles Schwab: Tax-Exempt | Tax-Exempt Money Market | 2,423.3 |
| Putnam NY Tax-Exempt Income; A | New York | 2,318.7 |
| Fidelity Institutional: Tax-Exempt Cash | Institutional Tax-Exempt | 2,298.7 |
| E. V. Marathon National Municipal | High Yield Municipal | 2,211.9 |

## 20 Best-Performing Tax-Exempt Funds, 1993

| Fund Name | Income Objective | 1993 Return ($) | 5-Year Return ($) |
|---|---|---|---|
| Fundamental: California Municipal | California Municipal | 16.76 | 53.46 |
| Evergreen Municipal: Ins. National | Insurance Municipal Debt | 15.97 | NA |
| Smith Barney/Shearson Mgd. Mutual; A | General Municipal | 15.90 | 67.79 |
| Executive Investment: Ins. Tax-Exempt | Insurance Municipal Debt | 15.75 | NA |
| Vankamp Tax-Free High; A | High Yield | 15.75 | 42.47 |
| Cambridge: Municipal Income; A | General Municipal | 15.61 | NA |
| UST Mstr. Tax-Exempt: Long | General Municipal | 15.60 | 71.22 |
| Lord Abbett Tax-Free: Michigan | Michigan | 15.58 | NA |
| Flagship Tax-Exempt: New York | New York | 15.47 | NA |
| Dreyfus Premium Municipal: Arizona; A | Arizona | 15.37 | NA |
| Smith Barney/Shearson Mgd. Mutual; B | General Municipal | 15.31 | NA |
| E. V. Marathon Los Angeles Tax-Free | Los Angeles | 15.26 | NA |
| First Investment Multi Ins.: Georgia | Georgia | 15.16 | NA |
| Transam Tax-Free Bond; A | General Municipal | 15.13 | NA |
| Sierra: National Municipal; A | General Municipal | 15.04 | NA |
| Vista: Tax-Free Income; A | General Municipal | 15.02 | 74.68 |
| E. V. Marathon Arizona Tax-Free | Arizona | 14.98 | NA |
| Cambridge: Municipal Income; B | General Municipal | 14.92 | NA |
| MAS Funds: PA Municipal Fixed | Pennsylvania | 14.90 | NA |
| Municipal Secs. Income: CA; Fortress | California Municipal | 14.90 | NA |

*Source: Lipper Analytical Services, Inc.*

*Tax-Exempt Funds (cont'd)*

## 20 Best-Performing Tax-Exempt Funds: 5-Year

| Fund Name | Income Objective | 5-Year Return ($) | 1993 Return ($) |
|---|---|---|---|
| Fidelity Adv. High Income Municipal | High Yield Municipal | 76.84 | 13.78 |
| Vista: Tax-Free Income; A | General Municipal | 74.68 | 15.02 |
| Dreyfus General Municipal Bond | General Municipal | 71.22 | 13.32 |
| UST Mstr. Tax-Exempt: Long | General Municipal | 71.22 | 15.60 |
| Flagship Tax-Exempt: America; A | General Municipal | 70.82 | 14.29 |
| Dreyfus Premium Municipal: Texas; A | Texas | 69.16 | 13.68 |
| Dreyfus Premium Municipal Bd.; A | General Municipal | 69.11 | 14.39 |
| Dreyfus Premium NY Municipal; A | New York | 68.62 | 14.09 |
| Smith Barney/Shearson Mgd. Mutual; A | General Municipal | 67.79 | 15.90 |
| Vanguard Municipal: Long-Term | General Municipal | 67.61 | 13.45 |
| Rochester Fd. Municipals | New York | 67.59 | 14.60 |
| Scudder High Yield Tax-Free | High Yield Municipal | 67.45 | 13.83 |
| Smith Barney Municipal: National; A | General Municipal | 67.17 | 13.46 |
| Vanguard Municipal: High Yield | High Yield Municipal | 67.05 | 12.66 |
| Dreyfus Premium Municipal: PA; A | Pennsylvania | 66.87 | 12.71 |
| First Investment Multi Ins.: Michigan | Michigan | 66.85 | 14.49 |
| United Municipal Bond | General Municipal | 66.70 | 14.31 |
| Kemper Tax-Free Income: New York | New York | 66.37 | 13.01 |
| Alliance Municipal: National; A | General Municipal | 66.30 | 13.28 |
| Vista: NY Income; A | New York | 66.24 | 13.80 |

*Source: Lipper Analytical Services, Inc.*

# Performance of Equity Fund Groups

## Overall Performance of Equity Fund Groups, 1993: 10-Year, 5-Year, 1-Year

| Type of Fund | Dec. 1993 Assets ($ mil.) | No. of Funds | 10-Year Return (%) | 5-Year Return (%) | 1-Year Return (%) |
|---|---|---|---|---|---|
| General Equity Funds Average | | | 245.58 | 78.69 | 5.43 |
| Capital Appreciation Funds | 39,792.4 | 154 | 249.27 | 83.12 | 8.34 |
| Growth Funds | 173,318.0 | 476 | 249.75 | 78.12 | 3.79 |
| Mid Cap Funds | 28,203.5 | 81 | 244.86 | 105.37 | 10.80 |
| Small Company Growth Funds | 29,770.8 | 219 | 258.32 | 97.83 | 11.13 |
| Growth & Income Funds | 174,989.4 | 362 | 240.43 | 70.07 | 3.30 |
| S & P 500 Objective Funds | 17,873.1 | 40 | 284.51 | 71.77 | 0.91 |
| Equity Income Funds | 60,740.8 | 100 | 224.17 | 61.51 | 2.80 |
| Health/Biotechnology Funds | 4,409.5 | 16 | 445.76 | 132.38 | 14.36 |
| Natural Resources Funds | 2,235.5 | 29 | 92.23 | 37.43 | 4.79 |
| Environmental Funds | 280.5 | 11 | 199.36 | 46.11 | 2.23 |
| Science & Technology Funds | 4,035.6 | 25 | 266.26 | 135.95 | 21.22 |
| Specialty/Miscellaneous Funds | 2,385.5 | 26 | 448.86 | 85.27 | 11.86 |
| Utility Funds | 27,248.1 | 73 | 248.61 | 74.28 | 2.50 |
| Financial Services Funds | 1,903.0 | 14 | 309.11 | 128.68 | 0.21 |
| Real Estate Funds | 970.4 | 11 | NA | 52.74 | 5.77 |
| World Equity Funds Average | | | 213.62 | 48.17 | 26.58 |
| Gold Oriented Funds | 5,774.7 | 34 | 32.65 | 30.49 | 40.05 |
| Global Funds | 32,039.9 | 97 | 286.59 | 57.48 | 19.32 |
| Global Small Company Funds | 4,833.4 | 15 | 195.18 | 70.24 | 25.49 |

*Performance of Equity Fund Groups (cont'd)*

| Type of Fund | Dec. 1993 Assets ($ mil.) | No. of Funds | 10-Year Return (%) | 5-Year Return (%) | I-Year Return (%) |
|---|---|---|---|---|---|
| International Funds | 45,275.2 | 165 | 278.96 | 52.49 | 24.75 |
| European Region Funds | 5,298.6 | 33 | NA | 46.99 | 21.36 |
| Pacific Region Funds | 11,322.9 | 41 | 317.23 | 56.42 | 33.09 |
| Emerging Markets Funds | 6,177.8 | 19 | 256.47 | 89.06 | 45.07 |
| Japanese Funds | 953.7 | 7 | 265.92 | 9.97 | 24.00 |
| Latin American Funds | 2,246.2 | 10 | NA | NA | 47.24 |
| Canadian Funds | 142.3 | 2 | NA | 33.65 | 16.14 |
| ALL EQUITY FUNDS AVERAGE | | | 243.17 | 75.62 | 9.54 |
| Flexible Portfolio Funds | 23,562.8 | 114 | 191.67 | 65.95 | 3.96 |
| Global-Flexible Portfolio Funds | 8,339.7 | 25 | 84.86 | 56.15 | 12.17 |
| Balanced Funds | 47,075.6 | 155 | 231.89 | 65.92 | 3.00 |
| Balanced Target Maturity Funds | 976.5 | 9 | NA | 71.43 | 3.20 |
| Convertible Securities Funds | 3,705.8 | 26 | 200.12 | 75.83 | 7.16 |
| Income Funds | 13,666.3 | 21 | 225.40 | 62.98 | 3.39 |
| World Income Funds | 34,508.7 | 156 | 172.46 | 58.18 | 4.50 |
| Fixed Income Funds | 344,469.3 | 1,135 | 171.96 | 56.84 | 3.04 |
| TOTAL | 1,158,525.5 | 3,701 | | | |
| AVERAGE | | | 225.76 | 68.85 | 6.84 |

## Top Performing Funds: Science & Technology

| Fund Name | 1993 Return ($) | 5-Year Return ($) | 10-Year Return ($) |
|---|---|---|---|
| Seligman Communication; A | 35.69 | 188.56 | 411.31 |
| Smith Barney/Shearson Tel. Gr.; A | 35.30 | 134.01 | 390.19 |
| Smith Barney/Shearson Tel. Gr.; B | 34.36 | NA | NA |
| Fidelity Select Software | 32.48 | 195.95 | NA |
| Fidelity Select Electronic | 32.16 | 178.86 | NA |
| J. Hancock Fr. Global Technology; A | 32.06 | 77.14 | 115.12 |
| Fidelity Select Development Comm. | 31.74 | NA | NA |
| Fidelity Select Telecommunications | 29.65 | 146.78 | NA |
| Fidelity Select Computer | 28.86 | 159.94 | NA |
| Fidelity Select Technology | 28.63 | 187.42 | 104.06 |

## Top Performing Funds: Health & Biotechnology

| Fund Name | 1993 Return ($) | 5-Year Return ($) | 10-Year Return ($) |
|---|---|---|---|
| Capstone Medical Research | 26.41 | 93.58 | NA |
| Vanguard Special: Health | 11.81 | 88.07 | NA |
| Franklin Global Health | 6.21 | NA | NA |
| Dean Witter Health Science | 5.63 | NA | NA |
| Fidelity Select Medical | 5.53 | 89.40 | NA |
| GT Global Health Care; A | 2.61 | 58.50 | NA |
| Fidelity Select Health | 2.42 | 92.79 | 471.65 |
| J. Hancock Fr. Global Rx. | 1.20 | NA | NA |
| Fidelity Select Biotechnology | 0.70 | 159.41 | NA |
| Putnam Health Sciences; A | -0.04 | 53.70 | 304.02 |

*Source: Lipper Analytical Services, Inc.*

*Performance of Equity Fund Groups (cont'd)*

## Top Performing Funds: Financial Services

| Fund Name | 1993 Return ($) | 5-Year Return ($) | 10-Year Return ($) |
|---|---|---|---|
| Fidelity Select Brokerage | 49.30 | 173.47 | NA |
| Fidelity Select Home Financial | 27.26 | 206.93 | NA |
| J. Hancock Fr. Reg. Bank; A | 21.11 | NA | NA |
| J. Hancock Fr. Reg. Bank; B | 20.54 | 171.17 | NA |
| Invesco Strategic: Financial | 18.50 | 232.25 | NA |
| Fidelity Select Financial | 17.60 | 145.14 | 339.27 |
| Retire. Plan America: GI Value | 14.87 | NA | NA |
| Fidelity Select Regional Banks | 11.04 | 174.72 | NA |
| PaineWebber Reg. Financial Growth; A | 10.33 | 170.05 | NA |
| PaineWebber Reg. Financial Growth; B | 9.57 | NA | NA |

*Source: Lipper Analytical Services, Inc.*

## Total Institutional Assets in Mutual Funds ($ billions)

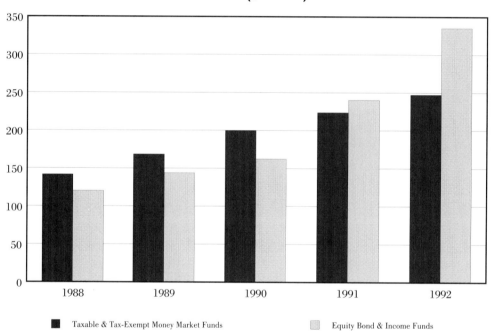

■ Taxable & Tax-Exempt Money Market Funds      ▧ Equity Bond & Income Funds

*Source: Mutual Fund Fact Book, Investment Company Institute,*
*Washington, DC, 1993. Reprinted with permission.*

*Delphi offers current commodities quotes from exchanges around the world. GO BUS COM.*

# Choosing a Mutual Fund

## 10 Questions to Ask About a Mutual Fund

### 1. Does this fund match my investment objectives?

Spend some time to determine your investment goals, then find a fund or funds that match them.

### 2. What is the load (fee) for purchasing shares?

Some funds charge an upfront fee (a load) for buying into a fund, while others don't. This can dramatically affect your real return.

### 3. Is there a redemption fee or a management fee?

Some funds charge you to redeem your shares. You should also check to see if the fund is liquid—making it easy to redeem your shares.

### 4. How often, and in what form, are reports generated?

If you're concerned about keeping very close tabs on your investment, ask to see sample reports.

### 5. Can I write checks against the fund?

This convenient feature makes it easy to remove money from a fund. Some funds charge a per-check fee, and others don't permit this at all.

### 6. Can I switch among a family of funds? Is there a charge?

Major fund providers, like Fidelity, give you the flexibility of switching from one fund to another by phone. This is convenient for those interested in short-range management of their money, and is less important to those seeking a long-term home for their cash.

### 7. Is the fund registered with the SEC?

While overseas funds may occasionally post tremendous profits, in the long run the oversight provided by the SEC provides an important safety net.

### 8. Is the fund leveraged?

Funds that borrow money to invest can post spectacular gains during bull markets. On the other hand, this strategy can virtually wipe out an investment if the market reacts poorly. Be aware of the risk to your principal as well as your interest.

### 9. What are the fund's philosophy and current holdings?

Closely examine a fund's approach to the market. You may be concerned about investments in certain industries or countries, or you may find the management of the fund too conservative or aggressive for your comfort.

### 10. What is the fund's long-term track record?

While there is little correlation between immediate past performance and future performance, there is some. Look for a fund that has consistently ranked in the top third or quarter of its category. This consistency makes it more likely that the firm will continue the policies that attracted you to it in the first place.

---

## The Top Reference Sources

*Morningstar Mutual Funds*, $395/year
225 W. Wacker Dr.
Chicago, IL 60606
(800) 876-6000

Morningstar is considered to be a watchdog organization for information on mutual funds. Its 32-page, biweekly updates cover over 1,200 mutual funds. The analysis provided includes a historical performance, information on fund managers and fees, ranking against other funds, top holdings, and quarterly returns. Morningstar also adds its own rating of risk and return so that the reader can analyze potential investments.

# Non-Stock Investments

IN ADDITION TO INVESTING IN STOCKS and bonds, commodities, futures, options, and all types of funds, people over time have invested their money in the pursuit of comfort and culture—in real estate, diamonds, paintings, and ceramics. While these investments can bring great personal and aesthetic pleasure, they are known to be notoriously volatile. Experts advise that you only purchase what you love. Here's how real estate and collectibles compare to more traditional investments:

## Compound Rates of Return on Various Investments

| Asset | 20 Years | | 10 Years | | 5 Years | | 1 Year | |
|---|---|---|---|---|---|---|---|---|
| | Return (%) | Rank | Return (%) | Rank | Return (%) | Rank | Return (%) | Rank |
| Stocks | 12.2 | 1 | 14.8 | 1 | 15.1 | 1 | 11.6 | 2 |
| Bonds | 9.8 | 2 | 13.2 | 2 | 13.1 | 2 | 14.8 | 1 |
| Stamps | 9.6 | 3 | -1.7 | 11 | 0.5 | 11 | 8.8 | 4 |
| 3-Month Treasury Bills | 8.8 | 4 | 7.3 | 4 | 6.6 | 4 | 3.3 | 8 |
| Diamonds | 8.5 | 5 | 5.9 | 5 | 4.3 | 5 | 1.5 | 11 |
| Oil | 7.5 | 6 | -4.7 | 12 | 1.7 | 9 | -6.3 | 12 |
| Gold | 6.9 | 7 | -1.0 | 9 | -4.2 | 12 | 9.6 | 3 |
| Housing | 6.7 | 8 | 4.4 | 7 | 3.7 | 7 | 1.8 | 10 |
| Consumer Price Index | 6.1 | 9 | 3.8 | 8 | 4.2 | 6 | 3.3 | 7 |
| Chinese Ceramics | 5.8 | 10 | 7.6 | 3 | 9.8 | 3 | -7.5 | 13 |
| U.S. Farmland | 5.4 | 11 | -1.2 | 10 | 2.1 | 8 | 2.3 | 9 |
| Foreign Exchange | 3.4 | 12 | 5.6 | 6 | 1.7 | 10 | 6.2 | 6 |
| Silver | 2.7 | 13 | -10.1 | 13 | -8.5 | 13 | 8.4 | 5 |

*Source: Salomon Brothers*

## The Top Reference Sources

Lipper Analytical Services
74 Trinity Pl.
New York, NY 10006
(212) 393-1300

Lipper Analytical Services is a publisher of statistical data covering the investment company industry in the U.S. and overseas. Lipper currently tracks the performance of over 8,600 investment companies, including those invested in by variable annuity and variable life contracts with assets in excess of $1.8 trillion.

The company also publishes specialized reports intended for investment managers. These include reports on fund performance, portfolio analysis, and fee and expense breakdown. Analysis of the brokerage firm industry is another specialized service.

# Retirement

FEDERAL INCOME TAX LAWS permit the establishment of a number of types of retirement plans, each of which may be funded with mutual fund shares.

## Individual Retirement Accounts

All wage-earners under the age of 70 1/2 may set up an Individual Retirement Account (IRA). The individual may contribute as much as 100 percent of his or her compensation each year, up to $2,000. Earnings are tax-deferred until withdrawal. The amount contributed each year may be wholly or partially tax-deductible. Under the Tax Reform Act of 1986, all taxpayers not covered by employer-sponsored retirement plans can continue to take the full deduction for IRA contributions. Those who are covered, or who are married to someone who is covered, must have an adjusted gross income of no more than $25,000 (single) or $40,000 (married, filing jointly) to take the full deduction. The deduction is phased out for incomes between $25,000 and $35,000 (single) and $40,000 and $50,000 (married, filing jointly). An individual who qualifies for an IRA and has a spouse who either has no earnings or elects to be treated as having no earnings, may contribute up to 100 percent of his or her income or $2,250, whichever is less.

## Simplified Employee Pensions (SEPs)

SEPs are employer-sponsored plans that may be viewed as an aggregation of separate IRAs. In an SEP, the employer contributes up to $30,000 or 15 percent of compensation, whichever is less, to an Individual Retirement Account maintained for the employee. SEPs established for employers with 25 or fewer employees may contain a "cash or deferred" arrangement allowing employees to make additional elective salary deferrals to the SEP. The cash or deferred arrangement for smaller employers is called a SARSEP, for salary reduction SEP.

## Corporate and Self-Employed Retirement Plans

Tax-qualified pension and profit-sharing plans may be established by corporations or self-employed individuals. Changes in the tax laws have made retirement plans for employees of corporations and those for self-employed individuals essentially comparable. Contributions to a plan are tax-deductible and earnings accumulate on a tax-sheltered basis.

The maximum annual amount which may be contributed to a defined contribution plan on behalf of an individual is limited to the lesser of 13 percent of the individual's compensation or $30,000.

Section 403(b)of the Internal Revenue Code permits employees of certain charitable organizations and public school systems to establish tax-sheltered retirement programs. These plans may be invested in either annuity contracts or mutual fund shares.

## Section 401(k) Plans

One particularly popular type of tax-qualified retirement plan which may be offered by either corporate or non-corporate entities is the 401(k) plan. A 401(k) plan is usually a profit-sharing plan that includes a "cash or deferred" arrangement. The cash or deferred arrangement permits employees to have a portion of their compensation contributed to a tax-sheltered plan on their behalf, or paid to them directly as additional taxable compensation. Thus, an employee may elect to reduce his or her taxable compensation with contributions to a 401(k) plan where those amounts will accumulate tax-free. Employers often "match" these amounts with employer contributions. The Tax Reform Act of 1986 established new, tighter anti-discrimination requirements for 401(k) plans and curtailed the amount of elective deferrals which may be made by all employees. Nevertheless, 401(k) plans remain excellent and popular retirement savings vehicles.

## Section 403(b) Plans

Section 403(b) of the Internal Revenue Code permits employees of certain charitable organizations and public school systems to establish tax-sheltered retirement programs. These plans may be invested in either annuity contracts or mutual fund shares.

*Source: Mutual Fund Fact Book, Investment Company Institute, Washington, DC, 1993. Reprinted with permission.*

## Recommended Resource

*Mutual Fund Fact Book*
Investment Company Institute, $25
P.O. Box 66140
Washington, DC 20035
(202) 326-5872

*Retirement (cont'd)*

## Growth in Mutual Fund IRA Plans ($ billions)

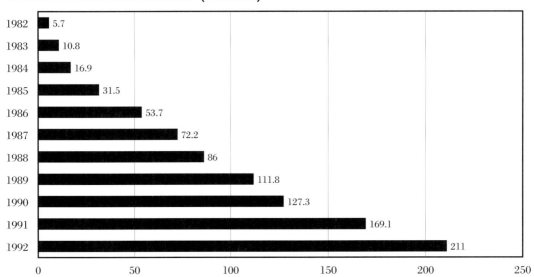

## Growth in Mutual Fund Self-Employed Retirement Plans ($ billions)

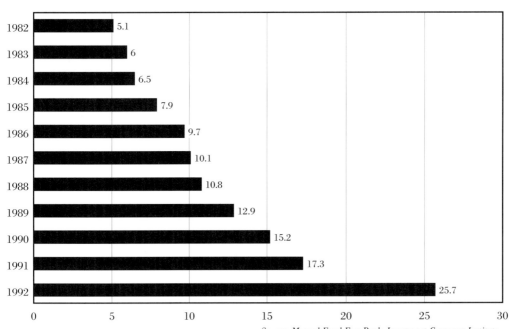

*Source: Mutual Fund Fact Book, Investment Company Institute,*
*Washington, DC, 1993. Reprinted with permission.*

# Actuaries

ACTUARIES USE MATHEMATICAL probability to project the financial effects that various events–birth, marriage, sickness, accident, fire, liability, retirement, death–have on insurance, benefit plans, and other financial security systems.

The American Academy of Actuaries is the best source of information on the actuarial profession. The Academy's *Fact Book* provides the most general information on the field, including assessments on the industry's past and future, and information on the academy programs and publications both for people inside and outside the field. The Academy's bi-monthly magazine, *Contingencies*, their monthly newsletter *The Actuarial Update*, and the *Enrolled Actuaries Report* (published 5 to 6 times yearly) explore current actuarial issues in-depth. Another publication, *The Issues Digest*, summarizes recent Washington legislative activities as they relate to the actuarial profession.

The *Directory of Actuarial Memberships*, published jointly by the two largest actuarial societies, the Academy and the Society of Actuaries (see below) lists all actuaries in North America, their professional affiliations, and qualifications.

## Recommended Resources

The American Academy of Actuaries
1720 I St., NW, 7th Floor
Washington, DC 20006
(202) 223-8196
    Represents actuaries in all practice specialties.

Society of Actuaries
475 N. Martingale Rd., Suite 800
Schaumburg, IL 60173
(708) 706-3500
    Represents actuaries working in the fields of life and health insurance, employee benefits, and pensions.

Casualty Actuarial Society
1100 N. Glebe Rd., Suite 600
Arlington, VA 22201
(703) 276-3100
    Represents actuaries specializing in property and liability insurance, workers' compensation, and liability coverage fields.

Conference of Actuaries in Public Practice
475 N. Martingale Rd., Suite 800
Schaumburg, IL 60173
(708) 706-3535
    Represents consulting actuaries in all fields of the practice.

American Society of Pension Actuaries
4350 N. Fairfax Dr., Suite 820
Arlington, VA 22203
(703) 516-9300
    Provides membership services to pension plan consultants and administrators.

# Financing a Business

INSTITUTIONS THAT OFFER VENTURE capital vary in size, scope of interest and qualification requirements. Although banking institutions do offer venture capital, much of this money is available through nonbank-related venture capital firms. Some offer start-up loans, while others lend money to established businesses. Some of these organizations have a minimum as low as $5,000 while others have a much larger minimum requirement. The following is a list representing venture capital firms around the country:

## Venture Capital Firms

| Company | City, State | Phone |
|---|---|---|
| ABS Ventures Limited Partnership | Baltimore, MD | (410) 783-3263 |
| Advanced Technology Ventures | Boston, MA | (617) 423-4050 |
| Allsop Venture Partners | Cedar Rapids, IA | (319) 363-8971 |
| Applied Technology | Lexington, MA | (617) 862-8622 |
| Arete Ventures | Rockville, MD | (301) 881-2555 |
| Asset Management | Palo Alto, CA | (415) 494-7400 |
| Austin Ventures | Austin, TX | (512) 479-0055 |
| BT Capital | New York, NY | (212) 454-1903 |
| Bradford Ventures | New York, NY | (212) 221-4620 |
| Capital Health Venture Partners | Chicago, IL | (312) 427-1227 |

*Financing a Business (cont'd)*

| Company | City, State | Phone |
| --- | --- | --- |
| Capital Southwest | Dallas, TX | (214) 233-8242 |
| The Centennial Funds | Denver, CO | (303) 298-9066 |
| Charter Venture Capital | Palo Alto, CA | (415) 325-6953 |
| Cherry Tree Ventures | Bloomington, MN | (612) 893-9012 |
| Cureton & Co. | Houston, TX | (713) 658-9806 |
| DSV Partners | Princeton, NJ | (609) 924-6420 |
| Edelson Technology Partners | Saddlebrook, NJ | (201) 843-4474 |
| First Analysis | Chicago, IL | (312) 258-1400 |
| Frontenac Company | Chicago, IL | (312) 368-0044 |
| Grace Ventures/Horn Venture Partners | Cupertino, CA | (408) 725-0774 |
| Hickory Venture Capital | Huntsville, AL | (205) 539-1931 |
| Horizon Partners | Milwaukee, WI | (414) 271-2200 |
| Houston Partners | Houston, TX | (713) 222-8600 |
| IEG Venture Management | Chicago, IL | (312) 993-7500 |
| Johnston Associates | Princeton, NJ | (609) 924-3131 |
| Lubar & Co. | Milwaukee, WI | (414) 291-9000 |
| M&I Ventures | Milwaukee, WI | (414) 765-7910 |
| Marquette Venture Partners | Deerfield, IL | (708) 940-1700 |
| Medical Innovation Partners | Minnetonka, MN | (612) 931-0154 |
| Meridian Venture Partners | Philadelphia, PA | (215) 254-2999 |
| Mesirow Private Equity Investments | Chicago, IL | (312) 670-6099 |
| Northwood Ventures | Syosset, NY | (516) 364-5544 |
| O'Donnell & Masur | Dallas, TX | (214) 692-8177 |
| P.R. Venture Partners, L.P. | Boston, MA | (617) 357-9600 |
| Palmer Partners L.P. | Woburn, MA | (617) 933-5445 |
| Paragon Venture Partners | Menlo Park, CA | (415) 854-8000 |
| Philadelphia Ventures | Philadelphia, PA | (215) 732-4445 |
| Phoenix Partners | Seattle, WA | (206) 624-8968 |
| Point Venture Partners | Pittsburgh, PA | (412) 261-1966 |
| Primus Venture Partners | Cleveland, OH | (216) 621-2185 |
| Rain Hill Group | New York, NY | (212) 752-2722 |
| S.R. One, Limited | Wayne, PA | (610) 293-3400 |
| Saugatuck Capital | Stamford, CT | (203) 348-6669 |
| Senmed Medical Ventures | Cincinnati, OH | (513) 563-3240 |
| Sierra Ventures | Menlo Park, CA | (415) 854-1000 |
| Society Venture Capital | Cleveland, OH | (216) 689-5776 |
| South Atlantic Venture Fund | Tampa, FL | (813) 253-2500 |
| Technology Partners | San Francisco, CA | (415) 435-1935 |
| Technology Venture Investors | Menlo Park, CA | (415) 854-7472 |
| Utah Ventures | Salt Lake City, UT | (801) 583-5922 |
| Venture Capital Fund of America | New York, NY | (212) 838-5577 |
| Venture Capital Fund of New England | Boston, MA | (617) 439-4646 |
| VIMAC | Boston, MA | (617) 574-0566 |
| Wind Point Partners | Chicago, IL | (312) 649-4000 |
| Wolfensohn | New York, NY | (212) 909-8100 |

*Financing a Business (cont'd)*

### Looking for Investors On-Line

Finding interested and appropriate investors for your company can be the greatest of all start-up challenges. Now a number of computer-based services are making the process of meeting and match-

ing much easier through the sharing of financial and investment information on-line. Subscribers to these services, both the company and the investor, pay a fee for listing their needs and criteria for investment.

### Sources for Investors On-Line

| Network | Area Served | Phone |
|---|---|---|
| Kentucky Investment Capital | National | (502) 564-4252 |
| Mid-Atlantic Investment Network | Mostly Mid-Atlantic | (301) 405-2149 |
| Northwest Capital | Oregon | (503) 282-6273 |
| Pacific Venture Capital Network | California | (714) 509-2990 |
| Private Investor | South Carolina | (803) 648-6851 |
| Texas Capital Network | National | (512) 794-9398 |
| Technology Capital Network | Mostly Northeast | (617) 253-7163 |

*Source: Inc. Magazine*

# Investment Banks/Brokerage Houses

## Top 10 Underwriters of Debt and Equity, 1993

| Managers | Proceeds ($ mil.) | Market Share |
|---|---|---|
| Merrill Lynch & Co. | 194,096.2 | 12.7 |
| Goldman Sachs | 152,382.1 | 10.0 |
| Lehman Brothers | 130,102.5 | 8.5 |
| CS First Boston/Credit Suisse | 116,292.1 | 7.6 |
| Salomon Brothers | 104,590.3 | 6.9 |
| Kidder Peabody | 102,861.4 | 6.7 |
| Morgan Stanley | 90,049.6 | 5.9 |
| Bear Stearns | 57,472.3 | 3.8 |
| Nomura Securities | 39,214.4 | 2.6 |
| Donaldson, Lufkin & Jenrette | 37,115.3 | 2.4 |

## Top 10 Underwriters of U.S. Debt and Equity, 1993

| Managers | Proceeds ($ mil.) | Market Share | No. of Issues |
|---|---|---|---|
| Merrill Lynch & Co. | 173,732.7 | 16.3 | 1,008 |
| Goldman Sachs | 127,787.2 | 12.0 | 636 |
| Lehman Brothers | 115,621.4 | 10.9 | 682 |
| Kidder Peabody | 94,755.7 | 8.9 | 312 |
| Salomon Brothers | 90,788.8 | 8.5 | 503 |
| CS First Boston | 89,761.8 | 8.4 | 452 |
| Morgan Stanley | 67,969.3 | 6.4 | 414 |
| Bear Stearns | 56,192.7 | 5.3 | 288 |
| Donaldson, Lufkin & Jenrette | 36,677.1 | 3.4 | 227 |
| PaineWebber | 30,115.9 | 2.8 | 180 |

*Source: Securities Data Company*

*Investment Banks/Brokerage Houses (cont'd)*

## Top 10 Underwriters of International Debt and Equity, 1993

| Managers | Proceeds ($ mil.) | Market Share | No. of Issues |
|---|---|---|---|
| CS First Boston/Credit Suisse | 26,530.2 | 5.7 | 165 |
| Nomura Securities | 25,356.4 | 5.5 | 120 |
| Goldman Sachs | 24,594.8 | 5.3 | 145 |
| Deutsche Bank AG | 23,781.2 | 5.1 | 76 |
| Morgan Stanley | 22,080.4 | 4.8 | 120 |
| Merrill Lynch & Co. | 20,363.5 | 4.4 | 161 |
| UBS Ltd/Union Bank Switzerland | 18,107.4 | 3.9 | 111 |
| Banque Paribas | 17,450.1 | 3.8 | 81 |
| Swiss Bank | 15,861.1 | 3.4 | 110 |
| Lehman Brothers | 14,481.1 | 3.1 | 117 |

## Top Markets of U.S. Debt and Equity, 1993

| Market | Amount ($ millions) | Top Ranked Manager |
|---|---|---|
| U.S. Domestic | 933.2 | Merrill Lynch |
| Straight Debt | 432.7 | Merrill Lynch |
| Convertible Debt | 9.3 | Merrill Lynch |
| Junk Bonds | 54.5 | Merrill Lynch |
| Investment Grade Debt | 378.2 | Merrill Lynch |
| Mortgage Debt | 420.7 | Kidder Peabody |
| Asset-Backed Debt | 59.5 | CS First Boston |
| Mortgage and Asset Backed Debt | 480.2 | Kidder Peabody |
| Preferred Stock | 28.4 | Merrill Lynch |
| Common Stock | 102.3 | Merrill Lynch |
| IPOs | 41.6 | Merrill Lynch |
| Closed-End Funds | 15.9 | Merrill Lynch |
| International Debt | 442.9 | Nomura Securities |
| International Equity | 18.9 | Merrill Lynch |

*Source: Securities Data Company*

## The Top Reference Sources

*Commodity Prices*
Gale Research, $69.50
(800) 877-4253

Encompassing 14,000 listings for 10,000 products and 200 sources, this book gives you specific information to lead you to the periodicals, yearbooks, and other sources that list commodity prices. The entries are arranged by commodity, and there is an extensive index.

# Alternative Financing

IN ADDITION TO BANKS, SBA loans, and traditional venture capital firms, there are a range of other, less traditional, financing alternatives available to entrepreneurs.

Here is a checklist of five alternatives, as assembled by Jay Levinson and Bruce Blechman, authors of *Guerrilla Financing*.

## Receivable Financing

Extending credit to your customers is similar to lending them money. You are essentially loaning them cash while they have your product or service.

Short-term revolving financing is provided by factors or receivable lenders. These firms recognize your receivables as a valuable asset, and are usually willing to lend against it, regardless of your company's financial position.

Factors will purchase your receivables (at a discount) and collect the money from your customers directly. For example, if a company sells $1,000,000 in clothing to Macy's, a factor might pay $900,000 for the receivable. It is then up to the factor to collect the entire invoice directly from Macy's.

A receivables lender will loan money against the invoice and hold it as collateral. Once the invoice is paid, your company repays the lender.

This is a common form of lending. Check your local yellow pages under Factors, or the Corporate Finance Sourcebook for firms that offer this service.

## Customer Financing

No one knows your business better than your customers. If your product or service is valuable and difficult to replace, many of your customers may be interested in financing your growth.

This is obviously a risky, time-consuming method of finding financing, but if the proper match is made, both parties can benefit.

## Equipment Financing

When purchasing expensive capital equipment, a company often has the opportunity to finance the purchase, or enter into a lease. In both cases, money is freed up, and the company gains the ability to use the machinery without sacrificing its cash position.

Many banks and manufacturers are willing to finance the purchase of capital equipment. They will lend your company money against the value of the equipment purchased, holding the equipment as collateral. The downside of this approach is that the loan appears on your balance sheet, affecting your company's leverage and your ability to borrow against the value of the company.

Leasing is an increasingly common method of financing. In this situation, the company never takes title to the equipment. Instead, the leasing company purchases the equipment and leases it to the company for a monthly fee. There are two significant advantages to this arrangement: the company doesn't need to dispose of the equipment at the end of the lease, and the lease is off balance sheet, meaning that since there is no loan, a company's debt load is not affected.

## Real Estate Financing

Many companies don't realize that their real estate is not fully leveraged. Banks prefer to make loans against land because they are more comfortable placing a value on it. Check the real estate section of the Sunday paper to find mortgage brokers in your area.

## Venture Capital Clubs

These clubs seek to eliminate the middleman by bringing small investors together with entrepreneurs in search of capital. These small organizations make it easy for a company to speak directly to a motivated lender. The downside is that these are people lending their own money, so there is often an emotional side to the process.

Connecticut Venture Capital Fund
200 Fisher Dr.
Avon, CT 06001
(203) 677-0183

Long Island Venture Group
Long Island University, CW Post Campus
College of Management
North Blvd., Worth Hall, Room 309
Brookville, NY 11548
(516) 299-3017

New Enterprise Forum
211 E. Herron, Suite 1
Ann Arbor, MI 48104
(313) 665-4433

Venture Association of New Jersey
177 Madison Ave.
P.O. Box CN 1982
Morristown, NJ 07960
(201) 267-4200, ext. 193

New York Venture Group
605 Madison Ave., Suite 300
New York, NY 10022
(212) 832-7300

Westchester Venture Capital Network
c/o Chamber of Commerce
222 Mamaroneck Ave.
White Plains, NY 10605
(914) 948-2110

*Alternative Financing (cont'd)*

Ohio Venture Association
1127 Euclid Ave., Suite 343
Cleveland, OH 44125
(216) 566-8884

Delaware Valley Venture Group
1234 Market St., Suite 1800
Philadelphia, PA 19107
(215) 972-3960

Southeastern Venture Capital
The Meyering Corporation
206 30 Harper Ave., Suite 103
Harper Woods, MI 48225
(313) 886-2331

Gold Coast Venture Capital Club
5820 North Federal, Suite 4
Boca Raton, FL 33478
(407) 997-6594

Mid-South Venture Group
5180 Park Ave., Suite 310
Memphis, TN 38119
(901) 761-3084

Florida Venture Group
2838 Kansas St.
Oviedo, FL 32765
(407) 365-5347

Venture Club of Iowa City
First Capital Development
325 E. Washington
Iowa City, IA 52240
(319) 354-3939

Grand Island Industrial Foundation
309 W. 2nd St.
P.O. Box 1486
Grand Island, NE 68802
(308) 382-9210

Birmingham Venture Club
(networking and education only)
P.O. Box 10127
Birmingham, AL 35202
(205) 323-5461

Louisiana Seed Capital
339 Florida St., Suite 525
Baton Rouge, LA 70801
(504) 383-1508

Great New Orleans Venture Capital Club
301 Camp St.
New Orleans, LA 70130
(800) 949-7890

Houston Venture Capital Association
1221 McKinney, Suite 2400
Houston, TX 77010
(713) 750-1500

Montana Private Capital Network
7783 Valley View Rd.
Poulson, MT 59860
(406) 883-5470

Mountainwest Venture Group
c/o Bonneville Research
48 Market St., Suite 200
Salt Lake City, Utah 84101
(801) 364-5300

Orange Coast Venture Group
c/p American Accounting
23011 Moulton Pkwy., F2
Languna Hills, CA 92653
(714) 859-3646

Orange County Venture Forum
P.O. Box 2011
Laguna Hills CA 92654
(714) 855-0652

Community Entrepreneurs Organization
P.O. Box 2781
San Rafael, CA 94912
(415) 435-4461

Northwest Venture Group
P.O. Box 21693
Seattle, WA 98111
(206) 746-1973

## Contact Option

For a complete list of venture capital clubs, contact
(by mail if possible):
Lisa Jones
Association of Venture Clubs
265 E. 100 South, #300
Salt Lake City, UT 84110
(801) 364-1100

## Recommended Resource

*Guerrilla Financing*
by Bruce Bleachman and Jay Conrad Levinson
Houghton Mifflin, $19.95
(800) 225-3362

# Insurance Companies

## Service Firms Ranked by Assets, 1992

| Rank | Company | Headquarters City | Phone |
|------|---------|-------------------|-------|
| 1 | Prudential of America | Newark, NJ | (201) 802-6000 |
| 2 | Metropolitan Life | New York | (212) 578-2211 |
| 3 | Teachers Insurance & Annuity | New York | (212) 490-9000 |
| 4 | Aetna Life | Hartford | (203) 273-0122 |
| 5 | New York Life | New York | (212) 576-7000 |
| 6 | Equitable Life Assurance | New York | (212) 554-1234 |
| 7 | Connecticut General Life | Bloomfield, CT | (203) 726-6000 |
| 8 | Northwestern Mutual Life | Milwaukee | (414) 299-7022 |
| 9 | John Hancock Mutual Life | Boston | (617) 572-6000 |
| 10 | Principal Mutual Life | Des Moines | (515) 247-5111 |
| 11 | Travelers | Hartford | (203) 277-0111 |
| 12 | Massachusetts Mutual Life | Springfield, MA | (413) 788-8411 |
| 13 | Lincoln National Life | Fort Wayne | (219) 455-2000 |
| 14 | IDS Life | Minneapolis | (612) 671-3131 |
| 15 | Hartford Life | Simsbury, CT | (203) 843-3492 |
| 16 | Allstate Life | Northbrook, IL | (708) 402-5000 |
| 17 | Nationwide Life | Columbus, OH | (614) 249-7111 |
| 18 | Variable Annuity Life | Houston | (713) 526-5251 |
| 19 | Mutual of New York | New York | (212) 708-2000 |
| 20 | New England Mutual Life | Boston | (617) 578-2000 |
| 21 | State Farm Life | Bloomington, IL | (309) 766-2311 |
| 22 | Aetna Life & Annuity | Hartford | (203) 273-0123 |
| 23 | Jackson National Life | Lansing, MI | (517) 394-3400 |
| 24 | New York Life & Annuity | New York | (212) 576-7000 |
| 25 | Pacific Mutual Life | Newport Beach, CA | (714) 640-3011 |

*Source: Fortune, May 31, 1993*

# Real Estate Advisers

## Real Estate Investment Advisers Ranked by Taxable/Tax-Exempt Assets

| Rank | Company | Total Assets ($ millions) | Tax-Exempt Assets ($ millions) |
|------|---------|---------------------------|-------------------------------|
| 1 | Equitable Real Estate | 39,383 | 10,877 |
| 2 | JMB Institutional Realty | 8,291 | 8,058 |
| 3 | Heilman Advisory | 7,251 | 6,852 |
| 4 | Copley Real Estate | 10,360 | 6,375 |
| 5 | Prudential Real Estate | 5,620 | 5,620 |
| 6 | Yarmouth Group | 6,450 | 4,875 |
| 7 | RREEF Funds | 5,377 | 4,699 |
| 8 | LaSalle Advisors | 7,600 | 4,541 |
| 9 | GE Investment | 4,514 | 4,514 |
| 10 | TCW Realty Advisors | 3,845 | 3,845 |
| 11 | Aetna Realty Investors | 3,553 | 3,553 |
| 12 | Aldrich, Eastman & Waltch | 4,560 | 3,390 |
| 13 | Jones Lang Wootton | 4,185 | 3,010 |
| 14 | Alex Brown Kleinwort Benson | 2,895 | 2,895 |
| 15 | Corporate Property Investors | 4,300 | 2,563 |

*Real Estate Advisers (cont'd)*

| Rank | Company | Total Assets ($ millions) | Tax-Exempt Assets ($ millions) |
|------|---------|---------------------------|--------------------------------|
| 16 | Mellon/McMahan Real Estate | 2,288 | 2,136 |
| 17 | L&B Real Estate Counsel | 2,098 | 2,035 |
| 18 | Hancock Timber Resource | 2,013 | 2,013 |
| 19 | Sentinel Real Estate | 2,274 | 1,939 |
| 20 | O'Connor Group | 2,105 | 1,906 |
| 21 | Grosvenor International | 1,740 | 1,740 |
| 22 | MIG Realty Advisors | 1,620 | 1,620 |
| 23 | J.P. Morgan | 1,690 | 1,609 |
| 24 | McMorgan | 1,500 | 1,500 |
| 25 | INVESCO Realty | 1,116 | 1,116 |
| 26 | Kennedy Associates | 1,070 | 1,070 |

*Source: Pensions and Investments, Sept. 20, 1993*

# Accounting Firms

## Accounting Firms Ranked by Sales, 1992

| Firm | City | Sales ($ millions) | Growth (%) |
|------|------|--------------------|------------|
| Arthur Andersen & Co., S.C. | Chicago | 2,921.9 | 9 |
| Ernst & Young | New York | 2,400.0 | 5 |
| Deloitte & Touche | Wilton, CT | 2,055.0 | 5 |
| KPMG Peat Marwick | New York | 1,822.0 | 1 |
| Coopers & Lybrand | New York | 1,642.0 | 5 |
| Price Waterhouse | New York | 1,430.0 | 4 |
| Grant Thornton | Chicago | 224.0 | 1 |
| McGladrey & Pullen | Davenport, IA | 196.6 | 4 |
| Kenneth Leventhal & Co. | Los Angeles | 192.7 | 2 |
| BDO Seidman | New York | 182.3 | 0 |
| Baird Kurtz & Dobson | Springfield, MO | 61.3 | 2 |
| Crowe, Chizek & Co. | South Bend, IN | 58.2 | 11 |
| Clifton Gunderson & Co. | Peoria, IL | 50.3 | -2 |
| Plante & Moran | Southfield, MI | 50.3 | 1 |
| Moss Adams | Seattle | 49.0 | 4 |
| Altschuler, Melvoin & Glasser | Chicago | 48.0 | -12 |
| Geo. S. Olive & Co. | Indianapolis | 38.0 | 6 |
| Richard A. Eisner & Co. | New York | 32.4 | 9 |
| IDS Financial Services | Minneapolis | 32.3 | 127 |
| Goldstein Golub Kessler & Co. | New York | 30.2 | 2 |
| Friedman, Eisenstein, Raemer & Schwartz | Chicago | 30.0 | 8 |
| Larson, Allen, Weishair & Co. | Minneapolis | 29.0 | 16 |
| J.H. Cohn & Co. | Roseland, NJ | 22.5 | -2 |
| Checkers Simon & Rosner | Chicago | 22.4 | 22 |
| Wipfli Ullrich Berterlson | Wausau, WI | 22.2 | 5 |
| David Berdon & Co. | New York | 22.0 | 9 |
| Campos & Stratis | Teaneck, NJ | 21.3 | 10 |
| Parente, Randolph, Orlando, Carey & Assoc. | Wilkes-Barre, PA | 21.1 | 10 |
| Cherry Bekaert & Holland | Richmond, VA | 20.6 | -13 |
| Thomas Havey & Co. | Chicago | 19.5 | 3 |

*Accounting Firms (cont'd)*

| Firm | City | Sales ($ millions) | Growth (%) |
|------|------|-------------------|------------|
| Reznick Fedder & Silverman | Bethesda, MD | 19.2 | 10 |
| Urbach, Kahn & Werlin | Albany, NY | 17.8 | -5 |
| M.R. Weiser & Co. | New York | 17.2 | 0 |
| Hausser & Taylor | Cleveland | 16.9 | 9 |
| Virchow Krause & Co. | Madison, WI | 15.8 | 6 |
| Schenck & Associates | Appleton, WI | 15.7 | 4 |
| Margolin Winer Evens | Garden City, NY | 15.0 | -16 |
| Mitchell/Titus & Co. | New York | 14.0 | 0 |
| Charles Bailly & Co. | Fargo, ND | 13.5 | -4 |
| Eide Helmeke & Co. | Fargo, ND | 13.5 | 5 |
| Kemper CPA Group | Robinson, IL | 13.2 | 1 |
| Blackman Kallick Bartelstein | Chicago | 13.0 | 0 |
| Kennedy & Coe | Salina, KS | 13.0 | -5 |
| Mahoney Cohen & Co. | New York | 13.0 | 8 |
| Dixon Odom & Co. | High Point, NC | 12.9 | 8 |
| Follmer, Rudzewicz & Co. | Southfield, MI | 12.8 | 5 |
| Rehmann Robson & Co. | Saginaw, MI | 12.6 | 3 |
| Weber Lipshie | New York | 12.6 | -9 |
| Mayer Hoffman McCann | Kansas City, MO | 12.5 | 6 |
| Rubin, Brown, Gornstein | St. Louis | 12.3 | 1 |
| Tofias, Fleishman, Shapiro & Co. | Cambridge, MA | 12.2 | 4 |
| Edward Isaacs & Co. | New York | 12.1 | 3 |
| Joseph Decosimo & Co. | Chattanooga, TN | 12.1 | 1 |
| Rothstein, Kass & Co. | Roseland, NJ | 12.0 | 9 |
| LeMaster & Daniels | Spokane, WA | 11.7 | 3 |
| Anchin, Block & Anchin | New York | 11.6 | 0 |
| Blue & Co. | Indianapolis | 11.4 | 21 |
| C.W. Amos & Co. | Baltimore | 11.0 | 10 |
| Habif, Arogeti & Wynne | Atlanta | 11.0 | 11 |
| Blum Shapiro & Co. | West Hartford, CT | 10.5 | 11 |

*Source: Accounting Today, Special Report, Dec., 1993*

## The Top Reference Sources

*Traders' Catalog & Resource Guide*
Crawford Associates, $39.50/year

This monthly 160-page publication is a combination of information about product and service vendors and a series of commentaries, reviews, and opinions all directed toward individual and institutional investors and traders. The magazine combines yellow- and white-page-style listings of tools for all kinds of market analysis, software for trading and system development, newsletters, rating services, hotlines, market timers, and brokerage services.

Other features included in the publication are book lists and reviews; magazines and periodicals, economic and financial glossaries; seminars, trade shows, workshops, and conferences; financial management; and brokerage consultants, accountants, and other professional services.

*Accounting Firms (cont'd)*

## Accountants' Favorite Software

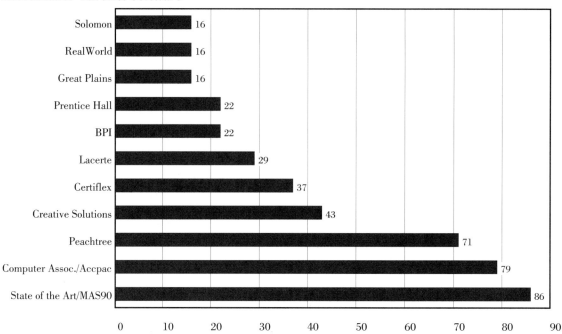

## Tax Preparers' Favorite Software

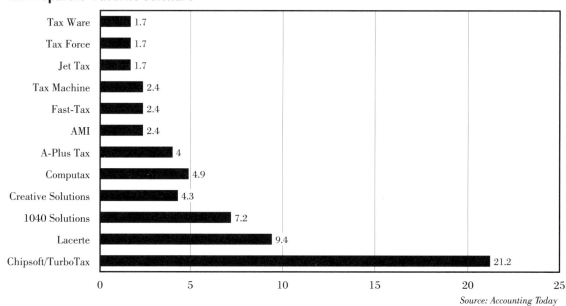

*Source: Accounting Today*

# Influential Accountants

## The 100 Most Influential People in Accounting

| Name | Position | Firm |
|------|----------|------|
| J. Mason Andres | Chairman, Private Co. Practice Section | AICPA |
| James F. Antonio | Chairman | Governmental Accounting Standards Board |
| Jerrell A. Atkinson | Managing Director | Atkinson & Co. |
| Andrew D. Bailey, Jr. | President | American Accounting Association |
| Dennis R. Beresford | Chairman | Financial Accounting Standards Board |
| William T. Bishop | President | Institute of Internal Auditors |
| Thomas M. Bloch | President, Chief Executive | H&R Block |
| L. Gary Boomer | Partner | Varney Mills Rogers Burnett & Associates |
| Michele R. Bourgerie | Chairwoman | New York State Board for Public Accountancy |
| Charles A. Bowsher | Comptroller General | U.S.Government Accounting Office |
| Abe Briloff | Partner | A.J. and L.A. Briloff CPAs |
| Milton Brown | First Vice President | National Society of Public Accountants |
| Robert Bunting | President | Moss Adams |
| John C. Burton | Ernst & Young Professor of Accounting | Columbia University |
| Jean Marie Caragher | President | Association for Accounting Marketing |
| Philip B. Chenok | President | AICPA |
| Shirley J. Cheramy | Chair, Women and Family Issues Committee | AICPA |
| Ronald S. Cohen | Managing Partner | Crowe, Chizek & Co. |
| Allison Conte | Executive Director | American Society of Women Accountants |
| J. Michael Cook | Chairman and Chief Executive | Deloitte & Touche |
| Scott D. Cook | President | Intuit |
| Beryl Davis | Member and Former Chairwoman | Florida Board of Accountancy |
| Stephen W. DeFilippis | Owner | West Suburban Income Tax Service |
| James Don Edwards | Professor of Accounting | J.M. Tull School of Accounting, Univ. of Georgia |
| Richard Eisner | Managing Partner | Richard A. Eisner & Co. |
| Robert K. Elliott | Assistant to the Chairman | KPMG Peat Marwick |
| Mark Ernst | Vice President, General Manager | IDS Financial Services |
| Richard E. Flaherty | Executive Director | Accounting Education Change Commission |
| Eugene Freedman | Chairman and Chief Executive | Coopers & Lybrand |
| Welling W. Fruehauf | President-Elect | National Assn. of State Boards of Accountancy |
| Carl George | Managing Partner | Clifton Gunderson & Co. |
| James Glauser | Managing Partner | Baird Kurtz & Dobson |
| Dan L. Goldwasser | Partner | Vedder Price Kaufman Kammholz & Day |
| Gerald L. Golub | Managing Partner | Goldstein Golub Kessler & Co. |
| John W. Goodhew III | President | Peachtree Software |
| Robert L. Gray | Executive Director | New York State Society of CPAs |
| John D. Harris | Managing Partner | George S. Olive |
| Nancy Marie Heimer | President | American Woman's Society of CPAs |
| John E. Hunnicutt | Group Vice President of Government Affairs | AICPA |
| Robert L. Israeloff | Vice Chairman | AICPA |
| Donald F. Istvan | President | D.F. Istvan Associates |
| Martin Ives | Vice Chairman and Director of Research | Governmental Accounting Standards Board |
| Edmund L. Jenkins | Managing Director, Accounting Principles | Arthur Andersen & Co. |
| Thomas P. Kelley | Vice President-Professional | AICPA |
| Sidney Kess | Educator | – |
| Stuart Kessler | Partner | Goldstein Golub Kessler & Co. |
| Noel Kirch | President | National Assn. of State Boards of Accountancy |
| James Kurtz | Executive Director | California Society of CPAs |
| Joseph LaGambina | Executive V.P. and Chief Administrative Officer | Financial Accounting Foundation |
| Charles Larson | Managing Director | Larson Consulting |

*Influential Accountants (cont'd)*

| Name | Position | Firm |
|------|----------|------|
| Philip A. Laskawy | Deputy Chairman | Ernst & Young |
| James Leisenring | Vice Chairman | Financial Accounting Standards Board |
| Norman W. Lipshie | Senior Partner | Weber Lipshie & Co. |
| Jon Madonna | Chairman | KPMG Peat Marwick |
| LeRoy E. Martin | Managing Partner | McGladrey & Pullen |
| Eli Mason | Senior Partner | Mason & Co. |
| Edward L. Massie | President and Chief Executive | CCH |
| William Matthews | Managing Partner | Plante & Moran |
| Patricia McConnell | Managing Director | Bear Stearns |
| Robert Mednick | Managing Partner, Prof. and Regulatory Matters | Arthur Andersen & Co. |
| James C. Metzler | Partner | Gaines Emhof Metzler & Kriner |
| Bert Mitchell | Chairman and Chief Executive | Mitchell Titus & Co. |
| Robert Nason | Executive Partner | Grant Thornton |
| Jay Nisberg | Management Consultant | Jay Nisberg & Assoc. |
| Shaun O'Malley | Chairman and Chief Executive | Price Waterhouse |
| Thomas Ochsenschlager | Partner | Grant Thornton |
| Alan Prahl | Executive Director | National Association of Tax Practitioners |
| William L. Raby | Tax Advisor | – |
| Margaret Milner Richardson | Commissioner | Internal Revenue Service |
| Gary C. Rohrs | President | National Society of Public Accountants |
| Martin Rosenberg | Executive Director | Illinois CPA Society |
| Stan Ross | Managing Partner | Kenneth Leventhal & Co. |
| P. Norman Roy | President | Financial Executives Institute |
| Ronnie Rudd | Chairman | Texas State Board of Public Accountancy |
| Eric Schindler | Vice President, Finance & Administration | Columbia Paint & Coatings |
| Donald B. Scholl | Consultant | D.B. Scholl |
| Walter Paul Schuetze | Chief Accountant | Securities and Exchange Commision |
| Abram Serotta | President | Serotta, Maddocks, Evans & Co. |
| Jerome P. Solomon | Director, Past President | National Assn. of State Boards of Accountancy |
| Stanley H. Stearman | Executive Vice President | National Society of Public Accountants |
| Irwin Steinberg | Managing Partner | Friedman, Eisenstein, Raemer & Schwartz |
| Howard Stone | Managing Partner, Chairman | Altschuler, Melvoin & Glasser |
| A. Marvin Strait | Partner | Baird Kurtz & Dobson |
| Norman N. Strauss | Chairman, Accounting Standards Committee | AICPA |
| John B. Sullivan | Director of Auditing Services | Deloitte & Touche |
| Dominic Tarantino | Chairman | AICPA |
| W.J. Tauzin | U.S. Congressman | – |
| Lloyd Turman | Executive Director | Florida Institute of CPAs |
| Bernie Valek | President | Alliance of Practicing CPAs |
| Herb D. Vest | Chairman and Chief Executive | H.D. Vest |
| Charles B. Wang | Chairman and Chief Executive | Computer Associates International |
| Lawrence Weinbach | Managing Partner, Chief Executive | Arthur Andersen & Co. |
| Melvyn I. Weiss | Senior Partner | Milberg Weiss Bershad Hynes & Lerach |
| Don Weldon | Executive Director | Texas Society of CPAs |
| Alan D. Westheimer | Adviser | Alan D. Westheimer CPA |
| Gary Wetstein | Chairman | BDO Seidman |
| Janice Wilson | President | California State Board of Accountancy |
| Stephen T. Winn | President and Chief Executive | Computer Language Research |
| Ronald T. Wyden | U.S. Congressman | – |
| Richard Ziegler | Chairman | Illinois Committee on Accountancy |

*Source: Accounting Today, Mar. 14, 1994*

# Tax Freedom Day

IN 1993, THE AVERAGE AMERICAN worker worked 123 days–from January 1 to May 3–to satisfy all federal, state, and local tax obligations for the year. Tax Freedom Day is that day on which the taxpayer stops working to earn the tax money he owes and starts working for himself–taking home his own paycheck for real. Over time, this day of freedom has fallen later and later in the year.

## Recommended Resource

*Public Accounting Report*
Strafford Publications, $197/year (24 issues)
1201 Peachtree St., NE, #1150
Atlanta, GA 30361
(404) 881-1141

## Tax Freedom Date

| Year | Date |
|------|------|
| 1960 | April 16 |
| 1965 | April 14 |
| 1970 | April 26 |
| 1975 | April 27 |
| 1980 | May 1 |
| 1985 | April 30 |
| 1990 | May 3 |
| 1991 | May 2 |
| 1992 | May 5 |
| 1993 | May 3 |

*Source: The 1994 Information Please Almanac*

## The Top Reference Sources

*Accounting Today*
Faulkner & Gray, $96
(212) 967-7000
This semi-monthly publication offers the inside scoop on the accounting field. Lively articles, news, and in-depth surveys offer the reader insight into the rules affecting accounting, and, more important, the intricacies of running a successful accounting practice.

 **Non-Performing Loans.** Request #279. See p. xi for instructions.
Table of the percentage of non-performing loans in each state (in FDIC-insured commercial banks).

# Choosing an Accountant

THE TERM ACCOUNTANT CAN MEAN many different things, depending on a company's size and needs. A huge company like IBM thinks of an accountant as not just one person but rather as a large professional team of consultants. The team may consist of specialists who audit financial statements, prepare tax returns, and give tax advice, or analyze and improve sophisticated computer and information systems.

A smaller company might need just one individual, probably a tax expert who periodically reviews the company's financial statements.

Finding an accountant whose specialties and interests match your needs is a critical step in setting up a long-term financial structure.

Here are 13 questions you can ask when interviewing a prospective accountant:

## I. Have you helped a client in a similar situation?

It saves time to work with an accountant who has already dealt with similar situations. Probe to discover exactly how he has dealt with problems similar to yours.

## 2. Will our firm be serviced by a partner or by junior accountants?

Many firms train new associates at the client's expense. Be sure that you get what you pay for.

## 3. What is the nature, scope, and timing of your work, and what will it cost me?

Often, an accountant's work plan can be more extensive and more expensive than you might expect. Get the accountant to be specific about what he or she will do, and get a detailed written engagement letter and cost estimate.

## 4. Can you give me two or three quick ideas on how you might be able to save our company money?

A good accountant should have sharp business acumen and be willing to be creative. A question like this can show whether the accountant can call on his or her many skills to truly help you to increase profits, improve productivity, trim costs, enhance return, and lower taxes.

## 5. Can you tell me a little about your practice, and your successes and failures?

Open-ended questions can elicit a wealth of information. Let the accountant talk. You will also learn a lot about the accountant's priorities, risk-tolerance levels, and various personality characteristics, all of which can be helpful in gauging compatibility.

## 6. How are your fees calculated? Will you be charging me for every phone discussion?

To avoid friction later, it is essential to discuss the accountant's fee structure, including the hourly rate of the accountant and staff, overhead expense reimbursement (how much should you pay for a fax?), and whether certain time is not billed.

## 7. What can I do to help you with your work and keep your fees to a minimum?

A great deal of your accountant's time can be saved by preparing information beforehand. Find out if your accountant is willing to work with you to offload this work to your firm.

## 8. How will you be communicating the results of your work to me?

The results of an audit usually take the form of an audit report, and tax return preparation yields tax returns. But this work also can lead to many suggestions by the accountant on how to cut taxes, increase income, restructure investments, build business, and improve information flow. Some accountants are more comfortable with interactive discussions and others prefer written action reports.

## 9. Do you perceive any conflicts of interest?

Accountants work for dozens of firms, and you should probe to see if any of your direct competition is represented by the firm. If so, inquire as to how this conflict is handled.

## 10. Are you a Certified Public Accountant, and what other licenses do you hold?

If the accountant is certified, you should inquire with the state CPA organization to discover if there have been any disciplinary actions entered. Some accountants also have credentials as financial planners, securities representatives, even lawyers.

## II. How well have you integrated computers into your practice, and has it enabled you to do more for clients at less cost?

Integrating your computer files with those of your accountant's can save time and money, and increase accuracy.

## 12. Will you need to overhaul our current system?

Your internal bookkeeping and cost-accounting systems are expensive to alter. Find out up front whether you can integrate with the firm's systems.

## 13. Are you conservative or aggressive in interpreting tax laws and regulations, and accounting and auditing standards?

Save yourself the hassle and be certain that your accountant approaches your books in the same way you would.

*Source: Frank Sisco*

# Mortgage Tables

TO COMPUTE A MORTGAGE PAYMENT, divide the amount borrowed by $100,000, then multiply that number by the number in the table.

| Rate | Length of Mortgage (years) | | | | | |
|------|------|------|------|------|------|------|
| | 5 | 10 | 15 | 20 | 25 | 30 |
| 5.0% | 1,887.12 | 1,060.66 | 790.79 | 659.96 | 584.59 | 536.82 |
| 5.5% | 1,910.12 | 1,085.26 | 817.08 | 687.89 | 614.09 | 567.79 |
| 6.0% | 1,933.28 | 1,110.21 | 843.86 | 716.43 | 644.30 | 599.55 |
| 6.5% | 1,956.61 | 1,135.48 | 871.11 | 745.57 | 675.21 | 632.07 |
| 7.0% | 1,980.12 | 1,161.08 | 898.83 | 775.30 | 706.78 | 665.30 |
| 7.5% | 2,003.79 | 1,187.02 | 927.01 | 805.59 | 738.99 | 699.21 |
| 8.0% | 2,027.64 | 1,213.28 | 955.65 | 836.44 | 771.82 | 733.76 |
| 8.5% | 2,051.65 | 1,239.86 | 984.74 | 867.82 | 805.23 | 768.91 |
| 9.0% | 2,075.84 | 1,266.76 | 1,014.27 | 899.73 | 839.20 | 804.62 |
| 9.5% | 2,100.19 | 1,293.98 | 1,044.22 | 932.13 | 873.70 | 840.85 |
| 10.0% | 2,124.70 | 1,321.51 | 1,074.61 | 965.02 | 908.70 | 877.57 |
| 10.5% | 2,149.39 | 1,349.35 | 1,105.40 | 998.38 | 944.18 | 914.74 |
| 11.0% | 2,174.24 | 1,377.50 | 1,136.60 | 1,032.19 | 980.11 | 952.32 |
| 11.5% | 2,199.26 | 1,405.95 | 1,168.19 | 1,066.43 | 1,016.47 | 990.29 |
| 12.0% | 2,224.44 | 1,434.71 | 1,200.17 | 1,101.09 | 1,053.22 | 1,028.61 |
| 12.5% | 2,249.79 | 1,463.76 | 1,232.52 | 1,136.14 | 1,090.35 | 1,067.26 |
| 13.0% | 2,275.31 | 1,493.11 | 1,265.24 | 1,171.58 | 1,127.84 | 1,106.20 |
| 13.5% | 2,300.98 | 1,522.74 | 1,298.32 | 1,207.37 | 1,165.64 | 1,145.41 |
| 14.0% | 2,326.83 | 1,552.66 | 1,331.74 | 1,243.52 | 1,203.76 | 1,184.87 |
| 14.5% | 2,352.83 | 1,582.87 | 1,365.50 | 1,280.00 | 1,242.16 | 1,224.56 |
| 15.0% | 2,378.99 | 1,613.35 | 1,399.59 | 1,316.79 | 1,280.83 | 1,264.44 |
| 15.5% | 2,405.32 | 1,644.11 | 1,433.99 | 1,353.88 | 1,319.75 | 1,304.52 |
| 16.0% | 2,431.81 | 1,675.13 | 1,468.70 | 1,391.26 | 1,358.89 | 1,344.76 |
| 16.5% | 2,458.45 | 1,706.42 | 1,503.71 | 1,428.90 | 1,398.24 | 1,385.15 |
| 17.0% | 2,485.26 | 1,737.98 | 1,539.00 | 1,466.80 | 1,437.80 | 1,425.68 |
| 17.5% | 2,512.22 | 1,769.79 | 1,574.58 | 1,504.94 | 1,477.53 | 1,466.33 |
| 18.0% | 2,539.34 | 1,801.85 | 1,610.42 | 1,543.31 | 1,517.43 | 1,507.09 |
| 18.5% | 2,566.62 | 1,834.17 | 1,646.52 | 1,581.90 | 1,557.48 | 1,547.94 |
| 19.0% | 2,594.06 | 1,866.72 | 1,682.88 | 1,620.68 | 1,597.68 | 1,588.89 |
| 19.5% | 2,621.64 | 1,899.52 | 1,719.47 | 1,659.66 | 1,638.01 | 1,629.92 |
| 20.0% | 2,649.39 | 1,932.56 | 1,756.30 | 1,698.82 | 1,678.45 | 1,671.02 |
| 20.5% | 2,677.29 | 1,965.82 | 1,793.35 | 1,738.15 | 1,719.01 | 1,712.18 |
| 21.0% | 2,705.34 | 1,999.32 | 1,830.61 | 1,777.64 | 1,759.66 | 1,753.40 |
| 21.5% | 2,733.54 | 2,033.03 | 1,868.08 | 1,817.28 | 1,800.41 | 1,794.67 |
| 22.0% | 2,761.89 | 2,066.97 | 1,905.76 | 1,857.06 | 1,841.24 | 1,835.98 |

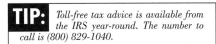

**TIP:** *Toll-free tax advice is available from the IRS year-round. The number to call is (800) 829-1040.*

# Business Incubators

BUSINESS INCUBATORS ARE FACILITIES that provide start-up and fledgling firms with business and management assistance, affordable space, and shared support services. They are an alternative to the office at home or the long-term lease.

A business incubator's services may include the following:

- Flexible space and flexible leases, often at below-market rates;

- Shared basic business services such as telephone answering, bookkeeping, word-processing and other secretarial help, receptionist services, and access to fax and copy machines, computers, and business libraries;

- Business and technical assistance through a combination of in-house expertise and a network of community support;

- Financing assistance, such as help in obtaining a bank loan or assistance in gaining access to federal and state R & D funds;

- A network of relationships with other business owners who provide support for each other and who may become customers or suppliers.

There are now about 500 business incubators in North America, up from about 15 in 1980. They are commonly operated by universities, colleges and community colleges, for-profit businesses and economic development agencies, local governments, or consortia of all of these organizations. They are often targeted to serve the needs of light manufacturing and service firms and those developing new products or engaged in research and development. Incubator tenants may also include construction-related, sales and marketing, or wholesale and distribution firms.

Incubators vary in the services they offer and in the charges to their tenants. Some items to consider when looking at a business incubator are:

- What are the charges for space and services? How do they compare to market rates in the area? What are the lease requirements? Is there room for business growth?

- What services does the incubator provide? Can the management offer on-site assistance and access to contacts and community business services? Does it provide seminar or training programs? Are some services provided free of charge?

- What is the experience of "incubator graduates," firms who have made use of the incubator for one to three years and then moved to their own space in the community? How about current tenants of the facility?

- What are the policies and procedures of the incubator? How long can a business remain a tenant? Is there a graduated structure as the business matures, or does the incubator take royalties or ownership right in its tenants in return for reduced charges? How simple is it to leave if the business fails?

- Does the incubator appear to be managed well? Does it have support from sponsoring organizations? Who are these sponsors and what are their goals and reasons for supporting the incubator?

*Source: National Business Incubation Association*

## Contact Options

National Business Incubation Association
One President St.
Athens, OH 45701
(614) 593-4331

Small Business Administration
Business Initiative, Education, and Training
409 3rd St., SW, 6th Floor
Washington, DC 20416
(202) 205-6665
Contact the above office or a local SBA office.

# Payroll Efficiency

## Direct Deposit

Experts estimate that the annual cost for generating payroll checks is about $200 per year for each employee. Direct deposit is a convenient way to reduce payroll time and expense. While larger companies with many employees experience a greater reduction in payroll processing expenses, even the smaller company will experience proportionate savings.

A secondary benefit is the reduction in lost time and productivity. Employees no longer have to leave work to deposit checks since funds are instantly available in the checking or savings accounts which are targeted to receive these deposits. Morale and productivity show improvement, particularly on paydays, since employees do not have to make time to personally deposit or cash payroll checks.

Additional cost-cutting strategies include reconsidering the company's payroll schedule. Corporate

*Payroll Efficiency (cont'd)*

studies show that companies can reduce payroll expenses by 20-40% by changing payroll schedules from weekly to bimonthly.

Information on direct deposit is available from the bank which handles a company's payroll account or from an organization which specializes in this service.

## Contact Option

National Automated Clearing House Association (NACHA)
607 Herndon Pkwy., Suite 200
Herndon, VA 22070
(703) 742-9190

## Payroll Processing

Processing a payroll for a large or small company can be time-consuming and requires careful attention to government regulations. Payroll efficiency can be affected by IRS requirements about depositing payroll taxes. Untimely payment errors can result in penalties and undesired attention from government taxation officials. One way to avoid such problems is to hire the services of specialists to process the corporation's payroll.

Automatic Data Processing (ADP), the largest of these payroll processing companies, offers a free, annually updated booklet on payroll information and IRS regulations. To obtain the booklet, call (800) 225-5237.

## Contact Options

ADP Response Center
335 Bishop Hollow Rd.
Newtown Square, PA 19073
(800) 225-5237

ADP Payroll Services
1 ADP Blvd.
Roseland, NJ 07068
(201) 994-5000
Local offices of ADP are available in the telephone directory.

Paychex
914 Panorama Trail
Rochester, NY 14625
(800) 322-7292
There are 90 nationwide locations for local Paychex offices. The main office will provide information and convenient locations for callers.

# Low-Cost Labor Alternatives

## Temporary Help

More and more corporations are finding that their workforce needs change with marketplace fluctuations and business cycles, special projects and vacation periods. During these times, employers need individuals with skills ranging from professional/technical to industrial and office/clerical skills, but do not want to increase their basic core of workers. Temporary service firms have changed to meet more specialized corporate needs. They provide the necessary screening, interviewing, and training needed to fulfill the wide variety of expertise requirements of the corporate community. The employer is relieved of these responsibilities as well as the expense of hiring, paying benefits, payroll taxes and other related bookkeeping.

For a free copy of *How to Buy Temporary Services*, which explains how to evaluate, select, and use temporary services, the interested individual should write to:

The National Association of Temporary Services
119 S. St. Asaph St.
Alexandria, VA 22314
(703) 549-6287

While the yellow pages of the local telephone book will provide the listing of temporary employment services, the following is a list of temporary

help companies which have at least 20 offices in ten different states in the U.S.

Ablest Service
810 N. Belcher Rd.
Clearwater, FL 34625
(813) 461-5656
26 offices: Industrial, Office/Clerical

Accountemps
service of Robert Half
2884 Sand Hill Rd.
Menlo Park, CA 94025
(415) 854-9700
150 offices: Technical/Professional

AccuStaff
2600 Potters Rd., P.O. Box 2218
Virginia Beach, VA 23452
(804) 431-2004
60 offices: Industrial, Office/Clerical, Technical/Professional

Adia Services
64 Willow Pl., P.O. Box 3044
Menlo Park, CA 94026
(415) 324-0696
582 offices: Industrial, Medical, Office/Clerical, Technical/Professional

*Low-Cost Labor Alternatives (cont'd)*

Alternative Resources
300 Tri-State International, Suite 270
Lincolnshire, IL 60069
(708) 317-1000
28 offices: Technical/Professional

Career Horizons
177 Crossways Park Dr.
Woodbury, NY 11797
(516) 496-2300
153 offices: Industrial, Office/Clerical, Technical/
Professional

Claims Overload Systems
11900 Olympic Blvd., Suite 720
Los Angeles, CA 90064
(310) 447-7144
29 offices: Office/Clerical, Technical/Professional

DayStar Temporary Services
1127 Euclid Ave., #910
Cleveland, OH 44115
(216) 696-1122
26 offices: Office/Clerical

Dunhill Temporary Systems
1000 Woodbury Rd.
Woodbury, NY 11797
(516) 364-8800
38 offices: Industrial, Office/Clerical

Express Personnel Services
6300 Northwest Expwy.
Oklahoma City, OK 73132
(800) 652-6400
194 offices: Industrial, Medical, Office/Clerical,
Technical/Professional

Hooper Holmes
170 Mount Airy Rd.
Basking Ridge, NJ 07920
(908) 953-6250
41 offices: Medical, Office/Clerical

Interim Services
2050 Spectrum Blvd.
Ft. Lauderdale, FL 33309-3008
(305) 938-7600
700 offices: Industrial, Medical, Office/Clerical,
Technical/Professional

Kelly Services
999 West Big Beaver Rd.
Troy, MI 48084
(313) 362-4444
850 Offices: Industrial, Office/Clerical, Technical/
Professional

Labor World of America
8000 N. Federal Hwy.
Boca Raton, FL 34487-1695
(407) 997-5000
40 offices: Industrial

MacTemps
66 Church St.
Cambridge, MA 02138
(617) 868-6800
21 offices: Office/Clerical, Technical/Professional

Manpower
5301 N. Ironwood Rd., P.O. Box 2053
Milwaukee, WI 53201-2053
(414) 961-1000
902 offices: Industrial, Office/Clerical, Technical/
Professional

Norrell
3535 Piedmont Rd., NE
Atlanta, GA 30305
(404) 240-3000
250 offices: Industrial, Medical, Office/Clerical

Office Specialists
Corporate Pl., 128 Audubon Rd.
Wakefield, MA 01880
(617) 246-4900
50 offices: Office/Clerical, Technical/Professional

The Olsten Corporation
One Merrick Ave.
Westbury, NY 11590
(516) 832-8200
1200 offices: Industrial, Medical, Office/Clerical

Pro Staff Personnel Services
920 2nd Ave. S., Suite 920
Minneapolis, MN 55402
(612) 339-2221
60 offices: Industrial, Office/Clerical, Technical/
Professional

Snelling and Snelling
12801 N. Central Expwy., Suite 700
Dallas, TX 75243
(214) 239-7575
200 offices: Industrial, Medical, Office/Clerical,
Technical/Professional

Stivers Temporary Personnel
200 W. Monroe St., Suite 1100
Chicago, IL 60606
(312) 558-3550
30 offices: Office/Clerical

TAC/TEMPS
109 Oak St., P.O. Box 9110
Newton Upper Falls, MA 02164
(617) 969-3100
49 offices: Office/Clerical

TAD Temporaries
158 Monroe Ave.
Rochester, NY 14607
(716) 546-1660
31 offices: Industrial, Office/Clerical

*Low-Cost Labor Alternatives (cont'd)*

Today's Temporary
18111 Preston Rd., #700
Dallas, TX 75252
(214) 380-9380
68 offices: Office/Clerical

TRC Staffing Services
100 Ashford Center N., Suite 500
Atlanta, GA 30338
(404) 392-1411
40 offices: Industrial, Office/Clerical

Talent Tree
9703 Richmond Ave.
Houston, TX 77042
(713) 789-1818
140 offices: Industrial, Medical, Office/Clerical,
Technical/Professional

Triad Personnel
One Tower Ln., Suite 2100
Oakbrook Terrace, IL 60181-4600
(708) 954-0455
23 offices: Office/Clerical

Uniforce Services
1335 Jericho Tpke.
New Hyde Park, NY 11040
(516) 437-3300
56 offices: Industrial, Office/Clerical, Technical/
Professional

Volt Temporary Services
2401 N. Glassell St., P.O. Box 13500
Orange, CA 92665
(714) 921-8800
95 offices: Industrial, Office/Clerical

Western Temporary Services
301 Lennon Ln.
Walnut Creek, CA 94598
(510) 930-5300
350 offices: Industrial, Medical, Office/Clerical,
Technical/Professional

## Telecommuting Employees

Companies are frequently in search of ways to offer a flexible work environment to their employees. Telecommuting is becoming more and more popular among large and small companies alike. No longer limited to high-powered executives, telecommuting is now well-used in a variety of employment situations, where the employee can perform work functions at home using a pc, modem, and telephone line to connect to a host computer in the workplace. To investigate the process of setting up and evaluating a program, several contact options are available.

## Recommended Resources

*Telecommuting Resource Guide*
Pacific Bell Telecommunications, free
(510) 901-6418

*Telecommuting Review*
Gil Gordon Associates, $157/year
(908) 329-2266
*Monthly Newsletter*

*Creating a Flexible Workplace*
by Barney Olmsted and Suzanne Smith
American Management Association
(AMACOM), $59.95
(800) 262-9699

# Cost Accounting Tips

## Telephone Accounting Codes

Cost accounting has always presented a challenge to companies. Tracking reimbursable expenses such as photocopies, mileage, postage and food continues to be a challenge. Telephone companies now provide services which track and list the costs of calls made to predetermined numbers. An accounting code number dialed with the telephone number called, enables the phone company to flag that call so that the user can quickly and easily identify the telephone expenses associated with a specific account. Call accounting code service information is available from the major companies.

## Contact Options

AT&T Call Manager
(800) 222-0400

Sprint Business Services
(800) 877-4020 or (800) 788-8981

MCI Business Services
(800) 800-2568

## Credit and Collection

All businesses have to deal with collection of payments from creditors. Finding creative and effective ways to collect on invoices can be a challenge to anyone responsible for a company's finances. There are organizations of experts available who produce publications, and standard credit forms as well as offering assistance and advice.

*Cost Accounting Tips (cont'd)*

## Contact Options

National Association of Credit Management
8815 Centre Park Dr., Suite 200
Columbia, MD 21045
(410) 740-5560

Dun & Bradstreet
Receivable Management Services
(800) 234-3867
For international collections:
(800) 274-6454

Dun & Bradstreet
Small Business Services
(800) 722-3867

TRW Business Credit Services National Hotline
(800) 344-0603

## Tax Deductions

Business tax deductions are available to organizations with excess inventory, new products which are not being used and in some cases older or surplus equipment such as computers. Several non-profit organizations distribute these corporate donations to other non-profit establishments such as schools, colleges, universities, groups serving disabled people or special needs students. These organizations are most willing to supply donation guidelines and information packets.

## Contact Options

National Exchange of Industrial
Resources (NAEIR)
P.O. Box 8076
560 McClure St.
Galesburg, IL 61402
(800) 562-0955
Accepts office supplies, computer accessories, tools and hardware, lab equipment, maintenance supplies, electrical and plumbing fixtures, appliance, paper products, books and other items for distribution to schools and charities around the country.

National Cristina Foundation
591 W. Putnam Ave.
Greenwich, CT 06830
(800) 274-7846 or
(203) 622-6000
Accepts surplus personal computers, software and related technology for distribution to disabled individuals, at risk-students, and the disadvantaged.

Gift-in-Kind Clearing House
P.O. Box 850
Davidson, NC 28036
(704) 892-7228
Accepts furniture, equipment, and merchandise from corporations for distribution to charities.

# Free Government Help

## Updating Mailing Lists

Mailing lists must continually be updated in order to ensure efficiency. Inaccurate address labels result in incomplete delivery, lost business and increased mailing expenses. Companies are faced with the dual task of weeding out bad addresses and updating zip codes to include the additional four digits now used by the U.S. Postal Service. The USPS now offers a one-time Diskette Coding Service which corrects most faulty street and city names and adds the 4-ditgit extension to the existing zip codes. By submitting a computer disk containing the mailing list, the interested user can obtain a one-time clean-up/update. Call the National Customer Support Center of the USPS at (800) 238-3150 for information and computer disk requirements for this useful service.

## Free Government Marketing Data

While marketing information companies provide vital demographics for corporate marketing needs, much of this information comes from agencies of the federal government which collects such data. By calling the appropriate department in several government agencies, the interested user can speak directly to an expert who knows and collects this information. Often these experts can direct the caller through the mire of government offices to locate an appropriate source for the precise information being sought.

## Contact Options

Economic and Demographic Statistics
Bureau of the Census
U.S. Dept. of Commerce
Data User Service Division
Customer Service
Washington, DC 20233
(301) 763-4100

Food and Agriculture Statistics
National Agriculture Statistics Service
Estimates Division, U.S. Dept. of Agriculture
Washington, DC 20250
(202) 720-3896

*Free Government Help (cont'd)*

National, Regional, and International Economics
Bureau of Economic Analysis
U.S. Dept. of Commerce
Washington, DC 20230
(202) 606-9900

Employment, Prices, Living Conditions, Productivity and Occupational Health and Safety
Bureau of Labor Statistics, U.S. Dept. of Labor
Washington, DC 20212
(202) 606-7828

Import and Export Statistics
World Trade Reference Room
U.S. Dept. of Commerce 20230
(202) 482-2185

The following are phone numbers of government hotlines which provide the latest economic statistics of topics ranging from selected interest rates to advance reports of retail trade. The information includes the best time of the month to call to get the most up-to-date information on the specific topic.

## Government Hotlines

| Topic | Government Agency | When to Call | Telephone |
|---|---|---|---|
| Aggregate Reserves of Depository Institutions | Federal Reserve Board | Thursdays | (202) 452-3206 |
| Collective Bargaining Sett. in Private Industry | Dept. of Commerce | Mid-month | (202) 606-7828, ext. 5 |
| Consumer Price Index | Bureau of Labor Statistics | Mid-month | (202) 606-7828, ext. 1 |
| Economic News Highlights | Dept. of Commerce | Daily | (202) 393-1847 |
| Foreign Exchange Rates | Federal Reserve Board | Mon.; 1st of mo. | (202) 452-3206 |
| Foreign Trade | Dept. of Commerce | End month | (202) 393-4100 |
| GNP | Dept. of Commerce | End month | (202) 898-2451 |
| Selected Interest Rates | Federal Reserve Board | Monday | (202) 452-3206 |
| Inventories and Sales, Manuf., and Trade | Dept. of Commerce | Mid-month | (301) 763-7077 |
| Leading Economic Indicators | Dept. of Commerce | Beginning month | (202) 606-5361 |
| Loans and Securities at Commercial Banks | Federal Reserve Board | 3rd wk. of mo. | (202) 452-3206 |
| Money Stock, Liq. Assets and Debt Measures | Federal Reserve Board | Thursdays | (202) 452-3206 |
| Mortgage Rates (Adjustable Rate Information) | Federal Housing Fin. Board | Mid-month | (202) 408-2940 |
| Mortgage Rates (30-Yield Fixed Rate Yields) | Fed. Natl. Mortgage Assn. | Daily | (800) 752-7020, ext. 3 |
| Mortgage Rates, (Fixed Intermed. Term Yields) | Fed. Natl. Mortgage Assn. | Daily | (800) 752-7020, ext 4 |
| Mortgage Rates (Adjustable Yields) | Fed. Natl. Mortgage Assn. | Daily | (800) 752-7020, ext. 5 |
| Personal Income and Outlays | Bureau of Labor Statistics | End month | (202) 606-7828 |
| Producer Price Index | Bureau of Labor Statistics | Mid-month | (202) 606-7828 |
| Retail Trade, Report of Previous Month | Dept. of Census | Mid-month | (202) 393-4100 |
| Treasury Sec. Purch. Notes, Bonds, and Bills | Dept. of Treasury | Daily | (202) 874-4000 |
| Wholesale Trade | Dept. of Commerce | Mid-month | (202) 606-7828, ext. 4 |

*The Government's Kimberly bulletin board is a terrific source of financial forecasts and data, Federal Reserve information, securities-auction results, and consumer-finance statistics. Modem (612) 340-2489.*

# HUMAN RESOURCES

# Business School Placement Offices

*Carnegie-Mellon University*
Career Opportunities Center
Graduate School of Industrial Administration
Schenley Park
Pittsburgh, PA 15213
(412) 268-2277

*Columbia University*
Columbia Business School
Office of Placement, 206 Uris Hall
New York, NY 10027
(212) 854-5471

*Cornell University*
Johnson Graduate School of Management
Placement Office
315 Malott Hall
Ithaca, NY 14853
(607) 255-4888

*Dartmouth University*
Amos Tuck School of Business Administration
Placement Office
100 Tuck Hall
Hanover, NH 03755
(603) 646-3820

*Duke University*
The Fuqua School of Business
Placement Office, Box 90120
Durham, NC 27708
(919) 660-7810

*Harvard University*
Graduate School of Business Administration
Placement Office
Soldiers Field
Boston, MA 02163
(617) 495-6232

*Indiana University at Bloomington*
Graduate School of Business
Business Placement Office
10th St. and Fee Lane
Bloomington, IN 47405
(812) 855-5317

*Massachusetts Institute of Technology*
Sloan School of Management
Placement Office
50 Memorial Dr.
Cambridge, MA 02139
(617) 253-6149

*New York University*
Graduate School of Business Administration
Office for Student Counseling & Career Placement
44 W. 4th St.
New York, NY 10012
(212) 998-0623

*Northwestern University*
Kellogg Graduate School of Management
Placement Office
2001 Sheridan Rd., Leverone Hall
Evanston, IL 60208
(708) 491-3168

*Purdue University*
Krannert Graduate School of Management
Placement Office
1310 Krannert Bldg., #160
West Lafayette, IN 47907
(317) 494-4377

*Stanford University*
Graduate School of Business
Career Management Center
Stanford, CA 94305
(415) 723-2151

*University of California at Berkeley (Haas)*
Graduate School of Business Administration
Placement Center
26 Barrows Hall
Berkeley, CA 94720
(510) 642-8124

*University of California at Los Angeles*
John E. Anderson Graduate School of Management
Career Management Services
405 Hilgard Ave., Suite 1349
Los Angeles, CA 90024
(310) 825-3325

*University of Chicago*
Graduate School of Business
Office of Career Services
1101 E. 58th St.
Chicago, IL 60637
(312) 702-7405

*University of Michigan*
School of Business Administration
Placement Office
701 Tappan
Ann Arbor, MI 48109
(313) 764-1372

*University of North Carolina-Chapel Hill*
Graduate School of Business Administration
Career Services
CB # 3490 Carroll Hall
Chapel Hill, NC 27599
(919) 962-2360

*Business School Placement Offices (cont'd)*

*University of Pennsylvania*
The Wharton School, Graduate Division
Career Development and Placement
102 Vance Hall
Philadelphia, PA 19104
(215) 898-4383

*University of Pittsburgh*
Joseph M. Katz Graduate School of Business
Placement and Career Services
201 Mervis Hall
Pittsburgh, PA 15260
(412) 648-1510

*University of Rochester*
William E. Simon Graduate School of Business
Career Services
Schlegel Hall
Rochester, NY 14627
(716) 275-4881

*University of Southern California*
MBA School of Business Administration
Career Services
Bridge Hall, #204
Los Angeles, CA 90089
(213) 740-0156

*University of Texas at Austin*
Graduate School of Business
Career Services Office
CBA 2.202
Austin, TX 78712
(512) 471-1739

*University of Virginia*
Darden Graduate School of Business Administration
Career Services and Placement Office
Box 6550
Charlottesville, VA 22906
(804) 924-7283

*Vanderbilt University*
Owen Graduate School of Management
Career Planning and Placement Office
401 21st Ave. S.
Nashville, TN 37203
(615) 322-4069

*Yale University*
Yale School of Organization and Management
Career Development Office
Box 208200
New Haven, CT 06520
(203) 432-5900

# MBA Schools Ranked

## Top 20 U.S. Business Schools

| Rank | School | Rank by Academics | Rank by CEOs | Placement Success | 1993 Median Starting Salary ($) |
|------|--------|-------------------|--------------|-------------------|---------------------------------|
| 1 | Stanford University | 1 | 2 | 3 | 65,000 |
| 2 | Massachusetts Institute of Technology (Sloan) | 3 | 8 | 1 | 65,000 |
| 3 | Harvard University | 3 | 1 | 2 | 65,000 |
| 4 | Pennsylvania (Wharton) | 3 | 4 | 5 | 62,000 |
| 5 | Northwestern University (Kellogg) | 1 | 3 | 6 | 60,000 |
| 6 | University of Chicago | 3 | 6 | 9 | 57,000 |
| 7 | Dartmouth (Tuck) | 7 | 10 | 7 | 60,000 |
| 8 | University of Michigan at Ann Arbor | 7 | 5 | 4 | 63,325 |
| 9 | Duke University (Fuqua) | 9 | 7 | 8 | 55,200 |
| 10 | U. of California at Los Angeles (Anderson) | 9 | 19 | 13 | 58,000 |
| 11 | Columbia University | 9 | 9 | 19 | 55,000 |
| 12 | U. of California at Berkeley (Haas) | 9 | 17 | 16 | 55,000 |
| 13 | University of Virginia (Darden) | 9 | 11 | 14 | 55,000 |
| 13 | Carnegie-Mellon | 14 | 18 | 10 | 56,000 |
| 15 | Cornell University | 14 | 13 | 17 | 56,000 |
| 16 | U. of No. Carolina at Chapel Hill (Kenan-Flagler) | 16 | 26 | 15 | 53,700 |
| 17 | New York University (Stern) | 16 | 20 | 11 | 55,000 |
| 18 | University of Texas at Austin | 19 | 15 | 25 | 48,000 |
| 19 | Yale University | 19 | 12 | 47 | 55,000 |
| 20 | University of Southern California | 24 | 21 | 36 | 50,000 |

*Source: U.S. News & World Report, March 21, 1994*

# Law School Placement Offices

*Boston College*
Law School
Placement Office
885 Centre St.
Newton, MA 02159
(617) 552-4345

*Columbia University*
School of Law
Career Services
435 W. 116th St.
New York, NY 10027
(212) 854-2683

*Cornell University*
Cornell Law School
Career Services
Myron Taylor Hall
Ithaca, NY 14853
(607) 255-5252

*Duke University*
School of Law
Career Services
Towerview and Science Dr.
Durham, NC 27708
(919) 684-5429

*Georgetown University*
Law Center
Career Services
600 New Jersey Ave., NW
Washington, DC 20001
(202) 662-9300

*George Washington University*
The National Law Center
Career Services
720 20th St., NW
Washington, DC 20052
(202) 994-7340

*Harvard University*
Harvard Law School
Career Services
Cambridge, MA 02138
(617) 495-3119

*New York University*
School of Law
Office of Placement Services
40 Washington Square S.
New York, NY 10012
(212) 998-6090

*Northwestern University*
School of Law
Placement Office
357 E. Chicago Ave.
Chicago, IL 60611
(312) 503-8438

*Stanford University*
Stanford Law School
Career Services and Placement
Crown Quadrangle
Stanford, CA 94305
(415) 723-3942

*University of California at Berkeley*
School of Law
Office of Career Services
291 Boalt Hall
Berkeley, CA 94720
(415) 642-4567

*University of California at Hastings*
College of Law
Career Services
200 MacAllister St., Suite 211
San Francisco, CA 94102
(415) 565-4619

*University of California at Los Angeles*
School of Law
Placement Office
405 Hilgard Ave.
Los Angeles, CA 90024
(310) 206-1117

*University of Chicago*
Law School
Placement Office
111 E. 60th St.
Chicago, IL 60637
(312) 702-9625

*University of Iowa*
College of Law
Placement Office
Boyd Law Building
Melrose and Byington Sts.
Iowa City, IA 52242
(319) 335-9011

*University of Michigan*
Law School
Office of Career Services
210 Hutchins Hall
625 S. State St.
Ann Arbor, MI 48109
(313) 764-0546

*Law School Placement Offices (cont'd)*

*University of Minnesota*
Law School
Career Services
229 19th Ave. S.
Minneapolis, MN 55455
(612) 625-1866

*University of Notre Dame*
Notre Dame Law School
Placement Office
Notre Dame, IN 46556
(219) 631-7542

*University of Pennsylvania*
Law School
Career Planning and Placement
3400 Chestnut St.
Philadelphia, PA 19104
(215) 898-7493

*University of Southern California*
Law Center
Career Services
University Park
Los Angeles, CA 90089
(213) 743-7397

*University of Texas at Austin*
School of Law
Career Services
727 E. 26th St.
Austin, TX 78705
(512) 471-4768

*University of Virginia*
School of Law
Placement Office
North Grounds
580 Massie Rd.
Charlottesville, VA 22903
(804) 924-7349

*Vanderbilt University*
School of Law
Career Services
Law Building, Room 127
Nashville, TN 37240
(615) 322-6192

*Yale University*
Law School
Career Development
P.O. Box 208330
New Haven, CT 06520
(203) 432-1676

# Law Schools Ranked

## Top 20 U.S. Law Schools

| Rank | School | Rank by Academics | Rank by Lawyers/Judges | Placement Success | 1993 Median Starting Salary ($) |
|------|--------|-------------------|------------------------|-------------------|--------------------------------|
| 1 | Yale University | 1 | 1 | 2 | 83,000 |
| 2 | Harvard University | 1 | 1 | 5 | 70,000 |
| 3 | Stanford University | 1 | 1 | 6 | 67,000 |
| 4 | University of Chicago | 1 | 1 | 4 | 70,000 |
| 5 | Columbia University | 1 | 6 | 3 | 83,000 |
| 6 | New York University | 7 | 11 | 1 | 83,000 |
| 7 | Duke University | 11 | 9 | 9 | 65,000 |
| 8 | University of Michigan at Ann Arbor | 1 | 1 | 7 | 63,283 |
| 9 | University of Pennsylvania | 7 | 9 | 8 | 70,000 |
| 10 | University of California at Berkeley | 7 | 6 | 17 | 65,000 |
| 11 | Cornell University | 11 | 11 | 10 | 68,550 |
| 12 | Northwestern University | 11 | 11 | 13 | 70,000 |
| 13 | Georgetown University | 15 | 11 | 15 | 70,000 |
| 14 | University of Virginia | 7 | 6 | 11 | 69,900 |
| 15 | Vanderbilt University | 19 | 17 | 14 | 58,125 |
| 16 | University of California at Los Angeles | 16 | 16 | 18 | 69,400 |
| 17 | University of Minnesota at Twin Cities | 17 | 20 | 21 | 53,000 |
| 18 | University of Southern California | 19 | 26 | 16 | 61,750 |
| 19 | University of Iowa | 19 | 26 | 27 | 45,500 |
| 20 | University of California at Hastings | 23 | 17 | 24 | 65,000 |

*Source: U.S. News & World Report, March 21, 1994*

# Business Co-Op Programs

COOPERATIVE EDUCATION BEGAN in 1906 at the University of Cincinnati in Ohio. The purpose then, as now, was to strengthen classroom learning with periods of study-related employment in companies outside of the academic environment. Cooperative students take part in a college program that alternates periods of study with periods of work, either on a full-time or part-time basis.

The goal of businesses that participate in cooperative learning programs is to enhance the education of college and university students through integrated, structured programs which combine academic study with paid, productive work experience. Co-op education can provide a cost-effective means of meeting recruiting goals, and training potential career employees, as well as providing an opportunity to influence the education process.

Co-op education is practiced in over 1,000 colleges and universities in the U.S., as well as in various countries around the world. It is found mostly in two- and four-year college programs but is also in a limited number of five-year programs. Co-op is available in virtually every college curriculum and is offered at all levels, from the associate to the doctoral degree. Age is no factor for participation. Co-op is open to both traditional and non-traditional college students. In most programs, students receive academic credit for work experience and are charged comparable tuition rates. In other programs, no academic credit is awarded and no tuition is charged.

Over 275,000 students are enrolled in co-op programs each year with over 50,000 employers. Although student earnings vary with college major, years in school, and geographic location, co-op students earn a national average of $7,000 per year.

## Where Co-Op Students Find Work

According to the National Commission for Cooperative Education, 80 percent of co-op students receive an offer for full-time employment from one of their co-op employers; 63 percent of co-op students receive an offer from their final co-op employer; 48 percent of the co-op students accept those offers; 40 percent find employment in fields directly related to their co-op assignments; and 15 percent enroll in graduate or professional programs.

## Recommended Resources

*Cooperative Education Association*
11710 Beltsville Dr., Suite 520
Beltsville, MD 20705
(301) 572-2329

This organization provides services for professionals who either hire or place cooperative education students. They publish *The Journal of Cooperative Education*, a research journal for educators; *Co-Op Experience* magazine for an audience of businesses and co-op students; and a newsletter and annual directory for educator and business members.

*National Commission for Cooperative Education*
360 Huntington Ave.
Boston, MA 02115
(617) 373-3778

This organization provides information on setting up co-op programs for businesses and educational institutions. Call for their *Cooperative Education Undergraduate Directory* which lists cooperative education programs by school and by state, and includes a list of cooperative education employers.

---

## The Top Reference Sources

*The College Blue Book: Occupational Education*
Macmillan, $48
(800) 257-5755

This extensive biennially updated directory has a complete listing of educational programs arranged

alphabetically by subject and by location. The book is available in the reference section of most public libraries.

# Colleges by Specialty Programs

## Top Undergraduate Business Administration Programs

Carnegie-Mellon University
Indiana University
Massachusetts Institute of Technology
New York University
University of California at Berkeley
University of Illinois
University of Michigan
University of Pennsylvania
University of Texas
University of Wisconsin

*Source: The Ultimate College Shopper's Guide*

## Top Undergraduate Accounting Programs

Arizona State University
Brigham Young University
James Madison University
Kansas State University
Miami University
Michigan State University
Northern Illinois University
Ohio State University
Oklahoma State University
Stanford University
Texas A&M University
University of Alabama
University of Florida
University of Georgia
University of Illinois
University of Michigan
University of Missouri
University of Notre Dame
University of Pennsylvania
University of Southern California
University of Tennessee
University of Texas
University of Virginia
University of Washington
University of Wisconsin
Wake Forest University

*Source: The Ultimate College Shopper's Guide*

# ESL Programs

TO FIND THE LOCATION of an English as a Second Language program, contact:

The National Literacy Hotline
(800) 228-8813
　　This hotline has a listing of available ESL programs in high schools, colleges, and universities throughout the United States and Canada.

## Contact Option

Institute of International Education
Information Center
809 United Nations Plaza
New York, NY 10017
(212) 883-8200
　　Provides information about English language and orientation programs in the United States.

## The Top Reference Sources

*The Idea-a-Day Guide to Super Selling
and Customer Service*
Dartnell, $19.95
(800) 621-5463

This excellent reference includes a self-diagnostic test to identify special selling needs; sections devoted to specific sales skills, techniques, and strategies; more than 100 tips, ideas and information sources, worksheets, and 250 practical money-making ideas for each working day of the year. The oversized format and easy-to-use design make it an excellent workbook.

# Correspondence Courses

THE FOLLOWING IS A LIST of selected programs that provide accredited home study programs. Most of them offer financial assistance through the G.I. Bill or through employee assistance programs.

*Accounting/Secretarial Computer*
North American Correspondence Schools
925 Oak St.
Scranton, PA 18515
(717) 342-7701

*Business/Engineering*
International Correspondence Schools
925 Oak St.
Scranton, PA 18515
(717) 342-7701

*Electronics/Computers*
McGraw-Hill Continuing Education Center
4401 Connecticut Ave., NW
Washington DC 20008
(202) 244-1600

*Electronics/Computers*
People's College of Independent Studies
233 Academy Dr.
P.O. Box 421768
Kissimmee, FL 34742
(407) 847-4444

*English Usage*
English Language Institute
925 Oak St.
Scranton, PA 18515
(717) 342-7701

*High School Diploma*
American School
850 E. 58 St.
Chicago, IL 60637
(312) 947-3300

*High School Diploma*
Cambridge Academy
1111 Southwest 17th St.
Ocala, FL 34474
(904) 620-2717

*High School Diploma*
Citizens' High School
188 College Dr.
Orange Park, FL 32067
(904) 276-1700

*High School Diploma*
ICS-Newport/Pacific High School
Scranton, PA 18515
(717) 342-7701

*Paralegal*
Paralegal Institute
3602 West Thomas Rd., Suite 9
Drawer 11408
Phoenix, AZ 85061-1408
(602) 272-1855

*Paralegal*
Southern Career Institute
164 W. Royal Palm Rd.
Boca Raton, FL 33432
(800) 669-2555

*Secretarial Training*
Laural School
2538 N. 8th St.
P.O. Box 5338
Phoenix, AZ 85010
(602) 994-3460

*Tax Training*
National Tax Training School
4 Melnick Dr.
P.O. Box 382
Monsey, NY 10952
(914) 352-3634

## Contact Option

National Home Study Council
1601 18 St., NW
Washington DC 20009
(202) 234-5100
    Produces listing of fully accredited home study programs.

# Executive Education

EXECUTIVE EDUCATION IS undergoing a series of changes as companies reconsider the most effective way to improve executive performance and make corporations more competitive. The biggest changes can be seen the the shift from traditional forms of educational programs to brief, expensive, but more needs-directed pragmatic courses offered by specialist consultants.

The largest public enrollment executive-education programs offered at universities and other educational institutions include the following:

## 20 Leading Institutions for Executive Education

| School | Location | Annual Revenues ($ millions) | (%) Customized Programs | Participants |
|--------|----------|------------------------------|-------------------------|--------------|
| Ashridge Management | Hertfordshire, U.K. | 10.5 | 55 | 4,420 |
| Babson | Babson Park, MA | 3.3 | 50 | 1,150 |
| Center for Creative Leadership | Greensboro, NC | 21.2 | 31 | 14,800 |
| Columbia | New York, NY | 8.0 | 29 | 1,800 |
| Dartmouth (Tuck) | Hanover, NH | 2.0 | 0 | 300 |
| Duke (Fuqua) | Durham, NC | 7.3 | 47 | 1,610 |
| Harvard | Cambridge, MA | 25.6 | 1 | 1,620 |
| I.M.D. | Lausanne, Switzerland | 15.8 | 20 | 2,000 |
| INSEAD | Fontainebleau, France | 20.2 | 30 | 2,490 |
| London Business School | London, England | 8.7 | 40 | 1,880 |
| MIT (Sloan) | Cambridge, MA | 9.0 | 5 | 1,010 |
| Michigan | Ann Arbor, MI | 19.0 | 20 | 5,170 |
| North Carolina (Kenan-Flagler) | Chapel Hill, NC | 2.8 | 36 | 1,280 |
| Northwestern (Kellogg) | Evanston, IL | 11.2 | 28 | 3,280 |
| Penn State (Smeal) | University Park, PA | 4.3 | 45 | 1,010 |
| Pennsylvania (Wharton) | Philadelphia, PA | 17.0 | 50 | 4,200 |
| Southern California | Los Angeles, CA | 3.5 | 28 | 3,410 |
| Stanford | Stanford, CA | 7.2 | 0 | 600 |
| UCLA (Anderson) | Los Angeles, CA | 4.0 | 25 | 1,220 |
| Virginia (Darden) | Charlottesville, VA | 9.3 | 20 | 2,000 |

*Source: Business Week, October 25, 1993*

A recent survey of major U.S. corporations conducted by *The Wall Street Journal* and *Bricker's International Directory* produced a list of popular executive-education programs in three core areas: general management programs, leadership programs, and human resources and organization programs. The best known programs in each of the three areas include the following:

## General Management Programs

| Institution | Program | Location | Telephone |
|-------------|---------|----------|-----------|
| Carnegie Mellon | Program for Executives | Pittsburgh, PA | (412) 268-2305 |
| European Institute of Bus. Admin. (INSEAD) | Advanced Mgmt. Program | Fontainebleau, France | [33] (60) 724000 |
| University of Virginia (Darden) | Executive Program | Charlottesville, VA | (804) 924-3000 |
| University of North Carolina (Kenan-Flagler) | Executive Program | Chapel Hill, NC | (919) 962-3123 |
| University of Michigan | Executive Program | Ann Arbor, MI | (313) 763-1003 |
| Dartmouth (Tuck) | Executive Program | Hanover, NH | (603) 646-2839 |
| University of California, Berkeley (Haas) | Executive Program | Berkeley, CA | (510) 642-1406 |
| University of Pennsylvania (Wharton) | Advanced Mgmt. Program | Philadelphia, PA | (215) 898-7722 |
| Stanford University | Stanford Executive Program | Palo Alto, CA | (415) 723-2921 |
| University of California, L.A. (Anderson) | UCLA Executive Program | Los Angeles, CA | (310) 825-2001 |
| Duke University (Fuqua) | Advanced Mgmt. Program | Durham, NC | (919) 660-6340 |

*Executive Education (cont'd)*

## Human Resources and Organization

| Institution | Program | Location | Telephone |
|---|---|---|---|
| University of Michigan | Strategic Human Resource Planning | Ann Arbor, MI | (313) 763-1003 |
| University of Michigan | Advanced Human Resource Executive Program | Ann Arbor, MI | (313) 763-1003 |
| University of Michigan | Human Resource Executive Program | Ann Arbor, MI | (313) 763-1003 |
| Penn State Univ. (Smeal) | Human Resource Management Program | University Park, PA | (814) 865-1263 |
| Columbia University | Human Res. Mgmt.: Effecting Change Beyond the 1990s | New York, NY | (212) 854-3395 |

## Leadership Programs

| Institution | Program | Location | Telephone |
|---|---|---|---|
| Center for Creative Leadership | Leadership at the Peak | Greensboro, NC | (910) 545-2810 |
| Center for Creative Leadership | Leadership Development Program | Greensboro, NC | (910) 545-2810 |
| Columbia University | Leading and Managing People | New York, NY | (212) 854-3395 |
| Boston University | Leadership Institute | Boston, MA | (617) 353-4217 |
| University of Virginia (Darden) | Creating the Future | Charlottesville, VA | (804) 924-3000 |

# Trainers and Seminars

ON-SITE TRAINING FOR PERSONNEL, whether in the form of books, audio cassettes, films, videotapes, software, or live seminars, is available through a wide range of human resources companies and consultants.

One of the most extensive sources for finding the right training program is published by the American Society for Training and Development. Their book offers a listing of companies and consultants that provide hardware, training facilities, and other training and equipment supplies. Also included is an alphabetized listing of companies and consultants and a listing of specialists who cater to industry-specific audiences. The directory features a subject index of companies and consultants who provide human resources development in areas as specific as: AIDS in the Workplace, Ergonomics, Quality Control, and Time Management Skills.

## Recommended Resource

*American Society For Training and Development Buyer's Guide and Consultant Directory*
$75
1640 King St., Box 1443
Alexandria, VA 22313
(703) 683-8100

## Contact Options

Personal Progress Library
7657 Winnetka Ave., #331
Winnetka, CA 91306
(800) 748-6245
America's largest cassette-lending library in the field.

*Training and Development Resource Catalogues:*

Blanchard Training and Development
125 State Pl.
Escondido, CA 92029
(800) 728-6000

CareerTrack
3085 Center Green Dr.
Boulder, CO 80301
(800) 423-3001

The Myers Method
P.O. Box 1526
Princeton, NJ 08542
(609) 737-6832

Nightingale-Conant
7300 N. Lehigh Ave.
Niles, IL 60714
(800) 323-5552

QCI International
P.O. Box 1503
1350 Vista Way
Red Bluff, CA 96080
(800) 527-6970

Sybervision Systems
1 Sansome St., #1610
San Francisco, CA 94104
(800) 888-9980

The Zig Ziglar Company
3330 Earhart #204
Carrollton, TX 75006
(800) 527-0306

# Executive Training

AUDIO RECORDINGS, VIDEOCASSETTES, training programs, and seminars designed to expand the skills of the corporate executive are a multi-billion dollar industry in this country.

There are several companies that design and present executive training programs that run anywhere from one day to several weeks. Seminars are offered in a wide array of topics ranging from quality control to stress reduction and from business writing to budget planning.

## Contact Options

*Executive Training Firms:*

CareerTrack
3085 Center Green Dr.
Boulder, CO 80301
(800) 423-3001

Fred Pryor Seminars
Pryor Resources
2000 Shawnee Mission Pkwy.
Shawnee Mission, KS 66205
(800) 255-6139

National Seminars Group
6901 W. 63 St.
Shawnee Mission, KS 66202
(800) 258-7246

First Seminar Service
600 Suffolk St.
Lowell, MA 01854
(800) 321-1990
For a fee, First Seminar will do a search and find all of the available seminars on a particular topic anywhere in the country over the course of the year.

## Recommended Resources

*The Corporate University Guide to Short Management Seminars*
The Corporate University Press, $69
A thorough listing of seminars available by topic, training organization, date, and location.

*Evaluation Guide to Executive Programs*
The Corporate University Press, $169
An in-depth evaluation of 170 of the best short programs available.

The Corporate University Press
124 Washington Ave.
Suite B2
Point Richard, CA
(510) 236-9400

# Speakers Bureaus

COMPANIES OFTEN NEED SPEAKERS, either to motivate a sales force or to entertain at a company event. For the right price, it's possible to hire anyone, from Henry Kissinger to a foreign expert on quality control, to lecture an audience of company personnel. A number of agencies exist whose sole function is to book speakers for corporate events.

## Contact Options

*Lecture Agents:*

Walters International Speakers Bureau
P.O. Box 1120
Glendora, CA 91740
(818) 335-8069

Washington Speakers Bureau
310 S. Henry St.
Alexandria, VA 22314
(703) 684-0555

The Harry Walker Agency
One Penn Plaza, Suite 2400
New York, NY 10119
(212) 563-0700

National Speakers Bureau
222 Wisconsin Ave.
Lake Forest, IL 60045
(708) 295-1122

Keppler Associates
4350 N. Fairfax Dr., Suite 700
Arlington, VA 22203
(703) 516-4000

## Recommended Resource

*Who's Who in Professional Speaking*
National Speakers Association, $25
(602) 968-2552
This directory lists names, addresses, and phone numbers of members alphabetically, geographically, and by specialty.

# Speech and Image Consultants

SEMINARS THAT ASSIST EXECUTIVES and managers in developing a solid professional image and effective presentation skills are available from a number of human resources consultants. These programs focus on effective communication styles for public speaking engagements.

## Contact Options

*Human Resource Consultants:*

Achievement Concepts
1963 Cynthia Ln.
P.O. Box 430
Merrick, NY 11566
(516) 868-5100

Anderson Management Group
413 Victoria Court, NW
Box 1745-A
Vienna, VA 22183
(703) 938-9672

Commocore
156 Fifth Ave., #701
New York, NY 10010
(212) 206-1003

Communication Resources
Harvard Square
P.O. Box 537
Cambridge, MA 02238
(617) 332-4334

Conrad Communications
6 Black Birch Ln.
Scarsdale, NY 10583
(914) 725-2360

Dale Carnegie & Associates
1475 Franklin Ave.
Garden City, NY 11530
(800) 231-5800

Decker Communications
44 Montgomery St., Suite 1700
San Francisco, CA 94104
(415) 391-5544

Kaufman Professional Image Consultants
233 S. 6th St., Suite 702
Philadelphia, PA 19106
(215) 592-9709

Parkhurst Communications
311 W. 75th St.
New York, NY 10023
(212) 580-9390

Tracy Presentation Skills
2414 Londonderry Rd., Suite 767
Alexandria, VA 22308
(703) 360-3222

# Top Business Speakers

## Cavett Award Winners

THE CAVETT AWARD is the top speaker's award given annually by the National Speakers Association:

1979 - Robert Cavett
1980 - Bill Gove
1981 - Dave Yoho
1982 - Ty Boyd
1983 - Joe Larson
1984 - Ira M. Hayes
1985 - Nido R. Qubein
1986 - Don Hutson
1987 - James "Doc" Blakely
1988 - Robert H. Henry
1989 - Jeanne Robertson
1990 - D. Michael Frank
1991 - Rosita Perez
1992 - D. John Hammond
1993 - Jim Cathcart

## Contact Option

National Speakers Association
1500 S. Priest Dr.
Tempe, AZ 85281
(602) 968-2552

# Coping With Illiteracy

**Training Costs, 1992**

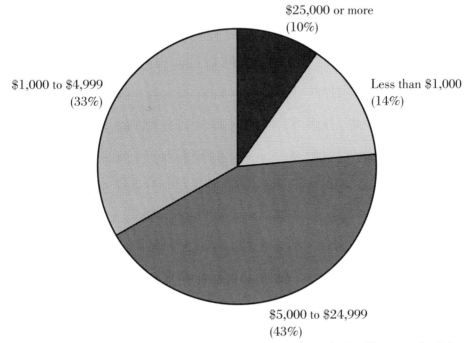

$25,000 or more (10%)

Less than $1,000 (14%)

$1,000 to $4,999 (33%)

$5,000 to $24,999 (43%)

*Source: American Management Association*

**Percentage of Companies that Provide Remedial Training Programs**

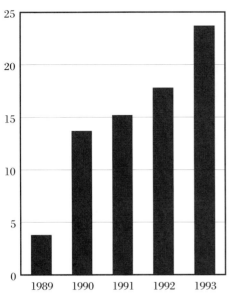

*Source: American Management Association*

**Percentage of Companies that Conduct Literacy and Math Testing**

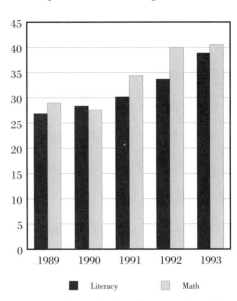

Literacy     Math

*Source: American Management Association*

# Skills Training

A NUMBER OF COMPANIES specialize in training programs to improve the reading and writing speeds and the efficiency of company personnel. These companies will conduct on-site seminars or provide materials for corporations to conduct their own courses.

## Contact Options

*Companies Specializing in Literacy Training:*

Aztec Software Associates
24 Tulip St., Box 863
Summit, NJ 07901
(908) 273-7443

Conover Company
P.O. Box 155
Omro, WI 54963
(800) 933-1933

Reading Development Resources
7201 S. Broadway, Suite 11
Littleton, CO 80122
(800) 328-5099

Writing Development Associates
254-39 Bates Rd.
Little Neck, NY 11363
(718) 279-3143

## Recommended Resource

National Literacy Hotline
P.O. Box 81826
Lincoln, NE 68501
(800) 228-8813

# Compensation and Benefits

A COMPANY NEEDING TO DESIGN a benefits package for its employees can contact a consulting firm that specializes in this field.

The following is a list of some of the largest U.S.-based consultants:

A. Foster Higgins & Co.
125 Broad St.
New York, NY 10004
(212) 574-9000

Alexander Consulting Group
125 Chubb Ave.
Lyndhurst, NJ 07071
(201) 460-6600

Buck Consultants
2 Penn Plaza, 23rd Floor
New York, NY 10121
(212)330-1000

Hewitt Associates
100 Half Day Rd.
Lincolnshire, IL 60069
(708) 295-5000

KPMG Peat Marwick
345 Park Ave.
New York, NY 10154
(212) 758-9700

Mercer Consulting Group
1166 Avenue of the Americas
New York, NY 10036
(212) 345-4500

Segal
One Park Ave.
New York, NY 10016
(212) 251-5000

Towers Perrin
245 Park Ave.
New York, NY 10167
(212) 309-3400

Wyatt
601 13th St., NW
Washington, DC 20005
(202) 624-0600

*Compensation and Benefits (cont'd)*

## Percentage of Firms Offering Health Benefits by Firm Size

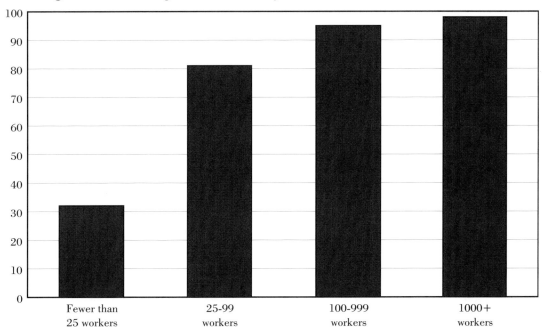

Source: *Health Insurance Association of America, Employer Survey*

A survey of over 1600 organizations produced this summary of plans offered by medium to large employers.

## Compensation and Benefits Offered

| Benefits Program | Total % With | Total % Without | Do Not Have But Are Considering |
|---|---|---|---|
| BASIC HEALTH-CARE PLANS | | | |
| Medical Insurance Coverage (excluding dental) | 97.7 | 2.3 | 0.0 |
| Health Maintenance Organization (HMO) | 74.5 | 23.3 | 2.2 |
| Preferred Provider Organization (PPO) | 60.8 | 29.3 | 9.9 |
| SPECIAL HEALTH-CARE PLANS (not included under Basic Health Care) | | | |
| Dental Coverage | 93.4 | 5.5 | 1.1 |
| Vision Coverage | 45.8 | 49.8 | 5.3 |
| Alcohol/Drug Program | 65.6 | 31.0 | 3.4 |
| Physical Fitness Program | 31.6 | 61.0 | 7.4 |
| Prescription Drug Coverage | 77.3 | 19.7 | 3.0 |
| Hearing Examination Coverage | 24.8 | 72.9 | 2.3 |
| OTHER EMPLOYEE BENEFITS | | | |
| Formal Training/Professional Development Program | 67.8 | 24.7 | 7.5 |
| Flextime (employee chooses alternative work schedules) | 48.1 | 45.6 | 6.3 |
| Group Term Life Insurance | 97.9 | 1.8 | 0.3 |
| Educational Assistance | 92.0 | 6.6 | 1.4 |
| Preretirement Counseling | 44.5 | 43.3 | 12.2 |
| Accidental Death and Dismemberment | 94.6 | 5.4 | 0.0 |
| Short-Term Disability Insurance | 83.0 | 14.7 | 2.3 |
| Long-Term Disability Insurance | 97.5 | 2.1 | 0.4 |
| Annual Computerized Benefits Statement | 60.5 | 24.9 | 14.6 |
| Group Personal Insurance (payroll deduction auto or homeowner's insurance) | 11.4 | 84.5 | 4.1 |
| Flexible Benefits (employee chooses from among various benefits plans) | 44.3 | 39.8 | 15.9 |
| Flexible Spending Account(s) (Section 125) | 68.6 | 24.0 | 7.4 |

*Compensation and Benefits (cont'd)*

| Benefits Program | Total % With | Total % Without | Do Not Have But Are Considering |
|---|---|---|---|
| **RETIREMENT INCOME** | | | |
| Pension Plan | 80.2 | 18.9 | 0.9 |
| Profit Sharing Plan | 29.3 | 68.3 | 2.4 |
| Thrift Plan | 19.3 | 79.4 | 1.3 |
| 401(k) Salary Reduction Plan | 85.6 | 13.2 | 1.2 |
| ESOP (Employee Stock Ownership Plan) | 22.6 | 75.2 | 2.2 |
| **EXECUTIVE STOCK PLANS** | | | |
| Incentive Stock Options | 36.2 | 61.6 | 2.2 |
| Nonqualified Stock Option Plan | 36.9 | 60.9 | 2.2 |
| Stock Appreciation Rights | 14.0 | 83.5 | 2.5 |
| Restricted Stock Award Plan | 26.7 | 71.5 | 1.8 |
| Performance Share Plan | 13.6 | 83.9 | 2.5 |
| **EXECUTIVE INCENTIVE PLANS** | | | |
| Performance Unit Plan | 22.9 | 75.4 | 1.7 |
| Annual Cash Incentive Plan | 69.4 | 29.6 | 1.0 |
| Medium-Term Cash Incentive Plan (2-3 yrs.) | 4.1 | 92.7 | 3.2 |
| Long-Term Cash Incentive Plan (3 yrs. or longer) | 19.6 | 76.2 | 4.2 |
| **SPECIAL EXECUTIVE BENEFIT PROGRAMS** | | | |
| Low/No Interest Loan Program | 7.9 | 91.4 | 0.7 |
| Executive Physical Examination | 65.8 | 33.2 | 1.0 |
| Executive Medical Reimbursement Plan | 17.4 | 81.5 | 1.1 |
| Executive Supplemental Disability Plan | 22.6 | 75.8 | 1.6 |
| Executive Supplemental Retirement Plan | 39.7 | 58.0 | 2.3 |
| Executive Supplemental Survivor Income Plan | 16.6 | 82.2 | 1.2 |
| Voluntary Deferred Compensation Plan | 39.1 | 57.9 | 3.0 |
| Executive Employment Contracts | 33.6 | 65.5 | 0.9 |
| Financial Counseling/Tax Planning | 35.5 | 61.4 | 3.1 |
| **COMPENSATION PROGRAMS** | | | |
| Formal Point-Factor Job Evaluation System | 56.5 | 39.1 | 4.4 |
| Formal Performance Appraisal | 95.1 | 3.3 | 1.6 |
| Special Project-Oriented Incentive for Engineers, Programmers, or Inventors | 7.7 | 88.2 | 4.1 |
| Other Group Incentives | 28.2 | 61.6 | 10.2 |
| Lump Sum Merit Increases | 31.5 | 62.8 | 5.7 |
| Gain Sharing | 10.7 | 81.1 | 8.2 |
| Specialized Compensation Software | 23.3 | 64.4 | 12.3 |

*Source: 1992 Human Resources Survey by William Mercer*

## The Top Reference Sources

*Fundamentals of Employee Benefit Programs*
Employee Benefit and Research Institute, $24.95
(202) 775-6341

A comprehensive and accessible primer on the whole range of employee benefits, including pension and retirement programs, profit-sharing plans, savings plans, life insurance plans, education assistance and legal services programs, dependent care benefits and all manner of healthcare benefits. This guide is a must for any employer creating or changing a company benefit program.

# Social Security

## Covered Employment, Earnings, and Contribution Rates

| Item | 1970 | 1980 | 1984 | 1985 | 1986 |
|---|---|---|---|---|---|
| WORKERS WITH INSURED STATUS (millions) | 105.7 | 137.4 | 147.0 | 148.7 | 150.6 |
| Male (millions) | 61.9 | 75.4 | 78.8 | 79.7 | 80.7 |
| Female (millions) | 43.8 | 62.0 | 68.2 | 69.0 | 69.9 |
| Under 25 years old (millions) | 17.7 | 25.5 | 23.1 | 22.3 | 21.9 |
| 25 to 34 years old (millions) | 22.3 | 34.9 | 39.7 | 39.9 | 40.0 |
| 35 to 44 years old (millions) | 19.0 | 22.4 | 27.2 | 28.5 | 29.8 |
| 45 to 54 years old (millions) | 19.0 | 18.6 | 18.8 | 19.0 | 19.3 |
| 55 to 59 years old (millions) | 7.8 | 9.2 | 9.1 | 9.1 | 9.0 |
| 60 to 64 years old (millions) | 6.3 | 7.9 | 8.6 | 8.7 | 8.8 |
| 65 to 69 years old (millions) | 5.1 | 6.7 | 7.1 | 7.3 | 7.5 |
| 70 years old and older (millions) | 8.5 | 12.1 | 13.4 | 13.9 | 14.3 |
| WORKERS REPORTED WITH | | | | | |
| Taxable earnings (millions) | 93.0 | 112.0 | 116.0 | 120.0 | 123.0 |
| Maximum earnings (millions) | 24.0 | 10.0 | 7.0 | 7.0 | 7.0 |
| Earnings in covered employment ($ billions) | 532.0 | 1,326.0 | 1,772.0 | 1,912.0 | 2,035.0 |
| Reported taxable ($ billions) | 416.0 | 1,176.0 | 1,609.0 | 1,724.0 | 1,844.0 |
| Percent of total (%) | 78.2 | 88.7 | 90.8 | 90.2 | 90.6 |
| AVERAGE PER WORKER | | | | | |
| Total earnings ($) | 5,711.0 | 11,817.0 | 15,260.0 | 15,955.0 | 16,587.0 |
| Taxable earnings ($) | 4,464.0 | 10,500.0 | 13,871.0 | 14,367.0 | 14,992.0 |
| Annual maximum taxable earnings ($) | 7,800.0 | 25,900.0 | 37,800.0 | 39,600.0 | 42,000.0 |
| Maximum tax ($) | 374.0 | 1,588.0 | 2,533.0 | 2,792.0 | 3,003.0 |

| Item | 1987 | 1988 | 1989 | 1990 | 1991 |
|---|---|---|---|---|---|
| WORKERS WITH INSURED STATUS (millions) | 152.7 | 155.4 | 158.0 | 161.1 | 163.6 |
| Male (millions) | 81.5 | 82.6 | 83.7 | 85.1 | 86.1 |
| Female (millions) | 71.2 | 72.8 | 74.3 | 76.0 | 77.4 |
| Under 25 years old (millions) | 21.3 | 21.3 | 21.1 | 21.3 | 21.2 |
| 25 to 34 years old (millions) | 40.6 | 41.0 | 41.3 | 41.6 | 41.5 |
| 35 to 44 years old (millions) | 31.2 | 32.3 | 33.5 | 34.8 | 36.3 |
| 45 to 54 years old (millions) | 19.8 | 20.5 | 21.4 | 22.2 | 22.8 |
| 55 to 59 years old (millions) | 8.9 | 8.8 | 8.7 | 8.7 | 8.7 |
| 60 to 64 years old (millions) | 8.7 | 8.7 | 8.7 | 8.6 | 8.7 |
| 65 to 69 years old (millions) | 7.6 | 7.7 | 7.9 | 8.0 | 8.1 |
| 70 years old and older (millions) | 14.7 | 15.0 | 15.4 | 15.8 | 16.3 |
| WORKERS REPORTED WITH | | | | | |
| Taxable earnings (millions) | 125.0 | 130.0 | 133.0 | 133.0 | 132.0 |
| Maximum earnings (millions) | 8.0 | 8.0 | 8.0 | 8.0 | 8.0 |
| Earnings in covered employment ($ billions) | 2,198.0 | 2,411.0 | 2,593.0 | 2,720.0 | 2,796.0 |
| Reported taxable ($ billions) | 1,960.0 | 2,101.0 | 2,243.0 | 2,363.0 | 2,428.0 |
| Percent of total (%) | 89.2 | 87.1 | 86.5 | 86.9 | 86.8 |
| AVERAGE PER WORKER | | | | | |
| Total earnings ($) | 17,584.0 | 18,610.0 | 19,494.0 | 20,442.0 | 21,131.0 |
| Taxable earnings ($) | 15,680.0 | 16,215.0 | 16,863.0 | 17,759.0 | 18,350.0 |
| Annual maximum taxable earnings ($) | 43,800.0 | 45,000.0 | 48,000.0 | 51,300.0 | 53,400.0 |
| Maximum tax ($) | 3,132.0 | 3,380.0 | 3,605.0 | 3,924.0 | 4,085.0 |

*Source: 1993 Statistical Abstract, Table No. 588*

*Social Security (cont'd)*

## Social Security: Beneficiaries, Annual Payments, and Average Monthly Benefit

| Year | Total Number of Beneficiaries (thousands) | Total Annual Payments ($ millions) | Average Monthly Benefit ($) |
|------|------|------|------|
| 1970 | 26,229 | 31,863 | 118 |
| 1980 | 35,585 | 120,472 | 341 |
| 1985 | 37,058 | 186,195 | 479 |
| 1986 | 37,703 | 196,692 | 489 |
| 1987 | 38,190 | 204,156 | 513 |
| 1988 | 38,627 | 217,214 | 537 |
| 1989 | 39,151 | 230,850 | 567 |
| 1990 | 39,832 | 247,796 | 603 |
| 1991 | 40,568 | 268,098 | 629 |

## Social Security: Beneficiaries, Annual Payments, and Average Monthly Benefit, by State

| Division, State, Other Area | Total Number of Beneficiaries (thousands) | Total Annual Payments ($ millions) | Average Monthly Benefits ($) |
|------|------|------|------|
| UNITED STATES | 39,621 | 264,049 | NA |
| New England | 2,182 | 14,955 | NA |
| Maine | 218 | 1,345 | 578 |
| New Hampshire | 167 | 1,127 | 632 |
| Vermont | 90 | 586 | 617 |
| Massachusetts | 989 | 6,719 | 632 |
| Rhode Island | 184 | 1,240 | 629 |
| Connecticut | 534 | 3,938 | 691 |
| Middle Atlantic | 6,375 | 45,320 | NA |
| New York | 2,868 | 20,451 | 673 |
| New Jersey | 1,242 | 9,125 | 689 |
| Pennsylvania | 2,265 | 15,744 | 648 |
| East North Central | 6,883 | 48,096 | NA |
| Ohio | 1,827 | 12,501 | 645 |
| Indiana | 919 | 6,387 | 655 |
| Illinois | 1,772 | 12,591 | 668 |
| Michigan | 1,515 | 10,793 | 672 |
| Wisconsin | 850 | 5,824 | 646 |
| West North Central | 3,054 | 20,052 | NA |
| Minnesota | 677 | 4,424 | 614 |
| Iowa | 527 | 3,522 | 631 |
| Missouri | 922 | 6,012 | 615 |
| North Dakota | 112 | 698 | 593 |
| South Dakota | 130 | 794 | 582 |
| Nebraska | 272 | 1,786 | 621 |
| Kansas | 414 | 2,816 | 645 |
| South Atlantic | 7,343 | 47,205 | NA |
| Delaware | 108 | 756 | 656 |
| Maryland | 625 | 4,204 | 628 |
| District of Columbia | 78 | 456 | 537 |
| Virginia | 857 | 5,387 | 595 |
| West Virginia | 373 | 2,409 | 622 |
| North Carolina | 1,111 | 6,858 | 588 |
| South Carolina | 558 | 3,415 | 588 |
| Georgia | 905 | 5,550 | 587 |
| Florida | 2,728 | 18,170 | 628 |

*Social Security (cont'd)*

## Social Security: Beneficiaries, Annual Payments, and Average Monthly Benefit, by State

| Division, State, Other Area | Total Number of Beneficiaries (thousands) | Total Annual Payments ($ millions) | Average Monthly Benefits ($) |
|---|---|---|---|
| East South Central | 2,685 | 16,086 | NA |
| Kentucky | 658 | 3,963 | 579 |
| Tennessee | 846 | 5,189 | 588 |
| Alabama | 722 | 4,357 | 581 |
| Mississippi | 459 | 2,577 | 546 |
| West South Central | 3,924 | 24,389 | NA |
| Arkansas | 473 | 2,791 | 565 |
| Louisiana | 663 | 3,989 | 584 |
| Oklahoma | 539 | 3,410 | 600 |
| Texas | 2,249 | 14,199 | 610 |
| Mountain | 2,013 | 13,090 | NA |
| Montana | 142 | 915 | 611 |
| Idaho | 161 | 1,035 | 611 |
| Wyoming | 64 | 426 | 628 |
| Colorado | 434 | 2,803 | 613 |
| New Mexico | 227 | 1,364 | 592 |
| Arizona | 609 | 4,066 | 637 |
| Utah | 198 | 1,288 | 635 |
| Nevada | 178 | 1,193 | 631 |
| Pacific | 5,161 | 34,856 | NA |
| Washington | 728 | 5,021 | 653 |
| Oregon | 509 | 3,437 | 641 |
| California | 3,738 | 25,200 | 643 |
| Alaska | 35 | 227 | 626 |
| Hawaii | 151 | 971 | 619 |
| Puerto Rico | 570 | 2,335 | 402 |
| Guam | 6 | 24 | 450 |
| American Samoa | 4 | 13 | 393 |
| Virgin Islands | 10 | 52 | 531 |
| Abroad | 361 | 1625 | 448 |

*Source: 1993 Statistical Abstract, Table No. 590*

## The Top Reference Sources

*Companies and Their Brands, 1994*
Gale, $390
(800) 877-4253

This valuable resource alphabetically lists the manufacturers, distributors, marketers, and im-

porters of 250,000 consumer products.
    Complete addresses, phone numbers, and fax numbers are provided for the 47,000 companies listed.

# Personnel Testing

## Physical Examinations

Physical examinations can be used to screen out applicants when the results indicate that job performance would be adversely affected. For example, jobs that require a great deal of physical force may require job applicants to receive back X-rays while desk jobs may not.

## Drug Testing

Drug testing for employees and job applicants has increased 250 percent since 1987. Perhaps as a result of increased testing and related educational programs, drug use among workers and job seekers has declined in recent years.

Only a handful of states presently outlaw drug testing for private sector businesses. Many government workers, on the other hand, are required to submit to random or periodic drug testing as mandated by the Federal Workplace Drug Testing Regulations.

Just about all drug testing is done by urinalysis which, when performed under the guidelines established by the Federal Workplace Drug Testing Regulations, offers a 99.9 percent accuracy rate.

## Contact Options

*Drug Testing and Program Management Firms:*

Drug Intervention Services of America
11200 Westheimer, Suite 630
Houston, Texas 77042
(713) 972-3472

National MRO
P.O. Box 261426
Lakewood, CO 80226
(303) 238-2000

Substance Abuse Management
Two Plaza East
330 E. Kilbourn Ave., Suite 1075
Milwaukee, WI 53202
(414) 273-7264

University Services
Arsenal Business Center
5301 Tacony St., Building 4
Philadelphia, PA 19137
(215) 743-4200

## Percentage of Drug Abuse Policies in the Workplace

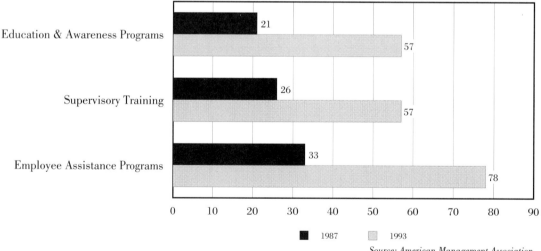

Source: American Management Association

---

**FAX**    **Family and Medical Leave.** Request #998. See p. xi for instructions.

Tables of percent of full-time employees by leave policy and duration of leave policy.

*Personnel Testing (cont'd)*

## Corporate Methods for Combating Drug Abuse

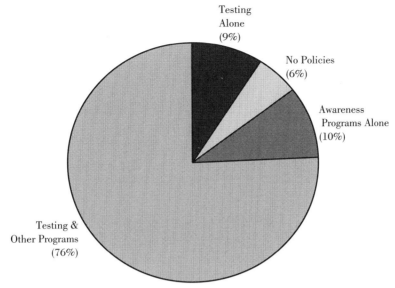

*Source: American Management Association*

## Percentage of Workplace Drug Testing 1989-1993

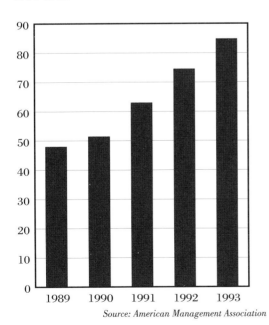

*Source: American Management Association*

## Percentage of Executives Who Say Drug Testing Is Effective

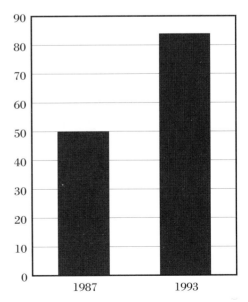

*Source: American Management Association*

*Personnel Testing (cont'd)*

## Polygraph Tests

With the passage of the Employee Polygraph Protection Act of 1988, employers are restricting their use of polygraph or lie detector tests. The law virtually outlaws the use of lie detectors in connection with employment, and covers all private employers in interstate commerce. Supporters of the law claim that the tests are accurate only two-thirds of the time and are far more likely to be inaccurate for honest employees. The new law restricts pre-employment screening and random use of the device.

The Employee Polygraph Protection Act allows polygraph tests to be used in connection with jobs in security, handling drugs, or in investigating a theft or other suspected crime. Before an employee can be required to take such a test as part of an investigation of an employment-related crime, however, the employee must be given a written notice stating that he or she is a suspect.

## AIDS

Employees with disabilities, including AIDS and HIV infection, are protected by law from discrimination in employment. In most cases, HIV testing of new or present employees for employment is prohibited by human rights laws. In the very few areas of employment where testing may be allowed, an employee may never be singled out for testing; tests must be required of all employees or none.

Because of the many sensitive legal issues involving privacy and discrimination, it is advised that employers develop a comprehensive "AIDS in the Workplace" policy, and should not require HIV screening as part of pre-employment or general workplace physical examination.

### Recommended Resource

*CDC Business Responds to AIDS Manager's Kit*
CDC National AIDS Clearinghouse, $25
(800) 458-5231
A terrific source for the straight scoop on developing a sensitive, effective policy on AIDS in the workplace.

*Sample Policies*
National Leadership Coalition on AIDS, $3
(202) 452-8845
This booklet offers a sampling of real company policies on AIDS in the workplace, and is a great place to start in determining your company's approach to AIDS.

# Family and Medical Leave

MORE THAN 70 PERCENT of all American women between the ages of 20 and 54 now work outside the home. The Family and Medical Leave Act of 1993 guarantees family leave for employees under certain circumstances. The FMLA requires private sector employers of 50 or more employees and public agencies to provide up to 12 weeks of unpaid, job-protected leave to "eligible" employees for certain family and medical reasons. Employees are "eligible" if they have worked for a covered employer for at least one year, and for 1,250 hours over the previous 12 months, and if there are at least 50 employees within 75 miles. Similar provisions may apply to federal and congressional employees. For more information on the new federal regulations, contact the nearest office of the Wage and Hour Division, listed in most telephone directories under U.S. Government, Department of Labor, Employment Standards Administration.

The following state regulations augment and supercede the federal requirements for employers:

### Alaska

Alaska's family leave law provides state and other public employees with up to 18 weeks of leave every 24 months to care for the serious health condition of a child, spouse, parent, or for the worker's own serious health condition. Additionally, the law provides 18 weeks of leave per year to care for a newborn or newly adopted child. It covers the state and political subdivisions of the state with at least 21 employees. Workers must work at least 35 hours per week for six consecutive months or 17.5 hours per week for 12 consecutive months to be eligible.

### California

California's family leave law provides up to 16 weeks of leave over two years for birth or adoption, or for the serious health condition of a child, spouse, or parent. It applies to employers of 50 or more; employees must be employed for 12 months to be eligible.

### Colorado

Colorado provides employees guarantees of "reasonable period" of leave for pregnancy, childbirth, and adoption.

### Connecticut

Connecticut provides 16 weeks of family and medical leave every two years for employers of 75 or more.

Employees must be employed for 1,000 hours in the 12-month period preceding the first day of leave to be eligible. Connecticut also provides state employees with a total of 24 weeks over two years for family or medical leave.

Connecticut's pregnancy disability law provides job-guaranteed leave for the period that a worker is

*Family and Medical Leave (cont'd)*

physically disabled due to pregnancy, childbirth, and related medical conditions. The law covers employers with three or more employees; certain family businesses are exempted.

## Delaware

Delaware provides state employees who have had one year of continuous employment with six weeks of family leave for adoption or birth of a child.

## District of Columbia

The District of Columbia's family and medical leave law provides up to 16 weeks of unpaid leave every two years to care for a newborn or newly adopted child or for a seriously ill family member. "Family member" is defined broadly to include a person related by blood, legal custody, or marriage, or a person with whom an employee shares a residence in the context of a committed relationship. Sixteen weeks of medical leave every two years is separately available for the employee's own serious health condition. Covers employers of 50 or more for the first three years after enactment; covers employers of 20 or more thereafter. Employees must have worked for the employer for at least 1,000 hours during the last 12 months to be eligible.

## Florida

Florida law grants up to six months of family leave per year to state employees for birth, adoption, or for the serious illness of a worker's spouse, child, or parent.

## Georgia

Georgia provides up to 12 weeks of family and medical leave per year for state employees. Employees must be employed for at least 12 months and 1,040 hours to be eligible.

## Hawaii

For state employees, and for private sector employers of 100 or more, Hawaii law provides employees four weeks of family leave for birth, adoption, or the serious health condition of a child, spouse, or parent.

Hawaii also provides pregnancy disability leave to all employees for the period that a worker is physically disabled by pregnancy, childbirth, or related medical conditions.

## Illinois

Illinois provides certain permanent, full-time state employees with family leave of up to one year for "bona fide family responsibilities" (including birth or adoption, or care of a seriously ill family member).

## Iowa

Iowa provides up to eight weeks pregnancy disability leave. Employers with four or more employees are covered.

## Kansas

Kansas provides pregnancy disability leave for the period that a worker is physically disabled by pregnancy, childbirth, or related medical conditions. Employers with four or more employees are covered.

## Kentucky

Kentucky provides all employees with six weeks leave for adopting a child under age seven.

## Louisiana

Louisiana provides up to four months of leave to employees who are temporarily disabled because of pregnancy, childbirth, or related medical conditions. Only six weeks of disability leave is generally available for normal pregnancy or childbirth. Employers with 26 or more employees are covered.

## Maine

Maine provides ten weeks of family and medical leave over a two-year period. Employers with 25 or more employees are covered. Employees must work for the same employer for 12 consecutive months to be eligible.

## Maryland

Maryland provides 12 weeks of leave for birth, adoption or family illness for state employees.

## Massachusetts

Female employees in Massachusetts are eligible for eight weeks of leave for birth or adoption of a child under age three. Employees are eligible after completing employer's initial probationary period or three consecutive months as a full-time employee. Covers employers of six or more employees.

## Minnesota

Minnesota employers with 21 or more employees must provide their employees with six weeks of leave for the birth or adoption of a child. Employees must work 12 months at 20 or more hours per week to be eligible.

## Missouri

Missouri provides equal leave for childbirth and adoption for state employees.

## Montana

Montana provides pregnancy disability leave for workers when temporarily disabled by pregnancy, childbirth, or related medical condition. Covers employers with one or more employees.

## New Hampshire

New Hampshire provides pregnancy disability leave for workers when temporarily disabled by pregnancy, childbirth, or related medical conditions. Covers employers of six or more.

*Family and Medical Leave (cont'd)*

### New Jersey

New Jersey provides 12 weeks of leave over a 24-month period for birth, adoption, or the serious health condition of a child, parent, or spouse. Employers of 50 or more are covered. Employee must have been employed at least 1,000 hours in the 12 months before the leave to be eligible.

### New York

New York provides equal leave for childbirth and adoption.

### North Carolina

North Carolina provides all state employees with pregnancy disability leave when temporarily disabled by pregnancy, childbirth, or related medical conditions.

### North Dakota

North Dakota provides state employees (with one-year minimum employment at an average of 20 hours per week) four months of leave per year for birth, adoption, or serious health condition of spouse, child, or parent.

### Oklahoma

Oklahoma provides state employees with 12 weeks of family leave per year for birth or adoption, or for the care of a critically ill child or dependent adult. Employees must work six months to be eligible.

### Oregon

Oregon's family leave law provides employees with 12 weeks of leave every two years for the illness of a child requiring "home care," or to care for a child, spouse, or parent suffering from "any mental or physical condition requiring constant care." Covers employers with 50 or more employees.

Oregon's parental leave law provides 12 weeks of leave for the birth of a child or for adopting a child up to age 12. This law covers employers of 25 or more employees; employees are eligible after 90 days of employment. Employees hired on a seasonal or temporary basis are not covered.

Oregon provides pregnancy disability leave for the period of physical disability if such leave can be reasonably accommodated.

### Rhode Island

Rhode Island provides up to 13 weeks of family medical leave over a two-year period. Covers private employers with 50 or more employees; city, town, or municipal agencies with 30 or more employees; and all state agencies. Employee must be employed for an average of 30 or more hours per week by same employer for 12 consecutive months to be eligible.

### Tennessee

Tennessee provides up to four months of leave for pregnancy disability and childbirth. Covers employees who have worked full-time for 12 consecutive months at companies with 100 or more employees.

### Texas

Texas provides state employees six weeks leave for childbirth or adoption.

### Vermont

Vermont provides 12 weeks of family and medical leave per year. Employers of ten or more must provide leave to care for a newborn or newly adopted child; employers of 15 or more must also provide leave to care for the serious health condition of a child, spouse, or parent, or for the worker's own serious health condition. Employees must work for at least one year for an average of 30 hours per week to be eligible.

### Virginia

Virginia provides state employees with six weeks of parental leave per year for birth or adoption.

### Washington

Washington's parental leave law provides 12 weeks of leave over a two-year period for the birth, adoption, or serious illness of a child. Employees must be employed 52 weeks at 35 or more hours per week to be eligible. Covers employers of 100 or more employees.

Effective October 28, 1973, Washington also provides pregnancy disability leave for the period of physical disability. Covers employees of eight or more.

### West Virginia

West Virginia provides state and school employees with 12 weeks of leave per year for the birth or adoption, or serious health condition of a spouse, child, or parent. Employees must have 12 consecutive weeks of employment to be eligible.

### Wisconsin

Wisconsin provides six weeks of leave for birth or adoption of a child; two weeks of leave for serious health condition of a child, spouse, or parent; and two weeks of medical leave for a worker's own serious health condition (including pregnancy disability). No more than ten weeks may be taken in a 12-month period for any combination of these reasons. Law covers employers with 50 or more employees; an employee must be employed for 52 consecutive weeks and have worked 1,000 hours to be eligible.

*Family and Medical Leave (cont'd)*

## Mothers Participating in Labor Force (%)

| Year | With Children Under 18 Years | With Children 6-17 Years | With Children Under 6 Years |
|------|------------------------------|--------------------------|------------------------------|
| 1955 | 27.0 | 38.4 | 18.2 |
| 1965 | 35.0 | 45.7 | 25.3 |
| 1975 | 47.4 | 54.8 | 38.9 |
| 1980 | 56.6 | 64.4 | 46.6 |
| 1985 | 62.1 | 69.9 | 53.5 |
| 1986 | 62.8 | 70.4 | 54.4 |
| 1987 | 64.7 | 72.0 | 56.7 |
| 1988 | 65.0 | 73.3 | 56.1 |
| 1989 | NA | NA | NA |
| 1990 | 66.7 | 74.7 | 58.2 |
| 1991 | 66.6 | 74.4 | 58.4 |
| 1992 | 67.2 | 75.9 | 58.0 |

*Source: 1994 Information Please Almanac*

## Family Friendly Companies

The Families and Work Institute (FWI) rigorously researched work-family problems and evaluated a range of work-family solutions.

The index measures the overall responsiveness to employees' family and personal needs in light of business objectives. It covers seven primary categories: flexible work arrangements, leaves, financial assistance, corporate giving/community service, dependent care services, management change, and work-family management.

The score for each work-family initiative is based on six criteria that the Families and Work Institute consider important:

- Impact: the program's capacity to reduce work-family conflicts.

- Coverage: the more widely available a program or services, the higher the score.

- Institutionalization: a policy that is formally written, thus sanctioning usage, will score higher.

- Commitment: a program that requires a great investment of resources in terms of money, people, time, or leadership will receive more points.

- Level of effort: the higher the complexity that the implementation of a program requires, the higher the score.

- Innovativeness: a program that is uniquely responsive scores higher.

The rankings are arranged in stages and are listed in descending order with the highest score (245) signifying the most family-friendly company in the study. Note: only companies that participated in the study are included. The top two stages of companies are listed here.

Rankings of companies within each stage of development are based on FWI Family-Friendly Index Scores.

## Most Friendly (Scores of 179+)

Aetna Life & Casualty
Corning
IBM
Johnson & Johnson

## Friendly (Scores of 100-178)

3M
AlliedSignal
Allstate Insurance
American Express
AT&T
Bank of America N.T. & S.A.
Campbell Soup
Champion International
Chase Manhattan
Citicorp
Coors Brewing
Digital Equipment
Dow Chemical U.S.A.
E.I. Du Pont de Nemours
Eastman Kodak
Equitable Life Assurance Society of the U.S.
Gannett
General Dynamics
Hewlett-Packard
Hoffmann-LaRoche
Honeywell
Household International
John Hancock Mutual Life Insurance
McDonnell Douglas
Merck
Metropolitan Life Insurance
Mobil
Norton
Polaroid
Procter & Gamble
Time
Travelers Insurance
US West
Warner-Lambert
Wells Fargo Bank

# Companies for Working Mothers

## The Working Mother 100
## Best Companies for Working Mothers

3M
Aetna Life & Casualty
Allstate Insurance
American Airlines
Amoco Corporation
Arthur Andersen
AT&T
Baptist Hospital of Miami
Barnett Banks
Bausch & Lomb
Baxter International
BE&K Engineering and Construction
Ben & Jerry's Homemade
Boston's Beth Israel Hospital
Bright Horizons Children's Centers
The Bureau of National Affairs
Leo Burnett USA
Burroughs Wellcome
Calvert Group
Champion International
Cigna Companies
Citibank
CMP Publications
Colgate-Palmolive
Consolidated Edison Company of New York
Corning
Dayton Hudson
Dow Chemical
DuPont
Eastman Kodak
Exxon
Federal National Mortgage Association (Fannie Mae)
Fel-Pro
Frontier Cooperative Herbs
Gannett
Glaxo
G.T. Water Products
Hallmark Cards
John Hancock Mutual Life Insurance
Hanna Andersson
Helene Curtis
Hewitt Associates
Hewlett Packard
Hoechst Celanese
Hoffmann-LaRoche
Home Box Office (HBO)
Honeywell
Household International
IBM

Johnson & Johnson
SC Johnson Wax
Lancaster Laboratories
Levi Strauss
Lincoln National
Lotus Development
LucasArts Entertainment
Lutheran General Hospital
The John D. and Catherine T. MacArthur Foundation
Marquette Electronics
Marriott
Mattel Toys
MBNA America Bank
Mentor Graphics
Merck
Morrison & Foerster
Motorola
Mutual of New York (MONY)
Nationsbank
Neuville Industries
Nike
Northern States Power
Northern Trust
NYNEX
Official Airline Guides
Patagonia
Phoenix Home Life
Pitney Bowes
Polaroid
Prudential Insurance
Quad/Graphics
Quaker Oats
Riverside Methodist Hospitals
The St. Paul Companies
The St. Petersburg Times
SAS Institute
Schering-Plough
The Seattle Times
Silicon Graphics
Syntex
Tom's of Maine
Toyota
The Travelers
United States Hosiery Corporation
United Technologies
UNUM Life Insurance
The USA Group
US West
Wegmans Food Markets
Work/Family Directions
Xerox

*Source: Working Mother, October, 1993*

# Affirmative Action

EMPLOYERS ALL OVER THE COUNTRY sign contracts with the federal government guaranteeing nondiscrimination and equal opportunity in all their employment practices. In these contracts, employers also agree to take affirmative action to hire and promote workers who traditionally have been discriminated against in the job market.

Each year, the U.S. Government awards hundreds of thousands of these contracts for supplies, services, use of property, and construction work, totaling over $200 billion. Construction contractors, banks, utilities, insurance and real estate companies, manufacturers, producers, builders, and universities are among those who do federal contract and subcontract work.

Under two statutes and one executive order, minorities, women, members of religious and ethnic groups, handicapped persons, and Vietnam and disabled veterans of all wars are protected by the Equal Employment Opportunity Commission (EEOC) and affirmative action requirements. These state that special efforts must be made by employers in outreach, recruitment, training, and other areas to help members of protected groups compete for jobs and promotions on equal footing with other applicants and employees. Affirmative action is not preferential treatment. Nor does it mean that unqualified persons should be promoted over other people. What affirmative action does mean is that positive steps must be taken to provide equal employment opportunity.

Enforcement of these contracts is carried out by the Office of Federal Contract Compliance Programs (OFCCP), a division of the U.S. Department of Labor's Employment Standards Administration. OFCCP's compliance officers regularly review the employment practices of federal contractors, subcontractors, and federally assisted construction contractors to determine whether or not they are fulfilling their EEOC and affirmative action obligations.

## Complaints of Discrimination

Individuals who are protected by the contract compliance programs may file complaints if they believe that they have been discriminated against by federal contractors, subcontractors, or federally assisted construction contractors or subcontractors. Complaints may also be filed by organizations or other individuals on behalf of the person or persons affected.

If a complaint filed under the Executive Order involves discrimination against only one person, OFCCP will refer it to the EEOC, an independent agency. Cases that involve groups of people or indicate patterns of discrimination are generally investigated by the OFCCP.

Complaints must be filed within 180 days from the date of the alleged discrimination, unless the time for filing is extended because of a good reason, which requires approval by the OFCCP director.

Persons filing complaints should include a description of the discrimination involved and any other related information which would assist in an investigation.

Complaints may be filed directly with the OFCCP in Washington, DC, or with any of the program's regional offices throughout the country.

## Enforcing Contract Compliance

When a complaint is filed, or a compliance review turns up problems, the OFCCP attempts to enter into a conciliation agreement with the contractor.

A conciliation agreement may include back pay, seniority credit, promotions, or other forms of relief for the victims of discrimination. It may also involve new training programs, special recruitment efforts, or other affirmative action measures.

The conciliation agreement allows the contractor to continue doing government business, and guarantees that employees' rights are protected.

When conciliation efforts are unsuccessful, the OFCCP moves to enforcement. Federal rules and regulations set forth administrative and judicial procedures to be followed when enforcement actions are necessary.

Contractors or subcontractors cited for violating their EEO and affirmative action requirements may have a formal hearing before an administrative law judge. If conciliation is not reached before or after the hearing, sanctions may be imposed. For example, contractors or subcontractors could lose their government contracts or subcontracts; they could have payments withheld by the government; or they could be declared ineligible for any federal contract work.

In some cases the Department of Justice, on behalf of the Department of Labor, may file suit in federal court against a contractor for violation of the contract requirements.

For more information about contract compliance, filing complaints, or special assistance, contact any of the OFCCP's ten regional offices, or get in touch with a program area office listed in telephone directories under U.S. Department of Labor, Employment Standards Administration, Office of Federal Contract Compliance Programs.

## Contact Option

The Office of Federal Contract
Compliance Programs
U.S. Department of Labor
200 Constitution Ave., NW
Washington, DC 20210
(202) 219-9430

# Unemployment Benefits

## Unemployment Insurance by State, 1991

| State | Beneficiaries' First Payments ($ thousands) | Benefits Paid ($ millions) | Avg. Weekly Unemployment Benefits ($) |
|---|---|---|---|
| TOTAL | 10,075 | 25,446 | 170 |
| AK | 45 | 110 | 170 |
| AL | 171 | 221 | 119 |
| AR | 103 | 176 | 140 |
| AZ | 98 | 199 | 143 |
| CA | 1,491 | 3,451 | 144 |
| CO | 83 | 176 | 173 |
| CT | 190 | 611 | 206 |
| DC | 31 | 135 | 221 |
| DE | 29 | 73 | 183 |
| FL | 353 | 823 | 158 |
| GA | 278 | 469 | 149 |
| HI | 30 | 81 | 214 |
| IA | 93 | 188 | 167 |
| ID | 48 | 81 | 153 |
| IL | 427 | 1,318 | 180 |
| IN | 168 | 215 | 112 |
| KS | 74 | 184 | 170 |
| KY | 145 | 273 | 145 |
| LA | 102 | 163 | 111 |
| MA | 318 | 1,313 | 222 |
| MD | 166 | 495 | 179 |
| ME | 71 | 176 | 164 |
| MI | 513 | 1,548 | 212 |
| MN | 148 | 436 | 194 |
| MO | 205 | 404 | 143 |
| MS | 85 | 127 | 116 |
| MT | 26 | 47 | 143 |
| NC | 332 | 510 | 157 |
| ND | 17 | 29 | 144 |
| NE | 34 | 47 | 126 |
| NH | 54 | 84 | 130 |
| NJ | 373 | 1,430 | 218 |
| NM | 33 | 71 | 135 |
| NV | 65 | 156 | 168 |
| NY | 737 | 2,650 | 190 |
| OH | 405 | 1,034 | 177 |
| OK | 60 | 130 | 153 |
| OR | 153 | 365 | 167 |
| PA | 560 | 1,725 | 197 |
| RI | 69 | 229 | 204 |
| SC | 148 | 235 | 141 |
| SD | 9 | 11 | 122 |
| TN | 221 | 333 | 118 |
| TX | 407 | 1,013 | 170 |
| UT | 39 | 74 | 168 |
| VA | 169 | 313 | 157 |
| VT | 31 | 73 | 153 |
| WA | 229 | 599 | 175 |
| WI | 239 | 498 | 176 |
| WV | 66 | 153 | 160 |
| WY | 11 | 25 | 161 |

*Source: 1993 Statistical Abstract, Table No. 598*

# Benefits Checklist

## Percent of Full-Time Employees Participating in Selected Employee Benefit Programs

| Employee Benefit Program | All Employees | Professional & Technical | Clerical & Sales | Production & Service |
|---|---|---|---|---|
| PAID | | | | |
| Vacations | 96 | 97 | 98 | 95 |
| Holidays | 92 | 93 | 94 | 90 |
| Jury duty leave | 86 | 92 | 88 | 82 |
| Funeral leave | 80 | 84 | 82 | 77 |
| Rest time | 67 | 58 | 67 | 71 |
| Military leave | 54 | 63 | 56 | 48 |
| Sick leave | 67 | 87 | 82 | 48 |
| Personal leave | 21 | 29 | 26 | 13 |
| Lunch time | 8 | 5 | 4 | 11 |
| Maternity leave | 2 | 3 | 2 | 1 |
| Paternity leave | 1 | 1 | 1 | 0 |
| UNPAID | | | | |
| Maternity leave | 37 | 43 | 38 | 33 |
| Paternity leave | 26 | 31 | 26 | 23 |
| INSURANCE PLANS | | | | |
| Medical care | 83 | 85 | 81 | 84 |
| Noncontributory | 41 | 38 | 35 | 46 |
| Hospital/room and board | 83 | 85 | 81 | 84 |
| Inpatient surgery | 83 | 85 | 81 | 84 |
| Mental health care | 81 | 83 | 79 | 82 |
| Dental | 60 | 67 | 60 | 57 |
| Extended care facility | 66 | 70 | 66 | 66 |
| Home health care | 67 | 71 | 66 | 66 |
| Hospice care | 46 | 48 | 45 | 45 |
| Vision | 23 | 21 | 21 | 25 |
| In HMO's | 14 | 15 | 15 | 12 |
| Alcohol abuse treatment | 82 | 83 | 80 | 82 |
| Inpatient detoxification | 81 | 82 | 79 | 81 |
| Inpatient rehabilitation | 64 | 63 | 63 | 66 |
| Outpatient | 64 | 66 | 63 | 64 |
| Drug abuse treatment | 81 | 83 | 79 | 80 |
| Inpatient detoxification | 80 | 82 | 79 | 80 |
| Inpatient rehabilitation | 63 | 62 | 62 | 65 |
| Outpatient | 62 | 65 | 62 | 61 |
| Life | 94 | 98 | 95 | 92 |
| Noncontributory | 80 | 83 | 82 | 77 |
| Accident/sickness | 45 | 32 | 35 | 57 |
| Noncontributory | 33 | 19 | 23 | 46 |
| Long-term disability | 40 | 61 | 49 | 24 |
| Noncontributory | 31 | 46 | 38 | 20 |
| RETIREMENT AND SAVINGS PLANS | | | | |
| Defined benefit pension | 59 | 60 | 56 | 59 |
| Earnings based formula (1) | 41 | 52 | 46 | 32 |
| Defined contribution | 48 | 57 | 53 | 39 |
| Savings and thrift | 29 | 38 | 35 | 20 |
| Employee stock ownership | 3 | 4 | 4 | 2 |
| Deferred profit sharing | 16 | 13 | 16 | 18 |
| Money purchase pension | 7 | 11 | 7 | 5 |

*Benefits Checklist (cont'd)*

## Percent of Full-Time Employees Participating in Selected Employee Benefit Programs

| Employee Benefit Program | All Employees | Professional & Technical | Clerical & Sales | Production & Service |
|---|---|---|---|---|
| ADDITIONAL BENEFITS | | | | |
| Parking | 88 | 86 | 85 | 92 |
| Educational assistance | 72 | 87 | 73 | 64 |
| Travel accident insurance | 42 | 55 | 47 | 32 |
| Severance Pay | 41 | 55 | 48 | 30 |
| Relocation allowance | 31 | 50 | 30 | 21 |
| Recreation facilities | 26 | 34 | 25 | 23 |
| Nonproduction bonuses, cash | 35 | 33 | 36 | 35 |
| Child care | 8 | 11 | 9 | 5 |
| Flexible benefits plans | 10 | 16 | 10 | 6 |
| Reimbursement accounts (2) | 36 | 48 | 40 | 26 |
| Eldercare | 9 | 11 | 12 | 6 |
| Long-term care insurance | 4 | 6 | 5 | 2 |
| Wellness programs | 35 | 47 | 34 | 28 |
| Employee assistance programs | 56 | 64 | 56 | 51 |

*Source: 1993 Statistical Abstract, Table No. 679*

## Sampling of Benefit Plans and Programs Offered by Employers

Accidental death and dismemberment insurance
Adoption benefits
Birthdays (time off)
Business and professional memberships
Cash profit-sharing
Civic activities (time off)
Club memberships
Company medical assistance
Company-provided or subsidized automobiles
Company-provided housing
Company-provided subsidized travel
Credit unions
Day-care centers
Death leave
Deferred bonus
Deferred compensation plan
Deferred profit-sharing
Dental and eye-care insurance
Discount on company products
Discount of other products
Educational activities (time off)
Education costs
Employment contract
Executive dining room
Financial counseling
Free or subsidized lunches
Group automobile insurance
Group homeowners insurance
Group legal insurance
Group life insurance

Health maintenance organization fees
Holidays
Home health care
Hospital-surgical-medical insurance
Interest-free loans
Layoff pay
Legal, estate planning, and other professional assistance
Loans of company equipment
Long-term disability benefits
Matching educational, charitable contributions
Nurseries
Nursing home care
Outside medical services
Paid attendance at business, professional, and other outside meetings
Parking facilities
Pension
Personal accident insurance
Personal counseling
Personal credit cards
Personal liability insurance
Physical examinations
Physical fitness programs
Political activities (time off)
Pre-retirement counseling
Price discount plan
Professional activities
Psychiatric services
Recreation facilities, sports activities
Resort facilities
Retirement gratuity

*Benefits Checklist (cont'd)*

Sabbatical leave
Salary continuation
Savings plan
Scholarships for dependents
Severance pay
Sickness and accident insurance
Social Security
Social service sabbaticals
Split-dollar insurance
State disability plans

Stock appreciation rights
Stock bonus plans
Stock option plans (qualified, nonqualified, tandem)
Stock purchase plans
Survivors benefits
Tax assistance
Training program
Travel accident insurance
Vacations
Weekly indemnity insurance

*Source: Buck Consultants*

# Quality of Work Life

THE DEFINITION OF SUCCESS is changing in the mind of the American worker. While earning a decent income is the primary purpose in having a paid job, recent studies indicate that the quality of work life is just as important as the traditional value of money. One recent study found that employees who have been with their current employers for less than five years have definite reasons for doing so.

Factors considered "very important" in deciding to take a job with current employer (by % of respondents) have shifted to a primary focus on the work environment.

## Important Factors in Choosing an Employer

| Factor | Percent |
|---|---|
| Open communications | 65 |
| Effect on personal/family life | 60 |
| Nature of work | 59 |
| Management quality | 59 |
| Supervisor | 58 |
| Gain new skills | 55 |
| Control over work content | 55 |
| Job security | 54 |
| Co-worker quality | 53 |
| Stimulating work | 50 |
| Job location | 50 |
| Family-supportive policies | 46 |

| Factor | Percent |
|---|---|
| Fringe benefits | 43 |
| Control of work schedule | 38 |
| Advancement opportunity | 37 |
| Salary/wage | 35 |
| Access to decision makers | 33 |
| No other offers | 32 |
| Management opportunity | 26 |
| Size of employer | 18 |

*Source: Families and Work Institute:*
*The Changing Workforce, 1993*

*Quality of Work Life (cont'd)*

## Most Frequently Mentioned Ways to Make Jobs More Satisfying (by % of respondents)

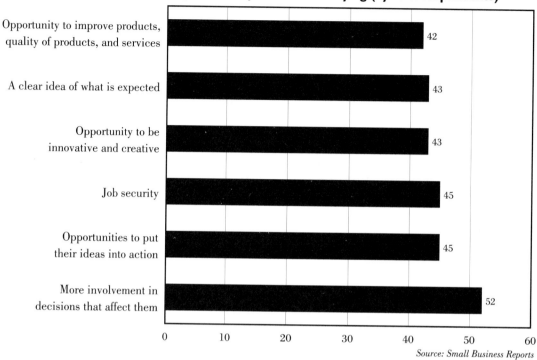

| | |
|---|---|
| Opportunity to improve products, quality of products, and services | 42 |
| A clear idea of what is expected | 43 |
| Opportunity to be innovative and creative | 43 |
| Job security | 45 |
| Opportunities to put their ideas into action | 45 |
| More involvement in decisions that affect them | 52 |

*Source: Small Business Reports*

# Childcare and Eldercare Services

ONE OF THE MOST IMPORTANT issues facing employers today involves "family responsive policies" in the workplace. Programs and policies are being established in many businesses as employers try to assist their employees in balancing the responsibilities of work and family. Under the auspices of the Women's Bureau of the U.S. Department of Labor, the Work and Family Clearinghouse was established to help employers identify the most appropriate policies for responding to the needs of employees and their dependents.

The Clearinghouse offers technical assistance to individualize the employees' needs, and guidance to both national and state information sources, bibliographic references, conference information, research, and statistics in five areas relating to child- and/or eldercare:

- Direct services such as onsite/offsite centers, consortium centers, after school/summer camps, family day care networks, emergency/sick childcare, "warmline" phones for school-age children;

- Information services such as resource and referral, parenting seminars, caregiver fairs, publications;

- Financial assistance such as vouchers/reimbursement, purchase of space discounts, flexible spending accounts, salary reduction plans, contributions to community resources;

- Cooperative policies such as flextime, job sharing, flexiplace, telecommuting, part-time, cafeteria-style benefits, maternity/parental leave;

- Public-private partnerships such as projects which address childcare and eldercare needs within communities.

Among the specific materials now available to employers are individual company "Program Profiles" which describe 100 employer-sponsored child- and/or eldercare programs in operation around the nation. "How-to" guides address 26 work/family options, including onsite and offsite child care centers, family day care networks, flexible leave policies, resource and referral services and the Dependent Care Assistance Program (DCAP).

The Clearinghouse responds to written or telephone inquiries from employers, unions, and other interested organizations.

*Childcare and Eldercare Services (cont'd)*

Another valuable resource is the Families and Work Institute, a non-profit research and planning organization committed to developing new approaches to balancing the needs of families with workplace productivity. The Institute deals with all issues from prenatal care to elder care, and management from the perspective of worker as well as manager.

This organization deals with four areas of interest:

- Policy research;

- Dissemination of information through conferences, seminars, publications, and public speaking;

- Strategic planning by advising government, business, and community organizations on the design, implementation, and evaluation of work-family solutions;

- Management training for corporations wishing to respond to work-family needs.

The Institute's 1993 report, *The Changing Workforce*, notes an increasing prevalence of family-friendly programs in the American workplace. The results of the study indicate that American companies are responding to the family needs of their workers.

## Contact Options

Women's Bureau Work and Family Clearinghouse
U.S. Department of Labor
200 Constitution Ave., NW
Washington, DC 20210
(202) 523-4486

Telephone hours are from 11:00 A.M. to 4:00 P.M. (EST) Monday through Thursday and from 11:00 A.M. to 3:00 P.M. on Friday.

Eldercare Locator
(800) 677-1116

Run by the National Association of Area Agencies on Aging, the Eldercare locator provides information services for Older People specific to the callers location.

## Recommended Resources

Families and Work Institute
330 Seventh Ave.
New York, NY 10001
(212) 465-2044

## Father-Friendly Companies

*Child Magazine* and The Families and Work Institute have identified ten companies who have made a real effort to support paternity leave, training on childbirth and development issues for dads, flexible and comprehensive on-site day care, and other father-friendly policies. The ten best are:

Apple Computer
AT&T
Ben & Jerry's
DuPont
Eastman Kodak
John Hancock Financial Services
Los Angeles Department of Water and Power
Peabody and Arnold
Sacramento County Sheriff's Department
Tom's of Maine

*Source: Child Magazine and The Fatherhood Project, Families and Work Institute*

**TIP:** *Every May brings a new edition of Job Hotlines USA, which features over 800 job hotlines operated by businesses nationwide. Call (800) 829-5220 to order.*

# Outplacement Firms & Headhunters

## Major Search Firms in the U.S.

| Firm | Headquarters | Number of Consultants | Number of Offices | Telephone Number |
|------|--------------|------------------------|--------------------|------------------|
| A.T. Kearney | Chicago | 52 | 13 | (312) 648-0111 |
| Battalia Winston | New York | 14 | 3 | (212) 308-8080 |
| D.E. Foster Partners | New York | 6 | 5 | (212) 872-6232 |
| DHR | Chicago | 45 | 6 | (312) 782-1581 |
| Diversified Search Companies | Philadelphia | 14 | 1 | (215) 732-6666 |
| Egan Zehnder | New York | 20 | 5 | (212) 838-9199 |
| Gilbert Tweed Assoc. | New York | 14 | 4 | (212) 758-3000 |
| Goodrich & Sherwood | New York | 25 | 5 | (212) 697-4131 |
| Gould & McCoy | New York | 4 | 1 | (212) 688-8671 |
| Handy HRM | New York | 12 | 1 | (212) 557-0400 |
| Heidrick & Struggles | Chicago | 165 | 30 | (312) 372-8811 |
| Howe-Lewis | New York | 13 | 2 | (212) 697-5000 |
| Korn/Ferry | New York | 150 | 48 | (212) 687-1834 |
| Lamalie Amrop | New York | 37 | 7 | (212) 953-7900 |
| Norman Broadbent | New York | 11 | 3 | (212) 953-6990 |
| Paul Ray Berndtson | Fort Worth | 133 | 31 | (817) 334-0500 |
| Russell Reynolds | New York | 175 | 25 | (212) 351-2000 |
| Sampson, Neill & Wilkins | Upper Montclair, NJ | 6 | 1 | (201) 783-9600 |
| Ward Howell | New York | 42 | 9 | (212) 697-3730 |
| Witt, Keiffer, Ford, Hadelman, Lloyd | Oakbrook, IL | 34 | 6 | (708) 990-1370 |

# Human Resource Software Systems

A NUMBER OF FIRMS MANUFACTURE low-cost, management software systems designed to assist corporations in employee selection, motivation, evaluation, and integration. Using a brief questionnaire, the software can create a comprehensive profile. The computer program is designed to analyze the individual's behavioral traits, stress and energy styles, and organizational skills.

## Contact Options

Consulting Psychologists Press
3803 E. Bayshore Rd.
Palo Alto, CA 94303
(415) 969-8901
   This company has an extensive catalogue of management software systems and training programs.

Professional Dynametric Programs
400 W. Highway 24, Suite 201
Woodland Park, CO 80866
(719) 687-6074
   This software manufacturer will also provide training in how to use and interpret the test results.

# Job Interview Tips

## Preparation

- Learn about the organization;
- Have a specific job or jobs in mind;
- Review your qualifications for the job;
- Prepare answers to broad questions about yourself;
- Review your résumé;
- Practice an interview with a friend or relative;
- Arrive before the scheduled time of your interview.

## Personal Appearance

- Be well groomed;
- Dress appropriately;
- Do not chew gum or smoke.

## The Interview

- Answer each question concisely;
- Respond promptly;
- Use good manners. Learn the name of your interviewer and shake hands as you meet;
- Use proper English and avoid slang;
- Be cooperative and enthusiastic;
- Ask questions about the position and the organization;
- Thank the interviewer and follow up with a letter.

## Test (if given)

- Listen closely to instructions;
- Read each question carefully;
- Write legibly and clearly;
- Budget your time wisely and don't dwell on one question.

## Information to Bring to an Interview

- Social Security number;
- Driver's license number;
- Résumé. Although not all employers require applicants to bring a résumé, you should be able to furnish the interviewer with information about your education, training, and previous employment;
- References. Usually an employer requires three references. Get permission from people before using their names, and make sure they will give you a good reference. Avoid using relatives. For each reference, provide the following information: name, address, telephone number, and job title.

*Source: U.S. Department of Labor, Bureau of Labor Statistics*

# Job Interview Questions

MANY MANAGERS ENCOUNTER a mental block when facing an interview. A checklist of questions makes it easier to elicit revealing answers from a job candidate.

Martin Yate, an employment analyst and best-selling author, has collected more than twenty questions that are of use in most interview settings.

According to Yate, some of the most important skill sets we can have for employees in the coming years are:

- analytical skills

- speed and mental processing

- ability to work with others

- an understanding of the necessity of taking direction.

The following questions will help you explore these areas with a job candidate:

- How would you describe the ideal job for you?

- What kind of work interests you most?

- How many levels of management did you interact with?

- What was the job's biggest challenge?

- If you were hiring for this position, what would you be looking for?

- What have you done that shows initiative and willingness to work?

- Why are you interviewing with us?

- What special characteristics should I consider about you?

- How do you plan your day?

- How do you plan your week?

- How do you determine your priorities?

- What happens when two priorities compete for your time?

- What's the toughest communication problem you faced?

- When have your verbal communications been important enough to follow up in writing?

- Tell me about the time when someone has lost his/her temper at you in a business environment.

- Have you ever worked in a place where it seemed to be just one crisis after another? And, obviously, there is a follow-up with that.

- How did you handle it? How did you feel?

- What do you see as some of your most pressing developmental needs?

- Define cooperation.

- What quality should a successful manager possess?

- How have past managers gotten the best out of you?

- A two-part question. Describe the best manager you've ever had. Describe the toughest manager you've ever had.

- And last, for what have you been most frequently criticized?

## The Top Reference Sources

*Hiring the Best*
Bob Adams Publishers, $9.95
(800) 872-5627

This fourth edition of Martin Yate's indispensable book includes over 400 interview questions. The book also includes a chapter on what constitutes a discriminatory, or perhaps illegal, interviewing question, an in-depth review of what it will take to recruit the best in the '90s, information on drug testing, plus four ready-to-use outlines for use as a starting point in critical interview areas: management, sales, recent graduates, and clerical.

# Employee Relocation Firms

MORE THAN HALF THE COMPANIES that relocate employees on a regular basis contract with a relocation firm that will help in the purchasing, managing, and disposing of the former homes of relocated employees. In general, the client company retains full ownership responsibilities for the homes during the time the employee agrees to accept the company's offer until the time of closing the sale. Home purchase firms charge a fee for their role in establishing a fair market value for the home, maintaining it after the employee has relocated, and managing the sale. The following relocation firms are among the largest in the country:

## Contact Options

Associates Relocation Management Company
250 E. Carpenter Freeway
Irving, TX 75062
(800) 241-6529 or (214) 541-6700

Coldwell Banker Relocation Services
27271 Las Ramblas
Mission Viejo, CA 92691
(714) 367-2500

PHH Homequity
249 Danbury Rd.
Wilton, CT 06897
(203) 834-8500

Prudential Relocation Management
200 Summit Lake Dr.
Valhalla, NY 10595
(914) 741-6111

Relocation Resources
(Eastern Operations Center)
120 Longwater Dr.
Norwell, MA 02061
(617) 871-4500

Relocation Resources
(Western Operations Center)
1099 Eighteenth St.,#1900
Denver, CO 80202
(303) 297-0500

## Average Annual Home Rental Costs in Most Expensive Locations Nationwide

| Location | Annual Rental Costs ($) | Index |
|---|---|---|
| Honolulu, HI | 12,480 | 244.7 |
| San Francisco, CA | 9,320 | 182.7 |
| Washington, DC | 8,920 | 174.9 |
| New York, NY | 8,810 | 172.7 |
| Boston, MA | 8,780 | 172.2 |
| Los Angeles, CA | 7,910 | 155.1 |
| Chicago, IL | 7,370 | 144.5 |
| Philadelphia, PA | 6,900 | 135.3 |
| Providence, RI | 6,900 | 135.3 |
| San Diego, CA | 6,840 | 134.1 |
| STANDARD CITY, U.S.A. | 5,100 | 100.0 |

*Source: Runzheimer International*

## Cost-of-Living Values in Selected Locations

| Location | Total Annual Costs ($) | Index |
|---|---|---|
| Los Angeles, CA | 75,975 | 126.6 |
| New York, NY | 74,028 | 123.4 |
| Washington, DC | 71,622 | 119.4 |
| Chicago, IL | 65,812 | 109.7 |
| Atlanta. GA | 63,494 | 105.8 |
| Syracuse, NY | 63,365 | 105.6 |
| Rochester, NY | 62,862 | 104.8 |
| Buffalo, NY | 62,638 | 104.4 |
| STANDARD CITY, U.S.A. | 60,000 | 100.0 |
| Dallas, TX | 58,768 | 97.9 |
| Denver, CO | 58,638 | 97.7 |
| Phoenix, AZ | 56,344 | 93.9 |

*Employee Relocation Firms (cont'd)*

## Average Annual Rental Costs in Least Expensive Locations Nationwide

| Location | Annual Rental Costs ($) | Index |
|---|---|---|
| Corbin, KY | 2,460 | 48.2 |
| Newport, TN | 2,760 | 54.1 |
| Hennessey, OR | 2,880 | 56.5 |
| Scottsboro, AL | 2,940 | 57.6 |
| Casper, WY | 3,000 | 58.8 |
| Midland, TX | 3,300 | 64.7 |
| Roanoke Rapids, NC | 3,360 | 65.9 |
| Rangely, CO | 3,480 | 68.2 |
| Hobbs, NM | 3,540 | 69.4 |
| Lafayette, LA | 3,600 | 70.6 |
| STANDARD CITY U.S.A. | 5,100 | 100.0 |

## Average Cost to Relocate Employees ($)

| Year | Homeowners | Renters | New Hires |
|---|---|---|---|
| 1986 | 34,984 | 9,218 | NA |
| 1987 | 36,253 | 10,503 | 12,847 |
| 1988 | 36,891 | 9,924 | 13,192 |
| 1989 | 40,939 | 10,666 | 13,937 |
| 1990 | 45,620 | 13,139 | 15,955 |
| 1991 | 44,804 | 13,358 | 17,903 |
| 1992 | 48,426 | 14,272 | 28,900 |

*Source: Runzheimer International*

## Five Lowest Car Cost Locations

| Location | Fixed Costs ($) | Operating Costs ($) | Total Annual Costs ($) |
|---|---|---|---|
| Sioux City, SD | 3,343 | 1,283 | 4,626 |
| Eau Claire, WI | 3,476 | 1,208 | 4,684 |
| Burlington, VT | 3,445 | 1,268 | 4,713 |
| Boise, ID | 3,479 | 1,238 | 4,717 |
| Billings, MT | 3,519 | 1,245 | 4,764 |

## Five Highest Car Cost Locations

| Location | Fixed Costs ($) | Operating Costs ($) | Total Annual Costs ($) |
|---|---|---|---|
| Los Angeles, CA | 6,074 | 1,455 | 7,529 |
| Philadelphia, PA | 5,118 | 1,418 | 6,536 |
| Detroit, MI | 5,081 | 1,343 | 6,424 |
| Boston, MA | 4,897 | 1,500 | 6,397 |
| Hartford, CT | 4,929 | 1,425 | 6,354 |

*Source: Runzheimer International*

# Sources for Interns

SEVERAL COMPANIES PUBLISH directories with extensive listings of internships available in a wide range of industries. Prospective interns may contact corporations listed therein. A few of these companies also provide access to data bases with listings of interns and internships, and will do an executive search for a small fee. Subscribing to one of these services may provide an inexpensive alternative to hiring a search firm or placing classified ads.

## Recommended Resources

National Society for Experiential Education
3509 Haworth Dr., Suite 207
Raleigh, NC 27609
(919) 787-3263
    This professional association of educators, career counselors, and employers who sponser interns is the best place to start if you want to explore

incorporating an internship into your business. This organization promotes internships by providing information referrals, publications, and consulting services to businesses and educational institutions. NSEE also publishes a directory of internships available across the country.

*Internships, 1994*
Peterson's, $29.95
202 Carnegie Center
P.O. Box 2123
Princeton, NJ 08543
(609) 243-9111

# Labor Union Directory

| Union | Phone |
|---|---|
| Actors' Equity Association | (212) 869-8530 |
| Amalgamated Clothing and Textile Workers Union | (212) 242-0700 |
| Amalgamated Transit Union | (202) 537-1645 |
| American Association of University Professors | (202) 737-5900 |
| American Federation of Government Employees | (202) 737-8700 |
| American Federation of Grain Millers | (612) 545-0211 |
| American Federation of Musicians of the United States and Canada | (212) 869-1330 |
| American Federation of State, County and Municipal Employees | (202) 429-1000 |
| American Federation of Teachers | (202) 879-4000 |
| American Federation of Television and Radio Artists | (212) 532-0800 |
| American Nurses' Association | (202) 554-4444 |
| American Postal Workers Union | (202) 842-4200 |
| Associated Actors and Artists of America | (212) 869-0358 |
| Association of Flight Attendants | (202) 328-5400 |
| Bakery, Confectionery, and Tobacco Workers' International Union | (301) 933-8600 |
| Brotherhood of Locomotive Engineers | (216) 241-2630 |
| Brotherhood of Maintenance of Way Employees | (313) 948-1010 |
| California School Employees Association | (408) 263-8000 |
| Communications Workers of America | (202) 434-1100 |
| Federation of Nurses and Health Professionals | (202) 879-4491 |
| Fraternal Order of Police | (614) 221-0180 |
| Glass, Molders, Pottery, Plastics and Allied Workers International Union | (215) 565-5051 |
| Graphic Communications International Union | (202) 462-1400 |
| Hotel Employees and Restaurant Employees International Union | (202) 393-4373 |
| Int'l Alliance of Theatrical Stage Employees & Moving Picture Machine Operators of the U.S. & Canada | (212) 730-1770 |
| International Association of Bridge, Structural and Ornamental Iron Workers | (202) 383-4800 |
| International Association of Fire Fighters | (202) 737-8484 |
| International Association of Machinists and Aerospace Workers | (301) 967-4500 |
| International Brotherhood of Boilermakers, Iron Ship Builders, Blacksmiths, Forgers and Helpers | (913) 371-2640 |
| International Brotherhood of Electrical Workers | (202) 833-7000 |
| International Brotherhood of Painters and Allied Trades of the United States and Canada | (202) 637-0700 |
| International Brotherhood of Teamsters, Chauffeurs, Warehousemen and Helpers of America | (202) 624-6800 |
| International Chemical Workers Union | (216) 867-2444 |
| International Federation of Professional and Technical Engineers | (301) 565-9016 |
| International Ladies' Garment Workers' Union | (212) 265-7000 |
| International Longshoremen's Association | (212) 425-1200 |
| International Union of Bricklayers and Allied Craftsmen | (202) 783-3788 |
| International Union of Electronic, Electrical, Salaried, Machine and Furniture Workers | (202) 296-1200 |
| International Union of Operating Engineers | (202) 429-9100 |
| International Union, Aluminum, Brick and Glass Workers | (314) 739-6142 |
| International Union, United Automobile, Aerospace and Agricultural Implement Workers of America | (313) 926-5000 |
| International Union, United Plant Guard Workers of America | (313) 772-7250 |
| International Woodworkers of America | (503) 656-1475 |
| Laborers' International Union of North America | (202) 737-8320 |
| National Association of Letter Carriers | (202) 393-4695 |
| National Education Association | (202) 833-4000 |
| National Federation of Federal Employees | (202) 862-4400 |
| National Marine Engineers' Beneficial Association | (202) 872-0902 |
| National Rural Letter Carriers' Association | (703) 684-5545 |
| National Treasury Employees Union | (202) 783-4444 |
| Office and Professional Employees International Union | (212) 675-3210 |
| Oil, Chemical and Atomic Workers International Union | (303) 987-2229 |
| Operative Plasterers' and Cement Masons' International Association of the United States and Canada | (202) 393-6569 |
| Retail, Wholesale and Department Store Union | (212) 684-5300 |
| Screen Actors Guild | (213) 954-1600 |

*Labor Union Directory (cont'd)*

| Union | Phone |
|---|---|
| Seafarers International Union of North America | (301) 899-0675 |
| Service Employees International Union | (202) 898-3200 |
| Sheet Metal Workers' International Association | (202) 783-5880 |
| State Employees Association of North Carolina | (919) 833-6436 |
| The Newspaper Guild | (301) 585-2990 |
| Transport Workers Union of America | (212) 873-6000 |
| Transportation Communications International Union | (202) 783-3660 |
| United Assn of Journeymen & Apprentices of the Plumbing & Pipe Fitting Industry of the U.S. & Canada | (202) 628-5823 |
| United Brotherhood of Carpenters and Joiners of America | (202) 546-6206 |
| United Electrical, Radio and Machine Workers of America | (412) 471-8919 |
| United Farm Workers of America | (805) 822-5571 |
| United Food and Commercial Workers International Union | (202) 223-3111 |
| United Garment Workers of America | (615) 889-9221 |
| United Mine Workers of America | (202) 842-7200 |
| United Paperworkers International Union | (615) 834-8590 |
| United Rubber, Cork, Linoleum and Plastic Workers of America | (216) 869-0320 |
| United Steelworkers of America | (412) 562-2400 |
| United Transportation Union | (216) 228-9400 |
| United Union of Roofers, Waterproofers and Allied Workers | (202) 638-3228 |
| Utility Workers Union of America | (202) 347-8105 |

*Source: Washington Directory of Labor Unions*

# Labor Unions Ranked

## Unions Ranked by Membership, 1993

| Union | Membership |
|---|---|
| National Education Association | 2,000,000 |
| International Brotherhood of Teamsters, Chauffeurs, Warehousemen and Helpers of America | 1,700,000 |
| American Federation of State, County and Municipal Employees | 1,300,000 |
| United Food and Commercial Workers, International Union | 1,300,000 |
| Service Employees International Union | 1,000,000 |
| International Union, United Automobile, Aerospace and Agricultural Implement Workers of America | 861,658 |
| International Brotherhood of Electrical Workers | 845,000 |
| American Federation of Teachers | 830,000 |
| Communications Workers of America | 600,000 |
| International Association of Machinists and Aerospace Workers | 550,000 |
| United Steelworkers of America | 550,000 |
| United Brotherhood of Carpenters and Joiners of America | 510,000 |
| Laborers' International Union of North America | 500,000 |
| International Union of Operating Engineers | 375,000 |
| American Postal Workers Union | 365,000 |
| United Association of Journeymen and Apprentices of the Plumbing and Pipe Fitting Industry | 315,000 |
| National Association of Letter Carriers | 307,000 |
| International Union, Hotel Employees and Restaurant Employees | 300,000 |
| Amalgamated Clothing and Textile Workers Union | 240,000 |
| United Paper Workers International Union | 250,000 |
| American Federation of Government Employees | 210,000 |
| American Nurses' Association | 204,000 |
| Graphic Communications International Union | 175,000 |
| International Association of Fire Fighters | 195,000 |

*Source: The 1994 Information Please Almanac*

# Collective Bargaining

## Major Collective Bargaining Agreements: Wage Rate Changes (%)

| Changes | 1975 | 1980 | 1985 | 1990 | 1991 | 1992 |
|---|---|---|---|---|---|---|
| AVERAGE WAGE RATE CHANGE (pro-rated over all workers) | 8.7 | 9.9 | 3.3 | 3.5 | 3.6 | 3.1 |
| SOURCE | | | | | | |
| Current settlements | 2.8 | 3.6 | 0.7 | 1.3 | 1.1 | 0.8 |
| Prior settlements | 3.7 | 3.5 | 1.8 | 1.5 | 1.9 | 1.9 |
| COLA provisions | 2.2 | 2.8 | 0.7 | 0.7 | 0.5 | 0.4 |
| INDUSTRY | | | | | | |
| Manufacturing | 8.5 | 10.2 | 2.8 | 4.4 | 3.7 | 3.1 |
| Nonmanufacturing | 8.9 | 9.7 | 3.6 | 3.0 | 3.5 | 3.1 |
| Construction | 8.1 | 9.9 | 3.0 | 3.4 | 3.4 | 3.4 |
| Transportation and public utilities | 9.7 | 10.8 | 3.6 | 2.2 | 3.3 | 2.7 |
| Wholesale and retail trade | 9.2 | 7.6 | 3.3 | 3.6 | 3.5 | 3.5 |
| Services | 6.4 | 8.1 | 5.1 | 4.3 | 4.9 | 3.7 |
| Nonmanufacturing, excluding construction | 9.3 | 9.6 | 3.7 | 2.9 | 3.6 | 3.0 |
| Average wage rate increase for workers receiving an increase | 9.0 | 10.1 | 4.2 | 4.2 | 4.0 | 3.7 |
| SOURCE | | | | | | |
| Current settlements | 10.2 | 9.4 | 4.1 | 4.1 | 4.2 | 3.6 |
| Prior settlements | 5.2 | 5.6 | 3.7 | 3.3 | 3.7 | 3.8 |
| COLA provisions | 4.8 | 7.7 | 2.2 | 2.7 | 2.0 | 2.0 |
| Total no. of workers receiving a wage rate increase (millions) | 9.7 | 8.9 | 5.5 | 4.9 | 5.1 | 4.7 |
| SOURCE (mil.) | | | | | | |
| Current settlements | 2.7 | 3.5 | 1.4 | 1.9 | 1.5 | 1.3 |
| Prior settlements | 7.3 | 5.6 | 3.4 | 2.7 | 3.0 | 2.8 |
| COLA provisions | 4.7 | 3.4 | 2.3 | 1.4 | 1.3 | 1.0 |
| No. of workers not receiving a wage rate increase (millions) | 0.4 | 0.2 | 1.5 | 1.0 | 0.5 | 0.9 |

*Source: 1993 Statistical Abstract, Table Nos. 680, 681*

# The Most Highly Paid Executives

## 15 Highest Compensated CEOs, 1993

| Company | CEO | Total Pay ($) |
|---|---|---|
| Disney | Michael Eisner | 203,011,000 |
| Travelers | Sanford Weill | 52,810,000 |
| Autozone | Joseph Hyde, III | 32,220,000 |
| International Game Technology | Charles Mathewson | 22,231,000 |
| Bear Stearns | Alan Greenberg | 15,915,000 |
| Blockbuster Entertainment | Wayne Huizenga | 15,557,000 |
| Brinker | Norman Brinker | 14,925,000 |
| Coca-Cola | Roberto Goizueta | 14,513,000 |
| Duracell | C. Robert Kidder | 14,172,000 |
| Georgia-Pacific | Thomas Kahn, Jr. | 13,680,000 |
| General Mills | H. Brewster Atwater Jr. | 13,177,000 |
| Applied Materials | James Morgan | 12,833,000 |
| Equitable | Richard Jenrette | 12,380,000 |
| Louisiana-Pacific | Harry Merlo | 12,051,000 |
| Sara Lee | John Bryan | 11,889,000 |

*Source: Business Week, April 25, 1994*

ACCORDING TO THE Wall Street Journal/William M. Mercer CEO Compensation Survey, the median CEO cash pay (salary and bonuses) for 1993 rose 8.1% and the CEO's median total compensation (salary, bonuses, long-term incentives, etc.) has reached an incredible high of $1,776,168, up from $1,095,000 in 1992.

Here is a sampling of salaries as reported by *The Wall Street Journal:*

## 1993 Salaries of 10 Selected CEOs

| Company | CEO | Base Salary ($) | Total Pay ($) |
|---|---|---|---|
| Occidental | Ray Irani | 1,900,000 | 4,959,000 |
| General Electric | John Welch, Jr. | 1,750,000 | 6,844,000 |
| ITT | Rand Araskog | 1,525,000 | 9,938,000 |
| Loews | Preston Tisch | 1,517,000 | 1,517,000 |
| IBM | Louis Gerstner, Jr. | 1,500,000 | 2,625,000 |
| Coca-Cola | Roberto Goizueta | 1,454,000 | 14,513,000 |
| GM | John Smith, Jr. | 1,375,000 | 1,420,000 |
| Bristol-Meyers | Richard Gelb | 1,240,000 | 3,973,000 |
| American | Maurice Greenberg | 1,232,000 | 7,779,000 |
| Citicorp | John Reed | 1,150,000 | 6,390,000 |

*The Most Highly Paid Executives (cont'd)*

*Working Woman* magazine produces an annual survey of the salaries of top-paid corporate women at the end of the year. According to the magazine's findings, the following are the highest paid female executives in the country (exclusive of privately held and Wall Street companies):

## 10 Highest Paid Female Executives, 1993

| Name | Position | Company | Salary ($ millions) |
|------|----------|---------|---------------------|
| Turi Josefson | Executive Vice President | U.S. Surgical | 26.70 |
| Rena Rowan | Executive Vice President of Design | Jones Apparel Group | 6.72 |
| Marion Sandler | Chairwoman and CEO | Golden West Financial | 6.44 |
| Sandra Kurtzig | Chairwoman | ASK Group | 3.60 |
| Jill Barad | President and COO | Mattel USA | 3.46 |
| Linda Wachner | Chairwoman and CEO | Warnaco | 3.16 |
| Sherry Lansing | Chairwoman | Paramount Motion Pictures | 3.00 |
| Jane Shaw | President and COO | Alza | 2.31 |
| Lucie Salhaney | Chairwoman | Fox Broadcasting | 1.50 |
| C.F. St. Mark | President, Logistics and Business Services | Pitney Bowes | 1.18 |

*Source: Working Woman, January, 1994*

## Executive Perks

| Perquisite | 1993 | 1991 | 1989 | 1987 | 1985 | % Change ('85–'93) |
|------------|------|------|------|------|------|---------------------|
| Executive dining rooms | 20 | 26 | 30 | 34 | 35 | -42.9 |
| Company plane | 53 | 56 | 63 | 67 | 66 | -19.7 |
| Reserved parking | 29 | 29 | 32 | 37 | 36 | -19.4 |
| Airline VIP clubs | 30 | 32 | 34 | 38 | 37 | -18.9 |
| Chauffeur service | 35 | 36 | 40 | 42 | 43 | -18.6 |
| Loans | 6 | 7 | 9 | 8 | 7 | -14.3 |
| First-class air travel | 57 | 60 | 62 | 66 | 66 | -13.6 |
| Club memberships | 62 | 63 | 71 | 73 | 70 | -11.4 |
| Company car | 63 | 63 | 68 | 70 | 71 | -11.3 |
| Physical exams | 85 | 89 | 91 | 93 | 94 | -9.6 |
| Financial counseling | 70 | 70 | 74 | 73 | 68 | 2.9 |
| Personal liability insurance | 47 | 46 | 50 | 48 | 42 | 11.9 |
| Home security system | 26 | 27 | 25 | 28 | 22 | 18.2 |
| Home computer | 9 | 7 | 6 | 5 | 6 | 50.0 |
| Cellular telephone | 45 | 37 | 22 | NA | NA | NA |

*Source: Hewitt Associates*

# 30 Most Overpaid CEOs

THE CRYSTAL 200 REPORT ANALYZES the salaries of over 200 top CEOs based on several criteria. The editors collect data on the Actual Total Compensation, which includes the CEO's base salary and bonuses. The Competitive Total Compensation is the compensation figure determined to be appropriate based on the company's size, performance, and salary averages and medians. The Deviation is the difference between the Total Current Compensation and the Competitive Total Compensation, or the amount by which it is believed the CEO is overpaid.

## Contact Option

Graef Crystal, Editor
*The Crystal Report*
564 Montecito Blvd.
Napa, CA 94559
(702) 832-3779

## 30 Most Relatively Overpaid CEOs According to the Crystal Report 200 Study, 1993

| Company | CEO | Actual Total Compensation | Competitive Total Compensation | Deviation |
|---|---|---|---|---|
| Primerica | Sanford I. Weill | 50,691,000 | 3,001,000 | 47,690 |
| Citizens Utilities | Leonard Tow | 21,345 ,000 | 1,982,000 | 19,363 |
| Bear Stearns Companies | Allan C. Greenberg | 16,032,000 | 2,110,000 | 13,922 |
| Chrysler | Lee A. Iacocca | 15,902,000 | 4,308,000 | 11,594 |
| Viacom | Frank J. Biondi, Jr. | 16,546,000 | 5,551,000 | 10,995 |
| General Electric | John F. Welch, Jr. | 15,525,000 | 4,570,000 | 10,955 |
| Intl Flavors & Fragrances | Eugene P. Grisanti | 11,525,000 | 2,248,000 | 9,277 |
| General Dynamics | William A. Anders | 16,249,000 | 8,324,000 | 7,925 |
| Grace (W.R.) & Co | J. Peter Grace | 9,568,000 | 1,929,000 | 7,639 |
| Philip Morris | Michael A. Miles | 13,958,000 | 8,181,000 | 5,777 |
| Occidental Petroleum | Ray R. Irani | 6,350,000 | 704,000 | 5,646 |
| Digital Equipment | Kenneth H. Olsen | 5,706,000 | 207,000 | 5,499 |
| Masco | Richard A. Manoogian | 6,641,000 | 1,344,000 | 5,297 |
| Freeport McMoran | James R. Moffett | 7,072,000 | 1,796,000 | 5,276 |
| Union Pacific | Drew Lewis | 7,962,000 | 3,053,000 | 4,909 |
| Capital Cities/ABC | Daniel B. Burke | 5,642,000 | 1,320,000 | 4,322 |
| Bankers Trust New York | Charles S. Sanford, Jr. | 6,980,000 | 2,756,000 | 4,224 |
| Merck & Co. | P. Roy Vagelos, M.D. | 9,191,000 | 5,247,000 | 3,944 |
| Texaco | James W. Kinnear | 7,080,000 | 3,249,000 | 3,831 |
| Morgan Stanley Group | Richard B. Fisher | 6,233,000 | 2,549,000 | 3,684 |
| Toys R Us | Charles Lazarus | 7,025,000 | 3,344,000 | 3,681 |
| Tenneco | Michael H. Walsh | 4,810,000 | 1,176,000 | 3,634 |
| Warner-Lambert | Melvin R. Goodes | 5,212,000 | 1,583,000 | 3,628 |
| Aluminum Co. of America | Paul H. O'Neill | 5,235,000 | 1,896,000 | 3,339 |
| Nationsbank | Hugh L. McColl, Jr. | 7,075,000 | 3,828,000 | 3,247 |
| Colgate-Palmolive | Reuben Mark | 7,831,000 | 4,679,000 | 3,152 |
| Paramount Communications | Martin S. Davis | 4,560,000 | 1,511,000 | 3,049 |
| Morgan (J.P.) & Co | Dennis Weatherstone | 6,095,000 | 3,088,000 | 3,007 |
| Gannett | John J. Curley | 4,731,000 | 1,782,000 | 2,948 |
| Citicorp | John S. Reed | 4,424,000 | 1,546,000 | 2,878 |

*Source: The Crystal Report, 1993*

# Wage Data

## Selected Occupations and Median Weekly Earnings

| Occupation (Male and Female) | 1993 Median Weekly Earnings ($) | % Change 1983–1993 |
|---|---|---|
| Accountants and auditors | 612 | 49.5 |
| Administrators & officials, public administration | 724 | 54.4 |
| Advertising and related sales | 590 | 64.8 |
| Airplane pilots and navigators | 1,086 | 76.6 |
| Architects | 694 | 39.4 |
| Bank tellers | 350 | 71.6 |
| Bookkeepers, accounting and auditing clerks | 375 | 49.4 |
| Chemical engineers | 996 | 58.1 |
| Clergy | 499 | 57.9 |
| Computer programmers | 747 | 58.0 |
| Computer systems analysts and scientists | 821 | 56.7 |
| Economists | 793 | 31.7 |
| Editors and reporters | 574 | 49.9 |
| Electricians | 549 | 30.1 |
| Engineers | 911 | 51.8 |
| Financial managers | 776 | 57.7 |
| Firefighters and fire prevention occupations | 614 | 54.7 |
| Insurance sales | 565 | 48.3 |
| Lawyers | 1,164 | 86.2 |
| Librarians, archivists, curators | 577 | 54.3 |
| Managers, marketing, advertising, public relations | 851 | 49.3 |
| Managers, properties and real estate | 511 | 52.1 |
| Mechanical engineers | 895 | 50.2 |
| Personnel and labor relations managers | 723 | 47.6 |
| Personnel, training, and labor relations specialists | 598 | 44.4 |
| Pharmacists | 913 | 81.9 |
| Physicians | 1,019 | 102.9 |
| Police and detectives, public service | 632 | 56.0 |
| Public relations specialists | 613 | 37.8 |
| Purchasing managers | 773 | 36.3 |
| Real estate sales | 610 | 58.9 |
| Receptionists | 316 | 49.8 |
| Secretaries | 386 | 53.2 |
| Securities and financial services sales | 783 | 50.9 |
| Social scientists and urban planners | 670 | 44.7 |
| Supervisors, general office | 548 | 55.2 |
| Supervisors, police and detectives | 750 | 49.1 |
| Teachers, secondary school | 625 | 60.7 |
| Telephone line installers and repairers | 664 | 37.2 |
| Telephone operators | 386 | 37.9 |
| Truck drivers, heavy | 445 | 36.5 |
| Waiters and waitresses | 230 | 42.0 |

*Source: Bureau of Labor Statistics*

*Wage Data (cont'd)*

## Percent Job Distribution of Non-Farm Establishments and Employees

| Year | Total Goods Prod. | Mining | Const. | Mfg. | Total Service Prod. | Trans. & Utilities | Wholesale Trade | Retail Trade | Finance | Svcs. | Gov't. |
|------|------|------|------|------|------|------|------|------|------|------|------|
| 1960 | 37.7 | 1.3 | 5.4 | 31.0 | 62.3 | 7.4 | 5.8 | 15.2 | 4.8 | 13.6 | 15.4 |
| 1965 | 36.1 | 1.0 | 5.3 | 29.7 | 63.9 | 6.6 | 5.7 | 15.2 | 4.9 | 14.9 | 16.6 |
| 1970 | 33.3 | 0.9 | 5.1 | 27.3 | 66.7 | 6.4 | 5.7 | 15.6 | 5.1 | 16.3 | 17.7 |
| 1975 | 29.4 | 1.0 | 4.6 | 23.8 | 70.6 | 5.9 | 5.8 | 16.4 | 5.4 | 18.1 | 19.1 |
| 1980 | 28.4 | 1.1 | 4.8 | 22.4 | 71.6 | 5.7 | 5.9 | 16.6 | 5.7 | 19.8 | 18.0 |
| 1985 | 25.5 | 1.0 | 4.8 | 19.7 | 74.5 | 5.4 | 5.9 | 17.8 | 6.1 | 22.6 | 16.8 |
| 1986 | 24.7 | 0.8 | 4.8 | 19.1 | 75.3 | 5.3 | 5.8 | 18.0 | 6.3 | 23.2 | 16.8 |
| 1987 | 24.2 | 0.7 | 4.9 | 18.6 | 75.8 | 5.3 | 5.7 | 18.1 | 6.4 | 23.7 | 16.6 |
| 1988 | 23.9 | 0.7 | 4.8 | 18.3 | 76.1 | 5.2 | 5.7 | 18.1 | 6.3 | 24.3 | 16.5 |
| 1989 | 23.4 | 0.6 | 4.8 | 17.9 | 76.6 | 5.2 | 5.7 | 18.0 | 6.2 | 25.0 | 16.4 |
| 1990 | 22.7 | 0.6 | 4.7 | 17.4 | 77.3 | 5.3 | 5.6 | 17.9 | 6.1 | 25.7 | 16.7 |
| 1991 | 22.0 | 0.6 | 4.3 | 17.0 | 78.0 | 5.3 | 5.6 | 17.8 | 6.2 | 26.1 | 17.0 |
| 1992 | 21.6 | 0.6 | 4.2 | 16.8 | 78.4 | 5.3 | 5.5 | 17.6 | 6.2 | 26.7 | 17.1 |

## Weekly Earnings of Non-Farm Employees ($)

| Year | Total | Total Goods Prod. | Mining | Const. | Mfg. | Total Svc. Prod. | Trans. & Utilities | Whsl. Trade | Retail Trade | Finance | Svcs. | Gov't. |
|------|------|------|------|------|------|------|------|------|------|------|------|------|
| 1960 | 81  | NA | 105 | 113 | 90  | NA | NA  | 91  | 58  | 75  | NA  | NA |
| 1965 | 95  | NA | 124 | 138 | 108 | NA | 125 | 106 | 67  | 89  | 74  | NA |
| 1970 | 120 | NA | 164 | 195 | 133 | NA | 156 | 137 | 82  | 113 | 97  | NA |
| 1975 | 164 | NA | 249 | 266 | 191 | NA | 233 | 182 | 109 | 148 | 135 | NA |
| 1980 | 235 | NA | 397 | 368 | 289 | NA | 351 | 267 | 147 | 210 | 191 | NA |
| 1985 | 299 | NA | 520 | 464 | 386 | NA | 450 | 351 | 175 | 289 | 256 | NA |
| 1986 | 305 | NA | 526 | 467 | 396 | NA | 459 | 358 | 176 | 304 | 266 | NA |
| 1987 | 313 | NA | 532 | 480 | 406 | NA | 472 | 365 | 179 | 317 | 276 | NA |
| 1988 | 322 | NA | 541 | 496 | 419 | NA | 476 | 380 | 184 | 325 | 289 | NA |
| 1989 | 334 | NA | 570 | 513 | 430 | NA | 490 | 395 | 189 | 341 | 306 | NA |
| 1990 | 345 | NA | 603 | 526 | 442 | NA | 505 | 411 | 194 | 357 | 319 | NA |
| 1991 | 354 | NA | 630 | 533 | 455 | NA | 512 | 425 | 199 | 371 | 331 | NA |
| 1992 | 364 | NA | 638 | 536 | 469 | NA | 523 | 435 | 206 | 387 | 343 | NA |

*Source: 1993 Statistical Abstract, Table No. 660*

**FAX**    **Longest Occupational Tenure.** Request #878. See p. xi for instructions.

Bar graph of the average number of years in occupation for the top 10 jobs.

# Job Outlook Data

## Change in Age Distribution (%) of the Labor Force, 1975 to Projected 2005

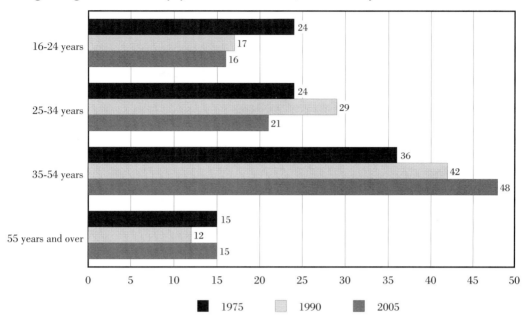

Source: U.S. Dept. of Labor, Bureau of Labor Statistics

## Proportion of Workers 25 and 64 Years Old With a College Background, 1975 vs. 1990

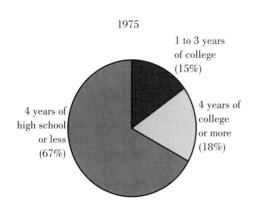

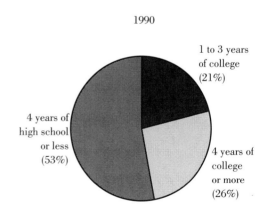

Source: U.S. Dept. of Labor, Bureau of Labor Statistics

*Job Outlook Data (cont'd)*

## Projected Percent Change in Employment by Industry, 1990 to 2005

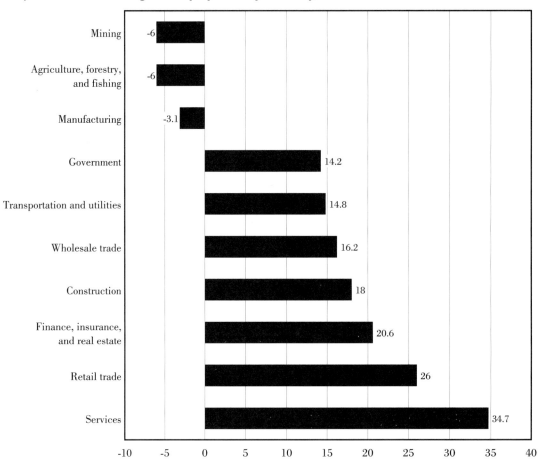

Source: U.S. Dept. of Labor, Bureau of Labor Statistics

*Job Outlook Data (cont'd)*

## Projected Percent Change in Employment by Broad Occupational Group, 1990 to 2005

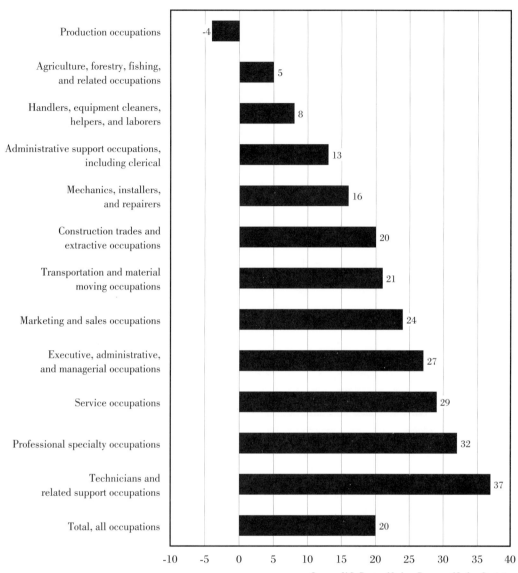

*Source: U.S. Dept. of Labor, Bureau of Labor Statistics*

# Job Outlook Information

STATE AND LOCAL JOB MARKET and career information is available from state employment security agencies and State Occupational Information Coordinating Committees (SOICCs). State employment security agencies develop occupational employment projections and other job market information. SOICCs provide or help locate labor market and career information. The following list provides the address and telephone number of state employment security agencies and SOICCs.

*Alabama*
Labor Market Information
Department of Industrial Relations
649 Monroe St., Room 422
Montgomery, AL 36130
(205) 242-8855

Occupational Information Coordinating Committee
401 Adams Ave., #424
Montgomery, AL 36103
(205) 242-2990

*Alaska*
Research and Analysis
Department of Labor
P.O. Box 25501
Juneau, AK 99802
(907) 465-4500

*Arizona*
Occupational Information Coordinating Committee
Department of Economic Security
P.O. Box 6123
Site Code 897J
Phoenix, AZ 85005
(602) 542-3680

*Arkansas*
State and Labor Market Information
Employment Security Division
P.O. Box 2981
Little Rock, AR 72203
(501) 682-1543

Occupational Information Coordinating Committee
Employment Security Division
Employment and Training Services
P.O. Box 2981
Little Rock, AR 72203
(501) 682-3159

*California*
Labor Market Information Division
Employment Development Department
P.O. Box 826880, MIC 57
Sacramento, CA 94280
(916) 262-2160

Occupational Information Coordinating Committee
P.O. Box 944222
Sacramento, CA 94244
(916) 323-6544

*Colorado*
Labor Market Information
393 S. Harlan St.
Lakewood, CO 80226
(303) 937-4935

*Connecticut*
Research and Information
Employment Security Division
Labor Department
200 Folly Brook Blvd.
Wethersfield, CT 06109
(203) 566-2120

Occupational Information Coordinating Committee
Connecticut Department of Education
25 Industrial Park Rd.
Middletown, CT 06457
(203) 638-4042

*Delaware*
Office of Occupational and
Labor Market Information
Delaware Department of Labor
University Plaza, Building D
P.O. Box 9029
Newark, DE 19702
(302) 368-6962

Office of Occupational and
Labor Market Information
Department of Labor
University Office Plaza
P.O. Box 9029
Newark, DE 19714
(302) 368-6963

*District of Columbia*
Labor Market Information
Department of Employment Services
500 C St., NW, Room 201
Washington, DC 20001
(202) 724-7214

Occupational Information Coordinating Committee
Department of Employment Security Services
500 C St., NW, Room 215
Washington, DC 20001
(202) 724-7238

*Job Outlook Information (cont'd)*

*Florida*
Bureau of Labor Market Information
Department of Labor Employment Security,
2012 Capitol Circle, SE, Room 200
Hartman Building
Tallahassee, FL 32399
(904) 488-1048

*Georgia*
Labor Information System
Department of Labor
148 International Blvd., Sussex Place
Atlanta, GA 30303
(404) 656-3177

Occupational Information Coordinating Committee
Department of Labor
148 International Blvd., Sussex Place
Atlanta, GA 30303
(404) 656-9639

*Hawaii*
Research and Statistics Office
Department of Labor and Industrial Relations
830 Punchbowl St., Room 304
Honolulu, HI 96813
(808) 586-8999

Occupational Information Coordinating Committee
830 Punchbowl St., Room 315
Honolulu, HI 96813
(808) 586-8750

*Idaho*
Research and Analysis
Department of Employment
317 Main St.
Boise, ID 83735
(208) 334-6169

Occupational Information Coordinating Committee
Len B. Jordan Bldg., Room 301
650 W. State St.
Boise, ID 83720
(208) 334-3705

*Illinois*
Economic Information and Analysis
Department of Employment Security
401 S. State St., 2 South
Chicago, IL 60605
(312) 793-2316

Occupational Information Coordinating Committee
217 E. Monroe, Suite 203
Springfield, IL 62706
(217) 785-0789

*Indiana*
Labor Market Information
Department of Employment and Training Services
10 N. Senate Ave.
Indianapolis, IN 46204
(317) 232-7460

Occupational Information Coordinating Committee
10 N. Senate Ave., Room SE 205
Indianapolis, IN 46204
(317) 232-8528

*Iowa*
Audit and Analysis
Department of Employment Services
1000 E. Grand Ave.
Des Moines, IA 50319
(515) 281-8181

Occupational Information Coordinating Committee
Department of Economic Development
200 E. Grand Ave.
Des Moines, IA 50309
(515) 242-4890

*Kansas*
Labor Market Information Services
Department of Human Resources
401 SW Topeka Blvd.
Topeka, KS 66603
(913) 296-2387

Occupational Information Coordinating Committee
401 Topeka Ave.
Topeka, KS 66603
(913) 296-1865

*Kentucky*
Labor Market Research and Analysis
Department for Employment Services
275 E. Main St.
Frankfort, KY 40621
(502) 564-7976

Occupational Information Coordinating Committee
275 E. Main St.
Frankfort, KY 40621
(502) 564-4258

*Louisiana*
Research and Statistics Division
Department of Employment and Training
P.O. Box 94094
Baton Rouge, LA 70804
(504) 342-3141

Occupational Information Coordinating Committee
P.O. Box 94094
Baton Rouge, LA 70804
(504) 342-5149

*Maine*
Division of Economic Analysis and Research
Bureau of Employment Security
20 Union St.
Augusta, ME 04330
(207) 287-2271

*Job Outlook Information (cont'd)*

*Maryland*
Office of Labor Market Analysis and Information
Department of Economic and
Employment Development
1100 N. Eutaw St., Room 601
Baltimore, MD 21201
(410) 333-5000

*Massachusetts*
Research Department
Massachusetts Division of Employment Security
19 Stamford St., 2nd Floor
Boston, MA 02114
(617) 626-5720

Occupational Information Coordinating Committee
Division of Employment Security
19 Stamford St.
Boston, MA 02114
(617) 626-5718

*Michigan*
Bureau of Research and Statistics
Employment Security Commission
7310 Woodward Ave.
Detroit, MI 48202
(313) 876-5445

Occupational Information Coordinating Committee
201 N. Washington Square, Box 30015
Lansing, MI 48909
(517) 373-0363

*Minnesota*
Research and Statistical Services
Department of Jobs and Training
390 N. Robert St., 5th Floor
St. Paul, MN 55101
(612) 296-6545

Occupational Information Coordinating Committee
Department of Economic Security
390 N. Robert St.
St. Paul, MN 55101
(612) 296-2072

*Mississippi*
Labor Market Information Department
Employment Security Commission
P.O. Box 1699
Jackson, MS 39215
(601) 961-7424

Department of Economic and
Community Development
Occupational Information Coordinating Committee
301 W. Pearl St.
Jackson, MS 39203
(601) 949-2002

*Missouri*
Research and Analysis
Division of Employment Security
P.O. Box 59
Jefferson City, MO 65104
(314) 751-3591

Occupational Information Coordinating Committee
400 Dix Rd.
Jefferson City, M0 65109
(314)751-3800

*Montana*
Research and Analysis
Department of Labor and Industry
P.O. Box 1728
Helena, MT 59624
(406) 444-2430

Occupational Information Coordinating Committee
P.O. Box 1728
Helena, MT 59624
(406) 444-2741

*Nebraska*
Labor Market Information
Department of Labor
P.O. Box 94600
Lincoln, NE 68509
(402) 471-9964

Occupational Information Coordinating Committee
P.O. Box 94600
Lincoln, NE 68509
(402) 471-9964

*Nevada*
Employment Security Research
500 E. Third St.
Carson City, NV 89713
(702) 687-4550

Occupational Information Coordinating Committee
1923 N. Carson St., Suite 211
Carson City, NV 89710
(702) 687-4577

*New Hampshire*
Labor Market Information
Department of Employment Security
10 West St.
Concord, NH 03301
(603) 228-4123

Occupational Information Coordinating Committee
64 Old Suncook Rd.
Concord, NH 03301
(603) 228-3349

*Job Outlook Information (cont'd)*

*New Jersey*
Policy and Planning
Department of Labor
John Fitch Plaza, Room 308
Trenton, NJ 08625
(609) 292-2643

Occupational Information Coordinating Committee
CN 056, Rm 307
Trenton, NJ 08625
(609) 292-2682

*New Mexico*
Economic Research and Analysis Bureau
Department of Labor
P.O. Box 1928
Albuquerque, NM 87103
(505) 841-8645

Occupational Information Coordinating Committee
P.O. Box 1928
Albuquerque, NM 87103
(505) 841-8455

*New York*
Division of Research and Statistics
Department of Labor
State Campus, Bldg. 12, Room 400
Albany, NY 12240
(518) 457-6181

Occupational Information Coordinating Committee
Department of Labor
State Campus, Bldg. 12, Room 400
Albany, NY 12240
(518) 457-6182

*North Carolina*
Labor Market Information Division
Employment Security Commission
P.O. Box 25903
Raleigh, NC 27611
(919) 733-2936

Occupational Information Coordinating Committee
P.O. Box 25903
Raleigh, NC 27611
(919) 733-6700

*North Dakota*
Research and Statistics
Job Service
P.O. Box 5507
Bismarck, ND 58502
(701) 224-2868

Occupational Information Coordinating Committee
P.O. Box 5507
Bismarck, ND 58502
(701) 224-2197

*Ohio*
Labor Market Information Division
Bureau of Employment Services
145 S. Front St.
Columbus, OH 43215
(614) 644-2689

Occupational Information Coordinating Committee
Bureau of Employment Services
145 S. Front St.
Columbus, OH 43215
(614) 466-11090

*Oklahoma*
Research Division
Employment Security Commission
308 Will Rogers Memorial Office Bldg.
Oklahoma City, OK 73105
(405) 557-7116

*Oregon*
Research and Statistics
Employment Division
875 Union St., NE
Salem, OR 97311
(503) 378-3220

Occupational Information Coordinating Committee
875 Union St., NE
Salem, OR 97311
(503) 378-5747

*Pennsylvania*
Research and Statistics Division
Department of Labor and Industry
300 Capitol Associates Bldg.
Harrisburg, PA 17120
(717) 787-3265

Occupational Information Coordinating Committee
Department of Labor and Industry
300 Capitol Associates Bldg.
Harrisburg, PA 17120
(717) 787-8646

*Rhode Island*
Labor Market Information and
Management Services
Department of Employment and Training
101 Friendship St.
Providence, RI 02903
(401) 277-3730

Occupational Information Coordinating Committee
22 Hayes St., Room 133
Providence, RI 02908
(401) 272-0830

*Job Outlook Information (cont'd)*

*South Carolina*
Labor Market Information
Employment Security Commission
P.O. Box 995
Columbia, SC 29202
(803) 737-2660

Occupational Information Coordinating Committee
P.O. Box 995
Columbia, SC 29202
(803) 737-2733

*South Dakota*
Labor Market Information Center
Department of Labor
P.O. Box 4730
Aberdeen, SD 57402
(605) 622-2314

*Tennessee*
Research and Statistics Division
Department of Employment Security
500 James Robertson Pkwy.,11th Floor
Nashville, TN 37245
(615) 741-2284

Occupational Information Coordinating Committee
500 James Robertson Pkwy., 11th Floor
Nashville, TN 37245
(615) 741-6451

*Texas*
Economic Research and Analysis
Employment Commission
15th and Congress Ave., Room 208T
Austin, TX 78778
(512) 463-2616

Occupational Information Coordinating Committee
3520 Executive Center Dr., Suite 205
Austin, TX 78731
(512) 502-3751

*Utah*
Labor Market Information and Research
Department of Employment Security
P.O. Box 45249
Salt Lake City, UT 84145
(801) 536-7810

*Vermont*
Policy and Information
Department of Employment and Training
P.O. Box 488
Montpelier, VT 05601
(802) 229-0311

Occupational Information Coordinating Committee
P.O. Box 488
Montpelier, VT 05601
(802) 828-4330

*Virginia*
Economic Information Service Division
Virginia Employment Commission
P.O. Box 1358
Richmond, VA 23211
(804) 786-7496

Occupational Information Coordinating Committee
Employment Commission
P.O. Box 1358
Richmond, VA 23211
(804) 786-7496

*Washington*
Labor Market Information
Washington Employment Security Department
P.O. Box 9026
Olympia, WA 98507
(206) 438-4800

Occupational Information Coordinating Committee
P.O. Box 9026
Olympia, WA 98507
(206) 438-4803

*West Virginia*
Labor and Economic Research
Bureau of Employment Programs
112 California Ave.
Charleston, WV 25305
(304) 558-2660

Occupational Information Coordinating Committee
West Virginia University
P.O. Box 6122
Morgantown, WV 26506
(304) 293-5314

*Wisconsin*
Labor Market Information Bureau
Department of Industry, Labor, and
Human Relations
P.O. Box 7944
Madison, WI 53707
(608) 266-5843

Occupational Information Coordinating Council
Division of Employment and Training Policy
P.O. Box 7944
Madison, WI 53707
(608) 266-8012

*Wyoming*
Research and Planning, Division of Administration
Department of Employment
P.O. Box 2760
Casper, WY 82602
(307) 265-6715

# National Labor Relations Board

## What Is the NLRB?

The National Labor Relations Board is an independent federal agency created in 1935 by Congress to administer the National Labor Relations Act, the basic law governing relations between labor unions and the employers whose operations affect interstate commerce.

The statute guarantees the right of employees to organize and to bargain collectively with their employers or to refrain from all such activity. Generally applying to all employers involved in interstate commerce–other than airlines, railroads, agriculture, and government–the Act implements the national labor policy of assuring free choice and encouraging collective bargaining as a means of maintaining industrial peace.

Through the years, Congress has amended the Act, and the Board and courts have developed a body of law drawn from the statute. This section is intended to give a brief explanation of the Act to employees, employers, unions, and the public.

## What Does It Do?

In its statutory assignment, the NLRB has two principal functions: (1) to determine, through secret ballot elections, the free democratic choice by employees as to whether or not they wish to be represented by a union in dealing with their employers and, if so, by which union; and (2) to prevent and remedy unlawful acts, called unfair labor practices, by either employers or unions.

The Act's election provisions provide the authority for conducting representation elections, which determine the views of the employees regarding representation by a labor union. Its unfair labor practice provisions place certain restrictions on actions of both employers and labor organizations in their relations with employees, as well as with each other.

The agency does not act on its own motion in either function. It processes only those charges of unfair labor practices and petitions for employee elections which are filed with the NLRB in one of its Regional, Subregional, or Resident Offices.

The staff in each office is available to assist the public with inquiries concerning the Act and to provide appropriate forms and other technical assistance to those who wish to file charges or petitions.

## What Does the Act Provide?

The Act sets forth the basic rights of employees as follows:

- To self-organize;

- To form, join, or assist labor organizations;

- To bargain collectively about wages and working conditions through representatives of their own choosing;

- To engage in other protected "concerted activities," that is, to act together for purposes of collective bargaining, or other mutual aid or protection;

- To refrain from any of these activities. (However, a union and employer may, in a state where such agreements are permitted, enter into a lawful union security clause.)

The Act prohibits both employers and unions from violating these employee rights. As an example, an employer may not discriminate against employees with regard to hiring, discharge, or working conditions because of their union activities. A union may not engage in acts of violence against employees who refrain from union activity. These examples are for illustration only.

For further information about employer and union unfair labor practices, refer to *The National Labor Relations Board and You: Unfair Labor Practices*, available from your nearest NLRB office. A related publication, *The National Labor Relations Board and You: Representation Cases*, describes the election process in more detail.

## What Is the NLRB's Structure?

The agency has two separate components. The Board itself has five members and primarily acts as a quasi-judicial body in deciding cases on the basis of formal records in administrative proceedings. Board members are appointed by the president to five-year terms, with Senate consent, the term of one member expiring each year. The general counsel, appointed by the President to a four-year term with Senate consent, is independent from the Board and is responsible for the investigation and prosecution of unfair labor practice cases and for the general supervision of the NLRB field offices in the processing of unfair labor practice and representation cases.

Each Regional Office is headed by a Regional Director who is responsible for making the initial determination in unfair labor practice and representation cases arising within the geographical area served by the Region (including any Resident or Subregional Offices within the Region).

## What Are the NLRB's Procedures?

*Representation Cases*

In a typical representation election case, a union employer or individual files a petition with the field office requesting that an election be held among a particular group of employees (referred to as a "bargaining unit") to determine whether the group wishes to be represented, or wishes to continue to be represented, by a union. A petition filed by a union or an individual must be supported by showing that at least 30 percent of affected employees desires an election. If the Region's investigation reveals that the

*National Labor Relations Board (cont'd)*

petition should be processed, attempts are made to secure agreement of the parties on the issues involved, including the appropriate unit and the time and place of the election. Over 80 percent of meritorious election petitions result in such agreements. If an agreement cannot be reached, the Region conducts a hearing. On the basis of the record of the hearing, the Regional Director issues a decision disposing of the issues. The Regional Director's decision may be appealed to the Board.

When an unfair labor practice charge is filed, the appropriate field office conducts an investigation to determine whether there is reasonable cause to believe the Act has been violated. If the Regional Director determines that the charge lacks merit, it will be dismissed, unless the charging party decides to withdraw the charge. A dismissal may be appealed to the General Counsel's office in Washington, DC.

If the Regional Director finds reasonable cause to believe a violation of the law has been committed, the Region seeks a voluntary settlement to remedy the alleged violations. If these settlement efforts fail, a formal complaint is issued, and the case goes to a hearing before an NLRB administrative law judge.

The judge issues a written decision which may be appealed to the Board for a final Agency determination. That final determination is subject to review in the Federal courts. More than 90 percent of the unfair labor practice cases filed with the NLRB are disposed of in an average of 45 days without the necessity of formal litigation before the Board. Only about four percent of the cases proceed to Board decision.

Since its establishment, the NLRB has processed more than 900,000 unfair labor practice charges and conducted in excess of 360,000 secret ballot elections. The Agency handles approximately 40,000 cases each year, including more than 7,000 representation petitions.

## For Additional Information

For further information, to determine the NLRB field office nearest to you, or to receive copies of the publications referred to here, contact the headquarters of the NLRB.

## Contact Option

The National Labor Realations Board
Office of Information
1099 14th St., NW
Washington, DC 20570-0001
(202) 273-1991

## Recommended Resources

*The National Labor Relations Board and You: Unfair Labor Practices*
National Labor Relations Board, free
(202) 273-1992
    Provides information about employer and union unfair labor practices

*The National Labor Relations Board and You: Representation Cases*
National Labor Relations Board, free
(202) 273-1992
    Describes the union election process in detail.

*A Guide to Basic Law and Procedures Under the National Labor Relations Act*
U.S. Government Printing Office, $2.50
(202) 783-3230

---

## The Top Reference Sources

*The Evaluation Guide to Corporate Wellness Programs*
The Corporate University Press, $119
(510) 236-9400

This looseleaf binder features more than 400 pages of in-depth evaluations of hundreds of corporate wellness seminars given around the country. These seminars offer executives an opportunity to learn how to control health costs through preventive techniques.
    This book is the preeminent resource on the topic.

# Time Management Techniques

## Ten Tips for Better Time Management

1. Any time you handle any piece of paper, limit your contact with it to one time. If it requires a response, respond now–not later. If it must be filed, file it now. If it might be better off in the wastebasket, toss it now.

2. Learn how to say no. This is not an easy word to say, and you'll have to say it to some of the nicest people in the world. Be nice, direct, and compassionate, but say it immediately. Don't leave people hanging and waste their time.

3. Respect your instincts and your mood. If you're not in the mood to do something, do something else, saving the original task for a time when you are more likely to tackle it efficiently.

4. Make a public commitment. If you want to complete a task by a certain hour, go public with your pronouncement. "I'll have that report to you by three o'clock," leaves you with little choice.

5. Take breaks. If you work straight through without any break at all, chances are your work will suffer. If you take brief breaks, you'll be better able to keep an attentive pace and your work will be more accurate.

6. Learn to tolerate your faults in an effort to overcome perfectionism. You'll have a far better time of almost anything in life if you strive for excellence rather than perfection.

7. Get things done right now. It is estimated that a minimum of 80 percent of the business coming across the desk of an efficient executive gets handled immediately, through either personal action or delegation.

8. Force yourself to be neat. Neatness leads to organization, and organization leads to time efficiency.

9. Do things one at a time. This simple mind-set can keep you well organized, because the main reason some people can't seem to organize anything is that they fear having to organize everything.

10. When negotiating, realize that the shortest route to an agreement isn't necessarily the straightest. It takes 90 percent of the total discussion time to resolve 10 percent of the issues, and the final 10 percent of the time to resolve the other 90 percent. By recognizing this fact of negotiation, you can save a great deal of valuable time.

*Source: Adapted from Jay Conrad Levinson's The 90-Minute Hour*

## Recommended Resources

*How to Get Organized When You Don't Have the Time*
by Stephanie Culp
Writer's Digest Books, $10.95
(800) 289-0963

*The Effective Executive*
by Peter Drucker
HarperCollins, $12
(800) 242-7737

*Working Smart*
by Michael Leboeuf
Warner Books, $5.50
(800) 222-6747

*The 90-Minute Hour*
by Jay Conrad Levinson
Plume, $9
(800) 253-6476

## The Top Reference Sources

*Business Rankings Annual*
Gale, $160
(800) 877-4253

This mammoth book (800+ pages) lists more than 4,000 top ten lists–from largest public companies to highest paid CEOs.

Covering more than 1,500 different topics, this volume is an excellent place to look for a wide breadth of information.

# First Aid

*The Information Please Business Almanac & Sourcebook is not responsible and assumes no responsibility for any action undertaken by anyone utilizing the first aid procedures which follow.*

## The Heimlich Maneuver for Choking

What to look for: victim cannot speak or breathe, turns blue, collapses.

To perform the Heimlich Maneuver when the victim is standing or sitting:

1. Stand behind the victim and wrap your arms around his or her waist.

2. Place the thumb side of your fist against the victim's abdomen, slightly above the navel and below the rib cage.

3. Grasp your fist with the other hand and press your fist into the victim's abdomen with a quick upward thrust. Repeat as often as necessary.

4. If the victim is sitting, stand behind the victim's chair and perform the maneuver in the same manner.

5. After the food is dislodged, have the victim see a doctor.

When the victim has collapsed and cannot be lifted:

1. Lay the victim on his or her back.

2. Face the victim and kneel astride his or her hips.

3. With one hand on top of the other, place the heel of your bottom hand on the abdomen slightly above the navel and below the rib cage.

4. Press into the victim's abdomen with a quick upward thrust. Repeat as often as necessary.

5. Should the victim vomit, quickly place on his or her side and wipe out the mouth to prevent aspiration (drawing of vomit into the throat).

6. After the food is dislodged, have the victim see a doctor.

NOTE: if you start to choke when alone, and help is not available, an attempt should be made to self-administer this maneuver.

## Burns

*First Degree:*

Signs/Symptoms: reddened skin.

Treatment: immerse quickly in cold water or apply ice until pain stops.

*Second Degree:*

Signs/Symptoms: reddened skin, blisters.

Treatment: (1) cut away loose clothing; (2) cover with several layers of cold, moist dressings or, if limb is involved, immerse in cold water for relief of pain; (3) treat for shock.

*Third Degree:*

Signs/Symptoms: skin destroyed, tissues damaged, charring.

Treatment: (1) cut away loose clothing (do not remove clothing adhered to skin); (2) cover with several layers of sterile, cold, moist dressings for relief of pain and to stop burning action; (3) treat for shock.

## Poisons

Treatment: (1) dilute by drinking large quantities of water; (2) induce vomiting except when poison is corrosive or a petroleum product; (3) call a Poison Control center or a doctor.

Poison Control Center: (800) 336-6997

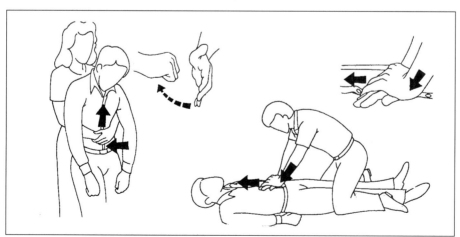

*Source: New York City Department of Health*

*First Aid (cont'd)*

## Shock

Shock may accompany any serious injury: blood loss, breathing impairment, heart failure, burns. Shock can kill, so treat as soon as possible and continue until medical aid is available.

Signs/Symptoms: (1) shallow breathing; (2) rapid and weak pulse; (3) nausea, collapse, vomiting; (4) shivering; (5) pale, moist skin; (6) mental confusion; (7) drooping eyelids, dilated pupils.

Treatment: (1) establish and maintain an open airway; (2) control bleeding; (3) keep victim lying down. Exception: head and chest injuries, heart attack, stroke, sun stroke. If no spine injury, victim may be more comfortable and breathe better in a semi-reclining position. If in doubt, keep the victim flat. Elevate the feet unless injury would be aggravated. Maintain normal body temperature. Place blankets under and over victim.

## Heat Cramps

Heat cramps affect people who work or do strenuous exercises in a hot environment. To prevent it, drink large amounts of cool water and add a pinch of salt to each glass of water.

Signs/Symptoms: (1) painful muscle cramps in legs and abdomen; (2) faintness; (3) profuse perspiration.

Treatment: (1) move victim to a cool place; (2) give him or her sips of salted drinking water (one teaspoon of salt to one quart of water); (3) apply manual pressure to the cramped muscle.

## Heat Exhaustion

Signs/Symptoms: (1) pale and clammy skin; (2) profuse perspiration; (3) rapid and shallow breathing; (4) weakness, dizziness, and headache.

Treatment: (1) care for victim as if he or she were in shock; (2) move victim to a cool area, do not allow chilling; (3) if body gets too cold, cover victim.

## Heat Stroke

Signs/Symptoms: (1) face is red and flushed; (2) victim rapidly loses consciousness; (3) skin is hot and dry with no perspiration.

Treatment: (1) lay victim down with head and shoulders raised; (2) apply cold applications to the body and head; (3) use ice and fan if available; (4) watch for signs of shock and treat accordingly; (5) get medical aid as soon as possible.

## Artificial Respiration

Artificial respiration is mouth-to-mouth breathing—in cases like drowning, electric shock, or smoke inhalation.

There is need for help when breathing movements stop or lips, tongue, and fingernails become blue. When in doubt, apply artificial respiration until you get medical help. No harm can result from its use, and delay may cost the patient his or her life. Start immediately. Seconds count. Clear mouth and throat of any obstructions with your fingers.

For adults: place patient on back with face up. Lift the chin and tilt the head back. If air passage is still closed, pull chin up by placing fingers behind the angles of the lower jaw and pushing forward. Take a deep breath, place your mouth over patient's mouth, making leak-proof seal. Pinch patient's nostrils closed. Blow into patient's mouth until you see his or her chest rise.

Repeat about 12 times a minute. (If the patient's stomach rises markedly, exert moderate hand pressure on the stomach just below the rib cage to keep it from inflating.)

For infants and small children: place your mouth over patient's mouth and nose. Blow into mouth and nose until you see patient's chest rise normally.

Repeat 20 to 30 times per minute. (Don't exaggerate the tilted position of an infant's head.)

NOTE: for emergency treatment of heart attack, cardiopulmonary resuscitation (CPR) is recommended. Instruction in CPR can be obtained through local health organizations or schools.

*Source: The Information Please Almanac, 1994*

# First-Aid Kit Contents

THE FEDERAL GOVERNMENT has no prescribed standard for the contents of an office first-aid kit. But, Johnson & Johnson, the leading manufacturer of first-aid kits, suggests that the following be included in a first-aid kit for an office:

150 or more mixed-size bandages, plastic and/or flexible fabric; sterile sponges, gauze, and eyepads; hypo-allergenic adhesive tape and an elastic bandage; antiseptic wipes, burn cream, and first-aid cream; instant cold packs; ophthalmic irrigating solution; Extra-Strength Tylenol®; scissors, tweezers, and disposable gloves; and a first-aid guide.

## Recommended Resource

Conney Safety Products
3202 Latham Dr.
P.O. Box 44190
Madison, WI 53744
(800) 356-9100

Conney Safety Products, one of the country's largest suppliers of first-aid, medical, and work safety products is a one-stop source for custom-assembled or standard first-aid kits for any size shop or office. Call for the catalogue.

# Dealing With Stress

ACCORDING TO *PERSONNEL* MAGAZINE, the cost of stress-related illnesses to American business is approximately 90 billion dollars a year. Being able to identify serious signs of stress and/or burnout in employees and co-workers, and alleviating the causes of stress where possible will increase productivity. In the long run, stress reduction can save millions of dollars in stress-related workers' compensation claims.

Stress is generally defined as any outside stimulus that disrupts the body's mental, physical, or chemical functioning.

Studies indicate that extreme forms of stress are characterized by restlessness, impatience, extreme competitiveness, and feelings of being under pressure. Furthermore, extreme stress can, over time, lead to deteriorating performance in the workplace as well as health problems such as: migraines, high blood pressure, arthritis, eczema, gastric and/or peptic ulcers, asthma, heart disease, and stroke.

The most common forms of workplace-related stress arise from one of the following conditions:

- Job changes that place new demands on a worker's time and personal or family relationships;

- Poor organizational climate and insufficient social support from friends or co-workers;

- Conflicts between workers' personal values and the values of the company;

- Frustrated career plans;

- Bad lighting, uncomfortable temperatures, noise, or other environmental factors.

An employee's ability to cope with stress is affected by the intensity and duration of one or more of the conditions listed above.

## Strategies Designed to Cope with Stress

- Physical maintenance
  Diet
  Sleep
  Exercise

- Internal assistance
  Relaxation response
  Biofeedback
  Autogenic training

- Personal organization
  Stress plan
  Delegation of responsibility
  Ability to choose or alternate environments
  Creative problem solving and decision making
  Goal setting
  Time management
  Conflict management
  Ability to restructure job
  Self-assessment measures

- Outside assistance
  Psychoanalysis
  Stress counseling
  Development program
  Behavior change techniques

- Stress-directed strategies
  Systematic desensitization
  Dynamic psychotherapy

- Situational and support group
  Assertiveness training and role-playing
  Development of supportive relationships

- Negative strategies
  Avoidance of substance abuse (alcohol, cigarettes, drugs)

*(Reprinted, by permission of publisher, from Personnel, August, 1989, copyright ©1989, American Management Association, New York. All rights reserved.)*

**TIP:** *Business owners who are interested in putting their business or career on a more environmental path can find information in a publication called Green at Work, which profiles environmental employment opportunities, and features a huge directory of environmental officers and resource contacts in over 230 companies. Call (800) 829-5220.*

*Dealing With Stress (cont'd)*

## 45 Elements of the Stress-Free Workplace

Northwestern National Life has created a simple questionnaire that allows workers to judge the level of stress they face at work. The basic principles behind this test are as follows:

1. Management is supportive of employees' efforts.

2. Management encourages work and personal support groups.

3. Management and employees talk openly.

4. Employees receive training when assigned new tasks.

5. Employees are recognized and rewarded for their contributions.

6. Work rules are published and are the same for everyone.

7. Employees have current and understandable job descriptions.

8. Management appreciates humor in the workplace.

9. Employees and management are trained in how to resolve conflicts.

10. Employees are free to talk with one another.

11. Workloads do not vary greatly for individuals or between individuals.

12. Employees have work spaces that are not crowded.

13. Employees have access to technology they need.

14. Opportunities for advancement are available.

15. Employees are given some control in how they do their work.

16. Employees generally are not physically isolated.

17. Mandatory overtime is seldom required.

18. Employees have some privacy.

19. Performance of work units is above average.

20. Personal conflicts on the job are not common.

21. Consequences of making a mistake on the job are not extremely severe.

22. Employees do not expect the organization will be sold or relocated.

23. There has been no major reorganization in the past 12 months.

24. Meal breaks are predictable.

25. Medical and mental health benefits are provided by the employer.

26. Employees are given information regularly on how to cope with stress.

27. Sick and vacation benefits are above that of similar organizations.

28. Employee benefits were not significantly cut in the past 12 months.

29. An employee assistance program (EAP) is offered.

30. Pay is above the going rate.

31. Employees can work flexible hours.

32. Employees have a place and time to relax during the workday.

33. Employer has a formal employee communications program.

34. Child care programs or referral services are available.

35. Referral programs or day care for elderly relatives are offered.

36. Special privileges are granted fairly based on an employee's level.

37. New machines or ways of working were introduced in the past year.

38. Employer offers exercise or other stress-reduction programs.

39. Work is neither sedentary nor physically exhausting.

40. Not all work is machine-paced or fast-paced.

41. Staffing or expense budgets are adequate.

42. Noise or vibration is low, or temperatures are not extreme or fluctuating.

43. Employees do not deal with a lot of red tape to get things done.

44. Downsizing or layoffs have not occurred in the past 12 months

45. Employees can put up personal items in their work area.

## Contact Option

Northwestern National Life
20 Washington Ave. S.
Minneapolis, MN 55401
(612) 372-5432

# Computer-Related Illnesses

THE APPLICATIONS OF COMPUTER technology and the use of video display terminals are revolutionizing the workplace. Along with their growing use, however, have come reports about adverse health effects for VDT operators.

For every potential hazard, health specialists recommend interventions that can be used both by employers and computer operators alike. Here is a list of the most commonly recognized harmful effects of frequent computer use and some suggested means of alleviating potential problems.

## Eyestrain

Visual problems, such as eyestrain and irritation are among the most frequently reported complaints by VDT operators. These visual problems can result from improper lighting, glare from the screen, poor positioning of the screen itself, or from copy that is difficult to read. These problems can usually be corrected by arranging workstations and lighting to avoid direct or reflected glare. VDT operators can also reduce eyestrain by taking vision breaks and by doing exercises that relax eye muscles.

## Radiation

Some workers, including pregnant women, are concerned that their health could be affected by X-rays or electromagnetic fields emitted from VDTs. To date, however, there is no conclusive evidence that the low levels of radiation emitted from VDTs pose a health risk. The issue is still being researched and studied. In the meantime, some workplace designs have incorporated changes such as increasing the distance between the operator and the terminal, and between workstations to reduce potential exposures to electromagnetic fields.

## Fatigue and Musculoskeletal Problems

Work performed at VDTs may require sitting still for considerable amounts of time and usually involves small frequent movements of the eyes, head, arms, and fingers. Retaining a fixed posture over long periods of time requires a significant static holding force, which causes fatigue. Proper workstation design is very important in eliminating these types of problems. An individual workstation should provide the operator with a comfortable sitting position sufficiently flexible to reach, use, and observe the display screen, keyboard, and document. Proper chair height and support to the lower region of the back are critical factors in reducing fatigue and related musculoskeletal complaints. Document holders also allow the operator to position and view material without straining the eyes or the muscles in the neck, shoulder, and back.

## Repetitive Stress Syndrome

VDT operators are also subject to a potential risk of developing various nerve or cumulative trauma disorders. Carpal tunnel syndrome (CTS), a commonly recognized cumulative trauma disorder, is caused by repetitive wrist-hand movement and exertion. CTS is the compression and entrapment of the median nerve where it passes through the wrist into the hand. When irritated, the tendons and their sheaths, housed inside the narrow carpal tunnel in the wrist, swell and press against the median nerve. The pressure causes tingling, numbness, or severe pain in the wrist and hand. CTS usually can be reduced by maintaining correct posture and by limiting the activity that aggravates the tendon and the median nerve. For correct posture, VDT operators should sit in an upright position at the keyboard, with arms parallel to the floor and wrists and forearms supported where possible. Additional exercises may help eliminate the problem. In extreme cases, surgery may be required.

## Ways to Help VDT Users Reduce Job-Related Stress

- Maintain a well-designed work area. (See next page).

- Limit continuous hours. The longer the time spent at a VDT, the higher the rate of health problems reported. Users should spend no more than four hours at one time for demanding work.

- Allow frequent breaks. Give workers the opportunity to get up and move about and give their eyes a chance to rest. A 15-minute break every two hours is recommended.

- Train workers thoroughly.

- Maintain variety. Limit the time workers spend on VDTs by giving staffers varied duties.

- Provide interaction or privacy as needed.

*Source: Office and Branch Managers Bulletin*

*Computer-Related Illnesses (cont'd)*

## VDT Workstation Checklist

- Does the workstation lend itself to proper posture considerations such as:
  - thighs horizontal;
  - lower legs vertical;
  - feet flat on floor or footrest;
  - wrists neutral or slightly extended?

- Does the chair in use:
  - adjust easily;
  - have a padded seat with a rounded front;
  - have a backrest which is adjustable;
  - provide lumbar support;
  - have casters?

- Is the keyboard worksurface:
  - height adjustable;
  - tilt adjustable?

- Is the keyboard detachable?

- Does keying require minimal force?

- Does the thickness of the keyboard affect wrist posture?

- Is there an adjustable document holder?

- Are armrests provided where needed?

- Are glare and reflections avoided?

- Do the VDTs have brightness and contrast controls?

- Is there proper distance between eyes and work?

- Is there sufficient space for knees and feet?

- Is the workstation biased toward right- or left-handed activity?

- Are adequate rest breaks provided for task demand?

- Are employees measured or rewarded by the number of keystrokes they type per minute?

- Is the employee's ability to maintain typing speed assisted by:
  - job rotation;
  - proper work methods;
  - when and how to adjust workstations;
  - how to get questions answered quickly?

*Source: OSHA: Ergonomic Program Management Recommendations for General Industry*

## Contact Options

Occupational Safety and Health Administration (OSHA)
U.S. Department of Labor
Technical Data Center, Room N2439
200 Constitution Ave., NW
Washington DC 20210
(202) 219-7500

U.S. Department of Health and Human Services
Public Health Service, Centers for Disease Control
National Institute for Occupational Safety and Health (NIOSH)
Robert A. Taft Laboratories
4676 Columbia Parkway
Cincinnati, OH 45226
(513) 533-8236

## Proper VDT Posture

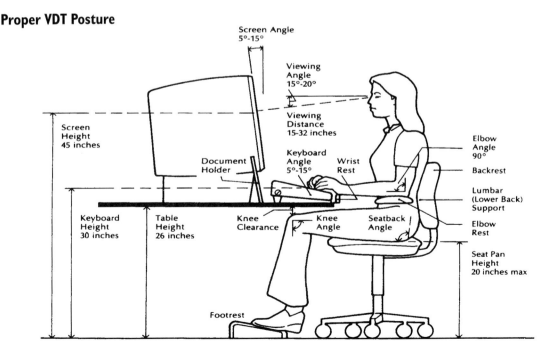

*Illustration courtesy of the Kemper National Insurance Companies*

# Accessibility for the Handicapped

THE AMERICANS WITH DISABILITIES ACT covers a broad range of topics relating to the working conditions of the disabled. All qualified handicapped workers are covered. An employer is not required to hire or retain an individual who is not qualified to perform a job. The regulations define a qualified individual with a disability as a person with a disability who "satisfies the requisite skills, experience, education, and other job-related requirements of the employment position such individual holds or desires, and who, with or without a reasonable accommodation, can perform the essential functions of such a position."

It is important that employers are familiar with the issues covered by ADA and with those discussed in Title I and Title III in particular.

## Title I

*Employment* deals specifically with employment. It prohibits discrimination against a qualified individual with a disability in regard to:

- Applications
- Testing
- Hiring
- Assignments
- Evaluation
- Disciplinary actions
- Training
- Promotion
- Medical examinations
- Layoff/recall
- Termination
- Compensation
- Leave
- Benefits.

## Title III

*Public Accommodations and Services Operated by Private Entities* prohibits discrimination in public accommodations and services operated by private entities. The term public accommodations means any business that provides goods or services to the general public. In general, persons with disabilities must be accorded the full and equal enjoyment of the goods, services, facilities, privileges, advantages, and accommodations by any person who owns, leases, or operates a place of public accommodation. To accomplish this end, this title requires:

- Provision of auxiliary aids and services;
- Removal of architectural and communications barriers in existing vehicles;
- Removal of transportation barriers in existing vehicles;
- Modifications in policies, practices, and procedures.

Many areas and items must be addressed in an accessibility audit of public accommodations. The following is a sample accessibility checklist:

- Accessible routes (paths or walks) at least 3 feet wide and with at least 80 inches of headroom;
- Ramps that are at least 3 feet wide and with a maximum slope equal to 1 to 12 inches and maximum rise equal to 30 inches;
- Stairs with treads at least 11 inches wide and having a tactile warning at the top of the stairs;
- Parking facilities with spaces at least 8 feet wide and having special reserved spaces for the handicapped;
- Passenger loading zone that is at least 4 feet wide and 20 feet long;
- Drinking fountain: spout 3 feet high or less;
- Public telephones that are controlled by push button;
- Seating and tables that are 27 to 34 inches wide and 19 inches deep;
- Corridors with carpet pile one half inch or less;
- Door openings at least 32 inches wide.

Employers with questions on how to accommodate applicants and employees with disabilities may contact the Job Accommodation Network (JAN). This free service, located at West Virginia University may be reached at (800) 526-7234.

## Recommended Resources

*The Employer's Guide to Understanding and Complying with the Americans with Disabilities Act*
Dartnell Publishing, $129
(800) 441-7878

*Americans with Disabilities Act Handbook, 2nd Edition*
John Wiley & Sons, $125
(800) 225-5945, ext. 2497

# Facts about AIDS

APPROXIMATELY ONE IN EVERY 250 Americans—most of whom are of working age—is living with HIV. What's more, nearly one in ten small employers already have employees who are living and working with HIV infection, including AIDS.

According to the American Red Cross, there is no danger in working with someone who is HIV-positive or who has AIDS. An individual cannot become infected through everyday work activities that do not involve contact with blood, semen, or vaginal fluids. Scientific studies from around the world have shown that HIV is not spread through ordinary employee, client, or public contact; nor through a handshake, a hug, or a social kiss.

For most workers, there is no need for special precautions. Scientific studies do not indicate any risk of HIV infection from contact with body fluids or waste—feces, nasal fluid, saliva, sweat, tears, urine, or vomit—unless these contain visible blood. Workers (such as sanitation workers) who may handle fluids and waste that sometimes contain blood should wear rubber or vinyl gloves. Furthermore, hairstylists, cosmetologists, electrologists, or any workers who use instruments that can penetrate the skin or become contaminated with blood should sterilize those instruments or throw them away after one use.

It is important that employees and employers alike are educated about HIV/AIDS and how to help support co-workers infected with the virus. An effective HIV/AIDS policy should address such issues as:

- Insurance and health care costs
- Productivity
- Work disruption
- Employee benefits
- Customer concern
- Employee morale
- Legal considerations
- Confidentiality and privacy
- Discrimination concerns
- Disability requirements
- Job accommodation.

## Reducing the Risk of Infection

- Avoid direct contact with blood. Use a barrier such as a clean cloth or wear disposable latex or vinyl gloves to protect yourself from any blood.
- Wash your hands with soap and water as soon as you can after giving first aid, whether or not you have worn gloves.
- If you perform rescue breathing, avoid contact with any blood.
- When cleaning someone's blood from surfaces, always wear rubber gloves and use a disinfectant solution. If a disinfectant is not available, you can make one by mixing 1/4 cup of liquid household chlorine bleach with one gallon of water. (This solution must be made fresh just prior to use and discarded each day.)

*Source: The American Red Cross*

## Responding to AIDS: Ten Principles for the Workplace

The Citizens Commission on AIDS of New York City and New Jersey suggests the following policies be adopted:

- People with HIV infection or AIDS are entitled to the same rights and opportunities as people with other serious or life-threatening illnesses.
- Employment policies must, at a minimum, comply with federal, state, and local laws and regulations.
- Employment policies should be based on the scientific and epidemiological evidence that people with HIV infection or AIDS do not pose a risk of transmission of the virus to co-workers through ordinary workplace contact.
- The highest levels of management and union leadership should unequivocally endorse nondiscriminatory employment policies and education programs about HIV/AIDS.
- Employers and unions should communicate their support of these policies clearly, simply, and unambiguously.
- Employers should provide employees with sensitive, accurate, and up-to-date education about risk reduction in their personal lives.
- Employers have a duty to protect the confidentiality of employees' medical information.
- To prevent work disruption and rejection by co-workers of employees with HIV infection or AIDS, employers and unions should undertake education for all employees before incidents occur and as needed thereafter.
- Employers should not require HIV screening as part of pre-employment or general workplace physical examinations.
- In those special occupational settings where there may be a potential risk of exposure to HIV, employers should provide specific ongoing education and training, as well as necessary equipment, to reinforce appropriate infection-control procedures and ensure that they are implemented.

# Alcohol and Substance Abuse

ALL ALCOHOL AND SUBSTANCE ABUSE programs in work settings are called Employee Assistance Programs or EAPs. According to the U.S. Department of Labor, the use of EAPs has grown dramatically over the last decade. Although there is no standardized EAP, most are based on the assumption that helping employees with alcohol and substance abuse problems will reduce employee turnover as well as reducing absenteeism, tardiness, accidents, and other problems that affect productivity. Many of these programs are also concerned with ensuring efficient health-care cost containment and providing a new benefit to enhance employee morale and company commitment. Most companies employ one of the following four types of EAP:

- Internal company programs staffed by a company employee who accepts referrals from supervisors as well as self-referrals, conducts initial assessments, and refers employees to community resources for professional counseling or treatment.

- External company programs in which companies contract with outside agencies to provide most services. These are more common in small- and medium-sized firms.

- Labor union programs which usually revolve around a peer referral process that encourages union members with alcohol-use problems to seek help.

- Professional association programs which are usually aimed at maintaining standards of professional conduct. Threats to withdraw licensure are frequently used to pressure members into seeking assistance.

In most EAPs, alcohol and substance abuse problems are defined by poor job performance. Supervisors should confront employees constructively, demanding improved job performance as a condition of continued employment. Studies reveal that constructive confrontation rather than more severe forms of discipline leads to improvement in employee work performance.

In the last few years, more and more small- and medium-sized companies have begun investing their own resources in EAPs without any outside regulatory pressure from the government. This suggests the growing recognition among employers of the value of these efforts. The average annual cost for an EAP ranges from $12 to $20 per employee. Statistics from the National Council on Alcoholism and Drug Dependence indicate that an employer saves anywhere from $5 to $16 for every dollar invested in an EAP.

Establishing an EAP, however, is only one part of the way that a company can deal with substance abuse in the workplace.

## Five Steps to a Workplace Substance Abuse Program

### I. Write a clear and comprehensive policy

- Let employees and applicants know that drug and alcohol use on the job, or any use that affects job performance, is not permitted.

- Explain that you are establishing the policy for workplace safety, worker health, product quality, productivity, public liability.

- Tell employees what will happen if they violate the policy.

### 2. Train your supervisors. Supervisors should be responsible for:

- Observing and documenting unsatisfactory work performance or behavior;

- Talking to employees about work problems and what needs to be done about them;

- Supervisors are *not* responsible for diagnosing or treating substance abuse problems.

### 3. Educate your employees. An employee education and awareness program:

- Explains your workplace substance abuse policy and the consequences of using drugs and alcohol on or off the job.

- Tells your employees how to get help with their drug and alcohol problems, including a description of services available to help employees by a representative of the EAP, if the company has one, or by a community resource.

- Informs employees on how drugs and alcohol actually affect the company's productivity, product quality, absenteeism, health care costs, or accident rates.

- Explains testing procedures—if drug testing is part of the program—with special attention to the consequences of testing positive, and procedures for ensuring accuracy and confidentiality.

### 4. Provide an employee assistance program

### 5. Start a drug testing program

Some companies must set up a drug testing program because of the kind of work they do. The Drug-Free Workplace Act of 1988 is a federal statute requiring certain federal contractors and grantees to maintain a drug-free workplace. Companies covered by the act must have a single contract with the Federal Government of $25,000 or more, or must receive

*Alcohol and Substance Abuse (cont'd)*

a grant from the Federal Government. Any company that sets up a drug testing program must make sure that the program explains the:

- Statutory or regulatory requirements;
- Disability discrimination provisions;
- Collective bargaining agreements;
- Any other requirements in effect.

*Source: An Employer's Guide to Dealing with Substance Abuse, U.S. Dept. of Labor, October, 1990*

## Alternative or Complementary Strategies to EAPs

- Alcohol education in the workplace, directed both toward information about the effects of drinking and identification of problem drinking and alcoholism;
- Alcohol control policies associated with work, such as prohibited lunchtime drinking, limiting availability of alcohol in executive dining rooms, excluding alcohol at company-sponsored functions, and prohibiting reimbursement of employee expenses for the purchase of alcohol for themselves and their clients;
- Wellness programs, including health-risk appraisals, blood-pressure screening, and counseling of employees regarding health risks associated with different drinking lifestyles.

*Source: Alcohol Health & Research World, Vol. 13*

## Ten Facts About Alcohol and Substance Abuse in the Workplace

- 12 percent of the American workforce reports heavy drinking, defined as drinking five or more drinks per occasion on five or more days in the past 30 days.
- Up to 40 percent of industrial fatalities and 47 percent of industrial injuries can be linked to alcohol consumption and alcoholism.
- 70 percent of all current adult illegal drug users are employed.
- 63 percent of firms responding to a 1991 survey were engaged in some sort of drug testing, a 200 percent increase since 1987.
- Absenteeism among alcoholics or problem drinkers is 3.8 to 8.3 times greater than normal and up to 16 times greater among all employees with alcohol and other drug-related problems. Drug-using employees use three times as many sick benefits as other workers. They are five times more likely to file a workers' compensation claim.

- Non-alcoholic members of alcoholic families use ten times as much sick leave as members of families in which alcoholism is not present.
- 43 percent of CEOs responding to one survey estimate that use of alcohol and other drugs cost them one percent to ten percent of their payroll.
- For every dollar they invest in an Employee Assistance Program, employers generally save anywhere from $5 to $16. The average annual cost for an EAP ranges from $12 to $20 per employee.
- While roughly 90 percent of the Fortune 500 companies have established EAPs, this percentage is much lower among smaller companies. Only nine percent of businesses with fewer than 50 employees have EAP programs. Fully 90 percent of U.S. businesses fall into this category.
- A recent survey reports that nearly nine out of ten employers limit benefits for alcoholism, other drug dependence, and mental disorders despite the fact that 52 percent of the survey participants could not say how much it cost them to provide treatment for these conditions.

*Source: National Council on Alcoholism and Drug Dependence*

## Contact Options

Dr. Richard K. Fuller
Division of Clinical and Prevention Research
National Institute on Alcohol Abuse and Alcoholism
Willco Bldg., #505
6000 Executive Blvd.
Rockville, MD 20892
(301) 443-1206

Center for Substance Abuse Prevention
Workplace Helpline
(800) 843-4971
  Provides information and publications that will help companies research and develop drug-free workplace programs.

The National Association of State Alcohol and Drug Abuse Directors (NASADAD)
Drug-Free Workplace Project
444 N. Capitol St., NW, Suite 642
Washington DC 20001
(202) 783-6868

Center for Substance Abuse Treatment
National Treatment Referral Hotline
(800) 662-HELP
  Refers callers to treatment programs locally and nationwide.

# Workers' Compensation

IF A WORKER IS INJURED ON THE JOB, he or she cannot sue the employer for negligence. The exclusive remedy is workers' compensation. The worker gets no more if the employer is to blame and no less if he or she is at fault. Instead, the worker is entitled to medical care, certain wage replacement, or indemnity benefits, and, often, vocational rehabilitation, regardless of fault.

This is a state program, and laws vary greatly from one state to another. All states except New Jersey, South Carolina, and Texas require that every employer provides workers' compensation coverage. Very large employers usually choose to be self-insured while others purchase insurance from insurance companies or, in some states, from funds sponsored by the state or trade associations. In most states the price of workers' compensation insurance is set by the state, but an increasing number of states are allowing varying forms of price competition.

Workers receive a portion of their wages (usually two thirds) while they are recovering from an injury. These are called temporary total benefits. Very often the employee returns to work and there is no further problem. If that does not happen, temporary total benefits continue until maximum medical improvement occurs, or until the worker is medically stable. At that point most states make an assessment of whether the worker has a permanent impairment, and award additional benefits based on its severity. About ten states, however, base continuing benefits on the amount of the worker's wage loss rather than his or her degree of impairment.

Originally this was intended to be a simple system in which there would be no need for lawyers or formal litigation. Recently, however, workers have come to rely more and more on attorneys and employers have found the system increasingly more costly. It has become very popular for politicians to attempt to "reform" state workers' compensation laws. In some cases these changes have been successful and in others they have not.

Research in Michigan has shown that there is much employers can do to control their workers' compensation experience regardless of the laws. A study conducted by the Upjohn Institute examined 5,000 employers in 29 different industries. It found that in each of the 29 industries some employers had ten times as many claims as others. What made the difference? Three things seemed to stand out: safety, disability management, and the corporate culture.

## Ed Welch's Suggestions for Controlling Costs

- Safety is the first and most important approach. Nothing reduces costs more than preventing injuries from occurring.

- Create an atmosphere in which safety is important. Du Pont has 100,000 employees in the United States and it averages 30 lost claims per year. Safety has always been the most important aspect of its corporate culture.

- Return workers to the job as quickly as possible. Most workers want to go back during the first few weeks or months after an injury but if they are allowed to sit idle for several months their attitude changes. They begin to view themselves as disabled people who can never return to work.

- Most successful employers have very aggressive return-to-work programs which are designed to keep the worker in the habit of "getting up and brushing his teeth every morning."

- Larger employers often find it best to become self-insured and to take more control over their workers' compensation program.

- Smaller employers need to demand more service from their insurance companies. This might include help with safety and return-to-work programs and more active claims management.

- Employers should find out if price competition is allowed in their state and shop for the best deal. Note, however, that good service may be more important than a small difference in price.

- Employers and insurers should work together. If you have more than a few open claims you should expect your insurance company to meet with you a few times each year to discuss those claims and to plan what should be done about them.

Ed Welch teaches continuing education courses and publishes a newsletter on workers' compensation. For more information, he can be contacted at:

*Ed Welch on Workers' Compensation*
2875 Northwind Dr., Suite 210-A
East Lansing, MI 48823
(517) 332-5266

---

**FAX**    **Employer Costs.** Request #431. See p. xi for instructions.

Tables of employer costs for employee compensation and employees with pension plans or group health plans.

# Insurance

## Work Fatalities and Injuries

| Year | Employed Labor Force (millions) | Fatalities | Fatalities per 100,000 Workers | Injuries (millions) | Injuries per 100,000 Workers |
|------|------|------|------|------|------|
| 1960 | 65.8 | 13,800 | 21.0 | 1,950 | 2,964 |
| 1970 | 78.7 | 13,800 | 17.5 | 2,200 | 2,795 |
| 1980 | 99.3 | 13,200 | 13.3 | 2,200 | 2,216 |
| 1983 | 100.8 | 11,700 | 11.6 | 1,900 | 1,885 |
| 1984 | 105.0 | 11,500 | 11.0 | 1,900 | 1,810 |
| 1985 | 107.2 | 11,500 | 10.7 | 2,000 | 1,866 |
| 1986 | 109.6 | 11,100 | 10.1 | 1,800 | 1,642 |
| 1987 | 112.4 | 11,300 | 10.1 | 1,800 | 1,601 |
| 1988 | 114.3 | 11,000 | 10.0 | 1,800 | 1,565 |
| 1989 | 116.7 | 10,700 | 9.0 | 1,700 | 1,449 |
| 1990 | 117.4 | 10,500 | 9.0 | 1,800 | 1,527 |
| 1991 | 116.4 | 9,300 | 8.0 | NA | NA |
| 1992 | 117.0 | 8,500 | 7.0 | NA | NA |

*Source: National Safety Council*

## Economic Losses From Work Accidents

| Year | Loss ($ millions) | Loss in 1992 Dollars ($ millions) | Cost per Worker 1992 Dollars ($) |
|------|------|------|------|
| 1960 | 4,400 | 20,853 | 324 |
| 1970 | 8,000 | 28,881 | 372 |
| 1980 | 28,000 | 47,700 | 483 |
| 1983 | 31,200 | 43,944 | 439 |
| 1984 | 30,800 | 41,565 | 399 |
| 1985 | 35,000 | 45,632 | 429 |
| 1986 | 32,800 | 41,997 | 386 |
| 1987 | 39,800 | 49,136 | 440 |
| 1988 | 44,500 | 52,788 | 462 |
| 1989 | 48,500 | 54,864 | 470 |
| 1990 | 63,800 | 68,455 | 587 |
| 1991 | 63,300 | 65,191 | 560 |
| 1992 | 111,700* | 111,700* | 955* |

*\*Loss figures have been revised by adding new components, benchmarks, and inflation factors and are not comparable to prior years*

*Source: Insurance Information Institute, The Fact Book, 1994*

## Contact Options

Insurance Information Institute
110 William St.
New York, NY 10038
(212) 669-9200
    Provides information, analysis, and referral on insurance subjects.

Insurance Fund Foundation
13555 S.E. 36th St., Suite 105
Bellevue, WA 98006
(206) 747-6631
    Provides educational materials and programs to teachers, students, and general public.

National Insurance Consumer HelpLine
(800) 942-4292
    Provides basic information on all types of insurance.

National Safety Council
1121 Spring Lake Dr.
Itasca, IL 60143
(708) 285-1121
    Provides national support and leadership in the field of safety; publishes safety materials of all kind.

Risk and Insurance Management Society, Inc.
205 E. 42nd St.
New York, NY 10017
(212) 286-9292
    Generates information for insurers about the insurance needs of business and industry.

# Insurance Rating Agencies

THERE ARE FOUR NATIONAL RATING agencies that monitor the status of the country's insurance companies. The ratings are no guarantee of an insurer's strength. Most experts agree, however, that if an insurance company receives either the highest or the second highest grade from two or more of the major rating companies and receives no grade below the fourth level from any of the raters, the insurance policy or annuity is relatively secure.

A company can call A.M. Best Co. and Standard & Poor's to order their reports or can find the Moody's and Duff & Phelps reports in some public libraries.

## Recommended Resources

*The Insurance Forum*
P.O. Box 245
Ellettsville, IN 47429
(812) 876-6502
This monthly newsletter costs $60 and reports thoroughly on the insurance industry. Each year *The Insurance Forum* publishes a special ratings issue, containing the listings of hundreds of life insurance companies and how they are rated by A.M. Best, Standard & Poor's, Moody's, and Duff & Phelps. *The Insurance Forum* special issue can be purchased for $10.

A.M. Best
Ambest Rd.
Old Wick, NJ 08858
(908) 439-2200
A custom-generated report of all insurance companies in a particular category for a fee dependent on the breadth of the report.

Duff & Phelps
Rating Hotline
55 E. Monroe St., 35th Floor
Chicago, IL 60603
(312) 629-3833
Besides the quick information available via the hotline, an annual subscription to the Duff & Phelps insurance company/claims paying ability report is available for $695 per year.

Moody's Investor Service
Corporate Ratings Desk
99 Church St.
New York, NY 10004
(212) 553-0377
A caller can inquire about a maximum of three insurance company ratings per call, but is invited to call as many times as desired.

Standard & Poor's
Ratings Information Department
25 Broadway
New York, NY 10004
(212) 208-1527
In addition to their ratings information telephone service, Standard & Poor's publishes the *S&P Insurer Solvency Review*, which gives the annual ratings of several hundred insurance companies and costs $95.

## The Top Reference Sources

*Insuring Your Business*
Insurance Information Institute, $22.50
(212) 669-9200

This is an essential reference for anyone who is planning to open and insure a business. There are, among others, chapters on property insur-

ance, liability insurance, workers' compensation, insuring key employees, and employee benefits insurance. There are also sections on specific types of businesses, such as restaurants, manufacturers, construction firms, and trading companies.

# Health Insurance Coverage

IN SPITE OF ALL THE HOOPLA surrounding the health care plan President Clinton proposed in 1993, whatever the fate of his plan, or whichever health care plan finally passes, the legislation won't take effect for a long time to come. Meanwhile, employee health insurance coverage is an expensive investment for small business owners, and worthy of their most informed attention.

Every small business owner has unique needs when it comes to selecting a health insurance policy for employees. That is why it is so important for you to make an informed decision about the health insurance coverage you choose for yourself and your employees.

This section discusses the small group market, defines the basic choices and provides a checklist to help you compare policies you consider. A glossary is included as an easy reference to health insurance terms and common benefits.

If you come across terms not defined, call the National Insurance Consumer Helpline at (800) 942-4242. The Helpline staff will try to explain them, and answer any other questions you may have about health insurance.

## Small Group Health Insurance

"Small group" refers to the number of employees (sometimes 1 or 2, but most often between 3 and 25) covered under a company's group insurance plan.

In the small group market, health insurance prices are based mainly upon two factors. The first is the expected cost of medical services in a given geographic area; the second is the projected utilization of services. Usually, insurers estimate the probability of an insured person using medical services based upon factors such as age, sex, and medical history. These factors influence an insurer's charges to you and your employees. Often, those individuals who are considered a greater risk due to age or other factors will pay a higher premium for insurance. Of course, the type of benefit plan chosen also affects the premium.

Most small group health insurance companies use a process known as medical underwriting, which enables them to better predict claims. An underwriter analyzes a number of risk factors, including the medical history of each individual, to determine the group's insurability.

The insurer's goal is to offer coverage at a price that is fair to the insured group and to assure adequate income to pay future claims and other expenses.

## Private Commercial Insurance Options

Today, there are many options for the small group employer. It is important to be aware of the pros and cons of each choice when selecting a plan. While premiums can vary among different carriers, recog-

nize that there can be substantial differences in the covered benefits and in what your employees must pay out-of-pocket for medical services.

### I. Fee-for-service plans

Fee-for-service is the traditional form of commercial health insurance. Fee-for-service plans enable you to choose your own physicians and hospitals. Most of these plans require deductible and co-insurance payments.

Simply put, coverage results from your insurer's paying "reasonable and customary" or usual charges (i.e., reasonable compared with other providers in the same geographic area) for physician and hospital services. Typically, fee-for-service coverage for employer-sponsored health insurance has been characterized by three major features:

- Employers and employees share the premiums in most cases;

- Employees have complete freedom to select any medical care provider;

- The insurance company pays the allowable claim.

Fee-for-service coverage has dominated employee benefits packages for many years. In the past, fee-for-service coverage often did not include cost containment provisions, and the major advantage of these plans was the freedom for the consumer to choose providers.

Today, however, many fee-for-service plans also offer a wide variety of cost containment features. These plans can hold down costs for both the insurance company and the business owner, as well as encourage consumers to be efficient users of medical services.

### 2. Managed care options

A managed care health insurance plan integrates both the financing and the delivery of appropriate health care services to covered individuals. Managed health care plans are becoming more common among small groups. Today, more than 70 percent of Americans who obtain health insurance through their employers are enrolled in some type of managed care plan. Most managed care plans have the following basic characteristics:

- Arrangements with selected doctors, hospitals, and other providers to furnish a comprehensive set of health care services to members;

- Explicit standards for the selection of health care providers;

- Formal programs for quality assurance and utilization review;

- Significant financial incentives when using the specific providers and procedures associated with the plan.

*Health Insurance Coverage (cont'd)*

### 3. Fee-for-service with managed care features

These plans combine some of the features of managed care plans with traditional fee-for-service insurance arrangements. They hold down costs and discourage unnecessary use of services. Examples of managed care features that may appear in a fee-for-service plan include:

- Case management
- Centers of excellence
- Employee assistance plans
- Pre-admission certification
- Second surgical opinion
- Special benefit networks
- Utilization review.

## Preferred Provider Organizations (PPO)

A PPO typically consists of groups of hospitals and providers that contract with employers, insurers, third-party administrators, or other sponsoring groups to provide health care services to covered persons and accept negotiated fees as payment for services rendered.

There are different sponsoring arrangements:

- Hospital-sponsored PPOs, which often include a network of institutions in order to cover a wider geographic area, as well as many of the physicians on their medical staffs;

- Physician-sponsored PPOs, which are developed by local medical societies, local professional associations or clinics, or groups of physicians;

- Third-party payer-sponsored PPOs, which include those initiated by commercial insurers and Blue Cross and Blue Shield plans;

- Entrepreneur-sponsored PPOs, which create a broker relationship, with the entrepreneur acting as an intermediary between the provider and the payer of service;

- Employer- or labor-sponsored PPOs, which contract directly with providers on behalf of their employees or members;

- Other provider-sponsored PPOs, which are developed by non-hospital and non-physician providers, such as dentists, optometrists, pharmacists, chiropractors, and podiatrists, through their professional associations, local groups, or clinics.

## Health Maintenance Organizations (HMO)

This was the original managed care arrangement, first emerging as prepaid group practices in the 1930s. The name "health maintenance organization" was coined in the early 1970s, and was given to 1973 federal legislation promoting its development. HMOs constitute an organized system for providing, or assuring delivery of, health care in a certain geo-graphic area; they provide an agreed-on set of basic and supplemental health-maintenance and treatment services to a voluntarily enrolled group of people.

In exchange for a set amount of premium or dues, HMOs provide all the agreed-on health services to their enrollees; there are generally no deductibles and no, or minimal, co-payments. The HMO bears the risk if the cost of providing the care exceeds the premium received. There are now several types of HMOs:

- The staff model, where providers are directly employed by the HMO;

- The group model, where medical groups contract with the HMO (Kaiser plans are the best-known example of this type);

- The independent practice association (IPA), where the HMO contracts with physicians in independent practice, or with associations of independent physicians. IPA physicians frequently have arrangements with more than one HMO;

- The network model, which contracts to cover two or more independent practices.

## Choosing Quality Coverage

Choosing health insurance can be confusing because the health care marketplace constantly changes. Finding a policy that provides quality coverage for you and your employees and stays within your budget can seem impossible. It doesn't have to be—you simply need to find an agent with whom you are comfortable, and a plan that is backed by a reputable insurance company.

### I. Choosing an insurance agent or broker

Agents and brokers are licensed by the state to solicit and negotiate contracts of insurance and serve policyholders. Agents may represent one company or several companies. They earn commissions based on the policies they sell.

When choosing an agent you should:

- Consult relatives, friends, and business associates for referrals;

- Make sure the agent has been licensed by your state insurance department and is a full-time agent;

- Look for an agent with special professional qualifications or many years' experience. The best agents have specialized training in health insurance and other related subjects.

Health insurance agents do more than just sell policies; they are paid to provide service to their clients. Services you should expect from your agent include:

- Advising you on the right insurance policy to fit your special needs. The agent should ask enough questions to understand your entire insurance picture before advising you;

*Health Insurance Coverage (cont'd)*

- Explaining the cost and coverage of a policy you are considering;

- Keeping you informed about the new insurance plans that may be of interest to you;

- Reviewing your insurance every year to consider changes in your employees' financial or family status which may change your insurance requirements;

- Helping you handle claims, answering your questions, and helping you resolve any other insurance problems.

## 2. Choosing an insurance company

When you purchase insurance, you are buying the insurer's promise to make the payments as specified in the policy if you incur covered medical expenses.

In order to satisfy this promise, the company must be able and willing to pay the claim. The best way to investigate a company's ability to pay the claim is to check on its financial stability. (See Company Reliability/Rating below).

Checking the company's willingness to pay claims can be more difficult. The best source for this kind of information is your agent or a personal referral from someone who has had a policy with the company for some time and has filed several claims. Either can give you a sense of the "friendliness" of the company, its willingness to answer questions, and resolve complaints or problems.

Another good source of information is your state insurance department. The state insurance department regulates insurers and collects information about the number of complaints received about a particular company. Local consumer groups, newspaper columnists and Better Business Bureaus may have additional information specific to your area.

## 3. Company reliability/rating

The financial stability of your insurance company is an important indicator of its ability to pay your future claims. A number of financial publishing firms investigate and report their findings on the financial standing of specific insurance companies. Some of these firms are A.M. Best Company, Moody's Investor Service, Duff & Phelps, and Standard & Poor's Corporation. These reports are expensive but often are available in the reference sections in business and public libraries.

If you have trouble finding published information about an insurance company, ask your agent for information or call or write the company home office and ask for a copy of its most recent annual report or report from a rating firm. The company's earnings or losses will be reported, along with information about its cash reserves and liabilities.

It is important to find out if the company and agent are licensed to do business in your state. Your state insurance department is the source for this information. It requires the companies it licenses to file yearly financial reports, maintain legally required reserve funds, undergo periodic inspection audits, and comply with state laws regarding fairness.

## A Final Note

Remember that price alone is not the sole factor of good insurance protection. The service provided by the company and agent you select is important, too. Therefore, in making your choice, personal knowledge of both the company's and agent's reputation for good service is a significant consideration.

Beware, also, that quite a few small employer health benefit plans are sold through a multiple-employer trust (MET) or a multiple employer welfare association (MEWA). Care should be exercised with such programs, as many are uninsured, i.e., don't have the backing of a financially sound life and health insurance company. Such plans present a high risk to employers as there may be no assurance that adequate funds will be set aside to pay future claims.

*Source: Health Insurance Association of America*

# Glossary of Health Insurance Terms

*Case Management*
This is a process for directing the ongoing course of treatment to be sure that it occurs in the most appropriate setting and that the best form of service is selected. Case management often can produce alternatives to institutional care that result in better patient outcomes as well as lower costs.

*Centers of Excellence*
These are hospitals that specialize in treating particular illnesses, such as cancer, or performing particular treatments, such as organ transplants.

*Co-insurance*
Sometimes called "co-payment," it is the portion of covered health care expenses an insured must pay in addition to a deductible. Co-insurance is usually described as a percentage. For example, on a standard 80/20 co-insurance plan, the insurance company will pay 80 percent of covered expenses and the insured employee will pay 20 percent.

*Concurrent Review*
See Utilization Review.

*Glossary of Health Insurance Terms (cont'd)*

### Deductible

A deductible is the amount of covered expenses that the insured must pay in each benefit period before the insurer pays for allowable claims. A higher deductible will usually result in a lower premium.

### Employee Assistance Program (EAP)

An EAP is a generic term for the variety of counseling services made available to employees (and frequently their families) through an employer-sponsored program. These programs often refer employees to appropriate treatment.

### Fee-for-Service

Fee-for-service is a method of charging, whereby a physician or other practitioner bills for each visit or service. Premium costs for fee-for-service agreements can increase if physicians or other providers increase their fees, increase the number of visits, or substitute more costly services for less expensive ones.

### Health Maintenance Organization (HMO)

HMOs constitute an organized system for providing, or assuring delivery of, health care in a certain geographic area; they provide an agreed-on set of basic and supplemental health-maintenance and treatment services to a voluntarily enrolled group of people. In exchange for a set amount of premium or dues, HMOs provide all the agreed-on health services to their enrollees; there are generally no deductibles and no, or minimal, co-payments. The HMO bears the risk if the cost of providing the care exceeds the premium received.

### Indemnity

An indemnity is a benefit paid by an insurance policy for an insured loss. Often it is used to refer to benefits paid directly to the insured.

### Insurance Department

Each state has an insurance department that is responsible for implementing state insurance laws and regulations.

### Limitations

Limitations describe conditions or circumstances under which the insurer will not pay or will limit payments. Detailed information about limitations and exclusions is found in the certificate of insurance. An employer gets a group policy, with all details of the contract. An employee gets a booklet on the insurance, which is a more concise presentation of the insurance contract.

### Major Medical

Major medical insurance plans provide broad coverage and substantial protection from large, unpredictable medical care expenses. They cover a wide range of medical care charges with few internal limits and a high overall maximum benefit.

### Maximum Out-of-Pocket

The maximum amount of money an insured will pay in a benefit period, in addition to regular premium payments, is called the maximum out-of-pocket. The out-of-pocket payment is usually the sum of the deductible and co-insurance payments. Non-covered expenses are the employee's responsibility in addition to out-of-pocket amounts.

### National Association of Insurance Commissioners (NAIC)

This national organization of state insurance commissioners promotes national uniformity in the regulation of insurance. Each state has an appointed or elected commissioner.

### Pre-Admission Certification

See Utilization Review.

### Pre-Admission Testing

Tests taken prior to a hospital admission are called pre-admission tests.

### Pre-Existing Condition

A medical condition that existed before obtaining insurance coverage for which a reasonably prudent person would seek medical treatment is called a pre-existing condition. Examples of pre-existing conditions include a sickness, injury, or complication of pregnancy for which an insured person received medical advice, consultation, prescription drugs, or treatment during a specified time period before the effective date of coverage.

### Preferred Provider Organization (PPO)

A PPO consists of hospitals and providers that contract with employers, insurers, third-party administrators, or other sponsoring groups to provide health care services to covered persons and accept negotiated fee schedules as payment for services rendered.

### Premium

A premium is a periodic payment made by a policyholder (employer, individual) for the cost of insurance.

### Reasonable and/or Customary Charge

A charge for health care that is consistent with the going rate or charge in a certain geographical area for the same or similar services is called a reasonable and/or customary charge.

### Retrospective Review

See Utilization Review.

### Second Surgical Opinion

See Utilization Review.

### Special Benefit Networks

Special networks of providers for a particular service, such as mental health, substance abuse, or prescription drugs are known as special benefit networks.

*Glossary of Health Insurance Terms (cont'd)*

### State-Mandated Benefits

Each state requires insurance policies sold in that state to include benefits for a variety of medical conditions or providers. These mandated benefits can add to costs greatly. For example, an insurance policy may have to cover mental health or podiatry services.

### Third-Party Administrator (TPA)

A TPA is a company or broker that handles the administration of an insurance plan. Depending on the terms of its agreement with an insurance plan, a TPA may collect premiums, pay claims, and handle routine underwriting and administrative functions. The TPA typically acts on guidelines that the insurance plan establishes.

### Underwriting

The process by which an insurer determines whether and on what basis it will accept an application for insurance is called underwriting.

### Utilization Review (UR)

UR is a process that assesses the delivery of medical services to determine if the care provided is appropriate, medically necessary, and of high quality. Utilization review may include review of appropriateness of admissions, services ordered and provided, length of stay and discharge practices, both on a concurrent and retrospective basis. For example:

- Pre-Admission Certification: determines whether a hospital should admit a patient and whether services can be provided on an outpatient basis; its goal is eliminating unnecessary non-emergency procedures.

- Concurrent Review: includes continued-stay review of hospital cases, discharge-planning efforts to include proper and efficient placement of the hospital patient on discharge and case management.

- Retrospective Review: follow-up analysis that ensures medical care services were necessary and appropriate (to detect and reduce the incidence of fraud and unnecessary services).

- Second Surgical Opinion: a process that requires patients to obtain an opinion from a second doctor before certain elective surgeries. Insurers rely on second surgical opinion to eliminate unnecessary surgical procedures.

## Explanation of Common Benefits

### Ambulatory Care

Also known as outpatient care, ambulatory care is medical, surgical, or diagnostic services provided in a non-hospital setting, not requiring an overnight stay.

### Dental Care

This coverage provides reimbursement of dental services and supplies, including preventive care. Benefits may be provided through a plan integrated with other medical insurance coverage, or a plan may be written separately from other coverage (non-integrated).

### Diagnostic X-Ray and Laboratory Examinations

This coverage provides reimbursement for outpatient diagnostic and laboratory examinations.

### Home Health Care

Home Health Care services are given at home to aged, disabled, sick, or convalescent individuals who do not need institutional care. The most common types of home care are visiting nurse services and speech, physical, occupational, and rehabilitation therapy. Home health agencies, hospitals, or other community organizations provide these services.

### Hospice Care

Hospices care for the terminally ill and their families, in the home or a non-hospital setting, emphasizing alleviating pain rather than medical cure.

### Hospital Care

Both in-patient medical care expenses and out-patient medical care expenses incurred in a hospital are reimbursed under this coverage.

### In-Patient Benefits

- Charges for room and board

- Charges for necessary services and supplies sometimes referred to as "hospital extras," "miscellaneous charges," and "ancillary charges."

### Out-Patient Benefits

- Surgical procedures

- Rehabilitation therapy

- Physical therapy.

### Physician Visits

This coverage provides reimbursement for physician's fees for visits in cases of injury or sickness. The two types of plans commonly offered are one covering in-hospital visits only and the other that covers visits in-hospital and doctor visits out of the hospital setting.

### Pregnancy Care

Federal maternity legislation, enacted in 1978, requires that employers with 15 or more employees who are engaged in interstate commerce provide the same benefits for pregnancy, childbirth, and related medical conditions as for any other sickness or injury. This includes all employers who are, or become, subject to Title VII of the Civil Rights Act of 1964.

*Glossary of Health Insurance Terms (cont'd)*

*Prescription Drug Plan*
Some prescription drug expense insurance plans are subject to the same deductible and co-payments as are other covered medical expenses. Other plans use a prescription drug card and cover these expenses with very little, if any, cost to the insured.

*Rehabilitation Care*
A program of care that provides physical and mental restoration of disabled insured individuals to maximum independence and productivity.

*Skilled Nursing Facility*
A licensed institution engaged in providing regular medical care and treatment to sick and injured persons is known as a skilled nursing facility. The institution maintains a daily medical record and requires that each patient be under the care of a licensed physician.

*Supplemental Accident*
Many plans contain supplemental accident insurance that provides first dollar coverage (no deductible or co-payments) when an injury is due to an accident. Another type of accident plan pays a fixed dollar amount–$5,000 or $10,000, for example–if a serious accidental injury occurs.

*Vision Care*
This coverage is designed to provide benefits for preventive and corrective eye care. Insurers usually offer vision care with basic coverage such as hospital, surgical, medical, or X-ray and laboratory benefits.

# Checklist for Comparing Plans

THIS CHECKLIST CAN GUIDE your discussions with your broker or agent.

## I. Evaluating your company's needs

- Number of employees
- Number of dependents
- Sex of employees
- Age of employees
- Employees and dependents of childbearing age
- Employees/dependents with pre-existing medical conditions
- Employees with health problems making them high-risk
- Employees insured elsewhere.

## 2. Covered medical services

- In-patient hospital services
- Out-patient surgery
- Psychiatric and mental health care
- Drug and alcohol abuse treatment
- Skilled nursing care
- Home health care visits
- Rehabilitation facility care
- Hospice care
- Dental care
- Maternity care
- Supplemental accident
- Prescription drugs
- Vision care
- Preventive care and checkups
- Chiropractic care
- Physician visits
- Medical tests and X-rays
- Mammograms.

## 3. Are there medical service limits, exclusions, or pre-existing conditions that will affect employees?

## 4. What cost-containment and quality assurance procedures are included? (i.e., utilization review, pre-certification, second surgical opinions)

## 5. What is the total cost of the policy?

- Cost for the employer
- Cost for employees
- Single deductible
- Family deductible
- Co-insurance
- Single out-of-pocket maximum per year
- Family out-of-pocket maximum per year
- Share of premium.

## 6. Is the rate guaranteed? For how long?

## 7. What is the policy's lifetime maximum amount of coverage?

*Checklist for Comparing Plans (cont'd)*

8. What has the rate history been for comparable groups over the past five years and how is it calculated?

9. What will happen to premiums if one of the employees has a major claim?

10. How will service needs be handled?

11. Will the agent/broker or a customer service representative be available to meet with employees and dependents?

12. How long will it take to process a claim?

13. How often will the employer be billed?

14. Is the agent or broker qualified in the small group market? Does the agent or broker know about small group insurance?

- Good references
- Licensed in my state
- Professional qualifications
- Experience in the small group market
- Doing business for at least three years
- Member of recognized professional organization.

## The Top Reference Sources

Infolink
(914) 736-1565

This group of researchers uses databases, computers, and libraries to track down obscure information on almost any topic.

For a rate of about $60 an hour, they will research any question you need answered, from competitive pricing and market share to the best ways to design a playground.

# INTERNATIONAL

# Foreign Investors in the U.S.

THE MAJOR FOREIGN INVESTOR IN THE UNITED STATES is Japan, followed by the United Kingdom and the Netherlands. The United Kingdom and the Netherlands concentrate on manufacturing and petroleum while Japan is focused on trade, real estate, and financial services.

## Foreign Direct Investment Position in the United States, Historical-Cost Basis by Account

| Location | 1992 Total ($) |
|---|---|
| WORLD | 419,526,000,000 |
| Petroleum | 38,545,000,000 |
| Manufacturing | 159,492,000,000 |
| Wholesale trade | 56,936,000,000 |
| Other | 164,553,000,000 |
| Canada | 38,997,000,000 |
| Petroleum | 1,342,000,000 |
| Manufacturing | 17,313,000,000 |
| Wholesale trade | 1,495,000,000 |
| Other | 18,848,000,000 |
| Europe | 248,461,000,000 |
| Petroleum | 30,015,000,000 |
| Manufacturing | 113,595,000,000 |
| Wholesale trade | 21,699,000,000 |
| Other | 83,151,000,000 |
| Netherlands | 61,341,000,000 |
| Petroleum | 12,373,000,000 |
| Manufacturing | 21,442,000,000 |
| Wholesale trade | 4,895,000,000 |
| Other | 22,631,000,000 |

| Location | 1992 Total ($) |
|---|---|
| United Kingdom | 94,718,000,000 |
| Petroleum | 11,863,000,000 |
| Manufacturing | 42,208,000,000 |
| Wholesale trade | 5,367,000,000 |
| Other | 35,280,000,000 |
| Japan | 96,743,000,000 |
| Petroleum | -13,000,000 |
| Manufacturing | 19,149,000,000 |
| Wholesale trade | 30,831,000,000 |
| Other | 46,776,000,000 |
| Other areas | 35,325,000,000 |
| Petroleum | 7,201,000,000 |
| Manufacturing | 9,435,000,000 |
| Wholesale trade | 2,911,000,000 |
| Other | 15,778,000,000 |

*Source: Survey of Current Business, July 1993*

## Foreign Direct Investment in the United States, Historical-Cost Basis ($ millions)

The foreign direct investment position is calculated from the equity in, and net outstanding loans to, subsidiaries in the United States owned by foreign corporations. This is the foreign corporation's contribution to subsidiary assets.

| Country | 1988 | 1989 | 1990 | 1991 | 1992 |
|---|---|---|---|---|---|
| ALL COUNTRIES | 314,754 | 368,924 | 394,911 | 414,358 | 419,526 |
| CANADA | 26,566 | 30,370 | 29,544 | 37,301 | 38,997 |
| EUROPE | 208,942 | 239,190 | 247,320 | 251,248 | 248,461 |
| Austria | 392 | 386 | 625 | 488 | 387 |
| Belgium | 3,471 | 3,799 | 3,900 | 3,089 | 4,066 |
| Denmark | 588 | 656 | 819 | 1,301 | 1,308 |
| Finland | 452 | 1,297 | 1,504 | 1,305 | 1,385 |
| France | 13,233 | 15,365 | 18,650 | 24,155 | 23,808 |
| Germany | 25,250 | 28,386 | 28,232 | 28,618 | 29,205 |
| Ireland | 725 | 1,416 | 1,340 | 1,823 | 2,273 |
| Italy | 752 | 1,436 | 1,524 | 2,705 | 571 |
| Liechtenstein | 181 | 177 | 167 | 110 | 40 |
| Luxembourg | -131 | 407 | 2,195 | 937 | 543 |
| Netherlands | 48,128 | 56,734 | 64,671 | 59,355 | 61,341 |
| Norway | 220 | 576 | 773 | 561 | 625 |

*Foreign Investors in the U.S. (cont'd)*

| Country | 1988 | 1989 | 1990 | 1991 | 1992 |
|---------|------|------|------|------|------|
| Spain | 511 | 601 | 792 | 1,155 | 1,290 |
| Sweden | 4,713 | 5,435 | 5,484 | 5,684 | 6,923 |
| Switzerland | 14,372 | 18,746 | 17,674 | 19,189 | 19,562 |
| United Kingdom | 95,698 | 103,458 | 98,676 | 100,386 | 94,718 |
| Other | 388 | 316 | 295 | 385 | 416 |
| LATIN AMERICA AND WESTERN HEMISPHERE | 11,243 | 16,218 | 20,168 | 17,665 | 18,895 |
| SOUTH AND CENTRAL AMERICA | 4,331 | 5,819 | 6,140 | 7,020 | 7,378 |
| Brazil | 286 | 428 | 377 | 478 | 502 |
| Mexico | 218 | 350 | 575 | 708 | 1,184 |
| Panama | 2,878 | 3,392 | 4,188 | 4,841 | 4,732 |
| Venezuela | 540 | 1,163 | 496 | 538 | 502 |
| Other | 409 | 486 | 504 | 455 | 456 |
| OTHER WESTERN HEMISPHERE | 6,911 | 10,399 | 14,028 | 10,646 | 11,518 |
| AFRICA | 441 | 505 | 505 | 643 | 635 |
| MIDDLE EAST | 6,570 | 7,588 | 4,425 | 4,771 | 4,813 |
| Israel | 587 | 630 | 640 | 1,147 | 1,131 |
| Kuwait | 3,954 | 4,280 | 1,805 | 1,891 | 1,893 |
| Lebanon | -7 | -9 | -16 | -23 | -29 |
| Saudi Arabia | 1,826 | 2,455 | 1,811 | 1,598 | 1,642 |
| United Arab Emirates | 111 | 112 | 99 | 99 | 121 |
| Other | 100 | 119 | 86 | 59 | 56 |
| ASIA AND PACIFIC | 60,992 | 75,053 | 92,948 | 102,730 | 107,725 |
| Australia | 7,171 | 4,962 | 6,542 | 6,083 | 7,140 |
| Hong Kong | 895 | 1,124 | 1,511 | 1,763 | 1,714 |
| Japan | 51,126 | 67,268 | 83,091 | 92,896 | 96,743 |
| Korea, Republic of | 505 | -307 | -1,009 | -618 | -496 |
| Malaysia | 42 | 29 | 56 | 41 | 54 |
| New Zealand | 154 | 166 | 157 | 113 | 108 |
| Philippines | 73 | 82 | 77 | 54 | 59 |
| Singapore | 510 | 934 | 1,289 | 870 | 847 |
| Taiwan | 329 | 476 | 836 | 1,142 | 1,154 |
| Other | 186 | 318 | 398 | 386 | 402 |

*Note: Values for 1990 and 1991 are restated.*            *Source: Survey of Current Business, July 1993*

## The Top Reference Sources

*Business America*
U.S. Government Printing Office, $61/year
(202) 783-3238

Published biweekly by the U.S. Department of Commerce, this informative magazine is focused on international trade issues. Features include articles on the U.S. trade balance, exporting to Japan, economic reforms in Africa, and the outlook for stronger commercial ties with North Africa and the Near East.

The many contact names and numbers for government support throughout each issue are extremely valuable.

**FAX** **Foreign Buyers of U.S. Companies.** Request #923. See p. xi for instructions.
Table of foreign buyers: number of transactions, by country.

*Foreign Investors in the U.S. (cont'd)*

## Sales of U.S. Companies to Foreign Buyers: By Industry ($ millions)

| Industry Classification of Seller | 1989 | 1990 | 1991 | 1992 | 1993 |
|---|---|---|---|---|---|
| Communications | 1,912.0 | 217.8 | 266.0 | 3,604.0 | 3,407.3 |
| Banking & Finance | 3,191.4 | 150.0 | 767.9 | 207.0 | 817.1 |
| Drugs, Medical Supplies, & Equipment | 1,679.9 | 3,844.0 | 1,309.7 | 118.9 | 766.5 |
| Mining & Minerals | 246.3 | 1,489.0 | 218.8 | 413.0 | 722.4 |
| Plastics & Rubber | 311.6 | 76.8 | 12.9 | 95.0 | 720.0 |
| Beverages | 296.0 | 21.0 | 103.0 | 0.0 | 645.3 |
| Oil & Gas | 1,400.0 | 1,522.0 | 558.8 | 261.9 | 589.4 |
| Broadcasting | 0.0 | 0.0 | 0.0 | 77.0 | 462.0 |
| Chemicals, Paints, & Coatings | 3,203.9 | 1,060.4 | 388.2 | 901.7 | 376.5 |
| Autos & Trucks | 0.0 | 340.1 | 99.8 | 0.0 | 337.0 |
| Wholesale & Distribution | 407.3 | 280.0 | 314.0 | 59.8 | 323.4 |
| Toys & Recreational Products | 202.9 | 20.0 | 0.0 | 0.0 | 314.2 |
| Textiles | 195.2 | 0.0 | 0.0 | 0.0 | 310.5 |
| Electrical Equipment | 316.5 | 26.5 | 2,828.2 | 146.2 | 301.3 |
| Computer Software, Supplies, & Services | 355.0 | 197.7 | 52.5 | 35.0 | 297.9 |
| Food Processing | 3,925.1 | 1,052.6 | 440.0 | 445.9 | 285.0 |
| Office Equipment & Computer Hardware | 1,212.6 | 362.6 | 10.0 | 8.0 | 237.4 |
| Auto Products & Accessories | 1,244.0 | 380.0 | 0.0 | 170.0 | 216.3 |
| Valves, Pumps, & Hydraulics | 100.0 | 640.2 | 0.0 | 0.0 | 207.0 |
| Industrial & Farm Equipment & Machinery | 450.6 | 254.1 | 225.7 | 79.0 | 154.8 |
| Electric, Gas, Water, & Sanitary Services | 0.0 | 0.0 | 643.2 | 95.0 | 150.0 |
| Fabricated Metal Products | 2,078.9 | 567.5 | 1,226.5 | 43.6 | 139.5 |
| Stone, Clay, & Glass | 153.5 | 2,323.3 | 0.0 | 38.0 | 133.6 |
| Leisure & Entertainment | 4,023.4 | 8,029.5 | 204.9 | 35.0 | 109.1 |
| Printing & Publishing | 2,562.2 | 285.0 | 32.0 | 1,059.5 | 76.6 |
| Construction, Mining & Oil Equip., & Mach. | 0.0 | 21.1 | 0.0 | 0.0 | 60.0 |
| Timber & Forest Products | 0.0 | 0.0 | 0.0 | 0.0 | 54.0 |
| Transportation | 89.8 | 234.8 | 96.7 | 30.4 | 27.4 |
| Brokerage, Investment, & Mgmt. Consulting | 122.0 | 11.0 | 357.7 | 0.0 | 23.6 |
| Miscellaneous Services | 2,084.8 | 622.1 | 122.6 | 16.5 | 23.0 |
| Construction Contractors & Eng. Svcs. | 55.6 | 7.6 | 10.7 | 64.7 | 16.3 |
| Primary Metal Processing | 88.2 | 785.5 | 0.0 | 203.7 | 15.0 |
| Retail | 208.2 | 701.6 | 125.0 | 275.0 | 14.0 |
| Miscellaneous Manufacturing | 0.0 | 5.5 | 0.0 | 4.0 | 6.5 |
| Insurance | 611.2 | 4,688.1 | 1,251.5 | 20.0 | 5.0 |
| Instruments & Photography Equipment | 38.0 | 100.0 | 180.0 | 8.0 | 4.1 |
| Electronics | 970.3 | 221.5 | 114.9 | 3.7 | 2.4 |
| Aerospace, Aircraft, & Defense | 498.5 | 103.0 | 0.0 | 115.6 | 0.0 |
| Agricultural Production | 4.9 | 131.7 | 0.0 | 0.0 | 0.0 |
| Apparel | 604.0 | 125.0 | 0.0 | 61.5 | 0.0 |
| Building Products & Materials | 0.0 | 40.0 | 0.0 | 0.0 | 0.0 |
| Conglomerate | 0.0 | 0.0 | 0.0 | 0.0 | 0.0 |
| Energy Services | 0.0 | 193.0 | 0.0 | 0.0 | 0.0 |
| Furniture | 0.0 | 0.0 | 0.0 | 0.0 | 0.0 |
| Health Services | 1,241.1 | 293.0 | 257.0 | 118.1 | 0.0 |
| Household Goods | 207.0 | 1,250.0 | 0.0 | 0.0 | 0.0 |
| Packaging & Containers | 416.8 | 0.0 | 0.0 | 0.0 | 0.0 |
| Paper | 0.0 | 275.5 | 0.0 | 41.0 | 0.0 |
| Real Estate | 1,065.3 | 2.0 | 0.0 | 2.0 | 0.0 |
| Toiletries & Cosmetics | 2,254.2 | 107.0 | 43.0 | 445.3 | 0.0 |

*Source: Mergerstat[SM] Review*

*Foreign Investors in the U.S. (cont'd)*

## Industries Attracting Foreign Buyers: By Number of Transactions

| Industry Classification of Seller | 1989 | 1990 | 1991 | 1992 | 1993 | Five-Year Cumulative |
|---|---|---|---|---|---|---|
| Computer Software, Supplies, & Service | 5 | 13 | 4 | 6 | 15 | 43 |
| Wholesale & Distribution | 12 | 4 | 6 | 4 | 15 | 41 |
| Mining & Minerals | 4 | 6 | 5 | 5 | 12 | 32 |
| Drugs, Medical Supplies, & Equipment | 12 | 18 | 9 | 13 | 11 | 63 |
| Oil & Gas | 10 | 4 | 3 | 9 | 9 | 35 |
| Office Equipment & Computer Hardware | 8 | 8 | 5 | 4 | 8 | 33 |
| Retail | 9 | 8 | 1 | 2 | 8 | 28 |
| Miscellaneous Services | 21 | 17 | 12 | 9 | 7 | 66 |
| Banking & Finance | 13 | 4 | 11 | 3 | 6 | 37 |
| Brokerage, Investment & Mgmt. Consulting | 9 | 10 | 10 | 1 | 6 | 36 |
| Communications | 4 | 4 | 6 | 3 | 6 | 23 |
| Autos & Trucks | 0 | 3 | 2 | 0 | 6 | 11 |
| Chemicals, Paints, & Coatings | 15 | 17 | 14 | 6 | 5 | 57 |
| Industrial & Farm Equipment & Machinery | 6 | 8 | 7 | 6 | 5 | 32 |
| Plastics & Rubber | 8 | 6 | 3 | 4 | 5 | 26 |
| Stone, Clay, & Glass | 3 | 6 | 1 | 3 | 5 | 18 |
| Printing & Publishing | 19 | 4 | 7 | 6 | 4 | 40 |
| Leisure & Entertainment | 11 | 11 | 7 | 4 | 4 | 37 |
| Electrical Equipment | 5 | 6 | 9 | 11 | 4 | 35 |
| Primary Metal Processing | 7 | 7 | 1 | 6 | 4 | 25 |
| Construction Contractors & Eng. Svcs. | 4 | 5 | 5 | 5 | 4 | 23 |
| Electric, Gas, Water, & Sanitary Services | 1 | 0 | 3 | 4 | 4 | 12 |
| Broadcasting | 0 | 1 | 0 | 3 | 4 | 8 |
| Electronics | 16 | 13 | 9 | 3 | 3 | 44 |
| Food Processing | 11 | 13 | 6 | 7 | 3 | 40 |
| Beverages | 6 | 2 | 2 | 1 | 3 | 14 |
| Transportation | 2 | 5 | 2 | 1 | 3 | 13 |
| Textiles | 3 | 2 | 1 | 0 | 3 | 9 |
| Toys & Recreational Products | 3 | 2 | 0 | 0 | 3 | 8 |
| Insurance | 6 | 10 | 14 | 5 | 2 | 37 |
| Instruments & Photographic Equipment | 4 | 6 | 7 | 3 | 2 | 22 |
| Fabricated Metal Products | 4 | 7 | 5 | 3 | 2 | 21 |
| Automotive Products & Accessories | 7 | 5 | 0 | 5 | 2 | 19 |
| Timber & Forest Products | 1 | 0 | 0 | 0 | 2 | 3 |
| Health Services | 6 | 5 | 7 | 3 | 1 | 22 |
| Apparel | 3 | 1 | 0 | 5 | 1 | 10 |
| Miscellaneous Manufacturing | 0 | 2 | 1 | 2 | 1 | 6 |
| Construction, Mining & Oil Equip. & Mach. | 2 | 1 | 1 | 1 | 1 | 6 |
| Valves, Pumps, & Hydraulics | 1 | 1 | 0 | 0 | 1 | 3 |
| Toiletries & Cosmetics | 7 | 3 | 1 | 4 | 0 | 15 |
| Aerospace, Aircraft, & Defense | 3 | 4 | 1 | 3 | 0 | 11 |
| Real Estate | 5 | 1 | 0 | 2 | 0 | 8 |
| Agricultural Production | 2 | 5 | 0 | 0 | 0 | 7 |
| Paper | 0 | 4 | 0 | 2 | 0 | 6 |
| Household Goods | 3 | 1 | 0 | 0 | 0 | 4 |
| Packaging & Containers | 3 | 0 | 0 | 0 | 0 | 3 |
| Energy Services | 0 | 2 | 0 | 0 | 0 | 2 |
| Building Products & Materials | 1 | 1 | 0 | 0 | 0 | 2 |
| Furniture | 0 | 0 | 0 | 0 | 0 | 0 |
| Conglomerate | 0 | 0 | 0 | 0 | 0 | 0 |
| TOTAL | 285 | 266 | 188 | 167 | 190 | 1096 |

*Source: Mergerstat<sup>SM</sup> Review*

*Foreign Investors in the U.S. (cont'd)*

## Largest Foreign Acquisitions of U.S. Companies, Jan. 1986-Dec. 1993*

| Date | Acquirer Name | Target Name | Value of Deal ($ mil.) |
|------|---------------|-------------|------------------------|
| 03/31/89 | Beecham Group | SmithKline Beckman | 7,922.0 |
| 09/24/90 | Matsushita Electric Industrial | MCA | 7,406.0 |
| 01/24/88 | Campeau | Federated Department Stores | 6,511.9 |
| 10/04/88 | Grand Metropolitan | Pillsbury | 5,757.9 |
| 11/21/88 | Pechiney (France) | Triangle Industries | 3,658.0 |
| 09/04/86 | Campeau | Allied Stores | 3,584.1 |
| 01/18/90 | Rhone-Poulenc (France) | Rorer Group | 3,476.0 |
| 06/02/93 | British Telecommunications | MCI Communications | 3,465.2 |
| 08/07/91 | Altus Finance | Executive Life Insurance–Junk Bond | 3,250.0 |
| 06/30/93 | Hanson | Quantum Chemical | 3,219.7 |

*\* excludes spin-offs*      *Source: Securities Data Company*

# Trade-Weighted Dollar Exchange Rate

THE TRADE-WEIGHTED DOLLAR represents the foreign currency price of the U.S. dollar or the export value of the U.S. dollar. When these index numbers increase, the value of the dollar increases, making it easier for Americans to afford imports, but making American exports more expensive to those in other countries.

## Trade-Weighted Dollar Index

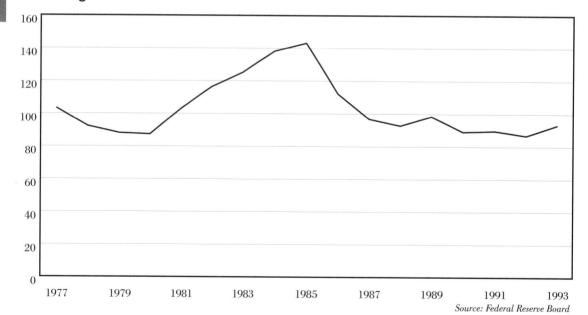

*Source: Federal Reserve Board*

**FAX** **Worldwide Gross Domestic Product.** Request #550. See p. xi for instructions.
Table of the gross domestic product for 24 major countries.

# Fortune's Top 50 Exporters

| 1992 Rank | Company | Major Exports | Exports ($ mil.) | % of Sales | Sales ($ mil.) |
|---|---|---|---|---|---|
| 1 | Boeing, Seattle, WA | Commerical aircraft | 17,486 | 58 | 30,414 |
| 2 | General Motors, Detroit, MI | Motor vehicles, parts | 14,045 | 11 | 132,775 |
| 3 | General Electric, Fairfield, CT | Jet engines, turbines, plastics, medical sys. | 8,200 | 13 | 62,202 |
| 4 | IBM, Armonk, NY | Computers, related equipment | 7,524 | 12 | 65,096 |
| 5 | Ford Motor, Dearborn, MI | Motor vehicles, parts | 7,220 | 7 | 100,786 |
| 6 | Chrysler, Highland Park, MI | Motor vehicles, parts | 7,052 | 19 | 36,897 |
| 7 | McDonnell Douglas, St. Louis, MO | Aerospace products, electronic systems | 4,983 | 29 | 17,513 |
| 8 | Philip Morris, NY | Tobacco, beverages, food products | 3,797 | 8 | 50,157 |
| 9 | Hewlett-Packard, Palo Alto, CA | Measurement and computation products | 3,720 | 23 | 16,427 |
| 10 | Du Pont, Wilmington, DE | Specialty chemicals | 3,509 | 9 | 37,386 |
| 11 | Motorola, Schaumburg, IL | Communications equipment, semiconductors | 3,460 | 26 | 13,341 |
| 12 | United Technologies, Hartford, CT | Jet engines, helicopters, cooling equipment | 3,451 | 16 | 22,032 |
| 13 | Caterpillar, Peoria, IL | Heavy machinery, engines, turbines | 3,341 | 33 | 10,194 |
| 14 | Eastman Kodak, Rochester, NY | Imaging, chemicals, health products | 3,220 | 16 | 20,577 |
| 15 | Archer Daniels Midland, Decatur, IL | Protein meals, vegetable oils, flour, grain | 2,700 | 29 | 9,344 |
| 16 | Intel, Santa Clara, CA | Microcomputer components, systems | 2,339 | 39 | 5,985 |
| 17 | Digital Equipment, Maynard, MA | Computers, related equipment | 1,900 | 14 | 14,027 |
| 18 | Allied-Signal, Morristown, NJ | Aircraft and automotive parts, chemicals | 1,810 | 15 | 12,089 |
| 19 | Unisys, Blue Bell, PA | Computers, related equipment | 1,796 | 21 | 8,422 |
| 20 | Sun Microsystems, Mtn. View, CA | Computers, related equipment | 1,784 | 49 | 3,628 |
| 21 | Raytheon, Lexington, MA | Electronic systems, engineering projects | 1,760 | 19 | 9,119 |
| 22 | Weyerhaeuser, Tacoma, WA | Pulp, newsprint, paperboard, logs, lumber | 1,500 | 16 | 9,260 |
| 23 | Merck, Rahway, NJ | Health care products, specialty chemicals | 1,490 | 15 | 9,801 |
| 24 | Minnesota Mining & Mfg., St. Paul, MN | Industrial, electronic, health care products | 1,433 | 10 | 13,883 |
| 25 | Westinghouse Electric, Pittsburgh, PA | Electrical products, electronic systems | 1,360 | 11 | 12,100 |
| 26 | IBP, Dakota City, NE | Fresh/frozen beef, pork, related by-products | 1,300 | 12 | 11,130 |
| 27 | Xerox, Stamford, CT | Copiers, printers, doc. processing, supplies | 1,292 | 7 | 18,089 |
| 28 | Dow Chemical, Midland, MI | Chemicals, plastics, consumer specialties | 1,247 | 7 | 19,080 |
| 29 | Textron, Providence, RI | Aerospace, commerical products | 1,244 | 15 | 8,348 |
| 30 | International Paper, Purchase, NY | Pulp, paperboard, wood products | 1,200 | 9 | 13,600 |
| 31 | RJR Nabisco Holdings, NY | Food, tobacco | 1,171 | 7 | 15,734 |
| 32 | Union Carbide, Danbury, CT | Chemicals, plastics | 1,125 | 18 | 6,167 |
| 33 | Compaq Computer, Houston, TX | Computers, related equipment | 1,104 | 27 | 4,132 |
| 34 | Hoechst Celanese, Bridgewater, NJ | Chemicals, plastics, fibers | 1,072 | 15 | 7,044 |
| 35 | FMC, Chicago, IL | Armored military vehicles, chemicals | 997 | 25 | 3,992 |
| 36 | Abbott Labs, Abbott Park, IL | Drugs, diagnostic equipment | 997 | 13 | 7,894 |
| 37 | Miles, Pittsburgh, PA | Chemicals, health care and imaging products | 956 | 15 | 6,499 |
| 38 | Apple Computer, Cupertino, CA | Computers, related equipment | 935 | 13 | 7,087 |
| 39 | Monsanto, St. Louis, MO | Food ingred., herbicides, chemicals, drugs | 927 | 11 | 8,485 |
| 40 | Bristol-Myers Squibb, New York, NY | Drugs, medical devices, consumer products | 915 | 8 | 11,805 |
| 41 | Exxon, Irving, TX | Petroleum, chemicals | 906 | 1 | 103,547 |
| 42 | Aluminum Co. of Amer., Pittsburgh, PA | Aluminum products | 886 | 9 | 9,588 |
| 43 | Georgia Pacific, Atlanta, GA | Pulp, building products, paper | 859 | 7 | 11,847 |
| 44 | Lockheed, Calabasas, CA | Aerospace products, missile systems | 831 | 10 | 10,138 |
| 45 | Honeywell, Minneapolis, MN | Building, industrial, aviation control systems | 830 | 13 | 6,254 |
| 46 | Cooper Industries, Houston, TX | Petroleum and industrial equipment | 805 | 13 | 6,159 |
| 47 | Cummins Engine, Columbus, OH | Diesel engines, diesel engine parts | 781 | 21 | 3,749 |
| 48 | Deere, Moline, IL | Farm, industrial equipment | 778 | 11 | 6,961 |
| 49 | Tenneco, Houston, TX | Farm, construction, auto equipment | 702 | 5 | 13,606 |
| 50 | Rockwell Intl., El Segundo, CA | Electronics, auto parts, printing presses | 701 | 6 | 10,995 |

*Source: Fortune, June 14, 1993, © Time, Inc. All rights reserved*

# Fastest-Growing Companies

## 50 Fastest-Growing American Companies with International Focus

| Company / Location / Phone | Type | 2-Year Growth (%) | 1992 Sales ($ mil.) | Foreign Markets | % Int'l |
|---|---|---|---|---|---|
| Electronics For Imaging<br>San Mateo, CA<br>(415) 286-8600 | Color processing software | 2,585.0 | 53.7 | Asia, Australia/New Zealand, Europe | 21.0 |
| Roberts Pharmaceutical<br>Eatontown, NJ<br>(908) 389-1182 | Pharmaceuticals | 1,471.4 | 33.0 | Canada, Europe | 28.5 |
| Reliv-International<br>Chesterfield, MO<br>(314) 537-9715 | Nutritional products | 1,368.2 | 32.3 | Australia/New Zealand, Canada | 22.6 |
| Cheyenne Software<br>Roslyn, NY<br>(516) 484-5110 | Networking software | 947.1 | 17.8 | Worldwide | 40.0 |
| Wellfleet Communications<br>Billerica, MA<br>(617) 275-2400 | Internetworking products | 734.3 | 85.1 | Asia, Canada, Europe | 25.0 |
| nView<br>Newport News, VA<br>(804) 873-1354 | Flat-screen projection systems | 536.4 | 28.0 | Asia, Canada, Europe, Latin America | 30.5 |
| Callaway Golf<br>Carlsbad, CA<br>(619) 931-1771 | Golf equipment | 514.4 | 132.1 | Asia, Australia/New Zealand, Canada, Europe, Latin America | 22.5 |
| Xircom<br>Calabasas, CA<br>(818) 878-7600 | Internetworking products | 479.4 | 59.1 | Worldwide | 42.0 |
| Cisco Systems<br>Menlo Park, CA<br>(415) 326-1941 | Internetworking products | 386.5 | 339.6 | Africa, Asia, Australia/New Zealand, Canada, Europe, Latin America, Middle East | 36.0 |
| Kaneb Services<br>Richardson, TX<br>(214) 699-4000 | Oil pipeline transportation | 331.0 | 176.7 | Europe | 49.5 |
| RHI Entertainment<br>New York, NY<br>(212) 977-9001 | Movies | 324.8 | 56.5 | Europe | 28.0 |
| Allied Research<br>Vienna, VA<br>(703) 847-5268 | Ammunition | 324.4 | 217.3 | Worldwide | 95.1 |
| Cannon Pictures<br>Beverly Hills, CA<br>(213) 966-5600 | Movies | 315.2 | 27.4 | Worldwide | 80.0 |
| Opti<br>Santa Clara, CA<br>(408) 980-8178 | Logic chips | 307.5 | 98.2 | Asia, Europe | 50.0 |
| PictureTel<br>Danvers, MA<br>(508) 762-5000 | Video communications | 282.2 | 141.4 | Africa, Asia, Australia/New Zealand, Europe, Latin America, Middle East | 35.0 |
| NetFRAME Systems<br>Milpitas, CA<br>(408) 944-0600 | Internetworking products | 258.7 | 39.1 | Asia, Europe | 33.0 |

*Fastest-Growing Companies (cont'd)*

| Company / Location / Phone | Type | 2-Year Growth (%) | 1992 Sales ($ mil.) | Foreign Markets | % Int'l |
|---|---|---|---|---|---|
| Bachman Info. Sys. Burlington, MA (617) 273-9003 | Software | 255.6 | 48.0 | Canada, Europe, Latin America, Middle East | 39.0 |
| CrossComm Marlborough, MA (508) 481-4060 | Internetworking products | 253.0 | 29.3 | Asia, Australia/New Zealand, E. Europe, Middle East, W. Europe | 22.5 |
| Trident Microsystems Mountain View, CA (415) 691-9211 | Semiconductors | 252.9 | 67.4 | Asia, Australia/New Zealand, Europe | 94.0 |
| Artisoft Tucson, AZ (602) 670-7100 | Networking software | 246.9 | 73.2 | Africa, Asia, Australia/New Zealand, Canada, Europe, Latin America | 26.5 |
| Parametric Technology Waltham, MA (617) 894-7111 | Mechanical design software | 240.0 | 86.7 | Asia, Australia/New, Zealand, Canada, E. Europe, W. Europe | 35.0 |
| SPI Pharmaceuticals Costa Mesa, CA (714) 545-0100 | Pharmaceuticals, medical instruments | 238.4 | 476.1 | Asia, Europe, Latin America, Middle East | 88.0 |
| Platinum Tech. Oakbrook Terrace, IL (708) 620-5000 | Software | 237.9 | 49.0 | Africa, Asia, Australia/New Zealand, Europe, Latin America, Middle East | 31.0 |
| Integrated Circuit Sys. Valley Forge, PA (215) 666-1900 | Semiconductors | 209.6 | 22.6 | Asia, Australia/New Zealand, Canada, Europe | 38.8 |
| VISX Santa Clara, CA (408) 733-2020 | Medical instruments | 207.6 | 20.3 | Asia, Canada, Europe | 72.0 |
| Chipcom Southborough, MA (508) 460-8900 | Internetworking products | 207.4 | 87.3 | Asia, Europe, Latin America | 41.3 |
| GulfMark International Houston, TX (713) 963-9522 | Pipeline engineering consulting | 206.7 | 23.0 | Asia, Europe, Latin America | 80.0 |
| Offshore Pipelines Houston, TX (713) 952-1000 | Pipeline services | 194.4 | 369.8 | Africa, Asia, Latin America, Middle East | 72.0 |
| Herbalife International Inglewood, CA (310) 410-9600 | Nutritional supplements | 188.9 | 214.4 | Asia, E. Europe, W. Europe | 78.7 |
| Standard Microsystems Hauppauge, NY (516) 273-3100 | Semiconductors | 187.9 | 250.5 | Asia, Canada, Europe | 43.9 |
| Synopsys Mountain View, CA (415) 962-5000 | CAD software | 185.1 | 63.0 | Asia, Canada, E. Europe, Middle East, W. Europe | 43.0 |
| VMARK Software Framingham, MA (508) 879-3311 | Systems software | 176.5 | 18.8 | Africa, Asia, Australia/New Zealand, Canada, Europe, Latin America, Middle East | 34.0 |
| Birtcher Medical Systems Irvine, CA (714) 753-9400 | Advanced surgical products | 172.9 | 52.4 | Asia, Europe, Latin America | 25.0 |
| Amtech Dallas, TX (214) 733-6600 | High-tech vehicle identification | 169.6 | 39.9 | Asia, Europe | 27.6 |

*Fastest-Growing Companies (cont'd)*

| Company / Location / Phone | Type | 2-Year Growth (%) | 1992 Sales ($ mil.) | Foreign Markets | % Int'l |
|---|---|---|---|---|---|
| Summit Technology Waltham, MA (617) 890-1234 | Medical instruments | 168.1 | 31.1 | Asia, Canada, Europe, Latin America | 50.8 |
| Microtest Phoenix, AZ (602) 957-6400 | Internetworking products | 167.7 | 26.5 | Worldwide | 32.0 |
| Amer. Power Conversion W. Kingston, RI (401) 789-5735 | PC power supplies, software | 166.0 | 157.5 | Asia, Canada, Europe, Latin America, Middle East | 32.0 |
| SSE Telecom McLean, VA (703) 790-0250 | Telecommun- ications | 157.1 | 23.4 | Asia, Australia/New Zealand, Canada, Europe, Latin America, Middle East | 67.0 |
| Sybase Emeryville, CA (510) 596-3500 | Database manage- ment software | 154.7 | 264.6 | Asia, Australia/New Zealand, Canada, Europe, Latin America | 23.0 |
| Ivax Miami, FL (305) 590-2200 | Chemicals, medical diagnostics | 153.8 | 451.0 | Africa, Asia, Europe, Middle East | 32.0 |
| Triconex Irvine, CA (714) 768-3709 | Safety-control software | 152.2 | 29.0 | Asia, Europe, Latin America, Middle East | 54.0 |
| Chiron Emeryville, CA (510) 655-8730 | Medical diagnostics | 150.5 | 248.2 | Asia, Europe | 23.5 |
| Digi International Eden Prairie, MN (612) 943-9020 | Data commun- ications | 149.1 | 57.8 | Worldwide | 26.0 |
| Netrix Herndon, VA (703) 742-6000 | Internetworking products | 145.3 | 31.4 | Africa, Asia, Australia/New Zealand, Canada, Europe, Latin America, Middle East | 62.0 |
| MicroTouch Systems Methuen, MA (508) 659-9000 | Touch-sensitive screens | 142.1 | 30.5 | Asia, Canada, Europe, Latin America | 32.0 |
| IDEXX Laboratories Westbrook, ME (207) 856-0300 | Medical diagnostics | 135.5 | 57.7 | Worldwide | 27.0 |
| Comverse Technology Woodbury, NY (516) 921-0470 | Fax, voice-mail messaging | 134.1 | 38.4 | Worldwide | 70.3 |
| Cabletron Systems Rochester, NH (603) 332-9400 | Internetworking products | 131.7 | 418.2 | Asia, Australia/New Zealand, Canada, Europe, Latin America | 29.5 |
| Computer Ntwk. Tech. Maple Grove, MN (612) 550-8000 | Internetworking products | 130.2 | 34.3 | Asia, Australia/New Zealand, Canada, Europe, Latin America | 23.0 |
| Network Comp. Devices Mountain View, CA (415) 694-0650 | Computer terminals | 130.0 | 120.3 | Africa, Asia, Australia/New Zealand, Canada, Europe, Latin America, Middle East | 34.0 |

*Note: Companies included generate more than 20% of sales internationally*　　　　*Source: International Business, January 1994*

# Exporting

GREAT POTENTIAL EXISTS for businesses in the United States to become more active in exporting. Only 15 percent of U.S. exporters account for 85 percent of the value of U.S.-manufactured exports. One-half of all exporters sell in only one foreign market. Fewer than 20 percent of exporters (less than three percent of U.S. companies) export to more than five markets.

Competing effectively abroad helps companies keep the edge they need at home. However, because there are real costs and risks associated with exporting, it is up to each company to weigh the necessary commitment against the potential benefit.

## Ten Recommendations for Successful Exporting

- Obtain qualified export counseling and develop a master international marketing plan before starting an export business. The plan should clearly define goals, objectives, and problems that may be encountered.

- Secure a commitment from top management to overcome the initial difficulties and financial requirements of exporting. Take a long-range view of this process.

- Select overseas distributors carefully. International communication and transportation require international distributors to act more independently than their domestic counterparts.

- Establish a basis for profitable operations and orderly growth. Unsolicited trade leads should not be ignored, but the successful exporter will not rely solely on these inquiries.

- Continue to pursue export business even when the U.S. market is healthy.

- Treat international distributors on an equal basis with domestic counterpart, offering similar advertising, special discounts, sales incentive programs, special credit terms, warranty offers, etc.

- Do not assume that a marketing technique that works in Japan will be equally successful in France. Treat each market individually to ensure maximum success.

- Be willing to adapt products to meet regulations or cultural preferences of other countries.

- Print service, sale, and warranty messages in local languages.

- Provide readily available servicing for the product.

*Source: A Basic Guide to Exporting*

---

 **FAX** **U.S. Direct Investment Abroad.** Request #227. See p. xi for instructions.

Tables of U.S. investment abroad, historical cost basis.

---

## The Top Reference Sources

*A Basic Guide to Exporting*
U.S. Government Printing Office, $9.50
(202) 783-3238
Stock #003-009-00604-0

This excellent publication of the U.S. Department of Commerce is designed to help companies learn the costs and risks associated with exporting and

develop a successful strategy. Reference appendixes include an export glossary, directory of federal export assistance, state and local sources of assistance, and U.S. and foreign contacts for major overseas markets. Topics discussed include preparing products for export, service exports, business travel, pricing, regulations, tax incentives, customs benefits, and financing.

# NAFTA

THE NORTH AMERICAN FREE TRADE Agreement was passed in November, 1993. Its objectives are:

- to eliminate barriers to trade in, and facilitate the cross border movement of, goods and services between the territories of the Parties [Canada, the United States, Mexico];

- to promote conditions of fair competition in the free trade area;

- to increase substantially investment opportunities in their territories;

- to provide adequate and effective protection and enforcement of intellectual property rights in each Party's territory;

- to create effective procedures for the implementation application of this Agreement, and for its joint administration and the resolution of disputes;

- to establish a framework for further trilateral, regional, and multilateral cooperation to expand and enhance the benefits of this Agreement.

*Source: Article 102, Objectives, North American Free Trade Agreement*

## NAFTA and Small Business

NAFTA provides the following for small businesses:

*Tariff reduction*
NAFTA removes Mexican tariffs on U.S. goods by the year 2009 (56 percent immediately and 98 percent by the year 2004) and Mexican customs users fees by 1999, allowing U.S. small businesses to export to Mexico more cheaply than before.

*Deregulation*
NAFTA removes regulations, such as licensing requirements, that hinder small businesses trying to enter the Mexican market.

*Intellectual property rights*
NAFTA enacts protection for intellectual property rights. The enforcement of these rights will help small business owners who are dependent on copyrights and patents.

*Customs regulations*
Under NAFTA, the United States, Canada and Mexico will all institute the same requirements for cus-

toms regulations, documentation, record keeping, and origin verification. This will make it easier and less expensive to export to Mexico and Canada.

*Services industries*
NAFTA will provide access to Mexico's $146 billion services market, including its financial, telecommunications and land transport sectors. The United States is the world's leading services provider—exporting $164 billion worth of services in 1991—and reducing trade barriers and modernizing the Mexican economy will accelerate Mexican consumer and business users needs for services.

*Government procurement*
NAFTA preserves U.S. minority and small business government procurement preferences and creates a trilateral commission to educate small and medium-sized businesses about the government procurement process and notify them of openings in each nation's market.

*Jobs*
NAFTA will remove trade barriers, allowing export-dependent jobs to grow. The Institute for International Economics predicts that by 1995, 1 million U.S. workers will owe their jobs to U.S. exports to Mexico.

*Latin America*
U.S. firms expanding into Mexico may increase their access to Central and South America as well through Mexico's existing linkages to Latin America.

*Source: The Small Business Advocate, Dec. 1993*

## Contact Options

U.S. Department of Commerce, Office of Canada
(202) 482-3103

U.S. Department of Commerce, Office of Mexico
(202) 482-0300

Flash Facts Canada (24-hour automated information line)
(202) 482-3101

Flash Facts Mexico (24-hour automated information line)
(202) 482-4464

# Small Business and Trade

NATIONAL SMALL BUSINESS UNITED and Arthur Andersen Enterprises Group conducted a survey of small and mid-sized businesses in June, 1993. The study focused in part on the businesses' position in the international market. The following graphs contain their findings:

## Scope of Marketplace

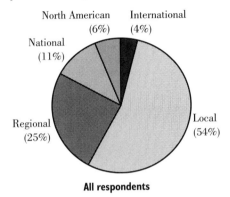

**All respondents**

## Businesses That Import

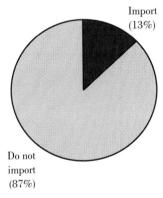

**All respondents**

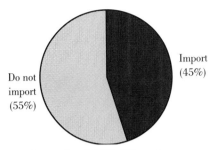

**Companies with 100–499 employees**

## Businesses That Export

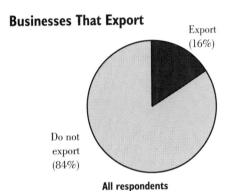

*Source: National Small Business United and Arthur Andersen Enterprises, June 1993*

*Small Business and Trade (cont'd)*

## Barriers to Exporting

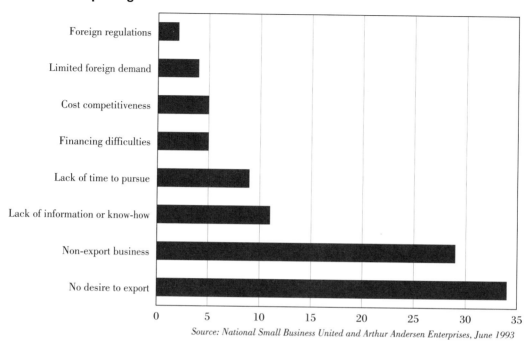

Source: National Small Business United and Arthur Andersen Enterprises, June 1993

# Top Ten Export Markets

## The United States' Top Ten Export Markets for Manufactured Goods

| Country | Cumulative to Date ($ billions) | Percent of Total |
|---|---|---|
| Canada | 100.2 | 21.55 |
| Japan | 47.9 | 10.32 |
| Mexico | 41.6 | 8.96 |
| United Kingdom | 26.4 | 5.68 |
| Germany | 19.0 | 4.08 |

| Country | Cumulative to Date ($ billions) | Percent of Total |
|---|---|---|
| Taiwan | 16.2 | 3.50 |
| South Korea | 14.8 | 3.18 |
| France | 13.3 | 2.85 |
| Netherlands | 12.8 | 2.76 |
| Singapore | 11.7 | 2.51 |

Source: U.S. Bureau of the Census, Foreign Trade Division, Dec. 1993

*SBA Online provides access to all kinds of information and downloadable files on Small Business Administration grants, loans, training programs, and seminars. Modem (800) 697-4636.*

# Methods of Payment Abroad

## Letters of Credit

The most secure and most often-used method of payment in export/import transactions is the documentary letter of credit. A letter of credit is a document issued by a bank on the instruction of a buyer of goods (importer), authorizing the seller (exporter) to draw a specified sum of money under specified terms, usually the receipt by the bank of certain documents within a given time.

Before payment, the bank responsible for making payment on behalf of the buyer verifies that all documents are exactly as required by the letter of credit.

If a U.S. exporter is unfamiliar with the credit risk of the foreign bank, or if there is concern about the political or economic risk associated with the country in which the bank is located, it is advised that a letter of credit issued by a foreign bank be *confirmed* by a U.S. bank. This means that the U.S. bank adds its pledge to pay to that of the foreign bank. Letters of credit that are not confirmed are called *advised* letters of credit. The local Department of Commerce district office or an international banker will help exporters determine whether a confirmed or advised letter of credit is appropriate for a particular transaction.

Letters of credit may be irrevocable (cannot be changed unless both the buyer and seller agree) or revocable (either party can make changes). An *at sight* letter of credit means that payment is made immediately upon presentation of documents. *Time* or *date* letters of credit specify when payment is to be made in the future.

Changes made to a letter of credit are called amendments. The fees charged by the banks involved in amending the letter of credit may be paid either by the buyer or the seller, but the letter of credit should specify which party is responsible. Since changes are costly and time-consuming, every effort should be made to get the letter of credit right the first time.

An exporter is usually not paid until the advising or confirming bank receives the funds from the issuing bank. To expedite the receipt of funds, wire transfers may be used. Bank practices vary, however, and the exporter may be able to receive funds by discounting the letter of credit at the bank, which involves paying a fee to the bank for this service. Exporters should consult with their international bankers about bank policy on these issues.

## Other Methods of Payment for International Transactions

### Cash in Advance (CIA)
Usually used only for small purchases and when the goods are built to order.

### Draft (or Bill of Exchange)
An unconditional order in writing from one person (the drawer) to another (the drawee), directing the drawee to pay a specified amount to a named drawer at a fixed or determinable future date. May be date, sight, or time draft.

### Credit cards
Used mainly in transactions where the dollar value of the items sold is low and shipment is to be made directly to the end-user.

### Open Account
The exporter bills the customer, who is expected to pay under agreed terms at a future date. Some of the largest firms abroad make purchases only on an open account, which is a convenient method of payment if the buyer is well established and has demonstrated a long and favorable payment record.

### Consignment Sales
Exporter delivers goods to an agent under agreement that the agent sell the merchandise for the account of the exporter. The agent sells the goods for commission and remits the net proceeds to the exporter.

### Countertrade/barter
Sale of goods or services that are paid for in whole or in part by the transfer of goods or services from a foreign country.

## Payment Problems

The best solution to a payment problem is to negotiate directly with the customer. If negotiations fail and the sum involved is large enough to warrant the effort, obtain the assistance of its bank, legal counsel, and other qualified experts. If both parties can agree to take their dispute to an arbitration agency, this step is faster and less costly than legal action. The International Chamber of Commerce handles the majority of international arbitrations and is usually acceptable to foreign companies because it is not affiliated with any single country.

*Source: A Basic Guide to Exporting*

## Contact Options

The International Chamber of Commerce
(212) 354-4480

American Arbitration Association
(212) 484-4000

Trade Remedy Assistance Office
International Trade Commission
(202) 205-2200

# U.S. Exports and Imports

## Exports and Imports by Principal SITC Commodity Groupings ($ millions)

| Item | 1993 Exports | 1993 Imports | 1992 Exports | 1992 Imports |
|---|---|---|---|---|
| TOTAL | 464,767.2 | 580,544.2 | 448,163.6 | 532,664.8 |
| AGRICULTURAL COMMODITIES | 41,820.8 | 23,646.3 | 42,237.7 | 23,374.9 |
| Animal feeds | 3,478.3 | 367.3 | 3,550.2 | 337.0 |
| Bulbs | 106.7 | 216.7 | 111.8 | 200.8 |
| Cereal flour | 1,072.1 | 801.8 | 924.4 | 723.9 |
| Cocoa | 39.2 | 739.3 | 30.6 | 774.4 |
| Coffee | 32.2 | 1,382.3 | 17.7 | 1,562.8 |
| Corn | 4,462.5 | 60.7 | 4,965.8 | 68.5 |
| Cotton, raw and linters | 1,540.7 | 12.4 | 2,014.6 | 11.4 |
| Dairy products, eggs | 774.6 | 544.0 | 710.5 | 506.3 |
| Furskins, raw | 96.7 | 59.0 | 95.4 | 61.3 |
| Grains, unmilled | 681.1 | 156.6 | 893.6 | 121.6 |
| Hides and skins | 1,188.8 | 119.7 | 1,252.8 | 124.0 |
| Live animals | 518.9 | 1,538.8 | 608.6 | 1,437.3 |
| Meat and preparations | 4,358.7 | 2,789.4 | 4,207.9 | 2,711.5 |
| Oils/fats, animal | 474.8 | 21.2 | 496.8 | 17.5 |
| Oils/fats, vegetable | 737.6 | 862.3 | 725.0 | 954.5 |
| Plants | 112.0 | 91.3 | 135.3 | 102.4 |
| Rice | 769.6 | 106.3 | 725.8 | 91.6 |
| Seeds | 298.2 | 154.4 | 302.4 | 152.8 |
| Soybeans | 4,626.5 | 22.2 | 4,462.8 | 15.8 |
| Sugar | 1.6 | 605.5 | 5.6 | 662.0 |
| Tobacco, unmanufactured | 1,306.1 | 943.6 | 1,649.1 | 950.8 |
| Vegetables and fruit | 6,010.3 | 5,665.6 | 5,736.3 | 5,697.6 |
| Wheat | 4,667.8 | 213.1 | 4,503.2 | 191.1 |
| Other agricultural | 4,465.8 | 6,172.8 | 4,111.6 | 5,897.9 |
| MANUFACTURED GOODS | 364,345.9 | 480,016.3 | 347,493.7 | 434,348.8 |
| ADP equip., office mach. | 27,167.2 | 43,182.3 | 26,999.9 | 36,377.1 |
| Airplane parts | 9,494.2 | 2,607.0 | 9,366.4 | 3,358.1 |
| Airplanes | 21,297.0 | 3,735.0 | 26,285.7 | 3,859.8 |
| Aluminum | 2,311.9 | 3,272.6 | 2,666.5 | 2,539.6 |
| Artwork/Antiques | 952.2 | 2,673.2 | 1,075.8 | 2,086.9 |
| Basketware, etc. | 1,644.7 | 2,391.1 | 1,522.0 | 2,188.8 |
| Chemicals | 6,821.2 | 2,940.6 | 6,264.6 | 2,622.4 |
| Chemicals–cosmetics | 3,043.0 | 1,809.3 | 2,631.5 | 1,711.4 |
| Chemicals–dyeing | 2,010.9 | 1,699.6 | 1,871.2 | 1,623.4 |
| Chemicals–fertilizers | 1,798.5 | 1,135.4 | 2,371.3 | 951.5 |
| Chemicals–inorganic | 3,812.9 | 3,285.2 | 4,122.8 | 3,305.0 |
| Chemicals–medicinal | 5,746.7 | 4,133.4 | 5,357.3 | 3,809.8 |
| Chemicals–organic | 11,090.2 | 9,316.0 | 10,992.6 | 9,408.1 |
| Chemicals–plastics | 10,742.4 | 4,846.7 | 10,257.9 | 4,292.0 |
| Clothing | 4,808.4 | 33,787.3 | 4,091.5 | 31,226.5 |
| Copper | 1,201.3 | 1,735.7 | 1,171.9 | 1,641.7 |
| Electrical machinery | 36,638.8 | 46,751.6 | 32,172.4 | 39,710.4 |
| Footwear | 604.3 | 11,175.9 | 603.4 | 10,163.4 |
| Furniture and parts | 2,770.9 | 6,249.4 | 2,553.0 | 5,502.5 |
| Gem diamonds | 152.9 | 5,098.6 | 368.7 | 4,147.8 |
| General industrial mach. | 19,519.0 | 17,083.8 | 18,479.6 | 15,519.7 |
| Glass | 1,321.0 | 1,004.2 | 1,213.1 | 849.7 |
| Glassware | 501.0 | 1,032.1 | 495.5 | 1,015.4 |
| Gold, non-monetary | 9,033.7 | 2,014.5 | 4,109.4 | 1,898.7 |
| Iron and steel mill prod. | 3,329.2 | 9,040.0 | 3,606.1 | 8,327.7 |
| Lighting, plumbing | 1,096.0 | 1,763.7 | 976.7 | 1,546.9 |
| Metal manufactures | 5,958.5 | 7,641.3 | 5,513.1 | 6,727.0 |
| Metalworking machinery | 3,262.0 | 3,674.5 | 3,033.9 | 3,187.0 |

*U.S. Exports and Imports (cont'd)*

| Item | 1993 Exports | 1993 Imports | 1992 Exports | 1992 Imports |
|---|---|---|---|---|
| Motorcycles, bicycles | 1,438.4 | 2,159.3 | 1,439.2 | 1,912.9 |
| Nickel | 199.3 | 685.7 | 195.6 | 797.0 |
| Optical goods | 796.0 | 1,682.5 | 766.4 | 1,645.1 |
| Paper and paperboard | 6,472.4 | 8,638.6 | 6,347.8 | 7,998.2 |
| Photographic equipment | 2,934.4 | 4,256.8 | 2,950.1 | 3,843.5 |
| Plastic articles | 2,987.5 | 3,935.2 | 2,776.9 | 3,571.9 |
| Platinum | 341.4 | 1,257.2 | 291.5 | 1,428.6 |
| Pottery | 110.2 | 1,433.8 | 103.4 | 1,404.2 |
| Power generating mach. | 19,132.4 | 17,162.7 | 17,994.7 | 15,888.1 |
| Printed materials | 3,982.2 | 2,027.3 | 3,803.3 | 1,875.3 |
| Records/magnetic media | 5,309.4 | 3,444.2 | 4,846.1 | 3,105.7 |
| Rubber articles | 673.8 | 1,014.2 | 621.8 | 877.7 |
| Rubber tires and tubes | 1,464.5 | 2,735.5 | 1,409.0 | 2,511.7 |
| Scientific instruments | 15,213.3 | 8,452.1 | 14,374.5 | 7,602.0 |
| Ships, boats | 978.4 | 969.3 | 1,421.0 | 319.4 |
| Silver and bullion | 202.3 | 391.1 | 209.4 | 449.2 |
| Spacecraft | 392.9 | 0.2 | 269.6 | 91.8 |
| Specialized ind. mach. | 17,634.5 | 13,545.9 | 16,688.5 | 11,814.4 |
| Telecommunications equip. | 13,070.7 | 27,302.5 | 11,247.8 | 25,802.8 |
| Textile yarn, fabric | 5,878.7 | 8,438.1 | 5,778.0 | 7,843.9 |
| Toys/games/sporting goods | 2,709.6 | 11,640.3 | 2,437.2 | 10,749.0 |
| Travel goods | 199.3 | 2,654.4 | 193.9 | 2,508.6 |
| Vehicles/chassis/bodies | 372.1 | 407.3 | 309.7 | 338.1 |
| Vehicles/new cars–Canada | 6,350.3 | 17,654.9 | 5,930.5 | 13,890.4 |
| Vehicles/new cars–Japan | 982.4 | 21,592.8 | 694.1 | 20,801.1 |
| Vehicles/new cars–Other | 4,976.3 | 12,055.3 | 5,095.3 | 11,561.3 |
| Vehicles/parts | 18,958.2 | 17,651.8 | 16,753.1 | 15,838.3 |
| Vehicles/trucks | 4,162.1 | 10,109.0 | 3,706.1 | 9,771.9 |
| Watches/clocks/parts | 235.4 | 2,549.0 | 207.6 | 2,320.1 |
| Wood manufactures | 1,475.8 | 2,868.5 | 1,389.4 | 2,409.7 |
| Zinc | 39.6 | 735.4 | 37.8 | 854.7 |
| Other manufactured goods | 26,542.1 | 35,485.4 | 27,030.7 | 32,923.9 |
| MINERAL FUEL | 9,735.6 | 55,582.3 | 11,254.1 | 55,255.6 |
| Coal | 3,198.4 | 512.7 | 4,427.0 | 419.1 |
| Crude oil | 20.2 | 38,437.6 | 32.4 | 38,553.1 |
| Electricity | 60.8 | 661.9 | 62.9 | 589.8 |
| Liquified propane/butane | 228.7 | 951.6 | 257.2 | 707.1 |
| Natural gas | 243.8 | 3,391.2 | 352.5 | 3,030.0 |
| Other mineral fuels | 2,062.0 | 831.1 | 2,110.8 | 679.5 |
| Petroleum preparations | 3,921.7 | 10,796.1 | 4,011.3 | 11,277.1 |
| SELECTED COMMODITIES | 2,984.6 | 5,820.2 | 3,382.9 | 5,657.3 |
| Alcoholic beverages, distilled | 2,769.2 | 1,687.1 | 2,800.6 | 1,596.9 |
| Cigarettes | 344.0 | 1,737.2 | 343.9 | 1,827.4 |
| Cork, wood, lumber | 2,986.2 | 1,886.9 | 3,859.2 | 2,129.4 |
| Crude fertilizers | 3,925.8 | 495.9 | 4,192.5 | 270.8 |
| Fish and preparations | 5,767.9 | 5,632.2 | 5,314.1 | 3,970.0 |
| Metal ores; scrap | 1,344.8 | 938.1 | 1,387.8 | 894.0 |
| Pulp and waste paper | 3,256.9 | 3,026.3 | 3,470.4 | 3,339.8 |
| ALL OTHER | 25,563.1 | NA | 22,426.7 | NA |
| RE-EXPORTS | 888.2 | NA | 893.2 | NA |

*Source: U.S. Bureau of the Census*

**FAX**   **U.S. Exports and Imports by Area.** Request #542. See p. ix for instructions.

Table of U.S. exports and imports for six major countries.

*U.S. Exports and Imports (cont'd)*

# Origin of Movement of U.S. Exports of Merchandise by State, 1993 ($ millions)

| Item | Manufactured Commodities | Non-Manufactured Commodities | Total Cumulative to Date |
|---|---|---|---|
| U.S. TOTAL | 423,200.9 | 41,566.1 | 464,767.2 |
| Alabama | 3,011.6 | 428.2 | 3,439.8 |
| Alaska | 983.4 | 1,528.5 | 2,511.9 |
| Arizona | 5,158.1 | 278.3 | 5,436.4 |
| Arkansas | 1,265.2 | 87.8 | 1,353.0 |
| California | 53,043.4 | 4,154.8 | 57,198.2 |
| Colorado | 2,962.5 | 102.7 | 3,065.2 |
| Connecticut | 5,152.3 | 366.7 | 5,519.0 |
| Delaware | 1,292.1 | 26.0 | 1,318.1 |
| Florida | 13,381.2 | 857.9 | 14,239.1 |
| Georgia | 6,176.4 | 646.1 | 6,822.5 |
| Hawaii | 208.8 | 51.0 | 259.8 |
| Idaho | 1,053.8 | 68.6 | 1,122.4 |
| Illinois | 15,804.3 | 619.2 | 16,423.5 |
| Indiana | 7,053.3 | 135.0 | 7,188.3 |
| Iowa | 2,604.9 | 174.2 | 2,779.1 |
| Kansas | 2,351.7 | 316.2 | 2,667.9 |
| Kentucky | 3,904.7 | 307.2 | 4,211.9 |
| Louisiana | 6,453.4 | 7,918.3 | 14,371.7 |
| Maine | 925.2 | 102.0 | 1,027.2 |
| Maryland | 4,141.8 | 234.6 | 4,376.4 |
| Massachusetts | 9,994.6 | 431.1 | 10,425.7 |
| Michigan | 22,780.2 | 418.1 | 23,198.3 |
| Minnesota | 5,714.7 | 513.7 | 6,228.4 |
| Mississippi | 1,603.6 | 83.6 | 1,687.2 |
| Missouri | 3,341.6 | 186.5 | 3,528.1 |
| Montana | 165.2 | 106.4 | 271.6 |
| Nebraska | 1,269.8 | 85.1 | 1,354.9 |
| Nevada | 510.9 | 28.0 | 538.9 |
| New Hampshire | 854.0 | 49.9 | 903.9 |
| New Jersey | 8,626.5 | 659.7 | 9,286.2 |
| New Mexico | 398.7 | 35.3 | 434.0 |
| New York | 26,590.0 | 1,779.9 | 28,369.9 |
| North Carolina | 8,910.9 | 978.1 | 9,889.0 |
| North Dakota | 327.4 | 80.9 | 408.3 |
| Ohio | 16,617.8 | 688.6 | 17,306.4 |
| Oklahoma | 2,029.9 | 70.8 | 2,100.7 |
| Oregon | 4,009.1 | 1,264.0 | 5,273.1 |
| Pennsylvania | 10,005.1 | 457.6 | 10,462.7 |
| Rhode Island | 759.6 | 133.0 | 892.6 |
| South Carolina | 4,378.3 | 136.3 | 4,514.6 |
| South Dakota | 235.5 | 18.6 | 254.1 |
| Tennessee | 5,254.1 | 343.1 | 5,597.2 |
| Texas | 42,255.0 | 3,035.1 | 45,290.1 |
| Utah | 2,044.3 | 323.0 | 2,367.3 |
| Vermont | 1,312.0 | 30.6 | 1,342.6 |
| Virginia | 7,448.0 | 1,604.1 | 9,052.1 |
| Washington | 23,982.8 | 2,641.3 | 26,624.1 |
| West Virginia | 932.2 | 491.0 | 1,423.2 |
| Wisconsin | 6,294.0 | 474.5 | 6,768.5 |
| Wyoming | 315.1 | 21.4 | 336.5 |
| Dist. of Columbia | 404.0 | 60.1 | 464.1 |
| Puerto Rico | 4,022.4 | 50.2 | 4,072.6 |
| U.S. Virgin Islands | 149.2 | 0.7 | 149.9 |

*Source: U.S. Bureau of the Census*

# Global High-Tech Markets

THE NATION'S COMPETITIVENESS in the global marketplace depends on its ability to sell products abroad and to compete against imports in the home market. According to studies by the National Science Foundation, the international market for high-tech goods is growing faster than that for other manufactured goods. The following charts provide a comparison of the leading three exporters.

## Global Market Share: Leading Exporters, by Industry (%), 1992

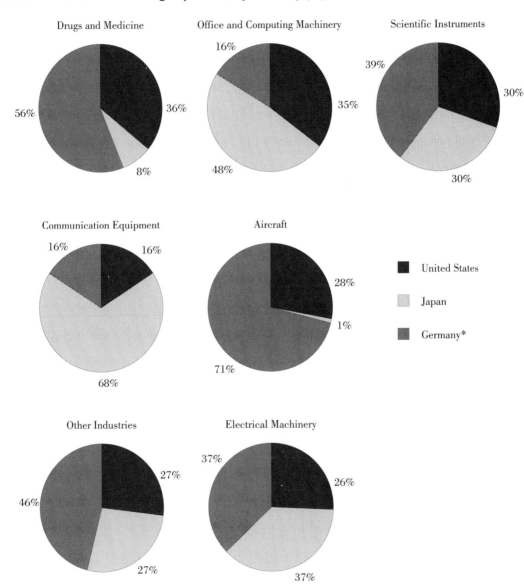

Drugs and Medicine

Office and Computing Machinery

Scientific Instruments

Communication Equipment

Aircraft

■ United States

▨ Japan

▩ Germany*

Other Industries

Electrical Machinery

*Germany refers to the former West Germany.

Note: Some figures do not add up to 100 due to rounding.

Source: National Science Board, Science & Engineering Indicators, 1993

*Global High-Tech Markets (cont'd)*

## Country Share of Global High-Tech Markets (%)

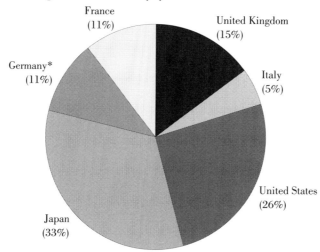

France
(11%)

United Kingdom
(15%)

Germany*
(11%)

Italy
(5%)

United States
(26%)

Japan
(33%)

*Germany refers to the former West Germany.*

*Source: National Science Board, Science & Engineering Indicators, 1993*

## Import Penetration of High-Tech Markets (% of home market supplied by imports), 1988

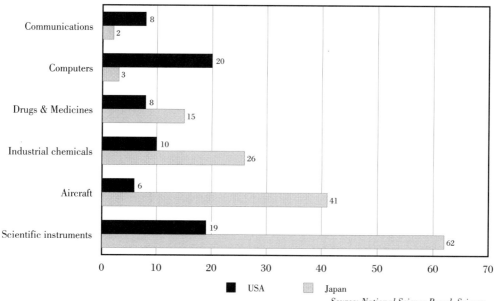

Communications — USA 8, Japan 2
Computers — USA 20, Japan 3
Drugs & Medicines — USA 8, Japan 15
Industrial chemicals — USA 10, Japan 26
Aircraft — USA 6, Japan 41
Scientific instruments — USA 19, Japan 62

■ USA    ▨ Japan

*Source: National Science Board, Science
& Engineering Indicators, 1992*

## The Top Reference Sources

*Journal of Commerce*, $325/year
(212) 837-7000

This daily magazine provides information on the
conditions and influences affecting national and
international commerce.

It covers a variety of topics including manufacturing, world trade, processing, shipping, foreign exchange, energy, and commodities. It also
reports on trade and investment studies within and
outside the U.S.

# Intellectual Property Exports

THE UNITED STATES IS A NET exporter of technology sold as intellectual property. Royalties and fees received from foreigners have been, on average, almost four times that paid out to foreigners by U.S. firms for access to their technology. Japan is the largest consumer of U.S. technology sold in this manner. While sales of technological know-how contribute positively to the balance sheets of U.S. firms and the U.S. economy in the short term, there has been ongoing controversy regarding the long-term consequences. The most recent statistics are reflected in the following graph.

## U.S. Royalties & License Fees Generated by the Exchange of Industrial Processes ($ millions)

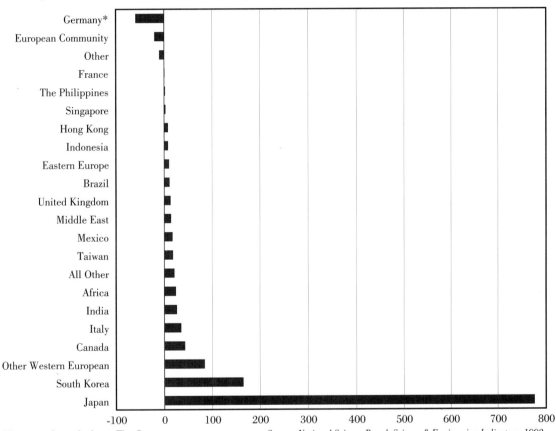

*Germany refers to the former West Germany.

Source: National Science Board, Science & Engineering Indicators, 1992

# Intellectual Property Protection

WHILE THE UNITED STATES HAS a long-standing tradition of protecting the intellectual property of its citizens, such protection is not offered by all foreign countries. The patents, trademarks, and copyrights of U.S. citizens are, at times, ignored in other countries and piracy and product counterfeiting result in a considerable loss of revenue for American companies.

Despite the efforts of the General Agreement on Tariffs and Trade (GATT), the Paris Convention for the Protection of Industrial Property (trademarks and patents), and the Berne Convention for the Protection of Literary and Artistic Works (copyrights), there is no uniform protection available to an individual whose invention, mark, literary works, or computer software might be used in foreign countries.

Property protection in a foreign country frequently is dependent upon the owner meeting the registration requirements of the individual country. Individual applications for patent protection, for example, must be filed in each country in which the patent owner desires protection, unless the country conforms to an international agreement. Usually a foreign patent agent or attorney is needed to execute the filing of the application in another country. The Patent Trade Office (PTO) will provide a list of individuals who are qualified to practice before the U.S. PTO and knowledgeable about foreign registration requirements.

More recent treaties, such as the Patent Cooperation Treaty, allow applicants from member countries to file one standardized international application to use in member countries in which intellectual property protection is desired.

Despite these strides in international cooperation, a number of countries are frequently cited as locations where property rights protection is often inadequate:

- Copyrights are inadequately protected in Brazil, China, India, Korea, Indonesia, Malaysia, Singapore, and Saudi Arabia.

- Patents are unprotected or inadequately protected in Indonesia, Mexico, Thailand, Brazil, India, Korea, Philippines, Singapore, Saudi Arabia, Taiwan, the United Arab Emirates, and China.

- Trademarks are inadequately protected in Brazil, India, Indonesia, Philippines, and Thailand.

- Product piracy and counterfeiting is a recurring problem in Taiwan, particularly with audio-visual materials.

A good source of information about protecting a business against foreign infringement of property rights is the U.S. and Foreign Commercial Service (US&FCS), which maintains 47 district offices and 20 branches in 67 cities around the United States. These offices are staffed by trade specialists and maintain business libraries of the latest reports of the Department of Commerce. For assistance, call the nearest Department of Commerce district office (see list this chapter) or call (800) 872-8723. The United States Patent Trademark Office will also provide additional information.

## Recommended Resources

*Copyrights, Patents & Trademarks*
by Hoyt L. Barber
Liberty Press, McGraw-Hill, $16.95
(800) 262-4729

*Exportise: An International Trade Source Book
for Smaller Company Executives*
The Small Business Foundation of America, $19.95
(202) 223-1103

---

## The Top Reference Sources

*The Multinational Executive Travel Companion*
Suburban Publishing, $60
(203) 324-6439

This is an indispensable resource for executives traveling overseas. Published annually, it includes 160 country profiles, with information on population, GNP, imports and exports, country affiliations, and trade groups.

The business traveler will also find listings of major companies' performances, weather conditions, time diffences, passport and visa requirements, postage, English-speaking physicians, embassies and consulates, tipping guidelines, travel and transportation tips, and more. Particularly useful are the listings of important addresses and phone numbers.

# Export Intermediaries

EXPORT MANAGEMENT COMPANIES and Export Trading Companies are firms that market American products and services abroad on behalf of manufacturers, farm groups, and distributors. These export intermediaries may handle products in a single sector, such as automotive equipment or clothing, or they may handle a variety of items from a number of different sectors. Intermediaries may service markets worldwide, or they may specialize in certain countries or regions.

Export Management Companies (EMC) help U.S. manufacturers establish an overseas market for the company's products, usually on an exclusive basis. The management company maintains a close relationship with its clients as well as with overseas distributors. Its business is supply-driven.

Management companies may take title to the products they sell, making a profit on the markup, or they may charge a commission, depending on the type of products being sold, the overseas market, or the manufacturer-client's needs. Export management companies may also work on a retainer basis.

In contrast, Export Trading Companies (ETC) most often act as independent distributors, bringing buyers and sellers together for a transaction. Business for ETCs is demand-driven and transaction-oriented. Most export trading companies take title to the products involved, but others may work on commission.

There are more than 1,500 ETCs and EMCs in the United States. Potential exporters should develop a list of those ETCs and EMCs which specialize in exporting the types of products proposed to be sold overseas.

For assistance in locating and selecting the proper ETC/EMC, contact the Commerce Department's Office of Export Trading Company Affairs, International Trade Administration, Washington, DC 20230, (202) 482-5131. Or, call a local office of the Small Business Administration or local World Trade Center (*see 402 and 404*).

*Source: Business America*

## Recommended Resources

*The Export Yellow Pages*
Office of Export Trading Company Affairs, free
International Trade Administration
Washington, DC 20230

This directory of more than 12,000 firms involved in foreign trade is designed to facilitate contact between producers of goods and services and firms providing export trade services. The directory is available free of charge from an ITA district office (*see 402*). Call the nearest Commerce Department district office to list your company in the next edition. For advertising information, call (800) 288-2582.

*Directory of Leading U.S. Export Management Companies*
Bergano Books, $49.50
P.O. Box 190
Fairfield, CT 06430
(203) 254-2054

Provides contacts, names, and addresses for 400 EMCs and 41 product categories. Geographic specialties and language capacities are also included. Lists export consultants. Cross-referenced by company name, state, and product category.

*Export Trading Company Guidebook, 1987*
U.S. Government Printing Office, $8.50
Washington, DC 20402
(202) 783-3238

*Export Profits*
Upstart Publishing, $19.95
Dover, NH 03820
(603) 749-5071

*Trading Company Sourcebook*
National Federation of Export Associations, $18
4905 Del Ray Ave., Suite 302
Bethesda, MD 20814
(301) 907-8647

Part yearbook of members of the Federation and part directory of EMCs and ETCs, this reference includes an index of companies by product specialization and specific examples of how these companies operate.

# Brokers and Forwarders

EVERY SHIPMENT ENTERING THE United States is subject to more than 500 pages of customs and tariff regulations. Customs brokers are import professionals, licensed by the U.S. Department of the Treasury, who have a thorough knowledge of these regulations, and who help clients choose the best modes of transportation, types of carriers, and shipping routes. Brokers also assist with exchange rates, appraisal, and determining proper classifications and duties. The broker's job often transcends the Customs Bureau, and involves contact with other government agencies such the USDA (for meat import questions), EPA (for vehicle emissions standards), or the FDA (product safety).

Ocean Freight Forwarders are licensed by the Federal Maritime Commission. Air Cargo or Air Transport Agents are accredited by the International Air Transportation Association. These freight forwarding professionals advise clients of the best rates, routings, and modes of transporting goods to or from any area in the world. Freight forwarders are experts on such items as foreign documentation requirements, hazardous materials regulations, special packaging or handling requirements, licensing provisions, etc.

The following licensed customs brokers and freight forwarders have been selected on the basis of range of services and the number of branch offices. The services provided include four or more of the following: Customs Broker (CB), Ocean Freight Forwarder (OFF), International Air Freight Forwarder (AFF), International Air Transport Agent (IATA), Container Station (CS), Drawback Specialist (DS), Steamship Agent (SA), Motor Property Broker (MPB), Non-Vessel Operating Common Carrier (NVO), Warehouseman (WH).

*Source: National Customs Brokers and Forwarders Association*

## Customs Brokers and Freight Forwarders in the United States

Air Express International
P.O. Box 1231
120 Tokeneke Rd.
Darien, CT 06820
AFF, CB, CS, IATA, OFF, WH
(203) 655-7900

Amerford International
One Cross Island Plaza
Rosedale, NY 11422
AFF, IATA, NVO, OFF
(718) 481-4200

Burlington Air Express
18200 Von Karman Ave.
Irvine, CA 92715
AFF, CB, DB, IATA, NVO, OFF, WH
(714) 752-1212

John V. Carr & Son
P.O. Box 33479
Detroit, MI 48232
AFF, CB, DB, IATA, MPB, NVO, OFF, WH
(313) 965-1540

Danzas
330 120th, NE
Bellevue, WA 98005
AFF, CB, IATA, MPB, NVO, OFF, WH
(206) 646-7171

A.N. Deringer
P.O. Box 1309
St. Albans, VT 05478
AFF, CB, CS, DB, IATA, MPB, NVO, OFF, WH
(802) 524-5975

Expeditors International of Washington
P.O. Box 69620
Seattle, WA 98168
AFF, CB, DB, IATA, MPB, NVO, OFF
(206) 246-3711

Fritz Companies
P.O. Box 7221
San Francisco, CA 94120
AFF, CB, DB, IATA, MPB, NVO, OFF, SA, WH
(415) 904-8200

The Harper Group
260 Townsend St.
San Francisco, CA 94107
AFF, CB, CS, DB, MPB, NVO, OFF, WH
(415) 978-0600

Intertrans
124 E. John Carpenter Freeway
Irving, TX 75062
AFF, CB, DB, IATA, MPB, NVO, OFF
(214) 830-8888

Norman G. Jensen
3050 Metro Dr., Suite 300
Minneapolis, MN 55425
AFF, CB, IATA, MPB, OFF
(612) 854-7363

The Myers Group
Myers Building
Rouses Point, NY 12979
AFF, CB, CS, DB, IATA, MPB, NVO, OFF, WH
(518) 297-2222

*Brokers and Forwarders (cont'd)*

Panalpina
Harborside Financial Center
Plaza Two, 34 Exchange Pl.
Jersey City, NJ 07311
AFF, CB, CS, DB, IATA, MP, NVO, OFF
(201) 451-4000

Schenkers International Forwarders
Exchange Place Centre
10 Exchange Pl., Suite 1500
Jersey City, NJ 07302
AFF, CB, IATA, MPB, NVO, OFF
(201) 434-5500

Tower Group International
128 Dearborn St.
Buffalo, NY 14207
AFF, CB, CS, DB, IATA, MPB, NVO, OFF, WH
(716) 874-1300

Yusen Air & Sea Service USA
60 E. 42nd St., Room 1915
New York, NY 10165
AFF, CB, IATA, OFF
(212) 983-1170

## Customs Brokers and Freight Forwarders Outside the United States

Affiliated Customs Brokers
411 Des Recollets
Montreal, PQ, Canada H2Y 1W3
AFF, CB, DB, IATA, OFF, WH
(514) 288-1211

Constantine Shipping and
International Services
10 Grafton St.
London, England W1X 3LA
AFF, OFF, SA
(01) 493-9484

Footwork-Hamacher GmbH
Martinistr. 24
P.O. Box 10 51 05
Bremen, Germany 1 2800
AFF, CB, CS, IATA, NVO, OFF, WH
421-33-77-60

A. Hartrodt GmbH & Co.
P.O. Box 10 29
Hamburg, Germany 1 0-200
AFF, CB, IATA, NVO, OFF
(040) 239-0383

Livingston Group
405 The West Mall, Suite 600
Toronto, ON, Canada M9C 5K7
AFF, CB, DB, IATA, MPB, NVO, OFF, WH
(416) 626-2828

Malenstein Rotterdam B.V.
Bergambachstraat 10
Rotterdam, Netherlands 3079 DA
AFF, CB, CS, DB, IATA, NVO, OFF, WH
010-492-8700

Naigai Nitto
38-8 Higashi-Shinagawa 1-Chome
Shinagawa-ku
Tokyo, Japan 140
AFF, CB, CS, IATA, MPB, NVO, OFF, SA, WH
(03) 3450-7400

Starber International
410 St. Nicholas St.
Montreal, PQ, Canada H2Y 2P5
AFF, CB, DB, IATA, NVO, OFF, WH
(514) 285-1500

Swift Freight International
Carrera (Bin Hendi Building)
Zabeel Road-Karama
P.O. Box 50177
Dubai, United Arab Emirates
AFF, CB, CS, IATA, NVO, OFF, WH
457 325

## Recommended Resource

*The Who's Who of Customs Brokers and International Freight Forwarders*
National Customs Brokers & Forwarders
Association of America, $20
One World Trade Center, Suite 1153
New York, NY 10048
(212) 432-0050

## Contact Options

U.S. Customs Service
1301 Constitution Ave., NW
Washington, DC 20229
(202) 927-2095

Federal Maritime Commission
800 N. Capitol St.
Washington, DC 20573
(202) 523-5725

International Air Transportation Association (IATA)
1001 Pennsylvania Ave., Suite 285N
Washington, DC 20004
(202) 624-2977

**TIP:** *The U.S. Department of Commerce has specialists from over 100 different industries who work with manufacturing and service industry associations and firms to identify trade opportunities and obstacles by product or service, industry sector, and market. Industry specialists develop export marketing plans and programs. Call (800) 872-8723 to contact a specialist.*

# Government Resources for Exporters

## Trade Information Center

Trade Information Center
Department of Commerce
Washington, DC 20230
(800) 872-8723

Established in the Department of Commerce, the Trade Information Center is the first point of contact for information on U.S. Government programs and activities that support exporting, including:

- Export counseling
- Seminars and conferences
- Overseas buyers and representatives
- Export financing
- Technical assistance.

## National Trade Data Bank

Department of Commerce
Washington, DC 20230
(202) 482-1986

Established by the Omnibus Trade and Competitiveness Act of 1988, the NTDB collects in one place the federal government's offerings of information on international trade, export promotion, trade contracts, country profiles, and other international economic data.

Each monthly NTDB disk sells for $35, and a 12-month subscription is available for $360.

## Trade with Eastern Europe and Selected Areas

The following offices have been established within the International Trade Administration to respond to the greatly expanded need for business information on new opportunities for trade and investment in selected parts of the world.

Eastern Europe Business Information Center
(202) 482-2645

The Baltics (Latvia, Lithuania, and Estonia) are now considered part of Eastern Europe.

Japan Export Information Center
(202) 482-2425

Latin America/Caribbean Business Dev. Center
(202) 482-0841

European Community Affairs
(202) 482-5276

The key Department of Commerce sources for information on trade potential for U.S. products in specific countries are the International Economic Policy Country Desk Officers. These specialists can identify the needs of an individual firm wishing to sell in a particular country in the full context of that country's economy, trade policies, political situation, and U.S. policies toward that country.

## Country Desk Officers

| Country | Desk Officer | Phone |
|---|---|---|
| Afghanistan | Timothy Gilman | (202) 482-2954 |
| Albania | Jeremy Keller | (202) 482-4915 |
| Algeria | Claude Clement | (202) 482-5545 |
| Angola | Finn Holm-Olsen | (202) 482-4228 |
| Anguilla | Michelle Brooks | (202) 482-2527 |
| Antigua/Barbuda | Michelle Brooks | (202) 482-2527 |
| Argentina | Randolph Mye | (202) 482-1548 |
| Armenia | Lynn Fabrizio | (202) 482-0988 |
| Aruba | Michelle Brooks | (202) 482-2527 |
| ASEAN | George Paine | (202) 482-3877 |
| Australia | Gary Bouck | (202) 482-2471 |
| Austria | Philip Combs | (202) 482-2920 |
| Azerbaijian | Lynn Fabrizio | (202) 482-0988 |
| Bahamas | Mark Siegelman | (202) 482-5680 |
| Bahrain | Claude Clement | (202) 482-5545 |
| Balkan States | Jeremy Keller | (202) 482-4915 |
| Bangladesh | John Simmons | (202) 482-2954 |
| Barbados | Michelle Brooks | (202) 482-2527 |
| Belarus | Christine Lucyk | (202) 482-1104 |
| Belgium | Simon Bensimon | (202) 482-5401 |

*Government Resources for Exporters (cont'd)*

| Country | Desk Officer | Phone |
|---|---|---|
| Belize | Michelle Brooks | (202) 482-2527 |
| Benin | Debra Henke | (202) 482-5149 |
| Bermuda | Michelle Brooks | (202) 482-2527 |
| Bhutan | Timothy Gilman | (202) 482-2954 |
| Bolivia | Rebecca Hunt | (202) 482-2521 |
| Botswana | Finn Holm-Olsen | (202) 482-4228 |
| Brazil | Larry Farris | (202) 482-3871 |
| Brunei | Raphael Cung | (202) 482-3877 |
| Bulgaria | Jeremy Keller | (202) 482-4915 |
| Burina Faso | Philip Michelini | (202) 482-4388 |
| Burma (Myanmar) | George Paine | (202) 482-3877 |
| Burundi | Philip Michelini | (202) 482-4388 |
| Cambodia | Hong-Phong B. Pho | (202) 482-3877 |
| Cameroon | Debra Henke | (202) 482-5149 |
| Canada | Jonathan Doh | (202) 482-3101 |
| Cape Verde | Philip Michelini | (202) 482-4388 |
| Caribbean Basin | Jay Dowling | (202) 482-1648 |
| Caymans | Michelle Brooks | (202) 482-2527 |
| Central African Rep. | Philip Michelini | (202) 482-4388 |
| Chad | Philip Michelini | (202) 482-4388 |
| Chile | Roger Turner | (202) 482-1435 |
| Colombia | Paul Moore | (202) 482-1659 |
| Comoros | Chandra Watkins | (202) 482-4564 |
| Congo | Debra Henke | (202) 482-5149 |
| Costa Rica | Mark Siegelman | (202) 482-5680 |
| Cuba | Mark Siegelman | (202) 482-5680 |
| Cyprus | Ann Corro | (202) 482-3945 |
| Czech Republic | Mark Mowrey | (202) 482-4915 |
| Denmark | Maryanne Kendall | (202) 482-3254 |
| Djibouti | Chandra Watkins | (202) 482-4564 |
| Dominica | Michelle Brooks | (202) 482-2527 |
| Dominican Republic | Mark Siegelman | (202) 482-5680 |
| East Caribbean | Michelle Brooks | (202) 482-2527 |
| Ecuador | Paul Moore | (202) 482-1659 |
| Egypt | Thomas Sams | (202) 482-1860 |
| El Salvador | Helen Lee | (202) 482-2528 |
| Equatorial Guinea | Philip Michelini | (202) 482-4388 |
| Eritrea | Chandra Watkins | (202) 482-4564 |
| Estonia | Pam Green | (202) 482-4915 |
| Ethiopia | Chandra Watkins | (202) 482-4564 |
| European Community | Charles Ludolph | (202) 482-5276 |
| Finland | Maryanne Kendall | (202) 482-3254 |
| France | Elena Mikalis | (202) 482-8008 |
| Gabon | Debra Henke | (202) 482-5149 |
| Gambia | Philip Michelini | (202) 482-4388 |
| Georgia | Lynn Fabrizio | (202) 482-0988 |
| Germany | Brenda Fisher | (202) 482-2435 |
| Ghana | Debra Henke | (202) 482-5149 |
| Greece | Ann Corro | (202) 482-3945 |
| Grenada | Michelle Brooks | (202) 482-2527 |
| Guadeloupe | Michelle Brooks | (202) 482-2527 |
| Guatemala | Helen Lee | (202) 482-2528 |
| Guinea | Philip Michelini | (202) 482-4388 |
| Guinea-Bissau | Philip Michelini | (202) 482-4388 |
| Guyana | Michelle Brooks | (202) 482-2527 |

*Government Resources for Exporters (cont'd)*

| Country | Desk Officer | Phone |
| --- | --- | --- |
| Haiti | Mark Siegelman | (202) 482-5680 |
| Honduras | Helen Lee | (202) 482-2528 |
| Hong Kong | Sheila Baker | (202) 482-3932 |
| Hungary | Brian Toohey | (202) 482-4915 |
| Iceland | Maryanne Kendall | (202) 482-3254 |
| India | John Simmons | (202) 482-2954 |
| Indonesia | Karen Goddin | (202) 482-3877 |
| Iran | Paul Thanos | (202) 482-1860 |
| Iraq | Thomas Sams | (202) 482-1860 |
| Ireland | Boyce Fitzpatrick | (202) 482-2177 |
| Israel | Paul Thanos | (202) 482-1860 |
| Italy | Boyce Fitzpatrick | (202) 482-2177 |
| Ivory Coast | Philip Michelini | (202) 482-4388 |
| Jamaica | Mark Siegelman | (202) 482-5680 |
| Japan | Edward A. Leslie | (202) 482-2425 |
| Jordan | Corey Wright | (202) 482-5508 |
| Kazakhstan | Pam Feodoroff | (202) 482-0360 |
| Kenya | Chandra Watkins | (202) 482-4564 |
| Korea | Jeffrey Donius | (202) 482-4390 |
| Kuwait | Corey Wright | (202) 482-5508 |
| Kyrgyzstan | Pam Feodoroff | (202) 482-0360 |
| Laos | Hong-Phong B. Pho | (202) 482-3877 |
| Latria | Pam Green | (202) 482-4915 |
| Lebanon | Thomas Sams | (202) 482-1860 |
| Lesotho | Finn Holm-Olsen | (202) 482-4228 |
| Liberia | Philip Michelini | (202) 482-4388 |
| Libya | Claude Clement | (202) 482-5545 |
| Lithuania | Pam Green | (202) 482-4915 |
| Luxembourg | Simon Bensimon | (202) 482-5401 |
| Macao | Sheila Baker | (202) 482-3932 |
| Madagascar | Chandra Watkins | (202) 482-4564 |
| Malawi | Finn Holm-Olsen | (202) 482-4228 |
| Malaysia | Raphael Cung | (202) 482-3877 |
| Maldives | John Simmons | (202) 482-2954 |
| Mali | Philip Michelini | (202) 482-4388 |
| Malta | Robert McLaughlin | (202) 482-3748 |
| Martinique | Michelle Brooks | (202) 482-2527 |
| Mauritania | Philip Michelini | (202) 482-4388 |
| Mauritius | Chandra Watkins | (202) 482-4564 |
| Mexico | Shawn Ricks | (202) 482-0300 |
| Moldova | Lynn Fabrizio | (202) 482-0988 |
| Mongolia | Sheila Baker | (202) 482-3932 |
| Montserrat | Michelle Brooks | (202) 482-2527 |
| Morocco | Claude Clement | (202) 482-5545 |
| Mozambique | Finn Holm-Olsen | (202) 482-4228 |
| Namibia | Finn Holm-Olsen | (202) 482-4228 |
| Nepal | Timothy Gilman | (202) 482-2954 |
| Netherlands | Simon Bensimon | (202) 482-5401 |
| Netherlands Antilles | Michelle Brooks | (202) 482-2527 |
| New Zealand | Gary Bouck | (202) 482-3647 |

*Government Resources for Exporters (cont'd)*

| Country | Desk Officer | Phone |
|---------|--------------|-------|
| Nicaragua | Jay Dowling | (202) 482-1648 |
| Niger | Philip Michelini | (202) 482-4388 |
| Nigeria | Debra Henke | (202) 482-5149 |
| Norway | James Devlin | (202) 482-4414 |
| Oman | Paul Thanos | (202) 482-1860 |
| Pacific Islands | Gary Bouck | (202) 482-2471 |
| Pakistan | Timothy Gilman | (202) 482-2954 |
| Panama | Helen Lee | (202) 482-2528 |
| Paraguay | Randolph Mye | (202) 482-1548 |
| People's Rep. of China | Cheryl McQueen | (202) 482-3932 |
| Peru | Rebecca Hunt | (202) 482-2521 |
| Philippines | George Paine | (202) 482-3877 |
| Poland | Audrey Zuck | (202) 482-4915 |
| Portugal | Mary Beth Double | (202) 482-4508 |
| Puerto Rico | Mark Siegelman | (202) 482-5680 |
| Qatar | Paul Thanos | (202) 482-1860 |
| Romania | Pam Green | (202) 482-4915 |
| Russia | Lynn Fabrizio | (202) 482-0988 |
| Rwanda | Philip Michelini | (202) 482-4388 |
| São Tomé & Principe | Philip Michelini | (202) 482-4388 |
| Saudi Arabia | Christopher Cerone | (202) 482-1880 |
| Senegal | Philip Michelini | (202) 482-4388 |
| Seychelles | Chandra Watkins | (202) 482-4564 |
| Sierra Leone | Philip Michelini | (202) 482-4388 |
| Singapore | Raphael Cung | (202) 482-3877 |
| Slovakia | Mark Mowrey | (202) 482-4915 |
| Somalia | Chandra Watkins | (202) 482-4564 |
| South Africa | Emily Solomon | (202) 482-5148 |
| Spain | Mary Beth Double | (202) 482-4508 |
| Sri Lanka | John Simmons | (202) 482-2954 |
| St. Barthélemy | Michelle Brooks | (202) 482-2527 |
| St. Kitts-Nevis | Michelle Brooks | (202) 482-2527 |
| St. Lucia | Michelle Brooks | (202) 482-2527 |
| St. Martin | Michelle Brooks | (202) 482-2527 |
| St. Vincent-Grenadines | Michelle Brooks | (202) 482-2527 |
| Sudan | Chandra Watkins | (202) 482-4564 |
| Suriname | Michelle Brooks | (202) 482-2527 |
| Swaziland | Finn Holm-Olsen | (202) 482-4228 |
| Sweden | James Devlin | (202) 482-4414 |
| Switzerland | Philip Combs | (202) 482-2920 |
| Syria | Corey Wright | (202) 482-5506 |
| Taiwan | Robert Ciro | (202) 482-4390 |
| Tajikistan | Pam Feodoroff | (202) 482-0360 |
| Tanzania | Finn Holm-Olsen | (202) 482-4228 |
| Thailand | Jean Kelly | (202) 482-3877 |
| Togo | Debra Henke | (202) 482-3317 |
| Trinidad & Tobago | Michelle Brooks | (202) 482-2527 |
| Tunisia | Corey Wright | (202) 482-5506 |
| Turkey | Anne Corro | (202) 482-3945 |
| Turks & Caicos Islands | Mark Siegelman | (202) 482-5680 |
| Uganda | Chandra Watkins | (202) 482-4564 |
| Ukraine | Christine Lucyk | (202) 482-1104 |
| United Arab Emirates | Claude Clement | (202) 482-5545 |
| United Kingdom | Robert McLaughlin | (202) 482-3748 |
| Uruguay | Roger Turner | (202) 482-1495 |

*Government Resources for Exporters (cont'd)*

| Country | Desk Officer | Phone |
|---|---|---|
| Uzbekistan | Pam Feodoroff | (202) 482-0360 |
| Venezuela | Laura Zeiger-Hatfield | (202) 482-4303 |
| Vietnam | Hong-Phong B. Pho | (202) 482-3877 |
| Virgin Islands (U.K.) | Michelle Brooks | (202) 482-2527 |
| Virgin Islands (U.S.) | Mark Siegelman | (202) 482-5680 |
| Yemen, Rep. of | Paul Thanos | (202) 482-1860 |
| Yugoslavia | Jeremy Keller | (202) 482-4915 |
| Zaire | Philip Michelini | (202) 482-4388 |
| Zambia | Finn Holm-Olsen | (202) 482-4228 |
| Zimbabwe | Finn Holm-Olsen | (202) 482-4228 |

## U.S. and Foreign Commercial Service

The US&FCS, a division of the U.S. Department of Commerce, maintains a network of locations throughout the world. Services for U.S. exporters include the following:

- Free General Export Support Services: includes product and/or country information, private counseling by appointment, trade statistics;

- Custom Support Services: may include surveys of potential sales representatives; interpreting and secretarial services; office space; market research; single-company promotional events; arranging appointments with local contacts;

- Product promotion (US&FCS will mail company brochures to potential clients and key industry associations);

- Customized Sales Survey (sales potential, competitors, normal sales channels, comparable product prices are all provided in a report on a particular product);

- Foreign Market Research (in-depth market data on selected products and industries, focusing on the best opportunities for U.S. goods);

- Agent/Distributor Service includes contacting potential agents and finally providing a list of six most interested and best-suited contacts for a specific product;

- Export Contact List Service (company profiles).

## Contact Options

U.S. and Foreign Commercial Service
Office of Domestic Operations
(202) 482-4767

U.S. and Foreign Commercial Service
Office of International Operations
(202) 482-6228

## US&FCS Overseas Posts

The following addresses are a combination of domestic and international information. Here are examples of ways to address an envelope depending on its origin and destination:

*Posts with APO/FPO Numbers:*

APO/FPO Address*
Organization
PSC or Unit number, Box number
APO AE 09080 or APO AA 34038 or
APO AP 96337

International Address**
American Embassy
P.O. Box 26431***
Manama, Bahrain

*Posts without APO/FPO Numbers:*

Diplomatic Pouch Address*
Name of Post
Department of State
Washington, DC 20521

International Address**
American Embassy
Jubilaeumstrasse 93***
3005 Bern, Switzerland

NOTE: Do not combine any of the above forms (e.g., international plus APO/FPO addresses). This will result in confusion and possible delays in delivery. Mail sent to the Department for delivery through its pouch system for posts with APO/FPO addresses cannot be accepted and will be returned to the sender.

\*  *Use domestic postage.*

\*\*  *Use international postage.*

\*\*\* *Use street address only when P.O. box is not supplied.*

*Albania*
(Tirane)
American Embassy Tirana Rruga
E. Elbansanit 103
PSC 59, Box 100 (A)
APO AE 09624
355-42-32875

*Algeria*
(Algiers)
4 Chemin Cheikh Bachir El-Ibrahimi
B.P. Box 549
Alger-Gare 16000
[213] (2) 601-425; 255; 186

*Government Resources for Exporters (cont'd)*

*Angola*
(Luanda)
Rua Major Kanhangulo
CP 6484
Pouch: American Embassy Luanda
Dept. of State, Washington, DC, 20521
[244] (2) 345-481

*Antigua and Barbuda*
(St. John's)
FPO AA34054-0001
(809) 462-3505/06

*Argentina*
(Buenos Aires)
4300 Colombia 1425
Unit 4334
APO AA 34034
[54] (1) 777-4533/4

*Armenia*
(Yerevan)
18 Gen Bagramian
7-8852-151-144

*Australia*
(Brisbane)
4th Floor
383 Wickham Terrace
Brisbane, Queensland 4000
Unit 11018
APO AP 96533-0002
[61] (7) 405-5555/6

(Canberra)
Moonah Pl.
Canberra, A.C.T. 2600
APO AP 96549
[61] (6) 270-5000

(Melbourne)
553 St. Kilda Rd.
P.O. Box 6722
Melbourne, Victoria 3004
Unit 11011
APO AP 96551-0002
[61] (3) 526-5900

(Perth)
13th Floor
16 St. Georges Terrace
Perth, WA 6000
Unit 11021
APO AP 96553-0002
[61] (2) 373-9200

(Sydney)
59th Floor, MLE Centre
19-29 Martin Pl.
Sydney N.S.W. 2000
Unit 11026
APO AP 96554-5000
[61] (2) 373-9200

*Austria*
(Vienna)
Boltzmanngasse 16
1-1091
Unit 27937
[43] (1) 313-39

U.S. Delegation to the Conference on Security
and Cooperation in Europe (CSCE)
Obersteinergasse 11
A-1190
[43] (1) 36-31-52

U.S. Mission to International
Organizations in Vienna (UNVIE)
Oberteinergasse 11
A-1190
[43] (1) 36-31-52

*Azerbaijan*
(Baku)
The Embassy is currently
located in the
Hotel Intourist
[7] 8922-92-63-06

*Bahamas*
(Nassau)
Queen St.
P.O. Box N-8197
(809) 322-1181

*Bahrain*
(Manama)
Building No. 979
Road 3119 (next to Al-Ahli Sports Club)
Zinj District
FPO AE 09834-5100
International Mail
P.O. Box 26431
[973] 273-300

*Bangladesh*
(Dhaka)
Diplomatic Enclave
Madani Ave.
Baridhara
G.P.O. Box 323
Dhaka 1212
[880] (2) 884700-22

*Barbados*
(Bridgetown)
P.O. Box 302
FPO AA 34055
(809) 436-4950

*Belarus*
(Minsk)
Starovilenskaya #46
[7] (172) 34-65-37

*Government Resources for Exporters (cont'd)*

*Belgium*
(Antwerp)
European Logistical Support Office
(ELSO)
Noorderlann 147
Bus 12A
B-2030
APO AE 09724
[32] (3) 542-4775

(Brussels)
27 Boulevard du Regent
B-1000
APO AE 09724
[32] (2) 513-3830

U.S. Mission to the European Communities (USEC)
40 Blvd. du Regent
B-1000
APO AE 09724
[32] (2) 513-4450

U.S. Mission to the North Atlantic Treaty
Organization (USNATO)
Autoroute de Zaventem
B-1110
APO AE 09724
[32] (2) 242-5280

(Lummen)
EURMAC
15 Klaverbladstraat
B-3560
APO AE 09724
[32] (013) 531-071

(Shape)
POLAD
B-7010
APO AE 09705
[32] (65) 4444471/4474

*Belize*
(Belize City)
Gabourel Land and Hutson St.
P.O. Box 286
APO Belize, Unit 7401
APO AA 34025
[501] (2) 77161

*Benin*
(Cotonou)
Rue Caporal Bernard Anani
B.P. 2012
[229] 30-06-50

*Bermuda*
(Hamilton)
Crown Hill, 16 Middle Road, Devonshire
P.O. Box HM325
Hamilton HMBX
PSC 1002
FPO AE 09727-1002
(809) 295-1342

*Bolivia*
(La Paz)
Banco Popular Del Peru Bldg.
Corner of Calles Mercado and Colon
P.O. Box 425
La Paz
APO AA 34032
[591] (2) 350251

*Bosnia-Herzegovina*
(Sarajevo)
AmEmbassy Bosnia
c/o AmEmbassy Vienna
Unit 27937
APO AE 09222
Vienna, Department of State
Washington, DC 20521
[43] (1) 31-399

*Botswana*
(Gaborone)
P.O. Box 90
[267] 353-982

*Brazil*
(Belem [CA and FCS Branch ])
Rua Osvaldo Cruz
165, 66017-090 Belem Para
[55] (91) 223-0800

(Belo Horizonte [USIS and FCS Branch, AV])
Alvares Cabral
1600 3 Andar - Belo Horizonte, MG
CEP 30170
[55] (31) 335-3555

(Brasilia)
Avenida das Nacoes
Lote 3
Unite 3500
APO AA 34030
[55] (61) 321-7272

(Fortaleza)
[55] (85) 252-1539

(Manaus)
Rue Recife 1010
Adrianopolois
CEP 69057-001
Manaus Amazonas
[55] (92) 234-4546

(Commerical Office)
Edifico Eloy Chaves Avenida
Paulista, 2439 Sao Paulo
APO AA 34030
[55] (11) 853-2011

*Government Resources for Exporters (cont'd)*

(Porto Alegre)
Rua Coronel Genuino
421 (9th Floor)
Unit 3504
APO AA 34030
[55] (51) 226-4288

(Recife)
Rua Goncalves Maia 163
APO AA 34030
[55] (81) 221-1412

(Rio de Janeiro)
Avendia Presidente Wilson 147
APO AA 34030
[55] (21) 297-7117

(Salvador da Bahia)
Av. Antonio Carlos Magalhaes
S/N - Ed. Cidadella Center 1
Sala 410
40275-440 Salvador, Bahia, Brazil
[55] (71) 358-9166

(São Paulo)
Rua Padre Joao Manoel, 933, 01411
P.O. Box 8063
APO AA 34030
[55] (11) 881-6511

*Brunei*
(Bandar Seri Begawan)
Third Floor-Teck Guan Plaza
Jalan Sultan
AMEMB Box B
APO AP 96440
[673] (2) 225-293

*Bulgaria*
(Sofia) 1 Saborna St., Unit 25402
APO AE 09213
[359] (2) 88-48-01

*Burkina Faso*
(Ouagadougou)
01 B.P. 35
[226] 30-67-23

*Burma*
(Rangoon)
581 Merchant St.
(GPO521)
AMEMB Box B
APO AP 96546
[95] (1) 82055

*Burundi*
(Bujumbura) B.P. 34
1720 Avenue des Etats-Unis
[257] 223-454

*Cambodia*
(Phnom Penh)
27 EO Street 240
Mail:
Box P
APO AP 96546
(855) 23-26436

*Cameroon*
(Yaounde)
Re Nachtigal
B.P. 817
[237] 23-40-14

*Canada*
(Calgary, Alberta)
Suite 1050
615 Macleod Trail S.E.
T2G 4T8
(403) 266-8962

(Halifax, Nova Scotia)
Suite 910
Cogswell Tower, Scotia Sq.
B3J 3K1
(902) 429-2480

(Montreal, Quebec)
P.O. Box 65
Postal Station Desjardins
H5B 1G1
P.O. Box 847
Champlain, NY 12919
(514) 398-9695

## The Top Reference Sources

*International Business*
American International Publishing, $48/ year
(914) 381-7700

This impressive magazine is loaded with information for businesses participating in the global marketplace. Features include articles on the use of bar codes to keep track of overseas shipments, why the weak dollar isn't helping U.S. export sales, and how Japan's recession has drastically cut Asian venture capital into U.S. companies.

A special highlight is *International Business'* Top 100, a ranking of America's fastest-growing mid-size international companies.

*Government Resources for Exporters (cont'd)*

U.S. Mission to the International Civil Aviation
Organization (ICAO)
1000 Sherbrooke St.
West Room 753
Montreal, Quebec
P.O. Box 847
Champlain, NY 12919
(514) 285-8304

(Ottawa, Ontario)
100 Wellington St.
K1P 5T1
P.O. BOX 5000
Ogdensburg, NY 13669
(613) 238-5335

(Quebec City, Quebec)
2 Place Terrasse Dufferin
C. P. 939
G1R 4T9
P.O. Box 1547
Champlain, NY 12919
(418) 692-2095

(Toronto, Ontario)
360 University Ave.
M5G 1S4
P.O. Box 135
Lewiston, NY 14092
(416) 595-1700

(Vancouver, British Columbia)
1095 West Pender St.
V6E 2M6
P.O. Box 5002
Point Roberts, WA 98281
(604) 685-4311

*Republic of Cape Verde*
(Praia)
Rua Abilio Macedo 81
C.P. 201
[238] 61-56-16

*Central African Republic*
(Bangui)
Avenue David Dacko
B.P. 924
[236] 61-02-00

*Chad*
(N'Djamena)
Ave. Felix Eboue
B.P. 413
[235] 51-62-18

*Chile*
(Santiago)
Codina Bldg.
Agustians 1343
Unit 4127
APO AA 34033
[56] (2) 671-0133

*China*
(Beijing)
Xiu Shui Bei Jie 3
100600
PSC 461, Box 50
FPO AP 96521-0002
[86] (1) 532-3831

(Chengdu)
Renmin Na Lu-Duan 4
Lingshiquan Lu
Chengdu 610041
PSC 461, Box 85
FPO AP 96521-0002
[86] (28) 582-2222

(Guangzhou)
No. 1 S. Shamian St.
Shamian Island
Guangzhou 510133
PSC 461, Box 100
FPO AP 96521-0002
[86] (20) 888-8911

(Shanghai)
1469 Huai Hai Middle Rd.
PSC 461, Box 200
FPO AP 96521-0002
[86] (21) 433-6880

(Shenyang)
52 14th Wei Rd.
Heping District 110003
PSC 461, Box 45
FPO AP 96521-0002
[86] (24) 282-0000

*Colombia*
(Barranquilla)
Calle 77 Carrera 68
Centro Comercial Mayorista
Apartado Aereo 51565
APO AA 34038
[57] (58) 45-8480

(Bogota)
Calle 38, No. 8-61
Apartado Aereo 3831
APO AA 34038
[57] (1) 320 1300

*Republic of the Congo*
(Brazzaville)
Avenue Amilcar Cabral
B.P. 1015
[242] 83-20-70

*Costa Rica*
(San Jose)
Pavas, San Jose
APO AA 34020
[506] 20-39-39

*Government Resources for Exporters (cont'd)*

*Cote D'Ivoire*
(formerly Ivory Coast)
(Abidjan)
5 Rue Jesse Owens
01 B.P. 1712
[225] 21-09-79

(African Development Bank/Fund)
Ave. Joseph Anoma
01 B.P. 1387
Agidjan 01
[225] 20-44-44

*Croatia*
(Zagreb)
Andrije Hebranga 2
Unit 25402
APO AE 09213
[38] (41) 444-800

*Cuba*
(Havana)
Swiss Embassy
Calzada Entre
LYM, Vedado
[53] 33-3551/9

*Cyprus*
(Nicosia)
Metochiou and Ploutarchou Streets
Engomi Nicosia, Cyprus
APO AE 09836
[357] (2) 465944

*Czech Republic*
(Prague)
(Int'l) Trziste 15
118 01Prague 1
Unit 25402
APO AE 09213
[42] (2) 536-641

*Denmark*
(Copenhagen)
Dag Hammarskjolds
Alle 24
2100 Copenhagen O or
APO AE 09716
[45] (31) 42-31-44

*Republic of Djibouti*
(Djibouti)
Plateau du Serpent, Blvd.
Marechal Joffre
B.P. 185
[253] 35-39-95

*Dominican Republic*
(Santo Domingo)
Corner of Calle Cesar Nicolas
Penson & Calle Leopoldo Navarro
Unit 5500
APO AA 34041
(809) 5412171

*Ecuador*
(Guayaquil)
9 de Octubre y Garcia Moreno
APO AA 34039
[593] (4) 323-570

(Quito)
Avenida 12 de Octubre y Avenida Patria
P.O. Box 358
Unit 5309
APO AA 34039-3420
[593] (2) 562-890

*Egypt*
(Cairo)
(North Gate)
8, Kamal El-Din Salah St.
Garden City
APO AE 09839-4900
[20] (2) 355-7371

*El Salvador*
(San Salvador)
Final Blvd.
Station Antiguo Cuscatlan
Unit 3116
APO AA 34023
(503) 98-1666

*Equatorial Guinea*
(Malabo)
Calle de Los Ministros
P.O. Box 597
[204] (9) 2815

*Eritera*
(Asmara)
34 Zera Yacob St.
P.O. Box 211
[291] (1) 123-720

*Estonia*
(Tallinn)
Kentamanni 20
EE 0001
[372] (6) 312-021

*Ethiopia*
(Addis Ababa)
Entoto St.
P.O. Box 1014
[251] (1) 550-666

*Fiji*
(Suva)
31 Loftus St.
P.O. Box 218
[679] 314-466

*Government Resources for Exporters (cont'd)*

*Finland*
(Helsinki)
Itainen Puistotie 14A
SF-00140
APO AE 09723
[358] (0) 171931

*France*
(Bordeaux)
22 Cours du Marechal Foch
33080 Bordeaux Cedex
Unit 21551
APO AE 09777
[33] (56) 52-65-95

(Lyon)
U.S. Commercial Office
45 Rue de la Bourse
Unit 21551
APO AE 09777
[33] (16) 72-40-58

(Marseille)
12 Boulevard Paul Peytral
13286 Marseille Cedex
Unit 21551
APO AE 09777
[33] (91) 549-200

(Nice)
U.S. Commercial Office
Rue du Marechal Joffre
c/o AMEMB Paris
Unit 21551
APO AE 09777
[33] (16) 93-88-89-55

(Paris)
2 Avenue Gabriel
75382 Paris Cedex 08
Unit 21551
APO AE 09777
[33] (1) 4296-12-02

U.S. Mission to the Organization for Economic
Cooperation and Development (USOECD)
19 Rue de Franqueville
75016
Unit 21551
APO AE 09777
[33] (1) 45-24-74-77

U.S. Observer Mission to the United Nations
Educational, Scientific, and Cultural Organization
(UNESCO)
2 Avenue Gabriel, 75382
CEDEX 08
Unit 21551
APO AE 09777
[33] (1) 42-96-12-02

(Strasbourg)
15 Ave. D'Alsace
67082 Strasbourg CEDEX or
Unit 21551
APO AE 09777
[33] (88) 35-31-04

*Gabon*
(Libreville)
Blvd. de la Mer
B.P. 4000
[214] 762003/4

*Gambia, The*
(Banjul)
Fajara
Kairaba Ave.
P.M.B. 19
Banjul
[220] 392-856

*Georgia*
(Tbilise)
#25 Antonely Str.
380026
[7] 8832-98-99-68

*Federal Republic of Germany*
(Berlin)
Neustaedtische Kirchstasse 4-5
10117 Berlin or
Unit 26738
APO AE 09235-5500
[49] 30-238-5174

(Bonn)
Deichmanns Aue 29
53170 Bonn
Unit 21701
APO AE 09080
[49] (228) 3391

(Dusseldorf)
U.S. Commercial Office
Emanuel-Leutz Str.
1B 40547 Dusseldorf
c/o AMEMB Bonn
Unit 21701, Box 30
APO AE 09080
[49] (211) 596-798

(Frankfurt Am Main)
Siesmayerstrasse 21
60323 Frankfurt
Unit 25401
APO AE 09213
[49] (69) 7535-0

(Hamburg)
Alsterufer 27/28
20354 Hamburg
[49] (40) 411710

*Government Resources for Exporters (cont'd)*

(Leipzig)
Wilhelm Seyfferth Strasse 4
04107 Leipzig
USEMB Berlin
Unit 26738
APO AE 09235-5500
[49] (341) 211-78-66

(Munich)
Koeniginstrasse 5
80539 Muenchen
Unit 24718
APO AE 09178
[49] (89) 28880

(Stuttgart)
Urbanstrasse 7
70182 Stuttgart
Unit 30607
APO AE 09154-0001
[49] (711) 21008-0

*Ghana*
(Accra)
Ring Road East
P.O. Box 194
Chancery
[233] (21) 775348/9

*Greece*
(Athens)
91 Vasilissis Sophias Blvd.
10160 Athens or
PSC 108
APO AE 09842
[30] (1) 721-2951

(Regional Trade Development Office)
91 Vasilissis Sophias Blvd.
(c/o Embassy)

(Thessaloniki)
59 Leoforos Nikis
GR-546-22
PSC 108, Box 37
APO AE 09842
[30] (31) 242905

*Grenada*
(St. George's)
P.O. Box 54
St. George's
Grenada, W.I.
(809) 444-1172/8

*Guatemala*
(Guatemala City)
7-01 Avenida de la Reforma
Zone 10
APO AA 34024
[502] (2) 31-15-41

*Guinea*
(Conakry)
2d Blvd. and 9th Ave.
B.P. 603
[224] 44-15-20

*Guinea-Bissau*
(Bissau)
Avenida Domingos Ramos
1067 Bissau Codex
Bissau, Guinea-Bissau
[245] 20-1139

*Guyana*
(Georgetown)
99-100 Young and Duke Sts.
Kingston, Georgetown, Guyana
P.O. Box 10507
[592] (2) 54900-9 or 57960-9

*Haiti*
(Port-au-Prince)
Harry Truman Blvd.
P.O. Box 1761
[509] 22-0354

*The Holy See*
(Vatican City)
Villino Pacelli
Via Aurelia 294
00165 Rome
PSC 59
APO AE 09624
[396] 46741

*Honduras*
(Tegucigalpa)
Avenido La Paz
Apartado Postal No. 3453
AMEMB Honduras
APO AA 34022
[504] 36-9320

*Hong Kong*
(Hong Kong)
26 Garden Rd.
PSC 464 Box 30
FPO AP 96522-0002
[852] 523-9011

*Hungary*
(Budapest)
V. Szabadsag Terrace 12
AmEmbassy
Unit 25402
APO AE 09213
[36] (1) 112-6450

*Government Resources for Exporters (cont'd)*

*Iceland*
(Reykjavik)
Laufasvegur 21 Box 40
USEMB
PSC 1003, Box 40
FPO AE 09728-0340
[354] (1) 629100

*India*
(Bombay)
Lincoln House
78 Bhulabhai Desai Rd.
400026
[91] (22) 363-3611

(Calcutta)
5/1 Ho Chi Minh Sarani
700071
[91] (33) 242-3611

(Madras)
220 Mount Rd.
600006
[91] (44) 825-0240

(New Delhi)
Shanti Path
Chanakyapuri 110021
[91] (11) 600651

*Indonesia*
(Jakarta)
Medan Merdeka Selatan 5, Box 1
APO AP 96520
[62] (21) 360-360

(Medan)
Jalan Imam Bonjol 13
APO AP 96520
[62] (610) 322200

(Surabaya)
Jalal Raya Dr. Sutomo 33
AMCONGEN, Box 18131
APO AP 96520-0002
[62] (31) 582287/8

*Iraq*
(Baghdad)
Opp. For. Ministry Club (Masbah Quarter)
P.O. Box 2447
Alwiyah Baghdad
[964] (1) 719-6138/9

*Ireland*
(Dublin)
42 Elgin Rd.
Ballsbridge
[353] (1) 6687122

*Israel*
(Jerusalem)
18 Agron Rd.
Jerusalem 94190
P.O. Box 290
PSC 98, Box 100
APO AE 09830
[972] (2) 253288

(Tel Aviv)
71 Hayarkon St.
PSC 98, Box 100
APO AE 09830
[972] (3) 517-4338

*Italy*
(Florence)
Lungarno Amerigo Vespucci, 38
50123 Firenze
APO AE 09613
[39] (55) 239-8276/7/8/9

(Milan)
Via Principe Amedo, 2/10
20121 Milano
c/o U.S. Embassy, Box M
PSC 59
APO AE 09624
[39] (2) 29-00-11-65

U.S. Information Service
Via Bigli 11/A
20121
[39] (2) 795051/2/3/4/5

(Naples)
Piazza della Repubblica
80122 Naples
Box 18, PSC 810
FPO AE 09619-0002
[39] (81) 761-4303

(Palermo)
Via Vaccarini 1
09143
APO AE 09624
(c/o AmEmbassy Rome-P)
[39] (91) 343-532

(Rome)
Via Veneto 119/A
00187-Rome
PSC 59, Box 100
APO AE 09624
[39] (6) 46741

*Government Resources for Exporters (cont'd)*

U.S. Mission to the United Nations Agencies for
Food and Agriculture (FODAG)
Via Aurelia 294/a
00165
c/o U.S. Embassy Rome
PSC 59, Box 100
APO AE 09624
[39] (6) 4674-4260, ext. 262

*Jamaica*
(Kingston)
Jamaica Mutual Life Center
2 Oxford Rd., 3rd Floor
(809) 929-4850

*Japan*
(Fukuoka)
5-26 Ohori 2-chome
Chuo-ku
Fukuoka-810 or
Unit 45004, Box 242
APO AP 96337-0001
[81] (92) 751-9331/4

(Nagoya)
Nishiki SIS Building 6F 10-33
Nishiki 3-chome Naka-ku
Nagoya 460
c/o AMEMB Tokyo
Unit 45004, Box 280
APO AP 96337-0001
[81] (52) 203-4011

(Naha, Okinawa)
2564 Nishihara
Urasoe City
Okinawa 90121
PSC 556, Box 840
Unit 45
FPO AP 96372-0840
[81] (98) 876-4211

(Osaka-Kobe)
11-5 Nishitenma 2-chome
Kita-Ku, Osaka 530
Unit 45004, Box 239
APO AP 96337-0002
[81] (6) 315-5900

(Sapporo)
Kita 1-Jo Nishi 28-chome
Chuo-ku
Sapporo 064
Unit 45004, Box 276
APO AP 96337-0003
[81] (11) 641-1115/7

(Tokyo)
10-5 Akasaka 1-chome
Minato-ku (107)
Unit 45004, Box 258
APO AP 96337-0001
[81] (3) 3224-5000

U.S. Trade Center
7th Fl., World Import Mart, 1-3
Higashi Ikebukuro 3-chome
Toshima-ku
Tokyo 170
[81] (3) 3987-2441

*Jordan*
(Amman)
P.O. Box 354
Amman 11118 or
APO AE 09892-0200
[962] (6) 820-101

*Kazakhstan*
(Almaty)
99/97 Furmanova St.
Almaty
Republic of Kazakhstan 480012
[7] 63-34-05

*Kenya*
(Nairobi)
Moi/Haile Selassie Ave.
P.O. Box 30137
Unit 64100
APO AE 09831
[254] (2) 334141

*Korea*
(Pusan)
24 2-Ka
Daechung-Dong
Chunk-ku
[82] (51) 246-7791

(Seoul)
82 Sejong-Ro
Chongro-ku
AMEMB, Unit 1550
APO AP 96205-0001
[82] (2) 397-4114

U.S. Export Development Office/
U.S. Trade Center
c/o U.S. Embassy
[82] (2) 397-4212

*Kuwait*
(Kuwait)
P.O. Box 77 SAFAT
13001 SAFAT
Unit 69000
APO AE 09880-9000
[965] 242-4151

*Kyrgyzstan*
(Bishkek)
Erkindik Prospekt #66
720002
[7] (3312) 22-29-20

*Government Resources for Exporters (cont'd)*

*Laos*
(Vientiane)
Rue Bartholonie
B.P. 114
Mail to AMEMB Vientiane Box V
APO AP 96546
[856] 2220

*Latvia*
(Riga)
Raina Blvd. 7
226050
[46] (9) 882-0046

*Lebanon*
(Beirut)
Antelias
P.O. Box 70-840 or
PSC 815, Box 2
FPO AE 09836-0001
[961] (1) 402-200

*Lesotho*
(Maseru)
P.O. Box 333
Maseru 100 Lesotho
[266] 312-666

*Liberia*
(Monrovia)
111 United Nations Dr.
P.O. Box 10-0098
Mamba Point
[231] 222-9991

*Lithuania*
(Vilnius)
Akmenu 6
232600
APO AE 09723
[370] (2) 223-031

*Luxembourg*
(Luxembourg)
22 Blvd. Emmanuel-Servais
2535 Luxembourg
PSC 11
APO AE 09132-5380
[352] 460123

*Madagascar*
(Antananarivo)
14-16 Rue Rainitovo
Antsahavola
B.P. 620
[261] (2) 212-57

*Malawi*
(Lilongwe)
P.O. Box 30016
Lilongwe 3
[265] 783-166

*Malaysia*
(Kuala Lumpur)
376 Jalan Tun Razak
50400 Kuala Lumpur
P.O. Box No. 10035
50700 Kuala Lumpur
APO AP 96535-8152
[60] (3) 248-9011

*Mali*
(Bamako)
Rue Rochester NY and
Rue Mohamed V
B.P. 34
[223] 225470

*Malta*
(Valetta)
2nd Floor
Development House
St. Anne
St. Floriana, Malta
P.O. Box 535
[356] 235960

*Republic of the Marshall Islands*
(Majuro)
P.O. Box 1379
96960-1379
[692] 247-4011

*Mauritius*
(Port Louis)
Rogers House
(4th Floor)
John Kennedy St.
[230] 280-9763

*Mexico*
(Ciudad Juarez)
Chihuahua Avenue Lopez
Mateos 924N
Mail:
Box 10545
El Paso, TX 79995
[52] (16) 134048

(Guadalajara)
JAL
Progreso 175
Mail:
Box 3088
Laredo, TX 78044
[52] (3) 625-2998

(Hermosillo)
Son
Monterrey 141
Mail:
Box 3598
Laredo, TX 78044
[52] (62) 17-2375

*Government Resources for Exporters (cont'd)*

(Matamoros)
Tamaulipas
Calle Primera 2002
Mail:
Box 633
Brownsville, TX 78522
[52] (891) 6-7270-2

(Merida)
Yucatan
Paseo Montejo 453
Mail:
Box 3087
Laredo, TX 78044
[52] (99) 25-5011

(Mexico City)
Paseo de la Reforma 305
Colonia Cuauhtemoc, 06500
D.F.
Mail:
P.O. Box 3087
Laredo, TX 78044
[52] (5) 211-0042

U.S. Export Development Office
Liverpool 31
06600 D.F.
[52] (5) 591-0155

U.S. Travel and Tourism Office
Plaza Comermex
M. Avila Camacho 1-402
11560 D.F.
[52] (5) 520-2101

(Monterrey)
Nuevo Leon
Avenida Constitucion 411 Poniente
64000 Monterrey, N.L.
Mail:
Box 3098
Laredo, TX 78044
[52] (83) 45-2120

(Nuevo Laredo)
Tamps
Calle Allende 3330
Col. Jardin
88260 Nuevo Laredo, Tamps
Mail:
Drawer 3089
Laredo, TX 78044
[52] (871) 4-0512

(Tijuana)
B.C.N.
Tapachula 96
Mail:
P.O. Box 439039
San Diego, CA 92143
[52] (66) 81-7400

*Micronesia*
(Kolonia)
P.O. Box 1286
Pohnpei
Federated States of Micronesia 96941
[691] 320-2187

*Moldova*
(Chisinau)
Strada Alexei Mateevici #103
[373] (2) 23-37-72

*Mongolia*
(Ulaanbaatar)
c/o American Embassy Beijing
Micro Region 11
Big Ring Rd.
PSC 461, Box 300
FPO AP 96521-0002
[976] (1) 329095

*Morocco*
(Casablanca)
9 Blvd. Moulay Youssef
APO AE 09718
[212] (2) 26-45-50

(Rabat)
2 Ave. De Marrakech
PSC 74, Box 003
APO AE 09718
[212] (7) 76 22 65

*Mozambique*
(Maputo)
Avenida Kenneth Kaunda 193
P.O. Box 783
[258] (1) 49-27-97

*Namibia*
(Windhoek)
Ausplan Building
14 Lossen St.
Private Bag 12029
Ausspannplatz Windhoek, Namibia
[264] (61) 221-601

*Nepal*
(Kathmandu)
Pani Pokhari
[977] (1) 411179

*Netherlands*
(Amsterdam)
Museumplein 19
1071 DJ Amsterdam
PSC 71, Box 1000
APO AE 09715
[31] (20) 5755 309

*Government Resources for Exporters (cont'd)*

(The Hague)
Lange Voorhout 103
2514 EJ The Hague
PSC 71 Box 1000
APO AE 09715
[31] (70) 310-9209

*Netherlands Antilles*
(Curaçao)
St. Anna Blvd. 19
P.O. Box 158
Willemstad
[599] (9) 613066

*New Zealand*
(Auckland)
4th Floor
Yorkshire General Building
Corner of Shortland and O'Connell Sts.
Auckland
Private Bag, 92022
PSC 467, Box 99
FPO AP 96531-1099
[64] (9) 303-2734

(Wellington)
29 Fitzherbert Terrace
Thorndon Wellington
P.O. Box 1190
PSC 467, Box 1
FPO AP 96531-1001
[64] (4) 472-2068

*Nicaragua*
(Managua)
Km 4-1/2 Carretera Sur
APO AA 34021
[505] (2) 666010

*Niger*
(Niamey)
Rue Des Ambassades
B.P. 11201
[227] 72-26-61

*Nigeria*
(Abuja [Branch Office])
11 Mambilla, Maitama District
P.O. Box 5760
Garki District
[234] (9) 523-0916

(Ibadan [USIS])
Bodija Estate
(022) 410-775

(Kaduna)
9 Maska Rd.
P.O. Box 170
[234] (62) 235990

(Lagos)
2 Eleke Crescent
P.O. Box 554
[234] (1) 261-0097

*Norway*
(Oslo)
Drammensveien 18
0244 Oslo 2 or
PSC 69, Box 1000
APO AE 09707
[47] 22-44-85-50

U.S. Information Office
Storgaten 92
9000 Tromso or AmEmbassy Oslo
PSC 69, Box 1000
APO AE 09707
[47] 77-68-37-45

*Oman*
(Muscat)
P.O. Box 202
Code No. 115
[968] 698-989

(Ruwi)
U.S. Delegation to the Oman/American Joint
Commission for Economic and
Technical Cooperation
P.O. Box 3001
Code No. 112
[968] 703-000

*Pakistan*
(Islamabad)
Diplomatic Enclave, Ramna 5
P.O. Box 1048
PSC 121, Box 2000
Unit 6220
APO AE 09812-2000
[92] (51) 86161

(Karachi)
8 Abdullah Haroon Rd.
PSC 1214, Box 2000
Unit 62400
APO AE 09814-2400
[92] (21) 5685170

(Lahore)
50 Sharah E-Bin Badees (50 Empress Rd.)
Simla Hills Lahore K
Unit 62216
APO AE 09812-2216
[92] 6365530

(Peshawar)
11 Hospital Rd.
Peshawar Cantt
AC Peshawar
Unit 62217
APO AE 09812-2217
[92] (521) 279801

*Government Resources for Exporters (cont'd)*

*Republic of Palau*
(Koror)
P.O. Box 6028
96940
[680] 488-2920

*Panama*
(Panama City)
Apartado 6959
Panama 5
AMEMB
Unit 0945
APO AA 34002
[507] 27-1777

U.S. Delegation to the Commission for the
Study of Alternatives to the Panama Canal (CASC)
c/o USEMB Panama
Apartado 6959
Panama 5
Unit 0945
APO AA 34002-0008
[507] 27-1777

*Papua New Guinea*
(Port Moresby)
Armit St.
P.O. Box 1492
APO AE 96533
[675] 211-455; 594; 654

*Paraguay*
(Asuncion)
1776 Mariscal Lopez Ave
Casilla Postal 402
Unit 4711
APO AA 34036-0001
[595] (21) 213-715

*Peru*
(Lima)
Corner Avenidas Inca Garcilaso de la
Vega and Espana
P.O. Box 1995
Lima 1 or
American Embassy (Lima)
APO AA 34031
[51] (41) 33-800

*Philippines*
(Cebu)
3rd Floor
PCI Bank Building
Gorordo Avenue
Lahug Cebu City 6000
APO AP 96440
[63] (32) 311-261

(Manila)
1201 Toxas Blvd.
Ermita Manila 1000
APO AP 96440
[63] (2) 521-7116

Asian Development Bank
#6 ADB Ave. Mandaluyong
Metro Manila
P.O. Box 789
APO AP 96440
[63] (2) 632-6050

*Poland*
(Krakow)
Ulica Stolarska 9
31043 Krakow
Unit 25402
APO AE 09213
[48] (12) 229764

(Poznan)
Ulica Chopina 4
61708 Poznan
Unit 25402
APO AE 09213
[48] (61) 551088

(Warsaw)
Aleje Ujazdowski 93/31
AmEmbassy Warsaw
Box 5010, Unit 25402
APO AE 09213-5010
[48] (2) 628-3041

U.S. Trade Center
Aleje Jerozolimskie 56C
IKEA Building, 2d floor
00-803 Warsaw
AmEmbassy Warsaw
Unit 25402
APO AE 09213
[48] (22) 21-45-15

*Portugal*
(American Business Center [Oporto])
Praca Conde de Samodaes 65
4000 Porto
APO AE 09726
[351] (2) 606-30-94

(Lisbon)
Avenida das Forcas Armadas
1600 Lisbon
PSC 83
APO AE 09726
[351] (1) 726-6600

(Ponta Delgada Sao Miguel Azores)
Avenida D. Henrique
PSC 76, Box 3000
APO AE 09720-0002
[351] (96) 22216/7/8/9

*Qatar*
(Doha)
149 Ali Bin Ahmed St.
Farig Bin Omran
P.O. Box 2399
[974] 864701/2/3

*Government Resources for Exporters (cont'd)*

*Romania*
(Bucharest)
Strada Tudor Arghezi 7-9 or
AmConGen (Buch)
Unit 25402
APO AE 09213
[40] (1) 312-0149

*Russia*
(Moscow)
Novinskiy Bul'var 19/23 or
APO AE 09721
[7] (095) 252-2451

U.S. Commercial Office
Novinskiy Bul'var 15
[7] (095) 956-4255

(St. Petersburg)
Furshtatskaya Ulitsa 15
St. Petersburg 191028
PSC 78 Box L
APO AE 09723
[7] (212) 275-1701

(Vladivostok)
Ulitsa Mordovtseva 12
[7] (4232) 268-458; 544

*Rwanda*
(Kigali)
Blvd. de la Revolution
B.P. 28
[250] 75601/2/3

*Saudi Arabia*
(Dhahran)
Between Armco Hdqrs. and Dhahran Int'l Airport
P.O. Box 81
Dhahran Airport, 31932 or
Unit 66803
APO AE 09858-6803
[966] (3) 891-3200

(Jeddah)
Palestine Rd.
Ruwais
P.O. Box 149
Jeddah 21411 or
Unit 6112
APO AE 09811-2112
[966] (2) 667-0080

(Riyadh)
Collector Road M.
Riyadh Dipolomatic Quarter
AMEMB
Unit 61307
APO AE 09803-1307
International Mail:
P.O. Box 94309
Riyadh, 11693
[966] (1) 488-3800

U.S. Rep. to the Saudi Arabian U.S. Joint
Commission on Economic Cooperation
(USREP/JECOR)
P.O. Box 5927
[966] (1) 464-0433

*Sengal*
(Dakar)
B.P. 49
Avenue Jean XXIII
[221] 23-42-96

*Serbia-Montenegro*
(Belgrade)
AmEmbassy Box 5070
Unit 25402
APO AE 09213-5070
[381] (11) 645-655

*Seychelles*
(Victoria)
Box 148
Unit 62501
APO AE 09815-2501 or
Victoria House
Box 251
Victoria Mahe, Seychelles
[248] 225256

*Sierra Leone*
(Freetown)
Corner of Walpole and Siaka Stevens Sts.
[232] (22) 226-481

*Singapore*
(AGR/ATO OFF)
541 Orchard Rd.
Unit 08-04
Liat Towers Bldg.
0923
[65] 737-1233

(FAA)
Changi Airport Terminal 2
South Finger, 4th Floor
Security Unit 048-002
International Area Office
Director and Field Office Unit 048-006
1781
[65] 543-1466

30 Hill St.
0617
FPO AP 96534
(65) 338-0251

(USAID/RIG/A)
111 North Bridge Rd.
No. 17-03
Peninsula Plaza
0617
[65] 334-2766

*Government Resources for Exporters (cont'd)*

(USIS/American Center MPH Building)
Level 4
71-77 Stamford Rd.
0617
[65] 334-0910

*Slovak Republic*
(Bratislava)
(Int'l) Hviezdoslavovo Namestie 4
81102 Bratislava
[42] (7) 330861

*Slovenia*
(Ljubljana)
Box 254
Prazakova 4
61000 Ljubljana
[386] (610 301-427/472/485

*South Africa*
(Cape Town)
Broadway Industries Centre
Heerengracht, Foreshore
[27] (21) 214-280

(Durban)
Durban Bay House, 29th Floor
333 Smith St.
[27] (31) 304-4737

(Johannesburg)
11th Floor
Kine Center
Commissioner and Kruis Sts.
P.O. Box 2155
[27] (11) 331-1681

(Pretoria)
877 Pretorius St.
P.O. Box 9536
[27] (12) 342-1048

*Spain*
(Barcelona)
Reina Elisenda 23
08034 Barcelona or
PSC 61, Box 0005
APO AE 09642
[34] (3) 280-2227

(Madrid)
Serrano 75
28006 Madrid or
APO AE 09642
[34] (1) 577-4000

*Sri Lanka*
(Colombo)
210 Galle Rd.
Colombo 3
P.O. Box 106
[94] (1) 448007

*Sudan*
(Khartoum)
Sharia Ali Abdul Latif
P.O. Box 699
APO AE 09829
[249] 74700

*Suriname*
(Paramaribo)
Dr. Sophie Redmondstraat 129
P.O. Box 1821
[597] 472900

*Swaziland*
(Mbabane)
Central Bank Building
Warner St.
P.O. Box 199
[268] 46441/5

*Sweden*
(Stockholm)
Strandvagen 101
S-115 89
[46] (8) 783-5300

*Switzerland*
(Bern)
Jubilaeumstrasse 93
3005 Bern
[41] (31) 357-7001

(Geneva)
U.S. Delegation to the Conference on
Disarmament
Botanic Building
1-3 Avenue De La paix
[41] (22) 749-5355

U.S. Mission to the European Office of the UN
and Other International Organizations
Mission Permanente Des Etats-Unis
Route de Pregny 11
1292 Chambesy-Geneva
[41] (22) 749-4111

U.S. Trade Representative (USTR)
Botanic Building
1-3 Avenue de la Paix
1202
[41] (22) 749-4111

(Zurich)
Zollikerstrasse 141
[41] (1) 422-25-66

*Syria*
(Damascus)
Abou Roumeneh
Al-Mansur St. No. 2
P.O. Box 29
[963] (11) 332-814

*Government Resources for Exporters (cont'd)*

*Tajikistan*
(Dushanbe)
Interim Chancery
#39 Ainii Street
Residences: Oktyabrskaya Hotel
[7] (3772)

*Tanzania*
(Dar Es Salaam)
36 Laibon Rd.
(off Bagamoyo Rd.)
P.O. Box 9123
[255] (51) 66010

*Thailand*
(Bangkok)
95 Wireless Rd.
APO AP 96546
[66] (2) 252-5040

(Chiang Mai)
Vidhayanond Rd.
Box C
APO AP 96546
[66] (53) 252-629

(Udorn)
35/6 Supakitjanya Rd.
Box UD
APO AP 96546
[66] (24) 244-270

*Togo*
(Lome)
Rue Pelletier Caventou and Rue Vauban
B.P. 852
[228] 21-77-17

*Trinidad and Tobago*
(Port of Spain)
15 Queen's Park West
P.O. Box 752
(809) 622-6372/6

Tunisia
(Tunis)
144 Ave. de la Liberte
1002 Tunis-Belvedere
[216] (1) 789-719

*Turkey*
(Adana)
Ataturk Caddesi
PSC 94
APO AE 09824
[90] (322) 453-9106

(Ankara)
110 Ataturk Blvd.
PSC 93, Box 5000
APO AE 09823
[90] (312) 468-6110

(Istanbul)
104-108 Mesrutiyet Caddesi, Tepebasi
PSC 97, Box 0002
APO AE 09827-002
[90] (212) 251 36 02

*Turkmenistan*
(Ashgabat)
Yubilenaya Hotel
[7] 36320 24-49-25

*Uganda*
(Kampala)
Parliament Ave.
P.O. Box 7007
[256] (41) 259792/3/5

*Ukraine*
(Kiev)
10 Yuria Kotsyubinskovo
252053 Kiev 53
[7] (044) 244-7349

*United Arab Emirates*
(Abu Dhabi)
Al-Sudan St.
P.O. Box 4009
Pouch: AmEmbassy Abu Dhabi
Department of State
Washington, DC 20521
[971] (2) 436-691

(Dubai)
Dubai International Trade Center, 21st Floor
P.O. Box 9343
[971] (4) 313-115

*United Kingdom*
(Belfast, Northern Ireland)
Queen's House
14 Queen St.
BT1 6EQ
PSC 801, Box 40
APO AE 09498-4040
[44] (232) 328239

(Edinburgh, Scotland)
3 Regent Terrace
EH7 5BW
PSC 801, Box 40
FPO AE 09498-4040
[44] (31) 556-8315

(London, England)
24/31 Grosvenor Sq.
W.1A 1AE
PSC 801, Box 40
FPO AE 09498-4040
[44] (71) 499-9000

*Government Resources for Exporters (cont'd)*

European Bank for Reconstruction
and Development
One Exchange Square
EC2A 2EH
[44] (71) 338-6502

*United States*
(New York, NY)
U.S. Mission to the United Nations
(USUN)
799 United Nations Plaza
10017
(212) 415-4050

(Washington, DC)
U.S. Mission to the Organization of American States
(USOAS)
Department of State
20520
(202) 647-9376

*Uruguay*
(Montevideo)
Lauro Muller 1776
APO AA 34035
[598] (2) 23-60-61

*Uzbekistan*
(Tashkent)
82 Chelanzanskaya
[7] (3712) 77-14-07; 11-32

*Venezuela*
(Caracas)
Avenida Francisco de Miranda and
Avenida Principal de la Floresta
P.O. Box 62291
Caracas 1060-A or
APO AA 34037
[58] (2) 285-2222

(Maracaibo)
Edificio Sofimara
Pisco 3
Calle 77 Con Avenida 13 or
Unit 4974
APO AA 34037
[58] (61) 83054/5

*Western Samoa*
(Apia)
5th Floor, Beach Rd.
P.O. Box 3430
[685] 21-631

*Republic of Yemen*
(Sanaa)
Dhahr Himyar Zone
Sheraton Hotel District
P.O. Box 22347
Sanaa Republic of Yemen or
Sanaa–Department of State
Washington, DC 20521
[967] (1) 238-843/52

*Zaire*
(Kinshasa)
310 Avenue des Aviateurs
Unit 31550
APO AE 09828
[243] (12) 21532; 21628

(Lubumbashi)
1029 Blvd. Kamanyola
B.P. 1196
APO AE 09828
[243] (11) 222324

*Zambia*
(Lusaka)
Corner of Independence and United Nations Aves.
P.O. Box 31617
[260] (1) 228-595

*Zimbabwe*
(Harare)
172 Herbert Chitepo Ave.
P.O. Box 3340
[263] (4) 794-521

---

## The Top Reference Sources

*Exportise: An International Trade Source Book
for Smaller Company Executives*
Small Business Foundation of America, $19.95
(202) 223-1103

This is a comprehensive source book on international trade for small business managers. It focuses primarily on exporting, but includes an expanded chapter on importing and foreign competition at home.

Topics covered include foreign markets, overseas marketing, channels of distribution, international finance, methods of payment, legal issues, regulations, taxation, and international communications. Also helpful are the country-by-country overviews that describe the potential for exports and list vital statistics.

# International Trade Administration

THE INTERNATIONAL TRADE Administration (ITA) is a branch of the Department of Commerce which deals with increasing international trade opportunities for U.S. businesses, both large and small. The District Offices are particularly useful because they are staffed by individuals who can advise the caller about national programs and assistance. In addition, they can direct the individual to state and local groups which may service his or her needs more directly.

## ITA District Offices

| State | City | Telephone |
|-------|------|-----------|
| AK | Anchorage | (907) 271-6237 |
| AL | Birmingham | (205) 731-1331 |
| AR | Little Rock | (501) 324-5794 |
| AZ | Phoenix | (602) 640-2513 |
| CA | Los Angeles | (310) 575-7105 |
| | Newport Beach | (714) 660-1688 |
| | San Diego | (619) 557-5395 |
| | San Francisco | (415) 705-2300 |
| | Santa Clara | (408) 291-7625 |
| CO | Denver | (303) 844-6622 |
| CT | Hartford | (203) 240-3530 |
| DC | Call Gaithersburg | (301) 975-3904 |
| DE | Call Philadelphia | (215) 962-4980 |
| FL | Miami | (305) 536-5267 |
| | Clearwater | (813) 461-0011 |
| | Orlando | (407) 648-6235 |
| | Tallahassee | (904) 488-6469 |
| GA | Atlanta | (404) 452-9101 |
| HI | Honolulu | (808) 541-1782 |
| IA | Des Moines | (515) 284-4222 |
| ID | Boise | (208) 334-3857 |
| IL | Chicago | (312) 353-4450 |
| | Wheaton | (312) 353-4332 |
| | Rockford | (815) 987-4347 |
| IN | Indianapolis | (317) 582-2300 |
| KS | Wichita | (316) 269-6160 |
| KY | Louisville | (502) 582-5066 |
| LA | New Orleans | (504) 589-6546 |
| MA | Boston | (617) 565-8563 |
| MD | Baltimore | (410) 962-3560 |
| | Gaithersburg | (301) 975-3904 |
| ME | Augusta | (207) 622-8249 |
| MI | Detroit | (313) 226-3650 |
| | Grand Rapids | (616) 456-2411 |
| MN | Minneapolis | (612) 348-1638 |
| MO | St. Louis | (314) 425-3302 |
| | Kansas City | (816) 426-3141 |
| MS | Jackson | (601) 965-4388 |
| MT | Call Portland | (503) 326-3001 |
| NC | Greensboro | (919) 333-5345 |

| State | City | Telephone |
|-------|------|-----------|
| ND | Call Omaha | (402) 221-3664 |
| NE | Omaha | (402) 221-3664 |
| NH | Portsmouth | (603) 334-6074 |
| NJ | Trenton | (609) 989-2100 |
| NM | Santa Fe | (505) 827-0350 |
| NV | Reno | (702) 784-5203 |
| NY | Buffalo | (716) 846-4191 |
| | Rochester | (716) 263-6480 |
| | New York | (212) 264-0634 |
| OH | Cincinnati | (513) 684-2944 |
| | Cleveland | (216) 522-4750 |
| OK | Oklahoma City | (405) 231-5302 |
| | Tulsa | (918) 581-7650 |
| OR | Portland | (503) 326-3001 |
| PA | Philadelphia | (215) 962-4980 |
| | Pittsburgh | (412) 644-2850 |
| PR | San Juan | (809) 766-5555 |
| RI | Providence | (401) 528-5104 |
| SC | Columbia | (803) 765-5345 |
| | Charleston | (803) 727-4361 |
| SD | Call Omaha | (402) 221-3664 |
| TN | Nashville | (615) 736-5161 |
| | Knoxville | (615) 545-4637 |
| | Memphis | (901) 544-4137 |
| TX | Dallas | (214) 767-0542 |
| | Austin | (512) 482-5939 |
| | Houston | (713) 229-2578 |
| UT | Salt Lake City | (801) 524-5116 |
| VA | Richmond | (804) 771-2246 |
| VT | Call Boston | (617) 565-8563 |
| WA | Seattle | (206) 553-5615 |
| | Tri-Cities | (509) 735-2751 |
| WI | Milwaukee | (414) 297-3473 |
| WV | Charleston | (304) 347-5123 |
| WY | Call Denver | (303) 844-6622 |

**TIP:** *An ITA District Office may be able to provide information on publications that are available in that particular state. For instance, the New York District Office has information on a free booklet produced by the state government called* Global New York, *which is a listing of useful numbers and services for businesses doing international trade from New York.*

# Export Financing Assistance

## Export-Import Bank of the United States

The Export-Import Bank, known as "Exim-bank," is an independent U.S. government agency with the primary purpose of facilitating the export of U.S. goods and services. Eximbank meets this objective by providing loans, guarantees, and insurance coverage to U.S. exporters and foreign buyers, normally on market-related credit terms.

Eximbank's insurance and guarantee programs encourage private financial institutions to fund U.S. exports by reducing the commercial and political risks exporters face. The financing made available under Eximbank's guarantees and insurance is generally on market terms, and most of the commercial and political risks are borne by Eximbank.

Eximbank's loan program is structured to neutralize interest rate subsidies offered by foreign governments. By responding with its own subsidized loan assistance, Eximbank enables U.S. financing to be competitive with that offered by foreign exporters.

## Contact Option

Export-Import Bank
Marketing and Program Division
811 Vermont Ave., NW
Washington, DC 20571
(800) 424-5201

## The Overseas Private Investment Corporation

The Overseas Private Investment Corporation (OPIC) is a U.S. government agency that provides project financing, investment insurance, and a variety of investor services in more than 130 developing nations and emerging economies throughout the world. OPIC assists U.S. investors through three principal programs:

- Financing of investments through direct loans and loan guarantees;

- Insuring investment projects against a broad range of political risks;

- Providing investor services including advisory services, country and regional information, computer assisted project/investor matching, investment missions, and outreach.

## Contact Option

Overseas Private Investment Corporation
1100 New York Ave., NW
Washington, DC 20537
(202) 336-8799

## Department of Agriculture

The Foreign Agriculture Service of the Department of Agriculture administers several programs to make U.S. exporters competitive in international markets and make U.S. products affordable to countries that have greater need than they have ability to pay. The Export Credit Guarantee program offers risk protection for U.S. exporters against non-payment by foreign banks.

## Contact Option

Foreign Agricultural Service
Export Credits
14th St. and Independence Ave., SW
Washington, DC 20250
(202) 720-3935

## State and Local Export Finance Programs

Several states and cities have export financing programs. To be eligible for assistance, an export sale must generally be made under a letter of credit or with credit insurance coverage. A certain percentage of state or local content may also be required. Some programs may require only that certain facilities, such as a state or local port, be used. Exporters should contact a Department of Commerce district office or state economic development agency for more information.

## Private Export Funding Corporation

The Private Export Funding Corporation (PEFCO) is owned by more than five-dozen investors, primarily commercial banks. PEFCO supplements the financing activities of commercial banks and Eximbank, lending only to finance the export of goods and services of U.S. manufacture and origin. PEFCO loans normally mature in the medium-term (181 days to five years), and all are unconditionally guaranteed by Eximbank with regard to payment of interest and repayment of principal.

## Contact Option

PEFCO
280 Park Ave.
New York, NY 10017
(212) 557-3100

# Export Assistance from the SBA

## U.S. Small Business Administration

The Small Business Administration is also involved in encouraging and supporting export activities of small businesses. Companies eligible for SBA programs include manufacturers with a maximum of 1,500 employees; wholesalers with maximum annual sales of $9.5 million; and service companies with maximum average annual sales for the past three years of $2 million.

## Specific Programs

*Management:*

- Counseling by volunteers with international trade experience;

- Counseling through Small Business Development Center Programs;

- Referral to other public or private sector organizations offering more in-depth international trade programs and services;

- International trade and export marketing publications;

- Business management training.

*Financial:*

- Pre-export financing of supply purchases, inventories, materials, and working capital needed for manufacture of export goods and for financing shipping costs, and receivable collection on exports;

- Activities to develop foreign markets, professional marketing advisors and services, foreign business travel, participation in trade shows, and other promotions overseas.

*Other:*

- Joint programs with the Commerce Department's International Trade Administration, the National Oceanic and Atmospheric Administration, and the Department of Agriculture.

## Contact Option

Small Business Administration
(800) 827-5722

## Small Business Administration Regional Offices

155 Federal St., 9th Floor
Boston, MA 02110
(617) 451-2023

26 Federal Plaza, Room 31-08
New York, NY 10007
(212) 264-1450

475 Allendale Rd., Suite 201
King of Prussia, PA 19406
(215) 962-3700

1375 Peachtree St., NE, 5th Floor
Atlanta GA 30367
(404) 347-2797

300 S. Riverside Plaza, Suite 1975S
Chicago, IL 60606
(312) 353-5000

8625 King George Dr., Building C
Dallas, TX 75235
(214) 767-7633

911 Walnut St., 13th Floor
Kansas City, MO 64106
(816) 426-3608

999 18th St., Suite 701
Denver, CO 80202
(303) 294-7186

71 Stevenson St., 20th Floor
San Francisco, CA 94105
(415) 744-6402

2615 Fourth Ave.
Seattle, WA 98121
(206) 553-5676

## Small Business Development Centers

Funded jointly by the Small Business Administration and private agencies, SBDCs also provide assistance in the area of international trade, including:

- Joint ventures/license programs;

- Assistance with overseas trade shows;

- Packaging international trade finance loans, language training;

- Translation services.

Contact one of the following state SBDCs, or:

Association of Small Business Development Centers
1313 Farnam St., Suite 132
Omaha, NE 68182
(402) 595-2387

*Export Assistance from the SBA (cont'd)*

**Alabama**
University of Alabama at Birmingham
Medical Towers Building
1717 11th Ave., Suite 419
Birmingham, AL 35294
(205) 934-7260

**Alaska**
University of Alaska at Anchorage
430 W. 7th Ave., Suite 110
Anchorage, AK 99501
(907) 274-7232

**Arizona**
2411 W. 14th St., Suite 132
Tempe, AZ 85281
(602) 731-8720

**Arkansas**
University of Arkansas at Little Rock
100 S. Main, Suite 401
Little Rock, AR 72201
(501) 324-9043

**California**
California Trade and Commerce Agency
801 K St., Suite 1700
Sacramento, CA 95814
(916) 324-5068

**Colorado**
Colorado Office of Business Development
1625 Broadway, Suite 1710
Denver, CO 80202
(303) 892-3809

**Connecticut**
University of Connecticut
368 Fairfield Rd., Box U-41, Room 422
Storrs, CT 06269
(203) 486-4135

**Delaware**
University of Delaware
Purnell Hall, Suite 005
Newark, DE 19716
(302) 831-1555

**District of Columbia**
Howard University
2600 6th St., Room 128
Washington, DC 20059
(202) 806-1550

**Florida**
19 W. Garden St.
Pensacola, FL 32501
(904) 444-2060

**Georgia**
University of Georgia
Chicopee Complex
180 E. Broad St.
Athens, GA 30602
(706) 542-6762

**Hawaii**
University of Hawaii at Hilo
200 W. Kawili St.
Hilo, HI 96720
(808) 933-3515

**Idaho**
Boise State University
1910 University Dr.
Boise, ID 83725
(208) 385-1640

**Illinois**
Department of Commerce and Community Affairs
620 E. Adams St., 3rd Floor
Springfield, IL 62701
(217) 524-5856

**Indiana**
Economic Development Council
One N. Capitol, Suite 420
Indianapolis, IN 46204
(317) 264-6871

**Iowa**
Iowa State University
137 Lynn Ave.
Ames, IA 50014
(515) 292-6351

**Kentucky**
University of Kentucky
Center for Business Development
225 Business and Economics Building
Lexington, KY 40506
(606) 257-7668

**Louisiana**
Northeast Louisiana University
College of Business Administration
700 University Ave., Adm. 2-57
Monroe, LA 71209
(318) 342-5506

**Maine**
University of Southern Maine
96 Falmouth St.
Portland, ME 04103
(207) 780-4420

*Export Assistance from the SBA (cont'd)*

*Maryland*
Department of Economic and Employment
Development
217 E. Redwood St., Suite 936
Baltimore, MD 21202
(410) 333-6995

*Massachusetts*
University of Massachusetts at Amherst
School of Management, Room 205
Amherst, MA 01003
(413) 545-6301

*Michigan*
2727 2nd Ave., Room 107
Detroit, MI 48201
(313) 577-4848

*Mississippi*
University of Mississippi
Old Chemistry Building, Suite 216
University, MS 38677
(601) 232-5001

*Missouri*
University of Missouri
300 University Place
Columbia, MO 65211
(314) 882-0344

*Montana*
Montana Department of Commerce
1424 Ninth Ave.
Helena, MT 59620
(406) 444-4780

*Nebraska*
University of Nebraska at Omaha
60th and Dodge Sts., CBA Room 407
Omaha, NE 68182
(402) 554-2521

*Nevada*
University of Nevada at Reno
College of Business Adminstration–032, Room 411
Reno, NV 89557
(702) 784-1717

*New Hampshire*
University of New Hampshire
15 College Rd., 108 McConnell Hall
Durham, NH 03824
(603) 862-2200

*New Jersey*
Rutgers University Graduate School of Management
180 University Ave., Ackerson Hall, 3rd Floor
Newark, NJ 07102
(201) 648-5950

*New Mexico*
Santa Fe Community College
P.O. Box 4187
Santa Fe, NM 87502
(505) 438-1362

*New York*
State University of New York
SUNY Central Plaza, S-523
Albany, NY 12246
(518) 443-5398

*North Carolina*
University of North Carolina at Chapel Hill
4509 Creedmoor Rd., Suite 201
Raleigh, NC 27612
(919) 571-4154

*North Dakota*
University of North Dakota
118 Gamble Hall, Box 7308
Grand Fork, ND 58202
(701) 777-3700

*Ohio*
77 S. High St., 28th Floor
P. O. Box 1001
Columbus, OH 43226
(614) 466-2711

*Oklahoma*
Southeastern Oklahoma State University
P.O. Box 2584, Station A
Durant, OK 74701
(405) 924-0277

*Oregon*
Lane Community College
99 W. 10th Ave., Suite 216
Eugene, OR 97401
(503) 726-2250

*Pennsylvania*
Wharton School of Business
University of Pennsylvania
423 Vance Hall
3733 Spruce St.
Philadelphia, PA 19104
(215) 898-1219

*Rhode Island*
Bryant College
1150 Douglas Pike
Smithfield, RI 02917
(401) 232-6111

*South Carolina*
University of South Carolina
College of Business Administration
Columbia, SC 29201
(803) 777-4907

*Export Assistance from the SBA (cont'd)*

*South Dakota*
University of South Dakota
414 E. Clark
Vermillion, SD 57069
(605) 677-5498

*Tennessee*
Memphis State University
Building 1, South Campus
Memphis, TN 38152
(901) 678-2500

*Texas*
Bill J. Priest Institute for Economic Development
1402 Corinth St.
Dallas, TX 75215
(214) 565-5835

University of Houston
1100 Louisiana, Suite 500
Houston, TX 77002
(713) 752-8444

Texas Tech University
2579 S. Loop 289, Suite 114
Lubbock, TX 79423
(806) 745-3973

University of Texas at San Antonio
1222 Main St., Suite 450
San Antonio, TX 78212
(210) 558-2450

*Utah*
University of Utah
102 W. 500 South, Suite 315
Salt Lake City, UT 84101
(801) 581-7905

*Vermont*
Vermont Technical College
P. O. Box 422
Randolph, VT 05060
(802) 728-9101

*Virginia*
1021 E. Cary St., 11th Floor
Richmond, VA 23219
(804) 371-8253

*Washington*
Washington State University
245 Todd Hall
Pullman, WA 99164
(509) 335-1576

*West Virginia*
1115 Virginia St., E
Charleston, WV 25301
(304) 558-2960

*Wisconsin*
University of Wisconsin
432 N. Lake St., Room 423
Madison, WI 53706
(608) 263-7794

# World Trade Centers

HEADQUARTERED IN NEW YORK, the World Trade Centers Association includes 241 affiliated organizations in 60 countries with a total membership of over 400,000 companies worldwide. World Trade Centers provide one-stop shopping in a region for international trade. The World Trade buildings usually house freight forwarders, customs brokers, international companies, and government agencies. Additional services include:

- Office space for the international trading community;

- Information and trade research services;

- Consumer/business services (hotels, restaurants, banks);

- Educational services (seminars, language training).

## Contact Option

World Trade Centers Association
1 World Trade Center, Suite 7701
New York, NY 10048
(212) 432-2626

## World Trade Centers

*Alaska*
World Trade Center
University of Alaska,–Anchorage
4201 Tudor Centre Dr., Suite 320
Anchorage, AK 99508
(907) 561-1615

*Arizona*
World Trade Center–Phoenix
34 W. Monroe, Suite 900
Phoenix, AZ 85003
(602) 495-6480

*World Trade Centers (cont'd)*

*California*
World Trade Center–Irvine
1 Park Plaza, Suite 150
Irvine, CA 92714
(714) 724-9822

Greater Los Angeles World Trade Center
One World Trade Center, Suite 295
Long Beach, CA 90831
(310) 495-7070

Los Angeles World Trade Center
350 S. Figueroa St., Suite 172
Los Angeles, CA 90071
(213) 680-1888

World Trade Center of San Francisco
110 Sutter St., Suite 408
San Francisco, CA 94104
(415) 392-2705

*Colorado*
World Trade Center–Denver
1625 Broadway, Suite 680
Denver, CO 80202
(303) 592-5760

*Connecticut*
Connecticut World Trade Association
177 State St., 4th Floor
Bridgeport, CT 06604
(203) 336-5353

*Costa Rica*
World Trade Center of San Jose, Costa Rica
1515 S. Federal Hwy., Suite 211
Boca Raton, FL 33432
(407) 394-9033

*Delaware*
World Trade Center–Delaware
1207 King St., P.O. Box 709
Wilmington, DE 19899
(302) 656-7905

*Florida*
World Trade Center–Fort Lauderdale
1100 Lee Wagener Blvd., P.O. Box 13065
Ft. Lauderdale International Airport
Fort Lauderdale, FL 33315
(305) 359-3615

Jacksonville World Trade Center Association
3 Independent Dr.
Jacksonville, FL 32202
(904) 366-6658

World Trade Center–Miami
One World Trade Plaza, Suite 1800
80 S.W. 8th St.
Miami, FL 33130
(305) 579-0064

World Trade Center–Orlando
122 E. Colonial Dr., Suite 102
Orlando, FL 32801
(407) 649-1899

World Trade Center–Tampa Bay
800 Second Ave. S., Suite 340
St. Petersburg, FL 33701
(813) 822-2492

*Georgia*
World Trade Center–Atlanta
240 Peachtree St., NE, Suite 2200
Atlanta, GA 30303
(404) 525-4144

*Hawaii*
Hawai World Trade Center–Honolulu
201 Merchant St., Suite 1510
P.O. Box 2359
Honolulu, HI 96804
(808) 587-2797

*Illinois*
Illinois World Trade Center–Chicago
One World Trade Center, 4th Floor
Chicago, IL 60654
(312) 467-0550

*Indiana*
World Trade Center–Indianapolis
P.O. Box 24427
Indianapolis, IN 46224
(317) 328-8928

*Iowa*
Iowa World Trade Center–Des Moines
3200 Ruan Center
666 Grand Ave.
Des Moines, IA 50309
(515) 245-2555

*Kansas*
World Trade Center–Wichita
Mid-America World Trade Center
350 W. Douglas
Wichita, KS 67202
(316) 262-3232

*Kentucky*
World Trade Center–Lexington
410 W. Vine St., Suite 290
Lexington, KY 40507
(606) 258-3139

*Louisiana*
World Trade Center–New Orleans
2 Canal St., Suite 2900
New Orleans, LA 70130
(504) 529-1601

*World Trade Centers (cont'd)*

*Maryland*
The World Trade Center–Baltimore
Suite 1355
Baltimore, MD 21202
(301) 576-0022

*Massachusetts*
World Trade Center–Boston
Executive Offices, Suite 50
Boston, MA 02210
(617) 439-5001

*Michigan*
World Trade Center–Detroit/Windsor
535 Griswold
Buhl Building, World Trade Center, Suite 1000
Detroit, MI 48226
(313) 965-6500

*Minnesota*
Minnesota World Trade Center–St. Paul
30 East 7th St., Suite 400
St. Paul, MN 55101
(612) 297-1580

*Missouri*
Greater Kansas City World Trade Center
2600 Commerce Tower
911 Main St.
Kansas City, MO 64105
(816) 221-2424

World Trade Center–St. Louis
121 S. Meramec, Suite 1111
St. Louis, MO 63105
(314) 854-6141

*Nevada*
Nevada World Trade Center–Las Vegas
6330 S. Eastern Ave., Suite 7
Las Vegas, NV 89119
(702) 795-8487

*New York*
Buffalo World Trade Center
Essex Investment Group
100 Corporate Woods, Suite 300
Rochester, NY 14623
(716) 272-2300

World Trade Center–New York
The Port Authority of New York and New Jersey
One World Trade Center, Suite 35 E
New York, NY 10048
(212) 435-8385

World Trade Center–Schenectady-Capital District
One Broadway Center, Suite 750
Schenectady, NY 12305
(518) 393-7252

*North Carolina*
World Trade Center–Piedmont Triad
Piedmont Triad Airport Authority, P.O. Box 35005
Greensboro, NC 27425
(919) 665-9657

Research Triangle World Trade Center
P.O. Box 13487
Research Triangle Park, NC 27709
(919) 544-8969

World Trade Center–Wilmington
Greater Wilmington Chamber of Commerce
P.O. Box 330
Wilmington, NC 28402
(919) 762-2611

*Ohio*
World Trade Center–Columbus
International Trade Development Office
Columbus Chamber of Commerce
37 N. High St.
Columbus, OH 43215
(614) 225-6907

*Oregon*
World Trade Center–Portland
One World Trade Center, Suite 250
121 Southwest Salmon St.
Portland, OR 97204
(503) 464-8888

*Pennsylvania*
Greater Philadelphia World Trade and
Financial Center
Carl Marks & Co.
135 E. 57th St.
New York, NY 10022
(212) 909-8400

World Trade Center–Pittsburgh
441 Smithfield St., 2nd Floor
Pittsburgh, PA 15146
(412) 355-4344

*Rhode Island*
World Trade Center–Rhode Island
Greater Providence
P.O. Box 1061, Bryant College
Smithfield, RI 02917
(401) 232-6400

*South Carolina*
South Carolina World Trade Center–Charleston
Charleston Trident Chamber of Commerce
81 Mary St.
P.O. Box 975
Charleston, SC 29402
(803) 577-2510 ext. 3029

*World Trade Centers (cont'd)*

The Greenville-Spartanburg World Trade Center
The Jenkins Companies
315 Old Boiling Springs Rd.
Greer, SC 29650
(803) 297-8600

*Tennessee*
World Trade Center–Chattanooga
1001 Market St.
Chattanooga, TN 37402
(615) 752-4316

*Texas*
The Alliance World Trade Center–Ft.Worth/Dallas
Hillwood Development
12377 Merit Dr., Suite 1700
Dallas, TX 75251
(214) 788-3050

Houston World Trade Association
1100 Milam, 25th Floor
Houston, TX 77002
(713) 651-2229

World Trade Center–Rio Grande Valley at McAllen
One Park Place, Suite 670
McAllen, TX 78503
(210) 686-1982

World Trade Center–San Antonio
118 Broadway
San Antonio, TX 78205
(210) 978-7600

*Virginia*
World Trade Center–Washington, DC
One Prince St., Suite 320
Alexandria, VA 22314
(703) 684-6630

*Washington*
World Trade Center–Seattle
The Greater Seattle World Trade Center Association
P.O. Box 61395
1420 5th Ave., Suite 2200
Seattle, WA 98121
(206) 224-7450

World Trade Center–Tacoma
3600 Port of Tacoma Rd., Suite 309
Tacoma, WA 98424
(206) 383-9474

*Wisconsin*
Wisconsin World Trade Center–Madison
8401 Greenway Blvd.
Middleton, WI 53562
(608) 831-0666

Wisconsin World Trade Center–Milwaukee
Pfister Hotel
424 E. Wisconsin Ave.
Milwaukee, WI 53202
(414) 274-3840

## The Top Reference Sources

*Nation's Business*
Chamber of Commerce of the United States,
$22/year
(202) 463-5650

This monthly publication is written for members
of the national business community concerned
with regional and national business and fractional
trends.

Sample features include tax planning ideas,
key professional investment opportunities, corporate
shifts and/or mergers, and association meetings
coverage.

# Organizations Focusing on Trade

THE FOLLOWING PRIVATE ORGANIZATIONS and associations are useful contacts for trade and export issues:

United States Council for International Business
1212 Avenue of the Americas
New York, NY 10036
(212) 354-4480
The Council is the official U.S. affiliate of the International Chamber of Commerce. In addition to addressing policy issues, the Council and the ICC provide a number of programs available for members:

- Court of Arbitration
- International Environmental Bureau
- Counterfeiting Intelligence Bureau
- Institute of International Business Law and Practice.

American Association for Exporters and Importers
11 W. 42nd St., 30th Floor
New York, NY 10036
(212) 944-2230

Committee for Small Business Exports
P.O. Box 6
Aspen, CO 81612
(303) 925-7567

Federation of International Trade Associations
1851 Alexander Bell Dr.
Reston, VA 22091
(703) 620-1588

International Trade Facilitation Council
1800 Diagonal Rd., Suite 220
Alexandria, VA 22314
(703) 519-0661
Helps importers and exporters to simplify the procedures and paperwork associated with world trade.

International Trade Council
3144 Circle Hill Rd.
Alexandria, VA 22305
(703) 548-1234
Conducts research and offers educational programs on topics such as market conditions abroad, transportation costs, and trade regulations.

National Foreign Trade Council
1625 K St., NW
Washington, DC 20006
(202) 887-0278
Trade association that deals exclusively with U.S. public policy affecting international trade and investment. Members are companies with substantial international operations or interests.

Small Business Foundation of America
1155 15th St., NW
Washington, DC 20005
(202) 223-1103
Export Opportunity Hotline: (800) 243-7232

# American Chambers of Commerce

THE AMERICAN CHAMBERS of Commerce abroad are voluntary associations of American business enterprises and individuals doing business in a given country, as well as firms of that country operating in the United States. American Chambers of Commerce Abroad will usually handle inquiries from any U.S. business. Detailed service, however, may be provided free of charge only for members of affiliated organizations. Some chambers have a set schedule of charges for services for non-members. Services available to U.S. companies may include:

- Briefings on market conditions;
- Export-import trade leads, business and government contacts;
- Periodic news bulletins and other publications on living and trading abroad;

- Information on customs duties, tariffs, and regulations;
- Clearinghouse of information on trade, investment, and commerce;
- Information on the host country business environment.

## American Chambers of Commerce Abroad

*Argentina*
Leandro N. Alem 1110, Piso 13
1001 Buenos Aires
[54] (1) 331-5420; 5126

*Australia*
Suite 4, Gloucester Walk, 88 Cumberland St.
Sydney, N.S.W. 2000
[61] (2) 241-1907

*American Chambers of Commerce (cont'd)*

Level 1, 123 Lonsdale St.
Melbourne, Victoria 3000
[61] (3) 663-2644

Level 23, 68 Queen St.
Brisbane, Queensland 4000
[61] (7) 221-8542

Level 6, 231 Adelaide Terrace
Perth, W.A. 6000
[61] (9) 325-9540

*Austria*
Porzellangasse 35
1090 Vienna
[43] (1) 319-5751

*Belgium*
Avenue des Arts 50, Boite 5
1040, Brussels
[32] (2) 513-6770/9

*Bolivia*
Casilla 8268, Avda. Area No. 2071
La Paz
[591] (2) 342-523

*Brazil*
C.P. 916, Praca Pio X-15, 5th Floor
20040 Rio de Janeiro, RJ
[55] (21) 203-2477

Rua da Espanha 2, Salas 604-606
40000 Salvador, Bahia
[55] (71) 242-0077; 5606

Rua Alexandre Dumas 1976
04717 São Paulo, SP
[55] (11) 246-9199

*Chile*
Av. Americo Vespucio Sur 80, 9 Pisco
82 Correo 34, Santiago
[56] (2) 208-4140; 3451

*China (PRC)*
Great Wall Sheraton Hotel, Room 301
North Donghuan Ave.
Beijing 100026
[86] (1) 500-5566 ext. 2271

*Colombia*
Apdo. Aereo 8008, Calle 35, No. 6-16
Bogota
[57] (1) 285-7800

Avenida 1N, No. 3N-97
Cali
[57] (23) 610-162; 572-993

Centro Comercial Bocagrande
Avda. San Martin, Of. 309
P.O. Box 15555
Cartagena
[57] (53) 657-724

*Costa Rica*
c/o Aerocasillas
P.O. Box 025216, Dept. # 1526
Miami, FL 33102
[506] 20-22-00

*Czech Republic*
Karlovo namest: 24
110 00 Prague 1
[42] (2) 299-887; 296-778

*Dominican Republic*
American Chamber EPS #A-528
P.O. Box 02-5256
Miami, FL 33102
(809) 544-2222

*Ecuador*
Edificio Multicentro, 4P
La Nina y Avda. 6 de Diciembre
Quito
[593] (2) 507-450

Edificio Banco del Pichincha
Manta
[593] (4) 621-699

*Egypt*
Cairo Marriott Hotel, Suite 1541
P.O. Box 33
Zamalek, Cairo
[20] (2) 340-8888

*El Salvador*
87 Ave. Norte, No. 720, Apt. A
Col. Escalon
San Salvador
(503) 23-3292; 24-3646

*France*
21 Avenue George V
75008 Paris
[33] (1) 47-23-70-28 or
[33] (1) 47-23-80-26

*Germany*
Rossmarkt 12, Postfach 100 162
60311 Frankfurt am Main 1
[49] (69) 28-34-01

Budapesterstrasse 29
W-1000 Berlin 30
[49] (30) 261-55-86

*Greece*
16 Kanari St., 3rd Floor
Athens 106 74
[30] (1) 36-18-385 ; 36-36-407

*American Chambers of Commerce (cont'd)*

*Guam*
102 Ada Plaza Center
P.O. Box 283
Agana, Guam 96910
[671] 472-6311; 8001

*Guatemala*
12 Calle 1-25, Zona 10
Edif. Geminis 10, Torre Norte
12 Nivel, Oficina 1206
Guatemala City
[502] (2) 353-355

*Honduras*
Hotel Honduras Maya, Ap. Pos. 1838
Tegucigalpa
[504] 32-70-43

Centro Bella Aurora
6 Avenida, 13-14 Calles, N.O.
San Pedro Sula
[504] 58-0164

*Hong Kong*
1030 Swire House, Chater Rd.
[852] 526-0165

*Hungary*
Dozsa Gyorgy ut. 84/A, Room 406
1068 Budapest
[36] (1) 142-9108

*Indonesia*
The Landmark Centre
22nd Floor, Suite 2204
JI. Jendral Sudirman, Jakarta
[62] (21) 571-0800 ext. 2222

*Ireland*
20 College Green
Dublin 2
[353] (1) 679-3733

*Israel*
35 Shaul Hamelech Blvd.
64927 Tel Aviv
[972] (3) 695-2341

*Italy*
Via Cantu 1
20123 Milano
[39] (2) 86-90-661

*Ivory Coast*
01 BP 3394
Abidjan 01
[225] 21-67-66; 44-68-48

*Jamaica*
The Wyndham Hotel
77 Knutsford Blvd.
Kingston 5
(809) 926-7866

*Japan*
Fukide Bldg., No. 2
4-1-21 Toranomon, Minato-ku
Tokyo 105
[81] (3) 3433-5381

P.O. Box 235
Okinawa City 904
[81] (9) 889-8935-2684

*Korea*
Room 307, Chosun Hotel
Seoul
[82] (2) 753-6471; 6516

*Malaysia*
15.01 Lev 15th Fl., Amoda
22 Jalan Imbi
55100 Kuala Lumpur
[60] (3) 248-2407; 2540

*Mexico*
P.O. Box 60326, Apdo. 113
Houston, TX 77205
[52] (57) 24-3800

Avda. Moctezuma #442
Col. Jardines del Sol
45050 Zapopan, Jalisco
[52] (36) 34-6606

Picachos 760, Despachos 4 y 6
Colonia Obispado
Monterrey, Nuevo Leon
[52] (83) 48-7141; 4749

*Netherlands*
Carnegieplein 5
2517 KJ The Hague
[31] (70) 3-65-98-08/9

*New Zealand*
P.O. Box 106-002 Downtown
Auckland 1001
[64] (9) 309-9140

*Nicaragua*
Apdo. 202
Managua
[505] (2) 67-30-99

*Pakistan*
NIC Building, 6th Floor
Abbasi Shaheed Road off Sharea Faisal
G.P.O. Box 1322
Karachi 74000
[92] (21) 526-436

*Panama*
Apdo. 168, Estafeta Balboa
Panama
[507] 69-3881

*American Chambers of Commerce (cont'd)*

*Paraguay*
Edif. El Faro International Piso 4
Asuncion
[595] (21) 442-135/6

*Peru*
Av. Ricardo Palma 836, Miraflores
Lima 18
[51] (14) 47-9349

*Philippines*
P.O. Box 1578, MCC
Manila
[63] (2) 818-7911

*Poland*
Plac Powstancow Warszawyl, 3rd Floor, Room 333
00-950 Warsaw
[48] (22) 26-39-60

*Portugal*
Rua de D. Estefania, 155, 5 Esq.
Lisbon P-1000
[351] (1) 57 25 61

*Saudi Arabia*
P.O. Box 88
Dhahran Airport 31932
[966] (3) 857-6464

Hyatt Regency–Jeddah
P.O. Box 8483
Jeddah 21482
[966] (2) 685-3335

P.O. Box 3050
Riyadh 11471, 07045
[966] (1) 477-7341

*Singapore*
1 Scotts Road, 16-07 Shaw Center, 0922
[65] 235-0077

*South Africa*
P.O. Box 62280
2107 Marshalltown
[27] 11-788-0265/6

*Spain*
Avda. Diagonal 477
08036 Barcelona
[34] (3) 405-266

Hotel EuroBuilding
Padre Damian 23
28036 Madrid
[34] (1) 458-6559

*Sri Lanka*
P.O. Box 1000, Lotus Rd.
Colombo Hilton, 3rd Floor
Colombo 1
[94] (1) 54-4644 ext. 2318

*Sweden*
Box 5512
114 85 Stockholm
[46] (8) 666-11-00

*Switzerland*
Talacker 41
8001 Zurich
[41] (1) 211-24-54

*Taiwan*
123-3, Ta-Pei Rd., 1st Floor #1-1
Niao Sung Hsiang
Kaohsiung County 83305
[886] (70) 731-3712

Room 1012, Chia Hsin Bldg. Annex
96 Chung Shan N. Rd., Section 2
Taipei
[886] (2) 581-7089

*Thailand*
P.O. Box 11-1095
140 Wireless Rd., 7th Floor
Kian Gwan Building, Bangkok
[66] (2) 251-9266

*Turkey*
Fahri Gizdem Sokak 22/5
80280 Gayrettepe, Istanbul
[90] (1) 274-2824; 288-6212

*Ukraine*
7 Kudriavsky Uzviv, 2nd Floor
Kiev 252053
[7] (44) 417-1413

*United Arab Emirates*
International Trade Center, Suite 1610
P.O. Box 9281, Dubai
[971] (4) 314-735

*United Kingdom*
75 Brook St.
London W1Y 2EB
[44] (71) 493-03-81

*Uruguay*
Calle Bartolome Mitre 1337
Cassilla de Correo 809
Montevideo
[598] (2) 9-590-59/48

*Venezuela*
Torre Credival, Piso 10
2da. Avenida de Campo Alegre
Campo Alegre, Apdo. 5181
Caracas 1010-A
[58] (2) 263-0833

# Trade Assistance

## Trade Adjustment Assistance

Trade adjustment assistance, part of the Commerce Department's Economic Development Administration, helps firms that have been harmed by imported products to adjust to international competition. Companies eligible for trade adjustment assistance may receive technical consulting to upgrade operations such as product engineering, marketing, information systems, export promotion, and energy management. The federal government may assume up to 75 percent of the cost of these services.

## Contact Option

Trade Adjustment Assistance Division
U.S. Department of Commerce
14th and Constitution Ave., Room 7023
Washington, DC 20230
(202) 482-3373

## Trade Remedy Assistance

The Trade Remedy Assistance Office, part of the U.S. International Trade Commission, will provide continuing technical assistance and legal support to certified small businesses pursuing remedies under the international trade laws.

For example, selling merchandise in another country at a price below the price at which the same merchandise is sold in the home market, or selling such merchandise below the costs incurred in production and shipment, is known as *dumping*. If a U.S. firm is adversely affected by a competitor's practices, a complaint may be filed with the Trade Remedy Assistance Office. In addition to information and assistance on anti-dumping laws, this office also provides remedies on countervailing duty laws (where subsidized foreign goods are sold in the U.S.); intellectual property laws (where articles imported into the U.S. infringe valid patents, trademarks, or copyrights); and investigations of situations where U.S. exports are subject to unfair restrictions in overseas markets.

## Contact Option

Trade Remedy Assistance Office
U.S. International Trade Commission
500 E St., SW
Washington, DC 20436
(800) 343-9822

## Port Import Export Reporting Service

Companies interested in finding out about their own market share, a competitor's exports and practices, who's dumping in which ports and cities, or where to find a new source of supply, can request such information from Port Import Export Reporting Service. For a fee, PIERS generates computer reports from original ships' manifests customized to meet an individual company's requirements.

PIERS reports provide product data, name and location of U.S. consignee/exporter, overseas shipper, country of origin or destination, quantities, weights, and other items.

## Contact Option

Denise Simms
PIERS
Two World Trade Center, 27th Floor
New York, NY 10048
(212) 837-7068

---

## The Top Reference Sources

*The Henry Holt International Desk Reference*
Henry Holt, $39.95
(212) 886-9200

Organized by geographical region and by country, this reference provides up-to-date information on the global community.

Each country listing is divided into sections such as agriculture, banking, business development, consultants and advisers, imports and exports, laws, politics, sales agents, social agents, and tourism.

The entries are highly annotated, with descriptions of services, addresses, telephone numbers, and background information.

# The President's "E" Award

ESTABLISHED BY AN EXECUTIVE order of the President in 1961, the "E" Certificate of Service is awarded to persons, firms, and organizations that may or may not export directly, but assist or facilitate export efforts through financing, transportation, market promotion, or other export-related services. In addition to manufacturers, other firms such as banks, utilities, chambers of commerce, trade associations, and individuals that promote and assist exporting may receive this award.

Applications must be submitted through the nearest Commerce Department district office. Award ceremonies may be held in conjunction with trade events, such as conventions, trade shows, conferences, and seminars. "E Star" Awards are presented to "E" Award winners to recognize continued superior performance in increasing or promoting exports.

## Contact Option

"E" Awards Program
Office of Domestic Operations
International Trade Administration
Room 3810
U.S. Department of Commerce
Washington, DC 20230
(202) 482-1289

## Recent "E Star" Award Recipients

| Company | Location | Type |
| --- | --- | --- |
| AJC International | Atlanta, GA | Exporter of frozen foodstuffs |
| AmSouth Bank | Birmingham, AL | Commercial bank |
| Direct Container Line | Carson, CA | Non-vessel operating common carrier |
| Gribetz International | Sunrise, FL | Quilting machinery manufacturer |
| Hampton Roads Maritime Assoc. | Norfolk, VA | Service organization supporting the port community |
| INDRESCO | Houston, TX | Pneumatic tools manufacturer |
| Paper Machinery | Milwaukee, WI | Machinery manufacturer for paper converting industry |
| Phifer Wire Products | Tuscaloosa, AL | Diversified product line manufacturer |
| Port of Tacoma | Tacoma, WA | Public port authority |
| Rotary | Glennville, GA | Lawnmower blades, parts, and accessories manufacturer |
| Systems Center | Reston, VA | Computer software developer |

## Recent "E" Award Recipients

| Company | Location | Type |
| --- | --- | --- |
| Bennett X-Ray | Copiague, NY | Diagnostic X-ray equipment manufacturer |
| Bruce Tool | Taylors, SC | Drilling tools manufacturer |
| California State World Trade Commission | Long Beach, CA | State export development agency |
| Diamond Chain Company | Indianapolis, IN | Precision roller chain and parts manufacturer |
| Diamond V Mills | Cedar Rapids, IA | Feed ingredients manufacturer |
| Export Advisory Service Extension | New York, NY | Educational trade promotion agency |
| Export Resource Associates | St. Paul, MN | International training and trade resource company |
| Fifth Third Bank | Cincinnati, OH | Commercial bank |
| Foreign Language and Culture Center | Savannah, GA | Provider of business support programs |
| Fulghum Industries | Wadley, GA | Wood processing machinery manufacturer |
| Hamilton Bank | Miami, FL | Commercial bank |
| International Pipe Machinery | Sioux City, IA | Concrete pipe construction machinery manufacturer |
| Kitchens Brothers Manufacturing | Utica, MS | Hardwood lumber manufacturer |
| Life Technologies | Gaithersburg, MD | Life science research products manufacturer |
| LIGHTNIN | Rochester, NY | Process equipment manufacturer |
| Martin Door Manufacturing | Salt Lake City, UT | Steel section garage doors manufacturer |
| National Assoc. of State Development Agencies | Washington, DC | National org. for state economic development agencies |
| North Carolina World Trade Association | Raleigh, NC | International trade promotion organization |
| PPM Cranes | Conway, SC | Cranes and parts manufacturer |
| Panalpina USA | Jersey City, NJ | Freight forwarder |

*The President's "E" Award (cont'd)*

| Company | Location | Type |
|---|---|---|
| Rock Valley College | Rockford, IL | Trade promotion partner |
| Rotoflow | Gardena, CA | Turboexpanders manufacturer for gas processing |
| SSE Technologies | Fremont, CA | Satellite communication equipment manufacturer |
| Sonix | Springfield, VA | Convertor circuit boards manufacturer |
| Square D | Oxford, OH | Electrical products for power distribution manufacturer |
| Tri-Chem | Harrison, NJ | Fabric paints manufacturer |
| Viasoft | Phoenix, AZ | Software manufacturer |
| Viracon | Owatonna, MN | Commercial glass manufacturer |
| Washex Machinery | Wichita Falls, TX | Industrial laundry and dyeing equipment |

# Cities for International Business

*WORLD TRADE* MAGAZINE publishes an annual ranking of the best cities for international business. They base their conclusions on a variety of scientific and qualitative criteria. Cities like Los Angeles and New York are not included because they are already clearly established as international trade meccas. The following table lists the top ten cities and how they ranked in several key indicators:

## Recommended Resource

*World Trade*
Freedom Newspapers, $24/year
(714) 640-7070 (CA office)

## Top Ten Cities for International Business

| City | Index* | No. of Foreign Banks | Foreign Employees (%) | Daily Int'l Flights | No. of Consulates | No. of Foreign Chambers of Commerce |
|---|---|---|---|---|---|---|
| Cleveland | 100 | 1 | 6.1 | 15-24 | 23 | 0 |
| Portland, OR | 92 | 5 | 3.9 | 5-9 | 15 | 0 |
| San Diego | 92 | 1 | 4.2 | 10-14 | 20 | 2 |
| Raleigh-Durham | 92 | 0 | 9.8 | 5-9 | 1 | 0 |
| Buffalo | 83 | 1 | 5.8 | <5 | 10 | 0 |
| St. Louis | 83 | 0 | 5.1 | 5-9 | 23 | 0 |
| Salt Lake City | 75 | 0 | 2.0 | <5 | 11 | 0 |
| Tucson | 67 | 1 | 2.5 | NA | NA | 0 |
| Oklahoma City | 67 | 0 | 5.7 | <5 | 4 | 0 |
| San Antonio | 67 | 0 | 3.8 | 5-9 | 5 | 1 |

*International Presence Index (New York City=158)*

Source: *World Trade, Oct. 1993*

# Export Regulations

EXPORT CONTROLS ARE ADMINISTERED by the Bureau of Export Administration (BXA) in the U.S. Department of Commerce, and are described in detail in the official *Export Administration Regulations (EAR)*. Whenever there is any doubt about how to comply with export regulations and licensing procedures, Department of Commerce officials or qualified professional consultants should be contacted for assistance.

The Department of Commerce controls exports for the following reasons:

- To restrict exports that would be detrimental to the national security of the United States;

- To advance the foreign policy of the United States, or to fulfill its declared international obligations;

- To protect the domestic economy from the excessive drain of materials that are in short supply and to reduce the serious inflationary impact of foreign demand.

Exports not controlled by the Department of Commerce are controlled by the following agencies:

- Department of State, Office of Defense Trade Controls (arms, ammunition and implements of war, and related technical data);

- Department of Justice, Drug Enforcement Administration (exports of certain narcotics and dangerous drugs);

- U.S. Maritime Administration (certain watercraft);

- Department of Agriculture (any tobacco seed and/or live tobacco plants);

- Department of the Interior (endangered fish and wildlife, migratory birds, and bald and golden eagles);

- Patent and Trademark Office (unclassified technical data contained in patent applications);

- Department of the Treasury, Office of Foreign Assets Control (certain business dealings involving U.S. persons and embargoed countries, and all exports to Libya).

In addition, exporters of food products should contact the Food and Drug Administration (FDA) Compliance Division, (301) 594-0054, to ensure that all foreign regulations, documents, and certification requirements are met.

## Export Licenses

An export license is the government document that permits the export of designated goods to certain destinations. All Commerce Department export licenses fall into two broad categories. *General licenses* do not require prior Commerce Department approval before shipment. *Validated licenses* are given to a particular exporter for a specified commodity to specified destinations for a specific end-use.

The majority of all exports leave the country under a general license authorization. A general license is a broad grant of authority by the government to all exporters for certain categories of products. Individual exporters do not need to apply for general licenses, since such authorization is already granted through *EAR*; they only need to know the authorization is available.

There are currently more than twenty different categories of general licenses. To qualify for a general license, an exporter must meet all of the described provisions and not violate any of the prohibitions listed in Part 771.2 of *EAR*. Violations of the *Export Administration Regulations* carry both civil and criminal penalties.

The procedure for applying for a validated license is to submit a completed application to: U.S. Department of Commerce, Office of Export Licensing, Herbert C. Hoover Building, Room 1093, Washington, DC 20230. Application forms may be ordered by sending a self-addressed mailing label to "Forms Request" at this same U.S. Department of Commerce address.

For assistance in determining the proper license, exporters may contact the Exporter Counseling Division of the Department of Commerce, Herbert C. Hoover Building, Room 1099B, Washington, DC 20230, (202) 482-4811. The exporter may also check with the local Department of Commerce district office.

## Contact Options

Bureau of Export Administration (BXA)
(202) 482-4811

BXA Eastern Regional Office
(603) 598-4300

BXA Western Regional Office
(714) 660-0144

Export Licensing Voice Information System (ELVIS)
(202) 482-4811

An automated attendant offers a range of licensing information and emergency handling procedures. Callers may order forms and publications or subscribe to the Office of Export Licensing (OEL) newsletter, called *OEL Insider*, which provides regulatory updates. Callers also will be given the option to speak to a consultant.

*Export Regulations (cont'd)*

## Recommended Resource

*A Basic Guide to Exporting*
Government Printing Office, $9.50
(202) 783-3238
    This comprehensive publication of the International Trade Administration helps businesses develop export strategies, find economic market research, ship overseas, complete export documentation, respond to overseas inquiries, and take advantage of available government export assistance programs.

*Export Administration Regulations*
Superintendent of Documents, $88/year
U.S. Government Printing Office
Washington, DC 20401
(202) 783-3238

## Import Regulations

    Import regulations imposed by foreign governments vary from country to country. Exporters should be aware of the regulations that apply to their own operations and transactions. Many governments require such items as consular invoices, certificates of inspection, health certification, and various other documents.

# Targeted Trade Barriers

TRADE BARRIERS CAN BE BROADLY DEFINED as government laws, regulations, policies, or practices that either protect domestic products from foreign competition or artificially stimulate exports of particular domestic products. While restrictive business practices sometimes have a similar effect, they are not usually regarded as trade barriers.

    The most common foreign trade barriers are government-imposed measures and policies that restrict, prevent, or impede the international exchange of goods and services. These include:

- Import policies such as tariffs, quantitative restrictions, import licensing, and customs barriers;

- Standards, testing, labeling, and certification in an unnecessarily restrictive application of standards;

- Export subsidies which offer export financing on preferential terms and displace U.S. exports in third country markets;

- Lack of intellectual property protection;

- Service barriers which regulate international data flow and foreign data processing;

- Investment barriers;

- Other barriers.

    The Office of the U.S. Trade Representative issues an annual report, called *Foreign Trade Barriers*, on 45 countries describing the trade barriers that exist in each country and estimating the impact on U.S. exports. Some of the countries included in the report are: Argentina, Brazil, Canada, China, Guatemala, India, Indonesia, Israel, Japan, Mexico, Nigeria, Singapore, Taiwan, Turkey, and Venezuela.

    *Foreign Trade Barriers* may be obtained through:

Office of the U.S. Trade Representative
Executive Office of the President
Washington, DC 20506
(202) 395-3230

    *Foreign Trade Barriers* may also be directly ordered from the Government Printing Office (GPO), (202) 783-3238, or one of the local offices.

    Other useful information may be obtained through the Trade Information Center, a one-stop information source on a multitude of federal export assistance programs. This service connects the caller with international trade specialists on a toll-free line.

Trade Information Center
Department of Commerce
14th St., NW, and Constitution Ave.
Washington, DC 20230
(800) 872-8723

# Import/Export Directories

*American Export Register*
Thomas Publishing Co., $120
5 Penn Plaza
New York, NY 10001
(212) 695-0500

This annual two-volume, 3,000-page directory features product listings in more than 4,200 categories. The reference also includes:

- Alphabetical listing of nearly 43,000 U.S. companies;

- Product listings in ten languages;

- Directory of import/export services (banks, cargo carriers, customs brokers, embassies, railroads).

*Directory of United States Importers*
*Directory of United States Exporters*
Journal of Commerce Business Directories,
$399 each, $599 both
445 Marshall St.
Phillipsburg, NJ 08865
(800) 222-0356

World trade directories featuring numerical product listings and company profile listings.

*Bergano's Register of International Importers*, $95
Bergano Books
P.O. Box 190
Fairfield, CT 06430
(203) 254-2054

A comprehensive resource of 2,000 leading distributors, dealers, agents, and representatives in over 75 important international markets.

# Making International Contacts

## Matchmaker Trade Delegations

Organized and led by Commerce Department personnel, Matchmaker trade delegations enable new-to-export and new-to-market firms to meet pre-screened prospects who are interested in their products or services in overseas markets. Matchmaker delegations usually target major markets in two countries and limit trips to a week or less. U.S. firms can interview a maximum number of prospective business partners with a minimum of time away from the office. Thorough briefings on market requirements and business practices and interpreters' services are provided. Delegation members pay their own expenses. For further information, call Export Promotion Services, International Trade Administration, (202) 482-3119.

## Trade Fairs and Exhibitions

About 80 international worldwide events are selected annually for recruitment by the Commerce Department or by the private sector under the Commerce's certification program. Exhibitors receive pre- and post-event logistical and transportation support, design and management of the USA pavilion, and extensive overseas market promotional campaigns to attract appropriate business audiences. For further information on trade fairs and exhibitions, call the Trade Information Center, (800) 872-8723.

The ITA also publishes *The Export Promotion Calendar*, a quarterly publication listing trade shows, trade fairs, seminars, and other events by industry, with dates and contact numbers.

---

## The Top Reference Sources

*Guide to Worldwide Postal-Code & Address Formats*
Marian Nelson, $99.50
(212) 362-9855

This postal guide is an extremely useful reference for anyone involved in using the mails to do business with a foreign country, from executives, to data managers to mailroom personnel.

The book includes practical tips for standardizing foreign addresses, including: city and county names, postal-code formats, abbreviations, sample addresses, information sources, and more. It is updated annually.

# International Price Indexes

THE U.S. EXPORT AND IMPORT PRICE indexes are general purpose indexes that measure changes in price levels within the foreign trade sector. The all-export index provides a measure of price change for domestically produced U.S. products shipped to other countries. The all-import index measures price change of goods purchased from other countries by U.S. residents.

## Import Price Indexes

|                | 1983  | 1984  | 1985  | 1986 | 1987 | 1988 | 1989 | 1990  | 1991  | 1992  | 1993  |
|----------------|-------|-------|-------|------|------|------|------|-------|-------|-------|-------|
| ALL COMMODITIES | 82.3  | 82.6  | 80.7  | 80.6 | 88.4 | 93.2 | 96.5 | 100.0 | 99.7  | 100.3 | 100.1 |
| Non-petroleum  | NA    | NA    | 76.9  | 88.3 | 89.7 | 96.8 | 98.5 | 100.0 | 101.2 | 102.6 | 103.2 |
| Petroleum      | 120.0 | 118.8 | 112.8 | 59.9 | 80.0 | 67.0 | 80.4 | 100.0 | 88.0  | 82.2  | 75.4  |

## Export Price Indexes

|                  | 1983 | 1984 | 1985 | 1986 | 1987 | 1988  | 1989  | 1990  | 1991  | 1992  | 1993  |
|------------------|------|------|------|------|------|-------|-------|-------|-------|-------|-------|
| ALL COMMODITIES  | NA   | 89.6 | 88.0 | 87.1 | 90.4 | 96.9  | 99.3  | 100.0 | 100.8 | 100.9 | 101.4 |
| Non-agricultural | NA   | NA   | 86.9 | 86.7 | 90.5 | 95.6  | 98.3  | 100.0 | 100.9 | 101.2 | 101.8 |
| Agricultural     | NA   | NA   | 92.5 | 85.6 | 87.0 | 103.3 | 106.2 | 100.0 | 99.0  | 98.1  | 99.9  |

*The average for the year 1990 is set to equal 100.*                              *Source: Bureau of Labor Statistics*

## The Top Reference Sources

*UNESCO Statistical Yearbook*
UNIPUB, $80
Order #U-2887
(301) 459-7666

Member states of the United Nations Education, Scientific and Cultural Organization report periodically on their laws, regulations, and statistics relating to educational, scientific, and cultural life. Statistics in this valuable yearbook include school enrollment ratios, educational expenditures, R&D expenditures, number of books, periodicals, and newspapers published, number of films imported, number of films produced, radio and television broadcasting revenues and expenditures, among others.

# Translation Services

THE TRANSLATION COMPANIES and language instruction services listed here all provide the following:

- Translation in all languages;

- All subjects (legal, technical, advertising, etc.);

- Interpreters (consecutive and simultaneous);

- Desktop publishing, typesetting, graphic arts;

- Film, video, and slide adaptations (narrative and voice-over).

## Contact Options

*Associations that Provide Referrals:*

American Society of Interpreters
P.O. Box 9603
Washington, DC 20016
(703) 883-0611

American Translators Association
1735 Jefferson Davis Hwy., Suite 903
Arlington, VA 22202
(703) 412-1500

*Translation Companies:*

Berlitz Translation Services
New York Center, 17th Floor
257 Park Ave. S
New York, NY 10010
(212) 777-7878
  Has 29 translation centers located in 18 countries worldwide.

Inlingua
551 Fifth Ave., Room 720
New York, NY 10176
(212) 682-8585
  Offers services in 250 offices worldwide.

The Language Lab
211 E. 43rd St.
New York, NY 10017
(212) 697-2891 or (800) 682-3126
  Also offers instruction services to corporations.

Berlitz International
293 Wall Street
Princeton, NJ 08540
(609) 924-8500 or (800) 257-9449
  Operates language centers in over 205 cities throughout the world, with training in all spoken languages.

Lingua Service Worldwide
2 West 45th Street, #500
New York, NY 10036
(800) 394-5327
(212) 768-2728

Modern Language Association of America
10 Astor Pl.
New York, NY 10003
(212) 475-9500
  Provides a list of language immersion and study programs (domestic and abroad).

## Over-the-Phone Interpretation

  AT&T Language Line offers 24-hour-a-day access to interpretations of over 140 languages, over the phone, within minutes. To reach an AT&T Language Line Services interpreter from the United States or Canada, call (800) 628-8486. Interpreter time costs $3.50 a minute, billable to major credit cards. The Language Line Service also provides software localization, translation and multinational document management services, and multilingual telephone marketing.

  MCI does not offer a general interpretation service, but provides translators for customer-service calls in Spanish, Japanese, Vietnamese, Korean, German, French, Italian, Cantonese, Tagalog, Portuguese and Mandarin. Call (800) 888-0800.

## Bilingual Business Cards

  In some countries, Japan especially, exchanging business cards at any first meeting is considered a basic part of good business etiquette. As a matter of courtesy, it is best to carry business cards printed both in English and in the language of the country being visited. There are many companies in the United States that translate and print bilingual business cards, among them:

Advantage
All languages
(212) 213-6464

Inlingua
All languages
(713) 622-1516

Oriental Printing
Japanese, Chinese, Korean
(708) 439-4822

Paramount Process Printing
All languages
(212) 691-3700

# Training for International Business

THE INCREASE IN INTERNATIONAL business opportunities has resulted in a need to train and prepare not only the global executive, but also the international regional director and the first-line supervisor. Overseas living requires cultural education, knowledge of the language, social, political, and economic institutions, as well as the business customs of a particular country. Corporate Human Resources are expanding to include programs which enhance the ability of the businessperson to cope and function in an alien environment and to facilitate the adjustment of spouses and children.

Experts point out that it is vital to prepare the international businessperson to deal with a new culture and thus reduce the incidence of failure in the overseas assignment. However, it is also critical to prepare the individual who has completed an extended assignment in a foreign land to return to the United States. Reassimilation into American culture after an extended absence or immersion in a radically different culture is an often neglected area of human resources and requires special attention and guidance.

The following are some current programs which focus on the needs of the international businessperson and his or her family:

## Contact Options

The Business Council for International
Understanding Institute (BCIU)
The American University
3301 New Mexico Ave., NW, Suite 244
Washington, DC 20016
(202) 686-2771
Works with over 400 major international corporations and 30,000 families relocating in 162 nations.

The International Society for Intercultural Education, Training and Research (SIETAR International)
1505 22nd St., NW
Washington, DC 20037
(202) 466-7883
Provides information on programs of intercultural education, training, and research. Over 2,000 members contribute to a bimonthly newsletter and calendar of events, as well as a quarterly journal dealing with issues to promote intercultural understanding through nonpolitical avenues.

Intercultural Press
P.O. Box 700
Yarmouth, ME 04096
(207) 846-5168
Produces an extensive list of titles on cross-cultural interaction and offers consultation services for issues such as communication and supervision in overseas settings. Call for a catalogue.

## Recommended Resources

*Do's and Taboos Around the World*
Edited by Roger E. Axtell
John Wiley & Sons, $12.95
(212) 850-6000

*International Business Practices*
Government Printing Office, $18
(202) 783-3238
Provides information about 117 countries including business organizations, exporting, regulatory agencies, foreign investment, and at least three useful contacts with phone numbers.

*The International Businesswoman of the 1990s: A Guide to Success in the Global Marketplace*
by Marlene L. Rossman
Praeger Publishers, $19.95
(203) 226-3571

*The Multinational Executive Travel Companion*
Suburban Publishing, $60
(203) 324-6439

*Delphi offers a translation service that can handle documents in more than 100 languages. GO MAI TRAN.*

# World Business Languages

## World Countries and Suggested Business Languages

| Country | Suggested Business Language(s) |
|---|---|
| Afghanistan | Russian, English |
| Albania | Albanian |
| Algeria | French, Arabic |
| Andorra | French, Spanish |
| Angola | Portuguese |
| Antigua and Barbuda | English |
| Argentina | Spanish |
| Australia | English |
| Austria | German |
| Bahamas | English |
| Bahrain | English, Arabic |
| Bangladesh | English |
| Barbados | English |
| Belgium | French, Dutch |
| Belize | English, Spanish |
| Benin | French |
| Bhutan | English |
| Bolivia | Spanish |
| Botswana | English |
| Brazil | Portuguese |
| Brunei | English |
| Bulgaria | Bulgarian |
| Burkina Faso (Upper Volta) | French |
| Burma | English |
| Burundi | French |
| Cambodia | French |
| Cameroon | French, English |
| Canada | English, French |
| Cape Verde | Portuguese |
| Central African Republic | French |
| Chad | French, Arabic |
| Chile | Spanish |
| China | English, Mandarin |
| Colombia | Spanish |
| Comoros | French, Arabic |
| Congo | French |
| Costa Rica | Spanish |
| Cuba | Spanish |
| Cyprus | English |
| The Czech Republic | Czech, Slovak |
| Denmark | Danish |
| Djibouti | French, Arabic |
| Dominica | English, French |
| Dominican Republic | Spanish |
| Ecuador | Spanish |

| Country | Suggested Business Language(s) |
|---|---|
| Egypt | English, Arabic |
| El Salvador | Spanish |
| Equatorial Guinea | Spanish |
| Ethiopia | English, Arabic |
| Fiji | English |
| Finland | Finnish, Swedish |
| France | French |
| Gabon | French |
| Gambia, The | English |
| Germany | German |
| Ghana | English |
| Gibraltar | English, Spanish |
| Greece | Greek |
| Grenada | English |
| Guatemala | Spanish |
| Guinea | French |
| Guinea-Bissau | Portuguese |
| Guyana | English |
| Haiti | French |
| Honduras | Spanish |
| Hong Kong | English, Cantonese |
| Hungary | Hungarian |
| Iceland | Icelandic |
| India | English |
| Indonesia | English |
| Iran | English, French |
| Iraq | English, Arabic |
| Irish Republic | English, Irish |
| Israel | English |
| Italy | Italian |
| Ivory Coast | French |
| Jamaica | English |
| Japan | English, Japanese |
| Jordan | English, Arabic |
| Kenya | English |
| Korea, North | English |
| Korea, South | English |
| Kuwait | English, Arabic |
| Laos | French |
| Lebanon | English, Arabic |
| Lesotho | English |
| Liberia | English |
| Libya | Arabic, English |
| Liechtenstein | German |
| Luxembourg | French, German |

*World Business Languages (cont'd)*

| Country | Suggested Business Language(s) |
|---------|-------------------------------|
| Madagascar | French |
| Malaysia | English |
| Maldives | English |
| Mali | French |
| Malta | English, Maltese |
| Mauritania | French, Arabic |
| Mauritius | English, French |
| Mexico | Spanish |
| Monaco | French |
| Mongolia | Russian |
| Morocco | French, Spanish, Arabic |
| Mozambique | Portuguese |
| Namibia | Afrikaans, German, Eng. |
| Nauru | English |
| Nepal | English |
| Netherlands, The | Dutch |
| New Zealand | English |
| Nicaragua | Spanish |
| Niger | French |
| Nigeria | English |
| Norway | Norwegian |
| Oman | English, Arabic |
| Pakistan | English |
| Panama | Spanish, English |
| Papua New Guinea | English |
| Paraguay | Spanish |
| Peru | Spanish |
| Philippines | English, Spanish |
| Poland | Polish |
| Portugal | Portuguese |
| Puerto Rico | English, Spanish |
| Qatar | English, Arabic |
| Romania | Romanian |
| Russia | Russian |
| Rwanda | French |
| St. Kitts & Nevis | English |
| St. Lucia | English, French |
| St. Vincent | English |
| San Marino | Italian |
| São Tomé and Principe | Portuguese |

| Country | Suggested Business Language(s) |
|---------|-------------------------------|
| Saudi Arabia | English, Arabic |
| Senegal | French |
| Seychelles | English, French |
| Sierra Leone | English |
| Singapore | English |
| Solomon Islands | English |
| Somalia | English, Italian, Arabic |
| South Africa | English, Afrikaans |
| South Yemen | English, Arabic |
| Spain | Spanish |
| Sri Lanka | English |
| Sudan | English, Arabic |
| Suriname | Dutch, English |
| Swaziland | English |
| Sweden | Swedish |
| Switzerland | German, French, Italian |
| Syria | English, Arabic |
| Taiwan | English, Mandarin |
| Tanzania | English |
| Thailand | English |
| Tonga | English |
| Trinidad and Tobago | English |
| Tunisia | French, Arabic |
| Turkey | Turkish |
| Tuvalu | English |
| Uganda | English |
| United Arab Emirates | English, Arabic |
| United Kingdom | English |
| United States of America | English |
| Uruguay | Spanish |
| Vatican City | Italian |
| Venezuela | Spanish |
| Vietnam | French |
| Western Samoa | English |
| Yemen | English, Arabic |
| Yugoslavia | Serbo-Croat |
| Zaire | French |
| Zambia | English |
| Zimbabwe | English |

# International Price Comparisons

## Price Comparisons of Selected Items, by City (in U.S. Dollars)

| Item | Amster-dam | Beijing | Berlin | Brussels | Dublin | Geneva | Hong Kong | London |
|---|---|---|---|---|---|---|---|---|
| Chocolate candy bar (150 g) | 1.36 | 3.66 | 0.94 | 1.31 | 0.93 | 1.62 | 0.00 | 1.13 |
| Carbonated soft drink (6 pack) | 2.47 | 3.26 | 2.67 | 2.98 | 2.92 | 3.76 | 0.00 | 2.68 |
| Bottled mineral water (1 liter) | 0.47 | 1.54 | 0.81 | 0.69 | 0.59 | 0.53 | 0.00 | 0.51 |
| Wine (750 ml) | 6.17 | 22.89 | 4.77 | 7.20 | 9.30 | 8.75 | 16.09 | 7.65 |
| Dry cleaning (man's suit–1 piece) | 10.89 | 5.17 | 11.63 | 12.42 | 8.05 | 14.89 | 7.96 | 11.85 |
| Woman's haircut–wash/dry | 47.80 | 36.51 | 45.45 | 46.03 | 25.08 | 50.81 | 73.01 | 53.28 |
| Toothpaste (100 ml) | 1.83 | 4.12 | 1.90 | 1.90 | 1.72 | 1.96 | 0.87 | 1.98 |
| Deodorant (155 ml) | 1.99 | 8.18 | 1.92 | 3.30 | 1.69 | 3.62 | 4.03 | 1.98 |
| Aspirin (20 units) | 12.29 | 14.72 | 13.56 | 6.64 | 3.46 | 16.91 | 7.16 | 3.38 |
| Blank video tape (1 unit) | 6.41 | 4.43 | 6.96 | 4.77 | 5.62 | 9.07 | 5.60 | 7.08 |
| Camera film (36 exposures) | 22.42 | 9.34 | 20.57 | 21.09 | 14.32 | 26.63 | 11.02 | 14.43 |
| Paperback book (1 unit) | 11.23 | 7.99 | 13.20 | 10.72 | 8.45 | 10.84 | 13.82 | 8.67 |
| Movie ticket (1 unit) | 7.43 | NA | 7.76 | 7.59 | 5.58 | 9.81 | 5.63 | 8.94 |
| Taxi ride (2 km) | 3.99 | 1.38 | 6.27 | 4.81 | 4.81 | 7.01 | 1.49 | 4.47 |
| Business lunch (for two) | 70.54 | 43.70 | 64.03 | 48.72 | 36.98 | 59.31 | 60.02 | 50.30 |
| Hotel (daily rate) | 174.27 | 187.00 | 208.38 | 329.22 | 162.16 | 206.90 | 307.98 | 310.65 |

| Item | Madrid | Moscow | Paris | Rome | São Paulo | Tokyo | Toronto | Vienna |
|---|---|---|---|---|---|---|---|---|
| Chocolate candy bar (150 g) | 0.96 | 2.00 | 1.40 | 1.27 | 1.12 | 3.85 | 2.18 | 1.48 |
| Carbonated soft drink (6 pack) | 4.22 | 5.23 | 2.21 | 2.65 | 2.82 | 7.98 | 4.27 | 2.31 |
| Bottled mineral water (1 liter) | 0.28 | 1.00 | 0.31 | 0.29 | 0.27 | 1.64 | 1.13 | 0.71 |
| Wine (750 ml) | 8.03 | 20.67 | 4.47 | 9.01 | 17.35 | 15.00 | 10.01 | 9.05 |
| Dry cleaning (man's suit–1 piece) | 11.52 | 28.74 | 21.05 | 8.65 | 16.08 | 25.47 | 10.45 | 12.92 |
| Woman's haircut–wash/dry | 35.01 | 35.70 | 51.77 | 37.14 | 23.18 | 87.20 | 44.65 | 44.22 |
| Toothpaste (100 ml) | 2.25 | 4.40 | 2.01 | 2.26 | 1.00 | 7.39 | 1.84 | 2.49 |
| Deodorant (155 ml) | 2.43 | 8.04 | 2.11 | 3.57 | 2.49 | 14.67 | 2.55 | 3.45 |
| Aspirin (20 units) | 7.49 | 12.60 | 9.36 | 13.33 | 7.37 | 23.78 | 4.39 | 10.42 |
| Blank video tape (1 unit) | 5.03 | 15.46 | 7.20 | 4.48 | 8.29 | 8.00 | 6.00 | 9.44 |
| Camera film (36 exposures) | 19.97 | 25.59 | 24.89 | 13.42 | 35.11 | 11.66 | 22.93 | 16.99 |
| Paperback book (1 unit) | 8.92 | 12.90 | 10.49 | 9.05 | 14.30 | 12.62 | 9.18 | 9.90 |
| Movie ticket (1 unit) | 4.25 | 7.35 | 7.47 | 5.97 | 3.54 | 21.88 | 8.00 | 7.38 |
| Taxi ride (2 km) | 2.34 | 6.48 | 3.57 | 5.79 | 0.54 | 5.71 | 5.20 | 4.10 |
| Business lunch (for two) | 29.89 | 50.00 | 66.07 | 49.20 | 34.00 | 63.72 | 41.85 | 68.05 |
| Hotel (daily rate) | 173.74 | 328.00 | 258.13 | 166.24 | 204.00 | 408.04 | 168.16 | 216.08 |

Note: Prices recorded between October, 1993 and February, 1994.

Source: Organization Resources Counselors

# International Cost of Living

THE FOLLOWING TABLE RANKS the relative cost of living in ten expensive cities worldwide. All locations are compared to Standard City, USA, which has an index of 1.00. Comparisons include housing, goods and services, and transportation costs, and assume an annual income of $60,000 and a family size of four.

| City | Index |
|------|-------|
| Cairo | 1.29 |
| Hong Kong | 3.10 |
| London | 1.81 |
| Manhattan | 2.06 |
| Mexico City | 1.83 |

| City | Index |
|------|-------|
| Moscow | 1.61 |
| Paris | 2.15 |
| São Paulo | 1.96 |
| Sydney | 1.39 |
| Tokyo | 4.62 |

*Source: Runzheimer International*

# The Newly Independent States

## BISNIS

Business Information Service for the Newly Independent States (BISNIS) assists U.S. firms interested in doing business in the Newly Independent States (NIS) of the former Soviet Union. It maintains current information on prevailing trade regulations and legislation, economic and industrial market data, up-to-date lists of NIS government officials, potential business contacts, available financing, trade promotion activities, and other practical market and business reports. The Flashfax BISNIS Bank is an automated information bank of fast-breaking trade leads and market information provided immediately by fax, 24 hours a day, seven days a week.

## Contact Option

Business Information Service for the Newly Independent States (BISNIS)
U.S. Department of Commerce
International Trade Administration
Room 7413
Washington, DC 20230
(202) 482-4655
Flashfax: (202) 482-3145

## The Top Reference Sources

*Export Profits*
Upstart Publishing Company, $19.95
(603) 749-5071

This very thorough reference, written by international trade consultant Jack S. Wolf, is essential reading for managers of small- and mid-size businesses who want to begin exporting.

With an extensive glossary, lists of resources, and sample documents, this book shows how to decide whether a business should export, find the right foreign markets for its products, choose distributors or agents, minimize currency risks, and cut through red tape.

Other topics discussed include pricing, shipping, finding a banker, property rights protection, and test marketing.

# Carnets

THE ATA CARNET IS a standardized international customs document used to obtain duty-free temporary admission of certain goods into the countries that are signatories to the ATA Convention. Under the ATA Convention, commmercial and professional travelers may take commercial samples, tools of the trade, advertising material, and cinematographic, audiovisual, medical, scientific, or other professional equipment into member countries temporarily without paying customs duties and taxes, or posting a bond at the border of each country to be visited.

Countries participating in the ATA Carnet System include: Australia, Austria, Belgium, Bulgaria, Canada, Cyprus, Denmark, Finland, France, Germany, Gibraltar, Greece, Hong Kong, Hungary, Iceland, India (commercial samples only), Iran, Ireland, Israel, Italy, Ivory Coast, Japan, Luxembourg, Mauritius, Netherlands, New Zealand, Norway, Poland, Portugal, Romania, Senegal, Singapore, Sri Lanka (certain professional equipment not accepted), South Africa, South Korea, Spain, Sweden, Switzerland, Turkey, United Kingdom, and United States.

Since other countries are continuously added to the ATA Carnet system, travelers should contact the U.S. Council for International Business if the country to be visited is not included in this list. Applications for carnets should also be made through the U.S. Council. The fee depends on the value of the goods to be covered. A bond, letter of credit, or bank guaranty of over 40 percent of the value of the goods is also required to cover duties and taxes that would be due if goods imported into a foreign country by carnet were not re-exported and the duties were not paid by the carnet holder. The carnets generally are valid for 12 months.

*Source: A Basic Guide to Exporting*

## Contact Option

U.S. Council for International Business
1212 Avenue of the Americas
New York, NY 10036
(212) 354-4480

# PAL, SECAM, NTSC Conversion

PAL, SECAM, and NTSC refer to the different kinds of video systems around the world. For a videotape to play in a foreign country's system, it must be converted to the correct format. Check the local Yellow Pages under Video Production Services, to find a local company that will convert U.S. tapes for viewing abroad and foreign tapes for viewing in the United States. Costs for this service vary according to the quality or definition required and the type of equipment used to make the conversions. Mid-range equipment conversions run from $40 to $70 for the first hour.

## Formats Used

*PAL*
Western Europe—excluding France—also, Australia, South Africa, parts of Asia, including India, China

*PAL-M*
Brazil

*PAL-N*
Argentina

*NTSC*
North America

*SECAM*
France, Eastern Bloc, and parts of the Middle East

# Electric Current Conversions

| Country | Cycles | Volts |
|---|---|---|
| Afghanistan | 50/60 | 220/380 |
| Algeria | 50 | 127/220 |
|  | 50 | 220/380 |
| Andorra | 50 | 110/130 |
|  | 50 | 220/380 |
| Angola | 50 | 220/380 |
| Antigua | 60 | 110/220 |
| Argentina | 50 | 220/380 |
| Australia | 50 | 220/250 |
| Austria | 50 | 220/380 |
| Bahamas | 60 | 120/208 |
|  | 60 | 120/240 |
| Bahrain | 50 | 230 |
| Bangladesh | 50 | 220/240 |
| Barbados | 50 | 110 |
| Belgium (Brussels) | 50 | 220/380 |
| Belize | 60 | 110/220 |
| Benin | 60 | 220 |
| Bermuda | 50 | 110/220 |
| Bolivia | 60 | 110/220 |
| Botswana | 50 | 230 |
| Brazil |  |  |
| (Belem) | 60 | 127/220 |
| (Brazilia) | 60 | 220/240 |
|  | 60 | 220/380 |
| (Recife) | 60 | 127/220 |
| (Rio de Janeiro) | 60 | 127/220 |
| (São Paulo) | 60 | 115/230 |
| Brunei | 50 | 240 |
| Bulgaria | 50 | 220/380 |
| Burkina Faso | 50 | 220 |
| Burma | 50 | 230/250 |
| Burundi | 50 | 220 |
| Cambodia | 50 | 220 |
| Cameroon | 50 | 110/220 |
| Canada | 60 | 120/240 & 110 |
| Central Afr. Rep. | 50 | 220/380 |
| Chad | 50 | 220/380 |
| Chile | 50 | 220/380 |
| China | 50 | 220/380 |
|  | 60 | 110/220 |
| Colombia | 60 | 110/120 |
| Bogota | 60 | 150/240 |
| Congo | 50 | 220 |
| Costa Rica | 60 | 120/240 & 110 |
| Cuba | 60 | 110/220 |
| Curacao | 50 | 127/220 |
| Cyprus | 50 | 220/240 |
|  | 50 | 240/415 |
| Czech Republic | 50 | 220/380 |

| Country | Cycles | Volts |
|---|---|---|
| Denmark | 50 | 220/380 |
| Dominica | 50 | 220/240 |
| Dominican Rep. | 60 | 110/220 |
| Ecuador | 60 | 120/208 |
|  | 60 | 120/240 |
|  | 60 | 110/220 |
|  | 60 | 121/210 |
| Egypt | 50 | 110/220/380 |
| El Salvador | 60 | 110 |
| Ethiopia | 50 | 220/380 |
| Finland | 50 | 220/380 |
| France | 50 | 220/380 |
|  | 50 | 110/115 |
|  | 50 | 127/220 |
| Gabon | 50 | 220 |
| Gambia | 50 | 230/400, 200 |
| Germany | 50 | 220/380 |
| Ghana | 50 | 220/400 |
| Great Britain | 50 | 240 & 240/415 |
| Greece | 50 | 220, 220/380/127 |
| Greenland | 50 | 220/380 |
| Grenada | 50 | 220/240 |
| Guatemala | 60 | 120/240, 110 |
| Guinea | 50 | 220/380 |
| Guyana | 60 | 110 |
| Haiti | 60 | 110/220 |
| Hawaii | 60 | 120 |
| Honduras | 60 | 110/220 |
| Hong Kong | 50 | 220, 200/346 |
| Hungary | 50 | 220/380 |
| Iceland | 50 | 220/380/ 240 |
| India | 50 | 230/400/ 220 |
| Indonesia | 50 | 127/220 |
| Iran | 50 | 220/380 |
| Iraq | 50 | 220/380 |
| Ireland | 50 | 220/380 |
| Israel | 50 | 230/400/ 220 |
| Italy | 50 | 220/380 |
|  | 50 | 127/220 |
| Ivory Coast | 50 | 220/380 |
| Jamaica | 50 | 110/220 |
| Japan | 50/60 | 100/200 |
| Jordan | 50 | 220/380 |
| Kenya | 50 | 240/415 |
| Kiribati | 50 | 240 |
| Korea | 60 | 110/220 |
| Kuwait | 50 | 240/415 |
| Laos | 50 | 220/380 |
| Lebanon | 50 | 110/190 |
|  | 50 | 220/380 |

*Electric Current Conversions (cont'd)*

| Country | Cycles | Volts |
|---|---|---|
| Lesotho | 50 | 220 |
| Liberia | 60 | 110,120/240 |
| | | 120/208 |
| Libya | 50 | 125/220 |
| Liechtenstein | 50 | 110/220 |
| Luxembourg | 50 | 120/208 |
| | 50 | 220/380 |
| Madagascar | 50 | 110/220 |
| Malawi | 50 | 230/400 |
| Malaysia | 50 | 230/240/415 |
| Mali | 50 | 220/380 |
| Malta | 50 | 240/415 |
| Mauritania | 50 | 220 |
| Mauritius | 50 | 230 |
| Mexico | 60 | varies |
| Federal District | 60 | 127/220 |
| Monaco | 50 | 220/380 |
| | 50 | 110/115 |
| Morocco | 50 | 115/200 |
| | 60 | 110/125 |
| Mozambique | 50 | 220/380 |
| Namibia | 50 | 220/240 |
| Nauru | 50 | 240 |
| Nepal | 50 | 220 |
| Netherlands | 50 | 220/380 |
| New Zealand | 50 | 230/400 |
| Nicaragua | 60 | 120/240/110 |
| Niger | 50 | 220/380 |
| Nigeria | 50 | 210/250 |
| | 50 | 230/415 |
| Norway | 50 | 220/230 |
| Oman | 50 | 220/240 |
| Pakistan | 50 | 220/230/400 |
| Panama | 60 | 110/120 |
| Papua New Guinea | 50 | 240/415 |
| Paraguay | 50 | 220 |
| Peru | 60 | 220 |
| Philippines | 60 | 110/220 |
| | 50 | 110/120 |
| Poland | 50 | 220/380 |
| Portugal | 50 | 220/380 |
| | 50 | 110/190 |
| Puerto Rico | 60 | 120/240 |
| Qatar | 50 | 220/240 |
| Romania | 50 | 220/380 |
| Russia | 50 | 127/220, 220 |
| Rwanda | 50 | 280/380 |
| St. Christopher & Nevis | 60 | 230 |
| St. Lucia | 50 | 220 |
| St. Vincent | 60 | 220/240 |

| Country | Cycles | Volts |
|---|---|---|
| Saudi Arabia | 60 | 110/120 |
| Mecca | 50 | 220 |
| Senegal | 50 | 110/220 |
| Sierra Leone | 50 | 220/400 |
| Singapore | 50 | 230/400 |
| Solomon Islands | 50 | 230/415 |
| Somalia | 50 | 200 |
| South Africa | 50 | 250 |
| Spain | 50 | 110/130 |
| | 50 | 220/380 |
| Sri Lanka | 50 | 230/400 |
| Sudan | 50 | 240/415 |
| | 60 | 127/220 |
| Suriname | 60 | 127/220 |
| Swaziland | 50 | 220 |
| Sweden | 50 | 220/380 |
| Switzerland | 50 | 110/220 |
| | 50 | 220/380 |
| Syria | 50 | 110/190 |
| | 50 | 220/380 |
| Tahiti | 60 | 220 & 110 |
| Taiwan | 60 | 110 |
| Tanzania | 50 | 230/400 |
| Thailand | 50 | 220/380 |
| Togo | 50 | 127/220 |
| | 50 | 220/380 |
| Tonga | 50 | 240 |
| Trinidad & Tobago | 60 | 115/220 |
| | 60 | 230/400 |
| Tunisia | 50 | 110/190 |
| | 50 | 220/380 |
| Turkey | 50 | 110/220 |
| | 50 | 220/380 |
| Uganda | 50 | 240/415 |
| United Arab Emirates | 50 | 220/240 |
| Uruguay | 50 | 220 |
| U.S. | 60 | 110 |
| Venezuela | 60 | 120/240 |
| Caracas | 50 | 120/208 |
| Vietnam | 50 | 120/127/220 |
| | 50 | 220/380 |
| Virgin Islands | 60 | 120/240 |
| Yugoslavia | 50 | 220/380 |
| Zaire | 50 | 220/380 |
| Zambia | 50 | 220/380 |
| Zimbabwe | 50 | 230 |

*Note: Pay particular attention to cycles when using any electronic or computer equipment.*

# Currencies of the World

| Country | Currency | Subcurrency |
|---|---|---|
| Afghanistan | afghani | 100 puls |
| Algeria | dinar | 100 centimes |
| Argentina | austral | 100 centavos |
| Australia | dollar | 100 cents |
| Austria | schilling | 100 groschen |
| Bahamas | dollar | 100 cents |
| Bahrain | dinar | 1,000 fils |
| Barbados | dollar | 100 cents |
| Belgium | franc | 100 centimes |
| Belize | dollar | 100 cents |
| Benin | franc | 100 centimes |
| Bolivia | boliviano | 100 centavos |
| Botswana | pula | 100 thebe |
| Brazil | cruzeiro | 100 centavos |
| Brunei | dollar | 100 cents |
| Bulgaria | lev | 100 stotinki |
| Cameroon | franc | 100 centimes |
| Canada | dollar | 100 cents |
| Cayman Islands | dollar | 100 cents |
| Central African Rep. | franc | 100 centimes |
| Chad | franc | 100 centimes |
| Chile | peso | 100 centesimos |
| China | yuan | 10 jiao |
| Colombia | peso | 100 centavos |
| Congo | franc | 100 centimes |
| Costa Rica | colon | 100 centimos |
| Cuba | peso | 100 centavos |
| Czechoslovakia | koruna | 100 halers |
| Denmark | krone | 100 ore |
| Djibouti | franc | 100 centimes |
| Dominican Rep. | peso | 100 centavos |
| Ecuador | sucre | 100 centavos |
| Egypt | pound | 100 piasters |
| El Salvador | colon | 100 centavos |
| Ethiopia | birr | 100 cents |
| Fiji | dollar | 100 cents |
| Finland | markka | 100 penni |
| France | franc | 100 centimes |
| Gabon | franc | 100 centimes |
| Gambia | dalasi | 100 butut |
| Germany | deutsche mark | 100 pfennigs |
| Ghana | cedi | 100 pesewa |
| Greece | drachma | 100 lepta |
| Guatemala | quetzel | 100 centavos |
| Guinea | franc | 100 centimes |
| Guyana | dollar | 100 cents |
| Haiti | gourde | 100 centimes |
| Honduras | lempira | 100 centavos |
| Hong Kong | dollar | 100 cents |
| Hungary | forint | 100 fillér |

| Country | Currency | Subcurrency |
|---|---|---|
| Iceland | krona | 100 aurer |
| India | rupee | 100 paise |
| Indonesia | rupiah | 100 sen |
| Iraq | dinar | 1,000 fils |
| Ireland | pound | 100 pence |
| Israel | shekel | 100 agorot |
| Italy | lira | 100 centesimi |
| Ivory Coast | franc | 100 centimes |
| Jamaica | dollar | 100 cents |
| Japan | yen | |
| Jordan | dinar | 1,000 fils |
| Kenya | shilling | 100 cents |
| Kuwait | dinar | 1,000 fils |
| Lebanon | pound | 100 piasters |
| Luxembourg | franc | 100 centimes |
| Malawi | kwacha | 100 tambala |
| Malaysia | ringgit | 100 sen |
| Maldives | rufilyaa | 100 larees |
| Malta | lira | 100 cents |
| Mauritania | ouguiya | 5 khoums |
| Mauritius | rupee | 100 cents |
| Mexico | peso | 100 centavos |
| Morocco | dirham | 100 centimes |
| Nepal | rupee | 100 paisas |
| Netherlands | guilder | 100 cents |
| New Zealand | dollar | 100 cents |
| Nicaragua | cordoba | 100 centavos |
| Niger | franc | 100 centimes |
| Nigeria | naira | 100 kobos |
| Norway | krone | 100 ore |
| Oman | riyal-omani | 1,000 baiza |
| Pakistan | rupee | 100 paisas |
| Papua New Guinea | kina | 100 toea |
| Paraguay | guarani | 100 centimos |
| Peru | inti | |
| Philippines | peso | 100 centavos |
| Poland | zloty | 100 groszy |
| Portugal | escudo | 100 centavos |
| Qatar | riyal | 100 dirhams |
| Romania | leu | 100 bani |
| Saudi Arabia | riyal | 20 qurush |
| Senegal | franc | 100 centimes |
| Seychelles | rupee | 100 cents |
| Sierra Leone | leone | 100 cents |
| Singapore | dollar | 100 cents |
| Solomon Islands | dollar | 100 cents |
| Somalia | shilling | 100 cents |
| South Africa | rand | 100 cents |
| South Korea | won | 100 chon |
| Spain | peseta | 100 centimos |

*Currencies of the World (cont'd)*

| Country | Currency | Subcurrency |
|---|---|---|
| Sri Lanka | rupee | 100 cents |
| Sudan | pound | 100 piasters |
| Suriname | guilder | 100 cents |
| Sweden | krona | 100 ore |
| Switzerland | franc | 100 centimes |
| Syria | pound | 100 piasters |
| Taiwan | dollar | 100 cents |
| Tanzania | shilling | 100 cents |
| Thailand | baht | 100 satang |
| Togo | franc | 100 centimes |
| Trinidad, Tobago | dollar | 100 cents |
| Tunisia | dinar | 1,000 millimes |
| Turkey | lira | 100 kurus |
| Uganda | shilling | 100 cents |
| United Arab Emir. | dirham | 1,000 fils |

| Country | Currency | Subcurrency |
|---|---|---|
| United Kingdom | pound | 100 pence |
| United States | dollar | 100 cents |
| Uruguay | peso | 100 centesimos |
| Venezuela | bolivar | 100 centimos |
| Western Samoa | tala | 100 sene |
| Yugoslavia | dinar | 100 para |
| Zambia | kwacha | 100 ngwee |
| Zimbabwe | dollar | 100 cents |

# World Temperatures

## Outside North America

| Location | December–March (high/low) | June–August (high/low) |
|---|---|---|
| Amsterdam | 40/32 | 69/53 |
| Athens | 58/44 | 90/72 |
| Bali | 90/74 | 94/76 |
| Bangkok | 89/70 | 90/75 |
| Bogotá | 67/48 | 64/50 |
| Buenos Aires | 87/62 | 57/40 |
| Cairo | 67/48 | 94/69 |
| Caracas | 77/57 | 78/63 |
| Dublin | 47/36 | 67/51 |
| Guam | 90/72 | 86/69 |
| Hong Kong | 68/57 | 87/59 |
| Israel | 57/41 | 90/65 |
| Istanbul | 48/38 | 80/64 |
| Kathmandu | 65/36 | 84/70 |
| Lima | 75/53 | 77/61 |
| Lisbon | 55/44 | 84/63 |

| Location | December–March (high/low) | June–August (high/low) |
|---|---|---|
| London | 44/35 | 70/52 |
| Manila | 87/70 | 90/75 |
| Montevideo | 84/72 | 77/70 |
| Munich | 36/23 | 73/53 |
| Nairobi | 77/54 | 69/51 |
| New Delhi | 71/43 | 96/80 |
| Panama City | 88/71 | 86/70 |
| Paris | 44/36 | 76/58 |
| Quito | 77/57 | 78/65 |
| Rio de Janeiro | 82/71 | 76/70 |
| Rome | 55/42 | 85/66 |
| Santiago | 86/70 | 78/69 |
| Seoul | 30/20 | 81/69 |
| Singapore | 88/74 | 87/73 |
| Taiwan | 70/61 | 90/72 |
| Tokyo | 47/32 | 81/69 |

**TIP:** *For up-to-date currency equivalents, call Thomas Cook at (212) 883-0400.*

*World Temperatures (cont'd)*

## North America

| Location | December–March (high/low) | June–August (high/low) |
|---|---|---|
| Acapulco | 87/70 | 89/75 |
| Albuquerque | 72/40 | 91/62 |
| Austin | 63/42 | 93/72 |
| Bermuda | 68/58 | 84/73 |
| Boston | 40/22 | 80/58 |
| Cancún | 87/70 | 89/75 |
| Chicago | 34/18 | 82/64 |
| Dallas | 58/37 | 92/72 |
| Denver | 43/17 | 85/57 |
| Dominican Rep. | 85/69 | 88/72 |
| Honolulu | 76/68 | 84/72 |
| Jackson Hole, WY | 36/11 | 80/52 |
| Lake Tahoe | 50/16 | 89/40 |
| Las Vegas | 65/34 | 103/71 |
| Los Angeles | 66/47 | 76/58 |
| Mexico City | 72/43 | 75/53 |

| Location | December–March (high/low) | June–August (high/low) |
|---|---|---|
| Miami | 76/59 | 88/75 |
| Montreal | 24/10 | 72/54 |
| Nassau | 77/67 | 88/76 |
| New Orleans | 65/48 | 90/76 |
| New York | 41/27 | 80/65 |
| Palm Beach | 79/43 | 95/73 |
| Philadelphia | 42/29 | 83/64 |
| Port au Prince | 86/68 | 70/73 |
| St. Thomas | 85/72 | 89/76 |
| San Juan | 82/72 | 87/76 |
| Tucson | 65/39 | 97/71 |
| Vancouver | 44/36 | 67/53 |
| Washington, DC | 45/29 | 85/64 |

*Source: National Weather Service*

## The Top Reference Sources

*The Economist Atlas*
Henry Holt, $47.50
(212) 886-9200

This revised edition of a bestselling reference provides a comprehensive, fully-illustrated portrait of the world today. Included are up-to-date political and economic analyses, plus 70 pages of full-color political and geographical maps for every country in the world.

There are also 37 pages of thematic maps which allow comparisons between countries on a variety of subjects, from defense spending to foreign debt to environmental pollution.

# MANUFACTURING

# Industrial Buying Guides

RESEARCH SHOWS THAT 97 percent of all industrial purchases are initiated by the buyer, not the seller. And most purchases, either of a new product or plant facility, a new component or material, are made with the help of a buying guide. The best known, most comprehensive and widely used industrial buying system is the *Thomas Register of Manufacturers*. More than $400 million in purchases of products or services are transacted each day through this system. The *Thomas Register* combines a product and services section, company directories, and a catalogue file section, in one multi-volume reference set. The location of a company's distributors, engineering or service offices, plants, and sales offices may be found in the company profiles section of this reference. Companies may advertise and/or distribute their catalogues in the *Thomas Register*.

## Recommended Resources

*Thomas Register of American Manufacturers*
Thomas Publishing, $240
(212) 290-7277

*Sweet's Catalogue*
McGraw-Hill
(800) 442-2258
     Distributes manufacturers' catalogues for con-struction-related products. Call to apply for this free publication.

*MacRae's Blue Book*
Business Research Publications, $140
(212) 673-4700
     National industrial directory listing manufacturers only.

*U.S. Industrial Directory*
Reed Reference Publishing, $179
(708) 390-2900
     Annual reference listing products and services for industrial manufacturing.

*Standard & Poor's Register of Corporations, Directors and Executives*
Standard & Poor's, $595
(212) 208-8786
     Descriptive listing of corporations, but not a buying guide.

# Manufacturers' Sales Agencies

MANUFACTURERS' AGENTS ARE independent contractors who work on commission for more than one company. Most manufacturers who have turned to agents in recent years have done so after first working with a salaried sales force of their own. Companies switch for a variety of reasons, but often because they want to trim sales costs and fixed overhead. Start-up companies with little knowledge of what to expect from different territories, and with no sales benchmarks, also use agents rather than establish their own sales force. Ideally, the manufacturer's agent will represent other manufacturers' products which are compatible, but not competitive, with the company's own products. Experienced agents will be able to provide information on what to expect in various territories, when and how to advertise, and what a competitor's efforts are likely to be. Sales agencies are paid commissions only when they make a sale.

     The source of first resort for manufacturers in search of a sales agent or independent contractor is the *Directory of Manufacturers' Sales Agencies*, the membership directory of the Manufacturers' Agents National Association. This reference of 9,000 member agents and agencies is organized in three sections: alphabetically by agency name, by state, and by product classification. Profiles of the agencies include the kinds of products sold, sales territories, names of key officials, warehousing facilities, size of sales staff, and location of branch offices.

## Contact Option

Manufacturers' Agents National Association
P.O. Box 3467
Laguna Hills, CA 92654
(714) 859-4040
     MANA also publishes the monthly *Agency Sales Magazine*, along with numerous special reports on making the agency decision, finding the right agent, negotiating the agreement, and so on.

# Overseas Manufacturing

TO ASSIST U.S. MANUFACTURERS in the areas of trade and import/export, the International Trade Administration assigns country desk officers to every country in the world. These specialists collect information on a specific country's regulations, tariffs, business practices, political and economic climate, and may provide selected industry sector analyses for that country as well. (*See also "Country Desk Officers" on page 380.*)

## Contact Options

*Hong Kong, Ireland, Canada, and Mexico are leading exporters of manufactured goods to the United States. For information on manufacturing, contact:*

Hong Kong Government Industrial Promotion Office
680 Fifth Ave., 22nd Floor
New York, NY 10019
(212) 265-7273
Industrial Promotion Unit/Hong Kong

Economic & Trade Office
222 Kearny St., Suite 402
San Francisco, CA 94108
(415) 956-4560

Irish Development Office
345 Park Ave., 17th Floor
New York, NY 10154
(212) 750-4300

Investment Canada
P.O. Box 2800, Postal Station D
Ottawa, Ontario
Canada K1P 6A5
(613) 995-0465

Trade Commission of Mexico
150 E. 58th St.
New York, NY 10155
(212) 826-2916

# New Techniques and Consultants

## The Manufacturing Technology Centers Program

The United States' long-dominant position in the world's marketplace is declining due to increasingly sophisticated foreign competition and swiftly changing technologies. There are more than 350,000 manufacturing firms in the U.S. with fewer than 500 employees. These firms employ 12 million workers and account for over 50 percent of the total of this country's value added to goods and services. While many small manufacturing firms have been able to maintain their competitive edge in smaller domestic markets and in special technology areas, they simply have not kept pace with the rapidly changing, computer-driven global marketplace of the past decade. To address this problem, the Omnibus Trade and Competitiveness Act established the Manufacturing Technology Centers (MTC) Program as a new initiative at the National Institute of Standards and Technology (NIST). The program, authorized by Congress in 1988, was created to improve U.S. industrial productivity and competitiveness in the growing international marketplace.

Each MTC's approach is unique, dictated by its location and the type of manufacturing in its client base. In general, the MTCs provide a wide range of services including:

- Individual project engineering

- Training courses

- Demonstrations

- Assistance in selecting and using software and equipment

- Factory survey visits

- Technical training

- Introduction of modern manufacturing equipment.

Seven MTCs have been established to date:

Great Lakes MTC (GLMTC)
2415 Woodland Ave.
Cleveland, OH 44115
(216) 987-3038

Northeast MTC (NEMTC)
Rensselaer Technology Park
385 Jordan Rd.
Troy, NY 12180
(518) 283-1010

Southeast MTC (SMTC)
P.O. Box 1149
Columbia, SC 29202
(803) 777-9595

Midwest MTC (MMTC)
P.O. Box 1485
Ann Arbor, MI 48106
(313) 769-4377

*New Techniques and Consultants (cont'd)*

Mid-America MTC (MAMTC)
10561 Barkley, Suite 602
Overland Park, KS 66212
(913) 649-4333

Upper Midwest MTC (UMMTC)
111 Third Ave. S., Suite 400
Minneapolis, MN 55401
(612) 338-7722

California MTC (CMTC)
13430 Hawthorne Blvd.
Hawthorne, CA 90250
(310) 355-3060

## Contact Option

Michael Baum
National Institute of Standards and Technology
Gaithersburg, MD 20899
(301) 975-2763

# The Federal Laboratory Consortium

THE FEDERAL LABORATORY Consortium is comprised of over 700 member research laboratories and centers from 16 federal departments. If a company has a specific technology need or question, one of the more than 100,000 scientists or engineers who work in the federal laboratories may have the solution. The FLC provides a link between the individual laboratory members and the potential users of government-developed technologies. The federal laboratories contain technologies, facilities, and expertise in all areas of science and engineering and offer opportunities such as:

• Technical assistance

• Cooperative research projects

• Employee exchange

• Exclusive or non-exclusive licensing

• Visits to laboratories

• Printed documentation

• Sponsored research

• Use of unique laboratory facilities

• Workshops, seminars, briefings.

The FLC Locator is part of the FLC network that assists companies in locating the appropriate laboratory or individual scientist or technician to handle a company's specific request. Once the contact is made, the specific technology transfer arrangements are made between the laboratory and the business.

To take advantage of the Federal Laboratory Consortium network and access the federal laboratories, contact one of the FLC Regional Coordinators in your region or the Locator Manager. The Regional Coordinator working with the FLC Locator will find the appropriate laboratory to meet specific requests.

FLC Laboratory Locator Network
Dr. Andrew Cowan, Manager
DelaBarre & Associates
P.O. Box 545
Sequim, WA 98382
(206) 683-1005

## Federal Laboratory Consortium Regional Contacts

*Mid-Atlantic*
Norma Vaught
ARL-Sensor, Signatures, Signal & Info Director
ATTN: AMSRL-CP-TT
2800 Powder Mill Rd.
Adelphi, MD 29783
(301) 394-2952

*Mid-Continent*
Douglas Blair
Air Force Armstrong Laboratory
AL/XPPO
Building 125, Room 260
Brooks AFB, TX 78235
(512) 536-3817

*Midwest*
Ted Schoenborn
HHS-National Institute for Occupational Safety & Health
4676 Columbia Pkwy., DPSE-R2
Cincinnati, OH 45226
(513) 841-4305

*Northeast*
Gary Conlon
Army Benet Laboratories
ATTN: SMCAR-CCB-T
Building 115, Room 224
Watervliet, NY 12189
(518) 266-4946

*Southeast*
Eric Greene
HHS/PHS-Centers for Disease Control
Technology Transfer Office MS-E67
1600 Clifton Rd., NE
Atlanta, GA 30333
(404) 639-6268

*The Federal Laboratory Consortium (cont'd)*

*Washington, DC*
Dr. Beverly Berger
1850 M St., NW Suite 800
Washington, DC 20036
(202) 331-4220

*West*
Geoffrey Phillips
Air Force Advanced Manufacturing Center
3237 Peacekeeper Way #13
McClellan AFB, CA 95652
(916) 643-1248

# Industry Studies

OPTIONS FOR INDUSTRY RESEARCH, from market analyses to forecasts, to planning and strategy, include producing studies internally, or commissioning an outside firm to do customized research. Given the prohibitive cost of customized research, companies are turning more and more to commercially available off-the-shelf studies produced by market research firms.

The most comprehensive guide to published market research reports, studies, and surveys is the *Findex* directory. This reference contains descriptions of consumer and industrial studies and surveys, syndicated and multi-client studies, audits and subscription research services, as well as published reports on general management and business topics. Individual reports may cover an entire industry, a specific segment of an industry, or an individual product or series of related products.

## Recommended Resource

*Findex*
Cambridge Information Group
Attn: Marketing Department
7200 Wisconsin Ave.
Bethesda, MD 20814
(800) 843-7751

## Contact Options

*Selected Market Research Firms:*

Business Trend Analysts
2171 Jericho Turnpike
Commack, NY 11725
(516) 462-5454

Leading Edge Reports
12417 Cedar Rd., Suite 29
Cleveland Heights, OH 44106
(800) 866-4648

The Freedonia Group
3570 Warrensville Center Rd.
Cleveland, OH 44122
(216) 921-6800

Frost & Sullivan
90 West St., Suite 1301
New York, NY 10006
(212) 233-1080

Euromonitor Plc
87-88 Turnmill St.
London EC1M 5QU
England
44-71-251-8024

Find/SVP
625 Avenue of the Americas
New York, NY 10011
(212) 645-4500

## The Top Reference Sources

*Directory of Manufacturers' Sales Agencies*
Manufacturers' Agents National Association,
$92.50
(714) 859-4040

This book offers the most efficient way to hire outside sales representatives. The directory includes informative articles on finding the best agents for your products, communication between agents,

manufacturers, and customers, and agent marketing, among others. Membership listings are cross-referenced and organized geographically and by product classification.

Listings include agency name, address, telephone number, branch offices, warehousing facilities, number of field salespeople, territory covered, and complete descriptions of the types of products sold.

# Environmental Issues

## Hazardous Waste

In 1976 the United States Congress passed a law called the Resource Conservation and Recovery Act (RCRA). Under RCRA, the United States Environmental Protection Agency has developed specific requirements for handling hazardous waste. These requirements control hazardous waste from the moment it is generated until its ultimate disposal. Since 1980, the EPA has been refining the hazardous waste program to further protect public health and the environment. As a result, the requirements were expanded to include small businesses that handle specified quantities of hazardous waste, and the number of wastes classified as hazardous has been increased.

## Defining Hazardous Waste

A waste is a solid or liquid material that is no longer used. EPA defines waste as hazardous if it has certain properties that could pose dangers to human health and the environment after it is discarded. EPA considers a waste to be hazardous if it possesses certain characteristics (ignitability, corrosivity, reactivity, or toxicity) or if it is on a list of specific wastes determined by the EPA to be hazardous. RCRA regulations, found in the Code of Federal Regulations (CFR) Title 40, Part 261, present the listed hazardous wastes, describe hazardous waste characteristics, and specify test methods for determining whether waste is hazardous.

Complete lists of wastes identified by the EPA as hazardous can also be obtained from the EPA's RCRA/Superfund Hotline at (800) 424-9346 or from the Regional EPA offices and state hazardous waste management agencies listed in this chapter.

In general, a business is likely to produce hazardous waste if it:

- Uses petroleum products;

- Uses dyes, paints, printing inks, thinners, solvents, or cleaning fluids;

- Uses pesticides or other related chemicals;

- Uses materials that dissolve metals, wood, paper, or clothing (acids and caustics);

- Uses flammable materials;

- Uses materials that burn or itch upon contact with skin;

- Uses materials that bubble or fume upon contact with water;

- Receives delivery of products accompanied by a shipping paper or label indicating that the product is hazardous.

## Waste Production Threshold

The EPA considers small-quantity generators to be producers of more than 220 and less than 2,200 pounds (more than 100 and less than 1,000 kilograms) of hazardous waste in a calendar month. Small-quantity generators are subject to hazardous waste requirements, and businesses should be aware that state agencies may have additional, or more restrictive requirements. Producers of 1,000 kilograms or more of hazardous waste in any calendar month, or more than one kilogram of certain acutely hazardous wastes (waste that is fatal to humans in small doses) are subject to the more extensive regulations that apply to large-quantity generators.

A business that produces hazardous waste and is regulated under the Federal Hazardous Waste Requirements must:

- Obtain an EPA identification number for each site at which hazardous waste is generated. To obtain an EPA identification number, contact the EPA regional office or your state hazardous waste management agency and ask for Form 8700-12.

- Properly handle waste on the company premises. A permit may be required if waste is stored, treated, or disposed of on site. Contact the regional EPA office, state agency or RCRA/ Superfund Hotline for information on permits, storing, and shipping of hazardous wastes.

*Source: U.S. Environmental Protection Agency*

## Emergency Planning and Community Right-to-Know Act

Established as part of the Superfund Amendments passed by Congress in 1986, the purpose of the Emergency Planning and Community Right-to-Know-Act (EPCRA) is to inform the public and community emergency-response services, such as fire departments, about the existence of certain toxic substances in area businesses. If toxic substances are being released into the air, land, or water while they are being manufactured, processed, or used in other ways, the EPCRA requires businesses to file a "Form R" with the EPA. (A list of more than 300 toxic substances is available from the EPA.)

Manufacturers should be aware that failure to submit a Form R is a felony, and even an unintentional violation of this law is a civil offense. The EPA estimates that compliance costs for businesses total $147 million dollars and acknowledges that small businesses are typically most burdened by these regulations.

For more information about environmental reporting laws, contact the EPCRA Hotline at (800) 535-0202 or your regional EPA office.

# EPA Regional Offices

**EPA Region 1**
*Connecticut, Maine, Massachusetts, New Hampshire, Rhode Island, Vermont*
JFK Federal Building
Boston, MA 02203
(617) 565-3420

**EPA Region 2**
*New Jersey, New York, Puerto Rico, Virgin Islands*
26 Federal Plaza
New York, NY 10278
(212) 264-2657

**EPA Region 3**
*Delaware, District of Columbia, Maryland, Pennsylvania, Virginia, West Virginia*
841 Chestnut St.
Philadelphia, PA 19107
(215) 597-9800

**EPA Region 4**
*Alabama, Florida, Georgia, Kentucky, Mississippi, North Carolina, South Carolina, Tennessee*
345 Courtland St., NE
Atlanta, GA 30365
(404) 347-4727

**EPA Region 5**
*Illinois, Indiana, Michigan, Minnesota, Ohio, Wisconsin*
77 West Jackson Blvd.
Chicago, IL 60604
(312) 353-2000

**EPA Region 6**
*Arkansas, Louisiana, New Mexico, Oklahoma, Texas*
1445 Ross Ave.
Dallas, TX 75202
(214) 655-6444

**EPA Region 7**
*Iowa, Kansas, Missouri, Nebraska*
726 Minnesota Ave.
Kansas City, KS 66101
(913) 551-7000

**EPA Region 8**
*Colorado, Montana, North Dakota, South Dakota, Utah, Wyoming*
999 18th St.
Denver, CO 80202
(303) 293-1603

**EPA Region 9**
*Arizona, California, Hawaii, Nevada, Guam, Marianas*
75 Hawthorne St.
San Francisco, CA 94105
(415) 744-1305

**EPA Region 10**
*Alaska, Idaho, Oregon, Washington*
1200 Sixth Ave.
Seattle, WA 98101
(206) 442-1200

## The Top Reference Sources

Manufacturers' Alliance for Productivity and Innovation
1200 18th St., NW
Washington, DC 20036
(202) 331-8430

This policy research organization is made up of over 500 member manufacturing companies in a broad range of industries. MAPI does research and analysis on economic, management, legal, and regulatory issues affecting the industrial sector. The organization produces some 75 subject-specific reports annually, and sponsors the Conference on Business and Economic Policies, an annual seminar series.

# Waste Management

## State Hazardous Waste Management Agencies

*Alabama*
Land Division
Department of Environmental Management
(205) 271-7730

*Alaska*
Department of Environmental Conservation
Division of Environmental Quality
(907) 465-5260

*Arizona*
Office of Waste and Water Quality Management
Department of Environmental Quality
(602) 257-2211

*Arkansas*
Hazardous Waste Division
Department of Pollution Control and Ecology
(501) 570-2872

*California*
Toxic Substances Control Division
Environmental Protection Agency
(916) 324-1826

*Colorado*
Waste Management Division
Department of Health
(303) 331-4830

*Connecticut*
Hazardous Materials Management Unit
Department of Environmental Protection
(203) 566-8476

*Delaware*
Hazardous Waste Management Section
Division of Air and Waste Management
(302) 739-3689

*District of Columbia*
Pesticides and Hazardous Materials Division
Department of Consumer and Regulatory Affairs
(202) 404-1167

*Florida*
Division of Waste Management (UST)
Department of Environmental Regulations
(904) 488-0190

*Georgia*
Land Protection Branch
Industrial and Hazardous Waste
(404) 656-2833

*Hawaii*
Department of Health
Hazardous Waste Program
(808) 586-4225

*Idaho*
Hazardous Materials Bureau
Department of Health and Welfare
(208) 334-5898

*Illinois*
Division of Land Pollution Control
Environmental Protection Agency
(217) 782-6760

*Indiana*
Department of Environmental Management
(317) 232-3210

*Iowa*
Air Quality and Solid Waste Protection
Department of Water, Air, and Waste Management
(515) 281-8693

*Kansas*
Bureau of Waste Management
Department of Health and Environment
(913) 296-1600

*Kentucky*
Division of Waste Management
Department of Environmental Protection
Cabinet for Natural Resources and
Environmental Protection
(502) 564-6716, ext. 214

*Louisiana*
Office of Solid and Hazardous Waste
Department of Environmental Quality
(504) 765-0355

*Maine*
Bureau of Oil and Hazardous Materials Control
Department of Environmental Protection
(207) 287-2651

*Maryland*
Waste Management Administration
Department of the Environment
(410) 631-3364

*Massachusetts*
Division of Solid and Hazardous Waste
Department of Environmental Protection
(617) 292-5589

*Waste Management (cont'd)*

*Michigan*
Waste Management Division
Environmental Protection Bureau
Department of Natural Resources
(517) 373-2730

*Minnesota*
Solid and Hazardous Waste Division
Pollution Control Agency
(612) 297-8503

*Mississippi*
Division of Solid and Hazardous Waste Management
Bureau of Pollution Control
Department of Natural Resources
(601) 961-5062

*Missouri*
Waste Management Program
Department of Natural Resources
(314) 751-3176

*Montana*
Solid and Hazardous Waste Bureau
Department of Health and Environmental Sciences
(406) 444-2821

*Nebraska*
Hazardous Waste Management Section
Department of Environmental Quality
(402) 471-4217

*Nevada*
Waste Management Program
Division of Environmental Protection
Department of Conservation and Natural Resources
(702) 687-4670

*New Hampshire*
Division of Public Health Services
Office of Waste Management
Department of Health and Welfare
(603) 271-2900

*New Jersey*
Hazardous Waste Regulations and Energy
Department of Environmental Protection
(609) 633-1418

*New Mexico*
Hazardous Waste Section
Health and Environment Department
(505) 827-4308

*New York*
Division of Solid and Hazardous Waste
Department of Environmental Conservation
(518) 457-6603

*North Carolina*
Solid and Hazardous Waste Management Branch
Division of Health Services
(919) 733-2178

*North Dakota*
Division of Hazardous Waste Management
Department of Health
(701) 221-5166

*Ohio*
Division of Solid and Hazardous Waste Management
Environmental Protection Agency
(614) 644-2917

*Oklahoma*
Waste Management Service
Department of Health
(405) 271-5338

*Oregon*
Hazardous and Solid Waste Division
Department of Environmental Quality
(503) 229-5913

*Pennsylvania*
Bureau of Waste Management
Department of Environmental Resources
(717) 787-9870

*Rhode Island*
Solid Waste Management Program
Department of Environmental Management
(401) 277-2797

*South Carolina*
Bureau of Solid and Hazardous Waste Management
Department of Health and Environmental Control
(803) 734-5200

*South Dakota*
Waste Management Program
Department of Water and Natural Resources
(605) 773-3153

*Tennessee*
Division of Solid Waste Management
Department of Public Health
(615) 532-0780

*Texas*
Hazardous and Solid Waste Division
Water Commission
(512) 239-2334

*Utah*
Bureau of Solid and Hazardous Waste Management
Department of Health
(801) 538-6170

*Waste Management (cont'd)*

*Vermont*
Waste Management Division
Agency of Environmental Conservation
(802) 241-3888

*Virginia*
Waste Management Division
Office of Environmental Quality
(804) 786-2378

*Washington*
Solid and Hazardous and Toxics Reduction Program
Department of Ecology
(206) 407-6702

*West Virginia*
Waste Management Division
Department of Natural Resources
(304) 558-5935

*Wisconsin*
Bureau of Solid Waste Management
Department of Natural Resources
(608) 266-1327

*Wyoming*
Solid Waste Management Program
Department of Environmental Quality
(307) 777-7752

## Largest Waste Management Companies

Attwoods
2601 S. Bay Shore Dr., Penthouse 2
Coconut Grove, FL 33133
(305) 856-4455

Browning-Ferris Industries
P.O. Box 3151
Houston, TX 77253
(713) 870-8100

Chambers Development
10700 Frankstown Rd.
Pittsburgh, PA 15235
(412) 242-6237

Laidlaw
3221 N. Service Rd.
P.O. Box 5028
Burlington, Ontario L7R 3Y8
(416) 336-5151

Waste Management
3003 Butterfield Rd.
Oak Brook, IL 60521
(708) 218-1500

Western Waste Industries
21061 S. Western Ave.
Torrance, CA 90501
(310) 328-0900

*Source: Waste Age*

## The Top Reference Sources

*The Information Please Environmental Almanac*
Houghton Mifflin, $11.95
(800) 225-3362

Compiled by the World Resources Institute, this informative book includes state, national, and global statistics on the environment, along with waste and clean-up information.

Articles of interest include green shopping, saving energy, toxins in food and water, recycling legislation, and facts on 145 countries.

Special highlights include the U.S. Green City rankings and comparisons.

# Corporate Environmental Awards

## National Corporate Environmental Awards

| Sponsor | Award/Recipient of 1993 Award | Telephone |
|---|---|---|
| American Marketing Association | Edison Award for Environmental Achievement<br>Green Paint Company<br>Wellman<br>Deja<br>Seventh Generation | (212) 255-3800 |
| Composting Council | Hi Kellogg Award<br>Jan Beyea/National Audubon Society | (703) 739-2401 |
| Council on Economic Priorities | Corporate Conscience Awards for Environmental Stewardship<br>S.C. Johnson & Son<br>Stonyfield Farm | (212) 420-1133 |
| Direct Marketing Association | Robert Rodale Environmental Achievement Award<br>L.L. Bean<br>Seventh Generation | (212) 768-7277 |
| Ecological Society of America | Corporate Award<br>Tampa Electric/Lewis Environmental Services | (202) 833-8773 |
| Environmental Exchange | Recognition, not an award per se<br>The Robbins Company | (202) 387-2182 |
| United Nations Environment Programme | Environmental Communications Award<br>Patagonia/Lost Arrow Design<br>Southern California Edison<br>Coors<br>Lake Michigan Federation<br>Texas Dept. Public Transportation<br>Texas Water Commission<br>Aveda/Time to Clear the Air<br>Molson Beer<br>Procter & Gamble/Pampers<br>Ciba Geigy<br>Amway<br>Recycle Minneapolis<br>Neal Aspinall<br>Shyam Madiraju/Leo Burnett | (801) 466-3600 |
| Flexible Packaging Association | Green Globe Award<br>American Packaging | (202) 842-3880 |
| Glass Packaging Institute | Clear Choice Awards<br>Enfancil Infant Formula | (202) 452-9450 |
| Keep America Beautiful | National Awards<br>Rubbermaid | (203) 323-8987 |
| National Arbor Day Foundation | Promise to the Earth<br>Pella Corporation<br>Country Living Magazine<br>Cinergi Productions and Hollywood Pictures Home Video | (402) 474-5655 |
| National Recycling Coalition | Fred Schmitt Award for Outstanding Leadership<br>Kash n' Karry | (202) 625-6406 |
| World Environment Center | Gold Medal Award<br>Xerox | (212) 683-4700 |

# Environmental Hotlines

MANY CLEARINGHOUSES, HOTLINES, and electronic bulletin boards have been developed by the Environmental Protection Agency (EPA) to respond to legislative initiatives requiring the agency to provide outreach, communications and technology transfer to businesses, individuals, and other organizations. Clearinghouses facilitate the exchange of critical information and are also useful as a central access point for hard-to-locate technical reports and documents. The following information clearinghouses and hotlines may be of particular interest to manufacturers:

## Air and Radiation

Control Technology Center (CTC)
U.S. Environmental Protection Agency
Air and Energy Research Laboratory
Research Triangle Park, NC 27711
(919) 541-0800
Provides information on air emissions and air pollution control technology for all air pollutants including air toxics emitted by stationary sources, and information on the Federal Small Business Assistance Program.

Emission Factor Clearinghouse
U.S. Environmental Protection Agency
Emission Factor Clearinghouse, MD-14
Research Triangle Park, NC 27711
(919) 541-5477
Provides information on air pollutant emission factors for criteria and toxic pollutants from stationary and area sources, as well as mobile sources.

Green Lights Program
The Bruce Company
1850 K St., NW, Suite 290
Washington, DC 20006
(202) 775-6650
Provides information on energy-efficient lighting and how companies can join and become a partner or ally with the Green Lights Program. Over 1,300 companies have joined, and 13 states have agreed to convert all state and government buildings to energy-efficient lighting in the next five years.

Indoor Air Quality Information Clearinghouse
P.O. Box 37133
Washington, DC 20013
(301) 585-9020 or (800) 438-4318
Provides access to a full range of information about indoor air quality problems.

National Air Toxics Information Clearinghouse
U.S. Environmental Protection Agency
Office of Air Quality Planning and Standards, MD-13
Research Triangle Park, NC 27711
(919) 541-0850
Collects, classifies, and disseminates air toxics

(noncriteria pollutant) information submitted by state and local air agencies, and makes the audience aware of published air toxics information from the EPA, other federal agencies, and similar relevant sources. State and local information includes general agency facts, regulatory program descriptions, acceptable ambient limits, permitted facilities, source testing data, emissions inventories, and monitoring.

National Radon Hotline
U.S. Environmental Protection Agency
Radon Division, ANR 464
401 M St., SW
Washington, DC 20460
(800) 767-7236
Provides information on radon health effects and testing for radon. Information seekers receive a brochure.

Office of Air Quality Planning and Standards Technology Transfer Network Bulletin Board System
Research Triangle Park, NC 27711
(919) 541-5742 or (919) 541-5384 (voice)
Provides information and technology exchange in areas of air pollution control ranging from emission test methods to regulatory air quality models.

## International

INFOTERRA
U.S. Environmental Protection Agency
USA National Focal Point, 3404
401 M St., SW, M 2904
Washington, DC 20460
(202) 260-5917
International environmental referral and research service made up of 140 countries coordinated by the United Nations Environment Programme in Nairobi, Kenya. The mission of the network is to link national and international institutions and experts in a cooperative venture to improve the quality of environmental decision-making worldwide.

## Pesticides and Toxic Substances

Toxic Substances Control Act Assistance
Information Service
U.S. Environmental Protection Agency
Environmental Assistance Division, 7408
401 M St., SW
Washington, DC 20460
(202) 554-1404
Provides information on TSCA regulations to industry, labor and trade organizations, environmental groups, and the public. Technical as well as general information is available.

*Environmental Hotlines (cont'd)*

National Pesticide Information Retrieval System
CERIS (NPIRS)
1231 Cumberland Ave., Suite A
West Lafayette, IN 47906
(317) 494-6614

Provides a database of information for membership of pesticide manufacturers and users, libraries, law firms, and state/federal agencies.

## Hazardous and Solid Waste

Emergency Planning and Community Right-to Know Information Hotline
Booz, Allen & Hamilton
1725 Jefferson Davis Highway
Arlington, VA 22202
(703) 920-9877 or (800) 535-0202

Provides regulatory, policy, and technical assistance to federal agencies, local, and state governments, the public, and the regulated community in response to questions related to the Emergency Planning and Community Right-to-Know Act (Title III of SARA).

Solid Waste Information Clearinghouse and Hotline
P.O. Box 7219
1100 Wayne Ave., #700
Silver Spring, MD 20910
(800) 67-SWICH

Developed and partially funded by the Solid Waste Association of North America and EPA, SWICH is comprised of a library system and an electronic bulletin board, and provides information on all aspects of solid waste management, including source reduction, recycling, composting, planning, education and training, legislation and regulation, waste combustion, collection, transfer, disposal, landfill gas, and special wastes.

Resource Conservation and Recovery
Act/Superfund/Underground
Storage Tank Hotline (RCRA/SF/OUST)
1725 Jefferson Davis Highway
Arlington, VA 22202
(703) 920-9810 or (800) 424-9346

Provides assistance to the public and regulated community in understanding the EPA's regulations pursuant to RCRA, UST, CERCLA, and Pollution Prevention/Waste Minimization.

Hazardous Waste Ombudsman Program
U.S. Environmental Protection Agency
401 M St., SW, Room SE 301
Washington, DC 20460
(800) 262-7937

The hazardous waste management program established under the RCRA is the most complex regulatory program developed by the EPA. It assists the public and regulated community in resolving problems concerning any program or requirement under the Hazardous Waste Program. The Ombudsman Program, located at Headquarters and in each Regional office (see listing in this chapter), handles complaints from citizens and the regulated community, obtains facts, sorts information, and substantiates policy.

National Response Center
U.S. Coast Guard Headquarters
2100 Second St., SW, Room 2611
Washington, DC 20593
(202) 267-2675 or (800) 424-8802

Receives reports of oil, hazardous chemical, biological, and radiological releases. The NRC then passes those reports to a predesignated federal On-Scene Coordinator who coordinates cleanup efforts with other responsible federal agencies.

Methods Information Communications
Exchange (MICE)
c/o SAIC
7600-A Lewisburg Pike
Falls Church, VA 22043
(703) 821-4789

Provides information on analytical test-methods for the characterization of hazardous waste in support of the Resource Conservation and Recovery Act (RCRA).

## Pollution Prevention

Stratospheric Ozone Information Hotline
The Bruce Company
501 3rd St., NW
Washington, DC 20001
(800) 296-1996

Provides consultation on ozone protection regulations and requirements under Title VI of the Clean Air Act Amendments (CAAA) of 1990. Title VI covers the following key aspects of the production, use, and safe disposal of ozone-depleting chemicals: (1) production and phase-out controls; (2) servicing of motor vehicle air conditioners; (3) recycling and emission reduction; (4) technician and equipment certification; (5) approval of alternatives; (6) ban of nonessential uses; (7) product labeling; and (8) federal procurement.

*Both Compuserve and GEnie feature TRW Business Profiles, a wealth of general business and credit information on over 13 million companies. GO TRWREPORT (Compuserve) or KEYWORD TRWPROFILES (GEnie).*

*Environmental Hotlines (cont'd)*

Pollution Prevention Information Clearinghouse
Science Applications International
7600A Leesburg Pike
Falls Church, VA 22043
(703) 821-4800
    Provides technical, policy, programmatic, legislative, and financial information dedicated to reducing industrial pollutants through technology transfer, education, and public awareness. It is a national and international communication network that targets multi-media source reduction and recycling opportunities.

## Water

National Small Flows Clearinghouse
West Virginia University
P.O. Box 6064
Morgantown, WV 26506
(800) 624-8301
    Distributes publications and videotapes, performs literature searches, operates a toll-free hotline, produces free newsletters, and operates a computer bulletin board.

## Small Business

Small Business Ombudsman Clearinghouse/Hotline
U.S. Environmental Protection Agency
Small Business Ombudsman, 1230C
401 M St., SW
Washington, DC 20460
(703) 305-5938
Fax: (703) 305-6462
    Apprises the trade associations representing small business interests of current regulatory developments.

## Recommended Resources

*Access EPA*
U.S. Environmental Protection Agency, $24
Public Information Center
(202) 260-2049
    A directory of U.S. Environmental Protection Agency and other public sector environmental information resources. First published in 1991, this annual directory provides information on documents, dockets, clearinghouses and hotlines, records, databases, models, EPA libraries, and state libraries.

# Environmental Organizations

SELECTED INDUSTRY AND ASSOCIATION contacts for further information on Recycling, Waste Management, and Environmental Issues, include:

Aluminum Association
900 19th St., NW, Suite 300
Washington, DC 20006
(202) 862-5100

Aluminum Recycling Association
1000 16th St., NW, Suite 400
Washington, DC 20036
(202) 785-0951

American Forest & Paper Association
1111 19th St., NW, #700
Washington, DC 20036
(202) 463-2700

American Petroleum Institute
1220 L St., NW
Washington, DC 20005
(202) 682-8000

American Plastics Council
1275 K Street, NW, Suite 500
Washington, DC 20005
(202) 371-5319

American Public Works Association
1301 Pennsylvania Ave., NW, Suite 501
Washington, DC 20004
(202) 393-2792

Association of Petroleum Re-Refiners
P.O. Box 605
Buffalo, NY 14205
(716) 855-2757

Association of State and Territorial
Solid Waste Management Officials
444 N. Capitol St.
Washington, DC 20001
(202) 624-5828

Can Manufacturers Institute
1625 Massachusetts Ave., NW
Washington, DC 20036
(202) 232-4677

Council on Packaging in the Environment
1001 Connecticut Ave., NW
Washington, DC 20036
(202) 789-1310

Environmental Action Foundation
6930 Carroll Ave., #600
Tacoma Park, MD 20912
(301) 891-1100

Environmental Defense Fund
1875 Connecticut Ave., NW, #1016
Washington, DC 20009
(202) 387-3500

*Environmental Organizations (cont'd)*

Glass Packaging Institute
1627 K St., NW, #800
Washington, DC 20006
(202) 887-4850

Institute of Clean Air Companies
1707 L St., NW, Suite 570
Washington, DC 20036
(202) 457-0911

Institute of Scrap Recycling Industries
1325 G St., NW, Suite 1000
Washington, DC 20005
(202) 466-4050

National Association for Plastic Container Recovery
100 No. Tryon St., #3770
Charlotte, NC 28202
(704) 358-8882

National Association of Chemical Recyclers
1200 G St., NW
Washington, DC 20005
(202) 434-8740

National Association of Counties
440 First St., NW
Washington, DC 20001
(202) 393-6226

National Association of Towns and Townships
1522 K St., NW, Suite 600
Washington, DC 20005
(202) 737-5200

National Governors Association
444 N. Capitol St., NW, Suite 267
Washington, DC 20001
(202) 624-5300

National League of Cities
1301 Pennsylvania Ave., NW
Washington, DC 20004
(202) 626-3000

National Recycling Coalition
1101 30th St., NW, Suite 305
Washington, DC 20007
(202) 625-6406

National Soft Drink Association
Solid Waste Management Dept.
1101 16th St., NW
Washington, DC 20036
(202) 463-6700

National Solid Wastes Management Association
4301 Connecticut Ave., NW, Suite 300
Washington, DC 20008
(202) 244-4700

National Tire Dealers and Retreaders Association
1250 I Street, NW, Suite 400
Washington, DC 20005
(202) 789-2300

Plastics Recycling Institute
Rutgers, The State University of New Jersey
Center for Plastics Recycling Research
Bldg. 3529, Busch Campus
Piscataway, NJ 08855
(908) 932-3632

Polystyrene Packaging Council
1025 Connecticut Ave., NW, Suite 515
Washington, DC 20036
(202) 822-6424

Rubber Manufacturers Association
1400 K St., NW, Suite 900
Washington, DC 20005
(202) 682-4800

The Society of the Plastics Industry
1275 K St., NW, Suite 400
Washington, DC 20005
(202) 371-5200

Solid Waste Association of North America
P.O. Box 7219
Silver Spring, MD 20910
(301) 585-2898

Steel Recycling Institute
Foster Plaza 10
680 Andersen Dr.
Pittsburgh, PA 15220
(412) 922-2772

Textile Fibers and By-Products Association
P.O. Box 11065
Charlotte, NC 28220
(704) 527-5593

U.S. Conference of Mayors
1620 I St., NW
Washington, DC 20006
(202) 293-7330

U.S. Department of Energy
Waste Material Management
1000 Independence Ave., SW
Washington, DC 20585
(202) 586-6750

The Vinyl Institute
Wayne Interchange Plaza II
155 Route 46 West
Wayne, NJ 07470
(201) 890-9299

*Source: List prepared in part by the Institute of Scrap Recycling Industries, Inc.*

# Labeling Regulations

ON FEBRUARY 11, 1993, CONGRESS issued the final ruling on Section 611 of the Clean Air Act, which requires labeling of products made with or containing class I and class II ozone-depleting substances (such as chlorofluorocarbons or CFCs). It also requires that containers containing class I or class II substances be labeled.

A product containing an adhesive for example, must be labeled as "containing." When that product is applied by a subsequent manufacturer in affixing a cushion to a seat, the seat must be labeled as a "product manufactured with" because the CFCs have been released. The subsequent sale of the seat to an automobile manufacturer, however, would not result in the labeling of a car based on that product.

All products made prior to May 15, 1993, are exempt from the labeling requirements if the manufacturer is able to show within 24 hours that its products were made before that date. Likewise, an importer, when so requested by the EPA, must be able to show that the products imported were manufactured before the deadline.

For additional information, including a complete list of class I and class II ozone-depleting chemicals, contact the Stratospheric Ozone Information Hotline at (800) 296-1996. To receive copies of the final rule and any follow-up notices regarding the labeling rule, see the Federal Register in a local university or government library.

*Source: Environmental Protection Agency*

# Waste Exchanges

THE IDEA BEHIND WASTE EXCHANGE is that one company's waste or unwanted material may be another company's resource. By promoting the reuse and recycling of industrial materials through waste exchanges, it is estimated that industry currently saves $27 million in raw material and disposal costs and the energy equivalent of more than 100,000 barrels of oil annually. With over 7 billion tons of industrial solid waste generated yearly, and only 6 million tons of waste currently on the exchange, there is an enormous potential for savings as more companies make use of waste exchanges.

Established in 1992, the National Materials Exchange Network is a partnership of industrial waste exchanges, supported in part by Congress and assisted by the Environmental Protection Agency, that increases recycling opportunities within industry. Materials listed on the Exchange include waste by-product, off-spec, overstock, obsolete, and damaged materials; used and virgin, solid and hazardous. Access to the National Materials Exchange Network is free with participation in your local exchange.

## Contact Option

National Materials Exchange Network
For computer modem access: (509) 466-1019
Canada only: (509) 325-1724
Direct assistance: (509) 466-1532

Solid Waste Assistance Program
1100 Wayne Ave.
Silver Spring, MD 20910
(800) 677-9424

## Waste Exchanges in North America

Alabama Waste Materials Exchange
404 Wilson Dam Ave.
Sheffield, AL 35660
(205) 760-4623

Alberta Waste Materials Exchange
Bldg. #350
6815 8th St., NE
Calgary, Alberta
Canada T2E 7H7
(403) 297-7505

Arizona Waste Exchange
4725 E. Sunrise Dr., Suite 215
Tucson, AZ 85718
(602) 299-7716

Arkansas Industrial Development Council
#1 Capitol Mall
Little Rock, AR 72201
(501) 682-1370

B.A.R.T.E.R.
2512 Delaware St., SE
Minneapolis, MN 55414
(612) 627-6811

Bourse Quebecoise des Matieres Secondaires
14 Place Du Commerce, Bureau 350
Le-Des-Squeurs, Quebec
Canada H3E 1T5
(514) 762-9012

*Waste Exchanges (cont'd)*

British Columbia Waste Exchange
102 1525 W. 8th Ave.
Vancouver, BC V6J 1T5
(604) 731-7222

Bureau of Solid Waste Management
P.O. Box 7921
Madison, WI 53707
(608) 266-2111

California Waste Exchange
P.O. Box 806
Sacramento, CA 95812
(916) 322-4742

CALMAX
909 12th St., Suite 205
Sacramento, CA 95826
(916) 255-2369

Canadian Chemical Exchange
P.O. Box 1135
Ste-Adele, Alberta
Canada J0R 1L0
(800) 561-6511

Canadian Waste Materials Exchange
2395 Speakman Drive
Mississauga, Ontario
Canada L5K 1B3
(416) 822-4111

Hawaii Waste Exchange
P.O. Box 1048
Paia, HI 96779
(808) 579-9109

Hudson Valley Materials Exchange
P.O. Box 550
1 Veterans Dr.
New Paltz, NY 12561
(914) 255-3749

Indiana Waste Exchange
P.O. Box 454
Carmel, IN 46032
(317) 574-6505

Industrial Materials Exchange (IMEX)
506 2nd Ave., Room 201
Seattle, WA 98104
(206) 296-4899

Industrial Materials Exchange Service
P.O. Box 19276
Springfield, IL 62794
(217) 782-0450

Intercontinental Waste Exchange
5200 Town Center Circle, #303
Boca Raton, FL 33486
(800) 541-0400

Iowa Waste Reduction Center
75 BRC, University of Northern Iowa
Cedar Falls, IA 50614
(319) 273-2079

Kansas Materials Exchange
P.O. Box 152
Hutchinson, KS 67504
(316)662-0551

Louisiana/Gulf Coast Waste Exchange
1419 CEBA
Baton Rouge, LA 70803
(504) 388-4594

Manitoba Waste Exchange
1812-330 Portage Ave.
Winnipeg, Manitoba
Canada R3C 0C4
(204) 942-7781

MISSTAP
P.O. Drawer CN
Mississippi State, MS 39762
(601) 325-8454

Minnesota Technical Assistance Program
1313 5th St., Suite 207
Minneapolis, MN 55414
(612) 627-4555

Missouri Environmental Improvement Authority
325 Jefferson St.
Jefferson City, MO 65101
(314) 751-4919

Montana Industrial Waste Exchange
Montana Chamber of Commerce
P.O. Box 1730
Helena, MT 59624
(406) 442-2405

New Hampshire Waste Exchange
122 N. Main St.
Concord, NH 03301
(603) 224-5388

New Jersey Materials Exchange
300 West Commercial Ave.
Moonachie, NJ 07074
(800) 676-2754

New Mexico Materials Exchange
P.O. Box 904
Farmington, NM 87499
(505) 325-2157

Northeast Industrial Waste Exchange
620 Erie Blvd., #211
Syracuse, NY 13202
(315) 422-6572

*Waste Exchanges (cont'd)*

Olmstead County Materials Exchange Program
Olmstead County Public Works
2122 Campus Dr., SE
Rochester, MN 55904
(507) 285-8231

Ontario Waste Exchange
ORTECH International
2395 Speakman Dr.
Mississauga, Ontario
Canada L5K 1B3
(416) 822-4111

Pacific Materials Exchange
4708 East Jaremko
Mead, WA 99021
(509) 466-1532

Portland Chemical Consortium
P.O. Box 751
Portland, OR 97207
(503) 725-3811

RENEW
Texas Water Commission
P.O. Box 13087
Austin, TX 78711
(512) 463-7773

SEMREX
171 W. 3rd St.
Winona, MN 55987
(507) 457-6460

Southeast Waste Exchange
Urban Institute
UNCC Charlotte
Charlotte, NC 28223
(704) 547-2307

Southern Waste Information Exchange
P.O. Box 960
Tallahassee, FL 32302
(800) 441-7949

Vermont Business Materials Exchange
P.O. Box 630
Montpelier, VT 05601
(802) 223-3441

Wastelink, Division of Tencon
140 Wooster Pike
Milford, OH 45150
(513) 248-0012

WasteNet
6907 Brookpark Rd.
Cleveland, OH 44129
(216) 749-2992

# Recycling

MOST AUTHORITIES AGREE THAT recycling can realistically reduce the amount of municipal solid waste by approximately 25 percent. Recycling allows discarded materials to be diverted from the waste stream and begins with separation and collection of recyclable material at the source.

## Easily Recycled Materials

- Aluminum: today we recycle more than 65,000 aluminum beverage cans every minute.

- Iron and steel: in 1989, the U.S. scrap processing industry prepared 60 million tons for recycling, double the amount of paper, nonferrous metals (aluminum, copper, lead, zinc, etc.), glass, and plastics combined.

- Plastics: currently, three principal types of plastics are being recycled:

  - PETE (polyethylene terephthalate) soft drink containers, especially the two-litre bottle, are the most common plastic containers manufactured—and discarded—today.

  - HDPE (high-density polyethylene) containers are used as milk and water jugs, base cups or bottoms of PET soft drink bottles, oil bottles, and detergent and other household cleaner bottles.

  - Polystyrene foam is used primarily to make fast-food carryout containers.

- Glass: the use of crushed glass, or cullet, in manufacturing offers economic advantages over virgin materials (sand, soda ash, limestone). Cullet melts at a lower temperature than the raw materials, so manufacturers can reduce energy usage as well as particulate emissions into the atmosphere. Today, 25 percent of any given glass container is made from recycled glass.

- Paper: paper and paperboard constitute the largest proportion of municipal solid waste. More than 30 percent of all the paper and paperboard used in the United States today is being collected and used as either a component to make recycled paper and paperboard or as an export to foreign nations.

*Source: Institute of Scrap Recycling Industries*

*Recycling (cont'd)*

## Products and Materials in the Waste Stream

| Product | Tons Generated (millions) | % of Waste Stream | Tons Recycled (millions) | % of Product Recycled |
|---|---|---|---|---|
| Yard waste | 31.6 | 17.6 | 0.5 | 1.6 |
| Corrugated boxes | 23.1 | 12.9 | 10.5 | 45.4 |
| Newspaper | 13.3 | 7.4 | 4.4 | 33.3 |
| Food waste | 13.2 | 7.4 | 0.0 | 0.0 |
| Consumer electronics | 10.6 | 5.9 | 0.1 | 0.7 |
| Furniture | 7.5 | 4.2 | 0.0 | 0.0 |
| Office paper | 7.3 | 4.1 | 1.6 | 22.5 |
| Glass beer & soft drink bottles | 5.4 | 3.0 | 1.1 | 20.0 |
| Books & magazines | 5.3 | 3.0 | 0.7 | 13.2 |
| Paper toys & games | 5.2 | 3.0 | 0.0 | 0.0 |
| Folding cartons | 4.4 | 2.4 | 0.3 | 7.7 |
| Junk mail | 4.1 | 2.3 | 0.6 | 14.6 |
| Clothing & shoes | 4.0 | 2.2 | 0.0 | 0.6 |
| Glass jars | 3.9 | 2.2 | 0.3 | 8.1 |
| Large appliances | 3.0 | 1.7 | 0.2 | 7.0 |
| Paper tissue & towels | 3.0 | 1.7 | 0.0 | 0.0 |
| Paper bags | 2.9 | 1.6 | 0.2 | 7.0 |
| Disposable diapers | 2.7 | 1.5 | 0.0 | 0.0 |
| Rocks & dirt | 2.7 | 1.5 | 0.0 | 0.0 |
| Steel food cans | 2.5 | 1.4 | 0.4 | 15.0 |
| Rubber tires | 2.2 | 1.2 | 0.1 | 4.8 |
| Wood crates & pallets | 2.1 | 1.2 | 0.0 | 0.0 |
| Glass wine & liquor bottles | 2.0 | 1.1 | 0.1 | 5.0 |
| Misc. plastic products | 1.7 | 1.0 | 0.0 | 0.0 |
| Lead-acid batteries | 1.6 | 0.9 | 1.5 | 90.0 |
| Aluminum beer & soft drink cans | 1.4 | 0.8 | 0.8 | 55.0 |
| Plastic wraps | 1.1 | 0.6 | 0.0 | 0.0 |
| Plastic bags | 0.8 | 0.4 | 0.0 | 0.0 |
| Paper plates & cups | 0.7 | 0.4 | 0.0 | 0.0 |
| Paper milk cartons | 0.5 | 0.3 | 0.0 | 0.0 |
| Plastic soft drink bottles | 0.4 | 0.2 | 0.1 | 21.0 |
| Plastic milk bottles | 0.4 | 0.2 | 0.0 | 0.0 |
| Other | 9.0 | 4.6 | 0.0 | 0.0 |
| TOTAL | 179.6 | 100.0 | 23.5 | 13.1 |

*Source: U.S. Environmental Protection Agency*

## The Top Reference Sources

*U.S. Industrial Outlook*
National Technical Information Service, $37.00
(703) 487-4650

This annual business report is a major publication of the International Trade Administration, U.S. Department of Commerce. The reference includes industry-by-industry overviews with economic analyses and projections for manufacturing, services, and high-technology industries.

Features include industry forecasts, five-year industry projections, 450 tables and charts, profiles of international competitiveness, international trade forecasts, and new environmental reviews.

# Recycled Content Mandates

TWELVE STATES NOW REQUIRE manufacturers to use recycled materials. Connecticut and California were the first states to enact these laws with mandates that responded to the glut of old newspapers in 1989. The following is a list of these 12 states and the amount of recycled materials that will be required in manufacturing:

- Arizona
  Newsprint: 50% by 2000.

- California
  Newsprint: 50% by 2000.
  Plastic containers: options similar to Oregon; see below.
  Glass containers: 65% by 2005.
  Trash bags: 30% by 1995.

- Connecticut
  Newsprint: 50% by 2000.
  Phone books: 40% by 2001.

- Illinois
  Newsprint: 45% by 1997.

- Maryland
  Newsprint: 40% by 1998.
  Phone books: 40% by 2000

- Missouri
  Newsprint: 50% by 2000.

- North Carolina
  Newsprint: 40% by 1997.

- Oregon
  Newsprint: 7.5% by 1995.
  Glass containers: 50% by 2000 (food/beverages).
  Plastic containers, options: made of 25% post-consumer material; recycled at 25% rate; reusable or refillable, or reduced 10% in content by 1995 (certain exemptions).

- Rhode Island
  Newsprint: 40% by 2000.

- Texas
  Newsprint: 30% by 2000.

- West Virginia
  Newsprint: highest "practicable" content; advisory committee created to determine rate.

- Wisconsin
  Newsprint: 45% by 2001.
  Plastic containers: 10% by 1995.

*Source: National Solid Wastes Management Association*

# Recycling Symbols

IN 1990, THE Society of the Plastics Industry introduced the Plastic Container Material Code System to assist plastic recyclers in sorting plastic bottles by resin type. The PBI coding system, comprised of those now familiar chasing arrows, is intended to encourage comprehensive bottle recycling by providing the means to obtain the highest value from all plastic bottles.

The system is meant for voluntary use by bottle and container producers, to be imprinted onto the bottom surface of plastic containers. These consistent national identification marks are designed to be most conveineint for those in the recycling industry who will sort containers, and is intended to avoid a complicated system which would require extensive worker training and possibly lead to missorting or confusion.

### Recommended Resource

*Recycled Plastic Products Source Book*
American Plastics Council
(800) 243-5790

This terrific source book is free of charge, and helps private and public sector buyers identify products made with recycled plastic. Organized by product category, with a supplementary Gray Pages section of alphabetized company listings, this book provides a wealth of leads and information on recycled plastic products. A Consumer's Edition of the Source Book is also available, and lists products that can be sold directly to the general public.

 1. Polyethylene terephthalate (PETE)

 2. High-Density Polyethylene (HDPE)

 3. Vinyl/Polyvinyl Chloride (V/PVC)

 4. Low-Density Polyethylene (LDPE)

 5. Polypropylene (PP)

 6. Polystyrene (PS)

 7. Other

# Tax Incentives for Recycling

IN ADDITION TO THE SPECIFICS listed below, many states have tax credits that apply to new business in general, to business expansions, or to businesses locating in certain pre-designated areas. In all cases, consult with state Commerce, Economic Development, or Tax Offices to learn the details of state law.

*Arizona*
Income tax credit of 10% of installed cost, up to lesser of 25% of total tax liability or $5,000.

*Arkansas*
30% tax credit on income/corporate taxes for purchase of equipment making products with at least 10% recycled content.

*California*
Banks and corporations may take a 40% tax credit for purchase of certain equipment to manufacture recycled products with minimum 50% secondary content and 10% post-consumer content. Development bonds for manufacturing products with recycled materials.

*Colorado*
Up to 20% tax credit for purchase of certain equipment to make products using post-consumer recycled materials. Special credits for plastic recycling.

*Delaware*
Corporate tax credits for investments and for job creation for use of minimum 25% secondary materials removed from in-state waste stream. Reductions in gross receipts tax also apply. Corporate tax credits also available for source reduction activities and for processors and collectors of recyclable materials.

*Florida*
Sales tax exemption on recycling machinery. Tax incentives to encourage affordable transportation of recycled goods from collection points to sites for processing and disposal.

*Illinois*
Sales tax exemption for manufacturing equipment.

*Indiana*
Property tax exemption for buildings, equipment, and land involved in converting waste into new products.

*Iowa*
Sales tax exemptions for recycling equipment.

*Kansas*
Tax abatement for equipment used to manufacture products made with at least 25% post-consumer material.

*Kentucky*
Property and income tax credits to encourage recycling industries.

*Louisiana*
Corporation and franchise tax credits for purchase of qualified recycling equipment; corporate and personal income tax credits for purchase of equipment to recycle CFCs used as refrigerants.

*Maine*
Corporate tax credits equal to 30% of cost of recycling equipment and machinery. Tax credits of up to $5.00 per ton of wood waste from lumber products used as fuel or to generate heat.

*Maryland*
Individual and corporate income credit for expenses incurred to convert a furnace to burn used oil or to buy and install equipment to recycle used freon.

*Minnesota*
Sales tax exemptions for recycling equipment.

*Montana*
25% tax credit on purchase of equipment to process recyclable materials, up to 5% off income taxes for purchase of business-related products made with recycled material.

*New Jersey*
50% investment tax credit for recycling vehicles and machinery. 6% sales tax exemption on purchases of recycling equipment.

*New Mexico*
Tax credits on equipment to recycle or use recycled materials in a manufacturing process.

*North Carolina*
Industrial and corporate income tax credits and exemptions for equipment and facilities.

*The Clean Air Act (cont'd)*

*Oklahoma*
15% income tax credit on purchase of equipment and facilities to use recyclable materials in a product.

*Oregon*
Individual and corporate income tax credits for capital investment in recycling equipment and facilities. Special credits for plastic recycling.

*South Carolina*
Scrap metal dealers defined as manufacturers for sales tax purposes and exempted from electricity and fuel sales taxes.

*Texas*
Sludge recycling corporations eligible for franchise tax exemptions.

*Virginia*
Individual and corporate income tax credits of 20% of the purchase price of machinery and equipment for processing recyclable materials. Manufacturing plants using recycled products are eligible for a 10% tax credit.

*Washington*
Motor vehicles are exempt from rate regulation when transporting recovered materials from collection to reprocessing facilities and manufacturers.

*West Virginia*
Disposal tax waivers for commercial recyclers who reduce their solid waste by 50%.

*Wisconsin*
Sales tax exemptions for waste reduction and recycling equipment and facilities; business property tax exemptions for same equipment.

*Source: National Solid Waste Management Association*

## Recommended Resources

*PaperMatcher: A Directory of Paper Recycling Resources*
American Forest & Paper Association, free
(800) 878-8878

*American Recycling Market Directory*, $175
(800) 267-0707

# The Clean Air Act

ENACTED TO CORRECT SERIOUS air pollution problems in the United States, the Clean Air Act Amendments of 1990 contain some of the most important elements of environmental legislation in recent years.

The Environmental Protection Agency estimates the new Clean Air Act will remove 56 billion pounds of pollution from the air each year. In human terms, these measures will significantly reduce lung disease, cancer, and other serious health problems caused by air pollution.

Air quality improvements mandated by the Clean Air Act Amendments include:

- Greatly reduced emissions of toxic air pollution and acid rain-causing pollutants

- Attainment of air quality standards nationwide by the year 2010

- Cleaner cars, fuels, factories, and power plants

- Less damage to lakes, streams, parks, and forests

- Reduced emissions of greenhouse gases

- Less damage to the stratospheric ozone layer.

The regulatory requirements of the CAAA will exact profound changes in many U.S. industries. For example, the amendments significantly affect the electric utility industry and, consequently, the coal industry. Sulfur emissions controls in the CAAA are divided into two phases. Phase I controls set out specific 1995 sulfur dioxide emissions limits for power plants built before 1978 (about 110 power plants). Phase II controls, set for the year 2000, generally limit sulfur dioxide emissions to the same level as for post-1978 power plants: 1.2 pounds of sulfur dioxide per million Btu. To achieve these emissions levels, plants will retrofit scrubbers, switch to low-sulfur coal, blend low-sulfur with high-sulfur coal, co-fire with natural gas, re-power with advanced technology boilers, or perhaps even close the plant. Plants may also trade emission allowance credits issued to them by the EPA.

The potential global climate change caused by so-called "greenhouse gases" is yet another environmental issue important to the coal industry. Carbon dioxide, which absorbs solar radiation and traps the sun's heat, has been steadily increasing in the earth's atmosphere. All fossil fuels emit carbon dioxide, but coal emits 80 percent more per unit of energy consumed than natural gas, and about 20 percent more carbon dioxide than fuel oil. Consequently, coal-fired power stations are prime candidates for controls on carbon dioxide emissions. While no actions affecting the coal industry are likely in the near future, the issue of global warming has far from disappeared.

*The Clean Air Act (cont'd)*

Passage of the CAAA also had a significant impact on the U.S. petroleum refining industry. The first oxygenated gasoline season began in November of 1992, and mandates that motor gasoline sold during at least four winter months in 39 areas of the country classified as moderate or serious carbon monoxide non-attainment areas must have a minimum oxygen content of 2.7 percent by weight (2 percent in California). Beginning January, 1995, the nine worst ozone non-attainment areas with populations in excess of 250,000 must begin using motor gasoline that meets mandated emissions and composition requirements. As a result of these and other mandates, U.S. refiners have had to closely examine their operations relative to the CAAA, committing considerable resources to plant additions and reconfigurations, product reformulations, and research and development to advance processing technologies.

The search for alternatives to CFC (chlorofluorocarbon) and HCFC (hydrofluorocarbon) refrigerants, as required by Title VI of the Clean Air Act, is one of the greatest challenges the air conditioning and refrigeration industry has ever faced. On July 1, 1992, Section 608 of the act prohibited intentional venting of CFCs and HCFCs during service, repair, or disposal of any air conditioning or refrigeration equipment. There will be controls on the sale of refrigerants and the disposition of recovered refrigerants, as well as mandatory certification of recovery/recycling equipment, technicians, and the purity of refrigerant recovered, reclaimed, and resold. Section 612 (list of safe alternatives to CFCs and HCFCs) and Section 611 (labeling of products containing or manufactured with controlled substances) regulations are also under development.

Paper and pulp mills are affected as the CAAA provides extensive changes to new and existing source requirements for ozone, carbon monoxide, and particulate matter. Paper companies will be required to demonstrate that they are in compliance with all existing air standards, or that the benefits of a mill outweigh the environmental and social costs of anti-pollution regulations.

Clean Air Act Amendments have created new markets in the United States for the general components industry, particularly valves and pipe fittings. Environmental and health concerns that are emerging abroad are also creating incipient markets for U.S. valve and pipe fitting companies, which are global leaders in the pollution control and pollution abatement industry.

## Industry Preparations

Large and small companies need to become aware of the many new clean air requirements and deadlines for compliance. Industry needs to know about the flexible options, pollution prevention incentives, programs that encourage technological innovation, and market-based programs that clean the air at a much lower cost. These programs include:

- *Early Reductions Program*: offers companies incentives to take early voluntary action to reduce emissions and, in so doing, receive a six-year deferral on new clean air requirements.

- *Allowance Trading System*: enables utilities to buy and sell emission credits among themselves, provided that total emissions reductions are achieved.

- *Fuel Averaging Program*: enables oil companies to meet tight new reformulated fuel standards by averaging the oxygen content in different grades of gasoline.

## Recommended Resource

*The Clean Air Act Amendments*
National Association of Manufacturers
Publications Coordinator
1331 Pennsylvania Ave., NW
Suite 1500, North Tower
Washington, DC 20004
(800) 637-3005

## Contact Options

*Government Agencies:*

Stratospheric Ozone Information Hotline
U.S. Environmental Protection Agency
(800) 296-1996

Clean Air Act Advisory Committee
U.S. Environmental Protection Agency
Office of Air & Radiation
(202) 260-7400

*State Air Quality Agencies:*

*Alabama*
Department of Environmental Management
Air Division
(205) 271-7861

*Alaska*
Department of Environmental Conservation
Air Quality Management Section
(907) 465-5100

*Arizona*
Department of Environmental Quality
Office of Air Quality
(602) 207-2308

*Arkansas*
Department of Pollution Control and Ecology
Air Division
(501) 570-2161

*The Clean Air Act (cont'd)*

*California*
Environmental Protection Agency
Air Resources Board
(916) 445-4383

*Colorado*
Department of Health
Air Pollution Control Division
(303) 692-3100

*Connecticut*
Department of Environmental Protection
Bureau of Air Management
(203) 566-2506

*Delaware*
Department of Natural Resources and
Environmental Control
Division of Air and Waste Management
Air Quality Management
(302) 739-4791

*District of Columbia*
Department of Consumer and Regulatory Affairs
Environmental Control Division
Air Quality Control and Monitoring Branch
(202) 404-1180

*Florida*
Department of Environmental Regulation
Air Resources Management
(904) 488-0114

*Georgia*
Department of Natural Resources
Environmental Protection Division
Air Protection Branch
(404) 363-7008

*Hawaii*
Department of Health
Clear Air Branch
(808) 586-4200

*Idaho*
Division of Environmental Quality
Air Quality Bureau
(208) 334-5898

*Illinois*
Environmental Protection Agency
Division of Air Radiation
(217) 782-7326

*Indiana*
Department of Environmental Management
Office of Air Management
(317) 232-8384

*Iowa*
Department of Natural Resources
Air Quality Section
(515) 281-8852

*Kansas*
Department of Health and Environment
Bureau of Air and Waste Management
(913) 296-1593

*Kentucky*
Department of Environmental Protection
Division for Air Quality
(502) 564-3382

*Louisiana*
Department of Environmental Quality
Office of Air Quality and Radiation Protection
Air Quality Division
(504) 765-0219

*Maine*
Department of Environmental Protection
Bureau of Air Quality Control
(207) 287-2437

*Maryland*
Department of the Environment
Air Management and Radiation
(410) 631-3255

*Massachusetts*
Department of Environmental Protection
Division of Air Quality Control
(617) 292-5630

*Michigan*
Department of Natural Resources
Air Quality Division
(517) 373-7023

*Minnesota*
Pollution Control Agency
Air Quality Division
(612) 296-7331

*Mississippi*
Department of Environmental Quality
Office of Pollution Control, Air Division
(601) 961-5171

*Missouri*
Department of Natural Resources
Division of Environmental Quality
Air Pollution Control Program
(314) 751-4817

*Montana*
Department of Health and Environmental Sciences
Air Quality Bureau
(406) 444-3454

*Nebraska*
Department of Environmental Control
Air Quality Control
(402) 471-2189

*The Clean Air Act (cont'd)*

*Nevada*
Division of Environmental Protection
Bureau of Air Quality
(702) 687-5065

*New Hampshire*
Air Resources Division
(603) 271-1370

*New Jersey*
Department of Environmental Protection
Division of Environmental Quality Air Program
(609) 292-6710

*New Mexico*
Environmental Protection Division
Air Quality Division
(505) 827-0070

*New York*
Department of Environmental Conservation
Division of Air Resources
(518) 457-7230

*North Carolina*
Department of Environment, Health, and
Natural Resources
Air Quality Section
(919) 733-3340

*North Dakota*
Department of Health
Division of Environmental Engineering
Air Quality Program
(701) 221-5188

*Ohio*
Environmental Protection Agency
Division of Air Pollution Control
(614) 644-2270

*Oklahoma*
State Department of Health
Air Quality Service
(405) 271-5220

*Oregon*
Department of Environmental Quality
Air Quality Control Division
(503) 229-5359

*Pennsylvania*
Department of Environmental Resources
Bureau of Air Quality Control
(717) 787-9702

*Rhode Island*
Department of Environmental Management
Air Resource Division
(401) 277-2808

*South Carolina*
Department of Health and
Environmental Control
Bureau of Air Quality Control
(803) 734-4750

*South Dakota*
Department of Environment and Natural Resources
Point Source Control Program
(605) 773-3351

*Tennessee*
Department of Environment and Conservation
Division of Air Pollution Control
(615) 532-0554

*Texas*
Natural Resource Conservation Commission
Air Quality Office
(512) 239-1457

*Utah*
Department of Environmental Quality
Division of Air Quality
(801) 536-4000

*Vermont*
Agency of Natural Resources
Air Pollution Control Division
(802) 241-3840

*Virginia*
Office of Environmental Quality
Air Division
(804) 786-2378

*Washington*
Department of Ecology
Air Program
(206) 407-6800

*West Virginia*
Division of EnvironmEntal Protection
Office of Air Quality
(304) 348-2275

*Wisconsin*
Department of Natural Resources
Bureau of Air Management
(608) 266-7718

*Wyoming*
Department of Environmental Quality
Air Quality Division
(307) 777-7391

# Productivity

PRODUCTIVITY EXPRESSES the relationship between the quantity of goods and services produced–output–and the quantity of labor, capital, land, energy, and other resources that produced it–input.

Productivity is a key element in analyzing an economy. It demonstrates both the efficiency of industry and the wealth-generating capability of the economy.

The best known measure of productivity relates output to the input of labor time: output per hour, or its reciprocal unit labor requirements. This kind of measure is used widely because labor productivity is relevant to the most economic analyses, and because labor is the most easily measured input. Relating output to labor input provides a tool not only for analyzing productivity but also for examining labor costs, real income, and employment trends.

## Trends in Productivity Growth

Productivity growth varies among individual industries. Large increases reflect many factors, including new technologies, advanced production methods, and increased output with economies of scale.

U.S. productivity growth has trailed that of other major industrial countries.

The absolute level of U.S. productivity, unlike its growth trend, is still ahead of that of other major industrial countries. Although the United States has the lowest rate of change in real domestic product per employed person among major industrialized countries, it still has the highest level of gross domestic product per employed person. The gap continues to shrink, however.

## Change in Output per Employee Hour (%), Selected Industries

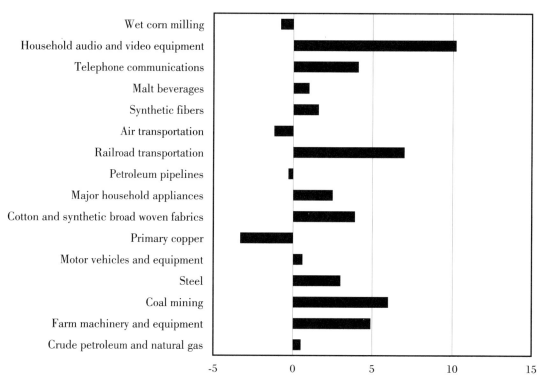

Note: The black bar indicates the average annual percent change from 1987 to 1992.

Source: Bureau of Labor Statistics

*Productivity (cont'd)*

## Relative Levels in Real Gross Domestic Product per Employed Person, Selected Countries

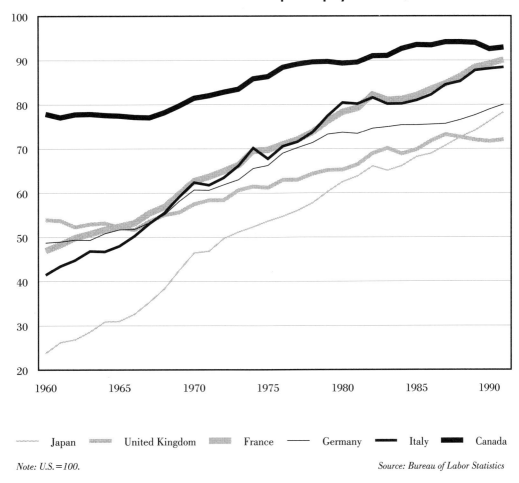

........... Japan    ▦ United Kingdom    ▦ France    —— Germany    ━━ Italy    ■■ Canada

*Note: U.S.=100.*                                    *Source: Bureau of Labor Statistics*

---

## The Top Reference Sources

*Who Knows What*
Henry Holt, $27.50
(800) 488-5233

Written by Daniel Starer, this 1,239-page reference contains names of thousands of experts and
organizations for business information on any sub-

ject, from abrasives to yarn.
    Organized alphabetically, sections provide
resource information for individual industries,
states, or selected topics. A subject index is provided, along with an index of associations, periodicals, and companies.

*Productivity (cont'd)*

## Trends in Real Gross Domestic Product per Employed Person, Selected Countries

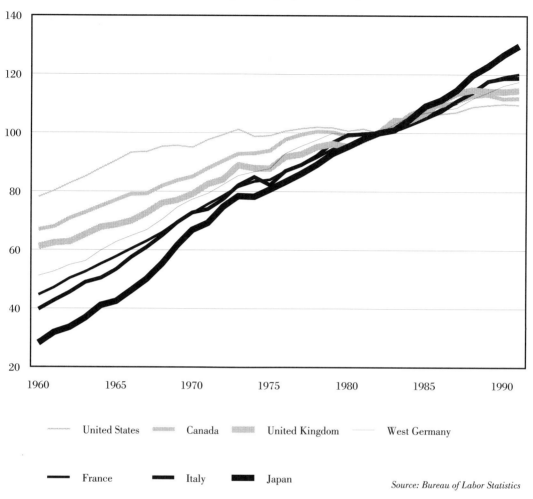

| ------ United States | ▨▨ Canada | ▨▨ United Kingdom | —— West Germany |
|---|---|---|---|

| ━━ France | ━━ Italy | ━━ Japan | |

*Source: Bureau of Labor Statistics*

---

### The Top Reference Sources

*Lesko's Info Power*
Information USA, $39.95
(800) 955-7693

Mathew Lesko's superb compilation of over 30,000 free and low-cost sources of information is an indispensable reference for use at home or at work.

Chapters provide information sources on consumer power, vacation and business travel, government financial help to individuals, investments and financial services, taxes, health and medicine, arts and humanities, housing and real estate, careers and workplace, law, science and technology, environment, patents, business and industry, and many more.

# Research & Development

GOVERNMENT FINANCING PROVIDED $25 billion for all industry R&D performance in 1991 (the most recent year for which data are available).

## Corporate and Government Spending on Research and Development ($ millions)

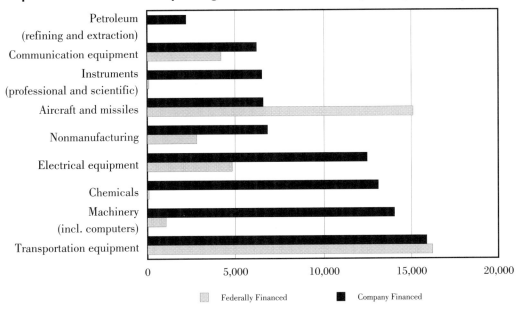

Federally Financed          Company Financed

## Percent of U.S. GDP Spent on Research and Development

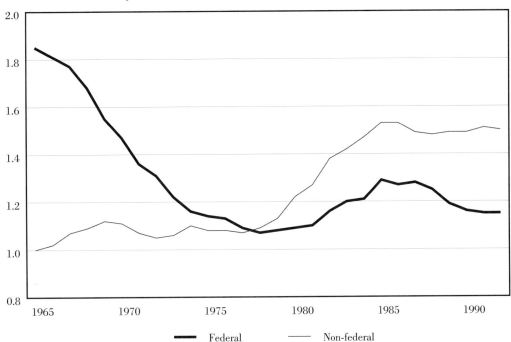

Federal          Non-federal

*Source: National Patterns of R&D Resources, National Science Foundation*

# Industry Growth Rates

MODEST GROWTH IS PROJECTED for basic materials industries, including rubber, chemicals, plastic products, and wood products. High-tech sectors, such as computers and semiconductors, have favorable outlooks, especially when the growth rates of individual industries are compared. Motor vehicles and parts industries are recovering, with much of the strength coming from rising sales of light trucks.

The aerospace industry will continue to decline in shipments as a result of defense spending reductions and a leveling off in backlogs for large commercial aircraft; however, production levels for large commercial aircraft will still be at relatively high levels. Consumer durables should continue to improve.

## Percent Change in Yearly Growth Rates for Selected Industries

| Sector | 1988-89 | 1989-90 | 1990-91 | 1991-92 | 1992-93 | 1993-94 (est.) |
|---|---|---|---|---|---|---|
| Construction | -1.3 | -2.9 | -9.2 | 7.3 | 3.0 | 1.9 |
| Food and beverages | -1.9 | 1.0 | 1.4 | 1.0 | 1.3 | 1.0 |
| Wood products | -1.1 | -3.0 | -5.9 | 4.9 | 0.2 | 2.3 |
| Paper and allied products | 1.7 | 0.2 | 0.0 | 1.0 | 0.5 | 3.0 |
| Chemicals | 1.1 | 3.6 | -2.6 | -0.6 | -0.1 | 1.4 |
| Rubber and plastic products | 2.7 | 2.4 | -1.5 | 1.2 | 3.6 | 4.7 |
| Construction materials | -0.1 | 0.8 | -8.0 | 3.3 | 0.4 | 0.8 |
| Steel mill products | -2.6 | -1.5 | -7.8 | 8.4 | 5.0 | 2.5 |
| Production machinery | 4.7 | -1.0 | -8.1 | -2.8 | 2.8 | 3.9 |
| Metal-working equipment | 7.4 | -1.7 | -9.7 | 0.1 | 7.4 | 5.7 |
| Electrical equipment | -0.5 | -2.5 | -6.3 | -1.2 | 2.0 | 3.8 |
| Electronic components | 4.3 | 3.4 | 8.8 | 13.4 | 13.1 | 11.1 |
| Computers | -4.8 | -1.3 | -7.3 | 6.1 | 7.8 | 5.9 |
| Telecommunications and navigation equipment | -4.7 | 5.5 | -2.9 | -2.9 | -2.2 | -2.6 |
| Motor vehicles and parts | -0.8 | -7.2 | -6.6 | 4.9 | 9.6 | 6.4 |
| Aerospace | 2.6 | 6.4 | 0.1 | -0.5 | -11.0 | -11.0 |
| Instruments, controls, and medical equipment | -1.2 | 1.5 | 3.0 | 4.1 | 5.0 | 5.2 |
| Durable consumer goods | 0.3 | -1.1 | -3.3 | 4.6 | 4.0 | 3.3 |
| Printing and publishing | -1.2 | 0.6 | -4.0 | -0.8 | 1.1 | 1.9 |

*Source: U.S. Industrial Outlook, 1994*

## 10 Fastest-Growing Manufacturing Industries (% change in yearly growth)

| Industry | % Change 1993-94 |
|---|---|
| Machine tools, metal cutting types | 12.8 |
| Electronic components and accessories | 11.1 |
| Surgical appliances | 10.0 |
| Mobile homes | 9.4 |
| Automotive parts and accessories | 7.7 |
| Surgical and medical instruments | 7.0 |
| Lighting fixtures | 6.6 |
| Mattresses and bedsprings | 6.4 |
| Leather tanning and finishing | 6.0 |
| Analytical instruments | 6.0 |

*Source: U.S. Industrial Outlook, 1994*

## 10 Slowest-Growing Manufacturing Industries (% change in yearly growth)

| Industry | % Change 1993-94 |
|---|---|
| Aircraft parts and equipment | -24.3 |
| Aircraft engines and engine parts | -20.0 |
| Aircraft | -11.3 |
| Search and navigation equipment | -6.6 |
| Ship building and repairing | -6.6 |
| Space propulsion units and parts | -5.3 |
| Personal leather goods | -5.2 |
| Manifold business forms | -5.0 |
| Phosphatic fertilizers | -4.8 |
| Space vehicle equipment | -3.9 |

*Source: U.S. Industrial Outlook, 1994*

*Industry Growth Rates (cont'd)*

## Forecast Growth Rates for Manufacturing Industries (Ranked by Compound Growth Rate)

| Rank | Industry | (%) Growth Rate 1993-94 | (%) Compound Annual Growth 1987-94 |
|------|----------|-------------------------|-------------------------------------|
| 1 | Fluid meters and counting devices | 1.0 | 11.4 |
| 2 | X-ray apparatus and tubes | 5.0 | 11.3 |
| 3 | Diagnostic substances | 2.0 | 10.9 |
| 4 | Electronic components and accessories | 11.1 | 9.3 |
| 5 | Motorcycles, bicycles, and parts | 2.6 | 8.7 |
| 6 | Surgical appliances and supplies | 10.0 | 7.9 |
| 7 | Space vehicle equipment | -3.9 | 7.6 |
| 8 | Plastic plumbing fixtures | 4.0 | 7.3 |
| 9 | Electromedical equipment | 0.2 | 7.1 |
| 10 | Medicinals and botanicals | 1.9 | 7.1 |
| 11 | Surgical and medical instruments | 7.0 | 6.1 |
| 12 | Analytical instruments | 6.0 | 6.0 |
| 13 | Biological products, except diagnostic | 1.9 | 5.9 |
| 14 | Household audio and video equipment | 2.0 | 5.6 |
| 15 | Household vacuum cleaners | 3.0 | 5.1 |
| 16 | Mobile homes | 9.4 | 5.0 |
| 17 | Sporting and athletic goods | 3.4 | 4.9 |
| 18 | Ophthalmic goods | 2.0 | 4.5 |
| 19 | Synthetic rubber | 3.0 | 4.1 |
| 20 | Soap and other detergents | 2.0 | 4.0 |
| 21 | Dental equipment and supplies | 3.5 | 3.8 |
| 22 | Radio and TV communications equipment | 2.2 | 3.7 |
| 23 | Household appliances | 4.1 | 3.3 |
| 24 | Packaging machinery | 3.9 | 3.3 |
| 25 | Mattresses and bedsprings | 6.4 | 3.3 |
| 26 | Reconstituted wood products | 4.0 | 3.3 |
| 27 | Oil and gas field machinery | 3.1 | 3.0 |
| 28 | Electric housewares and fans | 2.4 | 2.9 |
| 29 | Optical instruments and lenses | 4.0 | 2.9 |
| 30 | Gypsum products | 1.6 | 2.9 |
| 31 | Measuring and controlling devices | 2.0 | 2.9 |
| 32 | Farm machinery and equipment | 2.5 | 2.8 |
| 33 | Special dies, tools, jigs, and fixtures | 4.0 | 2.5 |
| 34 | Process control instruments | 5.0 | 2.5 |
| 35 | Computers and peripherals | 5.9 | 2.5 |
| 36 | Screw machine products | 6.0 | 2.4 |
| 37 | Platemaking services | 3.5 | 2.4 |
| 38 | Industrial inorganic chemicals, except pigments | 1.2 | 2.3 |
| 39 | Steel mill products | 2.5 | 2.3 |
| 40 | Fabricated rubber products | 3.0 | 2.3 |
| 41 | Miscellaneous plastic products except bottles and plumbing | 5.0 | 2.2 |
| 42 | Upholstered household furniture | 4.3 | 2.2 |
| 43 | Ceramic wall and floor tile | 3.0 | 2.2 |
| 44 | Household laundry equipment | 4.0 | 2.2 |
| 45 | Plastic materials and resins | 6.0 | 2.2 |
| 46 | Automotive parts and accessories | 7.7 | 2.1 |
| 47 | Dolls, toys, and games | 2.0 | 2.1 |
| 48 | Book publishing | 3.7 | 2.1 |
| 49 | Household refrigerators and freezers | 4.4 | 2.1 |
| 50 | Agricultural chemicals | 2.5 | 2.0 |

*Source: U.S. Industrial Outlook, 1994*

# Government Industry Specialists

THESE U.S. GOVERNMENT SPECIALISTS, under the auspices of the Department of Commerce, will provide advice on industry analysis, trade promotion, and trade policy development:

| Industry | Contact | Telephone |
|---|---|---|
| Aerospace | Sally Bath, Clayton Mowry, Ronald Green | (202) 482-4222 |
| Apparel | Joanne Tucker | (202) 482-4058 |
| Automotive parts | Mary Anne Slater | (202) 482-1418 |
| Bicycles, motorcycles, boat building, sporting goods | John Vanderwolf | (202) 482-0348 |
| CAD/CAM/CAE | Vera Swann | (202) 482-0396 |
| Chemicals | Fred Siesseger | (202) 482-0128 |
| Computer networking | Mary Davin | (202) 482-0572 |
| Computers | Timothy Miles | (202) 482-2990 |
| Construction | Patrick MacAuley | (202) 482-0132 |
| Construction materials | Charles Pitcher | (202) 482-0132 |
| Consumer electronics | Howard Fleming | (202) 482-5163 |
| Dairy, bakery, candy & other products; bottled & canned drinks | William Janis | (202) 482-2250 |
| Drugs & biotechnology | William Hurt | (202) 482-0128 |
| General industrial components | Richard Reise | (202) 482-3489 |
| Household appliances | John Harris | (202) 482-1178 |
| Household furniture | Donald Hodgen | (202) 482-3346 |
| Industrial & analytical instruments | Marguerite Nealon | (202) 482-3411 |
| Jewelry & musical instruments | John Harris | (202) 482-1178 |
| Lawn & garden | John Vanderwolf | (202) 482-0348 |
| Leather and leather products | James Byron | (202) 482-4034 |
| Meat, poultry, fruits, vegetables & spec. alcoholic beverages | William Janis | (202) 482-2250 |
| Medical equipment/instruments | Matthew Edwards | (202) 482-0550 |
| Medical, dental instruments & supplies | Victoria Kader | (202) 482-4073 |
| Metal industries | David Cammarota | (202) 482-5157 |
| Metalworking equipment | Megan Pilaroscia | (202) 482-0609 |
| Microelectronics | Margaret Donnelly | (202) 482-5466 |
| Midrange portables | Jonathan Streeter | (202) 482-0480 |
| Motor vehicles | Randy Miller | (202) 482-0669 |
| Paper products | Gary Stanley | (202) 482-0132 |
| Personal computers | R. Clay Woods | (202) 482-3013 |
| Photographic equipment & supplies | John McPhee | (202) 482-0571 |
| Plastics & rubber | Ray Pratt | (202) 482-0128 |
| Printing & publishing | Rose-Marie Bratland | (202) 482-0380 |
| Production machinery | Edward Abrahams | (202) 482-0312 |
| Semiconductor mfg. equipment | Rob Scott | (202) 482-3360 |
| Semiconductors | Dorthea Blouin | (202) 482-1333 |
| Semiconductors and related devices | Judee Mussehhl-Aziz | (202) 482-0429 |
| Software | Mary Smolenski | (202) 482-2053 |
| Supercomputers | Jonathan Streeter | (202) 482-0572 |
| Superconductors | Roger Chiarodo | (202) 482-0402 |
| Telecommunications and navigation equipment | Alexis Kemper | (202) 482-1512 |
| Telecommunications services | Dan Edwards | (202) 482-4331 |
| Textiles | Basil Kiwan | (202) 482-4058 |
| Textiles (man-made fibers) | Maria Corey | (202) 482-4058 |
| Wood products | Barbara Wise | (202) 482-0375 |

# Critical Technologies

THE DEPARTMENT OF COMMERCE defines a critical technology as one in which research has progressed far enough to indicate a high probability of technical success for new products and applications that might have substantial markets within approximately ten years.

Some critical technologies—usually self-contained products such as new medicines, or processes, such as X-ray lithography—have important, but focused, impacts. Others substantially affect the economy by advancing the technical infrastructure or by improving the quality and efficiency of the manufacturing process. Examples are components of a computer-integrated manufacturing system, such as robots or machining centers or the factory control system itself.

Critical technologies are also important because they will drive the next generation of research and development and spin-off applications. When an industry uses a new technology to design or improve a product, and successfully carries it to the marketplace, that new or improved product becomes the starting point for development of the next generation of products or services.

The Commerce Department has identified the following as critical technologies:

## Materials
Advanced Materials
Superconductors

## Electronics and Information Systems
Advanced Semiconductor Devices
Digital Imaging Technology
High-Density Data Storage
High-Performance Computing
Optoelectronics

## Manufacturing Systems
Artificial Intelligence
Flexible Computer-Integrated Manufacturing
Sensor Technology

## Life-Sciences Applications
Biotechnology
Medical Devices and Diagnostics

# The Advanced Technology Program

MANAGED BY THE TECHNOLOGY Administration's National Institute of Standards and Technology, the Advanced Technology Program is an industry-driven, cooperative partnership between government and the private sector to advance the nation's competitive position. The purpose of the program, now in its third year, is to assist U.S. companies in creating and applying "generic technology" and research results to help commercialize new technology more quickly and improve manufacturing processes.

The ATP Awards are based on merit as determined through a full and open competition. In December, 1992, twenty-one new awards were announced, two-thirds of which were for small busi-

nesses. The projects cover a broad spectrum of technology areas, including machine tools, biotechnology, electronics, optics, materials engineering, lighting technology, and refrigeration.

Any business or industrial joint venture may apply for these grants.

## Contact Option
Advanced Technology Program
Administration Building, Room A430
Rt. 270 & Quince Orchard Rd.
Gaithersburg, MD 20899
(301) 975-2636

*The Advanced Technology Program (cont'd)*

## 1993 ATP Awards

| Company | Location | ATP Award ($ thousands) |
| --- | --- | --- |
| 3M* | St. Paul, MN | 3,229 |
| IBM* | Yorktown Heights, NY | |
| Lexmark* | Lexington, KY | |
| Philips Laboratories | Briarcliff Manor, NY | 2,000 |
| American Display Consortium | Beaverton, OR | 6,464 |
| Caterpillar | Peoria, IL | 1,995 |
| Perception | Farmington Hills, MI | 1,219 |
| Hughes Aircraft | Torrance, CA | 1,255 |
| Integra Life Sciences | Plainsboro, NJ | 1,999 |
| Diamond Tool Consortium | Menlo Park, CA | 1,801 |
| Hercules | Wilmington, DE | 1,671 |
| Bio Hybrid Technologies* | Shrewsbury, MA | 4,262 |
| Synergy Research* | Hanover, NH | |
| Kurzweil Applied Intelligence | Waltham, MA | 1,777 |
| Allied Signal | Morristown, NJ | 2,000 |
| Thomas Electronics | Wayne, NJ | 718 |
| United States Biochemical | Cleveland, OH | 1,558 |
| Vitesse Semiconductor | Camarillo, CA | 2,000 |
| IBM | Yorktown Heights, NY | 1,988 |
| Advanced Power Technology | Bend, OR | 1,904 |
| Micron Optics | Atlanta, GA | 1,895 |
| Air Products and Chemicals | Allentown, PA | 1,998 |
| FED | Research Triangle Park, NC | 2,000 |
| IBC Advanced Technologies | Provo, UT | 2,000 |
| MicroFab Technologies | Plano, TX | 1,639 |
| M&M Precision Systems | West Carrollton, OH | 1,951 |
| Physical Optics | Torrance, CA | 850 |
| Communication Intelligence | Redwood Shores, CA | 1,480 |
| Amoco | Napierville, IL | 1,250 |
| National Center for Manufacturing Science | Ann Arbor, MI | 3,479 |
| Gen Pharm International | Mountain View, CA | 1,998 |
| Bio Traces | Greenbelt, MD | 1,718 |

*\* joint project*

## The Top Reference Sources

*American Demographics*
Dow Jones, $62/12 issues
(800) 828-1133

Published monthly, this extremely informative magazine is must-reading for businesses, especially their sales, marketing, and advertising departments.

Based primarily on census data, sample features include articles on aging, black suburbs, consumer confidence, influential Americans, market-driven companies, the real Hispanic market, the 1950s, and how market research can increase marketing efficiency.

The editors do a great job of making a dry topic extremely interesting.

# Producer Price Index

PRODUCER PRICE INDEXES measure average changes in prices received by domestic producers of commodities in all stages of processing. Most of the information used in calculating the indexes is obtained through the systematic sampling of nearly every industry in the manufacturing and mining sectors of the economy. Because producer price indexes are designed to measure only the change in prices received for the output of domestic industries, imports are not included. The stage-of-processing indexes organize products by class of buyer and degree of fabrication.

Within the stage-of-processing system, finished goods are commodities that will not undergo further processing and are ready for sale to the final individual or business consumer. Finished goods include unprocessed foods such as eggs and fresh vegetables, as well as processed foods such as bakery products and meats. Other finished consumer goods include durable goods such as automobiles, household furniture, and appliances, and nondurable goods such as apparel and home heating oil. Producer durable goods include heavy motor trucks, tractors, and machine tools.

Intermediate materials consist partly of commodities that have been processed but require further processing, such as flour, cotton yarn, steel mill products, and lumber. Nondurables in this category include diesel fuel, paper boxes, and fertilizers. Crude materials are products entering the market for the first time that have not been manufactured and that are not sold directly to consumers, such as grains and livestock. Raw cotton, crude petroleum, coal, hides and skins, iron and steel scrap are examples of nonfood crude materials. The following chart shows that industrial prices have risen only incrementally in the last couple of years, due mainly to foreign competition and the recession.

## Producer Price Indexes by Major Commodity Groups

| Commodity | 1975 | 1980 | 1985 | 1990 | 1991 | 1992 | 1993 |
|---|---|---|---|---|---|---|---|
| All commodities | 58.4 | 89.8 | 103.2 | 116.3 | 116.5 | 117.2 | 118.9 |
| Farm products | 77.0 | 102.9 | 95.1 | 112.2 | 105.7 | 103.6 | 107.0 |
| Processed foods and feeds | 72.6 | 95.9 | 103.5 | 121.9 | 121.9 | 122.1 | 124.0 |
| Textile products and apparel | 67.4 | 89.7 | 102.9 | 114.9 | 116.3 | 117.8 | 118.1 |
| Hides, skins, and leather products | 56.5 | 94.7 | 108.9 | 141.7 | 138.9 | 140.4 | 143.6 |
| Fuels and related products and power | 35.4 | 82.8 | 91.4 | 82.2 | 81.2 | 80.4 | 80.0 |
| Chemicals and allied products | 62.0 | 89.0 | 103.7 | 123.6 | 125.6 | 125.9 | 128.2 |
| Rubber and plastic products | 62.2 | 90.1 | 101.9 | 113.6 | 115.1 | 115.1 | 116.0 |
| Lumber and wood products | 62.1 | 101.5 | 106.6 | 129.7 | 132.1 | 146.6 | 174.0 |
| Pulp, paper, and allied products | 59.0 | 86.3 | 113.3 | 141.3 | 142.9 | 145.2 | 147.3 |
| Metals and metal products | 61.5 | 95.0 | 104.4 | 123.0 | 120.2 | 119.2 | 119.2 |
| Machinery and equipment | 57.9 | 86.0 | 107.2 | 120.7 | 123.0 | 123.4 | 124.0 |
| Furniture and household durables | 67.5 | 90.7 | 107.1 | 119.1 | 121.2 | 122.2 | 123.6 |
| Nonmetallic mineral products | 54.4 | 88.4 | 108.6 | 114.7 | 117.2 | 117.3 | 120.0 |
| Transportation equipment | 56.7 | 82.9 | 107.9 | 121.5 | 126.4 | 130.4 | 133.7 |
| Miscellaneous products | 53.4 | 93.6 | 109.4 | 134.2 | 140.8 | 145.3 | 145.5 |

*Note: The average for the year 1982 is set to equal 100*          *Source: Department of Commerce, Bureau of Economic Analysis*

---

**FAX** **Producer Price Indexes.** Request #443. See p. xi for instructions.

Table of producer price indexes, selected commodities.

# Purchasing Benchmarks

PURCHASING PERFORMANCE AND effectiveness has become one of the most closely watched economic indicators. The following chart is a comparison of select companies' total purchasing (dollars spent with vendors) as a percent of corporate sales in selected industries. For complete data on purchasing benchmarks, contact the Center for Advanced Purchasing Studies, an affiliate of the National Association of Purchasing Management, at (602) 752-2277.

### Recommended Resource

Tompkins Associates
2809 Millbrook Rd., #200
Raleigh, NC 27604
(919) 876-3667

## Total Purchasing Dollars as a Percent of Sales, Selected Industries

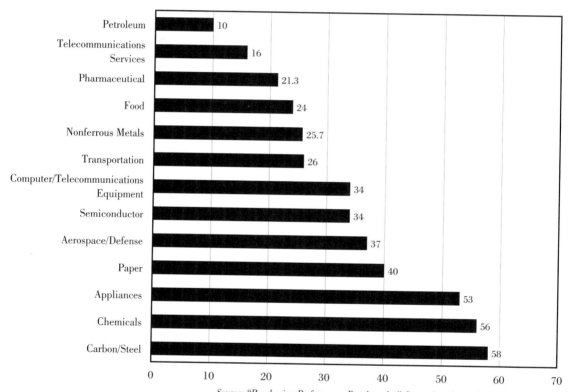

Source: "Purchasing Performance Benchmarks," Center for Advanced Purchasing Studies

**TIP:** *Robert Morris Associates and the American Institute of CPAs has developed a 32-page credit information package that could expedite the loan process for business borrowers. Call (215) 851-0585.*

# Warehousing

A NATIONAL STUDY BY Tompkins Associates reveals a number of interesting trends and conditions:

- Warehousing is still a very labor-intensive industry with great room for productivity improvements.

- The average warehouse is approximately 50,000 square feet with an average clear height of 22 feet.

- The age of the average warehouse is 19 years. New construction is prohibitively expensive.

- Few warehouses have ventured beyond basic material handling and storage methods.

- The pressure to computerize the warehouse is great, but the level of understanding of need, benefit, and specific requirements is low. A total of 85 percent of warehouses responding in the Tompkins Associates survey maintain inventory data on computer and 68 percent have a computerized stock location system. And 33 percent of warehouses surveyed use bar codes.

*Source: Tompkins Associates*

## The Public Warehouse Alternative

As warehousing costs continue to rise, public warehouses are more and more seen as a viable alternative. Jim McBride, President of Affiliated Warehouse Companies, estimates that public warehousing accounts for 16 percent of current warehousing needs. Criteria to be evaluated in selecting a public warehouse include:

- Financial stability
- Management depth
- Sanitation
- Facilities
- Rates
- Interest in the account
- Reputation
- Delivery capabilities
- Consolidations
- Ownership
- Similar accounts
- Building ownership
- Labor
- Security
- Data processing capabilities
- Contents insurance rate
- Legal liability insurance
- Taxes
- Location.

*Source: Affiliated Warehouse Companies*

## Average Warehouse Rates in Major Cities as of 4th Quarter, 1993

| Market | Price/sq. ft. ($) | Rent/sq. ft. ($) |
|--------|------------------|------------------|
| Atlanta | 25.82 | 3.23 |
| Baltimore | 31.62 | 3.76 |
| Boston | 38.26 | 5.13 |
| Chicago | 37.00 | 5.46 |
| Cincinnati | 26.28 | 3.69 |
| Cleveland | 25.18 | 4.01 |
| Columbus | 28.23 | 3.52 |
| Dallas | 28.38 | 3.92 |
| Denver | 26.48 | 3.32 |
| Detroit | 30.03 | 4.81 |
| Indianapolis | 28.82 | 3.62 |
| Los Angeles | 33.49 | 4.32 |
| Miami | 36.70 | 4.23 |
| Milwaukee | 28.81 | 4.19 |
| Minneapolis | 31.42 | 5.44 |
| New York | 35.82 | 4.89 |
| Norfolk | 31.20 | 4.34 |
| N. New Jersey | 38.21 | 5.46 |
| Philadelphia | 36.81 | 4.38 |
| Phoenix | 26.34 | 3.39 |
| Pittsburgh | 29.16 | 3.81 |
| Portland | 28.79 | 4.21 |
| Sacramento | 30.77 | 3.38 |
| St. Louis | 27.33 | 4.06 |
| San Antonio | 18.57 | 2.62 |
| San Diego | 43.75 | 5.05 |
| San Francisco | 42.33 | 5.09 |
| Seattle | 42.73 | 5.22 |
| Tampa | 27.94 | 4.10 |
| Washington, DC | 37.77 | 4.97 |

*Source: The National Real Estate Index Market Monitor*

Prices and rents above represent Class A (i.e. space built or substantially renovated in the preceding ten years) warehouse/distribution space at the metropolitan level. Reported rents are effective gross (i.e., after concessions, if any). New York rates are for Nassau-Suffolk counties.

## Contact Option

National Real Estate Index
1900 Powell St.
Emeryville, CA 94608
(800) 992-7257

# Recommended Trade Journals

THE FOLLOWING IS AN INCOMPLETE list of trade magazines in various fields. For a more complete listing, consult *Who Knows What* by Daniel Starer, published by Henry Holt.

*Adhesives Age*
Argus Business
6151 Powers Ferry Rd., NW
Atlanta, GA 30339
(404) 955-2500

*Advanced Material and Processes*
ASM International
Metals Park, OH 44073
(216) 338-5151

*American Printer*
Maclean Hunter Publishing
29 N. Wacker Dr.
Chicago, IL 60606
(312) 726-2802

*Appliance Manufacturer*
5900 Harper Rd., Suite 105
Solon, OH 44139
(216) 349-3060

*Automotive Industries*
Chilton
Chilton Way
Radnor, PA 19089
(215) 964-4245

*Automotive News*
Crain Communications
1400 Woodbridge
Detroit, MI 48207
(313) 446-6000

*Aviation Week and Space Technology*
P.O. Box 503
Hightstown, NJ 08520
(800) 257-9402

*Bakery Production and Marketing*
Cahners Publishing
455 N. Cityfront Plaza Dr.
Chicago, IL 60611
(312) 222-2000

*Beverage Industry*
Stagnito Publishing
1935 Shermer Rd., Suite 100
Northbrook, IL 60062
(708) 205-5660

*Chemical Engineering News*
American Chemical Society
1155 16th St., NW
Washington, DC 20036
(202) 872-4600

*Chilton's Food Engineering*
Chilton
Chilton Way
Radnor, PA 19089
(215) 964-4445

*Datamation*
Cahners Publishing
275 Washington St.
Newton, MA 02158
(617) 964-3030

*Designfax*
29100 Aurora Rd., #200
Solon, OH 44139
(216) 248-1125

*Distribution*
Chilton
Chilton Way
Radnor, PA 19089
(215) 964-4383

*Electronic Design*
Penton Publishing
611 Route 46 W
Hasbrouck Heights, NJ 07604
(201) 393-6060

*EDN (Electronic Design Engineering)*
Cahners Publishing
275 Washington St.
Newton, MA 02158
(617) 964-3030

*Electronic Products*
645 Stewart Ave.
Garden City, NY 11530
(516) 227-1300

*Food Processing*
Putnam Publishing
301 Erie St.
Chicago, IL 60611
(312) 644-2020

*Industrial Engineering*
Institute of Industrial Engineers
25 Technology Park
Norcross, GA 30092
(404) 449-0461

*Recommended Trade Journals (cont'd)*

*Industrial Maintenance and Plant Operation*
Chilton
Chilton Way
Radnor, PA 19089
(215) 964-4041

*Industrial Product Bulletin*
Gordon Publications
301 Gibraltar Dr.
Morris Plains, NJ 07950
(201) 361-9060

*Instrumentation and Automation News*
Chilton
Chilton Way
Radnor, PA 19089
(215) 964-4401

*Industry Week*
Penton Publishing
1100 Superior Ave.
Cleveland, OH 44114
(216) 696-7000

*Iron Age*
Hitchcock-Chilton
191 S. Gary Ave.
Carol Stream, IL 60188
(708) 665-1000

*Journal of Manufacturing Systems*
Society of Manufacturing Engineers
P.O. Box 930
Dearborn, MI 48121
(313) 271-1500

*Machine Design*
Penton Publishing
1100 Superior Ave.
Cleveland, OH 44114
(216) 696-7000

*Materials Handling Engineering*
Penton Publishing
1100 Superior Ave.
Cleveland, OH 44114
(216) 696-7000

*Mechanical Engineering*
American Society of Mechanical Engineers
345 E. 47th St.
New York, NY 10017
(800) 843-2763

*Metal Fabricating News*
P.O. Box 1178
Rockford, IL 61105
(815) 965-4031

*Mining Engineering*
8307 Shaffer Pkwy.
Littleton, CO 80127
(303) 973-9550

*Modern Materials Handling*
Cahners Publishing
275 Washington St.
Newton, MA 02158
(617) 964-3030

*Modern Plastics*
P.O. Box 602
Hightstown, NJ 08520
(800) 257-9402

*New Equipment Digest*
Penton Publishing
1100 Superior Ave.
Cleveland, OH 44114
(216) 696-7000

*Packaging*
Cahners Publishing
1350 E. Touhy Ave.
P.O. Box 5080
Des Plaines, IL 60017
(708) 635-8800

*Packaging Digest*
Cahners Publishing
455 N. Cityfront Plaza Dr.
Chicago, IL 60611
(312) 222-2000

*Paper Maker*
Maclean Hunter Publishing
57 Executive Park S.
Atlanta, GA 30329
(404) 325-9153

*Plant Engineering*
Cahners Publishing
1350 E. Touhy Ave.
P.O. Box 5080
Des Plaines, IL 60017
(708) 635-8800

*Prepared Foods*
Cahners Publishing
455 N. Cityfront Plaza Dr.
Chicago, IL 60611
(312) 222-2000

*Pulp and Paper*
Miller Freeman Publications
600 Harrison St.
San Francisco, CA 94107
(415) 905-2200

*Recommended Trade Journals (cont'd)*

*Purchasing Magazine*
Cahners Publishing
275 Washington St.
Newton, MA 02158
(216) 696-7000

*Quality Progress*
ASQC
611 E. Wisconsin Ave.
Milwaukee, WI 53202
(414) 272-8575

*Textile World*
Maclean Hunter Publishing
4170 Ashford-Dunwoody Road, Suite 420
Atlanta, GA 30319
(404) 847-2770

*Wood Technology*
Miller Freeman Publications
600 Harrison St.
San Francisco, CA 94107
(415) 905-2200

# Major Standards Developers

THE NATIONAL CENTER FOR Standards and Certification Information (NCSCI) is part of the National Institute of Standards and Technology, and provides information on national and voluntary standards, government regulations, and rules of certification for nonagricultural products. The Center serves as a referral service in the United States for information about standards and standards-related matters. It contributes to the Institute's goals of improving U.S. competitiveness in domestic and world markets by advancing the use of the nation's science and technology through providing up-to-date information on standards and certification programs. According to the Center, the following are among the major standards developers in the country:

Aerospace Industries Association
1250 I St., NW, Suite 1100
Washington, DC 20005
(202) 371-8400

American Association of Cereal Chemists
3340 Pilot Knob Rd.
St. Paul, MN 55121
(612) 454-7250

American Association of State Highway and
Transportation Officials
444 N. Capitol St., NW, Suite 249
Washington, DC 20001
(202) 624-5800

American Conference of Governmental
Industrial Hygienists
6500 Glenway Ave., Bldg. D-7
Cincinnati, OH 45211
(513) 661-7881

American National Standards Institute
11 W. 42nd St., 13th Floor
New York, NY 10036
(212) 642-4900

American Oil Chemists' Society
1608 Broadmoor Dr.
Champaign, IL 61821
(217) 359-2344

American Petroleum Institute
1220 L St., NW
Washington, DC 20005
(202) 682-8000

American Railway Engineering Association
50 F St., NW, Suite 7702
Washington, DC 20001
(202) 639-2190

American Society of Mechanical Engineers
345 E. 47th St.
New York, NY 10017
(212) 705-7722

American Society for Testing and Materials
1916 Race St.
Philadelphia, PA 19103
(215) 299-5585

Association of Official Analytical Chemists
2200 Wilson Blvd., Suite 400
Arlington, VA 22201
(703) 522-3032

Cosmetic, Toiletry and Fragrance Association
1101 17th St., Suite 300
Washington, DC 20036
(202) 331-1770

Electronic Industries Association
c/o Global Engineering
2805 McGraw Ave.
P.O. Box 19539
Irvine, CA 92714
(800) 854-7179

*Major Standards Developers (cont'd)*

Institute of Electrical and Electronics Engineers
445 Hoes Lane
P.O. Box 1331
Piscataway, NJ 08855
(908) 562-3800

National Fire Protection Association
One Batterymarch Park
P.O. Box 9101
Quincy, MA 02269
(617) 770-3000

SAE International
400 Commonwealth Dr.
Warrendale, PA 15096
(412) 776-4841

Technical Association of the Pulp and
Paper Industry
15 Technology Parkway
P.O. Box 105113
Norcross, GA 30092
(404) 446-1400

U.S. Pharmacopeial Convention
12601 Twinbrook Parkway
Rockville, MD 20852
(301) 881-0666

Underwriters Laboratories
333 Pfingsten Rd.
Northbrook, IL 60062
(708) 272-8800

## Contact Option

The National Center for Standards and
Certification Information
National Institute of Standards and Technology
Bldg. 411, Room A163
Gaithersburg, MD 20899
(301) 975-4040

## The Top Reference Sources

*The Directory to Industrial Design
in the United States*
Van Nostrand Reinhold, $47.95
(800) 842-3636

This directory is a comprehensive reference
to the field of industrial design. The information

presented allows readers to make discriminating
choices among consulting firms, design departments, schools, institutions, organizations and
resources listed.

Detailed information is carried in the profiles;
product category and name entries are cross refer-
enced with the profiles.

# Major Industrial Design Awards

## Industrial Design Excellence Awards

Presented each year by the Industrial Designers Society of America and sponsored by *Business Week* magazine, the IDEA is the nation's most coveted annual accolade for industrial design–from computers to packaging, toys to cars. A list of the most recent winners is included in this chapter.

IDEA/IDSA
1142 Walker Rd., Suite E
Great Falls, VA 22066
(703) 759-0100

## I.D. Annual Design Review

*I.D. (International Design) Magazine* presents this most comprehensive design award in categories such as consumer products, graphics, environments, furniture, equipment, packaging, surfaces, concepts, and student work.

*I.D. Magazine*
Design Review Editor
440 Park Ave. S.
New York, NY 10016
(212) 947-1400

## Nesté Forma Finlandia Plastics Design

Prizes include a First Prize of FIM 300,000 (about US$70,000) in this popular international plastics design competition, sponsored by Nesté, one of Scandinavia's largest companies. Entries are considered in two categories: "Tomorrow's Challengers," for new, previously unpublished plastics product ideas; and "The World's Best Plastic Products," recognizing products that have been on the market for less than three years. The "working language" of the competition is English.

Nesté Forma Finlandia 3
P.O. Box 20
02151 Espoo, Finland
358-0-450-5044

## International Design Competition, Osaka

This biennial competition sponsored by the Japan Design Foundation aims to question "the role of design in clarifying visions of the future of humankind in the 21st century" by inviting designers to enter imaginative works from a broad range of design fields. Each competition focuses on a singular theme, such as "wind," "air," or "terra." Prizes include a Grand Prize/Prime Minister's Prize of US $35,000. Official languages for the award are Japanese and English.

International Design Competition, Osaka
Japan Design Foundation
3-1-800 UMEDA 1 Chome
Kita-ku, Osaka 530
Japan
81-6-346-2611

## 1993 IDEA Gold Award Winners

*Deskjet Portable Printer*–Hewlett-Packard, Boise, ID

*PowerBook Duo System*–Apple Computer, Cupertino, CA

*3495 Tape Library Dataserver*–IBM, Tucson, AZ

*LiveBoard*–Xerox, Palo Alto, CA

*Thermal Electrical Grill*–The Thermos Co., Schaumburg, IL

*Macintosh Color Classic*–Apple Computer, Cupertino, CA

*Palmate*–Go-Video, Scottsdale, AZ

*Sensor for Women*–The Gillette Co., Boston, MA

*FM560 Motorized Stairclimber*–Fitness Master, Waconia, MN

*Softouch Scissors*–Fiskars, Inc., Wausau, WI

*First Play*–PlayWorld Systems/Play Designs, New Berlin, PA

*My First Sony*–Sony Corp., Park Ridge, NJ

*Leapfrog*–IBM Corp., Stamford, CT

*Retractable Wall Cord*–Steiner Design, Greenwich, CT

*Single-Burner Portable Cooker*–Tong Yang Magic, Seoul, Korea

*Metaform Personal Hygiene System*–Herman Miller Research, Ann Arbor, MI

*ImageRING*–Pratt Institute, Brooklyn, NY

*Peak 10 Campstove*–California State University, Long Beach, CA

*Anthrometron*–Boeing, Seattle, WA

*Highlander Concept Vehicle*–Chevrolet, Warren MI

*Birmingham Civil Rights Institute Exhibit*–City of Birmingham, AL

*Edge Lit Exit Sign*–At-Lite Lighting Equipment, Inc., Maspeth, NY

*Genesis Softside Easyturn Luggage*–American Tourister, Warren, RI

*Tutor Training Table System*–Howe Furniture, Norwalk, CT

*Major Industrial Design Awards (cont'd)*

*Silhouette Window Shadings*–Hunter Douglas, Broomfield, CO

*670 Perimeter*–Tomey Technology, Cambridge, MA

*Biojector*–Bioject, Portland, OR

*LAISer II*–LAIS Advanced Interventional Systems, Irvine, CA

*Pill Dispenser Package*–Alnamar Corp., Beaverton, OR

*LH Midsize Models* (Dodge Intrepid, Eagle Vision and Chrysler Concorde)–Chrysler Corp., Detroit, MI

*Northstar V-8 Engine*–Cadillac, Detroit, MI

## 1993 I.D. Annual Design Review Winners (Best of Category)

*Consumer Products*
Laerdal Family CPR Trainer, Laerdal

*Environments*
25 Brush Place, Jim Jennings Arkhitekture
LEF Foundation, LEF Foundation

*Packaging*
Book Jackets, Alfred A. Knopf

*Furniture*
Kinderlink, Skools
Zip-Light, Goods!

*Concepts/Students*
The Media Blanket, Cranbrook Academy of Art
Fingerspelling Hand, Palo Alto VA Medical Center

*Equipment*
Apple Adjustable Keyboard, Apple Computer
EPT Blazer Catheter, E.P. Technologies

## Recommended Resources

*Deadlines*
P.O. Box 3449
Alexandria, VA 22302
(703) 578-4918
    This monthly newsletter publishes announcements and deadline information for all national and international design competitions and award programs open to U.S. architects and designers.

Design Access
National Building Museum
401 F St., NW
Washington, DC 20001
(202) 272-5427 or (202) 272-5432
    Newly established by the National Endowment for the Arts and the National Building Museum, the Design Access database maintains information on all aspects of design, including industrial and product design, architecture, urban design and planning, graphic design, historic preservation, and landscape architecture.

## The Top Reference Sources

*Hoover's Handbook of American Business*
The Reference Press, $38.95
(800) 486-8666

This annual reference book profiles 500 business enterprises based in the United States. The book should be of interest to anyone who invests in, buys from, sells to, competes with, interviews with, or works for a large company in the U.S.
    The profiles include brief histories, names of officers and human resources contacts, headquarters address and telephone numbers, sales figures, income, markets, stock prices, products, affiliates and subsidiaries, key competitors, and rankings.

# Patent Licensors

LICENSING IS THE PROCESS of transferring intellectual property (copyrights, patents, trademarks, trade secrets, business information, etc.) from one business, individual, or organization to another. The Licensing Executive Society, Inc., is a professional society of over 3,200 members (scientists, engineers, lawyers, marketers, and licensing consutants), most of whom are actively engaged on behalf of their employers or clients in the transfer of intellectual property. These licensing professionals may provide a number of business services, including:

- Identifying potential markets and licenses;
- Evaluating and packaging licensable intellectual property;
- Funding research and development of intellectual property;
- Protecting the intellectual property to be licensed;
- Monitoring the flow of intellectual property and the payment of royalties;
- Determining what intellectual property rights should be licensed;
- Negotiating reasonable terms between the licensor (seller) and licensee (buyer) and drafting an appropriate license agreement which authorizes the use of intellectual property rights.

*Source: Licensing Executive Society*

## Contact Options

*The following consultants have been selected based on technical interests and the range of services provided. Each is a member of the Licensing Executive Society:*

Denton Anderson
Sheldon & Mak
225 S. Lake Ave., Suite 800
Pasadena, CA 91101
(818) 796-4000
*Medical technology, mechanical devices*

James D. Donovan
Executive Vice President
Intercon Research Associates
6865 Lincoln Ave.
Lincolnwood, IL 60646
(708) 982-1101
*Pharmaceutical, chemical, and medical*

C. Richard Goodlet, Vice President
UC Industries
137 East Ave., P.O. Box 395
Tallmadge, OH 44278
(216) 633-1105
*Plastics, building materials, specialized machinery*

George W. K. King
King Associates
1050 Eagle Rd.
Newtown, PA 18940
(215) 968-4483
*Mechanical, electronics, plastics*

James E. Malackowski
IPC Group
101 N. Wacker Dr., Suite 1600
Chicago, IL 60606
(312) 641-0051
*Automotive, electronics*

William R. Mattson, Jr., President
The Mattson Jack Group
9 The Pines Court, Suite A
St. Louis, MO 63141
(314) 469-7600
*Pharmaceuticals, over-the-counter products*

Jerry S. Oakes, CEO
Synergy Consultants
2915 LBJ, Suite 254
Dallas, TX 75234
(214) 243-1000
*Software, manufacturing*

Edward G. Tutle, President
Tutle International Technology Marketing
2601 Seabreeze Court
Orlando, FL 32805
(407) 423-8016
*Manufacturing, communications technology*

Richard Wechsler, President & C.E.O.
BIEC International
3400 Bath Pike, Park Plaza
Bethlehem, PA 18017
(215) 694-7597
*Steelmaking*

Dominic Yen, Director
Yen Enterprises
1360 W. 9th St., #210
Cleveland, OH 44113
(216) 621-5515
*Industrial machinery, automotive products, chemicals*

# Manufacturing Apprenticeships

WHILE A NUMBER OF GOVERNMENT programs are now in place to make the school-to-work transition a more productive process for American workers and industry, a few U.S. companies may be said to be at the forefront of an industry-driven apprenticeship movement. Among them, are:

Robert Bosch Corporation
38000 Hills Tech Dr.
Farmington Hills, MI 48331
(313) 553-9000

Corning
MP-PS-O2-7
Corning, NY 14831
(607) 974-9000

Milford Fabricating
19200 Glendale Ave.
Detroit, MI 48223
(313) 272-8400

Remmele Engineering
1211 Pierce Butler Route
St. Paul, MN 55104
(612) 642-5689

Siemens Corporation
1301 Avenue of the Americas
New York, NY 10019
(212) 258-4046

## Jobs for the Future

Jobs for the Future is a non-profit group which promotes workforce quality and helps to sponsor youth apprenticeship sites, along with state, school district, and industry support. The following programs are current and may be of particular interest to manufacturers:

Craftsmanship 2000
616 S. Boston
Tulsa, OK 74119
(918) 585-1201

Pennsylvania Youth Apprenticeship Program
Pennsylvania Department of Education
333 Market St., 10th Floor
Harrisburg, PA 17126
(717) 843-2898

Cornell Youth and Work Program
Cornell University
Department of Human Development and
Family Studies
Martha Van Rensselaer Hall
Ithaca, NY 14853
(607) 255-8394

Pickens County Youth Apprenticeship Initiative
School District of Pickens County
1348 Griffin Mill Rd.
Easley, SC 29640
(803) 855-8150

Roosevelt Renaissance 2000
Roosevelt High School
6941 N. Central St.
Portland, OR 97203
(503) 280-5138

Gwinett County Youth Apprenticeship
610 West Crogan St.
Lawrenceville, GA 30245
(404) 822-6421

Manufacturing Technology Partnership Program
Flint Board of Education
GASC Technology Center
G-5081 Torrey Rd.
Flint, MI 48507
(313) 760-1444

Illinois Youth Apprenticeship Program
Illinois State Board of Education
100 N. 1st St.
Springfield, IL 62777
(217) 782-4620

## Contact Options

CDS International
330 Seventh Ave.
New York, NY 10001
(212) 760-1400

Cushman Phillips
19010 Rio Vista Dr.
Fairhope, AL 36532
(205) 928-3211

Jobs for the Future
1815 Massachusetts Ave.
Cambridge, MA 02140
(617) 661-3411

U.S. Department of Labor
Training Policy Unit
200 Constitution Ave., NW, Room N-4663
Washington, DC 20210
(202) 219-5281

# ISO 9000 Quality Standards

IN 1987, THE INCREASED FOCUS on global quality issues led the International Organization for Standardization, or ISO, headquartered in Geneva, Switzerland, to establish a series of international quality standards. Called the ISO 9000 Series of Standards, the series is not specific to any one industry, but when used with proper industry-specific standards, helps build a strong foundation for a quality system. The idea behind ISO is to promote standardization which will facilitate the international exchange of goods and services.

Currently, ISO 9000 certification is voluntary and not required or mandated in any country. However, the European community has recently required that quality systems of many suppliers of products related to health, safety, and the environment be formally registered, by a third party, according to the ISO 9000 Series standard. This action has made adoption of the ISO standards a virtual prerequisite for doing business in Europe. Countries in Asia, Africa, and South America are more and more considering adoption of these standards as a means to increased trade among themselves and the United States. Over 20,000 companies have been registered worldwide, and at least 52 nations are implementing the standards. In its January, 1993, issue, the newsletter *Quality Systems Update* reports that a total of 621 companies, from 45 states, are registered in the United States.

In the United States, the ISO 9000 Series of Standards was adopted verbatim as the ANSI/ASQC Q90 series of standards. The series is comprised of five individual, but related, international standards on quality management and quality assurance, known as ISO 9000, 9001, 9002, 9003, and 9004. For a company's quality system to become registered in one or more of these standards involves having an accredited, independent third party conduct an audit of the company's operations against the requirements of the ISO 9000 standards. Upon successful completion of this audit, the company will receive a registration certificate that identifies its quality system as being in compliance with ISO 9000 standards.

## Accredited Registrars in the United States

ABS Quality Evaluations
16855 Northchase Dr.
Houston, TX 77060
(713) 873-9400

A.G.A. Quality
8501 E. Pleasant Valley Rd.
Cleveland, OH 44131
(216) 524-4990

American European Services (AES)
1054 31st St., NW, Suite 120
Washington, DC 20007
(202) 337-3214

American Association for Laboratory Accreditation
656 Quince Orchard Rd., #620
Gaithersburg, MD 20878
(301) 670-1377

American Society of Mechanical Engineers
United Engineering Center
345 E. 47th Street
New York, NY 10017
(212) 605-4796

AT&T Quality Registrar
650 Liberty Ave.
Union, NJ 07083
(908) 851-3058

AV Qualité
2900 Wilcrest, Suite 300
Houston, TX 77042
(713) 465-2850

Bellcore Quality Registration
6 Corporate Place, Room 1-A230
Piscataway, NJ 08854
(908) 699-3739

Bureau Veritas Quality International
509 N. Main St.
Jamestown, NY 14701
(716) 484-9002

DLS Quality Technology Associates
108 Hallmore Dr.
Camillus, NY 13031
(315) 468-5811

DNV Industry
16340 Park Ten Pl., Suite 100
Houston, TX 77084
(713) 579-9003

Electronic Industries Quality Registry
2001 Pennsylvania Ave., NW
Washington, DC 20006
(202) 457-4970

Entela
3033 Madison Ave., SE
Grand Rapids, MI 49548
(616) 247-0515

Intertek
9900 Main St., Suite 500
Fairfax, VA 22031
(703) 476-9000

*ISO 9000 Quality Standards (cont'd)*

KEMA Registered Quality
4379 County Line Rd.
Chalfont, PA 18914
(215) 822-4258

KPMG Quality Registrar
Three Chestnut Ridge Rd.
Montvale, NJ 07645
(201) 307-7900

Lloyd's Register Quality Assurance
33-41 Newark St.
Hoboken, NJ 07030
(201) 963-1111

MET Laboratories
916 W. Patapsco Ave.
Baltimore, MD 21230
(410) 354-3300

National Quality Assurance
1146 Massachusetts Ave.
Boxborough, MA 01719
(508) 635-9256

Quality Systems Registrars
13873 Park Center Rd.
Herndon, VA 22701
(703) 478-0241

SGS International Certification Services
1415 Park Ave.
Hoboken, NJ 07030
(800) 777-8378

Smithers Quality Assessments
425 W. Market St.
Akron, OH 44303-2099
(216) 762-4231

Steel Related Industries Quality System Registars
2000 Corporate Dr., Suite 450
Wexford, PA 15090
(412) 935-2844

TRA Certification
700 E. Beardsley Ave.
P.O. Box 1081
Elkhart, IN 46515
(219) 264-0745

Tri-Tech Services
4700 Clairton Boulevard
Pittsburgh, PA 15236
(412) 884-2290

TUV America–Hartford Steam Boiler
5 Cherry Hill Dr.
Danvers, MA 01923
(508) 777-7999

TUV Rheinland of North America
12 Commerce Rd.
Newtown, CT 06470
(203) 426-0888

Underwriters Laboratories
1285 Walt Whitman Rd.
Melville, NY 11747
(516) 271-6200, ext. 284

## Contact Options

American National Standards Institute
11 W. 42nd. St.
New York, NY 10036
(212) 692-4900
    The American National Standards Institute (ANSI), an influential member of the ISO, is a non-government voluntary organization which provides a process for accrediting standards-writing bodies. The ISO 9000 Series is available from ANSI (The ANSI/ASQC Q90 Series is identical to the ISO 900 Series.)

American Society for Quality Control
P.O. Box 3005
Milwaukee, WI 53201-3005
(800) 952-6587
    The American Society for Quality Control (ASQC) is an accredited standards-writing body. The ANSI/ASQC Q90 series is available from the customer service department of ASQC.

CEEM Information Services
P.O. Box 200
Fairfax Station, VA 22039
(800) 745-5565
    Publishes *Quality Systems Update* newsletter, ISO 9000 handbook, and a directory of registered companies.

National Institute of Standards and Technology
U.S. Department of Commerce
Gaithersburg, MD 20899
(301) 975-2000

*Consultants:*

Booz, Allen & Hamilton
4330 E. West Highway
Bethesda, MD 20814
(301)951-2200

Du Pont ISO 9000 Services
1007 Market St.
Wilmington, DE 19898
(800) 441-8040

Perry Johnson
3000 Town Center, Suite 2960
Southfield, MI 48075
(313) 356-4410

# Malcolm Baldrige Quality Award

THE MALCOLM BALDRIGE NATIONAL Quality Award is widely acknowledged as having raised overall quality awareness and practice in U.S. manufacturing. According to David A. Garvin, Robert and Jane Cizik Professors of Business Administration at the Harvard Business School, the award "has become the most important catalyst for transforming American business."

Established in 1987 by the Malcolm Baldrige National Quality Improvement Act, the award is administered by the Secretary of Commerce and the National Institute of Standards and Technology, with cooperation and financial support from the private sector. The Malcolm Baldrige National Quality Award is the highest level of national recognition for quality that a U.S. company can receive.

Officially, the Baldrige Award has three goals: to promote an understanding of quality excellence, to recognize the quality achievements of U.S. businesses, and to publicize successful quality strategies. Awards are presented to qualifying companies in manufacturing, service, and small business categories. A maximum of two awards per category may be given each year. Recipients of the award are allowed to publicize and advertise receipt of the award, in return for agreement to share their successful quality strategies with other U.S. organizations.

Applicants for the award are judged on these seven criteria:

• Leadership

• Information and analysis

• Strategic quality planning

• Human resource development and management

• Management of process quality

• Quality and operational results

• Customer focus and satisfaction.

The information submitted in each of these criteria must demonstrate that the applicant's approaches could be replicated or adapted by other companies.

The award has achieved such high status that many large manufacturers encourage their supplier base to participate. And, since all applicants, win or lose, receive feedback from the award's Board of Examiners, many of these companies find the application process itself a worthwhile exercise. For others, the time and expense is not justified. Indeed, a report prepared by the Grant Thornton Survey of Manufacturers in 1992 reveals that midsized U.S. manufacturers may have become disenchanted with the Malcolm Baldrige Award. Sixty percent of companies responding in the Grant Thornton study agree that the award needs to address more substance (the quality, integrity, or innovativeness of a company's products) than form (the quality of a company's control procedures).

## Number of Completed Applications/ Registrants Each Year
1988–66
1989–40
1990–97
1991–106
1992–90
1993–76

## Previous Award Winners

### 1993
*Manufacturing*
Eastman Chemical, Kingsport, TN

*Small Business*
Ames Rubber, Hamburg, NJ

### 1992
*Manufacturing*
AT&T Network Systems Group, Morristown, NJ.
Texas Instruments, Dallas, TX

*Service*
AT&T Universal Card Services, Jacksonville, FL
The Ritz-Carlton Hotel, Atlanta, GA

*Small Business*
Granite Rock, Watsonville, CA

### 1991
*Manufacturing*
Solectron, San Jose, CA
Zytec, Eden Prairie, MN

*Small Business*
Marlow Industries, Dallas, TX

### 1990
*Manufacturing*
Cadillac Motor Car, Detroit, MI
IBM Rochester, Rochester, MN

*Service*
Federal Express, Memphis, TN

*Small Business*
Wallace, Houston, TX

### 1989
*Manufacturing*
Milliken & Company, Spartanburg, IL
Xerox Business Products and Systems, Stamford, CT

*Malcolm Baldrige Quality Award (cont'd)*

## Malcolm Baldrige Award Application Fees

A nonrefundable Eligibility Determination Fee of $50 is required of all applicants. Additional fees for 1993 applicants covering all expenses associated with distribution of applications, review of applications, and development of feedback reports are $4,000 for Manufacturing and Service company categories and $1,200 for the Small Business category. Site visit review fees are established when the visits are scheduled.

Individual copies of the Award Criteria and application forms and instructions may be obtained free of charge from:

Malcolm Baldrige National Quality Award
National Institute of Standards and Technology
Route 270 and Quince Orchard Rd.
Administration Building, Room A537
Gaithersburg, MD 20899
(301) 975-2036

Multiple copies of the Award Criteria may be ordered in packets of 10 (Item Number T997) for $29.95 per packet from:

American Society for Quality Control
Customer Service Department
P.O. Box 3066
Milwaukee, WI 53201
(800) 248-1946

## Consultants for Malcolm Baldrige National Quality Award

The application for the Baldrige Award is sufficiently complicated that many companies rely on outside consultants for help in completing it. Here is a partial list, recommended by the Association of Management Consulting Firms:

Coopers & Lybrand
1251 Avenue of the Americas
New York, NY 10020
(212) 536-2000

K.W. Tunnell
900 E. Eighth Ave., Suite 106
King of Prussia, PA 19406
(215) 337-0820

Rath & Strong
92 Hayden Ave.
Lexington, MA 02173
(617) 861-1700

Robert E. Nolan
90 Hopmeadow St.
Simsbury, CT 06070
(203) 658-1941

## Contact Options

Association of Management Consulting Firms
521 Fifth Ave.
New York, NY 10175
(212) 697-9693

# Quality Benchmarking

BENCHMARKING, THE PROCESS of learning from the best practices of others, is increasing rapidly in the U.S. due to growing foreign competition, limited resources, and even the requirements of the Malcolm Baldrige National Award criteria. To assist firms, nonprofit organizations, and government agencies in the process of benchmarking, the American Productivity & Quality Center established an International Benchmarking Clearinghouse in 1992 as a source of information about "best practices" for a large number of organizational processes. The Clearinghouse provides standards of conduct, conducts in-depth secondary research, and collects and disseminates best practices through databases, case studies, publications, seminars, conferences, videos, and other media. The Clearinghouse also provides training and consulting.

## Contact Options

International Benchmarking Clearinghouse
American Productivity & Quality Center
123 North Post Oak Ln., #300
Houston, TX 77024
(713) 681-4020

International Quality and Productivity Center
P.O. Box 43155
Upper Montclair, NJ 07043
(800) 882-8684

The IQPC has sponsored numerous workshops and seminars on benchmarking practices.

# MARKETING

# Ad Agencies Ranked

## The 30 Hottest Agencies in the U.S., 1993

| Rank | Agency | Adweek Performance Index | 1993 Billings ($ thousands) | Increase in Billings 1993-92 ($ thousands) | % Increase in Billings 1993-92 |
|---|---|---|---|---|---|
| 1 | Houston Effler & Partners, Boston | 883 | 103,100 | 46,949 | 83.6 |
| 2 | Yaffe & Co., Southfield, MI | 551 | 84,212 | 28,885 | 52.2 |
| 3 | Hammeroff/Milenthal/Spence, Columbus, OH | 384 | 81,700 | 21,700 | 36.2 |
| 4 | Deutsch/Dworin, New York | 378 | 180,000 | 45,000 | 33.3 |
| 5 | Kirshenbaum & Bond, New York | 368 | 140,000 | 35,000 | 33.3 |
| 6 | BBDO, New York | 359 | 1,857,338 | 222,570 | 13.6 |
| 7 | Goodby Berlin & Silverstein, San Francisco | 348 | 216,000 | 49,555 | 29.8 |
| 8 | Anderson & Lembke, New York | 330 | 101,450 | 23,750 | 30.6 |
| 9 | Ammirati & Puris, New York | 326 | 405,000 | 80,000 | 24.6 |
| 10 | Fogarty Klein & Partners, Houston | 322 | 113,791 | 26,014 | 29.6 |
| 11 | Bernstein-Rein, Kansas City | 314 | 202,200 | 43,088 | 27.1 |
| 12 | Dahlin Smith White, Salt Lake City | 296 | 84,876 | 18,457 | 27.8 |
| 13 | Mullen, Wenham MA | 294 | 137,000 | 28,700 | 26.5 |
| 14 | The Martin Agency, Richmond, VA | 266 | 182,438 | 34,395 | 23.2 |
| 15 | Grey Advertising, New York | 264 | 1,885,700 | 166,700 | 9.7 |
| 16 | MVBMS/EURO RSCG, New York | 264 | 588,500 | 87,865 | 17.6 |
| 17 | Goldberg Moser O'Neill, San Francisco | 260 | 111,000 | 21,400 | 23.9 |
| 18 | GSD&M, Austin | 248 | 242,600 | 41,517 | 20.6 |
| 19 | Ackerman McQueen, Oklahoma City | 243 | 97,585 | 17,945 | 22.5 |
| 20 | J. Walter Thompson, New York | 225 | 2,092,700 | 148,700 | 7.6 |
| 21 | Fallon McElligott, Minneapolis | 224 | 150,000 | 24,902 | 19.9 |
| 22 | Lowe & Partners SMS, New York | 196 | 500,000 | 60,000 | 13.6 |
| 23 | Foote, Cone & Belding, Chicago | 195 | 2,424,538 | 136,069 | 5.9 |
| 24 | Bozell, New York | 185 | 935,000 | 85,000 | 10.0 |
| 25 | Meldrum & Fewsmith, Cleveland | 178 | 138,900 | 19,073 | 15.9 |
| 26 | McCann-Erickson, New York | 174 | 1,673,700 | 105,900 | 6.8 |
| 27 | Rotando Lerch & Iafeliece, Stamford, CT | 154 | 114,300 | 14,000 | 14.0 |
| 28 | Griffin Bacal, New York | 150 | 205,809 | 23,209 | 12.7 |
| 29 | Jordan McGrath Case & Taylor, New York | 148 | 410,000 | 40,000 | 10.8 |
| 30 | Margeotes Fertitta Donaher & Weiss, New York | 147 | 138,000 | 16,000 | 13.1 |

*Source: Adweek*

## The Top Reference Sources

*Guerrilla Marketing for the '90s*
Houghton Mifflin, $9.95
(800) 352-5455

One in a series of marketing books by best-selling author Jay Conrad Levinson, this book provides

100 affordable marketing weapons for maximizing profits from your small business.

Levinson has created an approach to marketing that relies on low cost, high impact techniques for identifying, reaching, and keeping customers.

*Ad Agencies Ranked (cont'd)*

## The Top 25 Agencies Worldwide, 1993

| Rank | Agency | Headquarters | 1993 Billings ($ thousands) | 1992 Billings ($ thousands) | % Change |
|------|--------|--------------|------------------------------|------------------------------|----------|
| 1 | Foote, Cone, & Belding | Chicago | 2,424,538 | 2,288,469 | 5.9 |
| 2 | Young & Rubicam | New York | 2,110,170 | 2,089,764 | 1.0 |
| 3 | Leo Burnett & Co. | Chicago | 2,106,403 | 2,104,073 | 0.1 |
| 4 | J. Walter Thompson | New York | 2,092,700 | 1,944,000 | 7.6 |
| 5 | D'Arcy, Masius, Benton & Bowles | New York | 1,974,105 | 1,928,837 | 2.3 |
| 6 | Grey Advertising | New York | 1,885,700 | 1,719,000 | 9.7 |
| 7 | BBDO | New York | 1,857,338 | 1,634,768 | 13.6 |
| 8 | DDB Needham | New York | 1,812,282 | 1,740,347 | 4.1 |
| 9 | Saatchi & Saatchi Advertising | New York | 1,770,000 | 1,800,000 | -1.7 |
| 10 | McCann-Erickson | New York | 1,673,700 | 1,567,800 | 6.8 |
| 11 | Ogilvy & Mather | New York | 1,553,000 | 1,522,000 | 2.0 |
| 12 | Lintas: USA | New York | 1,293,909 | 1,269,936 | 1.9 |
| 13 | Campbell Mithun Esty | Minneapolis | 1,072,000 | 1,008,542 | 6.3 |
| 14 | Backer Spielvogel Bates | New York | 1,018,348 | 976,029 | 4.3 |
| 15 | Bozell | New York | 935,000 | 850,000 | 10.0 |
| 16 | Wells Rich Greene BDDP | New York | 882,600 | 919,900 | -4.1 |
| 17 | Chiat/Day | Venice, CA | 827,000 | 807,200 | 2.5 |
| 18 | Ayer | New York | 780,998 | 855,300 | -8.7 |
| 19 | Ketchum | Pittsburgh | 600,000 | 612,400 | -2.0 |
| 20 | MVBMS/EURO RSCG | New York | 588,500 | 500,635 | 17.6 |
| 21 | Lowe & Partners SMS | New York | 500,000 | 440,000 | 13.6 |
| 22 | Temerlin McClain | Dallas | 440,000 | 405,000 | 8.6 |
| 23 | Jordan McGrath Case & Taylor | New York | 410,000 | 370,000 | 10.8 |
| 24 | Earle Palmer Brown | Bethesda | 409,600 | 382,200 | 7.2 |
| 25 | Ammirati & Puris | New York | 405,000 | 325,000 | 24.6 |

## The 15 Largest Agency Holding Companies, 1993

| Rank | Agency | Headquarters | 1993 Billings ($ thousands) | 1992 Billings ($ thousands) | % Change |
|------|--------|--------------|------------------------------|------------------------------|----------|
| 1 | WPP Group PLC | London | 19,710,000 | 18,954,900 | 4.0 |
| 2 | The Interpublic Group of Companies | New York | 14,273,575 | 13,544,527 | 5.3 |
| 3 | Omnicom | New York | 14,022,867 | 13,440,561 | 4.3 |
| 4 | Saatchi & Saatchi Co. PLC | London | 11,755,000 | 11,755,000 | 0.0 |
| 5 | Dentsu | Tokyo | 11,149,374 | 10,495,609 | 6.2 |
| 6 | Young & Rubicam | New York | 7,653,885 | 7,878,994 | -2.9 |
| 7 | FCB-Publicis | Chicago | 6,764,207 | 6,554,000 | 3.2 |
| 8 | Euro RSCG | Paris | 6,518,086 | 6,647,137 | -1.9 |
| 9 | Hakuhodo | Tokyo | 5,458,713 | 5,086,449 | 7.3 |
| 10 | Grey Advertising | New York | 5,083,400 | 4,835,000 | 5.1 |
| 11 | D'Arcy, Masius, Benton & Bowles | New York | 4,770,054 | 4,700,689 | 1.5 |
| 12 | Leo Burnett | Chicago | 4,223,482 | 4,304,343 | -1.9 |
| 13 | BDDP | Paris | 2,207,633 | 2,294,354 | -3.8 |
| 14 | Bozell Jacobs Kenyon & Eckhardt | New York | 1,850,000 | 1,720,000 | 7.6 |
| 15 | Ayer | New York | 931,382 | 1,375,056 | -32.3 |

*Source: Adweek*

*Ad Agencies Ranked (cont'd)*

## The Top 10 Direct Response Agencies, 1993

| Rank | Agency | Headquarters | 1993 Billings ($ thousands) | 1992 Billings ($ thousands) | % Change |
|------|--------|--------------|------------------------------|------------------------------|----------|
| 1 | Wunderman Cato Johnson Worldwide | New York | 536,635 | 483,564 | 11.0 |
| 2 | Ogilvy & Mather Direct | New York | 440,000 | 390,000 | 12.8 |
| 3 | Rapp Collins Worldwide | New York | 418,847 | 333,231 | 25.7 |
| 4 | Bronner Slosberg | Boston | 305,154 | 301,024 | 1.4 |
| 5 | Barry Blau | Fairfield, CT | 204,259 | 151,419 | 34.9 |
| 6 | Kobs & Draft | Chicago | 201,230 | 174,200 | 15.5 |
| 7 | DIMAC Direct | Bridgeton, MO | 176,106 | 163,485 | 7.7 |
| 8 | Grey Direct | New York | 161,000 | 135,000 | 19.3 |
| 9 | Chapman Direct | New York | 154,254 | 153,272 | 0.6 |
| 10 | Customer Development Corp. | Peoria, IL | 150,580 | 138,432 | 8.8 |

*Source: Adweek*

## The Top Reference Sources

*SRDS Direct Mail List Rates and Data*
Standard Rate and Data Service, $354/6 issues
(708) 256-6067

Virtually every mailing list available for rent to marketers is catalogued in this cumbersome volume.

This is a complete resource for direct mail users that includes a subject/market classification index, title/list index, suppliers, and services directory. Also included are mailing list brokers, compilers and managers, business lists, business co-ops and package insert programs, consumer lists, farm lists, consumer co-ops and package insert programs, and alternate delivery systems.

# Major Ad Award Winners

## Starch Awards

SINCE 1988, ROPER STARCH, a market research firm, has presented the Starch Award. The award is given to the print ads that achieved the highest recognition scores among consumers during the previous year. Winners are culled from more than 50,000 face-to-face interviews with consumers annually.

## 1989 Starch Winners

| Agency | Category | Client/Product |
|---|---|---|
| AC&R Advertising | Women's Toiletries | Estée Lauder |
| FCB/Leber Katz Partners | Beer, Wine, and Liquor | Bolla |
| Ogilvy & Mather | Confectionery, Snacks | Hershey's Kisses |
| D'Arcy, Masius, Benton & Bowles | Household Accessories | Charmin |
| CRK Advertising | Men's Toiletries | Calvin Klein/Obsession |
| Deutsch | Household Materials | Oneida |
| Foote, Cone & Belding | Automotive | Mazda |
| Ogilvy & Mather | Financial | American Express |
| Rick Bennett Agency | Computers | Oracle |
| Ammirati & Puris | Insurance and Real Estate | Aetna |
| Sales Aid International | Food | Swanson |
| Eric Michelson | Apparel, Footwear | Evan-Picone |
| BBDO | Freight | Federal Express |
| Backer Spielvogel Bates | Electronic Entertainment | Magnavox |

## 1990 Starch Winners

| Agency | Category | Client/Product |
|---|---|---|
| Hakuhodo Advertising America | Electronic Entertainment | Hitachi |
| Deutsch | Household Materials | Oneida |
| Geer, DuBois | Automotive | Jaguar |
| Levine, Huntley, Vick & Beaver | Financial | Dreyfus |
| Tracy-Locke | Travel | Embassy Suites Hotels |
| Ogilvy & Mather | Beer, Wine, and Liquor | Seagram's Seven |
| DCA Advertising | Office Equipment | Canon |
| Ad Group | Sportswear | Gitano |
| Saatchi & Saatchi | Computers | Hewlett-Packard |
| BBDO | Floor Coverings | Armstrong |
| D'Arcy, Masius, Benton & Bowles | Food | Kraft Foods Cool Whip |
| Lawner Reingold Britton & Partners | Sporting Goods, Toys | Pinnacle Golf Balls |
| Revlon Professional Products (in-house) | Hair Products | Revlon |
| Bozell | Lingerie | Vanity Fair |
| PR+ | Sportswear | Zena |

*Major Ad Award Winners (cont'd)*

## 1991 Starch Winners

| Agency | Category | Client/Product |
|---|---|---|
| Lintas | Hair Products | Johnson's Baby Shampoo |
| TBWA Advertsing | Beer, Wine and Liquor | Absolut |
| Hakuhodo Advertsing | Electronic Entertainment | Hitachi |
| D'Arcy, Masius, Benton & Bowles | Food | Cool Whip |
| BBDO | Floor Coverings | Armstrong |
| Eisaman, Johns & Law Advertising | Women's Toiletries | Giorgio Beverly Hills |
| Young & Rubicam | Automotive | Mercury |
| Bizell | Lingerie | Vanity Fair |
| Avrett, Free & Ginsberg | Tobacco Products | Kent Cigarettes |
| Ogilvy & Mather | Financial | American Express |
| FCB/ Leber Katz Partners | Bakery Goods | Chips Ahoy |
| Waring & LaRosa | Sporting Goods, Toys | Fisher-Price |
| DDB Needham | Computers | NEC |
| Young & Rubicam | Insurance and Real Estate | MetLife |
| Carlson & Partners | Sportswear | Ralph Lauren |

## 1992 Starch Winners

| Agency | Category | Client/Product |
|---|---|---|
| Bozell | Automotive | Chrysler |
| Ogilvy & Mather | Confectionary and Snacks | Hershey |
| Saatchi & Saatchi | Soaps and Detergents | Tide |
| BBDO | Floor Coverings and Fibers | Armstrong |
| George McWilliams Associates | Financial | Transamerica |
| Severin Group (in-house) | Jewelry | Gucci |
| Guess Advertising (in-house) | Apparel | Guess |
| Greengage Associates | Resorts and Travel | St. Croix, St. John, St. Thomas |
| Howard, Merrell & Partners | Pets and Pet Supplies | Defend |
| J. Walter Thompson | Cooking Products | Miracle Whip |
| Lintas | Computer Publications | OS/2-IBM |
| Walt Disney Home Video (in-house) | Pre-Recorded Records and Tapes | Disney |
| Stein Robaire Helm | Computers, Office Equipment, and Stationery | Day Runner |
| Falk Communications | Medical Publications | Esgicplus |
| Brugnatelli & Partners | Medicines | Baby Orajel |
| Eisaman, Johns & Co. | Liquor | Kahlua |
| CRK Advertising (in-house) | Cosmetics and Beauty Aids | Calvin Klein/Obsession |

*Source: Roper Starch*

*GEnie's Trade Names Database is a searchable reference for over 280,000 consumer brand names. KEYWORD TRADENAMES.*

*Major Ad Award Winners (cont'd)*

## The Kelly Awards

The Magazine Publishers of America give the annual Kelly Award to the print ad which best demonstrates the ability to capture and hold the reader's attention.

| Year | Agency | Client | Product/Campaign |
|------|--------|--------|------------------|
| 1981 | Ogilvy & Mather | Par Parfums | Paco Rabanne Cologne |
| 1982 | Ogilvy & Mather | International Paper | International Paper |
| 1983 | Doyle Dane Bernbach Group | Foodways National | Weight Watchers Frozen Foods |
| 1984 | Chiat/Day | Nike | Nike Apparel |
| 1985 | Ogilvy & Mather | American Express | Retail |
| 1986 | McKinney & Silver | North Carolina Travel & Tourism | Travel |
| 1987 | Ogilvy & Mather | American Express | "Green" Card |
| 1988 | TBWA Advertising | Carillon Importers | Absolut Vodka |
| 1989 | Wieden & Kennedy | Nike | Emotional Running |
| 1990 | TBWA Advertising | Carillon Importers | Absolut Vodka |
| 1991 | Wieden & Kennedy | Nike | Women's Fitness Campaign |
| 1992 | Wieden & Kennedy | Nike | Women's Fitness Campaign |

*Source: Magazine Publishers of America*

## The EFFIE Awards

The EFFIE Award is presented annually by the New York City Chapter of the American Marketing Association to advertisers and advertising agencies in recognition of those campaigns judged to be the most effective. Print, television, and radio campaigns are judged in over 30 categories.

| Year | Agency | Client | Category | Product |
|------|--------|--------|----------|---------|
| 1980 | Ally & Gargano | Federal Express | Business Products and Services | Federal Express |
|      | Advertising to Women | Gillette | Women's Toiletries | Silkience Conditioner |
| 1981 | BBDO | G.E. | Household Durables | G.E. Products |
|      | Doyle Dane Bernbach Group | Volkswagen | Automotive | Volkswagen Autos |
| 1982 | Doyle Dane Bernbach Group | Polaroid | Recreational Products | Sun Camera |
| 1983 | Della Femina, Travisano & Partners | AAA | Automotive Related | AAA, Auto Club |
| 1984 | SCC & B | Coca-Cola | Beverages: Non-Alcoholic | Diet Coke |
|      | Ally & Gargano | Federal Express | Business Products and Services | Federal Express |
| 1985 | Chiat/Day | Apple Computer | Bus. Computers: Software | Apple Computer |
| 1986 | Chiat/Day | Pizza Hut | Restaurants | Pizza Hut |
| 1987 | Chiat/Day | NYNEX | Telecommunications Services | Yellow Pages |
| 1988 | Jordan, McGrath, Case & Taylor | Quaker Oats | Breakfast Food | Quaker Oatmeal |
| 1989 | Chiat/Day | NYNEX | Media: Non-Newspaper | Yellow Pages |
| 1990 | TBWA Advertising | Carillon Importers | Distilled Spirits: Non-Wine | Absolut Vodka |
| 1991 | Northwoods Advertising | Senator Wellstone | Political | Senator Wellstone |
| 1992 | Hill Holiday Conners Cosmopulos | Reebok | Fashion Apparel | Blacktop Sneakers |
| 1993 | BBDO/Los Angeles | Apple Computer | Computers | Power Book Intro. |
| 1994 | Boodby Berlin & Silverstein | Burrell Comm. | Inner-City Drug Campaign | Partnership for a Drug-Free America |

*Source: American Marketing Association, NY Chapter*

*Major Ad Award Winners (cont'd)*

## The Clio Awards

The Clio Awards are presented annually for creative excellence in advertising to agencies throughout the world. Previously awarded by product category, the new and improved Clios are now awarded in media categories only, as judged by a panel of advertising professionals.

## 1993 Television Hall of Fame Award Recipients

| Product | Title | Entrant |
|---|---|---|
| Diet Pepsi | Apartment 10G | BBDO, New York |
| Hamlet Cigars | Photo Booth | Rose Hackney, London |
| Partnership for a Drug-Free America | Waking Up | Giraldi Suarez, New York |

## Campaign Award Recipients

| Campaign | Product | Entrant |
|---|---|---|
| Print—Local | Seattle Supersonics | Livingston & Company, Seattle |
| Print—Regional | New York State Lottery | DDB Needham Worldwide, New York |
| Print—National | Asia Dairies | Saatchi & Saatchi Advertising, Singapore |
| Radio—Regional | Utz Quality Foods | Gray Kirk/VanSant Advertising, Baltimore |
| TV—Local | Mystic Lake Casino | Hunt Murray, Minneapolis |
| TV—Regional | New York State Lottery | DDB Needham Worldwide, New York |
| TV—National | Bank of New Zealand | Colenso Communications, Wellington |

*Source: Clio Awards*

## Contact Option

Clio Awards
276 Fifth Ave., Suite 401
New York, NY 10001
(212) 683-4300

## AAAA A+ Creative Awards

The A+ Creative Awards, established by the American Association of Advertising Agencies, are awarded to advertising agencies rather than to a particular ad campaign. Each agency in the competition was asked to submit ten ads in any combination of media that ran for the first time the previous year.

| Year | Agency | Location |
|---|---|---|
| 1991 | Carmichael Lynch | Minneapolis |
| 1992 | Cliff Freeman and Partners | New York |
| 1993 | Carmichael Lynch | Minneapolis |

*Source: AAAA*

*Major Ad Award Winners (cont'd)*

## The One Show Awards–Best in Show

The One Show Awards, gold, silver, and bronze, have been given each year since 1973 by The One Club for Art & Copy. The award is given to print, television, and radio ad campaigns in a variety of categories on the basis of effectiveness.

## Best in Show

| Year | Agency | Client |
|------|--------|--------|
| 1990 | Wieden & Kennedy, Portland, OR | Nike |
| 1991 | GGK, London | Electricity Association |
| 1992 | Saatchi & Saatchi, London | British Airways |
| 1993 | Streetsmart Advertising | Coalition for the Homeless |

## 1993 One Show Winners

| Category | Agency | Client |
|----------|--------|--------|
| Newspaper Over 600 Lines: Single | Fallon McElligott | Jim Beam Brands |
| Newspaper Over 600 Lines: Campaign | The Martin Agency | Poe Museum |
| Newspaper 600 Lines or Less: Single | Fallon McElligott | Porsche Cars |
| Newspaper 600 Lines or Less: Campaign | The Ball Partnership | Yet Con Restaurant |
| Magazine B/W 1 Page or Spread: Single | Fallon McElligott | J.D. Hoyt's |
| Magazine Color 1 Page or Spread: Single | Franklin Stoorza | Taylor Guitar |
| Magazine B/W 1 Page or Spread: Campaign | The Ball Partnership | Gallery 13 |
| Magazine Color 1 Page or Spread: Campaign | Wieden & Kennedy | Nike |
| Magazine Less Than a Page: Single | Livingston & Keye | JBL |
| Outdoor: Single | The Richards Group | Tabu Lingerie |
| Outdoor: Campaign | The Richards Group | Tabu Lingerie |
| Trade B/W 1 Page or Spread: Single | RM&K | Mark Segal Photography |
| Trade Color 1 Page or Spread: Single | Goodby Berlin & Co. | The New Yorker Silverstein |
| Trade Less Than a Page B/W or Color: Single | Leo Burnett | Singapore Convention Bureau |
| Trade Any Size B/W or Color: Campaign | Goodby Berlin & Co. | The New Yorker Silverstein |
| Collateral Brochures Other Than By Mail | Cole & Weber | Klein Bikes |
| Collateral Direct Mail: Single | Ogilvy & Mather | Jaguar Cars |
| Collateral Direct Mail: Campaign | The Richards Group | Tabu Lingerie |
| Collateral P.O.P. | Think Tank | The Bell Pub |
| Public Service Newspaper: Single | DDB Needham | Lake Michigan Federation |
| Public Service Newspaper: Campaign | The Martin Agency | Perot for President |
| Public Service Outdoor: Single | Borders Perrin & Norrander | Oregon Donor Program |
| Consumer Radio: Single | The Martin Agenchy | Richmond Symphony |
| Public Service Radio | Hill Holliday Connors Cosmopulos | Pine Street Inn |
| Consumer TV Over :30 Single | Wieden & Kennedy | Nike |
| Consumer TV Over :30 Campaign | Wieden & Kennedy | McKenzie River Corporation |
| Consumer TV :30/:25 Single | DDB Needham | New York State Lottery |
| Consumer TV :30/:25 Campaign | Cliff Freeman & Partners | Little Caesar Enterprises |
| Consumer TV :20 and Under Single | Leo Burnett | Guinness Publishing |
| Consumer TV :20 and Under Campaign | Williams & Rockwood | Utah Film & Video Festival |
| Consumer TV Varying Lengths Campaign | Collett Dickenson & McEwans | Pearce |
| Consumer TV Under $50,000 Budget Single | Williams & Rockwood | Utah Film & Video Festival |
| Public Service/Political Television: Single | Streetsmart | Coalition for the Homeless |
| Public Service/Political Television: Campaign | Martin/Williams | American Humane Association |
| Non-Broadcast Cinema/Video | Chiat/Day | Reebok |
| Int'l Foreign Language Commercial | Nordskar & Thorkildsen Leo Burnett | Braathens S.A.F.E. |
| College Competition | East Texas State University | East Texas State University |

*Source: One Club for Art & Copy*

# Choosing an Ad Agency

ANY COMPANY THAT SPENDS more than $500,000 on advertising should seriously consider employing an agency to facilitate its advertising needs.

*Adweek* and *Advertising Age* are the two magazines that thoroughly cover the advertising industry. These sources, combined with the tips listed below, may help narrow the range of what you should be looking for and clarify how to evaluate what you've seen.

Finding the agency that is best suited to your company's needs can be a tricky business. Many agencies do a better job of selling themselves than the companies they represent, and the burden falls on the client to find a selection process that works.

## 10 Questions to Ask Yourself Before Hiring an Ad Agency:

- Are we more interested in creative or in short-term market share results?

- Does our agency need a media-buying capability or will we handle that separately?

- Do we want to pay our agency a flat fee or a percentage of our budget?

- Are we looking for a particular campaign or for a company?

- How important is it to have regular access to the head of the agency we choose?

- Which medium do we need our agency to handle?

- Do we need our agency to handle existing projects only or new product launches as well?

- Does it matter if our agency is conveniently located?

- Do we want a company with a particular philosophy or one that is willing to work with the philosophy of its clients?

- Whom do we want to be in charge?

## Evaluate Each Agency by Asking the Following:

- Does it understand our company's objectives?

- Does it address our company's objectives?

- Does it have the necessary credentials and experience?

- Does it have a knowledge of our business?

- Does it have an interest in our business?

- Does it have a knowledge of our competitive situation?

- Does it present sound marketing strategies?

- Does it present clear, creative solutions?

- Does it have good internal resources?

- Does it have a strong account management team?

- Can we work together?

*Source: Small Business Reports*

## Contact Options

The American Association of Advertising Agencies
666 Third Ave.
New York, NY 10017
(212) 682-2500
*Industry Association*

*Selection Agencies:*

Advertising Agency Register
155 E. 55th St., Suite 6A
New York, NY 10022
Leslie Winthrop
(212) 644-0790

Advertising Agency Search Service
30 E. Huron, Suite 1910
Chicago, IL 60611
Mary Jane Rumminger
(312) 649-1148

Bismark
30 Bismark Way
Dennis, MA 02638
William Weilbacher
(508) 385-6889

Dorward & Associates
150 Grand Ave., Suite 200
Oakland, CA 94612
Don Dorward
(510) 452-0587

EBJ Management Consultants
7229 S. Janmar Circle
Dallas, TX 75230
Eugene Jacobson
(214) 361-1427

Neal Gilliatt
1 Rockefeller Plaza, Suite 1510
New York, NY 10020
(212) 262-0660

*Choosing an Ad Agency (cont'd)*

Jones-Lundin Associates
625 N. Michigan Ave., Suite 500
Chicago, IL 60611

    Bob Lundin (Chicago)
    (312) 751-3470

    Kenneth Caffrey (New York)
    (212) 765-1986

    Jack McBride (California)
    (209) 577-1464

Horace Malfa
Malfa Enterprises
15 Country Rd.
Mamaroneck, NY 10543
(914) 698-4927

Robert Marker
10555 SE Terrapin Pl., #101
Tequesta, FL 33469
(407) 747-3237

Morgan, Anderson & Co.
136 W. 24th St.
New York, NY 10011
Lee Anne Morgan; Arthur Anderson
(212) 741-0777

New England Consulting Group
55 Green Farms Rd.
Westport, CT 06880
Gary Stibel
(203) 226-9200

Pile & Company
535 Boylston
Boston, MA 02116
"Skip" Pile
(617) 267-5000

Richard Roth Associates
73 Cross Ridge Rd.
Chappaqua, NY 10514
Richard Roth
(914) 238-9206

Wanamaker Associates
3060 Peachtree Rd., NW
Atlanta, GA 30305
Ken Bowes
(404) 233-3029

Herb Zeltner
R.D. #1
North Salem, NY 10560
(914) 669-8530

# Talent Agencies

MOST OF THE BIG TALENT NAMES are concentrated in a handful of top talent agencies.

Creative Artists Agency (CAA)
(615) 383-8787

The William Morris Agency
(212) 586-5100

International Creative Management (ICM)
(212) 556-5600

United Talent Agency
(310) 273-6700

The Gersh Agency
(310) 274-6611

Shapiro-Lichtman
(310) 859-8877

The Writers and Artists Agency
(310) 824-6300

## Recommended Resource

*Pacific Coast Studio Directory*
Published by Jack and Harry Reitz
P.O. Box V
Pine Mountain, CA 93222
(805) 242-2722
    This is a triannual reference on the film and television industries.

# Video Retention Rankings

## Top 10 Television Campaigns of 1993

| 1993 | 1992 | Brand | Ad Agency |
|------|------|-------|-----------|
| 1 | 5 | McDonald's | Leo Burnett |
| 2 | 2 | Pepsi | BBDO |
| 3 | 9 | Coca-Cola | Creative Artists Agency |
| 4 | 3 | Nike | Wieden & Kennedy |
| 5 | 1 | Little Caesar's Pizza | Cliff Freeman & Partners |
| 6 | 7 | Budweiser | DMB&B |
| 7 | – | Taco Bell | Foote, Cone & Belding |
| 8 | 10 | Taster's Choice | McCann-Erickson |
| 9 | 4 | DuPont Stainmaster | BBDO |
| 10 | 16 | Lexus | Team One |

*Source: Video Storyboard Tests*

# Top Advertising Industries

| Rank | Category | 1993 Spending ($) | % Change | 1992 Rank |
|------|----------|-------------------|----------|-----------|
| 1 | Direct Response Companies | 1,081,900,000 | 8.6 | 2 |
| 2 | Automotive | 1,079,200,000 | 1.1 | 1 |
| 3 | Toiletries and Cosmetics | 837,900,000 | 8.5 | 3 |
| 4 | Business and Consumer Services | 646,600,000 | 15.9 | 4 |
| 5 | Apparel, Footwear, and Accessories | 539,800,000 | 1.6 | 5 |
| 6 | Foods and Food Products | 511,200,000 | 0.8 | 6 |
| 7 | Travel, Hotels, and Resorts | 406,100,000 | 6.3 | 7 |
| 8 | Drugs & Remedies | 401,200,000 | 18.5 | 9 |
| 9 | Computers, Office Equipment, and Stationery | 371,600,000 | 3.7 | 8 |
| 10 | Retail | 275,400,000 | 7.5 | 10 |
| 11 | Cigarettes, Tobacco, and Accessories | 231,300,000 | -7.5 | 11 |
| 12 | Publishing and Media | 222,700,000 | 4.5 | 12 |
| 13 | Sporting Goods, Toys, and Games | 174,900,000 | -1.5 | 14 |
| 14 | Jewelry, Optical Goods, and Cameras | 173,300,000 | 3.7 | 16 |
| 15 | Liquor | 172,200,000 | -12.7 | 13 |

*Source: Adweek*

## The Top Reference Sources

*Zig Ziglar's Secrets of Closing the Sale*
Berkeley, $10
(800) 631-8571

This best-selling book is must reading for anyone who is serious about wanting to improve as a salesperson. Ziglar's inspiring work includes over 100 successful closings for every kind of persua-sion; over 700 questions that will open your eyes to new possibilities you may have overlooked; how to paint word pictures and use your imagination to get results; plus tips from America's 100 most successful salespeople.

This is one of the most important books on the topic—every salesperson should own a copy.

# Leading National Advertisers

| Rank | Advertiser | Ad Spending ($ millions) |
|------|-----------|--------------------------|
| 1 | Procter & Gamble | 2,165.6 |
| 2 | Philip Morris | 2,024.1 |
| 3 | General Motors | 1,333.6 |
| 4 | Sears, Roebuck & Co. | 1,204.6 |
| 5 | PepsiCo | 928.6 |
| 6 | Ford Motor | 794.5 |
| 7 | Warner-Lambert | 757.5 |
| 8 | Chrysler | 756.6 |
| 9 | McDonald's | 743.6 |
| 10 | Nestlé SA | 733.4 |
| 11 | Eastman Kodak | 686.0 |
| 12 | Grand Metropolitan | 680.2 |
| 13 | Unilever NV | 672.8 |
| 14 | Johnson & Johnson | 659.6 |
| 15 | Toyota Motor | 648.9 |
| 16 | Time Warner | 637.9 |
| 17 | Kellogg | 630.3 |
| 18 | AT&T | 623.7 |
| 19 | General Mills | 571.2 |
| 20 | Anheuser-Busch | 555.8 |
| 21 | Kmart | 551.1 |
| 22 | J.C. Penny | 537.4 |
| 23 | American Home Products | 531.6 |
| 24 | Walt Disney | 524.6 |
| 25 | Sony | 507.9 |
| 26 | RJR Nabisco | 422.2 |
| 27 | Ralston Purina | 411.5 |
| 28 | Coca-Cola | 392.0 |
| 29 | May Department Stores | 390.9 |
| 30 | Hershey Foods | 383.0 |
| 31 | Nissan Motor | 370.7 |
| 32 | Sara Lee | 356.9 |
| 33 | Honda Motor | 349.1 |
| 34 | U.S. Government | 331.0 |
| 35 | Mars | 320.4 |
| 36 | Colgate-Palmolive | 315.5 |
| 37 | Matsushita Electric Industrial | 304.2 |
| 38 | H.J. Heinz | 301.1 |
| 39 | American Express | 294.3 |
| 40 | Bristol-Myers Squibb | 280.1 |
| 41 | R.H. Macy & Co. | 270.4 |
| 42 | Circuit City Store | 261.1 |
| 43 | Smith Kline Beecham | 257.3 |
| 44 | Quaker Oats | 256.2 |
| 45 | General Electric | 250.7 |
| 46 | Hasbro | 245.3 |
| 47 | Dayton Hudson | 230.9 |
| 48 | Nike | 230.8 |
| 49 | Federated Department Stores | 225.9 |
| 50 | Wal-Mart Stores | 222.4 |

| Rank | Advertiser | Ad Spending ($ millions) |
|------|-----------|--------------------------|
| 51 | Mazda Motor | 215.4 |
| 52 | Schering-Plough | 214.0 |
| 53 | Levi Strauss & Co. | 211.9 |
| 54 | Campbell Soup | 209.7 |
| 55 | American Brands | 208.6 |
| 56 | S.C. Johnson & Son | 208.0 |
| 57 | Sprint | 207.6 |
| 58 | American Stores | 205.1 |
| 59 | ITT | 203.5 |
| 60 | Adolph Coors | 195.0 |
| 61 | U.S. dairy farmers | 189.6 |
| 62 | Helene Curtis Industries | 189.5 |
| 63 | Dow Chemical | 186.6 |
| 64 | ConAgra | 185.7 |
| 65 | IBM | 185.5 |
| 66 | Tandy | 185.1 |
| 67 | News Corp. | 181.3 |
| 68 | Goodyear Tire & Rubber | 178.1 |
| 69 | Ciba-Geigy | 177.6 |
| 70 | Joh. A. Benckiser | 172.0 |
| 71 | Montgomery Ward | 169.9 |
| 72 | Carter Hawley Hale Stores | 166.4 |
| 73 | Paramount | 166.3 |
| 74 | Gillette | 164.6 |
| 75 | Philips NV | 161.5 |
| 76 | Clorox | 161.4 |
| 77 | MCI | 156.2 |
| 78 | Marriott | 151.8 |
| 79 | Delta Air Lines | 147.1 |
| 80 | CPC International | 145.4 |
| 81 | Reebok International | 143.0 |
| 82 | Wendy's International | 142.6 |
| 83 | AMR | 139.4 |
| 84 | Upjohn | 138.0 |
| 85 | UAL | 136.9 |
| 86 | Wm. Wrigley Jr. | 134.0 |
| 87 | Dillard's Department Stores | 133.6 |
| 88 | Roll International | 133.1 |
| 89 | Revlon Group | 131.7 |
| 90 | Hewlett-Packard | 131.2 |
| 91 | Loews | 128.8 |
| 92 | Bayer AG | 127.4 |
| 93 | Mattel | 125.3 |
| 94 | Slim-Fast Foods | 122.0 |
| 95 | Bell Atlantic | 117.7 |
| 96 | U.S. Shoe | 117.3 |
| 97 | Dr Pepper/Seven-Up | 115.3 |
| 98 | Brown-Forman | 113.7 |
| 99 | Seagram | 113.1 |
| 100 | Nynex | 112.6 |

*Source: Ad Age, September 29, 1993*

# Music Permissions

A COMPANY SEEKING TO USE popular music or lyrics, either for commercial advertising or for an in-house corporate video, will have to get permission to do so.

Obtaining music permissions can be done simply and cheaply by purchasing music that comes with an automatic license for use, but the choice of music available will be significantly limited. On the other hand, obtaining permission to use protected music, which includes just about any song currently available in local music stores, can be costly and lead to extensive litigation since the copyright law protecting the use of current, popular music is very strict.

When choosing protected music, it is best to get a lawyer or an expert to help determine the appropriate legal procedures and to keep the following information in mind.

To use music that is protected by copyright in any way, it is necessary to obtain permission from the copyright owners in writing. These include the music publisher who represents the composer of the music and of the lyrics and the record company that owns the recording and represents the performer who made the recording.

A fee is generally charged by the copyright owners for permission, and the amount varies depending upon how it is used. Using a piece of protected music for a television or radio commercial is the most expensive. For a commercial in one state or city, the fees may be in the low thousands. For a national television commercial for one year, fees can range from $40,000 to $200,000 each to the music publisher and the record company.

Once a piece of music has been chosen, a company may either use an already recorded piece of music by a known artist or obtain the rights to use the music and rerecord it with other artists.

In the case of a performance by a known artist, for example, it may be necessary to pay various fees such as union new-use fees, which can enhance costs. On the other hand, hiring unknowns to perform a hit song will still require obtaining permission from the music publisher, who then pays the original talent. Union fees may be incurred, depending upon the arrangements made with the talent.

If using protected music seems too expensive or too complicated, the alternative may be to use a stock music library or similar music service. These services provide hundreds of CDs containing appropriate background music recorded by professional musicians.

The cost of purchasing these CDs is nominal, averaging $20 per CD. Additional licensing fees are also nominal, depending upon use. A company may pay a blanket fee of several hundred dollars to cover the music used throughout a video, or what's called a "needle drop" fee for each use of a piece of music within a video. These fees generally range from $15 to $75 per needle drop.

Listed below are the telephone numbers and addresses of key rights organizations and several stock music libraries.

## Contact Options

Barbara Zimmerman
B Z Rights and Permissions
125 W. 72nd St.
New York, NY 10023
(212) 580-0615
*Rights consultant*

BMI
320 W. 57th St.
New York, NY 10019
(212) 586-2000
*Trade association*

The American Society of Composers, Authors and Publishers (ASCAP)
1 Lincoln Plaza
New York, NY 10023
(212) 621-6000
*Trade association*

*Music Libraries:*

Associated Production Music
6255 Sunset Blvd., #820
Hollywood, CA 90026
(800) 543-4276

Firstcom
13747 Montfort Dr., Suite 220
Dallas, TX 75240
(800) 858-8880

De Wolfe Music Library
25 W. 45th St.
New York, NY 10036
(800) 221-6713

TRF Production Music Libraries
747 Chestnut Ridge Rd., Suite 301
Chestnut Ridge, NY 10977
(800) 899-6874

# Green Marketing

A STUDY PUBLISHED in the newsletter *Green Market-Alert* forecast that for four key consumer product markets (household products, health and beauty aids, food, and beverages), sales of "green" products would be more than 16 percent of total sales in those markets (almost $100 billion in green product sales).

Guidelines for the use of environmental marketing claims such as "recyclable," "biodegradable," "compostable," etc., have been established by the Federal Trade Commission, but the guides themselves are not enforceable regulations, nor do they have the force and effect of law. These guides specifically address the application of Section 5 of the Federal Trade Commission Act—which makes deceptive acts and practices in or affecting commerce unlawful—to environmental advertising and marketing practices. Guides for the Use of Environmental Marketing Claims provide the basis for voluntary compliance with such laws by members of industry, and are available from the EPA and the FTC.

## Contact Option

Carol C. Weisner
Environmental Protection Specialist
Municipal & Industrial Solid Waste Division
United States Environmental Protection Agency
401 M St., SW (OS-301)
Washington, DC 20460
(202) 260-4489

## Recommended Resource

*Green MarketAlert*
345 Wood Creek Rd.
Bethlehem, CT 06751
(203) 266-7209
Provides information about the impact of green consumerism on businesses.

## FTC Environmental Marketing Guidelines

In 1992, the Federal Trade Commission issued their Guides for the Use of Environmental Marketing Claims, which are based on data from FTC investigations, hearings, and public input. While these guides are not legally enforceable, they provide guidance to marketers in conforming with legal requirements. The guides apply to advertising, labeling, and other forms of marketing to consumers, and do not preempt state or local laws or regulations.

The FTC guides specify that any time marketers make objective environmental claims—whether explicit or implied—they must be substantiated by competent and reliable evidence. The guides outline four general concerns that apply to all environmental claims:

- Qualifications and disclosures should be clear and prominent to prevent deception.

- Environmental claims should make clear whether they apply to the product, the package, or a component of either. Claims need not be qualified with regard to minor, incidental components of the product or package.

- Environmental claims should not overstate the environmental attribute or benefit. Marketers should avoid implying a significant environmental benefit where the benefit is, in fact, negligible.

- A claim comparing the environmental attributes of one product with those of another product should make the basis for the comparison sufficiently clear and should be substantiated.

Certain environmental marketing claims are addressed specifically:

### General Environmental Benefit Claims

In general, unqualified general environmental claims are difficult to interpret, and may have a wide range of meanings to consumers. Every express and material implied claim conveyed to consumers about an objective quality should be substantiated. Unless they can be substantiated, broad environmental claims should be avoided or qualified.

### Degradable, Biodegradable, and Photodegradable

In general, unqualified degradability claims should be substantiated by evidence that the product will completely break down and return to nature, that is, decompose into elements found in nature within a reasonably short period of time after consumers dispose of it in the customary way. Such claims should be qualified to the extent necessary to avoid consumer deception about: (a) the product or package's ability to degrade in the environment where it is customarily disposed; and (b) the extent and rate of degradation.

### Compostable

In general, unqualified compostable claims should be substantiated by evidence that all the materials in the product or package will break down into, or otherwise become a part of, usable compost (e.g., soil-conditioning material, mulch) in a safe and timely manner in an appropriate composting program or facility, or in a home compost pile or device. Compostable claims should be qualified to the extent necessary to avoid consumer deception: (1) if municipal composting facilities are not available to a substantial majority of consumers or communities where the product is sold; (2) if the claim misleads consumers about the environmental benefit provided when the product is disposed of in a landfill; or (3) if consumers misunderstand the claim to mean that the package can be safely composted in their home compost pile or device, when in fact it cannot.

*Green Marketing (cont'd)*

### Recyclable

In general, a product or package should not be marketed as recyclable unless it can be collected, separated, or otherwise recovered from the solid waste stream for use in the form of raw materials in the manufacture or assembly of a new product or package. Unqualified recyclable claims may be made if the entire product or package, excluding incidental components, is recyclable.

Claims about products with both recyclable and non-recyclable components should be adequately qualified. If incidental components significantly limit the ability to recycle product, the claim would be deceptive. If, because of its size or shape, a product is not accepted in recycling programs, it should not be marketed as recyclable. Qualification may be necessary to avoid consumer deception about the limited availability of recycling programs and collection sites if recycling collection sites are not available to a substantial majority of consumers or communities.

### Recycled Content

In general, claims of recycled content should only be made for materials that have been recovered or diverted from the solid waste stream, either during the manufacturing process (pre-consumer) or after consumer waste (post-consumer). An advertiser should be able to substantiate that pre-consumer content would otherwise have entered the solid waste stream. Distinctions made between pre- and post-consumer content should be substantiated. Unqualified claims may be made if the entire product or package, excluding minor, incidental components, is made from recycled material. Products or packages only partially made of recycled material should be qualified to indicate the amount, by weight, in the finished product or package.

### Source Reduction

In general, an unqualified refillable claim should not be asserted unless a system is provided for: (1) the collection and return of the package for refill; or (2) the later refill of the package by consumers with product subsequently sold in another package. The claim should not be made if it is up to consumers to find ways to refill the package.

### Ozone Safe and Ozone Friendly

In general, a product should not be advertised as "ozone safe," "ozone friendly," or as not containing CFCs if the product contains any ozone-depleting chemical. Claims about the reduction of a product's ozone-depletion potential may be made if adequately substantiated.

*Source: FTC News, Summary of FTC Environmental Marketing Guidelines*

### Recommended Resource

For copies of the FTC Environmental Marketing Guidelines in their entirety, as well as the environmental assessment of these guidelines, and news releases on FTC cases in the green marketing area, contact:

FTC Public Reference Branch
Room 130
6th St. and Pennsylvania Ave., NW
Washington, DC 20580
(202) 326-2222

# Sources for Marketing Information

THE FOLLOWING ARE a few of the "Best 100 Sources for Marketing Information" as rated by *American Demographics' 1994 Directory:*

ACCRA (American Chamber of Commerce Research Association)
(703) 998-0072

American Business Information
(402) 593-4500

CACI Marketing Systems
(800) 292-2224

Donnelley Marketing Information Services
(203) 353-7223

Find/SVP
(212) 633-4510

Information Resources
(312) 726-1221

Mediamark Research (MRI)
(212) 599-0444

National Opinion Research Center
(312) 753-7500

The Roper Organization
(212) 599-0700

# Top Grossing Licenses

**Distribution of Licensed Product Sales by Property Type ($ billions), 1993**

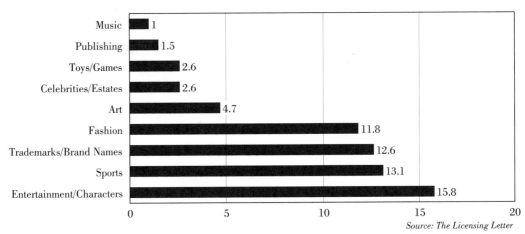

| Property Type | Value |
|---|---|
| Music | 1 |
| Publishing | 1.5 |
| Toys/Games | 2.6 |
| Celebrities/Estates | 2.6 |
| Art | 4.7 |
| Fashion | 11.8 |
| Trademarks/Brand Names | 12.6 |
| Sports | 13.1 |
| Entertainment/Characters | 15.8 |

*Source: The Licensing Letter*

## Recommended Resources

*The Licensing Letter*
EPM Communications, $275/12 issues

An indispensable source of data and information on the $91.1 billion licensing industry. Includes statistics, new property tips, and exclusive industry surveys and forecasts.

*EPM Licensing Business Sourcebook*
EPM Communications, $295

This annual directory is invaluable to anyone in –or wanting to get into–the licensing community. It's a comprehensive guide to more than 4,000 licensors, licensing agents, licensees, trade associations, consultants and other essential service providers. Also included are details on properties owned and agents used by licensors; properties represented by licensing agents; and licenses held and products manufactured by licensees.

## Contact Option

EPM Communications
488 E. 18th St.
Brooklyn, NY 11226
(718) 469-9330

---

 **Top Brands.** Request 852. See p. xi for instructions.

SuperBrands' 1994 list of top brands.

# Top Consumer Brands

*FINANCIAL WORLD* ANNUALLY EVALUATES major consumer brands, computing the value of the brand if it were to be sold.

## Cash Value of Major Consumer Brands

| Brand | Company | Value ($ millions) | 1992 Revenue ($ millions) | % Change (1991-92) |
|---|---|---|---|---|
| Marlboro cigarettes | Philip Morris | 39,469 | 10,688 | -6.3 |
| Coca-Cola soft drinks | Coca-Cola | 33,446 | 9,090 | 37.1 |
| Intel microchips | Intel | 17,810 | 3,969 | 106.7 |
| Kellogg's cereals | Kellogg | 9,678 | 5,391 | 8.4 |
| Nescafé coffee | Nestlé | 9,174 | 5,073 | 4.2 |
| Budweiser beer | Anheuser-Busch | 8,243 | 5,332 | -8.1 |
| Pepsi soft drinks | PepsiCo | 7,502 | 5,881 | -2.7 |
| Gillette razors and blades | Gillette | 7,147 | 1,978 | 14.1 |
| Pampers diapers | Procter & Gamble | 5,924 | 4,300 | -2.3 |
| Bacardi rum | Bacardi | 5,494 | 1,360 | - |
| Winston cigarettes | RJR Nabisco | 5,229 | 2,689 | -32.6 |
| Levi's clothing | Levi Strauss | 4,811 | 3,400 | - |
| Newport cigarettes | Loews | 4,590 | 1,288 | - |
| Motorola microchips | Motorola | 4,134 | 1,330 | 40.9 |
| Kodak films | Eastman Kodak | 4,122 | 2,660 | -3.8 |
| Camel cigarettes | RJR Nabisco | 3,647 | 1,813 | -24.1 |
| Nike shoes | Nike | 3,497 | 2,829 | 17.5 |
| Campbell's soups | Campbell Soup | 3,447 | 2,550 | -11.5 |
| L'Oréal cosmetics | L'Oréal | 3,403 | 2,933 | 39.8 |
| Hennessey cognac | LVMH | 3,398 | 882 | 8.4 |
| Avon cosmetics | Avon Products | 2,763 | 3,662 | 5.9 |
| Guinness beer | Guinness | 2,737 | 1,943 | 48 |
| Louis Vuitton Luggage | LVMH | 2,674 | 805 | 9.5 |
| Barbie toys | Mattel | 2,666 | 965 | 20.2 |
| Hershey chocolates | Hershey Foods | 2,530 | 2,560 | 9.6 |
| Nestlé chocolates | Nestlé | 2,378 | 4,575 | -13.9 |
| Michelin tires | Michelin | 2,363 | 7,087 | -24.7 |
| Kraft cheese and cheese products | Philip Morris | 2,273 | 2,905 | 3.8 |
| Heinz condiments | HJ Heinz | 2,266 | 1,279 | 17.6 |
| Reebok shoes | Reebok Int'l | 2,251 | 2,301 | 15 |
| Dannon yogurt | BSN | 2,229 | 3,544 | - |
| Tylenol pain reliever | Johnson & Johnson | 2,209 | 850 | - |
| Duracell batteries | Duracell | 2,135 | 1,617 | - |
| Nabisco cookies and crackers | RJR Nabisco | 2,117 | 3,450 | - |
| Goodyear tires | Goodyear Tire & Rubber | 2,002 | 5,240 | 20.8 |
| Smirnoff Vodka | Grand Metropolitan | 1,892 | 1,009 | -14.4 |
| Johnnie Walker Red Scotch whiskey | Guinness | 1,866 | 715 | 1.3 |
| Chivas Regal Scotch whiskey | Seagram | 1,769 | 540 | - |
| Tampax tampons | Tambrands | 1,725 | 663 | 27.5 |
| Wrigley's chewing gum | Wm. Wrigley Jr. | 1,660 | 1,132 | 14.2 |
| General Mills cereals | General Mills | 1,629 | 2,010 | - |
| Heineken beer | Heineken | 1,625 | 2,284 | -14.7 |
| Estée Lauder cosmetics | Estée Lauder | 1,619 | 1,100 | 10 |
| Cadbury's chocolates | Cadbury-Schweppes | 1,494 | 1,447 | - |
| Gerber baby foods | Gerber Products | 1,440 | 8,030 | - |

*Top Consumer Brands (cont'd)*

| Brand | Company | Value ($ millions) | 1992 Revenue ($ millions) | % Change (1991-92) |
|-------|---------|-------------------|--------------------------|---------------------|
| Huggies diapers | Kimberly Clark | 1,436 | 2,200 | - |
| Channel fashion | Channel | 1,418 | 890 | 2 |
| Colgate toothpaste | Colgate-Palmolive | 1,398 | 1,200 | 15.9 |
| Eveready batteries | Ralston-Purina | 1,382 | 1,798 | - |
| Purina pet food | Ralston-Purina | 1,333 | 1,734 | - |
| Knorr soups and sauces | CPC International | 1,313 | 2,036 | - |
| Bic razors, pens, lighters | Bic | 1,301 | 905 | - |
| Polaroid film | Polaroid | 1,236 | 1,590 | -10.2 |
| Dole produce and juices | Dole Food | 1,219 | 3,375 | - |
| Schweppes soft drinks | Cadbury-Schweppes | 1,107 | 1,031 | -1.2 |
| Playtex tampons | Playtex Family Products | 1,058 | 210 | - |
| Miller beer | Philip Morris | 1,018 | 2,174 | - |
| Tropicana juices | Seagrams | 1,016 | 1,203 | - |

*Source: Financial World, September 1, 1993*

## The Top Reference Sources

*News Media Yellow Book*
Monitor Publishing, $160/2 editions per year
104 Fifth Ave.
New York, NY 10011
(212) 627-4140

One of the best of Monitor's Yellow Book Refer-

ence series, the *News Media Yellow Book* is an invaluable resource for anyone looking to establish solid media contacts and make informed public relation maneuvers.

# Network and Cable TV Data

## Advertising Volume in the United States ($ millions)

| Year | Total Ad Volume | TV Ad Volume | % in TV |
|------|------|------|------|
| 1982 | 66,580 | 14,636 | 22.0 |
| 1983 | 75,850 | 16,759 | 22.1 |
| 1984 | 87,820 | 19,848 | 22.6 |
| 1985 | 94,750 | 21,022 | 22.2 |
| 1986 | 102,140 | 22,881 | 22.4 |
| 1987 | 109,650 | 23,904 | 21.8 |
| 1988 | 118,050 | 26,686 | 21.8 |
| 1989 | 123,930 | 26,891 | 21.7 |
| 1990 | 128,640 | 28,405 | 22.1 |
| 1991 | 126,400 | 27,402 | 21.7 |
| 1992 | 131,290 | 29,409 | 22.4 |

## Television Advertising Volume ($ millions)

| Year | Network | Spot | Local | Total |
|------|------|------|------|------|
| 1982 | 6,144 | 4,364 | 3,765 | 14,636 |
| 1983 | 6,955 | 4,827 | 4,345 | 16,759 |
| 1984 | 8,318 | 5,488 | 5,084 | 19,848 |
| 1985 | 8,060 | 6,004 | 5,714 | 21,022 |
| 1986 | 8,342 | 6,570 | 6,514 | 22,881 |
| 1987 | 8,500 | 6,846 | 6,833 | 23,904 |
| 1988 | 9,172 | 7,147 | 7,270 | 25,686 |
| 1989 | 9,110 | 7,354 | 7,612 | 26,891 |
| 1990 | 9,383 | 7,788 | 7,856 | 28,405 |
| 1991 | 8,933 | 7,110 | 7,565 | 27,402 |
| 1992 | 9,549 | 7,551 | 8,079 | 29,409 |

*Sources: TVB 1992-93 & McCann-Erickson*

## Avg. cost per :30 Commercial 1993 ($ thous.)

| | |
|------|------|
| Daytime (M-F 10 A.M.-4:30 P.M.) | 20.2 |
| Early News (M-F 6:30-7:30 P.M.) | 64.6 |
| Prime Time (M-S 8-11 P.M.) | 133.8 |
| Late Eve. (M-F 11:30 PM-1 A.M.) | 36.5 |

## Cost per TV Home Rating Point ($) 1993

| | |
|------|------|
| Daytime (M-F 10 A.M.-4:30 P.M.) | 4,073 |
| Early News (M-F 6:30-7:30 P.M.) | 6,019 |
| Prime Time (M-S 8-11 P.M.) | 11,192 |
| Late Eve. (M-F 11:30 P.M.-1 A.M.) | 8,792 |

*Source: Marketer's Guide to Media*

## Time Spent Viewing per TV Home per Day

| Year | Average Viewing Time |
|------|------|
| 1980 | 6 hours, 36 minutes |
| 1981 | 6 hours, 45 minutes |
| 1983 | 7 hours, 2 minutes |
| 1985 | 7 hours, 10 minutes |
| 1989 | 7 hours, 1 minutes |
| 1990 | 6 hours, 53 minutes |
| 1991 | 6 hours, 56 minutes |
| 1992 | 7 hours, 4 minutes |
| 1993 | 7 hours, 12 minutes |

*Sources: TVB & Nielsen Media Research*

*Network and Cable TV Data (cont'd)*

## Network Commercial Activity by Commercial Length (% of total)

| Year | :10 | :15 | :20 | :30 | :45 | :60 | :90+ | Total |
|------|-----|-----|-----|-----|-----|-----|------|-------|
| 1980 | 0.7 | - | - | 94.6 | 2.7 | 1.9 | 0.1 | 100 |
| 1981 | 0.9 | 0.1 | - | 94.2 | 3.2 | 1.5 | 0.1 | 100 |
| 1982 | 0.9 | 0.1 | - | 93.7 | 3.7 | 1.5 | 0.1 | 100 |
| 1983 | 0.9 | 0.2 | - | 93.8 | 2.9 | 1.8 | 0.4 | 100 |
| 1984 | 1.0 | 5.2 | - | 89.2 | 2.0 | 2.1 | 0.5 | 100 |
| 1985 | 1.3 | 10.1 | 0.8 | 83.5 | 1.7 | 2.2 | 0.4 | 100 |
| 1986 | 0.5 | 20.9 | 1.2 | 73.6 | 1.4 | 1.8 | 0.6 | 100 |
| 1987 | 0.2 | 30.9 | 1.0 | 65.1 | 0.9 | 1.5 | 0.4 | 100 |
| 1989 | 0.3 | 37.9 | 1.2 | 57.4 | 1.0 | 1.8 | 0.4 | 100 |
| 1990 | 0.1 | 35.4 | 1.4 | 60.1 | 1.0 | 1.7 | 0.3 | 100 |
| 1991 | 0.1 | 33.6 | 0.8 | 62.5 | 0.9 | 1.7 | 0.4 | 100 |
| 1992 | 0.1 | 31.9 | 0.9 | 63.1 | 1.0 | 1.7 | 1.3 | 100 |

*Sources: TVB & Arbitron, annual average*

## Commercial Television Stations

| Year | Total | VHF | UHF |
|------|-------|-----|-----|
| 1980 | 734 | 516 | 218 |
| 1981 | 756 | 519 | 237 |
| 1982 | 777 | 517 | 260 |
| 1983 | 813 | 519 | 294 |
| 1984 | 841 | 523 | 318 |
| 1985 | 883 | 520 | 363 |
| 1986 | 919 | 522 | 397 |
| 1987 | 968 | 524 | 444 |
| 1988 | 1,028 | 539 | 489 |
| 1989 | 1,061 | 545 | 516 |
| 1990 | 1,092 | 547 | 545 |
| 1991 | 1,099 | 547 | 552 |
| 1992 | 1,118 | 551 | 567 |
| 1993 | 1,137 | 552 | 585 |

*Sources: TVB & Television Digest*

## Top 10 ADI's for Television by Market: 4th Quarter, 1993

| Markets | TV Households (thousands) | % U.S. |
|---------|---------------------------|--------|
| New York | 6,760 | 7.3 |
| Los Angeles | 4,962 | 5.3 |
| Chicago | 3,024 | 3.3 |
| Philadelphia | 2,660 | 2.9 |
| San Francisco–Oakland–San Jose | 2,237 | 2.4 |
| Boston | 2,121 | 2.3 |
| Washington, DC | 1,813 | 2.0 |
| Dallas–Ft. Worth | 1,803 | 1.9 |
| Detroit | 1,728 | 1.9 |
| Atlanta | 1,483 | 1.6 |

*Source: SQAD Report Projections as of September, 1993*

*Network and Cable TV Data (cont'd)*

## Growth of Cable TV Penetration by County Size (%)

| Year | % of TV Homes with Cable | County Size "A" | County Size "B" | County Size "C" | County Size "D" |
|------|--------------------------|-----------------|-----------------|-----------------|-----------------|
| 1969 | 5 | 1 | 3 | 14 | 9 |
| 1974 | 14 | 4 | 10 | 26 | 15 |
| 1979 | 23 | 8 | 19 | 35 | 22 |
| 1981 | 34 | 24 | 40 | 49 | 36 |
| 1983 | 42 | 31 | 50 | 58 | 43 |
| 1985 | 49 | 39 | 57 | 60 | 46 |
| 1986 | 48 | 41 | 55 | 57 | 43 |
| 1987 | 51 | 45 | 59 | 58 | 48 |
| 1988 | 56 | 48 | 61 | 61 | 48 |
| 1989 | 59 | 52 | 64 | 63 | 48 |
| 1990 | 61 | 58 | 67 | 66 | 51 |
| 1991 | 64 | 62 | 67 | 70 | 56 |
| 1992 | 65 | 64 | 69 | 72 | 58 |

*Source: Nielsen*

## TV Network Telephone Directory

| Network | Telephone Number |
|---------|------------------|
| A.C. Nielsen | (212) 708-7500 |
| Arbitron | (212) 887-1300 |
| Arts & Entertainment (A&E) | (212) 661-4500 |
| Black Entertainment TV (BET) | (212) 697-5500 |
| Cable News Network (CNN) | (212) 852-6900 |
| Capital Cities/ABC | (212) 456-7777 |
| CBS Network | (212) 975-4146 |
| CNBC | (212) 664-7920 |
| Comedy Central | (212) 767-8647 |
| Country Music Television (CMT) | (212) 916-1000 |
| Court TV | (212) 973-2800 |
| The Discovery Channel (DSC) | (212) 751-2120 |
| Entertainment Television (E!) | (212) 852-5100 |
| ESPN Sales | (212) 916-9200 |
| The Family Channel (FAM) | (212) 997-1710 |
| Fox TV | (212) 452-5555 |
| Group W Broadcasting | (212) 307-3000 |
| Headline News | (212) 852-6600 |
| The Learning Channel (TLC) | (212) 751-2120 |
| LIFETIME | (718) 482-4000 |
| MTV/ VH-1/ NICKELODEON/ NICK AT NIGHT | (212) 258-8000 |
| The Nashville Network (TNN) | (212) 916-1000 |
| NBC Network | (212) 664-4444 |
| Prevue | (800) 447-7388 |
| Prime Network | (212) 935-5931 |
| SportsChannel America (SCA) | (212) 664-7920 |
| TBS | (212) 692-6900 |
| Telemundo | (212) 492-5500 |
| The Travel Channel | (212) 308-3055 |
| Turner Broadcasting | (212) 852-6600 |
| Turner Network Television (TNT) | (212) 692-6900 |
| USA | (212) 408-9100 |
| The Weather Channel (TWC) | (212) 308-3055 |

*Network and Cable TV Data (cont'd)*

## Advertising Expenditures by Media, 1992

| Category | Expenditures ($ millions) | % Change (1991-92) | Media as % of Total |
|---|---|---|---|
| Network TV | 10,732.8 | 6.2 | 8.2 |
| Local newspapers | 9,920.1 | 0.7 | 7.6 |
| Spot TV | 9,399.6 | 7.4 | 7.2 |
| Consumer magazines | 7,104.8 | 9.0 | 5.4 |
| Cable TV networks | 1,590.5 | 12.6 | 1.2 |
| Syndicated TV | 1,306.4 | 8.4 | 1.0 |
| Spot radio | 1,092.4 | -4.3 | 0.8 |
| Sunday magazines | 941.9 | 18.6 | 0.7 |
| Outdoor | 655.0 | -4.2 | 0.5 |
| Network radio | 549.1 | -5.1 | 0.4 |
| Measured media | 43,292.4 | 5.5 | 33.0 |
| Estimated unmeasured | 87,997.6 | 3.1 | 67.0 |

*Note: Measured media include above listed. Unmeasured include direct mail, promotion, co-op, couponing, catalogues, business and farm publications, and special events, to name a few.*

*Source: AdAge/CMR, Robert J. Coen, McCann-Erickson*

# Radio Data

## Radio's Top National Advertisers, 1992

| Rank | Company | Network | Spot | Total |
|---|---|---|---|---|
| 1 | Sears, Roebuck & Co. | 59,221 | 8,361 | 67,582 |
| 2 | AT&T | 26,649 | 9,252 | 35,901 |
| 3 | General Motors | 10,929 | 18,958 | 29,887 |
| 4 | American Home Products | 28,154 | 295 | 28,449 |
| 5 | Chrysler | 7,951 | 20,332 | 28,852 |
| 6 | Philip Morris (KGF, Miller) | 4,043 | 21,655 | 25,609 |
| 7 | Anheuser-Busch | 6,197 | 18,655 | 24,852 |
| 8 | Kmart | 7,791 | 14,885 | 22,676 |
| 9 | News Corp. (Fox TV) | 2,515 | 15,844 | 18,359 |
| 10 | Himmel Group | 17,895 | 28 | 17,924 |

*Source: Radio Fact Book/LNA/Arbitron/RER 1992 Report*

## Radio Audience by Location of Listening (% all radio reach)

| | Men 18+ | Women 18+ | Teens 12-17 |
|---|---|---|---|
| At home | 74.3 | 80.1 | 93.0 |
| In car | 84.3 | 77.2 | 78.2 |
| Other | 46.7 | 39.8 | 48.5 |

*Source: RADAR®, copyrighted© by Statistical Research, Inc., Spring, 1993*

## Radio Usage (average daily time spent listening)

| By Age | Men (hr:min) | Women (hr:min) |
|---|---|---|
| 18+ | 3:05 | 2:53 |
| 18-24 | 3:03 | 2:45 |
| 25-34 | 3:26 | 2:57 |
| 35-49 | 3:19 | 2:54 |
| 50+ | 2:35 | 2:52 |

*Source: Calculated from RADAR®, copyrighted© by Statistical Research, Inc., Spring, 1993*

*Radio Data (cont'd)*

## Profile of Daily Listeners of Radio Stations by Format

| Format | % Male | % Female | Median Age | Median Income ($ thousands) | % 1+Yrs. of College |
|---|---|---|---|---|---|
| Adult Contemporary | 41 | 59 | 37.3 | 39,100 | 29 |
| All News | 62 | 38 | 49.0 | 45,100 | 24 |
| Album-Oriented Rock | 63 | 37 | 30.4 | 40,500 | 32 |
| Black/R&B | 50 | 50 | 39.4 | 26,400 | 33 |
| Classic Rock | 64 | 36 | 30.9 | 41,800 | 32 |
| CHR/Rock | 44 | 56 | 30.6 | 36,600 | 27 |
| Classical | 56 | 44 | 46.4 | 44,400 | 22 |
| Country | 48 | 52 | 40.0 | 33,500 | 26 |
| Beautiful | 55 | 45 | 50.3 | 43,500 | 30 |
| Golden Oldies | 49 | 51 | 40.3 | 42,200 | 27 |
| MOR/Nostalgia | 49 | 51 | 59.8 | 37,500 | 23 |
| News/Talk | 60 | 40 | 49.2 | 40,300 | 23 |
| Religious | 41 | 59 | 41.5 | 31,200 | 22 |
| Urban Contemporary | 43 | 57 | 33.8 | 25,500 | 26 |

*Source: Simmons, Study of Media Markets, 1993*

## Radio Network Telephone Directory

| Station | Telephone Number |
|---|---|
| ABC Radio Network | (212) 456-5200 |
| AFN/ASRN/BRN | (719) 528-7040 |
| American Urban Radio | (212) 714-1000 |
| Arbitron | (212) 887-1300 |
| Banner Radio | (212) 424-6160 |
| CBS Radio Network | (212) 975-5354 |
| CBS Spot Sales | (212) 975-1877 |
| CMN Radio Network | (212) 532-1900 |
| Christal | (212) 424-6500 |
| DNR | (212) 309-9000 |
| Eastman | (212) 424-6000 |
| Katz | (212) 424-6000 |
| Katz & Powell | (212) 545-0600 |
| Keystone Broadcasting System | (518) 789-9000 |
| MBC Mutual | (212) 237-2500 |
| McGavern Guild | (212) 916-0500 |
| NBC Radio Networks | (212) 237-2500 |
| Radio Advertising Bureau | (212) 254-4800 |
| Radio Network Association | (212) 777-0045 |
| Roslin | (212) 486-0720 |
| Savalli Broadcast | (212) 239-3288 |
| StandardNews/Standard Broadcasting Network | (804) 523-7269 |
| Torbet | (212) 355-7705 |
| Unistar Network | (212) 247-1600 |
| USA Radio Network | (214) 484-3900 |
| Wall St./Dow Jones | (212) 416-2380 |
| Westwood One | (212) 237-2500 |

*Source: Marketer's Guide to Media*

# Magazine Data

## Adweek's 10 Hottest Small Magazines

| Rank | Magazine | Revenue Up ($ millions) | Ad Pages Up (%) | Circulation Up (%) |
|---|---|---|---|---|
| 1 | Martha Stewart Living | 3.8 | 34 | 24 |
| 2 | Worth | 3.0 | 24 | 18 |
| 3 | Discover | 3.8 | 37 | 2 |
| 4 | Snow Country | 4.8 | 24 | 23 |
| 5 | Backpacker | 2.2 | 31 | 1 |
| 6 | The Walking Magazine | 1.2 | 20 | 3 |
| 7 | Traditional Home | 2.7 | 26 | 8 |
| 8 | Golf for Women | 1.2 | 10 | 1 |
| 9 | Natural History | 1.8 | 33 | -1 |
| 10 | Audubon | 0.9 | 16 | -1 |

*Source: Adweek, February 28, 1994*

## Top Magazine Spending by Company

| Rank | Company | Magazines | Media Total | % in Magazines |
|---|---|---|---|---|
| 1 | General Motors | 313.2 | 1,111.2 | 28 |
| 2 | Ford | 222.2 | 728.3 | 31 |
| 3 | Philip Morris | 212.0 | 999.3 | 21 |
| 4 | Procter & Gamble | 201.8 | 1,299.9 | 16 |
| 5 | Chrysler | 148.1 | 611.3 | 24 |
| 6 | Nestlé | 126.0 | 408.2 | 31 |
| 7 | Roll International | 125.0 | 129.7 | 96 |
| 8 | Sony | 123.8 | 372.6 | 33 |
| 9 | Toyota Motor | 111.1 | 484.0 | 23 |
| 10 | Unilever | 109.0 | 462.2 | 24 |
| 11 | Bradford Exchange | 86.9 | 89.3 | 97 |
| 12 | Grand Metropolitan | 71.6 | 301.5 | 24 |
| 13 | National Syndications | 67.2 | 67.3 | 100 |
| 14 | Time Warner | 65.7 | 353.8 | 19 |
| 15 | RJR Nabisco | 64.3 | 294.1 | 22 |
| 16 | Nissan | 62.9 | 327.2 | 19 |
| 17 | American Express | 59.5 | 228.7 | 26 |
| 18 | Bertelsmann | 58.7 | 64.0 | 92 |
| 19 | Johnson & Johnson | 57.3 | 381.0 | 15 |
| 20 | Benckiser | 55.9 | 98.9 | 57 |
| 21 | Brown-Forman | 51.7 | 63.0 | 82 |
| 22 | MBI | 51.1 | 53.5 | 96 |
| 23 | Honda | 49.9 | 252.8 | 20 |
| 24 | Esteé Lauder | 49.6 | 75.2 | 66 |
| 25 | IBM | 47.8 | 97.3 | 49 |

*Source: Adweek, February 28, 1994*

*Magazine Data (cont'd)*

## Top 50 Magazines in Paid Circulation

| Rank | Magazine | Average Paid Circulation, 1993 | % Change vs. 1992 |
|---|---|---|---|
| 1 | Modern Maturity | 22,398,630 | -0.7 |
| 2 | Reader's Digest | 16,261,968 | 0.0 |
| 3 | TV Guide | 14,122,915 | -2.6 |
| 4 | National Geographic | 9,390,787 | -3.3 |
| 5 | Better Homes | 7,600,960 | -5.0 |
| 6 | Good Housekeeping | 5,162,597 | 0.5 |
| 7 | Ladies' Home Journal | 5,153,565 | 2.2 |
| 8 | Family Circle | 5,114,030 | -3.2 |
| 9 | Woman's Day | 4,858,625 | 1.0 |
| 10 | McCall's | 4,605,441 | -2.1 |
| 11 | Time | 4,103,772 | -2.4 |
| 12 | People Weekly | 3,446,569 | -1.7 |
| 13 | Playboy | 3,402,617 | 0.0 |
| 14 | Sports Illustrated | 3,356,729 | -2.2 |
| 15 | Redbook | 3,345,451 | -1.5 |
| 16 | Prevention | 3,220,763 | -0.4 |
| 17 | Newsweek | 3,156,192 | -2.6 |
| 18 | Cosmopolitan | 2,627,491 | -2.9 |
| 19 | Southern Living | 2,368,678 | -0.2 |
| 20 | Glamour | 2,304,769 | 10.6 |
| 21 | U.S. News | 2,281,369 | -1.1 |
| 22 | Smithsonian | 2,212,418 | 0.0 |
| 23 | Money | 2,100,039 | -2.2 |
| 24 | Field & Stream | 2,007,901 | 0.0 |
| 25 | Ebony | 1,994,570 | 5.6 |
| 26 | Country Living | 1,977,214 | 7.5 |
| 27 | Seventeen | 1,940,601 | 1.3 |
| 28 | Popular Science | 1,815,819 | 0.2 |
| 29 | Parents | 1,776,470 | 1.6 |
| 30 | YM | 1,701,615 | 26.9 |
| 31 | Popular Mechanics | 1,656,951 | 0.9 |
| 32 | Life | 1,625,096 | -8.6 |
| 33 | Outdoor Life | 1,502,676 | 0.0 |
| 34 | Golf Digest | 1,461,566 | 2.8 |
| 35 | Sunset | 1,441,506 | -0.7 |
| 36 | Soap Opera Digest | 1,437,758 | 3.0 |
| 37 | Self | 1,314,315 | -6.7 |
| 38 | New Woman | 1,314,294 | 0.1 |
| 39 | Bon Appetit | 1,294,945 | 5.2 |
| 40 | Boys' Life | 1,265,024 | -1.8 |
| 41 | Consumers Digest | 1,254,468 | 25.0 |
| 42 | Vogue | 1,250,008 | -2.7 |
| 43 | Rolling Stone | 1,236,525 | 2.1 |
| 44 | Golf | 1,221,554 | 3.2 |
| 45 | Mademoiselle | 1,218,985 | 0.0 |
| 46 | Penthouse | 1,201,692 | -4.2 |
| 47 | Sesame Street | 1,187,862 | -2.5 |
| 48 | Teen | 1,170,842 | -1.5 |
| 49 | Vanity Fair | 1,157,725 | 0.5 |
| 50 | Cooking Light | 1,119,811 | 9.2 |

## Top 50 Magazines in Ad Revenues

| Rank | Magazine | 1993 Revenues ($ millions) | % Change vs. 1992 |
|---|---|---|---|
| 1 | Parade | 410.7 | -8.6 |
| 2 | People Weekly | 367.4 | -0.2 |
| 3 | Time | 344.2 | 0.4 |
| 4 | TV Guide | 322.2 | 16.6 |
| 5 | Sports Illustrated | 302.0 | -3.9 |
| 6 | Newsweek | 260.7 | 0.9 |
| 7 | Business Week | 217.5 | 2.2 |
| 8 | Good Housekeeping | 206.9 | 6.8 |
| 9 | U.S. News | 202.1 | 2.7 |
| 10 | Better Homes | 188.7 | 0.1 |
| 11 | USA Weekend | 182.7 | 6.7 |
| 12 | Forbes | 173.8 | 0.1 |
| 13 | Family Circle | 163.2 | 3.0 |
| 14 | Fortune | 149.2 | 11.6 |
| 15 | Woman's Day | 146.3 | 11.8 |
| 16 | Cosmopolitan | 140.8 | 3.8 |
| 17 | Reader's Digest | 131.3 | 9.1 |
| 18 | Ladies' Home Journal | 127.8 | 9.0 |
| 19 | Vogue | 112.1 | 5.1 |
| 20 | NY Times Magazine | 110.7 | 8.9 |
| 21 | McCall's | 102.5 | 9.5 |
| 22 | Glamour | 102.0 | 0.9 |
| 23 | Redbook | 94.5 | 21.7 |
| 24 | Money | 94.3 | -0.6 |
| 25 | Southern Living | 87.7 | 11.4 |
| 26 | Golf Digest | 84.4 | 5.8 |
| 27 | Rolling Stone | 71.5 | -3.6 |
| 28 | The New Yorker | 70.6 | 26.4 |
| 29 | Parents | 68.1 | -4.7 |
| 30 | Country Living | 64.9 | 26.1 |
| 31 | Car and Driver | 60.2 | 5.5 |
| 32 | Bride's | 59.7 | 1.5 |
| 33 | Vanity Fair | 57.3 | -9.3 |
| 34 | Harper's Bazaar | 57.3 | 94.3 |
| 35 | Inc. | 54.5 | 0.0 |
| 36 | Elle | 54.0 | -2.3 |
| 37 | Modern Maturity | 52.2 | 13.1 |
| 38 | Sunset | 52.0 | 4.9 |
| 39 | Travel & Leisure | 51.2 | -4.8 |
| 40 | Modern Bride | 50.5 | 7.9 |
| 41 | Entertainment Weekly | 48.8 | 38.4 |
| 42 | Mademoiselle | 48.7 | -1.0 |
| 43 | Golf | 48.3 | 6.4 |
| 44 | GQ | 47.2 | -1.9 |
| 45 | National Geographic | 46.8 | 8.6 |
| 46 | Playboy | 46.0 | 6.1 |
| 47 | Self | 45.0 | 8.3 |
| 48 | New York Magazine | 43.4 | 9.8 |
| 49 | House Beautiful | 42.8 | 26.5 |
| 50 | Seventeen | 40.1 | 14.3 |

*Source: Adweek, February 28, 1994*

*Magazine Data (cont'd)*

## Magazine Ad Department Telephone Directory

| Magazine Ad Departments | NY Telephone | Magazine Ad Departments | NY Telephone |
|---|---|---|---|
| American Health | (212) 366-8900 | Motor Trend | (212) 935-9150 |
| American Way | (212) 455-6200 | National Enquirer | (212) 979-4810 |
| Architectural Digest | (212) 880-8194 | National Geographic | (212) 974-1700 |
| Automobile | (212) 332-0200 | National Geographic Traveler | (212) 974-8172 |
| Barron's | (212) 808-7200 | Nation's Business | (212) 370-1440 |
| Better Homes & Gardens | (212) 557-6600 | Natural History | (212) 599-5555 |
| Black Enterprise | (212) 242-8000 | New Choices | (212) 366-8800 |
| Bon Appetit | (212) 880-8800 | New York Magazine | (212) 880-0700 |
| Boys' Life | (212) 532-0985 | New York Times Magazine | (212) 556-5854 |
| Business Week | (212) 512-2700 | The New Yorker | (212) 840-3800 |
| Cable Guide | (212) 683-6116 | Newsweek | (212) 350-4000 |
| Chicago Tribune | (212) 682-3033 | Omni | (212) 496-6100 |
| Colonial Homes | (212) 830-2900 | Outdoor Life | (212) 779-5000 |
| Condé Nast Publications | (212) 880-8800 | Parade | (212) 573-7000 |
| Cosmopolitan | (212) 649-3570 | Parenting | (212) 840-4200 |
| Country America | (212) 551-7128 | Parents | (212) 878-8700 |
| Country Home | (212) 551-7117 | Penthouse | (212) 496-6100 |
| Country Living | (212) 649-3192 | People | (212) 522-2028 |
| Ebony | (212) 397-4500 | Playboy | (212) 261-5000 |
| Elle | (212) 767-6044 | Popular Mechanics | (212) 649-3133 |
| Endless Vacation | (212) 362-7654 | Popular Photography | (212) 767-6086 |
| Entertainment Weekly | (212) 522-5206 | Popular Science | (212) 779-5000 |
| Esquire | (212) 649-2000 | Prevention | (212) 697-2040 |
| Family Circle | (212) 463-1000 | Reader's Digest | (212) 953-0030 |
| Field & Stream | (212) 779-5450 | Redbook | (212) 649-3357 |
| Financial World | (212) 594-5030 | Rolling Stone | (212) 484-1616 |
| Food & Wine | (212) 382-5618 | Sassy | (212) 551-9363 |
| Forbes | (212) 620-2200 | Scientific American | (212) 754-0550 |
| Fortune | (212) 522-5203 | Scouting | (212) 532-0985 |
| GQ | (212) 880-8085 | Self | (212) 880-8814 |
| Glamour | (212) 880-7999 | Seventeen | (212) 407-9700 |
| Golf Digest | (212) 789-3000 | Smithsonian | (212) 490-2510 |
| Golf Magazine | (212) 779-5000 | Soap Opera Digest | (212) 332-0250 |
| Good Housekeeping | (212) 649-2556 | Southern Living | (212) 986-9010 |
| Gourmet | (212) 880-2769 | Spin | (212) 633-8200 |
| Harper's Bazaar | (212) 903-5370 | Sporting News | (212) 779-5600 |
| Home | (212) 767-5519 | Sports Afield | (212) 649-4302 |
| Home Mechanix | (212) 779-5250 | Sports Illustrated | (212) 522-1212 |
| House Beautiful | (212) 903-5100 | Sunset | (212) 986-3810 |
| Inc. | (212) 326-2600 | Tennis | (212) 789-3000 |
| Inside Sports | (212) 687-1130 | Time | (212) 522-1212 |
| Insight | (212) 599-1730 | Town & Country | (212) 903-5000 |
| Jet | (212) 397-4500 | Travel & Leisure | (212) 382-5600 |
| Kiplinger's Personal Finance | (212) 398-6320 | Travel Holiday | (212) 366-8700 |
| Ladies' Home Journal | (212) 351-3500 | TV Guide | (212) 852-7500 |
| Life Magazine | (212) 522-1212 | US | (212) 484-1616 |
| Los Angeles Times Magazine | (212) 692-7170 | U.S. News & World Report | (212) 830-1500 |
| Mademoiselle | (212) 880-7971 | Vanity Fair | (212) 880-8194 |
| McCall's | (212) 463-1000 | Victoria | (212)649-3700 |
| Metropolitan Home | (212) 767-6000 | Vogue | (212) 880-8405 |
| Modern Maturity | (212) 599-1880 | Woman's Day | (212) 767-6000 |
| Money | (212) 522-4829 | Working Mother | (212) 551-9500 |

*Source: Marketer's Guide to Media*

# Newspaper Data

## Top 25 National Newspaper Advertisers

| Rank | Advertiser | 1992 Spending ($) | % Change from 1991 |
|------|------------|-------------------|--------------------|
| 1 | Fidelity Investments | 29,700,000 | 35.0 |
| 2 | General Motors | 28,700,000 | 12.2 |
| 3 | Dreyfus | 18,100,000 | 37.2 |
| 4 | IBM | 17,600,000 | 71.0 |
| 5 | AT&T | 16,900,000 | -16.9 |
| 6 | American Express | 15,000,000 | 5.9 |
| 7 | Ford | 14,700,000 | 46.7 |
| 8 | Dow Jones | 14,600,000 | 12.1 |
| 9 | Toyota | 14,500,000 | 23.1 |
| 10 | Hewlett-Packard | 13,200,000 | 3.0 |
| 11 | Compaq Computer | 11,900,000 | 37.3 |
| 12 | Merrill Lynch | 11,700,000 | 27.5 |
| 13 | Damark International | 10,600,000 | 21.1 |
| 14 | Marriott | 10,300,000 | 10.6 |
| 15 | Chrysler | 9,800,000 | 11.0 |
| 16 | Apple Computer | 8,900,000 | 59.2 |
| 17 | Daimler-Benz AG | 8,100,000 | 80.3 |
| 18 | Franklin Distributors | 8,000,000 | -1.4 |
| 19 | Chemical Banking | 7,700,000 | 139.5 |
| 20 | BMW AG | 7,300,000 | -48.9 |
| 21 | AMR | 6,700,000 | 0.8 |
| 22 | ITT | 6,600,000 | 50.6 |
| 23 | U.S. Government | 6,500,000 | 28.4 |
| 24 | Delta Air Lines | 6,200,000 | 16.8 |
| 25 | Sprint | 6,000,000 | 136.9 |

*Source: Ad Age, September 29, 1993*

## The Top Reference Sources

*Marketer's Guide to Media*
Adweek, $60/$100
(800) 468-2395

This semiannual publication from the folks at *Adweek* gives a terrific overview of the current effectiveness of advertising. The statistics, facts, and trends presented here are illuminating, and the book is a useful telephone, address, and contact directory for the major media.

*Newspaper Data (cont'd)*

## Newspaper Advertising Departments

| Newspaper | Telephone |
|---|---|
| Albuquerque Journal/Tribune | (505) 823-3311 |
| Arizona Republic/Phoenix Gazette | (602) 271-8498 |
| Atlanta Journal-Constitution | (404) 577-5772 |
| Baltimore Sun | (410) 783-1800 |
| Boston Globe | (617) 929-2100 |
| Boston Herald | (617) 426-3000 |
| Buffalo News | (716) 849-3411 |
| Charlotte Observer | (704) 358-5420 |
| Chicago Sun Times | (312) 321-2350 |
| Chicago Tribune | (312) 222-4150 |
| Christian Science Monitor | (617) 450-2652 |
| Cincinnati Enquirer/Post | (513) 768-8220 |
| Cleveland Plain Dealer | (216) 999-4360 |
| Columbus Dispatch | (614) 461-5500 |
| Dallas Morning News | (214) 977-8511 |
| Denver Post | (303) 820-1434 |
| (Denver) Rocky Mountain News | (303) 892-5411 |
| Detroit Free Press/News | (313) 222-2700 |
| Grand Rapids Press | (616) 459-1552 |
| Greensboro News & Record | (910) 373-7150 |
| Greenville News/Piedmont | (803) 298-4216 |
| Hartford Courant | (203) 241-6221 |
| Houston Chronicle | (713) 220-2680 |
| Houston Post | (713) 840-5134 |
| Indianapolis Star/News | (317) 633-1143 |
| Kansas City Star | (816) 234-4150 |
| Los Angeles Times | (213) 237-7291 |
| Louisville Courier-Journal/Times | (502) 582-4711 |
| Memphis Commercial Appeal | (901) 529-2251 |
| Miami Herald | (305) 376-2820 |

| Newspaper | Telephone |
|---|---|
| Milwaukee Journal/Sentinel | (414) 224-2498 |
| Minneapolis Star-Tribune | (612) 673-7777 |
| Nashville Banner/Tennessean | (615) 259-8338 |
| New Orleans Times-Picayune | (504) 826-3000 |
| New York Daily News | (212) 949-1971 |
| New York Newsday | (718) 343-9000 |
| New York Times | (800) 223-7437 |
| Newark Star Ledger | (201) 877-4072 |
| Norfolk Ledger-Star/Virginia Pilot | (804) 446-2450 |
| (Oklahoma City) Daily Oklahoman | (405) 475-3338 |
| Orlando Sentinel | (407) 420-5191 |
| Philadelphia Inquirer/News | (215) 854-2000 |
| Pittsburgh Post Gazette | (412) 263-1333 |
| Portland Oregonian | (503) 221-8334 |
| Providence Journal/Bulletin | (401) 277-7060 |
| Raleigh News & Observer | (919) 829-4646 |
| Richmond Times-Dispatch | (804) 649-6251 |
| Sacramento Bee | (916) 321-1476 |
| (Salt Lake City) Tribune | (801) 237-2900 |
| San Antonio Express/News | (210) 351-7482 |
| San Diego Union/Tribune | (619) 293-1578 |
| San Francisco Chronicle | (415) 777-7777 |
| Seattle Times/Post-Intelligencer | (206) 464-2111 |
| St. Louis Post-Dispatch | (314) 340-8500 |
| St. Petersburg Times | (813) 893-8725 |
| Tampa Tribune | (813) 259-7746 |
| USA Today | (212) 715-5350 |
| USA Weekend | (212) 715-2100 |
| Wall Street Journal | (212) 808-6700 |
| Washington Post | (202) 334-7642 |

# Alternative Newspapers

WITH ORIGINS AMONG THE counter-culture publications of the sixties, alternative newspapers have come a long way. The Association of Alternative Newsweeklies counts 87 members, and a collective readership of over thirteen million—a distinct opportunity for the appropriate advertisers.

## Contact Options

Association of Alternative Newsweeklies
Helene Seisel, Administrative Director
1201 East Jefferson
Suite A-260

Phoenix, AZ 85034
(602) 229-8487
　　Call for membership roster, which includes addresses, telephone numbers, staff information, as well as helpful circulation and demographic data.

Alternative Press Center
P.O. Box 33109
Baltimore, MD 21218
(410) 243-2471
　　Produces the quarterly Alternative Press Index, a selection of articles indexed by subject.

*Alternative Newspapers (cont'd)*

## Alternative Newspapers

| Newspaper | Telephone |
| --- | --- |
| Austin Chronicle | (512) 454-5766 |
| Baltimore City Paper | (410) 523-2300 |
| Boston Phoenix | (617) 536-5390 |
| Chicago Reader | (312) 828-0350 |
| City Pages (Minneapolis) | (612) 375-1015 |
| Creative Loafing (Atlanta) | (800) 950-5623 |
| Creative Loafing (Tampa) | (813) 286-1600 |
| Dallas Observer | (214) 757-9000 |
| Fairfield/Westchester Weekly | (203) 226-4242 |
| Houston Press | (713) 624-1400 |
| Los Angeles Reader | (213) 965-7430 |
| LA Weekly | (213) 465-4414 |
| Metro (San Jose) | (408) 298-8000 |
| Metro Times (Detroit) | (313) 961-4060 |
| Miami New Times | (305) 372-0004 |
| New York Press | (212) 941-1130 |
| Philadelphia City Paper | (215) 735-8444 |
| Phoenix New Times | (602) 271-0040 |
| The Riverfront Times | (314) 231-6666 |
| Sacramento News & Review | (916) 737-1234 |
| San Diego Reader | (619) 235-3000 |
| San Francisco Bay Guardian | (415) 255-3100 |
| SF Weekly | (415) 541-0700 |
| Twin Cities Reader | (612) 591-2500 |
| The Village Voice (New York) | (212) 475-3300 |
| Washington City Paper | (202) 332-2100 |
| Westword (Denver) | (303) 296-7744 |
| Willamette Week (Portland) | (503) 243-2122 |

*Note: All newspapers are over 70,000 circulation*

# College Newspaper Advertising

THE AVERAGE COLLEGE NEWSPAPER issue is read by 62 percent of the students in its market. If a company wants to reach that market by placing ads in college newspapers, it may be easier and more cost-efficient to contact one of the few existing college newspaper advertising syndicates.

These organizations will ship your company's copy to thousands of college newspapers and then collect tearsheets and monitor advertising performance. They can also match your company's specific needs to particular college newspapers, based on categories such as college enrollment, circulation, cost to attend, or college degrees offered.

It is not necessary to pay these syndicates for placing ads. They are commissioned by college newspapers to represent them to advertisers.

## Contact Options

American Passage Media
1114 Ave. of the Americas
New York, NY 10036
(212) 382-0560
*Newspaper syndicate*

Cass Communications
1800 Sherman Pl.
Evanston, IL 60201
(708) 475-8800
*Newspaper syndicate*

# Outdoor Advertising

ACCORDING TO THE OUTDOOR Advertising Association of America, billboards and posters are the most cost-effective way of reaching the consumer.

The billboard, the most commonly used form of outdoor advertising, comes in two standard forms, the 30-sheet poster and the bulletin.

## The 30-Sheet Poster

These are lithographed or silk-screened by a printer and shipped to an outdoor advertising company. They are then prepasted and applied in sections to the poster panel's face on location. Standard 30-sheet posters measure approximately 12 feet high by 24 feet wide.

## The Bulletin

This can be hand-painted in an outdoor company's studio and erected in sections on location, painted directly at the location, or produced by computer. Most measure 14 feet high by 48 feet wide. The majority of painted bulletins in the United States are rotary panels, which can be dismantled and moved to a different location every 30–60 days. Permanent bulletins are placed at extremely high traffic locations and remain at a fixed location for the duration of an advertiser's contract.

## Other Types of Outdoor Advertising

- 8-sheet posters or junior panels
- Transit exteriors
- Painted walls
- Telephone kiosks
- Truck displays
- Taxi tops
- Transit/rail platforms
- Airport/bus terminal displays
- Transit clock platforms
- Bus shelter displays
- Shopping mall displays
- In-store clock and aisle displays.

In recent years, advertisers from various product categories have increased their use of outdoor advertising because of its relative cost-efficiency. Billboards are permitted in all states except Maine, Vermont, Hawaii, and Alaska. In fact, in 1991, the industry fared better than any other form of advertising. The chart below reveals the top ten spending categories for the outdoor advertising industry.

The actual billboard design is generally developed by a company's ad agency which then contacts one of the many outdoor companies operating throughout the country.

The cost of an outdoor ad will largely depend upon location. Unlike print advertising, which charges a space rate, billboard advertising sells by "showings." There are three types of showings, a 100, a 50, and a 25. A 50 showing, for example, is seen approximately 14 times a month by approximately 90 percent of the area's population. The billboard company will help distinguish the location that attracts the particular demographic population a company is trying to reach. The charts below may provide a general sense of what costs to expect.

To visualize how a billboard will appear from 300 feet away, cut out the rectangular frame below or cut a frame that is 3 inches wide by 1 inch, frame your artwork and hold it at arm's length.

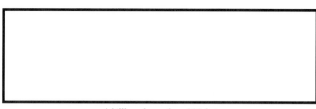

*A billboard seen from 300 feet*

*Outdoor Advertising (cont'd)*

## Billboard Reach (Frequency): Women

| Age | #100 Showing | #50 Showing | #25 Showing |
|---|---|---|---|
| 18-24 | 90.6 (23.98) | 85.8 (12.53) | 74.2 (7.05) |
| 18-34 | 89.0 (26.45) | 84.3 (13.84) | 75.3 (7.56) |
| 18-49 | 90.4 (27.87) | 86.1 (14.49) | 78.6 (7.82) |
| 25-34 | 88.1 (27.89) | 83.5 (14.61) | 76.0 (7.84) |
| 35-44 | 92.7 (29.71) | 88.4 (15.53) | 82.6 (8.24) |
| 45-54 | 90.7 (28.19) | 87.6 (14.14) | 80.7 (7.65) |
| 55-64 | 87.4 (24.31) | 80.4 (13.08) | 73.2 (7.30) |
| 65 + | 80.1 (18.65) | 70.1 (10.13) | 58.0 (6.15) |

*Source: Simmons Market Research Bureau*

## Billboard Reach (Frequency): Men

| Age | #100 Showing | #50 Showing | #25 Showing |
|---|---|---|---|
| 18-24 | 91.0 (33.79) | 86.8 (17.66) | 84.0 (9.27) |
| 18-34 | 90.8 (32.77) | 87.2 (17.07) | 83.5 (9.01) |
| 18-49 | 90.4 (33.71) | 87.5 (17.52) | 83.3 (9.19) |
| 25-34 | 90.6 (32.21) | 87.5 (16.75) | 83.2 (8.86) |
| 35-44 | 89.7 (34.78) | 88.1 (17.87) | 83.2 (9.39) |
| 45-54 | 90.8 (34.82) | 87.0 (18.33) | 82.5 (9.54) |
| 55-64 | 85.8 (33.99) | 83.2 (17.76) | 79.8 (9.30) |
| 65 + | 85.9 (24.01) | 80.6 (12.57) | 71.1 (7.02) |

*Source: Simmons Market Research Bureau*

## Top Ten Outdoor Advertisers

| Rank | Advertiser | 1992 Outdoor Spending ($ millions) | 1991 Outdoor Spending ($ millions) | % Change |
|---|---|---|---|---|
| 1 | Philip Morris | 59.9 | 70.1 | -14.5 |
| 2 | RJR Nabisco | 29.1 | 51.7 | -43.7 |
| 3 | Loews | 26.4 | 35.0 | -24.7 |
| 4 | McDonald's | 12.5 | 6.9 | 79.8 |
| 5 | American Brands | 11.7 | 12.5 | -6.1 |
| 6 | Anheuser-Busch | 10.9 | 11.6 | -6.2 |
| 7 | B.A.T. Industries | 10.5 | 24.3 | -57.0 |
| 8 | Grand Metropolitan | 5.7 | 7.7 | -26.0 |
| 9 | Seagram | 5.2 | 7.7 | -32.2 |
| 10 | BankAmerica | 5.1 | 5.7 | -9.8 |

*Source: Ad Age/Competitive Media Reporting*

For a free booklet containing illustrations of the annual Obie Award-winning billboards, contact:

Outdoor Advertising Association of America
Marketing Division
12 E. 49th St., Floor 22
New York, NY 10017
(212) 688-3667

## Contact Options

*Several of the largest outdoor companies:*

Ackerley Communications
3601 6th Ave. S.
Seattle, WA 98134
(206) 624-2888

Gannett Outdoor Group
666 Third Ave., 4th Floor
New York, NY 10017
(212) 297-6400

Naegele Outdoor Advertising
1700 W. 78th St.
Richfield, MN 55423
(612) 869-1900

Patrick Media Group
338 N. Washington Ave.
Scranton, PA 18503
(717) 347-7100

3M National Advertising
6850 S. Harlem Ave.
Bedford Park, IL 60501
(708) 496-6500

# Banners

MOST BANNERS ARE MADE of a vinyl- or acrylic-coated fabric. They average 3 feet by 5 feet in size but can be made 4 feet by 60 feet or even larger. The following is a partial listing of companies that provide stock banners carrying generic messages such as Grand Opening or Clearance Sale. These companies will also custom-make banners to any specifications.

## Contact Options

*Banner Producers:*

American Banner
9810-A E. 58 St.
Tulsa, OK 74146
(918) 254-6151

Best Buy Banner
6750-C Central Ave.
Riverside, CA 92504
(800) 624-1691

Davey Enterprises
44 Clinton St.
Newton, NJ 07860
(201) 579-5889

Eastern Banner Supply
2582 Spring Lake Rd.
Mooresville, IN 46158
(317) 831-6055

Royal Wholesale Banner
4801 E. 39th Ave.
Denver, CO 80207
(303) 320-0308

McCullough Manufacturing
27 Miller St.
Strasburg, PA 17579
(800) 423-8204

# Blimps

CORPORATIONS LOOKING FOR an innovative way to advertise may now contact several companies that sell and/or lease small airships to advertisers who can't afford the likes of Goodyear Aerospace's 192-foot-long blimps.

The advantages of advertising on one of the new breed of airships that patrols the country's stadiums, golf courses, and racetracks are two-fold. First, they are seen by the large crowds that attend sporting events. Second, because the airship companies request network coverage in exchange for providing aerial camera platforms, they are seen by the even larger audiences that watch the televised events. What's more, a poll conducted by Opinion Research revealed that consumer preference for a product rises by 19 percent after a blimp appearance.

## Contact Options

*Airship Advertising Brokers:*

Airship International
7380 Sand Lake Rd., Suite 350
Orlando, FL 32819
(407) 351-0011

Skyrider Airships
2840 Wilderness Pl., Suite E
Boulder, CO 80301
(303) 449-2190

## The Top Reference Sources

*Who's Who in Professional Speaking*
National Speakers Association, $25 (free to meeting planners)
(602) 968-2552

This membership directory of the National Speakers Association contains the most recent information on more than 3,100 professional speakers. Listings include individual speakers, what topics they address, and how to get in touch with them. The directory is organized alphabetically and includes a geographic index.

Most speakers are happy to provide references and a tape to prospective clients.

# Media Buying Services

ONE WAY FOR A COMPANY TO save money on advertising costs is to use a media buying service.

Many companies use an outside advertising agency and pay them a fee to design their ad campaign and place it in the media. That fee generally includes a fee of 15 percent of the cost of the ads that the ad agency charges to get the campaign placed in the various media outlets that carry the campaign. Since an accredited agency receives a 15 percent discount from the media, however, that 15 percent fee is generally profit for the advertising agency.

To reduce that 15 percent fee to a 5 percent fee, a company can hire an independent marketing consultant and art director and use a media buying service. A free-lance marketing consultant is paid a flat fee to help a company develop a marketing plan. The art director, also for a flat fee, will design the logo, ads, brochures, and everything else that needs designing. The media buying service will then place all of the ads in the media for a charge of from 3 to 5 percent of the cost of the ads, amounting to a 10 percent savings for the client.

## Contact Options

Western International Media
8544 Sunset Blvd.
Los Angeles, CA 90069
(310) 659-5711

Corinthian Media
600 Madison Ave.
New York, NY 10022
(212) 371-5225

MBS International
104 Fifth Ave.
New York, NY 10011
(212) 206-0600

DeWitt Media
460 Park Avenue S.
New York, NY 10016
(212) 545-0120

# Graphic Artists and Designers

FINDING THE RIGHT PHOTOGRAPHER, graphic designer, illustrator, or printer to design a brochure or package, or any other marketing tool is relatively simple.

Most art and office supply stores carry a substantial selection of graphic design portfolios. These books provide the names, addresses, and phone numbers of a varied assortment of working professionals. The catalogues are broken down by specialty and offer samples of each artist's work.

## Recommended Resource

*PrintBooks*
PRINT, $79
(800) 222-2654

## Contact Options

*Designers and Design-Related Organizations:*

*National Firms*
American Center for Design
233 E. Ontario St., Suite 500
Chicago, IL 60611
(312) 787-2018 (in-state)
(800) 257-8657

American Institute of Graphic Arts
164 Fifth Ave.
New York, NY 10010
(212) 752-0813

Association of Professional Design Firms
685 High St., Suite 5
Worthington, OH 43085
(614) 888-3301

Graphic Artists Guild
11 W. 20th St.
New York, NY 10011
(212) 463-7730

Society of Environmental Graphic Designers
1 Story St.
Cambridge, MA 02138
(617) 868-3381

Society of Illustrators
128 E. 63rd St.
New York, NY 10021
(212) 838-2560

Society of Publication Designers
Lincoln Building
60 E. 42nd St., # 721
New York, NY 10165
(212) 983-8585

*Graphic Artists and Designers (cont'd)*

University and College Designers Association
61S Roosevelt Rd., Suite 2
Walkerton, IN 46574
(219) 586-2988

Art Directors Club
250 Park Ave. S.
New York, NY 10003
(212) 674-0500

Art Directors Club of Cincinnati
c/o South-Western Publishing
5101 Madison Rd.
Cincinnati, OH 45227
(513) 241-4591

Art Directors Club of Los Angeles
7060 Hollywood Blvd., Suite 614
Los Angeles, CA 90028
(213) 465-8707

Creative Forum Nashville
P.O. Box 23512
Nashville, TN 37202
(615) 244-4220

Creative Club of Atlanta
P.O. Box 77244
Atlanta, GA 30309
(404) 881-9991

Dayton Advertising Club
P.O. Box 513
Dayton, OH 45409
(513) 436-9672

Graphic Arts Service
1612 Grand
Kansas City, MO 64108
(816) 421-3879

Western Art Directors Club
P.O. Box 996
Palo Alto, CA 94302
(415) 321-4196

# Packaging

FOR A COMPANY NEEDING TO LOCATE professionals to design packaging, there are a number of alternatives. The Package Design Council publishes an annual membership directory that lists the names, addresses, and phone numbers of packaging professionals, broken down by design and industry specialty. The reference costs $125 and is published in January.

Also available is *Packaging Magazine*'s annual *Supplier Source Guide*, which provides an alphabetical listing of suppliers, associations, contract packagers, consultants, and design firms.

## Recommended Resources

*Package Design Council Membership Directory*
Package Design Council International, $125
481 Carlisle Dr.
Herndon, VA 22070
(703) 318-7225

*Packaging*
Cahners Publishing
1350 E. Touhy Ave.
Des Plaines, IL 60017
(708) 635-8800

## The Top Reference Sources

*Who's Who and What's What in Packaging*
Institute of Packaging Professionals, $125
(800) 432-4085

More than just the usual association membership directory, this is a terrific source of leads and

information on all aspects of packaging–including lists of companies and their areas of packaging expertise, packaging and packaging-related professional organizations, educational institutions that offer packaging courses, and executive placement firms that specialize in packaging.

# Packaging Award Winners

## 1993 Institute of Packaging Professionals AmeriStar Packaging Award Winners

| Category | Product | Designer |
|---|---|---|
| Food | Big Mac Clamshell | Perseco |
| Beverage | Reclosable Aseptic Carton | Combibloc |
| Medical Device | Waste Blood Disposal Unit | Prent Corporation |
| Pharmaceutical | Physician Sample Blister Package | G.D. Searle |
| Health & Beauty Aids | Parfums de Coeur Package | Rexham |
| Household & Garden Supplies | Award 25# Package | Ciba-Geigy |
| Other Retail Products | Decorative Mirror Package | Sealed Air Corporation |
| Electronics | Computer Accessory Tray | Apple Computer |
| Regulated Packaging | Hazardous Materials Reusable Drum | Greif Bros. |
| Industrial | Collapsible Tubes Packaging Box | E&S Enterprises |

*Source: Institute of Packaging Professionals*

## Top Purchasers of Packaging in 1993

| Rank | Company | Expenditures ($ millions) |
|---|---|---|
| 1 | Coca-Cola | 856.25 |
| 2 | PepsiCo | 754.25 |
| 3 | Procter & Gamble | 682.72 |
| 4 | Anheuser-Busch | 484.25 |
| 5 | Kraft USA | 412.50 |
| 6 | Campbell Soup | 400.31 |
| 7 | Coca-Cola Foods | 358.00 |
| 8 | Kraft General Foods | 331.50 |
| 9 | General Mills | 312.26 |
| 10 | Miller Brewing | 282.50 |
| 11 | Tropicana | 269.50 |
| 12 | Kellogg | 266.70 |
| 13 | Nabisco Foods | 265.73 |
| 14 | P&G Beverages | 261.00 |
| 15 | Dr Pepper/7-Up | 236.15 |
| 16 | Quaker Oats | 206.93 |
| 17 | Ocean Spray Cranberries | 195.37 |
| 18 | Carnation | 180.32 |
| 19 | Frito-Lay | 179.40 |
| 20 | Nestlé Beverage | 157.08 |
| 21 | Adolph Coors | 147.15 |
| 22 | Ralston Purina | 134.48 |
| 23 | Lever Brothers | 128.35 |
| 24 | Hunt-Wesson | 119.55 |
| 25 | Clorox | 115.52 |

| Rank | Company | Expenditures ($ millions) |
|---|---|---|
| 26 | Oscar Mayer | 114.60 |
| 27 | Pillsbury | 112.99 |
| 28 | Best Foods | 112.40 |
| 29 | Del Monte | 109.59 |
| 30 | Nestlé USA | 96.15 |
| 31 | Star-Kist Seafood | 90.38 |
| 32 | Philip Morris | 89.73 |
| 33 | Thomas Lipton | 87.30 |
| 34 | Pet | 86.93 |
| 35 | Continental Baking | 86.25 |
| 36 | Keebler | 85.80 |
| 37 | Ross Laboratories | 85.17 |
| 38 | Armour Food | 84.20 |
| 39 | Borden | 82.80 |
| 40 | Cadbury Beverages | 82.72 |
| 41 | S.C. Johnson & Son | 81.56 |
| 42 | Stouffer Foods | 81.53 |
| 43 | Hershey Chocolate | 81.23 |
| 44 | Colgate-Palmolive | 78.16 |
| 45 | Green Giant | 76.96 |
| 46 | American Home Foods | 70.65 |
| 47 | Kal Kan Foods | 69.90 |
| 48 | Stroh Brewery | 66.86 |
| 49 | R.J. Reynolds Tobacco | 65.61 |
| 50 | Royal Crown | 63.98 |

*Source: Packaging Magazine, January, 1994*

# Celebrity Booking Services

IT MAY SEEM IMPOSSIBLE for a company to get Meryl Streep to appear at its annual convention or have Bill Cosby endorse its newest product at the local mall, but, in reality, many well-known celebrities are available for corporate appearances at a relatively reasonable cost.

A number of agencies are available whose job it is to book celebrities either to make a speech, perform, or simply appear at corporate conventions, publicity events, or charity benefits. These booking services cater to companies that believe that contact with major television, movie, music, and sports personalities will enhance their company's image. They rely on the fact that many celebrities are interested in getting alternative exposure and income.

These companies will contact a personality, present him or her with a company's proposal and negotiate a deal, usually within a day or two.

## Contact Options

*Celebrity Booking Services:*

Celebrity Service International
1780 Broadway, Suite 300
New York, NY 10019
(212) 245-1460

Washington Speakers Bureau
310 S. Henry St.
Alexandria, VA 22314
(703) 684-0555

Ingels
7080 Hollywood Blvd., 11th Fl.
Hollywood, CA 90028
(213) 464-0800

## Recommended Resources

*Earl Blackwell's Celebrity Register*
Gale Research, $89
(800) 776-6265

*Celebrity Service International Contact Book*
Celebrity Service International, $45
(212) 245-1460

*Cavalcade of Acts and Attractions*
Amusement Business, $55
(615) 321-4250

# Clipping Services

VERY OFTEN A COMPANY wants to monitor its own or a competitor's press coverage or needs to do subject research for a public relations campaign or a company presentation. The best solution may be the services of one of several clipping services available across the country.

For a fee that averages $200 per month, these companies will read the country's major daily and weekly newspapers, magazines, and trade publications and monitor the wire services, radio, and network and cable television news broadcasts. They will clip all articles or transcribe or tape every broadcast that mentions any subject requested by their client company.

Clips may be received on a daily or weekly basis. Companies may find them useful when they need to know the exact words written or spoken by politicians, executives, or public figures either for background research or for a company briefing, press release, daily news update, or public relations campaign.

Most of these clipping services offer a range of services, including day-of-publication delivery, historical research, news clip analysis of public relations performance, advertising analysis of competitors, and foreign press monitoring.

## Contact Options

*Press Clipping Services:*

Allen's Press Clipping Bureau
215 W. 6th St., Room 1100
Los Angeles, CA 90013
(213) 628-4214

Bacon's Information
332 S. Michigan Ave.
Chicago, IL 60604
(312) 922-2400

Burrelle's Information Services
75 E. Northfield Rd.
Livingston, NJ 07039
(201) 992-6600

Luce Press Clippings
420 Lexington Ave.
New York, NY 10170
(212) 889-6711

# Hiring a Copywriter

ANY TIME A COMPANY NEEDS TO disseminate information to the public, it's a good idea to hire a copywriter to ensure clean, effective, professional copy.

Herschell Gordon Lewis, author of *Direct Mail Copy That Sells*, suggests the following procedure for choosing a copywriter:

- Advertise for a copywriter listing enough specifics about the job to keep novices away.

- Ask for samples; then ask questions about the samples to validate authorship. If the candidate is boastful or seems more concerned with ego defense than with any admission of participation by others . . . beware.

- Conduct a convivial personal interview in which you lead the candidate to believe he or she actually has the job and the conversation is just a formality. Pay close attention to the degree of literacy. Look for two Achilles' heels (a) phony sincerity, and (b) contempt for whatever you're selling. Disqualify any candidate on either basis.

- Have the candidate take a timed writing test assignment. Pepper the instructions with weak words from the list below. If the writer regurgitates more than a couple of those words or uses platitudes and clichés, this person is not an original thinker.

- Give the top three candidates an actual, for-pay assignment. You'll find your writer.

A number of sources are available to help you find the writer that best suits your company's needs. The classified sections in AdWeek and Advertising Age, for example, are probably the best places to find the names of copywriters or place an advertisement.

Finally, it's always a good idea to check with a headhunter who specializes in advertising.

## Recommended Resources

Dial-A-Writer
1501 Broadway, Suite 302
New York, NY 10036
(212) 398-1934

Dial-A-Writer connects more than 800 well-published, independent, free-lance writers with anyone needing a skilled professional.

The One Club for Art and Copy
3 W. 18th St.
New York, NY 10011
(212) 979-1900

The One Club boasts a membership of some 700 advertising art directors and copywriters and is another good referral source for professional writers.

## Contact Options

*Headhunters:*

Baedar Chiu
9538 Brighton Way, Suite 306
Beverly Hills, CA 90210
(310) 274-0051

Greenberg & Associates
1133 Broadway, Room 1204
New York, NY 10010
(212) 463-0020

Howsam & Weingarten
275 Madison Ave.
New York, NY 10016
(212) 682-5151

Sandy Wade
101 E. Ontario
Chicago, IL 60611
(312) 280-9036

The Watts Group
225 Santa Monica Blvd., Suite 1111
Santa Monica, CA 90401
(310) 576-7925

Westerfield & Associates
5150 S. Florida Ave., #307
Lakeland, FL 33813
(813) 644-1216

## Weak Words

| | | |
|---|---|---|
| administration | facilitate | product |
| affinity | features | purchase |
| amendment | fond | quality |
| approximately | formulate | replacement |
| attractive | humorous | requested |
| configuration | indeed | respond |
| constructed | merchant | rethink |
| contradictory | moderate | service |
| "Dear Friend" | needs (as a noun) | standards |
| define | pamphlet | utilize |
| dispatch | peruse | value |
| earn | prearranged | work |

# Printers

CATALOGUES, BROCHURES, LABELS, and a host of other business printing needs can be arranged without ever leaving the office. A number of companies now provide fast, high-quality, full-color professional printing services nationwide based on specifics that the client can provide by mail, fax, or telephone.

## Contact Options

*Printing Companies:*

Multiprint
5555 W. Howard St.
Skokie, IL 60077
(800) 858-9999

Service Webb Offset Corporation
2500 S. Dearborn St.
Chicago, IL 60616
(800) 621-1567

Econocolor
7405 Industrial Rd.
Florence, KY 41042
(800) 877-7405

## Recommended Resource

*Graphic Arts Bluebook*
A.F. Lewis & Co., $80
(212) 679-0770

# Product Placement Firms

AFTER E.T. FOUND HIS HUMAN friend, Elliot, through a trail of Reese's Pieces, sales of the candy leaped 66 percent in three months.

When Tom Cruise sported Ray-Ban sunglasses in *Top Gun*, sales of the company's aviator-style glasses jumped 40 percent in seven months.

The use of these brand name products and many others on film and television is negotiated by companies called product placement firms. For a fee that can run as high as $50,000, these firms will provide their corporate clients with promotional consultation and placement of their products in television series, feature films, and even game shows. These deals enable corporations to market their products by using the entertainment industry, and allow filmmakers to cut production costs by getting free products and services in exchange for their placement.

Product placement firms are hired by corporate clients to review upcoming scripts and determine: what products will be needed, whether they should be handled visually or simply mentioned in dialogue; evaluate whether the film is aimed at the correct target audience for the product, and negotiate a mutually beneficial deal for both the corporate client and the cost-conscious studios.

## Contact Options

*Product Placement Firms:*

AIM Promotions
Kaufman Astoria Studios
34-12 36th St.
Astoria, NY 11106
(718) 729-9288

Ventura Media Group
11466 San Vicente
Los Angeles, CA 90049
(310) 820-0607

Creative Entertainment Services
1015 N. Hollywood Way, Suite 101
Burbank, CA 91505
(818) 842-9119

Motion Picture Placement
9250 Wilshire Blvd., #412
Beverly Hills, CA 90212
(310) 858-1115

Rogers & Cowan
3701 W. Oak St.
Burbank, CA 91505
(818) 954-6944

UPP Entertainment Marketing
10865 Burbank Blvd.
North Hollywood, CA 91601
(818) 508-8877

*Compuserve's PR and Marketing Forum offers contacts and info for PR, marketing, and corporate communications. GO PRSIG*

# Working with the Press

WORKING WITH THE PRESS IS a sales process. And like any other sales process, it is important for a company to establish clear goals and create ongoing relationships with the press with which they are dealing. Here are several guidelines that should help:

## 1. Set your objectives
The key to successful interviews is to know what you want to accomplish before entering into a conversation with the press. Never enter into an interview process without knowing your objectives. If you get a spontaneous phone call from a reporter, the best way to handle it is to call the person back after you've had a chance to think about the key company objectives.

## 2. Know your key message
Find every opportunity during a conversation with a reporter to underline the company's key objectives.

## 3. Manage the conversation
Try to drive an interview rather than let it be driven for you. Answer questions by bringing them back to the points you want to emphasize. The goal is to communicate information rather than load the listener with data he or she may not understand.

## 4. Be responsive to your audience
Different types of press have different needs. Try to understand their needs, either by getting advice from your public relations firm beforehand, or by taking the first few minutes of your interview to chat with the interviewer to understand his or her concerns. Then, present your material as effectively as possible to meet those needs.

## 5. Respect deadlines
Press people are often under deadline pressure. Since the purpose of taking the time to do an interview is to develop a rapport, try to get an understanding of what deadline pressures the interviewer is under and be responsive to those pressures.

## 6. Remember the First Amendment
Every interview may not result in a story and every story that gets written may not be exactly the story the company wants to see published. Members of the press are entitled to freedom of the press. Remember that if you want something to be "off the record," you need to get agreement from the person you are speaking with before you are guaranteed anonymity.

## Contact Option
Abigail Johnson
Roeder-Johnson
655 Skyway, Suite 130
San Carlos, CA 94070
(415) 802-1850

# Publicity Services

BELOW ARE LISTED SEVERAL services that will, for a fee, take a company's press release or other publicity material and present it to media outlets:

*Radio-TV Interview Report*
Bradley Communications
135 E. Plumstead Ave.
Landsdowne, PA 19050
(215) 259-1070
This bimonthly magazine lists project pitches and is mailed to over 5,000 radio-TV talk show and TV news programming executives nationwide.

*Publicity Express*
2646 Appian Way, #31
Pinole, CA 94564
(800) 541-2897
This monthly magazine lists projects and pitches and is mailed to over 5,000 electronic media outlets.

PR Newswire (PRN)
Harborside Financial Center
806 Plaza 3
Jersey City, NJ 07311
(800) 832-5522 or (212) 832-9400
This is a daily service that provides news releases and camera-ready photo transmissions to the world's largest media telecommunications network through satellite, fax, mail, and database.

News Broadcast Network
149 Madison Ave., No. 804
New York, NY 10016
(212) 889-0888
This is a daily radio feed servicing 2,000 news and talk radio stations and all AP and UPI audio feed wire service subscribers.

*Publicity Services (cont'd)*

Derus Media
500 N. Dearborn, No. 516
Chicago, IL 60601
(312) 644-4360

    This is a monthly distributor of multimedia script and slide packages to radio and television outlets. They are the only service to offer a full-service division for the Hispanic market.

News USA
4601 Eisenhower Ave.
Alexandria, VA 22304
(800) 355-9500

    This company distributes media releases and editorial feature camera-ready art in a monthly package by mail, discs, and computer hook-ups to 10,000 newspapers.

Metro Publicity Services
33 W. 34th St.
New York, NY 10001
(212) 947-5100

    This service mails to 7,000 newspapers monthly. They offer monthly theme sections 22 times a year featuring subject matter for targeted audiences.

## Recommended Resources

    Three newsletters list the new columns, shows, and magazines, and what they are looking for. They also report on free-lance project needs and provide names and addresses.

*Bulldog Reporter*
2115 Fourth St.
Berkeley, CA 94710
(800) 327-9893

*Contacts*
35-20 Broadway
Astoria, NY 11106
(718) 721-0508

*Partyline*
35 Sutton Pl.
New York, NY 10022
(212) 755-3487

*Bacon's Media Directories*
(Newspaper/Magazine, Radio/TV, Media Calendar, International Media)
Bacon's Information, Inc., $230-$250 per edition
332 S. Michigan Ave.
Chicago, IL 60604
(800) 621-0561 or (312) 922-2400

*Burrelle's Media Directory*
Burrelle's Media Information Systems
$400/4 updates per year
75 E. Northfield Rd.
Livingston, NJ 07039
(800) 631-1160

*Marketer's Guide to Media*
BPI: BPI Media Services $100/2 editions per year
1515 Broadway
New York, NY 10036
(800) 284-4915 or (212) 536-5263

*Power Media Selects*
Broadcast Interview Source $166.50/year
2233 Wisconsin Ave., NW
Washington, DC 20007
(202) 333-4904

# Selecting a Public Relations Firm

THOUGH THEY ARE OFTEN CONFUSED, public relations and advertising are not the same thing. A public relations firm is responsible for determining the way an organization is perceived by the public.

    The first thing to consider when choosing a public relations firm is whether you want that firm to handle your company's entire public relations program or just its publicity. A firm that handles publicity sees to it that a company's products or services receive media coverage in the form of articles or radio and television broadcasts. When a firm handles public relations as a whole, its job is to help craft a company's image. Most PR firms do both. Here are some of the other ways they can help an organization:

- Provide an outside viewpoint or perspective;

- Increase an organization's overall visibility;

- Support a product or an overall marketing effort;

- Counsel in a crisis;

- Communicate with employees;

- Inform investors;

- Strengthen community relations;

- Act as a liaison with government agencies;

- Measure and evaluate existing public relations programs;

*Selecting a Public Relations Firm (cont'd)*

- Research public attitudes and behavior;

- Stage media events.

Once you have determined the specific communication needs of your organization, choosing the right public relations firm involves a certain amount of investigation. Begin by looking through the magazines in which you would like to have coverage, call the companies that are written about and find out which firm those companies employ.

When you have narrowed down your options, interview several firms. Don't assume that a large company is necessarily better equipped to handle your organization's needs. While advertising often requires a large staff of people to create and develop a campaign, public relations can usually be handled by a smaller team that is responsible for writing press releases and getting them out to an appropriate contact list.

Before deciding on a firm, consider the following questions:

- Does the firm have expertise in your company's field and understand your particular needs?

- Do you want greater awareness for your product nationally or in a targeted market?

- Do you want to pay your firm a flat fee, a retainer fee, a minimum monthly fee, or a project fee?

- What is your company's objective?

- How important is it to have regular access to the agency head and who is the backup?

- Which of the media do you need your agency to handle?

- How long will it take to learn about your account?

- What reporting/measurement methods are used?

- Must you have easy access to your firm's offices?

- Do you want a company with a particular philosophy or one that is willing to work with the philosophy of its clients?

- Whom do you want to be in charge?

If, after meeting with key people, you are still undecided, ask each to send a written proposal outlining how it would provide the public relations services your organization needs. When you have decided upon a firm, get references from other clients, and work out a reasonable budget so there are no surprises down the line.

## Contact Option

Public Relations Society of America
33 Irving Plaza
New York, NY 10003
(212) 995-2230

## Recommended Resource

*O'Dwyer's Directory of Public Relations*
J.R. O'Dwyer, $125
271 Madison Ave.
New York, NY 10016
(212) 679-2471

Lists most existing public relations firms, noting their rank, specialties, number of employees, and clients.

# Leading Public Relations Firms

## Top Fifteen PR Firms by Net Fees

| Agency | 1991 Net Fees ($) | 1992 Net Fees ($) | % Change 1991 to 1992 |
|---|---|---|---|
| Burson-Marsteller | 199,818,000 | 203,638,000 | 1.93 |
| Shandwick | 72,970,000 | 166,100,000 | -3.93 |
| Hill and Knowlton | 173,500,000 | 149,100,000 | -14.00 |
| Omnicom PR Network | 63,948,548 | 65,569,433 | 2.50 |
| Edelman Public Relations Worldwide | 52,791,480 | 59,814,538 | 13.30 |
| Fleishman-Hillard | 52,228,000 | 58,651,000 | 12.30 |
| Ketchum Public Relations | 41,800,000 | 45,600,000 | 9.10 |
| The Rowland Company | 48,000,000 | 44,000,000 | -8.30 |
| Ogilvy Adams & Rinehart | 56,917,000 | 36,124,000 | -36.50 |
| Manning, Selvage & Lee | 30,346,000 | 31,424,000 | 3.60 |
| GCI Group | 29,584,296 | 28,095,400 | -1.00 |
| Ruder Finn | 28,234,066 | 27,076,769 | -4.10 |
| Robinson, Lake, Lerer & Montgomery | 20,733,000 | 21,200,000 | 3.00 |
| Cohn & Wolfe | 15,521,000 | 14,200,000 | -0.85 |
| Financial Relations Board | 8,815,745 | 10,263,134 | 16.40 |

*Source: J.R. O'Dwyer Company*

*Leading Public Relations Firms (cont'd)*

## Leading PR Firms by Specialty

### Agriculture

| Firm | 1992 Fee Income ($) |
|---|---|
| Shandwick | 4,107,000 |
| Gibbs and Soeil | 3,928,000 |
| Bader Rutter and Assoc. | 2,529,430 |
| Morgan & Myers | 2,515,919 |
| Fleishman-Hillard | 2,430,000 |

### Beauty/Fashion

| Firm | 1992 Fee Income ($) |
|---|---|
| Hill and Knowlton | 7,700,000 |
| The Rowland Co. | 4,664,000 |
| Burson-Marsteller | 3,058,000 |
| Shandwick | 2,569,000 |
| Porter/Novelli (Omnicom) | 2,367,000 |

### Entertainment/Cultural

| Firm | 1992 Fee Income ($) |
|---|---|
| Shandwick | 14,273,000 |
| Dennis Davidson Associations | 3,842,000 |
| Ruder Finn | 2,700,000 |
| The Rowland Co. | 2,288,000 |
| Manning, Selvage & Lee | 2,017,000 |

### Environmental

| Firm | 1992 Fee Income ($) |
|---|---|
| Burson-Marsteller | 19,000,000 |
| Ketchum Public Relations | 14,200,000 |
| Hill and Knowlton | 12,850,000 |
| Shandwick | 11,225,000 |
| Fleishman-Hillard | 8,600,000 |

### Financial PR/Investor Relations

| Firm | 1992 Fee Income ($) |
|---|---|
| Hill and Knowlton | 33,800,000 |
| Burson-Marsteller | 26,502,000 |
| Ogilvy Adams and Rinehart | 16,600,000 |
| Fleishman-Hillard | 14,879,000 |
| Financial Relations Board | 10,263,134 |

### Foods & Beverages

| Firm | 1992 Fee Income ($) |
|---|---|
| Burson-Marsteller | 36,696,000 |
| Hill and Knowlton | 23,000,000 |
| Shandwick | 18,090,000 |
| Fleishman-Hillard | 12,150,000 |
| Ketchum Public Relations | 12,100,000 |

### Health Care

| Firm | 1992 Fee Income ($) |
|---|---|
| Burson-Marsteller | 41,793,000 |
| Hill and Knowlton | 15,000,000 |
| Edelman PR Worldwide | 10,492,013 |
| Ruder Finn | 9,500,000 |
| Porter/Novelli (Omnicom) | 9,113,000 |

### High Tech

| Firm | 1992 Fee Income ($) |
|---|---|
| Shandwick | 27,178,000 |
| Hill and Knowlton | 22,000,000 |
| Burson-Marsteller | 14,271,000 |
| Cunningham Communications | 7,002,817 |
| Fleishman-Hillard | 6,555,000 |

### Sports

| Firm | 1992 Fee Income ($) |
|---|---|
| Cohn & Wolfe | 2,941,000 |
| Shandwick | 2,652,000 |
| Burson-Marsteller | 2,600,000 |
| Manning, Selvage & Lee | 2,267,000 |
| Hill and Knowlton | 1,900,000 |

### Travel

| Firm | 1992 Fee Income ($) |
|---|---|
| Hill and Knowlton | 12,000,000 |
| Shandwick | 7,636,000 |
| Burson-Marsteller | 7,135,000 |
| Fleishman-Hillard | 3,400,000 |
| The Rowland Company | 3,124,000 |

*Source: O'Dwyer's Directory of PR Firms, 1993*

**TIP:** *Advertising Age produces a Marketing with Video Kit, which includes an idea guide featuring more than 20 detailed case histories, a packaging guide, production tips, and more. Call (800) 218-2233.*

# VNR and Industrial Video

A VIDEO NEWS RELEASE IS basically a press release in video form–typically a 90-second video piece that is paid for by corporate sponsors and then distributed, via satellite or mail, to stations around the country to be included in local newscasts. They are, in effect, paid advertisements in a news format. When they are well made, it is almost impossible to distinguish them from a regular national news segment.

Presidential candidates use them for air time on local news channels. Fortune 500 companies create them to inform the public about their latest product research. And, in the last decade, a growing number of small companies have begun to use them as an effective public relations tool.

There are two basic categories of VNR: timely and "evergreen."

A timely VNR takes advantage of a newsworthy event to get across a company's ideas or products to the public. For example, the 3M Company provided a high-tech coating for American luges in the 1988 Winter Olympics and produced a VNR featuring action race shots and experts applying the coating. The advantage of a timely VNR is that there's a good chance it will be picked up by stations that may be looking for news fillers. The disadvantage to a timely VNR is that it may become obsolete very quickly.

The "evergreen" VNR, on the other hand, is produced to have a longer shelf life, typically dealing with human interest stories that can be used by stations on a slow news day. Recent studies conducted by Nielsen Media Research, however, reveal that "evergreens" were preferred by 25 percent of all news producers, while just under 50 percent preferred timely pieces.

Most commonly, VNRs try to tie a company's new products and/or services to one of the following topics:

- Health tips
- Consumer affairs
- Community services
- Government issues
- New regulations
- Public service messages.

Creating an effective VNR can cost $20,000 or more including production, distribution, and follow-up costs.

The emphasis should be on the video's newsworthiness. Also effective are issue-oriented videos. The Insurance Institute for Highway Safety, for instance, transmitted a hard-hitting VNR on seatbelt safety by focusing on a car manufacturer whose seatbelts were not well designed.

A Medialink-Nielsen survey suggests the following rules to keep in mind when producing a video news release:

- Create a package containing a news-story type release and a few minutes of background tape or B-Roll.
- Time your VNR to be approximately 90 seconds.
- Place audio signals on separate channels so that news producers may insert their own voice-overs on one sound channel with the natural sound of your VNR tape on the other.
- When distributing a VNR, always clearly identify it as a public relations service in the materials provided.

Nick Peters, Medialink vice-president, suggests the following "litmus test" when choosing a production firm to create your VNR:

- Ask your own or another public relations firm that has had experience with VNRs to recommend a production company.
- Ask the production company whether it has done any VNRs before and for whom. Ask what results it has had and how those results have been documented.
- Make sure the company has past experience in television news.
- Ask to see a demo reel.

For further information, contact Medialink, a major satellite distributor of VNRs and other video public relations services. Medialink has a variety of free reference books about VNR as well as a listing of production companies nationwide.

## Contact Options

*Medialink Locations:*

708 Third Ave.
New York, NY 10017
(212) 682-8300

1401 New York Ave., Suite 520
Washington, DC 20005
(202) 628-3800

6430 Sunset Blvd., Suite 1506
Los Angeles, CA 90028
(213) 465-0111

The Time and Life Building
541 N. Fairbanks Ct.
Chicago, IL 60611
(312) 222-9850

*VNR and Industrial Video (cont'd)*

For a price that most experts say averages $2,000 per minute, it is possible to create an in-house company video that uses the same sophisticated techniques common to most television broadcasts.

## Contact Options

*Production Companies Specializing in VNR and Industrial Video:*

Perri Pharris Productions
4590 MacArthur Blvd., Suite 620
Newport Beach, CA 92660
(714) 263-3737

Washington Independent Productions
400 N. Capitol St., NW, Suite 183
Washington, DC 20001
(202) 638-3400

Doug Manning Productions
300 W. Washington St. Suite 706
Chicago, IL 60606
(312) 782-2700

VNR-1
5639 Wembley Downs
Arlington, TX 76017
(817) 784-9920

The "A" Team
425 E. 79th St.
New York, NY 10021
(212) 737-8492

Reality Productions
6161 Kingsberry
St. Louis, MO 63112
(314) 725-3838

# Infomercials

INFOMERCIALS ARE PROGRAM-LENGTH TV commercials that are devoted solely to one product. These programs are designed to heighten public awareness, develop brand-name identification, and create a consumer market for a product by providing potential customers with all the information they will need about the product.

## Contact Options

*Among the Largest Infomercial Production Companies:*

American Telecast
16 Industrial Blvd.
Paoli, PA 19301
(215) 251-9933

National Media
1700 Walnut St.
Philadelphia, PA 19103
(215) 772-5000

Regal Group
355 Lexington Ave., 18th Floor
New York, NY 10017
(212) 682-6000

USA Direct
12701 Whitewater Dr.
Minnetonka, MN 55343
(612) 945-4391

Gunthy-Renker
41550 Eclectic, Suite 1200
Palm Desert, CA 92260
(619) 773-9022

## Recommended Resource

*Infomercial Marketing Report*
11533 Thurston Circle
Los Angeles, CA 90049
(310) 472-5253

The PLAY (Program Length Advertisement of the Year) Awards are given by *Infomercial Marketing Report*.

## The 1994 PLAY Awards

| Award | Title (Show) | Recipient |
| --- | --- | --- |
| Most Innovative New Product | Proform Crosswalk | Proform Fitness/Tyee Productions |
| Most Innovative Use of an Infomercial | The Great Wall | Philips Consumer Electronics/ Tyee Productions |
| Most Effective Home Fitness/ Health Product Infomercial | The Gravity Edge | SLM, Inc./Tyee Productions |
| Most Effective Beauty Product Infomercial | The Thinking Man's Guide to Hair Restoration | Bosley Medical Institute/ Tyee Productions |

*Infomercials (cont'd)*

| Award | Title (Show) | Recipient |
|---|---|---|
| Most Effective Household Appliance/ Consumer Electronics Infomercial | Jet Stream Oven 3000T | American Harvest/Stan Jacobs |
| Most Effective Entertainment Product Infomercial | The Great Wall | Philips Consumer Electronics/ Tyee Productions |
| Most Effective Self-Help Infomercial | Hidden Keys to Loving Relationships | Steve Scott & Frank Kovacs |
| Most Effective Retail Campaign Infomercial | The Great Wall | Philips Consumer Electronics/ Tyee Productions |
| Most Effective Campaign for an Established Product or Product Line | The Flying Lure III | Langer Technologies/Jim Caldwell |

*Source: Infomercial Marketing Report*

# Direct Response Fulfillment Houses

APPROXIMATELY 80 PERCENT of the calls generated by commercials and infomercials occur within the first five minutes after the commercial has aired. These "call spikes" make setting up an in-house center for receiving telephone orders impractical and expensive.

"800" service bureaus that specialize in handling spot TV and half-hour infomercial-generated calls present the advertiser with an effective and relatively inexpensive resource for handling a high volume of calls.

In selecting an inbound call center or fulfillment house, the advertiser must determine if the number of lines and staff available at the times when specific ads are scheduled to run are sufficient to handle the expected number of calls. Advertisers should expect to pay the following costs:

- A one time set-up fee that will include normal program set-up and any unique programming or training that may be necessary.

- Call-processing fees based upon a negotiated per-call charge or actual usage, per minute, of on-phone conversation.

- A monthly minimum fee credited against call charges.

- Special transaction fees such as output, payment processing, etc.

## Contact Options

*Operator Centers with More Than 400 Workstations:*

MATRIXX Marketing
2121 N. 117th Ave.
Omaha, NE 68164-3000
(402) 498-4000

West Telemarketing
9910 Maple St.
Omaha, NE 68134
(402) 571-7700

*Operator Centers with 100–400 Workstations:*

AT&T American Transtech
8000 Baymeadows Way
Jacksonville, FL 32256
(904) 636-1000

Neodata
833 W. South Boulder Rd.
Louisville, CO 80027
(303) 666-7000

Precision Response
4300 N.W. 135th St.
Miami, FL 33054
(305) 681-1188

The Product Line
2370 S. Trenton Way
Denver, CO 80231
(303) 671-8000

Sitel
5601 N. 103rd St.
Omaha, NE 68134
(402) 498-6810

Teletech
15355 Morrison St.
Sherman Oaks, CA 91403
(818) 501-5595

# Greeting Card Suppliers

## Contact Options

*Major Holiday Card Suppliers:*

New England Art-Birchcraft
10 Railroad St.
Abington, MA 02351
(617) 878-5151

Century Engraving and Embossing
1500 W. Monroe
Chicago, IL 60607
(312) 666-8686

Handshake Greeting Cards
P.O. Box 9027
Columbus, GA 31908
(800) 634-2134

Masterpiece Studios
5400 W. 35 St.
Chicago, IL 60650
(708) 656-4000

# Gift Baskets, Gift Brokers, Flowers

## Contact Options

*Gift Brokers:*

Dial-A-Gift
(800) 453-0428

800 Spirits
(800) 238-4373

The Peterson Nut Company
(800) 367-6887

Popcorn World
(800) 443-8226

Calyx & Corolla
(800) 800-7788

Phillips' Flower Shops
(800) 356-7257

# Premium Sources

MANY COMPANIES PROVIDE catalogues with a wide range of personalized premium or specialty advertising items, ranging from key rings and mugs to calendars, pens, pads, and other office items.

Total industry sales in 1992 were $5.2 billion, up 30 percent since 1987.

## Contact Options

Promotional Products Association
3125 Skyway Circle N.
Irving, TX 75038
(214) 252-0404

The association will provide free advice on developing a cost-efficient promotional plan and will provide a list of specialty advertising distributors by location. To find a local specialty advertising distributor, check the Yellow Pages under Advertising Specialties.

Promotion and Marketing Association of America
257 Park Ave., S.
New York, NY 10010
(212) 420-1100
*Trade association*

## Licensed Product Category Sales by Large Distributors

| Product | % Sales |
|---|---|
| Wearables | 22.4 |
| Writing Instruments | 14.0 |
| Office Accessories | 9.3 |
| Recognition Awards | 9.2 |
| Glassware/Ceramics | 8.8 |
| Calendars | 8.2 |
| Sporting Goods/ Leisure Products | 6.7 |
| Buttons, Badges, Ribbons/ Stickers, Magnets | 5.8 |
| Automotive Accessories | 4.5 |

*Source: The Specialty Advertising Association*

# Mailing Lists

DIRECT MAIL MARKETERS RELY on mailing lists to target the particular geographical and demographical market they are trying to reach. It is possible to rent or purchase mailing lists that include the names, addresses, and telephone numbers of people in categories as specific as museum curators, tax shelter investors, or people who have recently moved.

Mailing lists are divided into two major categories:

- Compiled lists, which are derived from directories, associations, government data, Yellow Pages registration, and public records.

- Response lists, which are comprised of individuals who have taken a direct action such as making a purchase, subscribing to a publication, or joining an organization. In general, these lists are more accurate since they are compiled from less general sources.

Anyone can obtain either kind of list directly from a mailing list company, or they can hire a list broker. Mailing list companies all provide free catalogues of their available lists and generally charge between $50 and $100 per 1,000 names for one-time use of a list. Overall, it is a better idea to use a broker than rent a list directly. It is not necessary to pay a broker since the broker receives a commission directly from the list owner, and will investigate, select, and order the list that is most suitable for each individual client.

## Recommended Resources

Standard Rate & Data Service
3004 Glenview Rd.
Wilmette, IL 60091
(708) 256-6067
This company publishes *Direct Mail List Rates and Data*, a directory of available mailing lists. The directory sells for $152 for a single issue, or $354 for a 6-issue annual subscription.

*Directory of Mailing List Companies*
Todd Publications
18 N. Greenbush Rd.
West Nyack, NY 10994
(914) 358-6213
This book sells for $25 and includes an alphabetical listing of the names, addresses, and telephone numbers of hundreds of mailing list brokers.

## Contact Options

*List Brokers:*

Abelow Response
181 S. Franklin Ave.
Valley Stream, NY 11581
(516) 791-7900

AZ Marketing Services
31 River Rd.
Cos Cob, CT 06807
(203) 629-8088

Direct Media
200 Pemberwick Rd.
Greenwich, CT 06830
(203) 532-1000

The Kaplan Agency
1200 High Ridge Rd.
Stamford, CT 06905
(203) 968-8800

Kleid Company
530 Fifth Ave., 17th Floor
New York, NY 10036
(212) 819-3400

Leon Henry
455 Central Ave.
Scarsdale, NY 10583
(914) 723-3176

Mal Dunn & Associates
Hardscrabble Rd.
Croton Falls, NY 10519
(914) 277-5558

Media Horizons
94 East Ave.
Norwalk, CT 06851
(203) 857-0770

Millard Group
10 Vose Farm Rd.
Peterborough, NH 03458
(603) 924-9262

Qualified Lists
1 American Ln.
Greenwich, CT 06831
(203) 552-6700

# Package Inserts and Co-ops

WITH THE RISE OF POSTAL RATES over the last decade, the direct mail industry has found increasing success in the use of alternative media such as package inserts, co-ops, and ride-alongs. These allow marketers to share the cost of direct mail advertising by sending their material out together in one package.

Package inserts are advertisements in the form of postcards, flyers, folders, or envelopes (either from the company selling the product or from outsiders) placed in packages delivered to mail order or retail buyers. The most popular format is a 5-by-8-inch one- or two-panel four-color advertisement.

The number of inserts enclosed will vary from four to eight. They are generally carried by an envelope or box that delivers an order sent by an established purveyor of mail-order merchandise, by a utility or credit card bill, or by a monthly bank statement. They can also be placed in an envelope containing photo-finishing, a package containing laundry or dry cleaning, a cereal box, a disposable diaper carton, or anything else bought retail. The average cost to direct marketers of package inserts is between $45 and $55 per thousand.

When non-competing advertisements are mailed together to reduce costs and reach the same prospective customers, it's called a co-op. These are generally carried in the same way or inserted in newspapers instead of being mailed.

When the mailing is run by a company with the primary purpose of mailing a catalogue or making an announcement, it's a ride-along. The average cost of such mailings is now edging above the $30 million mark.

The most obvious advantage to using these alternative media is the low initial cost relative to the benefits, particularly after a successful format has been created.

## Leon Henry's Ten Rules for the Most Effective Alternative Media Ad Placement

### I. Choose the right distribution program

Look for demographics that are geared to your product or service, and try to insure that the merchandise that your package insert accompanies will heighten the response to your offer.

### 2. Test at least ten programs at a time

Out of every ten programs tested, however, you will have an average of three losers. Experiment with new inserts to get an accurate measure of success.

### 3. Go with the maximum size

Different programs have different physical limitations. Go with the maximum size allowed by each program to prevent your insert from being lost in the shuffle.

### 4. Test with copy that you know works

Do not write new copy, create new graphics, or introduce a new offer when you first test your insert. Test what you already know works in direct mail or space advertising. If your program fails, you'll know it was the program and not your copy or offer that was at fault.

### 5. Be patient when evaluating a program

Inserts that accompany retail merchandise may take six months before they are fully distributed. Calculate a final cost-per-order you can be comfortable with, and as long as you come in under that number, you can consider your insert program a success.

### 6. Try to transform marginal performers into new profit makers

By reducing printing costs, changing layout, or changing stock, color, or copy, you might be able to manipulate the cost of participation in a program. and turn a marginal program into a real success.

### 7. Always key every insert package

Using a five- or six-digit code, mark every insert you send out with a key that will allow you to identify what package it was part of. It's better to pay the extra money to stop the press and change keys than it is to be unsure of your results.

### 8. Include an appropriate number of inserts

Unless you have at least 10,000 inserts in each program you test, your returns may not be statistically reliable. On the other hand, if the number of inserts you put in one program is too high, it will force you to wait too long a time until all of your inserts have been distributed and you can evaluate the results. You might break up a large number of inserts into several keys and evaluate them as you go along.

### 9. Choose a dependable broker

Many inserts miss the program they were intended for because of foul-ups in production or shipping. Your broker must make sure your materials are printed accurately, shipped to where they're supposed to go, received by the appropriate people, and inserted in the right program.

### 10. Always re-test favorable returns

If you don't, a competitor may jump in and pre-empt you from profiting from your success. On the other hand, you should maintain sizeable reserves of pre-keyed inserts to take advantage of a new program or a competitor's failure to re-test promptly.

## Contact Option

Leon Henry
455 Central Ave.
Scarsdale, NY 10583
(914) 723-3176

# Color Marketing

EFFECTIVE USE OF COLOR is the mission of The Color Marketing Group, an international non-profit association of 1,300 design and color professionals. The group forecasts color directions one to three years ahead in all industries, including consumer, contract, transportation, fashion, graphics, office, and health care. The Color Marketing Group provides a forum for the exchange of non-competitive information on all phases of color marketing, including color trends and combinations; styling and design; merchandising and sales; education and research.

Each year the Color Marketing Group selects emerging color preferences such as Ensign Blue, Plantation Shutter, and Canyon Rose for industry groups like exterior home, kitchen and bath, and retail.

## Contact Option

The Color Marketing Group
5904 Richmond Highway, #408
Alexandria, VA 22203
(703) 329-8500

# Classic Marketing Books

BOOKS ABOUT MARKETING account for a large percentage of the greatest business books ever written. Here is an idiosyncratic list of some of the most useful books on the topic.

*Direct Mail Copy That Sells*
by Herschell Gordon Lewis
Prentice Hall, $12.95
(800) 947-7700

*How to Write a Good Advertisement*
by Victor O. Schwab
Wilshire Book Company, $20
(818) 765-8579

*The Copy Workshop*
by Bruce Bendinger
The Copy Workshop, $33
(312) 871-1179

*Positioning*
by Trout & Reis
McGraw-Hill, $24.95
(800) 882-8158

*Tested Advertising Methods*
by John Caples
Prentice Hall, $9.95
(800) 947-7700

## The Top Reference Sources

*1994 Mail Order Business Directory*
B. Klein Publications, $85
(305) 752-1708

This directory is an essential tool for reaching the 9,500 most active mail order firms. This book also includes a very good summary of the mail order

market. Companies are listed by product categories, and all entries include company name, address, and telephone number.

Foreign mail order companies are also included.

# Typical Sales Rep Territories

| No. | Regions |
|---|---|
| 1 | Eastern Massachusetts, Rhode Island, New Hampshire, Maine |
| 2 | Connecticut, western Massachusetts, Vermont |
| 3 | New York City, Long Island, Westchester County, New Jersey north of Trenton |
| 4 | Upstate New York |
| 5 | New Jersey, Trenton and south, Pennsylvannia east of Harrisburg |
| 6 | Maryland, Delaware, District of Columbia, Northern Virginia |
| 7 | Southern Virginia, North Carolina, South Carolina, eastern Tennessee |
| 8 | Georgia and Alabama |
| 9 | Florida |
| 10 | Western Pennsylvania to Harrisburg, West Virginia |
| 11 | Ohio north of Route 40 |
| 12 | Ohio south of Route 40, Kentucky |
| 13 | Indiana except northwestern counties |
| 14 | Michigan and Toledo, Ohio |
| 15 | Illinios, north of Route 36 and Lake, Porter and LaPorte counties of Indiana |

| No. | Regions |
|---|---|
| 16 | Wisconsin and northwestern Michigan (area northwest of Lake Michigan) |
| 17 | Minnesota, may include North and South Dakota and all or part of Iowa and Nebraska |
| 18 | Eastern Missouri, southern Illinois |
| 19 | Western Missouri, Kansas |
| 20 | Louisiana, Mississippi, Arkansas, western Tennessee |
| 21 | Texas and Oklahoma |
| 22 | Colorado, Utah, may include Montana, Idaho, Wyoming |
| 23 | California, Bakersfield and south, Arizona, southern Nevada, and New Mexico |
| 24 | California north of Bakersfield, part of Nevada |
| 25 | Washington and Oregon |
| 26 | Alaska |
| 27 | Hawaii and Guam |
| 28 | Puerto Rico and the Caribbean |
| 29 | Eastern Canada |
| 30 | Western Canada |

*Source: Manufacturers' Agents National Association*

# Trade Shows and Conventions

## Convention Dates and Cities

*American Booksellers Association Convention and Trade Exchange*
American Booksellers Association 1995 Chicago 6/3 to 6/6
(914) 591-2665

*American Chemical Society National Expo*
American Chemical Society 1995 Anaheim 4/2 to 4/6
(202) 872-4485 Chicago 8/20 to 8/24

*American Financial Services Association Expo*
American Financial Services Association 1995 New Orleans 5/17 to 5/20
(202) 296-5544

*American Hospital Association*
American Hospital Association 1995 San Francisco 8/21 to 8/23
(312) 280-6711

*American International Toy Fair*
Toy Manufacturers of America 1995 New York 2/17 to 2/20
(212) 675-1141

*Amusement and Music Operators Association*
Smith, Bucklin and Associates 1995 New Orleans 9/21 to 9/23
(312) 644-6610

*Architectural Woodwork Institute Convention and Trade Show*
Architectural Woodwork Institute 1995 New Orleans September
(703) 222-1100

*ASCD Annual Conference and Exhibit Show*
Assn. for Supervision and Curriculum Development 1995 San Francisco 3/25 to 3/28
(703) 549-9110

*Associated General Contractors of America*
Associated General Contractors of America 1995 San Diego 3/5 to 3/10
(202) 393-2040

*Association of Broadcasters Convention*
National Association of Broadcasters 1995 Las Vegas 4/10 to 4/13
(202) 429-5300

*ASTA's World Travel Congress*
American Society of Travel Agents 1995 Philadelphia 11/5 to 11/10
(703) 739-2782

*The Builders Show*
National Association of Home Builders 1995 Houston 1/27 to 1/30
(202) 822-0200

*Building Owners and Managers Association Convention*
Building Owners & Managers Association (BOMA) 1995 Denver 6/25 to 6/28
(202) 408-2662

*Consumer Electronics Show*
Electronic Industries Association 1995 Las Vegas 1/6 to 1/9
(202) 457- 4900 Philadelphiaa Early May

*Converting Machinery and Materials Conference & Expo*
Blenheim Group 1995 Chicago 8/28 to 8/30
(201) 346-1400

*Trade Shows and Conventions (cont'd)*

*COMDEX*

| | | | | |
|---|---|---|---|---|
| The Interface Group (617) 449-6600 | 1995 | Atlanta Las Vegas | 4/24 to 4/27 11/13 to 11/17 |

*Frankfurt Book Fair*

| | | | |
|---|---|---|---|
| Ausstellungs-und Messe-GmbH (069) 2102-219 | 1995 | Frankfurt | 10/11 to 10/16 |

*Insurance Accounting and Systems Association Conference*

| | | | |
|---|---|---|---|
| Insurance Accounting & Systems Association (919) 489-0991 | 1995 | New Orleans | 6/4 to 6/7 |

*International Craft Expo*

| | | | |
|---|---|---|---|
| Offinger Management (614) 452-4541 | 1995 | Chicago | 7/21 to 7/24 |

*International Fashion Boutique Show*

| | | | |
|---|---|---|---|
| The Larkin Group (617) 964-5100 | 1995 | New York | 1/7 to 1/10 3/18 to 3/21 6/3 to 6/6 8/26 to 8/29 10/14 to 10/17 |

*International Housewares Show*

| | | | |
|---|---|---|---|
| National Housewares Manufacturers Association (708) 292-4200 | 1995 | Chicago | 1/15 to 1/18 |

*International Kids Fashion Show*

| | | | |
|---|---|---|---|
| The Larkin Group (212) 594-8556 | 1995 | New York | 1/15 to 1/17 3/19 to 3/22 8/6 to 8/9 10/15 to 10/18 |

*Internat'l Woodworking, Machinery and Furniture Supply Fair*

| | | | |
|---|---|---|---|
| Cahners Expo Group (708) 299-9311 | 1995 | Atlanta | 8/22 to 8/25 |

*The Licensing Show*

| | | | |
|---|---|---|---|
| International Licensing Industry Merchandising Association (212) 244-1944 | 1995 | New York | 6/20 to 6/22 |

*Medical Group Management Association Conference*

| | | | |
|---|---|---|---|
| Medical Group Management Association (303) 799-1111 | 1995 | New Orleans | 10/8 to 10/11 |

*Nat'l Cable Television Association Annual Convention*

| | | | |
|---|---|---|---|
| Dobson & Associates (202) 463-7905 | 1995 | Dallas | 5/7 to 5/10 |

*Nat'l Healthcare and American Hospital Association Convention*

| | | | |
|---|---|---|---|
| American Healthcare Association & American Hospital Association (202) 842-4444 | 1995 | Honolulu | 8/21 to 8/26 |

*National Association of Realtors Annual Conference*

| | | | |
|---|---|---|---|
| National Association of Realtors (312) 329-8200 | 1995 | Atlanta | 11/9 to 11/14 |

*National Business Aircraft Association Meeting and Convention*

| | | | |
|---|---|---|---|
| National Business Aircraft Association (202) 783-9000 | 1995 | Las Vegas | 9/27 to 9/29 |

*National Education Association*

| | | | |
|---|---|---|---|
| CEPI (813) 530-0405 | 1995 | Minneapolis | 6/30 to 7/2 |

*Trade Shows and Conventions (cont'd)*

*Nat'l Environmental Health Association Educational Conference*
National Environmental Health Association          1995          Denver          6/24 to 6/28
(303) 756-9090

*National Food Distributors Associaation Convention*
Smith Buklin & Associates          1995          Orlando          1/20 to 1/22
(312) 644-6610                                            New Orleans          7/22 to 7/21

*National Hardware Show*
Association of Expositions and Services          1995          Chicago          8/13 to 8/16
(203) 325-5099

*National Home Center Show*
Marvin Park & Association          1995          Dallas          3/12 to 3/14
(708) 823-2151

*National Home Health Care Expositions*
SEMCO Productions          1995          Atlanta          11/15 to 11/18
(404) 998-9800

*National Merchandise Show*
Miller Freeman          1995          New York          9/9 to 9/12
(212) 869-1300

*Nat'l Office Products Association Convention and Exhibit*
National Office Products Association          1995          Atlanta          8/23 to 8/26
(703) 549-9040

*National Restaurant, Hotel/Motel Show*
National Restaurant Association          1995          Chicago          5/20 to 5/24
(312) 853-2525

*National Stationery Show*
George Little Management          1995          New York          5/20 to 5/23
(914) 421-3200

*NATPE*
National Association of TV Programming Executives          1995          Las Vegas          1/23 to 1/26
(310) 453-4440

*New Music Seminar*
New Music Seminar          1995          New York          7/18 to 7/22
(212) 473-4343

*New York International Gift Fair*
George Little Management          1995          New York          1/22 to 1/26
(914) 421-3200

*PACK Expo*
Packaging Machinery Manufacturing Institute          1995          Las Vegas          10/9 to 10/12
(202) 347-3838

*PC Expo in New York*
Blenheim Group          1995          New York          6/20 to 6/22
(201) 346-1400                                            Chicago          10/17 to 10/19

*Premium and Incentive Show*
Miller Freeman          1995          New York          5/2 to 5/4
(212) 869-1300

*SUPERCOMM*
E.J. Krause & Associates          1995          Anaheim          3/20 to 3/23
(301) 986-7800

*Trade Shows and Conventions (cont'd)*

*The Super Show*
        The Super Show                                1995        Atlanta          2/4 to 2/6
        (305) 893-8771

*Variety Merchandise Show*
        Miller Freeman                            1995        New York       2/18 to 2/21
        (212) 869-1300

## Recommended Resource

*1994-95 Trade Show & Convention Guide*
Amusement Business, $85
(615) 321-4250

# Best Places to Start a Business

CHOOSING A LOCATION for a new business is critical to its success. *Entrepreneur* magazine conducted a survey to determine the ideal locations for new businesses. Their results were determined based on the availability of an educated labor pool, labor costs, growth in personal income and real estate costs. The following 20 cities in 4 regional areas were ranked as ideal locations for the average new business.

## Top 20 Cities (By Region)

| | 1992 Pop. | Estimated 1997 Pop. | % with College Degree | Average Clerical Salary | % Change in Income 1980-93 | Average Office Real Estate Cost (Per Square Foot) |
|---|---|---|---|---|---|---|
| Northeast | | | | | | |
| New Haven, CT | 533,235 | 823,000 | 27.4 | 19,717 | 41.64 | 14.00 |
| Worcester, MA | 441,683 | 751,000 | 23.4 | 18,705 | 35.29 | 15.00 |
| Hartford, CT | 773,934 | 1,131,000 | 28.1 | 18,956 | 42.91 | 17.75 |
| Middlesex, NJ | 1,046,058 | 1,055,000 | 30.2 | 20,866 | 63.32 | 17.25 |
| Boston, MA | 2,857,064 | 3,865,000 | 33.1 | 21,013 | 38.27 | 19.75 |
| South | | | | | | |
| Ft. Worth, TX | 1,407,445 | 1,404,000 | 22.6 | 16,357 | 52.79 | 13.50 |
| Columbia, SC | 466,673 | 497,000 | 25.3 | 16,784 | 50.22 | 13.75 |
| Austin, TX | 832,909 | 911,000 | 32.2 | 17,678 | 77.37 | 15.00 |
| Raleigh-Durham, NC | 772,978 | 841,000 | 34.8 | 17,813 | 77.38 | 17.25 |
| Dallas, TX | 2,679,134 | 2,710,000 | 27.6 | 17,280 | 47.30 | 14.00 |
| Midwest | | | | | | |
| Wichita, KS | 495,450 | 481,000 | 21.5 | 16,097 | 22.19 | 14.50 |
| Omaha, NE | 632,509 | 671,000 | 22.8 | 17,023 | 29.39 | 17.57 |
| Indianapolis, IN | 1,283,984 | 1,397,000 | 21.1 | 16,898 | 27.93 | 17.50 |
| Kansas City, MO | 1,599,338 | 1,693,000 | 23.4 | 17,727 | 30.19 | 18.38 |
| Minneapolis, MN | 2,546,689 | 2,746,000 | 27.1 | 18,434 | 38.81 | 21.55 |
| West | | | | | | |
| Albuquerque, NM | 496,251 | 548,000 | 26.7 | 17,195 | 44.34 | 14.25 |
| Phoenix, AZ | 2,224,211 | 2,416,000 | 22.1 | 17,519 | 65.53 | 16.14 |
| Tucson, AZ | 688,139 | 769,000 | 23.3 | 18,547 | 49.91 | 17.50 |
| San Diego, CA | 2,616,354 | 2,772,000 | 25.3 | 19,779 | 56.00 | 17.70 |
| Salt Lake City, UT | 1,115,354 | 1,233,000 | 22.9 | 16,488 | 34.35 | 15.00 |

*Source: Entrepreneur Magazine, October, 1993*

# Top Franchises

FRANCHISING IS A METHOD of distributing products or services as a result of an agreement between two parties. The franchisor is the parent company whose owner desires to expand his or her operations without maintaining additional stores. The franchisee, in return for an initial fee or a continuing royalty payment based on sales, assumes the right to operate the franchise, maintaining the products, services and quality of the original operation.

The franchisor benefits from the ability to more rapidly expand his or her operations, while the franchisee enters the retail world, bolstered by the established procedures, training, advice, and guidance of the parent company. The franchisor generally offers limited or expanded plan packages to the franchisee which may include support services such as: site selection, guidelines for decor and design, management training and consulting, employee training, advertising and merchandising support, and financial assistance.

The types of franchised businesses range from auto and truck dealerships to soft drink bottlers, with a wide variety of establishments in between. While statistics can direct the entrepreneur to businesses displaying growth and financial opportunity, the International Franchise Association emphasizes that it is critical to consider financial growth and analyze the track record of any prospective franchisor. A pattern of rapid growth may indicate a lack of sound support systems, whereas a long, steady growth pattern suggests a solid foundation in business franchising

According to IFA reports, the number of franchises grew from 542,496 in 1991 to 558,125 in 1992. Other experts report that the largest (number of outlets) franchise chains are as follows:

| Rank | Franchise Chains | Number of Outlets |
|------|------------------|-------------------|
| 1 | McDonald's | 12,643 |
| 2 | 7-Eleven Convenience Stores | 12,469 |
| 3 | H&R Block | 9,228 |
| 4 | KFC Corp. | 8,187 |
| 5 | Radio Shack | 7,000 |
| 6 | Subway | 6,862 |
| 7 | Burger King | 6,490 |
| 8 | Century 21 Real Estate | 6,150 |
| 9 | Pizza Hut | 5,745 |
| 10 | Dairy Queen | 5,347 |
| 11 | Domino's | 5,154 |
| 12 | Jazzercise | 4,782 |
| 13 | Little Caesars | 4,117 |
| 14 | ServiceMaster | 4,076 |
| 15 | Snap-On Tools | 4,000 |

When contemplating a new business, the entrepreneur's first concern is how much money it will require and how to obtain that money. Sources for start-up capital include:

- Bank loans;

- Life insurance policies that may allow borrowing on the cash value of the policy while charging a lower interest rate than banks;

- Equipment suppliers who will allow a new business to pay for equipment on an installment plan or offer similar short-term credit;

- Small Business Administration (see below for a description of this service);

- Private investors who are willing to commit money to a business in return for a percentage of the business's profits during a predetermined time period or during the life of the business. Limited partnerships are one form of private investing in which the partners are investors only and do not contribute to the management of the business;

- SBICs—Small Business Investment Companies that are licensed by the Small Business Administration to provide venture capital to small businesses. Venture capitalists are frequently prepared to wait for a considerable length of time for profits to begin and will charge a rate of 15 percent and higher on their investment. These investors, however, will require a higher percentage of ownership in the new company, as much as 51 percent. In addition to financing, they often provide marketing and product ideas and management consultation.

The Federal Trade Commission offers a free packet of information for individuals interested in franchises. It contains information regarding the pros and cons of franchising, a detailed explanation of the information required by the franchisor in fulfillment of the disclosure rule. Call (202) 326-3142.

## Recommended Resources

*Entrepreneur Magazine*
Entrepreneur Group
2329 Morse Ave.
Irvine, CA 92714
(714) 261-2325
Publishes an issue on franchises in January of each year.

*Franchise Opportunities Guide 1993 Edition*
International Franchise Association
1350 New York Ave., NW, Suite 900
Washington, DC 20005
(202) 628-8000

*Top Franchises (cont'd)*

## Success Magazine's Top 10 Franchises

| Rank | Franchise | Product/Service | No. of Locations |
|------|-----------|-----------------|------------------|
| 1 | Sonic Drive-Ins | Retail food | 1,191 |
| 2 | Coldwell Banker | Real estate | 2,136 |
| 3 | CleanNet USA | Maintenance, cleaning, sanitation | 887 |
| 4 | Travel Network | Travel | 310 |
| 5 | Merry Maids | Maid services, home cleaning | 703 |
| 6 | Interim Services | Employment, personnel | 657 |
| 7 | The Krystal Co. | Retail food | 259 |
| 8 | Decorating Den | Retail nonfood products, services | 1,247 |
| 9 | Voice-Tel Voice Messaging Network | Voice messaging | 120 |
| 10 | Mail Boxes Etc. | Business, financial services | 2,005 |

*Source: Success Magazine, November, 1993*

*Entrepreneur* Magazine's 15th Annual Franchise 500 issue (January, 1994) was devoted exclusively to the top franchises in the United States. These companies were ranked using a formula which included the following objective criteria: length of time in business, number of years franchising, number of franchised units and company-owned operating units, start-up costs, growth rate, percentage of terminations, and financial stability of the company.

## Entrepreneur Magazine's Top 50 Franchises

| Rank | Company | Rank | Company |
|------|---------|------|---------|
| 1 | Subway | 26 | Century 21 Real Estate |
| 2 | McDonald's | 27 | Miracle Ear |
| 3 | Burger King | 28 | Electronic Realty Associates |
| 4 | 7-Eleven | 29 | Super 8 Motels |
| 5 | Mail Boxes Etc. | 30 | Decorating Den |
| 6 | Little Caesars Pizza | 31 | Blimpie |
| 7 | Chem-Dry Carpet Drapery & Upholstery | 32 | Uniglobe Travel |
| 8 | Jani-King | 33 | The Medicine Shoppe |
| 9 | Snap-On Tools | 34 | Sonic Drive-In Restuarants |
| 10 | Coverall North America | 35 | Matco Tools |
| 11 | Hardee's | 36 | Fantastic Sam's |
| 12 | Re/Max Int'l | 37 | Play It Again sports |
| 13 | ServiceMaster | 38 | CleanNet USA |
| 14 | Jazzercise Inc. | 39 | ABC Seamless |
| 15 | Midas Int'l | 40 | Jackson Hewitt Tax Service |
| 16 | Dairy Queen | 41 | Merry Maids |
| 17 | Baskin-Robbins | 42 | Thrifty Rent-A-Car |
| 18 | Choice Hotels Int'l | 43 | Denny's |
| 19 | KFC | 44 | O.P.E.N. Cleaning Systems |
| 20 | Arby's | 45 | Meineke Discount Mufflers |
| 21 | Coldwell Banker Residential Affiliates | 46 | Pearle Vision |
| 22 | GNC Franchising | 47 | Tower Cleaning Systems |
| 23 | Holiday Inn Worldwide | 48 | Sir Speedy Printing |
| 24 | Budget Rent-A-Car | 49 | Servpro |
| 25 | Dunkin' Donuts | 50 | Ben Franklin Stores |

*Source: Entrepreneur Magazine, January, 1994*

*Top Franchises (cont'd)*

As the accompanying tables illustrate, franchising is becoming an increasingly popular form of business in the United States. The International Franchise Association (IFA), the industry regulator, recently noted that over 30% of total retail sales in the U.S. were made by retail franchise businesses.

## Domestic and International Franchising Summary: 1980 to 1991

| Item | 1983 | 1984 | 1985 | 1986 | 1987 | 1988 | 1989 | 1990 | 1991 |
|---|---|---|---|---|---|---|---|---|---|
| **DOMESTIC** | | | | | | | | | |
| No. of franchises est. (thousands) | 442 | 444 | 455 | 462 | 479 | 481 | 493 | 521 | 542 |
| Company-owned (thousands) | 86 | 87 | 86 | 88 | 89 | 94 | 95 | 97 | 100 |
| Franchisee-owned (thousands) | 355 | 357 | 369 | 374 | 390 | 387 | 398 | 424 | 442 |
| Sales of prod. & svcs. ($ billions) | 423 | 492 | 543 | 569 | 599 | 648 | 678 | 714 | 758 |
| Company-owned ($ billions) | 59 | 64 | 68 | 85 | 90 | 98 | 107 | 117 | 127 |
| Franchisee-owned ($ billions) | 364 | 428 | 475 | 484 | 509 | 550 | 570 | 597 | 631 |
| Avg. sales per est. ($ thousands) | 958 | 1,108 | 1,193 | 1,231 | 1,251 | 1,348 | 1,376 | 1,369 | 1,399 |
| Employment (thousands) | 5,165 | 5,671 | 6,283 | 6,501 | NA | NA | NA | NA | NA |
| **INTERNATIONAL** | | | | | | | | | |
| U.S.-operated foreign outlets | 305 | 328 | 342 | 354 | NA | 374 | NA | NA | NA |
| Foreign outlets (thousands) | 26 | 27 | 30 | 32 | NA | 35 | NA | NA | NA |

*Source: 1993 Statistical Abstract, Table No. 1313*

## Domestic Franchising by Number of Establishments (thousands): 1980 to 1991

| Franchised Businesses | 1980 | 1985 | 1987 | 1988 | 1989 | 1990 | 1991 |
|---|---|---|---|---|---|---|---|
| TOTAL FRANCHISING | 442.4 | 455.2 | 479.1 | 480.8 | 492.5 | 521.2 | 542.5 |
| Auto and truck dealers | 29.4 | 27.5 | 27.6 | 27.8 | 26.9 | 26.8 | 26.5 |
| Restaurants (all types) | 60.0 | 73.9 | 83.3 | 90.3 | 92.0 | 99.3 | 103.3 |
| Gasoline service stations | 158.5 | 124.6 | 115.9 | 113.2 | 111.5 | 107.5 | 107.0 |
| Retailing (non-food) | 35.2 | 45.1 | 47.9 | 46.2 | 50.0 | 54.4 | 57.0 |
| Auto, truck rental services | 7.3 | 11.2 | 10.0 | 9.5 | 9.8 | 10.7 | 11.1 |
| Automotive products & services | 40.2 | 36.5 | 39.3 | 34.7 | 36.2 | 39.2 | 42.2 |
| Business aids & services | | | | | | | |
| Employment services | 4.4 | 4.8 | 6.1 | 6.5 | 6.6 | 7.5 | 8.3 |
| Tax preparation services | 9.2 | 8.1 | 8.5 | 8.3 | 8.2 | 8.3 | 8.5 |
| Accounting, credit, collection | 2.4 | 2.1 | 2.0 | 1.7 | 1.7 | 1.8 | 1.9 |
| Real estate | 17.3 | 13.9 | 15.2 | 15.3 | 15.8 | 16.4 | 18.2 |
| Printing & copying | 2.8 | 4.5 | 5.6 | 5.9 | 6.3 | 6.8 | 7.4 |
| Other business aids | 4.8 | 16.4 | 19.4 | 17.9 | 19.5 | 23.6 | 25.3 |
| Construction, home improvement, maint. | 14.3 | 17.5 | 21.7 | 22.0 | 24.1 | 27.4 | 30.6 |
| Convenience stores | 15.6 | 15.1 | 16.3 | 17.2 | 17.6 | 17.2 | 17.3 |
| Educational products & services | 3.2 | 8.2 | 9.6 | 11.6 | 11.1 | 12.5 | 13.9 |
| Equipment rental services | 2.2 | 2.5 | 2.8 | 3.0 | 2.6 | 2.7 | 2.9 |
| Food retailing | 15.5 | 18.7 | 20.5 | 21.6 | 21.1 | 24.5 | 25.4 |
| Hotels & motels | 6.4 | 7.5 | 9.3 | 9.3 | 10.1 | 11.0 | 11.4 |
| Laundry, dry cleaning services | 3.4 | 2.3 | 2.2 | 2.3 | 3.0 | 3.2 | 3.5 |
| Recreation, entertainment, travel | 4.6 | 7.8 | 8.2 | 8.8 | 9.8 | 10.9 | 11.6 |
| Soft drink bottlers | 1.9 | 1.4 | 1.1 | 0.9 | 0.8 | 0.8 | 0.8 |
| Miscellaneous | 3.6 | 5.5 | 6.8 | 6.9 | 7.6 | 8.4 | 8.6 |

*Source: 1993 Statistical Abstract, Table No. 1314*

*Top Franchises (cont'd)*

## Domestic Franchising by Sales ($ billions): 1980 to 1991

| Franchised Businesses | 1980 | 1985 | 1987 | 1988 | 1989 | 1990 | 1991 |
|---|---|---|---|---|---|---|---|
| TOTAL FRANCHISING SALES | 336.2 | 543.0 | 599.4 | 648.1 | 677.9 | 713.8 | 757.8 |
| Auto and truck dealers | 143.9 | 282.6 | 319.7 | 345.1 | 351.0 | 345.9 | 354.5 |
| Restaurants (all types) | 27.9 | 47.7 | 56.8 | 64.3 | 70.1 | 77.9 | 85.5 |
| Gasoline service stations | 94.5 | 100.8 | 89.2 | 101.9 | 109.4 | 128.6 | 143.2 |
| Retailing (non-food) | 10.5 | 20.6 | 25.4 | 23.3 | 26.7 | 29.3 | 31.4 |
| Auto, truck rental services | 3.1 | 5.7 | 6.5 | 6.6 | 6.9 | 7.5 | 8.0 |
| Automotive products & services | 7.1 | 10.7 | 12.3 | 11.4 | 12.5 | 13.9 | 15.5 |
| Business aids & services | 6.7 | 12.0 | 14.7 | 15.7 | 16.9 | 18.6 | 20.8 |
| Employment services | 1.6 | 2.7 | 3.7 | 4.7 | 5.0 | 5.7 | 6.4 |
| Tax preparation services | 0.3 | 0.4 | 0.5 | 0.6 | 0.7 | 0.7 | 0.7 |
| Accounting, credit, collection | 0.1 | 0.2 | 0.2 | 0.2 | 0.2 | 0.2 | 0.2 |
| Real estate | 3.6 | 4.6 | 5.6 | 5.9 | 6.2 | 6.8 | 7.7 |
| Printing & copying | 0.4 | 0.9 | 1.2 | 1.5 | 1.6 | 1.8 | 2.0 |
| Other business aids | 0.8 | 3.1 | 3.5 | 3.0 | 3.4 | 3.5 | 3.8 |
| Construction, home improvement, maint. | 1.5 | 4.1 | 5.2 | 5.3 | 5.8 | 6.5 | 7.1 |
| Convenience stores | 7.8 | 10.8 | 12.3 | 13.9 | 14.3 | 14.3 | 15.0 |
| Educational products & services | 0.3 | 0.8 | 1.0 | 1.7 | 1.7 | 2.0 | 2.3 |
| Equipment rental services | 0.4 | 0.7 | 0.7 | 0.7 | 0.7 | 0.7 | 0.8 |
| Food retailing | 7.4 | 10.1 | 11.1 | 10.2 | 10.0 | 11.7 | 12.2 |
| Hotels & motels | 9.5 | 14.8 | 17.7 | 19.7 | 21.6 | 23.8 | 26.0 |
| Laundry, dry cleaning services | 0.3 | 0.3 | 0.3 | 0.3 | 0.4 | 0.4 | 0.5 |
| Recreation, entertainment, travel | 0.5 | 2.3 | 4.0 | 3.5 | 3.5 | 4.2 | 4.8 |
| Soft drink bottlers | 14.4 | 18.3 | 20.9 | 22.7 | 24.6 | 26.2 | 28.0 |
| Miscellaneous | 0.4 | 0.9 | 1.5 | 1.7 | 2.0 | 2.3 | 2.6 |

*Source: 1993 Statistical Abstract, Table No. 1314*

# Franchise Law

FRANCHISES ARE BECOMING INCREASINGLY popular with the aspiring small business owner. To protect the interests of the inexperienced entrepreneur, the Federal Trade Commission (FTC) requires every franchisor to provide an extensive disclosure document to prospective franchisees prior to making any purchases. This statement must contain information about the following:

- Required fees;

- Basic investment;

- Bankruptcy;

- Litigation history of the company;

- Expected term of the franchise;

- Audited financial statement of the franchisor including bankruptcy history;

- Earnings claims;

- List of directors, trustees or partners, and principal officers of the franchisor; history of the franchisor, its directors and key executives;

- Description of the franchise requirements, its directors and key executives and their business experience, and ongoing continuing expenses required of the franchisee to be paid to the franchisor;

- A list of individuals who are part of the franchisor or its affiliates and with whom the franchisee is required to do business, including real estate, services, equipment required to be purchased, and the names of those with whom these agreements must be made;

- Celebrity involvement in the franchise and a list of royalties and/or commissions paid to such third party individuals by the franchisee, and statistical information about the rate of termination;

- Obligations of franchisee to purchase or lease from approved suppliers;

- Obligations of the franchisor to the franchisee, namely, types of assistance and charges associated with these services;

*Franchise Law (cont'd)*

- Conditions of renewal, extension, termination of franchise;

- The number, names, addresses, and phone numbers of franchisees;

- A copy of all agreements to be signed before the purchase of the franchise.

On the federal level, the FTC allows the franchisors to distribute this information through a Uniform Franchise Offering Circular (UFOC). Fourteen individual states (California, Hawaii, Illinois, Indiana, Maryland, Michigan, Minnesota, New York, North Dakota, Rhode Island, South Dakota, Virginia, Washington, and Wisconsin) have disclosure laws similar to those required by the FTC. Write to the franchise division of the department of commerce of any of the state offices to request copies of the disclosure agreements of a specific company. While the forms vary from state to state, the essence of the reporting is the same. New York will send its report anywhere in the country:

New York State
Bureau of Investor and Protection Securities
120 Broadway
New York, NY 10271
(212) 416-8236

The next page provides a sample form for request of disclosure documents regarding any franchisor. Simply fill in the name of the franchise, complete the form and send the request to the above address.

The franchisee must, in turn, sign a franchise agreement. There should be clear, concise statements regarding the following items:

- Franchise fee;

- Advertising fees;

- Royalty fees;

- Hidden costs such as equipment and supplies;

- Quotas;

- Franchise term;

- Assignment or permission to transfer franchise agreement to another individual;

- Termination rights of franchisor and franchisee;

- Competition.

The International Franchise Association (IFA) is the industry's regulatory agency. Members must maintain a satisfactory financial condition and are expected to comply with franchise law. The association continually updates its membership regarding changes in franchise law as well as methods of improving cooperative advertising, public relations, marketing, and field operations.

The IFA recommends that any individual considering a franchise, should carefully discuss the disclosure materials, and the history and reputation of both the company and its officers, with both an accountant and an attorney. The organization also strongly suggests that the franchisee discuss the franchise with a number of other franchisees of the target organization.

## Contact Option

International Franchise Association
1350 New York Ave. NW, Suite 900
Washington, DC 20005
(202) 628-8000

## Recommended Resources

*The Legal Guide for Starting and Running a Small Business*
by Fred S. Steingold
Nolo Press, $22.95
(800) 992-6656 or (510) 549-1976

*Nation's Business*
Chamber of Commerce of the United States
$22/12 issues
(202) 463-5650
This outstanding publication includes four annual inserts specifically devoted to franchise trends, financing, seminars and expos, conversion, growth forecasts, and other related topics.

## Franchise Disclosure

Many states require franchises doing business within the state to file complete background information, including financial facts about their companies. A potential investor should request disclosure of such information from the state office of the Bureau of Investor Protection. A sample freedom of information request form for New York state can be found on the following page.

---

## The Top Reference Sources

*Franchise Opportunities Guide*
International Franchise Association, $15
(202) 628-8000

This reference provides a comprehensive listing of more than 2,000 franchises and contains answers to the most frequently asked questions about franchising. Special features include sources for legal advice and franchise consultants, and information on how to finance your franchise.

*Franchise Law (cont'd)*

# FREEDOM OF INFORMATION REQUEST

I HEREBY APPLY TO INSPECT THE FOLLOWING RECORD:

 

| NAME | REPRESENTING |
|------|-------------|
| MAILING ADDRESS | TELEPHONE NUMBER |
| SIGNATURE | DATE |

### FOR AGENCY USE ONLY

APPROVED _____

DENIED (for reason(s) checked below)
_____ Confidential disclosure
_____ Unwarranted invasion of personal privacy
_____ Record of which this agency is legal custodian cannot be found
_____ Record is not maintained by this agency
_____ Exempted by statute other than the Freedom of Information Act
_____ Request has been referred to department which has custody or control of original record
_____ Part of investigatory files
_____ Other (specify) _____

| SIGNATURE | TITLE | DATE |
|-----------|-------|------|

NOTE: YOU HAVE THE RIGHT TO APPEAL A DENIAL OF THIS APPLICATION TO HEAD OF THIS AGENCY

| NAME | BUSINESS ADDRESS |
|------|-----------------|

WHO MUST FULLY EXPLAIN HIS REASONS FOR WHICH DENIAL IN WRITING WITHIN SEVEN WORKING DAYS OF RECEIPT OF AN APPEAL.

I HEREBY APPEAL:

| SIGNATURE | DATE |
|-----------|------|

# OFFICE MANAGEMENT

# Auto Leasing

**Number of Cars Leased for Business Use\* (millions)**

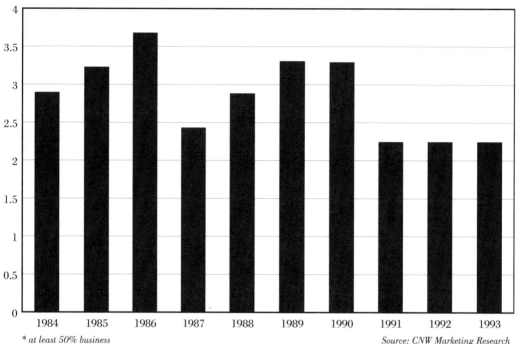

\* at least 50% business          Source: CNW Marketing Research

---

## The Top Reference Sources

*Consumer Reports Travel Letter*
Consumers Union, $37/year
(800) 272-0722

The *Travel Letter* is a monthly newsletter that helps track down the best travel values. It presents strategies for finding the best airfares, hotel rates, and car rental rates. Features include warnings about frauds and scams, ways to avoid hassles, and other timely guidance for travelers.

Comsumer Reports Books, a division of Consumers Union, publishes the *Travel Buying Guide*, an annual book that provides valuable information and evaluation of airfares, hotels, car rentals, and other items of interest to the traveler. It is available for $8.99.

# Auto Theft and Damage

## Motor Vehicle Registrations and Thefts, 1983–1992

| Year | Motor Vehicle Registrations | Estimated Thefts | Vehicles Stolen: Registered | Thefts per 100,000 Registrations |
|------|------------------------------|-------------------|-------------------------------|-----------------------------------|
| 1983 | 167,718,000 | 1,007,900 | 1:166 | 601 |
| 1984 | 169,446,281 | 1,032,200 | 1:164 | 609 |
| 1985 | 175,709,000 | 1,102,900 | 1:159 | 628 |
| 1986 | 181,890,000 | 1,224,100 | 1:149 | 673 |
| 1987 | 186,137,000 | 1,288,700 | 1:144 | 692 |
| 1988 | 183,930,000 | 1,432,900 | 1:128 | 779 |
| 1989 | 188,981,016 | 1,564,800 | 1:121 | 828 |
| 1990 | 194,582,000 | 1,661,700 | 1:117 | 853 |
| 1991 | 194,897,000 | 1,661,700 | 1:117 | 853 |
| 1992 | 193,775,000 | 1,610,800 | 1:120 | 831 |

*Source: Federal Bureau of Investigation*

## Average Loss Payment per Insured Vehicle Year*

*Best*

| Model | Size | Index |
|-------|------|-------|
| Subaru Loyale station wagon | Small | 10 |
| Ford Escort station wagon | Small | 13 |
| Saturn SL | Midsize | 13 |
| Volvo 240 station wagon | Midsize | 15 |
| Buick Park Avenue | Large | 17 |

*Worst*

| Model | Size | Index |
|-------|------|-------|
| Mercedes SL Series | Small | 1,800 |
| Volkswagen Cabriolet | Small | 1,192 |
| Volkswagen Golf/GTI | Small | 873 |
| Chevrolet Corvette convertible | Small | 763 |
| Ford Mustang convertible | Midsize | 747 |

## Claim Frequency*

*Best*

| Model | Size | Index |
|-------|------|-------|
| Mercury Sable station wagon | Midsize | 25 |
| Mercury Sable 4-door | Midsize | 27 |
| Chevrolet Cavalier station wagon | Midsize | 27 |
| Mazda MPV Van 4WD | Large | 28 |
| Oldsmobile Toronado | Midsize | 29 |

*Worst*

| Model | Size | Index |
|-------|------|-------|
| Volkswagen Golf/GTI | Small | 868 |
| Volkswagen Cabriolet | Small | 529 |
| Volkswagen Jetta 4-door | Small | 517 |
| Volkswagen Golf 4-door | Small | 483 |
| Cadillac DeVille 2-door | Large | 388 |

## Average Loss Payment per Claim*

*Best*

| Model | Size | Index |
|-------|------|-------|
| Buick LeSabre | Large | 22 |
| Mercury Tracer station wagon | Small | 23 |
| Volvo 240 station wagon | Midsize | 24 |
| Cadillac DeVille 4-door | Large | 26 |
| Subaru Loyale station wagon | Small | 26 |

*Worst*

| Model | Size | Index |
|-------|------|-------|
| Mercedes SL Series | Small | 1,108 |
| Chevrolet Corvette convertible | Small | 647 |
| BMW 525i/535i | Midsize | 555 |
| Infiniti Q45 | Large | 506 |
| Lincoln Mark VII | Midsize | 500 |

\* For 1990-92 passenger cars. Index numbers are relative; 100 represents the average for all passenger cars.

*Source: Highway Loss Data Institute*

 **FAX** **Fleet Cars.** Request #429. See p. xi for instructions.
Explanation of fleet cars and contact numbers.

# Electronic Surveillance

A FEW STORES SPECIALIZE in state-of-the-art electronic surveillance and security equipment. For prices that can run into the thousands, it is possible to purchase everything from hidden camera and alarm systems to anti-bugging and wiretapping equipment, to telephone and fax scramblers, weapons detectors, and surveillance vehicles. Briefcases equipped with covert microphones and miniature cameras and other specialized executive accessories are also sold.

## Contact Options

*Electronic Surveillance Sources:*

The Spy Store
164 Christopher St.
New York, NY 10014
(212) 366-6466

Communication Control Systems of New York
675 Third Ave.
New York, NY 10001
(212) 268-4779

Eavesdropping Detection Equipment
2480 Niagra Falls Blvd.
Tonawanda, NY 14150
(716) 691-3476

Sheffield Electronics
P.O. Box 377785
Chicago, IL 60637
(312) 643-4928

# Security and Bodyguards

## Contact Options

*National Companies Providing Corporate Security:*

Advance Security
2964 Peachtree Rd., Suite 200
Atlanta, GA 30305
(800) 241-0267

Burn's International Security Services
2 Campus Dr.
Parsippany, NJ 07054
(201) 397-2000

Guardsmark
22 S. Second St.
Memphis, TN 38103
(901) 522-6000

Orion Protective Services
1410 Gunston Rd.
Bel Air, MD 21015
(410) 515-7353

Pinkerton Security and Investigation Services
15910 Ventura Blvd., Suite 900
Encino, CA 91436
(818) 380-8800

## Recommended Resources

The American Society for Industrial Security
1655 N. Fort Myer Dr., Suite 1200
Arlington, VA 22209
(703) 522-5800

*The Security Industry Buyer's Guide 1995*
The American Society for Industrial Security and
Phillips Publishing, $169
(800) 777-5006 or (301) 424-3338
    Lists all products and services available in the security industry alphabetically and by product and location.

National Council of Investigation and Security Services
P.O. Box 449
Severna Park, MD 21146
(800) 445-8408
    Provides the names, addresses, and telephone numbers of companies providing security services in locations across the country.

    Also check the Yellow Pages under Guard and Patrol Services.

# Alarm Systems

## Largest Security Installation Companies Based on Revenue, 1992

| Firm | Location | 1992 Revenue ($ millions) | No. of Accounts |
|------|----------|---------------------------|-----------------|
| ADT Security Systems | Parsippany, NJ | 600.0 | 580,000 |
| Wells Fargo Alarm Services | King of Prussia, PA | 203.5 | 115,000 |
| Honeywell | Minneapolis, MN | 200.0 | 160,000 |
| National Guardian | Greenwich, CT | 177.0 | 180,000 |
| Emergency Networks | Dallas, TX | 90.0 | NA |
| Thorn Automated Systems | Westlake, OH | 75.0 | 10,000 |
| Brink's Home Security | Carrollton, TX | 70.8 | 217,000 |
| The Alert Center | Englewood, CO | 70.0 | 200,000 |
| Westinghouse Security Systems | Linthicum, MD | 69.0 | 115,000 |
| Automated Security Holdings | Culver City, CA | 64.8 | 33,300 |
| Rollins Protective Services | Atlanta, GA | 63.0 | 107,148 |
| Westec Security | Irvine, CA | 61.0 | 57,000 |
| Holmes Protection Group | New York, NY | 57.0 | 32,000 |
| SecurityLink | Oak Brook, IL | 38.0 | 98,000 |
| Kastle Systems | Arlington, VA | 33.0 | 45,000 |

*Source: Security Distributing & Marketing, May, 1993*

## Market Share of Monitored Alarm Security Systems

Firms ranked here either sell, install, service, and/or monitor residential and commercial alarm systems that produce recurring contracted revenue. To qualify, they must own the asset value of their customer contracts and provide the monitoring from their own facilities.

| Firm Name | 1991 Gross Revenue ($ millions) |
|-----------|----------------------------------|
| ADT | 577 |
| Honeywell | 203 |
| National Guardian | 177 |
| Wells Fargo | 168 |
| Alert Center | 80 |
| Westec/Secom | 63 |
| Holmes Protection | 60 |
| Rollins | 60 |
| SecurityLink | 60 |
| Brink's | 56 |
| API Alarms | 48 |
| Network/PSI | 48 |

| Firm Name | 1991 Gross Revenue ($ millions) |
|-----------|----------------------------------|
| Bay Alarm | 29 |
| AFA Protective | 26 |
| Intercap Monitoring | 23 |
| Guardian-Detroit | 20 |
| Consolidated Southern | 18 |
| Sonitrol Management | 18 |
| Comsec/Narragansett | 16 |
| Denver Burglar Alarm | 16 |
| PC Security/Westec | 15 |
| Protection One | 14 |
| Smith-Dallas | 14 |
| Westinghouse | 11 |

*Reprinted from Security Dealer Magazine, April, 1992,*
*Support Services Group, San Clemente, CA*

*Prodigy has an executive travel column.*
*JUMP BUSINESS TRAVEL.*

# Corporate Charge Cards

EXPERTS ESTIMATE THAT COMPANIES spent a total of $120 billion on travel and entertainment (T&E) in 1992. What's more, T&E is the third largest controllable expense, after salaries and data processing, for most companies.

In an effort to serve this growing business as well as other corporate needs, major credit card companies currently provide their corporate clients with a wide range of services—from expense management, to disability insurance, to protection plans, to travel benefits and discounts, to billing options.

Below is a list of numbers to contact to obtain corporate credit cards. In general, the more cards a company orders for its employees, the lower the card's annual fee.

## Contact Options

American Express Corporate Card
(800) 528-2122

Citibank Diner's Club Corporate Card
(800) 525-5289

Visa and MasterCard may be obtained through individual banks.

# Office Machinery Buyers Guide

BUYERS LABORATORY, an independent provider of critical evaluations of office products and procedures, gives its "Line of the Year" and "Pick of the Year" awards to the manufacturers of copiers, printers, and facsimile machines that excelled in the company's extensive in-house testing.

## Buyers Laboratory 1993 Awards

| Device | Category | Company | Model |
| --- | --- | --- | --- |
| All | Line of the Year | Lanier Worldwide | All |
| Copier | Low-volume | Sharp | SF-2022 |
| Copier | Mid-volume | Minolta | EP5320 Pro Series |
| Copier | Mid-volume | Minolta | EP5420 Pro Series |
| Copier | Technical achievement | Canon | CJ10, CJ7 |
| Copier | Outstanding value | Oce | 2400 |
| Copier | Overall outstanding | Sharp | SD-3075 |
| Printer | Page printer | Hewlett-Packard | Laser Jet 4M |
| Printer | High-volume page | Hewlett-Packard | Laser Jet 4SiMX |
| Printer | Outstanding page value | Kyocera | ECOSYS a-SiFS-1500A |
| Printer | Outstanding dot matrix value | Star Micronics | XR-1520 Multi-Font |
| Facsimile | High-volume plain paper | Canon | FAX-L785 |
| Facsimile | High-volume plain paper value | JetFax | 8000D |
| Facsimile | Mid-volume plain paper | Sharp | FO-5400 |
| Facsimile | Low-volume thermal | Ricoh | FAX240 |

*Source: Buyers Laboratory*

## The Top Reference Sources

*Buyers Laboratory Test Reports for Office Equipment*
Buyers Laboratory, $635/year
(201) 488-0404

Buyers Laboratory provides testing information to business consumers in much the same way as *Consumer Reports* provides information to the general public. Each test report is based on actual testing conducted by Buyers Laboratory test technicians. The Office Products subscription service provides reports on copiers, copier supplies, facsimile equipment, swivel chairs, file cabinets, typewriters, paper shredders, desks, printers, and postage meter machines, among others. A good source for critical, unbiased evaluations of business equipment.

# Voice Mail

VOICE MAIL HAS PROGRESSED from prerecorded answering machine messages to sophisticated systems that use applications of computer-telephone integration. Current and future technological developments in this facet of telecommunications include interactive voice response, and enhanced information services in combination with traditional office communications media such as facsimile and electronic messaging.

## Contact Options

*Companies Providing Voice Messaging Systems:*

Digital Equipment
(800) 332- 4636, ext. 705

InterVoice
(214) 497-8862

MacroTel International
(407) 997-5500

Toshiba America Information Systems
(714) 583-3000

Voice Professionals
(800) 868-3684

Voice Technologies Group
(716) 689-6700

Voicetek
(508) 250-9393

The local phone company may also provide voice messaging systems.

## Recommended Resources

Association of Telemessaging Services International
1150 S. Washington St., Suite 150
Alexandria, VA 22314
(703) 684-0016

*Voice Processing*, $39/year
131 W. First St.
Duluth, MN 55802
(800) 346-0085, ext. 477
This publication reports on the latest developments in computer-telephone integration and voice automation.

# MCI's Tips on Preventing Toll Fraud

MCI COMMUNICATIONS HAS A LIST of recommendations for limiting your risk of toll fraud. These will sound familiar to those managing file servers and other network services, but make sure the PBX administrator knows them, too.

- Learn all the capabilities of your PBX, particularly any you may not be aware of now. The vendor who sells or services your equipment is the most logical source for this information.

- Delete all authorization codes that were programmed into your PBX for testing or initial servicing.

- Audit and change all active codes in your PBX frequently and de-activate those not authorized.

- Treat authorization codes as you would credit card numbers. Each code should be assigned individually and employees' codes kept confidential.

- Assign the longest possible authorization numbers your PBX can handle. And select codes at random: do not use telephone extension numbers, so-

cial security numbers, employee identification numbers, and the like.

- Be alert during PBX-related conversations to the possibility that the person on the other end may be an impersonator; it may be a thief trying to learn about your phone system in order to defraud you.

- Tailor access to your PBX to conform strictly with the needs of your company. Block access to international and long-distance domestic numbers that your company does not call.

- Use an unpublished number for the Remote Access Unit/Direct Inward System Access and program the PBX to wait at least five rings before responding to the call.

- Review carefully all billing information to identify unauthorized calling patterns.

- Avoid a steady tone as the prompt for inputting an authorization code. Instead, use a voice recording or no prompt, which will minimize your vulnerability to unauthorized activity.

# Telecommunications Services

THERE ARE FOUR MAJOR CRITERIA a business must weigh when selecting telecommunications services. These are: quality, service, reliability, and price. Some questions to ask a company are:

- Can you cut my telecommunications costs? How?

- Why should I choose your company?

- In what ways can your program for small business be tailored to my needs?

- What kinds of incentives do you offer?

- What kinds of guarantees do you offer?

- How do I change my local or long distance carrier?

- How long does it take to change carriers?

- Will changing long distance carriers disrupt my service?

In addition, businesses may ask for the following:

- An appointment to discuss specific requirements;

- Reimbursement of local telephone company charges, when changing long distance carriers (called "PIC fees," usually $5.00 per telephone line);

- A list of the carrier's recurring "service" or "management" fees and installation charges (a standard "switched" service program should have no service or installation fees);

- Specifics on any minimum billing requirements (there is often a monthly "minimum usage requirement" associated with long distance programs. If a business does not meet this dollar amount, it may be charged the difference. Some carriers require businesses to commit to an annual amount of spending and will charge severe penalties if these minimums are not met);

- A written statement of penalties for breaking a "Term Agreement" or changing carriers (one-, two-, and three-year agreements can be signed in exchange for significant price discounts. Otherwise, there should be no charge or penalty for changing long distance carriers);

- A local account representative who can make on-site visits;

- A 24-hour, toll-free number for all service issues;

- Information about a carrier's disaster-recovery and re-routing capabilities;

- Information about a carrier's fraud-protection policies.

*Source: Sprint*

## Contact Options

AT&T
(800) 222-0400

MCI
(800) 888-0800

Sprint
(800) 877-2000

Tele-Trend Communications
(800) 848-1400

## The Top Reference Sources

*The Executive Desk Register of Publicly Held Corporations*
Demand Research, $59.95
(312) 664-6500
73207.3434@compuserve.com or
dresearch@aol.com

The *Register* is a database that contains approximately 5,500 domestic corporations and financial institutions. It is updated daily and published monthly on IBM PC diskettes.

The database includes executives in human resources, marketing, sales, manufacturing, and other areas, as well as computer and telecommunications companies. Portions of the database are released periodically as shareware.

# Business & Office Supplies by Mail

BELOW IS A BRIEF LISTING OF SELECTED mail order business dealers. For a more complete listing, consult the *Mail Order Product Guide* or the *Mail Order Business Directory*.

## Recommended Resources

*Mail Order Product Guide*
Todd Publications, $20
18 N. Greenbush Rd.
West Nyack, NY 10994
(914) 358-6213

*Mail Order Business Directory*
B. Klein Publications, $85
P.O. Box 8503
Coral Springs, FL 33075
(305) 752-1708

## Contact Options

*Office Equipment:*

Allied Business Machines
9281 Earl St.
La Mesa, CA 92041
(619) 461-6361

American Printing Equipment
42-25 9th St.
Long Island City, NY 11101
(718) 729-5779

Longacre Office Machines
20 E. 40th St.
New York, NY 10016
(212) 684-2471

Pitney Bowes
World Headquarters
Stamford, CT 06926
(203) 356-5000

Viking Office Products
13809 S. Figueroa St.
Los Angeles, CA 90061
(800) 421-1222

*Office Supplies:*

Adirondack Direct
31-01 Vernon Blvd.
Long Island City, NY 11106
(718) 932-4003

Charrette
31 Olympia Ave.
Woburn, MA 01888
(617) 935-6000

City Office Supply
156 N. Jefferson St.
Chicago, IL 60661
(312) 559-0100

Modern Service Office Supply
19315 E. San Jose Ave.
City of Industry, CA 91748
(800) 672-6767

Staples
100 Pennsylvania Ave.
Framingham, MA 01701
(800) 333-3330

Wholesale Supply
P.O. Box 23437
Nashville, TN 37202
(800) 962-9162

*Stationery:*

Atlas Pen and Pencil
3040 N. 29 Ave.
Hollywood, FL 33022
(305) 920-4444

Day Timers
One Willow Lane
East Texas, PA 18046
(215) 398-1151

Forms
P.O. Box 1109
La Jolla, CA 92038
(619) 454-5759

Standard Stationery
10 Furniture Row
Milford, CT 06460
(203) 874-1608

The Stationery House
1000 Florida Ave.
Hagerstown, MD 21740
(301) 739-4487

# Office Furniture by Mail

## Contact Options

*Mail Order Furniture Companies:*

A.T.D. American
135 Greenwood Ave.
Wyncote, PA 19095
(800) 523-2300

Business & Institutional Furniture
611 N. Broadway
Milwaukee, WI 53202
(414) 272-6080

Carl Manufacturing
P.O. Box 488
110 W. Washington St.
Lisbon, OH 44432
(216) 424-5363

Foster Manufacturing
414 N. 13 St.
Philadelphia, PA 19108
(215) 625-0500

National Business Furniture
222 E. Michigan St.
Milwaukee, WI 53202
(800) 558-1010

Office Furniture Center
135 Beaver St.
Waltham, MA 02154
(800) 343-4222

Standard Equipment
601 Concord Ave.
Williston Park, NY 11596
(800) 782-6866

# Color Printing

A NUMBER OF COMPANIES will provide four-color brochures, catalogues, sales sheets, posters, and other computer-generated color graphics by mail order quickly and inexpensively.

## Contact Options

*Companies Specializing in Color Printing:*

Color Impressions
1642 N. Besly Ct.
Chicago, IL 60622
(800) 626-1333

Multiprint
5555 W. Howard St.
Skokie, IL 60077
(800) 858-9999

Scangraphics
5300 Newport Dr.
Rolling Meadows, IL 60008
(708) 392-3980

# Catalogue Sources

A WIDE RANGE OF BUSINESS-RELATED articles–from office furniture to stationery to heavy machinery–can be efficiently purchased by mail. These publications profile a wide variety of catalogues.

## Recommended Resources

*The Directory of Mail Order Catalogues*
Grey House Publishing, $145
P.O. Box 1866
Pocket Knife Square
Lakeville, CT 06039
(203) 435-0868

*Mail Order Business Directory*
B. Klein Publications, $85
P.O. Box 8503
Coral Springs, FL 33065
(305) 752-1708

# Airlines Ranked by Size

## Domestic Airlines Ranked by Revenue

| Sales Rank | Company | Location | 1992 Revenue ($ thousands) | Load Factor (%) | # of Major Airports Served |
|---|---|---|---|---|---|
| 1 | American | D/FW Airport, TX | 13,581,102 | 63.7 | 215 |
| 2 | United | Chicago, IL | 12,724,577 | 67.4 | 169 |
| 3 | Delta | Atlanta, GA | 11,639,080 | 61.3 | 197 |
| 4 | Northwest | St. Paul, MN | 7,963,785 | 65.3 | NA |
| 5 | USAir | Arlington, VA | 6,235,622 | 58.8 | 126 |
| 6 | Continental | Houston, TX | 5,209,639 | 63.5 | 143 |
| 7 | TWA | Mount Kisco, NY | 3,569,922 | 64.6 | 110 |
| 8 | Southwest | Dallas, TX | 1,685,250 | 64.5 | 34 |
| 9 | America West | Phoenix, AZ | 1,302,632 | 61.1 | 44 |
| 10 | Alaska Airlines | Seattle, WA | 922,343 | 57.6 | 38 |
| 11 | American Trans Air | Indianapolis, IN | 421,790 | 70.3 | NA |
| 12 | Hawaiian Airlines | Honolulu, HI | 395,075 | 70.8 | 18 |
| 13 | Mesa Air | Farmington, NM | 316,615 | 50.3 | 55 |
| 14 | Comair | Cincinnati, OH | 238,000 | 45.0 | 55 |
| 15 | Atlantic Southeast | Atlanta, GA | 235,579 | 51.8 | NA |
| 16 | Aloha Airlines | Honolulu, HI | 226,400 | 57.5 | 6 |
| 17 | Air Wisconsin | Chicago, IL | 217,100 | 48.5 | 35 |
| 18 | Horizon Air | Seattle, WA | 208,149 | 53.6 | 34 |
| 19 | Skywest | St. George, UT | 151,509 | 43.5 | 42 |
| 20 | Shuttle | New York, NY | 147,184 | 46.0 | 4 |
| 21 | Midwest Express | Milwaukee, WI | 133,946 | 55.7 | 20 |
| 22 | Mesaba | Minneapolis, MN | 102,389 | 51.5 | 45 |
| 23 | MGM Grand Air | El Segundo, CA | 50,005 | 52.4 | 2 |
| 24 | Reno Air | Reno, NV | 27,092 | 50.3 | NA |
| 25 | Kiwi | Newark, NJ | 7,925 | 53.0 | NA |

*Source: Business Travel News, May 24, 1993*

## The Top Reference Sources

*FAA Statistical Handbook of Aviation, 1991*
The National Technical Information Service, $27
(703) 487-4650

This report presents statistical information pertaining to the Federal Aviation Administration,

The National Airspace System, airports, airport activity, U.S. Civil Air Carrier Fleet, U.S. Civil Air Carrier Operating Data, aircraft accidents, and aeronautical production. Also included are imports/exports, general aviation aircraft, and a glossary of terms.

# Domestic Airline Hubs

| Company | Major Hub(s) |
|---|---|
| American | Chicago, Dallas/Fort Worth, Miami, Nashville, Raleigh/Durham, San Jose, San Juan |
| United | Chicago, Denver, Orlando, San Francisco |
| Delta | Atlanta, Cincinnati, Dallas/Fort Worth, Salt Lake City |
| Northwest | Detroit, Memphis, Minneapolis |
| USAir | Baltimore, Charlotte, Indianapolis, Philadelphia, Pittsburgh |
| Continental | Cleveland, Denver, Houston, Newark |
| TWA | New York, St. Louis |
| Southwest | Dallas, Houston |
| America West | Columbus, Las Vegas, Phoenix |
| Alaska Airlines | Anchorage, Portland, Seattle |
| American Trans Air | Indianapolis |
| Hawaiian Airlines | Honolulu |
| Mesa Air | Denver |
| Comair | Cincinnati, Orlando |
| Atlantic Southeast | Atlanta |
| Aloha Airlines | Honolulu |
| Air Wisconsin | Chicago |
| Horizon Air | Portland, Seattle |
| Skywest | Los Angeles, Salt Lake City |
| Shuttle | New York |
| Midwest Express | Milwaukee |
| Mesaba | Minneapolis |
| MGM Grand Air | Los Angeles, New York |
| Reno Air | Reno |
| Kiwi | Newark |

*Source: Business Travel News, May 24, 1993*

# Special Meals on Airlines

| Airline | Meals | Notice Required |
|---|---|---|
| American | Bland and soft, child, gluten-free, Hindu, kosher, low-cholesterol, Muslim, low calorie, lactose free, low carbohydrate, low sodium, ovo-lacto vegetarian | 12 hours for kosher meal, 6 hours for others |
| Continental | Child, diabetic, fruit plate, Hindu, infant, kosher, low cholesterol/low fat, low sodium, Muslim, ovo-lacto vegetarian, seafood, vegetarian | 6 hours |
| Delta | Asian vegetarian, baby, bland, child, diabetic, fruit plate, gluten free, Hindu, kosher, low calorie/low cholesterol, low sodium, ovo-lacto vegetarian, Muslim, cold seafood, hot seafood, toddler, vegetarian | 12 hours for Asian, Hindu, kosher meals, 6 hours for others |
| Northwest | Baby, bland, child, diabetic, fruit, gluten free, Hindu, Japanese, kosher, low calorie, low carbohydrate, low sodium, Muslim, ovo-lacto vegetarian, seafood, soft diet, sulfite free, vegetarian | 12 hours |
| TWA | Child, cold seafood, kosher, low calorie, low cholesterol/low fat, low sodium, low carbohydrate/low sugar, ovo-lacto vegetarian, vegetarian | 24 hours |
| United | Bland, dietary (diabetic-hypoglycemic), McDonald's child's platter, gluten-free, high fiber, infant, low calorie/low carbohydrate, low protein, low purin, ovo-lacto vegetarian, Lighter Choice (chef's salad, fruit plate, or cold seafood), Muslim, non-lactose | 6 hours |
| USAir | Asian vegetarian, baby, bland, child, diabetic, fruit plate, gluten-free, high fiber, high protein, Hindu, kosher, low calorie, low fat/low cholesterol, low protein, low purin, low sodium, Muslim, non-lactose, Oriental, ovo-lacto vegetarian, raw vegetables, vegetarian, seafood | 6 hours |

# The Business Traveler

THE MAGAZINE *FREQUENT FLYER* conducts a poll of its readers annually. Included in this survey are questions about choice of airlines, frequent flyer plans, inflight experience, car rental, choice of hotels, and other relevant topics.

64 percent of the respondents said that their company has a corporate travel policy. The following chart shows their responses to the question, "How does your company's corporate travel policy affect your business travel?"

## Corporate Travel Policy

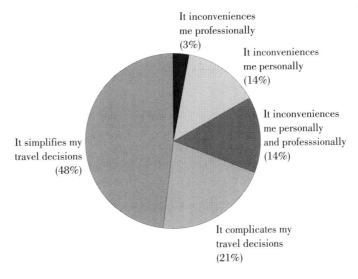

The following chart shows the responses to the question, "How many free tickets did you actually claim in the last twelve months?"

## Frequent Flyer Tickets

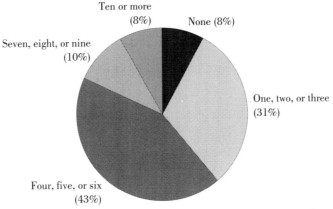

*Source: Frequent Flyer, Dec., 1993*

*The Business Traveler (cont'd)*

The following chart shows the responses to the question, "How do you fly most frequently when traveling internationally?"

**Ticket Type**

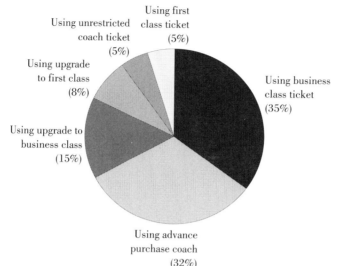

Using first class ticket (5%)

Using unrestricted coach ticket (5%)

Using upgrade to first class (8%)

Using business class ticket (35%)

Using upgrade to business class (15%)

Using advance purchase coach (32%)

*Source: Frequent Flyer, Dec., 1993*

# Airline Quality Ratings

THE NATIONAL INSTITUTE for Aviation Research at Wichita State University produces an evaluation of the major U.S. airlines each year. Using data from the Department of Transportation, they give each airline an Airline Quality Rating. This rating is based on a variety of factors, including: on-time percentage, load factor, number of accidents, frequent flier awards, mishandled baggage, fares, customer service, ticketing/boarding, financial stability, and average seat-mile cost.

The results for 1993 are summarized in the table to the right. The graphs on the next page show the airlines' scores on two key factors, denied boarding and baggage mishandling.

### Airlines Ranked by Quality

| Rank | Airline |
|------|---------|
| 1 | Southwest |
| 2 | American |
| 3 | United |
| 4 | Delta |
| 5 | USAir |
| 6 | Northwest |
| 7 | Trans World |
| 8 | America West |
| 9 | Continental |

*Source: National Institute for Aviation Research*

**FAX** **Largest Airlines Worldwide.** Request #888. See p. xi for instructions.
Fortune's ranking by revenue of the top 25 airlines worldwide.

*Airline Quality Ratings (cont'd)*

## Denied Boarding

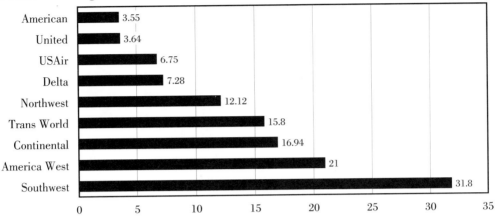

## Mishandled Baggage

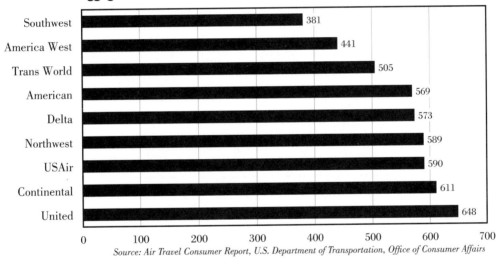

*Source: Air Travel Consumer Report, U.S. Department of Transportation, Office of Consumer Affairs*

# Frequent Flyer Programs

## InsideFlyer's Ratings of Frequent Flyer Programs

| Rank | Program | Ease of Earning Awards Dom. | Int'l | Service All | Blackouts Dom. | Int'l | Seat Availability Dom. | Int'l | Hotel Partners All | # Travel Awards 1992 All |
|------|---------|------|------|------|------|------|------|------|------|------|
| 1 | Northwest | B+ | A | A– | B | A | A | C | B | 1,000,000 |
| 2 | American | B+ | C | C | A | C | A | C | C | 1,474,000 |
| 3 | USAir | B | B | B | A | C | A | C | A | 540,000 |
| 4 | United | B+ | C | A– | B | C | A | C | A | 1,400,000 |
| 5 | America West | B | A | A– | B | B | A | C | B– | 106,000 |
| 6 | Alaska | B | B | B– | B+ | C | A– | C | B | NA |
| 7 | Continental | B+ | B | A– | C | D+ | B | C | A | 500,000 |
| 8 | Delta | B | C– | A– | C | D | A | C | A | 3,100,000 |
| 9 | TWA | B+ | C | B | C | D | B | C | C | 623,000 |
| 10 | Southwest | C | NA | A– | A | NA | A | NA | F | 209,000 |

*Ratings: A = Best; F = Worst*

*Source: InsideFlyer, 1993*

*Frequent Flyer Programs (cont'd)*

## Airline, Hotel, Car Rental, Credit Card Partners

| Airline | Car Rentals | Credit Cards | Hotels | Airlines |
|---|---|---|---|---|
| *American*<br>AAdvantage | Avis<br>Hertz | Citibank Visa<br>MCI | Fairmont<br>Forte<br>Intercontinental<br>Hilton<br>Holiday Inn<br>Marriott<br>Sheraton<br>Wyndham | American Eagle<br>Canadian<br>Cathay Pacific<br>Qantas<br>Reno Air<br>Singapore<br>TWA<br>South African |
| *Continental*<br>One Pass | Dollar<br>Eurocar<br>National<br>Thrifty<br>Tilden | American Express | Aston<br>Camino Real<br>Canadian Pacific<br>Doubletree<br>Marriott<br>Melia<br>Radisson<br>Sheraton | Aer Lingus<br>Air Canada<br>Alitalia<br>Austria<br>Big Sky<br>BWIA<br>Cayman<br>Continental Express<br>Iberian<br>KLM Royal Dutch<br>Lan Chile<br>Malaysia<br>Qantas<br>SAS |
| *Northwest*<br>WorldPerks | Budget<br>Hertz<br>National | MCI<br>First Bank<br>WorldPerks (Visa) | Colony<br>Holiday Inn<br>Hyatt<br>Marriott<br>New Ohtani<br>Radisson<br>Shangri La<br>Westin | Alaska<br>America West (int'l)<br>USAir (int'l)<br>KLM Royal Dutch |
| *TWA*<br>Frequent Flight<br>Bonus Program | Avis<br>Dollar | – | Adam's Mark<br>Doubletree<br>Forte<br>Marriott<br>Radisson | Air India<br>Alaska<br>American<br>Philippine<br>Trans World Express |
| *United*<br>Mileage Plus | Alamo<br>Dollar<br>Hertz<br>National | Mileage Plus First<br>Card (Visa) | Hilton<br>Holiday Inn<br>Hyatt<br>Intercontinental<br>Ritz-Carlton<br>Sheraton<br>Westin | Air Canada<br>Air France<br>Alitalia<br>ALM Antillean<br>Aloha<br>Ansett<br>British Midland<br>Emirates<br>Lufthansa<br>Scandinavian<br>Trans Brazil<br>TWA Express<br>United Express |
| *USAir*<br>Frequent Traveler<br>Program | Alamo<br>Hertz<br>National<br>Tilden | Nationsbank (Visa) | Hilton<br>Hyatt<br>Marriott<br>Omni<br>Radisson<br>Stouffer<br>Westin | Air France<br>Lufthansa<br>British Airways<br>Northwest (int'l)<br>Swissair<br>Air New Zealand<br>Sabena World<br>KLM<br>Alitalia<br>ANA |

# Airline Directory

| Airline | 800 Number |
|---|---|
| Aer Lingus | (800) 223-6537 |
| Aeromexico | (800) 237-6639 |
| Air Canada | (800) 776-3000 |
| Air France | (800) 237-2747 |
| Alaska Airlines | (800) 426-0333 |
| Alitalia | (800) 223-5730 |
| All Nippon Airways | (800) 235-9262 |
| America West | (800) 235-9292 |
| American Airlines | (800) 433-7300 |
| Austrian Airlines | (800) 843-0002 |
| Avianca | (800) 284-2622 |
| British Airways | (800) 247-9297 |
| British Caledonian | (800) 231-0270 |
| Canadian Airlines | (800) 426-7000 |
| Cathay Pacific Airways | (800) 233-2742 |
| China Airlines | (800) 227-5118 |
| Continental Airlines | (800) 525-0280 |
| Delta Airlines | (800) 221-1212 |
| Finn Air | (800) 950-5000 |
| Iberia Airlines | (800) 221-9741 |
| Iceland Air | (800) 223-5500 |
| Japan Airlines | (800) 525-3663 |
| KLM Royal Dutch Airlines | (800) 374-7747 |
| Korean Airlines | (800) 438-5000 |
| Lan-Chile Airlines | (800) 735-5526 |

| Airline | 800 Number |
|---|---|
| Lufthansa | (800) 645-3880 |
| Midwest Express Airlines | (800) 452-2022 |
| Northwest Airlines (dom.) | (800) 225-2525 |
| Northwest Airlines (int'l.) | (800) 447-4747 |
| Olympic Airways | (800) 223-1226 |
| Qantas | (800) 227-4500 |
| Royal Jordanian | (800) 223-0470 |
| Sabena | (800) 873-3900 |
| Scandinavian Air | (800) 221-2350 |
| Scandinavian Airlines | (800) 221-2350 |
| Singapore Airlines | (800) 742-3373 |
| Skyway Airlines | (800) 452-2022 |
| Swissair | (800) 221-4750 |
| TAP Air Portugal | (800) 221-7370 |
| Thai Airways | (800) 426-5042 |
| Transbrazil Airlines | (800) 872-3153 |
| TWA (dom.) | (800) 221-2000 |
| TWA (int'l.) | (800) 892-4141 |
| United Airlines | (800) 241-6522 |
| USAir | (800) 428-4322 |
| Varig Brazilian Airlines | (800) 468-2744 |

# Airline Clubs

## Domestic Airline Clubs: Fees and Services

| Airline | Club | Phone | Annual Fee ($) | Enrollment Fee ($) | No. of Locations | Bar | Guests Permitted* |
|---|---|---|---|---|---|---|---|
| Alaska | The Board Room | (800) 654-5669 | 150 | 100 | 5 | Free | 2 |
| America West | Phoenix Club | (602) 693-4072 | 100 | 50 | 2 | Free | 2 |
| American | Admirals Club | (800) 237-7971 | 250 | 100 | 41 | Cash | 2 |
| Continental | Presidents Club | (800) 322-2640 | 150 | 50 | 17† | NA | 2 |
| Delta | Crown Room | (404) 715-6615 | 150 | – | 66 | Free | 2 |
| Northwest | WorldClub | (800) 225-2525 | 150 | 50 | 26 | Free | 2 |
| TWA | Ambassadors Club | (800) 527-1468 | 150 | – | 19 | NA | 2 |
| United | Red Carpet Club | (800) 241-6522 | 175 | 100 | 31 | Cash | 2 |
| USAir | USAir Club | (800) 828-8522 | 150 | 50 | 26 | Cash | 2 |

*not including family members; they may enter at any time*

*† also affiliated with Air Canada*

# Paging at Major U.S. Airports

THE FOLLOWING IS A LIST of paging numbers at most U.S. airports, by airport and airline. When no number is listed, call the airline and ask that the passenger be paged.

## Paging Phone Numbers at Major U.S. Airports

| Airport | Airline | Telephone |
|---|---|---|
| Atlanta International | Northwest | (404) 530-3960 |
| | TWA | (404) 530-2620 |
| | Delta | (404) 714-7250 |
| | USAir | (404) 530-3300 |
| | Continental | (404) 530-3530 |
| Baltimore/Washington Intl., Baltimore | All | (410) 859-7111 |
| Logan Airport, Boston | All | (617) 568-8408 |
| | American | (800) 433-7300 |
| | Delta | (617) 561-2550 |
| | United | (800) 241-6522 |
| | Continental | (617) 561-2132 |
| | USAir | (617) 561-6721 |
| | Northwest | (617) 561-5310 |
| O'Hare, Chicago | All | (312) 686-2868 |
| | United | (312) 601-3100 |
| | American | (312) 686-4477 |
| | Northwest | (312) 686-5575 |
| | Continental | (312) 601-5305 |
| | Delta | (312) 686-8635 |
| | TWA | (312) 686-5080 |
| | America West | (312) 686-5670 |
| | USAir | (312) 686-7171 |
| Midway, Chicago | All | (312) 767-0500 |
| | Northwest | (312) 471-4692 |
| Greater Cincinnati International | Northwest | (606) 283-3144 |
| | TWA | (606) 283-3526 |
| | Delta | (606) 283-3427 |
| | United | (606) 283-3691 |
| | USAir | (606) 283-3645 |
| | Continental | (606) 283-3202 |
| Cleveland International, Cleveland | All | (216) 265-6030 |
| Columbus, OH | Northwest | (614) 239-4381 |
| | TWA | (614) 239-4082 |
| | Delta | (614) 239-4476 |
| | USAir | (614) 238-7500 |
| | Cleveland | (614) 239-4082 |
| Dallas | All | (214) 574-6673 |
| | Delta | (214) 574-2247 |
| | United | (214) 574-6673 |
| | USAir | (214) 574-6673 |
| | American | (214) 425-2477 |
| | Continental | (214) 574-6673 |
| Stapleton International, Denver | Northwest | (303) 270-1000 |
| | TWA | (303) 270-1300/1310 |
| | Delta | (303) 270-1300 |

*Paging at Major U.S. Airports (cont'd)*

| Airport | Airline | Telephone |
| --- | --- | --- |
| Stapleton International, Denver (cont'd) | United | (800) 247-2336 |
| | USAir | (303) 270-1300 |
| | American | (303) 270-1310 |
| | Continental | (303) 270-1300 |
| Detroit | Northwest | (313) 942-4268 |
| | TWA | (313) 942-3406 |
| | Delta | (313) 942-2640 |
| | USAir | (313) 942-2460 |
| | Continental | (313) 955-1797 |
| Houston Intercontinental | All | (713) 230-3000 |
| | Northwest | (713) 845-3500 |
| Indianapolis International | Northwest | (317) 248-7243 |
| | TWA | (317) 487-7243 |
| | Delta | (317) 248-7243 |
| | United | (317) 248-7243 |
| | USAir | (317) 487-7243 |
| | American | (317) 487-7243 |
| | Continental | (317) 487-7243 |
| Los Angeles | Northwest | (310) 646-7711/3517 |
| | TWA | (310) 646-2424 |
| | Delta | (310) 646-5802 |
| | United | (310) 646-3116 |
| | USAir | (310) 646-2020 |
| | American | (310) 646-3533 |
| | Continental | (310) 568-3131 |
| Miami International | All | (305) 876-7000, ext. 35 |
| Milwaukee | Northwest | (414) 747-4740; 4604 |
| | TWA | (414) 747-4670 |
| | United | (414) 747-4920 |
| | USAir | (414) 747-4713 |
| | Continental | (414) 747-4572 |
| Minneapolis | Delta | (612) 725-4931 |
| | Northwest | (612) 726-3007; 7981 |
| | TWA | (612) 726-5642 |
| | USAir | (612) 726-5373 |
| | Continental | (612) 726-5818 |
| John F. Kennedy, New York | Northwest | (718) 244-5604 |
| | TWA | (718) 244-2000 |
| | Delta | (718) 632-4180 |
| | USAir | (718) 656-2100 |
| LaGuardia, New York | Northwest | (718) 476-7191 |
| | TWA | (718) 803-6810 |
| | Delta | (718) 565-3940 |
| | United | (718) 476-4966 |
| | USAir | (718) 533-2634 |
| | Continental | (718) 334-7132 |
| Norfolk | TWA | (804) 857-3210 |
| | Delta | (804) 857-3245 |
| | United | (804) 857-3330 |
| | USAir | (804) 857-3318 |
| | Continental | (804) 857-3584 |

*Paging at Major U.S. Airports (cont'd)*

| Airport | Airline | Telephone |
|---|---|---|
| Philadelphia | All | (215) 492-3222 |
| Phoenix | All | (602) 273-3455 |
| Pittsburgh | Northwest | (412) 472-5450 |
| | TWA | (412) 472-5380 |
| | Delta | (412) 472-3209 |
| | United | (412) 472-5126 |
| | USAir | (412) 472-2527 |
| | American | (412) 472-5321 |
| | Continental | (412) 262-4405 |
| Portland, OR | All | (503) 335-1040 |
| Sacramento | Northwest | (916) 929-5411 |
| | Delta | (916) 922-7730 |
| | United | (916) 929-5411 |
| | USAir | (916) 929-5411 |
| | American | (916) 929-5411 |
| | Continental | (916) 929-5411 |
| Lambert/St. Louis International | All | (314) 426-8000 |
| | Northwest | (314) 427-5357 |
| | TWA | (314) 429-9400 |
| | Delta | (314) 426-9201 |
| | USAir | (314) 423-3757 |
| | Continental | (314) 423-6376 |
| San Antonio International | All | (512) 821-3411 |
| Lindbergh Field Intl., San Diego | All | (619) 231-2294 |
| | Northwest | (619) 231-7314 |
| Seattle | TWA | (206) 433-5722 |
| | Delta | (206) 433-4324 |
| | United | (206) 433-4343 |
| | USAir | (206) 433-7850 |
| | Continental | (206) 433-5545 |
| Tampa | All | (813) 870-8770 |
| Washington, DC, Dulles | Northwest | (703) 661-3356 |
| | TWA | (703) 834-1969 |
| | Delta | (703) 661-5577 |
| | American | (703) 661-5299 |
| | Continental | (703) 661-8636 |
| Washington, DC, National | Northwest | (703) 769-6100 |
| | TWA | (703) 684-6441 |
| | Delta | (703) 271-6150 |
| | USAir | (703) 892-7164 |
| | Continental | (703) 769-6745 |

**TIP:** *There are discount hotel reservations services for business travelers. They work on commissions from the hotels, so they do not charge the customer. Hotel Reservations Network, (800) 964-6835, and Quikbook, (800) 221-3531 are two such services.*

# Transportation from Airport to City

## Taxi Fares from Airport to City: Domestic

| City | Airport | Code | Mileage | Approx. Taxi Fare ($U.S.) |
|------|---------|------|---------|---------------------------|
| Atlanta | Atlanta Int'l. | ATL | 8 mi SW | 15.00 |
| Baltimore | Baltimore/Washington | BWI | 10 mi S | 16.00 |
| Boston | Logan Int'l. | BOS | 3 mi NE | 10.00 |
| Chicago | O'Hare Int'l. | ORD | 18 mi NW` | 24.00 |
| Chicago | Midway | MDW | 10 mi SW | 17.00 |
| Cincinnati | Greater Cincinnati Int'l. | CVG | 13 mi SW | 20.00 |
| Cleveland | Cleveland/Hopkins Int'l. | CLE | 10 mi SW | 15.00 |
| Columbus, OH | Port Columbus Int'l. | CMH | 7 mi NE | 15.00 |
| Dallas | Dallas/Ft. Worth Int'l. | DFW | 21 mi NW | 27.00 |
| Denver | Stapleton Int'l. | DEN | 7 mi NE | 10.00 |
| Detroit | Detroit Metropolitan | DTW | 19 mi SW | 28.00 |
| Houston | Houston Intercontinental | IAH | 22 mi N | 29.00 |
| Indianapolis | Indianapolis Int'l. | IND | 8 mi SW | 14.00 |
| Los Angeles | Los Angeles Int'l. | LAX | 15 mi SW | 27.00 |
| Miami | Miami Int'l. | MIA | 6 mi NW | 14.00 |
| Milwaukee | General Mitchell Int'l. | MKE | 7 mi S | 14.00 |
| Minneapolis | Minneapolis/St. Paul | MSP | 13 mi SE | 20.00 |
| New York | JFK Int'l. | JFK | 15 mi SE | 24.00 |
| New York | LaGuardia | LAG | 8 mi NE | 14.00 |
| Norfolk | Norfolk Int'l. | ORF | 6 mi NE | 15.00 |
| Philadelphia | Philadelphia Int'l. | PHL | 8 mi SW | 22.00 |
| Phoenix | Phoenix Sky Harbor Int'l. | PHX | 4 mi SE | 7.00 |
| Pittsburgh | Greater Pittsburgh Int'l. | PIT | 17 mi W | 25.00 |
| Portland, OR | Portland Int'l. | POX | 9 mi NE | 19.00 |
| Sacramento | Metropolitan | SMF | 11 mi NW | 25.00 |
| St. Louis | Lambert/St. Louis Int'l. | STL | 13 mi NW | 18.00 |
| San Antonio | San Antonio Int'l. | SAT | 8 mi N | 12.00 |
| San Diego | San Diego Int'l. | SAN | 3 mi NW | 7.00 |
| San Francisco | San Francisco Int'l. | SFO | 14 mi S | 29.00 |
| Seattle | Seattle/Tacoma Int'l. | SEA | 13 mi S | 22.00 |
| Tampa | Port Columbus Int'l. | TPA | 7 mi NE | 15.00 |
| Washington, DC | Dulles Int'l. | IAD | 26 mi W | 38.00 |
| Washington, DC | National | DCA | 4 mi S | 9.00 |

## Taxi Fares from Airport to City: International

| City | Airport | Mileage | Approx. Taxi Fare ($U.S.) |
|------|---------|---------|---------------------------|
| Amsterdam, Netherlands | Schiphol | 9 mi SW | 25-28 |
| Beijing, China | Beijing Capital | 18 mi NE | 8 |
| Berlin, Germany | Tegel | 4 mi NW | 10-11 |
| Brussels, Belgium | Brussels National Airport | 7.5 mi NE | 29 |
| Paris, France | Charles De Gaulle | 15 mi NE | 7-31 |
| Paris, France | Orly | 8 mi S | 22-60 |
| Rome, Italy | Leonardo Da Vinci | 18 mi SW | 40 |
| Dublin, Ireland | Dublin | 18 mi N | 12 |
| Geneva, Switzerland | Cointrin | 2.5 mi NW | 17-25 |
| Hong Kong | Hong Kong Int'l. | 3 mi NE | 5 |
| London, England | Heathrow | 15 mi W | 50 |
| London, England | Gatwick | 28 mi S | 75 |
| Madrid, Spain | Barajas | 7.5 mi NE | 15-17 |
| São Paulo, Brazil | São Paulo Int'l. | 18 mi NE | 22 |
| Tokyo, Japan | Narita Airport | 42 mi W | 150 |
| Toronto, Ontario | Lester B. Pearson Int'l. | 20 mi NW | 30 |
| Vienna, Austria | Schwecat | 10 mi SE | 27 |

# Busiest Airports

## Airports Ranked by Number of Passengers, 1992

| Rank | Airport | Passengers |
|---|---|---|
| 1 | Chicago (O'Hare) | 29,987,059 |
| 2 | Dallas/Ft. Worth | 25,963,239 |
| 3 | Los Angeles | 22,942,945 |
| 4 | Atlanta | 20,966,165 |
| 5 | San Francisco | 15,259,820 |
| 6 | Denver | 14,489,862 |
| 7 | New York (JFK) | 13,457,175 |
| 8 | Miami | 12,587,420 |
| 9 | Newark | 12,002,142 |
| 10 | Honolulu | 11,224,612 |

| Rank | Airport | Passengers |
|---|---|---|
| 11 | Detroit | 10,991,691 |
| 12 | Boston (Logan) | 10,974,082 |
| 13 | Phoenix | 10,958,285 |
| 14 | Minneapolis/St. Paul | 10,639,116 |
| 15 | St. Louis (Lambert) | 10,476,861 |
| 16 | Orlando | 9,989,092 |
| 17 | Las Vegas (McCarran) | 9,883,375 |
| 18 | New York (La Guardia) | 9,853,796 |
| 19 | Pittsburgh | 9,350,221 |
| 20 | Charlotte (Douglas) | 9,099,577 |

*Source: Federal Aviation Administration*

**FAX** **Basic Airline Fare Codes.** Request #684. See p. xi for instructions.

List of common airline abbreviations and their definitions.

**TIP:** *Timezone's "No Jet Lag" software is a program that explains how to minimize jet lag. Users simply enter their flight date and destination. It costs $70 and can be obtained by calling (714) 675-9588.*

# Best Times to Fly

## Departure: Best Hour to Go

| Airport | Best Hour | On-Time Percentage | Worst Hour | On-Time Percentage |
|---|---|---|---|---|
| Atlanta | 6-7 A.M. | 90.2 | 4-5 P.M. | 65.7 |
| Boston | 9-10 P.M. | 82.1 | 6-7 P.M. | 36.4 |
| Chicago | 6-7 A.M. | 81.4 | 6-7 P.M. | 53.6 |
| Cincinnati | 10-11 A.M. | 81.7 | 5-6 P.M. | 62.5 |
| Dallas | 7-8 A.M. | 92.8 | 6-7 P.M. | 64.5 |
| Denver | 7-8 A.M. | 95.2 | 4-5 P.M. | 64.6 |
| Houston | 10-11 P.M. | 96.8 | 8-9 P.M. | 68.0 |
| Los Angeles | 6-7 A.M. | 92.2 | 2-3 P.M. | 75.9 |
| Miami | 6-7 A.M. | 92.5 | 8-9 P.M. | 51.6 |
| Minneapolis | 6-7 A.M. | 85.7 | 8-9 P.M. | 70.3 |
| New York: Kennedy | 10-11 P.M. | 100.0 | 8-9 P.M. | 45.5 |
| New York: LaGuardia | 9-10 P.M. | 79.0 | 11 P.M.-6 A.M. | 50.0 |
| Philadelphia | 6-7 A.M. | 82.8 | 7-8 P.M. | 46.4 |
| Phoenix | 6-7 A.M. | 92.9 | 5-6 P.M. | 73.7 |
| Pittsburgh | 11 P.M.-6 A.M. | 76.7 | 7-8 P.M. | 34.1 |
| St. Louis | 7-8 A.M. | 86.9 | 6-7 P.M. | 54.9 |
| San Diego | 11 P.M.-6 A.M. | 90.6 | 10-11 P.M. | 65.4 |
| San Francisco | 10-11 P.M. | 91.6 | 1-2 P.M. | 63.4 |
| Seattle | 7-8 A.M. | 88.8 | 1-2 P.M. | 73.5 |
| Tampa | 10-11 P.M. | 100.0 | 9-10 P.M. | 51.9 |
| Washington (Dulles) | 6-7 A.M. | 83.6 | 8-9 P.M. | 59.7 |

## Arrival: Best Hour to Land

| Airport | Best Hour | On-Time Percentage | Worst Hour | On-Time Percentage |
|---|---|---|---|---|
| Atlanta | 7-8 A.M. | 85.6 | 6-7 A.M. | 53.8 |
| Boston | 6-7 A.M. | 77.6 | 7-8 P.M. | 34.8 |
| Chicago | 11 P.M.-6 A.M. | 81.0 | 7-8 A.M. | 45.6 |
| Cincinnati | 4-5 P.M. | 80.4 | 10-11 P.M. | 56.3 |
| Dallas | 6-7 A.M. | 90.9 | 6-7 P.M. | 61.1 |
| Denver | 8-9 A.M. | 79.9 | 10-11 P.M. | 55.6 |
| Houston | 10-11 A.M. | 86.9 | 10-11 P.M. | 58.6 |
| Los Angeles | 7-8 A.M. | 86.1 | 8-9 P.M. | 67.9 |
| Miami | 6-7 A.M. | 100.0 | 8-9 P.M. | 54.9 |
| Minneapolis | 6-7 A.M. | 86.4 | 8-9 P.M. | 60.5 |
| New York: Kennedy | 9-10 A.M. | 94.4 | 7-8 A.M. | 38.9 |
| New York: LaGuardia | 7-8 A.M. | 86.1 | 6-7 P.M. | 67.9 |
| Philadelphia | 6-7 A.M. | 78.0 | 7-8 P.M. | 51.2 |
| Phoenix | 7-8 A.M. | 100.0 | 8-9 P.M. | 71.9 |
| Pittsburgh | 6-7 A.M. | 87.1 | 9-10 P.M. | 49.2 |
| St. Louis | 11 P.M.-6 A.M. | 87.4 | 8-9 P.M. | 56.2 |
| San Diego | 8-9 A.M. | 93.8 | 11 P.M.-6 A.M. | 60.8 |
| San Francisco | 6-7 A.M. | 94.3 | NOON-1 P.M. | 55.2 |
| Seattle | 6-7 A.M. | 86.7 | 10-11 P.M. | 60.7 |
| Tampa | 7-8 A.M. | 88.2 | 7-8 P.M. | 47.9 |
| Washington (Dulles) | 11 A.M.-NOON | 76.9 | 6-7 P.M. | 56.0 |

*Source: Department of Transportation Report, March 1994*

# Travel Agencies

## Agencies Ranked by U.S. Sales

| Agency | 1992 Sales ($ thous.) |
|---|---|
| American Express | 4,250,000 |
| Carlson | 1,900,000 |
| Thomas Cook | 1,311,000 |
| Rosenbluth | 1,200,000 |
| USTravel | 913,000 |
| Maritz | 704,000 |
| IVI | 650,000 |
| Wagons-lits Travel USA | 319,000 |
| Omega World Travel | 318,000 |
| World Travel Partners | 250,000 |
| Northwestern Travel Service | 232,060 |
| Travel and Transport | 232,000 |
| VTS | 226,832 |
| TravelOne | 195,320 |
| Associated Travel Services | 164,100 |
| Travel Incorporated | 153,000 |
| McDonnell Douglas Travel | 152,545 |
| Total Travel Management | 151,000 |
| Corporate Travel Consultants | 151,000 |
| Garber | 136,263 |
| World Wide Travel | 132,450 |
| Arrington | 130,000 |
| Morris Travel | 130,000 |
| Supertravel | 129,000 |
| Worldtek | 118,000 |

## Agencies Ranked by Number of Offices

| Agency | Offices |
|---|---|
| American Express | 720 |
| Carlson | 400 |
| Thomas Cook | 387 |
| Rosenbluth | NA |
| USTravel | 242 |
| Omega World Travel | 202 |
| Travel and Transport | 116 |
| Northwestern Travel Service | 98 |
| Wagons-lits Travel USA | 89 |
| Maritz | 84 |
| Garber | 77 |
| Supertravel | 66 |
| Associated Travel Services | 65 |
| IVI | 62 |
| World Travel Partners | 62 |
| Direct Travel | 56 |
| TravelOne | 52 |
| Morris Travel | 51 |
| Travel Incorporated | 46 |
| Total Travel Management | 43 |
| World Wide Travel | 42 |
| Hoy & Eckdall Tours | 42 |
| Worldtek | 40 |
| AAA Auto Club South | 38 |

*Source: Business Travel News, May 24, 1993*

---

 **FAX** **Top 50 Airport Car Rental Markets.** Request #321. See p. xi for instructions.

Table of the top airport car rental markets by revenue and percent share.

---

## The Top Reference Sources

Runzheimer International
Runzheimer Park
Rochester, Wisconsin 53167
(800) 558-1702

Runzheimer International is a management consulting firm that specializes in travel and living costs, serving over 2,000 businesses and government agencies worldwide. Areas of special knowledge include employee relocation, business driving programs, and travel management.

*Runzheimer Reports on Travel Management*, a monthly newsletter, contains information on airline ticket costs, city highlights, business travel price indexes, and other topics of interest to travel managers. A one-year subscription is $295.

# Auto Rental Companies

## Top Companies by Revenue

| Company | 1992 Revenue ($) | Telephone |
|---------|------------------|-----------|
| Hertz | 4,200,000 | (800) 654-3131 |
| Avis | 3,200,000 | (800) 831-2847 |
| Budget | 2,200,000 | (800) 527-0770 |
| National | 2,000,000 | (800) 227-7368 |
| Alamo | 900,000 | (800) 327-9633 |
| Enterprise | 850,000 | (800) 325-8007 |
| Dollar | 650,000 | (800) 800-4000 |
| Thrifty | 411,200 | (800) 367-2277 |
| Agency | 290,000 | (800) 321-1972 |
| Carey | 183,000 | – |
| Rent A Wreck | 96,000 | (800) 822-1662 |
| U-Save | 55,000 | (800) 438-2300 |
| Payless | 48,000 | (800) 237-2804 |
| Advantage | 38,000 | (800) 777-5500 |
| Airways | 28,000 | (800) 952-9200 |
| Practical | 9,350 | (800) 233-1663 |

## Top Companies by Number of Locations

| Company | No. of Locations |
|---------|------------------|
| Hertz | 5,400 |
| Avis | 4,800 |
| National | 4,650 |
| Budget | 3,118 |
| Enterprise | 1,400 |
| Dollar | 1,362 |
| Thrifty | 822 |
| Agency | 700 |
| U-Save | 503 |
| Rent A Wreck | 426 |
| Carey | 390 |
| Payless | 200 |
| Alamo | 125 |
| Practical | 111 |
| Advantage | 60 |
| Airways | 39 |

*Source: Business Travel News, May 24, 1993*

# Per Diems by City

THE PER DIEM TOTALS SHOWN BELOW represent average costs for the typical business traveler, and include breakfast, lunch, and dinner in business-class restaurants and single-rate lodging in business-class hotels and motels. Data is from the *Runzheimer Meal-Lodging Cost Index*, and was gathered between the second half of 1993 and the first quarter of 1994.

## High-Priced Locations (Domestic)

| Location | Total Cost per Diem ($) |
|----------|-------------------------|
| New York, NY | 330 |
| Washington DC | 247 |
| Honolulu, HI | 240 |
| Chicago, IL | 229 |
| Boston, MA | 216 |

## High-Priced Locations (International)

| Location | Total Cost per Diem ($) |
|----------|-------------------------|
| Tokyo | 455 |
| Paris | 353 |
| Hong Kong | 348 |
| Moscow | 328 |
| London | 316 |

## Low-Priced Locations (Domestic)

| Location | Total Cost per Diem ($) |
|----------|-------------------------|
| Wheeling, WV | 76 |
| Augusta, GA | 76 |
| Johnson/Tri City, TN | 80 |
| Fayetteville, NC | 81 |
| Beaumont, TX | 81 |

## Low-Priced Locations (International)

| Location | Total Cost per Diem ($) |
|----------|-------------------------|
| Abidjan, Ivory Coast | 85 |
| London, Ontario, Canada | 99 |
| Panama City, Panama | 109 |
| Bordeaux, France | 118 |
| Guangzhou, China | 121 |

*Source: Runzheimer International*

*Per Diems by City (cont'd)*

The IRS has a maximum deduction for travel expenses. Any expenses over these amounts are the responsiblity of the corporation, and cannot be deducted from income taxes.

## IRS-Approved Allowances for Travel on or After January 1, 1994

| City | Lodging ($) | Meals & Incidentals ($) | Combined ($) |
|---|---|---|---|
| Atlanta | 81 | 38 | 119 |
| Baltimore | 78 | 38 | 116 |
| Boston | 101 | 38 | 139 |
| Chicago | 104 | 38 | 142 |
| Cincinnati | 62 | 30 | 92 |
| Cleveland | 78 | 38 | 116 |
| Columbus | 69 | 34 | 103 |
| Dallas | 71 | 34 | 105 |
| Denver | 77 | 38 | 115 |
| Detroit | 80 | 38 | 118 |
| Houston | 78 | 38 | 116 |
| Indianapolis | 71 | 34 | 105 |
| Los Angeles | 102 | 38 | 140 |
| Miami | 73 | 34 | 107 |
| Milwaukee | 67 | 30 | 97 |
| Minneapolis | 64 | 34 | 98 |
| New York City | 142 | 38 | 180 |
| Norfolk | | | |
|   May 1–Sep. 30 | 83 | 34 | 117 |
|   Oct. 1–Apr. 30 | 61 | 34 | 95 |
| Philadelphia | 89 | 34 | 123 |
| Phoenix | | | |
|   Dec. 1–Apr. 30 | 87 | 34 | 121 |
|   May 1–Nov. 30 | 61 | 34 | 95 |
| Pittsburgh | 75 | 34 | 109 |
| Portland | 67 | 30 | 97 |
| Sacramento | 67 | 34 | 101 |
| St. Louis | 74 | 38 | 112 |
| San Antonio | 67 | 30 | 97 |
| San Diego | 78 | 38 | 116 |
| San Francisco | 96 | 38 | 134 |
| Seattle | 79 | 34 | 113 |
| Tampa | 57 | 26 | 83 |
| Washington | 113 | 38 | 151 |

*Source: Compensation & Benefits Manager's Report*

# Tourism in American Business

THE U.S. TRAVEL AND TOURISM Administration's 1994 Outlook report projects that a total of 46.5 million foreign visitors will spend time in the United States this year. The report notes that over the past six years international visitors' spending has increased 72% from $46.9 billion to a projected $80.9 billion, opening vast opportunities for American businesses.

Valuable marketing information is available from this organization's in-flight surveys of international travelers. These surveys offer a clear profile of the international traveler, his or her purpose for travel, needs, and spending habits.

## Countries of Origin of U.S. Visitors

| Travelers' Residence | No. of Travelers |
|---|---|
| TOTAL | 17,791,000 |
| Western Europe | 8,055,000 |
| United Kingdom | 2,824,000 |
| Germany | 1,692,000 |
| France | 795,000 |
| Italy | 590,000 |
| Spain | 344,000 |
| Netherlands | 342,000 |
| Switzerland | 322,000 |
| Sweden | 262,000 |
| Eastern Europe | 207,000 |
| Caribbean | 1,004,000 |
| Bahamas | 287,000 |
| South America | 1,770,000 |
| Brazil | 475,000 |
| Venezuela | 372,000 |
| Argentina | 342,000 |
| Central America | 481,000 |
| Asia (Far East) | 5,097,000 |
| Japan | 3,653,000 |
| South Korea | 341,000 |
| Taiwan | 321,000 |
| Oceania | 654,000 |
| Australia | 487,000 |
| Middle East | 373,000 |
| Africa | 150,000 |

*Note: Numbers do not add up to regional totals since countries with less than 2% of total overseas travelers to the U.S. are not included.*

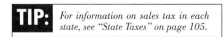

**TIP:** *For information on sales tax in each state, see "State Taxes" on page 105.*

## Purpose of U.S. Trip

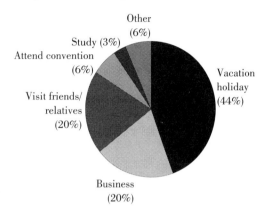

Other (6%)
Study (3%)
Attend convention (6%)
Visit friends/relatives (20%)
Vacation holiday (44%)
Business (20%)

## Type and Size of Traveling Party

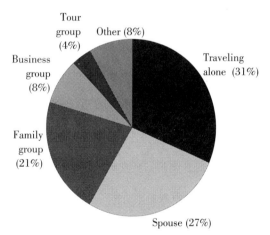

Tour group (4%)
Other (8%)
Business group (8%)
Traveling alone (31%)
Family group (21%)
Spouse (27%)

*Note: Figures do not add up to 100 due to rounding.*

*Source: U.S. Travel and Tourism Administration, October 1993*

## Recommended Resources

U.S. Travel and Tourism Administration
Main Commerce Bldg.
Washington, DC 20230
(202) 482-4752

U.S. Travel Data Center
2 Lafayette Centre
1133 21st St., NW
Washington, DC 20036
(202) 293-1040

Provides domestic travel statistical information and the economic impact on the travel and tourism industry.

# U.S. Passport Agencies

*Boston*
Thomas P. O'Neill Federal Building
10 Causeway St., Room 247
Boston, MA 02222
(617) 565-6698*
(617) 565-6990

*Chicago*
Kluczynski Federal Office Building
230 S. Dearborn St., Suite 380
Chicago, IL 60604
(312) 353-7155*

*Honolulu*
New Federal Building
300 Ala Moana Blvd., Room C-06
Honolulu, HI 96850
(808) 541-1919*
(808) 541-1918

*Houston*
Mickey Leland Federal Building
1919 Smith St., Suite 1100
Houston, TX 77002
(713) 653-3153*

*Los Angeles*
11000 Wilshire Blvd.
Room 13100
West Los Angeles, CA 90024
(213) 575-7070

*Miami*
Claude Pepper Federal Office Building
51 S.W. 1st Ave., 3rd Floor
Miami, FL 33130
(305) 536-4681*

*New Orleans*
Postal Service Building
701 Loyola Ave.
Room T-12005
New Orleans, LA 70113
(504) 589-6728*
(504) 589-6161/61/68

*New York City*
Rockefeller Center
630 Fifth Ave., Room 270
New York, NY 10111
(212) 399-5290*

*Philadelphia*
Federal Office Building
600 Arch St., Room 4426
Philadelphia, PA 19106
(215) 597-7480*

*San Francisco*
Tishman Speyer Building
525 Market St., Suite 200
San Francisco, CA 94105
(415) 744-4010*
(415) 744-4444

*Seattle*
Federal Office Building
915 Second Ave.
Room 992
Seattle, WA 98174
(206) 553-7941/42/43*
(206) 553-7945/46

*Stamford*
One Landmark Square
Broad and Atlantic Sts.
Stamford, CT 06901
(203) 325-4401/02*
(203) 325-3530/38/39

*Washington, DC*
1425 K St., NW
Washington, DC 20522
(202) 647-0518*

* 24-hour information line

It also may be possible to apply at the local post office or another designated location. Check the government listings in the phone book under Department of State or Passport Services.

# The Best Restaurants

## The Top 5 Rated Restaurants in Selected U.S. Metro Areas, Ranked by The Zagat Survey

| Restaurant | Type* |
| --- | --- |
| *Atlanta* | |
| The Dining Room | NAm |
| Ciboulette | FB |
| Pano's and Paul's | Co |
| Chops | St |
| The Hedgerose Heights Inn | Co |
| *Baltimore* | |
| The Prime Rib | AT |
| Milton Inn | Co |
| Hamptons | NAm |
| Tio Pepe | Sp |
| Linwood's Cafe Grille | NAm |
| *Boston* | |
| Olives | NAm |
| Aujourd'hui | Ca/F |
| Julien | FC |
| L'Espalier | NF |
| Jasper's | AR |
| *Chicago* | |
| Le Français | FC |
| Carlos' | FC |
| Ambria | NF |
| Jimmy's Place | F/J |
| Tallgrass | NF |
| *Cincinnati* | |
| The Palace | AR |
| Maisonette | FC |
| The Precinct | St |
| Orchids at Palm Court | AR |
| Barresi's Italian Restaurant | I |
| *Cleveland* | |
| Parker's | NAm |
| Johnny's Bar on Fulton | Co/I |
| Classics | Co |
| The Baricelli Inn | I |
| Hyde Park Grille | St |
| *Columbus* | |
| Rigsby's Cuisine Volatile | A/M |
| Handke's Cuisine | NAm |
| Carolyn's | NAm |
| The Refectory Restaurant | FC/NF |
| Restaurant Japan | J |
| *Dallas* | |
| The Riviera | M |
| Mansion on Turtle Creek | So |
| The French Room | FC |
| York Street | Co |
| Del Frisco's Double Eagle Steakhouse | St |

| Restaurant | Type* |
| --- | --- |
| *Denver* | |
| European Café–Boulder | F/NAm |
| Piñons | NAm |
| Morton's of Chicago | St |
| Wildflower | E |
| Sweet Basil | NAm |
| *Houston* | |
| Chez Nous | FB |
| DeVille | AR |
| Tony's | Co/I |
| Rotisserie for Beef and Bird | NAm |
| Ruggles Grill | NAm |
| *Los Angeles* | |
| Patina | Ca/F |
| Matsuhisa | PNW |
| Shiro | PNW |
| Sushi Nozawa | PNW |
| Chinois on Main | PNW |
| *Miami* | |
| Mark's Place | NAm |
| Chef Allen's | NAm |
| Grand Cafe | Co |
| The Fish Market | Se |
| Casa Larios | Cu |
| *Milwaukee* | |
| Sally's Steakhouse | St |
| Grenadier's | Co |
| The English Room | AT/F |
| Karl Ratzsch's | G |
| The Immigrant Room | AT |
| *New York* | |
| Bouley | NF |
| Aureole | NAm |
| Chanterelle | NF |
| Le Bernardin | F/Se |
| Le Cirque | NF |
| *Philadelphia* | |
| Le Bec-Fin | FC |
| The Fountain | In |
| Evermay on the Delaware | A/F |
| The Green Hills Inn | A/F |
| Le Bar Lyonnais | FB |
| *Phoenix* | |
| Vincent Guerithault on Camelback | So |
| Franco's Trattoria | NI |
| Yamakasa | J |
| Marquesa | Sp |
| Christopher's and The Bistro | NAm/NF |

*The Best Restaurants (cont'd)*

| Restaurant | Type* |
|---|---|
| *Portland* | |
| Genoa | NI |
| Cafe des Amis | FB |
| Winterborne | Se |
| Zefiro | M |
| Heathman | No |
| *St. Louis* | |
| Tony's | Co/I |
| Fio's La Fourchette | FC |
| Cafe de France | FC |
| Andria's | St |
| Giovanni's | NI |
| *San Diego* | |
| WineSellar/Brasserie | NF |
| Mille Fleurs | Ca/F |
| El Bizcocho | FC |
| Marius | NF |
| Belgian Lion | B/F |
| *San Francisco* | |
| Masa's | NF |
| Fleur de Lys | FC |
| La Folie | NF |
| Chez Panisse | Ca |
| Erna's Elderberry House | FC |

| Restaurant | Type* |
|---|---|
| *Seattle* | |
| The Herbfarm | A/No |
| Rover's | F/No |
| Shoalwater Restaurant | No |
| Saleh al Lago | NI |
| Szmania | G/No |
| *Tampa* | |
| Euphemia Haye | E |
| Armani's | NI |
| Bern's Steak House | St |
| Cafe L'Europe | Co |
| Mise en Place | NAm |
| *Washington, DC* | |
| Inn at Little Washington | NAm |
| Le Lion d'Or | FC |
| Jean-Louis | NF |
| L'Auberge Chez François | FC |
| The Prime Rib | St |

\* *A–American; AR–American Regional; AT–American Traditional; B–Belgian; Ca–Californian; Co–Continental; Cu–Cuban; E–Eclectic; F–French; FB–French Bistro; FC–French Classic; G–German; In–International; I–Italian; J–Japanese; M–Mediterranean; NAm–New American; NF–New French; NI–Northern Italian; No–Northwest; PNW–Pacific New Wave; Se–Seafood; So–Southwestern; Sp–Spanish; St–Steakhouse*

*Source: Zagat Survey, America's Top Restaurants 1994*

## The Top Reference Sources

*America's Top Restaurants*
Zagat Survey, $12.95
(212) 977-6000

This coat-pocket-sized book contains information on the top restaurants in 34 cities nationwide. Each entry includes the restaurant name, cuisine type, address, phone number, ratings on food, decor, and service, average meal price, and additional comments. The reviewers are volunteers.

The Zagat Survey also publishes 24 city/area restaurant guides as well as *America's Best Meal Deals* and *U.S. Hotel, Resort, and Spa Survey.*

# Guide to Audio-Visual Rentals

WHEN YOU ARE TRAVELING to another city to give a presentation, your firm can save money by using a local company to provide multimedia equipment like televisions, slide projectors, or computers. This city-by-city listing highlights selected firms around the country.

| Company | Telephone |
|---|---|
| *Atlanta* | |
| Atlanta Sound & Lighting | (404) 455-7695 |
| Projexions Video Supply | (404) 872-6247 |
| Total Audio Visual Services | (404) 875-7555 |
| *Baltimore* | |
| American Audio-Video | (410) 837-1339 |
| Audio Recording Services | (410) 643-4220 |
| Chesapeake Audio/Visual Communications | (410) 796-0040 |
| Crew Works | (410) 235-2037 |
| Total Audio-Visual Systems | (410) 625-4700 |
| *Boston* | |
| Immediate Connections | (617) 783-1599 |
| Media 1 | (617) 254-0770 |
| Projection Video Services | (617) 254-6693 |
| Audio Services | (617) 424-0065 |
| *Chicago* | |
| Artistic Communication Center | (312) 280-0808 |
| LeGrand Services | (800) 252-6222 |
| Video Replay | (312) 822-0221 |
| Williams Gerard Productions | (312) 467-5560 |
| *Cincinnati* | |
| Cavalier Audio Visual Services | (513) 784-0055 |
| CSI/Clarity Systems | (513) 784-1200 |
| Visual Aids Electronics | (513) 684-0800 |
| *Cleveland* | |
| CPS Meetings | (216) 771-7711 |
| Colortone | (216) 581-5055 |
| Eighth Day Sound | (216) 961-2900 |
| Presentation Services | (216) 241-2777 |
| *Columbus* | |
| Brite Lights | (614) 272-1404 |
| Mills James Productions | (614) 777-9933 |
| United States Audio Visuals | (614) 461-8444 |
| *Dallas* | |
| Bauer Audio Visual | (214) 630-6700 |
| SAV Communications | (214) 423-5874 |
| Brad Young Multi-Image | (214) 528-4888 |
| Arapaho Audio Visual | (214) 458-1468 |
| S Audio Visual | (214) 637-0581 |
| *Denver* | |
| Colorado Visual Aids | (303) 733-9910 |
| Ceavco Audio Visual Company | (303) 238-0443 |
| Colorado Audio Visual | (303) 925-8508 |
| Spectrum Audio-Visual | (303) 477-4456 |

| Company | Telephone |
|---|---|
| *Detroit* | |
| Audio Visual Wholesalers | (612) 559-9666 |
| Blumberg Communications | (612) 521-8225 |
| Showtech Presentation Systems | (313) 547-8880 |
| *Gaithersburg, MD* | |
| CPR Multimedia Solutions | (800) 825-4277 |
| *Houston* | |
| A/V Texas | (713) 526-3687 |
| Aves Audio Visual Systems | (713) 783-3440 |
| Image in Action | (713) 932-9779 |
| Photo & Sound | (713) 956-9566 |
| *Indianapolis* | |
| Dodd Technologies | (317) 842-4905 |
| Markey's Audio Visual | (317) 783-1155 |
| United States Audio-Visuals | (317) 632-2527 |
| *Los Angeles* | |
| Bauer/Southam Audio Video | (310) 815-8817 |
| Jacobs Audio Visual Systems | (213) 882-8577 |
| Studio Instrument Rental | (213) 848-3660 |
| Video Equipment Rentals of Southern California | (818) 956-0212 |
| *Miami* | |
| Blumberg Communications | (305) 594-3939 |
| Metro Audio Visual | (305) 623-1300 |
| Miami Audio Visual | (305) 757-5000 |
| Southern Audio/Video & Business Rental | (305) 591-3888 |
| Total Audiovisual | (407) 859-3399 |
| *Milwaukee* | |
| Audio Visual of Milwaukee | (414) 258-1077 |
| Midwest Visual Equipment | (414) 784-5880 |
| Studio Gear | (414) 223-4884 |
| United States Audio-Visuals | (414) 276-8688 |
| *Minneapolis* | |
| Audio-Visual and Video Resources | (612) 456-9033 |
| Twin City Audio-Visual Services | (612) 869-4501 |
| *New York* | |
| Ace Audio Visual | (212) 685-3344 |
| Bauer Audio Video | (212) 714-9648 |
| Executive Audio-Visual Services | (212) 575-2500 |
| *Norfolk* | |
| Craft-Work Sound | (804) 436-2577 |
| Atlantic Audio Visual | (804) 422-5252 |

*Guide to Audio-Visual Rentals (cont'd)*

| Company | Telephone |
|---|---|
| *Philadelphia* | |
| Audio Visual Center | (215) 563-6872 |
| Bauer Audio Video | (215) 625-0885 |
| Visual Sound | (215) 544-8700 |
| *Phoenix* | |
| A.V. Concepts | (602) 894-6642 |
| Southwest Audio Visual | (602) 258-4911 |
| *Pittsburgh* | |
| Corporate Video Creations | (412) 281-2662 |
| Pro-Com Systems | (412) 621-1950 |
| Visual Aids Center of Pittsburgh | (412) 566-1800 |
| Willowglen Productions | (412) 828-7777 |
| *Portland, OR* | |
| Audio-Visual Rentals & Services | (503) 222-1664 |
| Rose City Sound | (503) 238-6330 |
| *Sacramento* | |
| Munday & Collins | (916) 451-6511 |
| Pacific Crest Picture | (916) 652-4466 |
| Photo & Sound | (916) 649-6999 |
| *St. Louis* | |
| Audio-Visual Alternatives | (314) 773-9155 |
| Audio-Visual Management | (314) 421-2862 |

| Company | Telephone |
|---|---|
| *San Francisco* | |
| AVTS | (415) 882-7766 |
| Concept Organization | (415) 495-6521 |
| Projection Video Services | (415) 826-2244 |
| *Seattle* | |
| Barr Audio Visual | (206) 763-7181 |
| Pro-Image | (206) 284-5000 |
| *Tampa* | |
| Advanced Visual Communications (AVCOM) | (813) 875-0888 |
| Audio Visual Support Service | (813) 872-7914 |
| Cypress Productions | (813) 289-6115 |
| Vaughn Broadcast Rentals | (813) 887-3141 |
| *Washington, DC* | |
| Chesapeake Audio/Video Communications | (301) 596-3900 |
| Crew Works | (410) 235-2037 |

# Visitor and Convention Bureaus

BELOW IS A LISTING of the names, addresses, and phone numbers of the Visitors and Convention Bureaus in 30 major cities. Any company in need of a trade show facilitator should contact the Visitors and Convention Bureau in the city hosting the event. The telephone numbers of a variety of facilitators are available through the convention services department of each bureau.

## Contact Options

*Atlanta*
233 Peachtree St., NE
Suite 2000
Atlanta, GA 30303
(404) 521-6600

*Baltimore*
USF&G Tower
100 Light St., 12th Floor
Baltimore, MD 21202
(410) 659-7300 or (800) 343-3468

*Boston*
Prudential Tower, 4th Floor, Suite 400
P.O. Box 490
Boston, MA 02199
(617) 536-4100

*Chicago*
McCormick Place On-The-Lake
2301 S. Lake Shore Dr.
Chicago, IL 60616
(312) 567-8500

*Cincinnati*
300 W. Sixth St.
Cincinnati, OH 45202
(513) 621-2142

*Cleveland*
3100 Terminal Tower
Tower City Center
Cleveland, OH 44113
(216) 621-4110 or (800) 321-1001

*Columbus*
One Columbus Building
10 W. Broad St., Suite 1300
Columbus, OH 43215
(614) 221-6623 or (800) 234-2657

*Dallas*
1201 Elm St., Suite 2000
Dallas, TX 75270
(214) 746-6677

*Visitor and Convention Bureaus (cont'd)*

*Denver*
370 17th St., Suite 5000
Denver, CO 80202
(303) 892-1112

*Detroit*
100 Renaissance Center, Suite 1950
Detroit, MI 48243
(313) 259-4333

*Houston*
3300 Main St.
Houston, TX 77002
(713) 523-5050 or (800) 231-7799

*Indianapolis*
One Hoosier Dome, Suite 100
Indianapolis, IN 46225
(317) 639-4282 or (800) 323-4639

*Los Angeles*
515 S. Figueroa, 11th Floor
Los Angeles, CA 90071
(213) 624-7300

*Miami*
701 Brickell Ave., Suite 2700
Miami, FL 33131
(305) 539-3000 or (800) 933-8448

*Milwaukee*
510 West Kilbourn Ave.
Milwaukee, WI 53203
(414) 273-3950 or (800) 231-0903

*Minneapolis*
1219 Marquette Ave.
Minneapolis, MN 55403
(612) 348-4313 or (800) 445-7412

*New York*
Two Columbus Circle
New York, NY 10019
(212) 484-1200

*Norfolk*
236 E. Plume St.
Norfolk, VA 23510
(804) 441-5266 or (800) 368-3097

*Philadelphia*
1515 Market St., Suite 2020
Philadelphia, PA 19102
(215) 636-3300

*Phoenix*
One Arizona Center
400 E. Van Buren St., Suite 600
Phoenix, AZ 85004
(602) 254-6500 or (800) 535-8898

*Pittsburgh*
Four Gateway Center, Suite 514
Pittsburgh, PA 15222
(412) 366-0093 or (800) 821-1888

*Portland*
Three World Trade Center
26 South West Salmon
Portland, OR 97204
(503) 275-9750

*Sacramento*
1421 K St.
Sacramento, CA 95814
(916) 264-7777

*St. Louis*
10 S. Broadway, Suite 1000
St. Louis, MO 63102
(314) 421-1023 or (800) 325-7962

*San Antonio*
121 Alamo Plaza (78205)
P.O. Box 2277
San Antonio, TX 78298
(512) 270-8700 or (800) 447-3372

*San Diego*
1200 Third Ave., Suite 824
San Diego, CA 92101
(619) 232-3101

*San Francisco*
201 Third St., Suite 900
San Francisco, CA 94103
(415) 974-6900

---

 **State Travel Information Centers.** Request #411. See p. xi for instructions.
Phone numbers of travel information offices nationwide.

*Visitor and Convention Bureaus (cont'd)*

*Seattle*
520 Pike St., Suite 1300
Seattle, WA 98101
(206) 461-5800

*Tampa*
111 Madison St., Suite 1010
P.O. Box 519
Tampa, FL 33602
(813) 223-1111

*Washington, DC*
1212 New York Ave., NW, Suite 600
Washington, DC 20005
(202) 789-7000

### Recommended Resource

International Association of Convention and
Visitors Bureaus
P.O. Box 6690
Champaign, IL 61826
(217) 359-8881

# Convention Centers

## Major Convention Centers in Selected Cities

| City | Convention Center | Telephone |
|------|-------------------|-----------|
| Atlanta | Georgia World Congress Center | (404) 223-4000 |
| Baltimore | Baltimore Convention Center | (410) 659-7000 |
| Boston | Hynes Convention Center | (617) 954-2000 |
| Chicago | McCormick Place | (312) 791-7000 |
| Cincinnati | Cincinnati Convention Center | (513) 352-3750 |
| Cleveland | International Exposition (I-X) Center | (216) 676-6000 |
| Columbus | Greater Columbus Convention Center | (614) 645-5000 |
| Dallas | Dallas Convention Center | (214) 939-2700 |
| Denver | Colorado Convention Center | (303) 640-8000 |
| Detroit | Cobo Conference/Exhibition Center | (313) 224-1015 |
| Houston | George R. Brown Convention Center | (713) 853-8000 |
| Indianapolis | Indiana Convention Center & Hoosier Dome | (317) 262-3410 |
| Los Angeles | Los Angeles Convention Center | (800) 448-7775 |
| Miami | Miami Beach Convention Center | (305) 673-7311 |
| Milwaukee | Mecca–Milwaukee Exposition & Convention Center | (414) 271-4000 |
| Minneapolis | Minneapolis Convention Center | (612) 335-6000 |
| New Orleans | Ernest N. Morial Convention Center | (504) 582-3000 |
| New York | Jacob K. Javits Convention Center | (212) 216-2000 |
| Norfolk | Norfolk Scope | (804) 441-2764 |
| Philadelphia | Pennsylvania Convention Center | (215) 418-4700 |
| Phoenix | Phoenix Civic Plaza | (602) 262-6225 |
| Pittsburgh | David L. Lawrence Convention Center | (412) 565-6000 |
| Portland, OR | Oregon Convention Center | (503) 235-7575 |
| Sacramento | Sacramento Convention Center | (916) 264-5291 |
| San Antonio | Henry B. Gonzalez Convention Center | (210) 299-8500 |
| San Diego | San Diego Convention Center | (619) 525-5000 |
| San Francisco | Moscone Convention Center | (415) 974-4000 |
| Seattle | Washington State Convention and Trade Center | (206) 447-5000 |
| St. Louis | Cervantes at America's Center | (314) 342-5036 |
| Tampa | Tampa Convention Center | (800) 426-5630 |
| Washington, DC | Washington Convention Center | (800) 368-9000 |

# Hotel & Resort Convention Centers

CONVENTION AND VISITORS BUREAUS are an invaluable aid to the meeting planners and provide "one-stop shopping" for information on facilities, services, and suppliers available in a particular locale. *Meetings and Conventions* magazine annually awards the Gold Service Award to the CVBs rated on overall helpfulness by the magazine's voting readership.

Over the last 15 years *Meetings and Conventions* magazine has annually awarded the Gold Key Awards to those meeting properties which are judged to meet seven criteria deemed vital to a successful convention. These are: meeting staff; meeting rooms; guest services; food and beverage service; reservations handling; A/V and other technical/support equipment; and–for resorts–recreational facilities.

## 1993 Gold Service Award Winners

*Alaska*
Anchorage Convention & Visitors Bureau

*Arizona*
Phoenix & Valley of the Sun
Convention & Visitors Bureau
Scottsdale Chamber of Commerce
Metropolitan Tucson Convention & Visitors Bureau

*California*
Palm Springs Desert Resorts
Convention & Visitors Bureau
San Diego Convention & Visitors Bureau
San Francisco Convention & Visitors Bureau

*Colorado*
Denver Metro Convention & Visitors Bureau

*Florida*
Orlando/Orange County Convention
& Visitors Bureau

*Georgia*
Atlanta Convention & Visitors Bureau

*Illinois*
Chicago Convention & Tourism Bureau

*Missouri*
Convention & Visitors Bureau of Greater
Kansas City

*Louisiana*
Greater New Orleans Tourist &
Convention Commission

*Nevada*
Las Vegas Convention & Visitors Authority
Reno-Sparks Convention & Visitors Authority

*New York*
New York Convention & Visitors Bureau

*Puerto Rico*
San Juan–Puerto Rico Convention Bureau

*Tennessee*
Nashville Convention & Visitors Bureau

*Texas*
Dallas Convention & Visitors Bureau
Irving Convention & Visitors Bureau
San Antonio Convention & Visitors Bureau

*Washington*
Seattle–King County Convention & Visitors Bureau

*Australia*
Australian Tourist Commission

*Bermuda*
Bermuda Department of Tourism

*Canada*
Metropolitan Toronto Convention &
Visitors Association

*Singapore*
The Singapore Convention Bureau

*Hawaii*
Hawaii Visitors Bureau

*Hong Kong*
Hong Kong Convention & Incentive Travel Bureau

## Gold Key Domestic Award Winners

*Arizona*
Arizona Biltmore
The Boulders Resort
The Crescent Hotel
Loews Ventana Canyon Resort
Marriott's Camelback Inn Resort, Golf Club & Spa
The Phoenician
The Pointe Hilton Resort at Tapatio Cliffs
Scottsdale Conference Resort
Scottsdale Plaza Resort
Scottsdale Princess
Sheraton El Conquistador Golf & Tennis Resort
Westin La Paloma
The Wigwam

*California*
Fairmont Hotel San Francisco
Four Seasons Hotel Newport
Hotel del Coronado
Hyatt Regency Irvine
La Quinta Hotel Golf & Tennis Resort

*Hotel & Resort Convention Centers (cont'd)*

Anaheim Marriott Hotel
Marriott's Desert Springs Resort & Spa
Santa Clara Marriott
San Diego Marriott Hotel & Marina
San Francisco Marriott
The Ritz-Carlton, Laguna Niguel
The Ritz-Carlton, Rancho Mirage
Sheraton Grand on Harbor Island
Sheraton Grand Torrey Pines
Westin St. Francis

*Colorado*
The Broadmoor
Cheyenne Mountain Conference Resort
Denver Marriott Hotel City Center

*Florida*
Amelia Island Plantation
Boca Raton Resort & Club
The Breakers
Buena Vista Palace
Disney's Grand Floridian Beach Resort
Doral Resort & Country Club
Hyatt Regency Grand Cypress
Marriott's Harbor Beach Resort
Marriott's Marco Island Resort and Golf Club
Marriott's Orlando World Center
The Registry Resort
The Ritz-Carlton, Naples
Saddlebrook Golf & Tennis Resort
Sanibel Harbor Resort & Spa
Stouffer Vinoy Resort
The Villas of Grand Cypress
Walt Disney World Dolphin

*Georgia*
The Cloister
Atlanta Airport Hilton and Towers
Atlanta Marriott Marquis
Stouffer Pineisle Resort

*Illinois*
Four Seasons Hotel Chicago
The Palmer House Hilton
Hyatt Regency Chicago
Chicago Marriott Downtown
O'Hare Marriott

*Louisiana*
New Orleans Marriott Hotel

*Maryland*
Hyatt Regency Baltimore on the Inner Harbor
Stouffer Harborplace Hotel

*Massachusetts*
Boston Marriott Copley Place
Sheraton Boston Hotel & Towers
The Westin Hotel, Copley Place Boston

*Michigan*
Grand Hotel

*Missouri*
Marriott's Tan-Tar-A Resort & Golf Club

*Nevada*
Las Vegas Hilton
The Mirage

*New York*
New York Marriott Marquis

*North Carolina*
Pinehurst Hotel & Country Club

*South Carolina*
Westin Resort Hilton Head Hotel

*Tennessee*
Opryland Hotel

*Texas*
Barton Creek Conference Resort
Four Seasons Hotel & Resort, Dallas at Las Colinas
Loews Anatole Hotel
San Antonio Marriott Rivercenter
San Antonio Marriott Riverwalk

*Virginia*
The Homestead
Kingsmill Resort & Conference Center
Crystal Gateway Marriott Hotel

*Washington, DC*
J.W. Marriott Hotel

*West Virginia*
The Greenbrier

---

## The Top Reference Sources

*Business Travel News*
*Corporate Travel*
(212) 626-2466

These two publications provide valuable information for business travel managers. *Business Travel News* reports and analyzes breaking events and trends in the travel industry and redefines the jobs of business travel managers and purchasers.

*Corporate Travel* provides the "who's who and how" of travel management. It gives a practical approach to the duties of corporate travel services decision makers.

Both publications are free to qualified subscribers.

# PERSONAL COMPUTING

# Product Awards

EVERY YEAR *PC COMPUTING* selects noteworthy IBM PC-compatible products in a variety of categories.

## PC Computing MVP Awards, 1993

| Category | Subcategory | Product |
|---|---|---|
| Systems | Desktop Systems | Gateway P5-60 |
| | Entry-Level Desktop Systems | AST Bravo LP Green |
| | Notebooks & Portable PCs | IBM ThinkPad 750C |
| | Subnotebooks | IBM ThinkPad 500 |
| | File Servers | Compaq ProLiant 2000 Pentium |
| Peripherals | Monitors | Nanao FlexScan F760iW |
| | Video Adapters | Number Nine GXE |
| | Printers | Hewlett-Packard LaserJet 4SiMX |
| | Color Printers | Tektronix Phaser 200i |
| | Storage Devices | Maxtor MXL-105-III |
| | Input Devices | Logitech MouseMan Cordless |
| Communications & Networking | Communications Software | Symantec Norton pcAnywhere for Windows |
| | Network Software | Novell NetWare 4.0 |
| | Communications Hardware | Intel SatisFaxtion |
| | Network Hardware | Telebit NetBlazer PN |
| Business Applications | Databases | Borland Paradox 4.5 for Windows, Workgroup Ed. |
| | Spreadsheets | Borland Quattro Pro 5.0 for Windows, Workgroup Ed. |
| | Word Processors | WordPerfect 6.0 for Windows |
| | Financial & Accounting Software | Intuit QuickBooks 2 for Windows |
| | Business Utilities | Folio Views 3.0 |
| | Presentation Graphics | Software Publishing Harvard Graphics 2.0 for Windows |
| | Desktop Publishing | Microsoft Publisher 2.0 |
| System Software | Operating Systems & Environments | IBM OS/2 2.1 |
| | System Utilities | Hewlett-Packard Dashboard 2.0 for Windows |
| | Application Development | Microsoft Visual C++ |
| Multimedia & Graphics | Multimedia Software | Adobe Premiere |
| | Multimedia Hardware | Pioneer CD-ROM Jukebox DRM-604X |
| | Paint & Draw Software | Virtus Walkthrough for Windows 1.1.1 |
| | Education & Entertainment | Virgin Games The 7th Guest |
| Innovation | Hardware Innovation | Intel Pentium Processor |
| | Software Innovation | Microsoft OLE 2.0 |

*Source: PC Computing*

Every year *MacUser* magazine gives the Eddy Awards, gold statuettes that honor the most innovative Macintosh products of the year. The first product in each category is the winner, and those that follow are the runners-up.

## MacUser Eddy Awards, 1993

| Category | Product | Company |
|---|---|---|
| Hardware Product of the Year | EtherWave | Farallon Computing |
| Software Product of the Year | After Effects 1.1 | CoSA |
| Breakthrough Technology of the Year | Newton Intelligence | Apple |
| Best New Presentation Product | Astound 1.0 | Gold Disk |
| | DeltaGraph Pro 3 | DeltaPoint |
| | Passport Producer Pro 1.0 | Passport Designs |
| Best New Accounting Package | Dynamics | Great Plains |
| | Best Books 1.0 | Teleware |

*Product Awards (cont'd)*

| Category | Product | Company |
|---|---|---|
| Best New Personal-Finance Program | Quicken 4 | Intuit |
| | CheckWriter Pro 6 | Aatrix |
| | WealthBuilder 3.0 | Reality Technologies |
| Best New Data-Management Product | Omnis 72 | Blyth Software |
| | Data Desk 4.1 | Data Description |
| | 4th Dimension 3.0 | ACI US |
| Best New Portable Computing Product | Hewlett-Packard DeskWriter 310 | Hewlett-Packard |
| | E-Machines Presenter Dock | E-Machines |
| | PowerPlate Series | Technöggin |
| Best New Input Device | JABRA EarPHONE Streamline AV | JABRA |
| | Abacus | Key Tronic |
| | Wacom ArtZ Tablet | Wacom |
| Best New Utility | QuicKeys 3.0 | CE Software |
| | Conflict Cather II | Casady & Greene |
| | MacTools 3.0 | Central Point Software |
| Best New Organizational Tool | Now Contact 1.0 | Now Software |
| | DayMaker Organizer 3.0 | Pastel Development |
| | Meeting Maker XP 1.0 | ON Technology |
| Best New Data Resource/Edutainment Product | How Computers Work | Time-Warner Interactive Group |
| | A Hard Day's Night | The Voyager Company |
| | Random House Unabridged Dictionary | Random House |
| Best New Publishing-Productivity Tool | Aldus Fetch 1.2 | Aldus |
| | Adobe Acrobat 1.0 | Adobe Systems |
| | Cirrus 2.0 | Canto Software |
| Best New Page-Design Program | Aldus Pagemaker 5.0 | Aldus |
| | FrameMaker 4.0 | Frame Technology |
| | Quark XPress 3.2 | Quark |
| Best New Visual Resource | Fontek DesignFonts Series | Letraset |
| | America Remembered 1.0 | Boraventures Publishing |
| | Volume 8: Backgrounds and Objects | PhotoDisc |
| Best New Illustration Program | Adobe Illustrator 5.0 | Adobe Systems |
| | addDepth 1.0 | Ray Dream |
| | Canvas 3.5 | Deneba |
| Best New Imaging Program | Painter 2.0 and X2 | Fractal Design |
| | artWORKS 1.0 | Deneba |
| | Adobe Photoshop 2.5.1 | Adobe Systems |
| Best New Typographic Product | Fontographer 4.0 | Altsys |
| | FontMixer 1.0 | Monotype |
| | Super ATM 1.0 | Adobe Systems |
| Best New 3-D Program | form•Z 2.3 | auto•des•sys |
| | MacroModel 1.5 | Macromedia |
| | StudioPro 1.0 | Strata |
| Best New Music/Sound Product | DECK II 2.02 | OSC Media Products |
| | ConcertWare Pro 1.0 | Great Wave Software |
| | Sound Engine | E-MU Systems |
| Best New Computer-Aided Visualization Program | WalkThrough Pro 1.0 | Virtus |
| | Design Workshop 1.05 | Artifice |
| | upFRONT 2.0 | Alias |
| Best New Desktop-Video Product | Avid Media Suite Pro 2.0 | Avid Technology |
| | Data Translation Media 100 1.0 | Data Translation |
| | RosterOps MoviePak Presenter | RosterOps |
| Best New Multimedia Software | Apple Media Kit 1.0 | Apple |
| | Adobe Premiere 3.0 | Adobe Systems |
| | VideoShop 2.0 | Avid Technology |

*Product Awards (cont'd)*

| Category | Product | Company |
|---|---|---|
| Best New Special-Effects Program | After Effects 1.1 | CoSA |
| | Meta Flo' 1.0 | The Valis Group |
| | VideoFusion 1.5 | VideoFusion |
| Best New Network Software | Retrospect Remote 2.0 | Dantz Development |
| | 4D Server 1.0.5 | ACI US |
| | Timbuktu 5.0 | Farallon Computing |
| Best New Development Tool | Resorcerer 1.2.4 | Mathemæsthetics |
| | BBEdit 2.5 | Bare Bones Software |
| | UpdateMaker 2.1 | AD Instruments |
| Best New Network-Management Product | GraceLAN Bundle | TechWorks |
| | EtherPEEK 2.0.3 | ag group |
| | LANsurveyor 1.0 | Neon Software |
| Best New Science/Engineering Product | LabView 3.0 | National Instruments |
| | HiQ 2.0 | National Instruments |
| | Working Model 1.0 | Knowledge Revolution |
| Best New Communications Product | First Class 2.4 | SoftArc |
| | SITcomm 1.0 | Aladdin Systems |
| | VersaTilities 1.1 | Synergy Software |
| Best New Network Hardware | EtherWave | Farallon Computing |
| | RICS•Router 3000E | Compatible Systems |
| | TribeStar | Tribe Computer Works |
| Best New Display Product | SuperMac PressView 21 Display System | SuperMac |
| | Apple AudioVision 14 Display | Apple |
| | Radius IntelliColor Display/20 | Radius |
| Best New Scanning Product | Nikon Coolscan | Nikon |
| | PixelCraft Pro Imager 7650c | PixelCraft |
| | La Cie Silverscanner II | La Cie |
| Best New Monochrome Printer | Hewlett-Packard LaserJet 4ML | Hewlett-Packard |
| | Apple LaserWriter Pro 630 | Apple |
| | GCC SelectPress 600 | GCC |
| Best New Accelerator Board | YARC Systems Turbo MacRageous | YARC Systems |
| | DayStar Turbo 040 | DayStar |
| | Extreme Systems Impact RGB | Extreme Systems |
| Best New Color Systems | Tektronix Phaser 200i | Tektronix |
| | Hewlett-Packard DeskJet 1200C/PS | Hewlett-Packard |
| | SuperMac ProofPositive | SuperMac |
| Best New Storage Product | APS SR 2000 Case | APS |
| | Alphatronix Inspire III GG | Alphatronix |
| | FWB SCSI JackHammer | FWB |
| Best New Desktop Diversion | Opus 'n' Bill Screen Saver 1.0 | Selrina |
| | ClickChange 2.0 | DublClick |
| | UnderWare 1.0 | Bit Jugglers |
| Best New Children's Program | Thinkin' Things 1.0 | Edmark |
| | The San Diego Zoo Presents–The Animals! | The Software Toolworks |
| | Putt-Putt Joins the Parade | Humungous Entertainment |
| Best New Game | Myst 1.0 | Brøderbund |
| | Eight Ball Deluxe | AMTEX |
| | Iron Helix 1.0 | Drew Picture |

*Source: MacUser, 1994*

*Product Awards (cont'd)*

*Windows* magazine chooses the top 100 Windows products each year.

## The Windows 100, 1993

| Category | Product | Company |
|---|---|---|
| Accounting/Financial Management | Quicken 3.0 | Intuit |
| | TaxCut | Meca Software |
| Alternative Desktops | Dashboard 2.0 | Hewlett-Packard |
| | Plug-In for Program Manager | Plannet Crafters |
| | Power Launcher 2.0 | hDC Computer |
| Applications Development/Languages | QuickPak Professional 2.03 | Crescent Software |
| | RoboHELP 2.0 | Blue Sky Software |
| | Visual C++ 1.0 | Microsoft |
| CD-ROM Drives | NEC MultiSpin 3X | NEC Technologies |
| | Texel DM3024 and DM5024 | Texel/Plextor |
| Communications Software | CommWorks | Traveling Software |
| | HyperACCESS 1.0 | Hilgraeve |
| Content Publishing | Bookshelf 93 | Microsoft |
| | Encarta Multimedia Encyclopedia | Microsoft |
| | New Grolier Multimedia Encyclopedia | Grolier Electronic Publishing |
| | TechNet CD-ROM | Microsoft |
| Databases | Approach 2.1 | Lotus Development |
| | FileMaker Pro | Claris |
| | InfoPublisher 2.0 | PageAhead Software |
| | Paradox | Borland International |
| | Q&A 4.0 | Symantec |
| Desktop Faxing | Eclipse Fax OCR 1.21 | Eclipse Systems |
| | FaxWorks Pro 3.0 | SofNet |
| Desktop Publishing | Acrobat | Adobe Systems |
| | FrameMaker 4.0 | Frame Technology |
| | PageMaker 5.0 | Aldus |
| | Publisher 2.0 | Microsoft |
| | Replica | Farallon Computing |
| E-Mail/On-Line | E-Mail Connection 1.0 | Connect Software |
| | Journalist 1.1 | PED Software |
| | MailPlus | Computer Mail Services |
| | WordPerfect Office 4.0 | WordPerfect |
| Graphics/Photo Tools | ColorUP 1.0 | Pantone |
| | HiJaak Pro | Inset Systems |
| | ImagePals 1.2 | U-Lead Systems |
| | Photoshop 2.5 | Adobe Systems |
| | Picture Publisher 4.0 | Micrografx |
| Illustration/CAD | ABC FlowCharter 2.0 | Micrografx |
| | AutoCAD 12 | Autodesk |
| | Canvas Windows | Deneba Software |
| | CorelDRAW! 4.0 | Corel |
| | Visio 2.0 | Shapeware |
| | WalkThrough | Virtus |
| Management | ManagePro 2.0 | Avantos Performance Systems |
| Microprocessors | Cyrix Cx486SRx2 and Cx486Dx2 | Cyrix |
| | Intel Pentium | Intel |
| Modems | Hayes Optima 144 + Fax144 Pocket Edition | Hayes Microcomputer Products |
| Monitors | Compaq Q-Vision 170 | Compaq Computer |
| | NEC MultiSyncFG | NEC Technologies |
| | ViewSonic 21 | ViewSonic |

*Product Awards (cont'd)*

| Category | Product | Company |
|---|---|---|
| Networking | Intel EtherExpress16 | Intel |
| | Shiva NetModem/E for Windows for Workgroups | Shiva |
| Operating Systems | MS-DOS 6.2 | Microsoft |
| | OS/2 2.1 | IBM |
| | Windows for Workgroups 3.11 | Microsoft |
| Personal Information Managers | ACT! 1.1 | Symantec |
| | Calendar Creator Plus 1.0 | Spinnaker Software |
| | ECCO Professional 1.1 | Arabesque Software |
| Pointing Devices | Altra Felix | Altra |
| | Kensington Expert Mouse 4.0 | Kensington Microware |
| | Microsoft Mouse 2.0 and Ballpoint Mouse | Microsoft |
| Portable Systems | Gateway 2000 Colorbook | Gateway 2000 |
| | Hewlett-Packard OmniBook Superportables | Hewlett-Packard |
| | Toshiba Dynapad T100X Pen Computer | Toshiba Computer Systems Division |
| | Toshiba Protege T3400C | Toshiba Computer Systems Division |
| | Toshiba Satellite T1900 | Toshiba Computer Systems Division |
| Presentation | Freelance Graphics 2.0 | Lotus Development |
| | Harvard Graphics 2.0 | Software Publishing |
| Printers | Canon BJC-600 | Canon Computer Systems |
| | Eastman Kodak ColorEase PS | Eastman Kodak |
| | Hewlett-Packard DeskJet 1200C | Hewlett-Packard |
| | Hewlett-Packard LaserJet 4L | Hewlett-Packard |
| | Hewlett-Packard PaintJet XL300 | Hewlett-Packard |
| | LaserMaster WinJet 1200 | LaserMaster |
| Scanners | Pacific Crest Card Grabber | Pacific Crest Technologies |
| | Recognita Roll and Read | Recognita |
| Sound | Powered Partners AV-622 | Acoustic Research |
| | Sound Blaster 16 Advanced Signal Processing | Creative Labs |
| | Logitech AudioMan | Logitech |
| | MultiSound Full Upgrade Kit | Turtle Beach Systems |
| Spreadsheets | 1-2-3 Release 4 | Lotus Development |
| | Improv 2.1 | Lotus Development |
| | Quattro Pro 5.0 | Borland International |
| Systems | Compaq Presario | Compaq Computer |
| | Zeos 486DX2-66 | Zeos International |
| Utilities | DAZzle Plus | Envelope Manager Software |
| | Folio VIEWS 3.0 | Folio |
| | NetRoom 3.0 | Helix Software |
| | Outside In 2.1 | Systems Compatability |
| | Rummage 2.1 | America Online |
| | Searcher Pro 2.0 | Cognitronix |
| | Stacker 3.1 | Stac Electronics |
| | Uninstaller 1.0 | MicroHelp |
| | WinScope 1.01 | The Periscope Company |
| Video Cards | Cardinal WARPspeed VL90 | Cardinal Technologies |
| | Diamond Viper VL | Diamond Computer Systems |
| | Hercules Graphite Card | Hercules Computer Technology |
| | Number Nine #9GXE | Number Nine Computer |
| | Word Processors | Word 6.0 |
| | WordPerfect 6.0 | WordPerfect |

*Source: Windows, Feb., 1994*

# Industry Data

PC RESEARCH COLLECTS DATA on the best-selling software products. Below are the top products for 1993:

## Top-Selling Business Software (MS-DOS)

| Product | Company |
|---|---|
| MS-DOS 6.2 | Microsoft |
| QEMM | Quarterdeck |
| WordPerfect 6.0 Upgrade | WordPerfect |
| Stacker | Stac Electronics |
| OS/2 | IBM |
| Norton Utilities 7.0 | Symantec |
| Quattro Pro | Borland International |
| ProComm Plus | Datastorm |
| QuickBooks | Intuit |
| WordPerfect 6.0 | WordPerfect |

| Product | Company |
|---|---|
| Microsoft Office | Microsoft |
| Key Cad | Softkey |
| Microsoft Word | Microsoft |
| Norton Utilities | Symantec |
| Symantec Antivirus (SAM) | Symantec |

## Top-Selling Business Software (Windows)

| Product | Company |
|---|---|
| Microsoft Windows 3.1 | Microsoft |
| WordPerfect for Windows Upgrade | WordPerfect |
| Microsoft Access | Microsoft |
| Quattro Pro for Windows | Borland |
| After Dark 2.0 for Windows | Berkeley |
| Paradox for Windows | Borland |
| Lotus 1-2-3 for Windows Upgrade | Lotus |
| Winfax Pro | Delrina |
| Microsoft Word Upgrade | Microsoft |
| CompuServe Windows Membership Kit | CompuServe |

## Top-Selling Personal Productivity Software (MS-DOS/Windows)

| Product | Company |
|---|---|
| Quicken for Windows | Intuit |
| Quicken 6.0 (MS-DOS) | Intuit |
| TurboTax (MS-DOS) | Chipsoft |
| TurboTax for Windows | Chipsoft |
| Print Shop Deluxe for Windows | Brøderbund |
| Floorplan Designer 3-D | Cosmi |
| Print Shop Deluxe (MS-DOS) | Brøderbund |
| Quicken Companion | Intuit |
| Microsoft Money | Microsoft |
| Expert Home Design for Windows | Expert |
| Swift Label Publisher | Cosmi |
| Easy Working Resume Creator | Spinnaker |
| Christmas for Windows | Wink Data Products |
| Calendar Creator Plus | Power Up |
| Prodigy Start-Up Kit | Prodigy |

## Top-Selling Business Software (Macintosh)

| Product | Company |
|---|---|
| Claris Works | Claris |
| After Dark | Berkeley |
| Microsoft Works | Microsoft |
| Key Fonts | Softkey |
| Disney Collection Screen Saver | Berkeley |

## Top-Selling Personal Productivity Software (Macintosh)

| Product | Company |
|---|---|
| Quicken | Intuit |
| Macintax | Chipsoft |
| Print Shop Deluxe | Brøderbund |
| Print Shop | Brøderbund |
| Managing Your Money | Meca |

*Source: PC Research*

## The Top Reference Sources

*Before & After*, $36/year
(916) 784-3880

Published bimonthly, *Before and After* is a four-color newsletter devoted to teaching amateur computer users to look like professionals in print.

Each issue has in-depth, step-by-step instructions on how to choose type, draw shadows, buttons, or logos, and use photos in articles. A consistently well-written, compellingly designed publication, *Before and After* is endlessly useful.

# Ordering by Mail

THE BEST PRICES, delivery, and support on computer hardware and software are often found from mail order dealers. Use a credit card to avoid delays.

## Contact Options

*Ordering Software and Peripherals by Mail:*

Computer Outfitters
(800) 367-4222

PC Connection
(800) 243-8088

Tiger Software
(800) 888-4437

*Ordering a Computer by Mail:*

Acer
(800) 239-2237

AST
(800) 876-4277

Comp USA Direct
(800) 932-2667

Dell
(800) 289-1210

Gateway 2000
(800) 523-2000

Zeos International
(800) 423-5891

# Networking

NETWORKING PERSONAL COMPUTERS seems easy. For many businesses, however, it often takes more time and money to establish a network than it does to purchase the computers in the first place.

There are several competing networking standards, including Appletalk, Ethernet, and Netware from Novell. For more information on each format, and to determine which is best for your organization, contact the Novell Netware hotline at (800) 638-9273. They publish a comprehensive buyer's guide and a general product guide to networking that is free on request.

Also available is an electronic faxback system that will automatically send information on a wide variety of topics to any fax machine. To access the system, dial (800) 638-9273 and press 1, then 1.

## Recommended Resource

Novell
122 E. 1700 S.
Provo, UT 84606
(800) 638-9273

---

### The Top Reference Sources

*The Macintosh Bible*
Peachpit Press, $35
(800) 283-9444

*The Macintosh Bible* is a mammoth collection of tips, techniques, tricks, and advice. There

should be a copy next to every Macintosh in the office.

Other books in the series include easy-to-use books on FileMaker, Excel, MacDraw, and a book called *What Do I Do Now?* that is ideal for novice users.

# Shareware

SHAREWARE IS AN ALTERNATIVE method of software distribution. Instead of packaging the product and offering it for sale through dealers or mail order vendors, the author of the software posts a copy on various electronic bulletin boards (e.g. CompuServe) and allows users to try it for free. If the software does what it claims, and you find it useful, you're expected to send the requested fee directly to the author.

The only downsides of shareware are the lack of uniformity in technical support and the sometimes unpolished nature of the software.

## The Top Windows Shareware Programs

Accesses (Utilities collection)
Almanac for Windows (Calendar)
ApiSpy (Windows development tool)
Atoms (Game)
Backgammon (Game)
BackMenu and BigDesk (Program manager and desk space enlarger)
BizWiz Financial Calculator (Calculator)
Castle of the Winds (Game)
CCIZip (File compression)
Chartist (Charts)
ClysBar (Program manager)
Cribbage (Game)
Destroyer for Windows (Game)
File Commander (File manager)
Fish! (Screen saver)
Folders (Program manager)
Hearts (Game)
Hi, Finance! (Calculator)
KBS: People Management System (Address book/ database)
Life 3000 (Game)
Mah Jongg for Windows (Game)
M-B Analyst (Calculator)
Mega Edit (Text editor)
MGWalk (Heap utility)
MicroLink (Communications)
Ms. Chomp (Game)
The Palace of Deceit (Game)
PixFolio (Image processor)
Plug-In for Program Manager (Program manager)
PostCrypt (Font)
Scan for Windows (Viruses)
SideBar Lite (Program manager)
Taipei! (Game)
Time & Chaos (Personal information manaager)
Warheads for Windows (Game)
Whiskers (Mouse program)
Whoop It Up! (Sound)
WinBatch (Windows automator)
Windows Reminder (Personal information manager)
WindSock (Utility collection)

WinPoem (Database)
WinPost (Onscreen message memos)
WinTrek (Game)
World Empire II (Game)

*Source: The Windows Shareware 500, John Hedtke, Ventana Press*

## The Top Mac Shareware Programs

AKA (Aliases)
Beatsville (Font)
DateKey (Date utility)
Disinfectant (Viruses)
11/22/63 EXTRA! (HyperCard stack)
FlashWrite II (Word processor)
Inigo Gets Out (HyperCard game)
KidPix (Painting program)
Maelstrom (Game)
Mariner (Spreadsheet)
MaxAppleZoom (Monitor enhancement)
NIH Image (Image processor)
PopChar (Key finder)
Programmer's Key (Interrupt switch)
Solarian II (Game)
SoundMaster (Sound)
StuffIt Lite (File compression)
Thomas (Font)
To Do! (Scheduler)
ZTerm (Communications)

*Source: The Mac Shareware 500, Ruffin Prevost and Rob Terrell, Ventana Press*

## Recommended Resources

CWI
(800) 777-5636

Public Brand Software
(800) 426-3475

Shareware Express
(800) 346-2842

Ziffnet on CompuServe
(800) 848-8199

America Online
(800) 827-6364

Educorp
(800) 843-9497

*Glossbrenner's Guide to Shareware for Small Businesses*
Windcrest/McGraw Hill, $37.95
(800) 822-8138

# Upgrading an Existing PC or Mac

AS PERSONAL COMPUTERS become more advanced, the chances that a company's PCs are "obsolete" increase. With the price of used computers plummeting, it usually makes more sense to upgrade than to replace an existing machine. Here are the ten most effective ways to get more out of a computer:

## I. Buy more memory.

No computer has enough. Buy memory (SIMMs) from a reputable company like Techworks or the Chip Merchant. On some machines, the memory is easy to install. On others, see a dealer. Remember: always buy as much as you can afford–the bigger memory chips are worth it.

## 2. Get a bigger screen.

Studies have shown that, depending on the task, a user's productivity can increase as much as 100% with a larger work area. The ideal screen size is 19 inches for most spreadsheet, graphics, and word processing users.

## 3. Install a bigger hard drive.

More complicated software (especially Windows or complex graphic modeling tools) use lots of disk space. The price of hard disk storage has declined significantly. Look for a brand of drive with at least two years of history in the market, and a warranty of at least two years.

## 4. Install a better/faster printer.

Buy a PostScript printer (for more fonts and better graphics), or a printer with greater resolution (measured in dpi or dots per inch). Owners of sophisticated printers should consider adding a color printer.

## 5. Get an accelerator board.

These boards work with (or replace) an existing computer chip to dramatically speed up the computer. Some accelerators can increase speed by as many as ten times (that means that an activity that took 60 seconds–like opening a large spreadsheet–now takes six). Daystar is the leader in the Mac market, while ATI is a leader in the PC market.

## 6. Buy a backup device.

No one likes to backup, but every competent user must. Tape drives or removable bulk storage make it more painless. Investigate digital audio tapes, cartridge, Bernoulli, or Syquest devices (available from many vendors) that make backup automatic and foolproof.

## 7. Take a training course.

Often the bottleneck isn't the computer, it's the user. Investigate courses that can help a user become even more expert at the software already in use.

## 8. Buy and use a macro program.

Macro programs remember keystrokes and make it easy to automate repetitive tasks. Type a return address with one keystroke, or reserve a function key to automatically open a file, print it out, update it, and save a backup. A popular tool for the Mac is Quickkeys, and there are several specialized ones available for the PC.

## 9. Get a very fast fax modem.

With prices falling every day, fax modems are an easy choice. Send a fax without printing the document and walking across the office to feed it into a busy machine. The built-in modem allows a user to access bulletin boards and gain free access to huge amounts of data. In addition, electronic mail will dramatically increase a user's ability to communicate with others.

## 10. Buy an Uninterruptible Power Supply.

A little box that resembles a surge supressor, sometimes called a UPS, can automatically protect a computer from blackouts or power surges.

## The Top Reference Sources

*MacWEEK*
Ziff Davis, Controlled
(609) 786-8230

*InfoWorld*
IDG, Controlled
(800) 227-8365

*MacWEEK* is the ultimate resource for the computer manager responsible for Macintoshes. Every week, the magazine offers fresh graphics, helpful advice, and the inside news on new technology.

*MacWEEK* is a controlled circulation magazine, so you must qualify to get a subscription.

*InfoWorld* focuses on the issues facing managers who deal with computers. The reviews are among the best in the industry, and the news is usually more current and specific than you'll find anywhere else.

# Used Computers

## Contact Options

*Used Computer Brokers:*

Boston Computer Exchange
P.O. Box 1177
Boston, MA 02103
(800) 262-6399

Solute
145 Palisade St.
Dobbs Ferry, NY 10522
(914) 674-6000

Rentex
337 Summer St.
Boston, MA 02210
(800) 545-2313

River Computer
14 Mill St.
Marlow, NH 03456
(800) 998-0090

*Note: The Classified Board on America Online adds more than 2,000 used computers for sale each day.*

# Technical Support

## Five Tips on Technical Support

1. Go to the bookstore and buy a third-party book. It is easier and faster than using the manual.

2. Use CompuServe. Post your message and look for an answer the next day.

3. Send a fax to tech support. Faxes are often given to the best adviser, and you're guaranteed not to spend time and money on the phone.

4. Turn off all TSRs, inits, and special software before calling. The tech support people usually won't help you until you prove that the problem is theirs.

5. If you have a modem, send your problem directly to the company's bulletin board.

## The Top Reference Sources

Ventana Press
P.O. Box 2468
Chapel Hill, NC 27515
(919) 942-0220

This publisher's list is loaded with the best sort of computer help-books—the truly useful kind.

Ventana features a number of titles especially for those in the desktop publishing mode. Call for a free catalogue.

# Computer Products and Services

| Company | Phone | Fax |
|---|---|---|
| Abacus Accounting Systems | (403) 488-8100 | (403) 488-8150 |
| Abacus Software | (800) 451-4319 | (616) 698-0325 |
| ABL Electronics | (800) 726-0610 | (410) 296-2125 |
| ABS-American Business Systems | (800) 356-4034 | (508) 250-8027 |
| Acculogic | (800) 234-7811 | (714) 756-9518 |
| Ace Software | (408) 451-0100 | (408) 437-1018 |
| AceCad | (800) 676-4223 | (408) 655-1919 |
| Acer America | (800) 733-2237 | (408) 922-2965 |
| Acme Electric | (800) 325-5848 | (716) 968-1420 |
| Action Plus Software | (800) 766-7229 | (801) 255-0642 |
| Acucobol | (800) 262-6585 | (619) 566-3071 |
| Adaptec | (408) 945-8600 | (408) 262-2533 |
| Addtron Technology | (800) 998-4638 | (510) 770-0171 |
| ADI Systems | (800) 228-0530 | (408) 944-0300 |
| Adobe Systems | (800) 833-6687 | (415) 235-0078 |
| Advanced Gravis Computer Technology | (800) 663-8558 | (604) 434-7809 |
| Advanced Logic Research | (800) 444-4257 | (714) 581-9240 |
| Advanced Matrix Technology | (800) 992-2264 | (805) 484-5482 |
| Advantage Memory | (800) 245-5299 | (714) 707-5493 |
| Aeronet Canada | (416) 441-9966 | (416) 441-9785 |
| Affinity | (800) 367-6771 | (303) 442-4999 |
| Agfa | (800) 424-8973 | (508) 657-8568 |
| AimTech | (800) 289-2884 | (603) 883-5582 |
| Alacrity Systems | (800) 252-2748 | (908) 813-2490 |
| Aladdin Systems | (408) 761-6200 | (408) 761-6206 |
| Aldus | (800) 333-2538 | (206) 343-4240 |
| Altec Lansing Multimedia | (800) 648-6663 | (717) 296-2213 |
| Altima Systems | (800) 356-9990 | (510) 356-2408 |
| Altsys | (214) 680-2060 | (214) 680-0537 |
| American Power Conversion | (800) 800-4272 | (401) 789-3710 |
| AMP | (800) 522-6752 | (717) 561-6110 |
| Amrel Technology | (800) 882-6735 | (818) 303-8538 |
| Analog & Digital Peripherals | (513) 339-2241 | (513) 339-0070 |
| Analog Devices | (800) 262-5643 | (617) 821-4273 |
| Analog Technology | (818) 357-0098 | (818) 303-4993 |
| Andromeda Systems | (818) 709-7600 | (818) 709-7407 |
| Antec | (510) 770-1200 | (510) 770-1288 |
| Antex Electronics | (800) 338-4231 | (310) 532-8509 |
| Apple Computer | (800) 538-9696 | (408) 974-1725 |
| Applied Micro Circuits | (619) 450-9333 | (619) 450-9885 |
| Appoint | (800) 448-1184 | (510) 417-0614 |
| Apricorn | (800) 458-5448 | (619) 271-4888 |
| Archive Software | (800) 821-8782 | (407) 263-3555 |
| Areal Technology | (408) 436-6800 | (408) 436-6844 |
| Aris Entertainment | (310) 821-0234 | (310) 821-6463 |
| Arnet | (800) 366-8844 | (615) 834-5399 |
| Artek Computer Systems | (510) 490-8402 | (510) 490-8405 |
| Artisoft | (800) 846-9726 | (602) 670-7359 |
| Asanté Technologies | (800) 662-9686 | (408) 432-7511 |
| askSam Systems | (800) 800-1997 | (904) 584-7481 |

*Computer Products and Services (cont'd)*

| Company | Phone | Fax |
|---|---|---|
| ASP Computer Products | (800) 952-6277 | (408) 746-2803 |
| Aspen Imaging International | (800) 955-5555 | (303) 665-2972 |
| AST Research | (800) 876-4278 | (714) 727-9355 |
| Asymetrix | (800) 448-6543 | (206) 637-1504 |
| ATI Technologies | (905) 882-2600 | (905) 882-0546 |
| Attachmate | (800) 426-6283 | (206) 747-9924 |
| Austin Computer Systems | (800) 752-1577 | (512) 339-3550 |
| Autodesk Incorporated | (800) 228-3601 | * |
| Avance Logic | (510) 226-9555 | (510) 226-8039 |
| Award Software | (415) 968-4433 | (415) 968-0274 |
| Axelen (USA) | (206) 643-2781 | (206) 643-4478 |
| Axis Communications | (508) 777-7957 | (508) 377-9905 |
| Baler Software | (800) 327-6108 | (708) 506-1808 |
| Beame & Whiteside Software | (800) 463-6637 | (416) 765-0815 |
| Beaver Computer | (800) 827-4222 | (408) 944-9001 |
| Behavior Tech Computer (USA) | (510) 657-3956 | (510) 657-3965 |
| Belkin Components | (800) 223-5546 | (310) 898-1111 |
| Bell & Howell | (800) 247-3724 | (708) 675-5019 |
| Berkeley Speech Technologies | (510) 841-5083 | (510) 841-5093 |
| Berkeley Systems | (800) 877-5535 | (510) 540-5115 |
| Best Data Products | (800) 632-2378 | (818) 773-9619 |
| Best Power Technology | (800) 356-5794 | (608) 565-2929 |
| Bit 3 Computer | (612) 881-6955 | (612) 881-9674 |
| Bits Technical | (713) 735-9900 | (713) 735-9999 |
| Blue Sky Software | (800) 677-4946 | (619) 459-6366 |
| Boca Research | (407) 997-6227 | (407) 997-0918 |
| Bold Data Technology | (510) 490-8296 | (510) 490-9428 |
| Borland International | (800) 331-0877 | (408) 439-9103 |
| BOS National | (214) 956-7722 | (214) 350-6688 |
| Brier Technology | (404) 564-5699 | (404) 381-2808 |
| Brøderbund Software | (415) 382-4400 | (415) 382-4419 |
| Brooks Power Systems | (800) 523-1551 | (215) 244-0160 |
| Brother International | (908) 356-8880 | (908) 469-5167 |
| Brysis Data | (818) 810-0355 | (818) 810-4555 |
| Bureau of Electronic Publishing | (800) 828-4766 | (201) 808-2676 |
| BusLogic | (408) 492-9090 | (408) 492-1542 |
| Byte Brothers | (206) 271-9567 | (206) 227-9702 |
| C-Power Products | (800) 800-2797 | (214) 771-0462 |
| CA Retail Solutions | (800) 668-3767 | (416) 451-9362 |
| Cache Computers | (510) 226-9922 | (510) 226-9911 |
| Caere | (800) 535-7226 | (408) 354-2743 |
| Calculus | (305) 481-2334 | (305) 481-1866 |
| Calera Recognition Systems | (800) 544-7051 | (408) 720-1330 |
| Camintonn/Z-Ram | (714) 454-1500 | (714) 660-8063 |
| Campbell Services | (800) 345-6747 | (810) 559-1034 |
| Canon USA | (800) 848-4123 | (516) 354-5805 |
| Cardiff Software | (800) 659-8755 | (619) 259-6450 |
| CarNel Enterprises | (800) 962-1450 | (714) 630-3180 |
| Carroll Touch | (512) 244-3500 | (512) 244-7040 |
| Casio | (800) 962-2746 | (201) 361-3819 |
| CBIS | (404) 446-1332 | (404) 446-9164 |
| CD Technology | (408) 752-8500 | (408) 752-8501 |
| Central Point Software | (800) 445-4208 | (503) 690-8083 |
| Centrepoint | (613) 235-7054 | (613) 238-6549 |
| Certified Management Software | (801) 534-1231 | (801) 363-3653 |

*Computer Products and Services (cont'd)*

| Company | Phone | Fax |
|---|---|---|
| CH Products | (800) 624-5804 | (619) 598-2524 |
| Champion Business Systems | (800) 243-2626 | (303) 792-0255 |
| Chaplet Systems U.S.A. | (408) 732-7950 | (408) 732-6050 |
| Cherry Electrical Products | (708) 662-9200 | (708) 360-3566 |
| Chicony America | (714) 380-0928 | (714) 380-9204 |
| Chinon America | (800) 441-0222 | (310) 533-1727 |
| Chipsoft | (619) 453-8722 | * |
| Chronocom | (418) 449-4378 | (418) 449-1278 |
| Chuck Atkinson Programs | (800) 826-5009 | (817) 560-8249 |
| Cimmetry Systems | (800) 361-1904 | (514) 735-6440 |
| Cipher Data Products | (800) 424-7437 | (619) 693-0491 |
| Cirrus Logic | (510) 623-8300 | (510) 226-2270 |
| Citizen America | (800) 477-4683 | (310) 453-7530 |
| Citrix Systems | (800) 437-7503 | (305) 341-6880 |
| Clarion Software | (800) 354-5444 | (305) 746-1650 |
| Claris | (800) 325-2747 | (408) 987-3932 |
| Clark Development | (800) 356-1686 | (801) 261-8987 |
| Clary | (800) 442-5279 | (818) 305-0254 |
| CMG Technology | (800) 426-3832 | (714) 455-1656 |
| CMS Enhancements | (714) 222-6000 | (714) 549-4004 |
| Codenoll Technology | (914) 965-6300 | (914) 965-9811 |
| Colorado Memory Systems | (303) 635-1500 | (303) 667-0997 |
| Command Communications | (800) 288-3491 | (303) 750-6437 |
| Commax Technologies | (800) 526-6629 | (408) 435-5020 |
| Commerical & Industrial Design | (714) 556-0888 | (714) 556-0889 |
| Commodore International | (800) 900-2332 | * |
| Compaq Computer | (800) 345-1518 | * |
| CompSee | (800) 628-3888 | (407) 723-2895 |
| CompuAdd | (800) 999-9901 | (512) 250-2629 |
| CompuLan Technology | (800) 486-8810 | (408) 954-8299 |
| CompuMedia Technology | (510) 656-9811 | (510) 656-9821 |
| CompuRegister | (314) 365-2050 | (314) 365-2080 |
| Computer Aided Technology | (214) 350-0888 | (214) 904-0888 |
| Computer Associates International | (800) 225-5224 | (516) 432-0614 |
| Computer Dynamics Sales | (800) 627-1218 | (803) 879-2030 |
| Computer Friends | (800) 547-3303 | (503) 643-5379 |
| Computer Law Systems | (800) 328-1913 | (612) 941-6085 |
| Computer Modules | (408) 496-1881 | (408) 496-1886 |
| Computer Peripherals | (800) 854-7600 | (805) 498-8360 |
| Computone | (800) 241-3946 | (404) 475-2707 |
| CompuTrend Systems | (818) 333-5121 | (818) 369-6803 |
| Comy Technology | (408) 437-1555 | (408) 456-0366 |
| Concurrent Controls | (800) 487-2249 | (415) 873-6091 |
| Connect Tech | (519) 836-1291 | (519) 836-4878 |
| Connect-Air International | (800) 247-1978 | (206) 939-4882 |
| Conner Peripherals | (408) 456-3167 | (408) 456-4501 |
| Consumer Technology NW | (800) 356-3983 | (503) 671-9066 |
| Contact Software International | (800) 365-0606 | (214) 919-9750 |
| Core International | (407) 997-6044 | (407) 997-6202 |
| Corel Systems | (800) 836-7274 | (613) 728-9790 |
| Corollary | (800) 338-4020 | (714) 250-4043 |
| Cougar Mountain Software | (800) 388-3038 | (208) 343-0267 |
| Covox | (503) 342-1271 | (503) 342-1283 |
| CPU Products | (800) 882-1842 | (316) 788-7428 |
| Creative Labs | (800) 998-5227 | (408) 428-6611 |

*Computer Products and Services (cont'd)*

| Company | Phone | Fax |
|---|---|---|
| Crystal Semiconductor | (512) 445-7222 | (512) 445-7581 |
| CrystalGraphics | (408) 496-6175 | (408) 496-6988 |
| CTX International | (800) 289-2189 | (909) 595-6293 |
| Cybex | (205) 430-4000 | (205) 534-0010 |
| CyCare Software Publishing | (800) 545-2488 | (602) 596-4466 |
| CYMA Systems | (800) 292-2962 | (602) 345-5703 |
| DacEasy | (800) 222-8778 | (214) 250-7905 |
| Dallas Semiconductor | (214) 450-8170 | (214) 450-0470 |
| Danpex | (408) 437-7557 | (408) 437-7559 |
| Dassault Automatismes et Telecommunications | (212) 909-0550 | (212) 909-0555 |
| Data Access | (800) 451-3539 | (305) 238-0017 |
| Data Entry Systems | (205) 430-3023 | (205) 430-0989 |
| Data General | (800) 328-2436 | (508) 366-1319 |
| Data I/O | (800) 247-5700 | (206) 622-5596 |
| Data Race | (800) 749-7223 | (512) 558-1929 |
| Data Technology | (408) 942-4000 | (408) 942-4052 |
| Databook | (716) 889-4204 | (607) 889-2593 |
| Datacap | (914) 332-7515 | (914) 332-7516 |
| Datacap Systems | (215) 699-7051 | (215) 699-6779 |
| Datalux | (800) 328-2589 | (703) 662-1682 |
| Datasouth Computer | (800) 476-2120 | (704) 523-9298 |
| DataSym | (519) 758-5800 | (519) 758-5600 |
| Dataware | (800) 426-4844 | (713) 432-1385 |
| Dauphin Technology | (800) 782-7922 | (708) 971-8353 |
| Daystar | (800) 962-2077 | (404) 967-3018 |
| DD & TT Enterprise USA | (213) 780-0099 | (213) 780-0419 |
| Dell Computer | (800) 289-3355 | (800) 950-1329 |
| DeLorme Mapping | (207) 865-4171 | (207) 865-9628 |
| Delrina Technology | (800) 268-6082 | (416) 441-0333 |
| DeltaPoint | (800) 367-4334 | (408) 648-4020 |
| Deltec Electronics | (800) 854-2658 | (619) 291-2973 |
| Deneba Software | (800) 622-6827 | (305) 477-5794 |
| Denistron | (310) 530-3530 | (310) 534-8419 |
| DeScribe | (800) 448-1586 | (916) 923-3447 |
| DesignCAD | (918) 825-4844 | (918) 825-6359 |
| Deskstation Technology | (913) 599-1900 | (913) 599-4024 |
| DFM Systems | (800) 223-4791 | (515) 225-0388 |
| Diamond Computer Systems | (408) 736-2000 | (408) 730-5750 |
| DigiBoard | (800) 344-4273 | (612) 943-5398 |
| Digicom Systems | (800) 833-8900 | (408) 262-1390 |
| Digital Communications Associates | (800) 348-3221 | (404) 442-4364 |
| Digital Equipment | (800) 332-4636 | (508) 493-8780 |
| Digital Products | (800) 243-2333 | (617) 647-4474 |
| Digital Vision | (800) 346-0090 | (617) 329-6286 |
| Digitalk | (800) 922-8255 | (714) 513-3120 |
| Digitan Systems | (408) 954-8270 | (408) 954-9641 |
| Discoversoft | (510) 769-2902 | (510) 769-0149 |
| Disctec | (407) 671-5500 | (407) 671-6606 |
| Distributed Processing Technology | (407) 830-5522 | (407) 260-5366 |
| DNA Networks | (800) 999-3622 | (215) 296-0691 |
| Dolch Computer Systems | (800) 538-7506 | (408) 263-6305 |
| Dover Electronics Manufacturing | (800) 848-1198 | (303) 776-1883 |
| Dragon Systems | (800) 825-5897 | (617) 527-0372 |
| DSK | (801) 224-4828 | (801) 224-5872 |
| DTK Computer | (800) 925-7318 | (818) 810-5233 |

*Computer Products and Services (cont'd)*

| Company | Phone | Fax |
| --- | --- | --- |
| Dual Group | (310) 542-0788 | (310) 214-0697 |
| Dubl-Click | (800) 266-9525 | (818) 888-5405 |
| Dycam | (818) 998-8008 | (818) 998-7951 |
| Dynapro | (800) 667-0374 | (604) 521-4629 |
| DynaTek Automation Systems | (416) 636-3000 | (416) 636-3011 |
| Eastman Kodak | (800) 242-2424 | (716) 726-3585 |
| Edimax Computer | (408) 496-1105 | (408) 980-1530 |
| EFA of America | (301) 670-6166 | (301) 670-6167 |
| EFI Electronics | (800) 877-1174 | (801) 977-0200 |
| Electro Products | (800) 423-0646 | (206) 859-9101 |
| Electrohome Limited | (800) 265-2171 | (519) 749-3151 |
| Electronic Arts | (800) 245-4525 | (415) 571-7995 |
| Electronic Frontier Foundation | (202) 347-5400 | (202) 393-5509 |
| Electronic Imagery | (800) 645-9657 | (305) 968-7319 |
| Elographics | (615) 482-4100 | (615) 482-6617 |
| Emigre | (916) 451-4344 | (916) 451-4351 |
| Empress Software | (301) 220-1919 | (301) 220-1997 |
| Emulex | (800) 854-7112 | (714) 668-6819 |
| Enable Software | (800) 888-0684 | (518) 877-5225 |
| Epson America | (800) 922-8911 | (310) 782-5220 |
| Ergotron | (800) 888-8458 | (612) 452-8346 |
| ETC Computer | (510) 226-6250 | (510) 226-6252 |
| ETEQ Microsystems | (408) 432-8147 | (408) 432-8146 |
| Everex Systems | (800) 821-0806 | (510) 651-0728 |
| Exabyte | (303) 442-4333 | (303) 442-4269 |
| Exide Electronics | (800) 554-3448 | (919) 870-3450 |
| ExperVision | (800) 732-3897 | (408) 456-0823 |
| Facit | (800) 879-3224 | (603) 647-2724 |
| Farallon Computing | (510) 814-5000 | (510) 814-5023 |
| FileNet | (714) 966-3400 | (714) 966-3490 |
| Folex Film Systems | (800) 631-1150 | (201) 575-4646 |
| Folio | (800) 543-6546 | (801) 344-3790 |
| FontBank | (708) 328-7370 | (708) 328-7432 |
| Fora | (800) 367-3672 | (408) 943-0642 |
| Foresight Resources | (800) 231-8574 | (816) 891-8018 |
| Franklin Quest Technologies | (800) 877-1814 | (801) 975-9995 |
| Free Computer Technology | (408) 945-1118 | (408) 945-0604 |
| Fuji Photo Film | (914) 789-8100 | (914) 682-4955 |
| Fujitsu America | (800) 626-4686 | (408) 432-1318 |
| Funk Software | (800) 828-4146 | (617) 547-1031 |
| Future Domain | (800) 879-7599 | (714) 253-0913 |
| FutureSoft Engineering | (713) 496-9400 | (713) 496-1090 |
| Futurus | (800) 327-8296 | (404) 392-9313 |
| Gazelle Systems | (800) 786-3278 | (801) 373-6933 |
| GEC Plessey Semiconductors | (408) 438-2900 | (408) 438-5576 |
| General Parametrics | (800) 223-0999 | (510) 524-9954 |
| General Ribbon | (800) 423-5400 | (818) 709-1209 |
| Genesis Integrated Systems | (800) 325-6582 | (612) 544-4347 |
| Genoa Systems | (800) 934-3662 | (408) 434-0997 |
| Genovation | (714) 833-3355 | (714) 833-0322 |
| Glenco Engineering | (800) 562-2543 | (708) 808-0313 |
| GMC Technology | (818) 401-3743 | (818) 401-2798 |
| Golden Power Systems | (805) 582-4400 | (805) 583-4411 |
| Goldstar Technology | (800) 777-1192 | (408) 432-6063 |
| Graphic Enterprises of Ohio | (800) 321-9874 | (216) 452-8417 |

*Computer Products and Services (cont'd)*

| Company | Phone | Fax |
|---|---|---|
| Great Plains Software | (800) 456-0025 | (701) 281-3752 |
| Group 1 Software | (800) 368-5806 | (301) 982-4069 |
| GVC Technologies | (800) 289-4821 | (201) 579-2702 |
| Hayes Microcomputer Products | (800) 426-7704 | (404) 449-0087 |
| Health Software | (216) 759-2103 | (216) 759-7563 |
| Hercules Computer Technology | (800) 532-0600 | (510) 623-1112 |
| Hewlett-Packard | (800) 752-0900 | * |
| Hitachi America | (800) 369-0422 | (404) 242-1414 |
| Hooleon | (800) 937-1337 | (602) 634-4620 |
| Horizons Technology | (619) 292-8320 | (619) 565-1175 |
| HyperData | (909) 468-2955 | (909) 468-2961 |
| Hyundai Electronics America | (408) 473-9200 | (408) 943-9567 |
| IBC/Integrated Business Computers | (800) 468-5847 | (818) 882-8353 |
| IBM | (800) 426-2486 | * |
| IMSI | (800) 222-4723 | (415) 454-8901 |
| In Focus Systems | (800) 327-7231 | (503) 692-4476 |
| Indiana Cash Drawer | (317) 398-6643 | (317) 392-0958 |
| Infomatic Power Systems | (310) 948-2217 | (310) 948-5264 |
| Intel | (800) 538-3373 | (503) 629-7580 |
| Intellicom | (800) 992-2882 | (818) 882-2409 |
| International Keytech | (909) 598-6219 | (909) 598-5959 |
| International Power Machines | (800) 527-1208 | (214) 494-2690 |
| Interphase | (214) 919-9000 | (214) 919-9200 |
| Intuit | (800) 624-8742 | (415) 852-9370 |
| Iomega | (800) 456-5522 | (801) 778-3450 |
| IPC America | (512) 339-3500 | (800) 752-4171 |
| Iterated Systems | (800) 437-2285 | (404) 840-0806 |
| J-Mark Computer | (818) 814-9472 | (818) 960-5937 |
| JetFax | (800) 753-8329 | (415) 326-6003 |
| JMR Electronics | (818) 993-4801 | (818) 993-9173 |
| Joindata Systems | (818) 330-6553 | (818) 330-6865 |
| Jovian Logic | (510) 651-4823 | (510) 226-8227 |
| JVC Company of America | (201) 808-2100 | (201) 808-1370 |
| K.S. Brotherbox | (818) 814-0516 | (818) 814-0323 |
| Kalok | (408) 747-1315 | (408) 747-1319 |
| KAO Infosystems | (800) 274-5520 | (508) 747-5521 |
| Kedwell Software | (603) 433-4777 | (603) 433-4222 |
| KentMarsh | (800) 325-3587 | (713) 522-8965 |
| Key Power | (310) 948-2084 | (310) 942-0536 |
| KeyTronic | (800) 262-6006 | (509) 927-5224 |
| KFC USA | (800) 253-2872 | (714) 546-0315 |
| Kingston Technology | (800) 845-2545 | (714) 435-2699 |
| Knowledge Adventure | (800) 542-4240 | (818) 542-4205 |
| KnowledgePoint | (800) 727-1133 | (707) 762-0802 |
| Kofax Image Products | (714) 727-1733 | (714) 727-3144 |
| Koutech Systems | (310) 699-5340 | (310) 699-0795 |
| Kraft Systems | (619) 724-7146 | (619) 941-1770 |
| KYE International | (800) 456-7593 | (909) 923-1469 |
| Kyocera Electronics | (800) 323-0470 | (908) 560-8380 |
| L.A. Computer | (310) 533-7177 | (310) 533-6955 |
| Labtec Enterprises | (206) 896-2000 | (206) 896-2020 |
| LANCAST | (800) 752-2768 | (603) 881-9888 |
| LaserTools | (800) 767-8004 | (510) 420-1150 |
| Leading Edge Products | (800) 874-3340 | (508) 836-4504 |
| Legacy Storage Systems | (800) 966-6442 | (905) 475-1088 |

*Computer Products and Services (cont'd)*

| Company | Phone | Fax |
| --- | --- | --- |
| Linco Computer | (714) 990-2288 | (310) 903-1266 |
| Link Technologies | (800) 448-5465 | (510) 651-8808 |
| Logical Operations | (800) 456-4677 | (716) 288-7411 |
| Logitech | (800) 231-7717 | (510) 792-8901 |
| Longshine Electronics | (310) 903-0899 | (310) 944-2201 |
| Lotus Development | (800) 343-5414 | (617) 225-1197 |
| Lucas Deeco | (510) 471-4700 | (510) 489-3500 |
| M. Bryce & Associates | (813) 786-4567 | (813) 786-4765 |
| MA Laboratories | (408) 954-8188 | (408) 954-0944 |
| Mag InnoVision | (800) 827-3998 | (714) 751-5522 |
| Magic Solutions | (201) 529-5533 | (201) 529-2955 |
| Mannesmann Tally | (800) 843-1347 | (206) 251-5520 |
| Manzanita Software Systems | (800) 447-5700 | (916) 781-3814 |
| MapInfo | (800) 327-8627 | (518) 275-6066 |
| Mass Memory Systems | (407) 629-1081 | (407) 628-3862 |
| Mass Optical Storage Technologies | (714) 898-9400 | (714) 373-9960 |
| Matrix Digital Products | (800) 227-5723 | (818) 566-1476 |
| Matrox Electronic Systems | (800) 361-1408 | (514) 685-2853 |
| Maxell of America | (800) 533-2836 | (201) 796-8790 |
| Maxoptix | (800) 848-3092 | (408) 954-9711 |
| Maxpeed | (415) 345-5447 | (415) 345-6398 |
| Maynard Electronics | (800) 821-8782 | (407) 263-3555 |
| Media Vision | (800) 845-5870 | (510) 770-9592 |
| MegaDrive Systems | (800) 332-4744 | (310) 247-8118 |
| Megahertz | (800) 527-8677 | (801) 272-6077 |
| Megatel Computer | (416) 245-2953 | (416) 245-8792 |
| Memory Media Products | (714) 669-1800 | (714) 669-0555 |
| Meridian Data | (800) 767-2537 | (408) 438-6816 |
| Mextel | (800) 888-4146 | (708) 595-4149 |
| Micro Design International | (800) 228-0891 | (407) 677-8365 |
| Micro Direct International | (714) 251-1818 | (714) 251-1877 |
| Micro Palm Computers | (800) 832-0512 | (813) 530-0738 |
| Micro Solutions Computer Products | (815) 756-3411 | (815) 756-2928 |
| Micro Star Software | (800) 444-1343 | (619) 931-4950 |
| Micro-Integration Bluelynx | (800) 642-5888 | (301) 777-3462 |
| Micrografx | (800) 733-3729 | (214) 234-2410 |
| MicroMat Computer Systems | (800) 829-6227 | (415) 897-3901 |
| MicroNet Computer Systems | (714) 453-6100 | (714) 453-6061 |
| Microprose | (410) 771-0440 | (410) 771-1174 |
| Microrim | (800) 628-6990 | (206) 746-9350 |
| MicroSlate | (514) 444-3680 | (514) 444-3683 |
| Microsoft | (800) 426-9400 | (206) 883-8101 |
| Microspeed | (800) 232-7888 | (510) 490-1665 |
| MicroStep | (818) 964-5048 | (818) 336-5170 |
| Microtek Lab | (800) 654-4160 | (310) 538-1193 |
| Microtest | (800) 526-9675 | (602) 957-6414 |
| MicroTouch Systems | (800) 866-6873 | (508) 659-9100 |
| Minuteman UPS | (800) 238-7272 | (214) 446-9011 |
| Mitsubishi Electronics America | (800) 843-2515 | (714) 236-6453 |
| Monterey Electronics | (408) 437-5496 | (408) 437-5499 |
| Moses Computers | (408) 358-1550 | (408) 356-9049 |
| Mountain Network Solutions | (800) 458-0300 | (408) 379-4302 |
| Multi-Industry Technology | (800) 366-6481 | (310) 802-9218 |
| Multi-Tech Systems | (800) 328-9717 | (612) 785-9874 |
| Mustang Software | (800) 999-9619 | (805) 395-0713 |

*Computer Products and Services (cont'd)*

| Company | Phone | Fax |
|---|---|---|
| Mylex | (800) 776-9539 | (510) 745-8016 |
| Myriad | (510) 659-8782 | (510) 659-8526 |
| Nanao USA | (800) 800-5202 | (310) 530-1679 |
| National Instruments | (800) 433-3488 | (512) 794-8411 |
| National Semiconductor | (800) 272-9959 | (800) 428-0065 |
| NCL America | (408) 737-2496 | (408) 744-0709 |
| NCR | (800) 531-2222 | (513) 445-4184 |
| NEC Technologies | (800) 632-4636 | (508) 264-8673 |
| Network Security Systems | (800) 755-7078 | (619) 552-9162 |
| New Media Graphics | (800) 288-2207 | (508) 663-6678 |
| Newer Technology | (800) 678-3726 | (316) 685-9368 |
| NewGen Systems | (800) 756-0556 | (714) 641-2800 |
| Nikon | (800) 645-6687 | (516) 547-0305 |
| Nisca | (800) 245-7226 | (214) 245-0942 |
| NMB Technologies | (800) 662-8321 | (818) 341-8207 |
| Northgate Computer Systems | (800) 548-1993 | (612) 943-6960 |
| Novell | (800) 638-9273 | (801) 429-3944 |
| Now Software | (800) 237-3611 | (503) 274-0670 |
| Ntergaid | (203) 380-1280 | (203) 380-1465 |
| Numonics | (800) 247-4517 | (215) 361-0167 |
| nView | (800) 736-8439 | (804) 873-2153 |
| OCR Systems | (800) 233-4627 | (215) 938-7465 |
| Ocron | (800) 933-1399 | (408) 980-5100 |
| Odyssey Development | (800) 992-4797 | (303) 394-0096 |
| Omnicomp Graphics | (713) 464-2990 | (713) 827-7540 |
| OnTrack Computer Systems | (800) 872-2599 | (612) 937-5750 |
| OPTi | (408) 980-8178 | (408) 980-8860 |
| Optibase | (800) 451-5101 | (214) 386-2295 |
| Optical Devices | (805) 987-8801 | (805) 388-1123 |
| Optima Technology | (714) 476-0515 | (714) 476-0613 |
| Orchid Technology | (800) 767-2443 | (510) 490-9312 |
| Orientec of America | (818) 442-1818 | (818) 442-8880 |
| Output Technology | (509) 536-0468 | (509) 533-1280 |
| Overland Data | (800) 729-8725 | (619) 571-0982 |
| Pacific Data Products | (619) 552-0880 | (619) 552-0889 |
| Pacific Magnetics | (619) 474-8216 | (619) 474-3979 |
| Pacific Rim Systems | (800) 722-7461 | (510) 782-1017 |
| Panamax | (800) 472-5555 | (415) 472-5540 |
| Panasonic Communications & Systems | (800) 742-8086 | (201) 392-4792 |
| Panduit | (800) 777-3300 | (708) 532-1811 |
| Parity Systems | (800) 514-4080 | (408) 378-1022 |
| Passport Designs | (415) 726-0280 | (415) 726-2254 |
| Passport Software | (800) 969-7900 | (708) 729-7909 |
| Peachtree Software | (800) 554-8900 | (404) 564-5888 |
| Pelikan | (615) 794-9000 | (615) 794-4425 |
| Perceptive Solutions | (800) 486-3278 | (214) 953-1774 |
| Percon | (800) 873-7266 | (503) 344-1399 |
| Peripheral Land | (800) 288-8754 | (510) 683-9713 |
| Phoenix Technologies | (800) 677-7300 | * |
| Physician Micro Systems | (206) 441-8490 | (206) 441-8915 |
| Pinnacle Micro | (800) 553-7070 | (714) 727-1913 |
| Pioneer Communications of America | (800) 527-3766 | (201) 327-9379 |
| Pivar Computing Services | (800) 266-8378 | (708) 459-6095 |
| PKware | (414) 354-8699 | (414) 352-3815 |
| Plasmaco | (914) 883-6800 | (914) 883-6867 |

*Computer Products and Services (cont'd)*

| Company | Phone | Fax |
|---|---|---|
| PowerCom America | (800) 288-9807 | (714) 252-8240 |
| Practical Peripherals | (800) 442-4774 | (805) 374-7216 |
| Prima Storage Solutions | (408) 727-2600 | (408) 727-2435 |
| Primavera Systems | (800) 423-0245 | (215) 667-7894 |
| Prime Portable Manufacturer | (800) 966-7237 | (818) 444-1027 |
| Procom Technology | (800) 800-8600 | (714) 549-0527 |
| Procomp USA | (216) 234-6387 | (216) 234-2233 |
| Progen Technology | (714) 549-5818 | (714) 549-8047 |
| Progress Software | (800) 327-8445 | (617) 275-4595 |
| Prolink Computer | (213) 780-7978 | (213) 780-7984 |
| Prometheus Products | (800) 477-3473 | (503) 624-0843 |
| Proxim | (800) 229-1630 | (415) 964-5181 |
| Proxima | (800) 447-7694 | (619) 457-9647 |
| PS Solutions | (214) 980-2632 | (214) 980-6720 |
| QMS | (800) 523-2696 | (205) 633-0116 |
| Qualitas | (800) 733-1377 | (301) 907-0905 |
| Quantum | (800) 624-5545 | (408) 922-0735 |
| Quantum Designs Computer | (310) 908-1029 | (310) 908-1033 |
| Quark | (303) 894-8888 | (303) 894-3398 |
| QuaTech | (800) 553-1170 | (216) 434-1409 |
| Quicksoft | (800) 888-8088 | (206) 286-8802 |
| Radiometrics Midwest | (708) 932-7262 | (708) 932-7271 |
| Radius | (800) 227-2795 | (408) 434-0770 |
| Rainbow Technologies | (800) 852-8569 | (714) 454-8557 |
| Rancho Technology | (909) 987-3966 | (909) 989-2365 |
| RCI | (908) 874-4072 | (908) 874-5274 |
| RealWorld | (800) 678-6336 | (603) 224-1955 |
| Recognita of America | (800) 255-4627 | (408) 241-6009 |
| Red Wing Business Systems | (800) 732-9464 | (612) 388-7950 |
| Regent Peripherals | (800) 827-8848 | (509) 662-8146 |
| Relialogic | (510) 770-3990 | (510) 770-3994 |
| Relisys | (408) 945-9000 | (408) 945-0587 |
| Remote Control International | (800) 992-9952 | (619) 481-0311 |
| Reply | (800) 955-5295 | (408) 942-4897 |
| Rexon/Tecmar | (800) 624-8560 | (216) 349-0851 |
| Ricoh | (800) 955-3453 | (408) 432-8372 |
| Riso | (508) 777-7377 | (508) 777-2517 |
| Rockwell International | (800) 436-9988 | (714) 833-4391 |
| Roland Digital Group | (213) 685-5141 | (213) 722-0911 |
| S-MOS Systems | (408) 954-0120 | (408) 922-0578 |
| Sampo of America | (404) 449-6220 | (404) 447-1109 |
| Sampson MIDI Source | (800) 726-6434 | (214) 328-1092 |
| Samsung Electronics America | (800) 624-8999, ext. 85 | (408) 434-5633 |
| Samtron | (800) 726-8766 | (310) 802-8820 |
| Santa Cruz Operation (SCO) | (800) 726-8649 | (408) 458-4227 |
| SBT | (800) 944-1000 | (415) 331-1951 |
| SCI Systems | (205) 882-4800 | (205) 882-4305 |
| Scitor | (415) 570-7700 | (415) 570-7807 |
| Seagate Technology | (800) 468-3472 | (408) 438-6172 |
| Security Microsystems | (800) 345-7390 | (718) 667-0131 |
| Shape Electronics | (800) 367-5811 | (708) 620-0784 |
| Sharp Electronics | (800) 237-4277 | (201) 529-9695 |
| Shiva | (617) 252-6300 | (800) 370-6917 |
| Shuttle Computer International | (408) 945-1480 | (408) 945-1481 |
| Silicon Graphics | (800) 800-7441 | (415) 961-0595 |

*Computer Products and Services (cont'd)*

| Company | Phone | Fax |
|---|---|---|
| Silicon Star International | (510) 623-0500 | (510) 623-1092 |
| Silicon Systems | (800) 624-8999 | (714) 573-6914 |
| Smart Technologies | (403) 245-0333 | (403) 245-0366 |
| Softkey/Spinnaker | (800) 227-5609 | * |
| SoftSolutions Technology | (801) 226-6000 | (801) 224-0920 |
| Software Directions | (800) 346-7638 | (201) 584-7771 |
| Software of the Future | (800) 433-5355 | (214) 262-7338 |
| Software Products International | (800) 937-4774 | (619) 450-1921 |
| Software Publishing | (800) 282-6003 | (408) 980-0729 |
| Software Toolworks, The | (800) 234-3088 | (415) 883-3303 |
| Sola Electric | (800) 879-7652 | (800) 626-6269 |
| Soletek Computer Supply | (800) 437-1518 | (619) 457-2681 |
| Sonera Technologies | (800) 932-6323 | (908) 747-4523 |
| Sony of America | (800) 582-7669 | (201) 930-7201 |
| SourceMate Information Systems | (800) 877-8896 | (415) 381-6902 |
| Sprite | (408) 773-8888 | (408) 773-8892 |
| SRW Computer Components | (800) 547-7766 | (714) 968-1543 |
| Stac Electronics | (800) 522-7822 | (619) 431-0880 |
| Star Gate Technologies | (800) 782-7428 | (216) 349-2056 |
| Star Micronics | (800) 227-8274 | (212) 286-9063 |
| Statpower Technologies | (604) 420-1585 | (604) 420-1591 |
| STB Systems | (800) 234-4334 | (214) 234-1306 |
| Storage Technology | (800) 733-7381 | (303) 673-5019 |
| Summit Micro Design | (408) 739-6348 | (408) 739-4643 |
| Sun Microsystems | (800) 872-4786 | (415) 969-9131 |
| Suncom Technologies | (708) 647-4040 | (708) 647-7827 |
| SuperMac | (800) 541-7680 | (408) 541-5008 |
| SuperTime | (905) 764-3530 | (905) 771-6170 |
| Supra | (800) 727-8772 | (503) 967-2401 |
| Symantec | (800) 441-7234 | (800) 554-4403 |
| Symphony Laboratories | (408) 986-1701 | (408) 986-1771 |
| Synchronics | (800) 852-5852 | (901) 683-8303 |
| Synergystex International | (216) 225-3112 | (216) 225-0099 |
| Syntel Communications | (908) 651-0415 | (908) 805-0596 |
| SyQuest Technology | (800) 245-2278 | (510) 226-4100 |
| Sysgration USA | (415) 306-7860 | (415) 306-7868 |
| Syspro Impact Software | (800) 369-8649 | (714) 541-0662 |
| Systems Plus | (800) 222-7701 | (415) 969-0118 |
| Systems Strategies | (212) 279-8400 | (212) 967-8368 |
| Tandberg Data | (800) 537-3866 | (805) 495-4186 |
| Tandy | (817) 390-3011 | (817) 390-2774 |
| Tatung Company of America | (800) 827-2850 | (310) 637-8484 |
| TDK Electronics | (516) 625-0100 | (516) 625-0651 |
| Teac America | (213) 726-0303 | (213) 727-7656 |
| Techmar Computer Products | (718) 997-6666 | (718) 520-0170 |
| Telex Communications | (612) 887-5531 | (612) 884-0043 |
| Texas Instruments | (800) 527-3500 | (512) 345-9509 |
| Texas Microsystems | (800) 627-8700 | (713) 933-1029 |
| TextWare | (801) 645-9600 | (801) 645-9610 |
| THEOS Software | (510) 935-1118 | (510) 935-1177 |
| Thomas-Conrad | (800) 332-8683 | (512) 836-2840 |
| TimeKeeping Systems | (216) 361-9995 | (216) 361-0030 |
| T/Maker | (415) 962-0195 | (415) 962-0201 |
| TMC Research | (408) 262-0888 | (408) 262-1082 |
| Toshiba America | (800) 334-3445 | (714) 583-3140 |

*Computer Products and Services (cont'd)*

| Company | Phone | Fax |
| --- | --- | --- |
| TOSOH USA | (800) 238-6764 | (415) 888-2800 |
| TouchStone Software | (800) 531-0450 | (714) 960-1886 |
| Trace Mountain | (408) 441-8040 | (408) 441-3399 |
| Transition Engineering | (800) 325-2725 | (612) 942-2322 |
| Transitional Technology | (800) 437-4884 | (714) 693-0225 |
| Traveling Software | (800) 662-2652 | (206) 487-1284 |
| Trident Microsystems | (415) 691-9211 | (415) 691-9265 |
| Tripp Lite Manufacturing | (312) 329-1777 | (312) 329-1363 |
| Triton Technologies | (800) 322-9440 | (908) 855-9608 |
| Truevision | (800) 344-8783 | (317) 576-7700 |
| Tseng Labs | (215) 968-0502 | (215) 860-7713 |
| Twelve Tone Systems | (800) 234-1171 | (617) 273-1494 |
| Twinhead | (800) 545-8946 | (408) 945-1080 |
| U.S. Robotics | (800) 342-5877 | (708) 982-5235 |
| UDP Fonts | (800) 888-4413 | (310) 782-1527 |
| UDS Motorola | (800) 631-4869 | (205) 430-8926 |
| Ultima Electronics | (510) 659-1580 | (510) 440-1217 |
| UltraStor | (714) 453-8170 | (714) 581-0826 |
| Unlimited Systems | (619) 622-1400 | (619) 550-7330 |
| Upsonic | (800) 877-6642 | (714) 258-0811 |
| US Logic/HM System | (800) 777-4875 | (619) 467-1011 |
| Varta Batteries | (914) 592-2500 | (914) 592-2667 |
| Ventura Software | (800) 772-6735 | (619) 673-7777 |
| Verbatim | (704) 547-6500 | (704) 547-6609 |
| Videomedia | (408) 227-9977 | (408) 227-6707 |
| Videx | (503) 758-0521 | (503) 752-5285 |
| ViewSonic | (800) 888-8583 | (909) 869-7958 |
| Vision Imaging | (714) 965-7122 | (714) 965-7118 |
| Visionetics International | (310) 316-7940 | (310) 316-7457 |
| VLSI Technology | (602) 752-8574 | (602) 752-6000 |
| Voyetra Technologies | (800) 233-9377 | (914) 738-6946 |
| Wallaby Software | (201) 934-9333 | (201) 934-5538 |
| WangDat | (714) 753-8900 | (714) 753-8863 |
| Wangtek | (800) 992-9916 | (805) 522-1576 |
| Wearnes Technology | (800) 822-8884 | (408) 456-8846 |
| WEBCORP | (707) 939-9626 | ((707) 939-9661 |
| Western Telematic | (800) 854-7226 | (714) 583-9514 |
| Westrex | (617) 254-1200 | (617) 254-6848 |
| Wolfram Research, Inc. | (800) 441-6284 | (217) 398-0747 |
| WordPerfect | (800) 451-5151 | (801) 222-5077 |
| WordStar International | (800) 227-5609 | (415) 382-4952 |
| XDB Systems | (800) 488-4948 | (301) 317-7701 |
| Xing Technology | (805) 473-0145 | (805) 473-0147 |
| Xircom | (800) 874-4428 | (818) 878-7630 |
| XyQuest | (410) 576-2040 | (410) 576-1968 |
| Y-E Data America | (708) 291-2340 | (708) 498-2430 |
| Yamaha Of America | (800) 543-7457 | (408) 437-8791 |
| Young Micro Systems | (310) 802-8899 | (310) 802-8889 |
| Z-Ram | (800) 368-4726 | (714) 863-9478 |
| Zedcor | (602) 881-8101 | (602) 881-1841 |
| Zenith Data Systems | (800) 582-0524 | (800) 582-8194 |
| Zentek Storage | (408) 946-4464 | (408) 946-4465 |
| Zoom Telephonics | (800) 631-3116 | (617) 423-9231 |
| ZSoft | (404) 428-0008 | (404) 427-1150 |
| Zyxel Communications | (800) 255-4101 | (714) 693-8811 |

*\* multiple fax numbers; users are requested to call first*

*Source: Computer Vendors Directory*

# Specialized Computer Resources

## Contact Options

*Insurance:*

Safeware
2929 N. High St.
Columbus, OH 43202
(800) 848-3469

The Computer Insurance Agency
6150 Old Millersport Rd., NE
Pleasantville, OH 43148
(800) 722-0385

*Typefaces:*

FontHaus
1375 Kings Hwy., E
Fairfield, CT 06430
(800) 942-9110

Monotype
150 S. Wacker Dr., #2630
Chicago, IL 60606
(800) 666-6897

*Off-Site Data Storage:*

Iron Mountain
745 Atlantic Ave.
Boston, MA 02111
(617) 357-6966

*Hard Disk Crash Recovery:*

Drivesavers
400 Bel Marin Keys Blvd.
Novato, CA 94949
(415) 883-4232

Data Recovery Technology
5029 Stavan Creek Blvd.
Santa Clara, CA 95051
(408) 943-9401

Computer Peripheral Repair
11440 Okeechobee Rd., Suite 200
Royal Palm Beach, FL 33411
(800) 765-9292

*Software Piracy:*

Software Publishers of America
1730 M St., NW, Suite 700
Washington, DC 20036
(800) 388-7478

*CD ROM:*

*CD–ROM Professional*
*Magazine for CD-ROM Publishers*
Pemberton Press
462 Danbury Rd.
Wilton, CT 06897
(203) 761-1466

*Specialized Software Directories:*

Redgate Communications
660 Beachland Blvd.
Vero Beach, FL 32963
(407) 231-6904

# Electronic Mail

USING ELECTRONIC MAIL (E-MAIL), a business can instantly send a message or computer file to an employee or customer anywhere in the world. Unlike faxes, e-mail permits the recipient to edit the message and work with the data sent.

Just like faxes, e-mail requires that both parties have the right equipment. There are several different e-mail services, but fortunately a common standard is developing which permits them to speak to each other.

All electronic bulletin boards and information services provide their users with access to e-mail within the system. It is a straightforward and simple task to send mail to anyone on the same system. For this reason, many companies are asking their employees and customers to join one system or another.

Inter-bulletin board communication is handled through the Internet. Once an Internet address is known, most information systems (and some bulletin boards) permit users to send mail through the internet. For example, to reach the editors of *The Information Please Business Almanac*, send mail from any service with Internet access to the Internet address: ALMANAC@SGP.COM.

*Electronic Mail (cont'd)*

## Contact Options

*Popular Electronic Mail Services:*

America Online
(800) 827-6364

ATT Mail
(800) 367-7225

CompuServe
(800) 848-8199

Delphi
(800) 544-4005

GEnie
(800) 638-9636

MCI Mail
(800) 444-6245

Prodigy
(800) 346-9759

## Recommended Resource

*The Electronic Mail Advantage: Applications and Benefits*
Electronic Mail Association, free
1655 N. Fort Myer Dr., #850
Arlington, VA 22209
(703) 524-5550

# The Internet

MORE THAN 20 YEARS AGO, DARPA, a division of the Pentagon, created a network of computers being used by its researchers. These computers were located at universities and research facilities around the world. The purpose of the network was to permit researchers at one facility to contact others, and to exchange information as well.

Once the protocol for this network was established, the number of users and number of uses skyrocketed. With more than five million people currently "on" the Internet, it has become the de facto standard for electronic mail.

In addition to a huge base of mail users, the Internet provides access to hundreds of millions of pieces of data. A quick search could find a state of the art paper on the uses of silicon in biomedical engineering, or an article spoofing the latest state of the union address.

In general, a user can only access the Internet through a provider. The following is a list of Internet access providers (as posted on the Internet):

## Contact Options

A2I COMMUNICATIONS
1211 Park Ave., #202
San Jose, CA 95126
Net address: info@rahul.net
Area served: San Jose, CA area (408 area code)
Services: Dialup e-mail, SunOS software development environment

**TIP:** *There are literally hundreds of computer magazines. As the roster of titles changes almost daily, the best strategy is to start at your local newsstand. Consistent favorites are* MacUser, PCWorld, Boardwatch, InfoWorld *and* Computer Shopper.

ADVANCED NETWORK AND SERVICES (ANS)
AND ANS CORE
2901 Hubbard Rd.
Ann Arbor, MI 48105
(800) 456-8267 or
(313) 677-7300
Net address: info@ans.net
Area served: U.S. and International
Services: Network connections

ALTERNET
3110 Fairview Park Dr., Suite 570
Falls Church, VA 22042
(800) 488-6384 or
(703) 204-8000
Net address: alternet-info@uunet.uu.net
Area served: U.S.
Services: Network connections

AMERICA ONLINE
8619 Westwood Center Dr.
Vienna, VA 22182
(800) 827-6364
Net address: info@aol.com
Area served: U.S. and Canada
Services: Dialup e-mail

BARRNET
Bay Area Regional Research Network
Pine Hall, Room 115
Stanford, CA 94305
(415) 723-3104
Net address: gd.why@forsythe.stanford.edu
Area served: San Francisco Bay Area,
Northern California
Services: Network connections, national dialup IP, dialup e-mail

*The Internet (cont'd)*

CERFNET
California Education and Research
Federation Network
P.O. Box 85608
San Diego, CA 92186
(800) 876-2373 or
(619) 455-3900
Net address: help@cerf.net
Area served: California and International
Services: Network connections, national dialup IP,
dialup e-mail

CICNET
Committee on Institutional Cooperation Network
ITI Building
2901 Hubbard Dr., Pod G
Ann Arbor, MI 48105
(313) 998-6103
Net address: info@cic.net
Area served: Minnesota, Wisconsin, Iowa, Illinois,
Indiana, Michigan, and Ohio
Services: Network connections

CLASS
Cooperative Agency for Library Systems
and Services
1415 Koll Circle, Suite 101
San Jose, CA 95112
(800) 488-4559 or
(408) 453-0444
Net address: class@class.org
Area served: U.S.
Services: Dialup access for libraries in the U.S.

COLORADO SUPERNET
Colorado SuperNet
CSM Computing Center
Colorado School Mines
1500 Illinois
Golden, Colorado 80401
(303) 273-3471
Net address: info@csn.org
Area served: Colorado
Services: Network connections, dialup IP

COMMUNITY NEWS SERVICE
1715 Monterey Rd.
Colorado Springs, CO 80910
(800) 592-1240 or
(719) 579-9120
Net address: info@cscns.com
Area served: Colorado Springs (719 area code)
Services: Dialup e-mail, other services

COMPUSERVE INFORMATION SYSTEM
5000 Arlington Center Boulevard
P.O. Box 20212
Columbus, OH 43220
(614) 457-0802 or
(800) 848-8990
Net address: postmaster@csi.compuserve.com
Area served: U.S. and International
Services: Dialup e-mail, other services

CONCERT
Communications for North Carolina Education,
Research, and Technology Network
P.O. Box 12889
3021 Cornwallis Rd.
Research Triangle Park, NC 27709
(919) 248-1404
Net address: sellers@concert.net
Area served: North Carolina
Services: Network connections, dialup e-mail,
dialup IP

DASNET
DA Systems
1053 East Campbell Ave.
Campbell, CA 95008
(408) 559-7434
Net address: help@das.net
Area served: California
Services: Dialup e-mail

EXPRESS ACCESS ONLINE
COMMUNICATIONS SERVICE
Digital Express Group
6006 Greenbelt Rd., Suite 228
Greenbelt, MD 20770
(301) 220-2020
Net address: info@ss1.digex.com
Area served: Northern VA; Baltimore, MD;
Washington, DC
(area codes 202, 310, 410, 703)
Services: Dialup e-mail, other services

EZ-E-MAIL
Shecora Associates
P.O. Box 7604
Nashua, NH 03060
(603) 672-0736
Net address: info@lemuria.sai.com
Area served: U.S. and Canada
Services: Dialup e-mail

HALCYON
Dataway
P.O. Box 555
Grapeview, WA 98546
(206) 455-3505
Net address: info@remote.halcyon.com
Area served: Seattle, WA
Services: Dialup e-mail

HOLONET
Information Access Technologies
46 Shattuck Sq., Suite 11
Berkeley, CA 94704
(510) 704-0160
Net address: info@holonet.mailer.net
Area served: U.S.
Services: Dialup e-mail

*The Internet (cont'd)*

**INFOLAN**
Infonet Service
2100 E. Grand Ave.
El Segundo, CA 90245
(310) 335-2600
Area served: International, including U.S., Europe,
Canada, Hong Kong, Japan, Singapore, and
Australia
Services: Network connections, dialup IP

**INSTITUTE FOR GLOBAL COMMUNICATIONS**
18 De Boom St.
San Francisco, CA 94107
(415) 442-0220
Net address: igc-infot@igc.apc.org
Area served: Worldwide
Services: Dialup e-mail

**JVNCNET**
Global Enterprise Service
John von Neumann Center Network
6 von Neumann Hall
Princeton University
Princeton, NJ 08544
Sergio F. Heker
(609) 897-7300 or
(800) 358-4437
Net address: market@jvnc.net
Area served: U.S. and International
Services: Network connections, dialup IP

**LOS NETTOS**
University of Southern California
Information Sciences Institute
4676 Admiralty Way
Marina del Rey, CA 90292
(310) 822-1511
Net address: los-nettos-request@isi.edu
Area served: Los Angeles Area, Southern
California
Services: Network connections

**MCI MAIL**
1133 19th St., NW, 7th Floor
Washington, DC 20036
(800) 444-6245 or
(202) 833-8484
Net address: 2671163@mcimail.com or
3248333@mcimail.com
Area served: U.S. and International
Services: Dialup e-mail

**MICHNET**
2200 Bonisteel Blvd.
Ann Arbor, MI 48109
(313) 764-9430
Net address: info@merit.edu
Area served: Michigan
Services: Network connections, dialup IP

**MIDNET**
Midwestern States Network
208 N. 8th, Suite 421
Lincoln, NE 68508
(402) 472-5032
Net address: nic@mid.net
Area served: Midwestern states including Iowa,
Kansas, Oklahoma, Arkansas, Missouri, South
Dakota, and Nebraska
Services: Network connections

**MILWAUKEE INTERNET XCHANGE**
Mix Communications
P.O Box 17166
Milwaukee, WI 53217
(414) 228-0739
Net address: info@mixcom.com
Area served: Milwaukee, WI
Services: Dialup e-mail

**MRNET**
Minnesota Regional Network
511 11th Avenue South, Box 212
Minneapolis, MN 55415
(612) 342-2570
Net address: info@mr.net
Area served: Minnesota
Services: Network connections

**MSEN**
628 Brooks St.
Ann Arbor, MI 48103
(313) 998-4562
Net address: info@msen.com
Area served: U.S.
Services: Network connections, dialup IP, dialup
e-mail

**NEARNET**
New England Academic and Research Network
BBN Systems and Technologies
10 Moulton St.
Cambridge, MA 02138
(617) 873-8730
Net address: nearnet-staff@nic.near.net
Area served: Maine, Vermont, New Hampshire,
Connecticut, Massachusetts, Rhode Island
Services: Network connections, dialup IP

**NETCOM ONLINE COMMUNICATION
SERVICES**
4000 Moorpark Ave., Suite 200
San Jose, CA 95117
(800) 501-8649 or
(408) 554-8649
Net address: info@netcom.com
Area served: California (area codes 213, 310, 408,
415, 510, 818)
Services: Dialup e-mail, dialup IP

*The Internet (cont'd)*

**NETILLINOIS**
University of Illinois
Computing Services Office
1304 W. Springfield
Urbana, IL 61801
(309) 677-3100
Net address: oconnor@illinois.net
Area served: Illinois
Services: Network connections

**NEVADANET**
University of Nevada System
Computing Services
4505 Maryland Pkwy.
Las Vegas, NV 89154
(702) 784-6133
Net address: braddlee@nevada.edu
Area served: Nevada
Services: Network connections

**NORTHWESTNET**
Northwestern States Network
NorthWestNet
2435 233rd Pl., NE
Redmond, WA 98053
(206) 562-3000
Net address: info@nwnet.net
Area served: Academic and research sites in Alaska, Idaho, Montana North Dakota, Oregon, Wyoming, and Washington
Services: Network connections

**NYSERNET**
New York State Education and Research Network
111 College Pl., Room 3-211
Syracuse, NY 13244
(315) 453-2912
Net address: info@nysernet.org
Area served: New York State and International
Services: Network connections, dialup e-mail, dialup IP

**OARNET**
Ohio Academic Research Network
Ohio Supercomputer Center
2455 Northstar Rd.
Columbus, Ohio 43221
(800) 627-8101 or
(614) 728-8100
Net address: info@oar.net
Area served: Ohio
Services: Network connections, dialup

**PANIX PUBLIC ACCESS UNIX**
110 Riverside Drive
New York, NY 10024
(212) 877-4854
Net address: alexis@panix.com
Area served: New York, NY (area codes 212, 718)
Services: Dialup e-mail

**PERFORMANCE SYSTEMS INTERNATIONAL**
11800 Sunrise Valley Dr.
Suite 1100
Reston, VA 22091
Net address: all-info@psi.com
(800) 827-7482 or
(703) 709-0300
FAX: 1 703 620-4586
Area served: U.S. and International
Services: Network connections, dialup e-mail, dialup IP

**PORTAL COMMUNICATIONS**
20863 Stevens Creek Blvd., Suite 200
Cupertino, CA 95014
(408) 973-9111
Net address: cs@cup.portal.com
info@portal.com
Area served: Northern California (area codes 408, 415)
Services: Dialup e-mail

**PREPNET**
Pennsylvania Research and Economic Partnership Network
305 South Craig St., 2nd Floor
Pittsburgh, PA 15213
(412) 268-7870
Net address: nic@prep.net
Area served: Pennsylvania
Services: Network connections, dialup IP

**PSCNET**
Pittsburgh Supercomputing Center Network
Pittsburgh Supercomputing Center
4400 5th Ave.
Pittsburgh, PA 15213
(412) 268-4960
Net address: pscnet-admin@psc.edu
Area served: Eastern U.S. (Pennsylvania, Ohio, and West Virginia)
Services: Network connections

**TIP:** *Many of the e-mail addresses in the list above give automated responses to queries. A user who has an e-mail address simply sends mail to the appropriate address, and in a short time, a response with all pertinent information about the provider, including services and rates, is sent back to the user.*

*The Internet (cont'd)*

RADIOMAIL
2600 Campus Dr.
San Mateo, CA 94403
(800) 597-6245
Net address: info@radiomail.net
Area served: U.S.
Services: RadioMail

RISCNET
InteleCom Data Systems
11 Franklin Rd.
East Greenwich, RI 02818
(401) 885-6855
Net address: info@nic.risc.net
Area served: Rhode Island, New England
Services: Network connections, dialup IP, dialup
e-mail

SESQUINET
Texas Sesquicentennial Network
Office of Networking and Computing Systems
Rice University
Houston, TX 77251
(713) 527-4988
Net address: farrell@rice.edu
Area served: Texas
Services: Network connections, dialup IP

SPRINT NSFNET ICM
Sprint NSFNET International Connections Manager
(703) 904-2230
Net address: rcollet@icm1.icp.net
Area served: International
Services: International network connections to
NSFNET; operates under cooperative agreement
with NSF and conforms to CCIRN guidelines

SPRINTLINK
Sprint
13221 Woodland Park Rd.
Herndon, VA 22071
(703) 904-2167
Net address: rdoyle@icm1.icp.net
Area served: U.S. and International
Services: Network connections, dialup IP

SURANET
Southeastern Universities Research Association
Network
1353 Computer Science Center
University of Maryland
College Park, Maryland 20742
(301) 982-4600
Net address: hahn@sura.net
Area served: Southeastern U.S. (Alabama, Florida,
Georgia, Kentucky, Louisiana, Mississippi, North
Carolina, South Carolina, Tennessee, Virginia, and
West Virginia)
Services: Network connections

THENET
Texas Higher Education Network
Computation Center
University of Texas
Austin, TX 78712
(512) 471-5046
Net address: tracy@utexas.edu
Area served: Texas
Services: Network connections

UUNET TECHNOLOGIES
3110 Fairview Park Dr., Suite 570
Falls Church, Va 22042
Net address: info@uunet.uu.net
(800) 488-6384 or
(703) 204-8000
FAX: (703) 204-8001
Area served: U.S.
Services: Network connections, dialup e-mail

VERNET
Virginia Education and Research Network
Academic Computing Center
Gilmer Hall
University of Virginia
Charlottesville, VA 22903
(804) 924-0616
Net address: net-info@ver.net
Area served: Virginia
Services: Network connections

WESTNET
Southwestern States Network
UCC
601 S. Howes, 6th Floor So.
Colorado State University
Fort Collins, CO 80523
(303) 491-7260
Net address: pburns@yuma.acns.colostate.edu
Area served: Western U.S. (Arizona, Colorado, New
Mexico, Utah, Idaho, and Wyoming)
Services: Network connections

WHOLE EARTH 'LECTRONIC LINK (WELL)
27 Gate Five Rd.
Sausalito, CA 94965
(415) 332-4335
Net address: info@well.sf.ca.us
Area served: San Francisco Bay Area (area code
415)
Services: Dialup e-mail, international access,
UNIX, Usenet

WISCNET
Madison Academic Computing Center
1210 W. Dayton St.
Madison, WI 53706
(608) 262-8874
Net address: tad@cs.wisc.edu
Area served: Wisconsin
Services: Network connections

*The Internet (cont'd)*

THE WORLD
Software Tool & Die
1330 Beacon St.
Brookline, MA 02146
(617) 739-0202
Net address: office@world.std.com
Area served: Boston (area code 617)
Services: Dialup e-mail, other services

WVNET
West Virginia Network for Educational
Telecomputing
837 Chestnut Ridge Rd.
Morgantown, WV 26505
(304) 293-5192
Net address: cc011041@wvnvms.wvnet.edu
Area served: West Virginia
Services: Network connections, dialup IP

# Online Services

## CompuServe

CompuServe is one of the oldest and largest online services. As the de facto standard, it offers a wide range of software and advice, allows users to send and receive electronic mail, and provides a wide range of non-computer related information.

CompuServe offers a nationwide network of local phone numbers, which can be easily accessed by anyone with a computer and a modem. To obtain a local access number, call (800) 848-8199, 24 hours a day.

Once connected to CompuServe, the user can get detailed information on more than 1,000 topics, from wood carving to Amiga computers.

Divided into forums, the CompuServe service has segmented its users into nearly 1,000 special interest areas. This specialization allows the user to post a message directly to the people most interested in the topic. It's not unusual to post a question about a piece of software and receive more than a dozen answers within an hour.

In addition to forums and access to free files, CompuServe offers access to the Ezey Sabre travel reservations system, as well as dozens of other commercial services and databases. CompuServe will also monitor the wire services on request, clipping any stories that contain the keywords that the user has identified. The easiest way to use Compuserve is to use the forums to explore areas of interest.

CompuServe
Box 20212
Columbus, OH 43220
(800) 848-8199

## Dialog

Dialog is an online service that provides access to hundreds of research databases and publications. Corporations use Dialog as a fast, easy way to search through the full text of thousands of publications.

By navigating through its occasionally difficult interface, a researcher can access all of these sources in seconds.

Research-oriented services like Dialog and Nexis are quite expensive. Investigate subscription pricing as an alternative.

A 30-page list of Dialog publications can be requested by contacting Dialog directly.

Dialog
3460 Hillview Ave.
Palo Alto, CA 94304
(800) 334-2564

## Nexis

Nexis is a nearly complete compendium of news. It features the full text of hundreds of magazines, ranging from *Time* to *Forbes* to obscure technical journals. It also contains every word that has passed through more than twenty newswires, including AP and the Xinhua News Agency.

Using Nexis, a business user can find every mention of a competitor or a topic over a given period of time. Far more efficient than a clipping service, Nexis allows users to perform complicated Boolean searches. For example, one could search for every instance of the word "wool" within three words of the phrase "cardigan sweaters." Within seconds, Nexis will find all relevant references. NOTE: of all the services listed here, Nexis is far and away the most expensive, with monthly fees beginning at $500.

For a complete listing, contact Nexis at the number given.

Nexis
Mead Data Central
9393 Springboro Pike
Dayton, OH 45401
(800) 346-9759

## Prodigy

Prodigy currently posts the largest membership of all electronic information services. Designed primarily for consumer use, Prodigy offers an excellent way to get basic information on a variety of sources. In addition, Prodigy's news and Wall Street services provide an extremely low-cost way to stay in touch with the world on a daily basis.

Prodigy
445 Hamilton Ave.
White Plains, NY 10601
(914) 993-8000 or (800) 776-3449

*Online Services (cont'd)*

## Dow Jones

Dow Jones News Retrieval is similar to Dialog and Nexis, in that it offers easy access to hundreds of publications. But Dow Jones focuses primarily on business, offering everything from *Barron's* to *Plastics World* online.

Dow Jones & Co.
P.O. Box 300
Princeton, NJ 08543
(609) 452-1511

## America Online

America Online (AOL) is a hybrid. It combines the friendly interface of Macintosh or Windows with a speedy and powerful information service. AOL provides extremely low-cost access to Internet messaging, as well as a large range of forums and information sources. AOL is highly recommended for first-time users of information services.

America Online
8619 Westwood Center Dr.
Vienna, VA 22182
(800) 827-6364

## Other Online Services

Delphi
1030 Massachusetts Ave.
Cambridge, MA 02139
(800) 544-4005

E-World
Apple Computer
20525 Mariani Ave., MS 36BC
Cupertino, CA 95014
(800) 775-4556

GEnie
General Electric
401 N. Washington St.
Rockville, MD 20849
(800) 638-9636

NewsNet
945 Haverford Rd.
Bryn Mawr, PA 19010
(800) 345-1301

## Recommended Resource

*Online Access*
900 N. Franklin St. #310
Chicago, IL 60610
(800) 366-6336

# Bulletin Boards

USING A COMPUTER AND A MODEM, you can reach more than 70,000 bulletin boards around the world. These boards allow you to exchange software and data, find help on an awesome variety of topics, or just visit electronically with other computer users.

While there are a handful of large commercial bulletin boards, most are run by small businesses and individuals.

The typical bulletin board offers a large collection of shareware programs, frequently updated. Many also specialize, ranging from "adult" material

to information on tropical fish. In addition, many give access to the Internet, allowing low-cost or free electronic mail around the world.

## Recommended Resource

*Boardwatch Magazine*, $36/year
8500 W. Bowles Ave.
Littleton, CO 80123
(303) 973-6038

## The Top Reference Sources

*Computer Vendors Directory*, cost varies
908 1st Ave., NW
Minot, ND 58701

The *Computer Vendors Directory* lists over 10,000 companies worldwide. It is updated frequently,

and is available on disk. With the computer industry growing continuously, this directory is a valuable resource. Listings include short descriptions of each company's focus as well as sales numbers, fax numbers, and tech support numbers.

*Bulletin Boards (cont'd)*

The following table contains bulletin boards of interest to business users in a variety of areas:

## Business Bulletin Boards

| Name | Description | Baud | Phone |
|------|-------------|------|-------|
| A-E Resource BBS | For architects, engineers, related professionals | 14400 | (205) 821-9700 |
| Acs Online | National new & used vehicle buying | 9600 | (513) 624-0552 |
| The Ad Connection | Classified ads, shopping mall, faxback services, government jobs | 2400 | (804) 978-3927 |
| Agri-Specialists BBS | Agricultural information | 9600 | (918) 255-6542 |
| America's Suggestion Box | For input on improving any product or service | 14400 | (516) 471-8606 |
| American Business Research Net | Business services and files | 2400 | (516) 754-9205 |
| Anomalous BBS | Support for inventors, esp. in aerospace areas | 14400 | (615) 952-5638 |
| Attention To Details | ASP hub BBS, for ASP catalogue | 14400 | (909) 681-6221 |
| Auction Action Online | Auction listings in OH, MI, and some national | 4800 | (216) 454-8003 |
| Auction Action Online | Auction schedules, related information | 2400 | (216) 454-8003 |
| Automobile Consumer Services | New car pricing reports and used car value reports | 9600 | (513) 624-0552 |
| Axcess-Emergency Medicine | Emergency medicine job opportunities | 2400 | (412) 363-7510 |
| Biz-Net 2000 On-Line | Business orientation; real estate, entreprenuer, multi-level marketing, telemarketing | 14400 | (313) 559-8604 |
| The Bizopps Connection | Business opps, franchise opps, moneymaking opps, venture capital sources, etc. | 14400 | (310) 677-7034 |
| Bizynet | Business-oriented BBS, ASP approved files | 14400 | (619) 283-1721 |
| The Board Room BBS | Business-oriented, best of business shareware | 14400 | (717) 393-2640 |
| Book BBS | Information on computer books | 9600 | (215) 657-6130 |
| Book Stacks Unlimited | On-line bookstore, reader's conference, over 600,000 titles | 9600 | (216) 861-0469 |
| The Business Center | Business; marketing of real estate, singles, jobs, foreign correspondence | 14400 | (707) 451-0393 |
| Business Network Source | Business, minority business information, discussions | 14400 | (201) 836-1844 |
| Business Online | For all interested in business, money, success, etc. | 2400 | (216) 332-2712 |
| Business Opportunity BBS | Free online ad placement, for business opportunities, sales, etc. | 14400 | (618) 423-2331 |
| The Bu$inessman's Special | Business files, online magazines, conferences | 9600 | (312) 736-5415 |
| The CPA's BBS | Tax, investment, financial accounting, personal financial planning issues | 14400 | (202) 882-9067 |
| Career Connections | Career opportunities for viewing, response | 14400 | (415) 917-2125 |
| Career Decisions BBS | Job ads, book reviews, recruiters, resume service, job profiles, salaries, relocation tips | 2400 | (909) 864-8287 |
| The Career Network | Job and resume posting | 19200 | (213) 629-1472 |
| Career Systems | Job listings for MIS, software engineering, data processing professionals | 14400 | (413) 592-9208 |
| Careers Online | Career placement for engineering, manufacturing, computer professionals | 38400 | (317) 873-6283 |
| Central Records | Online criminal records, missing persons search, skiptracing, missing heirs, etc. | 9600 | (916) 443-8470 |
| Chicago Syslink | Online games, Bell business report, files, chat, online magazines, etc. | 14440 | (708) 795-4442 |
| City Senders BBS | Business, community advertising, business referral | 2400 | (216) 734-1477 |
| Computer Security BBS | For computer security and law enforcement professionals | 19200 | (303) 962-9536 |
| The Crafts Board | For crafters, craft vendors | 14400 | (205) 339-7022 |
| Crescendo | Music and musicians | 28800 | (301) 490-4775 |

*Bulletin Boards (cont'd)*

| Name | Description | Baud | Phone |
|------|-------------|------|-------|
| Cruise Trek's SuperBBS | Cruise and tours discounts | 19200 | (505) 525-8626 |
| Cyberia | Small business section, USA Today, Boardwatch, etc. | 57600 | (717) 840-1444 |
| DFG Financial BBS | For individuals & small businesses; information on money management, more | 14411 | (205) 745-0579 |
| Dallas Remote Imaging Group | For professionals in remote sensing, satellite communications, satellite imagery, etc. | 28800 | (214) 394-7438 |
| The "Delight the Customer" BBS | Networking, productivity-enhancing files, jobs database, vendor exhibits | 9600 | (517) 797-3740 |
| EDN Magazine BBS | For electrical engineering professionals | 9600 | (617) 558-4241 |
| Electronic Publishers BBS | USA Today, closing stock quotes, other online publications | 14000 | (503) 624-4966 |
| Energy/Recycling BBS | Engineering, energy management, waste recycling | 2400 | (704) 547-3114 |
| Entrenet | For business owners | 9600 | (908) 647-2202 |
| Evergreen BBS | Product sales, business opportunities | 14400 | (201) 398-2373 |
| Evergreen BBS | Product sales, business opportunities | 19200 | (201) 398-2373 |
| Farm Net USA | Ag-oriented; USA Today, newsbytes, etc. | 14400 | (805) 339-0945 |
| Fifth Estate BBS | For broadcast and media professionals | 14400 | (702) 898-9684 |
| Fjob | Information on federal jobs | 9600 | (912) 757-3100 |
| Free Financial Network | Largest financial bbs in the world | 14400 | (212) 752-8660 |
| Good Sam BBS | Business accounting software, geared to MAS90, add-on, facts, open systems | 38400 | (714) 957-2881 |
| Greenhill Comp/Line BBS | Shopping, files, multimedia, printing, etc. | 144 | (215) 441-8812 |
| Home Automation BBS | Brand-name, custom-made home automation products | 9600 | (416) 471-6776 |
| Horseman's BBS | For horse lovers or business people, extensive classified ad section | 14400 | (517) 769-2230 |
| Infomarket Express | Information bought and sold online | 14400 | (908) 879-7209 |
| Information Odyssey | Sales, marketing, usenet groups, general business information for metro Portland | 14400 | (503) 650-2992 |
| Investors Online Data | Online investment, stock market information, tech analysis | – | (206) 285-5359 |
| Jobbs | Online job listings, 2186 technical positions, 10,000 corporations | – | (404) 992-8937 |
| Kimberlely BBS | Prime rate, fed funds, t-bill discount rate, economic data | 9600 | (612) 340-2489 |
| Labor & Insurance Law BBS | Text files discussing workers compensation, labor, insurance law issues | 14400 | (805) 495-9911 |
| Leisure & Business BBS | Business, leisure subjects | 19200 | (516) 293-7540 |
| Linking Rings Systems | Business oriented; focus on Louisiana business development | 14400 | (318) 449-4824 |
| The Market BBS | Finance, investment, business related topics | 14400 | (201) 467-3269 |
| Max Ule | Online brokerage with competitive rates | 9600 | (212) 809-1160 |
| Mechanix Choice | For home mechanics, tradespeople, consumers | 14400 | (215) 887-0171 |
| The Meeting Works | For meetings, seminars, trade exhibits planners | 14400 | (212) 737-6932 |
| Moneyline Express | Home business ideas, consultation, legal documents | 2400 | (718) 816-5502 |
| "My Favorite BBS" | For computer resellers; hardware and software | 14400 | (916) 381-2851 |
| The Nonprofit Network | Supports nonprofit organizations | 2400 | (609) 261-5772 |
| Online Opportunities | Free resume database and job listing bbs for job seekers, mostly in Philadelphia | 14400 | (215) 873-7170 |

*Bulletin Boards (cont'd)*

| Name | Description | Baud | Phone |
|------|-------------|------|-------|
| Opm Mainstreet | Federal personnel information, forums with bulletins, files, e-mail | 9600 | (202) 606-4800 |
| Opportunity BBS | 6000+files, conferences | 24000 | (804) 588-4031 |
| Patent Hotline/Phl(Tm) | Over 3,400 patents for sale or license, how-to tips, etc. | 38400 | (619) 723-4413 |
| Pitstar BBS | Business, financial; daily updated commodities quotes, market indexes, etc. | 57600 | (708) 687-4413 |
| The Professional's BBS | For professional programmers and novices | 2400 | (716) 728-3896 |
| Propnet | Advice on competitive proposal development, government contracts | 14400 | (202) 244-9291 |
| RCR BBS & Computers | Sales of computers, other items | 2400 | (305) 823-3852 |
| RIRBBS | Commerce Business Daily, more | 14400 | (301) 309-1808 |
| The Resume File | Resume evaluation, review | 2400 | (805) 581-6210 |
| Sales Automation Success | Reviews, discussions of leading contact managers, sales automation programs | 144 | (206) 392-8943 |
| $ales Force | Nationwide business directory, net mail, database | 14400 | (817) 847-9255 |
| Sarte Collection | Entrepreneur offers | 9600 | (407) 881-0358 |
| SBA Online | Small Business Administration; management, financial issue advice | 9600 | (800) 697-4636 |
| Search BBS | High-tech company database, job listings | 2400 | (206) 253-5213 |
| Six Sigma BBS | PC software, text procedures for quality systems, list of local consultants | 14400 | (314) 349-7616 |
| Sleuth BBS | Business-oriented; online publications, file library, storage | 14400 | (818) 727-7639 |
| The Software Store | Professional business related software | 9600 | (516) 589-4984 |
| Solutions | Waste management service for industry, environmental technology issues | 2400 | (407) 321-6119 |
| Sourcery | For purchasing professionals; bid specs, vendor sources, professional dev. opportunties | 14400 | (702) 256-6050 |
| Stat Agline! | Agricultural market information, statistics, international trade leads | 2400 | (604) 531-8818 |
| Strictly Business! | For entrepreneurs, managers, business professionals | 2400 | (614) 538-9250 |
| Support U. | Technical support, program updates, etc. | 14400 | (314) 227-6746 |
| The TQM BBS | Information on total quality management | 14400 | (301) 585-1164 |
| Tech BBS | Tech support for pc compatibles | 9600 | (219) 654-3210 |
| Town Center Info Exchange | Business- and community-oriented local & international message areas | 14440 | (410) 995-1809 |
| The Vacation Source | Colorado vacation ideas | 14400 | (800) 868-7555 |
| Vertech's Graphic Connection | CAD, animation, rendering, graphics, material, texture files | 14400 | (503) 591-8412 |
| Virtual Office Complex | Cyberspace office center; Farm Net USA, summit software services, etc. | 14400 | (805) 339-0945 |
| The Wall Street Connection | Investing, finance, business | 14400 | (808) 521-4356 |
| World Class Software BBS | Business software | 14400 | (210) 656-7939 |

## The Top Reference Sources

*Microcomputer Market Place*
Random House Electronics Publishing, $30
(212) 751-2600

This new publication is a comprehensive guide to PC software and hardware vendors, service providers, and information sources. Thousands of listings are included such as software and hardware companies, new equipment sources (mail order and retail), secondary market sources, associations and organizations, information and media resources, computer safety and product information sources, and more.

# DOS Commands

DOS IS THE OPERATING SYSTEM used by more than 100 million computers around the world. Here are 28 common DOS commands, together with a brief description of their functions:

| | |
|---|---|
| BACKUP | Archives data |
| BREAK | Turns cntrl–c on and off |
| CD | Change directory |
| CHKDSK | Checks a disk |
| CLS | Clear screen |
| COMP | Compares two files |
| COPY | Copy a file |
| DATE | Sets the date |
| DEL | Delete |
| DIR | Directory |
| DISKCOPY | Copy all files on a disk |
| FIND | Searches for text in a file |
| FORMAT | Wipes a disk and prepares for use |
| MD | Makes a directory |
| MEM | Describes memory status |
| MODE | Sets defaults |
| MORE | Pauses the printout of a text file |
| PATH | Accesses other subdirectories |
| PROMPT | Changes the C: prompt |
| REN | Rename |
| RESTORE | Opposite of backup |
| SYS | Makes a disk bootable |
| TIME | Sets the time |
| TYPE | Prints a text file to the screen |
| VER | Lets you know what version of DOS is running |
| VERIFY | Double-checks all disk writes |
| VOL | Tells you a disk's volume |
| XCOPY | Better than Copy |

# The Hayes Command Set

VIRTUALLY ALL MODEMS for personal computers are Hayes-compatible modems. These modems can be controlled using an arcane code–speaker volume, auto answer, speed, and other features can be easily set once you know the proper code.

| Code | Modem Operation |
|---|---|
| ATA | Answer phone immediately |
| ATDT | Tone dial the phone |
| ATH0 | Hang up |

| Code | Modem Operation |
|---|---|
| ATL1 | Make speaker soft |
| ATL3 | Make speaker loud |
| ATM0 | Turn monitor speaker (dial tone) off |
| ATDP | Pulse dial the phone |
| ATS0=1 | Auto answer on one ring |
| ATS8=4 | Set the pause for a comma in the phone number to 4 seconds |
| ATZ | Reset the modem |

# Smileys

WHEN SENDING ELECTRONIC MAIL, users often want to express more emotion than the keyboard allows. These "smileys" can be more easily understood if you tilt your head to the left.

| Smiley | Meaning |
|---|---|
| :-) | Your basic smiley |
| :) | Midget smiley |
| ,-) | Winking happy smiley |
| (-: | Left-handed smiley |
| (:-) | Smiley big-face |
| (:-( | Very unhappy smiley |
| ,-} | Wry and winking smiley |
| '-) | Winking smiley |

| Smiley | Meaning |
|---|---|
| :-# | My lips are sealed |
| :-* | Kiss |
| :-/ | Skeptical smiley |
| :-> | Sarcastic smiley |
| :-@ | Screaming smiley |
| :-V | Shouting smiley |
| :-X | A big wet kiss! |
| :-\ | Undecided smiley |
| :-] | Smiley blockhead |
| ;-( | Crying smiley |
| >;-> | A very lewd remark was just made |

*Source: The Smiley Dictionary*

# Program Templates

## WordPerfect Commands

| Key | Function |
|---|---|
| F1 | Cancel |
| Alt F1 | Thesaurus |
| Shift F1 | Setup |
| Ctrl F1 | Shell |
| F2 | Search Forward |
| Alt F2 | Replace |
| Shift F2 | Search Backward |
| Ctrl F2 | Spell |
| F3 | Help |
| Alt F3 | Reveal Codes |
| Shift F3 | Switch |
| Ctrl F3 | Screen |
| F4 | Indent Right |
| Alt F4 | Block |
| Shift F4 | Indent Both Sides |
| Ctrl F4 | Move |
| F5 | List Files |
| Alt F5 | Mark Text |
| Shift F5 | Date/Outline |
| Ctrl F5 | Text In/Out |
| F6 | Bold |
| Alt F6 | Flush Right |
| Shift F6 | Center |
| Ctrl F6 | Tab Align |
| F7 | Exit |
| Alt F7 | Columns/Table |
| Shift F7 | Print |
| Ctrl F7 | Footnote |
| F8 | Underline |
| Alt F8 | Style |
| Shift F8 | Format |
| Ctrl F8 | Font |
| F9 | Merge R |
| Alt F9 | Graphics |
| Shift F9 | Merge Codes |
| Ctrl F9 | Merge/Sort |
| F10 | Save |
| Alt F10 | Macro |
| Shift F10 | Retrieve |
| Ctrl F10 | Macro Define |

## XyWrite Commands

| Key | Function |
|---|---|
| F1 | Begin/End Text Define |
| Alt F1 | Begin/End Column Define |
| Shift F1 | — |
| Ctrl F1 | — |
| F2 | Make or Load Save/Gets |
| Alt F2 | Display All Save/Gets |
| Shift F2 | Append to a Save/Get |
| Ctrl F2 | Displays Save/Get on one key |
| F3 | Release Define |
| Alt F3 | Undelete |
| Shift F3 | — |
| Ctrl F3 | Open a Footnote or Header |
| F4 | Define Line |
| Alt F4 | Define Word |
| Shift F4 | Define Paragraph |
| Ctrl F4 | Define Sentence |
| F5 | Clear Command Line |
| Alt F5 | Delete Line |
| Shift F5 | — |
| Ctrl F5 | — |
| F6 | Clear Command Line |
| Alt F6 | Delete Define |
| Shift F6 | — |
| Ctrl F6 | — |
| F7 | Copy Defined Block |
| Alt F7 | — |
| Shift F7 | — |
| Ctrl F7 | — |
| F8 | Move Defined Block |
| Alt F8 | — |
| Shift F8 | — |
| Ctrl F8 | — |
| F9 | Execute Command |
| Alt F9 | Help |
| Shift F9 | Show Page and Line Numbers |
| Ctrl F9 | Normal or Expanded Display |

**TIP:** *When buying a computer book, start from the back. Good computer books never have skimpy indexes. Look up a familiar technique and see if the explanation makes sense. Finally, don't be influenced by price. Sometimes the cheapest books are the best.*

# MAPS

# Atlanta

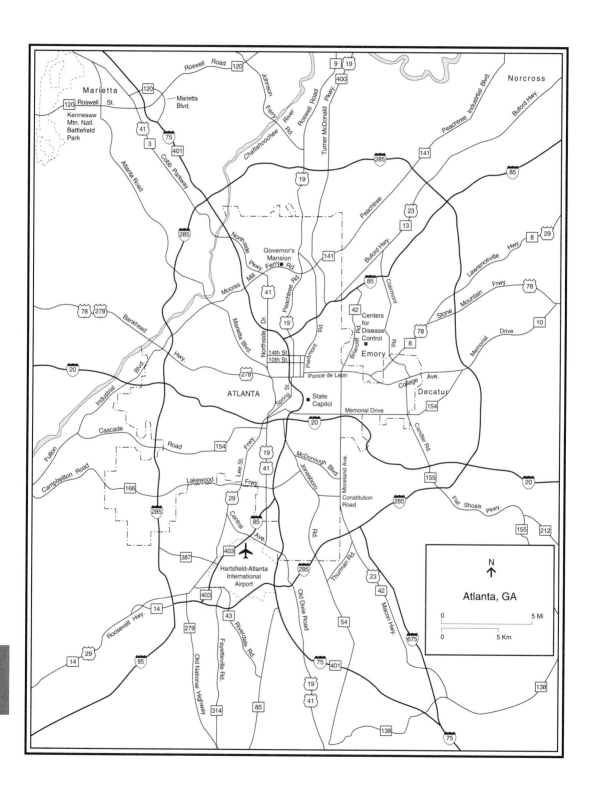

# Boston

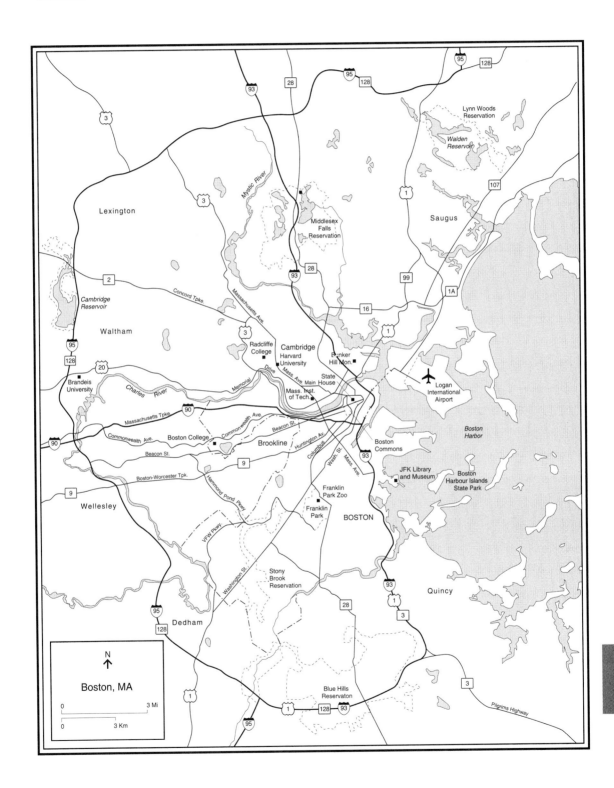

# Chicago

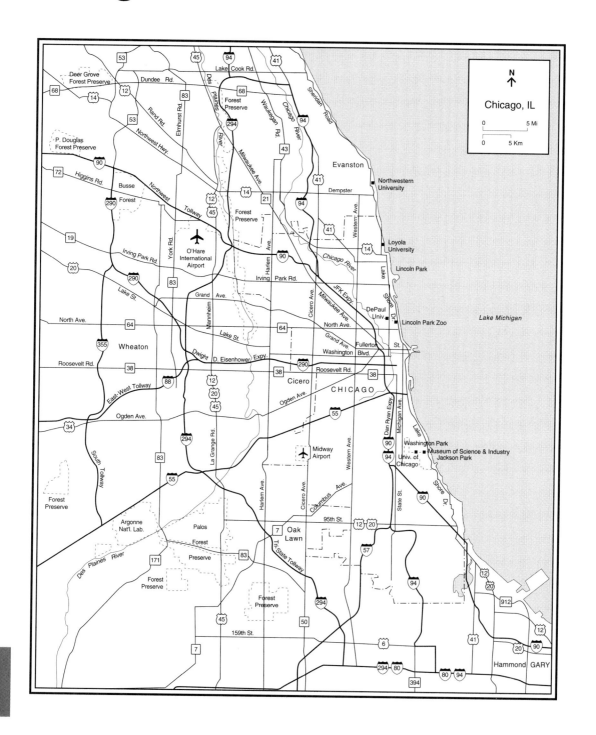

# Cleveland

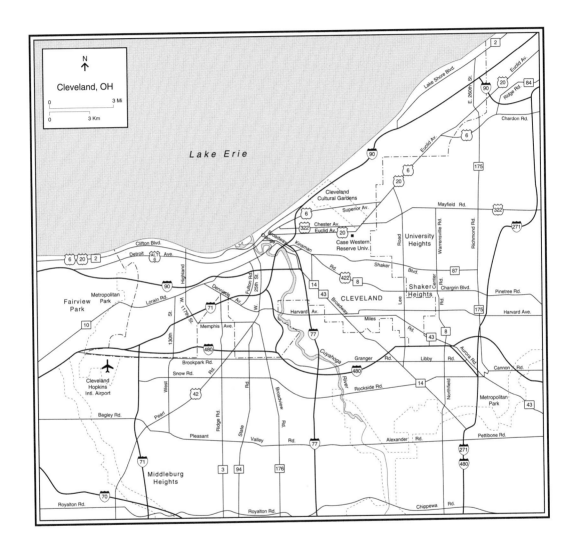

Cleveland, OH

N

0          3 Mi
0       3 Km

*Lake Erie*

Lake Shore Blvd.

Euclid Av.

E. 260th St.

Ridge Rd.

Chardon Rd.

Euclid Av.

Mayfield Rd.

Cleveland
Cultural Gardens

Superior Av.

Clifton Blvd.

Detroit Av.

Chester Av.
Euclid Av.

Case Western
Reserve Univ.

University
Heights

Warrensville Rd.

Richmond Rd.

Broadway
Kinsman

Road

Shaker

Blvd.

Chargrin Blvd.

Pinetree Rd.

Highland

Denison

Fulton Rd.

25th St.

Shaker
Heights

Lee

Center

Rd.

Harvard Ave.

Fairview
Park

Metropolitan
Park

Lorain Rd.

130th St.

W. 117th St.

Memphis  Ave.

CLEVELAND

Miles

Rd.

Harvard  Av.

Broadway

Cuyahoga

Granger      Rd.

Libby        Rd.

Aurora Rd.

Cannon    Rd.

Brookpark Rd.

Snow Rd.

Rockside Rd.

Northfield

Metropolitan
Park

Cleveland
Hopkins
Intl. Airport

West

Ridge Rd.

State Rd.

Broadview

River

Rd.

Alexander   Rd.

Pettibone Rd.

Bagley Rd.

Pearl

Pleasant

Valley

Rd.

Middleburg
Heights

Royalton Rd.

Royalton Rd.

Chippewa   Rd.

# Columbus

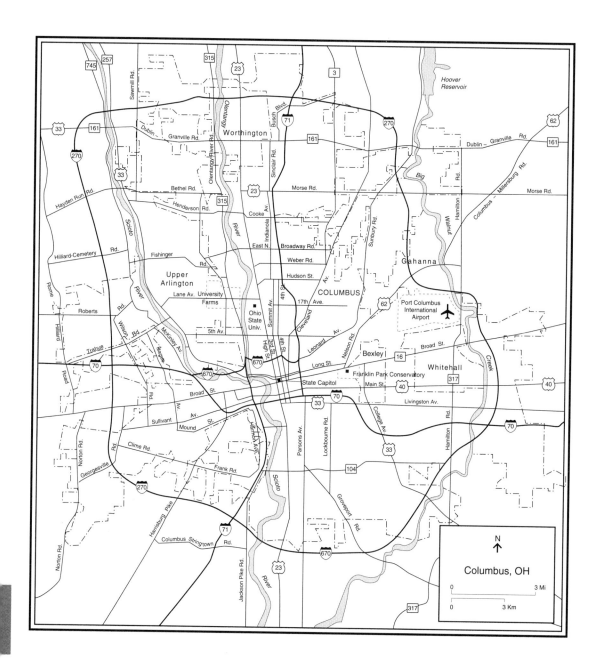

Columbus, OH

N

0                          3 Mi

0                          3 Km

# Dallas–Fort Worth

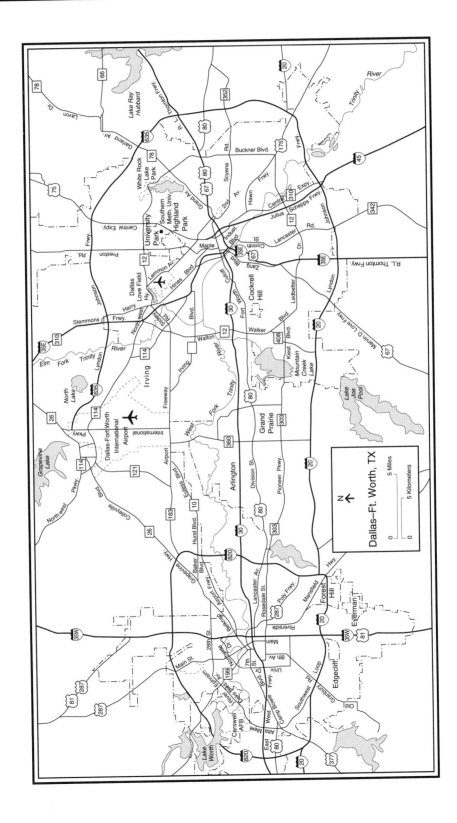

# Denver

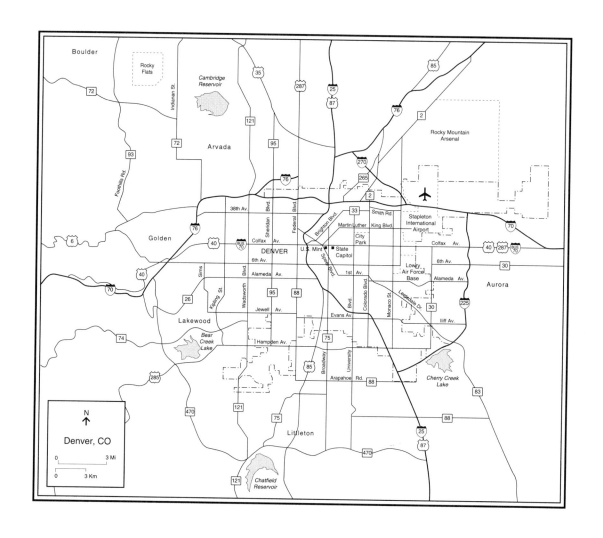

# Detroit

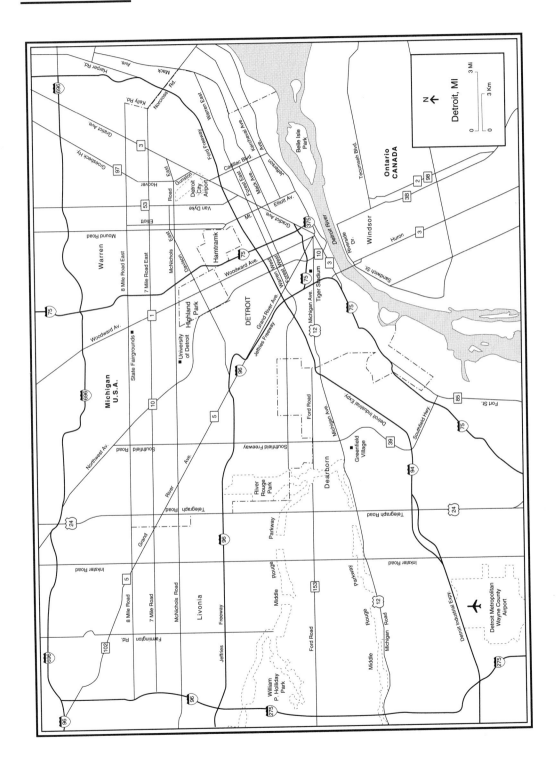

# Honolulu

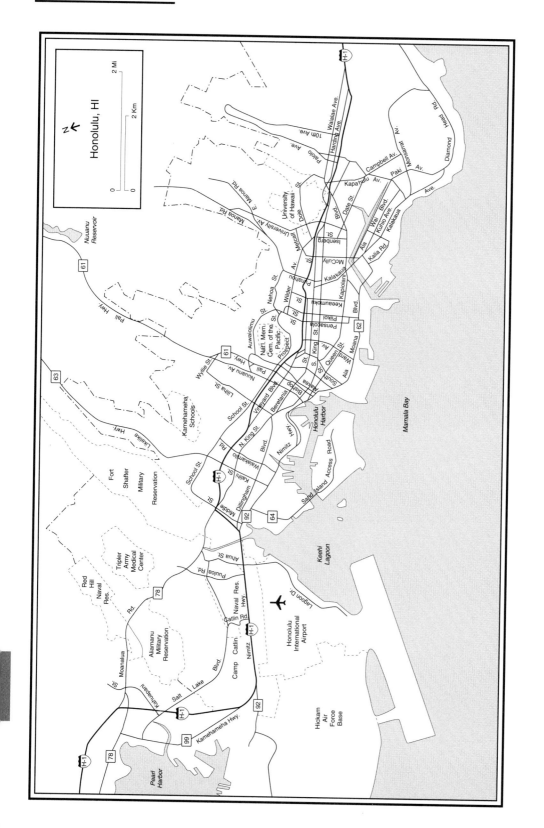

# Houston

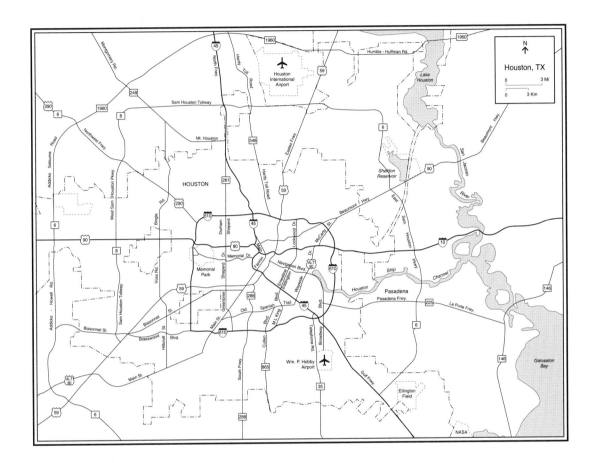

# Indianapolis

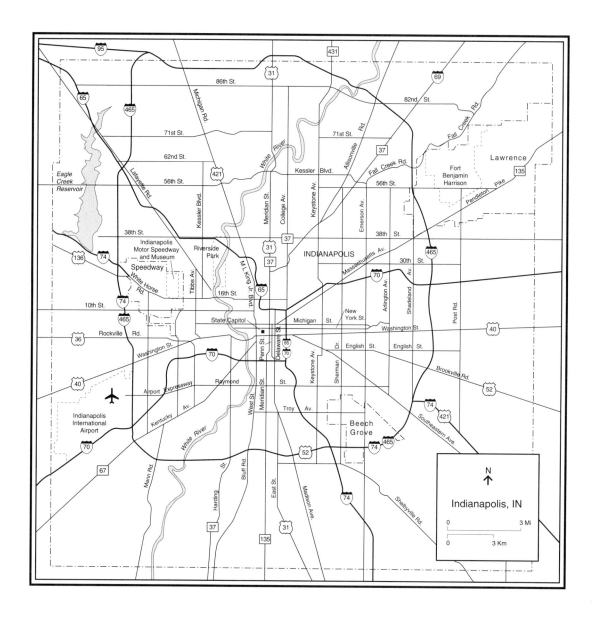

Indianapolis, IN

N

0            3 Mi

0          3 Km

# Kansas City

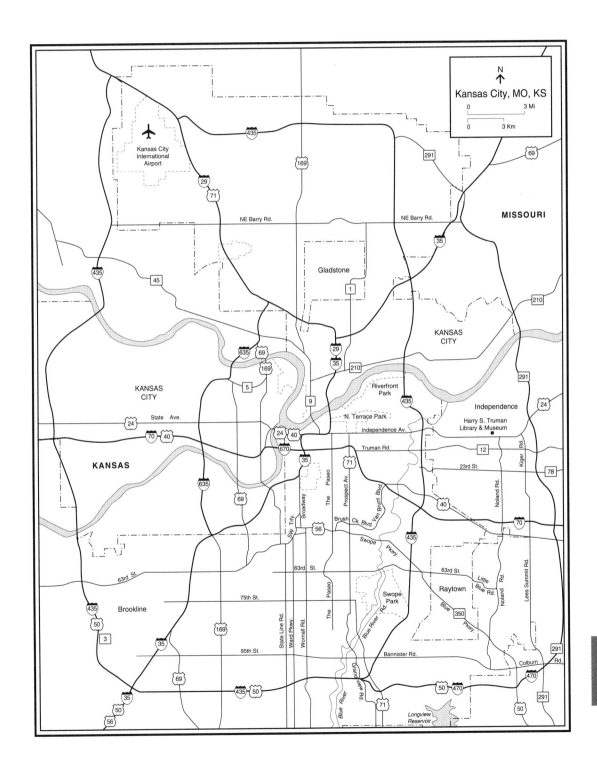

N
Kansas City, MO, KS

0 — 3 Mi
0 — 3 Km

Kansas City International Airport

MISSOURI

NE Barry Rd.   NE Barry Rd.

Gladstone

KANSAS CITY

KANSAS CITY

Riverfront Park

Independence

Harry S. Truman Library & Museum

State   Ave.

N. Terrace Park

Independence Av.

Truman Rd.

23rd St.

KANSAS

Brush   Ck. Blvd.

Swope   Pkwy.

63rd St.   63rd St.

Brookline

75th St.

Swope Park

Raytown

95th St.

Bannister Rd.

Colburn   Rd.

Longview Reservoir

State Line Rd.
Ward Pkwy.
Wornall Rd.
Broadway
Sw. Trfy.
The   Paseo
Prospect Av.
Van Brunt Blvd.
Blue River Rd.
Grand view Rd.
Blue   Pkwy.
Blue   River
Little Blue Rd.
Noland Rd.
Lees Summit Rd.
Kiger Rd.
Noland Rd.

# Los Angeles

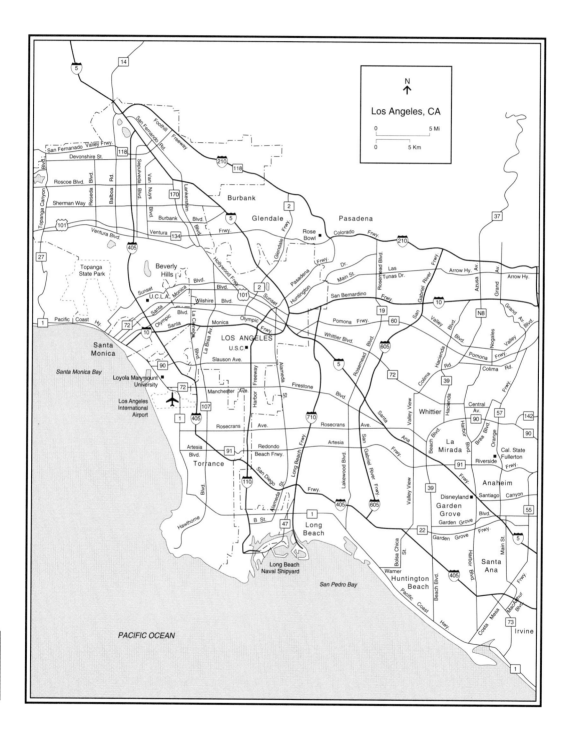

# Miami

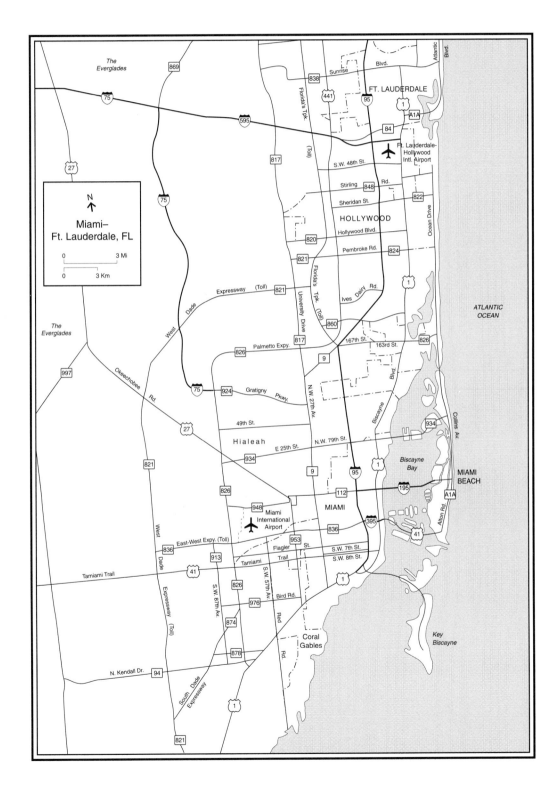

Miami–
Ft. Lauderdale, FL

# Minneapolis

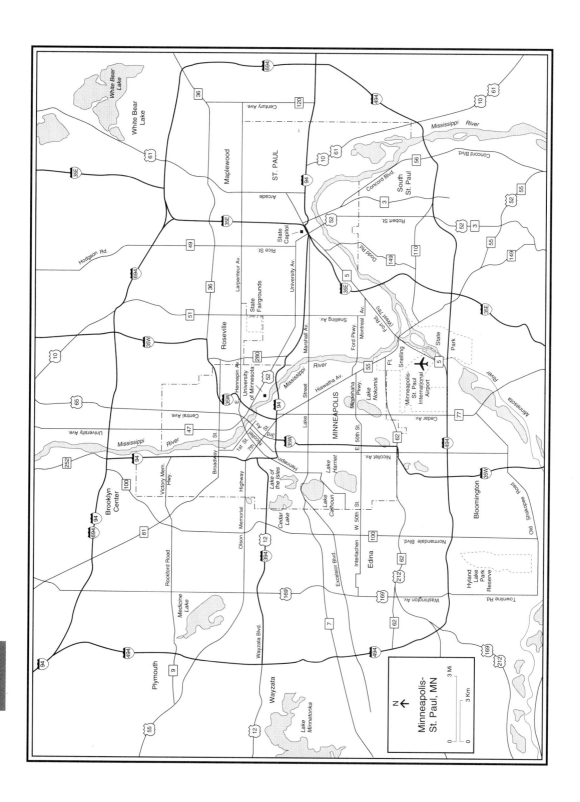

# New Orleans

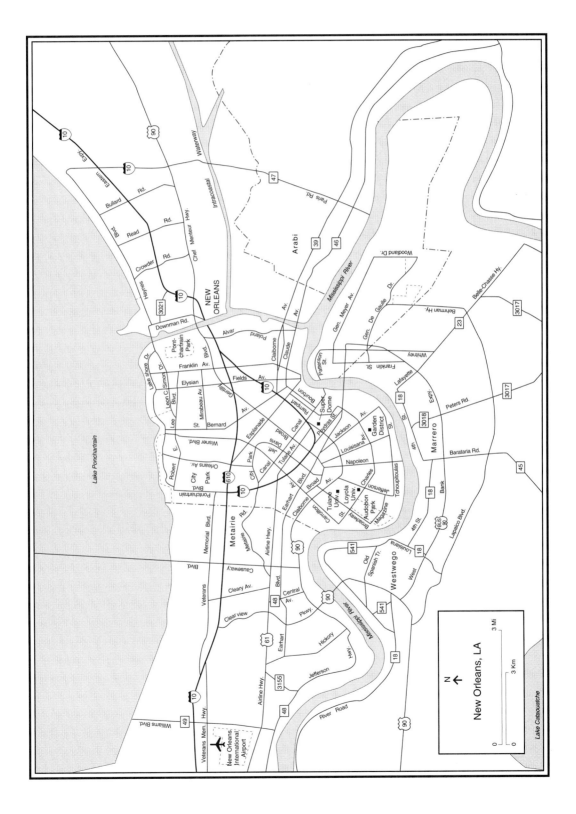

# New York

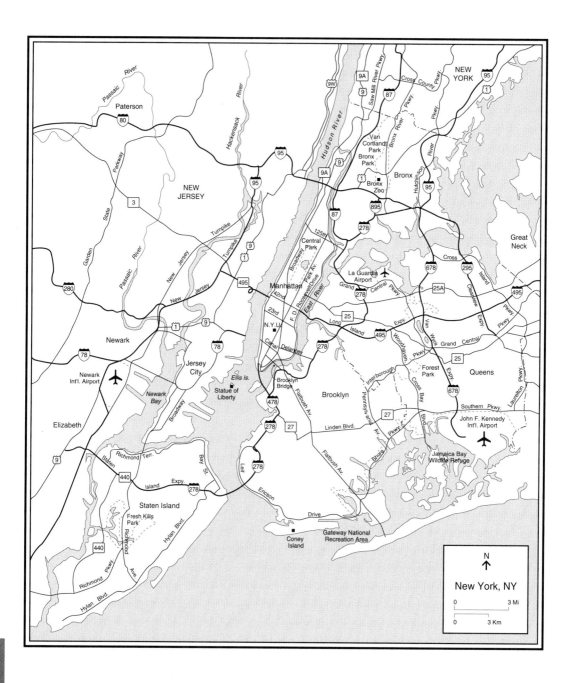

# Philadelphia

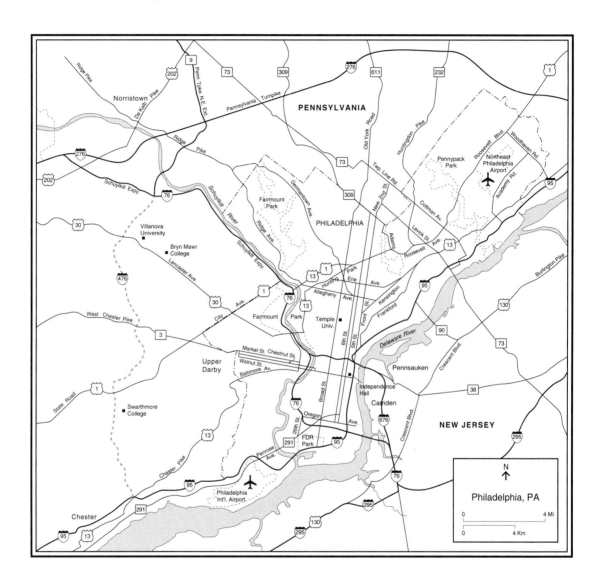

# Phoenix

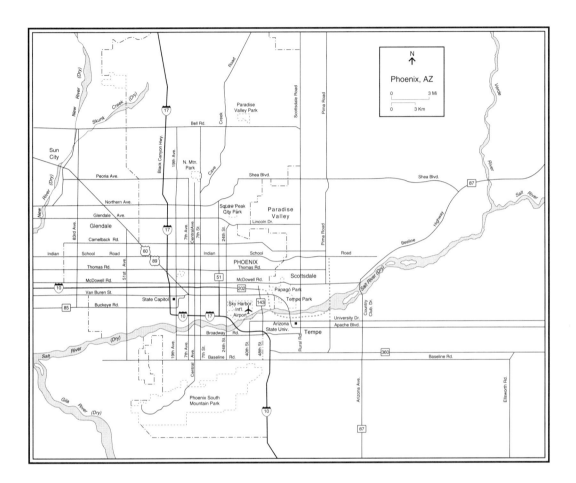

# Pittsburgh

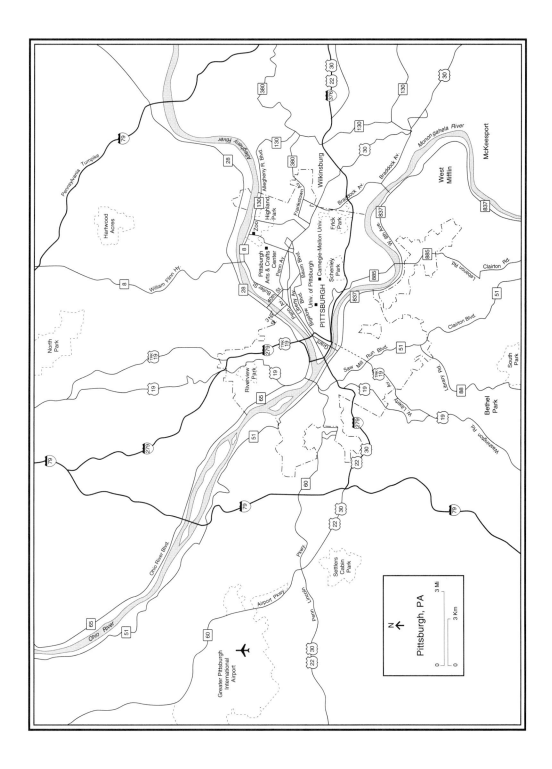

# St. Louis

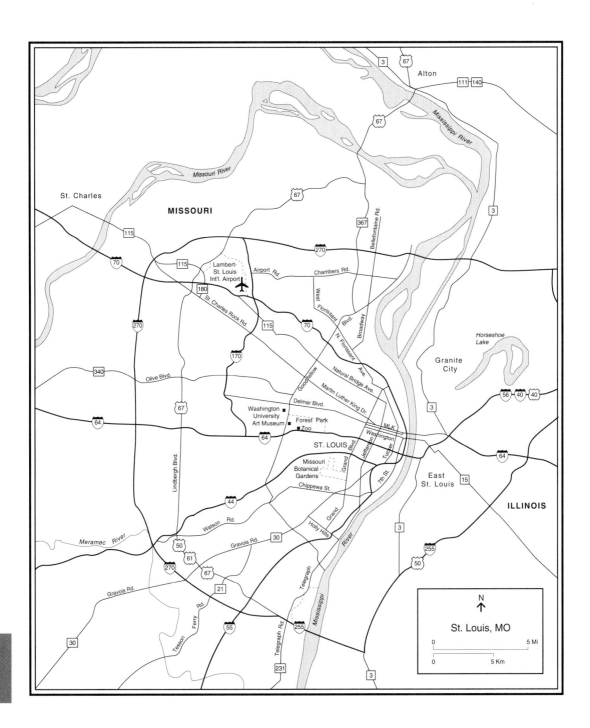

# San Diego

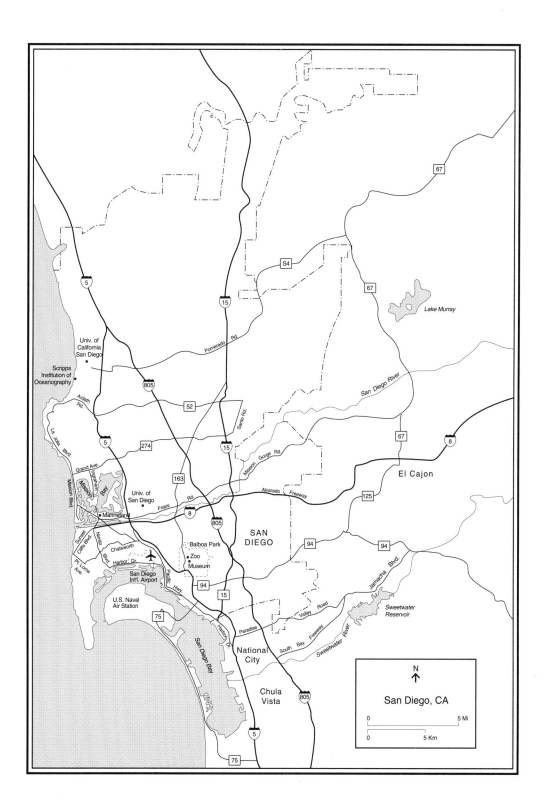

Univ. of California San Diego

Scripps Institution of Oceanography

Ardath Rd.

La Jolla Blvd.

Grand Ave.

Ingraham

Mission Blvd.

Mission Bay

Sunset Cliffs Blvd.

Nimitz Blvd.

Pt. Loma Ave.

Chatsworth

Harbor Dr.

San Diego Int'l. Airport

U.S. Naval Air Station

San Diego Bay

Pacific Hwy.

Harbor Dr.

Paradise

National City

Chula Vista

Univ. of San Diego

Marineland

Friars Rd.

Balboa Park

Zoo

Museum

SAN DIEGO

Pomerado Rd.

Santo Rd.

Mission Gorge Rd.

Alvarado Freeway

Mission Gorge Rd.

San Diego River

Lake Murray

El Cajon

Jamacha Blvd.

Sweetwater Reservoir

Sweetwater River

South Bay Freeway

Valley Road

5 805 15 52 274 163 8 94 75 67 S4 125

N

San Diego, CA

0 — 5 Mi

0 — 5 Km

# San Francisco

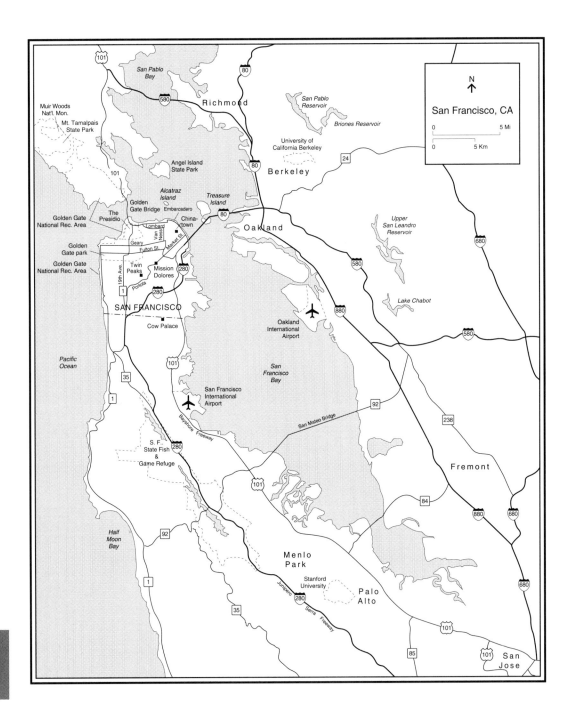

# Seattle

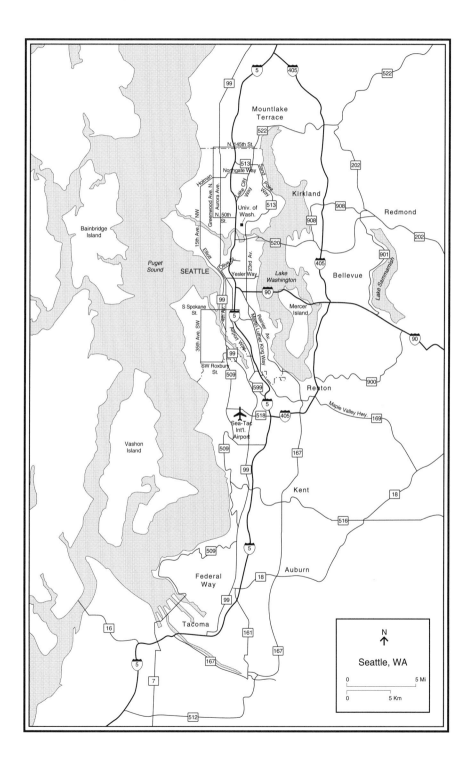

N

Seattle, WA

0               5 Mi

0         5 Km

# Washington, DC

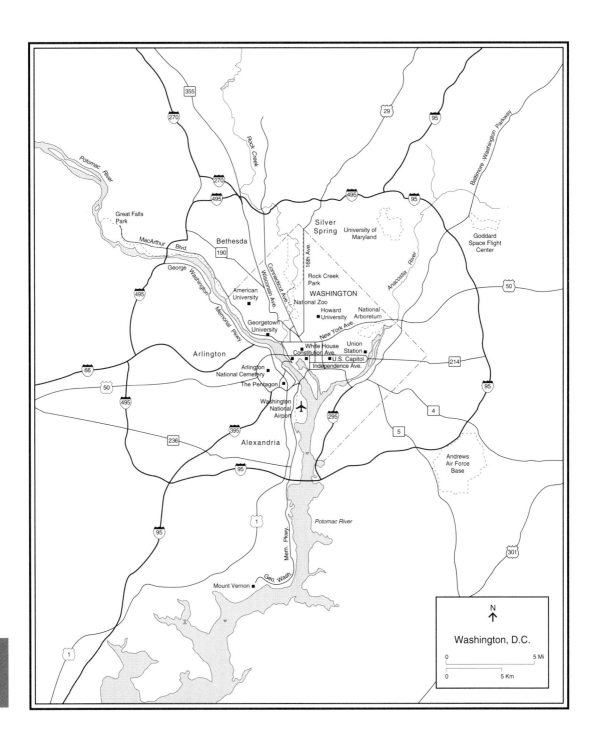

Potomac River

355

270

Rock Creek

29

95

Great Falls
Park

270

495

495

95

Silver
Spring

University of
Maryland

Baltimore - Washington Parkway

Goddard
Space Flight
Center

MacArthur      Blvd.

Bethesda

190

George   Washington

495

American
University

Wisconsin Ave.

Connecticut Ave.

16th Ave.

Rock Creek
Park

WASHINGTON

National Zoo

Howard
University

Anacostia River

National
Arboretum

50

Memorial Pkwy.

Georgetown
University

New York Ave.

Arlington

White House
Constitution Ave.

Union
Station

66

50

Arlington
National Cemetery

The Pentagon

U.S. Capitol
Independence Ave.

214

95

495

236

395

Washington
National
Airport

295

4

5

Alexandria

95

Andrews
Air Force
Base

1

Potomac River

301

95

Mem. Pkwy.

Geo. Wash.

Mount Vernon

1

N

Washington, D.C.

0                    5 Mi

0            5 Km

# Africa

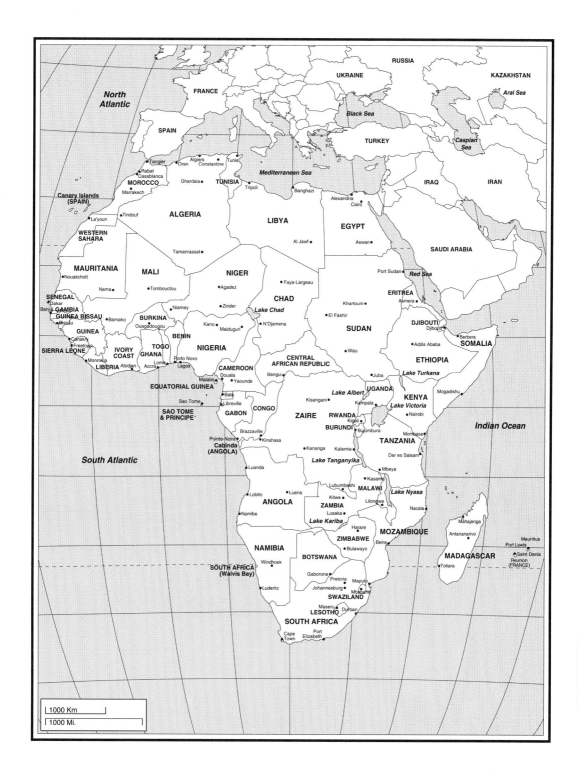

North Atlantic

RUSSIA

UKRAINE

KAZAKHSTAN

FRANCE

Aral Sea

Black Sea

SPAIN

TURKEY

Caspian Sea

Mediterranean Sea

Tangier
Oran Algiers Constantine Tunis
Rabat
Casablanca
MOROCCO
Ghardaia
TUNISIA
Tripoli
Banghazi

IRAQ

IRAN

Marrakech

Alexandria
Cairo

Canary Islands (SPAIN)

La'youn
Tindouf

ALGERIA

LIBYA

EGYPT

SAUDI ARABIA

WESTERN SAHARA

Al Jawf

Aswan

MAURITANIA

Nouakchott

MALI

Tamanrasset

NIGER

Port Sudan
Red Sea

Nema

Tombouctou

Agadez

Faya-Largeau

ERITREA
Asmera

SENEGAL
Dakar
GAMBIA
Banjul
GUINEA BISSAU
Bissau
GUINEA
Conakry
Freetown
SIERRA LEONE
Monrovia
LIBERIA Abidjan

Niamey

Zinder

CHAD
Lake Chad

Khartoum

El Fashir

DJIBOUTI
Djibouti

Bamako

BURKINA
Ouagadougou

Kano
Maiduguri

N'Djamena

Berbera
SOMALIA

BENIN

NIGERIA

SUDAN

Addis Ababa

ETHIOPIA

IVORY
COAST
GHANA
Porto Novo
Accra
Lome
Lagos

TOGO

CAMEROON
Douala
Yaounde

CENTRAL AFRICAN REPUBLIC

Wau

Juba

Lake Turkana

EQUATORIAL GUINEA
Bata
Malabo

Bangui

Kisangani

Lake Albert
UGANDA
Kampala
Lake Victoria

KENYA

Mogadishu

SAO TOME & PRINCIPE
Sao Tome
Libreville

GABON

CONGO

ZAIRE

RWANDA
Kigali
BURUNDI
Bujumbura

Nairobi

Indian Ocean

Brazzaville

Kananga

Kalemie

Mombasa

Pointe-Noire
Kinshasa
Cabinda (ANGOLA)

TANZANIA

Dar es Salaam

Lake Tanganyika

Mbeya

South Atlantic

Luanda

Kasama

Lubumbashi
MALAWI
Lake Nyasa

Lobito
Luena
Luena

Kitwe
ZAMBIA
Lusaka

Lilongwe

Nacala

ANGOLA

Namibe

Lake Kariba

Harare

MOZAMBIQUE

Mahajanga

Antananarivo

ZIMBABWE
Bulawayo

Beira

Mauritius
Port Lewis

NAMIBIA

BOTSWANA

Windhoek

MADAGASCAR

Saint Denis
Reunion (FRANCE)

SOUTH AFRICA (Walvis Bay)

Gaborone
Pretoria
Maputo

Toliara

Luderitz

Johannesburg
SWAZILAND
Mbabane

Maseru
LESOTHO
Durban

SOUTH AFRICA

Cape Town
Port Elizabeth

| 1000 Km |
| 1000 Mi. |

# Asia

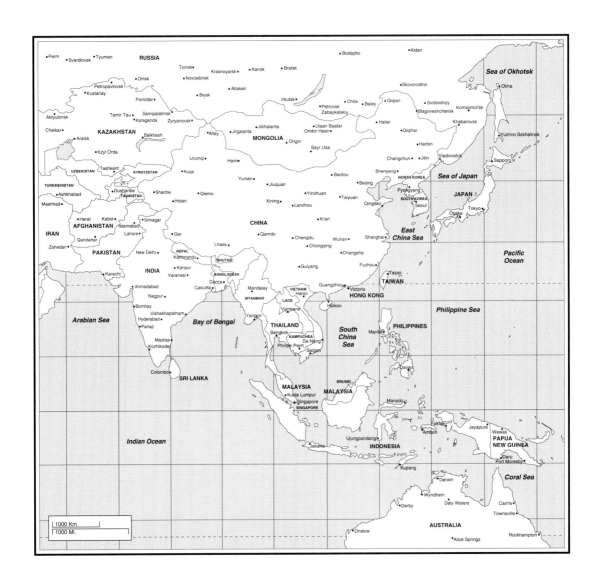

# Australia

# Canada

RUSSIA

*Arctic Ocean*

*Beaufort Sea*

GREENLAND (DENMARK)

ICELAND

UNITED STATES

*Baffin Bay*

• Dawson

Victoria Island

*Yukon Territory*

*Great Bear Lake*

Baffin Island

*Pacific Ocean*

• Whitehorse

*Northwest Territories*

*Great Slave Lake*  • Yellowknife

*Labrador Sea*

*British Columbia*

*Lake Athabasca*

*Alberta*

Churchill •

*Hudson Bay*

Newfoundland

Edmonton •

*Saskatchewan*

*Manitoba*

St. John's •

Victoria • • Vancouver

• Calgary

• Saskatoon

*Quebec*

*P.E.I.* • Sydney

Regina •

*Lake Winnipeg*

*Ontario*

New Brunswick

Winnipeg •

Thunder Bay •

*Lake Superior*

Quebec •

Fredericton •

• Halifax

*Nova Scotia*

Montreal •

*Lake Huron*

Ottawa ⊛

*Lake Michigan*

Toronto •

*Lake Ontario*

*Atlantic Ocean*

UNITED STATES

*Lake Erie*

## Canada

⊛  National Capital

Calgary •  City

———  International Boundary

- - - -  Provincial Boundary

*Quebec*  Province Name

0    Miles    500

# Europe

Reykjavik
ICELAND

Hammerfest
Murmansk

Kiruna

Norwegian
Sea

Oulu

SWEDEN

FINLAND

North
Atlantic
Ocean

Trondheim

NORWAY

Sundsvall
Gulf
of
Bothnia

Tampere

Helsinki

St. Petersburg

RUSSIA

Bergen

Oslo

Gavle

Moscow

Stockholm

Tallinn

ESTONIA

Aberdeen

North
Sea

Goteborg

Riga

LATVIA

Belfast
Edinburgh

IRELAND
Dublin

Newcastle

DENMARK

Baltic
Sea

LITHUANIA

Vilnius

Minsk

Liverpool

Copenhagen

Tver

U. K.

Rostock

Gdansk

BYELARUS

NETH.

Hamburg

Cardiff

London

Amsterdam
Hannover
Berlin

Poznan

Warsaw

English Channel

BELGIUM
Bruxelles

Bonn

GERMANY
Leipzig

POLAND

Kyiv

Le Havre

LUX.

Frankfurt

Prague

Krakow

Lviv

UKRAINE

Paris

Strasbourg

CZECH

Nantes

Munich

SLOVAKIA

MOLDOVA

FRANCE

Vienna
Bratislava

Chisinau
Odessa

Bern
SWITZERLAND

AUSTRIA

Budapest

Bordeaux

Geneva

HUNGARY

Cluj-Napoca

Bay of Biscay

Lyon

Ljubljana
SLOVENIA
Zagreb
CROATIA

Pecs

ROMANIA

Milan

Venice

Bilbao

Marseille

Florence

BOSNIA
Sarajevo

Belgrade

SERBIA

Bucharest

Constanta

Varna

Black
Sea

Porto

ANDORRA

ITALY

BULGARIA

PORTUGAL

Madrid

Barcelona

Rome

MONTENEGRO

Titograd
Adriatic

Sofiya

Skopje
MACEDONIA
Tirana
Thessaloniki
ALBANIA

Istanbul

Lisbon

SPAIN

Valencia

Naples

Tyrrhenian
Sea

TURKEY

Sevilla

Cagliari

GREECE
Aegean

Malaga

Mediterranean Sea

Ionian
Sea

Palermo

Patrai
Athens

CYPRUS

250 Km

250 Mi.

CRETE

# Mexico

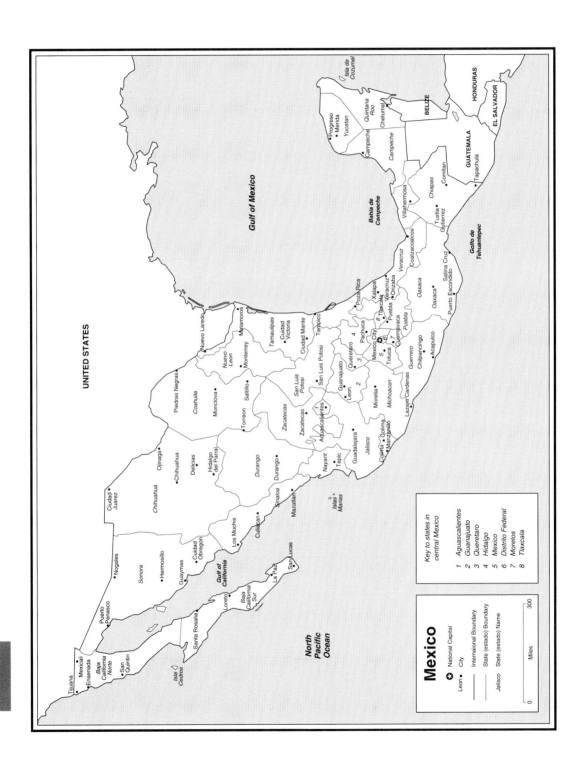

# Russia

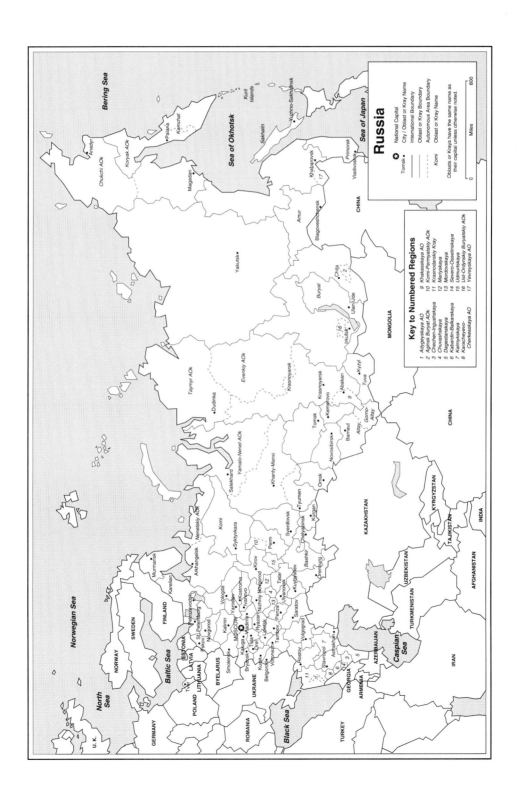

**Russia**

⊛ National Capital
Tomsk • City / Oblast or Kray Name
International Boundary
Oblast or Kray Boundary
Autonomous Area Boundary
Komi Oblast or Kray Name

Oblasts or Krays have the same name as their capital unless otherwise noted.

0        Miles        800

**Key to Numbered Regions**

1 Adygeyskaya AO
2 Aginsk Buryat AOk
3 Chechen-Ingushskaya
4 Chuvashskaya
5 Dagestanskaya
6 Kabardin-Balkarskaya
7 Kalmykskaya
8 Karacheyevo-
Cherkesskaya AO
9 Khakasskaya AO
10 Komi-Permyatsky AOk
11 Krasnodarsky Kray
12 Mariyskaya
13 Mordovskaya
14 Severo-Ossetinskaya
15 Udmurtskaya
16 Ust-Ordynskiy Buryatskiy AOk
17 Yevreyskaya AO

# South America

# United States

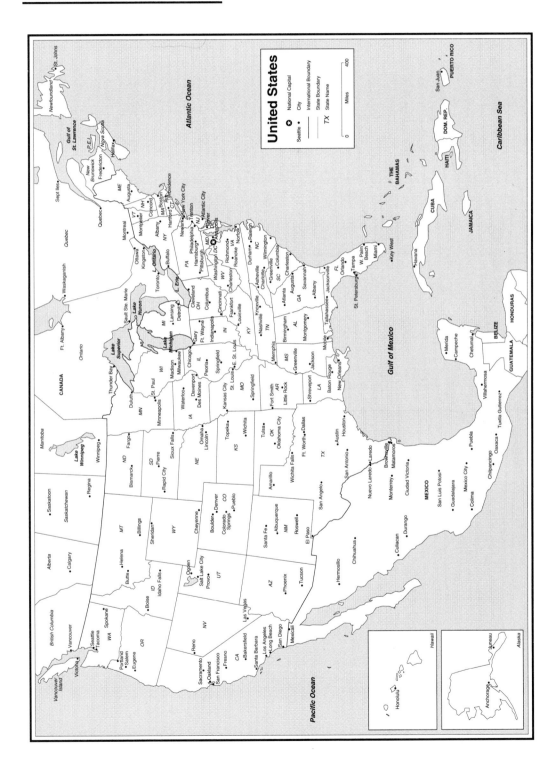

# Mileage Table

| | Atlanta | Baltimore | Boston | Chicago | Cincinnati | Cleveland | Columbus, OH | Dallas | Denver | Detroit | Houston | Indianapolis | Los Angeles | Miami | Milwaukee | Minneapolis | New York | Norfolk | Philadelphia | Phoenix | Pittsburgh | Portland, OR | Sacramento | St. Louis | San Antonio | San Diego | San Francisco | Seattle | Tampa | Washington, DC |
|---|---|---|---|---|---|---|---|---|---|---|---|---|---|---|---|---|---|---|---|---|---|---|---|---|---|---|---|---|---|---|
| Atlanta | | | | | | | | | | | | | | | | | | | | | | | | | | | | | | |
| Baltimore | 576 | | | | | | | | | | | | | | | | | | | | | | | | | | | | | |
| Boston | 945 | 368 | | | | | | | | | | | | | | | | | | | | | | | | | | | | |
| Chicago | 606 | 619 | 864 | | | | | | | | | | | | | | | | | | | | | | | | | | | |
| Cincinnatti | 374 | 428 | 750 | 264 | | | | | | | | | | | | | | | | | | | | | | | | | | |
| Cleveland | 555 | 313 | 561 | 314 | 221 | | | | | | | | | | | | | | | | | | | | | | | | | |
| Columbus, OH | 569 | 411 | 767 | 354 | 110 | 147 | | | | | | | | | | | | | | | | | | | | | | | | |
| Dallas | 728 | 1213 | 1557 | 800 | 810 | 1019 | 1046 | | | | | | | | | | | | | | | | | | | | | | | |
| Denver | 1204 | 1497 | 1761 | 898 | 1076 | 1209 | 1277 | 644 | | | | | | | | | | | | | | | | | | | | | | |
| Detroit | 596 | 407 | 630 | 233 | 229 | 94 | 209 | 984 | 1132 | | | | | | | | | | | | | | | | | | | | | |
| Houston | 693 | 1243 | 1605 | 945 | 885 | 1105 | 1228 | 247 | 884 | 1091 | | | | | | | | | | | | | | | | | | | | |
| Indianapolis | 434 | 514 | 814 | 177 | 98 | 260 | 178 | 760 | 984 | 230 | 862 | | | | | | | | | | | | | | | | | | | |
| Los Angeles | 1939 | 2321 | 2601 | 1739 | 1893 | 2045 | 2252 | 1230 | 846 | 1971 | 1385 | 1808 | | | | | | | | | | | | | | | | | | |
| Miami | 595 | 946 | 1258 | 1197 | 949 | 1081 | 1198 | 1118 | 1712 | 1147 | 953 | 1022 | 2334 | | | | | | | | | | | | | | | | | |
| Milwaukee | 669 | 639 | 857 | 67 | 317 | 327 | 455 | 852 | 905 | 237 | 1004 | 237 | 1749 | 1259 | | | | | | | | | | | | | | | | |
| Minneapolis | 906 | 933 | 1120 | 333 | 595 | 620 | 762 | 852 | 691 | 527 | 1057 | 501 | 1531 | 1501 | 296 | | | | | | | | | | | | | | | |
| New York | 761 | 185 | 184 | 730 | 583 | 417 | 567 | 1385 | 1626 | 500 | 1425 | 658 | 2460 | 1097 | 736 | 1017 | | | | | | | | | | | | | | |
| Norfolk | 515 | 160 | 467 | 714 | 484 | 434 | 577 | 1209 | 1558 | 528 | 1206 | 580 | 2362 | 803 | 745 | 1042 | 296 | | | | | | | | | | | | | |
| Philadelphia | 665 | 89 | 281 | 675 | 505 | 361 | 473 | 1298 | 1563 | 452 | 1332 | 584 | 2392 | 1013 | 688 | 976 | 97 | 212 | | | | | | | | | | | | |
| Phoenix | 1581 | 1992 | 2293 | 1436 | 1564 | 1732 | 1917 | 866 | 589 | 1666 | 1017 | 1485 | 368 | 1966 | 1456 | 1274 | 2141 | 2023 | 2068 | | | | | | | | | | | |
| Pittsburgh | 526 | 209 | 494 | 411 | 255 | 106 | 185 | 1064 | 1297 | 201 | 1129 | 323 | 2127 | 1013 | 724 | 430 | 333 | 329 | 266 | 1808 | | | | | | | | | | |
| Portland, OR | 2165 | 2349 | 2528 | 1733 | 1968 | 2038 | 2439 | 1611 | 982 | 1946 | 1839 | 1870 | 833 | 2693 | 1711 | 1420 | 2436 | 2445 | 2397 | 1009 | 2140 | | | | | | | | | |
| Sacramento | 2085 | 2386 | 2627 | 1776 | 1970 | 2090 | 2200 | 1427 | 895 | 2006 | 1619 | 1877 | 373 | 2545 | 1512 | 1772 | 2505 | 2453 | 2448 | 646 | 2183 | 477 | | | | | | | | |
| St. Louis | 483 | 735 | 1043 | 258 | 307 | 485 | 433 | 550 | 777 | 439 | 688 | 229 | 1586 | 1068 | 317 | 447 | 885 | 782 | 810 | 1258 | 551 | 1702 | 1673 | | | | | | | |
| San Antonio | 872 | 1404 | 1759 | 1041 | 1022 | 1239 | 1327 | 247 | 793 | 1213 | 191 | 984 | 1206 | 1140 | 1097 | 1095 | 1582 | 1492 | 1378 | 97 | 1273 | 1711 | 1459 | 785 | | | | | | |
| San Diego | 1885 | 2287 | 2578 | 1718 | 1858 | 2019 | 2255 | 1167 | 837 | 1949 | 1308 | 1777 | 109 | 2260 | 1733 | 1528 | 2432 | 2322 | 2361 | 302 | 2099 | 933 | 481 | 1551 | 1126 | | | | | |
| San Francisco | 2131 | 2447 | 2693 | 1839 | 2029 | 2153 | 2457 | 1459 | 952 | 2071 | 1619 | 1937 | 337 | 2577 | 1584 | 1582 | 2569 | 2509 | 2510 | 649 | 2245 | 550 | 85 | 1728 | 1478 | 446 | | | | |
| Seattle | 2175 | 2325 | 2485 | 1713 | 1956 | 2012 | 2460 | 1655 | 1015 | 1919 | 1889 | 1858 | 953 | 2717 | 1393 | 1305 | 2402 | 2428 | 2368 | 1105 | 2116 | 130 | 605 | 1703 | 1771 | 1050 | 678 | | | |
| Tampa | 406 | 843 | 1184 | 1012 | 773 | 928 | 999 | 926 | 1510 | 983 | 779 | 838 | 2150 | 205 | 1075 | 1305 | 1011 | 716 | 919 | 1782 | 873 | 2490 | 2351 | 868 | 969 | 2079 | 2384 | 2513 | | |
| Washington, DC | 546 | 30 | 398 | 609 | 409 | 309 | 407 | 1188 | 1482 | 405 | 1216 | 498 | 2302 | 920 | 632 | 928 | 214 | 141 | 118 | 1972 | 204 | 2341 | 2372 | 716 | 1377 | 2268 | 2433 | 2320 | 813 | |

# REFERENCE

# Glossary

Absolute net lease—Lease in which the tenant agrees to pay the landlord or owner a basic rent and also agrees to pay separately for all maintenance, operating, and other building expenses.

Abuse of process—The misuse of legal procedures for the benefit of an individual or business. For instance, suing someone simply in the hopes of frightening them into meeting one's demands.

Accounts payable—The amount of money owed to suppliers and vendors that is generally due within the next 30 days.

Accounts receivable—The amount of money due a business from its customers which is anticipated during the next 30 days.

Affidavit—A written statement certified by a notary public as to its authenticity.

Aggregate rent—Total dollar value of a lease.

Air rights—Space or air over a piece of property that legally belongs to, or is attached to, the property and can be transferred, sold, or rented. Frequently sold to permit a larger-than-zoned building on another property.

Amortize—Dividing a loan payment into a series of equal smaller payments to be made on a regular basis, thereby extending the payback over a longer period of time. A residential mortgage is generally amortized over a 30-year period, requiring monthly mortgage payments.

Annualized—Converting a monthly or daily figure to an annual basis.

Anticipatory breach—Notifying an individual or business that is part of a contract that another individual cannot meet the terms, thereby rendering the contract invalid.

Apparent authority—The situation in which a principal (individual or company) states or indicates that another individual or business may act on his or her behalf. The principal is then liable for the actions of the other individual, who is acting on his/her authority.

Arbitrage—Buying something in one market and selling it in another, profiting on the small differences between the two market prices.

Asset—Everything owned by a corporation that has value, including physical items, real estate, trademarks, and goodwill.

Assignment—Ability to transfer benefits and obligations of a contract or lease to another party.

Assumpsit—Reference to a contractual agreement made verbally or in writing with an individual or business that is not certified.

Assumption of risk—The situation that arises when an individual agrees to perform certain duties knowing that they could be potentially dangerous. Frequently,this claim is made in legal suits by the defendant, often an employer, in arguing that the plaintiff, often an employee, assumed the risk by agreeing to perform certain duties, such as on-the-job activities, despite the knowledge that they would be risky.

Attornment—Lease provision whereby the tenant agrees in advance to accept and pay rent or other required payments to a new landlord or legal owner.

Attorney-in-fact, subordination clause—Lease provision that permits the landlord to submit, on the tenant's behalf, without further approval, a certificate of subordination to a lender, trustee, or financing institution.

Bailor—An individual who delivers property to another individual who either owns the property or who holds it until it is claimed by the owner. Leaving your coat in a check room makes you a bailor.

Bait and switch pricing—An illegal sales tactic used by unscrupulous companies. Customers are lured into a store with advertising promises of low prices for an item. However, when the customer arrives at the store, the item is reported unavailable and an alternate, often higher-priced or lower-quality product, is recommended in its place.

Balance of trade—The difference between the amount of goods a country exports and imports. When the value of exports exceeds imports, the balance is positive. In the reverse, the balance is negative.

Balance sheet—An overview of a company's assets, liabilities, and owner's equity at a specific point in time.

Balloon payment—The term for the last payment on a loan if it is substantially larger than the previous series of payments. Generally, a balloon payment is negotiated when a large sum of money is anticipated before the payoff date, making such a payment possible.

Barter—An agreement between two individuals or firms where products or services of equal value are exchanged, with no cash changing hands.

*Glossary (cont'd)*

Basis—The original cost of an investment that must be reported to the IRS when it is sold, in order to calculate capital gains.

Basis point—The smallest measure used in quoting bond yields, .01%. When changes in bond yields are reported, the values are in basis points.

Bear market—A prolonged period of declining stock prices. Opposite of bull market.

Bearer bond—A type of bond that can be redeemed by whoever has possession. No proof of ownership is required. The opposite of a registered security.

Beta—A measure of a stock's volatility or changes in price, as compared with changes in other stocks. Stocks with a high beta are more likely to change dramatically.

Big Blue—Slang for International Business Machines Corp. (IBM).

Big Board—Slang for the New York Stock Exchange (NYSE).

Big Eight—Originally, the eight largest accounting firms in the U.S. Through mergers, they are now the Big Six: Arthur Andersen, Ernst & Young, Deloitte & Touche, KPMG Peat Marwick, Price Waterhouse, Coopers & Lybrand.

Binding letter of intent—Letter of intent that a court of law would uphold as the actual leasing of space, regardless of whether a lease document exists.

Black-Scholes model—A formula created by Fisher Black and Myron Scholes for evaluating stock option values.

Block trade—Buying or selling 10,000 or more shares of stock or $200,000 or more in bonds.

Blue sky laws—State laws governing the issuance and trading of securities established in order to prevent fraudulent transactions.

Board of directors—A group of advisors elected by stockholders to oversee the management of a public company. The Chief Executive Officer receives direction from the board.

Bond rating—A ranking system used to assess the financial solvency of bond issuers. The better the rating, the less the likelihood that the bond issuer will default.

Book value—The value of an asset or an entire business calculated by subtracting cumulative depreciation from the original purchase price.

Brainstorm—A group idea-generation technique. Ideas and problem-solving suggestions are offered by group members until no more are forthcoming. Then the group evaluates and considers each idea, looking for ways to combine and enhance ideas with those offered by other group members.

Brand—The name, symbol, packaging, and promotional theme surrounding a product that create an identity for that product, separate from the parent company's name and identity.

Brand extension—The addition of a new product to a family of similar products using the same brand name. Ivory Shampoo is a classic example.

Breach—The failure to perform certain duties as outlined in a contract, so that the contract is not fulfilled.

Break-even—The point at which revenues from a product exactly equal the cost to produce it. This calculation is frequently used to assess whether it is worth producing a product.

Break-even pricing—A pricing technique that provides for all costs to be covered but no profit realized.

Bridge loan—A short-term loan provided while longer-term financing is being finalized. Allows for business to proceed uninterrupted.

Bucket shop—A brokerage firm that accepts customer buy and sell orders, but does not immediately execute them as the SEC requires. Instead, the firm waits until the price has increased or decreased to the point of allowing the firm to buy or sell the stock and pocket the difference. In extreme cases, the firm just takes the money, with no intention of executing the order. Such practices are illegal.

Building standard workletter—Detailed specifications of the construction items that the developer will provide and use in building a tenant's office space. Available before a lease is executed, it should be included in the lease.

Bull market—A prolonged period of rising stock prices. Opposite of bear market.

Bylaws—The rules for running a company which are drafted when the business is incorporated. Items covered include the election of a board of directors, their responsibilities, and other committees to be established to assist in managing the company.

Call—The option to purchase shares of a stock at a specified price within a certain time frame. If a stock's price rises above the option price during the option period, there is an immediate financial advantage to making the purchase.

*Glossary (cont'd)*

**Capital assets**—Capital consists of property, inventory, cash on hand, accounts receivable, and other items of value owned by a company.

**Capital expenditure**—Money spent to purchase or repair a capital asset, such as a plant and machinery.

**Capital gains/losses**—The difference between an asset's purchase price and selling price. If the difference is positive, it is considered a capital gain and is taxable. If the difference is negative, it is a capital loss and can result in a tax reduction.

**Capital stock**—Stock sold by a corporation, rather than resold by an investor.

**Capitalization**—The amount of money used to start a company.

**Carryforward**—A tax benefit allowing a company to apply losses realized in a previous year to future years' revenue in order to reduce taxes.

**Cartel**—A group of businesses or countries that agree to work together to affect the pricing and availability of certain products that they produce. OPEC is a classic example.

**Cash cow**—Business that has had strong sales, generating revenue consistently. In most cases, cash cows are based on products with a strong brand name that generate repeat buying.

**Cash discount**—A discount offered to buyers who pay their bills within a specified time period. A prompt payment incentive.

**Cash flow**—The actual cash in and out of a corporation. Companies can secure paper profits but go bankrupt because of negative cash flow.

**Channel of distribution**—The means of getting a product into a customer's hands. This might include retail stores, direct salespeople, wholesalers, and distributors.

**Chapter 11**—A bankruptcy status that provides time for reorganizing a company in order to make it profitable and able to pay off its debts.

**Chapter 7**—A bankruptcy status that allows for liquidation of all of a company's assets in order to pay off creditors.

**Churn**—Unnecessary and excessive trading on a customer's brokerage account, thereby generating fee income for a broker without adding value to the investments. While this practice is illegal, it is also difficult to prove.

**Class action**—A suit filed by one or more individuals on behalf of a larger group of people who have been treated similarly by a situation. Once the suit has been filed and the court has approved its class action status, all people who may benefit from a ruling (the parties to the suit) must be notified.

**Clifford Trust**—A trust established for more than 10 years that allows the transfer of assets from one individual or organization to another and then back again when the trust expires. Before new regulations were established in 1986, these trusts were a popular means of transferring income-producing assets to children, who would be taxed at a lower tax rate. The assets were typically reclaimed when the child reached the age of 18.

**Cognitive dissonance**—A psychological state that occurs when an individual questions an action s/he has taken, such as a purchase s/he has made, and seeks reassurance that s/he has indeed made the right decision.

**Cold call**—A marketing technique that involves a salesperson placing a telephone call to a potential client without having had any previous contact.

**Collateral**—An item of value that is used to guarantee a loan. If the borrower fails to repay the loan, the lender keeps the asset pledged as collateral.

**Commodity**—Bulk goods, such as crops, food, and metals, that are traded on the commodities exchange. Such items are generally used as raw materials in other products.

**Common areas**—Portions of a building used by more than one tenant, such as hallways, elevators, and restrooms.

**Common carrier**—A business that specializes in providing transport of goods and services.

**Common market**—The group of European nations working cooperatively to establish a unified monetary and trading policy. Also called the European Economic Community (EEC).

**Common stock**—A class of stock that enables the owner to participate in management of the public corporation that has issued the stock, but which receives proceeds last in the case of bankruptcy.

**Comparative advantage**—The theory that if two countries specialize in manufacturing different products and each can sell its product at a relative price advantage, then trade between the countries results in more products at lower prices.

**Compound interest**—Interest that is earned on the original amount invested plus any additional interest earned.

**Consideration**—An item of value given from one individual or business to another in return for a promise or agreement to do something or sell

*Glossary (cont'd)*

something. In a contract, there must be consideration for both sides.

**Constant dollar**—A measurement tool used to gauge fluctuations in consumer purchasing power. The dollar in the base year is valued at $1, with its value being expressed over future years relative to the base year.

**Consumer price index**—The U.S. Department of Labor's measure of change in the U.S. cost of living. A survey is conducted monthly to gauge the cost of various consumer goods, such as food, housing, and transportation. Costs are tracked over time to monitor overall living expenses.

**Contempt of court**—An act that interferes with the ability of the court to conduct normal business, or which insults the court's authority.

**Contest**—A game of skill used to get consumers interested in a company's product. A prize is offered to the winner, who is selected based on criteria described in the contest guidelines.

**Contingent agreement**—Agreement between two parties in which lease, sale, purchase, or payment depends on a special condition usually involving a third party.

**Contract**—An agreement, signed by two individuals or businesses, outlining goods or services to be exchanged, and on what terms.

**Convertible security**—A security, such as a bond or preferred stock, that a stockholder can convert to common stock at any time.

**Copyright**—The legal right of artists, authors, and creative individuals to determine who can use works that they have created.

**Corporate culture**—The values, beliefs, and ways of doing business that affect the way employees act, think, and feel about their employer.

**Corporation**—A form of doing business that establishes a separate legal entity for transacting business, providing for limited liability on the part of the owners, easy transfer of ownership through the use of shares of stock, and continued existence following the death of the owner(s).

**Cost per thousand (CPM)**—The cost quoted in advertising to reach one thousand people using a promotional method. Allows comparison of various promotional methods by standardizing the way costs are reported.

**Cost-plus contract**—A type of contract negotiated that provides for full payment of all expenses incurred in fulfilling a contract, plus an additional percentage of the total costs as the profit margin. Cost-plus contracts are common in government work, where there are situations in which there is no way to accurately gauge upfront what a product will actually cost to produce, such as in the development of new weapons technology.

**Custodian**—An individual or institution that has the responsibility for overseeing the financial management of a group of assets.

**Debenture**—An unsecured bond that has a maturity of 15 years or more.

**Default judgment**—A court's decision to grant a plaintiff's motion or request without a trial simply because the defendant failed to appear in court to provide any debate on the subject.

**Deferred compensation**—Salary and earnings to be received at some point in the future, rather than when they are earned. Deferring payment often has tax advantages.

**Deflation**—A widespread decline in prices. The opposite of inflation.

**Demographics**—Characteristics of individuals, such as age, education level, and marital status, that are used to better target marketing efforts to appropriate groups of consumers.

**Depreciation**—An asset's decline in value due to usage or obsolescence.

**Devaluation**—Lowering a country's currency relative to the price of gold or to another country's currency.

**Dilution**—The decline in value of earnings per share and stock price when new shares are issued by a company.

**Direct marketing**—A marketing method that involves mailing brochures and promotional materials to a group of consumers believed to have a need for, or interest in, a company's product.

**Discount rate**—The rate used to calculate the time value of money; the value of future cash if it were to be received today.

**Disposable income**—Income available to consumers after expenses for food, clothing, shelter, and other debts have been covered. Also known as discretionary income.

**Divestiture**—The act of selling off an asset or business, typically because it is underperforming financially or no longer fits within a company's strategic plan.

**Dividend**—The distribution of a company's earnings to its shareholders.

**Dividend yield**—The amount of a company's annual dividend for one share of stock divided by the current price of one share.

*Glossary (cont'd)*

Dog—A product or service with minimal sales in a low-growth market. Generally, companies attempt to rid themselves of dogs, which can be a drain on cash flow.

Domicile—An individual's permanent address or where s/he consistently returns for periods of time, but does not necessarily reside.

Dow Jones Industrial Average—An index of 30 actively traded stocks of selected companies that is used to gauge overall price changes in the stock market.

Drawee—The individual or institution who has been instructed to pay another individual out of funds on deposit. Generally, when a check is written by an individual, the bank on which the check is drawn is the drawee.

Drawer—The individual or institution that has written the check or has requested that payment be made by the drawee.

Dumping—Selling large numbers of shares of a stock, despite the fact that such a large-scale sale may cause the share price to drop or the market to decline in response. Also used to define the act of selling goods at below cost to force competitors out of the market.

Dutch auction—A sale in which the price of an item is lowered until it reaches a price at which someone is willing to buy it.

Early adopters—The small group of consumers most likely to purchase new products immediately after they are made available on the market. The majority of consumers will wait for the reaction of the early adopters before making the decision of whether to purchase the product. Early adopters are most often mentioned with regard to the electronics market.

Earnings per share—A company's annual earnings divided by the total number of shares outstanding.

Easement—An agreement providing one individual or business with the right to use land owned by someone else. In the case of real estate transactions, long-term easements can affect the value of a property if they interfere with the potential usage of the land. One example of an easement is an agreement between a landowner and the telephone company to permit the installation of telephone poles on the land.

Economies of scale—The improvements in a company's operational efficiency as a result of savings from purchasing inventory in volume, the division of labor, and the learning curve.

80-20 rule—Business experience that indicates that 80% of a company's revenue will come from just 20% of its total customer base.

Elasticity of demand—A measure of the responsiveness of buyers to changes in a product's price. Demand is elastic if it increases due to price reductions or decreases due to price increases. Luxury items are generally more elastic, because consumers can wait for price changes before purchasing. Cigarette demand, on the other hand, is virtually inelastic.

Encumbrance—Any agreement involving the use of land that does not prohibit its sale, but which may reduce its value. An easement is one type of encumbrance. Other common encumbrances include liens and mortgages.

Equity—The value of common and preferred stock owned by stockholders.

Equity financing—Raising money by issuing stock, thereby offering part ownership in the company in return for an investment.

ERISA—The Employee Retirement Income Security Act, enacted in 1973 to set standards for how company pensions and retirement accounts are managed.

Escalator(s)—A clause in an agreement that increases prices or rents over time.

Escrow money—Assets held by a third party until the conditions of a contract are satisfied, at which time they are paid out.

ESOP—An Employee Stock Ownership Plan, a program to encourage employee investment in company stock.

Estoppel—A legal situation barring one individual or business from denying the existence of contracts or agreements when it is clear that a contract exists. Such situations can arise after one individual realizes that the terms of a signed contract is detrimental to his or her business and claims that the contract is invalid. An estoppel comes into play when the court recognizes that the contract exists and prevents the individual from trying to deny its existence as part of a legal suit.

Exchange rate—The price at which one country's currency can be converted to another currency.

Experience curve—The efficiency gains realized in production as more products are manufactured.

Fannie Mae—Federal National Mortgage Association. A publicly owned organization that purchases mortgages from banks and resells them on the open market to investors.

FASB—Financial Accounting Standards Board. A governing body established in 1973 to define and monitor the usage of generally accepted accounting principles.

*Glossary (cont'd)*

FDIC— Federal Deposit Insurance Corporation, the federal agency that guarantees deposits made by consumers in member banks.

Federal funds rate—The interest rate charged by Federal Reserve district banks for short-term, overnight loans to banks who cannot meet reserve cash requirements.

Federal Reserve Board—The governing body of the Federal Reserve System; seven presidential appointees who establish and oversee the U.S. money supply through its banking system.

Federal Reserve System—An organization established by the Federal Reserve Act of 1913 to regulate the U.S. banking system. Twelve regional Federal Reserve Banks and 24 branches oversee all of its member banks nationwide.

Fee—In real estate, property that is owned by an individual without any restrictions on its use.

FIFO—First In, First Out, a method of accounting for inventory that assumes that the first item to be produced was the first item sold. The opposite of LIFO.

Fixed cost—Production costs that do not vary, even when sales volumes change. Expenses such as rent, interest, and executive compensation are considered fixed costs.

Float—The time lag between when a check is deposited and when it clears.

Floor area ratio (F.A.R.)—Ratio between floor area and height.

Focus group—A non-scientific market research technique involving a group of 8 to 12 individuals who are brought together to provide feedback on such issues as new products, advertising campaigns, and a company's reputation.

Forward contract—An agreement to conduct business on a future date.

Franchise—The sale of the license and rights to establish and manage a business under a recognized name using set business practices. McDonald's, one of the most famous franchises, sells the rights to operate a restaurant within a specific geographic area provided all operating standards are maintained.

Franchisee—The individual or company that purchases the rights to operate a business from the owner or franchisor.

Franchisor—The owner of the rights to a business concept who sells them to the franchisee.

Fraudulent conveyance—The transfer of funds or property from one individual or business to another in order to avoid having to turn over such assets to creditors. A form of hiding assets.

Free on board (FOB)—Shipping arrangements that indicate exactly when the buyer assumes responsibility for the transport of a product. The location specified on an invoice as FOB Anywhere is the point to which the seller will assume responsibility for transport. Beyond that point, it is the buyer's responsibility.

Frequency—The calculation of how many times an advertisement has been seen by a specific population. An ad with a frequency of four, reaches each consumer four times. The higher the frequency, the better the chances that an ad will be noticed.

Full faith and credit—The requirement that legal judgments issued in one state be upheld and recognized by all other states.

Futures contract— An agreement made between traders on the floor of the commodity exchange regarding the purchase of commodities on a specific date in the future for an agreed-upon price.

GATT—General Agreement on Tariffs and Trade. A multinational trade agreement regarding trade issues and policies.

Generic—A non-branded product sold at prices generally below those of name-brand products.

Gold standard—A national monetary standard using gold as the basis.

Golden handcuffs—An employment contract between employer and employee that provides lucrative compensation and benefits during an employee's tenure with the firm. However, if the employee leaves, s/he is liable for repayment of the compensation and benefits received during his or her employment.

Golden parachute—A lucrative severance package negotiated for a top executive in the event of a takeover.

Goodwill—The intangible assets of a business that impact its overall value. Such assets might include company reputation, loyal customer base, brand recognition, and employee morale.

Greenmail—Repurchase of company stock from a potential acquirer in return for assurances that the acquirer will not pursue the takeover of the company. Generally, the purchase price of the stock is inflated by the acquirer.

Gross profit—The amount remaining after the cost to produce a product (cost of goods sold) is subtracted from the net sales.

*Glossary (cont'd)*

Gross rating point—A measure of the size of an audience watching a television program during a certain time period, reported in percentages of the total audience size.

Guaranty—An agreement to be responsible for the obligations of another individual or business.

Hedge—An investment tactic in which securities are purchased on both sides of a risk, so that any loss in one security is countered by gains in the other securities.

Holder in due course—An individual or business that accepts a check or form of payment in exchange for merchandise or property without noticing that the check is invalid. The individual accepting the check is the holder in due course and has the right to pursue full payment from the person who wrote the check.

Holding company—A company whose sole purpose is to hold stock in other companies, rather than creating a product or service itself.

Holdover rent—High rent that penalizes a tenant for staying beyond the term of a lease.

Horizontal market—A market with a wide range of customers–the market for sneakers, for example. As opposed to a vertical market, which might include people buying equipment for brain surgery.

In camera—The act of reviewing legal documents and motions in a judge's chambers, rather than in a public courtroom. In the case of sensitive information that could be publicly embarrassing or damaging to people involved in a suit, the information is often reviewed privately by a judge to decide whether it should become public through a court action.

Income statement—A summary of a company's revenue and expenses for a specified period of time, usually one year. This, and the balance sheet, make up a company's financial statements. Also known as a profit and loss statement.

Inelastic demand—A demand for products that remains relatively constant despite any changes in price. Basic needs for food and utilities, for instance, cannot be put off until prices drop.

Inflation—Widespread rise in prices that causes an overall increase in the cost of living.

Initial Public Offering—The first offering of a stock for sale to the public.

Injunction—A court order barring a defendant from doing something that would harm the plaintiff. If the defendant ignores the order, s/he may face fines, penalties, or formal charges.

Innovators—Consumers who are some of the first to try a new product.

Insider trading—Illegal trading of securities based on confidential information from internal company sources. Since such information would not be generally available to the public, the trader has an unfair advantage.

Intangible asset—Non-physical company assets such as patents, technical know-how, and trademarks.

Interest—Fees paid by a borrower to a lender for the use of the lender's money.

Internal rate of return (IRR)—The discount rate at which an investment has a net present value of $0.

Inventory turnover—The rate at which a firm's inventory is totally depleted over a period of time, usually a year. A company's average inventory divided by its annual sales will give you its inventory turnover.

Joint venture—An agreement between two or more groups to work together on a specific project.

Judgment debtor—An individual who owes an individual or business money following a legal judgment. The individual or business to whom the money is owed is the judgment creditor.

Junk bond—A bond with a rating of BB or worse that is considered to be more volatile than higher rated bonds. In return for the higher risk of default, the bonds promise higher yields.

Just-in-time purchasing—A purchasing method that schedules delivery of raw materials just at the point in the production when they are needed. Such arrangements reduce the cost of holding the inventory in-house and increase pressure on suppliers to create top quality materials.

Keogh plan—A pension program specifically for the self-employed.

Laches—The extended delay in processing a legal matter in which the defendant is placed at a disadvantage in proving his/her innocence because evidence no longer exists, witnesses are no longer living, or difficulties have occurred.

Laissez faire—The belief that government intervention in business should be minimal.

Latent defect—A problem or defect that cannot be discovered through normal examination and that is not noticed by the seller when turning the product or service over to the buyer. Such defects often become noticeable after a product or service has been delivered. Assets such as real estate, automobiles, and machinery most frequently have latent defects because it

*Glossary (cont'd)*

is difficult to check every possible source of future problems before the sale to the new owner.

**Leading economic indicator**—Twelve ratios tracked by the U.S. Department of Commerce as indications of economic activity.

**Lease**—A long-term rental agreement.

**Lease term**—Length of time a lease is in full force.

**Lease year**—Any period of 12 consecutive months, starting from the first day of a month.

**Lessee**—Tenant who pays rent in return for the right to use office space.

**Lessor**—Landlord who receives payment for renting out office space.

**Letter of credit**—A document provided by a bank on behalf of a customer guaranteeing that a debt will be paid up to a certain amount. Such letters are often necessary in international dealings.

**Letter of intent**—Good faith agreement signed by tenant and landlord prior to lease, setting forth major terms and conditions.

**Letter of representation**—Agreement between tenant and broker giving broker exclusive rights to locate and negotiate for office space.

**Leveraged buyout**—A purchase method that uses the existing assets of a company to finance its purchase by an outside investor.

**Lien**—A lender's claim to assets, usually as a guarantee against a loan.

**LIFO**—Last In, First Out. An accounting method for valuing inventory that assumes that the last or most recently produced item is the next item to be sold.

**Limited partnership**—A form of a partnership composed of a general manager responsible for the day-to-day management of the business and several limited partners who invest money but who have limited involvement in the management of the firm and, hence, limited liability for its financial obligations.

**Line of credit**—An agreement between a lender and borrower allowing the borrower to draw on a pool of money up to an established limit.

**Liquid**—Easily converted into cash.

**Liquidated damages**—The amount of money one individual or business agrees to pay another in the event that they breach a contract signed by both parties. Liquidated damages are calculated as part of the contract, so that both parties know at the outset what it will cost them if they are responsible for a breach of contract.

**Load**—The sales charge paid by an investor for the privilege of buying shares in a mutual fund.

**Loss leader**—Products sold at a loss as a means of drawing customers into a store. For example, Toys R Us toy store sells childrens' diapers at an extreme discount in order to draw parents into the store on a regular basis, hoping that once they are in the store, they will buy something else.

**M1**—The amount of U.S. currency in circulation at any given point in time, plus consumer bank deposits.

**M2**—M1 plus overnight European transactions, savings, and money market mutual fund transactions.

**M3**—A broad measure of the money supply, including M1, M2, and time deposits over $100,000 in value.

**Manufacturer's agent**—An independent salesperson representing a manufacturing firm or firms on a non-exclusive basis. Such arrangements reduce the need for manufacturers to keep large sales forces on staff.

**Margin**—Money borrowed from a brokerage house in order to purchase more securities.

**Marginal cost**—The cost of producing one more unit of a product or service beyond the planned quantity.

**Marginal revenue**—The change in total revenues for a firm from the sale of one more product.

**Market rent**—Current rental rates for similar kinds of office space.

**Market share**—The percentage of total industry sales that one company is responsible for. For instance, XYZ Co. has $10 million in sales in the widget industry, which has a total of $100 million in sales from all companies in the industry. So, XYZ has a 10% market share.

**Marketing mix**—The tools used to market a product or service, including the price, channels of distribution, promotional methods, and the product features.

**Markup**—The difference between the cost to produce a product and its selling price.

**Material**—Information relevant to a particular matter that may affect the outcome of a legal suit.

**Mean**—The average of a set of numbers. Calculated by adding several numbers together, counting how many numbers are being added, and then dividing by that number.

**Median**—The middle point in a series of numbers where half the numbers are higher and half are lower. For example, 3 is the median between 1 and 5.

*Glossary (cont'd)*

**Mitigation of damages**—The legal requirement that an individual who has been negatively affected by the action of another and who has been repaid for that action must make every effort not to hold the other responsible for any self-inflicted aggravation to the situation.

**Mode**—The number appearing most frequently in a series of numbers. For instance in the series 1,2,5,2,7,2,8, 2 is the mode, appearing more frequently than any of the other numbers.

**Monetarism**—The economic perspective that the federal money supply has great impact on the growth of the economy and should be handled carefully.

**Monetary policy**—Decisions made by the Federal Reserve Board regarding the amount of money in circulation at a given point. By supplying more credit to the banking system or withdrawing credit, the Federal Reserve Board can affect the growth of the economy.

**Money market**—The market for safe, short-term investments.

**Monopoly**—A market with one firm in control of the manufacture and supply of a product. Until the advent of Federal Express, the Postal Service was a monopoly.

**Monopsony**—A market with just one buyer for a product or service and many sellers.

**Mortgage**—A loan to purchase real estate, with the property used as collateral to guarantee the loan.

**Mortgage REIT**—A real estate investment trust that invests in real estate mortgages. Instead of investing in one or two properties, investors can buy shares in an REIT, which owns many different types of properties.

**Multinational**—A company with branch offices in many countries.

**Mutual fund**—A diversified portfolio of investments purchased in shares through brokers.

**Naked option**—The situation in which an investor has purchased a put or call, but does not own any shares. If the share price rises, there is the potential for great gains, without having to invest large sums of money to actually purchase shares. However, if the price drops and the investor has to replace the shares "borrowed" for the transaction, the cash outlay can be huge.

**Nationalization**—Action by the government to acquire ownership in a company or industry.

**Negotiable**—Investments that can be easily transferred to another form.

**Negotiable instrument**—A document, promising to pay an amount of money to another individual or business, that can be transferred to someone else and still be valid. A check is the most common form of a negotiable instrument.

**Net present value**—Today's discounted value of a string of cash inflows in the future.

**Net sales**—Gross sales minus such costs as cash discounts, shipping charges, and inventory returns.

**Net worth**—An individual's or business's total asset value minus all obligations.

**No par**—Stocks issued without a specific face value.

**Non-callable**—Securities that issuers cannot redeem before the date of maturity.

**Non-conforming use**—Changes in zoning requirements that occur after a structure has been built and is in use and that now make the structure noncompliant. A non-conforming use permits continued use of the structure, but requires that any future changes to it be approved by the zoning board.

**Offering circular**—Brief marketing materials describing a new stock issue.

**Oligopoly**—A market in which there are several firms, none of which is dominant enough to control the entire market through its actions.

**Operating income**—Income generated from day-to-day operations of a firm.

**Opinion**—A written evaluation of the accuracy of a firm's financial statements provided by the firm's certified public accounting firm.

**Opportunity cost**—The cost of giving up one opportunity in order to invest in another. For instance, the opportunity cost of eating a hot fudge sundae is the brownie you could have had instead.

**Option**—The purchased right to buy or sell securities at a set price for a specified period of time. Key executives often receive options to purchase company stock at an advantageous price as part of their compensation package.

**Original equipment manufacturer (OEM)**—A manufacturer that supplies its product to other firms who sell it as part of their product line, often under a different brand name.

**Over the counter (OTC)**—The market for securities that are not bought and sold over the major exchanges. Penny stocks are one example of securities that are only available over the counter.

**Overdraft**—A situation in which the amount of money deposited in an account does not adequately cover the obligations on the account.

*Glossary (cont'd)*

Overreaching—The advantage that one business acquires when it cheats or defrauds another business. Any agreements or contracts that arise from overreaching are invalid.

Owner's equity—The total value of a company's shares of stock minus obligations.

Paper—Short-term obligations issued for terms of 2 to 270 days. Such investments are targeted to investors with large amounts of cash available on a short-term basis.

Par value—The value of a security printed on the certificate.

Parking—Investing funds temporarily in short-term, safe havens while longer-term investment options are considered.

Partial breach—A minor breach of contract that does not affect an agreement to a major extent. As a result, the contract is maintained. An example of a partial breach would be if a business is a day late in delivering some materials necessary for a contract. If a one day delay has no material affect on the ability of the other business to hold up its part of the bargain, then it is only a partial breach.

Partnership—A firm owned by two or more people who are jointly liable for the assets and obligations of the firm.

Patent—A legal claim to a new process or device that provides protection from theft by other companies or individuals for 17 years. Patents must be registered in order to be protected.

Penny stock—A stock with an initial offering price of less than one dollar, available through over-the-counter markets and considered a high risk investment.

Pension fund—An investment fund established by a corporation or organization to manage retirement benefits and investments for its employees.

PERT—Program Evaluation and Review Technique, a scheduling method that graphically shows when certain project tasks must be completed before other activities can begin.

Piercing the corporate veil—The process of suing individuals involved in the management of a corporation. Since corporations generally shield individuals from liability, such action can only be taken if it can be proven that there is a good reason to disregard the corporate entity.

Point-of-purchase promotion—A piece of marketing literature that is placed in a store where a customer is likely to be making a purchase decision about a product.

Poison pill—A resolution passed by a company's board of directors that makes it difficult or impossible to stage an unfriendly takeover.

Ponzi scheme—A pyramid marketing program in which the proceeds from new investors are used to pay off existing investors. The last wave of investors is left with nothing.

Portfolio—Several securities owned by one individual or institution. A variety of securities reduces investment risk, so a diversified portfolio is the goal.

Position—The amount of money an individual has invested in a particular security; a company's stake.

Positioning—The way a company wants to be perceived by its public. The position is supported by investments in advertising, direct marketing, and public relations.

Power of acceptance—An individual's right and ability to accept or reject the terms of a contract.

Power of attorney—Appointing an individual to make important decisions for another individual.

Preferred stock—A class of stock that receives its dividends before common stock. Common stock dividends cannot be paid until and unless preferred stockholders have been paid.

Premium—The additional amount a stock is worth relative to other stocks. When one stock is selling at a higher price than another it is said to be selling at a premium of X%.

Pre-paid expense—Paying for an expense in advance, usually for tax or accounting reasons.

Price-earnings ratio (P/E ratio)—Current share price divided by a stock's earnings per share. Stocks in similar industries often have similar P/E ratios. Any differences reflect investor anticipation of the company's prospects.

Prime rate—The interest rate banks offer to their best commercial customers.

Principal—The base amount of money borrowed as part of a loan on which interest will be charged.

Private placement—Offering securities directly to private investors, rather than through a public offering.

Privileged communication—Discussions that take place between an attorney and his/her client that may not be forcibly divulged in court proceedings.

Product life cycle—The stages through which a product progresses in the marketplace. This

*Glossary (cont'd)*

normally includes introduction, acceptance, growth, and maturity.

Product portfolio—All the products a company has to sell.

Profit margin—The selling price of an item less all variable costs.

Profit-sharing plan—A plan that provides for the division of a portion of the company's profits, part of which are generally deposited into a tax-deferred account. The funds are paid out when the employee retires or leaves the company.

Program trading—Computerized buying and selling of stocks, bonds, and commodities.

Progressive tax—A type of tax that takes a larger proportion of income from those with higher incomes.

Promotion—Marketing tactics that communicate product and company information to the public through such vehicles as newsletters, advertisements, sweepstakes, and brochures.

Proprietorship—A type of business that is controlled and managed by one person.

Prospecting—The marketing practice of seeking out and classifying potential clients in terms of their likelihood to buy.

Prospectus—A summary of the registration statement for a security that has been filed with the SEC.

Protectionism—Government policy of establishing barriers to entry for foreign products, making domestic products more desirable. Such barriers protect domestic firms and products by making foreign products more expensive.

Proxy—Written authorization to act on behalf of someone else in a specific capacity, such as with stock voting rights.

Public relations—Activities on behalf of a company or organization that increase the company's exposure in the community through media coverage, sponsorships, and community involvement.

Put—An option to sell a specific stock for a specified price within a set time frame.

Pyramid—An illegal investment practice that involves soliciting investors by promising them high returns, but then using their invested funds to pay earlier investors, rather than actually investing those funds in securities.

Quantum meruit—The right to sue for payment resulting from an implied or existing contract. When individuals or businesses provide goods or services through an implied contract but are not paid, they can sue the other party in quantum meruit in order to be paid.

Question mark—A classification of a product line that is in a high growth market, but which isn't yet performing as well as anticipated. Such ventures can either yield great returns by acquiring a large share of the growing market, or they can lose money by falling behind.

Quick ratio—A measure of liquidity calculated by subtracting inventory values from current assets and dividing that figure by current liabilities.

Raider—An investor who aims to take control of a company by purchasing a majority stake in the firm.

Real estate—Land and property, including any building and structures on a parcel of land.

Real estate investment trust (REIT)—A real estate investment trust that invests in a variety of real estate properties. Instead of investing in one or two properties, investors can buy shares in a REIT, which owns many different types of properties, and reduce their risk.

Real income—Income adjusted for inflation, which is considered to be a truer measure of purchasing power than income itself.

Receiver—A court-appointed individual who is responsible for managing the day-to-day affairs of a company involved in bankruptcy proceedings. The receiver does not own the company and is not liable for the company's obligations, but simply keeps the company running until a determination is made on the bankruptcy claim.

Recession—Several months of decline in business activity.

Recoupment—A discount or reduction negotiated by a buyer or defendant in a legal matter.

Red herring—A preliminary prospectus issued before SEC approval for a security sale. Identified by the red band across the first page.

Registration statement—A document prepared prior to the public offering of securities, detailing the financial situation of the company, its history and background, and the qualifications of the business managers.

Regression analysis—A statistical tool used to look at past events and determine cause and effect.

Regressive tax—A type of tax that takes a larger proportion of income from those with lower incomes.

Re-insurance—The practice of spreading the risk of insuring someone across several insurance companies, in return for a portion of the pre-

*Glossary (cont'd)*

mium payment. Lloyd's of London is a re-insurance marketplace.

Release—A document that certifies that an individual or business has given up a claim to something.

Rent abatement—Reducing rent by omitting payments for a number of months to induce tenants to lease office space.

Replacement cost—The cost of replacing an asset with the same asset if the original were to break or malfunction.

Reserve requirement—The percentage of funds the Federal Reserve Board requires that member banks maintain on deposit at all times.

Retained earnings—Earnings that are left after dividends are paid out.

Retention—The number of units retained by an investment banker during the process of underwriting a securities sale, minus the units set aside for institutional sales.

Return on equity (ROE)—The return investors receive on their investment in a security, expressed as a percentage.

Royalty—Payment made to the owner of an asset in return for its use in generating income. Such payments are made to patent holders who grant permission to use the patent, as well as to authors, who are paid royalties based on book sales.

Sale and leaseback—The sale of an asset which is immediately leased from the new owner. Such a transaction helps to increase short-term cash flow for the seller, and can provide tax advantages.

Sallie Mae—Student Loan Marketing Association. A government-funded agency that guarantees student loans, purchasing them from financial institutions and selling them on the secondary market.

Scrip—A document issued by a corporation to represent a fractional share of stock. Scrip may be collected and presented for full shares.

Sector—Stocks from one particular industry. Stocks from firms in the automotive industry are in the automotive sector, for instance. Brokerage firms may specialize in tracking particular sectors.

Securities and Exchange Commission (SEC)—The government agency responsible for monitoring the issuance and sale of securities.

Security interest—The right to collateral in return for granting some form of financing. A creditor has a security interest in assets that have been pledged as collateral on a loan.

Segment—A grouping of customers within a market with similarities in their purchasing needs or preferences.

Self-liquidating premium—A premium paid in part or in full by the buyer. Includes gimmicks offered on the side of cereal boxes.

Senior debt—Debt that must be paid before subordinated debt, such as common stock, can be paid. This is a consideration in bankruptcy situations.

Service of process—The action of delivering or communicating information on a legal proceeding to the plaintiff or defendant in a suit.

Settlement—Completing a transaction by paying all obligations.

Seven sisters—The seven major international oil companies: British Petroleum, Chevron, Exxon, Gulf, Mobil, Shell, and Texaco.

Shakeout—The shutdown or closing of several firms in an industry, leaving only a few dominant players.

Share—One unit of stock in a corporation.

Shark repellent—Provisions established by a corporation to discourage unwanted takeover attempts by making it more expensive and difficult to purchase the company.

Short hedge—Hedges taken to lessen or eliminate the financial loss occurring from falling share prices.

Short position—A stock purchase procedure that involves "borrowing" shares of stock through a broker, selling them, and repurchasing them when the price has dropped. The buyer never actually takes possession of the shares and can make a profit if the shares are repurchased for less than what they were "borrowed" for. However, if the stock price rises, the buyer must pay to buy back the shares, thereby losing money.

Shrinkage—Losses experienced from worker and customer shoplifting.

Simple interest—Interest earned only on the initial capital investment. Unlike compound interest, which continues to accrue on both the capital and the earned interest, simple interest only applies to the capital.

Simulation—The process of creating an investment model in order to adjust certain variables to see their effect on investments. This type of learning can help brokers make decisions regarding where to place their clients' money.

Sixteenth—Reference to one sixteenth of a point change in the price of stocks, bonds, and options.

*Glossary (cont'd)*

Small-capitalization stock—Shares of stock issued by small firms with little equity or stock outstanding.

Smokestack industry—Basic manufacturing industries that have experienced minimal growth during the past decades.

Sovereign risk—Risk that lenders assume when making loans to foreign governments due to the fact that a change in the national power structure could cause the country to default on its commitments.

Specialist—A member of the securities exchange responsible for executing securities trades on a particular stock.

Spinoff—Separating a corporate division from the parent company and establishing it as its own independent operating unit.

Split—Increasing the number of shares outstanding without increasing the shareowner's equity, causing a drop in the share price proportional to the number of new shares.

Sponsor—A trader, generally an institution or brokerage firm, whose large scale purchases influence the purchases of other traders. The demand for a stock can be significantly affected by the actions of a sponsor.

Spread—The difference between yields of various maturities. For instance, the spread between a 3-month CD of 3% and a 5-year CD of 6% is 3 percentage points.

Stagflation—The economic condition of slowed economic growth and rising unemployment coupled with rising prices.

Standard deviation—A statistical measure used to assess variability.

Standard Metropolitan Statistical Area (SMSA)—A geographical area consisting of at least 50,000 residents. Used in marketing to determine potential sales and advertising costs for an area.

Star—A business or product line with growth potential—a market leader in a fast-growing market. Stars can become a cash cow or a question mark, depending on their performance.

Stock—Units of ownership in a publicly-held company.

Stock dividend—A dividend paid in shares of stock instead of cash.

Stock option—The opportunity to purchase shares of stock at a specified price and within a specified time period.

Stop order—An order given to a broker to buy or sell a security when it reaches a certain price.

Straight-life annuity—A series of payments that continues only while the recipient is alive.

Straight-line depreciation—A method of depreciating an asset by reducing its value in equal amounts each year.

Strategic business unit (SBU)—An organizational unit within a company that is typically focused on selling to one market segment or specializing in one type of product.

Strategic plan—A long-term road map for a company, spelling out its financial and operational objectives for the next 3-5 years.

Strip—The practice of dividing a bond into a series of lesser-valued zero-coupon bonds.

Strong dollar—When the foreign exchange rate results in the U.S. dollar being able to purchase foreign goods more cheaply.

Subordinated debenture—Debt which is paid out after preferred stock and bonds.

Supply-side economics—Economic policy that supports reduction in taxes as a means of improving the long-term growth of the economy.

Sweepstakes—A type of contest that encourages participants to purchase a product in order to be considered for free prizes. A lottery, which is illegal, requires a payment for a game of chance. A sweepstakes offers an alternative means of entry, eliminating the cost to play.

Syndicate—A group of individuals who have formed a joint venture to undertake a project they would have been unable to complete individually.

Synergy—A theory that states that businesses or groups merged into a large organization will be more productive and successful than the businesses were individually; the whole is greater than the sum of its parts.

Takeover—The action of assuming control of a business, usually by a raider.

Tangible asset—Physical assets, such as land, buildings, and machinery, that can be sold separately from the business entity.

Target market—A group of consumers or businesses believed to have a need for a company's products that the company attempts to communicate with through advertising.

Tariff—A tax levied on imported products that makes them more expensive, and hence less desirable, than domestic products.

Tax haven—A geographic location that charges little or no taxes on businesses in the area.

Technical correction—An unexplained drop in stock prices after several days of increases.

*Glossary (cont'd)*

10-K—An annual report filed with the SEC on behalf of any company that has stock issued, providing information on revenues and income.

Tenancy—Possession or occupancy of real estate by title, under a lease, or on payment of rent, with or without a written lease.

Tenant—Individual or entity paying rent to use or occupy property owned by another.

Tender offer—An offer made by one company seeking to buy another company by purchasing its shares of stock at a price above the current market price.

Term-to-maturity—The amount of time that will elapse before an obligation becomes due.

Time value of money—A dollar received today is worth more than a dollar received at some point in the future, considering the fact that rising prices will mean that a dollar will buy even less in the future.

Tombstone—A form of advertisement announcing the issuance of a security by a particular firm or group of firms.

Tout—To promote a firm or security to a group of clients by praising it.

Trade deficit—The difference between the amount of exports and imports a country has. When there are more imports than exports, a trade deficit exists for the country receiving the imports.

Trade secrets—Secret ideas, processes, or ways of doing business that give a firm an advantage but which are not patented. Businesses try to protect such information from being given to the competition.

Trade surplus—When a country's exports exceed its imports.

Trademark—A registered symbol, theme, mark, or identification related to a person or company. Only that company can use or grant the use of a trademarked item.

Transfer pricing—The cost to sell a company's product to another division or department internally. Since there is no need for markup and external distribution costs with an internal sale, the transfer price is typically less than the retail price.

Trend—A series of occurrences that indicate a pattern.

Triple witching hour—The hour before the market closes on a day when both stock options and futures expire.

Trust—A relationship established that gives one individual, the trustee, responsibility for the management and care of assets on behalf of another individual, the beneficiary.

Undercapitalized—A situation in which a business does not have the necessary funds to transact normal business.

Undervalued—When a share is trading at a price lower than its market value.

Underwrite—The process of purchasing securities from the issuer in order to sell them back to the public.

Unfriendly takeover—The acquisition of a business under protest from the current managers and/or owners.

Unrealized loss—A loss that has occurred on paper through a drop in price but which has not yet been realized because the security has not yet been sold.

Value-added tax—A tax levied at each stage in the production cycle, when another feature is added to the functioning of the product.

Variable cost—Production costs involving raw materials, labor, and utilities that vary according to the production quantity.

Venture capital—Capital provided by a pool of investors for use by firms just starting or expanding, in return for an equity position in the venture.

Voting rights—The opportunity to vote on issues of importance to the company. Owners of common stock acquire voting rights.

Warrant—A type of security that gives the owner the right to purchase a certain number of shares of stock at a price slightly higher than the market price at issuance. The warrant is usually good for several years, however, providing time for the stock price to appreciate.

Wasting asset—An asset that declines in value.

Workout—The process of renegotiating a loan package.

Yield curve—A graph showing the various bond maturities and corresponding yields. When the shorter-term bond rates are higher than the longer-term rates, the yield curve is negative. And when the shorter-term bond rates are lower than the longer-term rates, the curve is positive.

# Weights and Measures

## Linear Measure

12 inches (in) = 1 foot (ft)
3 feet = 1 yard (yd)
5 1/2 yards = 1 rod (rd), pole, or perch (16 1/2 ft)
40 rods = 1 furlong (fur) = 220 yds = 660 ft
8 furlongs = 1 statute mile (mi) = 1,760 yds = 5,280 ft
3 land miles = 1 league
5,280 feet = 1 statute or land mile
6,076.11549 feet = 1 international nautical mile

## Area Measure

144 square inches = 1 sq ft
9 square feet = 1 sq yd = 1,296 sq in.
30 1/4 square yards = 1 sq rd = 272 1/4 sq ft
160 square rods = 1 acre = 4,840 sq yds = 43,560 sq ft
640 acres = 1 sq mi
1 mile square = 1 section (of land)
6 miles square = 1 township = 36 sections = 36 sq mi

## Cubic Measure

1,728 cubic inches = 1 cu ft
27 cubic feet = 1 cu yd

## Liquid Measure

2 pints = 1 quart (qt) ( = 57.75 cu in.)
4 quarts = 1 gallon (gal) ( = 231 cu in.) = 8 pts

## Apothecaries' Fluid Measure

60 minims (min.) = 1 fluid dram (fl dr)
8 fluid drams = 1 fluid ounce (fl oz)
16 fluid ounces = 1 pt
2 pints = 1 qt
4 quarts = 1 gal

## Dry Measure

2 pints = 1 qt ( = 67.20 cu in.)
8 quarts = 1 peck (pk) ( = 537.60 cu in.) = 16 pts
4 pecks = 1 bushel (bu) ( = 2,150.42 cu in.) = 32 qts

## Avoirdupois Weight

27 11/32 grains = 1 dram (dr)
16 drams = 1 oz = 437 1/2 grains
16 ounces = 1 lb = 256 drams = 7,000 grains
100 pounds = 1 hundredweight (cwt)1
20 hundredweights = 1 ton(tn) = 2,000 lbs 1

## Units of Circular Measure

Minute (') = 60 seconds
Degree (°) = 60 minutes
Right angle = 90 degrees
Straight angle = 180 degrees
Circle = 360 degrees

## Troy Weight

24 grains = 1 pennyweight (dwt)
20 pennyweights = 1 ounce troy (oz t)12 ounces troy = 1 pound (lb t)

## Metric and U.S. Equivalents

1 angstrom (light wave measurement) = 0.1 millimicron
1 angstrom = 0.0000001 millimeter
1 angstrom = 0.0000004 inch
1 cable's length = 120 fathoms
1 cable's length = 720 feet
1 cable's length = 219.45 meters
1 centimeter = 0.39 inch
1 chain (Gunter's or surveyor's) = 66 feet
1 chain (Gunter's or surveyor's) = 20.11 meters
1 decimeter = 3.93 inches
1 dekameter = 32.80 feet
1 fathom = 6 feet
1 fathom = 1.82 meters
1 foot = 0.30 meter
1 furlong = 10 chains (surveyor's)
1 furlong = 660 feet
1 furlong = 220 yards
1 furlong = 1/8 statute mile
1 furlong = 201.16 meters
1 inch = 2.54 centimeters
1 kilometer = 0.62 mile
1 league (land) = 3 statute miles
1 league (land) = 4.82 kilometers
1 link (Gunter's or surveyor's) = 7.92inches
1 link (Gunter's or surveyor's) = 0.201168 meter
1 meter = 39.37 inches
1 meter = 1.09 yards
1 micron = 0.00 millimeter
1 micron = 0.00003937 inch
1 mil = 0.00 inch
1 mil = 0.02 millimeter
1 mile (statute or land) = 5,280 feet
1 mile (statute or land) = 1.60 kilometers
1 mile (nautical international) = 1.85 kilometers
1 mile (nautical international) = 1.15 statute miles
1 mile (nautical international) = 0.99 U.S. nautical miles
1 millimeter = 0.03937 inch
1 millimicron = 0.00 micron
1 millimicron − 0.00000003937 inch
1 nanometer = 0.00 micrometer
1 nanometer = 0.00000003937 inch
1 point (typography) = 0.013837 inch
1 point (typography) = 1/72 inch
1 point (typography) = 0.35 millimeter
1 yard = 0.91 meter

## Areas or Surfaces

1 acre = 43,560 square feet
1 acre = 4,840 square yards
1 acre = 0.40 hectare
1 hectare = 2.47 acres

*Weights and Measures (cont'd)*

1 square centimeter = 0.15 square inch
1 square decimeter = 15.5 square inches
1 square foot = 929.03 square centimeters
1 square inch = 6.45 square centimeters
1 square kilometer = 0.38 square mile
1 square kilometer = 247.10 acres
1 square meter = 1.19 square yards
1 square meter = 10.76 square feet
1 square mile = 258.99 hectares
1 square millimeter = 0.00 square inch
1 square rod, square pole or square perch = 25.29 square meters
1 square yard = 0.83 square meters

## Capacities or Volumes

1 cord (firewood) = 128 cubic feet
1 cubic centimeter = 0.06 cubic inch
1 cubic decimeter = 61.02 cubic inches
1 cubic foot = 7.48 gallons
1 cubic foot = 28.31 cubic decimeters
1 cubic inch = 0.55 fluid ounce
1 cubic inch = 4.43 fluid drams
1 cubic inch = 16.38 cubic centimeters
1 cubic meter = 1.30 cubic yards
1 cubic yard = 0.76 cubic meter
1 cup, measuring = 8 fluid ounces
1 cubic inch = 1/2 liquid pint
1 dram, fluid or liquid (U.S.) = 1/8 fluid ounce
1 dram, fluid or liquid (U.S.) = 0.22 cubic inch
1 dram, fluid or liquid (U.S.) = 3.69 milliliters
1 dram, fluid or liquid (U.S.) = 1.04 British fluid drams
1 dekaliter = 2.64 gallons
1 dekaliter = 1.13 pecks
1 gallon (U.S.) = 231 cubic inches
1 gallon (U.S.) = 3.78 liters
1 gallon (U.S.) = 0.83 British gallon
1 gallon (U.S.) = 128 U.S. fluid ounces
1 gallon (British Imperial) = 277.42 cubic inches
1 gallon (British Imperial) = 1.20 U.S. gallons
1 gallon (British Imperial) = 4.54 liters
1 gallon (British Imperial) = 160 British fluid ounces
1 liter = 1.05 liquid quarts
1 liter = 0.90 dry quart
1 milliliter = 0.27 fluid dram
1 ounce, fluid or liquid (U.S.) = 1.80 cubic inch
1 ounce, fluid or liquid (U.S.) = 29.57 milliliters
1 ounce, fluid or liquid (U.S.) = 1.04 British fluid ounces
1 peck = 8.81 liters
1 pint, dry = 0.55 liter
1 pint, liquid = 0.47 liter
1 quart, dry (U.S.) = 1.10 liters
1 quart, liquid (U.S.) = 0.94 liter
1 quart (British) = 1.03 U.S. dry quarts
1 quart (British) = 1.20 U.S. liquid quarts
1 tablespoon, measuring = 3 teaspoons
1 tablespoon, measuring = 4 fluid drams
1 tablespoon, measuring = 1/2 fluid ounce

1 teaspoon, measuring = 1/3 tablespoon
1 teaspoon, measuring = 1 1/3 fluid drams
1 assay ton = 29.16 grams
1 carat = 200 milligrams
1 carat = 3.08 grains
1 dram, apothecaries' = 60 grains
1 dram, apothecaries' = 3.88 grams
1 gram = 15.43 grains
1 kilogram = 2.20 pounds
1 microgram (μg) = 0.000001 gram
1 milligram = 0.01 grain
1 ounce, avoirdupois = 437.5 grains
1 ounce, avoirdupois = 0.91 troy or apothecaries' ounce
1 ounce, avoirdupois = 28.35 grams
1 pennyweight = 1.55 grams
1 point = 0.01 carat
1 point = 2 milligrams
1 ton = 2,240 pounds
1 ton, gross = 1.12 net tons
1 ton, gross = 1.01 metric tons
1 ton, metric = 2,204.62 pounds
1 ton, metric = 0.98 gross ton

## Miscellaneous Units of Measure

Acre–An area of 43,560 square feet. Originally, the area a yoke of oxen could plow in one day.

Agate–Originally a measurement of type size (5 1/2 points). Now equal to 1/12 inch. Used in printing for measuring column length.

Ampere–Unit of electrical current.

Astronomical Unit (A.U.)–93,000,000 miles, the average distance of the earth from the sun.

Bale–A large bundle of goods (hay, cotton).

Board Foot (fbm)–144 cubic inches (12 in. x 12 in. x 1 in.). Used for lumber.

Bolt–40 yards. Used for measuring cloth.

Btu–British thermal unit. Amount of heat needed to increase the temperature of one pound of water by one degree Fahrenheit (252 calories).

Carat (c)–200 milligrams or 3.08 grains troy (precious stones). See also Karat.

Chain (ch)–A chain 66 feet or one-tenth of a furlong in length, divided into 100 parts called links. One mile is equal to 80 chains. Cubit – 18 inches or 45.72 cm.

Decibel–Unit of relative loudness. One decibel is the smallest amount of change detectable by the human ear.

Freight, Ton (also called Measurement Ton) – 40 cubic feet of merchandise (cargo freight).

Great Gross–12 gross or 1,728 pieces.

*Weights and Measures (cont'd)*

Gross–12 dozen or 144 pieces.

Hand–4 inches or 10.16 cm. Derived from the width of the hand. Used for measuring the height of horses at withers.

Hertz–Modern unit for measurement of electromagnetic wave frequencies (equivalent to "cycles per second").

Horsepower–The power needed to lift 33,000 pounds a distance of one foot in one minute. Used mostly for measuring power of engines.

Karat (kt)–A measure of the purity of gold, indicating how many parts out of 24 are pure. For example – 18 karat gold is 3/4 pure. See also, carat.

Knot–The rate of speed of one nautical mile per hour.

League–Usually estimated at 3 miles in English-speaking countries.

Light-Year–5,880,000,000,000 miles, the distance light travels in a vacuum in a year at the rate of 186,281.7 miles (299.79 kilometers) per second. (If an astronomical unit were represented by one inch, a light-year would be represented by about one mile.) Used for measurements in interstellar space.

Magnum–Two-quart bottle. Used for measuring wine.

Ohm–Unit of electrical resistance. A circuit in which a potential difference of one volt produces a current of one ampere has a resistance of one ohm.

Parsec–Approximately 3.26 light-years or 19.2 million miles. Used for measuring interstellar distances.

Pi ($\pi$)–3.14159+. The ratio of the circumference of a circle to its diameter. The value is usually rounded to 3.1416

Pica–1/6 inch or 12 points. Used in printing for measuring column width, etc.

Point–0.013837 (approximately 1/72) inch or 1/12 pica.

Quire–25 sheets of paper.

Ream– 500 sheets of paper.

Roentgen–International unit of radiation exposure produced by X-rays.

Score–20 units.

Sound, speed of–1,088 ft per second at 32°F at sea level.

Span–9 inches or 22.86 cm.

Square–100 square feet. Used in building.

Therm–100,000 Btu's.

Tun–252 gallons, but often larger. Used for measuring wine and other liquids.

Watt–Unit of power. The power used by a current of one ampere across a potential difference of one volt equals one watt.

# Public Library Reference Contacts

THE LIBRARIES LISTED BELOW are delighted to answer almost any question by phone. Librarians are usually able to find the answer to a question in just a few minutes—longer searches may require a personal visit. The Brooklyn Business Library is an excellent source for business information, and the Honolulu library is great for after hours research.

| City | Phone |
| --- | --- |
| Atlanta | (404) 730-1700 |
| Baltimore | (410) 396-5430 |
| Boston | (617) 536-5400 |
| Brooklyn Business Library | (718) 722-3333 |
| Buffalo | (716) 858-8900 |
| Chicago | (312) 747-4090 |
| Cincinnati | (513) 369-6900 |
| Cleveland | (216) 623-2800 |
| Columbus | (614) 645-2800 |
| Dallas | (214) 670-1400 |
| Denver | (303) 640-8800 |
| Detroit | (313) 833-1000 |
| Hartford | (203) 293-6000 |
| Honolulu | (808) 586-3704 |
| Houston | (713) 247-2700 |
| Indianapolis | (317) 269-1700 |
| Jacksonville | (904) 630-1994 |
| Los Angeles | (310) 940-8462 |
| Memphis | (901) 725-8855 |
| Miami | (305) 375-2665 |

| City | Phone |
| --- | --- |
| Milwaukee | (414) 278-3020 |
| Minneapolis | (612) 372-6500 |
| Nashville | (615) 862-5800 |
| New Orleans | (504) 596-2550 |
| New York City | (212) 340-0849 |
| Norfolk | (804) 441-2887 |
| Orlando | (407) 425-4694 |
| Philadelphia | (215) 686-5300 |
| Phoenix | (602) 262-6451 |
| Pittsburgh | (412) 622-3100 |
| Portland, OR | (503) 248-5402 |
| St. Louis | (314) 241-2288 |
| Salt Lake City | (801) 943-4636 |
| San Antonio | (512) 299-7790 |
| San Deigo | (916) 440-5926 |
| San Francisco | (415) 557-4400 |
| Seattle | (206) 386-4100 |
| Tampa | (813) 223-8868 |
| Washington, DC | (202) 727-1101 |

# Industry Newsletters

## Advertising

*Ad Business Report*
Executive Communications
411 Lafayette St., Suite 3
New York, NY 10003
(212) 254-1823

*Ad Change*
Reed Reference Publishing
129 Chanolin Rd.
New Providence, NJ 07974
(800) 521-8110

*AD/PR Agency Report*
Pen & Inc.
P.O. Box 5350
Woodland Hills, CA 91364
(818) 222-6262

*Briefings*
National Business Services
1120 Wheeler Way
Langhorne, PA 19047
(215) 752-4200

*Broadcast Investor Charts*
Paul Kagan Associates
126 Clock Tower Pl.
Carmel, CA 93923
(408) 624-1536

*Broadcast Stats*
Paul Kagan Associates
126 Clock Tower Pl.
Carmel, CA 93923
(408) 624-1536

*Bulldog Reporter*
InfoCom
2115 4th St.
Berkeley, CA 94710
(510) 549-4300

*Channels*
PR Publishing
P.O. Box 600
Exeter, NH 03833
(603) 778-0514

*Directory MarketPlace*
Todd Publications
18 N. Greenbush Rd.
West Nyack, NY 10994
(914) 358-6213

*Levin's Public Relations Report*
Levin Public Relations & Marketing
30 Glenn St.
White Plains, NY 10603
(914) 993-0900

*Media Industry Newsletter*
Phillips Publishing
305 Madison Ave., Suite 4417
New York, NY 10165
(212) 983-5170

*Media Matters*
Media Dynamics
18 E. 41st St., Suite 1806
New York, NY 10017
(212) 683-7895

*The Multinational PR Report*
Pigafetta Press
P.O. Box 39244
Washington, DC 20016
(202) 244-2580

*The Nido Qubein Letter*
Creative Services
P.O. Box 6008
High Point, NC 27262
(919) 889-3010

*On Achieving Excellence*
Tom Peters Group
555 Hamilton Ave., Suite 500
Palo Alto, CA 94301
(800) 367-4310

*Partyline, The PR Media Newsletter*
Partyline Publishing
35 Sutton Pl.
New York, NY 10022
(212) 755-3487

*Peak Performance Selling*
Bureau of Business Practice
24 Rope Ferry Rd.
Waterford, CT 06386
(203) 442-4365

*PR Marcom Jobs West*
Rachel PR Services
513 Wilshire Blvd., Suite 238
Santa Monica, CA 90401
(310) 326-2661

*PR Reporter*
PR Publishing
P.O. Box 600
Exeter, NH 03833
(603) 778-0514

*Industry Newsletters (cont'd)*

*The Pricing Advisor*
3277 Roswell Rd., Suite 620
Atlanta, GA 30305
(404) 252-5708

*Public Relations News*
Phillips Business Information
1201 Seven Locks Rd.
Potomac, MD 20854
(800) 777-5006

*Publisher's Multinational Direct*
Direct International
150 E. 74th St.
New York, NY 10021
(212) 861-4188

*Radio Business Report*
P.O. Box 782
Springfield, VA 22150
(703) 866-9300

*Television & Radio Newsletter*
Restivo Communications
107 S. West St., Suite 199
Alexandria, VA 22314
(703) 793-5226

*Tested Copy*
Starch INRA Hooper
566 E. Boston Post Rd.
Mamaroneck, NY 10543
(914) 698-0800

*Video Marketing News*
Phillips Publishing
1201 Seven Locks Rd.
Potomac, MD 20854
(301) 340-2100

## Air Travel

*Airline Newsletter*
Roadcap Aviation Publications
1030 S. Green Bay
Lake Forest, IL 60045
(708) 234-4730

*Airport Highlights*
Airport Operators Council International
1775 K St., NW, Suite 500
Washington, DC 20006
(202) 293-8500

*Aviation Daily*
McGraw-Hill
1200 G St., Suite 200
Washington, DC 20005
(202) 383-2369

*The Business Flyer*
Holcon
P.O. Box 276
Newton Centre, MA 02159
(203) 782-2155 or
(800) 359-3774

## Automobiles

*Automotive Parts International*
International Trade Services
P.O. Box 5950
Bethesda, MD 20814
(202) 857-8454

*Automotive Week*
Automotive Week Publishing
P.O. Box 3495
Wayne, NJ 07474
(201) 694-7792; 6076

*Car Rental/Leasing Insider*
United Communications Group
11300 Rockville Pike, Suite 1100
Rockville, MD 20852
(301) 816-8950

## Banking

*Bank Bailout Litigation News*
Buraff Publications
1350 Connecticut Ave., NW, Suite 1000
Washington, DC 20036
(202) 862-0990

*Bank Mergers & Acquisitions*
SNL Securities LP
P.O. Box 2124
Charlottesville, VA 22902
(804) 977-1600

*Bank Securities Monthly*
SNL Securities LP
P.O. Box 2124
Charlottesville, VA 22902
(804) 977-1600

*Eximbank Letter*
International Business Affairs
4938 Hampden Ln., #346
Bethesda, MD 20814
(301) 907-8647

## Business Law

*Antitrust FOIA Log*
Washington Regulatory Reporting Assocs.
P.O. Box 356
Basye, VA 22810
(703) 856-2216

*Industry Newsletters (cont'd)*

*Bankruptcy Alert*
155 Pfingsten Rd.
Deerfield, IL 60015
(800) 323-1336

*Bankruptcy Law Letter*
Warren, Gorham & Lamont
31 St. James Ave.
Boston, MA 02116
(800) 950-1205

*BNA's Bankruptcy Law Reporter*
Bureau of National Affairs
1231 25th St., NW
Washington, DC 20037
(202) 452-4200

*BNA's Corporate Counsel Weekly*
Bureau of National Affairs
1231 25th St., NW
Washington, DC 20037
(202) 452-4200

*BNA's Patent, Trademark & Copyright Journal*
Bureau of National Affairs
1231 25th St., NW
Washington, DC 20037
(202) 452-4200

*Cable TV and New Media Law & Finance*
Leader Publications
345 Park Ave S.
New York, NY 10010
(212) 779-9200

*Futures Law Letter*
Commodities Law Press Associates
40 Broad St., Suite 2000
New York, NY 10004
(212) 612-9545

*Commodities Litigation Reporter*
Andrews Publications
P.O. Box 1000
Westtown, PA 19395
(215) 399-6600

*Corporate Control Alert*
American Lawyer Media
600 3rd Ave., 3rd Floor
New York, NY 10016
(212) 973-2800

*Europe 1992 Law & Strategy*
Leader Publications
345 Park Ave. S.
New York, NY 10010
(212) 779-9200

*FTC:Watch-FTC Freedom Of Information Log*
Washington Regulatory Reporting Assocs.
P.O. Box 356
Bayse, VA 22810
(703) 856-2216 or
(703) 856-8331

*Indoor Pollution Law Report*
Leader Publications
345 Park Ave. S.
New York, NY 10010
(212) 779-9200

*Liability Reporter*
Americans for Effective Law Enforcement
5519 N. Cumberland Ave., Suite 1008
Chicago, IL 60656
(312) 763-2800

*Licensing Law and Business Report*
155 Pfingsten Rd.
Deerfield, IL 60015
(800) 221-9428

*Manager's Legal Bulletin*
Alexander Hamilton Institute
70 Hilltop Rd.
Ramsay, NJ 07446
(201) 825-3377

*National Bankruptcy Litigation Reporter*
Andrews Publications
P.O. Box 1000
Westtown, PA 19395
(215) 399-6600

*Product Safety Letter*
Washington Business Information
1117 N. 19th St., Suite 200
Arlington, VA 22209
(703) 247-3423

*Product Safety News*
Institute for Product Safety
P.O. Box 1931
Durham, NC 27702
(919) 489-2357

*Securities Regulation & Law Report*
Bureau of National Affairs
1231 25th St., NW
Washington, DC 20037
(202) 452-4200

*Work In America*
Buraff Publications
1350 Connecticut Ave., NW, Suite 1000
Washington, DC 20036
(202) 862-0990

*Industry Newsletters (cont'd)*

*Worker's Compensation Law Bulletin*
Quinlan Publishing Company
131 Beverly St.
Boston, MA 02114
(617) 542-0048

*You & The Law*
National Institute of Business Management
P.O. Box 25287
Alexandria, VA 22313
(800) 543-2055

## Cellular Phones

*Cellular Technology*
Paul Kagan Associates
126 Clock Tower Pl.
Carmel, CA 93923
(408) 624-1536

## Collectibles

*Car Collecting & Investing*
Insightful Investor
175 Great Neck Rd., Suite 307
Great Neck, NY 11021
(516) 466-7788

*Connoisseur's Guide to California Wines*
P.O. Box V
Alameda, CA 94501
(510) 865-3150

*Jukebox Collector Newsletter*
2545 S.E. 60th Ct.
Des Moines, IA 50317
(515) 265-8324

*Kovels on Antiques and Collectibles*
P.O. Box 420235
Palm Coast, FL 32142
(800) 829-9158

*The Photograph Collector*
Photographic Arts Center
163 Amsterdam Ave., Suite 201
New York, NY 10023
(212) 838-8640

*The Print Collector's Newsletter*
119 E. 79th St.
New York, NY 10021
(212) 988-5959

*The Rosen Numismatic Advisory*
Numismatic Counseling
P.O. Box 38
Plainview, NY 11803
(516) 433-5800

*The Wine Investor/Buyer's Guide*
Wine Investor
3284 Barham Blvd., Suite 201
Los Angeles, CA 90068
(213) 876-7590

*The Wine Investor-Executive Edition*
3284 Barham Blvd., Suite 201
Los Angeles, CA 90068
(213) 876-7590

## Colleges

*Administrator: The Management Newsletter
for Higher Education*
Magna Publications
2718 Dryden Dr.
Madison, WI 53704
(608) 246-3580

*MBA Newsletter*
79 Verbena Ave.
Floral Park, NY 11001
(516) 488-2010

## Communications

*Communications Daily*
Warren Publishing
2115 Ward Ct., NW
Washington, DC 20037
(202) 872-9200

*Communications Industries Report*
Int'l Communications Industries Association
3150 Spring St.
Fairfax, VA 22031
(703) 273-7200

*Communications Product Reports*
Management Information
P.O. Box 5062
1111 Marlkress Rd.
Cherry Hill, NJ 08003
(609) 424-1100

*Current News on File*
Facts on File
460 Park Ave. S.
New York, NY 10016
(212) 683-2244

*Disaster Trends Update*
QW Communications
P.O. Box 6591
Concord, NH 03303
(603) 648-2629

*Trends in Communications Policy*
Economics and Technology
1 Washington Mall
Boston, MA 02108
(617) 227-0900

*Industry Newsletters (cont'd)*

## Computers

*Computer & Communications Buyer*
Technology News of America
110 Greene St.
New York, NY 10012
(212) 334-9750

*Computer Industry Report*
International Data
P.O. Box 955
5 Speen St.
Framingham, MA 01701
(508) 872-8200

*Computer Price Guide*
Computer Merchants
22 Saw Mill River Rd.
Hawthorne, NY 10532
(914) 592-1060

*Electronic Services Update*
Link Resources
79 5th Ave.
New York, NY 10003
(212) 627-1500

*Information Industry Alert*
Industry News Service
P.O. Box 457
Wilton, CT 06897
(203) 762-3206

*Information Industry Bulletin*
Digital Information Group
P.O. Box 110235
Stamford, CT 06911
(203) 348-2751

*ISDN News*
Phillips Business Information
1201 Seven Locks Rd.
Potomac, MD 20854
(301) 340-2100

*National Report on Computers & Health*
United Communications Group
11300 Rockville Pike, Suite 1000
Rockville, MD 20852
(301) 816-8950

*Packaged Software Reports*
Management Information
PO Box 5062
401 E. Rte. 70
Cherry Hill, NJ 08034
(609) 428-1020

*Software Digest*
National Software Testing Laboratories
Plymouth Corporate Center, Box 1000
Plymouth Meeting, PA 19462
(215) 941-9600

*Software Industry Bulletin*
Digital Information Group
51 Bank St.
Stamford, CT 06901
(203) 348-2751

*Software-Industry Report*
Millin Publishing Group
3918 Prosperity Ave., Suite 310
Fairfax, VA 22031
(703) 573-8400

*Word Processing: Quality Clinic*
Bureau of Business Practice
24 Rope Ferry Rd.
Waterford, CT 06386
(203) 442-4365

## Construction

*Construction Market Data*
4126 Pleasantdale Rd.
Atlanta, GA 30340
(404) 447-6633

*Economic Development*
Wakeman/Walworth
300 N. Washington St., Suite 204
Alexandria, VA 22314
(703) 549-8606

## Consulting

*Consulting Opportunities Journal*
Consultants National Resource Center
P.O. Box 430
Clear Spring, MD 21722
(301) 791-9332

*Management Consultant International*
Lafferty Publications
420 Lexington Ave., Suite 1745
New York, NY 10170
(212) 557-6729

*Professional Consultant &
Information Marketing Report*
123 N.W. 2nd Ave., Suite 403
Portland, OR 97209
(503) 224-8834

## Consumer Trends

*Buying Strategy Forecast*
Cahners Publishing
275 Washington St.
Newton, MA 02158
(617) 964-3030

*Industry Newsletters (cont'd)*

*Consumer Trends*
Interantional Credit Association
243 N. Lindbergh Blvd.
St Louis, MO 63141
(314) 991-3030

*Shopper Report*
Consumer Network
3624 Market St.
Philadelphia, PA 19104
(215) 386-5890

## Credit

*Credit Risk Management Report*
Phillips Business Information
1201 Seven Locks Rd.
Potomac, MD 20854
(301) 340-2100

## Dangerous Substances

*Job Safety and Health*
Bureau of National Affairs
1231 25th St., NW
Washington, DC 20037
(202) 452-4200

## Economic Indicators

*Blue Chip Economic Indicators*
Capitol Publications
1101 King St., Suite 444
Alexandria, VA 22314
(703) 683-4100

*Charting the Economy*
P.O. Box 829
New Haven, CT 06504
(203) 666-8664

*Economic Education Bulletin*
American Institute for Economic Research
Division St.
Great Barrington, MA 01230
(413) 528-1216

*Inside the Economy*
Statistical Indicator Associates
P.O. Box 187
North Egremont, MA 01252
(413) 528-3280

## Electronic Mail

*Electronic Messaging News*
Phillips Business Information
1201 Seven Locks Rd.
Potomac, MD 20854
(301) 340-2100

*EMMS–Electronic Mail &Message Systems*
Telecom Reports
65 Bleecker St., 5th Floor
New York, NY 10012
(202) 842-0520

*ISDN Newsletter*
Information Gatekeepers
214 Harvard Ave.
Boston, MA 02134
(617) 232-3111 or
(800) 323-1088

## Facsimile

*Facsimile and Voice Services*
Probe Research
3 Wing Dr., Suite 240
Cedar Knolls, NJ 07927
(201) 285-1500

*Fax Reporter*
Buyers Laboratory
20 Railroad Ave.
Hackensack , NJ 07601
(201) 488-0404

*Faxpaper*
Hartford Courant
285 Broad St.
Hartford, CT 06115
(203) 241-6200

## Electronics

*Henderson Electronic Market Forecast*
Henderson Ventures
101 1st St., #444
Los Altos, CA 94022
(415) 961-2900

*Industrial Communications*
Phillips Business Inormation
1201 Seven Locks Rd.
Potomac, MD 20854
(301) 340-2100

## Environment

*Business & The Environment*
Cutter Information
37 Broadway
Arlington, MA 02174
(617) 648-8700

*Environment Report*
Trends Publishing
1079 National Press Building
Washington, DC 20045
(202) 393-0031

*Industry Newsletters (cont'd)*

*Environment Reporter*
Bureau of National Affairs
1231 25th St., NW
Washington, DC 20037
(202) 452-4200

*Environmental Manager*
Executive Enterprises
22 W. 21st St., 10th Floor
New York, NY 10010
(212) 645-7880

*Environmental Manager's Compliance Advisor*
Business & Legal Reports
39 Academy St.
Madison, CT 06443
(203) 245-7448

## Finance

*Accounting & Tax Highlights*
Warren Gorham & Lamont
31 St. James Ave.
Boston, MA 02116
(800) 950-1216

*The Advisory Letter for Concerned Investors*
Franklin Research and Development
1711 Atlantic Ave., 5th Floor
Boston, MA 02111
(617) 423-6655

*Blue Chip Financial Forecasts*
Capitol Publications
1101 King St., Suite 444
Alexandria, VA 22314
(703) 683-4100

*Bondweek*
Institutional Investor
488 Madison Ave., 16th Floor
New York, NY 10022
(212) 303-3233

*Buy Low–Sell High*
Securities Investment Management
1224 Vallecita Dr.
Santa Fe, NM 87501
(505) 989-9224

*Commodity Price Charts*
Futures Magazine
P.O. Box 6
219 Parkade
Cedar Falls, IA 50613
(319) 277-6341

*CPA Digest*
CPA Services
16800 W. Greenfield Ave.
Brookfield, WI 53005
(414) 797-9999

*The CPA Letter*
American Institute of CPAs
1211 Ave. of the Americas
New York, NY 10036
(212) 596-6200

*Financial Market Trends*
Organization for Economic
Cooperation and Development
2001 L St., NW, Suite 700
Washington, DC 20036
(202) 785-6323

*Futures Market Service*
Knight-Ridder Financial Publishing
P.O. Box 94513
Chicago, IL 60690
(800) 621-5271

*GOOD MONEY Newsletter*
Good Money Publications
P.O. Box 363
Worcester, VT 05682
(800) 535-3551

*IBC/Donoghue's Quarterly Report on Money Fund Performance*
P.O. Box 91004
290 Eliot St.
Ashland, MA 01721
(508) 881-2800 or
(800) 343-5413

*Investment Guide*
American Investment Services
Division St.
Great Barrington, MA 02130
(413) 528-1216

*IRS Practice Alert*
Warren Gorham & Lamont
31 St. James Ave.
Boston, MA 02116
(800) 922-0066

*The Jacobs Report on Asset Protection Strategies*
Research Press
4500 W. 72nd Terrace
Shawnee Mission, KS 66208
(913) 362-9667

*Letters of Credit Report*
Executive Enterprises
22 W. 21st St., 10th Floor
New York, NY 10010
(212) 645-7880

*Long Term Investing*
Concept Publishing
P.O. Box 203
York, NY 14592
(716) 243-3148

*Industry Newsletters (cont'd)*

*Making Ends Meet*
Pascit Publications
P.O. Box 1125
Traverse City, MI 49685
(616) 929-7227

*Marketing Timing Report*
P.O. Box 225
Tucson, AZ 85702
(602) 795-9552

*Marple's Business Newsletter*
Newsletter Publishing
117 W. Mercer St., Suite 200
Seattle, WA 98119
(206) 281-9609

*Mutual Fund Investing*
Phillips Publishing
1201 Seven Locks Rd.
Potomac, MD 20854
(301) 340-2100

*O.T.C. Growth Stock Watch*
O.T.C. Research
1040 Great Plain Ave.
Needham, MA 02192
(617) 444-6100

*Penny Stocks Newsletter*
31731 Outer Highway 10
Redlands, CA 92373
(909) 794-0313

*Plain Talk Investor*
1500 Skokie Blvd., #203
Northbrook, IL 60062
(708) 564-1955

*Platinum Perspective*
Henry Gammage & Co.
2846 Redding Rd.
Atlanta, GA 30319
(404) 261-7744

*Real Estate Tax Ideas*
Warren Gorham & Lamont
31 St. James Ave.
Boston, MA 02116
(617) 423-2026 or
(800) 950-1205

*The Review of Securities & Commodities Regulation*
Standard & Poor's
25 Broadway
New York, NY 10004
(212) 208-8650

*SEC Today*
Washington Service Bureau
655 15th St., NW
Washington, DC 20005
(202) 508-0600

*Securities Week*
McGraw-Hill
1221 Avenue of the Americas
New York, NY 10020
(212) 997-3144

*The Small Business Tax Review*
A/N Group
17 Scott Dr.
Melville, NY 11747
(516) 549-4090

*The Tax Adviser*
Harborside Financial Center
201 Plaza III
Jersey City, NJ 07311
(201) 938-3447

*Taxwise Money*
Agora
824 E. Baltimore St.
Baltimore, MD 21202
(410) 234-0691

*Tax Haven Reporter*
Thomas P. Azzara
P.O. Box CB 11552
Nassau, Bahamas
(809) 327-7359

*Tax Management Compensation Planning Journal*
*Tax Management Estates, Gifts and Trusts Journal*
*Tax Management Financial Planning*
*Tax Management Financial Planning Journal*
*Tax Management Foreign Income Portfolios*
*Tax Management International Journal*
*Tax Management Real Estate Journal*
*Tax Management Washington Tax Review*
Tax Management
1231 23rd St., NW
Washington, DC 20037
(202) 833-7240

*Technical Trends*
P.O. Box 792
Wilton, CT 06897
(203) 762-0229 or
(800) 736-0229

## General Business

*Association's Report*
Galloway Publications
2940 N.W. Circle Blvd.
Corvallis, OR 97330
(503) 754-7464

*The Bruce Report*
Bruce Consulting Group
2865 Broderick
San Francisco, CA 94123
(415) 346-7230

*Industry Newsletters (cont'd)*

*Business & Acquisition Newsletter*
Newsletters International
2600 S. Gessner Rd.
Houston, TX 77063
(713) 783-0100

*Business Ideas*
Dan Newman
1051 Bloomfield Ave.
Clifton, NJ 07012
(201) 778-6677

*Homebased Business News Report*
1151 N.E. Todd George Rd.
Lee's Summit, MO 64086
(816) 525-4484

*Business Newsletter*
Business Newsletter
537 E. Vine St.
Owatonna, MN 55060
(507) 455-3220

*The Business Publisher*
JK Publishing
P.O. Box 71020
Milwaukee, WI 53211
(414) 332-1625

*BusinessGram*
BusinessGram
P.O. Box 273390
Tampa, FL 33688
(813) 968-2979

*Economic Development*
Wakeman/Walworth
300 N. Washington St., Suite 204
Alexandria, VA 22314
(703) 549-8606

*The Entrepreneurial Economy*
Corporation for Enterprise Development
777 N. Capital St., NE, #801
Washington, DC 20002
(202) 408-9788

*Forecaster*
Forecaster Pub
19623 Ventura Blvd.
Tarzana, CA 91356
(818) 345-4421

*General Trends–From the State Capitals*
Wakeman/Walworth
300 N. Washington St., Suite 204
Alexandria, VA 22314
(703) 549-8606

*Global Report*
Center for War/Peace Studies
218 E. 18th St.
New York, NY 10003
(212) 475-1077

*Industry Forecast*
Jerome Levy Economic Institute of Bard College
P.O. Box 26
223 N. Greeley Ave.
Chappaqua, NY 10514
(914) 238-3665

*The Main Report Business & Executive Letter*
Main Report Publications
P.O. Box 1046
47 Birmingham Dr.
Christchurch, New Zealand 8000
[64] 3-338-6068

*The TJFR Business News Reporter*
TJFR Publishing
545 N. Maple Ave., 2nd Floor
Ridgewood, NJ 07450
(201) 444-6061

*Working Smart*
National Institute of Business Management
P.O. Box 25287
Alexandria, VA 22313
(800) 543-2049

*The Yellow Sheet*
Communications Management
13523 Barrett Parkway Dr., Suite 221
Ballwin, MO 63021
(314) 882-0555

## Gold and Precious Metals

*The Powell Gold Industry Guide*
Reserve Research
P.O. Box 4135, Station A
Portland, ME 04101
(207) 774-4971

*Precious Metals Data Base*
Moneypower
P.O. Box 22644
Minneapolis, MN 55422
(612) 537-8096

## Graphics

*Board Report For Graphic Artists*
P.O. Box 300789
Denver, CO 80203
(717) 774-5413

*Industry Newsletters (cont'd)*

*Plus Business*
Metro Creative Graphics
33 W. 34th St.
New York, NY 10001
(212) 947-5100

## Health

*Benefits Today*
Bureau of National Affairs
1231 25th St., NW
Washington, DC 20037
(202) 452-4200

*Employee Assistance Program Management Letter*
American Business Publishing
3100 Hwy. 138
P.O. Box 1442
Wall Township, NJ 07719
(908) 681-1133

*Employee Health & Fitness*
American Health Consultants
P.O. Box 740056
Atlanta, GA 30374
(404) 262-7436

*The Executive Report on Managed Care*
American Business Publishing
3100 Highway 138
P.O. Box 1442
Wall Township, NJ 07719
(908) 681-1133

*OSHA Compliance Advisor (OCA)*
Business & Legal Reports
39 Academy St.
Madison, CT 06443
(203) 245-7448

*OSHA Compliance Advisor
(with Encyclopedia) (OCB)*
Business & Legal Reports
39 Academy St.
Madison, CT 06443
(203) 245-7448

*Safety Compliance Letter*
Bureau of Business Practice
24 Rope Ferry Rd.
Waterford, CT 06386
(203) 442-4365

## Human Resources

*Coursetrends*
Learning Resources Network
1554 Hayes Dr.
Manhattan, KS 66502
(913) 539-5376

*Creative Training Techniques*
Lakewood Publications
50 S. Ninth St.
Minneapolis, MN 55402
(612) 333-0471

*Discipline and Grievances*
Bureau of Business Practice
24 Rope Ferry Rd.
Waterford, CT 06386
(203) 442-4365

*EEOC Compliance Manual*
Bureau of National Affairs
1231 25th St., NW
Washington, DC 20037
(202) 452-4200

*Employee Assistance Program Management Letter*
American Business Publishing
3100 Highway 138
P.O. Box 1442
Wall Township, NJ 07719
(908) 681-1133

*Employee Benefit Notes*
Employee Benefit Research Institute
2121 K St., NW, Suite 600
Washington, DC 20037
(202) 659-0670

*Employee Benefits Cases*
Bureau of National Affairs
1231 25th St., NW
Washington, DC 20037
(202) 452-4200

*Employee Relations and Human Resources Bulletin*
Bureau of Business Practice
24 Rope Ferry Rd.
Waterford, CT 06386
(800) 243-0876

*Employee Security Connection*
National Security Institute
57 E. Main St., Suite 217
Westbourough, 01581
(508) 366-5800

*Employers' Health Benefits Management Letter*
American Business Publishing
3100 Hwy. 138
P.O. Box 1442
Wall Township, NJ 07719
(908) 681-1133

*Equal Employment Compliance Update*
Callaghan & Co.
155 Pfingsten Rd.
Deerfield, IL 60015
(708) 948-7000 or
(800) 323-1336

*Industry Newsletters (cont'd)*

*Fair Employment Practices*
Bureau of National Affairs
1231 25th St., NW
Washington, DC 20037
(202) 452-4200

*Government Employee Relations Report*
Bureau of National Affairs
1231 25th St., NW
Washington, DC 20047
(202) 452-4200

*Hiring & Firing*
Carswell
2075 Kennedy Rd.
Scarborough, Ontario Canada MIT 3V4
(416) 609-3800

*Individual Employment Rights*
Bureau of National Affairs
1231 25th St., NW
Washington, DC 20037
(202) 452-4200

*Job Finder*
Western Governmental Research Association
10900 Los Alamitos Blvd., Suite 201
Los Alamitos, CA 90720
(310) 795-6694

*The Office Professional*
Professional Training Associates
210 Commerce Blvd.
Round Rock, TX 78664
(512) 255-6006

*The Personnel Alert*
Alexander Hamilton Institute
70 Hilltop Rd.
Ramsay, NJ 07446
(201) 825-3377

*Personnel Management*
Bureau of National Affairs
1231 25th St., NW
Washington, DC 20037
(202) 452-4200

*Personnel Update*
Dartnell
4660 N. Ravenswood Ave.
Chicago, IL 60640
(312) 561-4000

*PPF Survey (Personnel Policies Forum)*
Bureau of National Affairs
1231 25th St., NW
Washington, DC 20037
(202) 452-4200

*Recruitment and Retention*
Magna Publications
2718 Dryden Dr.
Madison, WI 53704
(608) 246-3580

*Training & Development Alert*
Advanced Personnel Systems
P.O. Box 1438
Roseville, CA 95678
(916) 781-2900; 2901

*Wages and Hours*
Bureau of National Affairs
1231 25th St., NW
Washington, DC 20037
(202) 452-4200

*What To Do About Personnel
Problems In (your state)*
Business & Legal Reports
39 Academy St.
Madison, CT 06443
(203) 245-7448

*What's Ahead in Human Resources*
Remy Publishing
350 W. Hubbard
Chicago, IL 60610
(312) 464-0300

*Work in America*
Buraff Publications
1350 Connecticut Ave., NW, Suite 1000
Washington, DC 20036
(202) 862-0990

## International

*Business Asia*
Economists Intelligence Unit
111 W. 57th St.
New York, NY 10019
(212) 554-0600

*East-West Technology Digest*
Welt Publishing
1413 K St., NW, Suite 800
Washington, DC 20005
(202) 371-0555

*Government Business Reports Worldwide*
P.O. Box 5997
Washington, DC 20016
(202) 244-7050

*The Harriman Institute Forum*
Harriman Institute, Columbia University
420 W. 118th St., 5th Floor
New York, NY 10027
(212) 854-6218

*Industry Newsletters (cont'd)*

*Inside US Trade*
Inside Washington Publishers
P.O. Box 7167, Ben Franklin Station
Washington, DC 20044
(703) 416-8500

*International Information Report*
Washington Researchers Publishing
2000 P St., Suite 301
Washington, DC 20036
(202) 333-3533

*International Money & Politics*
MM
420 S. Orlando Ave.
Winter Park, FL 32789
(407) 629-9229

*International Trade and Investment Letter*
International Business Affairs
4938 Hampden Ln., Suite 346
Bethesda, MD 20814
(301) 907-8647

*International Trade Reporter Current Reports*
Bureau of National Affairs
1231 25th St., NW
Washington, DC 20037
(202) 452-4200

*Japan Financial Market Report*
Japan Market Research
609 Columbus Ave.
New York, NY 10024
(212) 496-6760

*Major Trends*
250 W. Coventry Ct.
Milwaukee, WI 53217
(414) 352-8460

*Market Europe*
W-Two Publications
202 The Commons, Suite 401
Ithaca, NY 14850
(607) 277-0934

*Mideast Report*
P.O. Box 2460, Grand Central Station
New York, NY 10163
(212) 714-3530

*Near East Report*
Near East Research
440 1st St., NW, Suite 607
Washington, DC 20001
(202) 639-5254

*Random Lengths Export Market Report*
Random Lengths Publications
P.O. Box 867
Eugene, OR 97440
(503) 686-9925

*Washington Export Letter*
International Business Affairs
4938 Hampden Ln., Suite 346
Bethesda, MD 20814
(301) 907-8647

*Washington Tariff & Trade Letter*
Gilston Communications Group
P.O. Box 467
Washington, DC 20044
(301) 570-4544

## Literacy

*Report on Literacy Programs*
Business Publishers
951 Pershing Dr.
Silver Spring, MD 20910
(301) 587-6300

## Management

*Academy of Management News*
Administration 3-17
Northeast Louisiana University
Monroe, LA 71209
(318) 342-1210

*Administration & Management*
National Technical Information Service
U.S. Department of Commerce
5285 Port Royal Rd.
Springfield, VA 22161
(703) 487-4630

*Advanced Management Report, English &
International*
Advanced Management Publishers
1357 Washington St.
Newton, MA 02165
(617) 964-5080

*Applied Management Newsletter*
National Association for Management
1617 Murray
Wichita, KS 67212
(316) 721-4684

*BNA's Employee Relations Weekly*
Bureau of National Affairs
1231 25th St., NW
Washington, DC 20037
(202) 452-4200

*Collective Bargaining Negotiations and Contracts*
Bureau of National Affairs
1231 25th St., NW
Washington, DC 20037
(202) 452-4200

*Industry Newsletters (cont'd)*

*Employer Advocate*
Independent Small Business Employers
520 S. Pierce, Suite 224
Mason City, IA 50401
(515) 424-3187

*The Entrepreneurial Manager's Newsletter*
Center for Entrepreneurial Management
180 Varick St., Penthouse
New York, NY 10014
(212) 633-0060

*From Nine To Five*
Dartnell
4660 N. Ravenswood Ave.
Chicago , IL 60640
(312) 561-4000

*Labor Notes*
Labor Education & Research Project
7435 Michigan Ave.
Detroit, MI 48210
(313) 842-6262

*Labor Relations*
Bureau of National Affairs
1231 25th St., NW
Washington, DC 20037
(202) 452-4200

*Labor Relations Reporter*
Bureau of National Affairs
1231 25th St., NW
Washington, DC 20037
(202) 452-4200

*Labor Relations–From The State Capitals*
Wakeman/Walworth
300 N. Washington St., Suite 204
Alexandria, VA 22314
(703) 549-8606

*Management Confidential*
Stonehart Publications
57-61 Mortimer St.
London, England W1N 7TD
[44] 81-597-7335

*Management Letter*
Bureau of Business Practice
24 Rope Ferry Rd.
Waterford, CT 06386
(203) 442-4365

*Management Matters*
Infoteam
P.O. Box 15640
Plantation, FL 33318
(305) 473-9560

*Management Report*
Executive Enterprises
22 W. 21st St., 10th Floor
New York, NY 10010
(212) 645-7880

*OSHA Compliance Advisor*
Business & Legal Reports
39 Academy St.
Madison, CT 06443
(203) 245-7448

*Union Labor Report*
Bureau of National Affairs
1231 25th St., NW
Washington, DC 20037
(202) 452-4200

*Update: The Executive's Purchasing Advisor*
Buyers Laboratory
20 Railroad Ave.
Hackensack, NJ 07601
(201) 488-0404

## Manufacturing

*American Industry*
Publications for Industry
21 Russell Woods Rd.
Great Neck, NY 11021
(516) 487-0990

*Industrial Purchasing Agent*
Publications for Industry
21 Russell Woods Rd.
Great Neck, NY 11021
(516) 487-0990

*Inside R&D*
Technical Insights
P.O. Box 1304
Fort Lee, NJ 07024
(201) 568-4744

*Quality Assurance Bulliten*
Bureau of Business Practice
24 Rope Ferry Rd.
Waterford, CT 06386
(203) 442-4635

## Marketing

*American Marketplace*
Business Publishers
951 Pershing Dr.
Silver Spring, MD 20910
(301) 587-6300

*Business Mailers Review*
1813 Shepherd St., NW
Washington, DC 20011
(202) 723-3397

*Industry Newsletters (cont'd)*

*Dartnell Sales and Marketing Executive Report*
Dartnell
4660 N. Ravenswood Ave.
Chicago, IL 60640
(312) 561-4000

*Frohlinger's Marketing Report*
Marketing Strategist Communications
7 Coppell Dr.
Tenafly, NJ 07670
(800) 962-7538 or
(201) 567-4447

*The Information Report*
Washington Researchers Publishing
2000 P St., NW, Suite 301
Washington, DC 20036
(202) 333-3533

*Inside Mass Marketing*
IMM Marketing Group
200 Boylston St., Suite 126
Chestnut Hill, MA 02167
(617) 969-4700

*Jack O'Dwyer's Newsletter*
J.R. O'Dwyer
271 Madison Ave.
New York, NY 10016
(212) 679-2471

*John Naisbitt's Trend Letter*
The Global Network
1101 30th St., NW, Suite 130
Washington, DC 20007
(202) 337-5960

*Marketing Breakthroughs*
World Business Publications
4th Floor, Britannia House
960 High Rd.
London, N12 9RY England
[44] 81-446-5141

*Marketing Insights*
WPI Communications
55 Morris Ave.
Springfield, NJ 07081
(800) 323-4995

*The Marketing Pulse*
Unlimited Positive Communications
11 N. Chestnut St.
New Paltz, NY 12561
(914) 255-2222, ext. 3130

## Marketing to Women

*About Women*
33 Broad St.
Boston, MA 02109
(617) 723-4337

*Marketing Update*
Predicasts
11001 Cedar Ave.
Cleveland, OH 44106
(216) 795-3000

*Professional Telephone Selling*
Bureau of Business Practice
24 Rope Ferry Rd.
Waterford, CT 06386
(203) 442-4365 or
(800) 243-0876

*Public Pulse*
Roper Organization
205 E. 42nd St.
New York, NY 10017
(212) 599-0700

*School Marketing Newsletter*
School Market Research Institute
P.O. Box 10
1721 Saybrook Rd.
Haddam, CT 06438
(203) 345-4018

*The SpeciaList's MarketPulse*
SpeciaLists
1200 Harbor Blvd., 9th Floor
Weehawken, NJ 07087
(201)865-5800

*TA Report*
Communications Trends
2 East Ave.
Larchmont, NY 10538
(914) 833-0600

*Telephone Selling Report*
Business By Phone
5301 S. 144th St.
Omaha, NE 68137
(402) 895-9399

## Miscellaneous

*Andrew Harper's Hideaway Report*
Harper Associates
P.O. Box 50
Sun Valley, ID 83353
(208) 622-3183

*Antitrust & Trade Regulation Report*
Bureau of National Affairs
1231 25th St., NW
Washington, DC 20037
(202) 452-4200

*Bottom Line Personal Incorporating*
*Privileged Information*
Boardroom Reports
330 W. 42nd St.
New York, NY 10036
(212) 239-9000

*Industry Newsletters (cont'd)*

*Business Information Alert*
Alert Publications
401 W. Fullerton Pkwy.
Chicago, IL 60614
(312) 525-7594

*Buyouts Newsletter*
Venture Economics
40 W. 57th St., 11th Floor
New York, NY 10019
(212) 765--5311

*Drugs In The Workplace*
Business Research Publications
65 Bleecker St., 5th Floor
New York, NY 10012
(212) 673-4700

*Executives' Digest*
Dartnell's Marketing Publications
286 Congress St.
Boston, MA 02110
(617) 451-7551 or
(800) 468-3038

*Hazardous Materials Transportation*
Washington Business Information
1117 N. 19th St., Suite 200
Arlington, VA 22209
(703) 247-3424

*Innovator's Digest*
Infoteam
P.O. Box 15640
Plantation, FL 33318
(305) 473-9560

*Kosher Business*
Kosher Business
P.O. Box 66136
Albany, NY 12206
(518) 438-9328

*The Licensing Journal*
GB Enterprises
P.O. Box 1169
Stamford, CT 06904
(203) 358-0848

*Metals Week*
McGraw-Hill
1221 Ave. of the Americas
New York, NY 10020
(212) 512-2823

*National Right To Work Newsletter*
8001 Braddock Rd.
Springfield, VA 22160
(703) 321-9820

*The Newsletter On Newsletters*
Newsletter Clearinghouse
P.O. Box 311
44 W. Market St.
Rhinebeck, NY 12572
(914) 876-2081

*Nutshell—A Digest of Employee Benefit Publications*
Country Press
P.O. Box 5880
Snowmass Village, CO 81615
(303) 923-3210

*The PresentFutures Report*
PresentFutures Group
101 Park Washington Ct.
Falls Church, VA 22046
(703) 538-6181

*Safety Management*
Bureau of Business Practice
24 Rope Ferry Rd.
Waterford, CT 06386
(203) 442-4365

*Taxation & Revenue Policies—From the State Capitals*
Wakeman/Walworth
300 N. Washington St., Suite 204
Alexandria, VA 22314
(703) 549-8606

*Tourist Business Promotion—From the State Capitals*
Wakeman/Walworth
300 N. Washington St., Suite 204
Alexandria, VA 22314
(703) 549-8606

*Travel Expense Management*
American Business Publishing
P.O. Box 1442
3100 Hwy. 138
Wall Township, NJ 07719
(908) 681-1133

*Washington Executive Travel Report*
1728 21st St., NW
Washington, DC 20009
(202) 328-0810

*The Worker's Compensation Review*
Carswell
2075 Kennedy Blvd.,
Scarborough, Ont. Canada M1T 3V4
(416) 609-3800

*Working At Home*
P.O. Box 200504
Cartersville, GA 30120
(404) 386-1257

*Industry Newsletters (cont'd)*

## Networking

*Linc: Linking Issue Networks for Cooperation*
Issue Action Publications
207 Lowdoin St., SE
Leesburg, VA 22075
(703) 777-8450

## Public Speaking

*The Executive Speechwriter Newsletter*
Words Ink
Emerson Falls
St. Johnsbury, VT 05819
(802) 748-4472

*Speechwriter's Newsletter*
Ragan Communications
212 W. Superior St., Suite 200
Chicago,, IL 60610
(312) 335-0037

## Publishing

*Publishing Trends & Trendsetters*
Oxbridge Communications
150 Fifth Ave.
New York, NY 10011
(212) 741-0231

## Real Estate

*Digest of State Land Sales Regulations*
Land Development Institute
1401 16th St., NW
Washington, DC 20036
(202) 232-2144

*Foreclosure Hotlist*
Foreclosure Research of America
P.O. Box 10236
Rockville, MD 20849
(301) 590-1177

*Housing Market Report*
CD Publications
8204 Fenton St., 2nd Floor
Silver Spring, MD 20910
(301) 588-6380

*Landlord–Tenant Relations Report*
CD Publications
8204 Fenton St., 2nd Floor
Silver Spring, MD 20910
(301) 588-6380

*Leasing Professional*
P.O. Box 5675
Scottsdale, AZ 85261
(602) 860-0659

*Managing Housing Letter*
CD Publications
8204 Fenton St., 2nd Floor
Silver Spring, MD 20910
(301) 588-6380

*People & Profits*
Lee Resources
P.O. Box 16711
Greenville, SC 29606
(800) 277-7888

*Professional Apartment Management*
Brownstone Publishers
149 5th Ave., 16th Floor
New York, NY 10010
(212) 473-8200

*Real Estate Digest*
InfoCom Group
2115 4th St.
Berkeley, CA 94710
(510) 549-4300

*Real Estate Insider*
Walker Communications
1541 Morris Ave.
Bronx, NY 10457
(718) 583-8060

*Real Estate Law Report*
Warren Gorham & Lamont
31 St. James Ave.
Boston, MA 02116
(800) 950-1205

*The Real Estate Tax Digest*
Matthew Bender & Co.
P.O. Box 22030
Albany, NY 12201
(800) 833-9844

*Span*
33300 Five Mile Rd., Suite 202
Livonia, MI 48154
(313) 422-6100

*Trade Dimensions*
236 Tresser Blvd., 5th Floor
Stamford, CT 06901
(203) 325-3500

## Reference

*Business Information From Your Public Library*
Administrator's Digest
P.O. Box 993
South San Francisco, CA 94080
(415) 573-5474

*Industry Newsletters (cont'd)*

*Census and You*
Superintendent of Documents
P.O. Box 371954
Pittsburgh, PA 15250
(202) 783-3238

*Current Events on File*
Facts on File
460 Park Ave. S.
New York, NY 10016
(212) 683-2244

*Home-Run-Business Newsletters*
IronGate Graphics
7627 Iron Gate Ln.
Frederick, MD 21702
(301) 473-4393

*The Morgan Report on Directory Publishing*
Morgan-Rand Publications
1800 Byberry St.
800 Mason's Mill II Business Park
Huntingdon Valley, PA 19006
(215) 938-5511

*Research Recommendations*
National Institute of Business Management
P.O. Box 25287
Alexandria, VA 22313
(800) 543-2051

## Sales

*Executive Compensation Report*
DP Publications
P.O. Box 7188
Fairfax Station, VA 22039
(703) 425-1322

*Professional Selling*
Bureau of Business Practice
24 Rope Ferry Rd.
Waterford, CT 06386
(203) 442-4365

*REP World*
Albee-Campbell
806 Penn Ave., Box 2087
Sinking Spring, PA 19608
(215) 678-3361

*Research Alert*
EPM Communications
488 E. 18th St.
Brooklyn, NY 11226
(718) 469-9330

*Sales Leads*
Sales Leads Publishing
705 Park Ave.
Lake Park, FL 33403
(407) 845-0133

*Sales Manager's Bulletin*
Bureau of Business Practice
24 Rope Ferry Rd.
Waterford, CT 06386
(203) 442-4365

*Salesman's Insider*
Marv Q. Modell Associates
P.O. Box 4111
Stanford, CA 94309
(408) 270-4526

*Salesmanship*
Dartnell
4660 N. Ravenswood Ave.
Chicago, IL 60640
(312) 561-4000

*Selling to Seniors*
CD Publications
8204 Fenton St., 2nd Floor
Silver Spring, MD 20910
(301) 588-6380

## Small Business

*SBANE Enterprise*
Smaller Business Association of
New England
204 2nd Ave.
Waltham, MA 02154
(617) 890-9070

## Venture Capital

*Venture Capital Journal*
Venture Economics
40 W. 57th St., 11th Floor
New York, NY 10019
(212) 765-5311

*Source: Almanac research and Hudson's Subscription Newsletter Directory*

## Recommended Resource

*Hudson's Subscription Newsletter Directory*
Hudson's, $118
(914) 876-2081

# Corporate Contact Directory

THE 1,000 MOST VALUABLE public companies in America, as ranked by *Business Week*.

| Rank | Company | Corporate Headquarters | Phone |
|---|---|---|---|
| 30 | Abbott Laboratories | One Abbott Park Rd., Abbott Park, IL 60064 | (708) 937-6100 |
| 818 | Acclaim Entertainment | 71 Audrey Ave., Oyster Bay, NY 11771 | (516) 624-8888 |
| 727 | Adaptec | 691 S. Milpitas Blvd., Milpitas, CA 95035 | (408) 945-8600 |
| 764 | ADC Telecommunications | 4900 W. 78th St., Minneapolis, MN 55435 | (612) 938-8080 |
| 634 | Adobe Systems | 1585 Charleston Rd., Mountain View, CA 94043 | (415) 961-4400 |
| 473 | Advanced Micro Devices | One AMD Pl., Sunnyvale, CA 94088 | (408) 732-2400 |
| 678 | Advanta | 300 Welsh Rd., Horsham, PA 19044 | (215) 657-4000 |
| 543 | AES | 1001 N. 19th St., Arlington, VA 22209 | (703) 522-1315 |
| 136 | Aetna Life & Casualty | 151 Farmington Ave., Hartford, CT 06156 | (203) 273-0123 |
| 331 | AFLAC | 1932 Wynnton Rd., Columbus, GA 31999 | (706) 323-3431 |
| 454 | Ahmanson (H.F.) | 4900 Rivergrade Rd., Irwindale, CA 91706 | (818) 960-6311 |
| 172 | Air Products & Chemicals | 7201 Hamilton Blvd., Allentown, PA 18195 | (215) 481-4911 |
| 991 | Airborne Freight | 3101 Western Ave., Seattle, WA 98111 | (206) 285-4600 |
| 122 | Albertson's | 250 Parkcenter Blvd., Boise, ID 83706 | (208) 385-6200 |
| 749 | ALC Communications | 30300 Telegraph Rd., Bingham Farms, MI 48025 | (313) 647-6920 |
| 382 | Alco Standard | 825 Duportail Rd., Wayne, PA 19087 | (215) 296-8000 |
| 139 | Alcoa | 426 6th Ave., Pittsburgh, PA 15219 | (412) 553-4545 |
| 905 | Alexander & Alexander | 1211 Ave. of the Americas, New York, NY 10036 | (212) 840-8500 |
| 690 | Alexander & Baldwin | 822 Bishop St., Honolulu, HI 96813 | (808) 525-6611 |
| 815 | Alleghany | 55 E. 52nd St., New York, NY 10055 | (212) 752-1356 |
| 638 | Allegheny Ludlum | 1000 Six PPG Pl., Pittsburgh, PA 15222 | (412) 394-2800 |
| 355 | Allegheny Power | 12 E. 49th St., New York, NY 10017 | (212) 752-2121 |
| 579 | Allergan | 2525 Dupont Dr., Irvine, CA 92713 | (714) 752-4500 |
| 77 | AlliedSignal | 101 Columbia Rd., Morristown, NJ 07962 | (201) 455-2000 |
| 707 | Allmerica Property | 440 Lincoln St., Worcester MA 01653 | (508) 855-1000 |
| 69 | Allstate | Allstate Plaza, Northbrook, IL 60062 | (708) 402-5000 |
| 686 | Alumax | 5655 Peachtree Pkwy., Norcross, GA 30092 | (404) 246-6600 |
| 182 | Alltel | One Allied Dr., Little Rock, AR 72202 | (501) 661-8000 |
| 495 | Alza | 950 Page Mill Rd., Palo Alto, CA 94303 | (415) 494-5000 |
| 586 | Ambac | One State St. Plaza, New York, NY 10004 | (212) 668-0340 |
| 231 | Amerada Hess | 1185 Ave. of the Americas, New York, NY 10036 | (212) 997-8500 |
| 137 | American Brands | 1700 E. Putnam Ave., Old Greenwich, CT 06870 | (203) 698-5000 |
| 253 | American Cyanamid | One Cyanamid Plaza, Wayne, NJ 07470 | (201) 831-2000 |
| 152 | American Electric | One Riverside Plaza, Columbus, OH 43215 | (614) 223-1000 |
| 54 | American Express | 200 Vesey St., World Financial Ctr., New York, NY 10285 | (212) 640-2000 |
| 160 | American General | 2929 Allen Pkwy., Houston TX 77019 | (713) 522-1111 |
| 452 | American Greetings | One American Rd., Cleveland, OH 44144 | (216) 252-7300 |
| 37 | American Home Products | 5 Giralda Farms, Madison, NJ 07940 | (201) 660-5000 |
| 20 | American International Group | 70 Pine St., New York, NY 10270 | (212) 770-7000 |
| 569 | American Medical | 8201 Preston Rd., Dallas, TX 75225 | (214) 360-6300 |
| 614 | American National | One Moody Plaza, Galveston, TX 77550 | (409) 763-4661 |
| 410 | American Power | 132 Fairgrounds Rd., West Kingston, RI 02892 | (401) 789-5735 |
| 656 | American Premier | One E. 4th St., Cincinnati, OH 45202 | (513) 579-6600 |
| 872 | American President | 1111 Broadway, Oakland, CA 94607 | (510) 272-8000 |
| 673 | American Re | 555 College Rd. E., Princeton, NJ 08543 | (609) 243-4200 |
| 297 | American Stores | 709 E.S. Temple, Salt Lake City, UT 84102 | (801) 539-0112 |
| 817 | American Water Works | 1025 Laurel Oak Rd., Voorhees, NJ 08043 | (609) 346-8200 |
| 33 | Ameritech | 30 S. Wacker Dr., Chicago IL 60606 | (312) 750-5000 |
| 163 | Amgen | 1840 De Havilland Dr., Thousand Oaks, CA 91320 | (805) 447-1000 |
| 22 | Amoco | 200 E. Randolph Dr., Chicago, IL 60601 | (312) 856-6111 |

*Corporate Contact Directory (cont'd)*

| Rank | Company | Corporate Headquarters | Phone |
|------|---------|------------------------|-------|
| 138 | AMP | 470 Friendship Rd., Harrisburg, PA 17111 | (717) 564-0101 |
| 204 | AMR | 4333 Amon Carter Blvd., Fort Worth, TX 76155 | (817) 963-1234 |
| 626 | Amsouth Bancorp. | 1900 5th Ave., N. Birmingham, AL 35203 | (205) 326-5120 |
| 386 | Anadarko Petroleum | 17001 Northchase Dr., Houston, TX 77060 | (713) 875-1101 |
| 620 | Analog Devices | One Technology Way, Norwood, MA 02062 | (617) 329-4700 |
| 914 | Andrew | 10500 W. 153rd St., Orland Park, IL 60462 | (708) 349-3300 |
| 50 | Anheuser-Busch | One Busch Pl., St. Louis, MO 63118 | (314) 577-2000 |
| 299 | AON | 123 N. Wacker Dr., Chicago, IL 60606 | (312) 701-3000 |
| 570 | Apache | 2000 Post Oak Blvd., Houston, TX 77056 | (713) 296-6000 |
| 233 | Apple Computer | 20525 Mariani Ave., Cupertino, CA 95014 | (408) 996-1010 |
| 264 | Applied Materials | 3050 Bowers Ave., Santa Clara, CA 95054 | (408) 727-5555 |
| 105 | Archer Daniels Midland | 4666 Faries Pkwy., Decatur, IL 62525 | (217) 424-5200 |
| 215 | Arco Chemical | 3801 W. Chester Pike, Newtown Square, PA 19073 | (215) 359-2000 |
| 933 | Argonaut Group | 1800 Ave. of the Stars, Los Angeles, CA 90067 | (310) 553-0561 |
| 811 | Arkla | 1600 Smith St., Houston, TX 77002 | (713) 654-5600 |
| 462 | Armstrong World | 313 W. Liberty St., Lancaster, PA 17604 | (717) 397-0611 |
| 616 | Arrow Electronics | 25 Hub Dr., Melville, NY 11747 | (516) 391-1300 |
| 760 | Asarco | 180 Maiden Ln., New York, NY 10038 | (212) 510-2000 |
| 406 | Ashland Oil | 1000 Ashland Dr., Russell, KY 41169 | (606) 329-3333 |
| 822 | Associated Communications | 200 Gateway Towers, Pittsburgh, PA 15222 | (412) 281-1907 |
| 798 | AST Research | 16215 Alton Pkwy., Irvine, CA 92713 | (714) 727-4141 |
| 3 | AT&T | 32 Ave. of the Americas, New York, NY 10013 | (212) 387-5400 |
| 689 | AT&T Capital | 44 Whippany Rd., Morristown, NJ 07960 | (201) 397-3000 |
| 868 | Atlanta Gas Light | 303 Peachtree St., NE, Atlanta, GA 30308 | (404) 584-4000 |
| 742 | Atlantic Energy | 6801 Black Horse Pike, Pleasantville, NJ 08232 | (609) 645-4100 |
| 44 | Atlantic Richfield | 515 S. Flower St., Los Angeles, CA 90071 | (213) 486-3511 |
| 725 | Atlantic Southeast Air | 100 Hartsfield Center Pkwy., Atlanta, GA 30354 | (404) 766-1400 |
| 814 | Atmel | 2125 O'Nel Dr., San Jose, CA 95131 | (408) 441-0311 |
| 615 | Autodesk | 2320 Marinship Way, Sausalito, CA 94965 | (415) 332-2344 |
| 123 | Automatic Data | One ADP Blvd., Roseland, NJ 07068 | (201) 994-5000 |
| 248 | Autozone | 3030 Poplar Ave., Memphis, TN 38111 | (901) 325-4600 |
| 517 | Avery Dennison | 150 N. Orange Grove Blvd., Pasadena, CA 91103 | (818) 304-2000 |
| 518 | Avnet | 80 Cutter Mill Rd., Great Neck, NY 11021 | (516) 466-7000 |
| 240 | Avon Products | 9 W. 57th St., New York, NY 10019 | (212) 546-6015 |
| 372 | Baker Hughes | 3900 Essex Ln., Houston, TX 77027 | (713) 439-8600 |
| 972 | Ball | 345 S. High St., Muncie, IN 47305 | (317) 747-6100 |
| 298 | Baltimore G&E | 39 W. Lexington, Baltimore, MD 21203 | (410) 234-5000 |
| 63 | Banc One | 100 E. Broad St., Columbus, OH 43271 | (614) 248-5800 |
| 631 | Bancorp Hawaii | 130 Merchant St., Honolulu, HI 96813 | (808) 537-8111 |
| 568 | Bandag | 2905 N. Hwy. 61, Muscatine, IA 52761 | (319) 262-1400 |
| 402 | Bank of Boston | 100 Federal St., Boston, MA 02106 | (617) 434-2200 |
| 183 | Bank of New York | 48 Wall St., New York, NY 10286 | (212) 495-1784 |
| 939 | Bank South | 55 Marietta St., NW, Atlanta, GA 30303 | (404) 529-4111 |
| 48 | Bankamerica | 555 California St., San Francisco, CA 94104 | (415) 622-3456 |
| 691 | Bankers Life | 222 Merchandise Mart Plaza, Chicago, IL 60624 | (312) 396-6000 |
| 141 | Bankers Trust N.Y. | 280 Park Ave., New York, NY 10017 | (212) 250-2500 |
| 757 | Banponce | 209 Munoz Riviera Ave., San Juan, PR 00918 | (809) 765-9800 |
| 967 | Banta | 225 Main St., Menasha WI 54952 | (414) 751-7777 |
| 590 | Bard (C.R.) | 730 Central Ave., Murray Hill, NJ 07974 | (908) 277-8000 |
| 246 | Barnett Banks | 50 N. Laura St., Jacksonville, FL 32202 | (904) 791-7720 |

*Corporate Contact Directory (cont'd)*

| Rank | Company | Corporate Headquarters | Phone |
|------|---------|------------------------|-------|
| 844 | Battle Mountain Gold | 333 Clay St., Houston, TX 77002 | (713) 650-6400 |
| 338 | Bausch & Lomb | One Lincoln First Square, Rochester, NY 14604 | (716) 338-6000 |
| 149 | Baxter International | One Baxter Pkwy., Deerfield, IL 60015 | (708) 948-2000 |
| 771 | BayBanks | 175 Federal St., Boston, MA 02110 | (617) 482-1040 |
| 819 | BB&T Financial | 223 W. Nash St., Wilson, NC 27893 | (919) 399-4111 |
| 371 | Bear Stearns | 245 Park Ave., New York, NY 10167 | (212) 272-2000 |
| 951 | Beckman Instruments | 2500 Harbor Blvd., Fullerton, CA 92634 | (714) 871-4848 |
| 342 | Becton, Dickinson | One Becton Dr., Franklin Lakes, NJ 07417 | (201) 847-6800 |
| 846 | Bed Bath & Beyond | 715 Morris Ave., Springfield NJ 07081 | (201) 379-1520 |
| 25 | Bell Atlantic | 1717 Arch St., Philadelphia, PA 19103 | (215) 963-6000 |
| 21 | Bellsouth | 1155 Peachtree St., NE, Atlanta, GA 30367 | (404) 249-2000 |
| 761 | Belo (A.H.) | 400 S. Record St., Dallas, TX 75202 | (214) 977-8730 |
| 702 | Bemis | 222 S. 9th St., Minneapolis, MN 55402 | (612) 376-3000 |
| 478 | Beneficial | 301 N. Walnut St., Wilmington, DE 19801 | (302) 425-2800 |
| 989 | Bergen Brunswig | 4000 Metropolitan Dr., Orange, CA 92668 | (714) 385-4000 |
| 38 | Berkshire Hathaway | 1440 Kiewit Plaza, Omaha, NE 68131 | (402) 346-1400 |
| 708 | Best Buy | 7075 Flying Cloud Dr., Eden Prarie, MN 55344 | (612) 947-2000 |
| 474 | Bethlehem Steel | 1170 8th Ave., Bethlehem, PA 18016 | (215) 694-2424 |
| 600 | Betz Laboratories | 4636 Somerton Rd., Trevose, PA 19053 | (215) 355-3300 |
| 660 | Beverly Enterprises | 1200 S. Waldron Rd., Fort Smith, AR 72903 | (501) 452-6712 |
| 456 | BHC Communications | 767 5th Ave., New York, NY 10153 | (212) 421-0200 |
| 602 | Biogen | 14 Cambridge Center, Cambridge, MA 02142 | (617) 252-9200 |
| 657 | Biomet | Airport Industrial Park, Warsaw, IN 46580 | (219) 267-6639 |
| 532 | Black & Decker | 701 E. Joppa Rd., Towson, MD 21286 | (410) 716-3900 |
| 198 | Block (H&R) | 4410 Main St., Kansas City, MO 64111 | (816) 753-6900 |
| 143 | Blockbuster Ent. | One Blockbuster Plaza, Fort Lauderdale, FL 33301 | (305) 832-3000 |
| 505 | BMC Software | 2101 City West Blvd., Houston, TX 77042 | (713) 918-8800 |
| 340 | Boatmen's Bancshares | 800 Market St., St. Louis, MO 63101 | (314) 466-6000 |
| 840 | Bob Evans Farms | 3776 S. High St., Columbus, OH 43207 | (614) 491-2225 |
| 47 | Boeing | 7755 E. Marginal Way S., Seattle, WA 98108 | (206) 655-2121 |
| 806 | Boise Cascade | One Jefferson Square, Boise, ID 83728 | (208) 384-6161 |
| 799 | Bombay | 550 Bailey Ave., Fort Worth, TX 76107 | (817) 347-8200 |
| 447 | Borden | 180 E. Broad St., Columbus, OH 43215 | (614) 225-4000 |
| 961 | Boston Chicken | 1804 Centre Point Dr., Naperville, IL 60563 | (708) 955-6100 |
| 674 | Boston Edison | 800 Boylston St., Boston, MA 02199 | (617) 424-2000 |
| 574 | Boston Scientific | 480 Pleasant St., Watertown, MA 02172 | (617) 923-1720 |
| 897 | Bowater | 55 E. Camperdown Way, Greenville, SC 29601 | (803) 271-7733 |
| 803 | Boyd Gaming | 2950 S. Industrial Rd., Las Vegas, NV 89109 | (702) 792-7200 |
| 874 | Breed Technologies | 5300 Old Tampa Hwy., Lakeland, FL 33811 | (813) 284-6000 |
| 663 | Briggs & Stratton | 12301 W. Wirth St., Wauwatosa, WI 53222 | (414) 259-5333 |
| 451 | Brinker International | 6820 LBJ Freeway, Dallas, TX 75240 | (214) 980-9917 |
| 18 | Bristol-Myers Squibb | 345 Park Ave., New York, NY 10154 | (212) 546-4000 |
| 675 | Brooklyn Union Gas | One MetroTech Center, Brooklyn, NY 11201 | (718) 403-2000 |
| 416 | Brown Forman | 850 Dixie Hwy., Louisville, KY 40210 | (502) 585-1100 |
| 195 | Browning-Ferris | 757 N. Eldridge, Houston, TX 77079 | (713) 870-8100 |
| 460 | Brunswick | One N. Field Ct., Lake Forest, IL 60045 | (708) 735-4700 |
| 946 | Buffets | 10260 Viking Dr., Eden Prairie, MN 55344 | (612) 942-9760 |
| 731 | Burlington Coat | 1830 Rte. 130, Burlington, NJ 08016 | (609) 387-7800 |
| 748 | Burlington Industries | 3330 W. Friendly Ave., Greensboro, NC 27420 | (919) 379-2000 |
| 164 | Burlington Northern | 777 Main St., Fort Worth, TX 76102 | (817) 333-2000 |

*Corporate Contact Directory (cont'd)*

| Rank | Company | Corporate Headquarters | Phone |
|------|---------|------------------------|-------|
| 166 | Burlington Resources | 999 3rd, Seattle, WA 98104 | (206) 467-3838 |
| 282 | Cabletron Systems | 35 Industrial Way, Rochester, NH 03867 | (603) 332-9400 |
| 588 | Cablevision Systems | One Media Crossways, Woodbury, NY 11797 | (516) 364-8450 |
| 813 | Cabot | 75 State St., Boston, MA 02109 | (617) 345-0100 |
| 607 | Caesars World | 1801 Century Park E., Los Angeles, CA 90067 | (310) 552-2711 |
| 680 | Callaway Golf | 2285 Rutherford Rd., Carlsbad, CA 92008 | (619) 931-1771 |
| 80 | Campbell Soup | Campbell Pl., Camden, NJ 08103 | (609) 342-4800 |
| 75 | Capital Cities/ABC | 77 W. 66th St., New York, NY 10023 | (212) 456-7777 |
| 288 | Capital Holding | 400 W. Market St., Louisville, KY 40202 | (502) 560-2000 |
| 572 | Cardinal Health | 655 Metro Pl. S., Dublin, OH 43017 | (614) 761-8700 |
| 563 | Caremark International | 2215 Sanders Rd., Northbrook, IL 60062 | (708) 559-4700 |
| 133 | Carnival Cruise Lines | 3655 N.W. 87th Ave., Miami, FL 33178 | (305) 599-2600 |
| 228 | Carolina Power & Light | 411 Fayetteville St. Mall, Raleigh, NC 27602 | (919) 546-6111 |
| 825 | Carter-Wallace | 1345 Ave. of the Americas, New York, NY 10105 | (212) 339-5000 |
| 74 | Caterpillar | 100 N.E. Adams St., Peoria, IL 61629 | (309) 675-1000 |
| 650 | CBI Industries | 800 Jorie Blvd., Oak Brook, IL 60521 | (708) 572-7000 |
| 207 | CBS | 51 W. 52nd St., New York, NY 10019 | (212) 975-4321 |
| 520 | Centerior Energy | 6200 Oak Tree Blvd., Independence, OH 44131 | (216) 447-3100 |
| 695 | Centex | 3333 Lee Pkwy., Dallas, TX 75219 | (214) 559-6500 |
| 178 | Central & South West | 1616 Woodall Rodgers Fwy., Dallas, TX 75202 | (214) 777-1000 |
| 713 | Central Fidelity Banks | 1021 E. Cary St., Richmond, VA 23219 | (804) 782-4000 |
| 973 | Central Newspapers | 135 N. Pennsylvania St., Indianapolis, IN 46204 | (317) 231-9200 |
| 841 | Century Communications | 50 Locust Ave., New Canaan, CT 06840 | (203) 972-2000 |
| 629 | Century Telephone | 100 Century Park Dr., Monroe, LA 71203 | (318) 388-9500 |
| 812 | Ceridian | 8100 34th Ave. S., Bloomington, MN 55425 | (612) 853-8100 |
| 343 | Champion International | One Champion Plaza, Stamford, CT 06921 | (203) 358-7000 |
| 628 | Charming Shoppes | 450 Winks Ln., Bensalem, PA 19020 | (215) 245-9100 |
| 155 | Chase Manhattan | One Chase Manhattan Plaza, New York, NY 10081 | (212) 552-2222 |
| 91 | Chemical Banking | 270 Park Ave., New York, NY 10017 | (212) 270-6000 |
| 482 | Chemical Waste | 3001 Butterfield Rd., Oak Brook, IL 60521 | (708) 218-1500 |
| 19 | Chevron | 225 Bush St., San Francisco, CA 94104 | (415) 894-7700 |
| 795 | Cheyenne Software | 3 Expressway Plaza, Roslyn Heights, NY 11577 | (516) 484-5110 |
| 684 | Chicago & North Western | 165 N. Canal St., Chicago, IL 60606 | (312) 559-7000 |
| 894 | Chiquita Brands Intl. | 250 E. 5th St., Cincinnati, OH 45202 | (513) 784-8000 |
| 399 | Chiron | 4560 Horton St., Emeryville, CA 94608 | (510) 655-8730 |
| 796 | Chris-Craft Industries | 767 5th Ave., New York, NY 10153 | (212) 421-0200 |
| 35 | Chrysler | 12000 Chrysler Dr., Highland Park, MI 48288 | (313) 956-5741 |
| 144 | Chubb | 15 Mountain View Rd., Warren, NJ 07059 | (908) 580-2000 |
| 211 | Cigna | One Liberty Pl., Philadelphia, PA 19192 | (215) 761-1000 |
| 751 | Cincinnati Bell | 201 E. 4th St., Cincinnati, OH 45201 | (513) 397-9900 |
| 365 | Cincinnati Financial | 6200 S. Gilmore Rd., Fairfield, OH 45014 | (513) 870-2000 |
| 441 | Cincinnati G&E | 139 E. 4th St., Cincinnati, OH 45202 | (513) 381-2000 |
| 930 | Cincinnati Milacron | 4701 Marburg Ave., Cincinnati, OH 45209 | (513) 841-8100 |
| 583 | Cintas | 6800 Cintas Blvd., Mason, OH 45040 | (513) 459-1200 |
| 815 | Cipsco | 607 E. Adams St., Springfield, IL 62739 | (217) 523-3600 |
| 498 | Circuit City Stores | 9950 Mayland Dr., Richmond, VA 23233 | (804) 527-4000 |
| 311 | Circus Circus | 2880 Las Vegas Blvd. S., Las Vegas, NV 89109 | (702) 734-0410 |
| 720 | Cirrus Logic | 3100 W. Warren Ave., Freemont, CA 94538 | (510) 623-8300 |
| 92 | Cisco Systems | 1525 O'Brien Dr., Menlo Park, CA 94025 | (415) 326-1941 |
| 45 | Citicorp | 399 Park Ave., New York, NY 10043 | (212) 559-1000 |

*Corporate Contact Directory (cont'd)*

| Rank | Company | Corporate Headquarters | Phone |
|------|---------|------------------------|-------|
| 337 | Citizens Utilities | High Ridge Park, Stamford, CT 06905 | (203) 329-8800 |
| 756 | Clark Equipment | 100 N. Michigan St., South Bend, IN 46634 | (219) 239-0100 |
| 640 | Clayton Homes | 4726 Airport Hwy., Louisville, TN 37777 | (615) 970-7200 |
| 348 | Clorox | 1221 Broadway, Oakland, CA 94612 | (510) 271-7200 |
| 740 | CML Group | 524 Main St., Acton, MA 01720 | (508) 264-4155 |
| 480 | CMS Energy | 330 Town Center Dr., Dearborn, MI 48126 | (313) 436-9200 |
| 232 | CNA Financial | CNA Plaza, Chicago, IL 60685 | (312) 822-5000 |
| 305 | Coastal | 9 Greenway Plaza, Houston, TX 77046 | (713) 877-1400 |
| 5 | Coca-Cola | One Coca-Cola Plaza, NW, Atlanta, GA 30313 | (404) 676-2121 |
| 423 | Coca-Cola Enterprises | One Coca-Cola Plaza, NW, Atlanta, GA 30313 | (404) 676-2100 |
| 982 | Coleman | 250 N. St. Francis, Wichita, KS 67202 | (316) 261-2100 |
| 86 | Colgate-Palmolive | 300 Park Ave., New York, NY 10022 | (212) 310-2000 |
| 612 | Coltec Industries | 430 Park Ave., New York, NY 10022 | (212) 940-0400 |
| 598 | Columbia Gas System | 20 Montchanin Rd., Wilmington, DE 19807 | (302) 429-5000 |
| 51 | Columbia/HCA Healthcare | 201 S. Main St., Louisville, KY 40201 | (502) 572-2000 |
| 223 | Comcast | 1234 Market St., Philadelphia, PA 19107 | (215) 665-1700 |
| 928 | Comdisco | 6111 N. River Rd., Rosemont, IL 60018 | (708) 698-3000 |
| 326 | Comerica | Renaissance Center, Detroit, MI 48275 | (313) 222-3300 |
| 783 | Commerce Bancshares | 1000 Walnut, Kansas City, MO 64199 | (816) 234-2000 |
| 161 | Commonwealth Edison | 10 S. Dearborn St., Chicago, IL 60603 | (312) 294-4321 |
| 953 | Community Psychiatric | 24502 Pacific Park Dr., Laguna Hills, CA 92656 | (714) 831-1166 |
| 106 | Compaq Computer | 20555 State Hwy. 249, Houston, TX 77070 | (713) 370-0670 |
| 888 | Compass Bancshares | 15 S. 20th St., Birmingham, AL 35233 | (205) 933-3000 |
| 154 | Computer Associates | One Computer Associates Plaza, Islandia, NY 11788 | (516) 342-5224 |
| 464 | Computer Sciences | 2100 E. Grand Ave., El Segundo, CA 90245 | (310) 615-0311 |
| 639 | Compuware | 31440 Northwestern Hwy., Farmington Hills, MI 48334 | (313) 737-7300 |
| 750 | Comsat | 6560 Rock Spring Dr., Bethesda, MD 20817 | (301) 214-3000 |
| 135 | ConAgra | One ConAgra Dr., Omaha, NE 68102 | (402) 595-4000 |
| 880 | Conner Peripherals | 3081 Zanker Rd., San Jose, CA 95134 | (408) 456-4500 |
| 197 | Conrail | 2001 Market St., Philadelphia, PA 19101 | (215) 209-2000 |
| 606 | Conseco | 11825 N. Pennsylvania St., Carmel, IN 46032 | (317) 573-6100 |
| 129 | Consolidated Edison | 4 Irving Pl., New York, NY 10003 | (212) 460-4600 |
| 827 | Consolidated Freightways | 3240 Hillview Ave., Palo Alto, CA 94304 | (415) 494-2900 |
| 247 | Consolidated Natural Gas | CNG Tower, 625 Liberty Ave., Pittsburgh, PA 15222 | (412) 227-1000 |
| 467 | Consolidated Papers | 231 1st Ave. N., Wisconsin Rapids, WI 54495 | (715) 422-3111 |
| 853 | Consolidated Stores | 300 Phillipi Rd., Columbus, OH 43228 | (614) 278-6800 |
| 540 | Contel Cellular | 245 Perimeter Center Pkwy., Atlanta, GA 30346 | (404) 391-8000 |
| 501 | Continental Bank | 231 S. LaSalle St., Chicago, IL 60697 | (312) 828-2345 |
| 609 | Continental | 180 Maiden Ln., New York, NY 10038 | (212) 440-3000 |
| 225 | Cooper Industries | 1001 Fannin, Houston, TX 77002 | (713) 739-5400 |
| 432 | Cooper Tire & Rubber | Lima & Western Aves., Findlay, OH 45840 | (419) 423-1321 |
| 994 | Coors (Adolph) | 12th & Ford Sts., Golden, CO 80401 | (303) 279-6565 |
| 334 | Corestates Financial | 1345 Chestnut St., Philadelphia, PA 19101 | (215) 973-3100 |
| 153 | Corning | Houghton Park, Corning, NY 14831 | (607) 974-9000 |
| 575 | Countrywide Credit | 155 N. Lake Ave., Pasadena, CA 91109 | (818) 304-8400 |
| 121 | CPC International | International Plaza, Englewood Cliffs, NJ 07632 | (201) 894-4000 |
| 560 | Cracker Barrel | Hartmann Dr., Lebanon, TN 37088 | (615) 444-5533 |
| 893 | Crane | 100 1st Stamford Pl., Stamford, CT 06902 | (203) 363-7300 |
| 942 | Cray Research | 655A Lone Oak Dr., Eagan, MN 55121 | (612) 452-6650 |
| 545 | Crestar Financial | 919 E. Main St., Richmond, VA 23219 | (804) 782-5000 |

*Corporate Contact Directory (cont'd)*

| Rank | Company | Corporate Headquarters | Phone |
|------|---------|------------------------|-------|
| 685 | Crompton & Knowles | One Station Pl., Stamford, CT 06902 | (203) 353-5400 |
| 302 | Crown Cork & Seal | 9300 Ashton Rd., Philadelphia, PA 19136 | (215) 698-5100 |
| 94 | CSX | One James Center, Richmond, VA 23219 | (804) 782-1400 |
| 303 | CUC International | 707 Summer St., Stamford, CT 06901 | (203) 324-9261 |
| 533 | Cummins Engine | 500 Jackson St., Columbus, IN 47202 | (812) 377-5000 |
| 361 | Cyprus Amax | 9100 E. Mineral Circle, Englewood, CO 80155 | (303) 643-5000 |
| 366 | Dana | 4500 Dorr St., Toledo, OH 43697 | (419) 535-4500 |
| 768 | Danaher | 1250 24th St., NW, Washington, DC 20037 | (202) 828-0850 |
| 995 | Dauphin Deposit | 213 Market St., Harrisburg, PA 17101 | (717) 255-2121 |
| 181 | Dayton Hudson | 777 Nicollet Mall, Minneapolis, MN 55402 | (612) 370-6948 |
| 651 | Dean Foods | 3600 N. River Rd., Franklin Park, IL 60131 | (708) 678-1680 |
| 150 | Dean Witter, Discover | 2 World Trade Center, New York, NY 10048 | (212) 392-2222 |
| 124 | Deere | John Deere Rd., Moline, IL 61265 | (309) 765-8000 |
| 832 | Dell Computer | 9505 Arboretum Blvd., Austin, TX 78759 | (512) 338-4400 |
| 671 | Delmarva Power | 800 King St., Wilmington, DE 19899 | (302) 429-3011 |
| 400 | Delta Air Lines | 10 Delta Blvd., Atlanta, GA 30320 | (404) 715-2600 |
| 358 | Deluxe | 1080 W. County Rd. F, Shoreview, MN 55126 | (612) 483-7111 |
| 794 | Dentsply International | 527 Colman Center Dr., Rockford, IL 61125 | (815) 395-9729 |
| 856 | Destec Energy | 2500 CityWest Blvd., Houston, TX 77042 | (713) 735-4000 |
| 242 | Detroit Edison | 2000 2nd Ave., Detroit, MI 48226 | (313) 237-8000 |
| 458 | Dial | 1850 N. Central Ave., Phoenix, AZ 85077 | (602) 207-4000 |
| 906 | Diamond Shamrock | 9830 Colonnade Blvd., San Antonio, TX 78230 | (210) 641-6800 |
| 734 | Diebold | 5995 Mayfair Rd., N. Canton OH 44720 | (216) 489-4000 |
| 252 | Digital Equipment | 146 Main St., Maynard, MA 01754 | (508) 493-5111 |
| 251 | Dillard Dept. Stores | 1600 Cantrell Rd., Little Rock, AR 72202 | (501) 376-5200 |
| 24 | Disney (Walt) | 500 S. Buena Vista St., Burbank, CA 91521 | (818) 560-1000 |
| 471 | Dole Food | 31355 Oak Crest Dr., Westlake Village, CA 91361 | (818) 879-6600 |
| 728 | Dollar General | 104 Woodmont Blvd., Nashville, TN 37205 | (615) 783-2000 |
| 128 | Dominion Resources | 901 E. Byrd St., Richmond, VA 23219 | (804) 775-5700 |
| 205 | Donnelley (R.R.) | 77 W. Wacker Dr., Chicago, IL 60601 | (312) 326-8000 |
| 287 | Dover | 280 Park Ave., New York, NY 10017 | (212) 922-1640 |
| 41 | Dow Chemical | 2030 Dow Center, Midland, MI 48674 | (517) 636-1000 |
| 255 | Dow Jones | 200 Liberty St., New York, NY 10281 | (212) 416-2000 |
| 455 | DPL | 1065 Woodman Dr., Dayton, OH 45432 | (513) 224-6000 |
| 537 | DQE | 301 Grant St., Pittsburgh, PA 15279 | (412) 393-6000 |
| 589 | Dr. Pepper-Seven-Up | 8144 Walnut Hill Ln., Dallas, TX 75231 | (214) 360-7000 |
| 254 | Dresser Industries | 2001 Ross Ave., Dallas, TX 75201 | (214) 740-6000 |
| 526 | Dreyfus | 200 Park Ave., New York, NY 10166 | (212) 922-6000 |
| 359 | DSC Communications | 1000 Coit Rd., Plano, TX 75075 | (214) 519-3000 |
| 112 | Duke Power | 422 S. Church St., Charlotte, NC 28242 | (704) 594-0887 |
| 82 | Dun & Bradstreet | 200 Nyala Farms Rd., Westport, CT 06880 | (203) 222-4200 |
| 10 | DuPont | 1007 Market St., Wilmington, DE 19898 | (302) 774-1000 |
| 202 | Duracell Intl. | Berkshire Corporate Park, Bethel, CT 06801 | (203) 796-4000 |
| 567 | E-Systems | 6250 LBJ Fwy., Dallas, TX 75240 | (214) 661-1000 |
| 293 | Eastman Chemical | 100 N. Eastman Rd., Kingsport, TN 37660 | (615) 229-2000 |
| 55 | Eastman Kodak | 343 State St., Rochester, NY 14650 | (716) 724-4000 |
| 243 | Eaton | 1111 Superior Ave. NNE, Cleveland, OH 44114 | (216) 523-5000 |
| 514 | Echlin | 100 Double Beach Rd., Branford, CT 06405 | (203) 481-5751 |
| 594 | Ecolab | 370 N. Wabasha, St. Paul, MN 55102 | (612) 293-2233 |
| 539 | Edwards (A.G.) | One N. Jefferson, St. Louis, MO 63103 | (314) 289-3000 |

*Corporate Contact Directory (cont'd)*

| Rank | Company | Corporate Headquarters | Phone |
|------|---------|------------------------|-------|
| 767 | EG&G | 45 William St., Wellesley, MA 02181 | (617) 237-5100 |
| 601 | El Paso Natural Gas | 304 Texas St., El Paso, TX 79901 | (915) 541-2600 |
| 665 | Electronic Arts | 1450 Fashion Island Blvd., San Mateo, CA 94404 | (415) 571-7171 |
| 276 | EMC | 171 South St., Hopkinton, MA 01748 | (508) 435-1000 |
| 52 | Emerson Electric | 8000 W. Florissant Ave., St. Louis, MO 63136 | (314) 553-2000 |
| 952 | Energy Service | 1445 Ross Ave., Dallas, TX 75202 | (214) 922-1500 |
| 378 | Engelhard | 101 Wood Ave., Iselin, NJ 08830 | (908) 205-6000 |
| 974 | Enquirer/Star Group | 600 S.E. Coast Ave., Lantana, FL 33462 | (407) 586-1111 |
| 117 | Enron | 1400 Smith St., Houston, TX 77002 | (713) 853-6161 |
| 294 | Enron Oil & Gas | 1400 Smith St., Houston, TX 77002 | (713) 853-6161 |
| 772 | Enserch | 300 S. St. Paul St., Dallas, TX 75201 | (214) 651-8700 |
| 158 | Entergy | 225 Baronne St., New Orleans, LA 70112 | (504) 529-5262 |
| 516 | Equifax | 1600 Peachtree St., NW, Atlanta, GA 30309 | (404) 885-8000 |
| 304 | Equitable | 787 7th Ave., New York, NY 10019 | (212) 554-1234 |
| 785 | Equitable of Iowa | 604 Locust St., Des Moines, IA 50309 | (515) 245-6911 |
| 654 | Equitable Resources | 420 Blvd. of the Allies, Pittsburgh, PA 15219 | (412) 261-3000 |
| 437 | Ethyl | 330 S. 4th St., Richmond, VA 23219 | (804) 788-5000 |
| 2 | Exxon | 225 E. Carpenter Fwy., Irving, TX 75062 | (214) 444-1000 |
| 829 | Family Dollar Stores | 10401 Old Monroe Rd., Matthews, NC 28105 | (704) 847-6961 |
| 31 | Fannie Mae | 3900 Wisconsin Ave., Washington, DC 20016 | (202) 752-7000 |
| 241 | Federal Express | 2005 Corporate Ave., Memphis, TN 38194 | (901) 369-3600 |
| 85 | Federal Home Loan | 8200 Jones Branch Dr., McLean, VA 22102 | (703) 903-2000 |
| 730 | Federal Paper Board | 75 Chestnut Ridge Rd., Montvale, NJ 07645 | (201) 391-1776 |
| 948 | Federal Realty | 4800 Hampden Ln., Bethesda, MD 20814 | (301) 652-3360 |
| 833 | Federal Signal | 1415 W. 22nd St., Oak Brook, IL 60521 | (708) 954-2000 |
| 664 | Federal-Mogul | 26555 Northwestern Hwy., Southfield, MI 48034 | (313) 354-7700 |
| 335 | Federated Department Stores | 7 W. 7th St., Cincinnati, OH 45202 | (513) 579-7000 |
| 784 | Ferro | 1000 Lakeside Ave., Cleveland, OH 44114 | (216) 641-8580 |
| 834 | FHP International | 9900 Talbert Ave., Fountain Valley, CA 92708 | (714) 963-7233 |
| 347 | Fifth Third Bancorp | 38 Fountain Square Plaza, Cincinnati, OH 45263 | (513) 579-5300 |
| 738 | Fina | 8350 N. Central Expwy., Dallas, TX 75206 | (214) 750-2400 |
| 637 | Fingerhut | 4400 Baker Rd., Minnetonka, MN 55343 | (612) 932-3100 |
| 655 | First Alabama | 417 N. 20th St., Birmingham, AL 35203 | (205) 326-7100 |
| 915 | First American | 300 Union St., Nashville, TN 37237 | (615) 748-2000 |
| 278 | First Bank System | 601 2nd Ave. S., Minneapolis, MN 55402 | (612) 973-1111 |
| 940 | First Brands | 83 Wooster Heights Rd., Danbury, CT 06813 | (203) 731-2300 |
| 236 | First Chicago | One First National Plaza, Chicago, IL 60670 | (312) 732-4000 |
| 644 | First Colony | 700 Main St., Lynchburg, VA 24504 | (804) 845-0911 |
| 935 | First Commerce | 210 Baronne St., New Orleans, LA 70112 | (504) 561-1371 |
| 203 | First Data | 200 Vesey St., New York, NY 10285 | (212) 640-2000 |
| 835 | First Empire State | One M&T Plaza, Buffalo, NY 14240 | (716) 842-4200 |
| 289 | First Fidelity Bancorp. | 550 Broad St., Newark, NJ 07102 | (201) 565-3200 |
| 283 | First Financial Mgmt. | 3 Corporate Square, Atlanta, GA 30329 | (404) 321-0120 |
| 885 | First Hawaiian | 1132 Bishop St., Honolulu, HI 96813 | (808) 525-7000 |
| 177 | First Interstate | 633 W. 5th St., Los Angeles, CA 90071 | (213) 614-3001 |
| 436 | First of America Bank | 211 S. Rose St., Kalamazoo, MI 49007 | (616) 376-9000 |
| 608 | First Security | 79 S. Main St., Salt Lake City, UT 84111 | (801) 246-6000 |
| 747 | First Tennessee National | 165 Madison Ave., Memphis, TN 38103 | (901) 523-4444 |
| 127 | First Union | One First Union Center, Charlotte, NC 28288 | (704) 374-6565 |
| 524 | First USA | 2001 Bryan Tower, Dallas, TX 75201 | (214) 746-8400 |

*Corporate Contact Directory (cont'd)*

| Rank | Company | Corporate Headquarters | Phone |
|---|---|---|---|
| 666 | First Virginia Banks | 6400 Arlington Blvd., Falls Church, VA 22042 | (703) 241-4000 |
| 463 | Firstar | 777 E. Wisconsin Ave., Milwaukee, WI 53202 | (414) 765-4321 |
| 945 | Fiserv | 255 Fiserv Dr., Brookfield, WI 53045 | (414) 879-5000 |
| 222 | Fleet Financial Group | 50 Kennedy Plaza, Providence, RI 02903 | (401) 278-5800 |
| 922 | Fleet Mortgage Group | 1333 Main St., Columbia, SC 29201 | (803) 929-7900 |
| 780 | Fleetwood Enterprises | 3125 Myers St., Riverside, CA 92513 | (909) 351-3500 |
| 826 | Fleming | 6301 Waterford Blvd., Oklahoma City, OK 73118 | (405) 840-7200 |
| 621 | Flightsafety Intl. | Marine Air Terminal, La Guardia Airport, Flushing, NY 11371 | (718) 565-4100 |
| 381 | Florida Progress | One Progress Plaza, St. Petersburg, FL 33701 | (813) 824-6400 |
| 273 | Fluor | 3333 Michelson Dr., Irvine, CA 92730 | (714) 975-2000 |
| 515 | FMC | 200 E. Randolph Dr., Chicago, IL 60601 | (312) 861-6000 |
| 354 | Food Lion | 2110 Executive Dr., Salisbury, NC 28144 | (704) 633-8250 |
| 14 | Ford Motor | The American Rd., Dearborn, MI 48121 | (313) 322-3000 |
| 440 | Forest Laboratories | 150 E. 58th St., New York, NY 10155 | (212) 421-7850 |
| 582 | Foster Wheeler | Perryville Corporate Park, Clinton, NJ 08809 | (908) 730-4000 |
| 746 | Foundation Health | 3400 Data Dr., Rancho Cordova, CA 95670 | (916) 631-5000 |
| 998 | Fourth Financial | 100 N. Broadway, Wichita, KS 67202 | (316) 261-4444 |
| 145 | FPL Group | 700 Universe Blvd., Juno Beach, FL 33408 | (407) 694-4000 |
| 963 | Franklin Quest | 2200 W. Pkwy. Blvd., Salt Lake City, UT 84119 | (801) 975-1776 |
| 272 | Franklin Resources | 777 Mariners Island Blvd., San Mateo, CA 94404 | (415) 312-2000 |
| 367 | Freeport-McMoran | 1615 Poydras St., New Orleans, LA 70112 | (504) 582-4000 |
| 176 | Freeport-McMoran C&G | 1615 Poydras St., New Orleans, LA 70112 | (504) 582-1640 |
| 426 | Fruit of the Loom | 233 S. Wacker Dr., Chicago, IL 60606 | (312) 876-7000 |
| 111 | Gannett | 1100 Wilson Blvd., Arlington, VA 22234 | (703) 284-6000 |
| 142 | Gap (The) | One Harrison, San Francisco, CA 94105 | (415) 952-4400 |
| 527 | Gateway 2000 | 610 Gateway Dr., N. Sioux City, SD 57049 | (605) 232-2000 |
| 919 | Gatx | 500 W. Munroe St., Chicago, IL 60661 | (312) 621-6200 |
| 425 | Gaylord Entertainment | 2802 Opryland Dr., Nashville, TN 37214 | (615) 885-1000 |
| 268 | Geico | 5260 Western Ave., Chevy Chase, MD 20815 | (301) 986-3000 |
| 162 | Genentech | 460 Pt. San Bruno Blvd., South San Francisco, CA 94080 | (415) 225-1000 |
| 344 | General Dynamics | 3190 Fairview Park Dr., Falls Church, VA 22042 | (703) 876-3000 |
| 1 | General Electric | 3135 Easton Tpke., Fairfield, CT 06431 | (203) 373-2211 |
| 352 | General Instrument | 181 W. Madison St., Chicago, IL 60602 | (312) 541-5000 |
| 99 | General Mills | One General Mills Blvd., Minneapolis, MN 55426 | (612) 540-2311 |
| 7 | General Motors | 3044 W. Grand Blvd., Detroit, MI 48202 | (313) 556-5000 |
| 737 | General Nutrition | 921 Penn Ave., Pittsburgh, PA 15222 | (412) 288-4600 |
| 306 | General Public Utilities | 100 Interpace Pkwy., Parsippany, NJ 07054 | (201) 263-6500 |
| 100 | General Re | 695 E. Main, Stamford, CT 06904 | (203) 328-5000 |
| 552 | General Signal | One High Ridge Park, Stamford, CT 06904 | (203) 357-8800 |
| 687 | Genetics Institute | 87 Cambridge Park Dr., Cambridge, MA 02140 | (617) 876-1170 |
| 210 | Genuine Parts | 2999 Circle 75 Pkwy., Atlanta, GA 30339 | (404) 953-1700 |
| 992 | Geon | 6100 Oak Tree Blvd., Cleveland, OH 44131 | (216) 447-6000 |
| 697 | Georgia Gulf | 400 Perimeter Center Terr., Atlanta, GA 30346 | (404) 395-4500 |
| 146 | Georgia-Pacific | 133 Peachtree St., NE, Atlanta, GA 30348 | (404) 652-4000 |
| 479 | Gerber Products | 445 State St., Fremont, MI 49413 | (616) 928-2000 |
| 564 | Giant Food | 6300 Sheriff Rd., Landover, MD 20785 | (301) 341-4100 |
| 878 | Giddings & Lewis | 142 Doty St., Fond du Lac, WI 54935 | (414) 921-9400 |
| 57 | Gillette | Prudential Tower Bldg., Boston, MA 02199 | (617) 421-7000 |
| 977 | Glatfelter (P.H.) | 228 S. Main St., Spring Grove, PA 17362 | (717) 225-4711 |
| 377 | Golden West Financial | 1901 Harrison St., Oakland, CA 94612 | (510) 446-6000 |

*Corporate Contact Directory (cont'd)*

| Rank | Company | Corporate Headquarters | Phone |
|------|---------|------------------------|-------|
| 762 | Goodrich (B.F.) | 3925 Embassy Pkwy., Akron, OH 44333 | (216) 374-2000 |
| 134 | Goodyear Tire & Rubber | 1144 E. Market St., Akron, OH 44316 | (216) 796-2121 |
| 239 | Grace (W.R.) | One Town Center Rd., Boca Raton, FL 33486 | (407) 362-2000 |
| 320 | Grainger (W.W.) | 5500 W. Howard St., Skokie, IL 60077 | (708) 982-9000 |
| 792 | Great A&P Tea | 2 Paragon Dr., Montvale, NJ 07645 | (201) 573-9700 |
| 845 | Great American Communications | One E. 4th St., Cincinnati, OH 45202 | (513) 562-8000 |
| 165 | Great Lakes Chemical | Great Lakes Blvd., West Lafayette, IN 47906 | (317) 497-6100 |
| 430 | Great Western | 9200 Oakdale Ave., Chatsworth, CA 91311 | (818) 775-3411 |
| 566 | Green Tree Financial | 345 St. Peter St., St. Paul, MN 55102 | (612) 293-3434 |
| 646 | Grumman | 1111 Stewart Ave., Bethpage, NY 11714 | (516) 575-0574 |
| 13 | GTE | One Stamford Forum, Stamford, CT 06904 | (203) 965-2000 |
| 577 | Gtech Holdings | 55 Technology Way, West Greenwich, RI 02817 | (401) 392-1000 |
| 280 | Halliburton | 500 N. Akard St., Dallas, TX 75201 | (214) 978-2600 |
| 899 | Hanna (M.A.) | 1301 E. 9th St., Cleveland, OH 44114 | (216) 589-4000 |
| 789 | Hannaford Brothers | 145 Pleasant Hill Rd., Scarborough, ME 04074 | (207) 883-2911 |
| 368 | Harcourt General | 27 Boylston St., Chestnut Hill MA 02167 | (617) 232-8200 |
| 988 | Harland (John H.) | 2939 Miller Rd., Decatur, GA 30035 | (404) 981-9460 |
| 490 | Harley-Davidson | 3700 W. Juneau Ave., Milwaukee, WI 53208 | (414) 342-4680 |
| 999 | Harnishfeger | 13400 Bishops Ln., Brookfield, WI 53005 | (414) 671-4400 |
| 459 | Harris | 1025 W. NASA Blvd., Melbourne, FL 32919 | (407) 727-9100 |
| 733 | Harsco | 350 Poplar Church Rd., Camp Hill, PA 17011 | (717) 763-7064 |
| 802 | Hartford Steam Boiler | One State St., Hartford, CT 06102 | (203) 722-1866 |
| 328 | Hasbro | 1027 Newport Ave., Pawtucket, RI 02862 | (401) 431-8697 |
| 848 | Hawaiian Electric | 900 Richards St., Honolulu, HI 96813 | (808) 543-5662 |
| 996 | Health & Rehabilitation | 400 Center St., Newton, MA 02158 | (617) 332-3990 |
| 907 | Health Care & Retirement | One Seagate, Toledo, OH 43604 | (419) 247-5600 |
| 924 | Health Care Property | 10990 Wilshire Blvd., Los Angeles, CA 90024 | (310) 473-1990 |
| 800 | Health Management | 5811 Pelican Bay Blvd., Naples, FL 33963 | (813) 598-3131 |
| 895 | Healthcare Compare | 3200 Highland Ave., Downers Grove, IL 60515 | (708) 241-7900 |
| 857 | Healthsource | 54 Regional Dr., Concord, NH 03302 | (603) 225-5077 |
| 891 | Healthsouth | 2 Perimeter Park S., Birmingham, AL 35243 | (205) 967-7116 |
| 422 | Healthtrust | 4525 Harding Rd., Nashville, TN 37201 | (615) 383-4444 |
| 555 | Heilig-Meyers | 2235 Staples Mill Rd., Richmond, VA 23230 | (804) 359-9171 |
| 108 | Heinz (H.J.) | 600 Grant St., Pittsburgh, PA 15219 | (412) 456-5700 |
| 212 | Hercules | 1313 N. Market St., Wilmington, DE 19894 | (302) 594-5000 |
| 219 | Hershey Foods | 100 Crystal A Dr., Hershey, PA 17033 | (717) 534-6799 |
| 29 | Hewlett-Packard | 3000 Hanover St., Palo Alto, CA 94304 | (415) 857-1501 |
| 341 | Hillenbrand Industries | 16 State Rte. 46 E., Batesville, IN 47006 | (812) 934-7000 |
| 292 | Hilton Hotels | 9336 Civic Center Dr., Beverly Hills, CA 90209 | (310) 278-4321 |
| 786 | Holnam | 6211 Ann Arbor Rd., Dundee, MI 48131 | (313) 529-2411 |
| 36 | Home Depot | 2727 Paces Ferry Rd., Atlanta, GA 30339 | (404) 433-8211 |
| 658 | Home Shopping Network | 2501 118th Ave. N., St. Petersburg, FL 33716 | (813) 572-8585 |
| 345 | Homestake Mining | 650 California St., San Francisco, CA 94108 | (415) 981-8150 |
| 824 | Hon Industries | 414 E. 3rd St., Muscatine, IA 52761 | (319) 264-7400 |
| 221 | Honeywell | Honeywell Plaza, Minneapolis, MN 55408 | (612) 951-1000 |
| 549 | Hormel (Geo. A.) | One Hormel Pl., Austin, MN 55912 | (507) 437-5611 |
| 641 | Hospitality Franchise | 339 Jefferson Rd., Parsippany, NJ 07054 | (201) 428-9700 |
| 599 | Host Marriot | Marriot Dr., Washington, DC 20058 | (301) 380-9000 |
| 310 | Household Intl. | 2700 Sanders Rd., Prospect Heights, IL 60070 | (708) 564-5000 |
| 175 | Houston Industries | 440 Post Oak Pkwy., Houston, TX 77027 | (713) 629-3000 |

*Corporate Contact Directory (cont'd)*

| Rank | Company | Corporate Headquarters | Phone |
|---|---|---|---|
| 507 | Hubbell | 584 Derby-Milford Rd., Orange, CT 06477 | (203) 799-4100 |
| 324 | Humana | 500 W. Main St., Louisville, KY 40202 | (502) 580-1000 |
| 838 | Hunt (J.B.) | 615 J.B. Hunt Dr., Lowell, AR 72745 | (501) 820-0000 |
| 417 | Huntington Bancshares | Huntington Center, Columbus, OH 43287 | (614) 463-8300 |
| 15 | IBM | Old Orchard Rd., Armonk, NY 10504 | (914) 765-1900 |
| 714 | IBP | IBP Ave., Dakota City, NE 68731 | (402) 494-2061 |
| 781 | Idaho Power | 1221 W. Idaho St., Boise, ID 83702 | (208) 383-2200 |
| 694 | IDB Communications | 10525 W. Washington Blvd., Culver City, CA 90232 | (213) 870-9000 |
| 923 | IES Industries | 200 1st St., SE, Cedar Rapids, IA 52401 | (319) 398-4411 |
| 571 | Illinois Central | 455 N. Cityfront Plaza Dr., Chicago, IL 60611 | (312) 755-7500 |
| 550 | Illinois Power | 500 S. 27th St., Decatur, IL 62525 | (217) 424-6600 |
| 200 | Illinois Tool Works | 3600 W. Lake Ave., Glenview, IL 60625 | (708) 724-7500 |
| 787 | IMC Fertilizer Group | 2100 Sanders Rd., Northbrook, IL 60062 | (708) 272-9200 |
| 351 | Imcera Group | 7733 Forsyth Blvd., Clayton, MO 63105 | (708) 564-8600 |
| 776 | Infinity Broadcasting | 600 Madison Ave., New York, NY 10022 | (212) 750-6400 |
| 573 | Informix | 4100 Bohannon Dr., Menlo Park, CA 94025 | (415) 926-6300 |
| 249 | Ingersoll-Rand | 200 Chestnut Ridge Rd., Woodcliff Lake, NJ 07675 | (201) 573-0123 |
| 619 | Inland Steel Industries | 30 W. Monroe St., Chicago, IL 60603 | (312) 346-0300 |
| 578 | Integra Financial | 4 PPG Pl., Pittsburgh, PA 15222 | (412) 644-7669 |
| 955 | Integrated Device | 2972 Stender Way, Santa Clara, CA 95054 | (408) 727-6116 |
| 16 | Intel | 2200 Mission College Blvd., Santa Clara, CA 95052 | (408) 765-8080 |
| 902 | Intelligent Electronics | 411 Eagleview Blvd., Exton, PA 19341 | (215) 458-5500 |
| 971 | Interco | 101 S. Hanley Rd., St. Louis, MO 63105 | (314) 863-1100 |
| 238 | International Flavors | 521 W. 57th St., New York, NY 10019 | (212) 765-5500 |
| 275 | International Game Technology | 520 S. Rock Blvd., Reno, NV 89502 | (702) 688-0100 |
| 96 | International Paper | 2 Manhattanville Rd., Purchase, NY 10577 | (914) 397-1500 |
| 407 | Interpublic Group | 1271 Ave. of the Americas, New York, NY 10020 | (212) 399-8000 |
| 669 | Ipalco Enterprises | 25 Monument Circle, Indianapolis, IN 46204 | (317) 261-8261 |
| 847 | Itel | 2 N. Riverside Plaza, Chicago, IL 60606 | (312) 902-1515 |
| 72 | ITT | 1330 Ave. of the Americas, New York, NY 10019 | (212) 258-1000 |
| 396 | Ivax | 8800 N.W. 36th St., Miami, FL 33178 | (305) 590-2200 |
| 562 | James River | 120 Tredegar St., Richmond, VA 23219 | (804) 644-5411 |
| 418 | Jefferson-Pilot | 100 N. Greene St., Greensboro, NC 27401 | (919) 691-3000 |
| 958 | John Alden Financial | 7300 Corporate Center Dr., Miami, FL 33126 | (305) 715-2000 |
| 855 | John Nuveen | 333 W. Wacker Dr., Chicago, IL 60606 | (312) 917-7700 |
| 23 | Johnson & Johnson | One Johnson & Johnson Plaza, New Brunswick, NJ 08933 | (908) 524-0400 |
| 414 | Johnson Controls | 5757 N. Green Bay Ave., Milwaukee, WI 53209 | (414) 228-1200 |
| 901 | Jones Apparel Group | 250 Rittenhouse Circle, Bristol, PA 19007 | (215) 785-4000 |
| 921 | Jostens | 5501 Norman Center Dr., Minneapolis, MN 55437 | (612) 830-3300 |
| 625 | Kansas City Power | 1201 Walnut, Kansas City, MO 64106 | (816) 556-2200 |
| 483 | Kansas City Southern | 114 W. 11th St., Kansas City, MO 64105 | (816) 556-0303 |
| 990 | Kaufman & Broad Home | 10877 Wilshire Blvd., Los Angeles, CA 90024 | (310) 443-8000 |
| 71 | Kellogg | One Kellogg Square, Battle Creek, MI 49016 | (616) 961-2000 |
| 770 | Kelly Services | 999 W. Big Beaver Rd., Troy, MI 48084 | (313) 362-4444 |
| 635 | Kemper | One Kemper Dr., Long Grove, IL 60049 | (708) 320-2000 |
| 898 | Kendall International | 15 Hampshire St., Mansfield, MA 02048 | (508) 261-8000 |
| 917 | Kenetech | 500 Sansome St., San Francisco, CA 94111 | (415) 398-3825 |
| 420 | Kerr-McGee | Kerr-McGee Ctr., Oklahoma City, OK 73125 | (405) 270-1313 |
| 118 | Keycorp | 127 Public Square, Cleveland, OH 44114 | (216) 689-3000 |
| 820 | Keystone International | 9600 W. Gulf Bank Rd., Houston, TX 77040 | (713) 466-1176 |

*Corporate Contact Directory (cont'd)*

| Rank | Company | Corporate Headquarters | Phone |
|------|---------|------------------------|-------|
| 97 | Kimberly-Clark | 545 E. Carpenter Fwy., Irving, TX 75062 | (214) 830-1200 |
| 954 | Kimco Realty | 1044 Northern Blvd., Roslyn, NY 11576 | (516) 484-5858 |
| 611 | King World | 830 Morris Tpke., Short Hills, NJ 07078 | (201) 376-1313 |
| 877 | KLA Instruments | 160 Rio Robles, San Jose, CA 95134 | (408) 434-4200 |
| 115 | Kmart | 3100 W. Big Beaver Rd., Troy, MI 48084 | (313) 643-1000 |
| 322 | Knight-Ridder | One Herald Plaza, Miami, FL 33132 | (305) 376-3800 |
| 493 | Kohl's | N54-W13600 Woodale Dr., Menomonee Falls, WI 53051 | (414) 783-5800 |
| 391 | Kroger | 1014 Vine St., Cincinnati, OH 45202 | (513) 762-4000 |
| 804 | Ku Energy | One Quality St., Lexington, KY 40507 | (606) 255-2100 |
| 938 | La Quinta Inns | 112 E. Pecan St., San Antonio, TX 78025 | (210) 302-6000 |
| 553 | Lafarge | 11130 Sunrise Valley Dr., Reston, VA 22091 | (703) 264-3600 |
| 904 | Lam Research | 4650 Cushing Pkwy., Fremont, CA 94538 | (510) 659-0200 |
| 791 | Lancaster Colony | 37 W. Broad St., Columbus, OH 43215 | (614) 224-7141 |
| 871 | Lands' End | Lands' End Ln., Dodgeville, WI 53595 | (608) 935-9341 |
| 314 | LDDs Communications | 515 E. Amite St., Jackson, MS 39201 | (601) 360-8600 |
| 890 | Lee Enterprises | 215 N. Main St., Davenport, IA 52801 | (319) 383-2100 |
| 887 | Legent | 575 Herndon Pkwy., Herndon, VA 22070 | (703) 708-3000 |
| 500 | Leggett & Platt | One Leggett Rd., Carthage, MO 64836 | (417) 358-8131 |
| 920 | Lennar | 700 N.W. 107th Ave., Miami, FL 33172 | (305) 559-4000 |
| 703 | Leucadia National | 315 Park Ave. S., New York, NY 10010 | (212) 460-1900 |
| 688 | LG&E Energy | 220 W. Main St., Louisville, KY 40202 | (502) 627-2000 |
| 336 | Liberty Media | 8101 E. Prentice Rd., Englewood, CO 80111 | (303) 721-5400 |
| 962 | Liberty National | 416 W. Jefferson St., Louisville, KY 40202 | (502) 566-2000 |
| 43 | Lilly (Eli) | Lilly Corporate Center, Indianapolis, IN 46285 | (317) 276-2000 |
| 126 | Limited (The) | 3 Limited Pkwy., Columbus, OH 43216 | (614) 479-7000 |
| 159 | Lin Broadcasting | 5295 Carillon Point, Kirkland, WA 98033 | (206) 828-1902 |
| 263 | Lincoln National | 1300 S. Clinton St., Fort Wayne, IN 46802 | (219) 455-2000 |
| 557 | Linear Technology | 1630 McCarthy Blvd., Milpitas, CA 95035 | (408) 432-1900 |
| 333 | Litton Industries | 360 N. Crescent Dr., Beverly Hills, CA 90210 | (310) 859-5000 |
| 494 | Liz Claiborne | 1441 Broadway, New York, NY 10018 | (212) 354-4900 |
| 244 | Lockheed | 4500 Park Granada Blvd., Calabasas, CA 91399 | (818) 876-2000 |
| 584 | Loctite | 10 Columbus Blvd., Hartford, CT 06106 | (203) 520-5000 |
| 157 | Loews | 667 Madison Ave., New York, NY 10021 | (212) 545-2000 |
| 882 | Lone Star Steakhouse | 224 E. Douglas, Wichita, KS 67202 | (316) 264-8899 |
| 389 | Long Island Lighting | 175 E. Old Country Rd., Hicksville, NY 11801 | (516) 755-6650 |
| 913 | Longs Drug Stores | 141 N. Civic Dr., Walnut Creek, CA 94596 | (510) 937-1170 |
| 782 | Longview Fibre | End of Fibre Way, Longview, WA 98632 | (206) 425-1550 |
| 313 | Loral | 600 3rd Ave., New York, NY 10016 | (212) 697-1105 |
| 332 | Lotus Development | 55 Cambridge Pkwy., Cambridge, MA 02142 | (617) 577-8500 |
| 661 | Louisiana Land | 909 Poydras St., New Orleans, LA 70112 | (504) 566-6500 |
| 206 | Louisiana-Pacific | 111 S.W. 5th Ave., Portland, OR 97204 | (503) 221-0800 |
| 199 | Lowe's | Hwy. 268 E., N. Wilkesboro, NC 28659 | (919) 651-4000 |
| 823 | LSI Logic | 1551 McCarthy Blvd., Milpitas, CA 95035 | (408) 433-8000 |
| 649 | LTV | 25 W. Prospect Ave., Cleveland, OH 44115 | (216) 622-5000 |
| 397 | Lubrizol | 29400 Lakeland Blvd., Wickliffe, OH 44092 | (216) 943-1200 |
| 502 | Lyondell Petrochemical | 1221 McKinney St., Houston, TX 77010 | (713) 652-7200 |
| 979 | Magma Power | 4365 Executive Dr., San Diego, CA 92121 | (619) 622-7800 |
| 548 | Manor Care | 10750 Columbus Pike, Silver Spring, MD 20901 | (301) 681-9400 |
| 613 | Manpower | 5301 N. Ironwood Rd., Milwaukee, WI 53217 | (414) 961-1000 |
| 753 | Manville | 717 17th St., Denver, CO 80202 | (303) 978-2000 |

*Corporate Contact Directory (cont'd)*

| Rank | Company | Corporate Headquarters | Phone |
|------|---------|------------------------|-------|
| 497 | Mapco | 1800 S. Baltimore Ave., Tulsa, OK 74119 | (918) 581-1800 |
| 218 | Marion Merrell Dow | 9300 Ward Pkwy., Kansas City, MO 64114 | (816) 966-4000 |
| 937 | Mark IV Industries | 501 Audubon Pkwy., Amherst, NY 14228 | (716) 689-4972 |
| 270 | Marriott International | 10400 Fernwood Rd., Bethesda, MD 20058 | (301) 380-3000 |
| 151 | Marsh & McLennan | 1166 Ave. of the Americas, New York, NY 10036 | (212) 345-5000 |
| 624 | Marshall & Ilsley | 770 N. Water St., Milwaukee, WI 53202 | (414) 765-7700 |
| 227 | Martin Marietta | 6801 Rockledge Dr., Bethesda, MD 20817 | (301) 897-6000 |
| 405 | Marvel Entertainment | 387 Park Ave. S., New York, NY 10016 | (212) 696-0808 |
| 174 | Masco | 21001 Van Born Rd., Taylor, MI 48180 | (313) 274-7400 |
| 682 | Mascotech | 21001 Van Born Rd., Taylor, MI 48180 | (313) 274-7400 |
| 220 | Mattel | 333 Continental Blvd., El Segundo, CA 90245 | (310) 524-2000 |
| 970 | Maxim Integrated | 120 San Gabriel Dr., Sunnyvale, CA 94086 | (408) 737-7600 |
| 76 | May Department Stores | 611 Olive St., St. Louis, MO 63101 | (314) 342-6300 |
| 491 | Maytag | 403 W. 4th St. N., Newton, IA 50208 | (515) 792-8000 |
| 394 | MBIA | 113 King St., Armonk, NY 10504 | (914) 273-4545 |
| 329 | MBNA | 400 Christiana Rd., Newark, DE 19713 | (800) 441-7048 |
| 81 | McCaw Cellular | 5400 Carillon Point, Kirkland, WA 98033 | (206) 827-4500 |
| 522 | McCormick | 18 Loveton Circle, Sparks, MD 21152 | (410) 771-7301 |
| 668 | McDermott International | 1450 Poydras St., New Orleans, LA 70112 | (504) 587-4411 |
| 34 | McDonald's | One McDonald's Plaza, Oak Brook, IL 60521 | (708) 575-3000 |
| 214 | McDonnell Douglas | J.S. McDonnell Blvd. & Airport Rd., Berkeley, MO 63134 | (314) 232-0232 |
| 290 | McGraw-Hill | 1221 Ave. of the Americas, New York, NY 10020 | (212) 512-2000 |
| 50 | MCI Communications | 1801 Pennsylvania Ave. NW, Washington, DC 20006 | (202) 872-1600 |
| 388 | McKesson | One Post St., San Francisco, CA 94104 | (415) 983-8300 |
| 722 | MCN | 500 Griswold St., Detroit, MI 48226 | (313) 256-5500 |
| 387 | Mead | Courthouse Plaza NE, Dayton, OH 45463 | (513) 222-6323 |
| 858 | Medical Care America | 13455 Noel Rd., Dallas, TX 75240 | (214) 701-2200 |
| 741 | Meditrust | 128 Technology Center, Waltham, MA 02154 | (617) 736-1500 |
| 217 | Medtronic | 7000 Central Ave. NE, Minneapolis, MN 55432 | (612) 574-4000 |
| 284 | Mellon Bank | One Melon Bank Center, Pittsburgh, PA 15258 | (412) 234-5000 |
| 245 | Melville | One Theall Rd., Rye, NY 10580 | (914) 925-4000 |
| 736 | Mercantile Bancorp. | 721 Locust St., St. Louis, MO 63101 | (314) 425-2525 |
| 884 | Mercantile Bankshares | 2 Hopkins Plaza, Baltimore, MD 21201 | (410) 237-5900 |
| 605 | Mercantile Stores | 9450 Seward Rd., Fairfield, OH 45014 | (513) 881-8000 |
| 8 | Merck | One Merck Dr., Whitehouse Station, NJ 08889 | (908) 423-1000 |
| 512 | Mercury Finance | 40 S. Skokie Blvd., Northbrook, IL 60062 | (708) 564-3720 |
| 936 | Mercury General | 4484 Wilshire Blvd., Los Angeles, CA 90010 | (213) 937-1060 |
| 558 | Meridian Bancorp | 35 N. 6th St., Reading, PA 19603 | (610) 655-2000 |
| 107 | Merrill Lynch | 250 Vesey St., North Tower, New York, NY 10281 | (212) 449-1000 |
| 1000 | Mesa Airlines | 2325 E. 30th St., Farmington, MN 87401 | (505) 327-0271 |
| 774 | Meyer (Fred) | 3800 S.E. 22nd Ave., Portland, OR 97202 | (503) 232-8844 |
| 469 | MFS Communications | 3555 Farnam St., Omaha, NE 68131 | (402) 271-2890 |
| 503 | Mgic Investment | 270 E. Kilbourn Ave., Milwaukee, WI 53202 | (414) 347-6480 |
| 561 | MGM Grand | 33799 Las Vegas Blvd. S., Las Vegas, NV 89109 | (702) 891-3333 |
| 807 | Michigan National | 27777 Inkster Rd., Farmington Hills, MI 48334 | (313) 473-3000 |
| 350 | Micron Technology | 2805 E. Columbia Rd., Boise, ID 83706 | (208) 368-4000 |
| 27 | Microsoft | One Microsoft Way, Redmond, WA 98052 | (206) 882-8080 |
| 941 | Mid Atlantic Medical | 4 Taft Court, Rockville, MD 20850 | (301) 762-8205 |
| 595 | Midlantic | 499 Thornall St., Edison, NJ 08837 | (908) 321-8000 |
| 859 | Midwest Resources | 666 Grand Ave., Des Moines, IA 50306 | (515) 242-4300 |

*Corporate Contact Directory (cont'd)*

| Rank | Company | Corporate Headquarters | Phone |
|------|---------|------------------------|-------|
| 896 | Miller (Herman) | 855 E. Main Ave., Zeeland, MI 49464 | (616) 654-3000 |
| 683 | Millipore | 80 Ashby Rd., Bedford, MA 01730 | (617) 275-9200 |
| 997 | Minerals Technologies | 405 Lexington Ave., New York, NY 10174 | (212) 878-1800 |
| 32 | Minnesota Mining & Mfg. | 3M Center, St. Paul, MN 55144 | (612) 733-1110 |
| 916 | Minnesota Power | 30 W. Superior St., Duluth, MN 55802 | (218) 722-2641 |
| 424 | Mirage Resorts | 3400 Las Vegas Blvd. S., Las Vegas, NV 89109 | (702) 791-7111 |
| 797 | Mitchell Energy | 2001 Timberloch Pl., The Woodlands, TX 77380 | (713) 377-5500 |
| 11 | Mobil | 3225 Gallows Rd., Fairfax, VA 22037 | (703) 846-3000 |
| 927 | Modine Manufacturing | 1500 De Koven Ave., Racine, WI 53403 | (414) 636-1200 |
| 433 | Molex | 2222 Wellington Court, Lisle, IL 60532 | (708) 969-4550 |
| 98 | Monsanto | 800 N. Lindbergh Blvd., St. Louis, MO 63167 | (314) 694-1000 |
| 652 | Montana Power | 40 E. Broadway, Butte, MT 59701 | (406) 723-5421 |
| 62 | Morgan (J.P.) | 60 Wall St., New York, NY 10260 | (212) 483-2323 |
| 193 | Morgan Stanley Group | 1251 Ave. of the Americas, New York, NY 10020 | (212) 703-4000 |
| 892 | Morrison Knudsen | 720 Park Blvd., Boise, ID 83729 | (208) 386-5000 |
| 849 | Morrison Restaurants | 4721 Morrison Dr., Mobile, AL 36609 | (205) 344-3000 |
| 179 | Morton International | 100 N. Riverside Plaza, Chicago, IL 60606 | (312) 807-2000 |
| 17 | Motorola | 1303 E. Algonquin Rd., Schaumburg, IL 60196 | (708) 576-5000 |
| 699 | Multimedia | 305 S. Main St., Greenville, SC 29601 | (803) 298-4373 |
| 509 | Murphy Oil | 200 Peach St., El Dorado, AR 71730 | (501) 862-6411 |
| 489 | Mylan Laboratories | 130 7th St., Pittsburgh, PA 15222 | (412) 232-0100 |
| 401 | Nalco Chemical | One Nalco Center, Naperville, IL 60563 | (708) 305-1000 |
| 250 | National City | 1900 E. 9th St., Cleveland, OH 44114 | (216) 575-2000 |
| 718 | National Fuel Gas | 10 Lafayette Square, Buffalo, NY 14203 | (716) 857-7000 |
| 903 | National Gypsum | 2001 Rexford Rd., Charlotte, NC 28211 | (704) 365-7300 |
| 701 | National Health Labs | 4225 Executive Square, La Jolla, CA 92037 | (619) 550-0600 |
| 390 | National Medical Ents. | 2700 Colorado Ave., Santa Monica, CA 90404 | (310) 998-8000 |
| 411 | National Semiconductor | 2900 Semiconductor Dr., Santa Clara, CA 95052 | (408) 721-5000 |
| 617 | National Service Inds. | 1420 Peachtree St., NE, Atlanta, GA 30309 | (404) 853-1000 |
| 60 | Nationsbank | 100 N. Tryon St., Charlotte, NC 28255 | (704) 386-5000 |
| 981 | Nationwide Health | 4675 MacArthur Ct., Newport Beach, CA 92660 | (714) 251-1211 |
| 506 | Navistar International | 455 N. Cityfront Plaza Dr., Chicago, IL 60611 | (312) 836-2000 |
| 216 | NBD Bancorp | 611 Woodward Ave., Detroit, MI 48226 | (313) 225-1000 |
| 866 | Nevada Power | 6226 W. Sahara Ave., Las Vegas, NV 89102 | (702) 367-5000 |
| 419 | New England Electric | 25 Research Dr., Westboro, MA 01582 | (508) 366-9011 |
| 721 | New Plan Realty Trust | 1120 Ave. of the Americas, New York, NY 10036 | (212) 869-3000 |
| 484 | New York State E&G | 4500 Vestal Pkwy. E., Binghamton, NY 13902 | (607) 729-2551 |
| 339 | New York Times | 229 W. 43rd St., New York, NY 10036 | (212) 556-1234 |
| 316 | Newell | 29 E. Stephenson St., Freeport, IL 61032 | (815) 235-4171 |
| 209 | Newmont Gold | One Norwest Bank Center, Denver, CO 80203 | (303) 863-7414 |
| 269 | Newmont Mining | One Norwest Bank Center, Denver, CO 80203 | (303) 863-7414 |
| 262 | Nextel Communications | 201 Rte. 17 N., Rutherford, NJ 07070 | (201) 438-1400 |
| 375 | Niagara Mohawk Power | 300 Erie Blvd. W., Syracuse, NY 13202 | (315) 474-1511 |
| 593 | Nicor | 1844 Ferry Rd., Naperville, IL 60563 | (708) 305-9500 |
| 260 | Nike | One Bowerman Dr., Beaverton, OR 97005 | (503) 671-6453 |
| 729 | Nine West | 9 W. Broad St., Stamford, CT 06902 | (203) 324-7567 |
| 472 | Nipsco Industries | 5265 Hohman Ave., Hammond, IN 46320 | (219) 853-5200 |
| 642 | Noble Affiliates | 110 W. Broadway, Ardmore, OK 73401 | (405) 223-4110 |
| 763 | Nordson | 28601 Clemens Rd., Westlake, OH 44145 | (216) 892-1580 |
| 315 | Nordstrom | 1501 5th Ave., Seattle, WA 98101 | (206) 628-2111 |

*Corporate Contact Directory (cont'd)*

| Rank | Company | Corporate Headquarters | Phone |
|------|---------|------------------------|-------|
| 89 | Norfolk Southern | 3 Commercial Pl., Norfolk, VA 23510 | (804) 629-2600 |
| 319 | Northeast Utilities | 107 Selden St., Berlin, CT 06037 | (203) 665-5000 |
| 363 | Northern States Power | 414 Nicollet Mall, Minneapolis, MN 55401 | (612) 330-5500 |
| 431 | Northern Trust | 50 S. LaSalle St., Chicago, IL 60675 | (312) 630-6000 |
| 477 | Northrop | 1840 Century Park E., Los Angeles, CA 90067 | (310) 553-6262 |
| 131 | Norwest | 6th St. & Marquette Ave., Minneapolis, MN 55479 | (612) 667-1234 |
| 711 | Novacare | 1016 W. 9th Ave., King of Prussia, PA 19406 | (215) 992-7200 |
| 113 | Novell | 122 E. 1700 S., Provo, UT 84606 | (801) 429-7000 |
| 186 | Nucor | 2100 Rexford Rd., Charlotte, NC 28211 | (704) 366-7000 |
| 929 | NWNL | 20 Washington Ave. S., Minneapolis, MN 55401 | (612) 372-5432 |
| 49 | NYNEX | 335 Madison Ave., New York, NY 10017 | (212) 370-7400 |
| 168 | Occidental Petroleum | 10889 Wilshire Blvd., Los Angeles, CA 90024 | (310) 208-8800 |
| 291 | Office Depot | 2200 Old Germantown Rd., Delray Beach, FL 33445 | (407) 278-4800 |
| 805 | Ogden | 2 Pennsylvania Plaza, New York, NY 10121 | (212) 868-6000 |
| 710 | Ohio Casualty | 136 N. 3rd St., Hamilton, OH 45025 | (513) 867-3000 |
| 323 | Ohio Edison | 76 S. Main St., Akron, OH 44308 | (216) 384-5100 |
| 603 | Oklahoma G&E | 101 N. Robinson Ave., Oklahoma City, OK 73102 | (405) 272-3000 |
| 653 | Old Kent Financial | One Vandenberg Center, Grand Rapids, MI 49503 | (616) 771-5000 |
| 993 | Old National Bancorp | 420 Main St., Evansville, IN 47708 | (812) 464-1434 |
| 667 | Old Republic International | 307 N. Michigan Ave., Chicago, IL 60601 | (312) 346-8100 |
| 830 | Olin | 120 Long Ridge Rd., Stamford, CT 06904 | (203) 356-2000 |
| 645 | Olsten | One Merrick Ave., Westbury, NY 11590 | (516) 832-8200 |
| 541 | Omnicom Group | 437 Madison Ave., New York, NY 10022 | (212) 415-3600 |
| 88 | Oracle Systems | 500 Oracle Pkwy., Redwood Shores, CA 94065 | (415) 506-7000 |
| 521 | Oryx Energy | 13155 Noel Rd., Dallas, TX 75240 | (214) 715-4000 |
| 735 | Outback Steakhouse | 550 N. Reo St., Tampa, FL 33609 | (813) 282-1225 |
| 960 | Overseas Shipholding | 1114 Ave. of the Americas, New York, NY 10036 | (212) 869-1222 |
| 523 | Owens-Corning | Fiberglas Tower, Toledo, OH 43659 | (419) 248-8000 |
| 580 | Owens-Illinois | One SeaGate, Toledo, OH 43666 | (419) 247-5000 |
| 801 | Oxford Health Plans | 800 Connecticut Ave., Norwalk, CT 06851 | (203) 852-1442 |
| 427 | Paccar | 777 106th Ave., NE, Bellevue, WA 98004 | (206) 455-7400 |
| 508 | Pacific Enterprises | 633 W. 5th St., Los Angeles, CA 90071 | (213) 895-5000 |
| 58 | Pacific Gas & Electric | 77 Beale St., San Francisco, CA 94177 | (415) 973-7000 |
| 790 | Pacific Telecom | 805 Broadway, Vancouver, WA 98668 | (206) 696-0983 |
| 28 | Pacific Telesis Group | 130 Kearny St., San Francisco, CA 94108 | (415) 394-3000 |
| 610 | Pacificare Health | 5995 Plaza Dr., Cypress, CA 90630 | (714) 952-1121 |
| 185 | Pacificorp | 700 N.E. Multnomah St., Portland, OR 97232 | (503) 731-2000 |
| 73 | Pactel | 2999 Oak Rd., Walnut Creek, CA 94596 | (510) 210-3900 |
| 604 | Paging Network | 4965 Preston Park Blvd., Plano, TX 75093 | (214) 985-4100 |
| 636 | Painewebber Group | 1285 Ave. of the Americas, New York, NY 10019 | (212) 713-2000 |
| 449 | Pall | 2200 Northern Blvd., East Hills, NY 11548 | (516) 484-5400 |
| 385 | Panhandle Eastern | 5400 Westheimer Court, Houston, TX 77056 | (713) 627-5400 |
| 481 | Parametric Technology | 128 Technology Dr., Waltham, MA 02154 | (617) 894-7111 |
| 95 | Paramount Communications | 15 Columbus Circle, New York, NY 10023 | (212) 373-8000 |
| 525 | Parker Hannifin | 17325 Euclid Ave., Cleveland, OH 44112 | (216) 531-3000 |
| 743 | Paul Revere | 18 Chestnut St., Worcester, MA 01608 | (508) 799-4441 |
| 698 | Paychex | 911 Panorama Trail S., Rochester, NY 14625 | (716) 385-6666 |
| 959 | Payless Cashways | 2300 Main St., Kansas City, MO 64141 | (816) 234-6000 |
| 156 | Peco Energy | 2301 Market St., Philadelphia, PA 19101 | (215) 841-4000 |
| 78 | Penney (J.C.) | 6501 Legacy Dr., Plano, TX 75024 | (214) 431-1000 |

*Corporate Contact Directory (cont'd)*

| Rank | Company | Corporate Headquarters | Phone |
|------|---------|------------------------|-------|
| 271 | Pennsylvania Power | 2 N. 9th St., Allentown, PA 18101 | (215) 774-5151 |
| 408 | Pennzoil | 700 Milam St., Houston, TX 77002 | (713) 546-4000 |
| 769 | Peoples Energy | 122 S. Michigan Ave., Chicago, IL 60603 | (312) 431-4000 |
| 529 | Pep Boys | 3111 W. Allegheny Ave., Philadelphia, PA 19132 | (215) 229-9000 |
| 12 | PepsiCo | 700 Anderson Hill Rd., Purchase, NY 10577 | (914) 253-2000 |
| 538 | Perkin-Elmer | 761 Main Ave., Norwalk, CT 06859 | (203) 762-1000 |
| 438 | Perrigo | 117 Water St., Allegan, MI 49010 | (616) 673-8451 |
| 465 | Pet | 400 S. 4th St., St. Louis, MO 63102 | (314) 622-7700 |
| 647 | Petrie Stores | 70 Enterprise Ave., Secaucus, NJ 07094 | (201) 866-3600 |
| 912 | Petsmart | 10000 N. 31st Ave., Phoenix, AZ 85051 | (602) 944-7070 |
| 39 | Pfizer | 235 E. 42nd St., New York, NY 10017 | (212) 573-2323 |
| 256 | Phelps Dodge | 2600 N. Central Ave., Phoenix, AZ 85004 | (602) 234-8100 |
| 6 | Philip Morris | 120 Park Ave., New York, NY 10017 | (212) 880-5000 |
| 125 | Phillips Petroleum | 4th & Keeler Sts., Bartlesville, OK 74004 | (918) 661-6600 |
| 837 | Phillips-Van Heusen | 1290 Ave. of the Americas, New York, NY 10104 | (212) 541-5200 |
| 773 | Physician Corporation | 5835 Blue Lagoon Dr., Miami, FL 33126 | (305) 267-6633 |
| 492 | Pinnacle West Capital | 400 E. Van Buren St., Phoenix, AZ 85004 | (602) 379-2500 |
| 309 | Pioneer Hi-Bred Intl. | 400 Locust St., Des Moines, IA 50309 | (515) 245-3500 |
| 130 | Pitney Bowes | One Elm Croft Rd., Stamford, CT 06926 | (203) 356-5000 |
| 726 | Pittston Services | 100 First Stamford Pl., Stamford, CT 06912 | (203) 978-5200 |
| 147 | Pnc Bank | 5th Ave. and Wood St., Pittsburgh, PA 15265 | (412) 762-2000 |
| 587 | Polaroid | 549 Technology Square, Cambridge, MA 02139 | (617) 386-2000 |
| 910 | Policy Management | I-77 & U.S. 21 N., Blythewood, SC 29016 | (803) 735-4000 |
| 873 | Portland General | 121 S.W. Salmon St., Portland, OR 97204 | (503) 464-8000 |
| 622 | Potlatch | One Maritime Plaza, San Francisco, CA 94111 | (415) 576-8800 |
| 360 | Potomac Electric Power | 1900 Pennsylvania Ave., NW, Washington, DC 20068 | (202) 872-2000 |
| 109 | PPG Industries | One PPG Pl., Pittsburgh, PA 15272 | (412) 434-3131 |
| 398 | Praxair | 39 Old Ridgebury Rd., Danbury, CT 06810 | (203) 794-3000 |
| 392 | Premark International | 1717 Deerfield Rd., Deerfield, IL 60015 | (708) 405-6000 |
| 439 | Premier Industrial | 4500 Euclid Ave., Cleveland, OH 44103 | (216) 391-8300 |
| 851 | Price (T. Rowe) | 100 E. Pratt St., Baltimore, MD 21202 | (410) 547-2000 |
| 229 | Price/Costco | 4649 Morena Blvd., San Diego, CA 92117 | (619) 581-4600 |
| 943 | Primadonna Resorts | Interstate 15, Jean, NV 89019 | (702) 382-1212 |
| 9 | Procter & Gamble | One Procter & Gamble Plaza, Cincinnati, OH 45202 | (513) 983-1100 |
| 409 | Progressive | 630 Wilson Mills Rd., Mayfield Village, OH 44143 | (216) 461-5000 |
| 187 | Promus | 1023 Cherry Rd., Memphis, TN 38117 | (901) 762-8600 |
| 831 | Property Trust | 7777 Market Center Ave., El Paso, TX 79912 | (915) 877-3900 |
| 643 | Provident Life | One Fountain Square, Chattanooga, TN 37402 | (615) 755-1011 |
| 504 | PS of Colorado | 1225 17th St., Denver, CO 80202 | (303) 571-7511 |
| 618 | PSI Resources | 1000 E. Main St., Plainfield, IN 46168 | (317) 839-9611 |
| 119 | Public Service Ent. | 80 Park Plaza, Newark, NJ 07101 | (201) 430-7000 |
| 596 | Puget Sound Power | 411 108th Ave. N.E., Bellevue, WA 98004 | (206) 454-6363 |
| 839 | Pulte | 33 Bloomfield Hills Pkwy., Bloomfield Hills, MI 48304 | (313) 647-2750 |
| 696 | Pyxis | 9380 Carroll Park Dr., San Diego, CA 92121 | (619) 625-3300 |
| 234 | Quaker Oats | 321 N. Clark St., Chicago, IL 60610 | (312) 222-7111 |
| 712 | Qualcomm | 6455 Lusk Blvd,, San Diego, CA 92121 | (619) 658-4400 |
| 984 | Quantum | 500 McCarthy Blvd., Milpitas, CA 95035 | (408) 894-4000 |
| 662 | Questar | 180 E. 1st S., Salt Lake City, UT 84111 | (801) 534-5000 |
| 496 | QVC Network | 1365 Enterprise Dr., West Chester, PA 19380 | (215) 430-1000 |
| 224 | Ralston Purina | Checkerboard Square, St. Louis, MO 63164 | (314) 982-1000 |

*Corporate Contact Directory (cont'd)*

| Rank | Company | Corporate Headquarters | Phone |
|---|---|---|---|
| 556 | Raychem | 300 Constitution Dr., Menlo Park, CA 94025 | (415) 361-3333 |
| 808 | Rayonier | 1177 Summer St., Stamford, CT 9 06904 | (203) 348-7000 |
| 104 | Raytheon | 141 Spring St., Lexington, MA 02173 | (617) 862-6600 |
| 192 | Reader's Digest | Reader's Digest Rd., Pleasantville, NY 10570 | (914) 238-1000 |
| 357 | Reebok International | 100 Technology Center Dr., Stoughton, MA 02072 | (617) 341-5000 |
| 879 | Reliance Electric | 6065 Parkland Blvd., Cleveland, OH 44124 | (216) 266-5800 |
| 374 | Republic New York | 452 5th Ave., New York, NY 10018 | (212) 525-5000 |
| 947 | Revco D.S. | 1925 Enterprise Pkwy., Twinsburg, OH 44087 | (216) 425-9811 |
| 765 | Reynolds & Reynolds | 115 S. Ludlow St., Dayton, OH 45402 | (513) 443-2000 |
| 330 | Reynolds Metals | 6601 W. Broad St., Richmond, VA 23230 | (804) 281-2000 |
| 191 | Rhone-Poulenc Rorer | 500 Arcola Rd., Collegeville, PA 19426 | (610) 454-8000 |
| 536 | Rite Aid | 30 Hunter Ln., Camp Hill, PA 17011 | (717) 761-2633 |
| 715 | Riverwood International | 3350 Cumberland Circle, Atlanta, GA 30339 | (404) 644-3000 |
| 114 | RJR Nabisco Holdings | 1301 Ave. of the Americas, New York, NY 10019 | (212) 258-5600 |
| 362 | Roadway Services | 1077 Gorge Blvd., Akron, OH 44309 | (216) 384-8184 |
| 862 | Rochester G&E | 89 East Ave., Rochester, NY 14649 | (716) 546-2700 |
| 585 | Rochester Telephone | 180 S. Clinton Ave., Rochester, NY 14646 | (716) 777-1000 |
| 93 | Rockwell International | 2201 Seal Beach Blvd., Seal Beach, CA 90740 | (310) 797-3311 |
| 261 | Rohm & Haas | Independence Mall W., Philadelphia, PA 19106 | (215) 592-3000 |
| 766 | Rollins | 2170 Piedmont Rd., NE, Atlanta, GA 30324 | (404) 888-2000 |
| 889 | Rouse | 10275 Little Patuxent Pkwy., Columbia, MD 21044 | (410) 992-6000 |
| 744 | RPM | 2628 Pearl Rd., Medina, OH 44258 | (216) 273-5090 |
| 201 | Rubbermaid | 1147 Akron Rd., Wooster, OH 44691 | (216) 264-6464 |
| 717 | Russell | One Lee St., Alexander City, AL 35010 | (205) 329-4000 |
| 530 | Rust International | 100 Corporate Pkwy., Birmingham, AL 35242 | (205) 995-7878 |
| 450 | Ryder System | 3600 N.W. 82nd Ave., Miami, FL 33166 | (305) 593-3726 |
| 277 | Safeco | Safeco Plaza, Seattle, WA 98185 | (206) 545-5000 |
| 860 | Safety-Kleen | 1000 N. Randall Rd., Elgin, IL 60123 | (708) 697-8460 |
| 404 | Safeway | 201 4th St., Oakland, CA 94660 | (510) 891-3000 |
| 265 | Sallie Mae | 1050 Thomas Jefferson St., NW, Washington, DC 20007 | (202) 333-8000 |
| 169 | Salomon | 7 World Trade Center, New York, NY 10048 | (212) 783-7000 |
| 370 | San Diego G&E | 101 Ash St., San Diego, CA 92101 | (619) 696-2000 |
| 911 | Santa Fe Energy | 1616 S. Voss, Houston, TX 77057 | (713) 783-2401 |
| 237 | Santa Fe Pacific | 1700 E. Golf Rd., Schaumburg, IL 60173 | (708) 995-6000 |
| 78 | Sara Lee | 3 First National Plaza, Chicago, IL 60602 | (312) 726-2600 |
| 444 | Scana | 1426 Main St., Columbia, SC 29201 | (803) 748-3000 |
| 110 | Scecorp | 2244 Walnut Grove Ave., Rosemead, CA 91770 | (818) 302-1212 |
| 865 | Scherer (R.P.) | 2075 W. Big Beaver Rd., Troy, MI 48084 | (313) 649-0900 |
| 70 | Schering-Plough | One Giralda Farms, Madison, NJ 07940 | (201) 822-7000 |
| 56 | Schlumberger | 277 Park Ave., New York, NY 10172 | (212) 350-9400 |
| 779 | Schulman (A.) | 3550 W. Market St., Akron, OH 44333 | (216) 666-3751 |
| 554 | Schwab (Charles) | 101 Montgomery St., San Francisco, CA 94104 | (415) 627-7000 |
| 793 | Scientific-Atlanta | One Technology Pkwy. South, Norcross, GA 30092 | (404) 903-5000 |
| 300 | Scott Paper | Scott Plaza, Philadelphia, PA 19113 | (215) 522-5000 |
| 448 | Scripps (E.W.) | 312 Walnut St., Cincinnati, OH 45202 | (513) 977-3000 |
| 867 | Scripps Howard | 312 Walnut St., Cincinnati, OH 45202 | (513) 977-3000 |
| 499 | Seagate Technology | 920 Disc Dr., Scotts Valley, CA 95066 | (408) 438-6550 |
| 864 | Seagull Energy | 1001 Fannin St., Houston, TX 77002 | (713) 951-4700 |
| 46 | Sears, Roebuck | 333 Beverly Rd., Hoffman Estates, IL 60179 | (708) 286-2500 |
| 442 | Sensormatic | 500 N.W. 12th Ave., Deerfield Beach, FL 33442 | (305) 427-9700 |

*Corporate Contact Directory (cont'd)*

| Rank | Company | Corporate Headquarters | Phone |
|------|---------|------------------------|-------|
| 429 | Service Corp. International | 1929 Allen Pkwy., Houston, TX 77019 | (713) 522-5141 |
| 925 | Service Merchandise | 7100 Service Merchandise Dr., Brentwood, TN 37027 | (615) 660-6000 |
| 470 | ServiceMaster | One ServiceMaster Way, Downers Grove, IL 60515 | (708) 964-1300 |
| 369 | Shaw Industries | 616 E. Walnut Ave., Dalton, GA 30720 | (706) 278-3812 |
| 466 | Shawmut National | 777 Main St., Hartford, CT 06115 | (203) 728-2000 |
| 325 | Sherwin-Williams | 101 Prospect Ave. NW, Cleveland, OH 44115 | (216) 566-2000 |
| 828 | Shoney's | 1727 Elm Hill Pike, Nashville, TN 37210 | (615) 391-5201 |
| 395 | Sigma-Aldrich | 3050 Spruce St., St. Louis, MO 63103 | (314) 771-5765 |
| 453 | Signet Banking | 7 N. 8th St., Richmond, VA 23219 | (804) 747-2000 |
| 312 | Silicon Graphics | 2011 N. Shoreline Blvd., Mountain View, CA 94039 | (415) 960-1980 |
| 949 | Sithe Energies | 450 Lexington Ave., New York, NY 10017 | (212) 450-9000 |
| 964 | Smith (A.O.) | 11270 W. Park Pl., Milwaukee, WI 53224 | (414) 359-4000 |
| 980 | Smucker (J.M.) | Strawberry Ln., Orrville, OH 44667 | (216) 682-3000 |
| 286 | Snapple Beverage | 175 N. Central Ave., Valley Stream, NY 11580 | (516) 872-4800 |
| 488 | Snap-On Tools | 2801 80th St., Kenosha, WI 53141 | (414) 656-5200 |
| 648 | Solectron | 847 Gibraltar Dr., Milpitas, CA 95035 | (408) 957-8500 |
| 376 | Sonat | 1900 5th., N. Birmingham, AL 35203 | (205) 325-3800 |
| 435 | Sonoco Products | N. 2nd St., Hartsville, SC 29550 | (803) 383-7000 |
| 852 | Sotheby's Holdings | 1334 York Ave., New York, NY 10021 | (212) 606-7000 |
| 461 | S. New England Tel. | 227 Church St., New Haven, CT 06510 | (203) 771-5200 |
| 61 | Southern | 64 Perimeter Center E., Atlanta, GA 30346 | (404) 393-0650 |
| 364 | Southern Pacific Rail | One Market Plaza, San Francisco, CA 94105 | (415) 541-1000 |
| 457 | Southland | 2711 N. Haskell Ave., Dallas, TX 75204 | (214) 828-7011 |
| 581 | Southtrust | 420 N. 20th St., Birmingham, AL 35203 | (205) 254-5000 |
| 208 | Southwest Airlines | 2702 Love Field Dr., Dallas, TX 75235 | (214) 904-4000 |
| 26 | Southwestern Bell | 175 E. Houston, San Antonio, TX 78205 | (210) 821-4105 |
| 709 | Southwestern PS | 600 S. Tyler St., Amarillo, TX 79101 | (806) 378-2121 |
| 428 | Spiegel | 3500 Lacey Rd., Downers Grove, IL 60515 | (708) 986-8800 |
| 65 | Sprint | 2330 Shawnee Mission, Westwood, KS 66205 | (816) 854-0903 |
| 985 | SPS Transaction | 2500 Lake Cook Rd., Riverwoods, IL 60015 | (708) 405-0900 |
| 547 | St. Joe Paper | 1650 Prudential Dr., Jacksonville, FL 32207 | (904) 396-6600 |
| 630 | St. Jude Medical | One Lillehei Plaza, St. Paul, MN 55117 | (612) 483-2000 |
| 285 | St. Paul | 385 Washington St., St. Paul, MN 55102 | (612) 221-7911 |
| 875 | Standard Federal Bank | 2600 W. Big Beaver Rd., Troy, MI 48084 | (313) 643-9600 |
| 485 | Stanley Works | 1000 Stanley Dr., New Britain, CT 06053 | (203) 225-5111 |
| 745 | Staples | 100 Pennsylvania Ave., Framingham, MA 01701 | (508) 370-8500 |
| 758 | Star Banc | 425 Walnut St., Cincinnati, OH 45202 | (513) 632-4000 |
| 356 | State Street Boston | 225 Franklin St., Boston, MA 02110 | (617) 786-3000 |
| 546 | Stewart & Stevenson | 2707 N. Loop W., Houston, TX 77008 | (713) 868-7700 |
| 732 | Stone Container | 150 N. Michigan Ave., Chicago, IL 60601 | (312) 346-6600 |
| 672 | Stop & Shop | 1358 Hancock Dr., Quincy, MA 02169 | (617) 380-8000 |
| 591 | Storage Technology | 2270 S. 88th St., Louisville, CO 80028 | (303) 673-5151 |
| 886 | Stride Rite | 5 Cambridge Center, Cambridge, MA 02142 | (617) 491-8800 |
| 559 | Stryker | 2725 Fairfield Rd., Kalamazoo, MI 49002 | (616) 385-2600 |
| 274 | Sun | 1801 Market St., Philadelphia, PA 19103 | (215) 977-3000 |
| 383 | Sun Microsystems | 2550 Garcia Ave., Mountain View, CA 94043 | (415) 960-1300 |
| 693 | Sunamerica | 1999 Ave. of the Stars, Los Angeles, CA 90067 | (310) 772-6000 |
| 565 | Sunbeam-Oster | 200 E. Las Olas Blvd., Ft. Lauderdale, FL 33301 | (305) 767-2100 |
| 576 | Sundstrand | 4949 Harrison Ave., Rockford, IL 61125 | (815) 226-6000 |
| 983 | Sungard Data Systems | 1285 Drummers Ln., Wayne, PA 19087 | (215) 341-8700 |

*Corporate Contact Directory (cont'd)*

| Rank | Company | Corporate Headquarters | Phone |
|------|---------|------------------------|-------|
| 167 | Suntrust Banks | 25 Park Pl., NE, Atlanta, GA 30303 | (404) 588-7711 |
| 373 | Supervalu | 11840 Valley View, Eden Prairie, MN 55344 | (612) 828-4000 |
| 677 | Superior Industries | 7800 Woodley Ave., Van Nuys, CA 91406 | (818) 781-4973 |
| 446 | Sybase | 6475 Christie Ave., Emeryville, CA 94608 | (510) 922-3500 |
| 975 | Sybron International | 411 E. Wisconsin Ave., Milwaukee, WI 53202 | (414) 274-6600 |
| 944 | Synopsys | 700 E. Middlefield Ave., Mountain View, CA 94043 | (415) 962-5000 |
| 551 | Synoptics Communications | 4401 Great American Pkwy., Santa Clara, CA 95052 | (408) 988-2400 |
| 700 | Synovus Financial | 901 Front Ave., Columbus, GA 31901 | (706) 649-2311 |
| 295 | Syntex | 3401 Hillview Ave., Palo Alto, CA 94304 | (415) 855-5050 |
| 189 | Sysco | 1390 Enclave Pkwy., Houston, TX 77077 | (713) 584-1390 |
| 883 | Takecare | 2300 Clayton Ave., Concord, CA 94520 | (510) 246-1300 |
| 759 | Talbots | 175 Beal St., Hingham, MA 02043 | (617) 749-7600 |
| 544 | Tambrands | 777 Westchester Ave., White Plains, NY 10604 | (914) 696-6000 |
| 535 | Tandem Computers | 19333 Vallco Pkwy., Cupertino, CA 95014 | (408) 285-6000 |
| 384 | Tandy | 1800 One Tandy Center, Fort Worth, TX 76102 | (817) 390-3700 |
| 415 | Teco Energy | 702 N. Franklin St., Tampa, FL 33602 | (813) 228-4111 |
| 705 | Tecumseh Products | 100 E. Patterson St., Tecumseh, MI 49286 | (517) 423-8411 |
| 926 | Tektronix | 26600 SW Pkwy., Wilsonville, OR 97070 | (503) 685-3180 |
| 83 | Tele-Communications | 5619 DTC Pkwy., Englewood, CO 80111 | (303) 267-5500 |
| 704 | Teledyne | 1901 Ave. of the Stars, Los Angeles, CA 90067 | (310) 277-3311 |
| 434 | Telephone & Data | 30 N. LaSalle St., Chicago, IL 60602 | (312) 630-1900 |
| 716 | Tellabs | 4951 Indiana Ave., Lisle, IL 60532 | (708) 969-8800 |
| 353 | Temple-Inland | 303 S. Temple Dr., Diboll, TX 75941 | (409) 829-5511 |
| 90 | Tenneco | 1010 Milam St., Houston, TX 77002 | (713) 757-2131 |
| 775 | Teradyne | 321 Harrison Ave., Boston, MA 02118 | (617) 482-2700 |
| 42 | Texaco | 2000 Westchester Ave., White Plains, NY 10650 | (914) 253-4000 |
| 120 | Texas Instruments | 13500 N. Central Expwy., Dallas, TX 75265 | (214) 995-2011 |
| 101 | Texas Utilities | 2001 Bryan St., Dallas, TX 75201 | (214) 812-4600 |
| 180 | Textron | 40 Westminster St., Providence, RI 02903 | (401) 421-2800 |
| 475 | Thermo Electron | 81 Wyman St., Waltham, MA 02254 | (617) 622-1000 |
| 592 | Thermo Instrument | 504 Airport Rd., Santa Fe, NM 87501 | (505) 438-3171 |
| 676 | Thomas & Betts | 1555 Linfield Rd., Memphis, TN 38119 | (901) 682-7766 |
| 486 | 3Com | 5400 Bayfront Plaza, Santa Clara, CA 95052 | (408) 764-5000 |
| 692 | Tidewater | 1440 Canal St., New Orleans, LA 70112 | (504) 568-1010 |
| 632 | TIG Holdings | 6300 Canoga Ave., Woodland Hills, CA 91367 | (818) 596-5000 |
| 53 | Time Warner | 75 Rockefeller Plaza, New York, NY 10019 | (212) 484-8000 |
| 226 | Times Mirror | Times Mirror Square, Los Angeles, CA 90053 | (213) 237-3700 |
| 739 | Timken | 1835 Dueber Ave., SW, Canton, OH 44706 | (216) 438-3000 |
| 476 | TJX | 770 Cochituate Rd., Framingham, MA 01701 | (508) 390-3000 |
| 965 | Tootsie Roll Industries | 7401 S. Cicero Ave., Chicago, IL 60629 | (312) 838-3400 |
| 321 | Torchmarx | 2001 3rd Ave S., Birmingham, AL 35233 | (205) 325-4200 |
| 810 | Tosco | 72 Cummings Point Rd., Stamford, CT 06902 | (203) 977-1000 |
| 900 | Total System Services | 1200 6th Ave., Columbus, GA 31901 | (706) 649-2310 |
| 79 | Toys 'R' Us | 461 From Rd., Paramus, NJ 07652 | (201) 262-7800 |
| 259 | Transamerica | 600 Montgomery St., San Francisco, CA 94111 | (415) 983-4000 |
| 752 | Transatlantic Holdings | 80 Pine St., New York, NY 10005 | (212) 770-2000 |
| 67 | Travelers | 65 E. 55th St., New York, NY 10022 | (212) 891-8900 |
| 258 | Tribune | 435 N. Michigan Ave., Chicago, IL 60611 | (312) 222-9100 |
| 778 | Trimas | 315 E. Eisenhower Pkwy., Ann Arbor, MI 48108 | (313) 747-7025 |
| 519 | Trinity Industries | 2525 Stemmons Frwy., Dallas TX 75207 | (214) 631-4420 |

*Corporate Contact Directory (cont'd)*

| Rank | Company | Corporate Headquarters | Phone |
|------|---------|------------------------|-------|
| 754 | Trinova | 3000 Strayer, Maumee, OH 43537 | (419) 867-2200 |
| 777 | Triton Energy | 6688 N. Central Expwy., Dallas, TX 75206 | (214) 691-5200 |
| 213 | TRW | 1900 Richmond Rd., Cleveland, OH 44124 | (216) 291-7000 |
| 230 | Turner Broadcasting | One CNN Center, Atlanta, GA 30348 | (404) 827-1700 |
| 627 | Twentieth Century Inds. | 6301 Owensmouth Ave., Woodland Hills, CA 91367 | (818) 704-3400 |
| 413 | Tyco International | One Tyco Park, Exeter, NH 03833 | (603) 778-9700 |
| 317 | Tyson Foods | 2210 Oaklawn Dr., Springdale, AR 72762 | (501) 290-4000 |
| 379 | U.S. Bancorp | 111 S.W. 5th Ave., Portland, OR 97204 | (503) 275-6111 |
| 443 | U.S. Cellular | 8410 W. Bryn Mawr Ave., Chicago, IL 60631 | (312) 399-8900 |
| 132 | U.S. Healthcare | 980 Jolly Rd., Blue Bell, PA 19422 | (215) 628-4800 |
| 809 | U.S. Surgical | 150 Glover Ave., Norwalk, CT 06856 | (203) 845-1000 |
| 307 | UAL | 1200 E. Algonquin Rd., Elk Grove Village, IL 60007 | (708) 952-4000 |
| 976 | UGI | 460 N. Gulph Rd., Valley Forge, PA 19482 | (215) 337-1000 |
| 623 | UJB Financial | 301 Carnegie Center, Princeton, NJ 08543 | (609) 987-3200 |
| 719 | Ultramar | 2 Pickwick Plaza, Greenwich, CT 06830 | (203) 622-7000 |
| 542 | Unifi | 7201 W. Friendly Rd., Greensboro, NC 27410 | (919) 294-4410 |
| 842 | Union Bank | 350 California St., San Francisco, CA 94104 | (415) 445-0200 |
| 301 | Union Camp | 1600 Valley Rd., Wayne, NJ 07470 | (201) 628-2000 |
| 279 | Union Carbide | 39 Old Ridgebury Rd., Danbury, CT 06817 | (203) 794-2000 |
| 267 | Union Electric | 1901 Chouteau Ave., St. Louis, MO 63103 | (314) 342-1000 |
| 66 | Union Pacific | 8th & Eaton Aves., Bethlehem, PA 18018 | (610) 861-3200 |
| 534 | Union Texas Petroleum | 1330 Post Oak Blvd., Houston, TX 77056 | (713) 623-6544 |
| 403 | Unisys | Township Line & Union Meeting Rds., Blue Bell, PA 19422 | (215) 986-4011 |
| 755 | United Asset Management | One International Pl., Boston, MA 02110 | (617) 330-8900 |
| 148 | United Healthcare | 9900 Bren Rd. E., Minnetonka, MN 55343 | (612) 936-1300 |
| 102 | United Technologies | United Technologies Bldg., Hartford, CT 06101 | (203) 728-7000 |
| 445 | Unitrin | One E.Wacker Dr., Chicago, IL 60601 | (312) 661-4600 |
| 881 | Universal Foods | 433 E. Michigan St., Milwaukee, WI 53202 | (414) 271-6755 |
| 140 | Unocal | 1201 W. 5th St., Los Angeles, CA 90017 | (213) 977-7600 |
| 235 | Unum | 2211 Congress St., Portland, ME 04122 | (207) 770-2211 |
| 188 | Upjohn | 7000 Portage Rd., Kalamazoo, MI 49001 | (616) 323-4000 |
| 40 | Us West | 7800 E. Orchard Rd., Englewood, CO 80111 | (303) 793-6500 |
| 679 | USF&G | 100 Light St., Baltimore, MD 21202 | (410) 547-3000 |
| 723 | USG | 125 S. Franklin St., Chicago, IL 60606 | (312) 606-4000 |
| 870 | USLife | 125 Maiden Ln., New York, NY 10038 | (212) 709-6000 |
| 171 | UST | 100 W. Putnam Ave., Greenwich, CT 06830 | (203) 661-1100 |
| 196 | USX-Marathon Group | 600 Grant St., Pittsburgh, PA 15219 | (412) 433-1121 |
| 327 | USX-U.S. Steel Group | 600 Grant St., Pittsburgh, PA 15219 | (412) 433-1121 |
| 670 | Utilicorp United | 911 Main St., Kansas City, MO 64105 | (816) 421-6600 |
| 931 | Valassis Communications | 2972 Stender Way, Livonia, MI 48150 | (313) 591-3000 |
| 821 | Valero Energy | 530 McCullough Ave., San Antonio, TX 78215 | (210) 246-2000 |
| 986 | Valley Bancorporation | 100 W. Lawrence St., Appleton, WI 54911 | (414) 738-3800 |
| 987 | Valley National | 1445 Valley Rd., Wayne, NJ 07470 | (201) 305-8800 |
| 861 | Valspar | 1101 3rd St. S., Minneapolis, MN 55415 | (612) 332-7371 |
| 724 | Value Health | 22 Waterville Rd., Avon, CT 06001 | (203) 678-3400 |
| 932 | Vanguard Cellular | 2002 Pisgah Church Rd., Greensboro, NC 27455 | (919) 282-3690 |
| 681 | Varian Associates | 3050 Hansen Way, Palo Alto, CA 94304 | (415) 493-4000 |
| 468 | Varity | 672 Delaware Ave., Buffalo, NY 14209 | (716) 888-8000 |
| 308 | VF | 1047 N. Park Rd., Wyomissing, PA 19610 | (215) 378-1151 |
| 257 | Viacom | 1515 Broadway, New York, NY 10036 | (212) 258-6000 |

*Corporate Contact Directory (cont'd)*

| Rank | Company | Corporate Headquarters | Phone |
|---|---|---|---|
| 836 | Viking Office Products | 13809 S. Figueroa St., Los Angeles, CA 90061 | (213) 321-4493 |
| 969 | Vishay | 63 Lincoln Hwy., Malvern, PA 19355 | (215) 644-1300 |
| 956 | Vons | 618 Michillinda Ave., Arcadia, CA 91007 | (818) 821-7000 |
| 950 | Vornado Realty | Park 80 W., Saddle Brook, NJ, 07662 | (201) 587-1000 |
| 510 | Vulcan Materials | One Metroplex Dr., Birmingham, AL 35209 | (205) 877-3000 |
| 170 | Wachovia | 301 N. Main St., Winston-Salem, NC 27102 | (910) 770-5000 |
| 4 | Wal-Mart Stores | 702 S.W. 8th St., Bentonville, AR 72716 | (501) 273-4000 |
| 190 | Walgreen | 200 Wilmot Rd., Deerfield, IL 60015 | (708) 940-2500 |
| 957 | Wallace Computer | 4600 W. Roosevelt Rd., Hillside, IL 60162 | (708) 449-8600 |
| 103 | Warner-Lambert | 201 Tabor Rd., Morris Plains, NJ 07950 | (201) 540-2000 |
| 876 | Washington Federal S&L | 425 Pike St., Seattle, WA 98101 | (206) 624-7930 |
| 908 | Washington Gas Light | 1100 H St., NW, Washington, DC 20080 | (703) 750-4440 |
| 633 | Washington Mutual | 1201 3rd Ave., Seattle, WA 98101 | (206) 461-2000 |
| 349 | Washington Post | 1150 15th St., NW, Washington, DC 20071 | (202) 334-6000 |
| 850 | Washington Water | E. 1411 Mission Ave., Spokane, WA 99202 | (509) 489-0500 |
| 909 | Watts Industries | 815 Chestnut St., North Andover, MA 01845 | (508) 688-1811 |
| 934 | Wausau Paper Mills | One Clark's Island, Wausau, WI 54402 | (715) 845-5266 |
| 788 | Weingarten Realty | 2600 Citadel Plaza Dr., Houston, TX 77008 | (713) 866-6000 |
| 706 | Weis Markets | 1000 S. 2nd St., Sunbury, PA 17801 | (717) 286-4571 |
| 412 | Wellfleet Communications | 8 Federal St., Billerica, MA 01821 | (508) 670-8888 |
| 296 | Wellpoint Health | 21555 Oxnard St., Woodland Hills, CA 91367 | (818) 703-4000 |
| 116 | Wells Fargo | 420 Montgomery St., San Francisco, CA 94163 | (415) 477-1000 |
| 511 | Wendy's International | 4288 W. Dublin-Granville Rd., Dublin, OH 43017 | (614) 764-3100 |
| 978 | Werner Enterprises | Interstate 80 & Hwy. 50, Omaha, NE 68137 | (402) 895-6640 |
| 863 | Wesco Financial | 301 E. Colorado Blvd., Pasadena, CA 91101 | (818) 585-6700 |
| 843 | West One Bancorp | 101 S. Capitol Blvd., Boise, ID 83702 | (208) 383-7165 |
| 966 | Western Gas Resources | 12200 N. Pecos St., Denver, CO 80234 | (303) 452-5603 |
| 487 | Western Resources | 818 Kansas Ave., Topeka, KS 66612 | (913) 575-6300 |
| 184 | Westinghouse Electric | 11 Stanwix St., Pittsburgh, PA 15222 | (412) 244-2000 |
| 421 | Westvaco | 299 Park Ave., New York, NY 10171 | (212) 688-5000 |
| 87 | Weyerhaeuser | 33663 Weyerhauser Way S., Federal Way, WA 98003 | (206) 923-2345 |
| 281 | Wheelabrator | 3003 Butterfield Rd., Oak Brook, IL 60521 | (708) 572-8800 |
| 194 | Whirlpool | 2000 M-63, Benton Harbor, MI 49022 | (616) 923-5000 |
| 528 | Whitman | 3501 Algonquin Rd., Rolling Meadows, IL 60008 | (708) 818-5000 |
| 318 | Willamette Industries | 1300 S.W. 5th Ave., Portland, OR 97201 | (503) 227-5581 |
| 393 | Williams | One Williams Center, Tulsa, OK 74172 | (918) 588-2000 |
| 854 | Wilmington Trust | 1100 N. Market St., Wilmington, DE 19890 | (302) 651-1000 |
| 266 | Winn-Dixie Stores | 5050 Edgewood Court, Jacksonville, FL 32254 | (904) 783-5000 |
| 380 | Wisconsin Energy | 231 W. Michigan St., Milwaukee, WI 53203 | (414) 221-2345 |
| 531 | Witco | 520 Madison Ave., New York, NY 10022 | (212) 605-3800 |
| 68 | WMX Technologies | 3003 Butterfield Rd., Oak Brook, IL 60521 | (708) 572-8800 |
| 346 | Woolworth | 233 Broadway, New York, NY 10279 | (212) 553-2000 |
| 513 | Worthington Industries | 1205 Dearborn Dr., Columbus, OH 43085 | (614) 438-3210 |
| 869 | WPL Holdings | 222 W. Washington Ave., Madison, WI 53703 | (608) 252-3311 |
| 173 | Wrigley (W.M.), Jr. | 410 N. Michigan Ave., Chicago, IL 60611 | (312) 644-2121 |
| 84 | Xerox | 800 Long Ridge Rd., Stamford, CT 06904 | (203) 968-3000 |
| 659 | Xilinx | 2100 Logic Dr., San Jose, CA 95124 | (408) 559-7778 |
| 968 | Xtra | 60 State St., Boston, MA 02109 | (617) 367-5000 |
| 918 | Yellow | 10777 Barkley, Overland Park, KS 66211 | (913) 967-4300 |
| 597 | York International | 631 S. Richland Ave., York, PA 17403 | (717) 771-7890 |

# INDEX

The following is an index of all companies, reference sources, table titles, and major concepts in the book. Reference sources are in italics, and table titles are in small capitals.

For a glossary of business terms, see pages 656-659. For a list of industry news-letters, see pages 674-690. For a list of the 1000 largest publicly-owned companies, see pages 691-710.

# A FREE BONUS FOR PURCHASING THE 1995 INFORMATION PLEASE® BUSINESS ALMANAC AND THE GUERRILLA MARKETING HANDBOOK

## BUY THIS . . .

## GET THIS FREE !

As a special bonus for purchasing *The 1995 Information Please® Business Almanac*, Houghton Mifflin offers you a special bonus. Buy a copy of *The Guerrilla Marketing Handbook* any time between November 1, 1994 and March 1, 1995, send us the proof of purchase from both books (1995 IPBA and the new GMH) and we will send you a copy of the classic *Guerrilla Marketing* ($11.95 retail value) absolutely FREE. We'll even pay for the postage.

*The Guerrilla Marketing Handbook* is the latest addition to the most acclaimed series of marketing books ever written. Jay Levinson and Seth Godin show you the ins and outs of getting the most out of every last dollar in your marketing budget. The book is so effective that it's guaranteed to work, or your money back.

**Please clip the bottom right corner of this page and send both original store receipts to:  Free Guerrilla Book, Houghton Mifflin Company, 222 Berkeley Street, 8th Floor, Boston, MA 02116. Be sure to include your name, street address, city, state and zip code.  Please print clearly.  Limit one per customer. No facsimiles or photocopies of receipts will be accepted.**

1995 IPBA
6-88738

## Business Law & Government

Pages 1 to 52

Includes:
Contracts
Intellectual Property
Working with the SBA
Federal Information Center
Finding a Lawyer
Regulatory Agencies
Alternate Dispute Resolution
Political Action Committees
OSHA
Members of Congress
U.S. Lawyers with Foreign Offices

## Communications

Pages 53 to 84

Includes:
Postal Abbreviations
Shipping
 UPS
 FEDEX
 USPS
Postal Answer Line
World Time Chart
International Dialing
Phone Cards on Other Systems
Time Zones
Area Codes

## Corporate Administration

Pages 85 to 164

Includes:
Supporters of the Arts & Charities
Corporate Social Responsibility
Demographics
Annual Reports
The Fortune 500
The Inc. 500
The Forbes 400
Business Plan Outline
Construction Starts
Mortgage Tables
BOMA Standards
Lease Negotiation Tips

## Manufacturing

Pages 435 to 484

Includes:
Industrial Buying Guides
Sales Agencies
The Federal Laboratory Consortium
Research & Development
EPA Regional Offices
Recycling
New Techniques
Environmental Issues
Productivity
Warehousing
Design Awards
Quality Standards

## Marketing

Pages 485 to 546

Includes:
Ad Agencies
Magazines
The Top Brands
College Newspaper Advertising
Infomercials
Product Placement Firms
Public Relations
Direct Marketing
Premium and Novelty Sources
The Sales Hall of Fame
Mailing Lists
Franchising
Trade Shows

*The Almanac is divided into twelve chapters, each focusing on a different area of business. The first page of each chapter lists the topics covered. There is also an index at the end of the book.*